Literature
Across Cultures

Literature
Across Cultures

Sheena Gillespie

Terezinha Fonseca

Carol Sanger

QUEENSBOROUGH COMMUNITY COLLEGE
CITY UNIVERSITY OF NEW YORK

ALLYN and BACON
Boston   London   Toronto   Sydney   Tokyo   Singapore

Copyright © 1994 by Allyn and Bacon
A Division of Simon & Schuster, Inc.
160 Gould Street
Needham Heights, MA 02194

Editor in Chief, Humanities: Joseph Opiela
Editorial Assistant: Brenda Conaway
Production Administrator: Rowena Dores
Editorial-Production Service: Tara L. Masih
Text Designer: Rita Naughton
Cover Administrator: Linda Dickinson
Manufacturing Buyer: Louise Richardson
Composition Buyer: Linda Cox

Library of Congress Cataloging-in-Publication Data

Gillespie, Sheena, [date]
   Literature across cultures / Sheena Gillespie, Terezinha Fonseca,
Carol Sanger.
    p. cm.
   Includes indexes.
   ISBN 0-205-13762-8 (pbk.)
   1. Literature—Collections. I. Fonseca, Terezinha. II. Sanger,
Carol. III. Title.
PN6014.G43 1994
808.8—dc20   93-30092
                                        CIP

This book is printed on
recycled, acid-free paper.

Acknowledgments

PART ONE

Edith Wharton. "Roman Fever" from *An Edith Wharton Treasury.* Copyright ©1950 by Appleton-Century Crofts.
   Reprinted by permission of Watkins/Loomis Agency, Inc.

(Acknowledgments continued on page 1080, which constitutes an extension of the copyright page)

Printed in the United States of America
10 9 8 7 6 5 4 3 2 1   98 97 96 95 94 93

To Amanda and Gabriel Stellman, the future.

In memory of Alair De Oliveira Gomes, a Brazilian with a vocatio
deep thought, beauty, and friendship.

In memory of my mother and father, Angelina and Michael Spica.

Contents

Part One: *Origins and Insights* *33*

Fiction

Poetry

Drama

Preface for Instructors

"Perhaps we should try to think of American culture as a conversation among different voices—even if it's a conversation that some of us weren't able to join until recently," Henry Louis Gates, Jr., has said. This anthology invites students to become acquainted with these new voices in their study of literature.

Our reading selections attempt to expose students to texts from diverse cultures and, through their study of and conversations with these traditional and modernist voices, provide them with broader contexts in which to discuss vital issues such as origins and insights, gender and identity, war and violence, race and difference, and individualism and community. The readings in these five thematic sections, grouped according to genre, suggest different ways of understanding and responding to traditional genres by exploring both their literary and cultural contexts.

In Part One, on origins and insights, students will find a diversity of literary texts from both familiar and new writers who speculate on topics such as the influence of tradition and culture, the degree to which the past informs the present, and the interaction of personal and cultural memories.

The gender and identity texts, in Part Two, provide a starting point for a more open debate between men and women on gender differences. They explore the woman question and the relations between women and men, as well as probe the crucial links between gender and identity.

The war and violence selections, in Part Three, pose questions about war as a cause and effect of the daily violence that erupts in homes and on the streets in communities around the world. They also suggest ways by which students may reevaluate heroic myths of war and examine new sensibilities promoting the merits of political negotiation and citing the misuses of power in a global, pluralistic society.

The race and difference texts, in Part Four, invite students to understand better the historical realities of personal indignities and social injustices resulting from individual and institutional attitudes toward sexual preference, ethnicity, gender, and class. Some voices in this part express anger and disillusionment about their sense of entrapment and exclusion from the North American mainstream. This chapter also includes texts from the literature of AIDS, as this condition finds emotional correlatives in the fiction, poetry, and drama of our time.

The individualism and community texts, in Part Five, explore the dialectic of self and society, examining the degree to which our ability to say "I" is predicated also on our need and willingness to say "we." Students will be asked to seek answers to questions such as these: What constitutes a community? How do the features of a community relate to individuals, some of whom submit and some of whom rebel? To what extent does the community promote the individual? What are an individual's responsibilities to the larger community?

Discussion questions follow each short story, cluster of poems, and play to assist students in making informed responses to the text. Their aim is to enrich the student's view of literary texts by suggesting multiple possibilities for the production of meaning. Specifically, the rationale we devised here links the expression of personal meanings in journal writing with meanings produced on textual, cultural, and collaborative levels. Writing assignments and research topics conclude each part.

The editorial apparatus includes a section on reading and writing about literature that addresses typical student reservations about the value of literature by approaching reading as a social act, in which students interact not only with the writers of the text but also through discussion with their peers.

A guided critical analysis of Kate Chopin's "The Story of an Hour" emphasizes the importance of close textual reading, as well as a discussion of the story's cultural contexts. This section also includes samples of student journal responses and summaries of their peer discussions of the text.

Using a sample student critical analysis of Sherwood Anderson's "Hands," another section takes students through the step-by-step process of writing a critical essay, beginning with interpreting a literary text, generating ideas for a critical paper, writing a first draft, learning from peer critiques, and revising the final draft.

The editorial apparatus also includes an appendix on interacting with the literary genres, as well as strategies for discussing the texts as cultural productions. This apparatus is intended to help students develop the analytical and critical skills they need to read and write about literature.

The appendix "Researching Literary Sources" includes information on using the library and locating critical sources, as well as a discussion of the research paper, MLA documentation, and two documented student essays.

The appendix "Critical Approaches: A Case Study of *Hamlet*" includes a discussion of several critical approaches to the play, including psychoanalytic, psychosocial, New Critical, feminist, reader-response, and New Historical.

"A Note About Film" discusses such elements within film as film and literature, psychology and character, and imagery and technique.

The apparatus also includes biographical endnotes that introduce the writers, plus a glossary of literary and cultural terms.

The text is accompanied by an instructor's manual, which includes strategies for discussing literature in an interactive classroom, selected critical bibliographies, a filmography for each unit, and selected audio and visual resources.

ACKNOWLEDGMENTS

We are grateful to Joe Opiela, our editor, who initiated and developed this project, and to his assistant, Brenda Conaway, who worked patiently with us throughout the process. For their help in preparing the manuscript for publication, we would like to thank Production Administrator Rowena Dores, and Production Editor Tara Masih. Our special thanks also to Tony Pipolo for his appendix on film as well as suggestions and filmographies in the instructor's manual.

Marlene dos Santos, Evelyn J. Kirstein, Ruth Kirstein, and Ellen Higgins, and Duane Crumb served as consultants. Our students offered invaluable criticism, and Devon McCabe and J. P. Lydon Fonseca made insightful suggestions for the instructor's manual.

Patricia D'Angeli and Isabel Pipolo contributed excellent research papers.

We acknowledge our gratitude to Margaret Cavanaugh and Kathy Howard for their generous assistance in the preparation of the manuscript, to Marge Caronna, Richard Crumb, and the library staff of Queensborough Community College for their help in securing outstanding permissions, and to Carole Pipolo for typing the instructor's manual.

We also thank the following reviewers: Lucien Agosta, California State University—Sacramento; Vivian R. Brown, Laredo Junior College; Mary Ellen Bryne, Ocean County College; Douglas E. Crowell, Texas Technical University; Robert Dees, Orange Coast College; James Egan, University of Akron; Ann O. Gebhard, SUNY—Cortland; Stephen Hahn, William Paterson College; Corrinne Hales, California State University—Fresno; John Iorio, University of South Florida; James O'Neil, Edison Community College; Melissa Pennell, University of Lowell; and Kathleen Tichnor, Brevard Community College.

Preface for Students

> People and their cultures perish in isolation, but they are born or reborn in contact with other men and women, with men and women of another culture, another creed, another race. If we do not recognize our humanity in others, we will not recognize it in ourselves.
>
> Carlos Fuentes

As teachers and students of literature, we believe that one of the most effective ways to understand people of other cultures, creeds, or races is through language; a person's words are the windows through which we gain access into his or her world. In this anthology, we invite you to travel with us to worlds beyond your own, to engage in a conversation among cultures, to explore unfamiliar traditions, and to evaluate human relationships in an attempt to better understand the meanings of community in our own pluralistic society and the multicultural society of the approaching twenty-first century.

We hope that as you listen to these voices, past and present, you will feel compelled to enter the conversation, to add your own voice and your own words. As you engage in dialogue with the selections, both in writing and in discussion with your fellow students, you will experiment with new ways of looking at yourself, enlarging the windows from which you view the world. The journey we invite you to share will be challenging—many of the voices, both classical and contemporary, expect you to respond.

In Part One, "Origins and Insights," you will encounter cultures with unfamiliar characteristics: the oral traditions and affinity with the worlds of nature and spirit of Native Americans, the love of language and pride in their history of Hispanics, the emphasis on kinship and music in the literature of African Americans, the cultural complexity and generational conflicts of Asian Americans, and the poignance of family loyalty among Italian Americans.

In Part Two, "Gender and Identity," you will be invited to examine traditional cross-cultural concepts of masculinity and femininity and to evaluate the degree to which they have affected both men and women in their individual quests for identity.

xix

Some of the voices in this part will ask you to decide whether gender conflicts should be confronted or avoided. Other voices will pose possibilities for freeing both sexes from the confines of traditional roles so that both men and women may become more dynamic and fulfilled.

In Part Three, "War and Violence," you will evaluate older heroic myths of war from other cultures as well as newer sensibilities advocating compromise as the desirable outcome of political conflict. You may also speculate on the misuses of power in a global, pluralistic society. Most of all, you will be asked to consider whether the recognition of our shared humanity will enable us to look beyond violence to peace.

In Part Four, "Race and Difference," you will be asked to reexamine many of the racial stereotypes with which we all have grown up. Some of these voices from diverse ethnic groups will invite you to share the anguish and anger of exclusion; others will challenge your preconceptions about race, class, and sexual preference; and still others will ask whether differences should be silenced or articulated, respected or shunned.

In Part Five, "Individualism and Community," you will confront the conflict experienced in every culture between the needs and desires of our individual selves and the needs and desires of the community. Many voices in this part debate the issue of individual freedom versus social responsibility; others advocate that solo voices join in the discord and harmony of the human chorus.

As you converse with the voices, both old and new, in this anthology, you will travel into uncharted territories, to real and imagined worlds where many of the familiar guideposts will no longer apply. But this is as it should be. Preparation for the global village of the twenty-first century requires your generation to sharpen its definition of an educated person. By adding your voice to the cultural conversations in this anthology, you will begin that process, perhaps leaving the familiar in favor of the unfamiliar.

Literature
Across Cultures

Reading and Writing as a Social Act

Why read literature? is the question many instructors pose during the first class session of Introduction to Literature.

Writer and critic Robert Scholes suggests that since students like writers who have stories to tell, "learning to read books—or pictures, or films—is not just a matter of learning to read, it is a matter of learning to read and write the texts of our lives."

Why do writers write? They write to be read; they write for you, their audience. Most writers value their relationship with their readers. For example, the well-known Russian writer Anton Chekov (1860–1904) has stated that "when I write, I reckon entirely upon the reader to add for himself the subjective elements that are lacking in the story." Similarly, the writer Grace Paley (b. 1922) reinforces the significance of the reader's role when she writes, "Maybe the reader of a particular story knows better than the writer what it means." Writers also write to communicate their insights to you in the hope that you will recognize aspects of your own thoughts and experiences in their stories.

Although many students express skepticism about finding meanings in the literature of the past, most acknowledge readily that human beings throughout history have had experiences in common. According to the novelist Albert Camus (1913–1960), "Every great work of art makes the human face more admirable and richer." His suggestion is that as we share in reading of the sufferings and joys of others, we better understand our own. The novelist James Baldwin (1924–1987) also reminds us of the continuity of human experiences in his short story "Sonny's Blues":

1

For while the tale of how we suffer, and how we are delighted, and how we may triumph is never new, it always must be heard. There isn't any other tale to tell. It's the only light we've got in all this darkness.

We invite you to approach the reading of the texts in this anthology from the vantage points suggested by Camus and Baldwin. Perhaps thinking about fiction, poetry, and drama as expressions of human suffering, delight, and triumph will make it possible for you to understand Medea's anger at being abandoned by her husband in favor of a younger woman; to empathize with Hamlet's attempt to find his real identity; and to share in the triumph of a nineteenth-century New England house-wife's revolt. You might even discover something about yourself. As the novelist Toni Morrison reminds us, interacting with literature is a dynamic process engaging both reader and writer: "The imagination that produces work which bears and invites rereading, which points to future readings as well as contemporary ones, implies a shareable world and an especially flexible language. Readers and writers both struggle to interpret and perform within a common language shareable imaginative worlds."

THE MEANING OF LITERATURE

What is literature? Traditionally set apart from other kinds of discourse, literature has been defined by the *Webster's Universal Unabridged Dictionary* as "all writings in prose or verse, especially those of an imaginative or critical character." Although this definition, like many others, has proved to be incomplete, it does highlight the presence of two major features of literature: its language and its imaginative charac-ter. When combined, these two elements produce a fictional world that reflects and evokes reality.

One story in this anthology can be used to illustrate this power of literature. The introduction to "The Sniper" transports us, not to the real world of urban guerrillas in Dublin, but to the fictional atmosphere of a Dublin that Liam O'Fla-herty especially re-created as a unique literary experience:

> The long June twilight faded into night, Dublin lay enveloped in darkness but for the dim light of the moon that shone through fleecy clouds, casting a pale light as of approaching dawn over the streets and the dark waters of the Liffey. Around the beleaguered Four Courts the heavy guns roared. Here and there through the city, machine-guns and rifles broke the silence of the night, spasmodically, like dogs barking on lone farms. Republicans and Free Staters were waging civil war.
>
> "The Sniper"

Although O'Flaherty might have modeled his portrayal of Dublin on a factual description of this Irish city caught in the civil war between the Republicans and Free Staters, his city, in strictly literary terms, is fictional. His text articulates imaginatively and creatively the significance of an actual historical event.

In O'Flaherty's text, atmosphere and imagery provide insights into events that we have not experienced directly. Characterization is another way literature can broaden our experience. You will observe, in other texts in this volume, how characters such as Antigone, Hamlet, J. Alfred Prufrock, and Karintha have dramatized across the centuries some of the most terrifying and stimulating possibilities of human experience. In this sense, literature can be defined as the enactment of human possibilities, or as a vehicle that will help us to discover more about ourselves and the meaning we can make of life. For the French philosopher Jean-Paul Sartre (1905–1980), the function of literature is to search for the meaning of life and to speculate about the role of human beings in the world.

Perhaps the best way to define literature is in practice, encountering the literary experience face-to-face through the readings in this anthology. In the process, you may notice that a literary work leads you to encounter not one precise, correct reading but a range of meanings evoked by the interaction of the text with your own experience as a reader. For instance, *Hamlet*, a work that is widely discussed from different critical perspectives, illustrates the variety of meanings that Shakespeare's readers have produced in the process of interpreting this play. In fact, one appendix in this anthology is devoted to exploring some of these various critical approaches and responses, known as psychoanalytic, formalist, reader-response, feminist, and New Historical (see the appendix "Critical Approaches").

THE FUNCTION OF LITERATURE

Following the literary tradition that the Latin poet Horace (65-8 B.C.) established for poetry, some scholars emphasize "to instruct" or "to delight," or both, as the major functions of literature. Recent scholarly opinion indicates that another function of literature is to actively shape our culture. For example, some literary historians believe that human beings learned how to cultivate a romantic idea of love only after reading works of literature that portrayed love in this light rather than as a social or sexual arrangement between a man and a woman. Both ancient and modern approaches emphasize two of literature's major functions: to construct and articulate sociocultural realities and to involve you as the reader in an invigorating interaction with these realities.

When you address the questions we formulate under "Cultural Contexts" in this anthology, you will be asked to interact with your classmates, to take sides, to make decisions, and to add your voice to various cultural and political issues related to class, race, gender, war, and violence. Consider, for instance, Wilfred Owen's poem "Disabled," in which his portrait of a disabled veteran stimulates our involvement in the violence perpetuated by World War I. By presenting such a viewpoint, literature can empower us—it can promote our active engagement with the world through our encounter with the poem's disclosure of the reality of violence caused by war. Thus, literature can fulfill a major cultural function in society.

STRATEGIES FOR READING LITERATURE:
A STEP-BY-STEP GUIDELINE

Reading literature is a process in which you, as a reader, should engage actively. To respond well to literature, you must take a critical approach that involves three major procedures: previewing, highlighting, and annotating.

Previewing

Even before you read a text, preview it by asking yourself some questions about the title, the writer, and the type of writing you are encountering:

- ◆ What does the title suggest?
- ◆ Have I heard of this author before?
- ◆ Does my anthology provide any information about this text?
- ◆ What type of text is this—a poem, a story, or a play?
- ◆ What kind of structure does it possess?
- ◆ How is the text organized? By paragraphs, stanzas, acts, scenes?

Highlighting

Read the text closely, and highlight—by underlining words or coloring them with a highlighting pen—the sections that particularly strike you from the point of view of style, structure, ideas, characterization, or any other key features you have observed as a reader. Notice, for example, in the passage below taken from James Joyce's short story "Eveline," the repetition of the verb form "used to" and some of its variants that indicate repeated action in the past. Identifying such a pattern enables you to discern the strong emotional links that Eveline has with the past. From this you may infer her psychological inability to accept change as a possibility for the future.

> One time there *used to* be a field there in which they *used to* play every evening with other people's children. Then a man from Belfast bought the field and built houses in it—not like the little brown houses but bright brick houses with shining roofs. The children of the avenue *used to* play together in that field—the Devines, the Waters, the Dunns, little Keogh the cripple, she and her brothers and sisters. Ernest, however, never played: he was too grown up. Her father *used* often *to* hunt them in out of the field with his blackthorn stick; but *usually* little Keogh *used to* keep **nix** and call out when he saw her father coming. Still they seemed to have been rather happy then . . .

Annotating

Annotating means making marginal notes on the book's pages, or using a pad or note cards. Once you reach this phase, you are involved in the critical process of selecting, summarizing, and annotating ideas. After a second and third reading, your notes will eventually lead you to respond to the literary and cultural impact of the text by identifying its words, imagery, and themes. Responding actively to the text therefore becomes a challenge for you as a reader, because you will interact with it and define its meanings on the basis of both the factual evidence that you find there and your own insights and experiences.

The following guided reading of Kate Chopin's "The Story of an Hour" should help you to understand what we mean by interaction between the reader and the text. After previewing, highlighting, and annotating the text, you might consider approaching your analysis of the "Textual Considerations" of "The Story of an Hour" as a detective trying to solve a crime. Arm yourself with a dictionary and thesaurus, and be on the alert for the many textual hints and clues that the writer has supplied for you. Pay close attention to the text by examining how the author uses nouns, adjectives, images, and symbols to construct plot and to build characterization.

Kate Chopin (1851–1904)

The Story of an Hour

"The Story of an Hour"

1. Knowing that **Mrs. Mallard** was afflicted with a heart trouble, great care was taken to break to her as gently as possible the news of her husband's death.

2. It was her sister Josephine who told her, in broken sentences, veiled hints that revealed in half concealing. Her husband's friend Richards was there, too, near her. It was he who had been in the newspaper office when intelligence of the railroad disaster was received, with Brently Mallard's name leading the list of "killed." He had only taken the time to assure himself of its truth by a second telegram, and had hastened to forestall any less careful, less tender friend in bearing the sad message.

Textual Considerations

What kinds of expectations does the opening paragraph raise in the reader about the protagonist and the plot of the story? Have you noticed that the protagonist is addressed as Mrs. Mallard and that the starting point of the story is "the news of her husband's death"?

Respond to Josephine's and Richards's attitude about breaking the news to Mrs. Mallard.

3. She did not hear the story as many women have heard the same, with a paralyzed inability to accept its significance. She wept at once, with sudden, **wild abandonment,** in her sister's arms. When the storm of grief had spent itself she went to her room alone. She would have no one follow her.

Focus on paragraph 3. What does the phrase "wild abandonment" suggest? Are you surprised by Mrs. Mallard's insistence on being left alone after hearing such bad news? Explain.

4. There stood, facing the open window, a comfortable, roomy armchair. Into this she sank, pressed down by a physical exhaustion that haunted her body and seemed to reach into her soul.

What examples do you find of images of freedom and repression in paragraphs 4 and 5? Comment on these examples.

5. She could see in the open square before her house the **tops of trees that were all aquiver with the new spring life. The delicious breath of rain was in the air.** In the street below a peddler was crying his wares. The notes of a distant song which some one was singing reached her faintly, and countless sparrows were twittering in the eaves.

Writers frequently use nature to open a symbolic level for the text. What is unusual about the text's emphasis on spring, given the events of the story thus far? What other aspects of nature emerge in paragraphs 5 and 6? What do they suggest about Mrs. Mallard's state of mind? What kind of expectations do they raise in the reader?

6. There were patches of blue sky showing here and there through the clouds that had met and piled above the other in the west facing her window.

7. She sat with her head thrown back upon the cushion of the chair quite motionless, except when a sob came up into her throat and shook her, as a child who has cried itself to sleep continues to sob in its dreams.

Characterize your response to paragraphs 7 and 8.

8. She was **young,** with a **fair,** calm face, whose **lines bespoke repression** and even a certain strength. But now there was a dull stare in her eyes, whose gaze was fixed away off yonder on one of those patches of blue sky. It was not

What new aspects of Mrs. Mallard's personality occur in paragraph 8? To what might "the lines of repression" be attributable? Consider the difference between a "glance of reflection" and a "suspension of intelligent thought."

a **glance of reflection,** but rather indicated a **suspension of intelligent thought.**

9. There was **something coming to her** and she was waiting for it, fearfully. What was it? She did not know; it was too subtle and elusive to name. But she felt it, creeping out of the sky, reaching toward her through the sounds, the scents, the color that filled the air.

What dramatic pattern is the text shaping in terms of plot (events, to rising action), characterization (Mrs. Mallard's reaction), and your own response as a reader? Focus on paragraphs 9 and 10.

10. Now her bosom rose and fell tumultuously. She was beginning to recognize this thing that was approaching to possess her, and she was striving to beat it back with her will—as powerless as her two white slender hands would have been.

11. When she abandoned herself a little word escaped her **slightly parted lips.** She said it over and over under her breath: "**Free,** free, free!" **The vacant stare** and the look of terror that had followed it went from her eyes. They stayed keen and bright. Her **pulses beat fast,** and the coursing **blood warmed** and relaxed every inch of her body.

What does "the vacant stare" suggest? What does "the look of terror" convey? Contrast the descriptions of Mrs. Mallard's bodily responses in paragraphs 4 and 11. To what extent are these physical and psychological reversals gender based (characteristic of women more than men)?

12. She did not stop to ask if it were not a **monstrous** joy that held her. A clear and exalted perception enabled her to dismiss the suggestion as trivial.

Check your thesaurus for various connotations of "monstrous." Speculate about Chopin's description of Mrs. Mallard's joy as "monstrous" in paragraph 12.

13. She knew that she would weep again when she saw the kind tender hands folded in death; the face that had never looked save with love upon her, fixed and gray and dead. But she saw beyond that **bitter moment a long procession of years to come** that would belong to her absolutely. And she opened and spread her arms out to them in welcome.

Notice how Mrs. Mallard contrasts the "bitter moment" of the present with "a long procession of years to come." To what extent does this contrast suggest her desire to rewrite her personal history? To what extent does the world of closed windows and fixed gender identities versus the evocations of freedom and self-discovery create narrative suspense?

14. There would be no one to live for during those coming years: **she would live for herself. There would be no powerful will bending her in** that blind persistence with which men and women believe they have a right to impose a private will upon a fellow-creature. A kind intention or a cruel intention made the act seem less a crime as she looked upon it in that brief moment of illumination.

Does Mrs. Mallard surprise you with her realistic portrait of male and female relations? What does this moment of illumination amount to?

15. And yet she had loved him—sometimes. Often she had not. What did it matter! What could love, the un-solved mystery, count for in face of this possession of self-assertion which she suddenly recognized as the strongest impulse of her being!

To what extent do you empathize with Mrs. Mallard's desire for autonomy and psychological space?

16. "Free! Body and soul free!" she kept whispering.

How do you characterize Mrs. Mallard's emotional outburst?

Explain why Chopin withholds the protagonist's first name until paragraph 17.

17. Josephine was kneeling before the closed door with her lips to the key-hole, imploring for admission. **"Louise,** open the door! I beg; open the door—you will make yourself ill. What are you doing, Louise? For heaven's sake open the door."

18. "Go away. I am not making myself ill." No; she was drinking in the very elixir of life through that open window.

Identify the two voices that interact in this paragraph.

19. Her fancy was running riot along **those days ahead of her.** Spring days, and summer days, and all sorts of days that would be her own. She breathed a quick prayer that life might be long. It was only **yesterday she** had thought with a shudder that life might be long.

React to the way the text juxtaposes the repression of the past and the possibilities of the future. Such a pattern culminates in paragraph 20 in the image that Mrs. Mallard "carries herself unwittingly like a goddess of Victory." To what extent does Chopin suggest that Mrs. Mallard's triumph will be transitory?

20. She arose at length and opened the door to her sister's importunities. There was a feverish triumph in her

eyes, and she carried herself un-wittingly like a goddess of Victory. She clasped her sister's waist, and together they descended the stairs. Richards stood waiting for them at the bottom.

21. Some one was opening the front door with a **latchkey.** It was Brently Mallard who entered, a little travel-stained, composedly carrying his **grip-sack** and **umbrella.** He had been far from the scene of the accident, and did not even know there had been one. He stood amazed at Josephine's pierc-ing cry: at Richards's quick motion to screen him from the view of his **wife.** But Richards was too late.

Read this paragraph carefully. Com-ment on the images of "latchkey," "gripsack," and "umbrella." What significance do you attach to Louise being referred to as "his wife"? To what extent does Richards's inability to protect Mrs. Mallard destabilize the action of the story? What kind of suspense or expecta-tion does this paragraph create in the reader?

22. When the doctors came they said that she had died of heart disease—**of joy that kills.**

How do you account for the ironic turn of the last sentence? Is it appropriate that the doctors misread the true cause of Mrs. Mallard's death? Explain.

Read "The Story of an Hour" again at least twice. More ideas will no doubt surface at each new reading, and you will react to more details concerning the arrangement of the events, Mrs. Mallard's reactions and expectations, and your own ability as a reader to produce more meanings in response to the text. As you deepen your understanding of the story, you will also become more aware of its cultural implications. To assist your interaction with the cultural possibilities of Chopin's text, you may discuss gender-related questions such as the ones listed in "Cultural Contexts" below.

Cultural Contexts

1. To what extent does "The Story of an Hour" reflect a feminist outlook on the roles of women? What evidence is there that the story is told from the perspective of a female narrator?
2. Consider what the text reveals about marriage as an institution. Is the concept of marriage that Chopin's text explores still applicable to contemporary gender relations?
3. Are men and women today more liberated than they were a century ago? Discuss the differences you see between then and now in the socially defined roles and "fixed gender identities" (identities determined by gender and social roles).

Following are some literature students' responses to the two literary and cultural topics listed below.

1. Respond to Kate Chopin's use of nature imagery in "The Story of an Hour."

2. React to the new meanings "The Story of an Hour" evokes as you think about the issues of gender and identity. Does this text reaffirm traditional ideas about gender relations, or does it provoke readers to discover different truths about gender relations?

In their responses to topic one, Chopin's use of nature imagery, the students previewed, highlighted, and annotated the text before they outlined how Chopin's suggestive use of imagery communicates Mrs. Mallard's new expectations about her future:

> Kate Chopin uses a great deal of imagery in "The Story of an Hour." Her description of "the tops of trees that were all aquiver with the new spring life" in paragraph 5 is a good example of her use of a nature image to communicate Mrs. Mallard's new feeling toward life, blooming, and rebirth.
>
> In paragraph 8, the image of "those patches of blue sky," showing that even though the dominant color of the sky might be gray it possesses "patches of blue," suggests that the color blue is also an indicator of new spring life. In spring the color of the sky is blue. However, it is important to realize that Chopin's reference to the clouds can function as a foreshadowing, indicating that the blue sky is as far off as Mrs. Mallard's expectations of freedom.
>
> Danielle Lucas

> Kate Chopin's reference to "the new spring life," "the notes of a distant song," "the delicious breath of rain," and "sparrows twittering" obviously suggests how Mrs. Mallard begins to respond to life. She is born again like new spring life, and she is ready to take in a new clean breath like "the delicious breath of rain." Her aspiration is to live her own life like the sparrow who is free to fly. Chopin uses the "patches of blue sky . . . through the clouds" as an image of a clearing in Mrs. Mallard's life. Gone is the husband with his "powerful will bending her in." There is a clearing of "blue sky" for her.
>
> Chopin says that Mrs. Mallard drinks in the very "elixir of life through the open window." Such an image supports the idea that Chopin uses nature imagery to show the freedom that Mrs. Mallard has now acquired.
>
> Mary Ellen Hogan

Two other students, Mike Lonergan and Robert Longstreet, also covered the preliminary reading strategies before they analyzed the issue of gender and identity as part of the larger cultural network Chopin's text evokes:

> "The Story of an Hour" by Kate Chopin reaffirms traditional ideas about gender relations with a riptide that illuminates the reader.
>
> Mr. and Mrs. Mallard portray a typical married couple of the late 1800s. Brently Mallard, the husband, is the head of the household, while Louise

Mallard, his wife, is his possession. To quote Emily Dickinson, Louise "rose to his requirement . . . to take the honorable work of women, and of wife" (Poem 172).

Like a typical wife of this era, Mrs. Mallard was supposed to obey her husband without any rebukes. Knowing nothing different, Mrs. Mallard accepted these social norms of her time.

However, Chopin's "The Story of an Hour" reveals the aged wrinkle in this status quo arrangement by showing how, subconsciously, Mrs. Mallard's inner self and soul were being repressed and sentenced to death by lack of use.

Mike Lonergan

"The Story of an Hour" is not a story that reaffirms traditional ideas about gender relations. In fact, Kate Chopin's text does just the opposite. It shows that no matter what your gender is, you should never lose your identity. The story suggests that instead of ignoring the restrictions of gender relations or hiding from them, you should try to eliminate them.

Robert Longstreet

WRITING AS A SOCIAL ACT

Even the best writers feel challenged and intimidated by public exposure of their texts. Geoffrey Chaucer (1343–1400), for instance, sent one of his books away with a plea for its favorable reception. Yet, although writing is in many ways a private activity, most of the writing you will do in your introductory course to literature will come out of a public context, in which your texts will be read, shared, critiqued, and evaluated by your peers and instructor. Often, too, you will have the chance to engage in group discussion and to record in written form the conclusions your group reaches about the interpretation of a text. On such occasions, your instructor will divide your class into small groups and ask you to compare your own interpretation of a text with those of your classmates. Finally, after the secretary of your group records the group's conclusions, your group will then proceed to revise and edit your writing. In such a collaborative context, writing becomes a social act.

The texts below show the results of some peer groups' invigorating discussions of Chopin's "The Story of an Hour." Notice that the discussion conducted by group one led the students to equate marriage with the loss of self:

The Mallards' marriage is the marriage of two to make up one. In fact, their marriage can be represented as A + B = C. As in the chemical reaction necessary to human survival, wherein a molecule of glucose must give up a portion of itself to become a part of a larger molecule (dehydration synthesis), so it is in marriage. One part of the self must be given up to form the sacred union of marriage. It is an unfortunate circumstance of marriage that identity and the self must be its sacrificial lamb.

Our group concluded that it is not possible to have a "successful" marriage without some loss of self. Mr. and Mrs. Mallard have just such a marriage: a "successful" one.

Recorded by Karen Digirolano

Unlike group one, whose overall observations about the loss of self in marriage offer insight into the Mallards' marriage, group two analyzes the evidence that the text provides about the Mallards as husband and wife:

Mr. Mallard was a typical husband, who never thought twice about his wife's thoughts or wishes. Neither did he think about the imposition of his own will over hers. Their marriage seemed a typical one. Mrs. Mallard, in fact, even "loved him—sometimes." For all intents and purposes, Mrs. Mallard seemed to have been a dutiful wife.

When informed of the news that her husband was dead, she acted as any woman would at her loss. However, when alone in her room, Mrs. Mallard came to know a feeling foreign to her: "There would be no one to live for during those coming years: she would live for herself. There would be no powerful will bending her in." She found herself looking forward to "those days ahead of her" which would truly be hers and no one else's. She even "spread her arms out to them in welcome."

The doctors were wrong when they said that Mrs. Mallard died of "the joy that kills." The shock to her weak heart was of sadness. When she saw her husband, she realized that her freedom was lost—once again.

Recorded by Rina Russo

Group three's analysis of Mrs. Mallard's life in the past, present, and future shows a sense of historical development:

When Mrs. Mallard moves away from the past and the present to think of the days ahead in the future, she is obviously elated. She prays to live a long life, whereas before her husband died she had prayed for a short one. Mrs. Mallard's first reactions show us that when her husband was alive, she had no optimistic outlook on the future. She only wanted to die.

After his death, she drinks from the elixir of the open window, or from all the freedom (the birds, the trees, and the blue sky) that she witnesses outside. Through all these revelations, we can see how Mrs. Mallard evaluates her life in the past, present, and future.

Recorded by Mary Ellen Hogan

Group four saw "The Story of an Hour" as a text that explores Mrs. Mallard's loss of freedom and her imprisonment in a marriage from which she could be set free only by death:

Mrs. Mallard is sketched as a young, good-looking woman with a heart condition whose husband "never looked save with love upon her." However, the fact that Mr. Mallard was a loving and kind husband had not been enough to keep his wife from dreading the thought of living a long life.

The enormity of Mrs. Mallard's "monstrous joy" on digesting the implications of Brently Mallard's death paints the picture of a woman feeling so imprisoned in her marriage that she cries out, "Free! Body and soul free!"

Mrs. Mallard dies when she sees her husband returning home. If, on one hand, the shock of her newly gained freedom, now lost again, destroys her, on the other hand her death sets her free from the imprisonment of her marriage.

Recorded by Doris Fleischer

After exploring the text and conducting a heated discussion about the Mallards and their marriage, group five concluded that Mr. and Mrs. Mallard were victims of their historical time:

We got the impression that even though Mrs. Mallard had an identity of her own, she was above all Mr. Mallard's wife. Thus, it was their nineteenth-century marriage that held Mrs. Mallard back from being the individual she really was: "She was young with a calm face whose lines bespoke repression."

Our group concluded that Mr. Mallard, like most husbands of his time, did not know how his wife felt. He probably thought he was a good husband to his wife. In fact, she sometimes loved him and "she knew that she would weep again when she saw the kind, tender hands folded in death." Our conclusion is that Mr. and Mrs. Mallard both were victims of the time they lived in.

Recorded by Damien Donohue

WRITING THE LITERARY ESSAY: A STEP-BY-STEP GUIDELINE

To help you achieve your goal of becoming an able writer, we provide six guidelines that student writer Yasuko Osahi followed as she completed an essay on a literary work. Yasuko's instructor asked her students to write about one of several short stories, using the theme "Individualism and the Community."

Yasuko chose to write her two-page essay on "Hands," by Sherwood Anderson, because she wanted to learn more about American life through reading the work of writers like Anderson. Besides providing her with the source of information she needed, Anderson's text (see pages 882–885) also stimulated her imagination because of the similarities it evoked between the communities portrayed in "Hands" and her mother's community in a small village in Japan.

Yasuko also knew that her *audience* (made up of her classmates and her instructor) and the *purpose* of her essay (to communicate to her audience her critical observations about "Hands") would control the development of her essay. And because she would be writing for a college audience, Yasuko knew also that she must organize her paper by presenting evidence from Anderson's text and following the conventions used to write a literary essay.

Guideline One: Techniques for Generating Ideas

Because writing is an act of discovery, Yasuko initially used some warm-up techniques to discover and generate ideas about her topic.

Brainstorming. First, Yasuko *brainstormed* her topic by jotting down on a piece of paper all the ideas that occurred to her from her reading of Anderson's story.

Biddlebaum: lived in two places
Pennsylvania and Winesburg, Ohio
Biddlebaum changes his real name.
New profession: berry picker
Carries the past with him
Afraid of people, but feels good with George Willard
How does the town react to him?
Do they see him as a threat to them?
They don't fear Biddblebaum, just make fun of him.
Pennsylvania and his past life
A victim of violence
The townspeople: ruthless, no pity for individuals
Almost killed him
Why?
Did they see Biddlebaum as a threat to them?
Why did they fear him? Who is to be blamed?

Journal Entry. Yasuko used her journal for *focused freewriting*—nonstop writing that flows freely, without concern for organization or editing of any kind. Freewriting should not be confused with disorganized writing, however. Freewriting is a focused kind of writing that helps you to get started by recalling any ideas or experiences as they occur to you. To keep her writing flowing, Yasuko asked questions related to *what, why, when, how, where, and who*. This technique helped her to relax and to establish a firm relationship with her topic. Occasionally, she got stuck. However, she persisted, continuing to write some of the key words related to her topic until her writing gained its own momentum. She did not use all the ideas she wrote down in her journal, but the entry below shows that through writing she learned how to associate ideas, to communicate her reactions about her topic, and to explore feelings and emotions.

I like "Hands," but can't relate the story to "Individualism-Community."
What does community really mean? The townspeople? Biddlebaum lived in
two places. I'll start with the first one. Violent people, like in my mother's village. You can't be different. A teacher. His real name was Adolph Myers. Myers, Myers, then Biddlebaum. A dreamer. Anderson says that his characters
are "grotesque." Look up this word. Individualism. Biddlebaum gives us an example of individualism. I like the story, and I sympathize with Biddlebaum.
The town's people see him as a threat. They fear him. Town's people and community. Community. Biddlebaum's community. Now I see the point. Biddlebaum's first community. Relationship: Biddlebaum-community. His second
community. Somebody in class said that if you don't understand the end of
the story, you'll miss the point. Bread. At the end he is just eating bread
crumbs. Why?

Clustering.   Since Yasuko responds well to visual texts and likes to relate them to
writing, she used *clustering* to develop and connect ideas about her topic. She
wrote down her topic in the middle of a page and circled it. Then she drew
connecting lines that radiated from the main topic to subtopics—ideas or words
that occurred to her. Next she circled the subtopics and continued to draw other
connecting lines to expose further ideas and relationships among them.

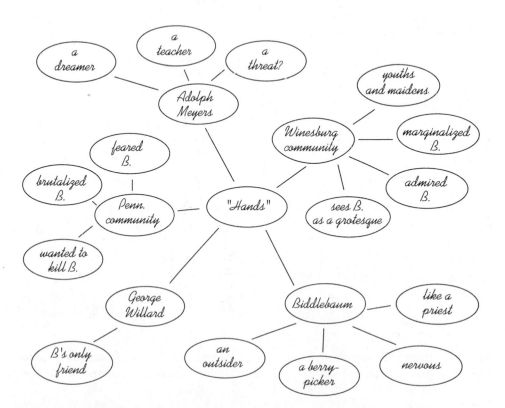

A Rough Outline. Yasuko continued to explore her topic by associating ideas and classifying them in a *rough outline*.

> *Biddlebaum: a teacher. Uses his hands*
> *to communicate. Dreams of ideal times.*
> *Pennsylvania community: people liars, brutes. Use*
> *violence. Biddlebaum as a threat? Do they fear him? Why?*
> *Winesburg community: isolated, new name, lonely,*
> *a grotesque, berry picker who sets a record.*
> *People don't fear him; just laugh at him;*
> *George Willard his only friend.*
> *The real Biddlebaum is like a priest: above the laugh of*
> *the community.*
> *Communities in "Hands" and Japanese communities.*
> *Similar in many ways. They hate people who*
> *threaten them because they are different.*
> *Why can't we accept individuals who are different?*

Guideline Two: Finding a Thesis

After examining the ideas in her brainstorming, journal entry, clustering, and rough outline, Yasuko noticed that her overall response to "Hands" was moving in the direction of one specific thesis statement or central idea. Gradually, as the pattern she was pursuing emerged, she was able to reinforce her sense of purpose and audience and to write a thesis statement. To formulate her thesis statement, Yasuko wrote down her topic and then expressed her opinion or commented on the topic.

Topic:

The conflict between individualism and community in "Hands."

+

Student's comment, opinion, or attitude about the topic:

Communities use violence only when they are under threat.

=

Thesis statement:

The conflict between individualism and community in "Hands" shows that communities, like Biddlebaum's Pennsylvania community, use violence only against individuals who pose a threat to their stability.

Yasuko's thesis statement shows how she narrowed her topic and phrased it using language that is clear, precise, and specific. It is important to remember, however, that even though your thesis statement functions as a contract that you sign with your readers, you might have to change or revise it as you move from draft to essay.

Guideline Three: Organizing the Paper

As the outline below shows, at this point Yasuko was ready to support her thesis statement on the basis of various ideas that she organized to build the body of her essay.

A Formal Outline

Thesis Statement

The conflict between individualism and community in "Hands" shows that communities, like Biddlebaum's Pennsylvania community, use violence only against individuals who pose a threat to their stability.

Supporting Ideas

I.   The Pennsylvania Community

    A. Biddlebaum as a threat to the community

        1. Biddlebaum: a real threat?

        2. The conflict of Biddlebaum-Pennsylvania community

    B. The community's reaction to Biddlebaum

        1. The community's disregard for individual rights

        2. The community's use of violence

II.   The Winesburg Community

    A. Biddlebaum as a member of the community

        1. Biddlebaum: a real member?

        2. Biddlebaum as an outsider

        3. Biddlebaum as a grotesque

    B. The community's reaction to Biddlebaum

        1. The community's view of Biddlebaum as a grotesque

        2. The community's acceptance of Biddlebaum

III. The Real Biddlebaum

    A. Neither a threat nor a grotesque

    B. A holy man above his community

A formal outline like Yasuko's may be used as a preliminary form of planning before you write your first draft, or during revision to check the organization of the draft. Either way, such an outline should serve as a guide, never a hindrance to making changes that improve your essay. Notice that in her outline Yasuko arranged the information in an order (Pennsylvania community, Winesburg community) that contrasts with the order (Winesburg, Pennsylvania) presented by Anderson in his short story. In her approach, Yasuko used a cause-and-effect pattern to show how the violent behavior of the Pennsylvania community accounts for the grotesque position that Biddlebaum occupies in Winesburg.

Yasuko's essay might be classified as an "analysis essay," or an essay that focuses on the study of one single element in relation to the whole. Her instructor might have considered other kinds of essays as well, such as the following examples:

1. A comparison-and-contrast essay discusses similarities and differences between elements in the same work or in different works.

    EXAMPLE: Compare and contrast the roles of the two communities in "Hands."

    or

    Compare and contrast the conflict between the individual and society in "Hands" and "Eveline."

2. A debate essay presents one or the other side of an argument.

    EXAMPLE: Take a position and explain whether individual rights should ever overshadow the claims of society. Support your arguments with examples from the texts discussed in class.

3. A reaction essay presents the reader's feelings and reactions about a work of literature or a literary issue.

    EXAMPLE: React to the statement that cities and places that are full of dislocated, grotesque people provide ideal settings for short stories. Use at least three of the texts discussed in class to support your arguments.

4. A combination essay combines several approaches. To write her analytical essay studying individualism and community in "Hands" (exploring one specific element in relation to the whole), Yasuko also used cause-and-effect (examination of the causes and the effects that are likely to result from them) as well as comparison and contrast (focus on the similarities and differences of two elements).

Guideline Four: Rough Draft with Peers' Comments

At this point, Yasuko wrote and revised several versions of her essay until she decided on a rough draft that she shared with some of her classmates. Here is Yasuko's essay, followed by an evaluation form supplied by her instructor and filled out by her peer editors.

Essay on Individualism and the Community

The conflict between individualism and community in "Hands" shows Biddlebaum's struggle against the two communities in which he lived: the Pennsylvania community and the Winesburg community. When viewed from this perspective, this conflict also shows that communities like Biddlebaum's Pennsylvania community use violence only against individuals who pose a threat to their stability. But what really happened in Pennsylvania was that one day one of Biddlebaum's students acted in a romantic way toward him, spreading rumors about his potential homosexuality. Then the boys' parents got together, and after making some inquiries about Biddlebaum's habits, hastily concluded that he was a threat to their youth. In my opinion, what happens to Biddlebaum in Pennsylvania throws some light on how communities respond to a potential threat against themselves.

It is a dissatisfied member of the community who leads his community in a hate-chase against Adolph Myers. No one in the Pennsylvania community dared to raise a voice in Biddlebaum's defense. Parents, in fact, disregarded Biddlebaum's individual rights. Ironically, even though Biddlebaum's hands become the focal point of his downfall, it's through them that Biddlebaum manages to communicate his love of humanity. Led by its violent rage against Biddlebaum, the community beat, kicked, and almost killed him.

After leaving Pennsylvania, twenty years later we find Biddlebaum settled in another community, the community of Winesburg in Ohio. He decided to go to Winesburg because he had an aunt who lived there. That is when he changed his original name of Adolph Myers to Biddlebaum, and made a living as a berry picker. After his aunt's death he lives completely alone. Biddlebaum was a berry picker who made only one friend, George Willard. In spite of their close relationship, there are times in which Biddlebaum and George do not feel comfortable with each other.

On one hand, the Winesburg community was proud of his ability to pick berries, but on the other hand, he was seen as weird and grotesque. However, the Winesburg community learns to accept Biddlebaum as a grotesque. This was shown in the opening paragraph of the story where Anderson presents Biddlebaum pacing up and down the veranda of his house.

Biddlebaum's mannerisms were made fun of by the youths and maidens, who managed to have a good laugh at his expense. At first the Winesburg community seems to react in a cruel way, but its reaction shows how Biddlebaum and his community unsettle each other.

From the point of view of the reader, who can see both communities, abusing and making fun of grotesque individuals like Biddlebaum made the Winesburg community feel confident and secure. However, unlike Biddlebaum's Winesburg community, his Pennsylvania community doesn't act in the same way. It is not violent. It is neither more sensitive nor enlightened than his Pennsylvania community. It would probably unleash the same kind of violence that his Pennsylvania community unleashed against him. The reason it didn't do so was that Biddlebaum never became a threat to that community. He isolated himself and was very careful not to mingle with anyone except George Willard.

My mother had also told me some stories about her small village in the Far East--horror tales about sons and daughters who were severely punished until they learned that individuals don't belong to themselves but to their communities. Such stories showed that what was at stake was not only the preservation of values and traditions, but also the community's defense of themselves against any kind of threat posed by their members.

Peer Editing Evaluation Form

WRITER: Yasuko Osahi

PEER EDITORS: Mary Anne Saboya, Gaby Jackson, Michael Hughes, Tony Spindola

1. *What does the writer want to say about the literary text in this paper? What aspects of the text does he or she focus on?*

    The writer wants to explore the conflict of individualism and community in "Hands." She focuses on how Biddlebaum relates to the two communities: the Winesburg and the Pennsylvania community.

2. *What kind of audience does the writer seem to be addressing? Which aspects of the paper might especially strike the audience? Why? Consider the writer's choice of subject, depth of information, point of view, tone, and voice.*

    Yasuko seems to be addressing her classmates and her instructors. Her thesis statement, "Communities use violence only against individuals who pose a threat to their stability," is powerful enough to strike her audience. Her choice of subject is good, but she needs to use more quotes to prove she is working close to the text. She also needs to soften the tone she uses in her essay.

3. *What are the strengths of the paper? How might the paper be revised to better fulfill the writer's purpose and meaning?*

    The strengths of the paper are Yasuko's choice of subject and her analysis of the two communities. Paragraphs 1, 3, and 4 need revision because at times she summarizes rather than interprets the story. Paragraphs 2 and 5 seem to go off track. Yasuko should rewrite them.

4. *Have you noticed any words and sentences that do not work? How would you rephrase them?*

    We noticed that in paragraph 5 she uses passive structures that are very vague. We would rephrase these sentences like this:
    - In the opening of the story, Anderson shows Biddlebaum pacing up and down the veranda of his house.
    - The youths and maidens made fun of him and managed to laugh at his expense.

5. *Other comments*

    Select a title that appeals to your readers.

Guideline Five: Revising

After reading her peers' comments on her rough draft, Yasuko knew that she would have to revise her paper and rewrite most of its paragraphs.

Yasuko revised her paper and handed it in to her instructor. A few days later, her instructor returned it with some marginal comments and an overall evaluation.

The Conflict of Individualism
and Community in "Hands"

*Be more
specific. See
"Strategies for
Revision" #5.*

*A powerful
thesis
statement. It
shows
psychological
depth.*

*Isn't your
opinion
implied in the
text? Have
you
considered the
role of the
narrator?*

*Is this
community
afraid of B.?
What does the
text suggest
about that?*

The conflict between individualism and community in "Hands" shows Biddlebaum's struggle against
two of the communities in which he lived: the Pennsylvania community and Winesburg community. When
viewed from this perspective, this conflict also
shows that communities like Biddlebaum's Pennsylvania community *tend to* use violence only against individuals who pose a threat to their stability. But
did Biddlebaum really pose a threat to the youth
of the Pennsylvania community? Does Anderson's
text present Biddlebaum as a homosexual who was
corrupting the Pennsylvania youth? Why is it that
Myers's Pennsylvania community reacted so violently
against him, while his second community, the one
in Winesburg, manages to establish a truce with
him? In my opinion, what happens to Biddlebaum in
Pennsylvania throws some light on how a community
responds to a potential threat against itself. *a new
¶?*

It is a dissatisfied member of the community
who leads his community in a hate-chase against
Adolph Myers. No one in the Pennsylvania
community dared to raise a voice in Biddlebaum's
defense. Parents, in fact, disregarded
Biddlebaum's individual rights. Led by its
violent rage against Biddlebaum, the community
beat, kicked, and almost killed him.

Anderson's text also suggests that it may be
fear or the spirit of preservation that controls
the action that the Pennsylvania townspeople take
against Biddlebaum. The community wanted to
defend itself against the schoolteacher. The
amount of violence it uses by "swearing and
throwing sticks and great balls of soft mud" at

him suggests that it feared Biddlebaum. If it got rid of him, it would also be able to eliminate the fear that he inspired. Once again the community would be able to restore its emotional balance.

Isn't this out of place? Either delete or rewrite it.

Ironically, even though Biddlebaum's hands become the focal point of his tragedy, and Biddlebaum himself "felt that the hands must be to blame" (292), it is through them that Biddlebaum manages to inspire his students to dream.

To consider Biddlebaum's position in Winesburg, Ohio, we have to ask whether Biddlebaum has really become a member of his community. The fact that he is a berry picker who contributes to the Winesburg economy does not seem to count because Biddlebaum "did not think of himself as in any way a part of the life of the town where he had lived for twenty years" (289). He was still an outsider who contrasted with the other berry pickers. However, unlike his Pennsylvania community, Biddlebaum's Winesburg community learns to accept him as "grotesque." In fact, Anderson's text opens with a description of how Adolph Myers, now Biddlebaum, an old and eccentric individual who nervously paces up and down the veranda of his shabby house, contrasts with the "youths and maidens" of Winesburg, Ohio.

This argument merits development. What about a quote?

Is there any thing in text that suggests that? Use quotes.

The fact that Biddlebaum and the "youths and maidens" unsettle each other seems to suggest that Biddlebaum will never become a real member of the Winesburg community. From the point of view of the reader, who can see both communities, abusing and making fun of grotesque individuals like Biddlebaum made the Winesburg community feel confident and secure. However, unlike Biddlebaum's Winesburg community, his Pennsylvania community

doesn't seem to act the same way. They are not
violent. They are neither more sensitive nor more
enlightened than his Pennsylvania community. They
would probably unleash the same kind of violence
that his Pennsylvania community unleashed against
him. The reason they don't do so is that
Biddlebaum never became a threat to the community.
He isolated himself and was very careful not to
mingle with anyone, except George Willard.

What about the ❡ on whom the real B. is? Check your outline.

My mother had also told me some stories about
her small village in the Far East––horror tales
about sons and daughters severely punished until
they learned that individuals don't belong to
themselves, but to their communities. Such

How does your conclusion tie in with "Hands?"

stories showed that what was at stake was not only
the preservation of values and traditions, but
also the community's defense of itself against any
kind of threat posed by its members.

Yasuko,
Even though you've made some good points in
your rough draft, your essay still needs a lot of
work. Put it aside for a day or two, but during
that time continue to read "Hands" to clarify
your ideas.
Start your revision by reading your text aloud.
Then develop your ❡/s more fully, use quotes to
support your arguments, and follow the
guidelines above.

After reading her instructor's comments, Yasuko rewrote and reorganized her paper. During this process, she consulted the strategies for revision described below.

Strategies for Revising the Literary Essay

1. **Select and Chose a Title Carefully**
    Select a title that describes or announces the topic without restating the thesis statement. Make sure that your title appeals to the reader.

2. **Replace Plot Summary with Analysis and Interpretation**
    Remember that all literary interpretations begin with critical observations. Thus, to avoid laying out a plot summary—or retelling the story—strive to use verbs that will assist you in achieving and maintaining the critical focus you need to write a literary essay.

explore	portray	include
analyze	argue	highlight
mention	refer	discuss
demonstrate	suggest	examine
show	illustrate	explain
reveal	emphasize	express
present	use	chronicle
write	indicate	outline

    EXAMPLE: In "Hands," Sherwood Anderson reveals how an individual becomes a potential threat to his community.

    "Hands" explores the conflict between individualism and society on several levels.

    Remember, however, that *purpose* and *audience* should always control your writing. Thus, if your presumed audience has not read the text, some plot summary would be necessary.

3. **Favor the Active Voice**
    The overuse of passive constructions—constructions with a subject that does not do the action or is acted upon—may weaken your sentences. Whenever possible, try to infuse energy and conviction into your sentences by using the active voice.

    PASSIVE: Biddlebaum's mannerisms are made fun of by the "youths and maidens" of Winesburg.

    ACTIVE: The "youths and maidens" of Winesburg make fun of Biddlebaum.

    PASSIVE: The conflict between the individual and society is explored in the opening of the story.

    ACTIVE: The opening of "Hands" explores the conflict between individual and society.

4. **Use the Present Tense to Analyze Literary Texts**
   Like other works of art, such as paintings, literary texts possess a time of their own. In a sense, they live forever, because they live outside time. Consequently, you should use the present tense to analyze texts and to describe the underlying action of their plots.

   EXAMPLE: **The Pennsylvania community in "Hands" feels more** confident and secure if it can eliminate individuals like Biddlebaum.

   "Hands" **presents** George Willard as Biddlebaum's only friend.

5. **Establish a Clear Context in Your First Paragraph**
   Identify the title, author, and characters in the work you are analyzing as if you were writing not only for your classmates and instructor but for a broader audience. This is especially important when you write the first paragraph of your essay.

   VAGUE: "Hands" portrays the tension that may arise between an individual and his community.

   REVISED: "Hands," one of Sherwood Anderson's stories in *Winesburg, Ohio,* portrays the tension that arises between an individual, Biddlebaum, and his community.

6. **Revise for Content and Organization**
   Your focus here should be the overall development of the essay. Concentrate on the title, thesis statement, supporting ideas, and organization.

   ◆ Is the title of your essay suggestive?
   ◆ Is the thesis clear and persuasive?
   ◆ Is your essay logically organized?

   Consider whether the opening paragraph introduces the topic and whether the conclusion summarizes the main ideas or offers an overall evaluation of the thesis. If necessary, rewrite your thesis statement and rearrange the major sections of your essay by adding, deleting, condensing, or changing the order of its various elements.

7. **Paragraph Organization**

   ◆ Relate each paragraph to the thesis of the essay.
   ◆ Make the main idea of each paragraph clear.
   ◆ See that the parts of the paragraph relate to each other.
   ◆ Make your paragraph more interesting by using rhetorical questions, quotations, examples, and illustrations that will keep the reader's attention.

8. **Revise for Purpose and Audience**
   Ask yourself whether your essay fulfills its purpose to inform, entertain, persuade, or call its readers to action.

◆ Who are your readers?
◆ Is your essay appropriate for your readers?

Put yourself in the intended reader's place, and check your paper for clarity and precision of meaning from the reader's point of view.

9. **Revise for Tone**

◆ What kind of attitude have you expressed in presenting your topic to your reader?
◆ Are you writing as an authority on your subject?
◆ Is your writing too formal or too informal? Is it ironic, direct?
◆ What kind of language are you using to express this tone?

Put yourself in the place of your intended reader, and listen to the sound of the speaking voice of your text.

Guideline Six: Editing and Preparing Your Manuscript

After revision, you may start to focus on the presentation of your essay. In this phase of the writing process, you should consider wordiness, redundancy, grammatical errors, mechanical problems (spelling, punctuation, capital letters, abbreviations), and the format required for preparing your manuscript. Bear in mind that the ear can detect flaws that the eye misses. Therefore, try reading your text aloud to catch mistakes that emerge not so much on the broader level of paragraph organization but on the more local level of the sentence or phrase.

See guidelines for title, margins, paging, source citations, in the section "Researching Literary Sources" (pages 1002–1025). If your school has a tutoring program, your instructor may ask you to work with a writing tutor to revise your text for clarity.

Writing the Final Draft

The final draft of Yasuko's essay on "Hands" follows. Do you consider her essay strong and effective enough? Would you suggest any further revision?

Osahi 1

Yasuko Osahi

Professor Jackson

English Composition II

May 27, 1994

The Conflict of Individualism

and Community in "Hands"

The conflict between individualism and community in Sherwood Anderson's short story
"Hands" shows the struggle of one individual--
the protagonist, Wing Biddlebaum, or Adolph
Myers--against two main communities: the Pennsylvania community and the Winesburg community.
When viewed from this perspective, this conflict also shows that communities like Biddlebaum's Pennsylvania community tend to use
violence against individuals who pose a threat
to their stability. But did Biddlebaum really
pose a threat to the youth of the Pennsylvania
community? Does Anderson's text present Biddlebaum as a homosexual who was corrupting the
Pennsylvania youth? Why is it that Myers's Pennsylvania community reacted so violently against
him, while his second community, the one in
Winesburg, manages to establish a truce with
him?

The narrator's description of what happened in Biddlebaum's Pennsylvania community
throws much light on how a community responds
to a potential threat against itself:

Osahi 2

> With lanterns in their hands a dozen
> men came to the door of the house
> where he lived alone and commanded
> that he dress and come forth. It
> was raining and one of the men had a
> rope in his hands. They had intended
> to hang the schoolmaster, but some-
> thing in his figure, so small, white,
> and pitiful, touched their hearts and
> they let him escape. (292)

It is through the narrator's eyes that we see
how any dissatisfied member of a community,
like one of Biddlebaum's students, can lead his
community in a hate-chase if he is clever
enough to unleash some of the community's covert fears:

> A half-witted boy of the school
> became enamored of the young master.
> . . . Strange, hideous accusations
> fell from his loose-hung lips.
> Through the Pennsylvania town went a
> shiver. Hidden, shadowy doubts that
> had been in men's minds concerning
> Adolph Myers were galvanized into be-
> liefs. (291)

Anderson's text also suggests that it may
be fear or the spirit of preservation that controls the action that the Pennsylvania townspeople take against Biddlebaum. The community
wanted to defend itself against the school-

Osahi 3

teacher. The amount of violence it uses by "swearing and throwing sticks and great balls of soft mud" at him suggests that it feared Biddlebaum. If it got rid of him, it would also be able to eliminate the fear that his hands inspired. Once again the community would be able to restore its emotional balance. Ironically, even though Biddlebaum's "hands" became the focal point of his tragedy, and Biddlebaum himself "felt that the hands must be to blame" (292), it is through them that Biddlebaum manages to inspire his students to dream: "under the caress of his hands doubt and disbelief went out of the minds of the boys and they began also to dream" (291).

To consider Biddlebaum's position in Winesburg, Ohio, we have to ask whether Biddlebaum has really become a member of his community. The fact that he is a berry picker who contributes to the Winesburg economy does not seem to count because Biddlebaum "did not think of himself as in any way a part of the life of the town where he had lived for twenty years" (289). He was still an outsider who contrasted with the other berry pickers. However, unlike his Pennsylvania community, Biddlebaum's Winesburg community learns to accept him as a "grotesque." In fact, Anderson's text opens with a description of how Adolph Myers, now Biddlebaum, an old and eccentric individual who

Osahi 4

nervously paces up and down the veranda of his
shabby house, contrasts with the "youths and
maidens" of Winesburg, Ohio. The fact that Biddlebaum and the "youths and maidens" unsettle
each other seems to suggest that Biddlebaum
will never become a real member of the Winesburg community.

From the point of view of the reader, who
can see the reality of both communities, the
Winesburg "youths and maidens" also seem to react in a cruel way, by making fun of Biddlebaum's mannerisms and by having a good laugh at
his expense. However, they don't seem to act
out of fear. Their critique of Biddlebaum
seems to give them just the sense of power
they need to feel confident and secure about
themselves: "'Oh, you Wing Biddlebaum, comb
your hair, it's falling into your eyes,' commanded the voice to the man, who was bald and
whose nervous little hands fiddled about the
bare white forehead as though arranging a mass
of tangled locks" (289). Biddlebaum, the weird
and eccentric outsider, seems to reaffirm the
feelings that they belong in their own community. In some ways, the Winesburg community is
neither better nor more civilized than Biddlebaum's Pennsylvania community. If driven by
the fear of a potential threat to its stability, it might probably unleash the same kind of
violence against people.

Osahi 5

Neither community ever learns who Biddlebaum really is. Through Anderson's narrator, however, the reader gets a good glimpse of his real personality. The narrator stresses Biddlebaum's childlike innocence and his love of humanity. Last, but not least, the narrator also casts Biddlebaum in the figure of a holy man. The religious images at the end of the text presenting Biddlebaum "like a priest engaged in some service of his church" (292) suggest that Biddlebaum possesses the sensibility of a religious man--one that neither community would be able to appreciate.

"Hands" brought to my mind some of my mother's stories about her small village in Japan. Those horror tales portrayed sons and daughters who were severely punished when they refused to conform. For me, such tales also show that what was at stake, as much in my mother's village as in the communities in "Hands," was not only the preservation of traditional values but the communities' defense of themselves against individuals who are different and who pose a threat to their stability.

Work Cited

Anderson, Sherwood. "Hands." <u>Literature Across Cultures.</u> Ed. Sheena Gillespie et al. Boston: Allyn and Bacon, 1993.

PART ONE

Origins and Insights

Fiction

Maggie: A Girl of the Streets, Stephen Crane ◆ *Roman Fever*, Edith Wharton ◆ *First Confession*, Frank O'Connor ◆ *A Power Struggle*, Bessie Head ◆ *The Watch*, Elie Wiesel ◆ *The Sky Is Gray*, Ernest J. Gaines ◆ *The Visit Home*, Rosemary Cho Leyson

Poetry

Chained Time, Luis Rodriguez ◆ *The Father Poem Two*, Sue Doro ◆ *The Hatmaker*, Keith Gilyard ◆ *Going Home*, Maurice Kenny ◆ *During a Son's Dangerous Illness*, Denise Levertov ◆ *Lost Sister*, Cathy Song ◆ *Song for My Name*, Linda Hogan ◆ *Moving Away [1]*, Gary Soto ◆ *Moving Away [2]*, Gary Soto ◆ *Runagate Runagate*, Robert Hayden ◆ *Nikki-Rosa*, Nikki Giovanni ◆ *The Jewish Cemetery at Newport*, Henry Wadsworth Longfellow ◆ *Fern Hill*, Dylan Thomas ◆ *A Breeze Swept Through*, Luci Tapahonso ◆ *This Is the Poem I Never Meant to Write*, Colleen J. McElroy ◆ *It's Something Our Family Has Always Done*, Wing Tek Lum ◆ *warm heart contains life*, Evangelina Vigil ◆ *Fishermen*, James A. Emanuel ◆ *What My Child Learns of the Sea*, Audre Lorde

Drama

The Tragedy of Hamlet, Prince of Denmark, William Shakespeare

The artist's imagination has always been captivated by the idea of the past and its relationship to the present. Stories from the oral traditions of ancient cultures as well as our own evoke the powers and mysteries of the past by portraying a time in which myths, fables, legends, and archetypes dictated the values of human actions within the community. The ritual of storytelling was an integral part of communal life, as tribe members from the oldest to the youngest listened to, recalled, or retold stories about creation, good and evil, war and peace, life and death.

How can we reach and understand the past? What can we learn from it? Why are memories an important part of our private and communal selves? Some writers in Part One begin with what the author Toni Morrison calls "sites of memory"—places that have affected these writers' lives because of emotional or sensory associations with them. The speaker in "Fern Hill," for example, takes us back to the Welsh landscapes and summer experiences that framed his childhood, and the speaker in "Moving Away" reminds his brother and sister of their first home and the family events there that shaped their present lives.

Historical places such as colonial Williamsburg, Ellis Island, and Martin Luther King's Memorial, or even photographs of a grandparent's birthplace, are also important sites of memory. They often motivate us to listen to the voices of the past or to search for our roots in an attempt to establish a dialogue with our past selves as we explore further our own terrain.

The past has been variously defined as a "foreign country," a "bucket of ashes," a "field of errors and ignorance," or a temporal continuum with the power "to delight and instruct." As you examine various aspects of the past in Part One texts, remember that we can try to understand our personal and historical pasts only with the aid of our memory and our imagination. As the writer Lynne Sharon Schwartz reminds us, "Memory is something we reconstruct, something we create. Memory is a story we make up from snatches of the past."

People who have influenced our lives are often important catalysts in reconstructing and understanding our stories. The protagonist in "First Confession," for instance, remembers with gratitude the Irish priest who offered him forgiveness instead of punishment, while the young son in "The Sky Is Gray" reflects on his mother's comment "You not a bum . . . You a Man."

To what extent is it important also to try to understand our collective pasts? Is it plausible to say that our identity and our individual lives are sometimes shaped by a fixed historical reality? Some of the writers in Part One speculate about these questions by examining the conditions under which people become particularly aware of historical identities. Robert Hayden's poem "Runagate Runagate," for example, reconstructs what it means to be a renegade caught in the grim historical reality that shaped the destiny of African slaves in the United States.

In "The Watch," Holocaust survivor Elie Wiesel explores his protagonist's attempt to retrieve a watch that symbolizes his past, "the soul and memory of that time" of war and holocaust. "Once more," says the protagonist as he attempts to defy time and to retrieve the past, "I am the bar mitzvah child. . . . I get ready to re-enact the scene my memory recalls."

The drama *Hamlet* offers another example of how men and women can identify themselves with the past. One major question you will explore is why the Danish prince wavers between remembering and forgetting the past that seems to link him and the political future of Denmark. What do people do when they realize that they carry the burden of the past with them or that the past can become an obstacle to their growth and to a redefinition of themselves?

In texts such as "A Power Struggle" and "Song for My Name," we encounter yet another aspect of the past in myths that attempt to voice the collective and private truths of humanity. Bessie Head's story of the Tlabina clan presents the origin of the power struggle between two brothers as a cosmological myth based on the primeval conflict between the principles of good and evil, and in Hogan's poem the speaker constructs a private myth to help her understand the terms of her existence—from her birth to the mystery of her death.

As you explore these and other selections from the sites of memory, consider them as catalysts for your own recollections and discoveries of your personal and communal past, for as writer Oscar Wilde reminds us, "Memory is the diary we carry about with us."

Stephen Crane

Maggie
A Girl of the Streets

1

A very little boy stood upon a heap of gravel for the honor of Rum Alley. He was throwing stones at howling urchins from Devil's Row who were circling madly about the heap and pelting at him.

His infantile countenance was livid with fury. His small body was writhing in the delivery of great, crimson oaths.

"Run, Jimmie, run! Dey'll get yehs," screamed a retreating Rum Alley child.

"Naw," responded Jimmie with a valiant roar, "dese micks can't make me run."

Howls of renewed wrath went up from Devil's Row throats. Tattered gamins on the right made a furious assault on the gravel heap. On their small, convulsed faces there shone the grins of true assassins. As they charged, they threw stones and cursed in shrill chorus.

The little champion of Rum Alley stumbled precipitately down the other side. His coat had been torn to shreds in a scuffle, and his hat was gone. He had bruises on twenty parts of his body, and blood was dripping from a cut in his head. His wan features wore a look of a tiny, insane demon.

On the ground, children from Devil's Row closed in on their antagonist. He crooked his left arm defensively about his head and fought with cursing fury. The little boys ran to and fro, dodging, hurling stones and swearing in barbaric trebles.

From a window of an apartment house that upreared its form from amid squat, ignorant stables, there leaned a curious woman. Some laborers, unloading a scow at a dock at the river, paused for a moment and regarded the fight. The engineer of a passive tugboat hung lazily to a railing and watched. Over on the Island,* a worm of yellow convicts came from the shadow of a grey ominous building and crawled slowly along the river's bank.

A stone had smashed into Jimmie's mouth. Blood was bubbling over his chin and down upon his ragged shirt. Tears made furrows on his dirt-stained cheeks. His thin legs had begun to tremble and turn weak, causing his small body to reel. His roaring curses of the first part of the fight had changed to a blasphemous chatter.

---

* Blackwell's Island, in the East River of Manhattan, on which New York City prisons were maintained.

In the yells of the whirling mob of Devil's Row children there were notes of joy like songs of triumphant savagery. The little boys seemed to leer gloatingly at the blood upon the other child's face.

Down the avenue came boastfully sauntering a lad of sixteen years, although the chronic sneer of an ideal manhood already sat upon his lips. His hat was tipped with an air of challenge over his eye. Between his teeth, a cigar stump was tilted at the angle of defiance. He walked with a certain swing of the shoulders which appalled the timid. He glanced over into the vacant lot in which the little raving boys from Devil's Row seethed about the shrieking and tearful child from Rum Alley.

"Gee!" he murmured with interest, "A scrap. Gee!"

He strode over to the cursing circle, swinging his shoulders in a manner which denoted that he held victory in his fists. He approached at the back of one of the most deeply engaged of the Devil's Row children.

"Ah, what deh hell," he said, and smote the deeply-engaged one on the back of the head. The little boy fell to the ground and gave a hoarse, tremendous howl. He scrambled to his feet, and perceiving, evidently, the size of his assailant, ran quickly off, shouting alarms. The entire Devil's Row party followed him. They came to a stand a short distance away and yelled taunting oaths at the boy with the chronic sneer. The latter, momentarily, paid no attention to them.

"What deh hell, Jimmie?" he asked of the small champion.

Jimmie wiped his blood-wet features with his sleeve.

"Well, it was dis way, Pete, see! I was goin' teh lick dat Riley kid and dey all pitched on me."

Some Rum Alley children now came forward. The party stood for a moment exchanging vainglorious remarks with Devil's Row. A few stones were thrown at long distances, and words of challenge passed between small warriors. Then the Rum Alley contingent turned slowly in the direction of their home street. They began to give, each to each, distorted versions of the fight. Causes of retreat in particular cases were magnified. Blows dealt in the fight were enlarged to catapultian power, and stones thrown were alleged to have hurtled with infinite accuracy. Valor grew strong again, and the little boys began to swear with great spirit.

"Ah, we blokies kin lick deh hull damn Row," said a child, swaggering.

Little Jimmie was striving to stanch the flow of blood from his cut lips. Scowling, he turned upon the speaker.

"Ah, where deh hell was yeh when I was doin' all deh fightin'?" he demanded. "Youse kids makes me tired."

"Ah, go ahn," replied the other argumentatively.

Jimmie replied with heavy contempt. "Ah, youse can't fight, Blue Billie!" I kin lick yeh wid one han'."

"Ah, go ahn," replied Billie again.

"Ah," said Jimmie threateningly.

"Ah," said the other in the same tone.

They struck at each other, clinched, and rolled over on the cobble stones.

"Smash 'im, Jimmie, kick deh damn guts out of 'im," yelled Pete, the lad with the chronic sneer, in tones of delight.

The small combatants pounded and kicked, scratched and tore. They began to weep and their curses struggled in their throats with sobs. The other little boys clasped their hands and wriggled their legs in excitement. They formed a bobbing circle about the pair.

A tiny spectator was suddenly agitated.

"Cheese it, Jimmy, cheese it! Here comes yer fader," he yelled.

The circle of little boys instantly parted. They drew away and waited in ecstatic awe for that which was about to happen. The two little boys fighting in the modes of four thousand years ago, did not hear the warning.

Up the avenue there plodded slowly a man with sullen eyes. He was carrying a dinner pail and smoking an apple-wood pipe.

As he neared the spot where the little boys strove, he regarded them listlessly. But suddenly he roared an oath and advanced upon the rolling fighters.

"Here, you Jim, git up, yer now, while I belt yer life out, you damned disorderly brat."

He began to kick into the chaotic mass on the ground. The boy Billie felt a heavy boot strike his head. He made a furious effort and disentangled himself from Jimmie. He tottered away, damning.

Jimmie arose painfully from the ground and confronting his father, began to curse him. His parent kicked him. "Come home, now," he cried, "an' stop yer jawin', er I'll lam the everlasting head off yehs."

They departed. The man paced placidly along with the apple-wood emblem of serenity between his teeth. The boy followed a dozen feet in the rear. He swore luridly, for he felt that it was degradation for one who aimed to be some vague soldier, or a man of blood with a sort of sublime license, to be taken home by a father.

2

Eventually they entered into a dark region where, from a careening building, a dozen gruesome doorways gave up loads of babies to the street and gutter. A wind of early autumn raised yellow dust from cobbles and swirled it against an hundred windows. Long streamers of garments fluttered from fire-escapes. In all unhandy places there were buckets, brooms, rags and bottles. In the street infants played or fought with other infants or sat stupidly in the way of vehicles. Formidable women, with uncombed hair and disordered dress, gossiped while leaning on railings, or screamed in frantic quarrels. Withered persons, in curious postures of submission to something, sat smoking pipes in obscure corners. A thousand odors of cooking food came forth to the street. The building quivered and creaked from the weight of humanity stamping about in its bowels.

A small ragged girl dragged a red, bawling infant along the crowded ways. He was hanging back, baby-like, bracing his wrinkled, bare legs.

The little girl cried out: "Ah, Tommie, come ahn. Dere's Jimmie and fader. Don't be a-pullin' me back."

She jerked the baby's arm impatiently. He fell on his face, roaring. With a second jerk she pulled him to his feet, and they went on. With the obstinacy of his order, he protested against being dragged in a chosen direction. He made heroic endeavors to keep on his legs, denounce his sister and consume a bit of orange peeling which he chewed between the times of his infantile orations.

As the sullen-eyed man, followed by the blood-covered boy, drew near, the little girl burst into reproachful cries. "Ah, Jimmie, youse bin fightin' agin."

The urchin swelled disdainfully.[2]

"Ah, what deh hell, Mag. See?"

The little girl upbraided him, "Youse allus fightin', Jimmie, an' yeh knows it puts mudder out when yehs come home half dead, an' it's like we'll all get a poundin'."

She began to weep. The babe threw back his head and roared at his prospects.

"Ah, what deh hell!" cried Jimmie. "Shut up er I'll smack yer mout'. See?"

As his sister continued her lamentations, he suddenly swore and struck her. The little girl reeled and, recovering herself, burst into tears and quaveringly cursed him. As she slowly retreated her brother advanced dealing her cuffs. The father heard and turned about.

"Stop that, Jim, d'yeh hear? Leave yer sister alone on the street. It's like I can never beat any sense into yer damned wooden head."

The urchin raised his voice in defiance to his parent and continued his attacks. The babe bawled tremendously, protesting with great violence. During his sister's hasty manoeuvres, he was dragged by the arm.

Finally the procession plunged into one of the gruesome doorways. They crawled up dark stairways and along cold, gloomy halls. At last the father pushed open a door and they entered a lighted room in which a large woman was rampant.

She stopped in a career[3] from a seething stove to a pan-covered table. As the father and children filed in she peered at them.

"Eh, what? Been fightin' agin, by Gawd!" She threw herself upon Jimmie. The urchin tried to dart behind the others and in the scuffle the babe, Tommie, was knocked down. He protested with his usual vehemence, because they had bruised his tender shins against a table leg.

The mother's massive shoulders heaved with anger. Grasping the urchin by the neck and shoulder she shook him until he rattled. She dragged him to an unholy sink, and, soaking a rag in water, began to scrub his lacerated face with it. Jimmie screamed in pain and tried to twist his shoulders out of the clasp of the huge arms.

The babe sat on the floor watching the scene, his face in contortions like that of a woman at a tragedy. The father, with a newly-ladened pipe in his mouth, crouched on a backless chair near the stove. Jimmie's cries annoyed him. He turned about and bellowed at his wife:

"Let the damned kid alone for a minute, will yeh, Mary? Yer allus poundin' 'im. When I come nights I can't git no rest 'cause yer allus poundin' a kid. Let up, d'yeh hear? Don't be allus poundin' a kid."

The woman's operations on the urchin instantly increased in violence. At last she tossed him to a corner where he limply lay cursing and weeping.

The wife put her immense hands on her hips and with a chieftain-like stride approached her husband.

"Ho," she said, with a great grunt of contempt. "An' what in the devil are you stickin' your nose for?"

The babe crawled under the table and, turning, peered out cautiously. The ragged girl retreated and the urchin in the corner drew his legs carefully beneath him.

The man puffed his pipe calmly and put his great mudded boots on the back part of the stove.

"Go teh hell," he murmured, tranquilly.

The woman screamed and shook her fists before her husband's eyes. The rough yellow of her face and neck flared suddenly crimson. She began to howl.

He puffed imperturbably at his pipe for a time, but finally arose and began to look out at the window into the darkening chaos of back yards.

"You've been drinkin', Mary," he said. "You'd better let up on the bot', ol' woman, or you'll git done."

"You're a liar. I ain't had a drop," she roared in reply.

They had a lurid altercation, in which they damned each other's souls with frequence.

The babe was staring out from under the table, his small face working in his excitement.

The ragged girl went stealthily over to the corner where the urchin lay.

"Are yehs hurted much, Jimmie?" she whispered timidly.

"Not a damn bit! See?" growled the little boy.

"Will I wash deh blood?"

"Naw!"

"Will I"—

"When I catch dat Riley kid I'll break 'is face! Dat's right! See?"

He turned his face to the wall as if resolved to grimly bide his time.

In the quarrel between husband and wife, the woman was victor. The man grabbed his hat and rushed from the room, apparently determined upon a vengeful drunk. She followed to the door and thundered at him as he made his way down stairs.

She returned and stirred up the room until her children were bobbing about like bubbles.

"Git outa deh way," she persistently bawled, waving feet with their dishevelled shoes near the heads of her children. She shrouded herself, puffing and snorting, in a cloud of steam at the stove, and eventually extracted a frying pan full of potatoes that hissed.

She flourished it. "Come teh yer suppers, now," she cried with sudden exasperation. "Hurry up, now, er I'll help yeh!"

The children scrambled hastily. With prodigious clatter they arranged themselves at table. The babe sat with his feet dangling high from a precarious infant chair and gorged his small stomach. Jimmie forced, with feverish rapidity, the grease-enveloped pieces between his wounded lips. Maggie with side glances of fear of interruption, ate like a small pursued tigress.

The mother sat blinking at them. She delivered reproaches, swallowed potatoes and drank from a yellow-brown bottle. After a time her mood changed and she wept as she carried little Tommie into another room and laid him to sleep with his fists doubled in an old quilt of faded red and green grandeur. Then she came and moaned by the stove. She rocked to and fro upon a chair, shedding tears and crooning miserably to the two children about their "poor mother" and "yer fader, damn 'is soul."

The little girl plodded between the table and the chair with a dishpan on it. She tottered on her small legs beneath burdens of dishes.

Jimmie sat nursing his various wounds. He cast furtive glances at his mother. His practised eye perceived her gradually emerge from a muddled mist of sentiment until her brain burned in drunken heat. He sat breathless.

Maggie broke a plate.

The mother started to her feet as if propelled.

"Good Gawd," she howled. Her eyes glittered on her child with sudden hatred. The fervent red of her face turned almost to purple. The little boy ran to the halls, shrieking like a monk in an earthquake.

He floundered about in darkness until he found the stairs. He stumbled, panic-stricken, to the next floor. An old woman opened a door. A light behind her threw a flare on the urchin's quivering face.

"Eh, Gawd, child, what is it dis time? Is yer fader beatin' yer mudder, or yer mudder beatin' yer fader?"

3

Jimmie and the old woman listened long in the hall. Above the muffled roar of conversation, the dismal wailings of babies at night, the thumping of feet in unseen corridors and rooms, mingled with the sound of varied hoarse shoutings in the street and the rattling of wheels over cobbles, they heard the screams of the child and the roars of the mother die away to a feeble moaning and a subdued bass muttering.

The old woman was a gnarled and leathery personage who could don, at will, an expression of great virtue. She possessed a small musicbox capable of one tune, and a collection of "God bless yehs" pitched in assorted keys of fervency. Each day she took a position upon the stones of Fifth Avenue, where she crooked her legs under her and crouched immovable and hideous, like an idol. She received daily a small sum in pennies. It was contributed, for the most part, by persons who did not make their homes in that vicinity.

Once, when a lady had dropped her purse on the sidewalk, the gnarled woman had grabbed it and smuggled it with great dexterity beneath her cloak. When she was arrested she had cursed the lady into a partial swoon, and with her aged limbs, twisted from rheumatism, had almost kicked the stomach out of a huge policeman whose conduct upon that occasion she referred to when she said: "The police, damn 'em."

"Eh, Jimmie, it's cursed shame," she said. "Go, now, like a dear an' buy me a can, an' if yer mudder raises 'ell all night yehs can sleep here."

Jimmie took a tendered tin-pail and seven pennies and departed. He passed into the side door of a saloon and went to the bar. Straining up on his toes he raised the pail and pennies as high as his arms would let him. He saw two hands thrust down and take them. Directly the same hands let down the filled pail and he left.

In front of the gruesome doorway he met a lurching figure. It was his father, swaying about on uncertain legs.

"Give me deh can. See?" said the man, threateningly.

"Ah, come off! I got dis can fer dat ol' woman an' it 'ud be dirt teh swipe it. See?" cried Jimmie.

The father wrenched the pail from the urchin. He grasped it in both hands and lifted it to his mouth. He glued his lips to the under edge and tilted his head. His hairy throat swelled until it seemed to grow near his chin. There was a tremendous gulping movement and the beer was gone.

The man caught his breath and laughed. He hit his son on the head with the empty pail. As it rolled clanging into the street, Jimmie began to scream and kicked repeatedly at his father's shins.

"Look at deh dirt what yeh done me," he yelled. "Deh ol' woman 'ill be raisin' hell."

He retreated to the middle of the street, but the man did not pursue. He staggered toward the door.

"I'll club hell outa yeh when I ketch yeh," he shouted, and disappeared.

During the evening he had been standing against a bar drinking whiskies and declaring to all comers, confidentially: "My home reg'lar livin' hell! Damndes' place! Reg'lar hell! Why do I come an' drin' whisk' here thish way? 'Cause home reg'lar livin' hell!"

Jimmie waited a long time in the street and then crept warily up through the building. He passed with great caution the door of the gnarled woman, and finally stopped outside his home and listened.

He could hear his mother moving heavily about among the furniture of the room. She was chanting in a mournful voice, occasionally interjecting bursts of volcanic wrath at the father, who, Jimmie judged, had sunk down on the floor or in a corner.

"Why deh blazes don' chere try teh keep Jim from fightin'? I'll break yer jaw," she suddenly bellowed.

The man mumbled with drunken indifference. "Ah, wha'deh hell. W'a's odds? Wha' makes kick?"

"Because he tears 'is clothes, yeh damn fool," cried the woman in supreme wrath.

The husband seemed to become aroused. "Go teh hell," he thundered fiercely in reply. There was a crash against the door and something broke into clattering fragments. Jimmie partially suppressed a howl and darted down the stairway. Below he paused and listened. He beard howls and curses, groans and shrieks, confusingly in chorus as if a battle were raging. With all was the crash of splintering furniture. The eyes of the urchin glared in fear that one of them would discover him.

Curious faces appeared in door-ways, and whispered comments, passed to and fro. "Ol' Johnson's raisin' hell agin."

Jimmie stood until the noises ceased and the other inhabitants of the tenement had all yawned and shut their doors. Then he crawled upstairs with the caution of an invader of a panther den. Sounds of labored breathing came through the broken door-panels. He pushed the door open and entered, quaking.

A glow from the fire threw red hues over the bare floor, the cracked and soiled plastering, and the overturned and broken furniture.

In the middle of the floor lay his mother asleep. In one corner of the room his father's limp body hung across the seat of a chair.

The urchin stole forward. He began to shiver in dread of awakening his parents. His mother's great chest was heaving painfully. Jimmy paused and looked down at her. Her face was inflamed and swollen from drinking. Her yellow brows shaded eye-lids that had grown blue. Her tangled hair tossed in waves over her forehead. Her mouth was set in the same lines of vindictive hatred that it had, perhaps, borne during the fight. Her bare, red arms were thrown out above her head in positions of exhaustion, something, mayhap, like those of a sated villain.

The urchin bended over his mother. He was fearful lest she should open her eyes, and the dread within him was so strong, that he could not forbear to stare, but hung as if fascinated over the woman's grim face.

Suddenly her eyes opened. The urchin found himself looking straight into that expression, which, it would seem, had the power to change his blood to salt. He howled piercingly and fell backward.

The woman floundered for a moment, tossed her arms about her head as if in combat, and again began to snore.

Jimmie crawled back in the shadows and waited. A noise in the next room had followed his cry at the discovery that his mother was awake. He grovelled in the gloom, the eyes from out his drawn face riveted upon the intervening door.

He heard it creak, and then the sound of a small voice came to him. "Jimmie! Jimmie! Are yehs dere?" it whispered. The urchin started. The thin, white face of his sister looked at him from the door-way of the other room. She crept to him across the floor.

The father had not moved, but lay in the same death-like sleep. The mother writhed in uneasy slumber, her chest wheezing as if she were in the agonies of strangulation. Out at the window a florid moon was peering over dark roofs, and in the distance the waters of a river glimmered pallidly.

The small frame of the ragged girl was quivering. Her features were haggard from weeping, and her eyes gleamed from fear. She grasped the urchin's arm in her little trembling hands and they huddled in a corner. The eyes of both were drawn, by some force, to stare at the woman's face, for they thought she need only to awake and all fiends would come from below.

They crouched until the ghost-mists of dawn appeared at the window, drawing close to the panes, and looking in at the prostrate, heaving body of the mother.

4

The babe, Tommie, died. He went away in a white, insignificant coffin, his small waxen hand clutching a flower that the girl, Maggie, had stolen from an Italian.

She and Jimmie lived.

The inexperienced fibres of the boy's eyes were hardened at an early age. He became a young man of leather. He lived some red years without laboring. During that time his sneer became chronic. He studied human nature in the gutter, and found it no worse than he thought he had reason to believe it. He never conceived a respect for the world, because he had begun with no idols that it had smashed.

He clad his soul in armor by means of happening hilariously in at a mission church where a man composed his sermons of "yous." While they got warm at the stove, he told his hearers just where he calculated they stood with the Lord. Many of the sinners were impatient over the pictured depths of their degradation. They were waiting for soup-tickets.

A reader of words of wind-demons might have been able to see the portions of a dialogue pass to and fro between the exhorter and his hearers.

"You are damned," said the preacher. And the reader of sounds might have seen the reply go forth from the ragged people: "Where's our soup?"

Jimmie and a companion sat in a rear seat and commented upon the things that didn't concern them, with all the freedom of English gentlemen. When they grew thirsty and went out their minds confused the speaker with Christ.

Momentarily, Jimmie was sullen with thoughts of a hopeless altitude where grew fruit. His companion said that if he should ever meet God he would ask for a million dollars and a bottle of beer.

Jimmie's occupation for a long time was to stand on streetcorners and watch the world go by, dreaming blood-red dreams at the passing of pretty women. He menaced mankind at the intersections of streets.

On the corners he was in life and of life. The world was going on and he was there to perceive it.[4]

He maintained a belligerent attitude toward all well-dressed men. To him fine raiment was allied to weakness, and all good coats covered faint hearts. He and his order were kings, to a certain extent, over the men of untarnished clothes, because these latter dreaded, perhaps, to be either killed or laughed at.

Above all things he despised obvious Christians and ciphers with the chrysan-themums[5] of aristocracy in their button-holes. He considered himself above both of these classes. He was afraid of neither the devil nor the leader of society.

When he had a dollar in his pocket his satisfaction with existence was the greatest thing in the world. So, eventually, he felt obliged to work. His father died and his mother's years were divided up into periods of thirty days.

He became a truck driver. He was given the charge of a painstaking pair of horses and a large rattling truck. He invaded the turmoil and tumble of the down-town streets and learned to breath maledictory defiance at the police who occasionally used to climb up, drag him from his perch and beat him.

In the lower part of the city he daily involved himself in hideous tangles. If he and his team chanced to be in the rear he preserved a demeanor of serenity, crossing his legs and bursting forth into yells when foot passengers took dangerous dives beneath the noses of his champing horses. He smoked his pipe calmly for he knew that his pay was marching on.

If in the front and the key-truck of chaos, he entered terrifically into the quarrel that was raging to and fro among the drivers on their high seats, and sometimes roared oaths and violently got himself arrested.

After a time his sneer grew so that it turned its glare upon all things. He became so sharp that he believed in nothing. To him the police were always actuated by malignant impulses and the rest of the world was composed, for the most part, of despicable creatures who were all trying to take advantage of him and with whom, in defense, he was obliged to quarrel on all possible occasions. He himself occupied a down-trodden position that had a private but distinct element of grandeur in its isolation.

The most complete cases of aggravated idiocy were, to his mind, rampant upon the front platforms of all of the street cars. At first his tongue strove with these beings, but he eventually was superior. He became immured like an African cow. In him grew a majestic contempt for those strings of street-cars that followed him like intent bugs.

He fell into the habit, when starting on a long journey, of fixing his eye on a high and distant object, commanding his horses to begin, and then going into a sort of a trance of observation. Multitudes of drivers might howl in his rear, and passengers might load him with opprobrium, he would not awaken until some blue policeman turned red and began to frenziedly tear bridles and beat the soft noses of the responsible horses.

When he paused to contemplate the attitude of the police toward himself and his fellows, he believed that they were the only men in the city who had no rights. When driving about, he felt that he was held liable by the police for anything that might occur in the streets, and was the common prey of all energetic officials. In revenge, he resolved never to move out of the way of anything, until formidable circumstances, or a much larger man than himself forced him to it.

Foot-passengers were mere pestering flies with an insane disregard for their legs and his convenience. He could not conceive their maniacal desires to cross the streets. Their madness smote him with eternal amazement. He was continually storming at them from his throne. He sat aloft and denounced their frantic leaps, plunges, dives and straddles.

When they would thrust at, or parry, the noses of his champing horses, making them swing their heads and move their feet, disturbing a solid dreamy repose, he swore at the men as fools, for he himself could perceive that Providence had caused it clearly to be written, that he and his team had the unalienable right to stand in the proper path of the sun chariot, and if they so minded, obstruct its mission or take a wheel off.

And, perhaps, if the god-driver had an ungovernable desire to step down, put up his flame colored fists and manfully dispute the right of way, he would have probably been immediately opposed by a scowling mortal with two sets of very hard knuckles.

It is possible, perhaps, that this young man would have derided, in an axle-wide alley, the approach of a flying ferry boat. Yet he achieved a respect for a fire-engine. As one charged toward his truck, he would drive fearfully upon a side-walk, threatening untold people with annihilation. When an engine would strike a mass of blocked trucks, splitting it into fragments, as a blow annihilates a cake of ice, Jimmie's team could usually be observed high and safe, with whole wheels, on the side-walk.The fearful coming of the engine could break up the most intricate muddle of heavy vehicles at which the police had been swearing for the half of an hour.

A fire-engine was enshrined in his heart as an appalling thing that he loved with a distant dog-like devotion. They had been known to overturn street-cars. Those leaping horses, striking sparks from the cobbles in their forward lunge, were creatures to be ineffably admired. The clang of the gong pierced his breast like a noise of remembered war.

When Jimmie was a little boy, he began to be arrested. Before he reached a great age, he had a fair record.

He developed too great a tendency to climb down from his truck and fight with other drivers. He had been in quite a number of miscellaneous fights, and in some general barroom rows that had become known to the police. Once he had been arrested for assaulting a Chinaman. Two women in different parts of the city, and entirely unknown to each other, caused him considerable annoyance by breaking forth, simultaneously, at fateful intervals, into wailings about marriage and support and infants.

Nevertheless, he had, on a certain star-lit evening, said wonderingly and quite reverently: "Deh moon looks like hell, don't it?"

5

The girl, Maggie, blossomed in a mud puddle. She grew to be a most rare and wonderful production of a tenement district, a pretty girl.

None of the dirt of Rum Alley seemed to be in her veins. The philosophers up-stairs, down-stairs and on the same floor, puzzled over it.

When a child, playing and fighting with gamins in the street, dirt disguised her. Attired in tatters and grime, she was unseen.

There came a time, however, when the young men of the vicinity, said: "Dat Johnson goil is a puty* good looker." About this period her brother remarked to her: "Mag, I'll tell yeh dis! See? Yeh've edder got teh go teh hel or go teh work!" Whereupon she went to work, having the feminine aversion of going to hell.

By a chance, she got a position in an establishment where they made collars and cuffs. She received a stool and a machine in a room where sat twenty girls of various shades of yellow discontent. She perched on the stool and treadled at her machine all day, turning out collars, the name of whose brand could be noted for its irrelevancy to anything in connection with collars. At night she returned home to her mother.

Jimmie grew large enough to take the vague position of head of the family. As incumbent of that office, he stumbled up-stairs late at night, as his father had done before him. He reeled about the room, swearing at his relations, or went to sleep on the floor.

The mother had gradually arisen to that degree of fame that she could bandy words with her acquaintances among the police-justices. Court-officials called her by her first name. When she appeared they pursued a course which had been theirs for months. They invariably grinned and cried out: "Hello, Mary, you here again?" Her grey head wagged in many a court. She always besieged the bench with voluble excuses, explanations, apologies and prayers. Her flaming face and rolling eyes were a sort of familiar sight on the Island.[6] She measured time by means of sprees, and was eternally swollen and dishevelled.

One day the young man, Pete, who as a lad had smitten the Devil's Row urchin in the back of the head and put to flight the antagonists of his friend, Jimmie, strutted upon the scene. He met Jimmie one day on the street, promised to take him to a boxing match in Williamsburg,* and called for him in the evening.

Maggie observed Pete.

He sat on a table in the Johnson home and dangled his checked legs with an enticing nonchalance. His hair was curled down over his forehead in an oiled bang. His rather pugged nose seemed to revolt from contact with a bristling moustache of short, wire-like hairs. His blue double-breasted coat, edged with black braid, buttoned close to a red puff tie, and his patent-leather shoes, looked like murder-fitted weapons.

His mannerisms stamped him as a man who had a correct sense of his personal superiority. There was valor and contempt for circumstances in the glance of his eye. He waved his hands like a man of the world, who dismisses religion and philosophy, and says "Fudge." He had certainly seen everything and with each curl of his lip, he declared that it amounted to nothing. Maggie thought he must be a very elegant and graceful bartender.

He was telling tales to Jimmie.

* Pretty

* A section in Brooklyn, a borough of New York City separated from the borough of Manhattan by the East River.

Maggie watched him furtively, with half-closed eyes, lit with a vague interest.

"Hully gee! Dey makes me tired," he said. "Mos' e'ry day some farmer comes in an' tries teh run deh shop. See? But deh gits t'rowed right out! I jolt dem right out in deh street before dey knows where dey is! See?"

"Sure," said Jimmie.

"Dere was a mug come in deh place deh odder day wid an idear he wus goin' teh own deh place! Hully gee, he wus goin' teh own deh place! I see he had a still on* an' I didn' wanna giv 'im no stuff, so I says: 'Git deh hell outa here an' don' make no trouble,' I says like dat! See? 'Git deh hell outa here an' don' make no trouble';[7] like dat. 'Git deh hell outa here,' I says. See?"

Jimmie nodded understandingly. Over his features played an eager desire to state the amount of his valor in a similar crisis, but the narrator proceeded.

"Well, deh blokie he says: 'T'hell wid it! I ain' lookin' for no scrap,' he says (See?) 'but' he says, 'I'm spectable citizen an' I wanna drink an' purtydamnsoon, too.' See? 'Deh hel,' I says. Like dat! 'Deh hel,' I says. See? 'Don' make no trouble,' I says. Like dat. 'Don' make no trouble.' See? Den deh mug he squared off an' said he was fine as silk wid his dukes (See?) an' he wanned a drink damnquick. Dat's what he said. See?"

"Sure," repeated Jimmie.

Pete continued. "Say, I jes' jumped deh bar an' deh way I plunked dat blokie was great. See? Dat's fight! In deh jaw! See? Hully gee, he t'rowed a spittoon true deh front windee. Say, I taut I'd drop dead. But deh boss, he comes in after an' he says, 'Pete, yehs done jes' right! Yeh've gota keep order an' it's all right.' See? 'It's all right,' he says. Dat's what he said."

The two held a technical discussion.

"Dat bloke was a dandy," said Pete, in conclusion, "but he had'n' oughta made no trouble. Dat's what I says teh dem: 'Don' come in here an' make no trouble,' I says, like dat. 'Don' make no trouble.' See?"[8]

As Jimmie and his friend exchanged tales descriptive of their prowess, Maggie leaned back in the shadow. Her eyes dwelt wonderingly and rather wistfully upon Pete's face. The broken furniture, grimy[9] walls, and general disorder and dirt of her home of a sudden appeared before her and began to take a potential aspect. Pete's aristocratic person looked as if it might soil. She looked keenly at him, occasionally, wondering if he was feeling contempt. But Pete seemed to be enveloped in reminiscence.

"Hully gee," said he, "dose mugs can't phase me. Dey knows I kin wipe up deh street wid any t'ree[10] of dem."

When he said, "Ah, what deh hell," his voice was burdened with disdain for the inevitable and contempt for anything that fate might compel him to endure.

Maggie perceived that here was the beau ideal of a man. Her dim thoughts were often searching for far away lands where, as God says, the little hills sing together in the morning. Under the trees of her dream-gardens there had always walked a lover.

---

* Was drunk.

6

Pete took note of Maggie.

"Say, Mag, I'm stuck on yer shape. It's outa sight," he said, parenthetically, with an affable grin.

As he became aware that she was listening closely, he grew still more eloquent in his descriptions of various happenings in his career. It appeared that he was invincible in fights.

"Why," he said, referring to a man with whom he had had a misunderstanding, "dat mug scrapped like a damn dago. Dat's right. He was dead easy. See? He taut[11] he was a scrapper! But he foun' out diff'ent! Hully gee."

He walked to and fro in the small room, which seemed then to grow even smaller and unfit to hold his dignity, the attribute of a supreme warrior. That swing of the shoulders that had frozen the timid when he was but a lad had increased with his growth and education at the ratio of ten to one. It, combined with the sneer upon his mouth, told mankind that there was nothing in space which could appall him. Maggie marvelled at him and surrounded him with greatness. She vaguely tried to calculate the altitude of the pinnacle from which he must have looked down upon her.

"I met a chump deh odder day way up in deh city," he said. "I was goin' teh see a frien' of mine. When I was a-crossin' deh street deh chump runned plump inteh me, an' den he turns aroun' an' says, 'Yer insolen' ruffin,' he says, like dat. 'Oh, gee,' I says, 'oh, gee, go teh hell and git off deh eart',' I says, like dat. See? 'Go teh hell an' git off deh eart',' like dat. Den deh blokie he got wild. He says I was a contempt'ble scoun'el, er someting like dat, an' he says I was doom' teh everlastin' pe'dition an' all like dat. 'Gee,' I says, 'gee! Deh hell I am,' I says. 'Deh hell I am,' like dat. An' den I slugged 'im. See?"

With Jimmie in his company, Pete departed in a sort of a blaze of glory from the Johnson home. Maggie, leaning from the window, watched him as he walked down the street.

Here was a formidable man who disdained the strength of a world[12] full of fists. Here was one who had contempt for brass-clothed power; one whose knuckles could defiantly ring against the granite of law. He was a knight.

The two men went from under the glimmering street-lamp and passed into shadows.

Turning, Maggie contemplated the dark, dust-stained walls, and the scant and crude furniture of her home. A clock, in a splintered and battered oblong box of varnished wood, she suddenly regarded as an abomination. She noted that it ticked raspingly. The almost vanished flowers in the carpet-pattern, she conceived to be newly hideous. Some faint attempts she had made with blue ribbon, to freshen the appearance of a dingy curtain, she now saw to be piteous.

She wondered what Pete dined on.

She reflected upon the collar and cuff factory. It began to appear to her mind as a dreary place of endless grinding. Pete's elegant occupation brought him, no doubt, into contact with people who had money and manners. It was probable that he had a large acquaintance of pretty girls. He must have great sums of money to spend.

To her the earth was composed of hardships and insults. She felt instant admiration for a man who openly defied it. She thought that if the grim angel of death should clutch his heart, Pete would shrug his shoulders and say: "Oh, ev'ryt'ing goes."

She anticipated that he would come again shortly. She spent some of her week's pay in the purchase of flowered cretonne for a lambrequin. She made it with infinite care and hung it to the slightly-careening mantel, over the stove, in the kitchen. She studied it with painful anxiety from different points in the room. She wanted it to look well on Sunday night when, perhaps, Jimmie's friend would come. On Sunday night, however, Pete did not appear.

Afterward the girl looked at it with a sense of humiliation. She was now convinced that Pete was superior to admiration for lambrequins.

A few evenings later Pete entered with fascinating innovations in his apparel. As she had seen him twice and he had different suits on each time, Maggie had a dim impression that his wardrobe was prodigiously extensive.

"Say, Mag," he said, "put on yer bes' duds Friday night an' I'll take yehs teh deh show. See?"

He spent a few moments in flourishing his clothes and then vanished, without having glanced at the lambrequin.

Over the eternal collars and cuffs in the factory Maggie spent the most of three days in making imaginary sketches of Pete and his daily environment. She imagined some half dozen women in love with him and thought he must lean dangerously toward an indefinite one, whom she pictured with great charms of person, but with an altogether contemptible disposition.

She thought he must live in a blare of pleasure. He had friends, and people who were afraid of him.

She saw the golden glitter of the place where Pete was to take her. An entertainment of many hues and many melodies where she was afraid she might appear small and mouse-colored.

Her mother drank whiskey all Friday morning. With lurid face and tossing hair she cursed and destroyed furniture all Friday afternoon. When Maggie came home at half-past six her mother lay asleep amidst the wreck of chairs and a table. Fragments of various household utensils were scattered about the floor. She had vented some phase of drunken fury upon the lambrequin. It lay in a bedraggled heap in the corner.

"Hah," she snorted, sitting up suddenly, "where deh hell yeh been? Why deh hell don' yeh come home earlier? Been loafin' 'round deh streets. Yer gettin' teh be a reg'lar devil."

When Pete arrived Maggie, in a worn black dress, was waiting for him in the midst of a floor strewn with wreckage. The curtain at the window had been pulled by a heavy hand and hung by one tack, dangling to and fro in the draft through the cracks at the sash. The knots of blue ribbons appeared like violated flowers. The fire in the stove had gone out. The displaced lids and open doors showed heaps of sullen grey ashes. The remnants of a meal, ghastly, like dead flesh, lay in a corner. Maggie's red mother, stretched on the floor, blasphemed and gave her daughter a bad name.

7

An orchestra of yellow silk women and bald-headed men on an elevated stage near the centre of a great green-hued hall, played a popular waltz. The place was crowded with people grouped about little tables. A battalion of waiters slid among the throng, carrying trays of beer glasses and making change from the inexhaustible vaults of their trousers pockets. Little boys, in the costumes of French chefs, paraded up and down the irregular aisles vending fancy cakes. There was a low rumble of conversation and a subdued clinking of glasses. Clouds of tobacco smoke rolled and wavered high in air about the dull gilt of the chandeliers.

The vast crowd had an air throughout of having just quitted labor. Men with calloused hands and attired in garments that showed the wear of an endless trudge for a living, smoked their pipes contentedly and spent five, ten, or perhaps fifteen cents for beer. There was a mere sprinkling of kid-gloved men who smoked cigars purchased elsewhere. The great body of the crowd was composed of people who showed that all day they strove with their hands. Quiet Germans, with maybe their wives and two or three children, sat listening to the music, with the expressions of happy cows. An occasional party of sailors from a warship, their faces pictures of sturdy health, spent the earlier hours of the evening at the small round tables. Very infrequent tipsy men, swollen with the value of their opinions, engaged their companions in earnest and confidential conversation. In the balcony, and here and there below, shone the impassive faces of women. The nationalities of the Bowery* beamed upon the stage from all directions.

Pete aggressively walked up a side aisle and took seats with Maggie at a table beneath the balcony.

"Two beehs!"

Leaning back he regarded with eyes of superiority the scene before them. This attitude affected Maggie strongly. A man who could regard such a sight with indifference must be accustomed to very great things.

It was obvious that Pete had been to this place many times before, and was very familiar with it. A knowledge of this fact made Maggie feel little and new.

He was extremely gracious and attentive. He displayed the consideration of a cultured gentleman who knew what was due.

"Say, what deh hell? Bring deh lady a big glass! What deh hell use is dat pony?"

"Don't be fresh, now," said the waiter, with some warmth, as he departed.

"Ah, git off deh eart'," said Pete, after the other's retreating form.

---

* A downtown, east-side Manhattan street, now the haunt of tramps and tenth-rate hotels and stores, but once filled with popular, inexpensive music-halls.

Maggie perceived that Pete brought forth all his elegance and all his knowledge of high-class customs for her benefit. Her heart warmed as she reflected upon his condescension.

The orchestra of yellow silk women and bald-headed men gave vent to a few bars of anticipatory music and a girl, in a pink dress with short skirts, galloped upon the stage. She smiled upon the throng as if in acknowledgment of a warm welcome, and began to walk to and fro, making profuse gesticulations and singing, in brazen soprano tones, a song, the words of which were inaudible. When she broke into the swift rattling measures of a chorus some half tipsy men near the stage joined in the rollicking refrain and glasses were pounded rhythmically upon the tables. People leaned forward to watch her and to try to catch the words of the song. When she vanished there were long rollings of applause.

Obedient to more anticipatory bars, she reappeared amidst the half-suppressed cheering of the tipsy men. The orchestra plunged into dance music and the laces of the dancer fluttered and flew in the glare of gas jets. She divulged the fact that she was attired in some half dozen skirts. It was patent that any one of them would have proved adequate for the purpose for which skirts are intended. An occasional man bent forward, intent upon the pink stockings. Maggie wondered at the splendor of the costume and lost herself in calculations of the cost of the silks and laces.

The dancer's smile of stereotyped enthusiasm was turned for ten minutes upon the faces of her audience. In the finale she fell into some of those grotesque attitudes which were at the time popular among the dancers in the theatres up-town, giving to the Bowery public the phantasies of the aristocratic theatre-going public, at reduced rates.

"Say, Pete," said Maggie, leaning forward, "dis is great."

"Sure," said Pete, with proper complacence.

A ventriloquist followed the dancer. He held two fantastic dolls on his knees. He made them sing mournful ditties and say funny things about geography and Ireland.

"Do dose little men talk?" asked Maggie.

"Naw," said Pete, "it's some damn fake. See?"

Two girls, on the bills as sisters, came forth and sang a duet that is heard occasionally at concerts given under church auspices. They supplemented it with a dance which of course can never be seen at concerts given under church auspices.

After the duettists had retired, a woman of debatable age sang a negro melody. The chorus necessitated some grotesque waddlings supposed to be an imitation of a plantation darkey, under the influence, probably, of music and the moon. The audience was just enthusiastic enough over it to have her return and sing a sorrowful lay, whose lines told of a mother's love and a sweetheart who waited and a young man who was lost at sea under the most harrowing circumstances. From the faces of a score or so in the crowd, the self-contained look faded. Many heads were bent forward with eagerness and sympathy. As the last distressing sentiment of the piece was brought forth, it was greeted by that kind of applause which rings as sincere.

As a final effort, the singer rendered some verses which described a vision of Britain being annihilated by America, and Ireland bursting her bonds. A carefully prepared crisis was reached in the last line of the last verse, where the singer threw out her arms and cried, "The starspangled banner." Instantly a great cheer swelled from the throats of the assemblage of the masses. There was a heavy rumble of booted feet thumping the floor. Eyes gleamed with sudden fire, and calloused hands waved frantically in the air.

After a few moments' rest, the orchestra played crashingly, and a small fat man burst out upon the stage. He began to roar a song and stamp back and forth before the footlights, wildly waving a glossy silk hat and throwing leers, or smiles, broadcast. He made his face into fantastic grimaces until he looked like a pictured devil on a Japanese kite. The crowd laughed gleefully. His short, fat legs were never still a moment. He shouted and roared and bobbed his shock of red wig until the audience broke out in excited applause.

Pete did not pay much attention to the progress of events upon the stage. He was drinking beer and watching Maggie.

Her cheeks were blushing with excitement and her eyes were glistening. She drew deep breaths of pleasure. No thoughts of the atmosphere of the collar and cuff factory came to her.

When the orchestra crashed finally, they jostled their way to the sidewalk with the crowd. Pete took Maggie's arm and pushed a way for her, offering to fight with a man or two.

They reached Maggie's home at a late hour and stood for a moment in front of the gruesome doorway.

"Say, Mag," said Pete, "give us a kiss for takin' yeh teh deh show, will yer?"

Maggie laughed, as if startled, and drew away from him.

"Naw, Pete," she said, "dat wasn't in it."

"Ah, what deh hell?" urged Pete.

The girl retreated nervously.

"Ah, what deh hell?" repeated he.

Maggie darted into the hall, and up the stairs. She turned and smiled at him, then disappeared.

Pete walked slowly down the street. He had something of an astonished expression upon his features. He paused under a lamp-post and breathed a low breath of surprise.

"Gawd," he said, "I wonner if I've been played fer a duffer."

8

As thoughts of Pete came to Maggie's mind, she began to have an intense dislike for all of her dresses.

"What deh hell ails yeh? What makes yeh be allus fixin' and fussin'? Good Gawd," her mother would frequently roar at her.

She began to note, with more interest, the well-dressed women she met on the avenues. She envied elegance and soft palms. She craved those adornments of person which she saw every day on the street, conceiving them to be allies of vast importance to women.

Studying faces, she thought many of the women and girls she chanced to meet, smiled with serenity as though forever cherished and watched over by those they loved.

The air in the collar and cuff establishment strangled her. She knew she was gradually and surely shrivelling in the hot, stuffy room. The begrimed windows rattled incessantly from the passing of elevated trains. The place was filled with a whirl of noises and odors.

She wondered as she regarded some of the grizzled women in the room, mere mechanical contrivances sewing seams and grinding out, with heads bended over their work, tales of imagined or real girl-hood happiness, past drunks, the baby at home, and unpaid wages. She speculated how long her youth would endure. She began to see the bloom upon her cheeks as valuable.

She imagined herself, in an exasperating future, as a scrawny woman with an eternal grievance. Too, she thought Pete to be a very fastidious person concerning the appearance of women.

She felt she would love to see somebody entangle their fingers in the oily beard of the fat foreigner who owned the establishment. He was a detestable creature. He wore white socks with low shoes.

He sat all day delivering orations, in the depths of a cushioned chair. His pocketbook deprived them of the power of retort.

"What een hell do you sink I pie fife dolla a week for? Play? No, py damn!"

Maggie was anxious for a friend to whom she could talk about Pete. She would have liked to discuss his admirable[13] mannerisms with a reliable mutual friend. At home, she found her mother often drunk and always raving.

It seems that the world had treated this woman very badly, and she took a deep revenge upon such portions of it as came within her reach. She broke furniture as if she were at last getting her rights. She swelled with virtuous indignation as she carried the lighter articles of household use, one by one under the shadows of the three gilt balls, where Hebrews chained them with chains of interest.

Jimmie came when he was obliged[14] to by circumstances over which he had no control. His well-trained legs brought him staggering home and put him to bed some nights when he would rather have gone elsewhere.

Swaggering Pete loomed like a golden sun to Maggie. He took her to a dime museum where rows of meek freaks astonished her. She contemplated their deformities with awe and thought them a sort of chosen tribe.

Pete, raking his brains for amusement, discovered the Central Park Menagerie and the Museum of Arts. Sunday afternoons would sometimes find them at these places. Pete did not appear to be particularly interested in what he saw. He stood around looking heavy, while Maggie giggled in glee.

Once at the Menagerie he went into a trance of admiration before the spectacle of a very small monkey threatening to thrash[15] a cageful because one of them had pulled his tail and he had not wheeled about quickly enough to discover who did it. Ever after Pete knew that monkey by sight and winked at him, trying to induce him to fight with other and larger monkeys.[16]

At the Museum, Maggie said, "Dis is outa sight."

"Oh hell," said Pete, "wait till next summer an' I'll take yehs to a picnic."

While the girl wandered in the vaulted rooms, Pete occupied himself in returning stony stare for stony stare, the appalling scrutiny of the watch-dogs of the treasures. Occasionally he would remark in loud tones: "Dat jay has got glass eyes," and sentences of the sort. When he tired of this amusement he would go to the mummies and moralize over them.

Usually he submitted with silent dignity to all which he had to go through, but at times, he was goaded into comment.

"What deh hell," he demanded once. "Look at all dese little jugs! Hundred jugs in a row! Ten rows in a case an' 'bout a t'ousand cases! What deh blazes use is dem?"

Evenings during the week he took her to see plays in which the brain-clutching heroine was rescued from the palatial home of her guardian, who is cruelly after her bonds, by the hero with the beautiful sentiments. The latter spent most of his time out at soak in pale-green snow storms, busy with a nickel-plated revolver, rescuing aged strangers from villains.

Maggie lost herself in sympathy with the wanderers swooning in snow storms beneath happy-hued church windows. And a choir within singing "Joy to the World." To Maggie and the rest of the audience this was transcendental realism. Joy always within, and they, like the actor, inevitably without. Viewing it, they hugged themselves in ecstatic pity of their imagined or real condition.

The girl thought the arrogance and granite-heartedness of the magnate of the play was very accurately drawn. She echoed the maledictions that the occupants of the gallery showered on this individual when his lines compelled him to expose his extreme selfishness.

Shady persons in the audience revolted from the pictured villainy of the drama. With untiring zeal they hissed vice and applauded virtue. Unmistakably bad men evinced an apparently sincere admiration for virtue.

The loud gallery was overwhelmingly with the unfortunate and the oppressed. They encouraged the struggling hero with cries, and jeered the villain, hooting and calling attention to his whiskers. When anybody died in the pale-green snow storms, the gallery mourned. They sought out the painted misery and hugged it as akin.

In the hero's erratic march from poverty in the first act, to wealth and triumph in the final one, in which he forgives all the enemies that he has left, he was assisted by the gallery, which applauded his generous and noble sentiments and confounded the speeches of his opponents by making irrelevant but very sharp remarks. Those actors who were cursed with villainy parts were confronted at every turn by the gallery. If one of them rendered lines containing the most subtle distinctions between right and wrong, the gallery was immediately aware if the actor meant wickedness, and denounced him accordingly.

The last act was a triumph for the hero, poor and of the masses, the representative of the audience, over the villain and the rich man, his pockets stuffed with bonds, his heart packed with tyrannical purposes, imperturbable amid suffering.

Maggie always departed with raised spirits from the showing places of the melodrama. She rejoiced at the way in which the poor and virtuous eventually surmounted the wealthy and wicked. The theater made her think. She wondered if the culture and refinement she had seen imitated, perhaps grotesquely, by the heroine on the stage, could be acquired by a girl who lived in a tenement house and worked in a shirt factory.

9

A group of urchins were intent upon the side door of a saloon. Expectancy gleamed from their eyes. They were twisting their fingers in excitement.

"Here she comes," yelled one of them suddenly.

The group of urchins burst instantly asunder and its individual fragments were spread in a wide, respectable half circle about the point of interest. The saloon door opened with a crash, and the figure of a woman appeared upon the threshold. Her[17] gray hair fell in knotted masses about her shoulders. Her face was crimsoned and wet with perspiration. Her eyes had a rolling glare.

"Not a damn cent more of me money will yehs ever get, not a damn cent. I spent me money here fer tree years an' now yehs tells me yeh'll sell me no more stuff! T'hell wid yeh, Johnnie Murckre! 'Disturbance'?[18] Disturbance be damned! T'hell wid yeh, Johnnie—"

The door received a kick of exasperation from within and the woman lurched heavily out on the sidewalk.

The gamins in the half-circle became violently agitated. They began to dance about and hoot and yell and jeer. Wide dirty grins spread over each face.

The woman made a furious dash at a particularly outrageous cluster of little boys. They laughed delightedly and scampered off a short distance, calling out over their shoulders to her. She stood tottering on the curbstone and thundered at them.

"Yeh devil's kids," she howled, shaking red fists. The little boys whooped in glee. As she started up the street they fell in behind and marched uproariously. Occasionally she wheeled about and made charges on them. They ran nimbly out of reach and taunted her.

In the frame of a gruesome doorway she stood for a moment cursing them. Her hair straggled, giving her crimson features a look of insanity. Her great fists quivered as she shook them madly in the air.

The urchins made terrific noises until she turned and disappeared. Then they filed quietly in the way they had come.

The woman floundered about in the lower hall of the tenement house and finally stumbled up the stairs. On an upper hall a door was opened and a collection of heads peered curiously out, watching her. With a wrathful snort the woman confronted the door, but it was slammed hastily in her face and the key was turned.

She stood for a few minutes, delivering a frenzied challenge at the panels.

"Come out in deh hall, Mary Murphy, damn yeh, if yehs want a row. Come ahn, yeh overgrown terrier, come ahn."

She began to kick the door with her great feet. She shrilly defied the universe to appear and do battle. Her cursing trebles brought heads from all doors save the one she threatened. Her eyes glared in every direction. The air was full of her tossing fists.

"Come ahn, deh hull damn gang of yehs, come ahn," she roared at the spectators. An oath or two, cat-calls, jeers and bits of facetious advice were given in reply. Missiles[19] clattered about her feet.

"What deh hell's deh matter wid yeh?" said a voice in the gathered gloom, and Jimmie came forward. He carried a tin[20] dinner-pail in his hand and under his arm a brown truckman's apron done in a bundle. "What deh hell's wrong?" he demanded.

"Come out, all of yehs, come out," his mother was howling. "Come ahn an' I'll stamp yer damn brains under me feet."

"Shet yer face, an' come home, yer damned old fool," roared Jimmie at her. She strided up to him and twirled her fingers in his face. Her eyes were darting flames of unreasoning rage and her frame trembled with eagerness for a fight.

"T'hell wid yehs! An' who deh hell are yehs? I ain't givin' a snap of me fingers fer yehs," she bawled at him. She turned her huge back in tremendous disdain and climbed the stairs to the next floor.

Jimmie followed, cursing blackly. At the top of the flight he seized his mother's arm and started to drag her toward the door of their room.

"Come home, damn yeh," he gritted between his teeth.

"Take yer hands off me! Take yer hands off me," shrieked his mother.

She raised her arm and whirled her great fist at her son's face. Jimmie dodged his head and the blow struck him in the back of the neck. "Damn yeh," gritted he again. He threw out his left hand and writhed his fingers about her middle arm. The mother and the son began to sway and struggle like gladiators.

"Whoop!" said the Rum Alley tenement house. The hall filled with interested spectators.

"Hi, ol' lady, dat was a dandy!"

"T'ree to one on deh red!"

"Ah, stop yer dam scrappin'!"

The door of the Johnson home opened and Maggie looked out. Jimmie made a supreme cursing effort and hurled his mother into the room. He quickly followed and closed the door. The Rum Alley tenement swore disappointedly and retired.

The mother slowly gathered herself up from the floor. Her eyes glittered menacingly upon her children.

"Here, now," said Jimmie, "we've had enough of dis. Sit down, an' don' make no trouble."

He grasped her arm, and twisting it, forced her into a creaking chair.

"Keep yer hands off me," roared his mother again.

"Damn yer ol' hide," yelled Jimmie, madly. Maggie shrieked and ran into the other room. To her there came the sound of a storm of crashes and curses. There was a great final thump and Jimmie's voice cried: "Dere,[21] damn yeh, stay still." Maggie opened the door now,[22] and went warily out. "Oh, Jimmie."

He was leaning against the wall and swearing. Blood stood upon bruises on his knotty fore-arms where they had scraped against the floor or the walls in the scuffle. The mother lay screeching on the floor, the tears running down her furrowed face.

Maggie, standing in the middle of the room, gazed about her. The usual upheaval of the tables and chairs had taken place. Crockery was strewn broadcast in fragments. The stove had been disturbed on its legs, and now leaned idiotically to one side. A pail had been upset and water spread in all directions.

The door opened and Pete appeared. He shrugged his shoulders. "Oh, Gawd," he observed.

He walked over to Maggie and whispered in her ear. "Ah, what deh hell, Mag? Come ahn and we'll have a hell of a time."

The mother in the corner upreared her head and shook her tangled locks.

"Teh hell wid him and you," she said, glowering at her daughter in the gloom. Her eyes seemed to burn balefully. "Yeh've gone teh deh devil, Mag Johnson, yehs knows yehs have gone teh deh devil. Yer a disgrace teh yer people, damn yeh. An' now, git out an' go ahn wid dat doe-faced jude* of yours. Go teh hell wid him, damn yeah, an' a good riddance. Go teh hell an' see how yeh likes it."

Maggie gazed long at her mother.

"Go teh hell now, an' see how yeh likes it. Git out. I won't have sech as yehs in me house! Get out, d'yeh hear! Damn yeah, git out!"

The girl began to tremble.

At this instant Pete came forward. "Oh, what deh hell, Mag, see," whispered he softly in her ear. "Dis all blows over. See? Deh ol' woman 'ill be all right in deh mornin'. Come ahn out wid me! We'll have a hell of a time."

The woman on the floor cursed. Jimmie was intent upon his bruised fore-arms. The girl cast a glance about the room filled with a chaotic mass of debris, and at the red, writhing body of her mother.

"Go teh hell an' good riddance."[23]

She went.

10

Jimmie had an idea it wasn't common courtesy for a friend to come to one's home and ruin one's sister. But he was not sure how much Pete knew about the rules of politeness.

The following night he returned home from work at rather a late hour in the evening. In passing through the halls he came upon the gnarled and leathery old woman who possessed the music box. She was grinning in the dim light that drifted through dust-stained panes. She beckoned to him with a smudged forefinger.

---

* Dough-faced dude.

"Ah, Jimmie, what do yehs tink I got onto las' night. It was deh funnies' ting I ever saw," she cried, coming close to him and leering. She was trembling with eagerness to tell her tale. "I was by me door las' night when yer sister and her jude feller came in late, oh, very late. An' she, the dear, she was a-cryin' as if her heart would break, she was. It was deh funnies' ting I ever saw. An' right out here by me door she asked him did he love her, did he. An' she was a-cryin' as if her heart would break, poor ting. An' him, I could see by[24] deh way what he said it dat she had been askin' orften, he says: 'Oh, hell, yes,' he says, says he, 'Oh, hell, yes.' "[25]

Storm-clouds swept over Jimmie's face, but he turned from the leathery old woman and plodded on up stairs.

" 'Oh, hell, yes,' "[26] called she after him. She laughed a laugh that was like a prophetic croak. " 'Oh, hell, yes,' he says, says he, 'Oh, hell, yes.' "

There was no one in at home. The rooms showed that attempts had been made at tidying them. Parts of the wreckage of the day before had been repaired by an unskilful hand. A chair or two and the table, stood uncertainly upon legs. The floor had been newly swept. Too, the blue ribbons had been restored to the curtains, and the lambrequin, with its immense sheaves of yellow wheat and red roses of equal size, had been returned, in a worn and sorry state, to its position at the mantel. Maggie's jacket and hat were gone from the nail behind the door.

Jimmie walked to the window and began to look through the blurred glass. It occurred to him to vaguely wonder, for an instant, if some of the women of his acquaintance had brothers.

Suddenly, however, he began to swear.

"But he was me frien'! I brought 'im here! Dat's deh hell of it!"

He fumed about the room, his anger gradually rising to the furious pitch.

"I'll kill deh jay! Dat's what I'll do! I'll kill deh jay!"

He clutched his hat and sprang toward the door. But it opened and his mother's great form blocked the passage.

"What deh hell's deh matter wid yeh?" exclaimed she, coming into the rooms.

Jimmie gave vent to a sardonic curse and then laughed heavily.

"Well, Maggie's gone teh deh devil! Dat's what! See?"

"Eh?" said his mother.

"Maggie's gone teh deh devil! Are yehs deaf?" roared Jimmie, impatiently.

"Deh hell she has," murmured the mother, astounded.

Jimmie grunted, and then began to stare out at the window. His mother sat down in a chair, but a moment later sprang erect and delivered a maddened whirl of oaths. Her son turned to look at her as she reeled and swayed in the middle of the room, her fierce face convulsed with passion, her blotched arms raised high in imprecation.

"May Gawd curse her forever," she shrieked. "May she eat nothin' but stones and deh dirt in deh street. May she sleep in deh gutter an' never see deh sun shine agin. Deh damn—"

"Here, now," said her son. "Take a drop on yourself."

The mother raised lamenting eyes to the ceiling.

"She's deh devil's own chil', Jimmie," she whispered. "Ah, who would tink such a bad girl could grow up in our fambly, Jimmie, me son. Many deh hour I've spent in talk wid dat girl an' tol' her if she ever went on deh streets I'd see her damned. An' after all her bringin' up an' what I tol' her and talked wid her, she goes teh deh bad, like a duck teh water."

The tears rolled down her furrowed face. Her hands trembled.

"An' den when dat Sadie MacMallister next door to us was sent teh deh devil by dat feller what worked in deh soap-factory, didn't I tell our Mag dat if she—"

"Ah, dat's anudder story," interrupted the brother. "Of course, dat Sadie was nice an' all dat—but—see—it ain't dessame as if—well, Maggie was diff'ent—see—she was diff'ent."

He was trying to formulate a theory that he had always unconsciously held, that all sisters, excepting his own, could advisedly be ruined.

He suddenly broke out again. "I'll go t'ump hell outa deh mug what did her deh harm. I'll kill 'im! He tinks he kin scrap, but when he gits me a-chasin' 'im he'll fin' out where he's wrong, deh damned duffer. I'll wipe up deh street wid 'im."

In a fury he plunged out of the doorway. As he vanished the mother raised her head and lifted both hands, entreating.

"May Gawd curse her forever," she cried.

In the darkness of the hallway Jimmie discerned a knot of women talking volubly. When he strode by they paid no attention to him.

"She allus was a bold thing," he heard one of them cry in an eager voice. "Dere wasn't a feller come teh deh house but she'd try teh mash 'im. My Annie says deh shameless t'ing tried teh ketch her feller, her own feller, what we useter know his fader."

"I could a' tol' yehs dis two years ago," said a woman, in a key of triumph. "Yesir, it was over two years ago dat I says teh my ol' man, I says, 'Dat Johnson girl ain't straight,' I says. 'Oh, hell,' he says. 'Oh, hell.' 'Dat's all right,' I says, 'but I know what I knows.' I says, 'an' it'll come out later. You wait an' see,' I says, 'you see.'"

"Anybody what had eyes could see dat dere was somethin' wrong wid dat girl. I didn't like her actions."

On the street Jimmie met a friend. "What deh hell?" asked the latter.

Jimmie explained. "An' I'll t'ump[27] 'im till he can't stand."

"Oh, what deh hell," said the friend. 'What's deh use! Yeh'll git pulled in! Everybody 'ill be onto it! An' ten plunks*! Gee!"

Jimmie was determined. "He t'inks he kin scrap, but he'll fin'out diff'ent."

"Gee," remonstrated the friend, "What deh hell?"

---

* Dollars. i.e., a ten-dollar fine.

11

On a corner a glass-fronted building shed a yellow glare upon the pavements. The open mouth of a saloon called seductively to passengers to enter and annihilate sorrow or create rage.

The interior of the place was papered in olive and bronze tints of imitation leather. A shining bar of counterfeit massiveness extended down the side of the room. Behind it a great mahogany-appearing sideboard reached the ceiling. Upon its shelves rested pyramids of shimmering glasses that were never disturbed. Mirrors set in the face of the sideboard multiplied them. Lemons, oranges and paper napkins, arranged with mathematical precision, sat among the glasses. Many-hued decanters of liquor perched at regular intervals on the lower shelves. A nickel-plated cash register occupied a position in the exact center of the general effect. The elementary senses of it all seemed to be opulence and geometrical accuracy.

Across from the bar a smaller counter held a collection of plates upon which swarmed frayed fragments of crackers, slices of boiled ham, dishevelled bits of cheese, and pickles swimming in vinegar. An odor of grasping, begrimed[28] hands and munching mouths pervaded.

Pete, in a white jacket, was behind the bar bending expectantly toward a quiet stranger. "A beeh," said the man. Pete drew a foam-topped glassful and set it dripping upon the bar.

At this moment the light bamboo doors at the entrance swung open and crashed against the siding. Jimmie and a companion entered. They swaggered unsteadily but belligerently toward the bar and looked at Pete with bleared and blinking eyes.

"Gin," said Jimmie.

"Gin," said the companion.

Pete slid a bottle and two glasses along the bar. He bended his head sideways as he assiduously polished away with a napkin at the gleaming wood. He had a look of watchfulness upon his features.

Jimmie and his companion kept their eyes upon the bartender and conversed loudly in tones of contempt.

"He's a dindy masher, ain't he, by Gawd?" laughed Jimmie.

"Oh, hell, yes," said the companion, sneering widely. "He's great, he is. Git onto deh mug on deh blokie. Dat's enough to make a feller turn hand-springs in 'is sleep."

The quiet stranger moved himself and his glass a trifle further away and maintained an attitude of oblivion.

"Gee! ain't he hot stuff!"

"Git onto his shape! Great Gawd!"

"Hey," cried Jimmie, in tones of command. Pete came along slowly, with a sullen dropping of the upper lip.

"Well," he growled, "what's eatin' yehs?"

"Gin," said Jimmie.

"Gin," said the companion.

As Pete confronted them with the bottle and the glasses, they laughed in his face. Jimmie's companion, evidently overcome with merriment, pointed a grimy forefinger in Pete's direction.

"Say, Jimmie," demanded he, "what deh hell is dat behind deh bar?"

"Damned if I knows," replied Jimmie. They laughed loudly. Pete put down a bottle with a bang and turned a formidable face toward them. He disclosed his teeth and his shoulders heaved restlessly.

"You fellers can't guy me," he said. "Drink yer stuff an' git out an' don' make no trouble."

Instantly the laughter faded from the faces of the two men and expressions of offended dignity immediately came.

"Who deh hell has said anyt'ing teh you," cried they in the same breath.

The quiet stranger looked at the door calculatingly.

"Ah, come off", said Pete to the two men. "Don't pick me up for no jay. Drink yer rum an' git out an' don' make no trouble."

"Oh, deh hell," airily cried Jimmie.

"Oh, deh hell," airily repeated his companion.

"We goes when we git ready! See!" continued Jimmie.

"Well," said Pete in a threatening voice, "don' make no trouble."

Jimmie suddenly leaned forward with his head on one side. He snarled like a wild animal.

"Well, what if we does? See?" said he.

Dark blood flushed into Pete's face, and he shot a lurid glance at Jimmie.

"Well, den we'll see whose deh bes' man, you or me," he said.

The quiet stranger moved modestly toward the door.

Jimmie began to swell with valor.

"Don' pick me up fer no tenderfoot. When yeh tackles me yeh tackles one of deh bes' men in deh city. See? I'm a scrapper, I am. Ain't dat right, Billie?"

"Sure, Mike," responded his companion in tones of conviction.

"Oh, hell," said Pete, easily. "Go fall on yerself."

The two men again began to laugh.

"What deh hell is dat talkin'?"[29] cried the companion.

"Damned if I knows," replied Jimmie with exaggerated contempt.

Pete made a furious gesture. "Git outa here now, an' don' make no trouble. See? Youse fellers er lookin' fer a scrap an' it's damn likely yeh'll fin' one if yeh keeps on shootin' off yer mout's. I know yehs! See? I kin lick better men dan yehs ever saw in yer lifes. Dat's right! See? Don' pick me up fer no stuff er yeh might be jolted out in deh street before yeh knows where yeh is. When I comes from behind dis bar, I t'rows yehs bot'[30] inteh deh street. See?"

"Oh, hell," cried the two men in chorus.

The glare of a panther came into Pete's eyes.[31] "Dat's what I said! Unnerstan'?"

He came through a passage at the end of the bar and swelled down upon the two men. They stepped promptly forward and crowded close to him.

They bristled like three roosters. They moved their heads pugnaciously and kept their shoulders braced. The nervous muscles about each mouth twitched with a forced smile of mockery.

"Well, what deh hell yer goin' teh do?" gritted Jimmie.

Pete stepped warily back, waving his hands before him to keep the men from coming too near.

"Well, what deh hell yer goin' teh do?" repeated Jimmie's ally. They kept close to him, taunting and leering. They strove to make him attempt the initial blow.

"Keep back, now! Don' crowd me," ominously said Pete.

Again they chorused in contempt. "Oh, hell!"

In a small, tossing group, the three men edged for positions like frigates contemplating battle.

"Well, why deh hell don' yeh try teh t'row us out?" cried Jimmie and his ally with copious sneers.

The bravery of bull-dogs sat upon the faces of the men. Their clenched fists moved like eager weapons.

The allied two jostled the bartender's elbows, glaring at him with feverish eyes and forcing him toward the wall.

Suddenly Pete swore redly. The flash of action gleamed from his eyes. He threw back his arm and aimed a tremendous, lightning-like blow at Jimmie's face. His foot swung a step forward and the weight of his body was behind his fist. Jimmie ducked his head, Bowery-like, with the quickness of a cat. The fierce, answering blows of him and his ally crushed on Pete's bowed head.

The quiet stranger vanished.

The arms of the combatants whirled in the air like flails. The faces of the men, at first flushed to flame-colored anger, now began to fade to the pallor of warriors in the blood and heat of a battle. Their lips curled back and stretched tightly over the gums in ghoul-like grins. Through their white, gripped teeth struggled hoarse whisperings of oaths. Their eyes glittered with murderous fire.

Each head was huddled between its owner's shoulders, and arms were swinging with marvelous rapidity. Feet scraped to and fro with a loud scratching sound upon the sanded floor. Blows left crimson blotches upon pale skin. The curses of the first quarter minute of the fight died away. The breaths of the fighters came wheezingly from their lips and the three chests were straining and heaving. Pete at intervals gave vent to low, labored hisses, that sounded like a desire, to kill. Jimmie's ally gibbered at times like a wounded maniac. Jimmie was silent, fighting with the face of a sacrificial priest. The rage of fear shone in all their eyes and their blood-colored fists swirled.

At a tottering moment a blow from Pete's hand struck the ally and he crashed to the floor. He wriggled instantly to his feet and grasping the quiet stranger's beer glass from the bar, hurled it at Pete's head.

High on the wall it burst like a bomb, shivering fragments flying in all directions. Then missiles[32] came to every man's hand. The place had heretofore appeared free of things to throw, but suddenly glass and bottles went singing through the air. They were thrown point blank at bobbing heads. The pyramid of shimmering glasses, that had never been disturbed, changed to cascades as heavy bottles were flung into them. Mirrors splintered to nothing.

The three frothing creatures on the floor buried themselves in a frenzy for blood. There followed in the wake of missiles[33] and fists some unknown prayers, perhaps for death.

The quiet stranger had sprawled very pyrotechnically out on the sidewalk. A laugh ran up and down the avenue for the half of a block.

"Dey've trowed a bloke inteh deh street."

People heard the sound of breaking glass and shuffling feet within the saloon and came running. A small group, bending down to look under the bamboo doors, watching the fall of glass, and three pairs of violent legs, changed in a moment to a crowd.

A policeman came charging down the sidewalk and bounced through the doors into the saloon. The crowd bended and surged in absorbing anxiety to see.

Jimmie caught first sight of the on-coming interruption. On his feet he had the same regard for a policeman that, when on his truck, he had for a fire engine. He howled and ran for the side door.

The officer made a terrific advance, club in hand. One comprehensive sweep of the long night stick threw the ally to the floor and forced Pete to a corner. With his disengaged hand he made a furious effort at Jimmie's coattails. Then he regained his balance and paused.

"Well, well, you are a pair of pictures. What in hell yeh been up to?"

Jimmie, with his face drenched in blood, escaped up a side street, pursued a short distance by some of the more law-loving, or excited individuals of the crowd.

Later, from a corner safely dark, he saw the policeman, the ally and the bartender emerge from the saloon. Pete locked the doors and then followed up the avenue in the rear of the crowd-encompassed policeman and his charge.

On first thoughts Jimmie, with his heart throbbing at battle heat, started to go desperately to the rescue of his friend, but he halted.

"Ah, what deh hell?" he demanded of himself.

12

In a hall of irregular shape sat Pete and Maggie drinking beer. A submissive orchestra dictated to by a spectacled man with frowsy hair and a dress suit, industriously followed the bobs of his head and the waves of his baton. A ballad singer, in a dress of flaming scarlet, sang in the inevitable voice of brass. When she vanished, men seated at the tables near the front applauded loudly, pounding the polished wood with their beer glasses. She returned attired in less gown, and sang again. She received another enthusiastic encore. She reappeared in still less gown and danced. The deafening rumble of glasses and clapping of hands that followed her exit indicated an overwhelming desire to have her come on for the fourth time, but the curiosity of the audience was not gratified.

Maggie was pale. From her eyes had been plucked all look of self-reliance. She leaned with a dependent air toward her companion. She was timid, as if fearing his anger or displeasure. She seemed to beseech tenderness of him.

Pete's air of distinguished valor had grown upon him until it threatened stupendous dimensions. He was infinitely gracious to the girl. It was apparent to her that his condescension was a marvel.

He could appear to strut even while sitting still and he showed that he was a lion of lordly characteristics by the air with which he spat.

With Maggie gazing at him wonderingly, he took pride in commanding the waiters who were, however, indifferent or deaf.

"Hi, you, git a russle on yehs! What deh hell yeh's lookin' at? Two more beehs, d'yeh hear?"

He leaned back and critically regarded the person of a girl with a straw-colored wig who upon the stage was flinging her heels in somewhat awkward imitation of a well-known danseuse.

At times Maggie told Pete long confidential tales of her former home life, dwelling upon the escapades of the other members of the family and the difficulties she had to combat in order to obtain a degree of comfort. He responded in tones of philanthropy. He pressed her arm with an air of reassuring proprietorship.

"Dey was damn jays," he said, denouncing the mother and brother.

The sound of the music which, by the efforts of the frowsy-headed leader, drifted to her ears through the smoke-filled[34] atmosphere, made the girl dream. She thought of her former Rum Alley environment and turned to regard Pete's strong protecting fists. She thought of the collar and cuff manufactory and the eternal moan of the proprietor: "What een hell do you sink I pie fife dolla a week for? Play? No, py damn." She contemplated Pete's man-subduing eyes and noted that wealth and prosperity was indicated by his clothes. She imagined a future, rose-tinted, because of its distance from all that she previously had experienced.

As to the present she perceived only vague reasons to be miserable. Her life was Pete's and she considered him worthy of the charge. She would be disturbed by no particular apprehensions, so long as Pete adored her as he now said he did. She did not feel like a bad woman. To her knowledge she had never seen any better.

At times men at other tables regarded the girl furtively. Pete, aware of it, nodded at her and grinned. He felt proud.

"Mag, yer a bloomin' good-looker," he remarked, studying her face through the haze. The men made Maggie fear, but she blushed at Pete's words as it became apparent to her that she was the apple of his eye.

Grey-headed men, wonderfully pathetic in their dissipation, stared at her through clouds. Smooth cheeked boys, some of them with faces of stone and mouths of sin, not nearly so pathetic as the grey heads, tried to find the girl's eyes in the smoke wreaths. Maggie considered she was not what they thought her. She confined her glances to Pete and the stage.

The orchestra played negro melodies and a versatile drummer pounded, whacked, clattered and scratched on a dozen machines to make noise.

Those glances of the men, shot at Maggie from under half-closed lids, made her tremble. She thought them all to be worse men than Pete.

"Come, let's go," she said.

As they went out Maggie perceived two women seated at a table with some men. They were painted and their cheeks had lost their roundness. As she passed them the girl, with a shrinking movement, drew back her skirts.

13

Jimmie did not return home for a number of days after the fight with Pete in the saloon. When he did, he approached with extreme caution.

He found his mother raving. Maggie had not returned home. The parent continually wondered how her daughter could come to such a pass. She had never considered Maggie as a pearl dropped unstained into Rum Alley from Heaven, but she could not conceive how it was possible for her daughter to fall so low as to bring disgrace upon her family. She was terrific in denunciation of the girl's wickedness.

The fact that the neighbors talked of it, maddened her. When women came in, and in the course of their conversation casually asked, "Where's Maggie dese days?" the mother shook her fuzzy head at them and appalled them with curses. Cunning hints inviting confidence she rebuffed with violence.

"An' wid all deh bringin' up she had, how could she?" moaningly she asked of her son.

"Wid all deh talkin' wid her I did an' deh t'ings I tol' her to remember? When a girl is bringed up deh way I bringed up Maggie, how kin she go teh deh devil?"

Jimmie was transfixed by these questions. He could not conceive how under the circumstances his mother's daughter and his sister could have been so wicked.

His mother took a drink from a squdgy[35] bottle that sat on the table. She continued her lament.

"She had a bad heart, dat girl did, Jimmie. She was wicked teh deh heart an' we never knowed it."

Jimmie nodded, admitting the fact.

"We lived in deh same house wid her an' I brought her up an' we never knowed how bad she was."

Jimmie nodded again.

"Wid a home like dis an' a mudder like me, she went teh deh bad," cried the mother, raising her eyes.

One day, Jimmie came home, sat down in a chair and began to wriggle about with a new and strange nervousness. At last he spoke shamefacedly.

"Well, look-a-here, dis ting queers us! See? We're queered! An' maybe it 'ud be better if I—well, I t'ink I kin look 'er up an'—maybe it 'ud be better if I fetched her home an'—"[36]

The mother started from her chair and broke forth into a storm of passionate anger.

"What! Let 'er come an' sleep under deh same roof wid her mudder agin! Oh, yes, I will, won't I? Sure? Shame on yehs, Jimmie Johnson, fer sayin' such a t'ing teh yer own mudder—teh yer own mudder! Little did I t'ink when yehs was a babby playin' about me feet dat ye'd grow up teh say sech a ting teh yer mudder—yer own mudder. I never taut—"

Sobs choked her and interrupted her reproaches.

"Dere ain't nottin teh raise sech hell about," said Jimmie. "I on'y says it 'ud be better if we keep dis t'ing dark, see? It queers us! See?"

His mother laughed a laugh that seemed to ring through the city and be echoed and reechoed by countless other laughs. "Oh, yes, I will, wont I! Sure!"

"Well, yeh must take me fer a damn fool," said Jimmie, indignant at his mother for mocking him. "I didn't say we'd make 'er inteh a little tin angel, ner nottin, but deh way it is now she can queer us! Don' che see?"

"Aye, she'll git tired of deh life atter a while an' den she'll wanna be a-comin' home, won' she, deh beast! I'll let 'er in den, won' I?"

"Well, I didn't mean none of dis prod'gal bus'ness anyway,"[37] explained Jimmie.

"It wasn't no prod'gal dauter, yeh damn fool," said the mother. "It was prod'gal son, anyhow."

"I know dat," said Jimmie.

For a time they sat in silence. The mother's eyes gloated on a scene her imagination could call before her. Her lips were set in a vindictive smile.

"Aye, she'll cry, won' she, an' carry on, an' tell how Pete, or some odder feller, beats 'er an' she'll say she's sorry an' all dat an' she ain't happy, she ain't, an' she wants to come home agin, she does."

With grim humor, the mother imitated the possible wailing notes of the daughter's voice.

"Den I'll take 'er in, won't I, deh beast. She kin cry 'er two eyes out on deh stones of deh street before I'll dirty deh place wid her. She abused an' ill-treated her own mudder—her own mudder what loved her an' she'll never git anodder chance dis side of hell."

Jimmie thought he had a great idea of women's frailty, but he could not understand why any of his kin should be victims.

"Damn her," he fervidly said.

Again he wondered vaguely if some of the women of his acquaintance had brothers. Nevertheless, his mind did not for an instant confuse himself with those brothers nor his sister with theirs. After the mother had, with great difficulty, suppressed the neighbors, she went among them and proclaimed her grief. "May Gawd forgive dat girl," was her continual cry. To attentive ears she recited the whole length and breadth of her woes.

"I bringed 'er up deh way a dauter oughts be bringed up an' dis is how she served me! She went teh deh devil deh first chance she got! May Gawd forgive her."

When arrested for drunkenness she used the story of her daughter's downfall with telling effect upon the police justices. Finally one of them said to her, peering down over his spectacles: "Mary, the records of this and other courts show that you are the mother of forty-two daughters who have been ruined. The case is unparalleled in the annals of this court, and this court thinks—"

The mother went through life shedding large tears of sorrow. Her red face was a picture of agony.

Of course Jimmie publicly damned his sister that he might appear on a higher social plane. But, arguing with himself, stumbling about in ways that he knew not, he, once, almost came to a conclusion that his sister would have been more firmly good had she better known why. However, he felt that he could not hold such a view. He threw it hastily aside.

14

In a hilarious hall there were twenty-eight tables and twenty-eight women and a crowd of smoking men. Valiant noise was made on a stage at the end of the hall by an orchestra composed of men who looked as if they had just happened in. Soiled waiters ran to and fro, swooping down like hawks on the unwary in the throng; clattering along the aisles with trays covered with glasses; stumbling over women's skirts and charging two prices for everything but beer, all with a swiftness that blurred the view of the cocoanut palms and dusty monstrosities painted upon the walls of the room. A bouncer, with an[38] immense load of business upon his hands, plunged about in the crowd, dragging bashful strangers to prominent chairs, ordering waiters here and there and quarrelling[39] furiously with men who wanted to sing with the orchestra.

The usual smoke cloud was present, but so dense that heads and arms seemed entangled in it. The rumble of conversation was replaced by a roar. Plenteous oaths heaved through the air. The room rang with the shrill voices of women bubbling o'er with drink-laughter. The chief element in the music of the orchestra was speed. The musicians played in intent fury. A woman was singing and smiling upon the stage, but no one took notice of her. The rate at which the piano, cornet and violins were going, seemed to impart wildness to the half-drunken crowd. Beer glasses were emptied at a gulp and conversation became a rapid chatter. The smoke eddied and swirled like a shadowy river hurrying toward some unseen falls. Pete and Maggie entered the hall and took chairs at a table near the door. The woman who was seated there made an attempt to occupy Pete's attention and, failing, went away.

Three weeks had passed since the girl had left home. The air of spaniel-like dependence had been magnified and showed its direct effect in the peculiar off-handedness and ease of Pete's ways toward her.

She followed Pete's eyes with hers, anticipating with smiles gracious looks from him.

A woman of brilliance and audacity, accompanied by a mere boy, came into the place and took seats near them.

At once Pete sprang to his feet, his face beaming with glad surprise.

"By Gawd, there's Nellie," he cried.

He went over to the table and held out an eager hand to the woman.

"Why, hello, Pete, me boy, how are you," said she, giving him her fingers.

Maggie took instant note of the woman. She perceived that her black dress fitted her to perfection. Her linen collar and cuffs were spotless. Tan gloves were stretched over her well-shaped hands. A hat of a prevailing fashion perched jauntily upon her dark hair. She wore no jewelry and was painted with no apparent paint. She looked clear-eyed through the stares of the men.

"Sit down, and call your lady-friend over," she said cordially to Pete. At his beckoning Maggie came and sat between Pete and the mere boy.

"I thought yeh were gone away fer good," began Pete, at once. "When did yeh git back? How did dat Buff'lo busness turn out?"

The woman shrugged her shoulders. "Well, he didn't have as many stamps as he tried to make out, so I shook him, that's all."

"Well, I'm glad teh see yehs back in deh city," said Pete, with awkward gallantry.

He and the woman entered into a long conversation, exchanging reminiscences of days together. Maggie sat still, unable to formulate an intelligent sentence upon the conversation and painfully aware of it.

She saw Pete's eyes sparkle as he gazed upon the handsome stranger. He listened smilingly to all she said. The woman was familiar with all his affairs, asked him about mutual friends, and knew the amount of his salary.

She paid no attention to Maggie, looking toward her once or twice and apparently seeing the wall beyond.

The mere boy was sulky. In the beginning he had welcomed with acclamations the additions.

"Let's all have a drink! What'll you take, Nell? And you, Miss what's-your-name. Have a drink, Mr. ——, you, I mean."

He had shown a sprightly desire to do the talking for the company and tell all about his family. In a loud voice he declaimed on various topics. He assumed a patronizing air toward Pete. As Maggie was silent, he paid no attention to her. He made a great show of lavishing wealth upon the woman of brilliance and audacity.

"Do keep still, Freddie! You gibber like an ape, dear," said the woman to him. She turned away and devoted her attention to Pete.

"We'll have many a good time together again, eh?"

"Sure, Mike," said Pete, enthusiastic at once.

"Say," whispered she, leaning forward, "let's go over to Billie's and have a heluva time."

"Well, it's dis way! See?" said Pete. "I got dis lady frien' here."

"Oh, t'hell with her," argued the woman.

Pete appeared disturbed.

"All right," said she, nodding her head at him. "All right for you! We'll see the next time you ask me to go anywheres with you."

Pete squirmed.

"Say," he said, beseechingly, "come wid me a minit an' I'll tell yer why."

The woman waved her hand.

"Oh, that's all right, you needn't explain, you know. You wouldn't come merely because you wouldn't come, that's all there is of it."

To Pete's visible distress she turned to the mere boy, bringing him speedily from a terrific rage. He had been debating whether it would be the part of a man to pick a quarrel with Pete, or would he be justified in striking him savagely with his beer glass without warning. But he recovered himself when the woman returned to renew her smilings. He beamed upon her with an expression that was somewhat tipsy and inexpressibly tender.

"Say, shake that Bowery jay," requested he, in a loud whisper.

"Freddie, you are so droll," she replied.

Pete reached forward and touched the woman on the arm.

"Come out a minit while I tells yeh why I can't go wid yer. Yer doin' me dirt, Nell! I never taut ye'd do me dirt, Nell. Come on, will yer?" He spoke in tones of injury.

"Why, I don't see why I should be interested in your explanations," said the woman, with a coldness that seemed to reduce Pete to a pulp.

His eyes pleaded with her. "Come out a minit while I tells yeh."

The woman nodded slightly at Maggie and the mere boy, "Scuse me."

The mere boy interrupted his loving smile and turned a shriveling glare upon Pete. His boyish countenance flushed and he spoke, in a whine, to the woman:

"Oh, I say, Nellie, this ain't a square deal, you know. You aren't goin' to leave me and go off with that duffer, are you? I should think—"

"Why, you dear boy, of course I'm not," cried the woman, affectionately. She bended over and whispered in his ear. He smiled again and settled in his chair as if resolved to wait patiently.

As the woman walked down between the rows of tables, Pete was at her shoulder talking earnestly, apparently in explanation. The woman waved her hands with studied airs of indifference. The doors swung behind them, leaving Maggie and the mere boy seated at the table.

Maggie was dazed. She could dimly perceive that something stupendous had happened. She wondered why Pete saw fit to remonstrate with the woman, pleading for forgiveness with his eyes. She thought she noted an air of submission about her leonine Pete. She was astounded.

The mere boy occupied himself with cocktails and a cigar. He was tranquilly silent for half an hour. Then he bestirred himself and spoke.

"Well," he said sighing, "I knew this was the way it would be." There was another stillness. The mere boy seemed to be musing.

"She was pulling m'leg. That's the whole amount of it," he said, suddenly. "It's a bloomin' shame the way that girl does. Why, I've spent over two dollars in drinks to-night. And she goes off with that plug-ugly who looks as if he had been hit in the face with a coin die.[40] I call it rocky treatment for a fellah like me. Here, waiter, bring me a cocktail and make it damned strong."

Maggie made no reply. She was watching the doors. "It's a mean piece of business," complained the mere boy. He explained to her how amazing it was that anybody should treat him in such a manner. "But I'll get square with her, you bet. She won't get far ahead of yours truly, you know," he added, winking. "I'll tell her plainly that it was bloomin' mean business. And she won't come it over me with any of her 'now-Freddie-dears.' She thinks my name is Freddie, you know, but of course it ain't. I always tell these people some name like that, because if they got onto your right name they might use it sometime. Understand? Oh, they don't fool me much."

Maggie was paying no attention, being intent upon the doors. The mere boy relapsed into a period of gloom, during which he exterminated a number of cock-tails with a determined air, as if replying defiantly to fate. He occasionally broke forth into sentences composed of invectives joined together in a long string.

The girl was still staring at the doors. After a time the mere boy began to see cobwebs just in front of his nose. He spurred himself into being agreeable and insisted upon her having a charlotte-russe and a glass of beer.

"They's gone," he remarked, "they's gone." He looked at her through the smoke wreaths. "Shay, lil' girl, we mightish well make bes' of it. You ain't such bad lookin' girl, y'know. Not half bad. Can't come up to Nell, though. No, can't do it! Well, I should shay not! Nell fine-lookin' girl! F–i–n–ine. You look damn bad longsider her, but by y'self ain't so bad. Have to do anyhow. Nell gone. On' y[41] you left. Not half bad, though."

Maggie stood up.

"I'm going home," she said.

The mere boy started.

"Eh? What? Home," he cried, struck with amazement. "I beg pardon, did hear say home?"

"I'm going home," she repeated.

"Great Gawd, what hava struck?"[42] demanded the mere boy of himself, stupefied.

In a semi-comatose state he conducted her on board an up-town car, ostentatiously paid her fare, leered kindly at her through the rear window and fell off the steps.

15

A forlorn woman went along a lighted avenue. The street was filled with people desperately bound on missions. An endless crowd darted at the elevated station stairs and the horse cars were thronged with owners of bundles.

The pace of the forlorn woman was slow. She was apparently searching for some one. She loitered near the doors of saloons and watched men emerge from them. She scanned furtively the faces in the rushing stream of pedestrians. Hurrying men, bent on catching some boat or train, jostled her elbows, failing to notice her, their thoughts fixed on distant dinners.

The forlorn woman had a peculiar face. Her smile was no smile. But when in repose her features had a shadowy look that was like a sardonic grin, as if some one had sketched with cruel forefinger indelible lines about her mouth.

Jimmie came strolling up the avenue. The woman encountered him with an aggrieved air.

"Oh, Jimmie, I've been lookin' all over fer yehs—," she began.

Jimmie made an impatient gesture and quickened his pace.

"Ah, don't bodder me! Good Gawd!" he said, with the savageness of a man whose life is pestered.

The woman followed him along the sidewalk in somewhat the manner of a suppliant.

"But, Jimmie," she said, "yehs told me ye'd—"

Jimmie turned upon her fiercely as if resolved to make a last stand for comfort and peace.

"Say, fer Gawd's sake, Hattie, don' foller me from one end of deh city teh deh odder. Let up, will yehs! Give me a minute's res', can't yehs? Yehs makes me tired, allus taggin' me. See? Ain' yehs got no sense? Do yehs want people teh get onto me? Go chase yerself, fer Gawd's sake."

The woman stepped closer and laid her fingers on his arm. "But, look-a here—"

Jimmie snarled. "Oh, go teh hell."

He darted into the front door of a convenient saloon and a moment later came out into the shadows that surrounded the side door. On the brilliantly lighted avenue he perceived the forlorn woman dodging about like a scout. Jimmie laughed with an air of relief and went away.

When he arrived home he found his mother clamoring. Maggie had returned. She stood shivering beneath the torrent of her mother's wrath.

"Well, I'm damned," said Jimmie in greeting.

His mother, tottering about the room, pointed a quivering forefinger.

"Lookut her, Jimmie, lookut her. Dere's yer sister, boy. Dere's yer sister. Lookut her! Lookut her!"

She screamed in scoffing laughter.

The girl stood in the middle of the room. She edged about as if unable to find a place on the floor to put her feet.

"Ha, ha, ha," bellowed the mother. "Dere she stands! Ain' she purty? Lookut her! Ain' she sweet, deh beast? Lookut her! Ha, ha, lookut her!"

She lurched forward and put her red and seamed hands upon her daughter's face. She bent down and peered keenly up into the eyes of the girl.

"Oh, she's jes' dessame as she ever was, ain' she? She's her mudder's purty darlin' yit, ain' she? Lookut her, Jimmie! Come here, fer Gawd's sake, and lookut her."

The loud, tremendous sneering of the mother brought the denizens of the Rum Alley tenement to their doors. Women came in the hall-ways. Children scurried to and fro.

"What's up? Dat Johnson party on anudder tear?"

"Naw! Young Mag's come home!"

"Deh hell yeh say?"

Through the open doors curious eyes stared in at Maggie. Children ventured into the room and ogled her, as if they formed the front row at a theatre. Women, without, bended toward each other and whispered, nodding their heads with airs of profound philosophy. A baby, overcome with curiosity concerning this object at which all were looking, sidled forward and touched her dress, cautiously, as if investigating a red-hot stove. Its mother's voice rang out like a warning trumpet. She rushed forward and grabbed her child, casting a terrible look of indignation at the girl.

Maggie's mother paced to and fro, addressing the doorful of eyes, expounding like a glib showman at a museum. Her voice rang through the building.

"Dere she stands," she cried, wheeling suddenly and pointing with dramatic finger. "Dere she stands! Lookut her! Ain' she a dindy? An' she was so good as to come home teh her mudder, she was! Ain' she a beaut'? Ain' she a dindy? Fer Gawd's sake!"

The jeering cries ended in another burst of shrill laughter.

The girl seemed to awaken. "Jimmie—"

He drew hastily back from her.

"Well, now, yer a hell of a t'ing, ain' yeh?" he said, his lips curling in scorn. Radiant virtue sat upon his brow and his repelling hands expressed horror of contamination.

Maggie turned and went.

The crowd at the door fell back precipitately. A baby failing down in front of the door, wrenched a scream like a wounded animal from its mother. Another woman sprang forward and picked it up, with a chivalrous air, as if rescuing a human being from an oncoming express train.

As the girl passed down through the hall, she went before open doors framing more eyes strangely microscopic, and sending broad beams of inquisitive light into the darkness of her path. On the second floor she met the gnarled old woman who possessed the music box.

"So," she cried, "'ere yehs are back again, are yehs? An' dey've kicked yehs out? Well, come in an' stay wid me teh-night. I ain' got no moral standin'."

From above came an unceasing babble of tongues, over all of which rang the mother's derisive laughter.

16

Pete did not consider that he had ruined Maggie. If he had thought that her soul could never smile again, he would have believed the mother and brother, who were pyrotechnic over the affair, to be responsible for it.

Besides, in his world, souls did not insist upon being able to smile. "What deh hell?"

He felt a trifle entangled. It distressed him. Revelations and scenes might bring upon him the wrath of the owner of the saloon, who insisted upon respectability of an advanced type.

"What deh hell do dey wanna[43] raise such a smoke about it fer?" demanded he of himself, disgusted with the attitude of the family. He saw no necessity for anyone's losing their equilibrium merely because their sister or their daughter had stayed away from home.

Searching about in his mind for possible reasons for their conduct, he came upon the conclusion that Maggie's motives were correct, but that the two others wished to snare him. He felt pursued.

The woman of brilliance and audacity whom he had met in the hilarious hall showed a disposition to ridicule him.

"A little pale thing with no spirit," she said. "Did you note the expression of her eyes? There was something in them about pumpkin pie and virtue. That is a peculiar way the left corner of her mouth has of twitching, isn't it? Dear, dear, my cloud-compelling Pete, what are you coming to?"

Pete asserted at once that he never was very much interested in the girl. The woman interrupted him, laughing.

"Oh, it's not of the slightest consequence to me, my dear young man. You needn't draw maps for my benefit. Why should I be concerned about it?"

But Pete continued with his explanations. If he was laughed at for his tastes in women, he felt obliged to say that they were only temporary or indifferent ones.

The morning after Maggie had departed from home, Pete stood behind the bar. He was immaculate in white jacket and apron and his hair was plastered over his brow with infinite correctness. No customers were in the place. Pete was twisting his napkined fist slowly in a beer glass, softly whistling to himself and occasionally holding the object of his attention between his eyes and a few weak beams of sunlight that had found their way over the thick screens and into the shaded room.

With lingering thoughts of the woman of brilliance and audacity, the bartender raised his head and stared through the varying cracks between the swaying bamboo doors. Suddenly the whistling pucker faded from his lips. He saw Maggie walking slowly past. He gave a great start, fearing for the previously-mentioned eminent respectability of the place.

He threw a swift, nervous glance about him, all at once feeling guilty. No one was in the room.

He went hastily over to the side door. Opening it and looking out, he perceived Maggie standing, as if undecided, on the corner. She was searching the place with her eyes.

As she turned her face toward him Pete beckoned to her hurriedly, intent upon returning with speed to a position behind the bar and to the atmosphere of respectability upon which the proprietor insisted.

Maggie came to him, the anxious look disappearing from her face and a smile wreathing her lips.

"Oh, Pete—," she began brightly.

The bartender made a violent gesture of impatience.

"Oh, my Gawd," cried he, vehemently. "What deh hell do yeh wanna hang aroun' here fer? Do yeh wanna git me inteh trouble?" he demanded with an air of injury.

Astonishment swept over the girl's features. "Why, Pete! yehs tol' me—"

Pete glanced profound irritation. His countenance reddened with the anger of a man whose respectability is being threatened.

"Say, yehs makes me tired. See? What deh hell deh yeh wanna tag aroun' atter me fer? Yeh'll git me inteh trouble wid deh ol' man an' dey'll be hell teh pay! If he sees a woman roun' here he'll go crazy an' I'll lose me job! See? Ain' yehs got no sense? Don' be allus bodderin' me. See? Yer brudder come in here an' raised hell an' deh ol' man hada put up fer it! An' now I'm done! See? I'm done."

The girl's eyes stared into his face. "Pete, don' yeh remem—"

"Oh, hell," interrupted Pete, anticipating.

The girl seemed to have a struggle with herself. She was apparently bewildered and could not find speech. Finally she asked in a low voice: "But where kin I go?"

The question exasperated Pete beyond the powers of endurance. It was a direct attempt to give him some responsibility in a matter that did not concern him. In his indignation he volunteered information.

"Oh, go teh hell," cried he. He slammed the door furiously and returned, with an air of relief, to his respectability.

Maggie went away.

She wandered aimlessly for several blocks. She stopped once and asked aloud a question of herself: "Who?"

A man who was passing near her shoulder, humorously took the questioning word as intended for him.

"Eh? What? Who? Nobody! I did'nt say anything," he laughingly said, and continued his way.

Soon the girl discovered that if she walked with such apparent aimlessness, some men looked at her with calculating eyes. She quickened her step, frightened. As a protection, she adopted a demeanor of intentness as if going somewhere.

After a time she left rattling avenues and passed between rows of houses with sternness[44] and stolidity stamped upon their features. She hung her head for she felt their eyes grimly upon her.

Suddenly she came upon a stout gentleman in a silk hat and a chaste black coat, whose decorous row of buttons reached from his chin to his knees. The girl had heard of the Grace of God and she decided to approach this man.

His beaming, chubby face was a picture of benevolence and kind-heartedness. His eyes shone good-will.

But as the girl timidly accosted him, he gave a convulsive movement and saved his respectability by a vigorous side-step. He did not risk it to save a soul. For how was he to know that there was a soul before him that needed saving?

17

Upon a wet evening, several months after the last chapter,[45] two interminable rows of cars, pulled by slipping horses, jangled along a prominent side-street. A dozen cabs, with coat-enshrouded drivers, clattered to and fro. Electric lights, whirring softly, shed a blurred radiance. A flower dealer, his feet tapping impatiently, his nose and his wares glistening with rain-drops, stood behind an array of roses and chrysanthemums. Two or three theatres emptied a crowd upon the storm-swept pavements. Men pulled their hats over their eyebrows and raised their collars to their ears. Women shrugged impatient shoulders in their warm cloaks and stopped to arrange their skirts for a walk through the storm. People having been comparatively silent for two hours burst into a roar of conversation, their hearts still kindling from the glowings of the stage.

The pavements became tossing seas of umbrellas. Men stepped forth to hail cabs or cars, raising their fingers in varied forms of polite request or imperative demand. An endless procession wended toward elevated stations.* An atmosphere of pleasure and prosperity seemed to hang over the throng, born, perhaps, of good clothes and of having just emerged from a place of forgetfulness.

In the mingled light and gloom of an adjacent park, a handful of wet wanderers, in attitudes of chronic dejection, was scattered among the benches.

A girl of the painted cohorts of the city went along the street. She threw changing glances at men who passed her, giving smiling invitations to men of rural or untaught pattern and usually seeming sedately unconscious of the men with a metropolitan seal upon their faces.

Crossing glittering avenues, she went into the throng emerging from the places of forgetness. She hurried forward through the crowd as if intent upon reaching a distant home, bending forward in her handsome cloak, daintily lifting her skirts and picking for her well-shod feet the dryer spots upon the pavements.

The restless doors of saloons, clashing to and fro, disclosed animated rows of men before bars and hurrying barkeepers.

A concert hall gave to the street faint sounds of swift, machinelike music, as if a group of phantom musicians were hastening.

A tall young man, smoking a cigarette with a sublime air, strolled near the girl. He had on evening dress, a moustache, a chrysanthemum, and a look of ennui, all of which he kept carefully under his eye. Seeing the girl walk on as if such a young man as he was not in existence, he looked back transfixed with interest. He stared glassily for a moment, but gave a slight convulsive start when he discerned that she was neither new, Parisian, nor theatrical. He wheeled about hastily and turned his stare into the air, like a sailor with a search-light.

A stout gentleman, with pompous and philanthropic whiskers, went stolidly by, the broad of his back sneering at the girl.

A belated man in business clothes, and in haste to catch a car, bounced against her shoulder. "Hi, there, Mary, I beg your pardon! Brace up, old girl." He grasped her arm to steady her, and then was away running down the middle of the street.

The girl walked on out of the realm of restaurants and saloons. She passed more glittering avenues and went into darker blocks than those where the crowd travelled.

A young man in light overcoat and derby hat received a glance shot keenly from the eyes of the girl. He stopped and looked at her, thrusting his hands in his pockets and making a mocking smile curl his lips. "Come, now, old lady," he said, "you don't mean to tell me that you sized me up for a farmer?"

---

* Stations of the elevated railways, now almost entirely demolished in Manhattan.

A laboring man marched along with bundles under his arms. To her remarks, he replied: "It's a fine evenin', ain't it?"

She smiled squarely into the face of a boy who was hurrying by with his hand buried in his overcoat, his blonde locks bobbing on his youthful temples, and a cheery smile of unconcern upon his lips. He turned his head and smiled back at her, waving his hands.

"Not this eve—some other eve!"

A drunken man, reeling in her pathway, began to roar at her. "I ain' ga no money, dammit," he shouted, in a dismal voice. He lurched on up the street, wailing to himself, "Dammit, I ain' ga no money. Damn ba' luck. Ain'ga no more money."

The girl went into gloomy districts near the river, where the tall black factories shut in the street and only occasional broad beams of light fell across the pavements from saloons. In front of one of these places, from whence came the sound of a violin vigorously scraped, the patter of feet on boards and the ring of loud laughter, there stood a man with blotched features.

"Ah, there," said the girl.

"I've got a date," said the man.

Further on in the darkness she met a ragged being with shifting, blood-shot eyes and grimy[46] hands. "Ah, what deh hell? T'ink I'm a millionaire?"

She went into the blackness of the final block. The shutters of the tall buildings were closed like grim lips. The structures seemed to have eyes[47] that looked over her, beyond her, at other things. Afar off the lights of the avenues glittered as if from an impossible distance. Street car bells jingled with a sound of merriment.

When almost to the river the girl saw a great figure. On going forward she perceived it to be a huge fat man in torn and greasy garments. His grey hair straggled down over his forehead. His small, bleared eyes, sparkling from amidst great rolls of red fat, swept eagerly over the girl's upturned face. He laughed, his brown, disordered teeth gleaming under a grey, grizzled moustache from which beer-drops dripped. His whole body gently quivered and shook like that of a dead jelly fish. Chuckling and leering, he followed the girl of the crimson legions.

At their feet the river appeared a deathly black hue. Some hidden factory sent up a yellow glare, that lit for a moment the waters lapping oilily against timbers. The varied sounds of life, made joyous by distance and seeming unapproachableness, came faintly and died away to a silence.

18

In a partitioned-off section of a saloon sat a man with a half dozen women, gleefully laughing, hovering about him. The man had arrived at that stage of drunkenness where affection is felt for the universe.

"I'm good f'ler, girls," he said, convincingly. "I'm damn good f'ler. An'body treats me right, I allus trea's zem right! See?"

The women nodded their heads approvingly. "To be sure," they cried in hearty chorus. "You're the kind of a man we like, Pete. You're outa sight! What yeh goin' to buy this time, dear?"

"An'thin' yehs wants, damn it," said the man in an abandonment of good will. His countenance shone with the true spirit of benevolence. He was in the proper mode of missionaries. He would have fraternized with obscure Hottentots. And above all, he was overwhelmed in tenderness for his friends, who were all illustrious.

"An'thing yehs wants, damn it," repeated he, waving his hands with beneficent recklessness. "I'm good f'ler, girls, an' if an' body treats me right I—here," called he through an open door to a waiter, "bring girls drinks, damn it. What 'ill yehs have, girls? An'thing yehs want, damn it!"

The waiter glanced in with the disgusted look of the man who serves intoxicants for the man who takes too much of them. He nodded his head shortly at the order from each individual, and went.

"Damn it," said the man, "we're havin' heluva time. I like you girls! Damn'd if I don't! Yer right sort! See?"

He spoke at length and with feeling, concerning the excellencies of his assembled friends.

"Don' try pull man's leg, but have a heluva time! Das right! Das way teh do! Now, if I sawght* yehs tryin' work me fer drinks, wouldn' buy damn t'ing! But yer right sort, damn it! Yehs know how ter treata a f'ler, an' I stays by yehs 'til spen' las' cent! Das right! I'm good f'ler an' I knows when an'body treats me right!"

Between the times of the arrival and departure of the waiter, the man discoursed to the women on the tender regard he felt for all living things. He laid stress upon the purity of his motives in all dealings with men in the world and spoke of the fervor of his friendship for those who were amiable. Tears welled slowly from his eyes. His voice quavered when he spoke to them.

Once when the waiter was about to depart with an empty tray, the man drew a coin from his pocket and held it forth.

"Here," said he, quite magnificently "here's quar.'"

The waiter kept his hands on his tray.

"I don' want yer money," he said.

The other put forth the coin with tearful insistence.

"Here, damn it," cried he, "tak't! Yer damn goo' f'ler an' I wan' yehs tak't!"

"Come, come, now," said the waiter, with the sullen air of a man who is forced into giving advice. "Put yer mon in yer pocket! Yer loaded an' yehs on'y makes a damn fool of yerself."

As the latter passed out of the door the man turned pathetically to the women.

"He don' know I'm damn goo' f'ler," cried he, dismally.

"Never you mind, Pete, dear," said a woman of brilliance and audacity, laying her hand with great affection upon his arm. "Never you mind, old boy! We'll stay by you, dear!"

"Das ri'," cried the man, his face lighting up at the soothing tones of the woman's voice. "Das ri', I'm damn goo' f'ler an' w'en anyone trea's me' ri', I treats zem ri'! Shee!"

---

* Probably should be "taght" for "thought," a word Crane earlier has rendered phonetically as "taut."

"Sure!" cried the women. "And we're not goin' back on you, old man."

The man turned appealing eyes to the woman of brilliance and audacity. He felt that if he could be convicted of a contemptible action he would die.

"Shay, Nell, damn it, I allus trea's yehs shquare, didn' I? I allus been goo' f'ler wi' yehs, ain't I, Nell?"

"Sure you have, Pete," assented the woman. She delivered an oration to her companions. "Yessir, that's a fact. Pete's a square fellah, he is. He never goes back on a friend. He's the right kind an' we stay by him, don't we, girls?"

"Sure," they exclaimed. Looking lovingly at him they raised their glasses and drank his health.

"Girlsh," said the man, beseechingly, "I allus trea's yehs ri', didn' I? I'm goo' f'ler, ain' I, girish?"

"Sure,"[48] again they chorused.

"Well," said he finally, "le's have nozzer drink, zen."

"That's right," hailed a woman, "that's right. Yer no bloomin' jay! Yer spends yer money like a man. Dat's right."

The man pounded the table with his quivering fists.

"Yessir," he cried, with deep earnestness, as if someone disputed him. "I'm damn goo' f'ler, an' w'en anyone trea's me ri', I allus trea's—le's have nozzer drink."

He began to beat the wood with his glass.

"Shay," howled he, growing suddenly impatient. As the waiter did not then come, the man swelled with wrath.

"Shay," howled he again.

The waiter appeared at the door.

"Bringsh drinksh," said the man.

The waiter disappeared with the orders.

"Zat f'ler dam fool," cried the man. "He insul' me! I'm ge'man! Can' stan' be insul'! I'm goin' lickim when comes!"

"No, no," cried the women, crowding about and trying to subdue him. "He's all right! He didn't mean anything! Let it go! He's a good fellah!"

"Din' he insul' me?" asked the man earnestly.

"No," said they. "Of course he didn't. He's all right!"

"Sure he didn' insul' me," demanded the man, with deep anxiety in his voice.

"No, no! We know him! He's a good fellah. He didn't mean anything."

"Well, zen," said the man, resolutely, "I'm go' 'pol'gize!"

When the waiter came, the man struggled to the middle of the floor.

"Girlsh shed you insul' me! I shay damn lie! I 'pol'gize!"

"All right," said the waiter.

The man sat down. He felt a sleepy but strong desire to straighten things out and have a perfect understanding with everybody.

"Nell, I allus trea's yeh shquare, din I? Yeh likes me, don' yehs, Nell? I'm goo' f'ler?"

"Sure," said the woman of brilliance and audacity.

"Yeh knows I'm stuck on yehs, don' yehs, Nell?"

"Sure," she repeated, carelessly.

Overwhelmed by a spasm of drunken adoration, he drew two or three bills from his pocket, and, with the trembling fingers of an offering priest, laid them on the table before the woman.

"Yehs knows, damn it, yehs kin have all got, 'cause I'm stuck on yehs, Nell, damn't, I—I'm stuck on yehs, Nell—buy drinksh 'damn't—we're havin' heleva time— w'en anyone trea's me ri'—I—damn't. Nell—we're havin' heluva—time."

Shortly he went to sleep with his swollen face fallen forward on his chest.

The women drank and laughed, not heeding the slumbering man in the corner. Finally he lurched forward and fell groaning to the floor.

The women screamed in disgust and drew back their skirts.

"Come ahn," cried one, starting up angrily, "let's get out of here."

The woman of brilliance and audacity stayed behind, taking up the bills and stuffing them into a deep, irregularly-shaped pocket. A gutteral snore from the recumbent man caused her to turn and look down at him.

She laughed. "What a damn fool," she said, and went.

The smoke from the lamps settled heavily down in the little compartment, obscuring the way out. The smell of oil, stifling in its intensity, pervaded the air. The wine from an overturned glass dripped softly down upon the blotches on the man's neck.

19

In a room a woman sat at a table eating like a fat monk in a picture.

A soiled, unshaven man pushed open the door and entered.

"Well," said he, "Mag's dead."

"What?" said the woman, her mouth filled with bread.

"Mag's dead," repeated the man.

"Deh hell she is," said the woman. She continued her meal. When she finished her coffee she began to weep.

"I kin remember when her two feet was no bigger dan yer t'umb[49] and she weared worsted boots," moaned she.

"Well, whata dat?" said the man.

"I kin remember when she weared worsted boots," she cried.

The neighbors began to gather in the hall, staring in at the weeping woman as if watching the contortions of a dying dog. A dozen women entered and lamented with her. Under their busy hands the rooms took on that appalling appearance of neatness and order with which death is greeted.

Suddenly the door opened and a woman in a black gown rushed in with out-stretched arms. "Ah, poor Mary," she cried, and tenderly embraced the moaning one.

"Ah, what ter'ble affliction is dis," continued she. Her vocabulary was derived from mission churches. "Me poor Mary, how I feel fer yehs! Ah, what a ter'ble affliction is a disobed'ent chile."

Her good, motherly face was wet with tears. She trembled in eagerness to express her sympathy. The mourner sat with bowed head, rocking her body heavily to and fro, and crying out in a high, strained voice that sounded like a dirge on some forlorn pipe.

"I kin remember when she weared worsted boots an' her two feets was no bigger dan yer t'umb[50] an' she weared worsted boots, Miss Smith," she cried, raising her streaming eyes.

"Ah, me poor Mary," sobbed the woman in black. With low, coddling cries, she sank on her knees by the mourner's chair, and put her arms about her. The other women began to groan in different keys.

"Yer poor misguided chil' is gone now, Mary, an' let us hope it's[51] fer deh bes'. Yeh'll fergive her now, Mary, won't yehs, dear, all her disobedience? All her t'ankless[52] behavior to her mudder an' all her badness? She's gone where her ter'ble sins will be judged."

The woman in black raised her face and paused. The inevitable sunlight came streaming in at the windows and shed a ghastly cheerfulness upon the faded hues of the room. Two or three of the spectators were sniffling, and one was loudly weeping. The mourner arose and staggered into the other room. In a moment she emerged with a pair of faded baby shoes held in the hollow of her hand.

"I kin remember when she used to wear dem," cried she. The women burst anew into cries as if they had all been stabbed. The mourner turned to the soiled and unshaven man.

"Jimmie, boy, go git yer sister! Go git yer sister an' we'll put deh boots on her feets!"

"Dey won't fit her now, yeh damn fool," said the man.

"Go git yer sister, Jimmie," shrieked the woman, confronting him fiercely.

The man swore sullenly. He went over to a corner and slowly began to put on his coat. He took his hat and went out, with a dragging, reluctant step.

The woman in black came forward and again besought the mourner.

"Yeh'll fergive her, Mary! Yeh'll fergive yer bad, bad chil'! Her life was a curse an' her days were black an' yeh'll fergive yer bad girl? She's gone where her sins will be judged."

"She's gone where her sins will be judged," cried the other women, like a choir at a funeral.

"Deh Lord gives and deh Lord takes away," said the woman in black, raising her eyes to the sunbeams.

"Deh Lord gives and deh Lord takes away," responded the others.

"Yeh'll fergive her, Mary!" pleaded the woman in black. The mourner essayed to speak but her voice gave way. She shook her great shoulders frantically, in an agony of grief. Hot tears seemed to scald her quivering face. Finally her voice came and arose like a scream of pain.

"Oh, yes, I'll fergive her! I'll fergive her!"

1893

[1]1893: can't fight. Blue Billie!

[2]1893: distainfully.

[3]1893: This may be a spelling error, for "careen"—denoting a lurching movement—is a more suitable word in the context.

[4]1893: perceive it

[5]1893: chrisanthemums

[6]1893: island.

[7]1893: trouble;' like

[8]1893: See."

[9]1893: grimey

[10]1893: tree

[11]1893: tau't

[12]1893: of world

[13]1893: admirable

[14]1893: obliged

[15]1893: trash

[16]1893: monkeys

[17]1893: He

[18]1893: 'Disturbance?'

[19]1893: Missles

[20] 1893: tin a

[21]1893: "Dere damn yeh,

[22]1893: now, door

[23]1893: riddance.

[24]1893: be

[25]1893: "Oh, hell, yes," he says, says he, "Oh, hell, yes."

[26]1893: "Oh, hell, yes,"

[27]1893: tump

[28]1893: begrimmed

[29]1893: talkin?"

[30]1893: boat

[31]1893: eyes

[32]1893: missles

[33]1893: missles

[34]1893: smoked-filled

[35]1893: squdgy: omitted in 1896 edition.

[36]1893: an—"

[37]1893: anyway, explained.

[38]1893: a

[39]1893: quarreling

[40]1893: coin-dye

[41]1893: gone O'ny

[42]1893: struck," demanded

[43]1893: wanna'

[44]1893: sterness

[45]1893: chapter two

[46]1893: grimey

[47]1893: eyet

[48]1893: "Sure." again

[49]1893: tumb

[50]1893: tumb

[51]1893: its

[52]1893: tankless

Journal Writing

React to the idea that "Maggie: A Girl of the Streets" explores the effects of the environment on human lives.

Textual Considerations

1. Make a list of some of the basic images Stephen Crane uses to describe Rum Alley and the Bowery. How do these images contribute to our understanding of Maggie, Jimmie, Mr. and Mrs. Johnson?
2. What does "home" mean to the protagonists in the story? How does home contrast with the world outdoors?

3. How is Maggie characterized? To what extent is she a victim of her environment? How do you account for Crane's assessment that Maggie possesses "none of the dirt of Rum Alley . . . in her veins"? To what extent do you empathize with her?
4. How does the dialect used in "Maggie" contribute to the authenticity of the story?

Cultural Contexts

1. Characterize the middle-class morality of the Johnsons. Discuss how and why their moral values centered on family life and respectability seem false and out of place at the Bowery.
2. To what extent would you consider "Maggie" a protest story? Make a list of the social injustices that the text explores and debate with your classmates whether these social situations, especially the ones underlining the problems of the American inner cities, have been corrected.

Edith Wharton

Roman Fever

I

From the table at which they had been lunching two American ladies of ripe but well-cared-for middle age moved across the lofty terrace of the Roman restaurant and, leaning on its parapet, looked first at each other, and then down on the outspread glories of the Palatine and the Forum, with the same expression of vague but benevolent approval.

As they leaned there a girlish voice echoed up gaily from the stairs leading to the court below. "Well, come along, then," it cried, not to them but to an invisible companion, "and let's leave the young things to their knitting"; and a voice as fresh laughed back: "Oh, look here, Babs, not actually *knitting*—" "Well, I mean figuratively," rejoined the first. "After all, we haven't left our poor parents much else to do. . . ." and at that point the turn of the stairs engulfed the dialogue.

The two ladies looked at each other again, this time with a tinge of smiling embarrassment, and the smaller and paler one shook her head and colored slightly.

"Barbara!" she murmured, sending an unheard rebuke after the mocking voice in the stairway.

The other lady, who was fuller, and higher in color, with a small determined nose supported by vigorous black eyebrows, gave a good-humored laugh. "That's what our daughters think of us!"

Her companion replied by a deprecating gesture. "Not of us individually. We must remember that. It's just the collective modern idea of Mothers. And you see—" Half-guiltily she drew from her handsomely mounted black handbag a twist of crimson silk run through by two fine knitting needles. "One never knows," she murmured. "The new system has certainly given us a good deal of time to kill; and sometimes I get tired just looking—even at this." Her gesture was now addressed to the stupendous scene at their feet.

The dark lady laughed again, and they both relapsed upon the view, contemplating it in silence, with a sort of diffused serenity which might have been borrowed from the spring effulgence of the Roman skies. The luncheon hour was long past, and the two had their end of the vast terrace to themselves. At its opposite extremity a few groups, detained by a lingering look at the outspread city, were gathering up guidebooks and fumbling for tips. The last of them scattered, and the two ladies were alone on the air-washed height.

"Well, I don't see why we shouldn't just stay here," said Mrs. Slade, the lady of the high color and energetic brows. Two derelict basket chairs stood near and she pushed them into the angle of the parapet, and settled herself in one, her gaze upon the Palatine. "After all, it's still the most beautiful view in the world."

"It always will be, to me," assented her friend Mrs. Ansley, with so slight a stress on the "me" that Mrs. Slade, though she noticed it, wondered if it were not merely accidental, like the random underlinings of old-fashioned letter writers.

"Grace Ansley was always old-fashioned," she thought; and added aloud, with a retrospective smile: "It's a view we've both been familiar with for a good many years. When we first met here we were younger than our girls are now. You remember?"

"Oh, yes, I remember," murmured Mrs. Ansley, with the same undefinable stress. "There's that headwaiter wondering," she interpolated. She was evidently far less sure than her companion of herself and of her rights in the world.

"I'll cure him of wondering," said Mrs. Slade, stretching her hand toward a bag as discreetly opulent-looking as Mrs. Ansley's. Signing to the headwaiter, she explained that she and her friend were old lovers of Rome, and would like to spend the end of the afternoon looking down on the view—that is, if it did not disturb the service? The headwaiter, bowing over her gratuity, assured her that the ladies were most welcome, and would be still more so if they would condescend to remain for dinner. A full-moon night, they would remember. . . .

Mrs. Slade's black brows drew together, as though references to the moon were out of place and even unwelcome. But she smiled away her frown as the headwaiter retreated. "Well, why not? We might do worse. There's no knowing, I suppose, when the girls will be back. Do you even know back from *where*? I don't!"

Mrs. Ansley again colored slightly. "I think those young Italian aviators we met at the Embassy invited them to fly to Tarquinia for tea. I suppose they'll want to wait and fly back by moonlight."

"Moonlight—moonlight! What a part it still plays. Do you suppose they're as sentimental as we were?"

"I've come to the conclusion that I don't in the least know what they are," said Mrs. Ansley. "And perhaps we didn't know much more about each other."

"No; perhaps we didn't."

Her friend gave her a shy glance. "I never should have supposed you were sentimental, Alida."

"Well, perhaps I wasn't." Mrs. Slade drew her lids together in retrospect; and for a few moments the two ladies, who had been intimate since childhood, reflected how little they knew each other. Each one, of course, had a label ready to attach to the other's name; Mrs. Delphin Slade, for instance, would have told herself, or anyone who asked her, that Mrs. Horace Ansley, twenty-five years ago, had been exquisitely lovely—no, you wouldn't believe it, would you? . . . though, of course, still charming, distinguished. . . . Well, as a girl she had been exquisite; far more beautiful than her daughter Barbara, though certainly Babs, according to the new standards at any rate, was more effective—had more *edge*, as they say. Funny where she got it, with those two nullities as parents. Yes; Horace Ansley was—well, just the duplicate of his wife. Museum specimens of old New York. Good-looking, irreproachable, exemplary. Mrs. Slade and Mrs. Ansley had lived opposite each other—actually as well as figuratively—for years. When the drawing-room curtains in No. 20 East 73rd Street were renewed, No. 23, across the way, was always aware of it. And of all the movings, buyings, travels, anniversaries, illnesses—the tame chronicle of an estimable pair. Little of it escaped Mrs. Slade. But she had grown bored with it by the time her husband made his big *coup* in Wall Street, and when they bought in upper Park Avenue had already begun to think: "I'd rather live opposite a speakeasy for a change; at least one might see it raided." The idea of seeing Grace raided was so amusing that (before the move) she launched it at a woman's lunch. It made a hit, and went the rounds—she sometimes wondered if it had crossed the street, and reached Mrs. Ansley. She hoped not, but didn't much mind. Those were the days when respectability was at a discount, and it did the irreproachable no harm to laugh at them a little.

A few years later, and not many months apart, both ladies lost their husbands. There was an appropriate exchange of wreaths and condolences, and a brief renewal of intimacy in the half-shadow of their mourning; and now, after another interval, they had run across each other in Rome, at the same hotel, each of them the modest appendage of a salient daughter. The similarity of their lot had again drawn them together, lending itself to mild jokes, and the mutual confession that, if in old days it must have been tiring to "keep up" with daughters, it was now, at times, a little dull not to.

No doubt, Mrs. Slade reflected, she felt her unemployment more than poor Grace ever would. It was a big drop from being the wife of Delphin Slade to being his widow. She had always regarded herself (with a certain conjugal pride) as his equal in social gifts, as contributing her full share to the making of the exceptional couple they were: but the difference after his death was irremediable. As the wife of the famous corporation lawyer, always with an international case or two on hand, every day brought its exciting and unexpected obligation: the impromptu entertaining of eminent colleagues from abroad, the hurried dashes on legal business to London, Paris or Rome, where the entertaining was so handsomely reciprocated;

the amusement of hearing in her wake: "What, that handsome woman with the good clothes and the eyes is Mrs. Slade—*the* Slade's wife? Really? Generally the wives of celebrities are such frumps."

Yes; being *the* Slade's widow was a dullish business after that. In living up to such a husband all her faculties had been engaged; now she had only her daughter to live up to, for the son who seemed to have inherited his father's gifts had died suddenly in boyhood. She had fought through that agony because her husband was there, to be helped and to help; now, after the father's death, the thought of the boy had become unbearable. There was nothing left but to mother her daughter; and dear Jenny was such a perfect daughter that she needed no excessive mothering. "Now with Babs Ansley I don't know that I *should* be so quiet," Mrs. Slade sometimes half-enviously reflected; but Jenny, who was younger than her brilliant friend, was that rare accident, an extremely pretty girl who somehow made youth and prettiness seem as safe as their absence. It was all perplexing—and to Mrs. Slade a little boring. She wished that Jenny would fall in love—with the wrong man, even; that she might have to be watched, out-maneuvered, rescued. And instead, it was Jenny who watched her mother, kept her out of drafts, made sure that she had taken her tonic. . . .

Mrs. Ansley was much less articulate than her friend, and her mental portrait of Mrs. Slade was slighter, and drawn with fainter touches. "Alida Slade's awfully brilliant; but not as brilliant as she thinks," would have summed it up; though she would have added, for the enlightenment of strangers, that Mrs. Slade had been an extremely dashing girl; much more so than her daughter, who was pretty, of course, and clever in a way, but had none of her mother's—well, "vividness," someone had once called it. Mrs. Ansley would take up current words like this, and cite them in quotation marks, as unheard-of audacities. No; Jenny was not like her mother. Sometimes Mrs. Ansley thought Alida Slade was disappointed; on the whole she had had a sad life. Full of failures and mistakes; Mrs. Ansley had always been rather sorry for her. . . .

So these two ladies visualized each other, each through the wrong end of her little telescope.

II

For a long time they continued to sit side by side without speaking. It seemed as though, to both, there was a relief in laying down their somewhat futile activities in the presence of the vast Memento Mori which faced them. Mrs. Slade sat quite still, her eyes fixed on the golden slope of the Palace of the Caesars, and after a while Mrs. Ansley ceased to fidget with her bag, and she too sank into meditation. Like many intimate friends, the two ladies had never before had occasion to be silent together, and Mrs. Ansley was slightly embarrassed by what seemed, after so many years, a new stage in their intimacy, and one with which she did not yet know how to deal.

Suddenly the air was full of that deep clangor of bells which periodically covers Rome with a roof of silver. Mrs. Slade glanced at her wristwatch. "Five o'clock already," she said, as though surprised.

Mrs. Ansley suggested interrogatively: "There's bridge at the Embassy at five." For a long time Mrs. Slade did not answer. She appeared to be lost in contemplation, and Mrs. Ansley thought the remark had escaped her. But after a while she said, as if speaking out of a dream: "Bridge, did you say? Not unless you want to. . . . But I don't think I will, you know."

"Oh, no," Mrs. Ansley hastened to assure her. "I don't care to at all. It's so lovely here; and so full of old memories, as you say." She settled herself in her chair, and almost furtively drew forth her knitting. Mrs. Slade took sideway note of this activity, but her own beautifully cared-for hands remained motionless on her knee.

"I was just thinking," she said slowly, "what different things Rome stands for to each generation of travelers. To our grandmothers, Roman fever; to our mothers, sentimental dangers—how we used to be guarded!—to our daughters, no more dangers than the middle of Main Street. They don't know it—but how much they're missing!"

The long golden light was beginning to pale, and Mrs. Ansley lifted her knitting a little closer to her eyes. "Yes; how we were guarded!"

"I always used to think," Mrs. Slade continued, "that our mothers had a much more difficult job than our grandmothers. When Roman fever stalked the streets it must have been comparatively easy to gather in the girls at the danger hour; but when you and I were young, with such beauty calling us, and the spice of disobedience thrown in, and no worse risk than catching cold during the cool hour after sunset, the mothers used to be put to it to keep us in—didn't they?"

She turned again toward Mrs. Ansley, but the latter had reached a delicate point in her knitting. "One, two, three—slip two; yes, they must have been," she assented, without looking up.

Mrs. Slade's eyes rested on her with a deepened attention. "She can knit—in the face of *this*! How like her. . . . "

Mrs. Slade leaned back, brooding, her eyes ranging from the ruins which faced her to the long green hollow of the Forum, the fading glow of the church fronts beyond it, and the outlying immensity of the Colosseum. Suddenly she thought: "It's all very well to say that our girls have done away with sentiment and moonlight. But if Babs Ansley isn't out to catch that young aviator—the one who's a Marchese—then I don't know anything. And Jenny has no chance beside her. I know that too. I wonder if that's why Grace Ansley likes the two girls to go everywhere together? My poor Jenny as a foil—!" Mrs. Slade gave a hardly audible laugh, and at the sound Mrs. Ansley dropped her knitting.

"Yes—?"

"I—oh, nothing. I was only thinking how your Babs carries everything before her. That Campolieri boy is one of the best matches in Rome. Don't look so innocent, my dear—you know he is. And I was wondering, ever so respectfully, you understand . . . wondering how two such exemplary characters as you and Horace had managed to produce anything quite so dynamic." Mrs. Slade laughed again, with a touch of asperity.

Mrs. Ansley's hands lay inert across her needles. She looked straight out at the great accumulated wreckage of passion and splendor at her feet. But her small profile was almost expressionless. At length she said: "I think you overrate Babs, my dear."

Mrs. Slade's tone grew easier. "No; I don't. I appreciate her. And perhaps envy you. Oh, my girl's perfect; if I were a chronic invalid I'd—well, I think I'd rather be in Jenny's hands. There must be times . . . but there! I always wanted a brilliant daughter . . . and never quite understood why I got an angel instead."

Mrs. Ansley echoed her laugh in a faint murmur. "Babs is an angel too."

"Of course—of course! But she's got rainbow wings. Well, they're wandering by the sea with their young men; and here we sit . . . and it all brings back the past a little too acutely."

Mrs. Ansley had resumed her knitting. One might almost have imagined (if one had known her less well, Mrs. Slade reflected) that, for her also, too many memories rose from the lengthening shadows of those august ruins. But no; she was simply absorbed in her work. What was there for her to worry about? She knew that Babs would almost certainly come back engaged to the extremely eligible Campolieri. "And she'll sell the New York house, and settle down near them in Rome, and never be in their way . . . she's much too tactful. But she'll have an excellent cook, and just the right people in for bridge and cocktails . . . and a perfectly peaceful old age among her grandchildren."

Mrs. Slade broke off this prophetic flight with a recoil of self-disgust. There was no one of whom she had less right to think unkindly than of Grace Ansley. Would she never cure herself of envying her? Perhaps she had begun too long ago.

She stood up and leaned against the parapet, filling her troubled eyes with the tranquilizing magic of the hour. But instead of tranquilizing her the sight seemed to increase her exasperation. Her gaze turned toward the Colosseum. Already its golden flank was drowned in purple shadow, and above it the sky curved crystal clear, without light or color. It was the moment when afternoon and evening hang balanced in mid-heaven.

Mrs. Slade turned back and laid her hand on her friend's arm. The gesture was so abrupt that Mrs. Ansley looked up, startled.

"The sun's set. You're not afraid, my dear?"

"Afraid—?"

"Of Roman fever or pneumonia? I remember how ill you were that winter. As a girl you had a very delicate throat, hadn't you?"

"Oh, we're all right up here. Down below, in the Forum, it does get deathly cold, all of a sudden . . . but not here."

"Ah, of course you know because you had to be so careful." Mrs. Slade turned back to the parapet. She thought: "I must make one more effort not to hate her." Aloud she said: "Whenever I look at the Forum from up here, I remember that story about a great-aunt of yours, wasn't she? A dreadfully wicked great-aunt?"

"Oh, yes; great-aunt Harriet. The one who was supposed to have sent her young sister out to the Forum after sunset to gather a night-blooming flower for her album. All our great-aunts and grandmothers used to have albums of dried flowers."

Mrs. Slade nodded. "But she really sent her because they were in love with the same man—"

"Well, that was the family tradition. They said Aunt Harriet confessed it years afterward. At any rate, the poor little sister caught the fever and died. Mother used to frighten us with the story when we were children."

"And you frightened *me* with it, that winter when you and I were here as girls. The winter I was engaged to Delphin."

Mrs. Ansley gave a faint laugh. "Oh, did I? Really frightened you? I don't believe you're easily frightened."

"Not often; but I was then. I was easily frightened because I was too happy. I wonder if you know what that means?"

"I—yes . . . " Mrs. Ansley faltered.

"Well, I suppose that was why the story of your wicked aunt made such an impression on me. And I thought: 'There's no more Roman fever, but the Forum is deathly cold after sunset—especially after a hot day. And the Colosseum's even colder and damper'."

"The Colosseum—?"

"Yes. It wasn't easy to get in, after the gates were locked for the night. Far from easy. Still, in those days it could be managed; it *was* managed, often. Lovers met there who couldn't meet elsewhere. You knew that?"

"I—I dare say. I don't remember."

"You don't remember? You don't remember going to visit some ruins or other one evening, just after dark, and catching a bad chill? You were supposed to have gone to see the moon rise. People always said that expedition was what caused your illness."

There was a moment's silence; then Mrs. Ansley rejoined: "Did they? It was all so long ago."

"Yes. And you got well again—so it didn't matter. But I suppose it struck your friends—the reason given for your illness, I mean—because everybody knew you were so prudent on account of your throat, and your mother took such care of you. . . . You *had* been out late sight-seeing, hadn't you, that night?"

"Perhaps I had. The most prudent girls aren't always prudent. What made you think of it now?"

Mrs. Slade seemed to have no answer ready. But after a moment she broke out: "Because I simply can't bear it any longer—!"

Mrs. Ansley lifted her head quickly. Her eyes were wide and very pale. "Can't bear what?"

"Why—your not knowing that I've always known why you went."

"Why I went—?"

"Yes. You think I'm bluffing, don't you? Well, you went to meet the man I was engaged to—and I can repeat every word of the letter that took you there."

While Mrs. Slade spoke Mrs. Ansley had risen unsteadily to her feet. Her bag, her knitting and gloves, slid in a panic-stricken heap to the ground. She looked at Mrs. Slade as though she were looking at a ghost.

"No, no—don't," she faltered out.

"Why not? Listen, if you don't believe me. 'My one darling, things can't go on like this. I must see you alone. Come to the Colosseum immediately after dark tomorrow. There will be somebody to let you in. No one whom you need fear will suspect'—but perhaps you've forgotten what the letter said?"

Mrs. Ansley met the challenge with an unexpected composure. Steadying herself against the chair she looked at her friend, and replied: "No; I know it by heart too."

"And the signature? 'Only *your* D.S.' Was that it? I'm right, am I? That was the letter that took you out that evening after dark?"

Mrs. Ansley was still looking at her. It seemed to Mrs. Slade that a slow struggle was going on behind the voluntarily controlled mask of her small quiet face. "I shouldn't have thought she had herself so well in hand," Mrs. Slade reflected, almost resentfully. But at this moment Mrs. Ansley spoke. "I don't know how you knew. I burnt that letter at once."

"Yes; you would, naturally—you're so prudent!" The sneer was open now. "And if you burnt the letter you're wondering how on earth I know what was in it. That's it, isn't it?"

Mrs. Slade waited, but Mrs. Ansley did not speak.

"Well, my dear, I know what was in that letter because I wrote it!"

"You wrote it?"

"Yes."

The two women stood for a minute staring at each other in the last golden light. Then Mrs. Ansley dropped back into her chair. "Oh," she murmured, and covered her face with her hands.

Mrs. Slade waited nervously for another word or movement. None came, and at length she broke out: "I horrify you."

Mrs. Ansley's hands dropped to her knee. The face they uncovered was streaked with tears. "I wasn't thinking of you. I was thinking—it was the only letter I ever had from him!"

"And I wrote it. Yes; I wrote it! But I was the girl he was engaged to. Did you happen to remember that?"

Mrs. Ansley's head drooped again. "I'm not trying to excuse myself . . . I remembered. . . . "

"And still you went?"

"Still I went."

Mrs. Slade stood looking down on the small bowed figure at her side. The flame of her wrath had already sunk, and she wondered why she had ever thought there would be any satisfaction in inflicting so purposeless a wound on her friend. But she had to justify herself.

"You do understand? I found out—and I hated you, hated you. I knew you were in love with Delphin—and I was afraid; afraid of you, of your quiet ways, your sweetness . . . your . . . well, I wanted you out of the way, that's all. Just for a few weeks; just till I was sure of him. So in a blind fury I wrote that letter . . . I don't know why I'm telling you now."

"I suppose," said Mrs. Ansley slowly, "it's because you've always gone on hating me."

"Perhaps. Or because I wanted to get the whole thing off my mind." She paused. "I'm glad you destroyed the letter. Of course I never thought you'd die."

Mrs. Ansley relapsed into silence, and Mrs. Slade, leaning above her, was conscious of a strange sense of isolation, of being cut off from the warm current of human communion. "You think me a monster!"

"I don't know. . . . It was the only letter I had, and you say he didn't write it?"

"Ah, how you care for him still!"

"I cared for that memory," said Mrs. Ansley.

Mrs. Slade continued to look down on her. She seemed physically reduced by the blow—as if, when she got up, the wind might scatter her like a puff of dust. Mrs. Slade's jealousy suddenly leapt up again at the sight. All these years the woman had been living on that letter. How she must have loved him, to treasure the mere memory of its ashes! The letter of the man her friend was engaged to. Wasn't it she who was the monster?

"You tried your best to get him away from me, didn't you? But you failed; and I kept him. That's all."

"Yes. That's all."

"I wish now I hadn't told you. I'd no idea you'd feel about it as you do; I thought you'd be amused. It all happened so long ago, as you say; and you must do me the justice to remember that I had no reason to think you'd ever taken it seriously. How could I, when you were married to Horace Ansley two months afterward? As soon as you could get out of bed your mother rushed you off to Florence and married you. People were rather surprised—they wondered at its being done so quickly; but I thought I knew. I had an idea you did it out of *pique*—to be able to say you'd got ahead of Delphin and me. Girls have such silly reasons for doing the most serious things. And your marrying so soon convinced me that you'd never really cared."

"Yes. I suppose it would," Mrs. Ansley assented.

The clear heaven overhead was emptied of all its gold. Dusk spread over it, abruptly darkening the Seven Hills. Here and there lights began to twinkle through the foliage at their feet. Steps were coming and going on the deserted terrace—waiters looking out of the doorway at the head of the stairs, then reappearing with trays and napkins and flasks of wine. Tables were moved, chairs straightened. A feeble string of electric lights flickered out. Some vases of faded flowers were carried away, and brought back replenished. A stout lady in a dust coat suddenly appeared, asking in broken Italian if anyone had seen the elastic band which held together her tattered Baedeker. She poked with her stick under the table at which she had lunched, the waiters assisting.

The corner where Mrs. Slade and Mrs. Ansley sat was still shadowy and deserted. For a long time neither of them spoke. At length Mrs. Slade began again: "I suppose I did it as a sort of joke—"

"A joke?"

"Well, girls are ferocious sometimes, you know. Girls in love especially. And I remember laughing to myself all that evening at the idea that you were waiting around there in the dark, dodging out of sight, listening for every sound, trying to get in— Of course I was upset when I heard you were so ill afterward."

Mrs. Ansley had not moved for a long time. But now she turned slowly toward her companion. "But I didn't wait. He'd arranged everything. He was there. We were let in at once," she said.

Mrs. Slade sprang up from her leaning position. "Delphin there? They let you in?—Ah, now you're lying!" she burst out with violence.

Mrs. Ansley's voice grew clearer, and full of surprise. "But of course he was there. Naturally he came—"

"Came? How did he know he'd find you there? You must be raving!"

Mrs. Ansley hesitated, as though reflecting. "But I answered the letter. I told him I'd be there. So he came."

Mrs. Slade flung her hands up to her face. "Oh, God—you answered! I never thought of your answering. . . . "

"It's odd you never thought of it, if you wrote the letter."

"Yes. I was blind with rage."

Mrs. Ansley rose, and drew her fur scarf about her. "It is cold here. We'd better go . . . I'm sorry for you," she said, as she clasped the fur about her throat.

The unexpected words sent a pang through Mrs. Slade. "Yes; we'd better go." She gathered up her bag and cloak. "I don't know why you should be sorry for me," she muttered.

Mrs. Ansley stood looking away from her toward the dusky secret mass of the Colosseum. "Well—because I didn't have to wait that night."

Mrs. Slade gave an unquiet laugh. "Yes; I was beaten there. But I oughtn't to begrudge it to you, I suppose. At the end of all these years. After all, I had everything; I had him for twenty-five years. And you had nothing but that one letter that he didn't write."

Mrs. Ansley was again silent. At length she turned toward the door of the terrace. She took a step, and turned back, facing her companion.

"I had Barbara," she said, and began to move ahead of Mrs. Slade toward the stairway.

Journal Entry

React to the idea that "when people talk about their pasts, tell their own stories, they are culling anecdotes from their stacks of memories, tapping certain of the past days on the shoulder."

Textual Considerations

1. Analyze the implications of Wharton's choice of Rome as the story's "site of memory." Consider, for example, how the glories of Roman architecture contribute to our awareness of the past and the degree to which the characters' lives are informed by their history.
2. Speculate as to the literal and figurative meanings of the story's title.
3. Contrast the attitudes of the protagonists toward aging and widowhood. To what extent are they reconciled to their present? How have their historical pasts affected their attitudes toward the present?

Cultural Contexts

1. "Roman Fever" explores the urge that human beings sometimes feel to return to the past in an attempt to reconcile its contradictions with the present. Working with your group, make a list of the features and traits that Mrs. Slade uses to unravel the mysteries and enigmas of the past.
2. To reach a consensus about the functions of gender and power in the story, consider not only the power struggles, both past and present, between Mrs. Ansley and Mrs. Slade but also the power struggle that males and females engage in through the game of courtship and marriage. How has each generation in the story rewritten the rules of power struggles among women and between the sexes? Consider, for example, the role of the daughters in the story.

Frank O'Connor

First Confession

All the trouble began when my grandfather died and my grandmother—my father's mother—came to live with us. Relations in the one house are a strain at the best of times, but, to make matters worse, my grandmother was a real old countrywoman and quite unsuited to the life in town. She had a fat, wrinkled face, and, to Mother's great indignation, went round the house in bare feet—the boots had her crippled, she said. For dinner she had a jug of porter and a pot of potatoes with—sometimes—a bit of salt fish, and she poured out the potatoes on the table and ate them slowly, with great relish, using her fingers by way of a fork.

Now, girls are supposed to be fastidious, but I was the one who suffered most from this. Nora, my sister, just sucked up to the old woman for the penny she got every Friday out of the old-age pension, a thing I could not do. I was too honest, that was my trouble; and when I was playing with Bill Connell, the sergeant-major's son, and saw my grandmother steering up the path with the jug of porter sticking out from beneath her shawl I was mortified. I made excuses not to let him come into the house, because I could never be sure what she would be up to when we went in.

When Mother was at work and my grandmother made the dinner I wouldn't touch it. Nora once tried to make me, but I hid under the table from her and took the bread-knife with me for protection. Nora let on to be very indignant (she wasn't, of course, but she knew Mother saw through her, so she sided with Gran) and came after me. I lashed out at her with the bread-knife, and after that she left me alone. I stayed there till Mother came in from work and made my dinner, but when Father came in later Nora said in a shocked voice: "Oh, Dadda, do you know what Jackie did at dinnertime?" Then, of course, it all came out; Father gave me a flaking; Mother interfered, and for days after that he didn't speak to me and Mother barely spoke to Nora. And all because of that old woman! God knows, I was heart-scalded.

Then, to crown my misfortunes, I had to make my first confession and communion. It was an old woman called Ryan who prepared us for these. She was about the one age with Gran; she was well-to-do, lived in a big house on Montenotte, wore a black cloak and bonnet, and came every day to school at three o'clock when we should have been going home, and talked to us of hell. She may have mentioned the other place as well, but that could only have been by accident, for hell had the first place in her heart.

She lit a candle, took out a new half-crown, and offered it to the first boy who would hold one finger—only one finger!—in the flame for five minutes by the school clock. Being always very ambitious I was tempted to volunteer, but I thought it might look greedy. Then she asked were we afraid of holding one finger—only one finger!—in a little candle flame for five minutes and not afraid of burning all over in roasting hot furnaces for all eternity. "All eternity! Just think of that! A whole lifetime goes by and it's nothing, not even a drop in the ocean of your sufferings." The woman was really interesting about hell, but my attention was all fixed on the half-crown. At the end of the lesson she put it back in her purse. It was a great disappointment; a religious woman like that, you wouldn't think she'd bother about a thing like a half-crown.

Another day she said she knew a priest who woke one night to find a fellow he didn't recognize leaning over the end of his bed. The priest was a bit frightened—naturally enough—but he asked the fellow what he wanted, and the fellow said in a deep, husky voice that he wanted to go to confession. The priest said it was an awkward time and wouldn't it do in the morning, but the fellow said that last time he went to confession, there was one sin he kept back, being ashamed to mention it, and now it was always on his mind. Then the priest knew it was a bad case, because the fellow was after making a bad confession and committing a mortal sin. He got up to dress, and just then the cock crew in the yard outside, and—lo and behold!— when the priest looked round there was no sign of the fellow, only a smell of burning timber, and when the priest looked at his bed didn't he see the print of two hands burned in it? That was because the fellow had made a bad confession. This story made a shocking impression on me.

But the worst of all was when she showed us how to examine our conscience. Did we take the name of the Lord, our God, in vain? Did we honor our father and our mother? (I asked her did this include grandmothers and she said it did.) Did we love our neighbors as ourselves? Did we covet our neighbor's goods? (I thought of the way I felt about the penny that Nora got every Friday.) I decided that, between one thing and another, I must have broken the whole ten commandments, all on account of that old woman, and so far as I could see, so long as she remained in the house I had no hope of ever doing anything else.

I was scared to death of confession. The day the whole class went I let on to have a toothache, hoping my absence wouldn't be noticed; but at three o'clock, just as I was feeling safe, along comes a chap with a message from Mrs. Ryan that I was to go to confession myself on Saturday and be at the chapel for communion with the rest. To make it worse, Mother couldn't come with me and sent Nora instead.

Now, that girl had ways of tormenting me that Mother never knew of. She held my hand as we went down the hill, smiling sadly and saying how sorry she was for me, as if she were bringing me to the hospital for an operation.

"Oh, God help us!" she moaned. "Isn't it a terrible pity you weren't a good boy? Oh, Jackie, my heart bleeds for you! How will you ever think of all your sins? Don't forget you have to tell him about the time you kicked Gran on the shin."

"Lemme go!" I said, trying to drag myself free of her. "I don't want to go to confession at all."

"But sure, you'll have to go to confession, Jackie," she replied in the same regretful tone. "Sure, if you didn't, the parish priest would be up to the house, looking for you. 'Tisn't, God knows, that I'm not sorry for you. Do you remember the time you tried to kill me with the bread-knife under the table? And the language you used to me? I don't know what he'll do with you at all, Jackie. He might have to send you up to the bishop."

I remember thinking bitterly that she didn't know the half of what I had to tell—if I told it. I knew I couldn't tell it, and understood perfectly why the fellow in Mrs. Ryan's story made a bad confession; it seemed to me a great shame that people wouldn't stop criticizing him. I remember that steep hill down to the church, and the sunlit hillsides beyond the valley of the river, which I saw in the gaps between the houses like Adam's last glimpse of Paradise.

Then, when she had maneuvered me down the long flight of steps to the chapel yard, Nora suddenly changed her tone. She became the raging malicious devil she really was.

"There you are!" she said with a yelp of triumph, hurling me through the church door. "And I hope he'll give you the penitential psalms, you dirty little caffler."

I knew then I was lost, given up to eternal justice. The door with the colored-glass panels swung shut behind me, the sunlight went out and gave place to deep shadow, and the wind whistled outside so that the silence within seemed to crackle like ice under my feet. Nora sat in front of me by the confession box. There were a couple of old women ahead of her, and then a miserable-looking poor devil came and wedged me in at the other side, so that I couldn't escape even if I had the courage. He joined his hands and rolled his eyes in the direction of the roof, muttering aspirations in an anguished tone, and I wondered had he a grandmother too. Only a grandmother could account for a fellow behaving in that heartbroken way, but he was better off than I, for he at least could go and confess his sins; while I would make a bad confession and then die in the night and be continually coming back and burning people's furniture.

Nora's turn came, and I heard the sound of something slamming and then her voice as if butter wouldn't melt in her mouth, and then another slam, and out she came. God, the hypocrisy of women! Her eyes were lowered, her head was bowed, and her hands were joined very low down on her stomach, and she walked up the aisle to the side altar looking like a saint. You never saw such an exhibition of devotion; and I remembered the devilish malice with which she had tormented me all the way from our door, and wondered were all religious people like that, really. It was my turn now. With the fear of damnation in my soul I went in, and the confessional door closed of itself behind me.

It was pitch-dark and I couldn't see priest or anything else. Then I really began to be frightened. In the darkness it was a matter between God and me, and He had all the odds. He knew what my intentions were before I even started; I had no chance. All I had ever been told about confession got mixed up in my mind, and I knelt to one wall and said: "Bless me, father, for I have sinned; this is my first confession." I waited for a few minutes, but nothing happened, so I tried it on the other wall. Nothing happened there either. He had me spotted all right.

It must have been then that I noticed the shelf at about one height with my head. It was really a place for grown-up people to rest their elbows, but in my distracted state I thought it was probably the place you were supposed to kneel. Of course, it was on the high side and not very deep, but I was always good at climbing and managed to get up all right. Staying up was the trouble. There was room only for my knees, and nothing you could get a grip on but a sort of wooden moulding a bit above it. I held on to the moulding and repeated the words a little louder, and this time something happened all right. A slide was slammed back; a little light entered the box, and a man's voice said: "Who's there?"

"'Tis me, father," I said for fear he mightn't see me and go away again. I couldn't see him at all. The place the voice came from was under the moulding, about level with my knees, so I took a good grip of the moulding and swung myself down till I saw the astonished face of a young priest looking up at me. He had to put his head on one side to see me, and I had to put mine on one side to see him, so we were more or less talking to one another upside-down. It struck me as a queer way of hearing confessions, but I didn't feel it my place to criticize.

"Bless me, father, for I have sinned; this is my first confession," I rattled off all in one breath, and swung myself down the least shade more to make it easier for him.

"What are you doing up there?" he shouted in an angry voice, and the strain the politeness was putting on my hold of the moulding, and the shock of being addressed in such an uncivil tone, were too much for me. I lost my grip, tumbled, and hit the door an unmerciful wallop before I found myself flat on my back in the middle of the aisle. The people who had been waiting stood up with their mouths open. The priest opened the door of the middle box and came out, pushing his biretta back from his forehead; he looked something terrible. Then Nora came scampering down the aisle.

"Oh, you dirty little caffler!" she cried. "I might have known you'd do it. I might have known you'd disgrace me. I can't leave you out of my sight for one minute."

Before I could even get to my feet to defend myself she bent down and gave me a clip across the ear. This reminded me that I was so stunned I had even forgotten to cry, so that people might think I wasn't hurt at all, when in fact I was probably maimed for life. I gave a roar out of me.

"What's all this about?" the priest hissed, getting angrier than ever and pushing Nora off me. "How dare you hit the child like that, you little vixen?"

"But I can't do my penance with him, father," Nora cried, cocking an outraged eye up at him.

"Well, go and do it, or I'll give you some more to do," he said, giving me a hand up. "Was it coming to confession you were, my poor man?" he asked me.

"'Twas, father," said I with a sob.

"Oh," he said respectfully, "a big hefty fellow like you must have terrible sins. Is this your first?"

"'Tis, father," said I.

"Worse and worse," he said gloomily. "The crimes of a lifetime. I don't know will I get rid of you at all today. You'd better wait now till I'm finished with these old ones. You can see by the looks of them they haven't much to tell."

"I will, father," I said with something approaching joy.

The relief of it was really enormous. Nora stuck out her tongue at me from behind his back, but I couldn't even be bothered retorting. I knew from the very moment that man opened his mouth that he was intelligent above the ordinary. When I had time to think, I saw how right I was. It only stood to reason that a fellow confessing after seven years would have more to tell than people that went every week. The crimes of a lifetime, exactly as he said. It was only what he expected, and the rest was the cackle of old women and girls with their talk of hell, the bishop, and the penitential psalms. That was all they knew. I started to make my examination of conscience, and barring the one bad business of my grandmother it didn't seem so bad.

The next time, the priest steered me into the confession box himself and left the shutter back the way I could see him get in and sit down at the further side of the grille from me.

"Well, now," he said, "what do they call you?"

"Jackie, father," said I.

"And what's a-trouble to you, Jackie?"

"Father" I said, feeling I might as well get it over while I had him in good humor, "I had it all arranged to kill my grandmother."

He seemed a bit shaken by that, all right, because he said nothing for quite a while.

"My goodness," he said at last, "that'd be a shocking thing to do. What put that into your head?"

"Father," I said, feeling very sorry for myself, "she's an awful woman."

"Is she?" he asked. "What way is she awful?"

"She takes porter, father," I said, knowing well from the way Mother talked of it that this was a mortal sin, and hoping it would make the priest take a more favorable view of my case.

"Oh, my!" he said, and I could see he was impressed.

"And snuff, father," said I.

"That's a bad case, sure enough, Jackie," he said.

"And she goes round in her bare feet, father," I went on in a rush of self-pity, "and she knows I don't like her, and she gives pennies to Nora and none to me, and my da sides with her and flakes me, and one night I was so heart-scalded I made up my mind I'd have to kill her."

"And what would you do with the body?" he asked with great interest.

"I was thinking I could chop that up and carry it away in a barrow I have," I said.

"Begor, Jackie," he said, "do you know you're a terrible child?"

"I know, father," I said, for I was just thinking the same thing myself. "I tried to kill Nora too with a bread-knife under the table, only I missed her."

"Is that the little girl that was beating you just now?" he asked.

"Tis, father."

"Someone will go for her with a bread-knife one day, and he won't miss her," he said rather cryptically. "You must have great courage. Between ourselves, there's a lot of people I'd like to do the same to but I'd never have the nerve. Hanging is an awful death."

"Is it, father?" I said with the deepest interest—I was always very keen on hanging. "Did you ever see a fellow hanged?"

"Dozens of them," he said solemnly. "And they all died roaring."

"Jay!" I said.

"Oh, a horrible death!" he said with great satisfaction. "Lots of the fellows I saw killed their grandmothers too, but they all said 'twas never worth it."

He had me there for a full ten minutes talking, and then walked out the chapel yard with me. I was genuinely sorry to part with him, because he was the most entertaining character I'd ever met in the religious line. Outside, after the shadow of the church, the sunlight was like the roaring of waves on a beach; it dazzled me; and when the frozen silence melted and I heard the screech of trams on the road my heart soared. I knew now I wouldn't die in the night and come back, leaving marks on my mother's furniture. It would be a great worry to her, and the poor soul had enough.

Nora was sitting on the railing, waiting for me, and she put on a very sour puss when she saw the priest with me. She was mad jealous because a priest had never come out of the church with her.

"Well," she asked coldly, after he left me, "what did he give you?"

"Three Hail Marys," I said.

"Three Hail Marys," she repeated incredulously. "You mustn't have told him anything."

"I told him everything," I said confidently.

"About Gran and all?"

"About Gran and all."

(All she wanted was to be able to go home and say I'd made a bad confession.)

"Did you tell him you went for me with the bread-knife?" she asked with a frown.

"I did to be sure."

"And he only gave you three Hail Marys?"

"That's all."

She slowly got down from the railing with a baffled air. Clearly, this was beyond her. As we mounted the steps back to the main road she looked at me suspiciously.

"What are you sucking?" she asked.

"Bullseyes."

"Was it the priest gave them to you?"

" 'Twas."

"Lord God," she wailed bitterly, "some people have all the luck! 'Tis no advantage to anybody trying to be good. I might just as well be a sinner like you."

Journal Entry

Discuss the conflict between punishment and forgiveness in "First Confession."

Textual Considerations

1. The story, a recollection of a childhood experience, is told in the past tense from a first-person point of view. What are the advantages of this narrative technique? How might the story differ if Nora were to tell it? Explain.
2. Focus on O'Connor's use of humor. How does it affect the story's meaning? Cite two passages, and explain how the humor is achieved.
3. Characterize Jackie and speculate as to why he is obsessed with making a bad confession. How does this first experience affect his attitude toward the church?

Cultural Contexts

1. Evaluate the role of religion in the life of this community. Can your group relate to Jackie's fear of the confessional? Why or why not? To what extent have personal and communal attitudes toward religion changed since this story was written?

2. Discuss with your group the role of the extended family in the story. To what extent are your childhood memories of family members similar to or different from Jackie's? How have they shaped your present?

Bessie Head

A Power Struggle

The universe had a more beautiful dream. It was not the law of the jungle or the survival of the fittest but a dream that had often been the priority of saints—the power to make evil irrelevant. All the people of Southern Africa had lived out this dream before the dawn of the colonial era. Time and again it shed its beam of light on their affairs although the same patterns of horror would arise like dark engulfing waves.

It was as though once people had lived in settled communities for any length of time, hostilities of an intolerable nature developed due to power struggles, rivalries and jealousies. Not all the stories were attractive or coherent; they were often so direct and brutal that it was almost like darkness destroying darkness and no rule was untainted by it. It was before these fierce passions for power that people often gave way and it formed the base of the tangled story of tribal movement and migration. When it was all over only a tree, a river bank, a hill or a mountain lingered in the memory as the dwelling place of a tribe.

There were two brothers of the Tlabina clan, Davhana and Baeli. In more ways than one Davhana was destined to rule. He was the born heir to the throne and in acknowledgement of this, the old chief, their father, had, once his health began to fail him, handed to Davhana the sacred rain-making apparatus—a symbol of his destiny. But Davhana was also a fearfully rich personality with glowing black eyes. There was about him the restless beauty of the earth in motion and he could laugh for so long and so loudly that his laughter was like the sound of the wind rushing across the open plains. He was tall and strongly-built with lithe, agile movements. People humorously accorded to him the formal and often meaningless titles a king held as his due such as "Beautiful One" or "Great Lion" but unlike other kings, Davhana earned them with his living personality. In spite of this his succession was not assured and his destiny took an unpredictable turn.

They were at the burial ceremony for their father when his brother, Baeli, abruptly threw down the first challenge to his succession. It was Davhana's right as his father's successor to turn the first sod in his grave. It was also a confirmation before the assembled people that he would rule. Davhana had his digging implement raised but his younger brother, Baeli, stepped in ahead of him and turned the first sod. The older brother stepped back instantly, his digging implement relaxed at his side. He flung his head back with an impatient gesture and stared at the horizon, his mouth curled down in contempt. The younger brother straightened up quietly. He too looked into the distance, a smile on his lips and menace in his eyes. The gestures were so unexpected that the assembled people stirred instinctively and stifled gasps of surprise swept through the crowd. There was not anyone present who did not know that the succession was open to dispute.

Immediately, the dispute did not concern the people. The real power struggle would take place in the inner circle of relatives and councillors. It was often an impersonal process as far as the mass of the people were concerned—what they respected was not so much a chief in person as the position he occupied. And yet, there seemed a contradiction in this. It was real men of passion who fought for that position and should an evil man gain the throne, people would suffer. People had a number of cynical attitudes to cover such events. One of their attitudes was: "We pay homage to all the chief's sons, since which one of them will finally become chief is uncertain. . . ." If things became too disruptive a large number of men would suddenly remember that they had not branded their cattle or attended to their everyday affairs.

The two young men of passion turned away from the funeral ceremony and walked side by side for some distance; Davhana purposefully keeping pace with his brother.

"Baeli," he asked in his direct way. "Why did you turn the first sod on father's grave? It was my duty by right! You have shamed me in front of all the people! Why did you do it?"

He listened with his whole body for his brother's reply but no reply was forthcoming—only the pacing of their feet walking in unison filled the silence. Davhana looked sideways at his brother's face. Baeli stared straight ahead; the smile still lingered around his mouth and there was an aloofness in his eyes. Had they in such an abrupt manner suddenly recognized that they were total strangers to each other? A day ago they had shared a youth together, hunted together and appeared to laugh at the same jokes. Only Davhana felt the pain. His personality radiated outwards, always reaching towards love and friendship. His brother's personality turned inwards into a whirlpool of darkness. He felt himself being dragged down into that whirlpool and instinctively he turned and walked off in his own direction.

Davhana walked until he reached a clearing outside the village. Evening was approaching. The night was warm. A full yellow moon arose behind a small hill in the distance. The atmosphere was deeply silent and still. The subdued murmurs of insects in the grass were peaceful and sweet. The young man settled himself on the earth and was soon lost in his own thoughts. Now and then he sighed deeply as though he were reaching a crossroad with himself, as though he were drawing to himself the scattered fragments of his youthful life. He had lived with the reckless generosity of his personality and nothing in his past seemed a high peak. He had lived, danced, eaten and sung in the full enjoyment of the pleasures of the moment. The events of the day cast their dark shadows over him.

Softly approaching footsteps stirred him out of his reverie. The moonlight outlined the form of one of the elders of the tribe. Davhana turned his head with his glowing look, inviting the old man to seat himself. The old man squatted low beside his reclining form and stared for some time in a detached way at the small hill behind which the moon had arisen.

"Do your thoughts trouble you, Beautiful One?" the old man asked at last. "I have stood here for some time and heard you sigh and sigh."

"Oh no, Uncle," the young man said, with a vigorous shake of his head. "Nothing troubles me. If I sigh it may be only for a carefree youth which I am about to lose."

The elder plucked at a few strands of grass and continued to stare at the distant hill.

"Everyone took note today of the awful deed your brother committed," he said. "It was the most awful breach of good manners and some of us are questioning its motive."

The young man curled his mouth in contempt again as though it were beneath him to recognize avarice and ambition.

"Baeli has always had strange tendencies," he said. "Though I have liked him as my brother."

The old man kept silent a while. When he spoke his voice was as sweet and peaceful as the subdued murmurs of the insects in the grass.

"I have come to teach you a few things about life," he said. "People have never been given a gift like you before, Beautiful One, and they look eagerly forward to your rule because they think that a time of prosperity and happiness lies before them. All these years you have lived with the people and your ways were good to them. When a man built his yard you stopped to tie a knot in the rafters and the hunting spoils you shared generously with all your men, never demanding an abundant share for yourself. You spread happiness and laughter wherever you travelled. People understand these qualities. They are the natural gifts of a good man. But these very gifts can be a calamity in a ruler. A ruler has to examine the dark side of human life and understand that men belong to that darkness. There are many men born with inadequate gifts and this disturbs them. They have no peace within themselves and once their jealousy is aroused they do terrible things. . . . "

The old man hesitated, uncertain of how to communicate his alarms and fears. A ruler could only reach the day of installation without bloodshed provided no other member of his family had declared his ambition publicly. Baeli had publicly declared his ambition and it needed only a little of that poison for all sorts of perverse things to happen. They had some horrible things in their history. They had been ruled by all sorts of lunatics and mental defectives who had mutually poisoned or assassinated each other. His grandfather had been poisoned by a brother who had in turn been assassinated by another brother. Not even Davhana's father's rule was untainted by it—there were several assassinations behind his father's peaceful and lengthy reign.

"You will soon find out the rules of life, Beautiful One," the old man murmured. "You will have to kill or be killed."

The young man said nothing in reply. The old man sat bathed in moonlight and the subdued murmurs of insects in the grass were peaceful and sweet.

The struggle that unfolded between Davhana and his brother was so subtle that it was difficult to deal with. It took place when men sat deep in council debating the issues of the day. There was always a point at which Baeli could command all the attention to himself and in doing so make his brother, Davhana, irrelevant. Baeli would catch a debate just at the point at which his brother had spoken and while a question or statement trembled in the air awaiting a reply, Baeli would step in and deflect men's thoughts in a completely new direction, thus making the previous point completely invalid. Some men began to enjoy this game and daily, Davhana rapidly lost ground with them. He refused at crucial points to assert his power and allowed dialogues to drift away from him. He indulged in no counter-intrigue when it became evident from the laughter of the men that his brother had begun to intrigue with them.

When they moved into the dark side of the moon, the most fearful massacre took place. Davhana alone escaped with his life and fled into the dark night. He had a wound in his right shoulder where a spear had pierced him as he lay asleep in his hut. He did not know who had stabbed him but in the confusion of the struggle in the dark he broke free of the hands that lunged at him and escaped.

Once, during his flight in the dark, Davhana paused again and took stock of his destiny. It was still scattered and fragmentary but the freshness and beauty of his youth lay on him like a protective mantle. If power was the unfocused demoniacal stare of his brother then he would have none of that world. Nothing had paralysed, frustrated and enraged him more than that stare.

"He can take all that he desires," Davhana thought. "I shall not go back there. I want to live."

He chose for himself that night the life of one who would take refuge where he could find it and so he continued his flight into the night.

The people of the Tlabina clan awoke the following morning to a new order. They had a murderer as their ruler. Baeli had slain whatever opposition he was likely to encounter and no one was immediately inclined to oppose him. The ritual of installation proceeded along its formal course. When Baeli appeared a chorus of adulation greeted him and everyone present made humble obeisance. The usual speeches were made to the impersonal office of kingship.

After three moons had waxed and waned word travelled back to the people that their ruler, Davhana, was alive and well and had sought refuge with a powerful Pedi clan. The people of the Tlabina clan began to vanish from their true home, sometimes in large groupings, sometimes in small trickles until they had abandoned Baeli. If the wild dogs ate him, who knows?

A power struggle was the great dialogue of those times and many aspects of the dialogue were touched by the grandeur of kings like Davhana. It was hardly impersonal as living men always set the dialogue in motion. They forced people under duress to make elaborate choices between good and evil. This thread of strange philosophical beauty was deeply woven into the history of the land and the story was repeated many times over so that it became the only history people ever knew.

With the dawn of the colonial era this history was subdued. A new order was imposed on life. People's kings rapidly faded from memory and became myths of the past. No choices were left between what was good and what was evil. There was only slavery and exploitation.

Journal Entry

Respond to the theme of sibling rivalry by comparing your family's experiences and those of the Tlabina clan brothers.

Textual Considerations

1. Analyze how the movement of the narrative voice throughout the text attempts to capture the interaction of dialogue and the sense of physical action.
2. Discuss the old man's premises about the conditions that make a good ruler.
3. Focus on Head's description of the Tlabina brothers on a realistic level. To what extent do they function also on the **symbolic** or **mythical** level? (See the glossary.)

Cultural Contexts

1. From classical works like *Oedipus Rex* to contemporary tales like "A Power Struggle," writers have wrestled with the idea that "should an evil man gain the throne, people would suffer." Analyze the political implications of this hypothesis in relation not only to "A Power Struggle" but to contemporary political events as well.
2. Bessie Head says: "A ruler has to examine the dark side of human life and understand that men belong to that darkness. There are many men born with inadequate gifts and this disturbs them. They have no peace within themselves and once their jealousy is aroused they do terrible things" (p. 102). Analyze the larger implication of Head's thesis, and apply it to power struggles in our own time.

Elie Wiesel

The Watch

For my bar mitzvah, I remember, I had received a magnificent gold watch. It was the customary gift for the occasion, and was meant to remind each boy that henceforth he would be held responsible for his acts before the Torah and its timeless laws.

But I could not keep my gift. I had to part with it the very day my native town became the pride of the Hungarian nation by chasing from its confines every single one of its Jews. The glorious masters of our municipality were jubilant: they were rid of us, there would be no more kaftans on the streets. The local newspaper was brief and to the point: from now on, it would be possible to state one's place of residence without feeling shame.

The time was late April, 1944.

In the early morning hours of that particular day, after a sleepless night, the ghetto was changed into a cemetery and its residents into gravediggers. We were digging feverishly in the courtyard, the garden, the cellar, consigning to the earth, temporarily we thought, whatever remained of the belongings accumulated by several generations, the sorrow and reward of long years of toil.

My father took charge of the jewelry and valuable papers. His head bowed, he was silently digging near the barn. Not far away, my mother, crouched on the damp ground, was burying the silver candelabra she used only on Shabbat eve; she was moaning softly, and I avoided her eyes. My sisters burrowed near the cellar. The youngest, Tziporah, had chosen the garden, like myself. Solemnly shoveling, she declined my help. What did she have to hide? Her toys? Her school notebooks? As for me, my only possession was my watch. It meant a lot to me. And so I decided to bury it in a dark, deep hole, three paces away from the fence, under a poplar tree whose thick, strong foliage seemed to provide a reasonably secure shelter.

All of us expected to recover our treasures. On our return, the earth would give them back to us. Until then, until the end of the storm, they would be safe.

Yes, we were naïve. We could not foresee that the very same evening, before the last train had time to leave the station, an excited mob of well-informed friendly neighbors would be rushing through the ghetto's wide-open houses and courtyards, leaving not a stone or beam unturned, throwing themselves upon the loot.

Twenty years later, standing in our garden, in the middle of the night, I remember the first gift, also the last, I ever received from my parents. I am seized by an irrational, irresistible desire to see it, to see if it is still there in the same spot, and if defying all laws of probability, it has survived—like me—by accident, not knowing how or why. My curiosity becomes obsession. I think neither of my father's money nor of my mother's candlesticks. All that matters in this town is my gold watch and the sound of its ticking.

Despite the darkness, I easily find my way in the garden. Once more I am the bar mitzvah child; here is the barn, the fence, the tree. Nothing has changed. To my left, the path leading to the Slotvino Rebbe's house. The Rebbe, though, had changed: the burning bush burned itself out and there is nothing left, not even smoke. What could he possibly have hidden the day we went away? His phylacteries? His prayer shawl? The holy scrolls inherited from his famous ancestor Rebbe Meirl of Premishlan? No, probably not even that kind of treasure. He had taken everything along, convinced that he was thus protecting not only himself but his disciples as well. He was proved wrong, the wonder rabbi.

But I mustn't think of him, not now. The watch, I must think of the watch. Maybe it was spared. Let's see, three steps to the right. Stop. Two forward. I recognize the place. Instinctively, I get ready to re-enact the scene my memory recalls. I fall on my knees. What can I use to dig? There is a shovel in the barn; its door is never locked. But by groping around in the dark I risk stumbling and waking the people sleeping in the house. They would take me for a marauder, a thief, and hand me over to the police. They might even kill me. Never mind, I'll have to manage without a shovel. Or any other tool. I'll use my hands, my nails. But it is difficult; the soil is hard, frozen, it resists as if determined to keep its secret. Too bad, I'll punish it by being the stronger.

Feverishly, furiously, my hands claw the earth, impervious to cold, fatigue and pain. One scratch, then another. No matter. Continue. My nails inch ahead, my fingers dig in, I bear down, my every fiber participates in the task. Little by little the hole deepens. I must hurry. My forehead touches the ground. Almost. I break out in a cold sweat, I am drenched, delirious. Faster, faster. I shall rip the earth from end to end, but I must know. Nothing can stop or frighten me. I'll go to the bottom of my fear, to the bottom of night, but I will know.

What time is it? How long have I been here? Five minutes, five hours? Twenty years. This night was defying time. I was laboring to exhume not an object but time itself, the soul and memory of that time. Nothing could be more urgent, more vital.

Suddenly a shiver goes through me. A sharp sensation, like a bite. My fingers touch something hard, metallic, rectangular. So I have not been digging in vain. The garden is spinning around me, over me. I stand up to catch my breath. A moment later, I'm on my knees again. Cautiously, gently I take the box from its tomb. Here it is, in the palm of my hand: the last relic, the only remaining symbol of everything I had loved, of everything I had been. A voice inside me warns: Don't open it, it contains nothing but emptiness, throw it away and run. I cannot heed the warning; it is too late to turn back. I need to know, either way. A slight pressure of my thumb and the box opens. I stifle the cry rising in my throat: the watch is there. Quick, a match. And another. Fleetingly, I catch a glimpse of it. The pain is blinding: could this thing, this object, be my gift, my pride? My past? Covered with dirt and rust, crawling with worms, it is unrecognizable, revolting. Unable to move, wondering what to do, I remain staring at it with the disgust one feels for love betrayed or a body debased. I am angry with myself for having yielded to curiosity. But disappointment gives way to profound pity: the watch too lived through war and holocaust, the kind reserved for watches perhaps. In its way, it too is a survivor, a ghost infested with humiliating sores and obsolete memories. Suddenly I feel the urge to carry it to my lips, dirty as it is, to kiss and console it with my tears, as one might console a living being, a sick friend returning from far away and requiring much kindness and rest, especially rest.

I touch it, I caress it. What I feel, besides compassion, is a strange kind of gratitude. You see, the men I had believed to be immortal had vanished into fiery clouds. My teachers, my friends, my guides had all deserted me. While this thing, this nameless, lifeless thing had survived for the sole purpose of welcoming me on my return and providing an epilogue to my childhood. And there awakens in me a desire to confide in it, to tell it my adventures, and in exchange, listen to its own. What had happened in my absence: who had first taken possession of my house, my bed? Or rather, no; our confidences could wait for another time, another place: Paris, New York, Jerusalem. But first I would entrust it to the best jeweler in the world, so that the watch might recover its luster, its memory of the past.

It is growing late. The horizon is turning a deep red. I must go. The tenants will soon be waking, they will come down to the well for water. No time to lose. I stuff the watch into my pocket and cross the garden. I enter the courtyard. From under the porch a dog barks. And stops at once: he knows I am not a thief, anything but a thief. I open the gate. Halfway down the street I am overcome by violent remorse: I have just committed my first theft.

I turn around, retrace my steps through courtyard and garden. Again I find myself kneeling, as at Yom Kippur services, beneath the poplar. Holding my breath, my eyes refusing to cry, I place the watch back into its box, close the cover, and my first gift once more takes refuge deep inside the hole. Using both hands, I smoothly fill in the earth to remove all traces.

Breathless and with pounding heart, I reach the still deserted street. I stop and question the meaning of what I have just done. And find it inexplicable.

In retrospect, I tell myself that probably I simply wanted to leave behind me, underneath the silent soil, a reflection of my presence. Or that somehow I wanted to transform my watch into an instrument of delayed vengeance: one day, a child would play in the garden, dig near the tree and stumble upon a metal box. He would thus learn that his parents were usurpers, and that among the inhabitants of his town, once upon a time, there had been Jews and Jewish children, children robbed of their future.

The sun was rising and I was still walking through the empty streets and alleys. For a moment I thought I heard the chanting of schoolboys studying Talmud; I also thought I heard the invocations of Hasidim reciting morning prayers in thirty-three places at once. Yet above all these incantations, I heard distinctly, but as though coming from far away, the tick-tock of the watch I had just buried in accordance with Jewish custom. It was, after all, the very first gift that a Jewish child had once been given for his very first celebration.

Since that day, the town of my childhood has ceased being just another town. It has become the face of a watch.

Journal Entry

Respond to the protagonist's comment that both he and his family were naive. In what ways does he indicate that he is less naive twenty years later?

Textual Considerations

1. What prompts Wiesel to dig up the watch twenty years later? What does he mean when he says that he was laboring to exhume "time itself, the soul and memory of that time"?
2. Discuss Wiesel's use of such literary devices as repetition, symbolism, and fragmented sentences to convey the narrator's attachment to his watch. Identify the climactic scene in the text, and speculate on the meaning that this scene indicates his watch has for the narrator.
3. Except for the opening section of the essay, most of the narrative is written in the present tense. Where in the account of his return to his native town does Wiesel revert to the past tense? Why does he do so? What effect does he achieve?

Cultural Contexts

1. Consider how "The Watch" explores the concept that human beings may personally be entrapped by a historical event. To what extent has the narrator in Wiesel's story come to terms with his historical past?
2. Discuss with your group the degree to which our personal past contributes to our present selves, and debate whether understanding our pasts is necessary for self-realization.

Ernest J. Gaines

The Sky Is Gray

1

Go'n be coming in a few minutes. Coming round that bend down there full speed. And I'm go'n get out my handkerchief and wave it down, and we go'n get on it and go.

I keep on looking for it, but Mama don't look that way no more. She's looking down the road where we just come from. It's a long old road, and far's you can don't see nothing but gravel. You got dry weeds on both sides, too, and you got trees on both sides, and fences on both sides, too. And you got cows in the pastures and they standing close together. And when we was coming out here to catch the bus I seen the smoke coming out of the cows's noses.

I look at my mama and I know what she's thinking. I been with Mama so much, just me and her, I know what she's thinking all the time. Right now it's home—Auntie and them. She's thinking if they got enough wood—if she left enough there to keep them warm till we get back. She's thinking if it go'n rain and if any of them have to go out in the rain. She's thinking 'bout the hog—if he go'n get out, and if

Ty and Val be able to get him back in. She always worry like that when she leaves the house. She don't worry too much if she leave me there with the smaller ones, 'cause she know I'm go'n look after them and look after Auntie and everything else. I'm the oldest and she say I'm the man.

I look at my mama and I love my mama. She's wearing that black coat and that black hat and she's looking sad. I love my mama and I want to put my arm round her and tell her. But I'm not supposed to do that. She say that's weakness and that's crybaby stuff, and she don't want no crybaby round her. She don't want you to be scared, either. 'Cause Ty's scared of ghosts and she's always whipping him. I'm scared of the dark, too, but I make 'tend I ain't. I make 'tend I ain't 'cause I'm the oldest, and I got to set a good sample for the rest. I can't ever be scared and I can't ever cry. And that's why I never said nothing 'bout my teeth. It's been hurting me and hurting me close to a month now, but I never said it. I didn't say it 'cause I didn't want act like a crybaby, and 'cause I know we didn't have enough money to go have it pulled. But, Lord, it been hurting me. And look like it wouldn't start till at night when you was trying to get yourself little sleep. Then soon's you shut your eyes—ummm-ummm, Lord, look like it go right down to your heartstring.

"Hurting, hanh?" Ty'd say.

I'd shake my head, but I wouldn't open my mouth for nothing. You open your mouth and let that wind in, and it almost kill you.

I'd just lay there and listen to them snore. Ty there, right 'side me, and Auntie and Val over by the fireplace. Val younger than me and Ty, and he sleeps with Auntie. Mama sleeps round the other side with Louis and Walker.

I'd just lay there and listen to them, and listen to that wind out there, and listen to that fire in the fireplace. Sometimes it'd stop long enough to let me get little rest. Sometimes it just hurt, hurt, hurt. Lord, have mercy.

2

Auntie knowed it was hurting me. I didn't tell nobody but Ty, 'cause we buddies and he ain't go'n tell anybody. But some kind of way Auntie found out. When she asked me, I told her no, nothing was wrong. But she knowed it all the time. She told me to mash up a piece of aspirin and wrap it in some cotton and jugg it down in that hole. I did it, but it didn't do no good. It stopped for a little while, and started right back again. Auntie wanted to tell Mama, but I told her, "Uh-uh." 'Cause I knowed we didn't have any money, and it just was go'n make her mad again. So Auntie told Monsieur Bayonne, and Monsieur Bayonne came over to the house and told me to kneel down 'side him on the fireplace. He put his finger in his mouth and made the Sign of the Cross on my jaw. The tip of Monsieur Bayonne's finger is some hard, I cause he's always playing on that guitar. If we sit outside at night we can always hear Monsieur Bayonne playing on his guitar. Sometimes we leave him out there playing on the guitar.

Monsieur Bayonne made the Sign of the Cross over and over on my jaw, but that didn't do no good. Even when he prayed and told me to pray some, too, that tooth still hurt me.

"How you feeling?" he say.

"Same," I say.

He kept on praying and making the Sign of the Cross and I kept on praying, too.

"Still hurting?" he say.

"Yes, sir."

Monsieur Bayonne mashed harder and harder on my jaw. He mashed so hard he almost pushed me over on Ty. But then he stopped.

"What kind of prayers you praying, boy?" he say.

"Baptist," I say.

"Well, I'll be—no wonder that tooth still killing him. I'm going one way and he pulling the other. Boy, don't you know any Catholic prayers?"

"I know 'Hail Mary,' " I say.

"Then you better start saying it."

"Yes, sir."

He started mashing on my jaw again, and I could hear him praying at the same time. And, sure enough, after awhile it stopped hurting me.

Me and Ty went outside where Monsieur Bayonne's two hounds was and we started playing with them. "Let's go hunting," Ty say. "All right," I say; and we went on back in the pasture. Soon the hounds got on a trail, and me and and Ty followed them all 'cross the pasture and then back in the woods, too. And then they cornered this little old rabbit and killed him, and me and Ty made them get back, and we picked up the rabbit and started on back home. But my tooth had started hurting me again. It was hurting me plenty now, but I wouldn't tell Monsieur Bayonne. That night I didn't sleep a bit, and first thing in the morning Auntie told me to go back and let Monsieur Bayonne pray over me some more. Monsieur Bayonne was in his kitchen making coffee when I got there. Soon's he seen me he knowed what was wrong.

"All right, kneel down there 'side that stove," he say. "And this time make sure you pray Catholic. I don't know nothing 'bout that Baptist, and I don't want know nothing 'bout him."

3

Last night Mama say, "Tomorrow we going to town."

"It ain't hurting me no more," I say. "I can eat anything on it."

"Tomorrow we going to town," she say.

And after she finished eating, she got up and went to bed. She always go to bed early now. 'Fore Daddy went in the Army, she used to stay up late. All of us sitting out on the gallery or round the fire. But now, look like soon's she finish eating she go to bed.

This morning when I woke up, her and Auntie was standing 'fore the fireplace. She say: "Enough to get there and get back. Dollar and a half to have it pulled. Twenty-five for me to go, twenty-five for him. Twenty-five for me to come back, twenty-five for him. Fifty cents left. Guess I get little piece of salt meat with that."

"Sure can use it," Auntie say. "White beans and no salt meat ain't white beans."

"I do the best I can," Mama say.

They was quiet after that, and I made 'tend I was still asleep.

"James, hit the floor," Auntie say.

I still made 'tend I was asleep. I didn't want them to know I was listening.

"All right," Auntie say, shaking me by the shoulder. "Come on. Today's the day."

I pushed the cover down to get out, and Ty grabbed it and pulled it back.

"You, too, Ty," Auntie said.

"I ain't getting no teef pulled," Ty say.

"Don't mean it ain't time to get up," Auntie say. "Hit it, Ty."

Ty got up grumbling.

"James, you hurry up and get in your clothes and eat your food," Auntie say. "What time y'all coming back?" she say to Mama.

"That 'leven o'clock bus," Mama say. "Got to get back in that field this evening."

"Get a move on you, James," Auntie say.

I went in the kitchen and washed my face, then I ate my breakfast. I was having bread and syrup. The bread was warm and hard and tasted good. And I tried to make it last a long time.

Ty came back there grumbling and mad at me.

"Got to get up," he say. "I ain't having no teefs pulled. What I got to be getting up for?"

Ty poured some syrup in his pan and got a piece of bread. He didn't wash his hands, neither his face, and I could see that white stuff in his eyes.

"You the one getting your teef pulled," he say. "What I got to get up for. I bet if I was getting a teef pulled, you wouldn't be getting up. Shucks; syrup again. I'm getting tired of this old syrup. Syrup, syrup, syrup. I'm go'n take with the sugar diabetes. I want me some bacon sometime."

"Go out in the field and work and you can have your bacon," Auntie say. She stood in the middle door looking at Ty. "You better be glad you got syrup. Some people ain't got that—hard's time is."

"Shucks," Ty say. "How can I be strong."

"I don't know too much 'bout your strength," Auntie say; "but I know where you go'n be hot at, you keep that grumbling up. James, get a move on you; your mama waiting."

I ate my last piece of bread and went in the front room. Mama was standing 'fore the fireplace warming her hands. I put on my coat and cap, and we left the house.

4

I look down there again, but it still ain't coming. I almost say, "It ain't coming yet," but I keep my mouth shut. 'Cause that's something else she don't like. She don't like for you to say something just for nothing. She can see it ain't coming. I can see it ain't coming, so why say it ain't coming. I don't say it, I turn and look at the river that's back of us. It's so cold the smoke's just raising up from the water. I see a bunch of pool-doos not too far out—just on the other side the lilies. I'm wondering if you can eat pool-doos. I ain't too sure, 'cause I ain't never ate none. But I done ate owls and blackbirds, and I done ate redbirds, too. I didn't want to kill the redbirds, but she made me kill them. They had two of them back there. One in my trap, one in Ty's trap. Me and Ty was go'n play with them and let them go, but she made me kill them 'cause we needed the food.

"I can't," I say. "I can't."

"Here," she say. "Take it."

"I can't," I say. "I can't. I can't kill him, Mama, please."

"Here," she say. "Take this fork, James."

"Please, Mama, I can't kill him," I say.

I could tell she was go'n hit me. I jerked back, but I didn't jerk back soon enough.

"Take it," she say.

I took it and reached in for him, but he kept on hopping to the back.

"I can't, Mama," I say. The water just kept on running down my face. "I can't," I say.

"Get him out of there," she say.

I reached in for him and he kept on hopping to the back. Then I reached in farther, and he pecked me on the hand.

"I can't, Mama," I say.

She slapped me again.

I reached in again, but he kept on hopping out my way. Then he hopped to one side and I reached there. The fork got him on the leg and I heard his leg pop. I pulled my hand out 'cause I had hurt him.

"Give it here," she say, and jerked the fork out of my hand.

She reached in and got the little bird right in the neck. I heard the fork go in his neck, and I heard it go in the ground. She brought him out and helt him right in front of me.

"That's one," she say. She shook him off and gived me the fork. "Get the other one."

"I can't, Mama," I say. "I'll do anything, but don't make me do that."

She went to the corner of the fence and broke the biggest switch over there she could find. I knelt 'side the trap, crying.

"Get him out of there," she say.

"I can't, Mama."

She started hitting me 'cross the back. I went down on the ground, crying.

"Get him," she say.

"Octavia?" Auntie say.

'Cause she had come out of the house and she was standing by the tree looking at us.

"Get him out of there," Mama say.

"Octavia," Auntie say, "explain to him. Explain to him. Just don't beat him. Explain to him."

But she hit me and hit me and hit me.

I'm still young—ain't no more than eight; but I know now; I know why I had to do it. (They was so little, though. They was so little. I 'member how I picked the feathers off them and cleaned them and helt them over the fire. Then we all ate them. Ain't had but a little bitty piece each, but we all had a little bitty piece, and everybody just looked at me 'cause they was so proud.) Suppose she had to go away? That's why I had to do it. Suppose she had to go away like Daddy went away? Then who was go'n look after us? They had to be somebody left to carry on. I didn't know it then, but I know it now. Auntie and Monsieur Bayonne talked to me and made me see.

5

Time I see it I get out my handkerchief and start waving. It's still 'way down there, but I keep waving anyhow. Then it come up and stop and me and Mama get on. Mama tell me go sit in the back while she pay. I do like she say, and the people look at me. When I pass the little sign that say "White" and "Colored," I start looking for a seat. I just see one of them back there, but I don't take it, 'cause I want my mama to sit down herself. She comes in the back and sit down, and I lean on the seat. They got seats in the front, but I know I can't sit there, 'cause I have to sit back of the sign. Anyhow, I don't want to sit there if my mama go'n sit back here.

They got a lady sitting 'side my mama and she looks at me and smiles little bit. I smile back, but I don't open my mouth, 'cause the wind'll get in and make that tooth ache. The lady take out a pack of gum and reach me a slice, but I shake my head. The lady just can't understand why a little boy'll turn down gum, and she reach me a slice again. This time I point to my jaw. The lady understands and smiles little bit, and I smile little bit, but I don't open my mouth, though.

They got a girl sitting 'cross from me. She got on a red overcoat and her hair's plaited in one big plait. First, I make 'tend I don't see her over there but then I start looking at her little bit. She make 'tend she don't see me, either, but I catch her looking that way. She got a cold, and every now and then she h'ist that little handkerchief to her nose. She ought to blow it, but she don't. Must think she's too much a lady or something.

Every time she h'ist that little handkerchief, the lady 'side her say something in her ear. She shakes her head and lays her hands in her lap again. Then I catch her kind of looking where I'm at. I smile at her little bit. But think she'll smile back? Uh-uh. She just turn up her little old nose and turn her head. Well, I show her both of us can turn us head. I turn mine too and look out at the river.

The river is gray. The sky is gray. They have pool-doos on the water. The water is wavy, and the pool-doos go up and down. The bus go round a turn, and you got plenty trees hiding the river. Then the bus go round another turn, and I can see the river again.

I look toward the front where all the white people sitting. Then I look at that little old gal again. I don't look right at her, 'cause I don't want all them people to know I love her. I just look at her little bit, like I'm looking out that window over there. But she knows I'm looking that way, and she kind of look at me, too. The lady sitting 'side her catch her this time, and she leans over and says something in her ear.

"I don't love him nothing," that little old gal says out loud.

Everybody back there hear her mouth, and all of them look at us and laugh.

"I don't love you, either," I say. "So you don't have to turn up your nose, Miss."

"You the one looking," she say.

"I wasn't looking at you," I say. "I was looking out that window, there."

"Out that window, my foot," she say. "I seen you. Everytime I turned round you was looking at me."

"You must of been looking yourself if you seen me all them times," I say.

"Shucks," she say, "I got me all kind of boyfriends."

"I got girlfriends, too," I say.

"Well, I just don't want you getting your hopes up," she say.

I don' say no more to that little old gal cause I don't want have to bust her in the mouth. I lean on the seat where Mama sitting, and I don't even look that way no more. When we get to Bayonne, she jugg her little old tongue out at me. I make 'tend I'm go'n hit her, and she duck down 'side her mama. And all the people laugh at us again.

6

Me and Mama get off and start walking in town. Bayonne is a little bitty town. Baton Rouge is a hundred times bigger than Bayonne. I went to Baton Rouge once—me, Ty, Mama, and Daddy. But that was 'way back yonder, 'fore Daddy went in the Army. I wonder when we go'n see him again. I wonder when. Look like he ain't ever coming back home. . . . Even the pavement all cracked in Bayonne. Got grass shooting right out the sidewalk. Got weeds in the ditch, too; just like they got at home.

It's some cold in Bayonne. Look like it's colder than it is home. The wind blows in my face, and I feel that stuff running down my nose. I sniff. Mama says use that handkerchief. I blow my nose and put it back.

We pass a school and I see them white children playing in the yard. Big old red school, and them children just running and playing. Then we pass a café, and I see a bunch of people in there eating. I wish I was in there 'cause I'm cold. Mama tells me keep my eyes in front where they belong.

We pass stores that's got dummies, and we pass another café, and then we pass a shoe shop, and that bald-head man in there fixing on a shoe. I look at him and I butt into that white lady, and Mama jerks me in front and tells me stay there.

We come up to the courthouse, and I see the flag waving there. This flag ain't like the one we got at school. This one here ain't got but a handful of stars. One at school got a big pile of stars—one for every state. We pass it and we turn and there it is—the dentist office. Me and Mama go in, and they got people sitting everywhere you look. They even got a little boy in there younger than me.

Me and Mama sit on that bench, and a white lady come in there and ask me what my name is. Mama tells her and the white lady goes on back. Then I hear somebody hollering in there. Soon's that little boy hear him hollering, he starts hollering too. His mama pats him and pats him, trying to make him hush up, but he ain't thinkin 'bout his mama.

The man that was hollering in there comes out holding his jaw. He is a big old man and he's wearing overalls and a jumper.

"Got it, hanh?" another man asks him.

The man shakes his head—don't want open his mouth.

"Man, I thought they was killing you in there," the other man says. "Hollering like a pig under a gate."

The man don't say nothing. He just heads for the door, and the other man follows him.

"John Lee," the white lady says. "John Lee Williams."

The little boy juggs his head down in his mama's lap and holler more now. His mama tells him go with the nurse, but he ain't thinking 'bout his mama. His mama tells him again, but he don't even hear her. His mama picks him up and takes him in there, and even when the white lady shuts the door I can still hear little old John Lee.

"I often wonder why the Lord let a child like that suffer," a lady says to my mama. The lady's sitting right in front of us on another bench. She's got on a white dress and a black sweater. She must be a nurse or something herself, I reckon.

"Not us to question," a man says.

"Sometimes I don't know if we shouldn't," the lady says.

"I know definitely we shouldn't," the man says. The man looks like a preacher. He's big and fat and he's got on a black suit. He's got a gold chain, too.

"Why?" the lady says.

"Why anything?" the preacher says.

"Yes," the lady says. "Why anything?"

"Not us to question," the preacher says.

The lady looks at the preacher a little while and looks at Mama again.

"And look like it's the poor who suffers the most," she says. "I don't understand it."

"Best not to even try," the preacher says. "He works in mysterious ways—wonders to perform."

Right then little John Lee bust out hollering, and everybody turn they head to listen.

"He's not a good dentist," the lady says. "Dr. Robillard is much better. But more expensive. That's why most of the colored people come here. The white people go to Dr. Robillard. Y'all from Bayonne?"

"Down the river," my mama says. And that's all she go'n say, 'cause she don't talk much. But the lady keeps on looking at her, and so she says, "Near Morgan."

"I see," the lady says.

7

"That's the trouble with the black people in this country today," somebody else says. This one here's sitting on the same side me and Mama's sitting, and he is kind of sitting in front of that preacher. He looks like a teacher or somebody that goes to college. He's got on a suit, and he's got a book that he's been reading. "We don't question is exactly our problem," he says. "We should question and question and question—question everything."

The preacher just looks at him a long time. He done put a toothpick or something in his mouth, and he just keeps on turning it and turning it. You can see he don't like that boy with that book.

"Maybe you can explain what you mean," he says.

"I said what I meant," the boy says. "Question everything. Every stripe, every star, every word spoken. Everything."

"It 'pears to me that this young lady and I was talking 'bout God, young man," the preacher says.

"Question Him, too," the boy says.

"Wait," the preacher says, "Wait now."

"You heard me right," the boy says. "His existence as well as everything else. Everything."

The preacher just looks across the room at the boy. You can see he's getting madder and madder. But mad or no mad, the boy ain't thinking 'bout him. He looks at that preacher just's hard's the preacher looks at him.

"Is this what they coming to?" the preacher says. "Is that what we educating them for?"

"You're not educating me," the boy says. "I wash dishes at night so that I can go to school in the day. So even the words you spoke need questioning."

The preacher just looks at him and shakes his head.

"When I come in this room and seen you there with your book, I said to myself, 'here's an intelligent man.' How wrong a person can be."

"Show me one reason to believe in the existence of a God," the boy says.

"My heart tells me," the preacher says.

" 'My heart tells me,' " the boy says. " 'My heart tells me.' Sure, 'My heart tells me.' And as long as you listen to what your heart tells you, you will have only what the white man gives you and nothing more. Me, I don't listen to my heart. The purpose of the heart is to pump blood throughout the body, and nothing else."

"Who's your paw, boy?" the preacher says.

"Why?"

"Who is he?"

"He's dead."

"And your mom?"

"She's in Charity Hospital with pneumonia. Half killed herself, working for nothing."

"And 'cause he's dead and she's sick, you mad at the world?"

"I'm not mad at the world. I'm questioning the world. I'm questioning it with cold logic sir. What do words like Freedom, Liberty, God, White, Colored mean? I want to know. That's why *you* are sending us to school, to read and to ask questions. And because we ask these questions, you call us mad. No sir, it is not us who are mad."

"You keep saying 'us'?"

" 'Us.' Yes—us. I'm not alone."

The preacher just shakes his head. Then he looks at everybody in the room—everybody. Some of the people look down at the floor, keep from looking at him. I kind of look 'way myself, but soon's I know he done turn his head, I look that way again.

"I'm sorry for you," he says to the boy.

"Why?" the boy says. "Why not be sorry for yourself? Why are you so much better off than I am? Why aren't you sorry for these other people in here? Why not be sorry for the lady who had to drag her child into the dentist office? Why not be sorry for the lady sitting on that bench over there? Be sorry for them. Not for me. Some way or the other I'm going to make it."

"No, I'm sorry for you," the preacher says.

"Of course, of course," the boy says, nodding his head. "You're sorry for me because I rock that pillar you're leaning on."

"You can't ever rock the pillar I'm leaning on, young man. It's stronger than anything man can ever do."

"You believe in God because a man told you to believe in God," the boy says. "A white man told you to believe in God. And why? To keep you ignorant so he can keep his feet on your neck."

"So now we the ignorant?" the preacher says.

"Yes," the boy says. "Yes." And he opens his book again.

The preacher just looks at him sitting there. The boy done forgot all about him. Everybody else make 'tend they done forgot the squabble, too.

Then I see that preacher getting up real slow. Preacher's great big old man and be got to brace himself to get up. He comes over where the boy is sitting. He just stands there a little while looking down at him, but the boy don't raise his head.

"Get up, boy," preacher says.

The boy looks up at him, then he shuts his book real slow and stands up. Preacher just hauls back and hit him in the face. The boy falls back 'gainst the wall, but be straightens himself up and looks right back at that preacher.

"You forgot the other cheek," he says.

The preacher hauls back and hit him again on the other side. But this time the boy braces himself and don't fall.

"That hasn't changed a thing," he says.

The preacher just looks at the boy. The preacher's breathing real hard like he just run up a big hill. The boy sits down and opens his book again.

"I feel sorry for you," the preacher says. "I never felt so sorry for a man before."

The boy makes 'tend he don't even hear that preacher. He keeps on reading his book. The preacher goes back and gets his hat off the chair.

"Excuse me," he says to us. "I'll come back some other time. Y'all, please excuse me."

And he looks at the boy and goes out the room. The boy h'ist his hand up to his mouth one time to wipe 'way some blood. All the rest of the time he keeps on reading. And nobody else in there say a word.

8

Little John Lee and his mama come out the dentist office, and the nurse calls somebody else in. Then little bit later they come out, and the nurse calls another name. But fast's she calls somebody in there, somebody else comes in the place where we sitting, and the room stays full.

The people coming in now, all of them wearing big coats. One of them says something 'bout sleeting, another one says he hope not. Another one says he think it ain't nothing but rain. 'Cause, he says, rain can get awful cold this time of year.

All round the room they talking. Some of them talking to people right by them, some of them talking to people clear 'cross the room, some of them talking to anybody'll listen. It's a little bitty room, no bigger than us kitchen, and I can see everybody in there. The little old room's full of smoke, 'cause you got two old men smoking pipes over by that side door. I think I feel my tooth thumping me some, and I hold my breath and wait. I wait and wait, but it don't thump me no more. Thank God for that.

I feel like going to sleep, and I lean back 'gainst the wall. But I'm scared to go to sleep. Scared 'cause the nurse might call my name and I won't hear her. And Mama might go to sleep, too, and she'll be mad if neither one of us heard the nurse.

I look up at Mama. I love my mama. I love my mama. And when cotton come I'm go'n get her a new coat. And I ain't go'n get a black coat, either. I think I'm go'n get her a red one.

"They got some books over there," I say. "Want read one of them?"

Mama looks at the books, but she don't answer me.

"You got yourself a little man there," the lady says.

Mama don't say nothing to the lady, but she must've smiled, 'cause I seen the lady smiling back. The lady looks at me a little while, like she's feeling sorry for me.

"You sure got that preacher out here in a hurry," she says to that boy.

The boy looks up at her and looks in his book again. When I grow up I want be just like him. I want clothes like that and I want to keep a book with me, too.

"You really don't believe in God?" the lady says.

"No," he says.

"But why?" the lady says.

"Because the wind is pink," he says.

"What?" the lady says.

The boy don't answer her no more. He just reads in his book.

"Talking 'bout the wind is pink," that old lady says. She's sitting on the same bench with the boy and she's trying to look in his face. The boy makes 'tend the old lady ain't even there. He just keeps on reading. "Wind is pink," she says again. "Eh, Lord, what children go'n be saying next?"

The lady 'cross from us bust out laughing.

"That's a good one," she says. "The wind is pink. Yes sir, that's a good one."

"Don't you believe the wind is pink?" the boy says. He keeps his head down in the book.

"Course I believe it, honey," the lady says. "Course I do." She looks at us and winks her eye. "And what color is grass, honey?"

"Grass? Grass is black."

She bust out laughing again. The boy looks at her.

"Don't you believe grass is black?" he says.

The lady quits her laughing and looks at him. Everybody else looking at him, too. The place quiet, quiet.

"Grass is green, honey," the lady says. "It was green yesterday, it's green today, and it's go'n be green tomorrow."

"How do you know it's green?"

"I know because I know."

"You don't know it's green," the boy says. "You believe it's green because someone told you it was green. If someone had told you it was black you'd believe it was black."

"It's green," the lady says. "I know green when I see green."

"Prove it's green," the boy says.

"Sure, now," the lady says. "Don't tell me it's coming to that."

"It's coming to just that," the boy says. "Words mean nothing. One means no more than the other."

"That's what it all coming to?" the old lady says. That old lady got on a turban and she got on two sweaters. She got a green sweater under a black sweater. I can see the green sweater 'cause some of the buttons on the other sweater's missing.

"Yes ma'am," the boy says. "Words mean nothing. Action is the only thing. Doing. That's the only thing."

"Other words, you want the Lord to come down here and show Hisself to you?" she says.

"Exactly, ma'am," he says.

"You don't mean that, I'm sure?" she says.

"I do, ma'am," he says.

"Done, Jesus," the old lady says, shaking her head.

"I didn't go 'long with that preacher at first," the other lady says; "but now—I don't know. When a person say the grass is black, he's either a lunatic or something's wrong."

"Prove to me that it's green," the boy says.

"It's green because the people say it's green."

"Those same people say we're citizens of these United States," the boy says.

"I think I'm a citizen," the lady says.

"Citizens have certain rights," the boy says. "Name me one right that you have. One right, granted by the Constitution, that you can exercise in Bayonne."

The lady don't answer him. She just looks at him like she don't know what he's talking 'bout. I know I don't.

"Things changing," she says.

"Things are changing because some black men have begun to think with their brains and not their hearts," the boy says.

"You trying to say these people don't believe in God?"

"I'm sure some of them do. Maybe most of them do. But they don't believe that God is going to touch these white people's hearts and change things tomorrow. Things change through action. By no other way."

Everybody sit quiet and look at the boy. Nobody says a thing. Then the lady 'cross the room from me and Mama just shakes her head.

"Let's hope that not all your generation feel the same way you do," she says.

"Think what you please, it doesn't matter," the boy says. "But it will be men who listen to their heads and not their hearts who will see that your children have a better chance than you had."

"Let's hope they ain't all like you, though," the old lady says. "Done forgot the heart absolutely."

"Yes ma'am, I hope they aren't all like me," the boy says. "Unfortunately, I was born too late to believe in your God. Let's hope that the ones who come after will have your faith—if not in your God, then in something else, something definitely that they can lean on. I haven't anything. For me, the wind is pink, the grass is black."

9

The nurse comes in the room where we all sitting and waiting and says the doctor won't take no more patients till one o'clock this evening. My mama jumps up off the bench and goes up to the white lady.

"Nurse, I have to go back in the field this evening," she says.

"The doctor is treating his last patient now," the nurse says. "One o'clock this evening."

"Can I at least speak to the doctor?" my mama asks.

"I'm his nurse," the lady says.

"My little boy's sick," my mama says. "Right now his tooth almost killing him."

The nurse looks at me. She's trying to make up her mind if to let me come in. I look at her real pitiful. The tooth ain't hurting me at all, but Mama says it is, so I make 'tend for her sake.

"This evening," the nurse says, and goes on back in the office.

"Don't feel 'jected, honey," the lady says to Mama. "I been round them a long time—they take you when they want to. If you was white, that's something else; but we the wrong color."

Mama don't say nothing to the lady, and me and her go outside and stand 'gainst the wall. It's cold out there. I can feel that wind going through my coat. Some of the other people come out of the room and go up the street. Me and Mama stand there a little while and we start walking. I don't know where we going. When we come to the other street we just stand there.

"You don't have to make water, do you?" Mama says.

"No, ma'am," I say.

We go on up the street. Walking real slow. I can tell Mama don't know where she's going. When we come to a store we stand there and look at the dummies. I look at a little boy wearing a brown overcoat. He's got on brown shoes, too. I look at my old shoes and look at his'n again. You wait till summer, I say.

Me and Mama walk away. We come up to another store and we stop and look at them dummies, too. Then we go on again. We pass a café where the white people in there eating. Mama tells me keep my eyes in front where they belong, but I can't help from seeing them people eat. My stomach starts to growling 'cause I'm hungry. When I see people eating, I get hungry; when I see a coat, I get cold.

A man whistles at my mama when we go by a filling station. She makes 'tend she don't even see him. I look back and I feel like hitting him in the mouth. If I was bigger, I say; if I was bigger, you'd see.

We keep on going. I'm getting colder and colder, but I don't say nothing. I feel that stuff running down my nose and I sniff.

"That rag," Mama says.

I get it out and wipe my nose. I'm getting cold all over now—my face, my hands, my feet, everything. We pass another little café, but this'n for white people, too, and we can't go in there, either. So we just walk. I'm so cold now I'm 'bout ready to say it. If I knowed where we was going I wouldn't be so cold, but I don't know where we going. We go, we go, we go. We walk clean out of Bayonne. Then we cross the street and we come back. Same thing I seen when I got off the bus this morning. Same old trees, same old walk, same old weeds, same old cracked pave— same old everything.

I sniff again.

"That rag," Mama says.

I wipe my nose real fast and jugg that handkerchief back in my pocket 'fore my hand gets too cold. I raise my head and I can see David's hardware store. When we come up to it, we go in I don't know why, but I'm glad.

It's warm in there. It's so warm in there you don't ever want to leave. I look for the heater, and I see it over by them barrels. Three white men standing round the heater talking in Creole. One of them comes over to see what my mama want.

"Got any axe handles?" she says.

Me, Mama and the white man start to the back, but Mama stops me when we come up to the heater. She and the white man go on. I hold my hands over the heater and look at them. They go all the way to the back, and I see the white man pointing to the axe handles 'gainst the wall. Mama takes one of them and shakes it like she's trying to figure how much it weighs. Then she rubs her hand over it from one end to the other end. She turns it over and looks at the other side, then she shakes it again, and shakes her head and puts it back. She gets another one and she does it just like she did the first one, then she shakes her head. Then she gets a brown one and do it that, too. But she don't like this one, either. Then she gets another one, but 'fore she shakes it or anything, she looks at me. Look like she's trying to say something to me, but I don't know what it is. All I know is I done got warm now and I'm feeling right smart better. Mama shakes this axe handle just like she did the others, and shakes her head and says something to the white man. The white man just looks at his pile of axe handles, and when Mama pass him to come to the front, the white man just scratch his head and follows her. She tells me come on and we go on and start walking again.

We walk and walk, and no time at all I'm cold again. Look like I'm colder now 'cause I can still remember how good it was back there. My stomach growls and I suck it in to keep Mama from hearing it. She's walking right 'side me, and it growls so loud you can hear it a mile. But Mama don't say a word.

10

When we come up to the courthouse, I look at the clock. It's got quarter to twelve. Mean we got another hour and a quarter to be out here in the cold. We go and stand 'side a building. Something hits my cap and I look up at the sky. Sleet's falling.

I look at Mama standing there. I want stand close 'side her, but she don't like that. She say that's crybaby stuff. She say you got to stand for yourself, by yourself.

"Let's go back to that office," she says.

We cross the street. When we get to the dentist office I try to open the door, but I can't. I twist and twist, but I can't. Mama pushes me to the side and she twist the knob, but she can't open the door, either. She turns 'way from the door. I look at her, but I don't move and I don't say nothing. I done seen her like this before and I'm scared of her.

"You hungry?" she says. She says it like she's mad at me, like I'm the cause of everything.

"No, ma'am," I say.

"You want eat and walk back, or you rather don't eat and ride?"

"I ain't hungry," I say.

I ain't just hungry, but I'm cold, too. I'm so hungry and cold I want to cry. And look like I'm getting colder and colder. My feet done got numb. I try to work my toes, but I don't even feel them. Look like I'm go'n die. Look like I'm go'n stand right here and freeze to death. I think 'bout home. I think 'bout Val and Auntie and Ty and Louis and Walker. It's 'bout twelve o'clock and I know they eating dinner now. I can hear Ty making jokes. He done forgot 'bout getting up early this morning and right now he's probably making jokes. Always trying to make somebody laugh. I wish I was right there listening to him. Give anything in the world if I was home round the fire.

"Come on," Mama says.

We start walking again. My feet so numb I can't hardly feel them. We turn the corner and go on back up the street. The clock on the courthouse starts hitting for twelve.

The sleet's coming down plenty now. They hit the pave and bounce like rice. Oh, Lord; oh, Lord, I pray. Don't let me die, don't let me die, don't let me die, Lord.

11

Now I know where we going. We going back of town where the colored people eat. I don't care if I don't eat. I been hungry before. I can stand it. But I can't stand the cold.

I can see we go'n have a long walk. It's 'bout a mile down there. But I don't mind. I know when I get there I'm go'n warm myself. I think I can hold out. My hands numb in my pockets and my feet numb, too, but if I keep moving I can hold out. Just don't stop no more, that's all.

The sky's gray. The sleet keeps on falling. Falling like rain now—plenty, plenty. You can hear it hitting the pave. You can see it bouncing. Sometimes it bounces two times 'fore it settles.

We keep on going. We don't say nothing. We just keep on going, keep on going.

I wonder what Mama's thinking. I hope she ain't mad at me. When summer come I'm go'n pick plenty cotton and get her a coat. I'm go'n get her a red one.

I hope they'd make it summer all the time. I'd be glad if it was summer all the time—but it ain't. We got to have winter, too. Lord, I hate the winter. I guess everybody hate the winter.

I don't sniff this time. I get out my handkerchief and wipe my nose. My hands's so cold I can hardly hold the handkerchief.

I think we getting close, but we ain't there yet. I wonder where everybody is. Can't see a soul but us. Look like we the only two people moving round today. Must be too cold for the rest of the people to move round in.

I can hear my teeth. I hope they don't knock together too hard and make that bad one hurt. Lord, that's all I need, for that bad one to start off.

I hear a church bell somewhere. But today ain't Sunday. They must be ringing for a funeral or something.

I wonder what they doing at home. They must be eating. Monsieur Bayonne might be there with his guitar. One day Ty played with Monsieur Bayonne's guitar and broke one of the strings. Monsieur Bayonne was some mad with Ty. He say Ty wasn't go'n ever 'mount to nothing. Ty can go just like Monsieur Bayonne when he ain't there. Ty can make everybody laugh when he starts to mocking Monsieur Bayonne.

I used to like to be with Mama and Daddy. We used to be happy. But they took him in the Army. Now, nobody happy no more. . . . I be glad when Daddy comes home.

Monsieur Bayonne say it wasn't fair for them to take Daddy and give Mama nothing and give us nothing. Auntie say, "Shhh, Etienne. Don't let them hear you talk like that." Monsieur Bayonne say, "It's God truth. What they giving his children? They have to walk three and a half miles to school hot or cold. That's anything to give for a paw? She's got to work in the field rain or shine just to make ends meet. That's anything to give for a husband?" Auntie say, "Shhh, Etienne, shhh." "Yes, you right," Monsieur Bayonne say. "Best don't say it in front of them now. But one day they go'n find out. One day." "Yes, I suppose so," Auntie say. "Then what, Rose Mary?" Monsieur Bayonne say. "I don't know, Etienne," Auntie say. "All we can do is us job, and leave everything else in His hand . . . "

We getting closer, now. We getting closer. I can even see the railroad tracks.

We cross the tracks, and now I see the café. Just to get in there, I say. Just to get in there. Already I'm starting to feel little better.

12

We go in. Ahh, it's good. I look for the heater; there 'gainst the wall. One of them little brown ones. I just stand there and hold my hands over it. I can't open my hands too wide 'cause they almost froze.

Mama's standing right 'side me. She done unbuttoned her coat. Smoke rises out of the coat, and the coat smells like a wet dog.

I move to the side so Mama can have more room. She opens out her hands and rubs them together. I rub mine together, too, 'cause this keep them from hurting. If you let them warm too fast, they hurt you sure. But if you let them warm just little bit at a time, and you keep rubbing them, they be all right every time.

They got just two more people in the café. A lady back of the counter, and a man on this side the counter. They been watching us ever since we come in.

Mama gets out the handkerchief and count up the money. Both of us know how much money she's got there. Three dollars. No, she ain't got three dollars 'cause she had to pay us way up here. She ain't got but two dollars and a half left. Dollar and a half to get my tooth pulled, and fifty cents for us to go back on, and fifty cents worth of salt meat.

She stirs the money round with her finger. Most of the money is change 'cause I can hear it rubbing together. She stirs it and stirs it. Then she looks at the door. It's still sleeting. I can hear it hitting 'gainst the wall like rice.

"I ain't hungry, Mama," I say.

"Got to pay them something for they heat," she says.

She takes a quarter out the handkerchief and ties the handkerchief up again. She looks over her shoulder at the people, but she still don't move. I hope she don't spend the money. I don't want her spending it on me. I'm hungry, I'm almost starving I'm so hungry, but I don't want her spending the money on me.

She flips the quarter over like she's thinking. She's must be thinking 'bout us walking back home. Lord, I sure don't want walk home. If I thought it'd do any good to say something, I'd say it. But Mama makes up her own mind 'bout things.

She turns 'way from the heater right fast, like she better hurry up and spend the quarter 'fore she change her mind. I watch her go toward the counter. The man and the lady look at her. She tells the lady something and the lady walks away. The man keeps on looking at her. Her back's turned to the man, and she don't even know he's standing there.

The lady puts some cakes and a glass of milk on the counter. Then she pours up a cup of coffee and sets it 'side the other stuff. Mama pays her for the things and comes on back where I'm standing. She tells me sit down at the table 'gainst the wall.

The milk and the cakes's for me; the coffee's for Mama. I eat slow and I look at her. She's looking outside at the sleet. She's looking real sad. I say to myself, I'm go'n make all this up one day. You see, one day, I'm go'n make all this up. I want say it now; I want tell her how I feel right now; but Mama don't like for us to talk like that.

"I can't eat all this," I say.

They ain't got but just three little old cakes there. I'm so hungry right now, the Lord knows I can eat a hundred times three. But I want my mama to have one.

Mama don't even look my way. She knows I'm hungry, she knows I want it. I let it stay there a little while, then I get it and eat it. I eat just on my front teeth, though, 'cause if cake touch that back tooth I know what'll happen. Thank God it ain't hurt me at all today.

After I finish eating I see the man go to the juke box. He drops a nickel in it, then he just stand there a little while looking at the record. Mama tells me keep my eyes in front where they belong. I turn my head like she say, but then I hear the man coming toward us.

"Dance, pretty?" he says.

Mama gets up to dance with him. But 'fore you know it, she done grabbed the little man in the collar and done heaved him 'side the wall.

He hit the wall so hard he stop the juke box from playing.

"Some pimp," the lady back of the counter says. "Some pimp."

The little man jumps up off the floor and starts toward my mama. 'Fore you know it, Mama done sprung open her knife and she's waiting for him.

"Come on," she says. "Come on. I'll gut you from your neighbo to your throat. Come on."

I go up to the little man to hit him, but Mama makes me come and stand 'side her. The little man looks at me and Mama and goes on back to the counter.

"Some pimp," the lady back of the counter says. "Some pimp." She starts laughing and pointing at the little man. "Yes sir, you a pimp, all right. Yes sir-ree."

13

"Fasten that coat, let's go," Mama says.

"You don't have to leave," the lady says. Mama don't answer the lady, and we right out in the cold again. I'm warm right now—my hands, my ears, my feet—but I know this ain't go'n last too long. It done sleet so much now you got ice everywhere you look.

We cross the railroad tracks, and soon's we do, I get cold. That wind goes through this little old coat like it ain't even there. I got on a shirt and a sweater under the coat, but that wind don't pay them no mind. I look up and I can see we got a long way to go. I wonder if we go'n make it 'fore I get too cold.

We cross over to walk on the sidewalk. They got just one sidewalk back here, and it's over there.

After we go just a little piece, I smell bread cooking. I look, then I see a baker shop. When we get closer, I can smell it more better. I shut my eyes and make 'tend I'm eating. But I keep them shut too long and I butt up 'gainst a telephone post. Mama grabs me and see if I'm hurt. I ain't bleeding or nothing and she turns me loose.

I can feel I'm getting colder and colder, and I look up to see how far we still got to go. Uptown is 'way up yonder. A half mile more, I reckon. I try to think of something. They say think and you won't get cold. I think of that poem, "Annabel Lee." I ain't been to school in so long—this bad weather—I reckon they done passed "Annabel Lee" by now. But passed it or not, I'm sure Miss Walker go'n make me recite it when I get there. That woman don't never forget nothing. I ain't never seen nobody like that in my life.

I'm still getting cold. "Annabel Lee" or no "Annabel Lee," I'm still getting cold. But I can see we getting closer. We getting there gradually.

Soon's we turn the corner, I seen a little old white lady up in front of us. She's the only lady on the street. She's all in black and she's got a long black rag over her head.

"Stop," she says.

Me and Mama stop and look at her. She must be crazy to be out in all this bad weather. Ain't got but a few other people out there, and all of them's men.

"Y'all done ate?" she says.

"Just finish," Mama says.

"Y'all must be cold then?" she says.

"We headed for the dentist," Mama says. "We'll warm up when we get there."

"What dentist?" the old lady says. "Mr. Bassett?"

"Yes, ma'am," Mama says.

"Come on in," the old lady says. "I'll telephone him and tell him y'all coming."

Me and Mama follow the old lady in the store. It's a little bitty store, and it don't have much in there. The old lady takes off her head rag and folds it up.

"Helena?" somebody calls from the back.

"Yes, Alnest?" the old lady says.

"Did you see them?"

"They're here. Standing beside me."

"Good. Now you can stay inside."

The old lady looks at Mama. Mama's waiting to hear what she brought us in here for. I'm waiting for that, too.

"I saw y'all each time you went by," she says. "I came out to catch you, but you were gone."

"We went back of town," Mama says.

"Did you eat?"

"Yes, ma'am."

The old lady looks at Mama a long time, like she's thinking Mama might just be saying that. Mama looks right back at her. The old lady looks at me to see what I have to say. I don't say nothing. I sure ain't going 'gainst my mama.

"There's food in the kitchen," she says to Mama. "I've been keeping it warm."

Mama turns right around and starts for the door.

"Just a minute," the old lady says. Mama stops. "The boy'll have to work for it. It isn't free."

"We don't take no handout," Mama says.

"I'm not handing out anything," the old lady says. "I need my garbage moved to the front. Ernest has a bad cold and can't go out there."

"James'll move it for you," Mama says.

"Not unless you eat," the old lady says. "I'm old, but I have my pride, too, you know."

Mama can see she ain't go'n beat this old lady down, so she just shakes her head.

"All right," the old lady says. "Come into the kitchen."

She leads the way with that rag in her hand. The kitchen is a little bitty little old thing, too. The table and the stove just 'bout fill it up. They got a little room to the side. Somebody in there layin 'cross the bed cause I can see one of his feet. Must be the person she was talking to: Ernest or Alnest—something like that.

"Sit down," the old lady says to Mama. "Not you," she says to me. "You have to move the cans."

"Helena?" the man says in the other room.

"Yes, Alnest?" the old lady says.

"Are you going out there again?"

"I must show the boy where the garbage is, Alnest," the old lady says.

"Keep your shawl over your head," the old man says.

"You don't have to remind me, Alnest. Come, Boy," the old lady says.

We go out in the yard. Little old back yard ain't no bigger than the store or the kitchen. But it can sleet here just like it can sleet in any big back yard. And 'fore you know it, I'm trembling.

"There," the old lady says, pointing to the cans. I pick up one of the cans and set it right back down. The can's so light. I'm go'n see what's inside of it.

"Here," the old lady says. "Leave that can alone."

I look back at her standing there in the door. She's got that black rag wrapped round her shoulders, and she's pointing one of her little old fingers at me.

"Pick it up and carry it to the front," she says. I go by her with the can, and she's looking at me all the time. I'm sure the can's empty. I'm sure she could've carried it herself—maybe both of them at the same time. "Set it on the sidewalk by the door and come back for the other one," she says.

I go and come back, and Mama looks at me when I pass her. I get the other can and take it to the front. It don't feel a bit heavier than that first one. I tell myself I ain't go'n be nobody's fool, and I'm go'n look inside this can to see just what I been hauling. First, I look up the street, then down the street. Nobody coming. Then I look over my shoulder toward the door. That little old lady done slipped up there quiet's a mouse, watching me again. Look like she knowed what I was go'n do.

"Ehh, Lord," she says. "Children, children. Come in here, boy, and go wash your hands."

I follow her in the kitchen. She points toward the bathroom, and I go in there and wash up. Little bitty old bathroom, but it's clean, clean. I don't use any of her towels; I wipe my hands on my pants legs.

When I come back in the kitchen, the old lady done dished up the food. Rice, gravy, meat—and she even got some lettuce and tomato in a saucer. She even got a glass of milk and a piece of cake there, too. It looks so good, I almost start eating 'fore I say my blessing.

"Helena?" the old man says.

"Yes, Alnest?"

"Are they eating?"

"Yes," she says.

"Good," he says. "Now you'll stay inside."

The old lady goes in there where he is and I can hear them talking. I look at Mama. She's eating slow like she's thinking. I wonder what's the matter now. I reckon she's thinking 'bout home.

The old lady comes back in the kitchen.

"I talked to Dr. Bassett's nurse," she says. "Dr. Bassett will take you as soon as you get there."

"Thank you, ma'am," Mama says.

"Perfectly all right," the old lady says. "Which one is it?"

Mama nods toward me. The old lady looks at me real sad. I look sad, too.

"You're not afraid, are you?" she says.

"No, ma'am," I say.

"That's a good boy," the old lady says. "Nothing to be afraid of. Dr. Bassett will not hurt you."

When me and Mama get through eating, we thank the old lady again.

"Helena, are they leaving?" the old man says.

"Yes, Alnest."

"Tell them I say good-bye."

"They can hear you, Alnest."

"Good-bye both mother and son," the old man says. "And may God be with you."

Me and Mama tell the old man good-bye, and we follow the old lady in the front room. Mama opens the door to go out, but she stops and comes back in the store.

"You sell salt meat?" she says.

"Yes."

"Give me two bits worth."

"That isn't very much salt meat," the old lady says.

"That's all I have," Mama says.

The old lady goes back of the counter and cuts a big piece off the chunk. Then she wraps it up and puts it in a paper bag.

"Two bits," she says.

"That looks like awful lot of meat for a quarter," Mama says.

"Two bits," the old lady says. "I've been selling salt meat behind this counter twenty-five years. I think I know what I'm doing."

"You got a scale there," Mama says.

"What?" the old lady says.

"Weigh it," Mama says.

"What?" the old lady says. "Are you telling me how to run my business?"

"Thanks very much for the food," Mama says.

"Just a minute," the old lady says.

"James," Mama says to me. I move toward the door.

"Just one minute, I said," the old lady says.

Me and Mama stop again and look at her. The old lady takes the meat out of the bag and unwraps it and cuts 'bout half of it off. Then she wraps it up again and juggs it back in the bag and gives the bag to Mama. Mama lays the quarter on the counter.

"Your kindness will never be forgotten," she says. "James," she says to me.

We go out, and the old lady comes to the door to look at us. After we go a little piece I look back, and she's still there watching us.

The sleet's coming down heavy, heavy now, and I turn up my coat collar to keep my neck warm. My mama tells me turn it right back down.

"You not a bum," she says. "You a man."

Journal Entry

What forces have formed the mother's character? Why does she raise her children as she does? Consider the incident with the redbirds as well as the last line of the story.

Textual Considerations

1. The title "The Sky Is Gray" obviously describes the weather. What does the title refer to on a symbolic level?
2. To what extent is Oscar Wilde's thesis that "memory is the diary we carry around with us" characteristic of the eight-year-old narrator of the story? In what ways does his memory help him in narrating the past? What limitations are placed on the author by his use of a young boy to re-create the story?
3. How does racial prejudice operate in the story? What are the implications of the inclusion of the old lady and her husband?

Cultural Contexts

1. To create a visual picture of the sociohistorical conditions before the civil rights movement in the United States, describe the town of Bayonne from the young narrator's point of view. Include the local bus and the café in your description.

2. Working with your group, select three narrative episodes in the story, including the debate between the preacher and the boy in the dentist's office, and discuss what light they shed on the narrator's cultural heritage.

Rosemary Cho Leyson

The Visit Home

Today the bus ride to her parents' house seems very long. Her body settles into her seat as if the seat is a part of her. It has been several months since she has gone to visit her family in the Mission. Today is special. It is time to celebrate the fall of Marcos and the first day of liberation in her home country.

Every time she visits her parents, it's as if she's going back into the past. A past filled with sorrow, shame and broken dreams, in a pit with no bottom or top. Her memories of growing up are a list of events poisoned and shot with indignities, malice and a feeling of nonexistence.

As she looks out the window her mind plays a flashback: Melinda is her name. A Puerto Rican girl who lived around the corner of the block. Didn't know why she wanted to be friends, and at that time, it didn't matter much. It just felt nice that someone wanted to be friends with me. She asked me to hold a watch for her. When I gave it back, she said it was broken and that if I didn't give her twenty bucks, she'd break my face and I'd be sorry I ever moved into the neighborhood.

Her body's reaction breaks the spell; the girl in this adult has surfaced. Her throat is dry and tight, her jaws clench and her body tenses from keeping in the tears. She has no hatred for Melinda—just confusion from trying to understand why she did it.

Pull yourself together, she interrupts herself. That was then. You're not going to let anyone push you around anymore. You have some power now, you've been here awhile. You're not the same girl who just came to the States from the Philippines. You can't change what happened then, but no one's gonna push you around and get away with it anymore.

She stands up, getting ready to hop off the bus, repeating to herself that no one had better mess with her and no one will. She carries her orange plastic bag and runs across the street looking straight ahead.

Everything looks the same. Same dirty streets, same kids who thought they were better than me. They say one stupid thing to me—I swear, I'll beat the shit out of them, she tells herself.

She finally reaches the steps to her parents' flat. Already she is upset. Nothing changes for the better around here, she thinks, as she observes the dried-out, split-up wood steps and the loose handrails attached to them. The stairs carry more meaning for her than what's in front of her. It's a reminder, another symbol of degradation that her parents have suffered while renting it as subsidized housing through the government.

She remembers it vividly through her ten-year-old eyes.

"Don't tell me you want to read it! I don't have time for this. Just sign the lease!"

Mom signed it without reading it or saying anything and I watched, trying to figure out what this lady was and then I knew what a devil must look like—tall, blonde, blue-eyed White woman from the Housing Authority. I vowed never to forget it, so that when I grow up I won't let them treat me or my parents that way. If mom knew English better, she wouldn't have let that bitch get away with it, she thinks to herself as she reaches the last step.

She knocks on the door, carefully listening to the footsteps approaching and guesses whose step patterns they are. Sounds like mom's, she thinks. Slowly, the door cracks open and a fair-skinned, short and stout woman appears at the door. Her face brightens to a modest smile. It's her mother. They both greet each other and then the daughter follows it with "It's me—Maree" in Korean. Her mom looks at her and replies "long time no see" in English.

By now, they've gone through the short, narrow hallway that serves as the kitchen and the daughter sets the bag on the cluttered kitchen table next to where her sister is sitting. They greet each other in English. Everything's the same, the same old gloomy way, she thinks. She tries to ignore it this time. She feels uneasy and disconnected speaking English in the house. Korean is her first language, even though her mom had banned it.

"How's things going?" she asks her mom and sister.

"Oh, the same."

"The usual."

They both reply simultaneously.

"That means it isn't good but it can't be worse than it already is. Is that what it means?" the visiting sister asks.

"You should know that by now," her little sister answers casually.

She is hoping maybe this one time it could be different.

"I brought roast duck and strawberry shortcake from Chinatown. Marcos is out—aren't you glad? Have to celebrate," she says, directing her words to no one in particular. It's no surprise to her that there is no response, or any sign of joy. After all, life is still the same miserable way it was and will be and what's the point of celebrating anything. In fact, she has no recollection of when they ever celebrated anything once they got to the States—except once. It was her mother's birthday and her mom's brother and sisters came. But that didn't turn out so well because they started to fight and that drove her mom to have a nervous breakdown on her birthday.

She walks over to the door of her dad's room. He's lying down watching television, an old black and white set he bought from Goodwill. The picture on the tube is so bad you can barely make out the faces. His room is cluttered, full of old bills. By his door is the dresser that he picked up from the street. There's a poster of a kitten next to the only window in the room.

"Hi, how are you feeling?" she asks her dad, concerned with his health since his drinking and smoking caught up to his heart and lungs, and his dishwashing job is aggravating the arthritis in his legs. The cataracts in his eyes, even after the surgery, have left him close to blind. He takes a couple of minutes to get his eyes focused and adjusted to the figure by the door.

He looks over at his daughter. "Oh, Maree, how are you?" he asks, his Filipino accent thick and his voice boisterous with joy for only a split second. His dark bushy eyebrows umbrella his deep-set eyes. His wrinkles are thick across his forehead but spread thin throughout his face.

"Aren't you glad Marcos left?" she asks gleefully.

"Oh—ya" he replies flatly. She frowns. If she was expecting anyone in the family to be a little happy, it was her dad. He's probably tired, she reasons. She tells him what she brought to celebrate and his only response is the terse chuckle he always gives when she mentions that she brought something. Almost always food.

He felt his guts twist and his heart sink into his bed. Why does she keep doing that? First she runs away from home, and now she keeps bringing food. What is she trying to tell me? I can't provide for my family? Was living here so bad she'd rather be with strangers in a runaway house? I kept warning her, don't go out. There are devils who want to hurt little girls. But she still didn't come home after what happened, he thinks as he shifts in his bed.

"Baby, get your mom to fix you something to eat."

She stares at him and thinks, is it too late for you to be happy about anything? She feels sad thinking about it.

"You don't want anything to eat, Dad?"

"You eat. Your mommy—she always yells at me if I ask her to do anything for me," he laughs. She can feel the pain in his voice.

"Okay, well I'll talk to you later," she says, opening the door.

"Okay, bye—call. I just want to know you're not dead, huh."

She walks back into the living room/kitchen area. Her mom is heating up the duck.

"Do you have any kimchee?" she asks in Korean.

"No, not for a long time," her mother answers in English. The visiting daughter sits down among the clutter, clearing up just enough space on the table to eat.

Even after all those times growing up when there was little to eat, there was something about eating at home. She reminisces about her early childhood in Manila, where except for her dad who was stateside, her family was together. They ate together and stuck up for each other. Nothing was ever the same after they came to the States.

The home her family made here is now a place saturated in painful and unhealed experiences of growing up in a country that didn't want her or her family. She was crushed between the constant hostility between her parents and the anger from each one not being what the other wanted them to be. They took the frustrations the world put upon them, swallowed them and turned them on themselves. They were unprepared and unable to cope with the reality of racism in a country they idealized as the great United States. They felt powerless in a country that ridiculed their accents and the color of their skin. Their presence handed them third class citizenship wherever they went. But her family, however disjointed they have become with each other from living in this country, is all she has to tell her who she is, what she is and where she was from.

The white, short-grained rice her mother scoops into her bowl never looked so precious sitting full along the top edge of the bowl ready to be eaten. She reaches for the pyrex bowl on the table and scoops a little bit of the content onto her bowl with her chopsticks. It is chut: salted baby shrimps, fermented Korean style with ferocious Korean chili powder, garlic and all sorts of other potent ingredients. Spread across a little bit of rice, it really hits the spot. She almost feels like crying as the sensation of the food sinks into her taste buds. It is an old familiar feeling, one too precious to ever take for granted. It is the only link she has to who she is and where she is from.

Silently, she eats with her sister as their mother cooks more rice. After she finishes eating, she takes her dishes to the sink and gets ready to leave. Her mother's face seems to get longer and more solemn each time she visits, though she never seems to age, a quality she knows her mother is proud of.

Reaching into her pocket, she hands her mom a bill and tells her it's pocket money, then she takes her jacket off the chair. She asks her mother if she wants to go to the Korean market. "When?" her mother asks, her eyes widening.

"Not this weekend, but I'll call you," the daughter replies. The mother helps her daughter with the jacket. My little girl is grown up. How did you ever go away from me? All my other children are here. Why did you feel you had to leave? her mother is thinking.

The daughter straightens out the collar on her jacket. Her mother carefully inspects her coat for unwanted objects and then picks a piece of lint off her right shoulder. The daughter feels an uneasiness in this ritual. Silence has taken over and it is about the only time she has stood so close to her mother that they can hear each other's breathing. For this reason she allows, and to an extent enjoys, this rare moment of her mother paying attention to her. The childhood feeling of neglect sends ripples into her heart. Her memories of girlhood consist of feelings of sorrow and anger and a helplessness that seemed devastating and eternal with no one by her side. But now, for a fleeting second, the sadness in her soul transforms into a healing glow.

She understands the damage to each of her family members and how it separates each one from the other. Even with this awareness, she still holds back from showing the love and understanding she has for her mother, the love that she wanted from her kin long ago when the only world around her was her family.

But she is no longer the little girl, the daughter is trying to convince herself. With that thought her body moves toward the door. She opens it and as she steps out, her breathing returns to normal. She thanks God she is able to keep from crying.

"Come again soon," her mother says.

She takes one last look at her mother. "Okay, bye. I'll call you about the market," she says as she jogs down the steps.

Journal Entry

List some of the factors that account for Maree's sense of cultural and social dislocation in the United States.

Textual Considerations

1. Define the meanings and connotations—historical and psychological—that words and phrases such as "Marcos," "Melinda," "the stairs," and "eating at home" acquire in Maree's private language.
2. "The Visit Home" is narrated by Maree primarily from a third-person point of view. Explain the effects of her shifting at times from the first- to the second-person pronouns to refer to herself. Consider, for example, how these shifts in point of view affect the interaction of the past and present in the story.
3. React to the following statement in Leyson's story: "Every time she visits her parents, it's as if she's going back into the past. A past filled with sorrow, shame and broken dreams, in a pit with no bottom or top."

Cultural Contexts

1. Debate with your group whether Maree's assessment "of growing up in a country that didn't want her or her family" reflects the experiences of many immigrants in the United States. Can you reach a consensus as to whether Maree's viewpoint reflects the reality of racism in this country?
2. Working with your group, investigate the socioeconomic situation of Maree's family. Starting with the physical portrait of her family's household, move to an analysis of their emotional and psychological states. How has their economic situation contributed to their sense of alienation? What other factors might you cite?

 **POETRY**

Luis Rodriguez

Chained Time

When history is stolen,
its heart wrenched from the meat of time,
it is like a missing orange-red mango
from a stained fruitbowl;
a still life of bruised apples, squashed grapes,   5
and brown bananas left behind.

History becomes that old DeSoto out in back
with peeling blue paint
and the parking-lot bondo job
coming apart in chucks;   10
weeds and foxtails hugging flattened tires.

It's a big brother who you admire
but who only comes around
to wrestle you to the ground.

History becomes a lost love in an old photograph;   15
still smiling, still with that look,
but fading like the colors,
the eyes—like the smile.

It is an old crescent wrench coming apart in sections:
A moss-covered anchor, a rusty machete   20
ready to slice into your head.
But when history is found—
because it may be stolen but nobody can destroy it—
it is a shiny new Excalibur
with a cloister of ivory horses on the handle,   25
beckoning like a gem in clear water,
to be held, to be swung, to render as it rises,
taking with it the fire, the purpose,
the dreams of humankind as a weapon
of chained time,   30
set free.

Sue Doro

The Father Poem Two

my father,
dark gray,
dusty factory father,
left with one lung
from filthy air,   5
aching with rheumatism,
from winter cold air
blowing on sweaty shoulders.

my father,
cursing your job, through us,   10
your family,
mean to my mother
my brother, my sister,
me.

yelling, coughing.   15
spitting angry yellow,
green and red.

my father, swallowing pills
to keep on your feet.
swallowing pills   20
to get to sleep.

my father,
two months into retirement,
an uncashed check
on the kitchen table,   25
found dead,
by the lady who ran
the downstairs tavern.

my father, dead,
your body melting   30
into the floor boards
near a shoe box
of assorted pills,
an empty brandy bottle,
and a bucket of spit   35
lined with newspaper.
your pain is finished now.

my father, dead but not gone,
alive but not living,
I remember you,   40
coming home
from a ten hour work day,
taking off your glasses
to reveal white circles
of sunken eyes   45
surrounded by soot,
because sometimes
you were too tired
to clean up at work,
in the washroom   50
your union fought for.

on those nights,
I remember
when the white circles
were around your eyes,   55
and your clothes
smelled like Johnnie's Bar,
you'd spit on the floor
and at mamma,
swearing, as you flung what was left   60
of your pay check,
and she would pick up the scattered bills,
the rolling coins,
and tuck them in her apron pocket,
while you kept on   65
cursing her for being there,
and I hid
behind the doorway,
not wanting to leave her
alone with you,   70
but too afraid
to stand next to her
and fight.

my father dead but not gone,
alive but not living,   75
were you always mean?
or were there days
I never knew?
lost years on a farm,
when you were a little boy,   80
summers gone loving
in the sun with the woman
who would become my mother.

days of slow drives to Milwaukee
in a truck full of fresh farm eggs   85
and sand stuffed chickens,
to make them weigh more when you got there.
old days when you were the man
my mother loved,
before you worked   90
in a rich man's factory,
and taverns became your second home.

potatoes-in-the-cellar days,
when both of you were young and new
and lived in Berlin, Wisconsin,   95
and went to band concerts in the park,
gathered hickory nuts,
and knew everyone in town.

what did you feel
when the depression   100
robbed you of your business?

how scared were you
to come to a big city
with a wife and 2 babies?
how guilty did you feel   105
for leaving your oldest child behind?

and how crazy did it make you
to be a family provider
who could not provide
in a system that demands it   110
as part of manhood?

my father,
a good welder,
proud to be
one of the best   115
in your department.
sealing seams
of World War II bombs,
from inside their smoky guts.
welding slabs of blue metal,   120
to create corn silos,
for farms you would only dream of,
frames for trucks
you could never afford.

how did it feel   125
when a time came,
and your shaky hands
and watering eyes
couldn't keep the torch steady?

on the day you collapsed at work,   130
the shop doctor gave you
a prescription for pain pills,
and a week of sick leave.
when you returned,
you found you'd been transferred   135
to the tool crib.

your use as a profit machine,
was over.
a welding career finished,
your new assignment: 140
to hand others their tools.

you were sick, and old at fifty-five,
and I feared and hated
and did not understand you.
did you feel bad   145
after swearing at me
for not emptying your bucket
fast enough?
did you feel ashamed
when you cursed and blamed me   150
for mamma's dying,
and your only son's death?
and for not being able

to breathe hear see
or walk without a cane?   155

after mamma died, you wanted me
to take her place.
I stayed late at school each night,
until the janitor made me leave.

you'd come home to sit in your red rocker   160
by the window,
looking out on Lisbon Avenue,
and you'd rock and talk
to yourself
about corn silos,   165
and dead relatives.

did you ever think
of the man you used to be?
did you ever question
the choices that you made?   170

were you sorry
for the pain
you put your family through,
the misery no child should endure?

did you wonder, as I do,   175
how much was from the rich man?
how much,
from you?

my father,
dark gray dusty factory father,   180
dead but not gone,
alive but not living,

for thirty years
you had a clock number.
a.o. smith company   185
knew you by it.

as for me,

I knew you
by your anger,
your choices,   190

and our communal pain.

Keith Gilyard

The Hatmaker
(for Mary Lewis Gilyard)

i
cold metal snake down
A snake
E snake
F snake
cold metal subway down   5
to the district
to make hats

fingers flipping through felt
rifling through ribbon
paste sequins mesh feathers   10
hard tight straw
didn't matter what style

hats since 1947

dark eyed dark faced momma
swept north of georgia on new hope   15
swept up to new york
new york, harbor of hope
swept to this big puzzle town
this half lit skyscraper town
this dazzle & dark mixed town   20
this dazzle & dull mixed town
this big rubik's cube town
hats since jackie was rookie of the year
hats to go see the black comet lose his
but not his head   25
big fun loving nerve wracked georgia boy
with flashy feet

fun loving georgia girl fan
with working fingers

hats since 1947   30
machines spilling hats since 1947

didn't matter what style
she didn't much wear em nohow

hustle bustle out hats
sewing machine foot stomp dance   35
hats for ladies in all styles

bosses doing finger tap dance
on the cash register
machine hum register jingle dance

great worker mary you are   40
good hatmaking girl you are
never sick
foot pedal machine stomp dance
since '47

tried to keep an eye on this big puzzle town   45
tried to get it rooted in this
slippery as a seal's back
big puzzle town

swept north
brown georgia girl   50
fingers molding material
into hats to sit atop
empty heads of ladies who could never
have her grace

hats since 1947   55
hats since 1947

didn't matter what style
she didn't wear em much nohow

machines sucking hats from her fingers
sucked hats of pain from her fingers   60

didn't matter

sew on saturday

didn't matter

do overtime

didn't matter what style   65

she had youth to pour into hats in '47
youth into hats 38 years ago
just a new mover making this move
trying to beat this big puzzle town
beat this big 1947 jackie robinson town   70

metal snake down
struggling & sewing & struggling
wiggling out hats since '47
fingers shedding hats since '47
didn't matter what style   75

hats don't keep off much chill nohow
in this cold metal big puzzle town

ii
as long as too many women of thick fingered greed
or thin fingered vanity
scooped them up   80
and kept retailers happy
hats dripped from her brow

motherhood wore a hat
her children wore hats on their backs
hats on their backs in this cold metal town   85
hats on their backs and knew
a brown georgia hatmaking girl would never
let them down

hats had her up at six
in bed by ten   90
then nine
then eight
even seven

hats in some pleasant dreams
hats in her greatest nightmares   95

hats since 1947
hats since 1947

hats get heavy since '47
hundreds of thousands of hats get
real heavy since '47   100
keeping four children in hats
gets real heavy

children get heavy

especially that son on the run
hardheaded boy   105
that do it his way boy
that in one ear out the other pants leg ripping

too hard on shoes boy
that disrupt class street running drug seeking
jail peeping sense leaking   110
boy

iii
maybe worked on a million hats since 1947
maybe a million heads wearing her fingers since '47
heads bobbing to the rhythm
of sewing machine madness   115

hats since 1947
hats since 1947

never mattered what style
she never wore em much nohow

fingers as wheels on limousines   120
a hard driving answer for this town
a hard driven answer for this town
a hard children in hats answer
for this big puzzle town
a can't cover all bases but   125
i'm doing the best i can answer
for this cold metal big puzzle town

hats since 1947
hats since 1947

didn't matter what style   130
never really for her nohow

and the boy could not go hatless
wore her pride as his main skimmer in this town
wore his mother as answer
in this big puzzle town   135
wears her even now on this
cold bitter night in this
cold metal town
this big puzzle
cold metal   140
snake metal
machine mad
son of a hatmaker's town

this son of a hatmaker's town

◆

Journal Entry

How does the past affect the present in "The Father Poem Two" or "The Hatmaker"?

Textual Considerations

1. Analyze the effects of repeating the lines "my father, dead but not gone, / alive but not living" throughout "The Father Poem Two." How does this repetition affect tone, mood, and theme?
2. Summarize what the speaker in "The Father Poem Two" has learned about herself through her attempts to analyze her father's personal history.
3. Examine the speaker's various definitions of "stolen history" in "Chained Time." Which do you find most compelling? How does the speaker's view of history compare with yours?
4. What portrait of the mother emerges in "The Hatmaker"? Characterize her influence on the poem's speaker.
5. How does the repetition of the phrase "hats since 1947" affect meaning in "The Hatmaker"?

Cultural Contexts

1. Discuss with your group the extent to which "The Father Poem Two" and "Chained Time" may be viewed as protest poems. Consider what each text implies about the theme of entrapment. To what extent are we trapped by our personal and collective histories?
2. In "The Hatmaker," Gilyard raises the issues of economic necessity and class differences. Discuss their implications with your group.

Kenny, Levertov, and Song

Maurice Kenny

Going Home

The book lay unread in my lap
snow gathered at the window
from Brooklyn it was a long ride
the Greyhound followed the plow
from Syracuse to Watertown   5

to country cheese and maples
tired rivers and closed paper mills
home to gossipy aunts . . .
their dandelions and pregnant cats . . .
home to cedars and fields of boulders   10
cold graves under willow and pine
home from Brooklyn to the reservation
that was not home
to songs I could not sing
to dances I could not dance   15
from Brooklyn bars and ghetto rats
to steaming horses stomping frozen earth
barns and privies lost in blizzards
home to a Nation, Mohawk
to faces, I did not know   20
and hands which did not recognize me
to names and doors
my father shut

Denise Levertov

During a Son's Dangerous Illness

You could die before me—
I've known it
always, the
dreaded worst, "unnatural" but
possible   5
in the play
of matter, matter and
growth and
fate.

•

My sister Philippa died   10
twelve years before I was born—
the perfect, laughing firstborn,
a gift to be cherished as my orphaned mother

had not been cherished. Suddenly:
death, a baby   15

cold and still.

                                    •

Parent, child—death ignores
protocol, a sweep of its cape brushes
this one or that one at random
into the dust, it was   20
not even looking.
                    What becomes
of the past if the future
snaps off, brittle,
the present left as a jagged edge   25
opening on nothing?

                                    •

Cathy Song

Lost Sister

1

In China,
even the peasants
named their first daughters
Jade—
the stone that in the far fields   5
could moisten the dry season,
could make men move mountains
for the healing green of the inner hills
glistening like slices of winter melon.

And the daughters were grateful: 10
they never left home.
To move freely was a luxury
stolen from them at birth.
Instead, they gathered patience,
learning to walk in shoes   15
the size of teacups,[1]

without breaking—
the arc of their movements
as dormant as the rooted willow,
as redundant as the farmyard hens.   20
But they traveled far
in surviving,
learning to stretch the family rice,
to quiet the demons,
the noisy stomachs.   25

2
There is a sister
across the ocean,
who relinquished her name,
diluting jade green
with the blue of the Pacific.   30
Rising with a tide of locusts,
she swarmed with others
to inundate another shore.
In America,
there are many roads   35
and women can stride along with men.

But in another wilderness,
the possibilities,
the loneliness,
can strangulate like jungle vines.   40
The meager provisions and sentiments
of once belonging—
fermented roots, Mah-Jongg[2] tiles and firecrackers—
set but a flimsy household
in a forest of nightless cities.   45
A giant snake rattles above,
spewing black clouds into your kitchen.
Dough-faced landlords
slip in and out of your keyholes,
making claims you don't understand,   50
tapping into your communication systems
of laundry lines and restaurant chains.

You find you need China:
your one fragile identification,
a jade link   55
handcuffed to your wrist.

You remember your mother
who walked for centuries,
footless—
and like her,   60
you have left no footprints,
but only because
there is an ocean in between,
the unremitting space of your rebellion.

---

[1] A reference to the practice of binding young girls' feet so that they remain small. This practice was common in China until the Communist revolution.

[2] Or mahjong, an ancient Chinese game played with dice and tiles.

Journal Entry

Record your associations with the phrase "going home."

Textual Considerations

1. To contrast the unique experiences that the speakers in "Lost Sister" and "Going Home" communicate through their narrative styles, identify words and images that define their sense of ethnic or racial identity.
2. Explain why the "lost sister" and her mother have "left no footprints" (l. 61).
3. Review Levertov's poem and discuss the implications of her comment that "death ignores protocol." To what extent does she succeed in addressing the threat of personal loss in a context that goes beyond her personal situation?

Cultural Contexts

1. "Lost Sister," "Going Home," and "During a Son's Dangerous Illness" portray some of the memories and ancestral ties that bind families in different cultures. Working with your group, make a list of the characteristics that emerge through the speakers' portraits of their family members.
2. In "Lost Sister," the speaker stresses her need for "one fragile identification" with her native country, China. Working with your group, suggest other kinds of identification that people need in order to explore their origins and their relation to the past. Consider the role played by both the family and the larger community.

Linda Hogan

Song for My Name

Before sunrise
think of brushing out an old woman's
dark braids.
Think of your hands,
fingertips on the soft hair.   5

If you have this name,
your grandfather's dark hands
lead horses toward the wagon
and a cloud of dust follows,
ghost of silence.   10

That name is full of women
with black hair
and men with eyes like night.
It means no money
tomorrow.   15

Such a name my mother loves
while she works gently
in the small house.
She is a white dove
and in her own land   20
the mornings are pale,
birds sing into the white curtains
and show off their soft breasts.

If you have a name like this,
there's never enough water.   25
There is too much heat.
When lightning strikes, rain
refuses to follow.
It's my name,
that of a woman living   30
between the white moon
and the red sun, waiting to leave.
It's the name that goes with me
back to earth
no one else can touch.   35

Gary Soto

Moving Away [1]

Remember that we are moving away brother
From those years
In the same house with a white stepfather
What troubled him has been forgotten

But what troubled us has settled   5
Like dirt
In the nests of our knuckles
And cannot be washed away

All those times you woke shivering
In the night   10
From a coldness I
Could not understand
And cupped a crucifix beneath the covers

All those summers we hoed our yard
In the afternoon sun   15
The heat waving across our faces
And we waved back wasps
While the one we hated
Watched us from under a tree and said nothing

We will remember those moments brother   20

And now that we are far
From one another
What I want to speak of
Is the quiet of a room just before daybreak
And you next to me sleeping   25

Gary Soto

Moving Away [2]

Remember that you are moving away   sister
From what was a summer
Of hunger
And of thorns deep in your feet
Prayers that unraveled   5
Like mama's stockings
At the day's end
When she came back from candling eggs

Those small things you knew on the old street
Have vanished   a holly bush   10
And its bright jays
The rocks you scratched
From the yard
And were your dolls   blond dolls
Given heartbeats   names   legs   15
The sighs of those
About to cry
                    Remember that you have left
Grandpa nodding like a tall weed
Over his patch of chilies and tomatoes   20
Left a jar of secrets
Buried in the vacant lot
On a hot day
And our family some distance
From your life   25
Remember

◆

Journal Entry

React to this statement: "The past that constitutes our identity cannot be erased."

Textual Considerations

1. Speculate on the meanings of Hogan's title, "Song for My Name." What significance do you attach to the speaker's not revealing her name?
2. How does Hogan explore the effects of color, sound, and rhythm to evoke recollections from the past?

3. What images most effectively convey the bonds of love between the brothers in Soto's poem? How does Soto use repetition to reinforce meaning?
4. Contrast the tones of Soto's poems. Of what significance is the speaker's use of the second-person pronoun throughout most of the poem about his sister? Analyze what the last stanza conveys about the sister's relation to the family.

Cultural Contexts

1. The speakers of these poems search for their origins in different ways. Explain how their memories of the past authenticate their narrative voices and contribute to their individual histories.
2. Speculate with your group about the implications of Gary Soto's gender-split poems. In how many ways can we read Soto's poems? How do these poems mirror each other? What kinds of effects do they create for you as reader?

Hayden and Giovanni

Robert Hayden

Runagate Runagate

I.

Runs falls rises stumbles on from darkness into darkness
and the darkness thicketed with shapes of terror
and the hunters pursuing and the hounds pursuing
and the night cold and the night long and the river
to cross and the jack-muh-lanterns beckoning beckoning   5
and blackness ahead and when shall I reach that somewhere
morning and keep on going and never turn back and keep on going

     Runagate
          Runagate
               Runagate   10

Many thousands rise and go
many thousands crossing over

               O mythic North
          O star-shaped yonder Bible city

Some go weeping and some rejoicing   15
some in coffins and some in carriages
some in silks and some in shackles

    Rise and go or fare you well

No more auction block for me
no more driver's lash for me   20

    If you see my Pompey, 30 yrs of age,
    new breeches, plain stockings, negro shoes;
    if you see my Anna, likely young mulatto
    branded E on the right cheek, R on the left,
    catch them if you can and notify subscriber,   25
    Catch them if you can, but it won't be easy.
    They'll dart underground when you try to catch them,
    plunge into quicksand, whirlpools, mazes,
    turn into scorpions when you try to catch them.

And before I'll be a slave   30
I'll be buried in my grave

    North star and bonanza gold
    I'm bound for the freedom, freedom-bound
    and oh Susyanna don't you cry for me

    Runagate   35

        Runagate

II.
Rises from their anguish and their power,

        Harriet Tubman,

        woman of earth, whipscarred,
        a summoning, a shining   40

    Mean to be free

And this was the way of it, brethren brethren,
way we journeyed from Can't to Can.

Moon so bright and no place to hide,
the cry up and the patterollers riding,   45
hound dogs belling in bladed air.
And fear starts a-murbling, Never make it,
we'll never make it. *Hush that now,*
and she's turned upon us, levelled pistol
glinting in the moonlight: 50
Dead folks can't jaybird-talk she says:
you keep on going now or die, she says.

Wanted Harriet Tubman alias The General
alias Moses Stealer of Slaves

In league with Garrison Alcott Emerson   55
Garrett Douglass Thoreau John Brown

Armed and known to be Dangerous

Wanted Reward Dead or Alive

Tell me, Ezekiel, oh tell me do you see
mailed Jehovah coming to deliver me?   60

Hoot-owl calling in the ghosted air,
five times calling to the hants in the air.
Shadow of a face in the scary leaves,
shadow of a voice in the talking leaves:

Come ride-a my train   65

Oh that train, ghost-story train
through swamp and savanna movering movering,
over trestles of dew, through caves of the wish,
Midnight Special on a sabre track movering movering,
first stop Mercy and the last Hallelujah.   70

Come ride-a my train

Mean mean mean to be free.

Nikki Giovanni

Nikki-Rosa

childhood remembrances are always a drag
if you're Black
you always remember things like living in Woodlawn[1]
with no inside toilet
and if you become famous or something   5
they never talk about how happy you were to have your mother
all to your self and
how good the water felt when you got your bath from one of those
big tubs that folk in chicago barbecue in
and somehow when you talk about home   10
it never gets across how much you
understood their feelings
as the whole family attended meetings about Hollydale
and even though you remember
your biographers never understand   15
your father's pain as he sells his stock
and another dream goes
and though you're poor it isn't poverty that
concerns you
and though they fought a lot   20
it isn't your father's drinking that makes any difference
but only that everybody is together and you
and your sister have happy birthdays and very good christmasses
and I really hope no white person ever has cause to write about me
because they never understand Black love is Black wealth and they'll   25
probably talk about my hard childhood and never understand that
all the while I was quite happy.

[1] A black suburb of Cincinnati, Ohio

Journal Entry

Respond to the idea that "we have to do with the past only as it is useful for the present and the future."

Textual Considerations

1. Discuss the effects of Giovanni's juxtaposition of short and long narrative lines. How does this structural pattern reinforce the speaker's meaning? How does it affect your response to the poem?

2. Cite two or three images in "Nikki-Rosa" that most vividly convey the speaker's feelings about her childhood. To what extent do you agree that family life can be happy despite economic hardship?
3. In "Runagate Runagate," Hayden uses the interaction of several voices to orchestrate the phonic meanings of the poem. Identify some of these voices, and extend your study of sound to explore how devices such as alliteration, onomatopoeia, rhyme, and meter contribute to the phonic pattern of the poem.
4. Consult a dictionary for various definitions of *runagate*. How does a better understanding of the meaning of the title affect your response to the powerful epic voice of the speaker in lines such as "and before I'll be a slave / I'll be buried in my grave"?

Cultural Contexts

1. To portray how "voiceless" people succeeded in constructing the history of the past, Hayden presents Harriet Tubman, Frederick Douglass, and others as models of individual heroism and courage. Identify each of these figures, and investigate how these "voiceless voices" from the past contributed to the collective history of the United States.

Longfellow and Thomas ◆

Henry Wadsworth Longfellow

The Jewish Cemetery at Newport[1]
(1854)

How strange it seems! These Hebrews in their graves,
    Close by the street of this fair seaport town,
Silent beside the never-silent waves,
    At rest in all this moving up and down!

The trees are white with dust, that o'er their sleep   5
    Wave their broad curtains in the south-wind's breath.
While underneath these leafy tents they keep
    The long, mysterious Exodus of Death[2]

And these sepulchral stones, so old and brown,
    That pave with level flags their burial-place,   10
Seem like the tablets of the Law, thrown down
    And broken by Moses at the mountain's base.[3]

The very names recorded here are strange,
    Of foreign accent, and of different climes;
Alvares and Rivera interchange   15
    With Abraham and Jacob of old times.[4]

"Blessed be God, for he created Death!"
    The mourners said, "and Death is rest and peace;"
Then added, in the certainty of faith,
    "And giveth Life that nevermore shall cease."   20

Closed are the portals of their Synagogue,
    No Psalms of David now the silence break,
No Rabbi reads the ancient Decalogue[5]
    In the grand dialect the Prophets spake.

Gone are the living, but the dead remain,   25
    And not neglected; for a hand unseen,
Scattering its bounty, like a summer rain,
    Still keeps their graves and their remembrance green.

How came they here? What burst of Christian hate,
    What persecution, merciless and blind,   30
Drove o'er the sea—that desert desolate—
    These Ishmaels and Hagars of mankind?[6]

They lived in narrow streets and lanes obscure,
    Ghetto and Judenstrass,[7] in mirk and mire;
Taught in the school of patience to endure   35
    The life of anguish and the death of fire.

All their lives long, with the unleavened bread
    And bitter herbs of exile and its fears,
The wasting famine of the heart they fed,
    And slaked its thirst with marah of their tears.   40

Anathema maranatha![8] was the cry
    That rang from town to town, from street to street;
At every gate the accursed Mordecai[9]
    Was mocked and jeered, and spurned by Christian feet.

Pride and humiliation hand in hand   45
    Walked with them through the world where'er they went;
Trampled and beaten were they as the sand,
    And yet unshaken as the continent.

For in the background figures vague and vast
    Of patriarchs and of prophets rose sublime,   50
And all the great traditions of the Past
    They saw reflected in the coming time.

And thus forever with reverted look
    The mystic volume of the world they read,
Spelling it backward, like a Hebrew book,   55
    Till life became a Legend of the Dead.

But ah! what once has been shall be no more!
   The groaning earth in travail and in pain
Brings forth its races, but does not restore,
   And the dead nations never rise again.   60

[1] The oldest synagogue in the U.S. is in Newport, Rhode Island.

[2] A reference to the second book of the Old Testament, which recounts the expulsion of the Jews from Egypt.

[3] See Exodus 32:19.

[4] The Jewish population in Newport was mostly of Spanish and Portuguese heritage.

[5] The Ten Commandments.

[6] Two exiles whose stories are recorded in Genesis.

[7] Literally, "Jew Street" (German). Jews lived in restricted areas, or ghettos.

[8] "Anathema" is an accursed person, or a formal curse; "Maranatha" means "O Lord, come." The combination is a powerful curse, calling on God to destroy the Jews. See 1 Corinthians 16:22.

[9] In the Book of Esther, Mordecai, Esther's uncle, sat at the king's gate, angering the chief minister, Haman, by refusing to bow before him. Haman plotted to kill Mordecai and all the Jews, but was executed.

Dylan Thomas

Fern Hill
(1946)

Now as I was young and easy under the apple boughs
About the lilting house and happy as the grass was green,
   The night above the dingle[1] starry,
     Time let me hail and climb
    Golden in the heydays of his eyes,   5
And honored among wagons I was prince of the apple towns
And once below a time I lordly had the trees and leaves
     Trail with daisies and barley
    Down the rivers of the windfall light.

And as I was green and carefree, famous among the barns   10
About the happy yard and singing as the farm was home,
     In the sun that is young once only,
        Time let me play and be
     Golden in the mercy of his means,
And green and golden I was huntsman and herdsman, the calves   15
Sang to my horn, the foxes on the hills barked clear and cold,
        And the sabbath rang slowly
     In the pebbles of the holy streams.

All the sun long it was running, it was lovely, the hay
Fields high as the house, the tunes from the chimneys, it was air   20
     And playing, lovely and watery
        And fire green as grass.
     And nightly under the simple stars
As I rode to sleep the owls were bearing the farm away,
All the moon long I heard, blessed among stables, the nightjars   25
     Flying with the ricks, and the horses
        Flashing into the dark.

And then to awake, and the farm, like a wanderer white
With the dew, come back, the cock on his shoulder: it was all
     Shining, it was Adam and maiden,   30
        The sky gathered again
     And the sun grew round that very day.
So it must have been after the birth of the simple light
In the first, spinning place, the spellbound horses walking warm
     Out of the whinnying green stable   35
        On to the fields of praise.

And honored among foxes and pheasants by the gay house
Under the new made clouds and happy as the heart was long,
     In the sun born over and over,
        I ran my heedless ways,   40
     My wishes raced through the house high hay
And nothing I cared, at my sky blue trades, that time allows
In all his tuneful turning so few and such morning songs
     Before the children green and golden
        Follow him out of grace,   45

Nothing I cared, in the lamb white days, that time would take me
Up to the swallow thronged loft by the shadow of my hand,
    In the moon that is always rising,
        Nor that riding to sleep
    I should hear him fly with the high fields   50
And wake to the farm forever fled from the childless land.
Oh as I was young and easy in the mercy of his means,
        Time held me green and dying
    Though I sang in my chains like the sea.

¹ Wooded valley.

Journal Entry

Explain the paradox in the last two lines of "Fern Hill."

Textual Considerations

1. Compare and contrast the speakers' attitudes toward time in these poems. To what extent do the speakers view time as benevolent, malevolent, or indifferent?
2. Discuss the effects of Longfellow's historical analysis of anti-Semitism in "The Jewish Cemetery at Newport." What can this poem teach new generations about the past?
3. Analyze how Dylan Thomas's use of color reinforces his theme in "Fern Hill." How do his references to music also contribute to the poem's meaning?
4. In stanza 4 in "Fern Hill," the speaker compares his own childhood to what other experience of newness and innocence?
5. That speaker sounds an ominous note for the first time in stanza 5. What foreshadowings of this danger can you find in earlier stanzas?

Cultural Contexts

1. What attitudes about the past do these poems elicit? Use evidence from the texts to describe Thomas's evocation of childhood and Longfellow's historical exploration of Judaism.
2. Is there a "site of memory" that has shaped your own historical past? Describe it to your group, and discuss the extent to which we are influenced by landscapes from the past.

Luci Tapahonso

A Breeze Swept Through

For my daughters, Lori Tazbah and Misty Dawn

The first born of dawn woman
slid out amid crimson fluid streaked with stratus clouds
    her body glistening August sunset pink
    light steam rising from her like rain on warm rocks
        (A sudden cool breeze swept through   5
        the kitchen and grandpa smiled then sang
        quietly knowing the moment.)
She came when the desert day cooled
and dusk began to move in
in that intricate changing of time   10
    she gasped and it flows from her now
    with every breath   with every breath
    she travels now
        sharing scarlet sunsets
        named for wild desert flowers   15
        her smile a blessing song.

And in mid-November
early morning darkness
after days of waiting pain
    the second one cried   wailing   20
    sucking first earth breath
    separating the heavy fog
    she cried and kicked   tiny brown limbs
    fierce movements as outside
    the mist lifted as   25
    the sun is born again.
        (East of Acoma, a sandstone boulder
        split in two—a sharp, clean crack.)
        She is born of damp mist and early sun.
        She is born again   woman of dawn.   30
        She is born knowing the warm smoothness of rock.
        She is born knowing her own morning strength.

Colleen J. McElroy

This Is the Poem I Never Meant to Write

my grandmother
raised me Georgia style
a broken mirror
spilled salt
a tattered hemline   5
all add up to bad spirits
when she died, I learned to worship
stranger things
a faded textbook full of bad theories
has no spirit at all   10
now I've gone full circle

in a town some still call Bahía
the drumbeat of the alabés
echoes my grandmother's warnings
I watch the daughters of the candomblé   15
dance to the rhythms of ancient spirits
as the ceremony begins
my lungs expand
like gas-filled dirigibles
stretched latex-thin   20

my grandmother spoke
the language of this scene
the mystery and magic
of rich colors in a tapestry
of brown and black skin   25
white candles
a small reed boat
six bloody gamecocks
all bind this church to its African source
I follow my people past spirit houses   30
past tight Spanish streets
where houses are painted blue and white
like any Moorish town
when we reach the sea
water seems to flow uphill   35
tropical landscapes turn mustard yellow
and above us the moon swallows the night

this is the poem
I never meant to write
I am learning to worship   40
my grandmother's spirits
an old woman
splinters of wood embedded
in her black leathery cheeks
three crosses tattooed   45
on the fleshy black skin
of her upper arms
draws my picture upon her palm
in blue ink
then tells me we are all strangers   50
bound by the same spirit
I have gone home
in the dim light
my grandmother smiles

Journal Entry

What do both poems imply about the influence of family origins?

Textual Considerations

1. Comment on the effectiveness of the speaker's use of nature imagery to describe her daughters in "A Breeze Swept Through." How are the daughters different from each other?
2. Speculate on the meaning of the title of Tapahonso's poem, "A Breeze Swept Through."
3. Analyze the implications of the title "This Is the Poem I Never Meant to Write." What insights has McElroy gained through rediscovering her grandmother?
4. McElroy defines poetry as "drama, music, and dance." What elements of each do you find in her poem?

Cultural Contexts

1. Characterize the speaker of each poem. What does each speaker reveal about her attitudes toward her ethnic heritage through the portrayal of family members?

Lum and Vigil-Pinon

Wing Tek Lum

It's Something Our Family Has Always Done

On every trip away from these islands
on the day of departure and on the day of return
we go to the graves, all seven of them,
but for one the sum total of all of our ancestors
who died in this place we call home.   5

The drive to the cemetery is only five minutes long.
Stopping by a florist adds maybe ten minutes more.
Yet my wife and I on the day of our flight
are so rushed with packing and last minute chores.
Why do we still make the time to go?   10

The concrete road is one lane wide.
We turn around at the circle up at the top,
always to park just to the side of the large banyan tree
as the road begins its slope back down.
I turn the wheels; we now lock our car.   15

As if by rote, we bring anthuriums,
at least two flowers for each of our dead.
On our way we stop to pay our respects to the "Old Man"
—that first one lain here, all wind and water before him—
who watches over this graveyard, and our island home.   20

Approaching my grandparents, we divide up our offering,
placing their long stems into the holes filled with sand.
Squatting in front of each marble tablet,
I make it a point to read off their names in Chinese.
My hands pull out crabgrass running over stone.   25

I stand erect, clutching palm around fist,
swinging the air three times up and down.
My wife from the waist bows once, arms at her sides.
I manage to whisper a few phrases out loud,
conversing like my father would, as if all could hear.   30

We do Grandfather, Grandmother, and my parents below them.
Following the same path we always take,
we make our way through the tombstones and mounds,
skirting their concrete borders, to the other two Lums
and to our Granduncle on the Chang side. 35

Back up the hill, we spend a few moments by the curb
picking off black, thin burrs from our cuffs and socks.
We talk about what errands we must do next.
I glance around us at these man-made gardens,
thrust upon a slope of earth, spirit houses rising to the sky. 40

As I get into our car, and look out at the sea,
I am struck with the same thought as always.
We spend so little time in front of these graves
asking each in turn to protect us when we are far away.
I question them all: what good does it really do? 45

I have read ancient poets who parted with sorrow
from family and friends, fearing never to return.
Our oral histories celebrate brave peasants
daring oceans and the lonely beds: they looked even more
to blessings at long distance from their spirit dead. 50

My father superstitious, even to the jet age,
still averred: but every little bit helps.
These sentiments I know, but I confess I do not feel.
Maybe it's for this loss that I still come here.
They are family, and I respect them so. 55

Evangelina Vigil

warm heart contains life
to our amás

warm heart contains life
heart's warmth
which penetrates through pen
lifeblood that reveals inner thoughts
subtly 5
like rustling leaves would secrets
to the winter wind

secrets collected
pressed between pages
to be kissed by lips red   10
protruding with warmth, desire
sometimes hurt, pain:

recuerdos
like that autumn leaf you singled out
and saved   15
pressed in-between the memories of your mind
diary never written
but always remembered, felt
scripted en tu mente—
your daughters will never read it   20
but they'll inherit it
and they'll know it
when they look into your eyes
shining luz de amor, corazón
unspoken, untold   25
keepsake for our treasure chests
que cargamos aquí adentro
radiant with jewels
sculpted by sentimientos y penas
y bastante amor: 30

    intuition tells us
    better having lived through pain
    than never having felt
    life's full intensity

Journal Entry

Respond to the concept of heritage in "It's Something Our Family Has Always Done" and in "warm heart contains life."

Textual Considerations

1. Characterize the speaker's emotions in Lum's poem as he visits the family burial grounds.
2. To what extent does the speaker answer his question, "What good does it really do?" (l. 45)?
3. Characterize the relation between the past and the future in Vigil's poem. To what extent does the speaker's bilingual text contribute to the poem's meaning? Explain.
4. Speculate on the implications of the title of Vigil's poem.

Cultural Contexts

1. In a text she edited in 1983 titled *Woman of Her Word: Hispanic Women Write,* Vigil describes the Latina writer: "As a person in the literature, the Latina is a woman of her word—*mujer de su palabra.* In this role, the Latina is self-sacrificing to her family as a mother and wife. She conveys values to her family members by way of example, and through the oral tradition, and, as such, she represents a tie to the cultural past." Discuss with your group how the oral tradition functions in Vigil's poem. Then review stanza 10 of Lum's poem. How has his oral tradition also contributed to his cultural heritage?

Emanuel and Lorde ◆

James A. Emanuel

Fishermen

When three, he fished these lakes,
Curled sleeping on a lip of rock,
Crib blankets tucked from ants and fishbone flies,
Twitching as the strike of bass and snarling reel
Uncoiled my shouts not quit   5
Till he jerked blinking up on all-fours,
Swaying with the winking leaves.
Strong awake, he shook his cane pole like a spoon
And dipped among the wagging perch
Till, tired, he drew his silver rubber blade   10
And poked the winding fins that tugged our string,
Or sprayed the dimpling minnows with his plastic gun,
Or, rainstruck, squirmed to my armpit in the poncho.

Ten years uncurled him, thinned him hard.
Now, far he casts his line into the wrinkled blue   15
And easy toes a rock, reel on his thigh
Till bone and crank cry out the strike
He takes with manchild chuckles, cunning
In his play of zigzag line and plunging silver.

Now fishing far from me, he strides through rain, shoulders   20
A spiny ridge of pines, and disappears
Near lakes that cannot be, while I must choose
To go or stay: bring blanket, blade, and gun,
Or stand a fisherman.

Audre Lorde

What My Child Learns of the Sea

What my child learns of the sea
Of the summer thunder
Of the bewildering riddle that hides at the vortex of spring
She will learn in my twilight
And childlike   5
Revise every autumn.

What my child learns
As her winters fall out of time
Ripened in my own body
To enter her eyes with first light.   10

This is why
More than blood,
Or the milk I have given
One day a strange girl will step
To the back of a mirror   15
Cutting my ropes
Of sea and thunder and sun.
Of the way she will taste her autumns
Toast-brittle, or warmer than sleep
And the words she will use for winter   20
I stand already condemned.

Journal Entry

State what "Fishermen" and "What My Child Learns of the Sea" imply about the relation between parents and child.

Textual Considerations

1. What will the child in Lorde's poem "revise every autumn"?
2. Discuss the significance of nature imagery in Lorde's poem.
3. Compare and contrast the three fishing trips in Emanuel's poem.
4. Why is the last word of Emanuel's poem "fisherman," whereas the title is "Fishermen"?

Cultural Contexts

1. Discuss with your group the meaning of the last line of Lorde's poem. To what extent does it also apply to Emanuel's poem? Is the process described in both poems inevitable? What did you discover about the role of parents from both poems?

William Shakespeare

The Tragedy of Hamlet Prince of Denmark

DRAMATIS PERSONAE

CLAUDIUS, *King of Denmark*
HAMLET, *son to the late, and nephew to the present, King*
POLONIUS, *Lord Chamberlain*
HORATIO, *friend to* HAMLET
LAERTES, *son to* POLONIUS
VOLTEMAND
CORNELIUS
ROSENCRANTZ
GUILDENSTERN ⎱ — *courtiers*
OSRIC
A GENTLEMAN
A PRIEST
MARCELLUS
BARNARDO ⎱ — *officers*
FRANCISCO
REYNALDO, *servant to* POLONIUS
Players
Two clowns, *gravediggers*
FORTINBRAS, *Prince of Norway*
A Norwegian captain
English ambassadors
GERTRUDE, *Queen of Denmark, mother to* HAMLET
OPHELIA, *daughter to* POLONIUS
GHOST *of* HAMLET'*s father*
Lords, Ladies, Officers, Soldiers, Sailors, Messengers, Attendants

SCENE. *Elsinore*

ACT I

SCENE I. *A guard platform of the castle.*

Enter BARNARDO *and* FRANCISCO, *two sentinels.*

BARNARDO. Who's there?
FRANCISCO. Nay, answer me. Stand and unfold° yourself.

SCENE I. 2. *unfold:* disclose.

170

BARNARDO. Long live the King!°
FRANCISCO. Barnardo?
BARNARDO. He.   5
FRANCISCO. You come most carefully upon your hour.
BARNARDO. 'Tis now struck twelve. Get thee to bed, Francisco.
FRANCISCO. For this relief much thanks. 'Tis bitter cold, And I am sick at heart.
BARNARDO. Have you had quiet guard?
FRANCISCO.   Not a mouse stirring.   10
BARNARDO. Well, good night.
  If you do meet Horatio and Marcellus,
  The rivals° of my watch, bid them make haste.

               Enter HORATIO *and* MARCELLUS.

FRANCISCO. I think I hear them. Stand, ho! Who is there?
HORATIO. Friends to this ground.
MARCELLUS.   And liegemen to the Dane.°   15
FRANCISCO. Give you° good night.
MARCELLUS.   O, farewell, honest soldier.
  Who hath relieved you?
FRANCISCO.   Barnardo hath my place.
  Give you good night. *Exit* FRANCISCO.
MARCELLUS.   Holla, Barnardo!
BARNARDO.   Say——
  What, is Horatio there?
HORATIO.   A piece of him.
BARNARDO. Welcome, Horatio. Welcome, good Marcellus.   20
MARCELLUS. What, has this thing appeared again tonight?
BARNARDO. I have seen nothing.
MARCELLUS. Horatio says 'tis but our fantasy,
  And will not let belief take hold of him
  Touching this dreaded sight twice seen of us;   25
  Therefore I have entreated him along
  With us to watch the minutes of this night,
  That, if again this apparition come,
  He may approve° our eyes and speak to it.
HORATIO. Tush, tush, 'twill not appear.
BARNARDO.   Sit down awhile,   30
  And let us once again assail your ears,
  That are so fortified against our story,
  What we have two nights seen.

---

3. *Long live the King:* (perhaps a password, perhaps a greeting). 13. *rivals:* partners.
15. *liegemen to the Dane:* loyal subjects to the King of Denmark. 16. *Give you:* God give you.
29. *approve:* confirm.

HORATIO.   Well, sit we down,
  And let us hear Barnardo speak of this.
BARNARDO. Last night of all,   35
  When yond same star that's westward from the pole°
  Had made his course t' illume that part of heaven
  Where now it burns, Marcellus and myself,
  The bell then beating one——

Enter GHOST.

MARCELLUS. Peace, break thee off. Look where it comes again.   40
BARNARDO. In the same figure like the king that's dead.
MARCELLUS. Thou art a scholar; speak to it, Horatio.
BARNARDO. Looks 'a not like the king? Mark it, Horatio.
HORATIO. Most like: it harrows me with fear and wonder.
BARNARDO. It would be spoke to.
MARCELLUS.   Speak to it, Horatio.   45
HORATIO. What art thou that usurp'st this time of night,
  Together with that fair and warlike form
  In which the majesty of buried Denmark°
  Did sometimes march? By heaven I charge thee, speak.
MARCELLUS. It is offended.
BARNARDO.   See, it stalks away.   50
HORATIO. Stay! Speak, speak, I charge thee, speak. *Exit* GHOST.
MARCELLUS. 'Tis gone and will not answer.
BARNARDO. How now, Horatio? You tremble and look pale.
  Is not this something more than fantasy?
  What think you on't?   55
HORATIO. Before my God, I might not this believe
  Without the sensible and true avouch°
  Of mine own eyes.
MARCELLUS.   Is it not like the King?
HORATIO. As thou art to thyself.
  Such was the very armor he had on   60
  When he the ambitious Norway° combated:
  So frowned he once, when, in an angry parle,°
  He smote the sledded Polacks° on the ice.
  'Tis strange.
MARCELLUS. Thus twice before, and jump° at this dead hour,   65
  With martial stalk hath he gone by our watch.

---

36. *pole:* polestar. 48. *buried Denmark:* the buried King of Denmark. 57. *sensible and true avouch:* sensory and true proof. 61. *Norway:* King of Norway. 62. *parle:* parley. 63. *sledded Polacks:* Poles in sledges. 65. *jump:* just.

HORATIO. In what particular thought to work I know not;
　　But, in the gross and scope° of my opinion,
　　This bodes some strange eruption to our state.
MARCELLUS. Good now, sit down, and tell me he that knows,　　　70
　　Why this same strict and most observant watch
　　So nightly toils the subject° of the land,
　　And why such daily cast of brazen cannon
　　And foreign mart° for implements of war,
　　Why such impress° of shipwrights, whose sore task　　　75
　　Does not divide the Sunday from the week,
　　What might be toward° that this sweaty haste
　　Doth make the night joint-laborer with the day?
　　Who is't that can inform me?
HORATIO.　　　　　　　　　　That can I.
　　At least the whisper goes so: our last king,　　　80
　　Whose image even but now appeared to us,
　　Was, as you know, by Fortinbras of Norway,
　　Thereto pricked on by a most emulate pride,
　　Dared to the combat; in which our valiant Hamlet
　　(For so this side of our known world esteemed him)　　　85
　　Did slay this Fortinbras, who, by a sealed compact
　　Well ratified by law and heraldry,°
　　Did forfeit, with his life, all those his lands
　　Which he stood seized° of, to the conqueror;
　　Against the which a moiety competent°　　　90
　　Was gagèd° by our King, which had returned
　　To the inheritance of Fortinbras,
　　Had he been vanquisher, as, by the same comart°
　　And carriage of the article designed,°
　　His fell to Hamlet. Now, sir, young Fortinbras,　　　95
　　Of unimprovèd° mettle hot and full,
　　Hath in the skirts° of Norway here and there
　　Sharked up° a list of lawless resolutes,°
　　For food and diet, to some enterprise
　　That hath a stomach in't;° which is no other,　　　100
　　As it doth well appear unto our state,
　　But to recover of us by strong hand

68. *gross and scope:* general drift. 72. *toils the subject:* makes the subjects toil. 74. *mart:* trading.
75. *impress:* forced service. 77. *toward:* in preparation. 87. *law and heraldry:* heraldic law
(governing the combat). 89. *seized:* possessed. 90. *moiety competent:* equal portion. 91. *gagèd:*
engaged, pledged. 93. *comart:* agreement. 94. *carriage of the article designed:* import of the
agreement drawn up. 96. *unimprovèd:* untried. 97. *skirts:* borders. 98. *Sharked up:* collected
indiscriminately (as a shark gulps its prey). 98. *resolutes:* desperadoes. 100. *hath a stomach in't:* i.e.,
requires courage.

And terms compulsatory, those foresaid lands
So by his father lost; and this, I take it,
Is the main motive of our preparations,   105
The source of this our watch, and the chief head°
Of this posthaste and romage° in the land.
BARNARDO. I think it be no other but e'en so;
  Well may it sort° that this portentous figure
  Comes armèd through our watch so like the King   110
  That was and is the question of these wars.
HORATIO.   A mote it is to trouble the mind's eye:
  In the most high and palmy state of Rome,
  A little ere the mightiest Julius fell,
  The graves stood tenantless, and the sheeted dead   115
  Did squeak and gibber in the Roman streets;°
  As stars with trains of fire and dews of blood,
  Disasters° in the sun; and the moist star,°
  Upon whose influence Neptune's empire stands,
  Was sick almost to doomsday with eclipse.   120
  And even the like precurse° of feared events,
  As harbingers° preceding still° the fates
  And prologue to the omen° coming on,
  Have heaven and earth together demonstrated
  Unto our climatures° and countrymen.   125

Enter GHOST.

But soft, behold, lo where it comes again!
I'll cross it,° though it blast me.—Stay, illusion.   *It spreads his° arms.*
If thou hast any sound or use of voice,
Speak to me.
If there be any good thing to be done   130
That may to thee do ease and grace to me,
Speak to me.
If thou art privy to thy country's fate,
Which happily° foreknowing may avoid,
O, speak!   135
Or if thou hast uphoarded in thy life
Extorted° treasure in the womb of earth,

106. *head:* fountainhead, origin. 107. *romage:* bustle. 109. *sort:* befit. 116. *Did squeak . . .*
Roman streets: (the break in the sense which follows this line suggests that a line has dropped out).
118. *Disasters:* threatening signs. 118. *moist star:* moon. 121. *precurse:* precursor, foreshadowing.
122. *harbingers:* forerunners. 122. *still:* always. 123. *omen:* calamity. 125. *climatures:* regions.
127. *cross it:* (1) cross its path, confront it (2) make the sign of the cross in front of it.
127. s.d. *his:* i.e., its, the ghost's (though possibly what is meant is that Horatio spreads his own
arms, making a cross of himself). 134. *happily:* haply, perhaps. 137. *Extorted:* ill-won.

For which, they say, you spirits oft walk in death,   *The cock crows.*
   Speak of it. Stay and speak. Stop it, Marcellus.
MARCELLUS.   Shall I strike at it with my partisan°?   140
HORATIO.   Do, if it will not stand.
BARNARDO.   'Tis here.
HORATIO.   'Tis here.
MARCELLUS.   'Tis gone.   *Exit* GHOST.
   We do it wrong, being so majestical,
   To offer it the show of violence,
   For it is as the air, invulnerable,   145
   And our vain blows malicious mockery.
BARNARDO.   It was about to speak when the cock crew.
HORATIO.   And then it started, like a guilty thing
   Upon a fearful summons. I have heard,
   The cock, that is the trumpet to the morn,   150
   Doth with his lofty and shrill-sounding throat
   Awake the god of day, and at his warning,
   Whether in sea or fire, in earth or air,
   Th' extravagant and erring° spirit hies
   To his confine; and of the truth herein   155
   This present object made probation.°
MARCELLUS.   It faded on the crowing of the cock.
   Some say that ever 'gainst° that season comes
   Wherein our Savior's birth is celebrated,
   This bird of dawning singeth all night long,   160
   And then, they say, no spirit dare stir abroad,
   The nights are wholesome, then no planets strike,°
   No fairy takes,° nor witch hath power to charm:
   So hallowed and so gracious is that time.
HORATIO.   So have I heard and do in part believe it.   165
   But look, the morn in russet mantle clad
   Walks o'er the dew of yon high eastward hill.
   Break we our watch up, and by my advice
   Let us impart what we have seen tonight
   Unto young Hamlet, for upon my life   170
   This spirit, dumb to us, will speak to him.
   Do you consent we shall acquaint him with it,
   As needful in our loves, fitting our duty?
MARCELLUS.   Let's do't, I pray, and I this morning know
   Where we shall find him most convenient.   *Exeunt.*   175

---

140. *partisan:* pike (a long-handled weapon).   154. *extravagant and erring:* out of bounds and
wandering.   156. *probation:* proof.   158. *'gainst:* just before.   162. *strike:* exert an evil influence.
163. *takes:* bewitches.

SCENE II. *The castle.*

Flourish.° *Enter* CLAUDIUS, *King of Denmark,* GERTRUDE *the Queen, Councilors,*
POLONIUS *and his son* LAERTES, HAMLET, *cum aliis*° [*including*
VOLTEMAND *and* CORNELIUS].

KING. Though yet of Hamlet our dear brother's death
   The memory be green, and that it us befitted
   To bear our hearts in grief, and our whole kingdom
   To be contracted in one brow of woe,
   Yet so far hath discretion fought with nature   5
   That we with wisest sorrow think on him
   Together with remembrance of ourselves.
   Therefore our sometime sister,° now our Queen,
   Th' imperial jointress° to this warlike state,
   Have we, as 'twere, with a defeated joy,   10
   With an auspicious° and a dropping eye,
   With mirth in funeral, and with dirge in marriage,
   In equal scale weighing delight and dole,
   Taken to wife. Nor have we herein barred
   Your better wisdoms, which have freely gone   15
   With this affair along. For all, our thanks.
   Now follows that you know young Fortinbras,
   Holding a weak supposal of our worth,
   Or thinking by our late dear brother's death
   Our state to be disjoint and out of frame,°   20
   Colleaguèd with this dream of his advantage,°
   He hath not failed to pester us with message,
   Importing the surrender of those lands
   Lost by his father, with all bands of law,
   To our most valiant brother. So much for him.   25
   Now for ourself and for this time of meeting.
   Thus much the business is: we have here writ
   To Norway, uncle of young Fortinbras—
   Who, impotent and bedrid, scarcely hears
   Of this his nephew's purpose—to suppress   30
   His further gait° herein, in that the levies,
   The lists, and full proportions° are all made
   Out of his subject;° and we here dispatch
   You, good Cornelius, and you, Voltemand,

SCENE II. s.d. *Flourish:* fanfare of trumpets. s.d. *cum aliis:* with others (Latin). 8. *our sometime sister:* my (the royal "we") former sister-in-law. 9. *jointress:* joint tenant, partner. 11. *auspicious:* joyful. 20. *frame:* order. 21. *advantage:* superiority. 31. *gait:* proceeding. 32. *proportions:* supplies for war. 33. *Out of his subject:* i.e., out of old Norway's subjects and realm.

For bearers of this greeting to old Norway,   35
Giving to you no further personal power
To business with the King, more than the scope
Of these delated articles° allow.
Farewell, and let your haste commend your duty.
CORNELIUS, VOLTEMAND. In that, and all things, will we show our duty.   40
KING. We doubt it nothing. Heartily farewell. *Exit* VOLTEMAND *and* CORNELIUS.
    And now, Laertes, what's the news with you?
    You told us of some suit. What is't, Laertes?
    You cannot speak of reason to the Dane
    And lose your voice.° What wouldst thou beg, Laertes,   45
    That shall not be my offer, not thy asking?
    The head is not more native° to the heart,
    The hand more instrumental to the mouth,
    Than is the throne of Denmark to thy father.
    What wouldst thou have, Laertes?
LAERTES.   My dread lord,   50
    Your leave and favor to return to France,
    From whence, though willingly I came to Denmark
    To show my duty in your coronation,
    Yet now I must confess, that duty done,
    My thoughts and wishes bend again toward France   55
    And bow them to your gracious leave and pardon.
KING. Have you your father's leave? What says Polonius?
POLONIUS. He hath, my lord, wrung from me my slow leave
    By laborsome petition, and at last
    Upon his will I sealed my hard consent.°   60
    I do beseech you give him leave to go.
KING. Take thy fair hour, Laertes. Time be thine,
    And thy best graces spend it at thy will.
    But now, my cousin° Hamlet, and my son——
HAMLET. [*Aside*] A little more than kin, and less than kind!°   65
KING. How is it that the clouds still hang on you?
HAMLET. No so, my lord. I am too much in the sun.°
QUEEN. Good Hamlet, cast thy nighted color off,
    And let thine eye look like a friend on Denmark.
    Do not forever with thy vailèd° lids   70
    Seek for thy noble father in the dust.

---

38. *delated articles:* detailed documents. 45. *lose your voice:* waste your breath. 47. *native:* related.
60. *Upon his . . . hard consent:* to his desire I gave my reluctant consent. 64. *cousin:* kinsman.
65. *kind:* (pun on the meanings "kindly" and "natural"; though doubly related—*more than kin*—Hamlet asserts that he neither resembles Claudius in nature nor feels kindly toward him).
67. *sun:* sunshine of royal favor (with a pun on "son"). 70. *vailèd:* lowered.

Thou know'st 'tis common; all that lives must die,
Passing through nature to eternity.
HAMLET.   Ay, madam, it is common.°
QUEEN.   If it be,
Why seem it so particular with thee?   75
HAMLET.   Seems, madam? Nay, it is. I know not "seems."
'Tis not alone my inky cloak, good mother,
Nor customary suits of solemn black,
Nor windy suspiration° of forced breath,
No, nor the fruitful river in the eye,   80
Nor the dejected havior of the visage,
Together with all forms, moods, shapes of grief,
That can denote me truly. These indeed seem,
For they are actions that a man might play,
But I have that within which passes show;   85
These but the trappings and the suits of woe.
KING.   'Tis sweet and commendable in your nature, Hamlet,
To give these mourning duties to your father,
But you must know your father lost a father,
That father lost, lost his, and the survivor bound   90
In filial obligation for some term
To do obsequious° sorrow. But to persever
In obstinate condolement° is a course
Of impious stubbornness. 'Tis unmanly grief.
It shows a will most incorrect to heaven,   95
A heart unfortified, a mind impatient,
An understanding simple and unschooled.
For what we know must be and is as common
As any the most vulgar° thing to sense,
Why should we in our peevish opposition   100
Take it to heart? Fie, 'tis a fault to heaven,
A fault against the dead, a fault to nature,
To reason most absurd, whose common theme
Is death of fathers, and who still hath cried,
From the first corse° till he that died today,   105
"This must be so." We pray you throw to earth
This unprevailing° woe, and think of us
As of a father, for let the world take note
You are the most immediate to our throne,

74. *common:* (1) universal, (2) vulgar.   79. *windy suspiration:* heavy sighing.   92. *obsequious:*
suitable to obsequies (funerals).   93. *condolement:* mourning.   99. *vulgar:* common.
105. *corse:* corpse.   107. *unprevailing:* unavailing.

And with no less nobility of love   110
Than that which dearest father bears his son
Do I impart toward you. For your intent
In going back to school in Wittenberg,
It is most retrograde° to our desire,
And we beseech you, bend you° to remain   115
Here in the cheer and comfort of our eye,
Our chiefest courtier, cousin, and our son.
QUEEN. Let not thy mother lose her prayers, Hamlet.
I pray thee stay with us, go not to Wittenberg.
HAMLET. I shall in all my best obey you, madam.   120
KING. Why, 'tis a loving and a fair reply.
Be as ourself in Denmark. Madam, come.
This gentle and unforced accord of Hamlet
Sits smiling to my heart, in grace whereof
No jocund health that Denmark drinks today,   125
But the great cannon to the clouds shall tell,
And the King's rouse° the heaven shall bruit° again,
Respeaking earthly thunder. Come away.   *Flourish. Exeunt all but* HAMLET.
HAMLET. O that this too too sullied° flesh would melt,
Thaw, and resolve itself into a dew,   130
Or that the Everlasting had not fixed
His canon° 'gainst self-slaughter. O God, God,
How weary, stale, flat, and unprofitable
Seem to me all the uses of this world!
Fie on't, ah, fie, 'tis an unweeded garden   135
That grows to seed. Things rank and gross in nature
Possess it merely.° That it should come to this:
But two months dead, nay, not so much, not two,
So excellent a king, that was to this
Hyperion° to a satyr, so loving to my mother   140
That he might not beteem° the winds of heaven
Visit her face too roughly. Heaven and earth,
Must I remember? Why, she would hang on him
As if increase of appetite had grown
by what it fed on; and yet within a month—   145
Let me not think on't; frailty, thy name is woman—

---

114. *retrograde:* contrary. 115. *bend you:* incline. 127. *rouse:* deep drink. 127. *bruit:* announce
noisily. 129. *sullied:* (Q2 has *sallied,* here modernized to *sullied,* which makes sense and is
therefore given; but the Folio reading, *solid,* which fits better with *melt,* is quite possibly correct).
132. *canon:* law. 137. *merely:* entirely. 140. *Hyperion:* the sun god, a model of beauty.
141. *beteem:* allow.

A little month, or ere those shoes were old
With which she followed my poor father's body
Like Niobe,° all tears, why she, even she—
O God, a beast that wants discourse of reason°   150
Would have mourned longer—married with my uncle,
My father's brother, but no more like my father
Than I to Hercules. Within a month,
Ere yet the salt of most unrighteous tears
Had left the flushing° in her gallèd eyes,   155
She married. O, most wicked speed, to post°
With such dexterity to incestuous° sheets!
It is not, nor it cannot come to good.
But break my heart, for I must hold my tongue.

        Enter HORATIO, MARCELLUS, *and* BARNARDO.

HORATIO. Hail to your lordship!
HAMLET.   I am glad to see you well.   160
  Horatio—or I do forget myself.
HORATIO. The same, my lord, and your poor servant ever.
HAMLET. Sir, my good friend, I'll change° that name with you.
  And what make you from Wittenberg, Horatio?
  Marcellus.   165
MARCELLUS. My good lord!
HAMLET. I am very glad to see you. [*To* BARNARDO] Good even, sir.
  But what, in faith, make you from Wittenberg?
HORATIO. A truant disposition, good my lord.
HAMLET. I would not hear your enemy say so,   170
  Nor shall you do my ear that violence
  To make it truster° of your own report
  Against yourself. I know you are no truant.
  But what is your affair in Elsinore?
  We'll teach you to drink deep ere you depart.   175
HORATIO. My lord, I came to see your father's funeral.
HAMLET. I prithee do not mock me, fellow student.
  I think it was to see my mother's wedding.
HORATIO. Indeed, my lord, it followed hard upon.
HAMLET. Thrift, thrift, Horatio. The funeral baked meats   180
  Did coldly furnish forth the marriage tables.
  Would I had met my dearest° foe in heaven

---

149. *Niobe:* (a mother who wept profusely at the death of her children). 150. *wants discourse of reason:* lacks reasoning power. 155. *left the flushing:* stopped reddening. 156. *post:* hasten.
157. *incestuous:* (canon law considered marriage with a deceased brother's widow to be incestuous).
163. *change:* exchange. 172. *truster:* believer. 182. *dearest:* most intensely felt.

Or ever I had seen that day, Horatio!
My father, methinks I see my father.
HORATIO. Where, my lord?
HAMLET.   In my mind's eye, Horatio.   185
HORATIO. I saw him once. 'A° was a goodly king.
HAMLET. 'A was a man, take him for all in all,
I shall not look upon his like again.
HORATIO. My lord, I think I saw him yesternight.
HAMLET. Saw? Who?   190
HORATIO. My lord, the King your father.
HAMLET.   The King my father?
HORATIO. Season your admiration° for a while
With an attent ear till I may deliver
Upon the witness of these gentlemen
This marvel to you.
HAMLET.   For God's love let me hear!   195
HORATIO. Two nights together had these gentlemen,
Marcellus and Barnardo, on their watch
In the dead waste and middle of the night
Been thus encountered. A figure like your father,
Armèd at point exactly, cap-a-pe,°   200
Appears before them, and with solemn march
Goes slow and stately by them. Thrice he walked
By their oppressed and fear-surprisèd eyes,
Within his truncheon's length,° whilst they, distilled°
Almost to jelly with the act° of fear,   205
Stand dumb and speak not to him. This to me
In dreadful° secrecy impart they did,
And I with them the third night kept the watch,
Where, as they had delivered, both in time,
Form of the thing, each word made true and good,   210
The apparition comes. I knew your father.
These hands are not more like.
HAMLET.   But where was this?
MARCELLUS. My lord, upon the platform where we watched.
HAMLET. Did you not speak to it?
HORATIO.   My lord, I did;
But answer made it none. Yet once methought   215
It lifted up it° head and did address
Itself to motion like as it would speak:

---

186. *'A:* he. 192. *Season your admiration:* control your wonder. 200. *cap-a-pe:* head to foot.
204. *truncheon's length:* space of a short staff. 204. *distilled:* reduced. 205. *act:* action.
207. *dreadful:* terrified. 216. *it:* its.

But even then the morning cock crew loud,
And at the sound it shrunk in haste away
And vanished from our sight.

HAMLET.   'Tis very strange.   220

HORATIO. As I do live, my honored lord, 'tis true,
And we did think it writ down in our duty
To let you know of it.

HAMLET. Indeed, indeed, sirs, but this troubles me.
Hold you the watch tonight?

ALL.   We do, my lord.   225

HAMLET. Armed, say you?

ALL. Armed, my lord.

HAMLET. From top to toe?

ALL.   My lord, from head to foot.

HAMLET. Then saw you not his face.

HORATIO. O, yes, my lord. He wore his beaver° up.   230

HAMLET. What, looked he frowningly?

HORATIO. A countenance more in sorrow than in anger.

HAMLET. Pale or red?

HORATIO. Nay, very pale.

HAMLET.   And fixed his eyes upon you?

HORATIO. Most constantly.

HAMLET.   I would I had been there.   235

HORATIO. It would have much amazed you.

HAMLET. Very like, very like. Stayed it long?

HORATIO. While one with moderate haste might tell° a hundred.

BOTH. Longer, longer.

HORATIO. Not when I saw't.

HAMLET.   His beard was grizzled,° no?   240

HORATIO. It was as I have seen it in his life,
A sable silvered.°

HAMLET.   I will watch tonight.
Perchance 'twill walk again.

HORATIO.   I warr'nt it will.

HAMLET. If it assume my noble father's person,
I'll speak to it though hell itself should gape   245
And bid me hold my peace. I pray you all,
If you have hitherto concealed this sight,
Let it be tenable° in your silence still,
And whatsoever else shall hap tonight,
Give it an understanding but no tongue;   250

---

230. *beaver:* visor, face guard. 238. *tell:* count. 240. *grizzled:* gray. 242. *sable silvered:* black
mingled with white. 248. *tenable:* held.

I will requite your loves. So fare you well.
Upon the platform 'twixt eleven and twelve
I'll visit you.

ALL.   Our duty to your honor.

HAMLET. Your loves, as mine to you. Farewell. *Exeunt [all but* HAMLET*]*.
 My father's spirit—in arms? All is not well.   255
 I doubt° some foul play. Would the night were come!
 Till then sit still, my soul. Foul deeds will rise,
 Though all the earth o'erwhelm them, to men's eyes. *Exit.*

SCENE III. *A room.*

Enter LAERTES *and* OPHELIA, *his sister.*

LAERTES. My necessaries are embarked. Farewell.
 And, sister, as the winds give benefit
 And convoy° is assistant, do not sleep,
 But let me hear from you.

OPHELIA.   Do you doubt that?

LAERTES. For Hamlet, and the trifling of his favor,   5
 Hold it a fashion and a toy° in blood,
 A violet in the youth of primy° nature,
 Forward,° not permanent, sweet, not lasting,
 The perfume and suppliance° of a minute,
 No more.

OPHELIA. No more but so?

LAERTES.   Think it no more.   10
 For nature crescent° does not grow alone
 In thews° and bulk, but as this temple° waxes,
 The inward service of the mind and soul
 Grows wide withal. Perhaps he loves you now,
 And now no soil nor cautel° doth besmirch   15
 The virtue of his will; but you must fear,
 His greatness weighed,° his will is not his own.
 For he himself is subject to his birth.
 He may not, as unvalued° persons do,
 Carve for himself; for on his choice depends   20
 The safety and health of this whole state;
 And therefore must his choice be circumscribed
 Unto the voice and yielding of that body
 Whereof he is the head. Then if he says he loves you,

---

256. *doubt:* suspect. SCENE III. 3. *convoy:* conveyance. 6. *toy:* idle fancy. 7. *primy:* springlike.
8. *Forward:* premature. 9. *suppliance:* diversion. 11. *crescent:* growing. 12. *thews:* muscles and
sinews. 12. *temple:* i.e., the body. 15. *cautel:* deceit. 17. *greatness weighed:* high rank considered.
19. *unvalued:* of low rank.

It fits your wisdom so far to believe it   25
As he in his particular act and place
May give his saying deed, which is no further
Than the main voice of Denmark goes withal.
Then weigh what loss your honor may sustain
If with too credent° ear you list his songs,   30
Or lose your heart, or your chaste treasure open
To his unmastered importunity.
Fear it, Ophelia, fear it, my dear sister,
And keep you in the rear of your affection,
Out of the shot and danger of desire.   35
The chariest maid is prodigal enough
If she unmask her beauty to the moon.
Virtue itself scapes not calumnious strokes.
The canker° galls the infants of the spring
Too oft before their buttons° be disclosed,   40
And in the morn and liquid dew of youth
Contagious blastments are most imminent.
Be wary then; best safety lies in fear;
Youth to itself rebels, though none else near.
OPHELIA. I shall the effect of this good lesson keep   45
As watchman to my heart, but, good my brother,
Do not, as some ungracious° pastors do,
Show me the steep and thorny way to heaven,
Whiles, like a puffed and reckless libertine,
Himself the primrose path of dalliance treads   50
And recks not his own rede.°

Enter POLONIUS.

LAERTES.   O, fear me not.
I stay too long. But here my father comes.
A double blessing is a double grace;
Occasion smiles upon a second leave.
POLONIUS. Yet here, Laertes? Aboard, aboard, for shame!   55
The wind sits in the shoulder of your sail,
And you are stayed for. There—my blessing with thee,
And these few precepts in thy memory
Look thou character.° Give thy thoughts no tongue,
Nor any unproportioned° thought his act.   60

---

30. *credent:* credulous. 39 *canker:* cankerworm. 40. *buttons:* buds. 47. *ungracious:* lacking grace.
51. *recks not his own rede:* does not heed his own advice. 59. *character:* inscribe.
60. *unproportioned:* unbalanced.

Be thou familiar, but by no means vulgar.
Those friends thou hast, and their adoption tried,
Grapple them unto thy soul with hoops of steel,
But do not dull thy palm with entertainment
Of each new-hatched, unfledged courage.° Beware   65
Of entrance to a quarrel; but being in,
Bear't that th' opposèd may beware of thee.
Give every man thine ear, but few thy voice;
Take each man's censure,° but reserve thy judgment.
Costly thy habit as thy purse can buy,   70
But not expressed in fancy; rich, not gaudy,
For the apparel oft proclaims the man,
And they in France of the best rank and station
Are of a most select and generous, chief in that.°
Neither a borrower nor a lender be,   75
For loan oft loses both itself and friend,
And borrowing dulleth edge of husbandry.°
This above all, to thine own self be true,
And it must follow, as the night the day,
Thou canst not then be false to any man.   80
Farewell. My blessing season this° in thee!
LAERTES. Most humbly do I take my leave, my lord.
POLONIUS. The time invites you. Go, your servants tend.°
LAERTES. Farewell, Ophelia, and remember well
 What I have said to you.
OPHELIA.   'Tis in my memory locked,   85
 And you yourself shall keep the key of it.
LAERTES. Farewell. *Exit* LAERTES.
POLONIUS. What is't, Ophelia, he hath said to you?
OPHELIA. So please you, something touching the Lord Hamlet.
POLONIUS. Marry,° well bethought.   90
 'Tis told me he hath very oft of late
 Given private time to you, and you yourself
 Have of your audience been most free and bounteous.
 If it be so—as so 'tis put on me,
 And that in way of caution—I must tell you   95
 You do not understand yourself so clearly
 As it behooves my daughter and your honor.
 What is between you? Give me up the truth.

---

65. *courage:* gallant youth. 69. *censure:* opinion. 74. *Are of . . . in that:* show their fine taste
and their gentlemanly instincts more in that than in any other point of manners (Kittredge).
77. *husbandry:* thrift. 81. *season this:* make fruitful this (advice). 83. *tend:* attend.
90. *Marry:* (a light oath, from "By the Virgin Mary").

OPHELIA. He hath, my lord, of late made many tenders°
    Of his affection to me.   100

POLONIUS. Affection pooh! You speak like a green girl,
    Unsifted° in such perilous circumstance.
    Do you believe his tenders, as you call them?

OPHELIA. I do not know, my lord, what I should think.

POLONIUS. Marry, I will teach you. Think yourself a baby.   105
    That you have ta'en these tenders for true pay
    Which are not sterling. Tender yourself more dearly,
    Or (not to crack the wind of the poor phrase)
    Tend'ring it thus you'll tender me a fool.°

OPHELIA. My lord, he hath importuned me with love   110
    In honorable fashion.

POLONIUS. Ay, fashion you may call it. Go to, go to.

OPHELIA. And hath given countenance to his speech, my lord,
    With almost all the holy vows of heaven.

POLONIUS. Ay, springes to catch woodcocks.° I do know,   115
    When the blood burns, how prodigal the soul
    Lends the tongue vows. These blazes, daughter,
    Giving more light than heat, extinct in both,
    Even in their promise, as it is a-making,
    You must not take for fire. From this time   120
    Be something scanter of your maiden presence.
    Set your entreatments° at a higher rate
    Than a command to parley. For Lord Hamlet,
    Believe so much in him that he is young,
    And with a larger tether may he walk   125
    Than may be given you. In few, Ophelia,
    Do not believe his vows, for they are brokers,°
    Not of that dye° which their investments° show,
    But mere implorators° of unholy suits,
    Breathing like sanctified and pious bonds,°   130
    The better to beguile. This is for all:
    I would not, in plain terms, from this time forth
    Have you so slander° any moment leisure
    As to give words or talk with the Lord Hamlet.
    Look to't, I charge you. Come you ways.   135

OPHELIA. I shall obey, my lord. *Exeunt.*

---

99. *tenders:* offers (in line 103 it has the same meaning, but in line 106 Polonius speaks of *tenders* in the sense of counters or chips; in line 109 *Tend'ring* means "holding," and *tender* means "give," "present"). 102. *Unsifted:* untried. 109. *tender me a fool:* (1) present me with a fool, (2) present me with a baby. 115. *springes to catch woodcocks:* snares to catch stupid birds. 122. *entreatments:* interviews. 127. *brokers:* procurers. 128. *dye:* i.e., kind. 128. *investments:* garments. 129. *implorators:* solicitors. 130. *bonds:* pledges. 133. *slander:* disgrace.

SCENE IV. *A guard platform.*

Enter HAMLET, HORATIO, *and* MARCELLUS.

HAMLET. The air bites shrewdly;° it is very cold.
HORATIO. It is a nipping and an eager° air.
HAMLET. What hour now?
HORATIO.   I think it lacks of twelve.
MARCELLUS. No, it is struck.
HORATIO. Indeed? I heard it not. It then draws near the season   5
  Wherein the spirit held his wont to walk.

A flourish of trumpets, and two pieces go off.

  What does this mean, my lord?
HAMLET. The King doth wake° tonight and takes his rouse,°
  Keeps wassail, and the swagg'ring upspring° reels,
  And as he drains his draughts of Rhenish° down   10
  The kettledrum and trumpet thus bray out
  The triumph of his pledge.°
HORATIO.   Is it a custom?
HAMLET. Ay, marry, is't,
  But to my mind, though I am native here
  And to the manner born, it is a custom   15
  More honored in the breach than the observance.
  This heavy-headed revel east and west
  Makes us traduced and taxed of° other nations.
  They clepe° us drunkards and with swinish phrase
  Soil our addition,° and indeed it takes   20
  From our achievements, though performed at height,
  The pith and marrow of our attribute.°
  So oft it chances in particular men
  That for some vicious mole° of nature in them,
  As in their birth, wherein they are not guilty,   25
  (Since nature cannot choose his origin)
  By the o'ergrowth of some complexion,°
  Oft breaking down the pales° and forts of reason,
  Or by some habit that too much o'erleavens°
  The form of plausive° manners, that (these men,   30

SCENE IV. 1. *shrewdly:* bitterly. 2. *eager:* sharp. 8. *wake:* hold a revel by night. 8. *takes his rouse:* carouses. 9. *upspring:* (a dance). 10. *Rhenish:* Rhine wine. 12. *The triumph of his pledge:* the achievement (of drinking a wine cup in one draught) of his toast. 18. *taxed of:* blamed by. 19. *clepe:* call. 20. *addition:* reputation (literally, "title of honor"). 22. *attribute:* reputation. 24. *mole:* blemish. 27. *complexion:* natural disposition. 28. *pales:* enclosures. 29. *o'erleavens:* mixes with, corrupts. 30. *plausive:* pleasing.

Carrying, I say, the stamp of one defect,
Being nature's livery, or fortune's star°)
Their virtues else, be they as pure as grace,
As infinite as man may undergo,
Shall in the general censure° take corruption   35
From that particular fault. The dram of evil
Doth all the noble substance of a doubt,
To his own scandal.°

Enter GHOST.

HORATIO.   Look, my lord, it comes.
HAMLET. Angels and ministers of grace defend us!
Be thou a spirit of health° or goblin damned,   40
Bring with thee airs from heaven or blasts from hell,
Be thy intents wicked or charitable,
Thou com'st in such a questionable° shape
That I will speak to thee. I'll call thee Hamlet,
King, father, royal Dane. O, answer me!   45
Let me not burst in ignorance, but tell
Why thy canonized° bones, hearsèd in death,
Have burst their cerements,° why the sepulcher
Wherein we saw thee quietly interred
Hath oped his ponderous and marble jaws   50
To cast thee up again. What may this mean
That thou, dead corse, again in complete steel,
Revisits thus the glimpses of the moon,
Making night hideous, and we fools of nature
So horridly to shake our disposition°   55
With thoughts beyond the reaches of our souls?
Say, why is this? Wherefore? What should we do?

GHOST *beckons* HAMLET.

HORATIO. It beckons you to go away with it,
As if it some impartment° did desire
To you alone.

---

32. *nature's livery, or fortune's star:* nature's equipment (i.e., "innate"), or a person's destiny determined by the stars. 35. *general censure:* popular judgment. 36–38. *The dram . . . own scandal:* (though the drift is clear, there is no agreement as to the exact meaning of these lines). 40. *spirit of health:* good spirit. 43. *questionable:* (1) capable of discourse, (2) dubious. 47. *canonized:* buried according to the canon or ordinance of the church. 48. *cerements:* waxed linen shroud. 55. *shake our disposition:* disturb us. 59. *impartment:* communication.

MARCELLUS.   Look with what courteous action   60
   It waves you to a more removèd ground.
   But do not go with it.
HORATIO.   No, by no means.
HAMLET.   It will not speak. Then I will follow it.
HORATIO.   Do not, my lord.
HAMLET.   Why, what should be the fear?
   I do not set my life at a pin's fee,   65
   And for my soul, what can it do to that,
   Being a thing immortal as itself?
   It waves me forth again. I'll follow it.
HORATIO.   What if it tempt you toward the flood, my lord,
   Or to the dreadful summit of the cliff   70
   That beetles° o'er his base into the sea,
   And there assume some other horrible form
   Which might deprive your sovereignty of reason°
   And draw you into madness? Think of it.
   The very place puts toys° of desperation,   75
   Without more motive, into every brain
   That looks so many fathoms to the sea
   And hears it roar beneath.
HAMLET.   It waves me still.
   Go on; I'll follow thee.
MARCELLUS.   You shall not go, my lord.
HAMLET.   Hold off your hands.   80
HORATIO.   Be ruled. You shall not go.
HAMLET.   My fate cries out
   And makes each petty artere° in this body
   As hardy as the Nemean lion's nerve.°
   Still am I called! Unhand me, gentlemen.
   By heaven, I'll make a ghost of him that lets° me!   85
   I say, away! Go on. I'll follow thee.   *Exit* GHOST *and* HAMLET.
HORATIO.   He waxes desperate with imagination.
MARCELLUS.   Let's follow. 'Tis not fit thus to obey him.
HORATIO.   Have after! To what issue will this come?
MARCELLUS.   Something is rotten in the state of Denmark.   90
HORATIO.   Heaven will direct it.
MARCELLUS.   Nay, let's follow him.   *Exeunt*.

---

71. *beetles:* juts out.   73. *deprive your sovereignty of reason:* destroy the sovereignty of your reason.
75. *toys:* whims, fancies.   82. *artere:* artery.   83. *Nemean lion's nerve:* sinews of the mythical lion
slain by Hercules.   85. *lets:* hinders.

SCENE V. *The battlements.*

Enter GHOST *and* HAMLET.

HAMLET. Whither wilt thou lead me? Speak; I'll go no further.
GHOST. Mark me.
HAMLET.   I will.
GHOST.   My hour is almost come,
    When I to sulf'rous and tormenting flames
    Must render up myself.
HAMLET.   Alas, poor ghost.
GHOST. Pity me not, but lend thy serious hearing   5
    To what I shall unfold.
HAMLET.   Speak. I am bound to hear.
GHOST. So art thou to revenge, when thou shalt hear.
HAMLET. What?
GHOST. I am thy father's spirit,
    Doomed for a certain term to walk the night,   10
    And for the day confined to fast in fires,
    Till the foul crimes° done in my days of nature
    Are burnt and purged away. But that I am forbid
    To tell the secrets of my prison house,
    I could a tale unfold whose lightest word   15
    Would harrow up thy soul, freeze thy young blood,
    Make thy two eyes like stars start from their spheres,°
    Thy knotted and combinèd locks to part,
    And each particular hair to stand an end
    Like quills upon the fearful porpentine.°   20
    But this eternal blazon° must not be
    To ears of flesh and blood. List, list, O, list!
    If thou didst ever thy dear father love——
HAMLET. O God!
GHOST. Revenge his foul and most unnatural murder.   25
HAMLET. Murder?
GHOST. Murder most foul, as in the best it is,
    But this most foul, strange, and unnatural.
HAMLET. Haste me to know't, that I, with wings as swift
    As meditation° or the thoughts of love,   30
    May sweep to my revenge.

SCENE V. 12. *crimes:* sins. 17. *spheres:* (in Ptolemaic astronomy, each planet was fixed in a hollow transparent shell concentric with the earth). 20. *fearful porpentine:* timid porcupine. 21. *eternal blazon:* revelation of eternity. 30. *meditation:* thought.

GHOST.   I find thee apt,
   And duller shouldst thou be than the fat weed
   That roots itself in ease on Lethe wharf,°
   Wouldst thou not stir in this. Now, Hamlet, hear.
   'Tis given out that, sleeping in my orchard,   35
   A serpent stung me. So the whole ear of Denmark
   Is by a forgèd process° of my death
   Rankly abused. But know, thou noble youth,
   The serpent that did sting thy father's life
   Now wears his crown.
HAMLET.   O my prophetic soul!   40
   My uncle?
GHOST. Ay, that incestuous, that adulterate° beast,
   With witchcraft of his wits, with traitorous gifts—
   O wicked wit and gifts, that have the power
   So to seduce!—won to his shameful lust   45
   The will of my most seeming-virtuous queen.
   O Hamlet, what a falling-off was there,
   From me, whose love was of that dignity
   That it went hand in hand even with the vow
   I made to her in marriage, and to decline   50
   Upon a wretch whose natural gifts were poor
   To those of mine.
   But virtue, as it never will be moved,
   Though lewdness° court it in a shape of heaven,
   So lust, though to a radiant angel linked,   55
   Will sate itself in a celestial bed
   And prey on garbage.
   But soft, methinks I scent the morning air;
   Brief let me be. Sleeping within my orchard,
   My custom always of the afternoon,   60
   Upon my secure° hour thy uncle stole
   With juice of cursed hebona° in a vial,
   And in the porches of my ears did pour
   The leperous distillment, whose effect
   Holds such an enmity with blood of man   65
   That swift as quicksilver it courses through
   The natural gates and alleys of the body,
   And with a sudden vigor it doth posset°

---

33. *Lethe wharf:* bank of the river of forgetfulness in Hades. 37. *forgèd process:* false account.
42. *adulterate:* adulterous. 54. *lewdness:* lust. 61. *secure:* unsuspecting. 62. *hebona:* a poisonous
plant. 68. *posset:* curdle.

And curd, like eager° droppings into milk,
The thin and wholesome blood. So did it mine,   70
And a most instant tetter° barked about
Most lazarlike° with vile and loathsome crust
All my smooth body.
Thus was I, sleeping, by a brother's hand
Of life, of crown, of queen at once dispatched,   75
Cut off even in the blossoms of my sin,
Unhouseled, disappointed, unaneled,°
No reck'ning made, but sent to my account
With all my imperfections on my head.
O, horrible! O, horrible! Most horrible!   80
If thou hast nature in thee, bear it not.
Let not the royal bed of Denmark be
A couch for luxury° and damnèd incest.
But howsomever thou pursues this act,
Taint not thy mind, nor let thy soul contrive   85
Against thy mother aught. Leave her to heaven
And to those thorns that in her bosom lodge
To prick and sting her. Fare thee well at once.
The glowworm shows the matin° to be near
And 'gins to pale his uneffectual fire.   90
Adieu, adieu, adieu. Remember me. *Exit.*
HAMLET.   O all you host of heaven! O earth! What else?
And shall I couple hell? O fie! Hold, hold, my heart,
And you, my sinews, grow now instant old,
But bear me stiffly up. Remember thee?   95
Ay, thou poor ghost, whiles memory holds a seat
In this distracted globe.° Remember thee?
Yea, from the table° of my memory
I'll wipe away all trivial fond° records,
All saws° of books, all forms, all pressures° past   100
That youth and observation copied there,
And thy commandment all alone shall live
Within the book and volume of my brain,
Unmixed with baser matter. Yes, by heaven!
O most pernicious woman!   105
O villain, villain, smiling, damnèd villain!
My tables—meet it is I set it down

---

69. *eager:* acid. 71. *tetter:* scab. 72. *lazarlike:* leperlike. 77. *Unhouseled, disappointed, unaneled:*
without the sacrament of communion, unabsolved, without extreme unction. 83. *luxury:* lust.
89. *matin:* morning. 97. *globe:* i.e., his head. 98. *table:* tablet, notebook. 99. *fond:* foolish.
100. *saws:* maxims. 100. *pressures:* impressions.

That one may smile, and smile, and be a villain.
At least I am sure it may be so in Denmark. [*Writes.*]
So, uncle, there you are. Now to my word: 110
It is "Adieu, adieu, remember me."
I have sworn't.
HORATIO AND MARCELLUS. [*Within*] My lord, my lord!

Enter HORATIO *and* MARCELLUS.

MARCELLUS.   Lord Hamlet!
HORATIO.   Heavens secure him!
HAMLET. So be it!
MARCELLUS. Illo, ho, ho,° my lord!   115
HAMLET. Hillo, ho, ho, boy! Come, bird, come.
MARCELLUS. How is't, my noble lord?
HORATIO.   What news, my lord?
HAMLET. O, wonderful!
HORATIO. Good my lord, tell it.
HAMLET.   No, you will reveal it.
HORATIO. Not I, my lord, by heaven.
MARCELLUS.   Nor I, my lord.   120
HAMLET. How say you then? Would heart of man once think it?
  But you'll be secret?
BOTH.   Ay, by heaven, my lord.
HAMLET. There's never a villain dwelling in all Denmark
  But he's an arrant knave.
HORATIO. There needs no ghost, my lord, come from the grave   125
  To tell us this.
HAMLET.   Why, right, you are in the right;
  And so, without more circumstance° at all,
  I hold it fit that we shake hands and part:
  You, as your business and desire shall point you,
  For every man hath business and desire   130
  Such as it is, and for my own poor part,
  Look you, I'll go pray.
HORATIO. These are but wild and whirling words, my lord.
HAMLET. I am sorry they offend you, heartily;
  Yes, faith, heartily.
HORATIO.   There's no offense, my lord.   135
HAMLET. Yes, by Saint Patrick, but there is, Horatio,
  And much offense too. Touching this vision here,
  It is an honest ghost,° that let me tell you.

---

115. *Illo, ho, ho:* (falconer's call to his hawk). 127. *circumstance:* details. 138. *honest ghost:* i.e., not
a demon in his father's shape.

For your desire to know what is between us,
O'ermaster't as you may. And now, good friends,   140
As you are friends, scholars, and soldiers,
Give me one poor request.
HORATIO. What is't, my lord? We will.
HAMLET. Never make known what you have seen tonight.
BOTH. My lord, we will not.
HAMLET.   Nay, but swear't.
HORATIO.   In faith,   145
My lord, not I.
MARCELLUS.   Nor I, my lord—in faith.
HAMLET. Upon my sword.
MARCELLUS.   We have sworn, my lord, already.
HAMLET. Indeed, upon my sword, indeed.

                    GHOST *cries under the stage.*

GHOST. Swear.
HAMLET. Ha, ha, boy, say'st thou so? Art thou there, truepenny?°   150
Come on. You hear this fellow in the cellarage.
Consent to swear.
HORATIO.   Propose the oath, my lord.
HAMLET. Never to speak of this that you have seen.
Swear by my sword.
GHOST. [*Beneath*] Swear.   155
HAMLET. *Hic et ubique?*° Then we'll shift our ground;
Come hither, gentlemen,
And lay your hands again upon my sword.
Swear by my sword
Never to speak of this that you have heard.   160
GHOST. [*Beneath*] Swear by his sword.
HAMLET. Well said, old mole! Canst work i' th' earth so fast?
A worthy pioner!° Once more remove, good friends.
HORATIO. O day and night, but this is wondrous strange!
HAMLET. And therefore as a stranger give it welcome.   165
There are more things in heaven and earth, Horatio,
Than are dreamt of in your philosophy.
But come:
Here as before, never, so help you mercy,
How strange or odd some'er I bear myself   170
(As I perchance hereafter shall think meet
To put an antic disposition° on),

---

150. *truepenny:* honest fellow. 156. *Hic et ubique:* here and everywhere (Latin). 163. *pioner:*
digger of mines. 172. *antic disposition:* fantastic behavior.

That you, at such times seeing me, never shall
With arms encumb'red° thus, or this headshake,
Or by pronouncing of some doubtful phrase,   175
As "Well, well, we know," or "We could, an if we would,"
Or "If we list to speak," or "There be, an if they might,"
Or such ambiguous giving out, to note
That you know aught of me—this do swear,
So grace and mercy at your most need help you.   180
GHOST. [*Beneath*] Swear. [*They swear.*]
HAMLET. Rest, rest, perturbèd spirit. So, gentlemen,
With all my love I do commend me° to you,
And what so poor a man as Hamlet is
May do t' express his love and friending to you,   185
God willing, shall not lack. Let us go in together,
And still your fingers on your lips, I pray.
The time is out of joint. O cursèd spite,
That ever I was born to set it right!
Nay, come, let's go together. *Exeunt.*   190

ACT II

SCENE I. *A room.*

Enter old POLONIUS, *with his man* REYNALDO.

POLONIUS. Give him this money and these notes, Reynaldo.
REYNALDO. I will, my lord.
POLONIUS. You shall do marvell's° wisely, good Reynaldo,
Before you visit him, to make inquire
Of his behavior.
REYNALDO.   My lord, I did intend it.   5
POLONIUS. Marry, well said, very well said. Look you sir,
Inquire me first what Danskers° are in Paris,
And how, and who, what means, and where they keep,°
What company, at what expense; and finding
By this encompassment° and drift of question   10
That they do know my son, come you more nearer
Than your particular demands° will touch it.
Take you as 'twere some distant knowledge of him,
As thus, "I know his father and his friends,
And in part him." Do you mark this, Reynaldo?   15
REYNALDO. Ay, very well, my lord.

174. *encumb'red:* folded. 183. *commend me:* entrust myself. SCENE I. 3. *marvell's:*
marvelous(ly). 7. *Danskers:* Danes. 8. *keep:* dwell. 10. *encompassment:* circling.
12. *demands:* questions.

POLONIUS. "And in part him, but," you may say, "not well,
  But if't be he I mean, he's very wild,
  Addicted so and so," And there put on him
  What forgeries° you please; marry, none so rank   20
  As may dishonor him—take heed of that—
  But, sir, such wanton, wild, and usual slips
  As are companions noted and most known
  To youth and liberty.
REYNALDO.   As gaming, my lord.
POLONIUS. Ay, or drinking, fencing, swearing, quarrelling,   25
  Drabbing.° You may go so far.
REYNALDO. My lord, that would dishonor him.
POLONIUS. Faith, no, as you may season it in the charge.
  You must not put another scandal on him,
  That he is open to incontinency.°   30
  That's not my meaning. But breathe his faults so quaintly°
  That they may seem the taints of liberty,
  The flash and outbreak of a fiery mind,
  A savageness in unreclaimèd blood,
  Of general assault.°
REYNALDO.   But, my good lord——   35
POLONIUS. Wherefore should you do this?
REYNALDO.   Ay, my lord,
  I would know that.
POLONIUS.   Marry, sir, here's my drift,
  And I believe it is a fetch of warrant.°
  You laying these slight sullies on my son
  As 'twere a thing a little soiled i' th' working,   40
  Mark you,
  Your party in converse, him you would sound,
  Having ever seen in the prenominate crimes°
  The youth you breathe of guilty, be assured
  He closes with you in this consequence:°   45
  "Good sir," or so, or "friend," or "gentleman"—
  According to the phrase or the addition°
  Of man and country—
REYNALDO.   Very good, my lord.
POLONIUS. And then, sir, does 'a° this—'a does—
  What was I about to say? By the mass, I was about   50
  to say something! Where did I leave?

---

20. *forgeries:* inventions. 26. *Drabbing:* wenching. 30. *incontinency:* habitual licentiousness.
31. *quaintly:* ingeniously, delicately. 35. *Of general assault:* common to all men. 38. *fetch of warrant:* justifiable device. 43. *Having . . . crimes:* if he has ever seen in the aforementioned crimes.
45. *He closes . . . this consequence:* he falls in with you in this conclusion. 47. *addition:* title.
49. *'a:* he.

REYNALDO. At "closes in the consequence," at "friend
  or so," and "gentleman."
POLONIUS. At "closes in the consequence"—Ay, marry!
  He closes thus: "I know the gentleman;   55
  I saw him yesterday, or t'other day,
  Or then, or then, with such or such, and, as you say,
  There was 'a gaming, there o'ertook in's rouse,
  There falling out at tennis"; or perchance,
  "I saw him enter such a house of sale,"   60
  Videlicet,° a brothel, or so forth.
  See you now—
  Your bait of falsehood take this carp of truth,
  And thus do we of wisdom and of reach,°
  With windlasses° and with assays of bias,°   65
  By indirections find directions out.
  So, by my former lecture and advice,
  Shall you my son. You have me, have you not?
REYNALDO. My lord, I have.
POLONIUS.   God bye ye, fare ye well.
REYNALDO. Good my lord.   70
POLONIUS. Observe his inclination in yourself.°
REYNALDO. I shall, my lord.
POLONIUS. And let him ply his music.
REYNALDO.   Well, my lord.
POLONIUS. Farewell. *Exit* REYNALDO.

                Enter OPHELIA.

          How now, Ophelia, what's the matter?
OPHELIA. O my lord, my lord, I have been so affrighted!   75
POLONIUS. With what, i' th' name of God?
OPHELIA. My lord, as I was sewing in my closet,°
  Lord Hamlet, with his doublet all unbraced,°
  No hat upon his head, his stockings fouled,
  Ungartered, and down-gyvèd° to his ankle,   80
  Pale as his shirt, his knees knocking each other,
  And with a look so piteous in purport,°
  As if he had been loosèd out of hell
  To speak of horrors—he comes before me.

---

61. *Videlicet:* namely. 64. *reach:* far-reaching awareness(?). 65. *windlasses:* circuitous
courses. 65. *assays of bias:* indirect attempts (metaphor from bowling; *bias* = curved course).
71. *in yourself:* for yourself. 77. *closet:* private room. 78. *doublet all unbraced:* jacket entirely
unlaced. 80. *down-gyvèd:* hanging down like fetters. 82. *purport:* expression.

POLONIUS. Mad for thy love?
OPHELIA.   My lord, I do not know,   85
    But truly I do fear it.
POLONIUS.   What said he?
OPHELIA. He took me by the wrist and held me hard;
    Then goes he to the length of all his arm,
    And with his other hand thus o'er his brow
    He falls to such perusal of my face   90
    As 'a would draw it. Long stayed he so.
    At last, a little shaking of mine arm,
    And thrice his head thus waving up and down,
    He raised a sigh so piteous and profound
    As it did seem to shatter all his bulk   95
    And end his being. That done, he lets me go,
    And, with his head over his shoulder turned,
    He seemed to find his way without his eyes,
    For out o' doors he went without their helps,
    And to the last bended their light on me.   100
POLONIUS. Come, go with me. I will go seek the King.
    This is the very ecstasy° of love,
    Whose violent property fordoes° itself
    And leads the will to desperate undertakings
    As oft as any passions under heaven   105
    That does afflict our natures. I am sorry.
    What, have you given him any hard words of late?
OPHELIA. No, my good lord; but as you did command,
    I did repel his letters and denied
    His access to me.
POLONIUS.   That hath made him mad.   110
    I am sorry that with better heed and judgment
    I had not quoted° him. I feared he did but trifle
    And meant to wrack thee; but beshrew my jealousy.°
    By heaven, it is as proper° to our age
    To cast beyond ourselves° in our opinions   115
    As it is common for the younger sort
    To lack discretion. Come, go we to the King.
    This must be known, which, being kept close, might move
    More grief to hide than hate to utter love.°
    Come. *Exeunt.*   120

---

102. *ecstasy:* madness. 103. *property fordoes:* quality destroys. 112. *quoted:* noted. 113. *beshrew my jealousy:* curse on my suspicions. 114. *proper:* natural. 115. *To cast beyond ourselves:* to be over-calculating. 117–119. *Come, go . . . utter love:* (the general meaning is that while telling the King of Hamlet's love may anger the King, more grief would come from keeping it secret).

SCENE II. *The castle.*

Flourish. Enter KING *and* QUEEN, ROSENCRANTZ, *and* GUILDENSTERN [*with others*].

KING. Welcome, dear Rosencrantz and Guildenstern.
　Moreover that° we much did long to see you,
　The need we have to use you did provoke
　Our hasty sending. Something have you heard
　Of Hamlet's transformation: so call it,　　　　　　　　　　　5
　Sith° nor th' exterior nor the inward man
　Resembles that it was. What it should be,
　More than his father's death, that thus hath put him
　So much from th' understanding of himself,
　I cannot dream of. I entreat you both　　　　　　　　　　　10
　That, being of so° young days brought up with him,
　And sith so neighbored to his youth and havior,°
　That you vouchsafe your rest° here in our court
　Some little time, so by your companies
　To draw him on to pleasures, and to gather　　　　　　　　15
　So much as from occasion you may glean,
　Whether aught to us unknown afflicts him thus,
　That opened° lies within our remedy.
QUEEN. Good gentlemen, he hath much talked of you,
　And sure I am, two men there is not living　　　　　　　　20
　To whom he more adheres. If it will please you
　To show us so much gentry° and good will
　As to expend your time with us awhile
　For the supply and profit of our hope,
　Your visitation shall receive such thanks　　　　　　　　　25
　As fits a king's remembrance.
ROSENCRANTZ. 　　　　　　　　Both your Majesties
　Might, by sovereign power you have of us,
　Put your dread pleasure more into command
　Than to entreaty.
GUILDENSTERN. 　　But we both obey,
　And here give up ourselves in the full bent°　　　　　　　30
　To lay our service freely at your feet,
　To be commanded.
KING. Thanks, Rosencrantz and gentle Guildenstern.
QUEEN. Thanks, Guildenstern and gentle Rosencrantz.

SCENE II. 2. *Moreover that:* beside the fact that. 6. *Sith:* since. 11. *of so:* from such.
12. *youth and havior:* behavior in his youth. 13. *vouchsafe your rest:* consent to remain.
18. *opened:* revealed. 22. *gentry:* courtesy. 30. *in the full bent:* entirely (the figure is of a bow bent to its capacity).

And I beseech you instantly to visit   35
My too much changèd son. Go, some of you,
And bring these gentlemen where Hamlet is.
GUILDENSTERN. Heavens make our presence and our practices
  Pleasant and helpful to him!
QUEEN.   Ay, amen!

Exeunt ROSENCRANTZ *and* GUILDENSTERN [*with some Attendants*]. *Enter* POLONIUS.

POLONIUS. Th' ambassadors from Norway, my good lord,   40
  Are joyfully returned.
KING. Thou still° hast been the father of good news.
POLONIUS. Have I, my lord? Assure you, my good liege,
  I hold my duty, as I hold my soul,
  Both to my God and to my gracious king;   45
  And I do think or else this brain of mine
  Hunts not the trail of policy so sure°
  As it hath used to do, that I have found
  The very cause of Hamlet's lunacy.
KING. O, speak of that! That do I long to hear.   50
POLONIUS. Give first admittance to th' ambassadors.
  My news shall be the fruit to that great feast.
KING. Thyself do grace to them and bring them in.   *Exit* POLONIUS.
  He tells me, my dear Gertrude, he hath found
  The head and source of all your son's distemper.   55
QUEEN. I doubt° it is no other but the main,°
  His father's death and our o'erhasty marriage.
KING. Well, we shall sift him.

Enter POLONIUS, VOLTEMAND, *and* CORNELIUS.

            Welcome, my good friends.
  Say, Voltemand, what from our brother Norway?
VOLTEMAND. Most fair return of greetings and desires.   60
  Upon our first,° he sent out to suppress
  His nephew's levies, which to him appeared
  To be a preparation 'gainst the Polack;
  But better looked into, he truly found
  It was against your Highness, whereat grieved,   65
  That so his sickness, age, and impotence
  Was falsely borne in hand,° sends out arrests
  On Fortinbras; which he, in brief, obeys,

42. *still:* always. 47. *Hunts not . . . so sure:* does not follow clues of political doings with such sureness. 56. *doubt:* suspect. 56. *main:* principal point. 61. *first:* first audience. 67. *borne in hand:* deceived.

Receives rebuke from Norway, and in fine,°
Makes vow before his uncle never more   70
To give th' assay° of arms against your Majesty.
Whereon old Norway, overcome with joy,
Gives him threescore thousand crowns in annual fee
And his commission to employ those soldiers,
So levied as before, against the Polack,   75
With an entreaty, herein further shown,   *Gives a paper.*
That it might please you to give quiet pass
Through your dominions for this enterprise,
On such regards of safety and allowance°
As therein are set down.
KING.   It likes us well;   80
And at our more considered time° we'll read,
Answer, and think upon this business.
Meantime, we thank you for your well-took labor.
Go to your rest; at night we'll feast together.
Most welcome home!   *Exeunt Ambassadors.*
POLONIUS.   This business is well ended.   85
My liege and madam, to expostulate°
What majesty should be, what duty is,
Why day is day, night night, and time is time.
Were nothing but to waste night, day, and time.
Therefore, since brevity is the soul of wit,°   90
And tediousness the limbs and outward flourishes,
I will be brief. Your noble son is mad.
Mad call I it, for, to define true madness,
What is't but to be nothing else but mad?
But let that go.
QUEEN.   More matter, with less art.   95
POLONIUS. Madam, I swear I use no art at all.
That he's mad, 'tis true: 'tis true 'tis pity,
And pity 'tis 'tis true—a foolish figure.°
But farewell it, for I will use no art.
Mad let us grant him then; and now remains   100
That we find out the cause of this effect,
Or rather say, the cause of this defect,
For this effect defective comes by cause.
Thus it remains, and the remainder thus.
Perpend.°   105

---

69. *in fine:* finally. 71. *assay:* trial. 79. *regards of safety and allowance:* i.e., conditions.
81. *considered time:* time proper for considering. 86. *expostulate:* discuss. 90. *wit:* wisdom,
understanding. 98. *figure:* figure of rhetoric. 105. *Perpend:* consider carefully.

I have a daughter: have, while she is mine,
Who in her duty and obedience, mark,
Hath given me this. Now gather, and surmise. [*Reads*] *the letter.*
"To the celestial, and my soul's idol, the most
beautified Ophelia"—   110
That's an ill phrase, a vile phrase; "beautified" is a
vile phrase. But you shall hear. Thus:
"In her excellent white bosom, these, &c."
QUEEN. Came this from Hamlet to her?
POLONIUS. Good madam, stay awhile. I will be faithful.   115
   "Doubt thou the stars are fire,
    Doubt that the sun doth move;
   Doubt° truth to be a liar,
    But never doubt I love.
O dear Ophelia, I am ill at these numbers.° I have   120
not art to reckon my groans; but that I love thee
best, O most best, believe it. Adieu.
 Thine evermore, most dear lady, whilst this
  machine° is to him, Hamlet."
This in obedience hath my daughter shown me,   125
And more above° hath his solicitings,
As they fell out by time, by means, and place,
All given to mine ear.
KING.   But how hath she
Received his love?
POLONIUS.   What do you think of me?
KING. As of man faithful and honorable.   130
POLONIUS. I would fain prove so. But what might you think,
When I had seen this hot love on the wing
(As I perceived it, I must tell you that,
Before my daughter told me), what might you,
Or my dear Majesty your Queen here, think,   135
If I had played the desk or table book,°
Or given my heart a winking,° mute and dumb,
Or looked upon this love with idle sight?
What might you think? No, I went round to work
And my young mistress thus I did bespeak: 140
"Lord Hamlet is a prince, out of thy star.°
This must not be." And then I prescripts gave her,

---

118. *Doubt:* suspect. 120. *ill at these numbers:* unskilled in verses.
124. *machine:* complex device (here, his body). 126. *more above:* in addition. 136. *played the desk or table book:* i.e., been a passive recipient of secrets. 137. *winking:* closing of the eyes.
141. *star:* sphere.

That she should lock herself from his resort,
Admit no messengers, receive no tokens.
Which done, she took the fruits of my advice,   145
And he, repellèd, a short tale to make,
Fell into a sadness, then into a fast,
Thence to a watch,° thence into a weakness,
Thence to a lightness,° and, by this declension,
Into the madness wherein now he raves,   150
And all we mourn for.
KING.   Do you think 'tis this?
QUEEN. It may be, very like.
POLONIUS. Hath there been such a time, I would fain know that,
  That I have positively said " 'Tis so,"
  When it proved otherwise?
KING.   Not that I know.   155
POLONIUS. [*Pointing to his head and shoulder*] Take this from this, if this be
  otherwise.
  If circumstances lead me, I will find
  Where truth is hid, though it were hid indeed
  Within the center.°
KING.   How may we try it further?
POLONIUS. You know sometimes he walks four hours together   160
  Here in the lobby.
QUEEN.   So he does indeed.
POLONIUS. At such a time I'll loose my daughter to him.
  Be you and I behind an arras° then.
  Mark the encounter. If he love her not,
  And be not from his reason fall'n thereon,   165
  Let me be no assistant for a state
  But keep a farm and carters.
KING.   We will try it.

Enter HAMLET *reading on a book.*

QUEEN. But look where sadly the poor wretch comes reading.
POLONIUS. Away, I do beseech you both, away. *Exit King and Queen.*
  I'll board him presently.° O, give me leave.   170
  How does my good Lord Hamlet?
HAMLET. Well, God-a-mercy.
POLONIUS. Do you know me, my lord?

148. *watch:* wakefulness. 149. *lightness:* mental derangement. 159. *center:* center of the earth.
163. *arras:* tapestry hanging in front of a wall. 170. *board him presently:* accost him at once.

HAMLET. Excellent well. You are a fishmonger.°

POLONIUS. Not I, my lord.   175

HAMLET. Then I would you were so honest a man.

POLONIUS. Honest, my lord?

HAMLET. Ay, sir. To be honest, as this world goes, it to be one man picked out of ten thousand.

POLONIUS. That's very true, my lord.   180

HAMLET. For if the sun breed maggots in a dead dog, being a good kissing carrion°——Have you a daughter?

POLONIUS. I have, my lord.

HAMLET. Let her not walk i' th' sun. Conception° is a blessing, but as your daughter may conceive, friend, look to't.   185

POLONIUS. [*Aside*] How say you by that? Still harping on my daughter. Yet he knew me not at first. 'A said I was a fishmonger. 'A is far gone, far gone. And truly in my youth I suffered much extremity for love, very near this. I'll speak to him again.—What do you read, my lord?

HAMLET. Words, words, words.   190

POLONIUS. What is the matter, my lord?

HAMLET. Between who?

POLONIUS. I mean that matter° that you read, my lord.

HAMLET. Slanders, sir; for the satirical rogue says here that old men have gray beards, that their faces are wrinkled, their eyes purging thick amber and plum- 195
tree gum, and that they have a plentiful lack of wit, together with most weak hams. All which, sir, though I most powerfully and potently believe, yet I hold it not honestly° to have it thus set down; for you yourself, sir, should be old as I am if, like a crab, you could go backward.

POLONIUS. [*Aside*] Though this be madness, yet there is method in't. Will you walk 200
out of the air, my lord?

HAMLET. Into my grave.

POLONIUS. Indeed, that's out of the air. [*Aside*] How pregnant° sometimes his replies are! A happiness° that often madness hits on, which reason and sanity could not so prosperously be delivered of. I will leave him and suddenly 205
contrive the means of meeting between him and my daughter.—My lord, I will take my leave of you.

HAMLET. You cannot take from me anything that I will more willingly part withal—except my life, except my life, except my life.

---

174. *fishmonger:* dealer in fish (slang for a procurer). 181–182. *a good kissing carrion:* (perhaps the meaning is "a good piece of flesh to kiss," but many editors emend *good* to *god*, taking the word to refer to the sun). 184. *Conception:* (1) understanding, (2) becoming pregnant.
193. *matter:* (Polonius means "subject matter," but Hamlet pretends to take the word in the sense of "quarrel"). 198. *honesty:* decency. 203. *pregnant:* meaningful. 204. *happiness:* apt turn of phrase.

Enter GUILDENSTERN *and* ROSENCRANTZ.

POLONIUS. Fare you well, my lord.   210
HAMLET. These tedious old fools!
POLONIUS. You go to seek the Lord Hamlet? There he is.
ROSENCRANTZ. [*To* POLONIUS] God save you, sir! *Exit* POLONIUS.
GUILDENSTERN. My honored lord!
ROSENCRANTZ. My most dear lord!   215
HAMLET. My excellent good friends! How dost thou, Guildenstern? Ah, Rosen-
     crantz! Good lads, how do you both?
ROSENCRANTZ. As the indifferent° children of the earth.
GUILDENSTERN. Happy in that we are not overhappy.
     On Fortune's cap we are not the very button.   220
HAMLET. Nor the soles of her shoe?
ROSENCRANTZ. Neither, my lord.
HAMLET. Then you live about her waist, or in the middle of her favors?
GUILDENSTERN. Faith, her privates° we.
HAMLET. In the secret parts of Fortune? O, most true! She is a strumpet. What 225
     news?
ROSENCRANTZ. None, my lord, but that the world's grown honest.
HAMLET. Then is doomsday near. But your news is not true. Let me question more
     in particular. What have you, my good friends, deserved at the hands of Fortune
     that she sends you to prison hither?   230
GUILDENSTERN. Prison, my lord?
HAMLET. Denmark's a prison.
ROSENCRANTZ. Then is the world one.
HAMLET. A goodly one, in which there are many confines, wards,° and dungeons,
     Denmark being one o' th' worst.   235
ROSENCRANTZ. We think not so, my lord.
HAMLET. Why, then 'tis none to you, for there is nothing either good or bad but
     thinking makes it so. To me it is a prison.
ROSENCRANTZ. Why then your ambition makes it one. 'Tis too narrow for your
     mind.   240
HAMLET. O God, I could be bounded in a nutshell and count myself a king of
     infinite space, were it not that I have bad dreams.
GUILDENSTERN. Which dreams indeed are ambition, for the very substance of the
     ambitious is merely the shadow of a dream.
HAMLET. A dream itself is but a shadow.   245
ROSENCRANTZ. Truly, and I hold ambition of so airy and light a quality that it is but
     a shadow's shadow.

---

218. *indifferent:* ordinary. 224. *privates:* ordinary men (with a pun on "private parts").
234. *wards:* cells.

HAMLET. Then are our beggars bodies, and our monarchs and outstretched heroes
the beggars' shadows.° Shall we to th' court? For, by my fay,° I cannot reason.

BOTH. We'll wait upon you.   250

HAMLET. No such matter. I will not sort you with the rest of my servants, for, to
speak to you like an honest man, I am most dreadfully attended. But in the
beaten way of friendship, what make you at Elsinore?

ROSENCRANTZ. To visit you, my lord; no other occasion.

HAMLET. Beggar that I am, I am even poor in thanks, but I thank you; and sure,   255
dear friends, my thanks are too dear a halfpenny.° Were you not sent for? Is it
your own inclining? Is it a free visitation? Come, come, deal justly with me.
Come, come; nay, speak.

GUILDENSTERN. What should we say, my lord?

HAMLET. Why anything—but to th' purpose. You were sent for, and there is a kind 260
of confession in your looks, which your modesties have not craft enough to
color. I know the good King and Queen have sent for you.

ROSENCRANTZ. To what end, my lord?

HAMLET. That you must teach me. But let me conjure you by the rights of our
fellowship, by the consonancy of our youth, by the obligation of our ever-pre- 265
served love, and by what more dear a better proposer can charge you withal, be
even and direct with me, whether you were sent for or no.

ROSENCRANTZ. [*Aside to Guildenstern*] What say you?

HAMLET. [*Aside*] Nay then, I have an eye of you.—If you love me, hold not off.

GUILDENSTERN. My lord, we were sent for.   270

HAMLET. I will tell you why; so shall my anticipation prevent your discovery,° and
your secrecy to the King and Queen molt no feather. I have of late, but
wherefore I know not, lost all my mirth, forgone all custom of exercises;
and indeed, it goes so heavily with my disposition that this goodly frame, the
earth, seems to me a sterile promontory; this most excellent canopy, the air,   275
look you, this brave o'erhanging firmament, this majestical roof fretted° with
golden fire: why, it appeareth nothing to me but a foul and pestilent con-
gregation of vapors. What a piece of work is a man, how noble in reason, how
infinite in faculties, in form and moving how express° and admirable, in action
how like an angel, in apprehension how like a god: the beauty of the world,   280
the paragon of animals; and yet to me, what is this quintessence of dust?
Man delights not me; nor woman neither, though by your smiling you seem to
say so.

ROSENCRANTZ. My lord, there was no such stuff in my thoughts.

HAMLET. Why did ye laugh then, when I said "Man delights not me"?   285

248–249 *Then are . . . beggars' shadows:* i.e., by your logic, beggars (lacking ambition) are substantial,
and great men are elongated shadows. 249. *fay:* faith. 256. *too dear a halfpenny:* i.e., nor worth a
halfpenny. 271. *prevent your discovery:* forestall your disclosure. 276. *fretted:* adorned.
279. *express:* exact.

ROSENCRANTZ. To think my lord, if you delight not in man, what lenten° entertainment the players shall receive from you. We coted° them on the way, and
hither are they coming to offer you service.

HAMLET. He that plays the king shall be welcome; his Majesty shall have tribute of
me; the adventurous knight shall use his foil and target;° the lover shall not sigh 290
gratis; the humorous man° shall end his part in peace; the clown shall make
those laugh whose lungs are tickle o' th' sere;° and the lady shall say her mind
freely, or° the blank verse shall halt° for't. What players are they?

ROSENCRANTZ. Even those you were wont to take such delight in, the tragedians of
the city. 295

HAMLET. How chances it they travel? Their residence, both in reputation and profit,
was better both ways.

ROSENCRANTZ. I think their inhibition° comes by the means of the late innovation.°

HAMLET. Do they hold the same estimation they did when I was in the city? Are
they so followed? 300

ROSENCRANTZ. No indeed, are they not.

HAMLET. How comes it? Do they grow rusty?

ROSENCRANTZ. Nay, their endeavor keeps in the wonted pace, but there is, sir, an
eyrie° of children, little eyases, that cry out on the top of question° and are most
tyrannically° clapped for't. These are now the fashion, and so berattle the 305
common stages° (so they call them) that many wearing rapiers are afraid of
goosequills° and dare scarce come thither.

HAMLET. What, are they children? Who maintains 'em? How are they escoted?° Will
they pursue the quality° no longer than they can sing? Will they not say
afterwards, if they should grow themselves to common players (as it is most 310
like, if their means are no better), their writers do them wrong to make them
exclaim against their own succession?°

ROSENCRANTZ. Faith, there has been much to-do on both sides, and the nation holds
it no sin to tarre° them to controversy. There was, for a while, no money bid
for argument° unless the poet and the player went to cuffs in the question. 315

HAMLET. Is't possible?

GUILDENSTERN. O, there has been much throwing about of brains.

HAMLET. Do the boys carry it away?

---

286. *lenten:* meager. 287. *coted:* overtook. 290. *target:* shield. 291. *humorous man:* i.e., eccentric
man (among stock characters in dramas were men dominated by a "humor" or odd trait).
292. *tickle o' th' sere:* on hair trigger (*sere* = part of the gunlock). 293. *or:* else. 293. *halt:* limp.
298. *inhibition:* hindrance. 298. *innovation:* (probably an allusion to the companies of child actors
that had become popular and were offering serious competition to the adult actors). 304. *eyrie:* nest.
304. *eyases, that . . . of question:* unfledged hawks that cry shrilly above others in matters of debate.
305. *tyrannically:* violently. 305–306. *berattle the common stages:* cry down the public theaters
(with the adult acting companies). 307. *goosequills:* pens (of satirists who ridicule the public theaters
and their audiences). 308. *escoted:* financially supported. 309. *quality:* profession of acting. 312.
succession: future. 314. *tarre:* incite. 315. *argument:* plot of a play.

ROSENCRANTZ. Ay, that they do, my lord—Hercules and his load° too.

HAMLET. It is not very strange, for my uncle is King of Denmark, and those that   320
would make mouths at him while my father lived give twenty, forty, fifty, a
hundred ducats apiece for his picture in little. 'Sblood,° there is something in
this more than natural, if philosophy could find it out. *A flourish.*

GUILDENSTERN. There are the players.

HAMLET. Gentlemen, you are welcome to Elsinore. Your hands, come then. Th'   325
appurtenance of welcome is fashion and ceremony. Let me comply° with you
in this garb,° lest my extent° to the players (which I tell you must show fairly
outwards) should more appear like entertainment than yours. You are welcome.
But my uncle-father and aunt-mother are deceived.

GUILDENSTERN. In what, my dear lord?   330

HAMLET. I am but mad north-northwest:° when the wind is southerly I know a
hawk from a handsaw.°

    Enter POLONIUS.

POLONIUS. Well be with you, gentlemen.

HAMLET. Hark you, Guildenstern, and you too; at each ear a hearer. That great baby
you see there is not yet out of his swaddling clouts.   335

ROSENCRANTZ. Happily° he is the second time come to them, for they say an old
man is twice a child.

HAMLET. I will prophesy he comes to tell me of the players. Mark it.—You say right,
sir; a Monday morning, 'twas then indeed.

POLONIUS. My lord, I have news to tell you.   340

HAMLET. My lord, I have news to tell you. When Roscius° was an actor in Rome——

POLONIUS. The actors are come hither, my lord.

HAMLET. Buzz, buzz.°

POLONIUS. Upon my honor——

HAMLET. Then came each actor on his ass——   345

POLONIUS. The best actors in the world, either for tragedy, comedy, history, pastoral, pastoral-comical, historical-pastoral, tragical-historical, tragical-comi-
cal-historical-pastoral; scene individable,° or poem unlimited.° Seneca° cannot
be too heavy, nor Plautus° too light. For the law of writ and the liberty,° these
are the only men.   350

---

319. *Hercules and his load:* i.e., the whole world (with a reference to the Globe Theatre, which had a
sign that represented Hercules bearing the globe). 322. *'Sblood:* by God's blood. 326. *comply:* be
courteous. 327. *garb:* outward show. 327. *extent:* behavior. 331. *north-northwest:* i.e., on one
point of the compass only. 332. *hawk from a handsaw* (*hawk* can refer not only to a bird but to a
kind of pickax; *handsaw*—a carpenter's tool—may involve a similar pun on "hernshaw," a heron).
336. *Happily:* perhaps. 341. *Roscius:* (a famous Roman comic actor). 343. *Buzz, buzz:* (an
interjection, perhaps indicating that the news is old). 348. *scene individable:* plays observing the
unities of time, place, and action. 348. *poem unlimited:* plays not restricted by the tenets of criticism.
348. *Seneca:* (Roman tragic dramatist). 349. *Plautus:* (Roman comic dramatist). 349 *For the law of
writ and liberty:* (perhaps "for sticking to the text and for improvising"; perhaps "for classical plays
and for modern loosely written plays").

HAMLET. O Jeptha, judge of Israel,° what a treasure hadst thou!
POLONIUS. What a treasure had he, my lord?
HAMLET. Why,
  "One fair daughter, and no more,
    The which he lovèd passing well." 355
POLONIUS. [*Aside*] Still on my daughter.
HAMLET. Am I not i' th' right, old Jeptha?
POLONIUS. If you call me Jeptha, my lord, I have a daughter that I love passing well.
HAMLET. Nay, that follows not.
POLONIUS. What follows, then, my lord? 360
HAMLET. Why,
      "As by lot, God wot,"
  and then, you know,
    "It came to pass, as most like it was."
The first row of the pious chanson° will show you 365
more, for look where my abridgment° comes.

Enter the Players.

You are welcome, masters, welcome, all. I am glad to see thee well. Welcome,
good friend. O, old friend, why, they face is valanced° since I saw thee last.
Com'st thou to beard me in Denmark? What, my young lady° and mistress?
By'r Lady, your ladyship is nearer to heaven than when I saw you last by the 370
altitude of a chopine.° Pray God your voice, like a piece of uncurrent gold, be
not cracked within the ring.°—Masters, you are all welcome. We'll e'en to't like
French falconers, fly at anything we see. We'll have a speech straight. Come,
give us a taste of your quality. Come, a passionate speech.
PLAYER. What speech, my good lord? 375
HAMLET. I heard thee speak me a speech once, but it was never acted, or if it was,
    not above once, for the play, I remember, pleased not the million; 'twas caviary
    to the general,° but it was (as I received it, and others, whose judgments in such
    matters cried in the top of° mine) an excellent play, well digested in the scenes,
    set down with as much modesty as cunning.° I remember one said there were 380
    no sallets° in the lines to make the matter savory; nor no matter in the phrase
    that might indict the author of affectation, but called it an honest method, as
    wholesome as sweet, and by very much more handsome than fine.° One speech

351. *Jeptha, judge of Israel:* (the title of a ballad on the Hebrew judge who sacrificed his daughter;
see Judges 11). 365. *row of the pious chanson:* stanza of the scriptural song. 366. *abridgment:* (1)
i.e., entertainers, who abridge the time, (2) interrupters. 368. *valanced:* fringed (with a beard).
369. *young lady:* i.e., boy for female roles. 371. *chopine:* thick-soled shoe. 371–372. *like a piece . . .
the ring:* (a coin was unfit for legal tender if a crack extended from the edge through the ring
enclosing the monarch's head. Hamlet, punning on *ring*, refers to the change of voice that the boy
actor will undergo). 377–378. *caviary to the general:* i.e., too choice for the multitude. 379. *in the
top of:* overtopping. 380 *modesty as cunning:* restraint as art. 381. *sallets:* salads, spicy jests.
383. *more handsome than fine:* well-proportioned rather than ornamented.

in't I chiefly loved. 'Twas Aeneas' tale to Dido, and thereabout of it especially
when he speaks of Priam's slaughter. If it live in your memory, begin at this 385
line—let me see, let me see:
    "The rugged Pyrrhus, like th' Hyrcanian
      beast°——"
'Tis not so; it begins with Pyrrhus:
    "The rugged Pyrrhus, he whose sable° arms,
    Black as his purpose, did the night resemble 390
When he lay couchèd in th' ominous horse,°
Hath now this dread and black complexion smeared
With heraldry more dismal.° Head to foot
Now is he total gules, horridly tricked°
With blood of father, mothers, daughters, sons, 395
Baked and impasted° with the parching streets,
Than lend a tyrannous and a damnèd light
To their lord's murder. Roasted in wrath and fire,
And thus o'ersizèd° with coagulate gore,
With eyes like carbuncles, the hellish Pyrrhus 400
Old grandsire Priam seeks."
    So, proceed you.
POLONIUS. Fore God, my lord, well spoken, with good accent and good discretion.
PLAYER.   "Anon he finds him,
Striking too short at Greeks. His antique sword, 405
Rebellious to his arm, lies where it falls,
Repugnant to command.° Unequal matched,
Pyrrhus at Priam drives, in rage strikes wide,
But with the whiff and wind of his fell sword
Th' unnervèd father falls. Then senseless Ilium,° 410
Seeming to feel this blow, with flaming top
Stoops to his base,° and with a hideous crash
Takes prisoner Pyrrhus' ear. For lo, his sword,
Which was declining on the milky head
Of reverend Priam, seemed i' th' air to stick. 415
So as a painted tyrant° Pyrrhus stood,
And like a neutral to his will and matter°
Did nothing.
But as we often see, against° some storm,
A silence in the heavens, the rack° stand still, 420

387. *Hyrcanian beast:* i.e., tiger (Hyrcania was in Asia). 389. *sable:* black. 391. *ominous horse:* i.e.,
wooden horse at the siege of Troy. 393. *dismal:* ill-omened. 394. *total gules, horridly
tricked:* all red, horridly adorned. 396. *impasted:* encrusted. 399. *o'ersizèd:* smeared over.
407. *Repugnant to command:* disobedient. 410. *senseless Ilium:* insensate Troy. 412. *Stoops to his
base:* collapses (*his* = its). 416. *painted tyrant:* tyrant in a picture. 417. *matter:* task.
419. *against:* just before. 420. *rack:* clouds.

The bold winds speechless, and the orb below
As hush as death, anon the dreadful thunder
Doth rend the region, so after Pyrrhus' pause,
A rousèd vengeance sets him new awork,
And never did the Cyclops' hammers fall   425
On Mars's armor, forged for proof eterne,°
With less remorse than Pyrrhus' bleeding sword
Now falls on Priam.
Out, out, thou strumpet Fortune! All you gods,
In general synod° take away her power,   430
Break all the spokes and fellies° from her wheel,
And bowl the round nave° down the hill of heaven,
As low as to the fiends."

POLONIUS. This is too long.

HAMLET. It shall to the barber's, with your beard.— Prithee say on. He's for a jig 435
   or a tale of bawdry, or he sleeps. Say on; come to Hecuba.

PLAYER. "But who (ah woe!) had seen the mobled° queen———"

HAMLET. "The mobled queen"?

POLONIUS. That's good. "Mobled queen" is good.

PLAYER. "Run barefoot up and down, threat'ning the flames   440
   With bisson rheum;° a clout° upon that head
   Where late the diadem stood, and for a robe,
   About her lank and all o'erteemèd° loins,
   A blanket in the alarm of fear caught up—
   Who this had seen, with tongue in venom steeped   445
   'Gainst Fortune's state would treason have pronounced.
   But if the gods themselves did see her then,
   When she saw Pyrrhus make malicious sport
   In mincing with his sword her husband's limbs,
   The instant burst of clamor that she made   450
   (Unless things mortal move then not at all)
   Would have made milch° the burning eyes of heaven
   And passion in the gods."

POLONIUS. Look, whe'r° he has not turned his color, and has tears in's eyes. Prithee
   no more.   455

HAMLET. 'Tis well, I'll have thee speak out the rest of this soon. Good my lord, will
   you see the players well bestowed?° Do you hear? Let them be well used, for
   they are the abstract and brief chronicles of the time. After your death you were
   better have a bad epitaph than their ill report while you live.

---

426. *proof eterne:* eternal endurance.   430. *synod:* council.   431. *fellies:* rims.   432. *nave:* hub.
437. *mobled:* muffled.   441. *bisson rheum:* blinding tears.   441. *clout:* rag.   443. *o'erteemèd:*
exhausted with childbearing.   452. *milch:* moist (literally, "milk-giving").   454. *whe'r:* whether.
457. *bestowed:* housed.

POLONIUS. My lord, I will use them according to their desert.   460

HAMLET. God's bodkin,° man, much better! Use every man after his desert, and
who shall scape whipping? Use them after your own honor and dignity. The
less they deserve, the more merit is in your bounty. Take them in.

POLONIUS. Come, sirs.

HAMLET. Follow him, friends. We'll hear a play tomorrow. [*Aside to Player*] Dost 465
thou hear me, old friend? Can you play *The Murder of Gonzago?*

PLAYER. Ay, my lord.

HAMLET. We'll ha't tomorrow night. You could for a need study a speech of some
dozen or sixteen lines which I would set down and insert in't, could you not?

PLAYER. Ay, my lord.   470

HAMLET. Very well. Follow that lord, and look you mock him not. My good friends,
I'll leave you till night. You are welcome to Elsinore. *Exeunt* POLONIUS *and
Players.*

ROSENCRANTZ. Good my lord. *Exeunt* ROSENCRANTZ *and* GUILDENSTERN.

HAMLET. Ay, so, God bye to you.—Now I am alone.

 O, what a rogue and peasant slave am I!   475
 Is it not monstrous that this player here,
 But in a fiction, in a dream of passion,°
 Could force his soul so to his own conceit°
 That from her working all his visage wanned,
 Tears in his eyes, distraction in his aspect,   480
 A broken voice, and his whole function° suiting
 With forms° to his conceit? And all for nothing!
 For Hecuba!
 What's Hecuba to him, or he to Hecuba,
 That he should weep for her? What would he do   485
 Had he the motive and the cue for passion
 That I have? He would drown the stage with tears
 And cleave the general ear with horrid speech,
 Make mad the guilty and appall the free,°
 Confound the ignorant, and amaze indeed   490
 The very faculties of eyes and ears.
 Yet I,
 A dull and muddy-mettled° rascal, peak
 Like John-a-dreams,° unpregnant of° my cause,
 And can say nothing. No, not for a king,   495
 Upon whose property and most dear life

---

461. *God's bodkin:* by God's little body. 477. *dream of passion:* imaginary emotion. 478. *conceit:*
imagination. 481. *function:* action. 482. *forms:* bodily expressions. 489. *appall the free:* terrify
(make pale?) the guiltless. 493. *muddy-mettled:* weak-spirited. 493–494. *peak/Like John-a-dreams:*
mope like a dreamer. 495. *unpregnant of:* unquickened by.

A damned defeat was made. Am I a coward?
Who calls me villain? Breaks my pate across?
Plucks off my beard and blows it in my face?
Tweaks me by the nose? Gives me the lie i' th' throat   500
As deep as to the lungs? Who does me this?
Ha, 'swounds,° I should take it, for it cannot be
But I am pigeon-livered° and lack gall
To make oppression bitter, or ere this
I should ha' fatted all the region kites°   505
With this slave's offal. Bloody, bawdy villain!
Remorseless, treacherous, lecherous, kindless° villain!
O, vengeance!
Why, what an ass am I! This is most brave,°
That I, the son of a dear father murdered,   510
Prompted to my revenge by heaven and hell,
Must, like a whore, unpack my heart with words
And fall a-cursing like a very drab,°
A stallion!° Fie upon't, foh! About,° my brains.
Hum——   515
I have heard that guilty creatures sitting at a play
Have by the very cunning of the scene
Been struck so to the soul that presently°
They have proclaimed their malefactions.
For murder, though it have no tongue, will speak   520
With most miraculous organ. I'll have these players
Play something like the murder of my father
Before mine uncle. I'll observe his looks,
I'll tent° him to the quick. If 'a do blench,°
I know my course. The spirit that I have seen   525
May be a devil, and the devil hath power
T' assume a pleasing shape, yea, and perhaps
Out of my weakness and my melancholy,
As he is very potent with such spirits,
Abuses me to damn me. I'll have grounds   530
More relative° than this. The play's the thing
Wherein I'll catch the conscience of the King.   *Exit.*

---

502. *'swounds:* by God's wounds. 503. *pigeon-livered:* gentle as a dove. 505. *region kites:*
kites (scavenger birds) of the sky. 507. *kindless:* unnatural. 509. *brave:* fine. 513. *drab:*
prostitute. 514. *stallion:* male prostitute (perhaps one should adopt the Folio reading,
scullion = kitchen wrench). 514. *About:* to work. 518. *presently:* immediately.
524. *tent:* probe. 524. *blench:* flinch. 531. *relative:* (probably "pertinent," but possibly
"able to be related plausibly").

ACT III

SCENE I. *The castle.*

Enter King, Queen, POLONIUS, OPHELIA, ROSENCRANTZ, GUILDENSTERN, Lords.

KING. And can you by no drift of conference°
  Get from him why he puts on this confusion,
  Grating so harshly all his days of quiet
  With turbulent and dangerous lunacy?
ROSENCRANTZ. He does confess he feels himself distracted,   5
  But from what cause 'a will by no means speak.
GUILDENSTERN. Nor do we find him forward to be sounded,°
  But with a crafty madness keeps aloof
  When we would bring him on to some confession
  Of his true state.
QUEEN.   Did he receive you well?   10
ROSENCRANTZ. Most like a gentleman.
GUILDENSTERN. But with much forcing of his disposition.°
ROSENCRANTZ. Niggard of question,° but of our demands
  Most free in his reply.
QUEEN.   Did you assay° him
  To any pastime?   15
ROSENCRANTZ. Madam, it so fell out that certain players
  We o'erraught° on the way; of these we told him,
  And there did seem in him a kind of joy
  To hear of it. They are here about the court,
  And, as I think, they have already order   20
  This night to play before him.
POLONIUS.   'Tis most true,
  And he beseeched me to entreat your Majesties
  To hear and see the matter.
KING. With all my heart, and it doth much content me
  To hear him so inclined.   25
  Good gentlemen, give him a further edge
  And drive his purpose into these delights.
ROSENCRANTZ. We shall, my lord. *Exeunt ROSENCRANTZ and GUILDENSTERN.*
KING.   Sweet Gertrude, leave us too,
  For we have closely° sent for Hamlet hither,
  That he, as 'twere by accident, may here   30
  Affront° Ophelia.

SCENE I. 1. *drift of conference:* management of conversation. 7. *forward to be sounded:* willing to be questioned. 12. *forcing of his disposition:* effort. 13. *Niggard of question:* uninclined to talk. 14. *assay:* tempt. 17. *o'erraught:* overtook. 29. *closely:* secretly. 31. *Affront:* meet face to face.

Her father and myself (lawful espials°)
Will so bestow ourselves that, seeing unseen,
We may of their encounter frankly judge
And gather by him, as he is behaved,   35
If't be th' affliction of his love or no
That thus he suffers for.
QUEEN.   I shall obey you.
  And for your part, Ophelia, I do wish
  That your good beauties be the happy cause
  Of Hamlet's wildness. So shall I hope your virtues   40
  Will bring him to his wonted way again,
  To both your honors.
OPHELIA.   Madam, I wish it may. *Exit Queen.*
POLONIUS. Ophelia, walk you here.—Gracious, so please you,
  We will bestow ourselves. [*To Ophelia*] Read on this book,
  That show of such an exercise may color°   45
  Your loneliness. We are oft to blame in this,
  'Tis too much proved, that with devotion's visage
  And pious action we do sugar o'er
  The devil himself.
KING.   [*Aside*] O, 'tis too true.
  How smart a lash that speech doth give my conscience!   50
  The harlot's cheek, beautied with plast'ring art,
  Is not more ugly to the thing that helps it
  Than is my deed to my most painted word.
  O heavy burden!
POLONIUS. I hear him coming. Let's withdraw, my lord. *Exeunt King and*   55
  POLONIUS.

                    Enter HAMLET.

HAMLET. To be, or not to be: that is the question:
  Whether 'tis nobler in the mind to suffer
  The slings and arrows of outrageous fortune,
  Or to take arms against a sea of troubles,
  And by opposing end them. To die, to sleep—   60
  No more—and by a sleep to say we end
  The heartache, and the thousand natural shocks
  That flesh is heir to! 'Tis a consummation
  Devoutly to be wished. To die, to sleep—
  To sleep—perchance to dream: ay, there's the rub,°   65
  For in that sleep of death what dreams may come

---

32. *espials:* spies. 45. *exercise may color:* act of devotion may give a plausible hue to (the book is one of devotion). 65. *rub:* impediment (obstruction to a bowler's ball).

When we have shuffled off this mortal coil,°
Must give us pause. There's the respect°
That makes calamity of so long life:°
For who would bear the whips and scorns of time,   70
Th' oppressor's wrong, the proud man's contumely,
The pangs of despised love, the law's delay,
The insolence of office, and the spurns
That patient merit of th' unworthy takes,
When he himself might his quietus° make   75
With a bare bodkin?° Who would fardels° bear,
To grunt and swear under a weary life,
But that the dread of something after death,
The undiscovered country, from whose bourn°
No traveler returns, puzzles the will,   80
And makes us rather bear those ills we have,
Than fly to others that we know not of?
Thus conscience° does make cowards of us all,
And thus the native hue of resolution
Is sickled o'er with the pale cast° of thought,   85
And enterprises of great pitch° and moment,
With this regard° their current turn awry,
And lose the name of action.—Soft you now,
The fair Ophelia!—Nymph, in thy orisons°
Be all my sins remembered.
OPHELIA.   Good my lord,   90
    How does your honor for this many a day?
HAMLET. I humbly thank you; well, well, well.
OPHELIA. My lord, I have remembrances of yours
    That I have longèd long to redeliver.
    I pray you now, receive them.
HAMLET.   No, not I.   95
    I never gave you aught.
OPHELIA. My honored lord, you know right well you did,
    And with them words of so sweet breath composed
    As made these things more rich. Their perfume lost,
    Take these again, for to the noble mind   100
    Rich gifts wax poor when givers prove unkind.
    There, my lord.

---

67. *coil:* (1) turmoil, (2) a ring of rope (here the flesh encircling the soul). 68. *respect:*
consideration. 69. *makes calamity of so long life:* (1) makes calamity so long-lived, (2) makes living
so long a calamity. 75. *quietus:* full discharge (a legal term). 76. *bodkin:* dagger. 76. *fardels:*
burdens. 79. *bourn:* region. 83. *conscience:* self-consciousness, introspection. 85. *cast:* color.
86. *pitch:* height (a term from falconry). 87. *regard:* consideration. 89. *orisons:* prayers.

HAMLET. Ha, ha! Are you honest?°

OPHELIA. My lord?

HAMLET. Are you fair? 105

OPHELIA. What means your lordship?

HAMLET. That if you be honest and fair, your honesty should admit no discourse to
your beauty.°

OPHELIA. Could beauty, my lord, have better commerce than with honesty?

HAMLET. Ay, truly; for the power of beauty will sooner transform honesty from what 110
it is to a bawd° than the force of honesty can translate beauty into his likeness.
This was sometime a paradox, but now the time gives it proof. I did love you
once.

OPHELIA. Indeed, my lord, you made me believe so.

HAMLET. You should not have believed me, for virtue cannot so inoculate° our old 115
stock but we shall relish of it.° I loved you not.

OPHELIA. I was the more deceived.

HAMLET. Get thee to a nunnery. Why wouldst thou be a breeder of sinners? I am
myself indifferent honest,° but yet I could accuse me of such things that it were
better my mother had not borne me: I am very proud, revengeful, ambitious, 120
with more offenses at my beck° than I have thoughts to put them in, imagination to give them shape, or time to act them in. What should such fellows as I
do crawling between earth and heaven? We are arrant knaves all; believe none
of us. Go thy ways to a nunnery. Where's your father?

OPHELIA. At home, my lord. 125

HAMLET. Let the doors be shut upon him, that he may play the fool nowhere but
in's own house. Farewell.

OPHELIA. O help him, you sweet heavens!

HAMLET. If thou dost marry, I'll give thee this plague for thy dowry: be thou as
chaste as ice, as pure as snow, thou shalt not escape calumny. Get thee to a 130
nunnery. Go, farewell. Or if thou wilt needs marry, marry a fool, for wise men
know well enough what monsters° you make of them. To a nunnery, go, and
quickly too. Farewell.

OPHELIA. Heavenly powers, restore him!

HAMLET. I have heard of your paintings, well enough. God hath given you one face, 135
and you make yourselves another. You jig and amble, and you lisp; you
nickname God's creatures and make your wantonness your ignorance.° Go to,
I'll no more on't; it hath made me mad. I say we will have no moe° marriage.
Those that are married already—all but one—shall live. The rest shall keep as
they are. To a nunnery, go. *Exit.* 140

103. *Are you honest:* (1) are you modest, (2) are you chaste, (3) have you integrity. 107–108 *your
honesty . . . to your beauty:* your modesty should permit no approach to your beauty. 111 *bawd:*
procurer. 115. *inoculate:* graft. 116. *relish of it:* smack of it (our old sinful nature).
119. *indifferent honest:* moderately virtuous. 121. *beck:* call. 132. *monsters:* horned beasts,
cuckolds. 137. *make your wantonness your ignorance:* excuse your wanton speech by pretending
ignorance. 138. *moe:* more.

OPHELIA. O what a noble mind is here o'erthrown!
  The courtier's, soldier's, scholar's, eye, tongue, sword,
  Th' expectancy and rose° of the fair state,
  The glass of fashion, and the mold of form,°
  Th' observed of all observers, quite, quite down!   145
  And I, of ladies most deject and wretched,
  That sucked the honey of his musicked vows,
  Now see that noble and most sovereign reason
  Like sweet bells jangled, out of time and harsh,
  That unmatched form and feature of blown° youth   150
  Blasted with ecstasy.° O, woe is me
  T' have seen what I have seen, see what I see!

Enter King and POLONIUS.

KING. Love? His affections° do not that way tend,
  Nor what he spake, though it lacked form a little,
  Was not like madness. There's something in his soul   155
  O'er which his melancholy sits on brood,
  And I do doubt° the hatch and the disclose
  Will be some danger; which for to prevent,
  I have in quick determination
  Thus set it down: he shall with speed to England   160
  For the demand of our neglected tribute.
  Haply the seas, and countries different,
  With variable objects, shall expel
  This something-settled° matter in his heart,
  Whereon his brains still beating puts him thus   165
  From fashion of himself. What think you on't?
POLONIUS. It shall do well. But yet do I believe
  The origin and commencement of his grief
  Sprung from neglected love. How now, Ophelia?
  You need not tell us what Lord Hamlet said;   170
  We heard it all. My lord, do as you please,
  But if you hold it fit, after the play,
  Let his queen mother all alone entreat him
  To show his grief. Let her be round° with him,
  And I'll be placed, so please you, in the ear   175
  Of all their conference. If she find him not,°

---

143. *expectancy and rose:* i.e., fair hope. 144. *The glass . . . of form:* the mirror of fashion, and the pattern of excellent behavior. 150. *blown:* blooming. 151. *ecstasy:* madness. 153. *affections:* inclinations. 157. *doubt:* fear. 164. *something-settled:* somewhat settled. 174. *round:* blunt. 176. *find him not:* does not find him out.

To England send him, or confine him where
Your wisdom best shall think.

KING.   It shall be so.
Madness in great ones must not unwatched go.   *Exeunt.*

SCENE II. *The castle.*

Enter HAMLET *and three of the Players.*

HAMLET. Speak the speech, I pray you, as I pronounced it to you, trippingly on the
tongue. But if you mouth it, as many of our players do, I had as lief the town
crier spoke my lines. Nor do now saw the air too much with your hand, thus,
but use all gently, for in the very torrent, tempest, and (as I may say) whirlwind
of your passion, you must acquire and beget a temperance that may give it 5
smoothness. O, it offends me to the soul to hear a robustious periwig-pated°
fellow tear a passion to tatters, to very rags, to split the ears of the groundlings,°
who for the most part are capable of° nothing but inexplicable dumb shows°
and noise. I would have such a fellow whipped for o'erdoing Termagant. It
out-herods Herod.° Pray you avoid it.   10

PLAYER. I warrant your honor.

HAMLET. Be not too tame neither, but let your own discretion be your tutor. Suit
the action to the word, the word to the action, with this special observance,
that you o'erstep not the modesty of nature. For anything so o'erdone is from°
the purpose of playing, whose end, both at the first and now, was and is, to 15
hold, as 'twere, the mirror up to nature; to show virtue her own feature, scorn
her own image, and the very age and body of the time his form and pressure.°
Now, this overdone, or come tardy off, though it makes the unskillful laugh,
cannot but make the judicious grieve, the censure of the which one must in
your allowance o'erweigh a whole theater of others. O, there be players that I 20
have seen play, and heard others praise, and that highly (not to speak it
profanely), that neither having th' accent of Christians, nor the gait of Christian,
pagan, nor man, have so strutted and bellowed that I have thought some of
Nature's journeymen° had made men, and not made them well, they imitated
humanity so abominably.   25

PLAYER. I hope we have reformed that indifferently° with us, sir.

HAMLET. O, reform it altogether! And let those that play your clowns speak no more
than is set down for them, for there be of them that will themselves laugh, to
set on some quantity of barren spectators to laugh too, though in the meantime
some necessary question of the play be then to be considered. That's villainous 30

SCENE II. 6. *robustious periwig-pated:* boisterous wig-headed. 7. *groundlings:* those who stood in
the pit of the theater (the poorest and presumably most ignorant of the audience). 8. *are capable of:*
are able to understand. 8. *dumb shows:* (it had been the fashion for actors to preface plays or parts of
plays with silent mime). 9–10. *Termagant . . . Herod:* (boisterous characters in the old mystery
plays). 14. *from:* contrary to. 17. *pressure:* image, impress. 24. *journeymen:* workers not yet
masters of their craft. 26. *indifferently:* tolerably.

and shows a most pitiful ambition in the fool that uses it. Go make you ready.
Exit Players.

Enter POLONIUS, GUILDENSTERN, *and* ROSENCRANTZ.

How now, my lord? Will the King hear this piece of work?
POLONIUS. And the Queen too, and that presently.
HAMLET. Bid the players make haste. *Exit* POLONIUS.
Will you two help to hasten them?   35
ROSENCRANTZ. ⎱
GUILDENSTERN. ⎰ Ay, my lord. *Exeunt they two.*
HAMLET. What, ho, Horatio!

Enter HORATIO.

HORATIO. Here, sweet lord, at your service.
HAMLET. Horatio, thou art e'en as just a man
As e'er my conversation coped withal.°   40
HORATIO. O, my dear lord——
HAMLET.   Nay, do you think I flatter.
For what advancement° may I hope from thee,
That no revenue hast but thy good spirits
To feed and clothe thee? Why should the poor be flattered?
No, let the candied° tongue lick absurd pomp,   45
And crook the pregnant° hinges of the knee
Where thrift° may follow fawning. Dost thou hear?
Since my dear soul was mistress of her choice
And could of men distinguish her election,
S' hath sealed thee° for herself, for thou hast been   50
As one, in suff'ring all, that suffers nothing,
A man that Fortune's buffets and rewards
Hast ta'en with equal thanks; and blest are those
Whose blood° and judgment are so well commeddled°
That they are not a pipe for Fortune's finger   55
To sound what stop she please. Give me that man
That is not passions' slave, and I will wear him
In my heart's core, ay, in my heart of heart,
As I do thee. Something too much of this—
There is a play tonight before the King.   60
One scene of it comes near the circumstance
Which I have told thee, of my father's death.
I prithee, when thou seest that act afoot,

---

40. *coped withal:* met with. 42. *advancement:* promotion. 45. *candied:* sugared, flattering.
46. *pregnant:* (1) pliant, (2) full of promise of good fortune. 47. *thrift:* profit. 50. *S'hath sealed
thee:* she (the soul) has set a mark on you. 54. *blood:* passion. 54. *commeddled:* blended.

Even with the very comment° of thy soul
Observe my uncle. If his occulted° guilt   65
Do not itself unkennel in one speech,
It is a damnèd ghost that we have seen,
And my imaginations are as foul
As Vulcan's stithy.° Give him heedful note,
For I mine eyes will rivet to his face,   70
And after we will both our judgments join
In censure of his seeming.°

HORATIO.   Well, my lord.
  If 'a steal aught the whilst this play is playing,
  And scape detecting, I will pay the theft.

Enter Trumpets and Kettledrums, King, Queen, POLONIUS, OPHELIA, ROSENCRANTZ,
GUILDENSTERN, *and other Lords attendant with his Guard carrying torches. Danish
March. Sound a Flourish.*

HAMLET. They are coming to the play: I must be idle;° Get you a place.   75
KING. How fares our cousin Hamlet?
HAMLET. Excellent, i' faith, of the chameleon's dish;° I eat the air, promise-
  crammed; you cannot feed capons so.
KING. I have nothing with this answer, Hamlet; these words are not mine.
HAMLET. No, nor mine now. [*To Polonius*] My lord, you played once i' th' uni   80
  versity, you say?
POLONIUS. That did I, my lord, and was accounted a good actor.
HAMLET. What did you enact?
POLONIUS. I did enact Julius Caesar. I was killed i' th' Capitol; Brutus killed me.
HAMLET. It was a brute part of him to kill so capital a calf there. Be the players ready? 85
ROSENCRANTZ. Ay, my lord they stay upon your patience.
QUEEN. Come hither, my dear Hamlet, sit by me.
HAMLET. No, good mother. Here's metal more attractive.°
POLONIUS. [*To the King*] O ho! Do you mark that?
HAMLET. Lady, shall I lie in your lap?   90

He lies at OPHELIA's *feet.*

OPHELIA. No, my lord.
HAMLET. I mean, my head upon your lap?
OPHELIA. Ay, my lord.
HAMLET. Do you think I meant country matters?°
OPHELIA. I think nothing, my lord.   95

---

64. *very comment:* deepest wisdom. 65. *occulted:* hidden. 69. *stithy:* forge, smithy. 72. *censure of
his seeming:* judgment on his looks. 75. *be idle:* play the fool. 77. *the chameleon's dish:* air (on
which chameleons were thought to live). 88. *attractive:* magnetic. 94. *country matters:* rustic
doings (with a pun on the vulgar word for the pudendum).

HAMLET. That's a fair thought to lie between maids' legs.

OPHELIA. What is, my lord?

HAMLET. Nothing.

OPHELIA. You are merry, my lord.

HAMLET. Who, I? 100

OPHELIA. Ay, my lord.

HAMLET. O God, your only jig-maker!° What should a man do but be merry? For look you how cheerfully my mother looks, and my father died within's two hours.

OPHELIA. Nay, 'tis twice two months, my lord. 105

HAMLET. So long? Nay then, let the devil wear black, for I'll have a suit of sables.° O heavens! Die two months ago, and not forgotten yet? Then there's hope a great man's memory may outlive his life half a year. But, by'r Lady, 'a must build churches then, or else shall 'a suffer not thinking on, with the hobby-horse,° whose epitaph is "For O, for O, the hobby-horse is forgot!" 110

The trumpets sound. Dumb show follows:

Enter a King and a Queen very lovingly, the Queen embracing him, and he her. She kneels; and makes show of protestation unto him. He takes her up, and declines his head upon her neck. He lies him down upon a bank of flowers. She, seeing him asleep, leaves him. Anon come in another man: takes off his crown, kisses it, pours poison in the sleeper's ears, and leaves him. The Queen returns, finds the King dead, makes passionate action. The poisoner, with some three or four, come in again, seem to condole with her. The dead body is carried away. The poisoner woos the Queen with gifts; she seems harsh awhile, but in the end accepts love. [Exeunt.]

OPHELIA. What means this, my lord?

HAMLET. Marry, this is miching mallecho;° it means mischief.

OPHELIA. Belike this show imports the argument° of the play.

Enter Prologue.

HAMLET. We shall know by this fellow. The players cannot keep counsel; they'll tell all. 115

OPHELIA. Will 'a tell us what this show meant?

HAMLET. Ay, or any show that you will show him. Be not you ashamed to show, he'll not shame to tell you what it means.

OPHELIA. You are naught,° you are naught; I'll mark the play. 120

PROLOGUE. For us, and for our tragedy,

---

102. *jig-maker:* composer of songs and dances (often a Fool, who performed them). 106. *sables:* (pun on "black" and "luxurious furs"). 109–110. *hobby-horse:* mock horse worn by a performer in the morris dance. 112. *miching mallecho:* sneaking mischief. 113. *argument:* plot. 119. *naught:* wicked, improper.

Here stooping to your clemency,
We beg your hearing patiently. [*Exit.*]
HAMLET. Is this a prologue, or the posy of a ring?°
OPHELIA. 'Tis brief, my lord.   125
HAMLET. As a woman's love.

Enter [*two* PLAYERS *as*] *King and Queen.*

PLAYER KING. Full thirty times hath Phoebus' cart° gone round
  Neptune's salt wash° and Tellus'° orbèd ground,
  And thirty dozen moons with borrowed sheen
  About the world have times twelve thirties been,   130
  Since love our hearts, and Hymen did our hands,
  Unite commutual in most sacred bands.
PLAYER QUEEN. So many journeys may the sun and moon
  Make us again count o'er ere love be done!
  But woe is me, you are so sick of late,   135
  So far from cheer and from your former state,
  That I distrust° you. Yet, though I distrust,
  Discomfort you, my lord, it nothing must.
  For women fear too much, even as they love,
  And women's fear and love hold quantity,   140
  In neither aught, or in extremity.°
  Now what my love is, proof° hath made you know,
  And as my love is sized, my fear is so.
  Where love is great, the littlest doubts are fear;
  Where little fears grow great, great love grows there.   145
PLAYER KING. Faith, I must leave thee, love, and shortly too;
  My operant° powers their functions leave to do:
  And thou shalt live in this fair world behind,
  Honored, beloved, and haply one as kind
  For husband shalt thou——   150
PLAYER QUEEN.   O, confound the rest!
  Such love must needs be treason in my breast.
  In second husband let me be accurst!
  None wed the second but who killed the first.
HAMLET. [*Aside*] That's wormwood.°
PLAYER QUEEN. The instances° that second marriage move°   155
  Are base respects of thrift,° but none of love.

---

124. *posy of a ring:* motto inscribed in a ring. 127. *Phoebus' cart:* the sun's chariot. 128. *Neptune's salt wash:* the sea. 128. *Tellus:* Roman goddess of the earth. 137. *distrust:* am anxious about. 140–141. *And women's . . . in extremity:* (perhaps the idea is that women's anxiety is great or little in proportion to their love. The previous line, unrhymed, may be a false start that Shakespeare neglected to delete). 142. *proof:* experience. 147. *operant:* active. 154. *wormwood:* a bitter herb. 155. *instances:* motives. 155. *move:* induce. 156. *respects of thrift:* considerations of profit.

A second time I kill my husband dead
When second husband kisses me in bed.
PLAYER KING. I do believe you think what now you speak,
    But what we do determine oft we break.   160
    Purpose is but the slave to memory,
    Of violent birth, but poor validity,°
    Which now like fruit unripe sticks on the tree,
    But fall unshaken when they mellow be.
    Most necessary 'tis that we forget   165
    To pay ourselves what to ourselves is debt.
    What to ourselves in passion we propose,
    The passion ending, doth the purpose lose.
    The violence of either grief or joy
    Their own enactures° with themselves destroy;   170
    Where joy most revels, grief doth most lament;
    Grief joys, joy grieves, on slender accident.
    This world is not for aye, nor 'tis not strange
    That even our loves should with our fortunes change,
    For tis a question left us yet to prove,   175
    Whether love lead fortune, or else fortune love.
    The great man down, you mark his favorite flies;
    The poor advanced makes friends of enemies;
    And hitherto doth love on fortune tend,
    For who not needs shall never lack a friend;   180
    And who in want a hollow friend doth try,
    Directly seasons him° his enemy.
    But, orderly to end where I begun,
    Our wills and fates do so contrary run
    That our devices still are overthrown;   185
    Our thoughts are ours, their ends none of our own.
    So think thou wilt no second husband wed,
    But die thy thoughts when thy first lord is dead.
PLAYER QUEEN. Nor earth to me give food, nor heaven light,
    Sport and repose lock from me day and night,   190
    To desperation turn my trust and hope,
    An anchor's° cheer in prison be my scope,
    Each opposite that blanks° the face of joy
    Meet what I would have well, and it destroy:
    Both here and hence pursue me lasting strife,   195
    If, once a widow, ever I be wife!
HAMLET. If she should break it now!

162. *validity:* strength. 170. *enactures:* acts. 182. *season him:* ripens him into.
192. *anchor's:* anchorite's, hermit's. 193. *opposite that blanks:* adverse thing that blanches.

PLAYER KING. 'Tis deeply sworn. Sweet, leave me here awhile;
My spirits grow dull, and fain I would beguile
The tedious day with sleep.
PLAYER QUEEN.   Sleep rock thy brain, [*He*] *sleeps.*   200
And never come mischance between us twain! *Exit.*
HAMLET. Madam, how like you this play?
QUEEN. The lady doth protest too much, methinks.
HAMLET. O, but she'll keep her word.
KING. Have you heard the argument?° Is there no offense in't?   205
HAMLET. No, no, they do but jest, poison in jest; no offense i' th' world.
KING. What do you call the play?
HAMLET. *The Mousetrap.* Marry, how? Tropically.° This play is the image of a murder
done in Vienna: Gonzago is the Duke's name; his wife, Baptista. You shall see
anon. 'Tis a knavish piece of work, but what of that? Your Majesty, and we that 210
have free° souls, it touches us not. Let the galled jade winch;° our withers are
unwrung.

     Enter LUCIANUS.

This is one Lucianus, nephew to the King.
OPHELIA. You are as good as a chorus, my lord.
HAMLET. I could interpret° between you and your love, if I could see the puppets 215
dallying.
OPHELIA. You are keen,° my lord, you are keen.
HAMLET. It would cost you a groaning to take off mine edge.
OPHELIA. Still better, and worse.
HAMLET. So you mistake° your husbands.—Begin, murderer. Leave thy damnable 220
faces and begin. Come, the croaking raven doth bellow for revenge.
LUCIANUS. Thoughts black, hands apt, drugs fit, and
time agreeing,
Confederate season,° else no creature seeing,
Thou mixture rank, of midnight weeds collected,   225
With Hecate's ban° thrice blasted, thrice infected,
Thy natural magic and dire property°
On wholesome life usurps immediately.

     Pours the poison in his ears.

HAMLET. 'A poisons him i' th' garden for his estate. His name's Gonzago. The story
is extant, and written in very choice Italian. You shall see anon how the 230
murderer gets the love of Gonzago's wife.

---

205. *argument:* plot. 208. *Tropically:* figuratively (with a pun on "trap"). 211. *free:* innocent.
211. *galled jade winch:* chafed horse wince. 215. *interpret:* (like a showman explaining the action
of puppets). 217. *keen:* (1) sharp, (2) sexually aroused. 220. *mistake:* err in taking.
224. *Confederate season:* the opportunity allied with me. 226. *Hecate's ban:* the curse of the
goddess of sorcery. 227. *property:* nature.

OPHELIA. The King rises.
HAMLET. What, frighted with false fire?°
QUEEN. How fares my lord?
POLONIUS. Give o'er the play.   235
KING. Give me some light. Away!
POLONIUS. Lights, lights, lights! *Exeunt all but* HAMLET *and* HORATIO.
HAMLET. Why, let the strucken deer go weep,
      The hart ungallèd play:
   For some must watch, while some must sleep;   240
      Thus runs the world away.
   Would not this, sir, and a forest of feathers°—if the rest of my fortunes turn
   Turk° with me—with two Provincial roses° on my razed° shoes, get me a
   fellowship in a cry° of players?
HORATIO. Half a share.   245
HAMLET. A whole one, I.
   For thou dost know, O Damon dear,
      This realm dismantled was
  Of Jove himself; and now reigns here
      A very, very—pajock.°   250
HORATIO. You might have rhymed.°
HAMLET. O good Horatio, I'll take the ghost's word for a thousand pound. Didst
   perceive.
HORATIO. Very well, my lord.
HAMLET. Upon the talk of poisoning?   255
HORATIO. I did very well note him.
HAMLET. Ah ha! Come, some music! Come, the recorders!°
   For if the King like not the comedy,
   Why then, belike he likes it not, perdy.°
  Come, some music!   260

Enter ROSENCRANTZ *and* GUILDENSTERN.

GUILDENSTERN. Good my lord, vouchsafe me a word with you.
HAMLET. Sir, a whole history.
GUILDENSTERN. The King, sir——
HAMLET. Ay, sir, what of him?
GUILDENSTERN. Is in his retirement marvelous distemp'red.   265
HAMLET. With drink, sir?
GUILDENSTERN. No, my lord, with choler.°

---

233. *false fire:* blank discharge of firearms. 242. *feathers:* (plumes were sometimes part of a costume). 242–243. *turn Turk:* i.e., go bad, treat me badly. 243. *Provincial roses:* rosettes like the roses of Provence (?). 243. *razed:* ornamented with slashes. 244. *cry:* pack, company. 250. *pajock:* peacock. 251. *You might have rhymed:* i.e., rhymed "was" with "ass." 257. *recorders:* flutelike instruments. 259. *perdy:* by God (French: *par dieu*). 267. *choler:* anger (but Hamlet pretends to take the word in its sense of "bilousness").

HAMLET. Your wisdom should show itself more richer to signify this to the doctor, for, for me to put him to his purgation would perhaps plunge him into more choler. 270

GUILDENSTERN. Good my lord, put your discourse into some frame,° and start not so wildly from my affair.

HAMLET. I am tame, sir; pronounce.

GUILDENSTERN. The Queen, your mother, in most great affliction of spirit hath sent me to you. 275

HAMLET. You are welcome.

GUILDENSTERN. Nay, good my lord, this courtesy is not of the right breed. If it shall please you to make me a wholesome answer, I will do your mother's command-ment: if not, your pardon and my return shall be the end of my business.

HAMLET. Sir, I cannot. 280

ROSENCRANTZ. What, my lord?

HAMLET. Make you a wholesome° answer; my wit's diseased. But, sir, such answer as I can make, you shall command, or rather, as you say, my mother. Therefore no more, but to the matter. My mother, you say——

ROSENCRANTZ. Then thus she says: your behavior hath struck her into amazement 285 and admiration.°

HAMLET. O wonderful son, that can so stonish a mother! But is there no sequel at the heels of this mother's admiration? Impart.

ROSENCRANTZ. She desires to speak with you in her closet ere you go to bed.

HAMLET. We shall obey, were she ten times our mother. Have you any further trade 290 with us?

ROSENCRANTZ. My lord, you once did love me.

HAMLET. And do still, by these pickers and stealers.°

ROSENCRANTZ. Good my lord, what is your cause of distemper? You do surely bar the door upon your own liberty, if you deny your griefs to your friend. 295

HAMLET. Sir, I lack advancement.°

ROSENCRANTZ. How can that be, when you have the voice of the King himself for your succession in Denmark?

Enter the Players with recorders.

HAMLET. Ay, sir, but "while the grass grows"—the proverb° is something musty. O, the recorders. Let me see one. To withdraw° with you—why do you go 300 about to recover the wind° of me as if you would drive me into a toil?°

GUILDENSTERN. O my lord, if my duty be too bold, my love is too unmannerly.°

HAMLET. I do not well understand that. Will you play upon this pipe?

---

271. *frame:* order, control. 282. *wholesome:* sane. 286. *admiration:* wonder. 293. *pickers and stealers:* i.e., hands (with reference to the prayer; "Keep my hands from picking and stealing"). 296. *advancement:* promotion. 299. *proverb:* ("While the grass groweth, the horse starveth"). 300. *withdraw:* speak in private. 301. *recover the wind:* get the windward side (as in hunting). 301. *toil:* snare. 302. *if my duty . . . too unmannerly:* i.e., if these questions seem rude, it is because my love for you leads me beyond good manners.

GUILDENSTERN. My lord, I cannot.
HAMLET. I pray you. 305
GUILDENSTERN. Believe me, I cannot.
HAMLET. I pray you.
GUILDENSTERN. Believe me, I cannot.
HAMLET. I do beseech you.
GUILDENSTERN. I know no touch of it, my lord. 310
HAMLET. It is as easy as lying. Govern these ventages° with your fingers and thumb,
    give it breath with your mouth, and it will discourse most eloquent music. Look
    you, these are the stops.
GUILDENSTERN. But these cannot I command to any utt'rance of harmony; I have
    not the skill. 315
HAMLET. Why, look you now, how unworthy a thing you make of me! You would
    play upon me; you would seem to know my stops; you would pluck out the
    heart of my mystery; you would sound me from my lowest note to the top of
    my compass;° and there is much music, excellent voice, in this little organ,° yet
    cannot you make it speak. 'Sblood, do you think I am easier to be played on 320
    than a pipe? Call me what instrument you will, though you can fret° me, you
    cannot play upon me.

        Enter POLONIUS.

    God bless you, sir!
POLONIUS. My lord, the Queen would speak with you, and presently.
HAMLET. Do you see yonder cloud that's almost in shape of a camel? 325
POLONIUS. By th' mass and 'tis, like a camel indeed.
HAMLET. Methinks it is like a weasel.
POLONIUS. It is backed like a weasel.
HAMLET. Or like a whale.
POLONIUS. Very like a whale. 330
HAMLET. Then I will come to my mother by and by. [*Aside*] They fool me to the
    top of my bent.°—I will come by and by.°
POLONIUS. I will say so. *Exit.*
HAMLET. "By and by" is easily said. Leave me, friends. *Exeunt all but* HAMLET.
    'Tis now the very witching time of night, 335
    When churchyards yawn, and hell itself breathes out
    Contagion to this world. Now could I drink hot blood
    And do such bitter business as the day
    Would quake to look on. Soft, now to my mother.
    O heart, lost not thy nature; let not ever 340

---

311. *ventages:* vents, stops on a recorder. 319. *compass:* range of voice. 319. *organ:* i.e., the
recorder. 321. *fret:* vex (with a pun alluding to the frets, or ridges, that guide the fingering on
some instruments). 331–332. *They fool . . . my bent:* they compel me to play the fool to the limit of
my capacity. 332. *by and by:* very soon.

The soul of Nero° enter this firm bosom.
Let me be cruel, not unnatural;
I will speak daggers to her, but use none.
My tongue and soul in this be hypocrites:
How in my words somever she be shent,°   345
To give them seals° never, my soul, consent!   *Exit.*

SCENE III.   *The castle.*

Enter King, ROSENCRANTZ, *and* GUILDENSTERN.

KING. I like him not, nor stands it safe with us
    To let his madness range. Therefore prepare you.
    I your commission will forthwith dispatch,
    And he to England shall along with you.
    The terms° of our estate may not endure   5
    Hazard so near's° as doth hourly grow
    Out of his brows.
GUILDENSTERN.   We will ourselves provide.
    Most holy and religious fear it is
    To keep those many many bodies safe
    That live and feed upon your Majesty.   10
ROSENCRANTZ. The single and peculiar° life is bound
    With all the strength and armor of the mind
    To keep itself from noyance,° but much more
    That spirit upon whose weal depends and rests
    The lives of many. The cess of majesty°   15
    Dies not alone, but with a gulf° doth draw
    What's near it with it; or it is a massy wheel
    Fixed on the summit of the highest mount,
    To whose huge spokes ten thousand lesser things
    Are mortised and adjoined, which when it falls,   20
    Each small annexment, petty consequence,
    Attends° the boist'rous ruin. Never alone
    Did the King sigh, but with a general groan.
KING. Arm° you, I pray you, to this speedy voyage,
    For we will fetters put about this fear,   25
    Which now goes too free-footed.
ROSENCRANTZ.   We will haste us.   *Exeunt Gentlemen.*

341. *Nero:* (Roman emperor who had his mother murdered). 345. *shent:* rebuked.
346. *give them seals:* confirm them with deeds. SCENE III. 5. *terms:* conditions. 6. *near's:* near us.
11. *peculiar:* individual, private. 13. *noyance:* injury. 15. *cess of majesty:* cessation (death) of a king.
16. *gulf:* whirlpool. 22. *Attends:* waits on, participates in.   24 *Arm:* prepare.

Enter POLONIUS.

POLONIUS. My lord, he's going to his mother's closet.°
    Behind the arras I'll convey myself
    To hear the process.° I'll warrant she'll tax him home,°
    And, as you said, and wisely was it said,   30
    'Tis meet that some more audience than a mother,
    Since nature makes them partial, should o'erhear
    The speech of vantage.° Fare you well, my liege.
    I'll call upon you ere you go to bed
    And tell you what I know.
KING.   Thanks, dear my lord.   *Exit* [POLONIUS].   35
    O, my offense is rank, it smells to heaven;
    It hath the primal eldest curse° upon't,
    A brother's murder. Pray can I not,
    Though inclination be as sharp as will.
    My stronger guilt defeats my strong intent,   40
    And like a man to double business bound
    I stand in pause where I shall first begin,
    And both neglect. What if this cursèd hand
    Were thicker than itself with brother's blood,
    Is there not rain enough in the sweet heavens   45
    To wash it white as snow? Whereto serves mercy
    But to confront° the visage of offense?
    And what's in prayer but this twofold force,
    To be forestallèd ere we come to fall,
    Or pardoned being down? Then I'll look up.   50
    My fault is past. But, O, what form of prayer
    Can serve my turn? "Forgive me my foul murder"?
    That cannot be, since I am still possessed
    Of those effects° for which I did the murder,
    My crown, mine own ambition, and my queen.   55
    May one be pardoned and retain th' offense?
    In the corrupted currents of this world
    Offense's gilded hand may shove my justice,
    And oft 'tis seen the wicked prize itself
    Buys out the law. But 'tis not so above.   60
    There is no shuffling;° there the action lies
    In his true nature, and we ourselves compelled,
    Even to the teeth and forehead of our faults,

---

27. *closet:* private room. 29. *process:* proceedings. 29. *tax him home:* censure him sharply.
33. *of vantage:* from an advantageous place. 37. *primal eldest curse:* (curse of Cain, who killed
Abel). 47. *confront:* oppose. 54. *effects:* things gained. 61. *shuffling:* trickery.

To give in evidence. What then? What rests?°
Try what repentance can. What can it not? 65
Yet what can it when one cannot repent?
O wretched state! O bosom black as death!
O limèd° soul, that struggling to be free
Art more engaged!° Help, angels! Make assay.°
Bow, stubborn knees, and, heart with strings of steel, 70
Be soft as sinews of the newborn babe.
All may be well. [*He kneels.*]

Enter HAMLET.

HAMLET. Now might I do it pat, now 'a is a-praying,
And now I'll do't. And so 'a goes to heaven,
And so am I revenged. That would be scanned.° 75
A villain kills my father, and for that
I, his sole son, do this same villain send
To heaven.
Why, this is hire and salary, not revenge.
'A took my father grossly, full of bread,° 80
With all his crimes broad blown,° as flush° as May;
And how his audit° stands, who knows save heaven?
But in our circumstance and course of thought,
'Tis heavy with him; and am I then revenged,
To take him in the purging of his soul, 85
When he is fit and seasoned for his passage?
No.
Up, sword, and know thou a more horrid hent.°
When he is drunk asleep, or in his rage,
Or in th' incestuous pleasure of his bed, 90
At game a-swearing, or about some act
That has no relish° of salvation in't—
Then trip him, that his heels may kick at heaven,
And that his soul may be as damned and black
As hell, whereto it goes. My mother stays. 95
This physic° but prolongs thy sickly days. *Exit.*
KING. [*Rises*] My words fly up, my thoughts remain below.
Words without thoughts never to heaven go. *Exit.*

---

64. *rests:* remains. 68. *limèd:* caught (as with birdlime, a sticky substance spread on boughs to snare birds). 69. *engaged:* ensnared. 69. *assay:* an attempt. 75. *would be scanned:* ought to be looked into. 80. *bread:* i.e., worldly gratification. 81. *crimes broad blown:* sins in full bloom. 81. *flush:* vigorous. 82. *audit:* account. 88. *hent:* grasp (here, occasion for seizing). 92. *relish:* flavor. 96. *physic:* (Claudius' purgation by prayer, as Hamlet thinks in line 85).

SCENE IV. *The Queen's closet.*

Enter [*Queen*] GERTRUDE *and* POLONIUS.

POLONIUS. 'A will come straight. Look you lay home° to him.
Tell him his pranks have been too broad° to bear with,
And that your Grace hath screened and stood between
Much heat and him. I'll silence me even here.
Pray you be round with him.   5
HAMLET. [*Within*] Mother, Mother, Mother!
QUEEN. I'll warrant you; fear me not. Withdraw; I hear him coming. [POLONIUS
hides behind the arras.]

Enter HAMLET.

HAMLET. Now, Mother, what's the matter?
QUEEN. Hamlet, thou hast thy father much offended.
HAMLET. Mother, you have my father much offended.   10
QUEEN. Come, come, you answer with an idle° tongue.
HAMLET. Go, go, you question with a wicked tongue.
QUEEN. Why, how now, Hamlet?
HAMLET.   What's the matter now?
QUEEN. Have you forgot me?
HAMLET.   No, by the rood,° not so!
You are the Queen, your husband's brother's wife,   15
And, would it were not so, you are my mother.
QUEEN. Nay, then I'll set those to you that can speak.
HAMLET. Come, come, and sit you down. You shall not budge.
You go not till I set you up a glass°
Where you may see the inmost part of you!   20
QUEEN. What wilt thou do? Thou wilt not murder me?
Help, ho!
POLONIUS. [*Behind*] What, ho! Help!
HAMLET. [*Draws*] How now? A rat? Dead for a ducat, dead!

[*Makes a pass through the arras and*] *kills* POLONIUS.

POLONIUS. [*Behind*] O, I am slain!
QUEEN.   O me, what has thou done?   25
HAMLET. Nay, I know not. Is it the King?
QUEEN. O, what a rash and bloody deed is this!
HAMLET. A bloody deed—almost as bad, good Mother,
As kill a king, and marry with his brother.
QUEEN. As kill a king?

SCENE IV. 1. *lay home:* thrust (rebuke) him sharply. 2. *broad:* unrestrained. 11. *idle:* foolish.
14. *rood:* cross. 19. *glass:* mirror.

HAMLET.   Ay, lady, it was my word.   30

Lifts up the arras and sees POLONIUS.

Thou wretched, rash, intruding fool, farewell!
I took thee for thy better. Take thy fortune.
Thou find'st to be too busy is some danger.—
Leave wringing of your hands. Peace, sit you down
And let me wring your heart, for so I shall   35
If it be made of penetrable stuff,
If damnèd custom have not brazed° it so
That it be proof° and bulwark against sense.°
QUEEN. What have I done that thou dar'st wag thy tongue
In noise so rude against me?
HAMLET.   Such an act   40
That blurs the grace and blush of modesty,
Calls virtue hypocrite, takes off the rose
From the fair forehead of an innocent love,
And sets a blister° there, makes marriage vows
As false as dicers' oaths. O, such a deed   45
As from the body of contraction° plucks
The very soul, and sweet religion makes
A rhapsody° of words! Heaven's face does glow
O'er this solidity and compound mass
With heated visage, as against the doom   50
Is thoughtsick at the act.°
QUEEN.   Ay me, what act,
That roars so loud and thunders in the index?°
HAMLET. Look here upon this picture, and on this,
The counterfeit presentment° of two brothers.
See what a grace was seated on this brow: 55
Hyperion's curls, the front° of Jove himself,
An eye like Mars, to threaten and command,
A station° like the herald Mercury
New lighted on a heaven-kissing hill—
A combination and a form indeed   60
Where every god did seem to set his seal
To give the world assurance of a man.
This was your husband. Look you now what follows.

---

37. *brazed:* hardened like brass. 38. *proof:* armor. 38. *sense:* feeling. 44. *sets a blister:* brands (as a
harlot). 46. *contraction:* marriage contract. 48. *rhapsody:* senseless string. 48–51. *Heaven's face . . .
the act:* i.e., the face of heaven blushes over this earth (compounded of four elements), the face hot,
as if Judgment Day were near, and it is thoughtsick at the act. 52. *index:* prologue. 54. *counterfeit
presentment:* represented image. 56. *front:* forehead. 58. *station:* bearing.

Here is your husband, like a mildewed ear
Blasting his wholesome brother. Have you eyes?   65
Could you on this fair mountain leave to feed,
And batten° on this moor? Ha! Have you eyes?
You cannot call it love, for at your age
The heyday° in the blood is tame, it's humble,
And waits upon the judgment, and what judgment   70
Would step from this to this? Sense° sure you have,
Else could you not have motion, but sure that sense
Is apoplexed,° for madness would not err,
Nor sense to ecstasy° was ne'er so thralled
But it reserved some quantity of choice   75
To serve in such a difference. What devil was't
That thus hath cozened you at hoodman-blind?°
Eyes without feeling, feeling without sight,
Ears without hands or eyes, smelling sans° all,
Or but a sickly part of one true sense   80
Could not so mope.°
O shame, where is thy blush? Rebellious hell,
If thou canst mutine in a matron's bones,
To flaming youth let virtue be as wax
And melt in her own fire. Proclaim no shame   85
When the compulsive ardor° gives the charge,
Since frost itself as actively doth burn,
And reason panders will.°
QUEEN.   O Hamlet, speak no more.
Thou turn'st mine eyes into my very soul,
And there I see such black and grainèd° spots   90
As will not leave their tinct.°
HAMLET.   Nay, but to live
In the rank sweat of an enseamèd° bed,
Stewed in corruption, honeying and making love
Over the nasty sty——
QUEEN.   O, speak to me no more.
These words like daggers enter in my ears.   95
No more, sweet Hamlet.
HAMLET.   A murderer and a villain,
A slave that is not twentieth part the tithe°
Of your precedent lord, a vice° of kings,

---

67. *batten:* feed gluttonously. 69. *heyday:* excitement. 71. *Sense:* feeling. 73. *apoplexed:* paralyzed.
74. *ecstasy:* madness. 77. *cozened you at hoodman-blind:* cheated you at blindman's buff. 79. *sans:*
without. 81. *mope:* be stupid. 86. *compulsive ardor:* compelling passion. 88. *reason panders will:*
reason acts as a procurer for desire. 90. *grainèd:* dye in grain (fast dyed). 91. *tinct:* color.
92. *enseamèd:* (perhaps "soaked in grease," i.e., sweaty; perhaps "much wrinkled"). 97. *tithe:* tenth
part. 98. *vice:* (like the Vice, a fool and mischief-maker in the old morality plays).

A cutpurse of the empire and the rule,
That from a shelf the precious diadem stole   100
And put it in his pocket——
QUEEN.   No more.

Enter GHOST.

HAMLET. A king of shreds and patches—
  Save me and hover o'er me with your wings,
  You heavenly guards! What would your gracious figure?
QUEEN. Alas, he's mad.   105
HAMLET. Do you not come your tardy son to chide,
  That, lapsed in time and passion, lets go by
  Th' important acting of your dread command?
  O, say!
GHOST. Do not forget. This visitation   110
  Is but to whet thy almost blunted purpose.
  But look, amazement on thy mother sits.
  O, step between her and her fighting soul!
  Conceit° in weakest bodies strongest works.
  Speak to her, Hamlet.
HAMLET.   How is it with you, lady?   115
QUEEN. Alas, how is't with you,
  That you do bend your eye on vacancy,
  And with th' incorporal° air do hold discourse?
  Forth at your eyes your spirits wildly peep,
  And as the sleeping soldiers in th' alarm   120
  Your bedded hair° like life in excrements°
  Start up and stand an end.° O gentle son,
  Upon the heat and flame of thy distemper
  Sprinkle cool patience. Whereon do you look?
HAMLET. On him, on him! Look you, how pale he glares!   125
  His form and cause conjoined, preaching to stones,
  Would make them capable.°—Do not look upon me,
  Lest with this piteous action you convert
  My stern effects.° Then what I have to do
  Will want true color; tears perchance for blood.   130
QUEEN. To whom do you speak this?
HAMLET.   Do you see nothing there?
QUEEN. Nothing at all; yet all that is I see.
HAMLET. Nor did you nothing hear?
QUEEN.   No, nothing but ourselves.

114. *Conceit:* imagination. 118. *incorporal:* bodiless. 121. *bedded hair:* hairs laid flat.
121. *excrements:* outgrowths (here, the hair). 122. *an end:* on end. 127. *capable:* receptive.
128–129. *convert/My stern effects:* divert my stern deeds.

HAMLET. Why, look you there! Look how it steals away!
    My father, in his habit° as he lived! 135
    Look where he goes even now out at the portal!   *Exit* GHOST.
QUEEN. This is the very coinage of your brain.
    This bodiless creation ecstacy
    Is very cunning in.
HAMLET.   Ecstacy?
    My pulse as yours doth temperately keep time 140
    And makes as healthful music. It is not madness
    That I have uttered. Bring me to the test,
    And I the matter will reword, which madness
    Would gambol° from. Mother, for love of grace,
    Lay not that flattering unction° to your soul, 145
    That not your trespass but my madness speaks.
    It will but skin and film the ulcerous place
    Whiles rank corruption, mining° all within,
    Infects unseen. Confess yourself to heaven,
    Repent what's past, avoid what is to come, 150
    And do not spread the compost° on the weeds
    To make them ranker. Forgive me this my virtue.
    For in the fatness of these pursy° times
    Virtue itself of vice must pardon beg,
    Yea, curb° and woo for leave to do him good. 155
QUEEN. O Hamlet, thou hast cleft my heart in twain.
HAMLET. O, throw away the worser part of it,
    And live the purer with the other half.
    Good night—but go not to my uncle's bed.
    Assume a virtue, if you have it not. 160
    That monster custom, who all sense doth eat,
    Of habits devil, is angel yet in this,
    That to the use° of actions fair and good
    He likewise gives a frock or livery°
    That aptly is put on. Refrain tonight, 165
    And that shall lend a kind of easiness
    To the next abstinence; the next more easy;
    For use almost can change the stamp of nature,
    And either° the devil, or throw him out
With wondrous potency. Once more, good night, 170

---

135. *habit:* garment (Q1, though a "bad" quarto, is probably correct in saying that at line 101 the ghost enters "in his nightgown," i.e., dressing gown). 144. *gambol:* start away. 145. *unction:* ointment. 148. *mining:* undermining. 151. *compost:* fertilizing substance. 153. *pursy:* bloated. 155. *curb:* bow low. 163. *use:* practice. 164. *livery:* characteristic garment (punning on "habits" in line 162). 169. *either:* (probably a word is missing after *either;* among suggestions are "master," "curb," and "house"; but possibly *either* is a verb meaning "make easier").

And when you are desirous to be blest,
I'll blessing beg of you.—For this same lord,
I do repent; but heaven hath pleased it so,
To punish me with this, and this with me,
That I must be their° scourge and minister.   175
I will bestow° him and will answer well
The death I gave him. So again, good night.
I must be cruel only to be kind.
Thus bad begins, and worse remains behind.
One word more, good lady.
QUEEN.   What shall I do?   180
HAMLET. Not this, by no means, that I bid you do:
Let the bloat King tempt you again to bed,
Pinch wanton on your cheek, call you his mouse,
And let him, for a pair of reechy° kisses,
Or paddling in your neck with his damned fingers,   185
Make you to ravel° all this matter out,
That I essentially am not in madness,
But mad in craft. 'Twere good you let him know,
For who that's but a queen, fair, sober, wise,
Would from a paddock,° from a bat, a gib,°   190
Such dear concernings hide? Who would do so?
No, in despite of sense and secrecy,
Unpeg the basket on the house's top,
Let the birds fly, and like the famous ape,
To try conclusions,° in the basket creep   195
And break your own neck down.
QUEEN. Be thou assured, if words be made of breath,
And breath of life, I have no life to breathe
What thou hast said to me.
HAMLET. I must to England; you know that?
QUEEN.   Alack,   200
I had forgot. 'Tis so concluded on.
HAMLET. There's letters sealed, and my two school fellows,
Whom I will trust as I will adders fanged,
They bear the mandate;° they must sweep my way
And marshall me to knavery. Let it work;   205
For 'tis the sport to have the enginer
Hoist with his own petar,° and 't shall go hard
But I will delve one yard below their mines

175. *their:* i.e., the heavens'. 176. *bestow:* stow, lodge. 184. *reechy:* foul (literally "smoky").
186. *ravel:* unravel, reveal. 190. *paddock:* toad. 190. *gib:* tomcat. 195. *To try conclusions:* to
make experiments. 204. *mandate:* command. 207. *petar:* bomb.

And blow them at the moon. O, 'tis most sweet
When in one line two crafts° directly meet.   210
This man shall set me packing:
I'll lug the guts into the neighbor room.
Mother, good night. Indeed, this counselor
Is now most still, most secret, and most grave,
Who was in life a foolish prating knave.   215
Come, sir, to draw toward an end with you.
Good night, Mother.

> [*Exit the Queen. Then*] *exit* HAMLET, *tugging in* POLONIUS.

ACT IV

SCENE I. The castle.

Enter King and Queen, with ROSENCRANTZ *and* GUILDENSTERN.

KING. There's a matter in these sighs. These profound heaves
   You must translate; 'tis fit we understand them.
   Where is your son?
QUEEN. Bestow this place on us a little while.

> *Exeunt* ROSENCRANTZ *and* GUILDENSTERN.

   Ah, mine own lord, what have I seen tonight!   5
KING. What, Gertrude? How does Hamlet?
QUEEN. Mad as the sea and wind when both contend
   Which is the mightier. In his lawless fit,
   Behind the arras hearing something stir,
   Whips out his rapier, cries, "A rat, a rat!"   10
   And in this brainish apprehension° kills
   The unseen good old man.
KING.   O heavy deed!
   It had been so with us, had we been there.
   His liberty is full of threats to all,
   To you yourself, to us, to every one.   15
   Alas, how shall this bloody deed be answered?
   It will be laid to us, whose providence°
   Should have kept short, restrained, and out of haunt°
   This mad young man. But so much was our love
   We would not understand what was most fit,   20
   But, like the owner of a foul disease,

---

210. *crafts:* (1) boats, (2) acts of guile, crafty schemes. SCENE I. 11. *brainish apprehension:* mad imagination. 17. *providence:* foresight. 18. *out of haunt:* away from association with others.

To keep it from divulging, let it feed
Even on the pith of life. Where is he gone?
QUEEN. To draw apart the body he hath killed;
  O'er whom his very madness, like some ore   25
  Among a mineral° of metals base,
  Shows itself pure. 'A weeps for what is done.
KING. O Gertrude, come away!
  The sun no sooner shall the mountains touch
  But we will ship him hence, and this vile deed   30
  We must will all our majesty and skill
  Both countenance and excuse. Ho, Guildenstern!

Enter ROSENCRANTZ *and* GUILDENSTERN.

Friends both, go join you with some further aid:
Hamlet in madness hath Polonius slain,
And from his mother's closet hath he dragged him.   35
Go seek him out; speak fair, and bring the body
Into the chapel. I pray you haste in this.   *Exeunt* ROSENCRANTZ *and*
    GUILDENSTERN.
Come, Gertrude, we'll call up our wisest friends
And let them know both what we mean to do
And what's untimely done . . .°   40
Whose whisper o'er the world's diameter,
As level as the cannon to his blank°
Transport his poisoned shot, may miss our name
And hit the woundless° air, O, come away!
My soul is full of discord and dismay.   *Exeunt.*   45

SCENE II. *The castle.*

Enter HAMLET.

HAMLET. Safely stowed.
GENTLEMEN. [*Within*] Hamlet! Lord Hamlet!
HAMLET. But soft, what noise? Who calls on Hamlet?
  O, here they come.

Enter ROSENCRANTZ *and* GUILDENSTERN.

ROSENCRANTZ. What have you done, my lord, with the dead body?   5
HAMLET. Compounded it with dust, whereto 'tis kin.
ROSENCRANTZ. Tell us where 'tis, that we may take it thence
  And bear it to the chapel.

25–26. *ore / Among a mineral:* vein of gold in a mine. 40. *Done . . . :* (evidently something has dropped out of the text. Capell's conjecture, "So, haply slander," is usually printed). 42. *Blank:* white center of a target. 44. *woundless:* invulnerable.

HAMLET. Do not believe it.

ROSENCRANTZ. Believe what? 10

HAMLET. That I can keep your counsel and not mine own. Besides, to be demanded
of° a sponge, what replication° should be made by the son of a king?

ROSENCRANTZ. Take you me for a sponge, my lord?

HAMLET. Ay, sir, that soaks up the King's countenance,° his rewards, his authorities.
But such officers do the King best service in the end. He keeps them, like an 15
ape, in the corner of his jaw, first mouthed, to be last swallowed. When he needs
what you have gleaned, it is but squeezing you and, sponge, you shall be dry
again.

ROSENCRANTZ. I understand you not, my lord.

HAMLET. I am glad of it: a knavish speech sleeps in a foolish ear. 20

ROSENCRANTZ. My lord, you must tell us where the body is and go with us to the
King.

HAMLET. The body is with the King, but the King is not with the body. The King
is a thing——

GUILDENSTERN. A thing, my lord? 25

HAMLET. Of nothing. Bring me to him. Hide fox, and all after.° *Exeunt.*

SCENE III. *The castle.*

Enter King, and two or three.

KING. I have sent to seek him and to find the body:
How dangerous is it that this man goes loose!
Yet must not we put the strong law on him:
He's loved of the distracted° multitude,
Who like not in their judgment, but their eyes, 5
And where 'tis so, th' offender's scourge is weighed,
But never the offense. To bear° all smooth and even,
This sudden sending him away must seem
Deliberate pause.° Diseases desperate grown
By desperate appliance are relieved, 10
Or not at all.

      Enter ROSENCRANTZ, GUILDENSTERN, *and all the rest.*

      How now? What hath befall'n?

ROSENCRANTZ. Where the dead body is bestowed, my lord,
We cannot get from him.

KING.   But where is he?

SCENE II. 11–12 *demanded of:* questioned by. 12. *replication:* reply. 14. *countenance:* favor.
26. *Hide fox, and all after:* (a cry in a game such as hide-and-seek; Hamlet runs from the stage).
SCENE III. 4. *distracted:* bewildered, senseless. 7. *bear:* carry out. 9. *pause:* planning.

ROSENCRANTZ. Without, my lord; guarded, to know your pleasure.
KING. Bring him before us.
ROSENCRANTZ.   Ho! Bring in the lord.   15

They enter.

KING. Now, Hamlet, where's Polonius?
HAMLET. At supper.
KING. At supper? Where?
HAMLET. Not where he eats, but where 'a is eaten. A certain convocation of politic°
worms are e'en at him. Your worm is your only emperor for diet. We fat all   20
creatures else to fat us, and we fat ourselves for maggots. Your fat king and your
lean beggar is but variable service° —two dishes, but to one table. That's the
end.
KING. Alas, alas!
HAMLET. A man may fish with the worm that hath eat of a king, and eat of the fish   25
that hath fed of that worm.
KING. What dost thou mean by this?
HAMLET. Nothing but to show you how a king may go a progress° through the guts
of a beggar.
KING. Where is Polonius?   30
HAMLET. In heaven. Send thither to see. If your messenger find him not there, seek
him i' th' other place yourself. But if indeed you find him not within this
month, you shall nose him as you go up the stairs into the lobby.
KING. [*To Attendants*] Go seek him there.
HAMLET. 'A will stay till you come. *Exeunt Attendants.*   35
KING. Hamlet, this deed, for thine especial safety,
Which we do tender° as we dearly grieve
For that which thou hast done, must send thee hence
With fiery quickness. Therefore prepare thyself.
The bark is ready and the wind at help,   40
Th' associates tend,° and everything is bent
For England.
HAMLET.   For England?
KING.   Ay, Hamlet.
HAMLET.   Good.
KING. So is it, if thou knew'st our purposes.
HAMLET. I see a cherub° that sees them. But come, for England! Farewell, dear
Mother.
KING. Thy loving father, Hamlet.   45
HAMLET. My mother—father and mother is man and wife, man and wife is one
flesh, and so, my mother. Come, for England! *Exit.*

---

19. *politic:* statesmanlike, shrewd. 22. *variable service:* different courses. 28. *progress:* royal journey.
37. *tender:* hold dear. 41. *tend:* wait. 44. *cherub:* angel of knowledge.

KING. Follow him at foot;° tempt him with speed aboard.
  Delay it not; I'll have him hence tonight.
  Away! For everything is sealed and done   50
  That else leans° on th' affair. Pray you make haste. *Exeunt all but the King.*
  And, England, if my love thou hold'st at aught—
  As my great power thereof may give thee sense,
  Since yet thy cicatrice° looks raw and red
  After the Danish sword, and thy free awe°   55
  Pays homage to us—thou mayst not coldly set
  Our sovereign process,° which imports at full
  By letters congruing to that effect
  The present° death of Hamlet. Do it, England,
  For like the hectic° in my blood he rages,   60
  And thou must cure me. Till I know 'tis done,
  Howe'er my haps,° my joys were ne'er begun. *Exit.*

SCENE IV. *A plain in Denmark.*

Enter FORTINBRAS *with his Army over the stage.*

FORTINBRAS. Go, Captain, from me greet the Danish king.
  Tell him that by his license Fortinbras
  Craves the conveyance of° a promised march
  Over his kingdom. You know the rendezvous.
  If that his Majesty would aught with us,   5
  We shall express our duty in his eye;°
  And let him know so.
CAPTAIN.   I will do't, my lord.
FORTINBRAS. Go softly° on. *Exeunt all but the Captain.*

Enter HAMLET, ROSENCRANTZ, &c.

HAMLET. Good sir, whose powers° are these?
CAPTAIN. They are of Norway, sir.   10
HAMLET. How purposed, sir, I pray you?
CAPTAIN. Against some part of Poland.
HAMLET. Who commands them, sir?
CAPTAIN. The nephew to old Norway, Fortinbras.
HAMLET. Goes it against the main° of Poland, sir,   15
  Or for some frontier?

---

48. *at foot:* closely. 51. *leans:* depends. 54. *cicatrice:* scar. 55. *free awe:* uncompelled submission. 56–57 *coldly set / Our sovereign process:* regard slightly our royal command. 59. *present:* instant. 60. *hectic:* fever. 62. *haps:* chances, fortunes. SCENE IV. 3. *conveyance of:* escort for. 6. *in his eye:* before his eyes (i.e., in his presence). 8. *softly:* slowly. 9. *powers:* forces. 15. *main:* main part.

CAPTAIN. Truly to speak, and with no addition,°
  We go to gain a little patch of ground
  That hath in it no profit but the name.
  To pay five ducats, five, I would not farm it,   20
  Nor will it yield to Norway or the Pole
  A ranker° rate, should it be sold in fee.°
HAMLET. Why, then the Polack never will defend it.
CAPTAIN. Yes, it is already garrisoned.
HAMLET. Two thousand souls and twenty thousand ducats   25
  Will not debate° the question of this straw.
  This is th' imposthume° of much wealth and peace,
  That inward breaks, and shows no cause without
  Why the man dies. I humbly thank you, sir.
CAPTAIN. God bye you, sir. [*Exit.*]
ROSENCRANTZ.   Will't please you go, my lord?   30
HAMLET. I'll be with you straight. Go a little before.   *Exeunt all but* HAMLET.
  How all occasions do inform against me
  And spur my dull revenge! What is a man,
  If his chief good and market° of his time
  Be but to sleep and feed? A beast, no more.   35
  Sure he that made us with such large discourse,°
  Looking before and after, gave us not
  That capability and godlike reason
  To fust° in us unused. Now, whether it be
  Bestial oblivion,° or some craven scruple   40
  Of thinking too precisely on th' event°—
  A thought which, quartered, hath but one part wisdom
  And ever three parts coward—I do not know
  Why yet I live to say, "This thing's to do,"
  Sith I have cause, and will, and strength, and means   45
  To do't. Examples gross° as earth exhort me.
  Witness this army of such mass and charge,°
  Led by a delicate and tender prince,
  Whose spirit, with divine ambition puffed,
  Makes mouths at the invisible event,°   50
  Exposing what is mortal and unsure
  To all that fortune, death, and danger dare,
  Even for an eggshell. Rightly to be great

---

17. *with no addition:* plainly. 22. *ranker:* higher. 22. *in fee:* outright. 26. *debate:* settle.
27. *imposthume:* abscess, ulcer. 34. *market:* profits. 36. *discourse:* understanding. 39. *fust:* grow
moldy. 40. *oblivion:* forgetfulness. 41. *event:* outcome. 46. *gross:* large, obvious. 47. *charge:*
expense. 50. *Makes mouths at the invisible event:* makes scornful faces (is contemptuous of) the
unseen outcome.

Is not° to stir without great argument,°
But greatly° to find quarrel in a straw   55
When honor's at the stake. How stand I then,
That have a father killed, a mother stained,
Excitements° of my reason and my blood,
And let all sleep, while to my shame I see
The imminent death of twenty thousand men   60
That for a fantasy and trick of fame°
Go to their graves like beds, fight for a plot
Whereon the numbers cannot try the cause,
Which is not tomb enough and continent°
To hide the slain? O, from this time forth,   65
My thoughts be bloody, or be nothing worth!   *Exit.*

SCENE V.   *The castle.*

Enter HORATIO, [*Queen*] GERTRUDE, *and a Gentleman.*

QUEEN.   I will not speak with her.
GENTLEMAN.   She is importunate, indeed distract.
   Her mood will needs be pitied.
QUEEN.   What would she have?
GENTLEMAN.   She speaks much of her father, says she hears
   There's tricks i' th' world, and hems, and beats her heart,   5
   Spurns enviously at straws,° speaks things in doubt°
   That carry but half sense. Her speech is nothing,
   Yet the unshapèd use of it doth move
   The hearers to collection;° they yawn° at it,
   And botch the words up fit to their own thoughts,   10
   Which, as her winks and nods and gestures yield them,
   Indeed would make one think there might be thought,
   Though nothing sure, yet much unhappily.
HORATIO.   'Twere good she were spoken with, for she may strew
   Dangerous conjectures in ill-breeding minds.   15
QUEEN.   Let her come in. [*Exit Gentleman.*]
   [*Aside*] To my sick soul (as sin's true nature is)
   Each toy seems prologue to some great amiss;°
   So full of artless jealousy° is guilt
   It spills° itself in fearing to be spilt.   20

54. *not:* (the sense seems to require "not not"). 54. *argument:* reason. 55. *greatly:* i.e., nobly. 58. *Excitement:* incentives. 61. *fantasy and trick of fame:* illusion and trifle of reputation. 64. *continent:* receptacle, container. SCENE V. 6. *Spurns enviously at straws:* objects spitefully to insignificant matters. 6. *in doubt:* uncertainly. 8–9 *Yet the . . . to collection:* i.e., yet the formless manner of it moves her listeners to gather up some sort of meaning. 9. *yawn:* gape (?). 18. *amiss:* misfortune. 19. *artless jealousy:* crude suspicion. 20. *spills:* destroys.

Enter OPHELIA [*distracted.*]

OPHELIA. Where is the beauteous majesty of Denmark?
QUEEN. How now, Ophelia?
OPHELIA. [*She sings.*] How should I your truelove know
      From another one?
    By his cockle hat° and staff   25
      And his sandal shoon.°
QUEEN. Alas, sweet lady, what imports this song?
OPHELIA. Say you? Nay, pray you mark.
    He is dead and gone, lady, [*Song*]
      He is dead and gone;   30
    At his head a grass-green turf,
      At his heels a stone,
 O, ho!
QUEEN. Nay, but Ophelia——
OPHELIA. Pray you mark.   35
  [*Sings.*] White his shroud as the mountain snow——

Enter King.

QUEEN. Alas, look here, my lord.
OPHELIA.   Larded° all with sweet flowers [*Song*]
    Which bewept to the grave did not go
      With truelove showers.   40
KING. How do you, pretty lady?
OPHELIA. Well, God dild° you! They say the owl was a baker's daughter.° Lord, we
    know what we are, but know not what we may be. God be at your table!
KING. Conceit° upon her father.
OPHELIA. Pray let's have not words of this, but when they ask you what it means, 45
    say you this:
    Tomorrow is Saint Valentine's day.° [*Song*]
      All in the morning betime,
    And I a maid at your window,
      To be your Valentine.   50

  Then up he rose and donned his clothes
    And dupped° the chamber door,
  Let in the maid, that out a maid
    Never departed more.

---

25. *cockle hat:* (a cockleshell on the hat was the sign of a pilgrim who had journeyed to shrines
overseas. The association of lovers and pilgrims was a common one). 26. *shoon:* shoes.
38. *Larded:* decorated. 42. *dild:* yield, i.e., reward. 42. *baker's daughter:* (an allusion to a tale of a
baker's daughter who begrudged bread to Christ and was turned into an owl). 44. *Conceit:*
brooding. 47. *Saint Valentine's day:* Feb. 14 (the notion was that a bachelor would become the
truelove of the first girl he saw on this day). 52. *dupped:* opened (did up).

KING.   Pretty Ophelia.   55
OPHELIA.   Indeed, la, without an oath, I'll make an end on't:
  [*Sings.*] By Gis° and by Saint Charity,
                  Alack, and fie for shame!
              Young men will do't if they come to't,   60
                  By Cock,° they are to blame.
              Quoth she, "Before you tumbled me,
                  You promised me to wed."
        He answers:
                  "So would I 'a' done, by yonder sun,   65
                  An thou hadst not come to my bed."
KING.   How long hath she been thus?
OPHELIA.   I hope all will be well. We must be patient, but I cannot choose but weep
    to think they would lay him i' th' cold ground. My brother shall know of it;
    and so I thank you for your good counsel. Come, my coach! Good night, ladies,   70
    good night. Sweet ladies, good night, good night.   *Exit.*
KING.   Follow her close; give her a good watch, I pray you. [*Exit* HORATIO.]
    O, this is the poison of deep grief; it springs
    All from her father's death—and now behold!
    O Gertrude, Gertrude,   75
    When sorrows come, they come not single spies,
    But in battalions: first, her father slain;
    Next, your son gone, and he most violent author
    Of his own just remove; the people muddied,°
    Thick and unwholesome in their thoughts and whispers   80
    For good Polonius' death, and we have done but greenly°
    In huggermugger° to inter him; poor Ophelia
    Divided from herself and her fair judgment,
    Without the which we are pictures or mere beasts;
    Last, and as much containing as all these,   85
    Her brother is in secret come from France,
    Feeds on his wonder,° keeps himself in clouds,
    And wants not buzzers° to infect his ear
    With pestilent speeches of his father's death,
    Wherein necessity, of matter beggared,°   90
    Will nothing stick° our person to arraign
    In ear and ear. O my dear Gertrude, this,
    Like to a murd'ring piece,° in many places
    Gives me a superfluous death.   *A noise within.*

---

57. *Gis:* (contraction of "Jesus"). 60. *Cock:* (1) God, (2) phallus. 79. *muddied:* muddled.
81. *greenly:* foolishly. 82. *huggermugger:* secret haste. 87. *wonder:* suspicion. 88. *wants not
buzzers:* does not lack talebearers. 90. *of matter beggared:* unprovided with facts. 91. *Will nothing
stick:* will not hesitate. 93. *murd'ring piece:* (a cannon that shot a kind of shrapnel).

Enter a Messenger.

QUEEN.   Alack, what noise is this?
KING. Attend, where are my Switzers?° Let them guard the door.   95
   What is the matter?
MESSENGER.   Save yourself, my lord.
  The ocean, overpeering of his list,°
  Eats not the flats with more impiteous haste
  Than your Laertes, in a riotous head,°
  O'erbears your officers. The rabble call him lord,   100
  And, as the world were now but to begin,
  Antiquity forgot, custom not known,
  The ratifiers and props of every word,
  They cry, "Choose we! Laertes shall be king!"
  Caps, hands, and tongues applaud it to the clouds,   105
  "Laertes shall be king! Laertes King!" *A noise within.*
QUEEN. How cheerfully on the false trail they cry!
  O, this is counter,° you false Danish dogs!

Enter LAERTES *with others.*

KING. The doors are broke.
LAERTES. Where is this king?—Sirs, stand you all without.   110
ALL. No, let's come in.
LAERTES.   I pray you give me leave.
ALL. We will, we will.
LAERTES. I thank you. Keep the door. [*Exeunt his Followers.*] O thou vile King,
  Give me my father.
QUEEN.   Calmly, good Laertes.
LAERTES. That drop of blood that's calm proclaims me bastard,   115
  Cries cuckold° to my father, brands the harlot
  Even here between the chaste unsmirchèd brow
  Of my true mother.
KING.   What is the cause, Laertes,
  That thy rebellion looks so giantlike?
  Let him go, Gertrude. Do not fear° our person.   120
  There's such divinity doth hedge a king
  That treason can but peep to° what it would,
  Acts little of his will. Tell me, Laertes,
  Why thou art thus incensed. Let him go, Gertrude.
  Speak, man.   125

---

95. *Switzers:* Swiss guards. 97. *list:* shore. 99. *in a riotous head:* with a rebellious force.
109. *counter:* (a hound runs counter when he follows the scent backward from the prey).
116. *cuckold:* man whose wife is unfaithful. 120. *fear:* fear for. 122. *peep to:* i.e., look at from a distance.

LAERTES. Where is my father?
KING.   Dead.
QUEEN.   But not by him.
KING. Let him demand his fill.
LAERTES. How came he dead? I'll not be juggled with.
   To hell allegiance, vows to the blackest devil,
   Conscience and grace to the profoundest pit!   130
   I dare damnation. To this point I stand,
   That both the worlds I give to negligence,°
   Let come what comes, only I'll be revenged
   Most throughly for my father.
KING.   Who shall stay you?
LAERTES. My will, not all the world's.   135
   And for my means, I'll husband them° so well
   They shall go far with little.
KING.   Good Laertes,
   If you desire to know the certainty
   Of your dear father, is't writ in your revenge
   That swoopstake° you will draw both friend and foe,   140
   Winner and loser?
LAERTES. None but his enemies.
KING.   Will you know them then?
LAERTES. To his good friends thus wide I'll ope my arms
   And like the kind life-rend'ring pelican°
   Repast° them with my blood.
KING.   Why, now you speak   145
   Like a good child and a true gentleman.
   That I am guiltless of your father's death,
   And am most sensibly° in grief for it,
   It shall as level to your judgment 'pear
   As day does to your eye.   150

             A noise within: "Let her come in."

LAERTES. How now? What noise is that?

                 Enter OPHELIA.

   O heat, dry up my brains; tears seven times salt
   Burn out the sense and virtue° of mine eye!
   By heaven, thy madness shall be paid with weight
   Till our scale turn the beam.° O Rose of May,   155

132. *That both . . . to negligence:* i.e., I care not what may happen (to me) in this world or the next.
136. *husband them:* use them economically. 140. *swoopstake:* in a clean sweep. 144. *pelican:*
(thought to feed its young with its own blood). 145. *Repast:* feed. 148. *sensibly:* acutely.
153. *virtue:* power. 155. *turn the beam:* weigh down the bar (of the balance).

Dear maid, kind sister, sweet Ophelia!
O heavens, is't possible a young maid's wits
Should be as mortal as an old man's life?
Nature is fine° in love, and where 'tis fine,
It sends some precious instance° of itself   160
After the thing it loves.
OPHELIA. They bore him barefaced on the bier [*Song*]
  Hey non nony, nony, hey nony
  And in his grave rained many a tear——
Fare you well, my dove!   165
LAERTES. Hadst thou thy wits, and didst persuade revenge,
 It could not move thus.
OPHELIA. You must sing "A-down a-down, and you call him a-down-a." O, how
 the wheel° becomes it! It is the false steward, that stole his master's daughter.
LAERTES. This nothing's more than matter.°   170
OPHELIA. There's rosemary, that's for remembrance. Pray you, love, remember. And
 there is pansies, that's for thoughts.
LAERTES. A document° in madness, thoughts and remembrance fitted.
OPHELIA. There's fennel° for you, and columbines. There's rue for you, and here's
 some for me. We may call it herb of grace o' Sundays. O, you must wear your   175
 rue with a difference. There's a daisy. I would give you some violets, but they
 withered all when my father died. They say 'a made a good end. [*Sings*]   For
 bonny sweet Robin is all my joy.
LAERTES. Thought and affliction, passion, hell itself,
 She turns to favor° and to prettiness.   180
OPHELIA. And will' a not come again? [*Song*]
  And will 'a not come again?
   No, no, he is dead,
   Go to thy deathbed,
  He never will come again.   185
  His beard was as white as snow,
  All flaxen was his poll.°
   He is gone, he is gone,
   And we cast away moan.
  God 'a' mercy on his soul!   190
And of all Christian souls, I pray God. God bye you. *Exit.*

---

159. *fine:* refined, delicate. 160. *instance:* sample. 169. *wheel:* (of uncertain meaning, but
probably a turn or dance of Ophelia's, rather than Fortune's wheel). 170. *This nothing's more than
matter:* this nonsense has more meaning than matters of consequence. 173. *document:* lesson.
174. *fennel:* (the distribution of flowers in the ensuing lines has symbolic meaning, but the meaning
is disputed. Perhaps *fennel,* flattery; *columbines,* cuckoldry; *rue,* sorrow for Ophelia and repentance
for the Queen; *daisy,* dissembling; *violets,* faithfulness. For other interpretations, see J. W. Lever in
Review of English Studies, New Series 3 [1952], pp. 123–129). 180. *favor:* charm, beauty.
187. *All flaxen was his poll:* white as flax was his head.

LAERTES. Do you see this, O God?
KING. Laertes, I must commune with your grief,
  Or you deny me right. Go but apart,
  Make choice of whom your wisest friends you will,   195
  And they shall hear and judge 'twixt you and me.
  If by direct or by collateral° hand
  They find us touched,° we will our kingdom give,
  Our crown, or life, and all that we call ours,
  To you in satisfaction; but if not,   200
  Be you content to lend your patience to us,
  And we shall jointly labor with your soul
  To give it due content.
LAERTES.   Let this be so.
  His means of death, his obscure funeral—
  No trophy, sword, nor hatchment° o'er his bones,   205
  No noble rite nor formal ostentation°—
  Cry to be heard, as 'twere from heaven to earth,
  That I must call't in question.
KING.   So you shall;
  And where th' offense is, let the great ax fall.
  I pray you go with me. *Exeunt.*   210

SCENE VI. The castle.

Enter HORATIO and others.

HORATIO. What are they that would speak with me?
GENTLEMAN. Seafaring men, sir. They say they have
  letters for you.
HORATIO. Let them come in. [*Exit Attendant.*]
  I do not know from what part of the world   5
  I should be greeted, if not from Lord Hamlet.

Enter Sailors.

SAILOR. God bless you, sir.
HORATIO. Let Him bless thee too.
SAILOR. 'A shall, sir, an't please Him. There's a letter for you, sir—it came from th'
  ambassador that was bound for England—if your name be Horatio, as I am let 10
  to know it is.
HORATIO. [*Reads the letter.*] "Horatio, when thou shalt have overlooked° this, give
  these fellows some means to the King. They have letters for him. Ere we were
  two days old at sea, a pirate of very warlike appointment° gave us chase. Finding

197. *collateral:* indirect. 198. *touched:* implicated. 205. *hatchment:* tablet bearing the coat of arms
of the dead. 206. *ostentation:* ceremony. SCENE VI. 12. *overlooked:* surveyed. 14. *appointment:*
equipment.

ourselves too slow of sail, we put on a compelled valor, and in the grapple I 15
boarded them. On the instant they got clear of our ship; so I alone became their
prisoner. They have dealt with me like thieves of mercy, but they knew what
they did: I am to do a good turn for them. Let the King have the letters I have
sent, and repair thou to me with as much speed as thou wouldest fly death. I
have words to speak in thine ear will make thee dumb; yet are they much too 20
light for the bore° of the matter. These good fellows will bring thee where I
am. Rosencrantz and Guildenstern hold their course for England. Of them I
have much to tell thee. Farewell.

         He that thou knowest thine, Hamlet."
Come, I will give you way for these your letters,   25
And do't the speedier that you may direct me
To him from whom you brought them. *Exeunt.*

SCENE VII. *The castle.*

Enter King and LAERTES.

KING. Now must your conscience my acquittance seal,
  And you must put me in your heart for friend,
  Sith you have heard, and with a knowing ear,
  That he which hath your noble father slain
  Pursued my life.
LAERTES.   It well appears. But tell me   5
  Why you proceeded not against these feats
  So criminal and so capital° in nature,
  As by your safety, greatness, wisdom, all things else,
  You mainly° were stirred up.
KING.   O, for two special reasons,
  Which may to you perhaps seem much unsinewed,°   10
  But yet to me they're strong. The Queen his mother
  Lives almost by his looks, and for myself—
  My virtue or my plague, be it either which—
  She is so conjunctive° to my life and soul,
  That, as the star moves not but in his sphere,   15
  I could not but by her. The other motive
  Why to a public count° I might not go
  Is the great love the general gender° bear him,
  Who, dipping all his faults in their affection,
  Would, like the spring that turneth wood to stone,°   20

---

21. *bore:* caliber (here, "importance"). SCENE VII. 7. *capital:* deserving death. 9. *mainly:*
powerfully. 10. *unsinewed:* weak. 14. *conjunctive:* closely united. 17. *count:* reckoning.
18. *general gender:* common people. 20. *spring that turneth wood to stone:* (a spring in
Shakespeare's county was so charged with lime that it would petrify wood placed in it).

Convert his gyves° to graces; so that my arrows,
Too slightly timbered° for so loud a wind,
Would have reverted to my bow again,
And not where I had aimed them.

LAERTES. And so have I a noble father lost,   25
A sister driven into desp'rate terms,°
Whose worth, if praises may go back again,°
Stood challenger on mount of all the age
For her perfections. But my revenge will come.

KING. Break not your sleeps for that. You must not think   30
That we are made of stuff so flat and dull
That we can let our beard be shook with danger,
And think it pastime. You shortly shall hear more.
I loved your father, and we love ourself,
And that, I hope, will teach you to imagine——   35

Enter a Messenger with letters.

How now? What news?
MESSENGER.   Letters, my lord, from Hamlet:
These to your Majesty; this to the Queen.
KING. From Hamlet? Who brought them?
MESSENGER. Sailors, my lord, they say; I saw them not.
They were given me by Claudio; he received them   40
Of him that brought them.
KING.   Laertes, you shall hear them.—
Leave us. *Exit Messenger.*
[*Reads.*] "High and mighty, you shall know I am set naked° on your kingdom.
Tomorrow shall I beg leave to see your kingly eyes; even when I shall (first
asking your pardon thereunto) recount the occasion of my sudden and more 45
strange return.

                        Hamlet."
What should this mean? Are all the rest come back?
Or is it some abuse,° and no such thing?
LAERTES. Know you the hand?
KING.   'Tis Hamlet's character.° "Naked"!   50
And in a postscript here, he says "alone."
Can you devise° me?
LAERTES. I am lost in it, my lord. But let him come.
It warms the very sickness in my heart
That I shall live and tell him to his teeth,   55
"Thus did'st thou."

---

21. *gyves:* fetters. 22. *timbered:* shafted. 26. *terms:* conditions. 27. *go back again:* revert to what
is past. 43. *naked:* destitute. 49. *abuse:* deception. 50. *character:* handwriting. 52. *devise:* advise.

KING.   If it be so, Laertes
 (As how should it be so? How otherwise?),
 Will you be ruled by me?
LAERTES.   Ay, my lord,
 So you will not o'errule me to a peace.
KING. To thine own peace. If he be now returned,   60
 As checking at° his voyage, and that he means
 No more to undertake it, I will work him
 To an exploit now ripe in my device,
 Under the which he shall not choose but fall;
 And for his death no wind of blame shall breathe,   65
 But even his mother shall uncharge the practice°
 And call it accident.
LAERTES.   My lord, I will be ruled;
 The rather if you could devise it so
 That I might be the organ.
KING.   It falls right.
 You have been talked of since your travel much,   70
 And that in Hamlet's hearing, for a quality
 Wherein they say you shine. Your sum of parts
 Did not together pluck such envy from him
 As did that one, and that, in my regard,
 Of the unworthiest siege.°
LAERTES.   What part is that, my lord?   75
KING. A very riband in the cap of youth,
 Yet needful too, for youth no less becomes
 The light and careless livery that it wears
 Than settled age his sables and his weeds,°
 Importing health and graveness. Two months since   80
 Here was a gentleman of Normandy.
 I have seen myself, and served against, the French,
 And they can° well on horseback, but this gallant
 Had witchcraft in't. He grew unto his seat,
 And to such wondrous doing brought his horse   85
 As had he been incorpsed and deminatured
 With the brave beast. So far he topped my thought
 That I, in forgery° of shapes and tricks,
 Come short of what he did.
LAERTES.   A Norman was't?
KING. A Norman.   90

---

61. *checking at:* turning away from (a term in falconry). 66. *uncharge the practice:* not charge the device with treachery. 75. *siege:* rank. 79. *sables and his weeds:* i.e., sober attire. 83. *can:* do 88. *forgery:* invention.

LAERTES. Upon my life, Lamord.

KING. The very same.

LAERTES. I know him well. He is the brooch° indeed
  And gem of all the nation.

KING. He made confession° of you,
  And gave you such a masterly report, 95
  For art and exercise in your defense,
  And for your rapier most especial,
  That he cried out 'twould be a sight indeed
  If one could match you. The scrimers° of their nation
  He swore that neither motion, guard, nor eye, 100
  If you opposed them. Sir, this report of his
  Did Hamlet so envenom with his envy
  That he could nothing do but wish and beg
  Your sudden coming o'er to play with you.
  Now, out of this——

LAERTES. What out of this, my lord? 105

KING. Laertes, was your father dear to you?
  Or are you like the painting of a sorrow,
  A face without a heart?

LAERTES. Why ask you this?

KING. Not that I think you did not love your father,
  But that I know love is begun by time, 110
  And that I see, in passages of proof,°
  Time qualifies° the spark and fire of it.
  There lives within the very flame of love
  A kind of wick or snuff° that will abate it,
  And nothing is at a like goodness still,° 115
  For goodness, growing to a plurisy,°
  Dies in his own too-much. That we would do
  We would do when we would, for this "would" changes,
  And hath abatements and delays as many
  As there are tongues, are hands, are accidents, 120
  And then this "should" is like a spendthrift sigh,°
  That hurts by easing. But to the quick° of th' ulcer—
  Hamlet comes back; what would you undertake
  To show yourself in deed your father's son
  More than in words?

---

92. *brooch:* ornament. 94. *confession:* report. 99. *scrimers:* fencers. 111. *passages of proof:* proved cases. 112. *qualifies:* diminishes. 114. *snuff:* residue of burnt wick (which dims the light). 115. *still:* always. 116. *plurisy:* fullness, excess. 121. *spendthrift sigh:* (sighing provides ease, but because it was thought to thin the blood and so shorten life it was spendthrift). 122. *quick:* sensitive flesh.

LAERTES.	To cut his throat i' th' church!	125

KING. No place indeed should murder sanctuarize;°
   Revenge should have no bounds. But, good Laertes,
   Will you do this? Keep close within your chamber.
   Hamlet returned shall know you are come home.
   We'll put on those° shall praise your excellence 130
   And set a double varnish on the fame
   The Frenchman gave you, bring you in fine° together
   And wager on your heads. He, being remiss,
   Most generous, and free from all contriving,
   Will not peruse the foils, so that with ease, 135
   Or with a little shuffling, you may choose
   A sword unbated,° and, in a pass of practice,°
   Requite him for your father.

LAERTES. I will do't,
   And for that purpose I'll anoint my sword.
   I bought an unction of a mountebank,° 140
   So mortal that, but dip a knife in it,
   Where it draws blood, no cataplasm° so rare,
   Collected from all simples° that have virtue°
   Under the moon, can save the thing from death
   That is but scratched withal, I'll touch my point 145
   With this contagion, that, if I gall him slightly,
   It may be death.

KING. Let's further think of this,
   Weigh what convenience both of time and means
   May fit us to our shape.° If this should fail,
   And that our drift look through° our bad performance. 150
   'Twere better not assayed. Therefore this project
   Should have a back or second, that might hold
   If this did blast in proof.° Soft, let me see.
   We'll make a solemn wager on our cunnings—
   I ha't! 155
   When in your motion you are hot and dry—
   As make your bouts more violent to that end—
   And that he calls for drink, I'll have prepared him
   A chalice for the nonce,° whereon but sipping,

---

126. *sanctuarize:* protect. 130. *We'll put on those:* we'll incite persons who. 132. *in fine:* finally.
137. *unbated:* not blunted. 137. *pass of practice:* treacherous thrust. 140. *mountebank:* quack.
142. *cataplasm:* poultice. 143. *simples:* medicinal herbs. 143. *virtue:* (power to heal).
149. *shape:* role. 150. *drift look through:* purpose show through. 153. *blast in proof:* burst (fail) in performance 159. *nonce:* occasion.

If he by chance escape your venomed stuck,°   160
Our purpose may hold there.—But stay, what noise?

Enter Queen.

QUEEN. One woe doth tread upon another's heel.
So fast they follow. Your sister's drowned, Laertes.
LAERTES. Drowned! O, where?
QUEEN. There is a willow grows askant° the brook,   165
That shows his hoar° leaves in the glassy stream:
Therewith° fantastic garlands did she make
Of crowflowers, nettles, daisies, and long purples,
That liberal° shepherds give a grosser name,
But our cold maids do dead men's fingers call them.   170
There on the pendent boughs her crownet° weeds
Clamb'ring to hang, an envious sliver° broke,
When down her weedy trophies and herself
Fell in the weeping brook. Her clothes spread wide,
And mermaidlike awhile they bore her up,   175
Which time she chanted snatches of old lauds,°
As one incapable° of her own distress,
Or like a creature native and indued°
Unto that element. But long it could not be
Till that her garments, heavy with their drink,   180
Pulled the poor wretch from her melodious lay
To muddy death.
LAERTES.   Alas, then she is drowned?
QUEEN. Drowned, drowned.
LAERTES. Too much of water hast thou, poor Ophelia,
And therefore I forbid my tears; but yet   185
It is our trick;° nature her custom holds,
Let shame say what it will: when these are gone,
The woman° will be out. Adieu, my lord.
I have a speech o'fire, that fain would blaze,
But that this folly drowns it.   *Exit.*
KING.   Let's follow, Gertrude.   190
How much I had to do to calm his rage!
Now fear I this will give it start again;
Therefore let's follow.   *Exeunt.*

---

160. *stuck:* thrust. 165. *askant:* aslant. 166. *hoar:* silver-gray. 167. *Therewith:* i.e., with willow
twigs. 169. *liberal:* free-spoken, coarse-mouthed. 171. *crownet:* coronet. 172. *envious silver:*
malicious branch. 176. *lauds:* hymns. 177. *incapable:* unaware. 178. *indued:* in harmony with.
186. *trick:* trait, way. 188. *woman:* i.e., womanly part of me.

ACT V

Scene I. *A churchyard.*

Enter two Clowns.°

CLOWN. Is she to be buried in Christian burial when she willfully seeks her own salvation?

OTHER. I tell thee she is. Therefore make her grave straight.° The crowner° hath sate on her, and finds it Christian burial.

CLOWN. How can that be, unless she drowned herself in her own defense? 5

OTHER. Why, 'tis found so.

CLOWN. It must be *se offendendo;*° it cannot be else. For here lies the point: if I drown myself wittingly, it argues an act, and an act hath three branches— it is to act, to do, to perform. Argal,° she drowned herself wittingly.

OTHER. Nay, but hear you, Goodman Delver. 10

CLOWN. Give me leave. Here lies the water—good. Here stands the man—good. If the man go to this water and drown himself, it is, will he nill he,° he goes; mark you that. But if the water come to him and drown him, he drowns not himself. Argal, he that is not guilty of his own death, shortens not his own life.

OTHER. But is this law? 15

CLOWN. Ay marry, is't—crowner's quest° law.

OTHER. Will you ha' the truth on't? If this had not been a gentlewoman, she should have been buried out o' Christian burial.

CLOWN. Why, there, thou say'st. And the more pity that great folk should have count'nance° in this world to drown or hang themselves more than their 20 even-Christen.° Come, my spade. There is no ancient gentlemen but gard'ners, ditchers, and gravemakers. They hold up° Adam's profession.

OTHER. Was he a gentleman?

CLOWN. 'A was the first ever bore arms.°

OTHER. Why, he had none. 25

CLOWN. What, art a heathen? How dost thou understand the Scripture? The Scripture says Adam digged. Could he dig without arms? I'll put another question to thee. If thou answerest me not to the purpose, confess thyself——

OTHER. Go to.

CLOWN. What is he that builds stronger than either the mason, the shipwright, or 30 the carpenter?

OTHER. The gallowsmaker, for that frame outlives a thousand tenants.

CLOWN. I like thy wit well, in good faith. The gallows does well. But how does it well? It does well to those that do ill. Now thou dost ill to say the gallows is

---

SCENE I. s.d. *Clowns:* rustics. 3. *straight:* straightway. 3. *crowner:* coroner. 7. *se offendendo:* (blunder for *se defendendo,* a legal term meaning "in self-defense"). 9. *Argal:* (blunder for Latin *ergo,* "therefore"). 12. *will he nill he:* will he or will he not (whether he will or will not). 16. *quest:* inquest. 20. *count'nance:* privilege. 21. *even-Christen:* fellow Christian. 22. *hold up:* keep up. 24. *bore arms:* had a coat of arms (the sign of a gentleman).

built stronger than the church. Argal, the gallows may do well to thee. To't 35
again, come.

OTHER. Who builds stronger than a mason, a shipwright, or a carpenter?

CLOWN. Ay, tell me that, and unyoke.°

OTHER. Marry, now I can tell.

CLOWN. To't. 40

OTHER. Mass,° I cannot tell.

Enter HAMLET *and* HORATIO *afar off.*

CLOWN. Cudgel thy brains no more about it, for your dull ass will not mend his
pace with beating. And when you are asked this question next, say "grave-
maker." The houses he makes lasts till doomsday. Go, get thee in, and fetch me
a stoup° of liquor. *Exit Other Clown.* 45
In youth when I did love, did love, [*Song*]
    Methought it was very sweet
To contract—O—the time for—a—my behove,°
    O, methought there—a—was nothing—a—meet.

HAMLET. Has this fellow no feeling of his business? 'A sings in gravemaking. 50

HORATIO. Custom hath made it in him a property of easiness.°

HAMLET. 'Tis e'en so. The hand of little employment hath the daintier sense.°

CLOWN. But age with his stealing steps [*Song*]
    Hath clawed me in his clutch,
  And hath shipped me into the land, 55
    As if I had never been such. *Throws up a skull.*

HAMLET. That skull had a tongue in it, and could sing once. How the knave jowls°
it to the ground, as if 'twere Cain's jawbone, that did the first murder! This
might be the pate of a politician, which this ass now o'erreaches,° one that
would circumvent God, might it not? 60

HORATIO. It might, my lord.

HAMLET. Or, of a courtier, which could say "Good morrow, sweet lord! How dost
thou, sweet lord?" This might be my Lord Such-a-one, that praised my Lord
Such-a-one's horse when 'a went to beg it, might it not?

HORATIO. Ay, my lord. 65

HAMLET. Why, e'en so, and now my Lady Worm's, chapless,° and knocked about
the mazzard° with a sexton's spade. Here's fine revolution, and we had the trick
to see't. Did these bones cost no more the breeding but to play at loggets° with
them? Mine ache to think on't.

---

38. *unyoke:* i.e., stop work for the day. 41. *Mass:* by the mass. 45. *stoup:* tankard. 48. *behove:*
advantage. 51. *in him a property of easiness:* easy for him. 52. *hath the daintier sense:* is more
sensitive (because it is not calloused). 57. *jowls:* hurls. 59. *o'erreaches:* (1) reaches over, (2) has the
advantage over. 66. *chapless:* lacking the lower jaw. 67. *mazzard:* head. 68. *loggets:* (a game in
which small pieces of wood were thrown at an object).

CLOWN. A pickax and a spade, a spade,   [*Song*]   70
    For and a shrouding sheet;
      O, a pit of clay for to be made
      For such a quest is meet.   *Throws up another skull.*

HAMLET. There's another. Why may not that be the skull of a lawyer? Where be his
    quiddities° now, his quillities,° his cases, his tenures,° and his tricks? Why does 75
    he suffer this mad knave now to knock him about the sconce° with a dirty
    shovel, and will not tell him of his action of battery? Hum! This fellow might
    be in's time a great buyer of land, with his statutes, his recognizances, his fines,°
    his double vouchers, his recoveries. Is this the fine° of his fines, and the recovery
    of his recoveries, to have his fine pate full of fine dirt? Will his vouchers vouch 80
    him no more of his purchases, and double ones too, than the length and
    breadth of a pair of indentures?° The very conveyances° of his lands will scarcely
    lie in this box, and must th' inheritor himself have no more, ha?

HORATIO. Not a jot more, my lord.

HAMLET. Is not parchment made of sheepskins?   85

HORATIO. Ay, my lord, and of calveskins too.

HAMLET. They are sheep and calves which seek out assurance° in that. I will speak
    to this fellow. Whose grave's this, sirrah?

CLOWN. Mine, sir.
    [*Sings.*]   O, a pit of clay for to be made   90
           For such a guest is meet.

HAMLET. I think it be thine indeed, for thou liest in't.

CLOWN. You lie out on't, sir, and therefore 'tis not yours. For my part, I do not lie
    in't, yet it is mine.

HAMLET. Thou dost lie in't, to be in't and say it is thine. 'Tis for the dead, not for 95
    the quick;° therefore thou liest.

CLOWN. 'Tis a quick lie, sir; 'twill away again from me to you.

HAMLET. What man dost thou dig it for?

CLOWN. For no man, sir.

HAMLET. What woman then?   100

CLOWN. For none neither.

HAMLET. Who is to be buried in't?

CLOWN. One that was a woman, sir: but, rest her soul, she's dead.

HAMLET. How absolute° the knave is! We must speak by the card,° or equivocation°
    will undo us. By the Lord, Horatio, this three years I have took note of it, the 105

---

75. *quiddities:* subtle arguments (from Latin *quidditas,* "whatness").   75. *quillities:* fine distinctions.
75. *tenures:* legal means of holding land.   76. *sconce:* head.   78. *his statutes, his recognizances, his*
fines: his documents giving a creditor control of a debtor's land, his bonds of surety, his documents
changing an entailed estate into fee simple (unrestricted ownership).   79. *fine:* end.   82. *indentures:*
contracts.   82. *conveyances:* legal documents for the transference of land.   87. *assurance:* safety.
96. *quick:* living.   104. *absolute:* positive, decided.   104. *by the card:* by the compass card, i.e.,
exactly.   104. *equivocation:* ambiguity.

age is grown so picked° that the toe of the peasant comes so near the heel of
the courtier he galls his kibe.° How long hast thou been a grave-maker?

CLOWN. Of all the days i' th' year, I came to't that day that our last king Hamlet
overcame Fortinbras.

HAMLET. How long is that since?   110

CLOWN. Cannot you tell that? Every fool can tell that. It was that very day that
young Hamlet was born—he that is mad, and sent into England.

HAMLET. Ay, marry, why was he sent into England?

CLOWN. Why, because 'a was mad. 'A shall recover his wits there; or, if 'a do not,
'tis no great matter there.   115

HAMLET. Why?

CLOWN. 'Twill not be seen in him there. There the men are as mad as he.

HAMLET. How came he mad?

CLOWN. Very strangely, they say.

HAMLET. How strangely?   120

CLOWN. Faith, e'en with losing his wits.

HAMLET. Upon what ground?

CLOWN. Why, here in Denmark. I have been sexton here, man and boy, thirty years.

HAMLET. How long will a man lie i' th' earth ere he rot?

CLOWN. Faith, if 'a be not rotten before 'a die (as we have many pocky corses°   125
nowadays that will scarce hold the laying in), 'a will last you some eight year or
nine year. A tanner will last you nine year.

HAMLET. Why he, more than another?

CLOWN. Why, sir, his hide is so tanned with his trade that 'a will keep out water a
great while, and your water is a sore decayer of your whoreson dead body.   130
Here's a skull now hath lien you i' th' earth three and twenty years.

HAMLET. Whose was it?

CLOWN. A whoreson mad fellow's it was. Whose do you think it was?

HAMLET. Nay, I know not.

CLOWN. A pestilence on him for a mad rogue! 'A poured a flagon of Rhenish on   135
my head once. This same skull, sir, was, sir, Yorick's skull, the King's jester.

HAMLET. This?

CLOWN. E'en that.

HAMLET. Let me see. [*Takes the skull.*] Alas, poor Yorick! I knew him, Horatio, a
fellow of infinite jest, of most excellent fancy. He hath borne me on his back a   140
thousand times. And now how abhorred in my imagination it is! My gorge rises
at it. Here hung those lips that I have kissed I know not how oft. Where be
your gibes now? Your gambols, your songs, your flashes of merriment that were
wont to set the table on a roar? Not one now to mock your own grinning?
Quite chapfall'n°? Now get you to my lady's chamber, and tell her, let her paint   145

---

106. *picked:* refined. 107. *kibe:* sore on the back of the heel. 125. *pocky corses:* bodies of persons
who had been infected with the pox (syphilis). 145. *chapfall'n:* (1) down in the mouth, (2) jawless.

an inch thick, to this favor° she must come. Make her laugh at that. Prithee,
    Horatio, tell me one thing.
HORATIO. What's that, my lord?
HAMLET. Dost thou think Alexander looked o' this fashion i' th' earth?
HORATIO. E'en so.   150
HAMLET. And smelt so? Pah! [*Puts down the skull.*]
HORATIO. E'en so, my lord.
HAMLET. To what base use we may return, Horatio! Why may not imagination trace
    the noble dust of Alexander till 'a find it stopping a bunghole?
HORATIO. 'Twere to consider too curiously,° to consider so.   155
HAMLET. No, faith, not a jot, but to follow him thither with modesty enough,° and
    likelihood to lead it; as thus: Alexander died, Alexander was buried, Alexander
    returneth to dust; the dust is earth; of earth we make loam; and why of that
    loam whereto he was converted might they not stop a beer barrel?
Imperious Caesar, dead and turned to clay,   160
Might stop a hole to keep the wind away.
O, that that earth which kept the world in awe
Should patch a wall t' expel th winter's flaw!°
But soft, but soft awhile! Here comes the King.

    Enter King, Queen, LAERTES, *and a coffin, with Lords attendant*
        [*and a Doctor of Divinity*].

The Queen, the courtiers. Who is this they follow?   165
And with such maimèd° rites? This doth betoken
The corse they follow did with desp'rate hand
Fordo it° own life. 'Twas of some estate.°
Couch° we awhile, and mark. [*Retires with Horatio.*]
LAERTES. What ceremony else?
HAMLET.   That is Laertes,   170
    A very noble youth. Mark.
LAERTES. What ceremony else?
DOCTOR. Her obsequies have been as far enlarged
    As we have warranty. Her death was doubtful,°
And, but that great command o'ersways the order,   175
She should in ground unsanctified been lodged
Till the last trumpet. For charitable prayers,
Shards,° flints, and pebbles should be thrown on her.
Yet here she is allowed her virgin crants,°
Her maiden strewments,° and the bringing home   180
Of bell and burial.

---

146. *favor:* facial appearance. 155. *curiously:* minutely. 156. *with modesty enough:* without
exaggeration. 163. *flaw:* gust. 166. *maimèd:* incomplete. 168. *Fordo it:* destroy its.
168. *estate:* high rank. 169. *Couch:* hide. 174. *doubtful:* suspicious. 178. *Shards:* broken pieces
of pottery. 179. *crants:* garlands. 180. *strewments:* i.e., of flowers.

LAERTES.   Must there no more be done?

DOCTOR.   No more be done.
   We should profane the service of the dead
   To sing a requiem and such rest to her
   As to peace-parted souls.

LAERTES.   Lay her i' th' earth,   185
   And from her fair and unpolluted flesh
   May violets spring! I tell thee, churlish priest,
   A minist'ring angel shall my sister be
   When thou liest howling!

HAMLET.   What, the fair Ophelia?

QUEEN.   Sweets to the sweet! Farewell.   *Scatters flowers.*   190
   I hoped thou shouldst have been my Hamlet's wife.
   I thought thy bride bed to have decked, sweet maid,
   And not have strewed thy grave.

LAERTES.   O, treble woe
   Fall ten times treble on that cursèd head
   Whose wicked deed thy most ingenious sense°   195
   Deprived thee of! Hold off the earth awhile,
   Till I have caught her once more in mine arms.   *Leaps in the grave.*
   Now pile your dust upon the quick and dead
   Till of this flat a mountain you have made
   T'o'ertop old Pelion° or the skyish head   200
   Of blue Olympus.

HAMLET.   [*Coming forward*] What is he whose grief
   Bears such an emphasis, whose phrase of sorrow
   Conjures the wand'ring stars,° and makes them stand
   Lake wonder-wounded hearers? This is I,
   Hamlet the Dane.

LAERTES.   The devil take thy soul!   *Grapples with him.*°   205

HAMLET.   Thou pray'st not well.
   I prithee take thy fingers from my throat,
   For, though I am not splenitive° and rash,
   Yet have I in me something dangerous,
   Which let they wisdom fear. Hold off thy hand.   210

KING.   Pluck them asunder.

195. *most ingenious sense:* finely endowed mind. 200. *Pelion:* (according to classical legend, giants
in their fight with the gods sought to reach heaven by piling Mount Pelion and Mount Ossa on
Mount Olympus). 203. *wand'ring stars:* planets. 205. s.d. *Grapples with him:* (Q1, a bad quarto,
presumably reporting a version that toured, has a previous direction saying "Hamlet leaps in after
Laertes." Possibly he does so, somewhat hysterically. But such a direction—absent from the two
good texts, Q2 and F—makes Hamlet the aggressor, somewhat contradicting his next speech.
Perhaps Laertes leaps out of the grave to attack Hamlet). 208. *splenitive:* fiery (the spleen was
thought to be the seat of anger).

QUEEN.   Hamlet, Hamlet!
ALL. Gentlemen!
HORATIO.   Good my lord, be quiet. *Attendants part them.*
HAMLET. Why, I will fight with them upon this theme
  Until my eyelids will no longer wag.
QUEEN. O my son, what theme?   215
HAMLET. I loved Ophelia. Forty thousand brothers
  Could not with all their quantity of love
  Make up my sum. What wilt thou do for her?
KING. O, he is mad, Laertes.
QUEEN. For love of God forbear him.   220
HAMLET. 'Swounds, show me what thou't do.
  Woo't weep? Woo't fight? Woo't fast? Woo't tear thyself?
  Woo't drink up eisel?° Eat a crocodile?
  I'll do't. Dost thou come here to whine?
  To outface me with leaping in her grave?   225
  Be buried quick with her, and so will I.
  And if thou prate of mountains, let them throw
  Millions of acres on us, till our ground,
  Singeing his pate against the burning zone,°
  Make Ossa like a wart! Nay, an thou'lt mouth,   230
  I'll rant as well as thou.
QUEEN.   This is mere madness;
  And thus a while the fit will work on him.
  Anon, as patient as the female dove
  When that her golden couplets are disclosed,°
  His silence will sit drooping.
HAMLET.   Hear you, sir.   235
  What is the reason that you use me thus?
  I loved you ever. But it is no matter.
  Let Hercules himself do what he may,
  The cat will mew, and the dog will have his day.
KING. I pray thee, good Horatio, wait upon him. *Exit* HAMLET *and* HORATIO.   240
  [*To* LAERTES] Strengthen your patience in our last night's speech.
  We'll put the matter to the present push.°
  Good Gertrude, set some watch over your son.
  This grave shall have a living° monument.
  An hour of quiet shortly shall we see;   245
  Till then in patience our proceeding be. *Exeunt.*

223. *eisel:* vinegar. 229. *burning zone:* sun's orbit. 234. *golden couplets are disclosed:* (the dove lays two eggs, and the newly hatched [disclosed] young are covered with golden down). 242. *present push:* immediate test. 244. *living:* lasting (with perhaps also a reference to the plot against Hamlet's life).

SCENE II. *The castle.*

Enter HAMLET *and* HORATIO.

HAMLET. So much for this, sir; now shall you see the other.
You do remember all the circumstance?
HORATIO. Remember it, my lord!
HAMLET. Sir, in my heart there was a kind of fighting
That would not let me sleep. Methought I lay   5
Worse than the mutines in the bilboes.° Rashly
(And praised be rashness for it) let us know,
Our indiscretion sometime serves us well
When our deep plots do pall,° and that should learn us
There's a divinity that shapes our ends,   10
Rough-hew them how we will.
HORATIO.   That is most certain.
HAMLET. Up from my cabin,
My sea gown scarfed about me, in the dark
Groped I to find out them, had my desire,
Fingered° their packet, and in fine° withdrew   15
To mine own room again, making so bold,
My fears forgetting manners, to unseal
Their grand commission; where I found, Horatio—
Ah, royal knavery!—an exact command,
Larded° with many several sorts of reasons,   20
Importing Denmark's health, and England's too,
With, ho, such bugs and goblins in my life,°
That on the supervise,° no leisure bated,°
No, not to stay the grinding of the ax,
My head should be struck off.
HORATIO.   Is't possible?   25
HAMLET. Here's the commission; read it at more leisure,
But wilt thou hear now how I did proceed?
HORATIO. I beseech you.
HAMLET. Being thus benetted round with villains,
Or° I could make a prologue to my brains,   30
They had begun the play. I sat me down,
Devised a new commission, wrote it fair.
I once did hold it, as our statists° do,
A baseness to write fair,° and labored much
How to forget that learning, but, sir, now   35

SCENE II. 6. *mutines in the bilboes:* mutineers in fetters. 9. *pall:* fail. 15. *Fingered:* stole.
15. *in fine:* finally. 20. *Larded:* enriched. 22. *such bugs and goblins in my life:* such bugbears and
imagined terrors if I were allowed to live. 23. *supervise:* reading. 23. *leisure bated:* delay allowed.
30. *Or:* ere. 33. *statists:* statesmen. 34. *fair:* clearly.

It did me yeoman's service. Wilt thou know
Th' effect° of what I wrote?
HORATIO.   Ay, good my lord.
HAMLET. An earnest conjuration from the King,
 As England was his faithful tributary,
 As love between them like the palm might flourish,   40
 As peace should still her wheaten garland wear
 And stand a comma° 'tween their amities,
 And many suchlike as's of great charge,°
 That on the view and knowing of these contents,
 Without debatement further, more or less,   45
 He should those bearers put to sudden death,
 Not shriving° time allowed.
HORATIO.   How was this sealed?
HAMLET. Why, even in that was heaven ordinant.°
 I had my father's signet in my purse,
 Which was the model° of that Danish seal,   50
 Folded the writ up in the form of th' other,
 Subscribed it, gave't th' impression, placed it safely,
 The changeling never known. Now, the next day
 Was our sea fight, and what to this was sequent
 Thou knowest already.   55
HORATIO. So Guildenstern and Rosencrantz go to't.
HAMLET. Why, man, they did make love to this employment.
 They are not near my conscience; their defeat
 Does by their own insinuation° grow.
 'Tis dangerous when the baser nature comes   60
 Between the pass° and fell° incensèd points
 Of might opposites.
HORATIO.   Why, what a king is this!
HAMLET. Does it not, think thee, stand me now upon°—
 He that hath killed my king, and whored my mother,
 Popped in between th' election° and my hopes,   65
 Thrown out his angle° for my proper life,°
 And with such coz'nage°—is't not perfect conscience
 To quit° him with this arm? And is't not to be damned
 To let this canker of our nature come
 In further evil?   70

---

37. *effect:* purport. 42. *comma:* link. 43. *great charge:* (1) serious exhortation, (2) heavy burden (punning on *as's* and "asses"). 47. *shriving:* absolution. 48. *ordinant:* ruling. 50. *model:* counterpart. 59. *insinuation:* meddling. 61. *pass:* thrust. 61. *fell:* cruel. 63. *stand me now upon:* become incumbent upon me. 65. *election:* (the Danish monarchy was elective). 66. *angle:* fishing line. 66. *my proper life:* my own life. 67. *coz'nage:* trickery. 68. *quit:* pay back.

HORATIO. It must be shortly known to him from England
    What is the issue of the business there.
HAMLET. It will be short; the interim's mine,
    And a man's life's no more than to say "one."
    But I am very sorry, good Horatio,   75
    That to Laertes I forgot myself,
    For by the image of my cause I see
    The portraiture of his. I'll court his favors.
    But sure the bravery° of his grief did put me
    Into a tow'ring passion.
HORATIO.   Peace, who comes here?   80

Enter young OSRIC, *a courtier.*

OSRIC. Your lordship is right welcome back to Denmark.
HAMLET. I humbly thank you, sir. [*Aside to Horatio*] Dost know this waterfly?
HORATIO. [*Aside to Hamlet*] No, my good lord.
HAMLET. [*Aside to Horatio*] Thy state is the more gracious, for 'tis a vice to know
    him. He hath much land, and fertile. Let a beast be lord of beasts, and his crib 85
    shall stand at the king's mess.° 'Tis a chough,° but, as I say, spacious° in the
    possession of dirt.
OSRIC. Sweet lord, if your lordship were at leisure, I should impart a thing to you
    from his Majesty.
HAMLET. I will receive it, sir, with all diligence of spirit. Put your bonnet to his right 90
    use. 'Tis for the head.
OSRIC. I thank your lordship, it is very hot.
HAMLET. No, believe me, 'tis very cold; the wind is northerly.
OSRIC. It is indifferent cold, my lord, indeed.
HAMLET. But yet methinks it is very sultry and hot for my complexion.°   95
OSRIC. Exceedingly, my lord; it is very sultry, as 'twere —I cannot tell how. But, my
    lord, his Majesty bade me signify to you that 'a has laid a great wager on your
    head. Sir, this is the matter——
HAMLET. I beseech you remember.

HAMLET *moves him to put on his hat.*

OSRIC. Nay, good my lord; for ease, in good faith. Sir, here is newly come to court 100
    Laertes—believe me, an absolute gentleman, full of most excellent differences,°
    of very soft society and great showing. Indeed, to speak feelingly°of him, he is
    the card° or calendar of gentry; for you shall find in him the continent° of what
    part of a gentleman would see.

---

79. *bravery:* bravado. 86. *mess:* table. 86. *chough:* jackdaw (here, chatterer).
86. *spacious:* well off. 95. *complexion:* temperament. 101. *differences:* distinguishing characteristics.
102. *feelingly:* justly. 103. *card:* chart. 103. *continent:* summary.

HAMLET. Sir, his definement° suffers no perdition° in you, though, I know, to divide   105
    him inventorially would dozy° th' arithmetic of memory, and yet but yaw
    neither in respect of his quick sail.° But, in the verity of extolment, I take him
    to be a soul of great article,° and his infusion° of such dearth and rareness as,
    to make true diction° of him, his semblable° is his mirror, and who else would
    trace him, his umbrage,° nothing more.   110
OSRIC. Your lordship speaks most infallibly of him.
HAMLET. The concernancy,° sir? Why do we wrap the gentleman in our more rawer
    breath?
OSRIC. Sir?
HORATIO. Is't not possible to understand in another tongue? You will to't,° sir,   115
    really.
HAMLET. What imports the nomination of this gentleman?
OSRIC. Of Laertes?
HORATIO. [*Aside to* HAMLET] His purse is empty already. All's golden words are
    spent.   120
HAMLET. Of him, sir.
OSRIC. I know you are not ignorant——
HAMLET. I would you did, sir; yet, in faith, if you did, it would not much approve°
    me. Well, sir?
OSRIC. You are not ignorant of what excellence Laertes is——   125
HAMLET. I dare not confess that, lest I should compare with him in excellence; but
    to know a man well were to know himself.
OSRIC. I mean, sir, for his weapon; but in the imputation° laid on him by them, in
    his meed° he's unfellowed.
HAMLET. What's his weapon?   130
OSRIC. Rapier and dagger.
HAMLET. That's two of his weapons—but well.
OSRIC. The King, sir, hath wagered with him six Barbary horses, against the which
    he has impawned,° as I take it, six French rapiers and poniards, with their
    assigns,° as girdle, hangers,° and so. Three of the carriages,° in faith, are very   135
    dear to fancy, very responsive° to the hilts, most delicate carriages, and of very
    liberal conceit.°
HAMLET. What call you the carriages?
HORATIO. [*Aside to* HAMLET] I knew you must be edified by the margent° ere you
    had done.   140

---

105. *definement:* description. 105. *perdition:* loss. 106. *dozy:* dizzy. 106–107. *and yet . . . quick
sail:* i.e., and yet only stagger despite all (*yaw neither*) in trying to overtake his virtues. 108. *article:*
(literally, "item," but here perhaps "traits" or "importance"). 108. *infusion:* essential quality.
109. *diction:* description. 109. *semblable:* likeness. 110. *umbrage:* shadow. 112. *concernancy:*
meaning. 115. *will to't:* will get there. 123. *approve:* commend. 128. *imputation:* reputation.
129. *meed:* merit. 134. *impawned:* wagered. 135. *assigns:* accompaniments. 135. *hangers:* straps
hanging the sword to the belt. 135. *carriages:* (an affected word for hangers). 136. *responsive:*
corresponding. 137. *liberal conceit:* elaborate design. 139. *margent:* i.e., marginal (explanatory)
comment.

OSRIC. The carriages, sir, are the hangers.

HORATIO. The phrase would be more germane to the matter if we could carry a cannon by our sides. I would it might be hangers till then. But on! Six Barbary horses against six French swords, their assigns, and three liberal-conceited carriages—that's the French bet against the Danish. Why is this all impawned, 145 as you call it?

OSRIC. The King, sir, hath laid, sir, that in a dozen passes between yourself and him he shall not exceed you three hits; he hath laid on twelve for nine, and it would come to immediate trial if your lordship would vouchsafe the answer.

HAMLET. How if I answer no? 150

OSRIC. I mean, my lord, the opposition of your person in trial.

HAMLET. Sir, I will walk here in the hall. If it please his Majesty, it is the breathing time of day with me.° Let the foils be brought, the gentleman willing, and the King hold his purpose. I will win for him an I can; if not, I will gain nothing but my shame and the odd hits. 155

OSRIC. Shall I deliver you e'en so?

HAMLET. To this effect, sir, after what flourish your nature will.

OSRIC. I commend my duty to your lordship.

HAMLET. Yours, yours. [*Exit* OSRIC.] He does well to commend it himself; there are no tongues else for's turn. 160

HORATIO. This lapwing° runs away with the shell on his head.

HAMLET. 'A did comply, sir, with his dug° before 'a sucked it. Thus has he, and many more of the same breed that I know the drossy age dotes on, only got the tune of the time and, out of an habit of encounter,° a kind of yeasty° collection, which carries them through and through the most fanned and 165 winnowed opinions; and do but blow them to their trial, the bubbles are out.°

Enter a Lord.

LORD. My lord, his Majesty commended him to you by young Osric, who brings back to him that you attend him in the hall. He sends to know if your pleasure hold to play with Laertes, or that you will take longer time.

HAMLET. I am constant to my purposes; they follow the King's pleasure. If his 170 fitness speaks, mine is ready; now or whensoever, provided I be so able as now.

LORD. The King and Queen and all are coming down.

HAMLET. In happy time.

LORD. The Queen desires you to use some gentle entertainment° to Laertes before you fall to play. 175

HAMLET. She well instructs me. [*Exit Lord.*]

152–153. *breathing time of day with me:* time when I take exercise. 161 *lapwing:* (the new-hatched lapwing was thought to run around with half its shell on its head). 162. *'A did comply, sir, with his dug:* he was ceremoniously polite to his mother's breast. 164. *out of an habit of encounter:* out of his own superficial way of meeting and conversing with people. 164. *yeasty:* frothy. 166. *the bubbles are out:* i.e., they are blown away (the reference is to the "yeasty collection"). 174. *to use some gentle entertainment:* to be courteous.

HORATIO. You will lose this wager, my lord.

HAMLET. I do not think so. Since he went into France I have been in continual practice. I shall win at the odds. But thou wouldst not think how ill all's here about my heart. But it is no matter.   180

HORATIO. Nay, good my lord——

HAMLET. It is but foolery, but it is such a kind of gaingiving° as would perhaps trouble a woman.

HORATIO. If your mind dislike anything, obey it. I will forestall their repair hither and say you are not fit.   185

HAMLET. Not a whit, we defy augury. There is a special providence in the fall of a sparrow.° If it be now, 'tis not to come; if it be not to come, it will be now; if it be not now, yet it will come. The readiness is all. Since no man of aught he leaves knows, what is't to leave betimes?° Let be.

*A table prepared. [Enter] Trumpets, Drums, and Officers with cushions;
King, Queen, [OSRIC,] and all the State, with foils, daggers, [and stoups of wine
borne in]; and LAERTES.*

KING. Come, Hamlet, come, and take this hand from me.   190

The King puts LAERTES*'s hand into* HAMLET*'s.*

HAMLET. Give me your pardon, sir. I have done you wrong,
But pardon't, as you are a gentleman.
This presence° knows, and you must needs have heard,
How I am punished with a sore distraction.
What I have done   195
That might your nature, honor, and exception°
Roughly awake, I here proclaim was madness.
Was't Hamlet wronged Laertes? Never Hamlet.
If Hamlet from himself be ta'en away,
And when he's not himself does wrong Laertes,   200
Then Hamlet does it not, Hamlet denies it.
Who does it then? His madness. If't be so,
Hamlet is of the faction° that is wronged;
His madness is poor Hamlet's enemy.
Sir, in this audience,   205
Let my disclaiming from a purposed evil
Free me so far in your most generous thoughts
That I have shot my arrow o'er the house
And hurt my brother.

---

182. *gaingiving:* misgiving. 186–187. *the fall of a sparrow:* (cf. Matthew 10:29 "Are not two sparrows sold for a farthing? and one of them shall not fall on the ground without your Father").
189. *betimes:* early. 193. *presence:* royal assembly. 196. *exception:* disapproval.
203. *faction:* party, side.

LAERTES.   I am satisfied in nature,
  Whose motive in this case should stir me most   210
  To my revenge. But in my terms of honor
  I stand aloof, and will no reconcilement
  Till by some elder master of known honor
  I have a voice and precedent° of peace
  To keep my name ungored. But till that time   215
  I do receive your offered love like love,
  And will not wrong it.
HAMLET.   I embrace it freely,
  And will this brother's wager frankly play,
  Give us the foils. Come on.
LAERTES.   Come, one for me.
HAMLET. I'll be your foil,° Laertes. In mine ignorance   220
  Your skill shall, like a star i' th' darkest night,
  Stick fiery off° indeed.
LAERTES.   You mock me, sir.
HAMLET. No, by this hand.
KING. Give me the foils, young Osric. Cousin Hamlet,
  You know the wager?
HAMLET.   Very well, my lord.   225
  Your grace has laid the odds o' th' weaker side.
KING. I do not fear it, I have seen you both;
  But since he is bettered,° we have therefore odds.
LAERTES. This is too heavy; let me see another.
HAMLET. This likes me well. These foils have all a length? *Prepare to play.*   230
OSRIC. Ay, my good lord.
KING. Set me the stoups of wine upon that table.
  If Hamlet give the first or second hit,
  Or quit° in answer of the third exchange,
  Let all the battlements their ordnance fire.   235
  The King shall drink to Hamlet's better breath,
  And in the cup an union° shall he throw
  Richer than that which four successive kings
  In Denmark's crown have worn. Give me the cups,
  And let the kettle° to the trumpet speak,   240
  The trumpet to the cannoneer without,
  The cannons to the heavens, the heaven to earth,
  "Now the King drinks to Hamlet." Come, begin. *Trumpets the while.*
  And you, the judges, bear a wary eye.

---

214. *voice and precedent:* authoritative opinion justified by precedent. 220. *foil:* (1) blunt sword, (2) background (of metallic leaf) for a jewel. 222. *Stick fiery off:* stand out brilliantly. 228. *bettered:* has improved (in France). 234. *quit:* repay, hit back. 237. *union:* pearl. 240. *kettle:* kettledrum.

HAMLET. Come on, sir.
LAERTES.   Come, my lord. *They play.*
HAMLET.   One.
LAERTES.   No.
HAMLET.   Judgment?   245
OSRIC. A hit, a very palpable hit.

          Drum, trumpets, and shot. Flourish; a piece goes off.

LAERTES.   Well, again.
KING. Stay, give me drink. Hamlet, this pearl is thine.
  Here's to thy health. Give him the cup.
HAMLET. I'll play this bout first; set it by awhile.
  Come. [*They play.*] Another hit. What say you?   250
LAERTES. A touch, a touch; I do confess't.
KING. Our son shall win.
QUEEN.   He's fat,° and scant of breath.
  Here, Hamlet, take my napkin, rub thy brows.
  The Queen carouses to thy fortune, Hamlet.
HAMLET. Good madam!
KING.   Gertrude, do not drink.   255
QUEEN. I will, my lord; I pray you pardon me. [*Drinks.*]
KING. [*Aside*] It is the poisoned cup; it is too late.
HAMLET. I dare not drink yet, madam—by and by.
QUEEN. Come, let me wipe thy face.
LAERTES. My lord, I'll hit him now.
KING.   I do not think't.   260
LAERTES. [*Aside*] And yet it is almost against my conscience.
HAMLET. Come for the third, Laertes. You do but dally.
  I pray you pass with your best violence;
  I am sure you make a wanton° of me.
LAERTES. Say you so? Come on. [*They*] *play.*   265
OSRIC. Nothing neither way.
LAERTES. Have at you now!

       In scuffling they change rapiers [*and both are wounded*].

KING.   Part them. They are incensed.
HAMLET. Nay, come—again! [*The Queen falls.*]
OSRIC.   Look to the Queen there, ho!
HORATIO. They bleed on both sides. How is it, my lord?
OSRIC. How is't, Laertes?   270

252. *fat:* (1) sweaty, (2) out of training. 264. *wanton:* spoiled child.

LAERTES. Why, as a woodcock to mine own springe,° Osric.
   I am justly killed with mine own treachery.
HAMLET. How does the Queen?
KING.   She sounds° to see them bleed.
QUEEN. No, no, the drink, the drink! O my dear Hamlet!
   The drink, the drink! I am poisoned. [*Dies.*]   275
HAMLET. O villainy! Ho! Let the door be locked.
   Treachery! Seek it out. [LAERTES *falls.*]
LAERTES. It is here, Hamlet. Hamlet, thou art slain;
   No med'cine in the world can do thee good.
   In thee there is not half an hour's life.   280
   The treacherous instrument is in thy hand,
   Unbated and envenomed. The foul practice°
   Hath turned itself on me, Lo, here I lie,
   Never to rise again. Thy mother's poisoned.
   I can no more. The King, the King's to blame.   285
HAMLET. The point envenomed too?
   Then, venom, to thy work. *Hurts the King.*
ALL. Treason! Treason!
KING. O, yet defend me, friends, I am but hurt.
HAMLET. Here, thou incestuous, murd'rous, damnèd Dane,   290
   Drink off his potion. Is thy union here?
   Follow my mother, *King dies.*
LAERTES.   He is justly served.
   It is a poison tempered° by himself,
   Exchange forgiveness with me, noble Hamlet.
   Mine and my father's death come not upon thee,   295
   Nor thine on me! *Dies.*
HAMLET. Heaven made thee free of it! I follow thee.
   I am dead, Horatio. Wretched Queen, adieu!
   You that look pale and tremble at this chance,
   That are but mutes° or audience to this act,   300
   Had I but time (as this fell sergeant,° Death,
   Is strict in his arrest) O, I could tell you—
   But let it be. Horatio, I am dead;
   Thou livest; report me and my cause aright
   To the unsatisfied.°
HORATIO.   Never believe it.   305
   I am more an antique Roman° than a Dane.
   Here's yet some liquor left.

271. *springe:* snare. 273. *sounds:* swoons. 282. *practice:* deception. 293. *tempered:* mixed.
300. *mutes:* performers who have no words to speak. 301. *fell sergeant:* dread sheriff's officer.
305. *unsatisfied:* uniformed. 306. *antique Roman:* (with reference to the old Roman fashion of suicide).

HAMLET.   As th' art a man,
  Give me the cup. Let go. By heaven, I'll ha't!
  O God, Horatio, what a wounded name,
  Things standing thus unknown, shall live behind me!   310
  If thou didst ever hold me in thy heart,
  Absent thee from felicity° awhile,
  And in this harsh world draw thy breath in pain,
  To tell my story. *A march afar off.* [*Exit* OSRIC.]
               What warlike noise is this?

Enter OSRIC.

OSRIC. Young Fortinbras, with conquest come from Poland,   315
  To th' ambassadors of England gives
  This warlike volley.
HAMLET.   O, I die, Horatio!
  The potent poison quite o'ercrows° my spirit.
  I cannot live to hear the news from England,
  But I do prophesy th' election lights   320
  On Fortinbras. He has my dying voice
  So tell him, with th' occurrents,° more and less,
  Which have solicited°—the rest is silence. *Dies.*
HORATIO. Now cracks a noble heart. Good night, sweet Prince,
  And flights of angels sing thee to thy rest. *March within.*   325
  Why does the drum come hither?

Enter FORTINBRAS, *with the Ambassadors with Drum, Colors, and Attendants.*

FORTINBRAS. Where is this sight?
HORATIO.   What is it you would see?
  If aught of woe or wonder, cease your search.
FORTINBRAS. This quarry° cries on havoc.° O proud Death,
  What feast is toward° in thine eternal cell   330
  That thou so many princes at a shot
  So bloodily has struck?
AMBASSADOR.   The sight is dismal;
  And our affairs from England come too late.
  The ears are senseless that should give us hearing
  To tell him his commandment is fulfilled,   335
  That Rosencrantz and Guildenstern are dead.
  Where should we have our thanks?

---

312. *felicity:* i.e., the felicity of death. 318. *o'ercrows:* overpowers (as a triumphant cock crows over
its weak opponent). 322. *occurrents:* occurrences. 323. *solicited:* incited. 329. *quarry:* heap of
slain bodies. 329. *cries on havoc:* proclaims general slaughter. 330. *toward:* in preparation.

HORATIO.   Not from his° mouth,
    Had it th' ability of life to thank you.
    He never gave commandment for their death.
    But since, so jump° upon this bloody question,   340
    You from the Polack wars, and you from England,
    Are here arrived, give order that these bodies
    High on a stage° be placèd to the view,
    And let me speak to th' yet unknowing world
    How these things came about. So shall you hear   345
    Of carnal, bloody, and unnatural acts,
    Of accidental judgments, casual° slaughters,
    Of deaths put on by cunning and forced cause,
    And, in this upshot, purposes mistook
    Fall'n on th' inventors' heads. All this can I   350
    Truly deliver.
FORTINBRAS.   Let us haste to hear it,
    And call the noblest to the audience.
    For me, with sorrow I embrace my fortune.
    I have some rights of memory° in this kingdom,
    Which now to claim my vantage doth invite me.   355
HORATIO.   Of that I shall have also cause to speak,
    And from his mouth whose voice will draw on° more.
    But let this same be presently performed,
    Even while men's minds are wild, lest more mischance
    On° plots and errors happen.
FORTINBRAS.   Let four captains   360
    Bear Hamlet like a soldier to the stage,
    For he was likely, had he been put on,°
    To have proved most royal; and for his passage°
    The soldiers' music and the rite of war
    Speak loudly for him.   365
    Take up the bodies. Such a sight as this
    Becomes the field,° but here shows much amiss.
    Go, bid the soldiers shoot.

Exeunt marching; after the which a peal of ordnance are shot off.

FINIS

Edited by Edward Hubler

---

337. *his:* (Claudius's).   340. *jump:* precisely.   343. *stage:* platform.   347. *casual:* not humanly planned, chance.   354. *rights of memory:* remembered claims.   357. *voice will draw on:* vote will influence.   360. *On:* on top of.   362. *put on:* advanced (to the throne).   363. *passage:* death. 367. *field:* battlefield.

Journal Entry

Discuss the difference between Ophelia's and Hamlet's madness.

Textual Considerations

1. In act 2, Hamlet tries to discover the facts about Claudius' guilt while the king attempts to uncover the truth about Hamlet's madness. Explain what their plans have in common.
2. Discuss the degree to which Hamlet's bitterness and sorrow are attributable to his mother's remarrying rather than to his father's death.
3. To what extent is Laertes a **foil** to Hamlet? (See the glossary.) Compare, for example, their responses to their fathers' murders.
4. Investigate the dramatic development of the play from its two extremes—the ghost's urge to disclose his story to Hamlet in act 1, scene 5, and Hamlet's urge to reveal his story to Horatio in act 5, scene 2. What do these scenes reveal about Old Hamlet's and Hamlet's attitudes toward their origins? How effectively do these scenes enhance the dramatic action of the play?
5. Review Hamlet's interview with Ophelia in act 3, scene 1. Consider what his comments reveal about the motives and attitudes that prompt him to cast Ophelia, rather than Claudius, as his antagonist.
6. Discuss how Hamlet's act of remembering and forgetting the ghost—or his ambivalence toward the ghost's narrative—informs his own private identity and his public responsibility to Denmark.

Cultural Contexts

1. What can we infer about Ophelia's and Gertrude's roles in *Hamlet*? Do these feminine characters merely fulfill the gender roles in the play, or do they also add to our understanding of Hamlet's character? Investigate also how Ophelia and Gertrude narrate the past, and how they establish a dramatic dialogue with the present and the future. How do Hamlet's attacks on these characters and on women in general affect your response to the drama?
2. Explore the father-son relationship in *Hamlet*. In your discussion, debate with your group whether Hamlet, by inheriting the past and his father's designs, is also forced to inherit his father's moral law.
3. Attempt a dramatic production of one of the scenes of *Hamlet*. To enlarge your understanding of the play, research some portrayals of Hamlet such as Laurence Olivier's and Mel Gibson's. Then discuss with your group how you would handle scenery, costumes, casting, theme, and characters.

PART ASSIGNMENTS

WRITING TOPICS

1. Several poems in Part One, such as "Fern Hill," "Song for My Name," and "Moving Away," illustrate how human beings evoke the powers of the past by re-creating their personal and communal pasts. Analyze how the poets' use of images helps to re-create their emotional and personal experiences.

2. Poems such as "During a Son's Dangerous Illness," "Moving Away," and "It's Something Our Family Has Always Done" explore the paradoxical relationship between past and present. To what extent do they suggest that past experiences affect the present?

3. Select at least one text each by a Native American, an Asian American, and a Latina, and discuss how the speakers communicate their sense of ethnic or racial identity.

4. Analyze how the themes of immigration, exile, and displacement are explored in the context of the American Dream of success in "The Visit Home" and "Lost Sister."

5. Discuss how Crane uses the theme of Maggie's origins as a motivating force influencing her actions. What details of plot and characterization are suggested by Maggie's origins?

6. Examine whether setting enhances characterization. Consider, for example, the interplay of indoor and outdoor settings in "Maggie." How do they affect characterization?

7. According to Lynne Sharon Schwartz, "memory is something we reconstruct, something we create. Memory is a story we make up from snatches of the past." Apply Schwartz's testimony to "Fern Hill," "The Sky Is Gray," "During a Son's Dangerous Illness," and/or "The Jewish Cemetery at Newport."

8. "The Watch," "Roman Fever," and "The Visit Home" communicate the validity of past experiences and explore the role that memory plays in the interaction of past and present. Discuss the role of memory in each story.

9. Consider how the attempt to retrieve the past affects the destiny of the characters in Edith Wharton's "Roman Fever" and Elie Wiesel's "The Watch."

10. Investigate whether texts such as "Nikki-Rosa" and "The Sky Is Gray" succeed in their attempt to challenge the social myths and stereotypes about African Americans.

11. Rewrite Hamlet's dilemma from Horatio's point of view, and discuss the degree to which his view corresponds with your own.

12. Hamlet and Ophelia's relationship is portrayed as problematic. Was Hamlet really in love with her? Why does he turn against her? To what extent is Hamlet to blame for Ophelia's madness and death? Write an essay analyzing their love affair.

PART ASSIGNMENTS

RESEARCH TOPICS

1. Carry out a research project on your family's history: tape interviews with family members, and collect old family photos, letters, diaries, memoirs, or any other family records that you might use as supporting evidence. Then check library sources, such as newspapers and magazines, to identify the major sociohistorical events that were part of your family's history. In writing the paper, consider assuming the personal voice of a family member and narrating your family history from his or her point of view.

2. Some novelists and intellectuals have shown a strong preference for "the pastness of the past"; others believe that only through a commitment to the present can a country re-create itself. Carry out research to demonstrate the advantages and/or disadvantages of both positions. You might explore, for instance, how African Americans or Native Americans had to come to terms with the burdens of the past, such as slavery and exploitation, in order to define their present and re-create themselves. Consult as your primary sources works by African Americans (Margaret Walker, Gwendolyn Brooks, and Robert Hayden); Native Americans (Linda Hogan, Maurice Kenny, Duane Niatum); and Asian Americans (Janice Mirikitani, Maxine Hong Kingston, Amy Tan).

3. Many critics have argued that *Hamlet* belongs to the literary tradition of the revenge tragedy—a type of drama whose literary conventions demand suspense, violence, and revenge for a murder. Research the conventions of the revenge play, and demonstrate the extent to which you would or would not apply such conventions to *Hamlet*.

PART TWO

Gender and Identity

Fiction

The Revolt of "Mother," Mary E. Wilkins Freeman ◆ *At Sea: A Sailor's Story,* Anton Chekhov ◆ *The Awakening,* Kate Chopin ◆ *The Yellow Wallpaper,* Charlotte Perkins Gilman ◆ *Karintha,* Jean Toomer ◆ *Another Evening at the Club,* Alifa Rifaat

Poetry

The Faithful Wife, Barbara L. Greenberg ◆ *Aunt Jennifer's Tigers,* Adrienne Rich ◆ *Ragazza,* Maryfrances Wagner ◆ *Petals of Silence,* Maria Mazziotti Gillan ◆ *Borders,* Pat Mora ◆ *Elena,* Pat Mora ◆ *Home Burial,* Robert Frost ◆ *The Harlem Dancer,* Claude McKay ◆ *What Lips My Lips Have Kissed,* Edna St. Vincent Millay ◆ *The Love Song of J. Alfred Prufrock,* T. S. Eliot ◆ *My Last Duchess,* Robert Browning ◆ *The Young Warrior,* Gayle Two Eagles ◆ *For My Lover, Returning to His Wife,* Anne Sexton ◆ *Bright Star,* John Keats ◆ *My Mistress' Eyes Are Nothing like the Sun,* William Shakespeare ◆ *She Proves the Inconsistency of the Desires and Criticism of Men Who Accuse Women of What They Themselves Cause,* Sor Juana Inés de la Cruz

Drama

Medea, Euripides ◆ *A Doll's House,* Henrik Ibsen

The culturally diverse texts in Part Two present a number of points of view on the relationships between men and women and their perceptions of each other. The writers ask, among other things, why various cultures have constructed different images of women at different points in their history, images as wide-ranging as goddess, rebel, warrior, sex object, mother, wife, and "other." Since most cultures have been dominated by men, the choice of female image no doubt projects a powerful representation of the male's own image. Many male and female writers included here invite you to evaluate the merit of sexual politics that promotes a male-dominated model of gender relationships.

Looking back, we discover several traditions that have created images of women to represent specific models of male-female relations. Major among these is the idealizing tradition, which portrays women as different and superior beings. For example, the Greek story of Pygmalion—the legendary sculptor who fell in love with the female statue he carved according to his own inspired view of beauty—illustrates an extreme idealization of the notion of woman. Such an idealization often transforms a woman into a love object that men can use to escape immediate reality. Other idealizing traditions, such as platonic love and courtly love, also explore the Pygmalion model of gender relations. Keats's sonnet "Bright Star" (1819), for example, evokes a romantic concept of women in the poet's transforming his mistress into an image of permanence essential to his orderly view of the world. Shakespeare's sonnet "My Mistress' Eyes Are Nothing like the Sun" playfully rejects the idealizing tradition of his poetic predecessors; he views his lover more realistically, in keeping with his Renaissance tradition.

Sor Juana Inés de la Cruz, in "She Proves the Inconsistency . . . ," addresses the mystique of gender relations through the Christian focus that polarizes the image of a woman into an "angel" or "demon." The poet protests against the tradition that debased women in seventeenth-century Mexico, reflecting the cultural oppression of "raw erotic play," or the game of male power and dominance in which, if a woman says no, "she has no heart," and if she says yes, "she's a whore." To keep pace with the social evolution of "the modern woman," we should perhaps ask what has happened to the polar image of "virgin-whore" in our own day. To what extent have women and men been able to overcome the "raw erotic play" that has tended to shape male-female relations in terms of male power and dominance?

Other texts focus on various aspects of marriage. Frost's poem "Home Burial" and Mora's "Elena" examine the difficulties men and women often encounter in trying to communicate their emotions to each other. Two short stories, "The Revolt of 'Mother'," set in nineteenth-century New England, and "Another Evening at the Club," which takes place in present-day Egypt, explore the extent to which the cult of feminine domesticity and financial dependence has perpetuated the power of the patriarchal system.

The selections by Millay, Sexton, Greenberg, and Toomer explore the question of women's sexuality, and Native American Gayle Two Eagles's poem raises the possibility that great warrior deeds, traditionally thought of as belonging to the world of men, can be successfully appropriated by women.

What have women done to claim their rights in face of male-dominated structures? How far have they gone in presenting a healthier model of gender relations and in helping to liberate men from male stereotypes of aggression and dominance? The drama selections in this part, *Medea* and *A Doll's House,* raise these questions. *Medea,* Euripides' classical Greek play, reinforces the myth of woman as femme fatale by dramatizing the story of a forsaken woman who resorts to an extreme revenge to reestablish her sense of justice. In Ibsen's nineteenth-century Norwegian play, *A Doll's House,* Nora, the protagonist, moves from negotiation to open confrontation with her husband. When Nora decides that her duties to herself are more important than those of wife or mother, to what extent is she pointing the way to freeing both men and women from the roles of the patriarchal tradition?

As you join the debate here between feminists and patriarchs in these and other texts from various cultures and traditions, you will be invited to speculate on questions such as the following: Are men rightly in charge of the family and tribe? Should women be accorded the same personal, political, and economic rights as men? How have men and women used traditional concepts of sexuality, femininity and masculinity to manipulate each other? To what extent has the ancient ideal of male supremacy been detrimental to men as well as women? How have traditional societal roles influenced gender identity? What new possibilities are there for healthier gender relationships and more fulfilled individual selves? For despite the difficulties involved in forming relationships, one theme in all these texts remains constant: We are social beings whose personal and cultural identities are rooted in our need for relatedness.

Mary E. Wilkins Freeman

The Revolt of "Mother"

"Father!"

"What is it?"

"What are them men diggin' over there in the field for?"

There was a sudden dropping and enlarging of the lower part of the old man's face, as if some heavy weight had settled therein; he shut his mouth tight, and went on harnessing the great bay mare. He hustled the collar on to her neck with a jerk.

"Father!"

The old man slapped the saddle upon the mare's back.

"Look here, father, I want to know what them men are diggin' over in the field for, an' I'm goin' to know."

"I wish you'd go into the house, mother, an' 'tend to your own affairs," the old man said then. He ran his words together, and his speech was almost as inarticulate as a growl.

But the woman understood; it was her most native tongue. "I ain't goin' into the house till you tell me what them men are doin' over there in the field," said she.

Then she stood waiting. She was a small woman, short and straight-waisted like a child in her brown cotton gown. Her forehead was mild and benevolent between the smooth curves of gray hair; there were meek downward lines about her nose and mouth; but her eyes, fixed upon the old man, looked as if the meekness had been the result of her own will, never of the will of another.

They were in the barn, standing before the wide open doors. The spring air, full of the smell of growing grass and unseen blossoms, came in their faces. The deep yard in front was littered with farm wagons and piles of wood; on the edges, close to the fence and the house, the grass was a vivid green, and there were some dandelions.

The old man glanced doggedly at his wife as he tightened the last buckles on the harness. She looked as immovable to him as one of the rocks in his pasture-land, bound to the earth with generations of blackberry vines. He slapped the reins over the horse, and started forth from the barn.

"*Father!*" said she.

The old man pulled up. "What is it?"

"I want to know what them men are diggin' over there in the field for."

"They're diggin' a cellar, I s'pose, if you've got to know."

"A cellar for what?"

"A barn."

"A barn? You ain't goin' to build a barn over there where we was goin' to have a house, father?"

The old man said not another word. He hurried the horse into the farm wagon, and clattered out of the yard, jouncing as sturdily on his seat as a boy.

The woman stood a moment looking after him, then she went out of the barn across a corner of the yard to the house. The house, standing at right angles with the great barn and a long reach of sheds and out-buildings, was infinitesimal compared with them. It was scarcely as commodious for people as the little boxes under the barn eaves were for doves.

A pretty girl's face, pink and delicate as a flower, was looking out of one of the house windows. She was watching three men who were digging over in the field which bounded the yard near the road line. She turned quietly when the woman entered.

"What are they digging for, mother?" said she. "Did he tell you?"

"They're diggin' for—a cellar for a new barn."

"Oh, mother, he ain't going to build another barn?"

"That's what be says."

A boy stood before the kitchen glass combing his hair. He combed slowly and painstakingly, arranging his brown hair in a smooth hillock over his forehead. He did not seem to pay any attention to the conversation.

"Sammy, did you know father was going to build a new barn?" asked the girl.

The boy combed assiduously.

"Sammy!"

He turned, and showed a face like his father's under his smooth crest of hair. "Yes, I s'pose I did," he said, reluctantly.

"How long have you known it?" asked his mother.

"'Bout three months, I guess."

"Why didn't you tell of it?"

"Didn't think 'twould do no good."

"I don't see what father wants another barn for," said the girl, in her sweet, slow voice. She turned again to the window, and stared out at the digging men in the field. Her tender, sweet face was full of a gentle distress. Her forehead was as bald and innocent as a baby's, with, the light hair strained back from it in a row of curl-papers. She was quite large, but her soft curls did not look as if they covered muscles.

Her mother looked sternly at the boy. "Is he goin' to buy more cows?" said she.

The boy did not reply; he was tying his shoes.

"Sammy, I want you to tell me if he's goin' to buy more cows."

"I s'pose he is."

"How many?"

"Four, I guess."

His mother said nothing more. She went into the pantry, and there was a clatter of dishes. The boy got his cap from a nail behind the door, took an old arithmetic from the shelf, and started for school. He was lightly built, but clumsy. He went out of the yard with a curious spring in the hips, that made his loose home-made jacket tilt up in the rear.

The girl went to the sink, and began to wash the dishes that were piled up there. Her mother came promptly out of the pantry, and shoved her aside. "You wipe 'em," said she; "I'll wash. There's a good many this mornin'."

The mother plunged her hands vigorously into the water, the girl wiped the plates slowly and dreamily. "Mother," said she, "don't you think it's too bad father's going to build that new barn, much as we need a decent house to live in?"

Her mother scrubbed a dish fiercely. "You ain't found out yet we're women-folks, Nanny Penn," said she. "You ain't seen enough of men-folks yet to. One of these days you'll find it out, an' then you'll know that we know only what men-folks think we do, so far as any use of it goes, an' how we'd ought to reckon men-folks in with Providence, an' not complain of what they do any more than we do of the weather."

"I don't care; I don't believe George is anything like that, anyhow," said Nanny. Her delicate face flushed pink, her lips pouted softly, is if she were going to cry.

"You wait an' see. I guess George Eastman ain't no better than other men. You hadn't ought to judge father, though. He can't help it, 'cause he don't look at things jest the way we do. An' we've been pretty comfortable here, after all. The roof don't leak—ain't never but once—that's one thing. Father's kept it shingled right up."

"I do wish we had a parlor."

"I guess it won't hurt George Eastman any to come to see you in a nice clean kitchen. I guess a good many girls don't have as good a place as this. Nobody's ever heard me complain."

"I ain't complained either, mother."

"Well, I don't think you'd better, a good father an' a good home as you've got. S'pose your father made you go out an' work for your livin'? Lots of girls have to that ain't no stronger an' better able to than you be."

Sarah Penn washed the frying-pan with a conclusive air. She scrubbed the outside of it as faithfully as the inside. She was a masterly keeper of her box of a house. Her one living-room never seemed to have in it any of the dust which the friction of life with inanimate matter produces. She swept, and there seemed to be no dirt to go before the broom; she cleaned, and one could see no difference. She was like an artist so perfect that he has apparently no art. To-day she got out a mixing bowl and a board, and rolled some pies, and there was no more flour upon her than upon her daughter who was doing finer work. Nanny was to be married in the fall, and she was sewing on some white cambric and embroidery. She sewed industriously while her mother cooked, her soft milk-white hands and wrists showed whiter than her delicate work.

"We must have the stove moved out in the shed before long," said Mrs. Penn. "Talk about not havin' things, it's been a real blessin' to be able to put a stove up in that shed in hot weather. Father did one good thing when he fixed that stove-pipe out there."

Sarah Penn's face as she rolled her pies had that expression of meek vigor which might have characterized one of the New Testament saints. She was making mince-pies. Her husband, Adoniram Penn, liked them better than any other kind. She baked twice a week. Adoniram often liked a piece of pie between meals. She hurried this morning. It had been later than usual when she began, and she wanted to have a pie baked for dinner. However deep a resentment she might be forced to hold against her husband, she would never fail in sedulous attention to his wants.

Nobility of character manifests itself at loop-holes when it is not provided with large doors. Sarah Penn's showed itself to-day in flaky dishes of pastry. So she made the pies faithfully, while across the table she could see, when she glanced up from her work, the sight that rankled in her patient and steadfast soul—the digging of the cellar of the new barn in the place where Adoniram forty years ago had promised her their new house should stand.

The pies were done for dinner. Adoniram and Sammy were home a few minutes after twelve o'clock. The dinner was eaten with serious haste. There was never much conversation at the table in the Penn family. Adoniram asked a blessing, and they ate promptly, then rose up and went about their work.

Sammy went back to school, taking soft sly lopes out of the yard like a rabbit. He wanted a game of marbles before school, and feared his father would give him some chores to do. Adoniram hastened to the door and called after him, but he was out of sight.

"I don't see what you let him go for, Mother," said he. "I wanted him to help me unload that wood."

Adoniram went to work out in the yard unloading wood from the wagon. Sarah put away the dinner dishes, while Nanny took down her curl-papers and changed her dress. She was going down to the store to buy some more embroidery and thread.

When Nanny was gone, Mrs. Penn went to the door. "Father!" she called.

"Well, what is it!"

"I want to see you jest a minute."

"I can't leave this wood nohow. I've got to git it unloaded an' go for a load of gravel afore two o'clock. Sammy had ought to helped me. You hadn't ought to let him go to school so early."

"I want to see you jest a minute."

"I tell ye I can't, nohow, mother."

"Father, you come here." Sarah Penn stood in the door like a queen; she held her head as if it bore a crown; there was that patience which makes authority royal in her voice. Adoniram went.

Mrs. Penn led the way into the kitchen, and pointed to a chair. "Sit down, father," said she; "I've got somethin' I want to say to you."

He sat down heavily; his face was quite stolid, but he looked at her with restive eyes. "Well, what is it, mother?"

"I want to know what you're buildin' that new barn for, father?"

"I ain't got nothin' to say about it."

"It can't be you think you need another barn?"

"I tell ye I ain't got nothin' to say about it, mother, an' I ain't goin' to say nothin'."

"Be you goin' to buy more cows?"

Adoniram did not reply; he shut his mouth tight.

"I know you be, as well as I want to. Now, father, look here"—Sarah Penn had not sat down; she stood before her husband in the humble fashion of a Scripture woman—"I'm goin' to talk real plain to you; I never have sence I married you, but I'm goin' to now. I ain't never complained, an' I ain't goin' to complain now, but I'm goin' to talk plain. You see this room here, father; you look at it well. You see there ain't no carpet on the floor, an' you see the paper is all dirty, an' droppin' off the walls. We ain't had no new paper on it for ten year, an' then I put it on myself, an' it didn't cost but ninepence a roll. You see this room, father; it's all the one I've had to work in an' eat in an' sit in sence we was married. There ain't another woman in the whole town whose husband ain't got half the means you have but what's got better. It's all the room Nanny's got to have her company in; an' there ain't one of her mates but what's got better, an' their fathers not so able as hers is. It's all the room she'll have to be married in. What would you have thought, father, if we had had our weddin' in a room no better than this? I was married in my mother's parlor, with a carpet on the floor, an' stuffed furniture, an' a mahogany card-table. An' this is all the room my daughter will have to be married in. Look here, father!"

Sarah Penn went across the room as though it were a tragic stage. She flung open a door and disclosed a tiny bedroom, only large enough for a bed and bureau, with a path between. "There, father," said she—"there's all the room I've had to sleep in forty year. All my children were born there— the two that died, an' the two that's livin'. I was sick with a fever there."

She stepped into another door and opened it. It led into the small, ill-lighted pantry. "Here," said she, "is all the buttery I've got—every place I've got for my dishes, to set away my victuals in, an' to keep my milk-pans in. Father, I've been takin' care of the milk of six cows in this place, an' now you're goin' to build a new barn, an' keep more cows, an' give me more to do in it."

She threw open another door. A narrow crooked flight of stairs wound upward from it. "There, father," said she. "I want you to look at the stairs that go up to them two unfinished chambers that are all the places our son an' daughter have had to sleep in all their lives. There ain't a prettier girl in town nor a more ladylike one than Nanny, an' that's the place she has to sleep in. It ain't so good as your horse's stall; it ain't so warm an' tight."

Sarah Penn went back and stood before her husband. "Now, father," said she, "I want to know if you think you're doin' right an' accordin' to what you profess. Here, when we was married, forty year ago, you promised me faithful that we should have a new house built in that lot over in the field before the year was out. You said you had money enough, an' you wouldn't ask me to live in no such place as this. It is forty year now, an' you've been makin' more money, an' I've been savin' of it for you ever since, an' you ain't built no house yet. You've built sheds an' cow-houses an' one new barn, an' now you're goin' to build another. Father, I want to know if you think it's right. You're lodgin' your dumb beasts better than you are your own flesh an' blood. I want to know if you think it's right."

"I ain't got nothin' to say."

"You can't say nothin' without ownin' it ain't right, father. An' there's another thing—I ain't complained; I've got along forty year, an' I s'pose I should forty more, if it wa'n't for that—if we don't have another house. Nanny she can't live with us after she's married. She'll have to go somewheres else to live away from us, an' it don't seem as if I could have it so, noways, father. She wa'n't ever strong. She's got considerable color, but there wa'n't never any backbone to her. I've always took the heft of everything off her, an' she ain't fit to keep house an' do everything herself. She'll be all worn out inside of a year. Think of her doin' all the washin' an' ironin' an' bakin' with them soft white hands an' arms, an' sweepin'! I can't have it so, noways, father."

Mrs. Penn's face was burning; her mild eyes gleamed. She had pleaded her little cause like a Webster;[1] she had ranged from severity to pathos; but her opponent employed that obstinate silence which makes eloquence futile with mocking echoes. Adoniram arose clumsily.

"Father, ain't you got nothin' to say?" said Mrs. Penn.

"I've got to go off after that load of gravel. I can't stan' here talkin' all day."

"Father, won't you think it over, an' have a house built there instead of a barn?"

"I ain't got nothin' to say."

Adoniram shuffled out. Mrs. Penn went into her bedroom. When she came out, her eyes were red. She had a roll of unbleached cotton cloth. She spread it out on the kitchen table, and began cutting out some shirts for her husband. The men over in the field had a team to help them this afternoon; she could hear their halloos. She had a scanty pattern for the shirts; she had to plan and piece the sleeves.

Nanny came home with her embroidery, and sat down with her needlework. She had taken down her curl-papers, and there was a soft roll of fair hair like an aureole over her forehead; her face was as delicately fine and clear as porcelain. Suddenly she looked up, and the tender red flamed all over her face and neck. "Mother," said she.

"What say?"

"I've been thinking—I don't see how we're goin' to have any—wedding in this room. I'd be ashamed to have his folks come if we didn't have anybody else."

"Mebbe we can have some new paper before then; I can put it on. I guess you won't have no call to be ashamed of your belongin's."

"We might have the wedding in the new barn," said Nanny, with gentle pettishness. "Why, mother, what makes you look so?"

Mrs. Penn had started, and was staring at her with a curious expression. She turned again to her work, and spread out a pattern carefully on the cloth. "Nothin'," said she.

---

[1] Daniel Webster (1782–1852) was an American orator, lawyer, and statesman.

Presently Adoniram clattered out of the yard in his two-wheeled dump cart, standing as proudly upright as a Roman charioteer. Mrs. Penn opened the door and stood there a minute looking out; the halloos of the men sounded louder.

It seemed to her all through the spring months that she heard nothing but the halloos and the noises of saws and hammers. The new barn grew fast. It was a fine edifice for this little village. Men came on pleasant Sundays, in their meeting suits and clean shirt bosoms, and stood around it admiringly. Mrs. Penn did not speak of it, and Adoniram did not mention it to her, although sometimes, upon a return from inspecting it, he bore himself with injured dignity.

"It's a strange thing how your mother feels about the new barn," he said, confidentially, to Sammy one day.

Sammy only grunted after an odd fashion for a boy; he had learned it from his father.

The barn was all completed ready for use by the third week in July. Adoniram had planned to move his stock in on Wednesday; on Tuesday he received a letter which changed his plans. He came in with it early in the morning. "Sammy's been to the post-office," said he, "an' I've got a letter from Hiram." Hiram was Mrs. Penn's brother, who lived in Vermont.

"Well," said Mrs. Penn, "what does he say about the folks?"

"I guess they're all right. He says he thinks if I come up country right off there's a chance to buy jest the kind of a horse I want." He stared reflectively out of the window at the new barn.

Mrs. Penn was making pies. She went on clapping the rolling-pin into the crust, although she was very pale, and her heart beat loudly.

"I dun' know but what I'd better go," said Adoniram. "I hate to go off jest now, right in the midst of hayin', but the ten-acre lot's cut, an' I guess Rufus an' the others can git along without me three or four days. I can't get a horse round here to suit me, nohow, an' I've got to have another for all that wood-haulin' in the fall. I told Hiram to watch out, an if he got wind of a good horse to let me know. I guess I'd better go."

"I'll get your clean shirt an' collar," said Mrs. Penn calmly.

She laid out Adoniram's Sunday suit and his clean clothes on the bed in the little bedroom. She got his shaving-water and razor ready. At last she buttoned on his collar and fastened his black cravat.

Adoniram never wore his collar and cravat except on extra occasions. He held his head high, with a rasped dignity. When he was all ready, with his coat and hat brushed, and a lunch of pie and cheese in a paper bag, he hesitated on the threshold of the door. He looked at his wife, and his manner was defiantly apologetic. "*If* them cows come to-day, Sammy can drive 'em into the new barn," said he, "an' when they bring the hay up, they can pitch it in there."

"Well," replied Mrs. Penn.

Adoniram set his shaven face ahead and started. When he had cleared the door-step, he turned and looked back with a kind of nervous solemnity. "I shall be back by Saturday if nothin' happens," said he.

"Do be careful, father," returned his wife.

She stood at the door with Nanny at her elbow and watched him out of sight. Her eyes had a strange, doubtful expression in them; her peaceful forehead was contracted. She went in, and about her baking again. Nanny sat sewing. Her wedding-day was drawing nearer, and she was getting pale and thin with her steady sewing. Her mother kept glancing at her.

"Have you got that pain in your side this mornin'?" she asked.

"A little."

Mrs. Penn's face, as she worked, changed, her perplexed forehead smoothed, her eyes were steady, her lips firmly set. She formed a maxim for herself, although incoherently with her unlettered thoughts. "Unsolicited opportunities are the guide-posts of the Lord to the new roads of life," she repeated in effect, and she made up her mind to her course of action.

"S'posin' I *had* wrote to Hiram," she muttered once, when she was in the pantry—"s'posin' I had wrote, an' asked him if he knew of any horse? But I didn't, an' father's goin' wa'n't none of my doin'. It looks like a providence." Her voice rang out quite loud at the last.

"What are you talkin' about, mother?" called Nanny.

"Nothin'."

Mrs. Penn hurried her baking; at eleven o'clock it was all done. The load of hay from the west field came slowly down the cart track, and drew up at the new barn. Mrs. Penn ran out. "Stop!" she screamed—"stop!"

The men stopped and looked; Sammy upreared from the top of the load, and stared at his mother.

"Stop!" she cried out again. "Don't you put the hay in that barn; put it in the old one."

"Why, he said to put it in here," returned one of the haymakers, wonderingly. He was a young man, a neighbor's son, whom Adoniram hired by the year to help on the farm.

"Don't you put the hay in the new barn; there's room enough in the old one, ain't there?" said Mrs. Penn.

"Room enough," returned the hired man, in his thick, rustic tones. "Didn't need the new barn, nohow far as room's concerned. Well, I s'pose he changed his mind." He took hold of the horses' bridles.

Mrs. Penn went back to the house. Soon the kitchen windows were darkened, and a fragrance like warm honey came into the room.

Nanny laid down her work. "I thought father wanted them to put the hay into the new barn?" she said wonderingly.

"It's all right," replied her mother.

Sammy slid down from the load of hay, and came in to see if dinner was ready.

"I ain't goin' to get a regular dinner to-day, as long as father's gone," said his mother. "I've let the fire go out. You can have some bread an' milk an' pie. I thought we could get along." She set out some bowls of milk, some bread, and a pie on the kitchen table. "You'd better eat your dinner now," said she. "You might jest as well get through with it. I want you to help me afterward."

Nanny and Sammy stared at each other. There was something strange in their mother's manner. Mrs. Penn did not eat anything herself. She went into the pantry, and they heard her moving dishes while they ate. Presently she came out with a pile of plates. She got the clothes-basket out of the shed, and packed them in it. Nanny and Sammy watched. She brought out cups and saucers, and put them in with the plates.

"What you goin' to do, mother?" inquired Nanny, in a timid voice. A sense of something unusual made her tremble, as if it were a ghost. Sammy rolled his eyes over his pie.

"You'll see what I'm goin' to do," replied Mrs. Penn. "If you're through, Nanny, I want you to go upstairs an' pack up your things; an' I want you, Sammy, to help me take down the bed in the bedroom."

"Oh, mother, what for?" gasped Nanny.

"You'll see."

During the next few hours a feat was performed by this simple, pious New England mother which was equal in its way to Wolfe's storming of the Heights of Abraham.[2] It took no more genius and audacity of bravery for Wolfe to cheer his wondering soldiers up those steep precipices, under the sleeping eyes of the enemy, than for Sarah Penn, at the head of her children, to move all their little household goods into the new barn while her husband was away.

Nanny and Sammy followed their mother's instructions without a murmur; indeed, they were overawed. There is a certain uncanny and superhuman quality about all such purely original undertakings as their mother's was to them. Nanny went back and forth with her light loads, and Sammy tugged with sober energy.

At five o'clock in the afternoon the little house in which the Penns had lived for forty years had emptied itself into the new barn.

Every builder builds somewhat for unknown purposes, and is in a measure a prophet. The architect of Adoniram Penn's barn, while he designed it for the comfort of four-footed animals, had planned better than he knew for the comfort of humans. Sarah Penn saw at a glance its possibilities. Those great box-stalls, with quilts hung before them, would make better bedrooms than the one she had occupied for forty years, and there was a tight carriage-room. The harness-room, with its chimney and shelves, would make a kitchen of her dreams. The great middle space would make a parlor, by-and-by, fit for a palace. Upstairs there was as much room as down. With partitions and windows, what a house would there be! Sarah looked at the row of stanchions before the allotted space for cows, and reflected that she would have her front entry there.

At six o'clock the stove was up in the harness-room, the kettle was boiling, and the table set for tea. It looked almost as home-like as the abandoned house across

---

[2] James Wolfe (1727–1759) was a British general whose troops stormed the French army on the Plains of Abraham above Quebec.

the yard had ever done. The young hired man milked, and Sarah directed him calmly to bring the milk to the new barn. He came gaping, dropping little blots of foam from the brimming pails on the grass. Before the next morning he had spread the story of Adoniram Penn's wife moving into the new barn all over the little village. Men assembled in the store and talked it over, women with shawls over their heads scuttled into each other's houses before their work was done. Any deviation from the ordinary course of life in this quiet town was enough to stop all progress in it. Everybody paused to look at the staid, independent figure on the side track. There was a difference of opinion with regard to her. Some held her to be insane; some, of a lawless and rebellious spirit.

Friday the minister went to see her. It was in the forenoon, and she was at the barn door shelling pease[3] for dinner. She looked up and returned his salutation with dignity, then she went on with her work. She did not invite him in. The saintly expression of her face remained fixed, but there was an angry flush over it.

The minister stood awkwardly before her, and talked. She handled the pease as if they were bullets. At last she looked up, and her eyes showed the spirit that her meek front had covered for a lifetime.

"There ain't no use talkin', Mr. Hersey," she said. "I've thought it all over an' over, an' I believe I'm doin' what's right. I've made it the subject of prayer, an' it's betwixt me an' the Lord an' Adoniram. There ain't no call for anybody else to worry about it."

"Well, of course, if you have brought it to the Lord in prayer, and feel satisfied that you are doing right, Mrs. Penn," said the minister, helplessly. His thin gray-bearded face was pathetic. He was a sickly man; his youthful confidence had cooled; he had to scourge himself up to some of his pastoral duties as relentlessly as a Catholic ascetic, and then he was prostrated by the smart.

"I think it's right jest as much as I think it was right for our forefathers to come over from the old country 'cause they didn't have what belonged to 'em," said Mrs. Penn. She arose. The barn threshold might have been Plymouth Rock from her bearing. "I don't doubt you mean well, Mr. Hersey," said she, "but there are things people hadn't ought to interfere with. I've been a member of the church for over forty year. I've got my own mind an' my own feet, an' I'm goin' to think my own thoughts an' go my own ways, an' nobody but the Lord is goin' to dictate to me unless I've a mind to have him. Won't you come in an' set down? How is Mis' Hersey?"

"She is well, I thank you," replied the minister. He added some more perplexed apologetic remarks; then he retreated.

He could expound the intricacies of every character study in the Scriptures, he was competent to grasp the Pilgrim Fathers and all historical innovators, but Sarah Penn was beyond him. He could deal with primal causes, but parallel ones worsted him. But, after all, although it was aside from his province, he wondered more how Adoniram Penn would deal with his wife than how the Lord would. Everybody

---

[3] Old or variant spelling of "peas."

shared the wonder. When Adoniram's four new cows arrived, Sarah ordered three to be put in the old barn, the other in the house shed where the cooking-stove had stood. That added to the excitement. It was whispered that all four cows were domiciled in the house.

Towards sunset on Saturday, when Adoniram was expected home, there was a knot of men in the road near the new barn. The hired man had milked, but he still hung around the premises. Sarah Penn had supper all ready. There were brown-bread and baked beans and a custard pie; it was the supper that Adoniram loved on a Saturday night. She had on a clean calico, and she bore herself imperturbably. Nanny and Sammy kept close at her heels. Their eyes were large, and Nanny was full of nervous tremors. Still there was to them more pleasant excitement than anything else. An inborn confidence in their mother over their father asserted itself.

Sammy looked out of the harness-room window. "There he is," he announced, in an awed whisper. He and Nanny peeped around the casing. Mrs. Penn kept on about her work. The children watched Adoniram leave the new horse standing in the drive while he went to the house door. It was fastened. Then he went around to the shed. That door was seldom locked, even when the family was away. The thought how her father would be confronted by the cow flashed upon Nanny. There was a hysterical sob in her throat. Adoniram emerged from the shed and stood looking about in a dazed fashion. His lips moved; he was saying something, but they could not hear what it was. The hired man was peeping around a corner of the old barn, but nobody saw him.

Adoniram took the new horse by the bridle and led him across the yard to the new barn. Nanny and Sammy slunk close to their mother. The barn doors rolled back, and there stood Adoniram, with the long mild face of the great Canadian farm horse looking over his shoulder.

Nanny kept behind her mother, but Sammy stepped suddenly forward, and stood in front of her.

Adoniram stared at the group. "What on airth you all down here for?" said he. "What's the matter over to the house?"

"We've come here to live, father," said Sammy. His shrill voice quavered out bravely.

"What"—Adoniram sniffled—"what is it smells like cooking?" said he. He stepped forward and looked in the open door of the harness-room. Then he turned to his wife. His old bristling face was pale and frightened. "What on airth does this mean, mother?" he gasped.

"You come in here, father," said Sarah. She led the way, into the harness-room and shut the door. "Now, father," said she, "you needn't be scared. I ain't crazy. There ain't nothin' to be upset over. But we've come here to live, an' we're goin' to live here. We've got jest as good a right here as new horses an' cows. The house wa'n't fit for us to live in any longer, an' I made up my mind I wa'n't goin' to stay there. I've done my duty by you forty year, an' I'm goin' to do it now; but I'm goin' to live here. You've got to put in some windows and partitions; an' you'll have to buy some furniture."

"Why, mother!" the old man gasped.

"You'd better take your coat off an' get washed—there's the wash-basin—an' then we'll have supper."

"Why, mother!"

Sammy went past the window, leading the new horse to the old barn. The old man saw him, and shook is head speechlessly. He tried to take off his coat, but his arms seemed to lack the power. His wife helped him. She poured some water into the tin basin, and put in a piece of soap. She got the comb and brush, and smoothed his thin gray hair after he had washed. Then she put the beans, hot bread, and tea on the table. Sammy came in, and the family drew up. Adoniram sat looking dazedly at his plate, and they waited.

"Ain't you goin' to ask a blessin', father?" said Sarah.

And the old man bent his head and mumbled.

All through the meal he stopped eating at intervals, and stared furtively at his wife; but he ate well. The home food tasted good to him, and his old frame was too sturdily healthy to be affected by his mind. But after supper he went out, and sat down on the step of the smaller door at the right of the barn, through which he had meant his Jerseys to pass in stately file, but which Sarah designed for her front house door, and he leaned his head on his hands.

After the supper dishes were cleared away and the milk-pans washed, Sarah went out to him. The twilight was deepening. There was a clear green glow in the sky. Before them stretched the smooth level of field; in the distance was a cluster of hay-stacks like the huts of a village; the air was very cool and calm and sweet. The landscape might have been an ideal one of peace.

Sarah bent over and touched her husband on one of his thin, sinewy shoulders. "Father!"

The old man's shoulders heaved: he was weeping.

"Why, don't do so, father," said Sarah.

"I'll—put up the—partitions, an'—everything you—want, mother."

Sarah put her apron up to her face; she was overcome by her own triumph.

Adoniram was like a fortress whose walls had no active resistance, and went down the instant the right besieging tools were used. "Why, mother," he said, hoarsely, "I hadn't no idee you was so set on't as all this comes to."

Journal Entry

Speculate on the relation between revolt and identity in "The Revolt of 'Mother'." Analyze the reaction of family members to Mother's "revolt."

Textual Considerations

1. Analyze the functions of setting in the story, including its relation to the conflict.
2. Freeman uses expressions such as "immovable as one of the rocks" or "meek vigor which might have characterized one of the New Testament saints" to describe Mrs. Penn. Identify other expressions that serve to sketch her physical and psychological portrait.

3. Explore the causes that motivate Mrs. Penn to break out of her socially defined role as an obedient wife. Include in your discussion the different ways in which she and her husband perceive the world. How effectively do they communicate with each other?

Cultural Contexts

1. Find examples and illustrations of feminine solidarity between Mrs. Penn and her daughter. Speculate on why Mother feels she must pass down to her daughter the feminine consciousness that "we know only what men-folks think we do."
2. To examine the power of the patriarchal traditions that dictate Mrs. Penn's social confinement, as well as the dynamics of gender relations in their household, comment on the reaction of the male community to Mrs. Penn's "revolt." Include the minister, Hersey, in your discussion.

Anton Chekhov

At Sea
A Sailor's Story

Only the dimming lights of the receding harbor were visible in an ink-black sky. We could feel the heavy storm clouds overhead about to burst into rain, and it was suffocating, in spite of the wind and cold.

Crowded together in the crew's quarters we, the sailors, were casting lots. Loud, drunken laughter filled the air. One of our comrades was playfully crowing like a cock. A slight shiver ran through me from the back of my heels, as if cold small shot were pouring down my naked body from a hole in the back of my head. I was shivering both from the cold and certain other causes, which I wish to describe.

In my opinion, man is, as a rule, foul; and the sailor can sometimes be the foulest of all the creatures of the earth—fouler than the lowest beast, which has, at least, the excuse of obeying his instincts. It is possible that I may be mistaken, since I do not know life, but it appears to me that a sailor has more occasion than anyone else to despise and curse himself. A man who at any moment may fall headlong from a mast to be forever hidden beneath a wave, a man who may drown, God alone knows when, has need of nothing, and one on dry land feels pity for him. We sailors drink a lot of vodka and are dissolute because we do not know what one needs virtue for at sea. However, I shall continue.

We were casting lots. There were twenty-two of us who, having stood watch, were now at liberty. Out of this number only two were to have the luck of enjoying a rare spectacle. On this particular night the honeymoon cabin was occupied, but the wall of the cabin had only two holes at our disposal. One of them I myself had made with a fine saw, after boring through with a corkscrew; the other had been cut out with a knife by one of my comrades. We had worked at it for more than a week.

"You got one hole?"

"Who?"

They pointed to me. "Who got the other?"

"Your father."

My father, a humpbacked old sailor with a face like a baked apple, came up to me and clapped me on the back. "Today, my boy, we're lucky!" he said. "Do you hear, boy? Luck came to us both at the same time. That means something." Impatiently he asked the time; it was only eleven o'clock.

I went up on deck, lit my pipe and gazed out to sea. It was dark, but it can be assumed that my eyes reflected what was taking place in my soul, as I made out images on the background of the night, visualizing what was so lacking in my own still young but already ruined life. . . .

At midnight I walked past the saloon and glanced in at the door. The bridegroom, a young pastor with a handsome blond head, sat at a table holding the Gospels in his hands. He was explaining something to a tall, gaunt Englishwoman. The bride, a very beautiful, shapely young woman, sat at her husband's side with her light blue eyes fixed on him. A tall, plump, elderly Englishman, a banker, with a repulsive red face, paced up and down the saloon. He was the husband of the middle-aged lady to whom the pastor was talking.

"Pastors have a habit of talking for hours," I thought. "He won't finish before morning." At one o'clock my father came to me, pulled me by the sleeve and said: "It's time. They've left the saloon."

In the twinkling of an eye I flew down the companionway and approached the familiar wall. Between this wall and the side of the ship there was a space where soot, water, and rats collected. I soon heard the heavy tread of the old man, my father. He cursed as he stumbled over a mat-sack and some kerosene cans. I felt for the hole in the wall and pulled out the square piece of wood I had so painstakingly sawed. I was looking at a thin, transparent muslin through which penetrated a soft, rosy light. Together with the light, my burning face was caressed by a delightful, sultry fragrance; this, no doubt, was the smell of an aristocratic bedroom. In order to see the room it was necessary to draw aside the muslin with two fingers, which I hastened to do. I saw bronze, velvet, lace, all bathed in a pink glow. About ten feet from my face stood the bed.

"Let me have your place," said my father, impatiently pushing me aside. "I can see better here." I did not answer him. "Your eyes are better than mine, boy, and it makes no difference to you if you look from far or near."

"Be quiet," I said, "they might hear us."

The bride sat on the side of the bed, dangling her little feet in a foot muff. She was staring at the floor. Before her stood her husband, the young pastor. He was telling her something, what I do not know; the noise of the steamer made it impossible for me to hear. He spoke passionately, with gestures, his eyes flashing. She listened and shook her head in refusal.

"The devil!" my father muttered. "A rat bit me!"

I pressed my chest to the wall, as if fearing my heart would jump out. My head was burning.

The bride and groom talked at great length. At last he sank to his knees and held out his arms, imploring her. She shook her head in refusal. He leaped to his feet, crossed the cabin, and from the expression on his face and the movements of his arms I surmised that he was threatening her. The young wife rose and went slowly towards the wall where I was standing. She stopped near the opening and stood motionless in thought. I devoured her face with my eyes. It seemed to me that she was suffering, struggling with herself, not knowing what to do; but at the same time her features expressed anger. I did not understand it.

We continued to stand there face to face for above five minutes, then she moved slowly away and, pausing in the middle of the cabin, nodded to the pastor—a sign of consent, undoubtedly. He smiled happily, kissed her hand and went out.

Within three minutes the door opened and the pastor reentered followed by the tall, plump Englishman whom I mentioned above. The Englishman went over to the bed and asked the beautiful woman a question. Pale, not looking at him, she nodded her head affirmatively. The banker then took out of his pocket a packet of some sort—evidently bank notes—and handed it to the pastor, who examined it, counted it, bowed and went out. The elderly Englishman locked the door after him.

I sprang away from the wall as if I had been stung. I was frightened. It seemed to me the wind was tearing our ship to pieces, that we were going down. My father, that drunken, debauched old man, took me by the arm and said: "Let's go away from here! You shouldn't see that. You're still a boy."

He was hardly able to stand. I carried him up the steep winding stairs. Above an autumn rain had begun to fall.

Translated by Ann Dunnigan

Journal Entry

Reflect on how you would have responded in either the husband's or the wife's situation, and cite your reasons for your response.

Textual Considerations

1. Comment on Chekhov's use of a narrator in "At Sea: A Sailor's Story." How does this device affect the tone of the story?
2. Analyze Chekhov's use of narrative devices such as suspense and expectation in the development of the story and in the creation of a dramatic climax.
3. Speculate on the circumstances that lead the wife to give in to her seducer. What kind of resistance does she put up against her husband's schemes?

Cultural Contexts

1. Comment on the fact that the sex traffic involving the wife in "At Sea: A Sailor's Story" was protected by religious and social institutions such as marriage.
2. Characterize your group's attitude toward this text, which attempts to record part of the social history of men and women. To what extent is Chekhov's portrayal of nineteenth-century marriage relevant to today's society? Consider, for example, whether men and women still seek to control and manipulate each other.

Kate Chopin

The Awakening

I

A green and yellow parrot, which hung in a cage outside the door, kept repeating over and over:

"*Allez vous-en! Allez vous-en! Sapristi!*[1] That's all right!"

He could speak a little Spanish, and also a language which nobody understood, unless it was the mocking-bird that hung on the other side of the door, whistling his fluty notes out upon the breeze with maddening persistence.

Mr. Pontellier, unable to read his newspaper with any degree of comfort, arose with an expression and an exclamation of disgust. He walked down the gallery and across the narrow "bridges" which connected the Lebrun cottages one with the other. He had been seated before the door of the main house. The parrot and the mocking-bird were the property of Madame Lebrun, and they had the right to make all the noise they wished. Mr. Pontellier had the privilege of quitting their society when they ceased to be entertaining.

He stopped before the door of his own cottage, which was the fourth one from the main building and next to the last. Seating himself in a wicker rocker which was there, he once more applied himself to the task of reading the newspaper. The day was Sunday; the paper was a day old. The Sunday papers had not yet reached Grand Isle.[2] He was already acquainted with the market reports, and he glanced restlessly over the editorials and bits of news which he had not had time to read before quitting New Orleans the day before.

Mr. Pontellier wore eye-glasses. He was a man of forty, of medium height and rather slender build; he stooped a little. His hair was brown and straight, parted on one side. His beard was neatly and closely trimmed.

---

[1] *Allez . . . Sapristi:* Go away! go away! For God's sake. [2] *Grand Isle:* a resort island fifty miles south of New Orleans.

Once in a while he withdrew his glance from the newspaper and looked about him. There was more noise than ever over at the house. The main building was called "the house," to distinguish it from the cottages. The chattering and whistling birds were still at it. Two young girls, the Farival twins, were playing a duet from "Zampa"[3] upon the piano. Madame Lebrun was bustling in and out, giving orders in a high key to a yard-boy whenever she got inside the house, and directions in an equally high voice to a dining-room servant whenever she got outside. She was a fresh, pretty woman, clad always in white with elbow sleeves. Her starched skirts crinkled as she came and went. Farther down, before one of the cottages, a lady in black was walking demurely up and down, telling her beads. A good many persons of the *pension*[4] had gone over to the *Chênière Caminada* in Beaudelet's lugger[5] to hear mass. Some young people were out under the water-oaks playing croquet. Mr. Pontellier's two children were there—sturdy little fellows of four and five. A quadroon nurse followed them about with a far-away, meditative air.

Mr. Pontellier finally lit a cigar and began to smoke, letting the paper drag idly from his hand. He fixed his gaze upon a white sunshade that was advancing at snail's pace from the beach. He could see it plainly between the gaunt trunks of the water-oaks and across the stretch of yellow camomile. The gulf looked far away, melting hazily into the blue of the horizon. The sunshade continued to approach slowly. Beneath its pink-lined shelter were his wife, Mrs. Pontellier, and young Robert Lebrun. When they reached the cottage, the two seated themselves with some appearance of fatigue upon the upper step of the porch, facing each other, each leaning against a supporting post.

"What folly! to bathe at such an hour in such heat!" exclaimed Mr. Pontellier. He himself had taken a plunge at daylight. That was why the morning seemed long to him.

"You are burnt beyond recognition," he added, looking at his wife as one looks at a valuable piece of personal property which has suffered some damage. She held up her hands, strong, shapely hands, and surveyed them critically, drawing up her lawn[6] sleeves above the wrists. Looking at them reminded her of her rings, which she had given to her husband before leaving for the beach. She silently reached out to him, and he, understanding, took the rings from his vest pocket and dropped them into her open palm. She slipped them upon her fingers; then clasping her knees, she looked across at Robert and began to laugh. The rings sparkled upon her fingers. He sent back an answering smile.

"What is it?" asked Pontellier, looking lazily and amused from one to the other. It was some utter nonsense; some adventure out there in the water, and they both tried to relate it at once. It did not seem half so amusing when told. They realized this, and so did Mr. Pontellier. He yawned and stretched himself. Then he got up, saying he had half a mind to go over to Klein's hotel and play a game of billiards.

---

[3] *"Zampa":* opera by Louis Hérold (1791–1833). In the opera, a lover dies at sea.   [4] *pension:* small hotel
[5] *lugger:* small boat   [6] *lawn:* fine cotton or linen.

"Come go along, Lebrun," he proposed to Robert. But Robert admitted quite frankly that he preferred to stay where he was and talk to Mrs. Pontellier.

"Well, send him about his business when he bores you, Edna," instructed her husband as he prepared to leave.

"Here, take the umbrella," she exclaimed, holding it out to him. He accepted the sunshade, and lifting it over his head descended the steps and walked away.

"Coming back to dinner?" his wife called after him. He halted a moment and shrugged his shoulders. He felt in his vest pocket; there was a ten-dollar bill there. He did not know; perhaps he would return for the early dinner and perhaps he would not. It all depended upon the company which he found over at Klein's and the size of "the game." He did not say this, but she understood it, and laughed, nodding good-by to him.

Both children wanted to follow their father when they saw him starting out. He kissed them and promised to bring back bonbons and peanuts.

II

Mrs. Pontellier's eyes were quick and bright; they were a yellowish brown, about the color of her hair. She had a way of turning them swiftly upon an object and holding them there as if lost in some inward maze of contemplation or thought.

Her eyebrows were a shade darker than her hair. They were thick and almost horizontal, emphasizing the depth of her eyes. She was rather handsome than beautiful. Her face was captivating by reason of a certain frankness of expression and a contradictory subtle play of features. Her manner was engaging.

Robert rolled a cigarette. He smoked cigarettes because he could not afford cigars, he said. He had a cigar in his pocket which Mr. Pontellier had presented him with, and he was saving it for his after-dinner smoke.

This seemed quite proper and natural on his part. In coloring he was not unlike his companion. A clean-shaved face made the resemblance more pronounced than it would otherwise have been. There rested no shadow of care upon his open countenance. His eyes gathered in and reflected the light and languor of the summer day.

Mrs. Pontellier reached over for a palm-leaf fan that lay on the porch and began to fan herself, while Robert sent between his lips light puffs from his cigarette. They chatted incessantly: about the things around them; their amusing adventure out in the water—it had again assumed its entertaining aspect; about the wind, the trees, the people who had gone to the *Chênière;* about the children playing croquet under the oaks, and the Farival twins, who were now performing the overture to "The Poet and the Peasant."[7]

Robert talked a good deal about himself. He was very young, and did not know any better. Mrs. Pontellier talked a little about herself for the same reason. Each was interested in what the other said. Robert spoke of his intention to go to Mexico in the autumn, where fortune awaited him. He was always intending to go to Mexico,

---

[7] *"The Poet and the Peasant"*: operetta by Franz von Suppé (1819–95).

but some way never got there. Meanwhile he held on to his modest position in a mercantile house in New Orleans, where an equal familiarity with English, French and Spanish gave him no small value as a clerk and correspondent.

He was spending his summer vacation, as he always did, with his mother at Grand Isle. In former times, before Robert could remember, "the house" had been a summer luxury of the Lebruns. Now, flanked by its dozen or more cottages, which were always filled with exclusive visitors from the "*Quartier Français,*"[8] it enabled Madame Lebrun to maintain the easy and comfortable existence which appeared to be her birthright.

Mrs. Pontellier talked about her father's Mississippi plantation and her girlhood home in the old Kentucky blue-grass country. She was an American woman, with a small infusion of French which seemed to have been lost in dilution. She read a letter from her sister, who was away in the East, and who had engaged herself to be married. Robert was interested, and wanted to know what manner of girls the sisters were, what the father was like, and how long the mother had been dead.

When Mrs. Pontellier folded the letter it was time for her to dress for the early dinner.

"I see Léonce isn't coming back," she said, with a glance in the direction whence her husband had disappeared. Robert supposed he was not, as there were a good many New Orleans club men over at Klein's.

When Mrs. Pontellier left him to enter her room, the young man descended the steps and strolled over toward the croquet players, where, during the half-hour before dinner, he amused himself with the little Pontellier children, who were very fond of him.

III

It was eleven o'clock that night when Mr. Pontellier returned from Klein's hotel. He was in an excellent humor, in high spirits, and very talkative. His entrance awoke his wife, who was in bed and fast asleep when he came in. He talked to her while he undressed, telling her anecdotes and bits of news and gossip that he had gathered during the day. From his trousers pockets he took a fistful of crumpled banknotes and a good deal of silver coin, which he piled on the bureau indiscriminately with keys, knife, handkerchief, and whatever else happened to be in his pockets. She was overcome with sleep, and answered him with little half utterances.

He thought it very discouraging that his wife, who was the sole object of his existence, evinced so little interest in things which concerned him, and valued so little his conversation.

Mr. Pontellier had forgotten the bonbons and peanuts for the boys. Notwithstanding he loved them very much, and went into the adjoining room where they slept to take a look at them and make sure that they were resting comfortably. The result of his investigation was far from satisfactory. He turned and shifted the

---

[8] *Quartier Français:* French Quarter, in New Orleans.

youngsters about in bed. One of them began to kick and talk about a basket full of crabs.

Mr. Pontellier returned to his wife with the information that Raoul had a high fever and needed looking after. Then he lit a cigar and went and sat near the open door to smoke it.

Mrs. Pontellier was quite sure Raoul had no fever. He had gone to bed perfectly well, she said, and nothing had ailed him all day. Mr. Pontellier was too well acquainted with fever symptoms to be mistaken. He assured her the child was consuming[9] at that moment in the next room.

He reproached his wife with her inattention, her habitual neglect of the children. If it was not a mother's place to look after children, whose on earth was it? He himself had his hands full with his brokerage business. He could not be in two places at once; making a living for his family on the street, and staying at home to see that no harm befell them. He talked in a monotonous, insistent way.

Mrs. Pontellier sprang out of bed and went into the next room. She soon came back and sat on the edge of the bed, leaning her head down on the pillow. She said nothing, and refused to answer her husband when he questioned her. When his cigar was smoked out he went to bed, and in half a minute he was fast asleep.

Mrs. Pontellier was by that time thoroughly awake. She began to cry a little, and wiped her eyes on the sleeve of her *peignoir*.[10] Blowing out the candle, which her husband had left burning, she slipped her bare feet into a pair of satin *mules* at the foot of the bed and went out on the porch, where she sat down in the wicker chair and began to rock gently to and fro.

It was then past midnight. The cottages were all dark. A single faint light gleamed out from the hallway of the house. There was no sound abroad except the hooting of an old owl in the top of a water-oak, and the everlasting voice of the sea, that was not uplifted at that soft hour. It broke like a mournful lullaby upon the night.

The tears came so fast to Mrs. Pontellier's eyes that the damp sleeve of her *peignoir* no longer served to dry them. She was holding the back of her chair with one hand; her loose sleeve had slipped almost to the shoulder of her uplifted arm. Turning, she thrust her face, steaming and wet, into the bend of her arm, and she went on crying there, not caring any longer to dry her face, her eyes, her arms. She could not have told why she was crying. Such experiences as the foregoing were not uncommon in her married life. They seemed never before to have weighed much against the abundance of her husband's kindness and a uniform devotion which had come to be tacit and self-understood.

An indescribable oppression, which seemed to generate in some unfamiliar part of her consciousness, filled her whole being with a vague anguish. It was like a shadow, like a mist passing across her soul's summer day. It was strange and unfamiliar; it was a mood. She did not sit there inwardly upbraiding her husband, lamenting at Fate, which had directed her footsteps to the path which they had

---

[9] *Consuming:* being consumed, i.e., feverish.   [10] *peignoir:* dressing gown.

taken. She was just having a good cry all to herself. The mosquitoes made merry over her, biting her firm, round arms and nipping at her bare insteps,

The little stinging, buzzing imps succeeded in dispelling a mood which might have held her there in the darkness half a night longer.

The following morning Mr. Pontellier was up in good time to take the rock-away[11] which was to convey him to the steamer at the wharf. He was returning to the city to his business, and they would not see him again at the Island till the coming Sunday. He had regained his composure, which seemed to have been somewhat impaired the night before. He was eager to be gone, as he looked forward to a lively week in Carondelet Street.[12]

Mr. Pontellier gave his wife half of the money which he had brought away from Klein's hotel the evening before. She liked money as well as most women, and accepted it with no little satisfaction.

"It will buy a handsome wedding present for Sister Janet!" she exclaimed, smoothing out the bills as she counted them one by one.

"Oh! we'll treat Sister Janet better than that, my dear," he laughed, as he prepared to kiss her good-by.

The boys were tumbling about, clinging to his legs, imploring that numerous things be brought back to them. Mr. Pontellier was a great favorite, and ladies, men, children, even nurses, were always on hand to say good-by to him. His wife stood smiling and waving, the boys shouting, as he disappeared in the old rockaway down the sandy road.

A few days later a box arrived for Mrs. Pontellier from New Orleans. It was from her husband. It was filled with *friandises*, with luscious and toothsome bits—the finest of fruits, *patés*, a rare bottle or two, delicious syrups, and bonbons in abundance.

Mrs. Pontellier was always very generous with the contents of such a box; she was quite used to receiving them when away from home. The *patés* and fruit were brought to the dining-room; the bonbons were passed around. And the ladies, selecting with dainty and discriminating fingers and a little greedily, all declared that Mr. Pontellier was the best husband in the world. Mrs. Pontellier was forced to admit that she knew of none better.

IV

It would have been a difficult matter for Mr. Pontellier to define to his own satisfaction or any one else's wherein his wife failed in her duty toward their children. It was something which he felt rather than perceived, and he never voiced the feeling without subsequent regret and ample atonement.

If one of the little Pontellier boys took a tumble whilst at play, he was not apt to rush crying to his mother's arms for comfort; he would more likely pick himself up, wipe the water out of his eyes and the sand out of his mouth, and go on playing.

---

[11] *rockaway:* horse-drawn carriage   [12] *Carondelet Street:* street in the financial district of New Orleans.

Tots as they were, they pulled together and stood their ground in childish battles with doubled fists and uplifted voices, which usually prevailed against the other brother-tots. The quadroon nurse was looked upon as a huge encumbrance, only good to button up waists and panties and to brush and part hair; since it seemed to be a law of society that their hair must be parted and brushed.

In short, Mrs. Pontellier was not a mother-woman. The mother-women seemed to prevail that summer at Grand Isle. It was easy to know them, fluttering about with extended, protecting wings when any harm, real or imaginary, threatened their precious brood. They were women who idolized their children, worshiped their husbands, and esteemed it a holy privilege to efface themselves as individuals and grow wings as ministering angels.

Many of them were delicious in the rôle; one of them was the embodiment of every womanly grace and charm. If her husband did not adore her, he was a brute, deserving of death by slow torture. Her name was Adèle Ratignolle. There are no words to describe her save the old ones that have served so often to picture the bygone heroine of romance and the fair lady of our dreams. There was nothing subtle or hidden about her charms; her beauty was all there, flaming and apparent; the spun-gold hair that comb nor confining pin could restrain; the blue eyes that were like nothing but sapphires; two lips that pouted, that were so red one could only think of cherries or some other delicious crimson fruit in looking at them. She was growing a little stout, but it did not seem to detract an iota from the grace of every step, pose, gesture. One would not have wanted her white neck a mite less full or her beautiful arms more slender. Never were hands more exquisite than hers, and it was joy to look at them when she threaded her needle or adjusted her gold thimble to her taper middle finger as she sewed away on the little night-drawers or fashioned a bodice or a bib.

Madame Ratignolle was very fond of Mrs. Pontellier, and often she took her sewing and went over to sit with her in the afternoons. She was sitting there the afternoon of the day the box arrived from New Orleans. She had possession of the rocker, and she was busily engaged in sewing upon a diminutive pair of night-drawers.

She had brought the pattern of the drawers for Mrs. Pontellier to cut out—a marvel of construction, fashioned to enclose a baby's body so effectually that only two small eyes might look out from the garment, like an Eskimo's. They were designed for winter wear, when treacherous drafts came down chimneys and insidious currents of deadly cold found their way through key-holes.

Mrs. Pontellier's mind was quite at rest concerning the present material needs of her children, and she could not see the use of anticipating and making winter night garments the subject of her summer meditations. But she did not want to appear unamiable and uninterested, so she had brought forth newspapers, which she spread upon the floor of the gallery, and under Madame Ratignolle's directions she had cut a pattern of the impervious garment.

Robert was there, seated as he had been the Sunday before, and Mrs. Pontellier also occupied her former position on the upper step, leaning listlessly against the post. Beside her was a box of bonbons, which she held out at intervals to Madame Ratignolle.

That lady seemed at a loss to make a selection, but finally settled upon a stick of nougat, wondering if it were not too rich; whether it could possibly hurt her. Madame Ratignolle had been married seven years. About every two years she had a baby. At that time she had three babies, and was beginning to think of a fourth one. She was always talking about her "condition." Her "condition" was in no way apparent, and no one would have known a thing about it but for her persistence in making it the subject of conversation.

Robert started to reassure her, asserting that he had known a lady who had subsisted upon nougat during the entire—but seeing the color mount into Mrs. Pontellier's face he checked himself and changed the subject.

Mrs. Pontellier, though she had married a Creole[13] was not thoroughly at home in the society of Creoles; never before had she been thrown so intimately among them. There were only Creoles that summer at Lebrun's. They all knew each other, and felt like one large family, among whom existed the most amicable relations. A characteristic which distinguished them and which impressed Mrs. Pontellier most forcibly was their entire absence of prudery. Their freedom of expression was at first incomprehensible to her, though she had no difficulty in reconciling it with a lofty chastity which in the Creole woman seems to be inborn and unmistakable.

Never would Edna Pontellier forget the shock with which she heard Madame Ratignolle relating to old Monsieur Farival the harrowing story of one of her *accouchements*,[14] withholding no intimate detail. She was growing accustomed to like shocks, but she could not keep the mounting color back from her cheeks. Oftener than once her coming had interrupted the droll story with which Robert was entertaining some amused group of married women.

A book had gone the rounds of the *pension*. When it came her turn to read it, she did so with profound astonishment. She felt moved to read the book in secret and solitude, though none of the others had done so—to hide it from view at the sound of approaching footsteps. It was openly criticized and freely discussed at table. Mrs. Pontellier gave over being astonished, and concluded that wonders would never cease.

V

They formed a congenial group sitting there that summer afternoon—Madame Ratignolle sewing away, often stopping to relate a story or incident with much expressive gesture of her perfect hands; Robert and Mrs. Pontellier sitting idle, exchanging occasional words, glances or smiles which indicated a certain advanced stage of intimacy and *camaraderie*.

He had lived in her shadow during the past month. No one thought anything of it. Many had predicted that Robert would devote himself to Mrs. Pontellier when

---

[13] *Creole:* aristocratic descendant of the French and Spanish settlers of New Orleans.
[14] *accouchements:* birthings

he arrived. Since the age of fifteen, which was eleven years before, Robert each summer at Grand Isle had constituted himself the devoted attendant of some fair dame or damsel. Sometimes it was a young girl, again a widow; but as often as not it was some interesting married woman.

For two consecutive seasons he lived in the sunlight of Mademoiselle Duvigné's presence. But she died between summers; then Robert posed as an inconsolable, prostrating himself at the feet of Madame Ratignolle for whatever crumbs of sympathy and comfort she might be pleased to vouchsafe.

Mrs. Pontellier liked to sit and gaze at her fair companion as she might look upon a faultless Madonna.

"Could any one fathom the cruelty beneath that fair exterior?" murmured Robert. "She knew that I adored her once, and she let me adore her. It was 'Robert, come; go; stand up; sit down; do this; do that; see if the baby sleeps; my thimble, please, that I left God knows where. Come and read Daudet[15] to me while I sew.'"

"*Par example!*[16] I never had to ask. You were always there under my feet, like a troublesome cat."

"You mean like an adoring dog. And just as soon as Ratignolle appeared on the scene, then it *was* like a dog. '*Passez! Adieu! Allez vous-en!*'"[17]

"Perhaps I feared to make Alphonse jealous," she interjoined, with excessive naïveté. That made them all laugh. The right hand jealous of the left! The heart jealous of the soul! But for that matter, the Creole husband is never jealous; with him the gangrene passion is one which has become dwarfed by disuse.

Meanwhile Robert, addressing Mrs. Pontellier, continued to tell of his one time hopeless passion for Madame Ratignolle; of sleepless nights, of consuming flames till the very sea sizzled when he took his daily plunge. While the lady at the needle kept up a little running, contemptuous comment:

"*Blageur—farceur—gros bête, va!*"[18]

He never assumed this serio-comic tone when alone with Mrs. Pontellier. She never knew precisely what to make of it; at that moment it was impossible for her to guess how much of it was jest and what proportion was earnest. It was understood that he had often spoken words of love to Madame Ratignolle, without any thought of being taken seriously. Mrs. Pontellier was glad he had not assumed a similar rôle toward herself. It would have been unacceptable and annoying.

Mrs. Pontellier had brought her sketching materials, which she sometimes dabbled with in an unprofessional way. She liked the dabbling. She felt in it satisfaction of a kind which no other employment afforded her.

She had long wished to try herself on Madame Ratignolle. Never had that lady seemed a more tempting subject than at that moment, seated there like some sensuous Madonna, with the gleam of the fading day enriching her splendid color.

Robert crossed over and seated himself upon the step below Mrs. Pontellier, that he might watch her work. She handled her brushes with a certain ease and

---

[15] *Daudet:* Alphonse Daudet (1840–87), French novelist.   [16] *Par example!:* Indeed!   [17] *Passez . . . vous-en!:* Go! Goodby! Go away!   [18] *Blaguer . . . va!:* Joker—clown—silly, cut it out!

freedom which came, not from long and close acquaintance with them, but from a natural aptitude. Robert followed her work with close attention, giving forth little ejaculatory expressions of appreciation in French, which he addressed to Madame Ratignolle.

"Mais ce n'est pas mal! Elle s'y connait, elle a de la force, oui."[19]

During his oblivious attention he once quietly rested his head against Mrs. Pontellier's arm. As gently she repulsed him. Once again he repeated the offense. She could not but believe it to be thoughtlessness on his part; yet that was no reason she should submit to it. She did not remonstrate, except again to repulse him quietly but firmly. He offered no apology.

The picture completed bore no resemblance to Madame Ratignolle. She was greatly disappointed to find that it did not look like her. But it was a fair enough piece of work, and in many respects satisfying.

Mrs. Pontellier evidently did not think so. After surveying the sketch critically she drew a broad smudge of paint across its surface, and crumpled the paper between her hands.

The youngsters came tumbling up the steps, the quadroon following at the respectful distance which they required her to observe. Mrs. Pontellier made them carry her paints and things into the house. She sought to detain them for a little talk and some pleasantry. But they were greatly in earnest. They had only come to investigate the contents of the bonbon box. They accepted without murmuring what she chose to give them, each holding out two chubby hands scoop-like, in the vain hope that they might be filled; and then away they went.

The sun was low in the west, and the breeze soft and languorous that came up from the south, charged with the seductive odor of the sea. Children, freshly befurbelowed,[20] were gathering for their games under the oaks. Their voices were high and penetrating.

Madame Ratignolle folded her sewing, placing thimble, scissors and thread all neatly together in the roll, which she pinned securely. She complained of faintness. Mrs. Pontellier flew for the cologne water and a fan. She bathed Madame Ratignolle's face with cologne, while Robert plied the fan with unnecessary vigor.

The spell was soon over, and Mrs. Pontellier could not help wondering if there were not a little imagination responsible for its origin, for the rose tint had never faded from her friend's face.

She stood watching the fair woman walk down the long line of galleries with the grace and majesty which queens are sometimes supposed to possess. Her little ones ran to meet her. Two of them clung about her white skirts, the third she took from its nurse and with a thousand endearments bore it along in her own fond, encircling arms. Though, as everybody well knew, the doctor had forbidden her to lift so much as a pin!

---

[19] *Mais . . . oui:* Not bad! She knows what's she doing, she's really good.   [20] *befurbelowed:* dressed in frills.

"Are you going bathing?" asked Robert of Mrs. Pontellier. It was not so much a question as a reminder.

"Oh, no," she answered with a tone of indecision. "I'm tired; I think not." Her glance wandered from his face away toward the Gulf, whose sonorous murmur reached her like a loving but imperative entreaty.

"Oh, come!" he insisted. "You mustn't miss your bath. Come on. The water must be delicious; it will not hurt you. Come."

He reached up for her big, rough straw hat that hung on a peg outside the door, and put it on her head. They descended the steps, and walked away together toward the beach. The sun was low in the west and the breeze was soft and warm.

VI

Edna Pontellier could not have told why, wishing to go to the beach with Robert, she should in the first place have declined, and in the second place have followed in obedience to one of the two contradictory impulses which impelled her.

A certain light was beginning to dawn dimly within her,—the light which, showing the way, forbids it.

At that early period it served but to bewilder her. It moved her to dreams, to thoughtfulness, to the shadowy anguish which had overcome her the midnight when she had abandoned herself to tears.

In short, Mrs. Pontellier was beginning to realize her position in the universe as a human being, and to recognize her relations as an individual to the world within and about her. This may seem like a ponderous weight of wisdom to descend upon the soul of a young woman of twenty-eight—perhaps more wisdom than the Holy Ghost is usually pleased to vouchsafe to any woman.

But the beginning of things, of a world especially, is necessarily vague, tangled, chaotic, and exceedingly disturbing. How few of us ever emerge from such beginning! How many souls perish in its tumult!

The voice of the sea is seductive; never ceasing, whispering, clamoring, murmuring, inviting the soul to wander for a spell in abysses of solitude; to lose itself in mazes of inward contemplation.

The voice of the sea speaks to the soul. The touch of the sea is sensuous, enfolding the body in its soft, close embrace.

VII

Mrs. Pontellier was not a woman given to confidences, a characteristic hitherto contrary to her nature. Even as a child she had lived her own small life all within herself. At a very early period she had apprehended instinctively the dual life—that outward existence which conforms, the inward life which questions.

That summer at Grand Isle she began to loosen a little the mantle of reserve that had always enveloped her. There may have been—there must have been— influences, both subtle and apparent, working in their several ways to induce her to do this; but the most obvious was the influence of Adèle Ratignolle. The excessive physical charm of the Creole had first attracted her, for Edna had a sensuous susceptibility to beauty. Then the candor of the woman's whole existence, which every one might read, and which formed so striking a contrast to her own habitual reserve—this might have furnished a link. Who can tell what metals the gods use in forging the subtle bond which we call sympathy, which we might as well call love.

The two women went away one morning to the beach together, arm in arm, under the huge white sunshade. Edna had prevailed upon Madame Ratignolle to leave the children behind, though she could not induce her to relinquish a diminutive roll of needlework, which Adèle begged to be allowed to slip into the depths of her pocket. In some unaccountable way they had escaped from Robert.

The walk to the beach was no inconsiderable one, consisting as it did of a long, sandy path, upon which a sporadic and tangled growth that bordered it on either side made frequent and unexpected inroads. There were acres of yellow camomile reaching out on either hand. Further away still, vegetable gardens abounded, with frequent small plantations of orange or lemon trees intervening. The dark green clusters glistened from afar in the sun.

The women were both of goodly height, Madame Ratignolle possessing the more feminine and matronly figure. The charm of Edna Pontellier's physique stole insensibly upon you. The lines of her body were long, clean and symmetrical; it was a body which occasionally fell into splendid poses; there was no suggestion of the trim stereotyped fashion-plate about it. A casual and indiscriminating observer, in passing, might not cast a second glance upon the figure. But with more feeling and discernment he would have recognized the noble beauty of its modeling, and the graceful severity of poise and movement, which made Edna Pontellier different from the crowd.

She wore a cool muslin that morning—white, with a waving vertical line of brown running through it; also a white linen collar and the big straw hat which she had taken from the peg outside the door. The hat rested any way on her yellow-brown hair, that waved a little, was heavy, and clung close to her head.

Madame Ratignolle, more careful of her complexion, had twined a gauze veil about her head. She wore doeskin gloves, with gauntlets that protected her wrists. She was dressed in pure white, with a fluffiness of ruffles that became her. The draperies and fluttering things which she wore suited her rich, luxuriant beauty as a greater severity of line could not have done.

There were a number of bath-houses along the beach, of rough but solid construction, built with small, protecting galleries facing the water. Each house consisted of two compartments, and each family at Lebrun's possessed a compartment for itself, fitted out with all the essential paraphernalia of the bath and whatever other conveniences the owners might desire. The two women had no intention of bathing; they had just strolled down to the beach for a walk and to be alone and near the water. The Pontellier and Ratignolle compartments adjoined one another under the same roof.

Mrs. Pontellier had brought down her key through force of habit. Unlocking the door of her bath-room she went inside, and soon emerged, bringing a rug, which she spread upon the floor of the gallery, and two huge hair pillows covered with crash,[21] which she placed against the front of the building.

The two seated themselves there in the shade of the porch, side by side, with their backs against the pillows and their feet extended. Madame Ratignolle removed her veil, wiped her face with a rather delicate handkerchief, and fanned herself with the fan which she always carried suspended somewhere about her person by a long, narrow ribbon. Edna removed her collar and opened her dress at the throat. She took the fan from Madame Ratignolle and began to fan both herself and her companion. It was very warm, and for a while they did nothing but exchange remarks about the heat, the sun, the glare. But there was a breeze blowing, a choppy, stiff wind that whipped the water into froth. It fluttered the skirts of the two women and kept them for a while engaged in adjusting, readjusting, tucking in, securing hair-pins and hat-pins. A few persons were sporting some distance away in the water. The beach was very still of human sound at that hour. The lady in black was reading her morning devotions on the porch of a neighboring bath-house. Two young lovers were exchanging their hearts' yearnings beneath the children's tent, which they had found unoccupied.

Edna Pontellier, casting her eyes about, had finally kept them at rest upon the sea. The day was clear and carried the gaze out as far as the blue sky went; there were a few white clouds suspended idly over the horizon. A lateen[22] sail was visible in the direction of Cat Island, and others to the south seemed almost motionless in the far distance.

"Of whom—of what are you thinking?" asked Adèle of her companion, whose countenance she had been watching with a little amused attention, arrested by the absorbed expression which seemed to have seized and fixed every feature into a statuesque repose.

"Nothing," returned Mrs. Pontellier, with a start, adding at once: "How stupid! But it seems to me it is the reply we make instinctively to such a question. Let me see," she went on, throwing back her head and narrowing her fine eyes till they shone like two vivid points of light. "Let me see. I was really not conscious of thinking of anything; but perhaps I can retrace my thoughts."

"Oh! never mind!" laughed Madame Ratignolle. "I am not quite so exacting. I will let you off this time. It is really too hot to think, especially to think about thinking."

"But for the fun of it," persisted Edna. "First of all, the sight of the water stretching so far away, those motionless sails against the blue sky, made a delicious picture that I just wanted to sit and look at it. The hot wind beating in my face made me think—without any connection that I can trace—of a summer day in Kentucky, of a meadow that seemed as big as the ocean to the very little girl walking through the grass, which was higher than her waist. She threw out her arms as if swimming when she walked, beating the tall grass as one strikes out in the water. Oh, I see the connection now!"

---

[21] *crash:* heavy linen [22] *lateen:* triangular.

"Where were you going that day in Kentucky, walking through the grass?"

"I don't remember now. I was just walking diagonally across a big field. My sun-bonnet obstructed the view. I could see only the stretch of green before me, and I felt as if I must walk on forever, without coming to the end of it. I don't remember whether I was frightened or pleased. I must have been entertained."

"Likely as not it was Sunday," she laughed; "and I was running away from prayers, from the Presbyterian service, read in a spirit of gloom by my father that chills me yet to think of."

"And have you been running away from prayer ever since, *ma chére?*" asked Madame Ratignolle, amused.

"No! oh, no!" Edna hastened to say. "I was a little unthinking child in those days, just following a misleading impulse without question. On the contrary, during one period of my life religion took a firm hold upon me; after I was twelve and until—until—why, I suppose until now, though I never thought much about it—just driven along by habit. But do you know," she broke off, turning her quick eyes upon Madame Ratignolle and leaning forward a little so as to bring her face quite close to that of her companion, "sometimes I feel this summer as if I were walking through the green meadow again; idly, aimlessly, unthinking and un-guided."

Madame Ratignolle laid her hand over that of Mrs. Pontellier, which was near her. Seeing that the hand was not withdrawn, she clasped it firmly and warmly. She even stroked it a little fondly, with the other hand, murmuring in an undertone, "*Pauvre chérie.*"[23]

The action was at first a little confusing to Edna, but she soon lent herself readily to the Creole's gentle caress. She was not accustomed to an outward and spoken expression of affection, either in herself or in others. She and her younger sister, Janet, had quarreled a good deal through force of unfortunate habit. Her older sister, Margaret, was matronly and dignified, probably from having assumed matronly and housewifely responsibilities too early in life, their mother having died when they were quite young. Margaret was not effusive: she was practical. Edna had had an occasional girl friend, but whether accidentally or not, they seemed to have been all of one type—the self-contained. She never realized that the reserve of her own character had much, perhaps everything, to do with this. Her most intimate friend at school had been one of rather exceptional intellectual gifts, who wrote fine-sounding essays, which Edna admired and strove to imitate; and with her she talked and glowed over the English classics, and sometimes held religious and political controversies.

Edna often wondered at one propensity which sometimes had inwardly disturbed her without causing any outward show or manifestation on her part. At a very early age—perhaps it was when she traversed the ocean of waving grass—she remembered that she had been passionately enamored of a dignified and sad-eyed cavalry officer who visited her father in Kentucky. She could not leave his presence

[23] *Pauvre chérie:* Poor dear.

when he was there, nor remove her eyes from his face, which was something like Napoleon's, with a lock of black hair falling across the forehead. But the cavalry officer melted imperceptibly out of her existence.

At another time her affections were deeply engaged by a young gentleman who visited a lady on a neighboring plantation. It was after they went to Mississippi to live. The young man was engaged to be married to the young lady, and they sometimes called upon Margaret, driving over of afternoons in a buggy. Edna was a little miss, just merging into her teens; and the realization that she herself was nothing, nothing, nothing to the engaged young man was a bitter affliction to her. But he, too, went the way of dreams.

She was a grown young woman when she was overtaken by what she supposed to be the climax of her fate. It was when the face and figure of a great tragedian began to haunt her imagination and stir her senses. The persistence of the infatuation lent it an aspect of genuineness. The hopelessness of it colored it with the lofty tones of a great passion.

The picture of the tragedian stood enframed upon her desk. Any one may possess the portrait of a tragedian without exciting suspicion or comment. (This was a sinister reflection which she cherished.) In the presence of others she expressed admiration for his exalted gifts, as she handed the photograph around and dwelt upon the fidelity of the likeness. When alone she sometimes picked it up and kissed the cold glass passionately.

Her marriage to Léonce Pontellier was purely an accident, in this respect resembling many other marriages which masquerade as the decrees of Fate. It was in the midst of her secret great passion that she met him. He fell in love, as men are in the habit of doing, and pressed his suit with an earnestness and an ardor which left nothing to be desired. He pleased her; his absolute devotion flattered her. She fancied there was a sympathy of thought and taste between them, in which fancy she was mistaken. Add to this the violent opposition of her father and her sister Margaret to her marriage with a Catholic, and we need seek no further for the motives which led her to accept Monsieur Pontellier for her husband.

The acme of bliss, which would have been a marriage with the tragedian, was not for her in this world. As the devoted wife of a man who worshiped her, she felt she would take her place with a certain dignity in the world of reality, closing the portals forever behind her upon the realm of romance and dreams.

But it was not long before the tragedian had gone to join the cavalry officer and the engaged young man and a few others; and Edna found herself face to face with the realities. She grew fond of her husband, realizing with some unaccountable satisfaction that no trace of passion or excessive and fictitious warmth colored her affection, thereby threatening its dissolution.

She was fond of her children in an uneven, impulsive way. She would sometimes gather them passionately to her heart; she would sometimes forget them. The year before they had spent part of the summer with their grandmother Pontellier in Iberville. Feeling secure regarding their happiness and welfare, she did not miss them except with an occasional intense longing. Their absence was a sort of relief, though she did not admit this, even to herself. It seemed to free her of a responsibility which she had blindly assumed and for which Fate had not fitted her.

Edna did not reveal so much as all this to Madame Ratignolle that summer day when they sat with faces turned to the sea. But a good part of it escaped her. She had put her head down on Madame Ratignolle's shoulder. She was flushed and felt intoxicated with the sound of her own voice and the unaccustomed taste of candor. It muddled her like wine, or like a first breath of freedom.

There was the sound of approaching voices. It was Robert, surrounded by a troop of children, searching for them. The two little Pontelliers were with him, and he carried Madame Ratignolle's little girl in his arms. There were other children beside, and two nurse-maids followed, looking disagreeable and resigned.

The women at once rose and began to shake out their draperies and relax their muscles. Mrs. Pontellier threw the cushions and rug into the bath-house. The children all scampered off to the awning, and they stood there in a line, gazing upon the intruding lovers, still exchanging their vows and sighs. The lovers got up, with only a silent protest, and walked slowly away somewhere else.

The children possessed themselves of the tent, and Mrs. Pontellier went over to join them.

Madame Ratignolle begged Robert to accompany her to the house; she complained of cramp in her limbs and stiffness of the joints. She leaned draggingly upon his arm as they walked.

VIII

"Do me a favor, Robert," spoke the pretty woman at his side, almost as soon as she and Robert had started on their slow, homeward way. She looked up in his face, leaning on his arm beneath the encircling shadow of the umbrella which he had lifted.

"Granted; as many as you like," he returned, glancing down into her eyes that were full of thoughtfulness and some speculation.

"I only ask for one; let Mrs. Pontellier alone."

"*Tiens!*" he exclaimed, with a sudden, boyish laugh. "*Voilá que Madame Ratignolle est jalouse!*"[24]

"Nonsense! I'm in earnest; I mean what I say. Let Mrs. Pontellier alone."

"Why?" he asked; himself growing serious at his companion's solicitation.

"She is not one of us; she is not like us. She might make the unfortunate blunder of taking you seriously."

His face flushed with annoyance, and taking off his soft hat he began to beat it impatiently against his leg as he walked. "Why shouldn't she take me seriously?" he demanded sharply. "Am I a comedian, a clown, a jack-in-the-box? Why shouldn't she? You Creoles! I have no patience with you! Am I always to be regarded as a feature of an amusing programme? I hope Mrs. Pontellier does take me seriously. I

---

[24] *Tiens . . . jalouse!*: Ah, so Madam Ratignolle is jealous!

hope she has discernment enough to find in me something besides the *blagueur*.[25] If I thought there was any doubt—"

"Oh, enough, Robert!" she broke into his heated outburst. "You are not thinking of what you are saying. You speak with about as little reflection as we might expect from one of those children down there playing in the sand. If your intentions to any married women here were ever offered with any attention of being convincing, you would not be the gentleman we all know you to be, and you would be unfit to associate with the wives and daughters of the people who trust you."

Madame Ratignolle had spoken what she believed to be the law and the gospel. The young man shrugged his shoulders impatiently.

"Oh! well! That isn't it," slamming his hat down vehemently upon his head. "You ought to feel that such things are not flattering to say to a fellow."

"Should our whole intercourse consist of an exchange of compliments? *Ma foi!*"[26]

"It isn't pleasant to have a woman tell you—" he went on, unheedingly, but breaking off suddenly: "Now if I were like Arobin—you remember Alcée Arobin and that story of the consul's wife at Biloxi?" And he related the story of Alcée Arobin and the consul's wife; and another about the tenor of the French Opera, who received letters which should never have been written; and still other stories, grave and gay, till Mrs. Pontellier and her possible propensity for taking young men seriously was apparently forgotten.

Madame Ratignolle, when they had regained her cottage, went in to take the hour's rest which she considered helpful. Before leaving her, Robert begged her pardon for the impatience—he called it rudeness—with which he had received her well-meant caution.

"You made one mistake, Adèle," he said, with a light smile; "there is no earthly possibility of Mrs. Pontellier ever taking me seriously. You should have warned me against taking myself seriously. Your advice might then have carried some weight and given me subject for some reflection. *Au revoir.* But you look tired," he added, solicitously. "Would you like a cup of bouillon? Shall I stir you a toddy? Let me mix you a toddy with a drop of Angostura."

She acceded to the suggestion of bouillon, which was grateful and acceptable. He went himself to the kitchen, which was a building apart from the cottages and lying to the rear of the house. And he himself brought her the golden-brown bouillon, in a dainty Sèvres cup, with a flaky cracker or two on the saucer.

She thrust a bare, white arm from the curtain which shielded her open door, and received the cup from his hands. She told him he was a *bon garçon*[27] and she meant it. Robert thanked her and turned away toward "the house."

The lovers were just entering the grounds of the *pension*. They were leaning toward each other as the water-oaks bent from the sea. There was not a particle of earth beneath their feet. Their heads might have been turned upside-down, so absolutely did they tread upon blue ether. The lady in black, creeping behind them,

---

[25] *blagueur:* joker. [26] *Ma foi!:* Good Lord! [27] *bon garçon:* (1) nice fellow; (2) good waiter.

looked a trifle paler and more jaded than usual. There was no sign of Mrs. Pontellier and the children. Robert scanned the distance for any such apparition. They would doubtless remain away till the dinner hour. The young man ascended to his mother's room. It was situated at the top of the house, made up of odd angles and a queer, sloping ceiling. Two broad dormer windows looked out toward the Gulf, and as far across it as man's eye might reach. The furnishings of the room were light, cool, and practical.

Madame Lebrun was busily engaged at the sewing-machine. A little black girl sat on the floor, and with her hands worked the treadle of the machine. The Creole woman does not take any chances which may be avoided of imperiling her health.

Robert went over and seated himself on the broad sill of one of the dormer windows. He took a book from his pocket and began energetically to read it, judging by the precision and frequency with which he turned the leaves. The sewing-machine made a resounding clatter in the room; it was of a ponderous, by-gone make. In the lulls, Robert and his mother exchanged bits of desultory conversation.

"Where is Mrs. Pontellier?"

"Down at the beach with the children."

"I promised to lend her the Goncourt.[28] Don't forget to take it down when you go; it's there on the bookshelf over the small table." Clatter, clatter, clatter, bang! for the next five or eight minutes.

"Where is Victor going with the rockaway?"

"The rockaway? Victor?"

"Yes; down there in front. He seems to be getting ready to drive away somewhere."

"Call him." Clatter, clatter!

Robert uttered a shrill, piercing whistle which might have been heard back at the wharf.

"He won't look up."

Madame Lebrun flew to the window. She called "Victor!" She waved a handkerchief and called again. The young fellow below got into the vehicle and started the horse off at a gallop.

Madame Lebrun went back to the machine, crimson with annoyance. Victor was the younger son and brother—a *tête montée*,[29] with a temper which invited violence and a will which no ax could break.

"Whenever you say the word I'm ready to thrash any amount of reason into him that he's able to hold."

"If your father had only lived!" Clatter, clatter, clatter, clatter, bang! It was a fixed belief with Madame Lebrun that the conduct of the universe and all things pertaining thereto would have been manifestly of a more intelligent and higher order had not Monsieur Lebrun been removed to other spheres during the early years of their married life.

---

[28] *the Goncourt:* novel by Edmond Goncourt (1822–96). [29] *tête montée:* impulsive fellow.

"What do you hear from Montel?" Montel was a middle-aged gentleman whose vain ambition and desire for the past twenty years had been to fill the void which Monsieur Lebrun's taking off had left in the Lebrun household. Clatter, clatter, bang, clatter!

"I have a letter somewhere," looking in the machine drawer and finding the letter in the bottom of the work-basket. "He says to tell you he will be in Vera Cruz the beginning of next month"—clatter, clatter!—"and if you still have the intention of joining him"—bang! clatter, clatter, bang!

"Why didn't you tell me so before, mother? You know I wanted—" Clatter, clatter, clatter!

"Do you see Mrs. Pontellier starting back with the children? She will be in late to luncheon again. She never starts to get ready for luncheon till the last minute." Clatter, clatter! "Where are you going?"

"Where did you say the Goncourt was?"

IX

Every light in the hall was ablaze; every lamp turned as high as it could be without smoking the chimney or threatening explosion. The lamps were fixed at intervals against the wall, encircling the whole room. Some one had gathered orange and lemon branches, and with these fashioned graceful festoons between. The dark green of the branches stood out and glistened against the white muslin curtains which draped the windows, and which puffed, floated, and flapped at the capricious will of a stiff breeze that swept up from the Gulf.

It was Saturday night a few weeks after the intimate conversation held between Robert and Mrs. Ratignolle on their way from the beach. An unusual number of husbands, fathers, and friends had come down to stay over Sunday; and they were being suitably entertained by their families, with the material help of Madame Lebrun. The dining tables had all been removed to one end of the hall, and the chairs ranged about in rows and in clusters. Each little family group had had its say and exchanged its domestic gossip earlier in the evening. There was now an apparent disposition to relax; to widen the circle of confidences and give a more general tone to the conversation.

Many of the children had been permitted to sit up beyond their usual bedtime. A small band of them were lying on their stomachs on the floor looking at the colored sheets of the comic papers which Mr. Pontellier had brought down. The little Pontellier boys were permitting them to do so, and making their authority felt.

Music, dancing, and a recitation or two were the entertainments furnished, or rather, offered. But there was nothing systematic about the programme, no appearance of prearrangement nor even premeditation.

At an early hour in the evening the Farival twins were prevailed upon to play the piano. They were girls of fourteen, always clad in the Virgin's colors, blue and white, having been dedicated to the Blessed Virgin at their baptism. They played a duet from "Zampa," and at the earnest solicitation of every one present followed it with the overture to "The Poet and the Peasant."

"*Allez vous-en! Sapristi!*" shrieked the parrot outside the door. He was the only being present who possessed sufficient candor to admit that he was not listening to these gracious performances for the first time that summer. Old Monsieur Farival, grandfather of the twins, grew indignant over the interruption, and insisted upon having the bird removed and consigned to regions of darkness. Victor Lebrun objected; and his decrees were as immutable as those of Fate. The parrot fortunately offered no further interruption to the entertainment, the whole venom of his nature apparently having been cherished up and hurled against the twins in that one impetuous outburst.

Later a young brother and sister gave recitations, which every one present had heard many times at winter evening entertainments in the city.

A little girl performed a skirt dance in the center of the floor. The mother played her accompaniments and at the same time watched her daughter with greedy admiration and nervous apprehension. She need have had no apprehension. The child was mistress of the situation. She had been properly dressed for the occasion in black tulle and black silk tights. Her little neck and arms were bare, and her hair, artificially crimped, stood out like fluffy black plumes over her head. Her poses were full of grace, and her little black-shod toes twinkled as they shot out and upward with a rapidity and suddenness which were bewildering.

But there was no reason why every one should not dance. Madame Ratignolle could not, so it was she who gaily consented to play for the others. She played very well, keeping excellent waltz time and infusing an expression into the strains which was indeed inspiring. She was keeping up her music on account of the children, she said; because she and her husband both considered it a means of brightening the home and making it attractive.

Almost every one danced but the twins, who could not be induced to separate during the brief period when one or the other should be whirling around the room in the arms of a man. They might have danced together, but they did not think of it.

The children were sent to bed. Some went submissively; others with shrieks and protests as they were dragged away. They had been permitted to sit up till after the ice-cream, which naturally marked the limit of human indulgence.

The ice-cream was passed around with cake—gold and silver cake arranged on platters in alternate slices; it had been made and frozen during the afternoon back of the kitchen by two black women, under the supervision of Victor. It was pronounced a great success—excellent if it had only contained a little less vanilla or a little more sugar, if it had been frozen a degree harder, and if the salt might have been kept out of portions of it. Victor was proud of his achievement, and went about recommending it and urging every one to partake of it to excess.

After Mrs. Pontellier had danced twice with her husband, once with Robert, and once with Monsieur Ratignolle, who was thin and tall and swayed like a reed in the wind when he danced, she went out on the gallery and seated herself on the low window-sill, where she commanded a view of all that went on in the hall and could look out toward the Gulf. There was a soft effulgence in the east. The moon was coming up, and its mystic shimmer was casting a million lights across the distant, restless water.

"Would you like to hear Mademoiselle Reisz play?" asked Robert, coming out on the porch where she was. Of course Edna would like to hear Mademoiselle Reisz play; but she feared it would be useless to entreat her.

"I'll ask her," he said. "I'll tell her that you want to hear her. She likes you. She will come." He turned and hurried away to one of the far cottages, where Mademoiselle Reisz was shuffling away. She was dragging a chair in and out of her room, and at intervals objecting to the crying of a baby, which a nurse in the adjoining cottage was endeavoring to put to sleep. She was a disagreeable little woman, no longer young, who had quarreled with almost every one, owing to a temper which was self-assertive and a disposition to trample upon the rights of others. Robert prevailed upon her without any too great difficulty.

She entered the hall with him during a lull in the dance. She made an awkward, imperious little bow as she went in. She was a homely woman, with a small weazened face and body and eyes that glowed. She had absolutely no taste in dress, and wore a batch of rusty black lace with a bunch of artificial violets pinned to the side of her hair.

"Ask Mrs. Pontellier what she would like to hear me play," she requested of Robert. She sat perfectly still before the piano, not touching the keys, while Robert carried her message to Edna at the window. A general air of surprise and genuine satisfaction fell upon every one as they saw the pianist enter. There was a settling down, and a prevailing air of expectancy everywhere. Edna was a trifle embarrassed at being thus signaled out for the imperious little woman's favor. She would not dare to choose, and begged that Mademoiselle Reisz would please herself in her selections.

Edna was what she herself called very fond of music. Musical strains, well rendered, had a way of evoking pictures in her mind. She sometimes liked to sit in the room of mornings when Madame Ratignolle played or practiced. One piece which that lady played Edna had entitled "Solitude." It was a short, plaintive, minor strain. The name of the piece was something else, but she called it "Solitude." When she heard it there came before her imagination the figure of a man standing beside a desolate rock on the seashore. He was naked. His attitude was one of hopeless resignation as he looked toward a distant bird winging its flight away from him.

Another piece called to her mind a dainty young woman clad in an Empire gown, taking mincing dancing steps as she came down a long avenue between tall hedges. Again, another reminded her of children at play, and still another of nothing on earth but a demure lady stroking a cat.

The very first chords which Mademoiselle Reisz struck upon the piano sent a keen tremor down Mrs. Pontellier's spinal column. It was not the first time she had heard an artist at the piano. Perhaps it was the first time she was ready, perhaps the first time her being was tempered to take an impress of the abiding truth.

She waited for the material pictures which she thought would gather and blaze before her imagination. She waited in vain. She saw no pictures of solitude, of hope, of longing, or of despair. But the very passions themselves were aroused within her soul, swaying it, lashing it, as the waves daily beat upon her splendid body. She trembled, she was choking, and the tears blinded her.

Mademoiselle had finished. She arose, and bowing her stiff, lofty bow, she went away, stopping for neither thanks nor applause. As she passed along the gallery she patted Edna upon the shoulder.

"Well, how did you like my music?" she asked. The young woman was unable to answer; she pressed the hand of the pianist convulsively. Mademoiselle Reisz perceived her agitation and even her tears. She patted her again upon the shoulder as she said:

"You are the only one worth playing for. Those others? Bah!" and she went shuffling and sidling on down the gallery toward her room.

But she was mistaken about "those others." Her playing had aroused a fever of enthusiasm. "What passion!" "What an artist!" "I have always said no one could play Chopin[30] like Mademoiselle Reisz!" "That last prelude! *Bon Dieu!*[31] It shakes a man!"

It was growing late, and there was a general disposition to disband. But some one, perhaps it was Robert, thought of a bath at that mystic hour and under that mystic moon.

X

At all events Robert proposed it, and there was not a dissenting voice. There was not one but was ready to follow when he led the way. He did not lead the way, however, he directed the way; and he himself loitered behind with the lovers, who had betrayed a disposition to linger and hold themselves apart. He walked between them, whether with malicious or mischievous intent was not wholly clear, even to himself.

The Pontelliers and Ratignolles walked ahead; the women leaning upon the arms of their husbands. Edna could hear Robert's voice behind them, and could sometimes hear what he said. She wondered why he did not join them. It was unlike him not to. Of late he had sometimes held away from her for an entire day, redoubling his devotion upon the next and the next, as though to make up for hours that had been lost. She missed him the days when some pretext served to take him away from her, just as one misses the sun on a cloudy day without having thought much about the sun when it was shining.

The people walked in little groups toward the beach. They talked and laughed; some of them sang. There was a band playing down at Klein's hotel, and the strains reached them faintly, tempered by the distance. There were strange, rare odors abroad—a tangle of the sea smell and of weeds and damp, new-plowed earth, mingled with the heavy perfume of a field of white blossoms somewhere near. But the night sat lightly upon the sea and the land. There was no weight of darkness,

---

[30] *Chopin:* Frédéric François Chopin (1810–49), Polish pianist and composer. [31] *Bon Dieu!:* Good Lord!

there were no shadows. The white light of the moon had fallen upon the world like the mystery and the softness of sleep.

Most of them walked into the water as though into a native element. The sea was quiet now, and swelled lazily in broad billows that melted into one another and did not break except upon the beach in little foamy crests that coiled back like slow, white serpents.

Edna had attempted all summer to learn to swim. She had received instructions from both the men and women; in some instances from the children. Robert had pursued a system of lessons almost daily; and he was nearly at the point of discouragement in realizing the futility of his efforts. A certain ungovernable dread hung about her when in the water, unless there was a hand near by that might reach out and reassure her.

But that night she was like the little tottering, stumbling, clutching child, who of a sudden realizes its powers, and walks for the first time alone, boldly and with over-confidence. She could have shouted for joy. She did shout for joy, as with a sweeping stroke or two she lifted her body to the surface of the water.

A feeling of exultation overtook her, as if some power of significant import had been given to her to control the working of her body and her soul. She grew daring and reckless, overestimating her strength. She wanted to swim far out, where no woman had swum before.

Her unlooked-for achievement was the subject of wonder, applause, and admiration. Each one congratulated himself that his special teachings had accomplished this desired end.

"How easy it is!" she thought. "It is nothing," she said aloud; "why did I not discover before that it was nothing? Think of the time I have lost splashing about like a baby!" She would not join the groups in their sports and bouts, but intoxicated with her newly conquered power, she swam out alone.

She turned her face seaward to gather in an impression of space and solitude, which the vast expanse of water, meeting and melting with the moonlit sky, conveyed to her excited fancy. As she swam she seemed to be reaching out for the unlimited in which to lose herself.

Once she turned and looked toward the shore, toward the people she had left there. She had not gone any great distance—that is, what would have been a great distance for an experienced swimmer. But to her unaccustomed vision the stretch of water behind her assumed the aspect of a barrier which her unaided strength would never be able to overcome.

A quick vision of death smote her soul, and for a second time appalled and enfeebled her senses. But by an effort she rallied her staggering faculties and managed to regain the land.

She made no mention of her encounter with death and her flash of terror, except to say to her husband, "I thought I should have perished out there alone."

"You were not so very far, my dear; I was watching you," he told her.

Edna went at once to the bath-house, and she had put on her dry clothes and was ready to return home before the others had left the water. She started to walk away alone. They all called to her and shouted to her. She waved a dissenting hand, and went on, paying no further heed to their renewed cries which sought to detain her.

"Sometimes I am tempted to think that Mrs. Pontellier is capricious," said Madame Lebrun, who was amusing herself immensely and feared that Edna's abrupt departure might put an end to the pleasure.

"I know she is," assented Mr. Pontellier; "sometimes, not often."

Edna had not traversed a quarter of the distance on her way home before she was overtaken by Robert.

"Did you think I was afraid?" she asked him, without a shade of annoyance.

"No; I knew you weren't afraid."

"Then why did you come? Why didn't you stay out there with the others?"

"I never thought of it."

"Thought of what?"

"Of anything. What difference does it make?"

"I'm very tired," she uttered, complainingly.

"I know you are."

"You don't know anything about it. Why should you know? I never was so exhausted in my life. But it isn't unpleasant. A thousand emotions have swept through me to-night. I don't comprehend half of them. Don't mind what I'm saying; I am just thinking aloud. I wonder if I shall ever be stirred again as Mademoiselle Reisz's playing moved me to-night. I wonder if any night on earth will ever again be like this one. It is like a night in a dream. The people about me are like some uncanny, half-human beings. There must be spirits abroad to-night."

"There are," whispered Robert. "Didn't you know this was the twenty-eighth of August?"

"The twenty-eighth of August?"

"Yes. On the twenty-eighth of August, at the hour of midnight, and if the moon is shining—the moon must be shining—a spirit that has haunted these shores for ages rises up from the Gulf. With its own penetrating vision the spirit seeks some one mortal worthy to hold him company, worthy of being exalted for a few hours into realms of the semi-celestials. His search has always hitherto been fruitless, and he has sunk back, disheartened, into the sea. But to-night he found Mrs. Pontellier. Perhaps he will never wholly release her from the spell. Perhaps she will never again suffer a poor, unworthy earthling to walk in the shadow of her divine presence."

"Don't banter me," she said, wounded at what appeared to be his flippancy. He did not mind the entreaty, but the tone with its delicate note of pathos was like a reproach. He could not explain; he could not tell her that he had penetrated her mood and understood. He said nothing except to offer her his arm, for, by her own admission, she was exhausted. She had been walking alone with her arms hanging limp, letting her white skirts trail along the dewy path. She took his arm, but she did not lean upon it. She let her hand lie listlessly, as though her thoughts were elsewhere—somewhere in advance of her body, and she was striving to overtake them.

Robert assisted her into the hammock which swung from the post before her door out to the trunk of a tree.

"Will you stay out here and wait for Mr. Pontellier?" he asked.

"I'll stay out here. Good-night."

"Shall I get you a pillow?"

"There's one here," she said, feeling about, for they were in the shadow.

"It must be soiled; the children have been tumbling it about."

"No matter." And having discovered the pillow, she adjusted it beneath her head. She extended herself in the hammock with a deep breath of relief. She was not a supercilious or an over-dainty woman. She was not much given to reclining in the hammock, and when she did so it was with no cat-like suggestion of voluptuous ease, but with a beneficent repose which seemed to invade her whole body.

"Shall I stay with you till Mr. Pontellier comes?" asked Robert, seating himself on the outer edge of one of the steps and taking hold of the hammock rope which was fastened to the post.

"If you wish. Don't swing the hammock. Will you get my white shawl which I left on the window-sill over at the house?"

"Are you chilly?"

"No; but I shall be presently."

"Presently?" he laughed. "Do you know what time it is? How long are you going to stay out here?"

"I don't know. Will you get the shawl?"

"Of course I will," he said, rising. He went over to the house, walking along the grass. She watched his figure pass in and out of the strips of moonlight. It was past midnight. It was very quiet.

When he returned with the shawl she took it and kept it in her hand. She did not put it around her.

"Did you say I should stay till Mr. Pontellier came back?"

"I said you might if you wished to."

He seated himself again and rolled a cigarette, which he smoked in silence. Neither did Mrs. Pontellier speak. No multitude of words could have been more significant than those moments of silence, or more pregnant with the first-felt throbbings of desire.

When the voices of the bathers were heard approaching, Robert said goodnight. She did not answer him. He thought she was asleep. Again she watched his figure pass in and out of the strips of moonlight as he walked away.

XI

"What are you doing out here, Edna? I thought I should find you in bed," said her husband, when he discovered her lying there. He had walked up with Madame Lebrun and left her at the house. His wife did not reply.

"Are you asleep?" he asked, bending down close to look at her.

"No." Her eyes gleamed bright and intense, with no sleepy shadows, as they looked into his.

"Do you know it is past one o'clock? Come on," and he mounted the steps and went into their room.

"Edna!" called Mr. Pontellier from within, after a few moments had gone by.

"Don't wait for me," she answered. He thrust his head through the door.

"You will take cold out there," he said irritably. "What folly is this? Why don't you come in?"

"It isn't cold; I have my shawl."

"The mosquitoes will devour you."

"There are no mosquitoes."

She heard him moving about the room; every sound indicating impatience and irritation. Another time she would have gone in at his request. She would, through habit, have yielded to his desire; not with any sense of submission or obedience to his compelling wishes, but unthinkingly, as we walk, move, sit, stand, go through the daily treadmill of the life which has been portioned out to us.

"Edna, dear, are you not coming in soon?" he asked again, this time fondly, with a note of entreaty.

"No; I am going to stay out here."

"This is more than folly," he blurted out. "I can't permit you to stay out there all night. You must come in the house instantly."

With a writhing motion she settled herself more securely in the hammock. She perceived that her will had blazed up, stubborn and resistant. She could not at that moment have done other than denied and resisted. She wondered if her husband had ever spoken to her like that before, and if she had submitted to his command. Of course she had; she remembered that she had. But she could not realize why or how she should have yielded, feeling as she then did.

"Léonce, go to bed," she said. "I mean to stay out here. I don't wish to go in, and I don't intend to. Don't speak to me like that again; I shall not answer you."

Mr. Pontellier had prepared for bed, but he slipped on an extra garment. He opened a bottle of wine, of which he kept a small and select supply in a buffet of his own. He drank a glass of wine and went out on the gallery and offered a glass to his wife. She did not wish any. He drew up a rocker, hoisted his slippered feet on the rail, and proceeded to smoke a cigar. He smoked two cigars; then he went inside and drank another glass of wine. Mrs. Pontellier again declined to accept a glass when it was offered to her. Mr. Pontellier once more seated himself with elevated feet, and after a reasonable interval of time smoked some more cigars.

Edna began to feel like one who awakens gradually out of a dream, a delicious, grotesque, impossible dream, to feel again the realities pressing into her soul. The physical need for sleep began to overtake her; the exuberance which had sustained and exalted her spirit left her helpless and yielding to the conditions which crowded her in.

The stillest hour of the night had come, the hour before dawn, when the world seems to hold its breath. The moon hung low, and had turned from silver to copper in the sleeping sky. The old owl no longer hooted, and the water-oaks had ceased to moan as they bent their heads.

Edna arose, cramped from lying so long and still in the hammock. She tottered up the steps, clutching feebly at the post before passing into the house.

"Are you coming in, Léonce?" she asked, turning her face toward her husband.

"Yes, dear," he answered, with a glance following a misty puff of smoke. "Just as soon as I have finished my cigar."

XII

She slept but a few hours. They were troubled and feverish hours, disturbed with dreams that were intangible, that eluded her, leaving only an impression upon her half-awakened senses of something unattainable. She was up and dressed in the cool of the early morning. The air was invigorating and steadied somewhat her faculties. However, she was not seeking refreshment or help from any source, either external or from within. She was blindly following whatever impulse moved her, as if she had placed herself in alien hands for direction, and freed her soul of responsibility.

Most of the people at that early hour were still in bed and asleep. A few, who intended to go over to the *Chênière* for mass, were moving about. The lovers, who had laid their plans the night before, were already strolling toward the wharf. The lady in black, with her Sunday prayer-book, velvet and gold-clasped, and her Sunday silver beads, was following them at no great distance. Old Monsieur Farival was up, and was more than half inclined to do anything that suggested itself. He put on his big straw hat, and taking his umbrella from the stand in the hall, followed the lady in black, never overtaking her.

The little negro girl who worked Madame Lebrun's sewing-machine was sweeping the galleries with long, absent-minded strokes of the broom. Edna sent her up into the house to awaken Robert.

"Tell him I am going to the *Chênière*. The boat is ready; tell him to hurry."

He had soon joined her. She had never sent for him before. She had never asked for him. She had never seemed to want him before. She did not appear conscious that she had done anything unusual in commanding his presence. He was apparently equally unconscious of anything extraordinary in the situation. But his face was suffused with a quiet glow when he met her.

They went together back to the kitchen to drink coffee. There was no time to wait for any nicety of service. They stood outside the window and the cook passed them their coffee and a roll, which they drank and ate from the window-sill. Edna said it tasted good. She had not thought of coffee nor of anything. He told her he had often noticed that she lacked forethought.

"Wasn't it enough to think of going to the *Chênière* and waking you up?" she laughed. "Do I have to think of everything?—as Léonce says when he's in a bad humor. I don't blame him; he'd never be in a bad humor if it weren't for me."

They took a short cut across the sands. At a distance they could see the curious procession moving toward the wharf—the lovers, shoulder to shoulder, creeping; the lady in black, gaining steadily upon them; old Monsieur Farival, losing ground inch by inch, and a young barefooted Spanish girl, with a red kerchief on her head and a basket on her arm, bringing up the rear.

Robert knew the girl, and he talked to her a little in the boat. No one present understood what they said. Her name was Mariequita. She had a round, sly, piquant face and pretty black eyes. Her hands were small, and she kept them folded over the handle of her basket. Her feet were broad and coarse. She did not strive to hide them. Edna looked at her feet, and noticed the sand and slime between her brown toes.

Beaudelet grumbled because Mariequita was there, taking up so much room. In reality he was annoyed at having old Monsieur Farival, who considered himself the better sailor of the two. But he would not quarrel with so old a man as Monsieur Farival, so he quarreled with Mariequita. The girl was deprecatory at one moment, appealing to Robert. She was saucy the next, moving her head up and down, making "eyes" at Robert and making "mouths" at Beaudelet.

The lovers were all alone. They saw nothing, they heard nothing. The lady in black was counting her beads for the third time. Old Monsieur Farival talked incessantly of what he knew about handling a boat, and of what Beaudelet did not know on the same subject.

Edna liked it all. She looked Mariequita up and down, from her ugly brown toes to her pretty black eyes, and back again.

"Why does she look at me like that?" inquired the girl of Robert.

"Maybe she thinks you are pretty. Shall I ask her?"

"No. Is she your sweetheart?"

"She's a married lady, and has two children."

"Oh! well! Francisco ran away with Sylvano's wife, who had four children. They took all his money and one of the children and stole his boat."

"Shut up!"

"Does she understand?"

"Oh, hush!"

"Are those two married over there—leaning on each other?"

"Of course not," laughed Robert.

"Of course not," echoed Mariequita, with a serious, confirmatory bob of the head.

The sun was high up and beginning to bite. The swift breeze seemed to Edna to bury the sting of it into the pores of her face and hands. Robert held his umbrella over her.

As they went cutting sidewise through the water, the sails bellied taut, with the wind filling and overflowing them. Old Monsieur Farival laughed sardonically at something as he looked at the sails, and Beaudelet swore at the old man under his breath.

Sailing across the bay to the *Chênière Caminada*, Edna felt as if she were being borne away from some anchorage which had held her fast, whose chains had been loosening—had snapped the night before when the mystic spirit was abroad, leaving her free to drift whithersoever she chose to set her sails. Robert spoke to her incessantly; he no longer noticed Mariequita. The girl had shrimps in her bamboo basket. They were covered with Spanish moss. She beat the moss down impatiently, and muttered to herself sullenly.

"Let us go to Grande Terre to-morrow," said Robert in a low voice.

"What shall we do there?"

"Climb up the hill to the old fort and look at the little wriggling gold snakes, and watch the lizards sun themselves."

She gazed away toward Grande Terre and thought she would like to be alone there with Robert, in the sun, listening to the ocean's roar and watching the slimy lizards writhe in and out among the ruins of the old fort.

"And the next day or the next we can sail to the Bayou Brulow," he went on.

"What shall we do there?"

"Anything—cast bait for fish."

"No; we'll go back to Grande Terre. Let the fish alone."

"We'll go wherever you like," he said. "I'll have Tonie come over and help me patch and trim my boat. We shall not need Beaudelet nor any one. Are you afraid of the pirogue?"[32]

"Oh, no."

"Then I'll take you some night on the pirogue when the moon shines. Maybe your Gulf spirit will whisper to you in which of these islands the treasures are hidden—direct you to the very spot, perhaps."

"And in a day we should be rich!" she laughed. "I'd give it all to you, the pirate gold and every bit of treasure we could dig up. I think you would know how to spend it. Pirate gold isn't a thing to be hoarded or utilized. It is something to squander and throw to the four winds, for the fun of seeing the golden specks fly."

"We'd share it, and scatter it together," he said. His face flushed.

They all went together up to the quaint little Gothic church of Our Lady of Lourdes, gleaming all brown and yellow with paint in the sun's glare.

Only Beaudelet remained behind, tinkering at his boat, and Mariequita walked away with her basket of shrimps, casting a look of childish ill-humor and reproach at Robert from the corner of her eye.

XIII

A feeling of oppression and drowsiness overcame Edna during the service. Her head began to ache, and the lights on the altar swayed before her eyes. Another time she might have made an effort to regain her composure; but her one thought was to quit the stifling atmosphere of the church and reach the open air. She arose, climbing over Robert's feet with a muttered apology. Old Monsieur Farival, flurried, curious, stood up, but upon seeing that Robert had followed Mrs. Pontellier, he sank back into his seat. He whispered an anxious inquiry of the lady in black, who did not

[32] *pirogue:* canoe.

notice him or reply, but kept her eyes fastened upon the pages of her velvet prayer-book.

"I felt giddy and almost overcome," Edna said, lifting her hands instinctively to her head and pushing her straw hat up from her forehead. "I couldn't have stayed through the service." They were outside in the shadow of the church. Robert was full of solicitude.

"It was folly to have thought of going in the first place, let alone staying. Come over to Madame Antoine's; you can rest there." He took her arm and led her away, looking anxiously and continuously down into her face.

How still it was, with only the voice of the sea whispering through the reeds that grew in the salt-water pools! The long line of little gray, weather-beaten houses nestled peacefully among the orange trees. It must always have been God's day on that low, drowsy island, Edna thought. They stopped, leaning over a jagged fence made of sea-drift, to ask for water. A youth, a mild-faced Acadian,[33] was drawing water from the cistern, which was nothing more than a rusty buoy, with an opening on one side, sunk in the ground. The water which the youth handed to them in a tin pail was not cold to taste, but it was cool to her heated face, and it greatly revived and refreshed her.

Madame Antoine's cot[34] was at the far end of the village. She welcomed them with all the native hospitality, as she would have opened her door to let the sunlight in. She was fat, and walked heavily and clumsily across the floor. She could speak no English, but when Robert made her understand that the lady who accompanied him was ill and desired to rest, she was all eagerness to make Edna feel at home and to dispose of her comfortably.

The whole place was immaculately clean, and the big, four-posted bed, snow-white, invited one to repose. It stood in a small side room which looked out across a narrow grass plot toward the shed, where there was a disabled boat lying keel upward.

Madame Antoine had not gone to mass. Her son Tonie had, but she supposed he would soon be back, and she invited Robert to be seated and wait for him. But he went and sat outside the door and smoked. Madame Antoine busied herself in the large front room preparing dinner. She was boiling mullets over a few red coals in the huge fireplace.

Edna, left alone in the little side room, loosened her clothes, removing the greater part of them. She bathed her face, her neck and arms in the basin that stood between the windows. She took off her shoes and stockings and stretched herself in the very center of the high, white bed. How luxurious it felt to rest thus in a strange, quaint bed, with its sweet country odor of laurel lingering about the sheets and mattress! She stretched her strong limbs that ached a little. She ran her fingers through her loosened hair for a while. She looked at her round arms as she held them straight up and rubbed them one after the other, observing closely, as if it were

---

[33] *Acadian:* descendant of French Canadians whom the British expelled from eastern Canada (Acadia) in 1775.   [34] *cot:* cottage.

something she saw for the first time, the fine, firm quality and texture of her flesh. She clasped her hands easily above her head, and it was thus she fell asleep.

She slept lightly at first, half awake and drowsily attentive to the things about her. She could hear Madame Antoine's heavy, scraping tread as she walked back and forth on the sanded floor. Some chickens were clucking outside the windows, scratching for bits of gravel in the grass. Later she half heard the voices of Robert and Tonie talking under the shed. She did not stir. Even her eyelids rested numb and heavily over her sleepy eyes. The voices went on—Tonie's slow, Acadian drawl, Robert's quick, soft, smooth French. She understood French imperfectly unless directly addressed, and the voices were only part of the other drowsy, muffled sounds lulling her senses.

When Edna awoke it was with the conviction that she had slept long and soundly. The voices were hushed under the shed. Madame Antoine's step was no longer to be heard in the adjoining room. Even the chickens had gone elsewhere to scratch and cluck. The mosquito bar was drawn over her; the old woman had come in while she slept and let down the bar. Edna arose quietly from the bed, and looking between the curtains of the window, she saw by the slanting rays of the sun that the afternoon was far advanced. Robert was out there under the shed, reclining in the shade against the sloping keel of the overturned boat. He was reading from a book. Tonie was no longer with him. She wondered what had become of the rest of the party. She peeped out at him two or three times as she stood washing herself in the little basin between the windows.

Madame Antoine had lain some coarse, clean towels upon a chair, and had placed a box of *poudre de riz*[35] within easy reach. Edna dabbed the powder upon her nose and cheeks as she looked at herself closely in the little distorted mirror which hung on the wall above the basin. Her eyes were bright and wide awake and her face glowed.

When she had completed her toilet she walked into the adjoining room. She was very hungry. No one was there. But there was a cloth spread upon the table that stood against the wall, and a cover was laid for one, with a crusty brown loaf and a bottle of wine beside the plate. Edna bit a piece from the brown loaf, tearing it with her strong, white teeth. She poured some of the wine into the glass and drank it down. Then she went softly out of doors, and plucking an orange from the low-hanging bough of a tree, threw it at Robert, who did not know she was awake and up.

An illumination broke over his whole face when he saw her and joined her under the orange tree.

"How many years have I slept?" she inquired. "The whole island seems changed. A new race of beings must have sprung up, leaving only you and me as past relics. How many ages ago did Madame Antoine and Tonie die? and when did our people from Grand Isle disappear from the earth?"

He familiarly adjusted a ruffle upon her shoulder.

---

[35] *poudre de riz:* talcum powder.

"You have slept precisely one hundred years. I was left here to guard your slumbers; and for one hundred years I have been out under the shed reading a book. The only evil I couldn't prevent was to keep a broiled fowl from drying up."

"If it has turned to stone, still will I eat it," said Edna, moving with him into the house. "But really, what has become of Monsieur Farival and the others?"

"Gone hours ago. When they found that you were sleeping they thought it best not to awake you. Any way, I wouldn't have let them. What was I here for?"

"I wonder if Léonce will be uneasy!" she speculated, as she seated herself at table.

"Of course not; he knows you are with me," Robert replied, as he busied himself among sundry pans and covered dishes which had been left standing on the hearth.

"Where are Madame Antoine and her son?" asked Edna.

"Gone to Vespers,[36] and to visit some friends, I believe. I am to take you back in Tonie's boat whenever you are ready to go."

He stirred the smoldering ashes till the broiled fowl began to sizzle afresh. He served her with no mean repast, dripping the coffee anew and sharing it with her. Madame Antoine had cooked little else than the mullets, but while Edna slept Robert had foraged the island. He was childishly gratified to discover her appetite, and to see the relish with which she ate the food which he had procured for her.

"Shall we go right away?" she asked, after draining her glass and brushing together the crumbs of the crusty loaf.

"The sun isn't as low as it will be in two hours," he answered.

"The sun will be gone in two hours."

"Well, let it go; who cares!"

They waited a good while under the orange trees, till Madame Antoine came back, panting, waddling, with a thousand apologies to explain her absence. Tonie did not dare to return. He was shy, and would not willingly face any woman except his mother.

It was very pleasant to stay there under the orange trees, while the sun dipped lower and lower, turning the western sky to flaming copper and gold. The shadows lengthened and crept out like stealthy, grotesque monsters across the grass.

Edna and Robert both sat upon the ground—that is, he lay upon the ground beside her, occasionally picking at the hem of her muslin gown.

Madame Antoine seated her fat body, broad and squat, upon a bench beside the door. She had been talking all the afternoon, and had wound herself up to the story-telling pitch.

And what stories she told them! But twice in her life she had left the *Chênière Caminada,* and then for the briefest span. All her years she had squatted and waddled there upon the island, gathering legends of the Baratarians[37] and the sea.

---

[36] *Vespers:* evening church service   [37] *Baratarians:* pirates (e.g., Jean Laffitte) in the Baratarian Bay (in the Mississippi delta).

The night came on, with the moon to lighten it. Edna could hear the whispering voices of dead men and the click of muffled gold.

When she and Robert stepped into Tonie's boat, with the red lateen sail, misty spirit forms were prowling in the shadows and among the reeds, and upon the water were phantom ships, speeding to cover.

XIV

The youngest boy, Etienne, had been very naughty, Madame Ratignolle said, as she delivered him into the hands of his mother. He had been unwilling to go to bed and had made a scene; whereupon she had taken charge of him and pacified him as well as she could. Raoul had been in bed and asleep for two hours.

The youngster was in his long white nightgown, that kept tripping him up as Madame Ratignolle led him along by the hand. With the other chubby fist he rubbed his eyes, which were heavy with sleep and ill humor. Edna took him in her arms, and seating herself in the rocker, began to coddle and caress him, calling him all manner of tender names, soothing him to sleep.

It was not more than nine o'clock. No one had yet gone to bed but the children.

Léonce had been very uneasy at first, Madame Ratignolle said, and had wanted to start at once for the *Chênière*. But Monsieur Farival had assured him that his wife was only overcome with sleep and fatigue, that Tonie would bring her safely back later in the day; and he had thus been dissuaded from crossing the bay. He had gone over to Klein's, looking up some cotton broker whom he wished to see in regard to securities, exchanges, stocks, bonds, or something of the sort, Madame Ratignolle did not remember what. He said he would not remain away late. She herself was suffering from heat and oppression, she said. She carried a bottle of salts and a large fan. She would not consent to remain with Edna, for Monsieur Ratignolle was alone, and he detested above all things to be left alone.

When Etienne had fallen asleep Edna bore him into the back room, and Robert went and lifted the mosquito bar that she might lay the child comfortably in his bed. The quadroon had vanished. When they emerged from the cottage Robert bade Edna good-night.

"Do you know we have been together the whole livelong day, Robert—since early this morning?" she said at parting.

"All but the hundred years when you were sleeping. Good-night."

He pressed her hand and went away in the direction of the beach. He did not join any of the others, but walked alone toward the Gulf.

Edna stayed outside, awaiting her husband's return. She had no desire to sleep or to retire; nor did she feel like going over to sit with the Ratignolles, or to join Madame Lebrun and a group whose animated voices reached her as they sat in conversation before the house. She let her mind wander back over her stay at Grand Isle; and she tried to discover wherein this summer had been different from any and every other summer of her life. She could only realize that she herself—her present self—was in some way different from the other self. That she was seeing with different eyes and making the acquaintance of new conditions in herself that colored and changed her environment, she did not yet suspect.

She wondered why Robert had gone away and left her. It did not occur to her to think he might have grown tired of being with her the livelong day. She was not tired, and she felt that he was not. She regretted that he had gone. It was so much more natural to have him stay when he was not absolutely required to leave her.

As Edna waited for her husband she sang low a little song that Robert had sung as they crossed the bay. It began with "Ah! *Si tu savais*,"[38] and every verse ended with "*si tu savais*."

Robert's voice was not pretentious. It was musical and true. The voice, the notes, the whole refrain haunted her memory.

XV

When Edna entered the dining-room one evening a little late, as was her habit, an unusually animated conversation seemed to be going on. Several persons were talking at once, and Victor's voice was predominating, even over that of his mother. Edna had returned late from her bath, had dressed in some haste, and her face was flushed. Her head, set off by her dainty white gown, suggested a rich, rare blossom. She took her seat at table between old Monsieur Farival and Madame Ratignolle.

As she seated herself and was about to begin to eat her soup, which had been served when she entered the room, several persons informed her simultaneously that Robert was going to Mexico. She laid her spoon down and looked about her bewildered. He had been with her, reading to her all the morning, and had never even mentioned such a place as Mexico. She had not seen him during the afternoon; she had heard some one say he was at the house, upstairs with his mother. This she had thought nothing of, though she was surprised when he did not join her later in the afternoon, when she went down to the beach.

She looked across at him, where he sat beside Madame Lebrun, who presided. Edna's face was a blank picture of bewilderment, which she never thought of disguising. He lifted his eyebrows with the pretext of a smile as he returned her glance. He looked embarrassed and uneasy.

"When is he going?" she asked of everybody in general, as if Robert were not there to answer for himself.

"To-night!" "This very evening!" "Did you ever!" "What possesses him!" were some of the replies she gathered, uttered simultaneously in French and English.

"Impossible!" she exclaimed. "How can a person start off from Grand Isle to Mexico at a moment's notice, as if he were going over to Klein's or to the wharf or down to the beach?"

"I said all along I was going to Mexico; I've been saying so for years!" cried Robert, in an excited and irritable tone, with the air of a man defending himself against a swarm of stinging insects.

---

[38] *Si tu savais:* "Could'st thou but know" (title and refrain of a song by Michael William Balfe [1808–70]).

Madame Lebrun knocked on the table with her knife handle.

"Please let Robert explain why he is going, and why he is going to-night," she called out. "Really, this table is getting to be more and more like Bedlam every day, with everybody talking at once. Sometimes—I hope God will forgive me—but positively, sometimes I wish Victor would lose the power of speech."

Victor laughed sardonically as he thanked his mother for her holy wish, of which he failed to see the benefit to anybody, except that it might afford her a more ample opportunity and license to talk herself.

Monsieur Farival thought that Victor should have been taken out in midocean in his earliest youth and drowned. Victor thought there would be more logic in thus disposing of old people with an established claim for making themselves universally obnoxious. Madame Lebrun grew a trifle hysterical; Robert called his brother some sharp, hard names.

"There's nothing much to explain, mother," he said; though he explained, nevertheless—looking chiefly at Edna—that he could only meet the gentleman whom he intended to join at Vera Cruz by taking such and such a steamer, which left New Orleans on such a day; that Beaudelet was going out with his lugger-load of vegetables that night, which gave him an opportunity of reaching the city and making his vessel in time.

"But when did you make up your mind to all this?" demanded Monsieur Farival.

"This afternoon," returned Robert, with a shade of annoyance.

"At what time this afternoon?" persisted the old gentleman, with nagging determination, as if he were cross-questioning a criminal in a court of justice.

"At four o'clock this afternoon, Monsieur Farival," Robert replied, in a high voice and with a lofty air, which reminded Edna of some gentleman on the stage.

She had forced herself to eat most of her soup, and now she was picking the flaky bits of a *court bouillon*[39] with her fork.

The lovers were profiting by the general conversation on Mexico to speak in whispers of matters which they rightly considered were interesting to no one but themselves. The lady in black had once received a pair of prayer-beads of curious workmanship from Mexico, with very special indulgence[40] attached to them, but she had never been able to ascertain whether the indulgence extended outside the Mexican border. Father Fochel of the Cathedral had attempted to explain it; but he had not done so to her satisfaction. And she begged that Robert would interest himself, and discover, if possible, whether she was entitled to the indulgence accompanying the remarkably curious Mexican prayer-beads.

Madame Ratignolle hoped that Robert would exercise extreme caution in dealing with the Mexicans, who, she considered, were a treacherous people, unscrupulous and revengeful. She trusted she did them no injustice in thus condemning them as a race. She had known personally but one Mexican, who made and sold excellent tamales, and whom she would have trusted implicitly, so soft-spoken was

---

[39] *court bouillon:* fish broth   [40] *indulgence:* power to reduce the punishment for sins.

he. One day he was arrested for stabbing his wife. She never knew whether he had been hanged or not.

Victor had grown hilarious, and was attempting to tell an anecdote about a Mexican girl who served chocolate one winter in a restaurant in Dauphine Street. No one would listen to him but old Monsieur Farival, who went into convulsions over the droll story.

Edna wondered if they had all gone mad, to be talking and clamoring at that rate. She herself could think of nothing to say about Mexico or the Mexicans.

"At what time do you leave?" she asked Robert.

"At ten," he told her. "Beaudelet wants to wait for the moon."

"Are you all ready to go?"

"Quite ready. I shall only take a hand-bag, and shall pack my trunk in the city."

He turned to answer some question put to him by his mother, and Edna, having finished her black coffee, left the table.

She went directly to her room. The little cottage was close and stuffy after leaving the outer air. But she did not mind; there appeared to be a hundred different things demanding her attention indoors. She began to set the toilet-stand to rights, grumbling at the negligence of the quadroon, who was in the adjoining room putting the children to bed. She gathered together stray garments that were hanging on the backs of chairs, and put each where it belonged in closet or bureau drawer. She changed her gown for a more comfortable and commodious wrapper. She rearranged her hair, combing and brushing it with unusual energy. Then she went in and assisted the quadroon in getting the boys to bed.

They were very playful and inclined to talk—to do anything but lie quiet and go to sleep. Edna sent the quadroon away to her supper and told her she need not return. Then she sat and told the children a story. Instead of soothing it excited them, and added to their wakefulness. She left them in heated argument, speculating about the conclusion of the tale which their mother promised to finish the following night.

The little black girl came in to say that Madame Lebrun would like to have Mrs. Pontellier go and sit with them over at the house till Mr. Robert went away. Edna returned answer that she had already undressed, that she did not feel quite well, but perhaps she would go over to the house later. She started to dress again, and got as far advanced as to remove her *peignoir*. But changing her mind once more she resumed the *peignoir*, and went outside and sat down before her door. She was over-heated and irritable, and fanned herself energetically for a while. Madame Ratignolle came down to discover what was the matter.

"All that noise and confusion at the table must have upset me," replied Edna, "and moreover, I hate shocks and surprises. The idea of Robert starting off in such a ridiculously sudden and dramatic way! As if it were a matter of life and death! Never saying a word about it all morning when he was with me."

"Yes," agreed Madame Ratignolle. "I think it was showing us all—you especially—very little consideration. It wouldn't have surprised me in any of the others; those Lebruns are all given to heroics. But I must say I should never have expected such a thing from Robert. Are you not coming down? Come on, dear; it doesn't look friendly."

"No," said Edna, a little sullenly. "I can't go to the trouble of dressing again; I don't feel like it."

"You needn't dress; you look all right; fasten a belt around your waist. Just look at me!"

"No," persisted Edna; "but you go on. Madame Lebrun might be offended if we both stayed away."

Madame Ratignolle kissed Edna good-night, and went away, being in truth rather desirous of joining in the general and animated conversation which was still in progress concerning Mexico and the Mexicans.

Somewhat later Robert came up, carrying his hand-bag.

"Aren't you feeling well?" he asked.

"Oh, well enough. Are you going right away?"

He lit a match and looked at his watch. "In twenty minutes," he said. The sudden and brief flare of the match emphasized the darkness for a while. He sat down upon a stool which the children had left out on the porch.

"Get a chair," said Edna.

"This will do," he replied. He put on his soft hat and nervously took it off again, and wiping his face with his handkerchief, complained of the heat.

"Take the fan," said Edna, offering it to him.

"Oh, no! Thank you. It does no good; you have to stop fanning some time, and feel all the more uncomfortable afterward."

"That's one of the ridiculous things which men always say. I have never known one to speak otherwise of fanning. How long will you be gone?"

"Forever, perhaps. I don't know. It depends upon a good many things."

"Well, in case it shouldn't be forever, how long will it be?"

"I don't know."

"This seems to me perfectly preposterous and uncalled for. I don't like it. I don't understand your motive for silence and mystery, never saying a word to me about it this morning." He remained silent, not offering to defend himself. He only said, after a moment:

"Don't part with me in an ill-humor. I never knew you to be out of patience with me before."

"I don't want to part in any ill-humor," she said. "But can't you understand? I've grown used to seeing you, to having you with me all the time, and your action seems unfriendly, even unkind. You don't even offer an excuse for it. Why, I was planning to be together, thinking of how pleasant it would be to see you in the city next winter."

"So was I," he blurted. "Perhaps that's the—" He stood up suddenly and held out his hand. "Good-by, my dear Mrs. Pontellier; good-by. You won't—I hope you won't completely forget me." She clung to his hand, striving to detain him.

"Write to me when you get there, won't you, Robert?" she entreated.

"I will, thank you. Good-by."

How unlike Robert! The merest acquaintance would have said something more emphatic than "I will, thank you; good-by," to such a request.

He had evidently already taken leave of the people over at the house, for he descended the steps and went to join Beaudelet, who was out there with an oar across his shoulder waiting for Robert. They walked away in the darkness. She could only hear Beaudelet's voice; Robert had apparently not even spoken a word of greeting to his companion.

Edna bit her handkerchief convulsively, striving to hold back and to hide, even from herself as she would have hidden from another, the emotion which was troubling—tearing—her. Her eyes were brimming with tears.

For the first time she recognized anew the symptoms of infatuation which she had felt incipiently as a child, as a girl in her earliest teens, and later as a young woman. The recognition did not lessen the reality, the poignancy of the revelation by any suggestion or promise of instability. The past was nothing to her; offered no lesson which she was willing to heed. The future was a mystery which she never attempted to penetrate. The present alone was significant; was hers, to torture her as it was doing then with the biting conviction that she had lost that which she had held, that she had been denied that which her impassioned, newly awakened being demanded.

XVI

"Do you miss your friend greatly?" asked Mademoiselle Reisz one morning as she came creeping up behind Edna, who had just left her cottage on her way to the beach. She spent much of her time in the water since she had acquired finally the art of swimming. As their stay at Grand Isle drew near its close, she felt that she could not give too much time to a diversion which afforded her the only real pleasurable moments that she knew. When Mademoiselle Reisz came and touched her upon the shoulder and spoke to her, the woman seemed to echo the thought which was ever in Edna's mind; or better, the feeling which constantly possessed her.

Robert's going had some way taken the brightness, the color, the meaning out of everything. The conditions of her life were in no way changed, but her whole existence was dulled, like a faded garment which seems to be no longer worth wearing. She sought him everywhere—in others whom she induced to talk about him. She went up in the mornings to Madame Lebrun's room, braving the clatter of the old sewing-machine. She sat there and chatted at intervals as Robert had done. She gazed around the room at the pictures and photographs hanging upon the wall, and discovered in some corner an old family album, which she examined with the keenest interest, appealing to Madame Lebrun for enlightenment concerning the many figures and faces which she discovered between its pages.

There was a picture of Madame Lebrun with Robert as a baby, seated in her lap, a round-faced infant with a fist in his mouth. The eyes alone in the baby suggested the man. And that was he also in kilts, at the age of five, wearing long curls and holding a whip in his hand. It made Edna laugh, and she laughed, too, at the portrait in his first long trousers; while another interested her, taken when he left for college, looking thin, long-faced, with eyes full of fire, ambition and great intentions. But there was no recent picture, none which suggested the Robert who had gone away five days ago, leaving a void and wilderness behind him.

"Oh, Robert stopped having his pictures taken when he had to pay for them himself! He found wiser use for his money, he says," explained Madame Lebrun. She had a letter from him, written before he left New Orleans. Edna wished to see the letter, and Madame Lebrun told her to look for it either on the table or the dresser, or perhaps it was on the mantelpiece.

The letter was on the bookshelf. It possessed the greatest interest and attraction for Edna; the envelope, its size and shape, the post-mark, the handwriting. She examined every detail of the outside before opening it. There were only a few lines, setting forth that he would leave the city that afternoon, that he had packed his trunk in good shape, that he was well, and sent her his love and begged to be affectionately remembered to all. There was no special message to Edna except a postscript saying that if Mrs. Pontellier desired to finish the book which he had been reading to her, his mother would find it in his room, among other books there on the table. Edna experienced a pang of jealousy because he had written to his mother rather than to her.

Every one seemed to take for granted that she missed him. Even her husband, when he came down the Saturday following Robert's departure, expressed regret that he had gone.

"How do you get on without him, Edna?" he asked.

"It's very dull without him," she admitted. Mr. Pontellier had seen Robert in the city, and Edna asked him a dozen questions or more. Where had they met? On Carondelet Street, in the morning. They had gone "in" and had a drink and a cigar together. What had they talked about? Chiefly about his prospects in Mexico, which Mr. Pontellier thought were promising. How did he look? How did he seem— grave, or gay, or how? Quite cheerful, and wholly taken up with the idea of his trip, which Mr. Pontellier found altogether natural in a young fellow about to seek fortune and adventure in a strange, queer country.

Edna tapped her foot impatiently, and wondered why the children persisted in playing in the sun when they might be under the trees. She went down and led them out of the sun, scolding the quadroon for not being more attentive.

It did not strike her as in the least grotesque that she should be making of Robert the object of conversation and leading her husband to speak of him. The sentiment which she entertained for Robert in no way resembled that which she felt for her husband, or had ever felt, or ever expected to feel. She had all her life long been accustomed to harbor thoughts and emotions which never voiced themselves. They had never taken the form of struggles. They belonged to her and were her own, and she entertained the conviction that she had a right to them and that they concerned no one but herself. Edna had once told Madame Ratignolle that she would never sacrifice herself for her children, or for any one. Then had followed a rather heated argument; the two women did not appear to understand each other or to be talking the same language. Edna tried to appease her friend, to explain.

"I would give up the unessential; I would give my money, I would give my life for my children; but I wouldn't give myself. I can't make it more clear; it's only something which I am beginning to comprehend, which is revealing itself to me."

"I don't know what you would call the essential, or what you mean by the unessential," said Madame Ratignolle, cheerfully; "but a woman who would give her life for her children could do no more than that—your Bible tells you so. I'm sure I couldn't do more than that."

"Oh, yes you could!" laughed Edna.

She was not surprised at Mademoiselle Reisz's question the morning that lady, following her to the beach, tapped her on the shoulder and asked if she did not greatly miss her young friend.

"Oh, good morning, Mademoiselle; is it you? Why, of course I miss Robert. Are you going down to bathe?"

"Why should I go down to bathe at the very end of the season when I haven't been in the surf all summer?" replied the woman, disagreeably.

"I beg your pardon," offered Edna, in some embarrassment, for she should have remembered that Mademoiselle Reisz's avoidance of the water had furnished a theme for much pleasantry. Some among them thought it was on account of her false hair, or the dread of getting the violets wet, while others attributed it to the natural aversion for water sometimes believed to accompany the artistic temperament. Mademoiselle offered Edna some chocolates in a paper bag, which she took from her pocket, by way of showing that she bore no ill feeling. She habitually ate chocolates for their sustaining quality; they contained much nutrient in small compass, she said. They saved her from starvation, as Madame Lebrun's table was utterly impossible; and no one save so impertinent a woman as Madame Lebrun could think of offering such food to people and requiring them to pay for it.

"She must feel very lonely without her son," said Edna, desiring to change the subject. "Her favorite son, too. It must have been quite hard to let him go."

Mademoiselle laughed maliciously.

"Her favorite son! Oh, dear! Who could have been imposing such a tale upon you? Aline Lebrun lives for Victor, and for Victor alone. She has spoiled him into the worthless creature he is. She worships him and the ground he walks on. Robert is very well in a way, to give up all the money he can earn to the family, and keep the barest pittance for himself. Favorite son, indeed! I miss the poor fellow myself, my dear. I liked to see him and to hear him about the place—the only Lebrun who is worth a pinch of salt. He comes to see me often in the city. I like to play to him. That Victor! hanging would be too good for him. It's a wonder Robert hasn't beaten him to death long ago."

"I thought he had great patience with his brother," offered Edna, glad to be talking about Robert, no matter what was said.

"Oh! he thrashed him well enough a year or two ago," said Mademoiselle. "It was about a Spanish girl, whom Victor considered that he had some sort of claim upon. He met Robert one day talking to the girl, or walking with her, or bathing with her, or carrying her basket—I don't remember what;—and he became so insulting and abusive that Robert gave him a thrashing on the spot that has kept him comparatively in order for a good while. It's about time he was getting another."

"Was her name Mariequita?" asked Edna.

"Mariequita—yes, that was it; Mariequita. I had forgotten. Oh, she's a sly one, and a bad one, that Mariequita!"

Edna looked down at Mademoiselle Reisz and wondered how she could have listened to her venom so long. For some reason she felt depressed, almost unhappy. She had not intended to go into the water; but she donned her bathing suit, and left Mademoiselle alone, seated under the shade of the children's tent. The water was growing cooler as the season advanced. Edna plunged and swam about with an abandon that thrilled and invigorated her. She remained a long time in the water, half hoping that Mademoiselle Reisz would not wait for her.

But Mademoiselle waited. She was very amiable during the walk back, and raved much over Edna's appearance in her bathing suit. She talked about music. She hoped that Edna would go to see her in the city, and wrote her address with the stub of a pencil on a piece of card which she found in her pocket.

"When do you leave?" asked Edna.

"Next Monday; and you?"

"The following week," answered Edna, adding, "It has been a pleasant summer, hasn't it, Mademoiselle?"

"Well," agreed Mademoiselle Reisz, with a shrug, "rather pleasant, if it hadn't been for the mosquitoes and the Farival twins."

XVII

The Pontelliers possessed a very charming home on Esplanade Street[41] in New Orleans. It was a large, double cottage, with a broad front veranda, whose round, fluted columns supported the sloping roof. The house was painted a dazzling white; the outside shutters, or jalousies, were green. In the yard, which was kept scrupulously neat, were flowers and plants of every description which flourish in South Louisiana. Within doors the appointments were perfect after the conventional type. The softest carpets and rugs covered the floors; rich and tasteful draperies hung at doors and windows. There were paintings, selected with judgment and discrimination, upon the walls. The cut glass, the silver, the heavy damask which daily appeared upon the table were the envy of many women whose husbands were less generous than Mr. Pontellier.

Mr. Pontellier was very fond of walking about his house examining its various appointments and details, to see that nothing was amiss. He greatly valued his possessions, chiefly because they were his, and derived genuine pleasure from contemplating a painting, a statuette, a rare lace curtain—no matter what—after he had bought it and placed it among his household goods.

On Tuesday afternoons—Tuesday being Mrs. Pontellier's reception day—there was a constant stream of callers—women who came in carriages or in the street cars,

---

[41] *Esplanade Street:* fashionable street in New Orleans.

or walked when the air was soft and distance permitted. A light-colored mulatto boy, in dress coat and bearing a diminutive silver tray for the reception of cards, admitted them. A maid, in white fluted cap, offered the callers liqueur, coffee, or chocolate, as they might desire. Mrs. Pontellier, attired in a handsome reception gown, remained in the drawing-room the entire afternoon receiving her visitors. Men sometimes called in the evening with their wives.

This had been the programme which Mrs. Pontellier had religiously followed since her marriage, six years before. Certain evenings during the week she and her husband attended the opera or sometimes the play.

Mr. Pontellier left his home in the mornings between nine and ten o'clock, and rarely returned before half-past six or seven in the evening—dinner being served at half-past seven.

He and his wife seated themselves at table one Tuesday evening, a few weeks after their return from Grand Isle. They were alone together. The boys were being put to bed; the patter of their bare, escaping feet could be heard occasionally, as well as the pursuing voice of the quadroon, lifted in mild protest and entreaty. Mrs. Pontellier did not wear her usual Tuesday reception gown; she was in ordinary house dress. Mr. Pontellier, who was observant about such things, noticed it, as he served the soup and handed it to the boy in waiting.

"Tired out, Edna? Whom did you have? Many callers?" he asked. He tasted his soup and began to season it with pepper, salt, vinegar, mustard—everything within reach.

"There were a good many," replied Edna, who was eating her soup with evident satisfaction. "I found their cards when I got home; I was out."

"Out!" exclaimed her husband, with something like genuine consternation in his voice as he laid down the vinegar cruet and looked at her through his glasses. "Why, what could have taken you out on Tuesday? What did you have to do?"

"Nothing. I simply felt like going out, and I went out."

"Well, I hope you left some suitable excuse," said her husband, somewhat appeased, as he added a dash of cayenne pepper to the soup.

"No, I left no excuse. I told Joe to say I was out, that was all."

"Why, my dear, I should think you'd understand by this time that people don't do such things; we've got to observe *les convenances*[42] if we ever expect to get on and keep up with the procession. If you felt that you had to leave home this afternoon, you should have left some suitable explanation for your absence.

"This soup is really impossible; it's strange that woman hasn't learned yet to make a decent soup. Any free-lunch stand in town serves a better one. Was Mrs. Belthrop here?"

"Bring the tray with the cards, Joe. I don't remember who was here."

The boy retired and returned after a moment, bringing the tiny silver tray, which was covered with ladies' visiting cards. He handed it to Mrs. Pontellier.

"Give it to Mr. Pontellier," she said.

[42] *les convenances:* the proprieties; social conventions.

Joe offered the tray to Mr. Pontellier, and removed the soup.

Mr. Pontellier scanned the names of his wife's callers, reading some of them aloud, with comments as he read.

"'The Misses Delasidas.' I worked a big deal in futures[43] for their father this morning; nice girls; it's time they were getting married. 'Mrs. Belthrop.' I tell you what it is Edna; you can't afford to snub Mrs. Belthrop. Why, Belthrop could buy and sell us ten times over. His business is worth a good, round sum to me. You'd better write her a note. 'Mrs. James Highcamp.' Hugh! the less you have to do with Mrs. Highcamp, the better. 'Madame Laforcé.' Came all the way from Carrolton, too, poor old soul. 'Miss Wiggs,' 'Mrs. Eleanor Boltons.'" He pushed the cards aside.

"Mercy!" exclaimed Edna, who had been fuming. "Why are you taking the thing so seriously and making such a fuss over it?"

"I'm not making any fuss over it. But it's just such seeming trifles that we've got to take seriously; such things count."

The fish was scorched. Mr. Pontellier would not touch it. Edna said she did not mind a little scorched taste. The roast was in some way not to his fancy, and he did not like the manner in which the vegetables were served.

"It seems to me," he said, "we spend money enough in this house to procure at least one meal a day which a man could eat and retain his self-respect."

"You used to think the cook was a treasure," returned Edna, indifferently.

"Perhaps she was when she first came; but cooks are only human. They need looking after, like any other class of persons that you employ. Suppose I didn't look after the clerks in my office, just let them run things their own way; they'd soon make a nice mess of me and my business."

"Where are you going?" asked Edna, seeing that her husband arose from table without having eaten a morsel except a taste of the highly-seasoned soup.

"I'm going to get my dinner at the club. Good night." He went into the hall, took his hat and stick from the stand, and left the house.

She was somewhat familiar with such scenes. They had often made her very unhappy. On a few previous occasions she had been completely deprived of any desire to finish her dinner. Sometimes she had gone into the kitchen to administer a tardy rebuke to the cook. Once she went to her room and studied the cookbook during an entire evening, finally writing out a menu for the week, which left her harassed with a feeling that, after all, she had accomplished no good that was worth the name.

But that evening Edna finished her dinner alone, with forced deliberation. Her face was flushed and her eyes flamed with some inward fire that lighted them. After finishing her dinner she went to her room, having instructed the boy to tell any other callers that she was indisposed.

It was a large, beautiful room, rich and picturesque in the soft, dim light which the maid had turned low. She went and stood at an open window and looked out upon the deep tangle of the garden below. All the mystery and witchery of the night

---

[43] *futures:* stocks or commodities bought or sold for future delivery (a form of speculation).

seemed to have gathered there amid the perfumes and the dusky and tortuous outlines of flowers and foliage. She was seeking herself and finding herself in just such sweet, half-darkness which met her moods. But the voices were not soothing that came to her from the darkness and the sky above and the stars. They jeered and sounded mournful notes without promise, devoid even of hope. She turned back into the room and began to walk to and fro down its whole length, without stopping, without resting. She carried in her hands a thin handkerchief, which she tore into ribbons, rolled into a ball, and flung from her. Once she stopped, and taking off her wedding ring, flung it upon the carpet. When she saw it lying there, she stamped her heel upon it, striving to crush it. But her small boot heel did not make an indenture, not a mark upon the little glittering circlet.

In a sweeping passion she seized a glass vase from the table and flung it upon the tiles of the hearth. She wanted to destroy something. The crash and clatter were what she wanted to hear.

A maid, alarmed at the din of breaking glass, entered the room to discover what was the matter.

"A vase fell upon the hearth," said Edna. "Never mind; leave it till morning."

"Oh! you might get some of the glass in your feet, ma'am," insisted the young woman, picking up bits of the broken vase that were scattered upon the carpet. "And here's your ring, ma'am, under the chair."

Edna held out her hand, and taking the ring, slipped it upon her finger.

XVIII

The following morning Mr. Pontellier, upon leaving for his office, asked Edna if she would not meet him in town in order to look at some new fixtures for the library.

"I hardly think we need new fixtures, Léonce. Don't let us get anything new; you are too extravagant. I don't believe you ever think of saving or putting by."

"The way to become rich is to make money, my dear Edna, not to save it," he said. He regretted that she did not feel inclined to go with him and select new fixtures. He kissed her good-by, and told her she was not looking well and must take care of herself. She was unusually pale and very quiet.

She stood on the front veranda as he quitted the house, and absently picked a few sprays of jessamine that grew upon a trellis near by. She inhaled the odor of the blossoms and thrust them into the bosom of her white morning gown. The boys were dragging along the banquette[44] a small "express wagon," which they had filled with blocks and sticks. The quadroon was following them with little quick steps, having assumed a fictitious animation and alacrity for the occasion. A fruit vendor was crying his wares in the street.

Edna looked straight before her with a self-absorbed expression upon her face. She felt no interest in anything about her. The street, the children, the fruit vender, the flowers growing there under her eyes, were all part and parcel of an alien world which had suddenly become antagonistic.

[44] *banquette:* sidewalk.

She went back into the house. She had thought of speaking to the cook concerning her blunders of the previous night; but Mr. Pontellier had saved her that disagreeable mission, for which she was so poorly fitted. Mr. Pontellier's arguments were usually convincing with those whom he employed. He left home feeling quite sure that he and Edna would sit down that evening, and possibly a few subsequent evenings, to a dinner deserving of the name.

Edna spent an hour or two in looking over some of her old sketches. She could see their shortcomings and defects, which were glaring in her eyes. She tried to work a little, but found she was not in the humor. Finally she gathered together a few of the sketches—those which she considered the least discreditable; and she carried them with her when, a little later, she dressed and left the house. She looked handsome and distinguished in her street gown. The tan of the seashore had left her face, and her forehead was smooth, white, and polished beneath her heavy, yellow-brown hair. There were a few freckles on her face, and a small, dark mole near the under lip and one on the temple, half-hidden in her hair.

As Edna walked along the street she was thinking of Robert. She was still under the spell of her infatuation. She had tried to forget him, realizing the inutility of remembering. But the thought of him was like an obsession, ever pressing itself upon her. It was not that she dwelt upon details of their acquaintance, or recalled in any special or peculiar way his personality; it was his being, his existence, which dominated her thought, fading sometimes as if it would melt into the mist of the forgotten, reviving again with an intensity which filled her with an incomprehensible longing.

Edna was on her way to Madame Ratignolle's. Their intimacy, begun at Grand Isle, had not declined, and they had seen each other with some frequency since their return to the city. The Ratignolles lived at no great distance from Edna's home, on the corner of a side street, where Monsieur Ratignolle owned and conducted a drug store which enjoyed a steady and prosperous trade. His father had been in the business before him, and Monsieur Ratignolle stood well in the community and bore an enviable reputation for integrity and clear-headedness. His family lived in commodious apartments over the store, having an entrance on the side within the *porte cochère*.[45] There was something which Edna thought very French, very foreign, about their whole manner of living. In the large and pleasant salon which extended across the width of the house, the Ratignolles entertained their friends once a fortnight with a *soirée musicale*,[46] sometimes diversified by card-playing. There was a friend who played upon the 'cello. One brought his flute and another his violin, while there were some who sang and a number who performed upon the piano with various degrees of taste and agility. The Ratignolles' *soirées musicales* were widely known, and it was considered a privilege to be invited to them.

Edna found her friend engaged in assorting the clothes which had returned that morning from the laundry. She at once abandoned her occupation upon seeing Edna, who had been ushered without ceremony into her presence.

[45] *porte cochère:* a roof supported by columns, serving to protect passengers who alight from a carriage
[46] *soirée musicale:* evening of music.

"'Cité can do it as well as I; it is really her business," she explained to Edna, who apologized for interrupting her. And she summoned a young black woman, whom she instructed, in French, to be very careful in checking off the list which she handed her. She told her to notice particularly if a fine linen handkerchief of Monsieur Ratignolle's, which was missing last week, had been returned; and to be sure to set to one side such pieces as required mending and darning.

Then placing an arm around Edna's waist, she led her to the front of the house, to the salon, where it was cool and sweet with the odor of great roses that stood upon the hearth in jars.

Madame Ratignolle looked more beautiful than ever there at home, in a négligée which left her arms almost wholly bare and exposed the rich, melting curves of her white throat.

"Perhaps I shall be able to paint your picture some day," said Edna with a smile when they were seated. She produced the roll of sketches and started to unfold them. "I believe I ought to work again. I feel as if I wanted to be doing something. What do you think of them? Do you think it worth while to take it up again and study some more? I might study for a while with Laidpore."

She knew that Madame Ratignolle's opinion in such a manner would be next to valueless, that she herself had not alone decided, but determined; but she sought the words of praise and encouragement that would help her to put heart into her venture.

"Your talent is immense, dear!"

"Nonsense!" protested Edna, well pleased.

"Immense, I tell you," persisted Madame Ratignolle, surveying the sketches one by one, at close range, then holding them at arm's length, narrowing her eyes, and dropping her head on one side. "Surely, this Bavarian peasant is worthy of framing; and this basket of apples! Never have I seen anything more lifelike. One might almost be tempted to reach out a hand and take one."

Edna could not control a feeling which bordered upon complacency at her friend's praise, even realizing, as she did, its true worth. She retained a few of the sketches, and gave all the rest to Madame Ratignolle, who appreciated the gift far beyond its value and proudly exhibited the pictures to her husband when he came up from the store a little later for his midday dinner.

Mr. Ratignolle was one of those men who are called the salt of the earth. His cheerfulness was unbounded, and it was matched by his goodness of heart, his broad charity, and common sense. He and his wife spoke English with an accent which was only discernible through its un-English emphasis and a certain carefulness and deliberation. Edna's husband spoke English with no accent whatever. The Ratignolles understood each other perfectly. If ever the fusion of two human beings into one has been accomplished on this sphere it was surely in their union.

As Edna seated herself at table with them she thought, "Better a dinner of herbs," though it did not take her long to discover that it was no dinner of herbs, but a delicious repast, simple, choice, and in every way satisfying.

Monsieur Ratignolle was delighted to see her, though he found her looking not so well as at Grand Isle, and he advised a tonic. He talked a good deal on various topics, a little politics, some city news and neighborhood gossip. He spoke with an animation and earnestness that gave an exaggerated importance to every syllable he uttered. His wife was keenly interested in everything he said, laying down her fork the better to listen, chiming in, taking the words out of his mouth.

Edna felt depressed rather than soothed after leaving them. The little glimpse of domestic harmony which had been offered her, gave her no regret, no longing. It was not a condition of life which fitted her, and she could see in it but an appalling and hopeless ennui. She was moved by a kind of commiseration for Madame Ratignolle,—a pity for that colorless existence which never uplifted its possessor beyond the region of blind contentment, in which no moment of anguish ever visited her soul, in which she would never have the taste of life's delirium. Edna vaguely wondered what she meant by "life's delirium." It had crossed her thought like some unsought extraneous impression.

XIX

Edna could not help but think that it was very foolish, very childish, to have stamped upon her wedding ring and smashed the crystal vase upon the tiles. She was visited by no more outbursts, moving her to such futile expedients. She began to do as she liked and to feel as she liked. She completely abandoned her Tuesdays at home, and did not return the visits of those who had called upon her. She made no ineffectual efforts to conduct her household *en bonne ménagère,*[47] going and coming as it suited her fancy, and, so far as she was able, lending herself to any passing caprice.

Mr. Pontellier had been a rather courteous husband so long as he met a certain tacit submissiveness in his wife. But her new and unexpected line of conduct completely bewildered him. It shocked him. Then her absolute disregard for her duties as a wife angered him. When Mr. Pontellier became rude, Edna grew insolent. She had resolved never to take another step backward.

"It seems to me the utmost folly for a woman at the head of a household, and the mother of children, to spend in an atelier[48] days which would be better employed contriving for the comfort of her family."

"I feel like painting," answered Edna. "Perhaps I shan't always feel like it."

"Then in God's name paint! but don't let the family go to the devil. There's Madame Ratignolle; because she keeps up her music, she doesn't let everything else go to chaos. And she's more of a musician than you are a painter."

"She isn't a musician, and I'm not a painter. It isn't on account of painting that I let things go."

"On account of what, then?"

"Oh! I don't know. Let me alone; you bother me."

---

[47] *en bonne ménagère:* as a good housewife. [48] *atelier:* studio.

It sometimes entered Mr. Pontellier's mind to wonder if his wife were not growing a little unbalanced mentally. He could see plainly that she was not herself. That is, he could not see that she was becoming herself and daily casting aside that fictitious self which we assume like a garment with which to appear before the world.

Her husband let her alone as she requested, and went away to his office. Edna went up to her atelier—a bright room in the top of the house. She was working with great energy and interest, without accomplishing anything, however, which satisfied her even in the smallest degree. For a time she had the whole household enrolled in the service of art. The boys posed for her. They thought it amusing at first, but the occupation soon lost its attractiveness when they discovered that it was not a game arranged especially for their entertainment. The quadroon sat for hours before Edna's palette, patient as a savage, while the house-maid took charge of the children, and the drawing-room went undusted. But the house-maid, too, served her term as model when Edna perceived that the young woman's back and shoulders were molded on classic lines, and that her hair, loosened from its confining cap, became an inspiration. While Edna worked she sometimes sang low the little air, "*Ah! si tu savais!*"

It moved her with recollections. She could hear again the ripple of the water, the flapping sail. She could see the glint of the moon upon the bay, and could feel the soft, gusty beating of the hot south wind. A subtle current of desire passed through her body, weakening her hold upon the brushes and making her eyes burn.

There were days when she was very happy without knowing why. She was happy to be alive and breathing, when her whole being seemed to be one with the sunlight, the color, the odors, the luxuriant warmth of some perfect Southern day. She liked then to wander alone into strange and unfamiliar places. She discovered many a sunny, sleepy corner, fashioned to dream in. And she found it good to dream and to be alone and unmolested.

There were days when she was unhappy, she did not know why,—when it did not seem worth while to be glad or sorry, to be alive or dead; when life appeared to her like a grotesque pandemonium and humanity like worms struggling blindly toward inevitable annihilation. She would not work on such a day, nor weave fancies to stir her pulses and warm her blood.

XX

It was during such a mood that Edna hunted up Mademoiselle Reisz. She had not forgotten the rather disagreeable impression left upon her by their last interview; but she nevertheless felt a desire to see her—above all, to listen while she played upon the piano. Quite early in the afternoon she started upon her quest for the pianist. Unfortunately she had mislaid or lost Mademoiselle Reisz's card, and looking up her address in the city directory, she found that the woman lived on Bienville Street, some distance away. The directory which fell into her hands was a year or more old, however, and upon reaching the number indicated, Edna discovered that the house was occupied by a respectable family of mulattoes who had *chambres gamies*[49] to let. They had been living there for six months, and knew absolutely nothing of a Mademoiselle Reisz. In fact, they knew nothing of any of their neighbors; their lodgers were all people of the highest distinction, they assured Edna. She did not linger to discuss class distinctions with Madame Pouponne, but hastened to a neighboring grocery store, feeling sure that Mademoiselle would have left her address with the proprietor.

He knew Mademoiselle Reisz a good deal better than he wanted to know her, he informed his questioner. In truth, he did not want to know her at all, or anything concerning her—the most disagreeable and unpopular woman who ever lived in Bienville Street. He thanked heaven she had left the neighborhood, and was equally thankful that he did not know where she had gone.

Edna's desire to see Mademoiselle Reisz had increased tenfold since these unlooked-for obstacles had arisen to thwart it. She was wondering who could give her the information she sought, when it suddenly occurred to her that Madame Lebrun would be the one most likely to do so. She knew it was useless to ask Madame Ratignolle, who was on the most distant terms with the musician, and preferred to know nothing concerning her. She had once been almost as emphatic in expressing herself upon the subject as the corner grocer.

Edna knew that Madame Lebrun had returned to the city, for it was the middle of November. And she also knew where the Lebruns lived, on Chartres Street.

Their home from the outside looked like a prison, with iron bars before the door and lower windows. The iron bars were a relic of the old *régime*,[50] and no one had ever thought of dislodging them. At the side was a high fence enclosing the garden. A gate or door opening upon the street was locked. Edna rang the bell at this side garden gate, and stood upon the banquette, waiting to be admitted.

It was Victor who opened the gate for her. A black woman, wiping her hands upon her apron, was close at his heels. Before she saw them Edna could hear them in altercation, the woman—plainly an anomaly—claiming the right to be allowed to perform her duties, one of which was to answer the bell.

Victor was surprised and delighted to see Mrs. Pontellier, and he made no attempt to conceal either his astonishment or his delight. He was a dark-browed, good-looking youngster of nineteen, greatly resembling his mother, but with ten times her impetuosity. He instructed the black woman to go at once and inform Madame Lebrun that Mrs. Pontellier desired to see her. The woman grumbled a refusal to do part of her duty when she had not been permitted to do it all, and started back to her interrupted task of weeding the garden. Whereupon Victor administered a rebuke in the form of a volley of abuse, which, owing to its rapidity and incoherence, was all but incomprehensible to Edna. Whatever it was, the rebuke was convincing, for the woman dropped her hoe and went mumbling into the house.

---

[49] *chambres garnies:* furnished rooms [50] *the old régime:* i.e., the days of the Spanish.

Edna did not wish to enter. It was very pleasant there on the side porch, where there were chairs, a wicker lounge, and a small table. She seated herself, for she was tired from her long tramp; and she began to rock gently and smooth out the folds of her silk parasol. Victor drew up his chair beside her. He at once explained that the black woman's offensive conduct was all due to imperfect training, as he was not there to take her in hand. He had only come up from the island the morning before, and expected to return next day. He stayed all winter at the island; he lived there, and kept the place in order and got things ready for the summer visitors.

But a man needed occasional relaxation, he informed Mrs. Pontellier, and every now and again he drummed up a pretext to bring him to the city. My! but he had had a time of it the evening before! He wouldn't want his mother to know, and he began to talk in a whisper. He was scintillant with recollections. Of course, he couldn't think of telling Mrs. Pontellier all about it, she being a woman and not comprehending such things. But it all began with a girl peeping and smiling at him through the shutters as he passed by. Oh! but she was a beauty! Certainly he smiled back, and went up and talked to her. Mrs. Pontellier did not know him if she supposed he was one to let an opportunity like that escape him. Despite herself, the youngster amused her. She must have betrayed in her look some degree of interest or entertainment. The boy grew more daring, and Mrs. Pontellier might have found herself, in a little while, listening to a highly colored story but for the timely appearance of Madame Lebrun.

That lady was still clad in white, according to her custom of the summer. Her eyes beamed an effusive welcome. Would not Mrs. Pontellier go inside? Would she partake of some refreshment? Why had she not been there before? How was that dear Mr. Pontellier and how were those sweet children? Had Mrs. Pontellier ever known such a warm November?

Victor went and reclined on the wicker lounge behind his mother's chair, where he commanded a view of Edna's face. He had taken her parasol from her hands while he spoke to her, and he now lifted it and twirled it above him as he lay on his back. When Madame Lebrun complained that it was so dull coming back to the city; that she saw so few people now; that even Victor, when he came up from the island for a day or two, had so much to occupy him and engage his time; then it was that the youth went into contortions on the lounge and winked mischievously at Edna. She somehow felt like a confederate in crime, and tried to look severe and disapproving.

There had been but two letters from Robert, with little in them, they told her. Victor said it was really not worth while to go inside for the letters, when his mother entreated him to go in search of them. He remembered the contents, which in truth he rattled off very glibly when put to the test.

One letter was written from Vera Cruz and the other from the City of Mexico. He had met Montel, who was doing everything toward his advancement. So far, the financial situation was no improvement over the one he had left in New Orleans, but of course the prospects were vastly better. He wrote of the City of Mexico, the buildings, the people and their habits, the conditions of life which he found there. He sent his love to the family. He inclosed a check to his mother, and hoped she would affectionately remember him to all his friends. That was about the substance of the two letters. Edna felt that if there had been a message for her, she would have received it. The despondent frame of mind in which she had left home began again to overtake her, and she remembered that she wished to find Mademoiselle Reisz.

Madame Lebrun knew where Mademoiselle Reisz lived. She gave Edna the address, regretting that she would not consent to stay and spend the remainder of the afternoon, and pay a visit to Mademoiselle Reisz some other day. The afternoon was already well advanced.

Victor escorted her out upon the banquette, lifted her parasol, and held it over her while he walked to the car[51] with her. He entreated her to bear in mind that the disclosures of the afternoon were strictly confidential. She laughed and bantered him a little, remembering too late that she should have been dignified and reserved.

"How handsome Mrs. Pontellier looked!" said Madame Lebrun to her son.

"Ravishing!" he admitted. "The city atmosphere has improved her. Some way she doesn't seem like the same woman."

XXI

Some people contended that the reason Mademoiselle Reisz always chose apartments up under the roof was to discourage the approach of beggars, peddlers and callers. There were plenty of windows in her little front room. They were for the most part dingy, but as they were nearly always open it did not make so much difference. They often admitted into the room a good deal of smoke and soot; but at the same time all the light and air that there was came through them. From her windows could be seen the crescent of the river, the masts of ships and the big chimneys of the Mississippi steamers. A magnificent piano crowded the apartment. In the next room she slept, and in the third and last she harbored a gasoline stove on which she cooked her meals when disinclined to descend to the neighboring restaurant. It was there also that she ate, keeping her belongings in a rare old buffet, dingy and battered from a hundred years of use.

When Edna knocked at Mademoiselle Reisz's front room door and entered, she discovered that person standing beside the window, engaged in mending or patching an old prunella gaiter.[52] The little musician laughed all over when she saw Edna. Her laugh consisted of a contortion of the face and all the muscles of the body. She seemed strikingly homely, standing there in the afternoon light. She still wore the shabby lace and the artificial bunch of violets on the side of her head.

"So you remembered me at last," said Mademoiselle. "I had said to myself, 'Ah, bah! she will never come.'"

"Did you want me to come?" asked Edna with a smile.

"I had not thought much about it," answered Mademoiselle. The two had seated themselves on a little bumpy sofa which stood against the wall. "I am glad, however, that you came. I have the water boiling back there, and was just about to make some coffee. You will drink a cup with me. And how is la *belle dame*? Always

---

[51] *car:* streetcar [52] *prunella gaiter:* ankle-high shoe, with the upper section made of cloth.

handsome! always healthy! always contented!" She took Edna's hand between her strong wiry fingers, holding it loosely without warmth, and executing a sort of double theme upon the back and palm.

"Yes," she went on; "I sometimes thought: 'She will never come. She promised as those women in society always do, without meaning it. She will not come.' For I really don't believe you like me, Mrs. Pontellier."

"I don't know whether I like you or not," replied Edna, gazing down at the little woman with a quizzical look.

The candor of Mrs. Pontellier's admission greatly pleased Mademoiselle Reisz. She expressed her gratification by repairing forthwith to the region of the gasoline stove and rewarding her guest with the promised cup of coffee. The coffee and the biscuit accompanying it proved very acceptable to Edna, who had declined refreshment at Madame Lebrun's and was now beginning to feel hungry. Mademoiselle set the tray which she brought in upon a small table near at hand, and seated herself once again on the lumpy sofa.

"I have had a letter from your friend," she remarked, as she poured a little cream into Edna's cup and handed it to her.

"My friend?"

"Yes, your friend Robert. He wrote to me from the City of Mexico."

"Wrote to *you?*" repeated Edna in amazement, stirring her coffee absently.

"Yes, to me. Why not? Don't stir all the warmth out of your coffee; drink it. Though the letter might as well have been sent to you; it was nothing but Mrs. Pontellier from beginning to end."

"Let me see it," requested the young woman, entreatingly.

"No; a letter concerns no one but the person who writes it and the one to whom it is written."

"Haven't you just said it concerned me from beginning to end?"

"It was written about you, not to you. 'Have you seen Mrs. Pontellier? How is she looking?' he asks. 'As Mrs. Pontellier says,' or 'as Mrs. Pontellier once said.' 'If Mrs. Pontellier should call upon you, play for her that Impromptu of Chopin's my favorite. I heard it here a day or two ago, but not as you play it. I should like to know how it affects her,' and so on, as if he supposed we were constantly in each other's society."

"Let me see the letter."

"Oh, no."

"Have you answered it?"

"No."

"Let me see the letter."

"No, and again, no."

"Then play the Impromptu for me."

"It is growing late; what time do you have to be home?"

"Time doesn't concern me. Your question seems a little rude. Play the Impromptu."

"But you have told me nothing of yourself. What are you doing?"

"Painting!" laughed Edna. "I am becoming an artist. Think of it!"

"Ah! an artist! You have pretensions, Madame."

"Why pretensions? Do you think I could not become an artist?"

"I do not know you well enough to say. I do not know your talent or your temperament. To be an artist includes much; one must possess many gifts—absolute gifts—which have not been acquired by one's own effort. And, moreover, to succeed, the artist must possess the courageous soul."

"What do you mean by the courageous soul?"

"Courageous, *ma foi!* The brave soul. The soul that dares and defies."

"Show me the letter and play for me the Impromptu. You see that I have persistence. Does that quality count for anything in art?"

"It counts with a foolish old woman whom you have captivated," replied Mademoiselle, with her wriggling laugh.

The letter was right there at hand in the drawer of the little table upon which Edna had just placed her coffee cup. Mademoiselle opened the drawer and drew forth the letter, the topmost one. She placed it in Edna's hands, and without further comment arose and went to the piano.

Mademoiselle played a soft interlude. It was an improvisation. She sat low at the instrument, and the lines of her body settled into ungraceful curves and angles that gave it an appearance of deformity. Gradually and imperceptibly the interlude melted into the soft opening minor chords of the Chopin Impromptu.

Edna did not know when the Impromptu began or ended. She sat in the sofa corner reading Robert's letter by the fading light. Mademoiselle had glided from the Chopin into the quivering love-notes of Isolde's song,[53] and back again to the Impromptu with its soulful and poignant longing.

The shadows deepened in the little room. The music grew strange and fantastic—turbulent, insistent, plaintive and soft with entreaty. The shadows grew deeper. The music filled the room. It floated out upon the night, over the housetops, the crescent of the river, losing itself in the silence of the upper air.

Edna was sobbing, just as she had wept one midnight at Grand Isle when strange, new voices awoke in her. She arose in some agitation to take her departure. "May I come again, Mademoiselle?" she asked at the threshold.

"Come whenever you feel like it. Be careful; the stairs and landings are dark; don't stumble."

Mademoiselle reentered and lit a candle. Robert's letter was on the floor. She stooped and picked it up. It was crumpled and damp with tears. Mademoiselle smoothed the letter out, restored it to the envelope, and replaced it in the table drawer.

---

[53] *Isolde's song:* i.e., the Liebestod ("Love-Death") sung by Isolde in *Tristan and Isolde* (1857–59) by the German composer Richard Wagner. Isolde, holding her dead lover in her arms, bids him farewell and then dies.

XXII

One morning on his way into town, Mr. Pontellier stopped at the house of his old friend and family physician, Doctor Mandelet. The Doctor was a semi-retired physician, resting, as the saying is, upon his laurels. He bore a reputation for wisdom rather than skill—leaving the active practice of medicine to his assistants and younger contemporaries—and was much sought for in matters of consultation. A few families, united to him by bonds of friendship, he still attended when they required the services of a physician. The Pontelliers were among these.

Mr. Pontellier found the Doctor reading at the open window of his study. His house stood rather far back from the street, in the center of a delightful garden, so that it was quiet and peaceful at the old gentleman's study window. He was a great reader. He stared up disapprovingly over his eye-glasses as Mr. Pontellier entered, wondering who had the temerity to disturb him at that hour of the morning.

"Ah! Pontellier! Not sick, I hope. Come and have a seat. What news do you bring this morning?" He was quite portly, with a profusion of gray hair, and small blue eyes which age had robbed of much of their brightness but none of their penetration.

"Oh! I'm never sick, Doctor. You know that I come of tough fiber—of that old Creole race of Pontelliers that dry up and finally blow away. I came to consult—no, not precisely to consult—to talk to you about Edna. I don't know what ails her."

"Madame Pontellier not well?" marveled the Doctor. "Why, I saw her—I think it was a week ago—walking along Canal Street, the picture of health, it seemed to me."

"Yes, yes; she seems quite well," said Mr. Pontellier, leaning forward and whirling his stick between his two hands; "but she doesn't act well. She's odd, she's not like herself. I can't make her out, and I thought perhaps you'd help me."

"How does she act?" inquired the doctor.

"Well, it isn't easy to explain," said Mr. Pontellier, throwing himself back in his chair. "She lets the housekeeping go to the dickens."

"Well, well; women are not all alike, my dear Pontellier. We've got to consider—"

"I know that; I told you I couldn't explain. Her whole attitude—toward me and everybody and everything—has changed. You know I have a quick temper, but I don't want to quarrel or be rude to a woman, especially my wife; yet I'm driven to it, and feel like ten thousand devils after I've made a fool of myself. She's making it devilishly uncomfortable for me," he went on nervously. "She's got some sort of notion in her head concerning the eternal rights of women; and—you understand—we meet in the morning at the breakfast table."

The old gentleman lifted his shaggy eyebrows, protruded his thick nether lip, and tapped the arms of his chair with his cushioned fingertips.

"What have you been doing to her, Pontellier?"

"Doing! *Parbleu!*"[54]

---

[54] *Parbleu!:* For heaven's sake!

"Has she," asked the Doctor, with a smile, "has she been associating of late with a circle of pseudo-intellectual women—super-spiritual superior beings? My wife has been telling me about them."

"That's the trouble," broke in Mr. Pontellier, "she hasn't been associating with any one. She has abandoned her Tuesdays at home, has thrown over all her acquaintances, and goes tramping about by herself, moping in the street-cars, getting in after dark. I tell you she's peculiar. I don't like it; I feel a little worried over it."

This was a new aspect for the Doctor. "Nothing hereditary?" he asked, seriously. "Nothing peculiar about her family antecedents, is there?"

"Oh, no indeed! She comes of sound old Presbyterian Kentucky stock. The old gentleman, her father, I have heard, used to atone for his weekday sins with his Sunday devotions. I know for a fact, that his race horses literally ran away with the prettiest bit of Kentucky farming land I ever laid eyes upon. Margaret— you know Margaret—she has all the Presbyterianism undiluted. And the youngest is something of a vixen. By the way, she gets married in a couple of weeks from now."

"Send your wife up to the wedding," exclaimed the Doctor, foreseeing a happy solution. "Let her stay among her own people for a while; it will do her good."

"That's what I want her to do. She won't go to the marriage. She says a wedding is one of the most lamentable spectacles on earth. Nice thing for a woman to say to her husband!" exclaimed Mr. Pontellier, fuming anew at the recollection.

"Pontellier," said the Doctor, after a moment's reflection, "let your wife alone for a while. Don't bother her, and don't let her bother you. Woman, my dear friend, is a very peculiar and delicate organism—a sensitive and highly organized woman, such as I know Mrs. Pontellier to be, is especially peculiar. It would require an inspired psychologist to deal successfully with them. And when ordinary fellows like you and me attempt to cope with their idiosyncrasies the result is bungling. Most women are moody and whimsical. This is some passing whim of your wife, due to some cause or causes which you and I needn't try to fathom. But it will pass happily over, especially if you let her alone. Send her around to see me."

"Oh! I couldn't do that; there'd be no reason for it," objected Mr. Pontellier.

"Then I'll go around and see her," said the Doctor. "I'll drop in to dinner some evening *en bon ami*."[55]

"Do! by all means," urged Mr. Pontellier. "What evening will you come? Say Thursday. Will you come Thursday?" he asked, rising to take his leave.

"Very well; Thursday. My wife may possibly have some engagement for me Thursday. In case she has, I shall let you know. Otherwise, you may expect me."

Mr. Pontellier turned before leaving to say:

"I am going to New York on business very soon. I have a big scheme on hand, and want to be on the field proper to pull the ropes and handle the ribbons.[56] We'll let you in on the inside if you say so, Doctor," he laughed.

[55] *en bon ami:* as a friend [56] *handle the ribbons:* control the reins, i.e., run things.

"No, I thank you, my dear sir," returned the Doctor. "I leave such ventures to you younger men with the fever of life still in your blood."

"What I wanted to say," continued Mr. Pontellier, with his hand on the knob; "I may have to be absent a good while. Would you advise me to take Edna along?"

"By all means, if she wishes to go. If not, leave her here. Don't contradict her. The mood will pass, I assure you. It may take a month, two, three months—possibly longer, but it will pass; have patience."

"Well, good-by, *à jeudi*," [57] said Mr. Pontellier, as he let himself out.

The doctor would have liked during the course of conversation to ask, "Is there any man in the case?" but he knew his Creole too well to make such a blunder as that.

He did not resume his book immediately, but sat for a while meditatively looking out into the garden.

XXIII

Edna's father was in the city, and had been with them several days. She was not very warmly or deeply attached to him, but they had certain tastes in common, and when together they were companionable. His coming was in the nature of a welcome disturbance; it seemed to furnish a new direction for her emotions.

He had come to purchase a wedding ring for his daughter, Janet, and an outfit for himself in which he might make a creditable appearance at her marriage. Mr. Pontellier had selected the bridal gift, as every one immediately connected with him always deferred to his taste in such matters. And his suggestions on the question of dress—which too often assumes the nature of a problem—were of inestimable value to his father-in-law. But for the past few days the old gentleman had been upon Edna's hands, and in his society she was becoming acquainted with a new set of sensations. He had been a colonel in the Confederate army, and still maintained, with the title, the military bearing which had always accompanied it. His hair and mustache were white and silky, emphasizing the rugged bronze of his face. He was tall and thin, and wore his coats padded, which gave a fictitious breadth and depth to his shoulders and chest. Edna and her father looked very distinguished together, and excited a good deal of notice during their perambulations. Upon his arrival she began by introducing him to her atelier and making a sketch of him. He took the whole matter very seriously. If her talent had been tenfold greater than it was, it would not have surprised him, convinced as he was that he had bequeathed to all of his daughters the germs of a masterful capability, which only depended upon their own efforts to be directed toward successful achievement.

Before her pencil he sat rigid and unflinching, as he had faced the cannon's mouth in days gone by. He resented the intrusion of the children, who gaped with wondering eyes at him, sitting so stiff up there in their mother's bright atelier. When they drew near he motioned them away with an expressive action of the foot, loath to disturb the fixed lines of his countenance, his arms, or his rigid shoulders.

---

[57] *à jeudi:* until Thursday.

Edna, anxious to entertain him, invited Mademoiselle Reisz to meet him, having promised him a treat in her piano playing; but Mademoiselle declined the invitation. So together they attended a *soirée musicale* at the Ratignolles'. Monsieur and Madame Ratignolle made much of the Colonel, installing him as the guest of honor and engaging him at once to dine with them the following Sunday, or any day which he might select. Madame coquetted with him in the most captivating and naïve manner, with eyes, gestures, and a profusion of compliments, till the Colonel's old head felt thirty years younger on his padded shoulders. Edna marveled, not comprehending. She herself was almost devoid of coquetry.

There were one or two men whom she observed at the *soirée musicale;* but she would never have felt moved to any kittenish display to attract their notice—to any feline or feminine wiles to express herself toward them. Their personality attracted her in an agreeable way. Her fancy selected them, and she was glad when a lull in the music gave them an opportunity to meet her and talk with her. Often on the street the glance of strange eyes had lingered in her memory, and sometimes had disturbed her.

Mr. Pontellier did not attend these *soirées musicales.* He considered them *bourgeois,* and found more diversion at the club. To Madame Ratignolle he said the music dispensed at her *soirées* was too "heavy," too far beyond his untrained comprehension. His excuse flattered her. But she disapproved of Mr. Pontellier's club, and she was frank enough to tell Edna so.

"It's a pity Mr. Pontellier doesn't stay home more in the evenings. I think you would be more—well, if you don't mind my saying it—more united, if he did."

"Oh! dear no!" said Edna, with a blank look in her eyes. "What should I do if he stayed home? We wouldn't have anything to say to each other."

She had not much of anything to say to her father, for that matter; but he did not antagonize her. She discovered that he interested her, though she realized that he might not interest her long; and for the first time in her life she felt as if she were thoroughly acquainted with him. He kept her busy serving him and ministering to his wants. It amused her to do so. She would not permit a servant or one of the children to do anything for him which she might do herself. Her husband noticed, and thought it was the expression of a deep filial attachment which he had never suspected.

The Colonel drank numerous "toddies" during the course of the day, which left him, however, imperturbed. He was an expert at concocting strong drinks. He had even invented some, to which he had given fantastic names, and for whose manufacture he required diverse ingredients that it devolved upon Edna to procure for him.

When Doctor Mandelet dined with the Pontelliers on Thursday he could discern in Mrs. Pontellier no trace of that morbid condition which her husband had reported to him. She was excited and in a manner radiant. She and her father had been to the race course, and their thoughts when they seated themselves at table were still occupied with the events of the afternoon, and their talk was still of the track. The Doctor had not kept pace with turf affairs. He had certain recollections of racing in what he called "the good old times" when the Lecompte stables flourished, and he drew upon this fund of memories so that he might not be left out and seem wholly devoid of the modern spirit. But he failed to impose upon the Colonel, and was even far from impressing him with this trumped-up knowledge of bygone days. Edna had staked her father on his last venture, with the most gratifying results to both of them. Besides, they had met some very charming people, according to the Colonel's impressions. Mrs. Mortimer Merriman and Mrs. James Highcamp, who were there with Alcée Arobin, had joined them and had enlivened the hours in a fashion that warmed him to think of.

Mr. Pontellier himself had no particular leaning toward horse-racing, and was even rather inclined to discourage it as a pastime, especially when he considered the fate of that blue-grass farm in Kentucky. He endeavored in a general way, to express a particular disapproval, and only succeeded in arousing the ire and opposition of his father-in-law. A pretty dispute followed, in which Edna warmly espoused her father's cause and the Doctor remained neutral.

He observed his hostess attentively from under his shaggy brows, and noted a subtle change which had transformed her from the listless woman he had known into a being who, for the moment, seemed palpitant with the forces of life. Her speech was warm and energetic. There was no repression in her glance or gesture. She reminded him of some beautiful, sleek animal waking up in the sun.

The dinner was excellent. The claret was warm and the champagne was cold, and under their beneficent influence the threatened unpleasantness melted and vanished with the fumes of the wine.

Mr. Pontellier warmed up and grew reminiscent. He told some amusing plantation experiences, recollections of old Iberville and his youth, when he hunted 'possum in company with some friendly darky; thrashed the pecan trees, shot the grosbec, and roamed the woods and fields in mischievous idleness.

The Colonel, with little sense of humor and of the fitness of things, related a somber episode of those dark and bitter days, in which he had acted a conspicuous part and always formed a central figure. Nor was the Doctor happier in his selection, when he told the old, ever new and curious story of the waning of a woman's love, seeking strange, new channels, only to return to its legitimate source after days of fierce unrest. It was one of the many little human documents which had been unfolded to him during his long career as a physician. The story did not seem especially to impress Edna. She had one of her own to tell, of a woman who paddled away with her lover one night in a pirogue and never came back. They were lost amid the Barataria Islands, and no one ever heard of them or found trace of them from that day to this. It was a pure invention. She said that Madame Antoine had related it to her. That, also, was an invention. Perhaps it was a dream she had had. But every glowing word seemed real to those who listened. They could feel the hot breath of the Southern night; they could hear the long sweep of the pirogue through the glistening moonlit water, the beating of birds' wings, rising startled from among the reeds in the salt-water pools; they could see the faces of the lovers, pale, close together, rapt in oblivious forgetfulness, drifting into the unknown.

The champagne was cold, and its subtle fumes played fantastic tricks with Edna's memory that night.

Outside, away from the glow of the fire and the soft lamplight, the night was chill and murky. The Doctor doubled his old-fashioned cloak across his breast as he strode home through the darkness. He knew his fellow-creatures better than most men; knew that inner life which so seldom unfolds itself to unanointed eyes. He was sorry he had accepted Pontellier's invitation. He was growing old, and beginning to need rest and an imperturbed spirit. He did not want the secrets of other lives thrust upon him.

"I hope it isn't Arobin," he muttered to himself as he walked. "I hope to heaven it isn't Alcée Arobin."

XXIV

Edna and her father had a warm, and almost violent dispute upon the subject of her refusal to attend her sister's wedding. Mr. Pontellier declined to interfere, to interpose either his influence or his authority. He was following Doctor Mandelet's advice, and letting her do as she liked. The Colonel reproached his daughter for her lack of filial kindness and respect, her want of sisterly affection and womanly consideration. His arguments were labored and unconvincing. He doubted if Janet would accept any excuse—forgetting that Edna had offered none. He doubted if Janet would ever speak to her again, and he was sure Margaret would not.

Edna was glad to be rid of her father when he finally took himself off with his wedding garments and his bridal gifts, with his padded shoulders, his Bible reading, his "toddies" and ponderous oaths.

Mr. Pontellier followed him closely. He meant to stop at the wedding on his way to New York and endeavor by every means which money and love could devise to atone somewhat for Edna's incomprehensible action.

"You are too lenient, too lenient by far, Léonce," asserted the Colonel. "Authority, coercion are what is needed. Put your foot down good and hard; the only way to manage a wife. Take my word for it."

The Colonel was perhaps unaware that he had coerced his own wife into her grave. Mr. Pontellier had a vague suspicion of it which he thought it needless to mention at that late day.

Edna was not so consciously gratified at her husband's leaving home as she had been over the departure of her father. As the day approached when he was to leave her for a comparatively long stay, she grew melting and affectionate, remembering his many acts of consideration and his repeated expressions of an ardent attachment. She was solicitious about his health and his welfare. She bustled around, looking after his clothing, thinking about heavy underwear, quite as Madame Ratignolle would have done under similar circumstances. She cried when he went away, calling him her dear, good friend, and she was quite certain she would grow lonely before very long and go to join him in New York.

But after all, a radiant peace settled upon her when she at last found herself alone. Even the children were gone. Old Madame Pontellier had come herself and carried them off to Iberville with their quadroon. The old Madame did not venture to say she was afraid they would be neglected during Léonce's absence; she hardly ventured to think so. She was hungry for them—even a little fierce in her attachment. She did not want them to be wholly "children of the pavement," she always said when begging to have them for a space. She wished them to know the country, with its streams, its fields, its woods, its freedom, so delicious to the young. She wished them to taste something of the life their father had lived and known and loved when he, too, was a little child.

When Edna was at last alone, she breathed a big, genuine sigh of relief. A feeling that was unfamiliar but very delicious came over her. She walked all through the house, from one room to another, as if inspecting it for the first time. She tried the various chairs and lounges, as if she had never sat and reclined upon them before. And she perambulated around the outside of the house, investigating, looking to see if windows and shutters were secure and in order. The flowers were like new acquaintances; she approached them in a familiar spirit, and made herself at home among them. The garden walks were damp, and Edna called to the maid to bring out her rubber sandals. And there she stayed, and stooped, digging around the plants, trimming, picking dead, dry leaves. The children's little dog came out, interfering, getting in her way. She scolded him, laughed at him, played with him. The garden smelled so good and looked so pretty in the afternoon sunlight. Edna plucked all the bright flowers she could find, and went into the house with them, she and the little dog.

Even the kitchen assumed a sudden interesting character which she had never before perceived. She went in to give directions to the cook, to say that the butcher would have to bring much less meat, that they would require only half their usual quantity of bread, of milk and groceries. She told the cook that she herself would be greatly occupied during Mr. Pontellier's absence, and she begged her to take all thought and responsibility of the larder upon her own shoulders.

That night Edna dined alone. The candelabra, with a few candles in the center of the table, gave all the light she needed. Outside the circle of light in which she sat, the large dining-room looked solemn and shadowy. The cook, placed upon her mettle, served a delicious repast—a luscious tenderloin broiled *à point*.[58] The wine tasted good; the *marron glacé*[59] seemed to be just what she wanted. It was so pleasant, too, to dine in a comfortable *peignoir*.

She thought a little sentimentally about Léonce and the children, and wondered what they were doing. As she gave a dainty scrap or two to the doggie, she talked intimately to him about Etienne and Raoul. He was beside himself with astonishment and delight over these companionable advances, and showed his appreciation by his little quick, snappy barks and a lively agitation.

Then Edna sat in the library after dinner and read Emerson until she grew sleepy. She realized that she had neglected her reading, and determined to start anew

[58] *à point:* to a turn   [59] *marron glacé:* glazed chestnuts

upon a course of improving studies, now that her time was completely her own to do with as she liked.

After a refreshing bath, Edna went to bed. And as she snuggled comfortably beneath the eiderdown a sense of restfulness invaded her, such as she had not known before.

XXV

When the weather was dark and cloudy Edna could not work. She needed the sun to mellow and temper her mood to the sticking point. She had reached a stage when she seemed to be no longer feeling her way, working, when in the humor, with sureness and ease. And being devoid of ambition, and striving not toward accomplishment, she drew satisfaction from the work in itself.

On rainy or melancholy days Edna went out and sought the society of the friends she had made at Grand Isle. Or else she stayed indoors and nursed a mood with which she was becoming too familiar for her own comfort and peace of mind. It was not despair; but it seemed to her as if life were passing by, leaving its promise broken and unfulfilled. Yet there were other days when she listened, was led on and deceived by fresh promises which her youth held out to her.

She went again to the races, and again. Alcée Arobin and Mrs. Highcamp called for her one bright afternoon in Arobin's drag.[60] Mrs. Highcamp was a worldly but unaffected, intelligent, slim, tall blonde woman in the forties, with an indifferent manner and blue eyes that stared. She had a daughter who served her as a pretext for cultivating the society of young men of fashion. Alcée Arobin was one of them. He was a familiar figure at the race course, the opera, the fashionable clubs. There was a perpetual smile in his eyes, which seldom failed to awaken a corresponding cheerfulness in any one who looked into them and listened to his good-humored voice. His manner was quiet, and at times a little insolent. He possessed a good figure, a pleasing face, not overburdened with depth of thought or feeling; and his dress was that of the conventional man of fashion.

He admired Edna extravagantly, after meeting her at the races with her father. He had met her before on other occasions, but she had seemed to him unapproachable until that day. It was at his instigation that Mrs. Highcamp called to ask her to go with them to the Jockey Club to witness the turf event of the season.

There were possibly a few track men out there who knew the race horse as well as Edna, but there was certainly none who knew it better. She sat between her two companions as one having authority to speak. She laughed at Arobin's pretensions, and deplored Mrs. Highcamp's ignorance. The race horse was a friend and intimate associate of her childhood. The atmosphere of the stable and the breath of the blue grass paddock revived in her memory and lingered in her nostrils. She did not perceive that she was talking like her father as the sleek geldings ambled in review before them. She played for very high stakes, and fortune favored her. The fever of

[60] *drag:* heavy carriage.

the game flamed in her cheeks and eyes, and it got into her blood and into her brain like an intoxicant. People turned their heads to look at her, and more than one lent an attentive ear to her utterances, hoping thereby to secure the elusive but everdesired "tip." Arobin caught the contagion of excitement which drew him to Edna like a magnet. Mrs. Highcamp remained, as usual, unmoved, with her indifferent stare and uplifted eyebrows.

Edna stayed and dined with Mrs. Highcamp upon being urged to do so. Arobin also remained and sent away his drag.

The dinner was quiet and uninteresting, save for the cheerful efforts of Arobin to enliven things. Mrs. Highcamp deplored the absence of her daughter from the races, and tried to convey to her what she had missed by going to the "Dante[61] reading" instead of joining them. The girl held a geranium leaf up to her nose and said nothing, but looked knowing and noncommittal. Mr. Highcamp was a plain, bald-headed man, who only talked under compulsion. He was unresponsive. Mrs. Highcamp was full of delicate courtesy and consideration toward her husband. She addressed most of her conversation to him at table. They sat in the library after dinner and read the evening papers together under the droplight; while the younger people went into the drawing-room near by and talked. Miss Highcamp played some selections from Grieg[62] upon the piano. She seemed to have apprehended all of the composer's coldness and none of his poetry. While Edna listened she could not help wondering if she had lost her taste for music.

When the time came for her to go home, Mr. Highcamp grunted a lame offer to escort her, looking down at his slippered feet with tactless concern. It was Arobin who took her home. The car ride was long, and it was late when they reached Esplanade Street. Arobin asked permission to enter for a second to light his cigarette—his match safe[63] was empty. He filled his match safe, but did not light his cigarette until he left her, after she had expressed her willingness to go to the races with him again.

Edna was neither tired nor sleepy. She was hungry again, for the Highcamp dinner, though of excellent quality, had lacked abundance. She rummaged in the larder and brought forth a slice of Gruyère and some crackers. She opened a bottle of beer which she found in the icebox. Edna felt extremely restless and excited. She vacantly hummed a fantastic tune as she poked at the wood embers on the hearth and munched a cracker.

She wanted something to happen—something, anything; she did not know what. She regretted that she had not made Arobin stay a half hour to talk over the horses with her. She counted the money she had won. But there was nothing else to do, so she went to bed, and tossed there for hours in a sort of monotonous agitation.

In the middle of the night she remembered that she had forgotten to write her regular letter to her husband; and she decided to do so next day and tell him about

---

[61] *Dante:* Dante Alighieri (1265–1321), Italian poet. [62] *Grieg:* Edvard Grieg (1843–1907), Norwegian composer. [63] *match safe:* noncombustible box to hold friction matches.

her afternoon at the Jockey Club. She lay wide awake composing a letter which was nothing like the one which she wrote next day. When the maid awoke her in the morning Edna was dreaming of Mr. Highcamp playing the piano at the entrance of a music store on Canal Street, while his wife was saying to Alcée Arobin, as they boarded an Esplanade Street car:

"What a pity that so much talent has been neglected! but I must go."

When, a few days later, Alcée Arobin again called for Edna in his drag, Mrs. Highcamp was not with him. He said they would pick her up. But as that lady had not been apprised of his intention of picking her up, she was not at home. The daughter was just leaving the house to attend the meeting of a branch Folk Lore Society, and regretted that she could not accompany them. Arobin appeared non-plused, and asked Edna if there were any one else she cared to ask.

She did not deem it worth while to go in search of any of the fashionable acquaintances from whom she had withdrawn herself. She thought of Madame Ratignolle, but knew that her fair friend did not leave the house, except to take a languid walk around the block with her husband after nightfall. Mademoiselle Reisz would have laughed at such a request from Edna. Madame Lebrun might have enjoyed the outing, but for some reason Edna did not want her. So they went alone, she and Arobin.

The afternoon was intensely interesting to her. The excitement came back upon her like a remittent fever. Her talk grew familiar and confidential. It was no labor to become intimate with Arobin. His manner invited easy confidence. The preliminary stage of becoming acquainted was one which he always endeavored to ignore when a pretty and engaging woman was concerned.

He stayed and dined with Edna. He stayed and sat beside the wood fire. They laughed and talked; and before it was time to go he was telling her how different life might have been if he had known her years before. With ingenuous frankness he spoke of what a wicked, ill-disciplined boy he had been, and impulsively drew up his cuff to exhibit upon his wrist the scar from a saber cut which he had received in a duel outside of Paris when he was nineteen. She touched his hand as she scanned the red cicatrice[64] on the inside of his white wrist. A quick impulse that was somewhat spasmodic impelled her fingers to close in a sort of clutch upon his hand. He felt the pressure of her pointed nails in the flesh of his palm.

She arose hastily and walked toward the mantel.

"The sight of a wound or scar always agitates and sickens me," she said. "I shouldn't have looked at it."

"I beg your pardon," he entreated, following her; "it never occurred to me that it might be repulsive."

He stood close to her, and the effrontery in his eyes repelled the old, vanishing self in her, yet drew all her awakening sensuousness. He saw enough in her face to impel him to take her hand and hold it while he said his lingering good night.

"Will you go to the races again?" he asked.

---

[64] *cicatrice:* scar.

"No," she said. "I've had enough of the races. I don't want to lose all the money I've won, and I've got to work when the weather is bright, instead of—"

"Yes; work; to be sure. You promised to show me your work. What morning may I come up to your atelier? To-morrow?"

"No!"

"Day after?"

"No, no."

"Oh, please don't refuse me! I know something of such things. I might help you with a stray suggestion or two."

"No. Good night. Why don't you go after you have said good night? I don't like you," she went on in a high, excited pitch, attempting to draw away her hand. She felt that her words lacked dignity and sincerity, and she knew that he felt it.

"I'm sorry you don't like me. I'm sorry I offended you. How have I offended you? What have I done? Can't you forgive me?" And he bent and pressed his lips upon her hand as if he wished never more to withdraw them.

"Mr. Arobin," she complained, "I'm greatly upset by the excitement of the afternoon; I'm not myself. My manner must have misled you in some way. I wish you to go, please." She spoke in a monotonous, dull tone. He took his hat from the table, and stood with eyes turned from her, looking into the dying fire. For a moment or two he kept an impressive silence.

"Your manner has not misled me, Mrs. Pontellier," he said finally. "My own emotions have done that. I couldn't help it. When I'm near you, how could I help it? Don't think anything of it, don't bother, please. You see, I go when you command me. If you wish me to stay away, I shall do so. If you let me come back, I—oh! you will let me come back?"

He cast one appealing glance at her, to which she made no response. Alcée Arobin's manner was so genuine that it often deceived even himself.

Edna did not care or think whether it were genuine or not. When she was alone she looked mechanically at the back of her hand which he had kissed so warmly. Then she leaned her head down on the mantelpiece. She felt somewhat like a woman who in a moment of passion is betrayed into an act of infidelity, and realizes the significance of the act without being wholly awakened from its glamour. The thought was passing vaguely through her mind, "What would he think?"

She did not mean her husband; she was thinking of Robert Lebrun. Her husband seemed to her now like a person whom she had married without love as an excuse.

She lit a candle and went up to her room. Alcée Arobin was absolutely nothing to her. Yet his presence, his manners, the warmth of his glances, and above all the touch of his lips upon her hand had acted like a narcotic upon her.

She slept a languorous sleep, interwoven with vanishing dreams.

XXVI

Alcée Arobin wrote Edna an elaborate note of apology, palpitant with sincerity. It embarrassed her; for in a cooler, quieter moment it appeared to her absurd that she should have taken his action so seriously, so dramatically. She felt sure that the significance of the whole occurrence had lain in her own self-consciousness. If she ignored his note it would give undue importance to a trivial affair. If she replied to it in a serious spirit it would still leave in his mind the impression that she had in a susceptible moment yielded to his influence. After all, it was no great matter to have one's hand kissed. She was provoked at his having written the apology. She answered in as light and bantering a spirit as she fancied it deserved, and said she would be glad to have him look in upon her at work whenever he felt the inclination and his business gave him the opportunity.

He responded at once by presenting himself at her home with all his disarming naïveté. And then there was scarcely a day which followed that she did not see him or was not reminded of him. He was prolific in pretexts. His attitude became one of good-humored subservience and tacit adoration. He was ready at all times to submit to her moods, which were as often kind as they were cold. She grew accustomed to him. They became intimate and friendly by imperceptible degrees, and then by leaps. He sometimes talked in a way that astonished her at first and brought the crimson into her face; in a way that pleased her at last, appealing to the animalism that stirred impatiently within her.

There was nothing which so quieted the turmoil in Edna's senses as a visit to Mademoiselle Reisz. It was then, in the presence of that personality which was offensive to her, that the woman, by her divine art, seemed to reach Edna's spirit and set it free.

It was misty, with heavy, lowering atmosphere, one afternoon, when Edna climbed the stairs to the pianist's apartments under the roof. Her clothes were dripping with moisture. She felt chilled and pinched as she entered the room. Mademoiselle was poking at a rusty stove that smoked a little and warmed the room indifferently. She was endeavoring to heat a pot of chocolate on the stove. The room looked cheerless and dingy to Edna as she entered. A bust of Beethoven, covered with a hood of dust, scowled at her from the mantelpiece.

"Ah! here comes the sunlight!" exclaimed Mademoiselle, rising from her knees before the stove. "Now it will be warm and bright enough; I can let the fire alone."

She closed the stove door with a bang, and approaching, assisted in removing Edna's dripping mackintosh.

"You are cold; you look miserable. The chocolate will soon be hot. But would you rather have a taste of brandy? I have scarcely touched the bottle which you brought me for my cold." A piece of red flannel was wrapped around Mademoiselle's throat; a stiff neck compelled her to hold her head on one side.

"I will take some brandy," said Edna, shivering as she removed her gloves and overshoes. She drank the liquor from the glass as a man would have done. Then flinging herself upon the uncomfortable sofa she said, "Mademoiselle, I am going to move away from my house on Esplanade Street."

"Ah!" ejaculated the musician, neither surprised nor especially interested. Nothing ever seemed to astonish her very much. She was endeavoring to adjust the bunch of violets which had become loose from its fastening in her hair. Edna drew her down upon the sofa, and taking a pin from her own hair, secured the shabby artificial flowers in their accustomed place.

"Aren't you astonished?"

"Passably. Where are you going? to New York? to Iberville? to your father in Mississippi? where?"

"Just two steps away," laughed Edna, "in a little four-room house around the corner. It looks so cozy, so inviting and restful, whenever I pass by; and it's for rent. I'm tired looking after that big house. It never seemed like mine, anyway—like home. It's too much trouble. I have to keep too many servants. I am tired bothering with them."

"That is not your true reason, *ma belle*. There is no use in telling me lies. I don't know your reason, but you have not told me the truth." Edna did not protest or endeavor to justify herself.

"The house, the money that provides for it, are not mine. Isn't that enough reason?"

"They are your husband's," returned Mademoiselle, with a shrug and a malicious elevation of the eyebrows.

"Oh! I see there is no deceiving you. Then let me tell you: It is a caprice. I have a little money of my own from my mother's estate, which my father sends me by driblets. I won a large sum this winter on the races, and I am beginning to sell my sketches. Laidpore is more and more pleased with my work; he says it grows in force and individuality. I cannot judge of that myself, but I feel that I have gained in ease and confidence. However, as I said, I have sold a good many through Laidpore. I can live in the tiny house for little or nothing, with one servant. Old Celestine, who works occasionally for me, says she will come stay with me and do my work. I know I shall like it, like the feeling of freedom and independence."

"What does your husband say?"

"I have not told him yet. I only thought of it this morning. He will think I am demented, no doubt. Perhaps you think so."

Mademoiselle shook her head slowly. "Your reason is not yet clear to me," she said.

Neither was it quite clear to Edna herself; but it unfolded itself as she sat for a while in silence. Instinct had prompted her to put away her husband's bounty in casting off her allegiance. She did not know how it would be when he returned. There would have to be an understanding, an explanation. Conditions would some way adjust themselves, she felt; but whatever came, she had resolved never again to belong to another than herself.

"I shall give a grand dinner before I leave the old house!" Edna exclaimed. "You will have to come to it, Mademoiselle. I will give you everything that you like to eat and drink. We shall sing and laugh and be merry for once." And she uttered a sigh that came from the very depths of her being.

If Mademoiselle happened to have received a letter from Robert during the interval of Edna's visits, she would give her the letter unsolicited. And she would seat herself at the piano and play as her humor prompted her while the young woman read the letter.

The little stove was roaring; it was red-hot, and the chocolate in the tin sizzled and sputtered. Edna went forward and opened the stove door, and Mademoiselle rising, took a letter from under the bust of Beethoven and handed it to Edna.

"Another! so soon!" she exclaimed, her eyes filled with delight. "Tell me, Mademoiselle, does he know that I see his letters?"

"Never in the world! He would be angry and would never write to me again if he thought so. Does he write to you? Never a line. Does he send you a message? Never a word. It is because he loves you, poor fool, and is trying to forget you, since you are not free to listen to him or to belong to him."

"Why do you show me his letters, then?"

"Haven't you begged for them? Can I refuse you anything? Oh! you cannot deceive me," and Mademoiselle approached her beloved instrument and began to play. Edna did not at once read the letter. She sat holding it in her hand, while the music penetrated her whole being like an effulgence, warming and brightening the dark places of her soul. It prepared her for joy and exultation,

"Oh!" she exclaimed, letting the letter fall to the floor. "Why did you not tell me?" She went and grasped Mademoiselle's hands up from the keys. "Oh! unkind! malicious! Why did you not tell me?"

"That he was coming back? No great news, *ma foi.* I wonder he did not come long ago."

"But when, when?" cried Edna, impatiently. "He does not say when."

"He says 'very soon.' You know as much about it as I do; it is all in the letter."

"But why? Why is he coming? Oh, if I thought—" and she snatched the letter from the floor and turned the pages this way and that way, looking for the reason, which was left untold.

"If I were young and in love with a man," said Mademoiselle, turning on the stool and pressing her wiry hands between her knees as she looked down at Edna, who sat on the floor holding the letter, "it seems to me he would have to be some *grand esprit;*[65] a man with lofty aims and ability to reach them; one who stood high enough to attract the notice of his fellow-men. It seems to me if I were young and in love I should never deem a man of ordinary caliber worthy of my devotion."

"Now it is you who are telling lies and seeking to deceive me, Mademoiselle; or else you have never been in love, and know nothing about it. Why," went on Edna, clasping her knees and looking up into Mademoiselle's twisted face, "do you suppose a woman knows why she loves? Does she select? Does she say to herself: 'Go to! Here is a distinguished statesman with presidential possibilities; I shall proceed to fall in love with him.' Or, 'I shall set my heart upon this musician, whose fame is on every tongue?' Or, 'This financier, who controls the world's money markets?'"

"You are purposely misunderstanding me, *ma reine.*[66] Are you in love with Robert?"

---

[65] *grand esprit:* noble soul [66] *ma reine:* my dear (literally, "my queen").

"Yes," said Edna. It was the first time she had admitted it, and a glow over-spread her face, blotching it with red spots.

"Why?" asked her companion. "Why do you love him when you ought not to?"

Edna, with a motion or two, dragged herself on her knees before Mademoiselle Reisz, who took the glowing face between her two hands.

"Why? Because his hair is brown and grows away from his temples; because he opens and shuts his eyes, and his nose is a little out of drawing; because he has two lips and a square chin, and a little finger which he can't straighten from having played baseball too energetically in his youth. Because—"

"Because you do, in short," laughed Mademoiselle. "What will you do when he comes back?" she asked.

"Do? Nothing, except feel glad and happy to be alive."

She was already glad and happy to be alive at the mere thought of his return. The murky, lowering sky, which had depressed her a few hours before, seemed bracing and invigorating as she splashed through the streets on her way home.

She stopped at a confectioner's and ordered a huge box of bonbons for the children in Iberville. She slipped a card in the box, on which she scribbled a tender message and sent an abundance of kisses.

Before dinner in the evening Edna wrote a charming letter to her husband, telling him of her intention to move for a while into the little house around the block, and to give a farewell dinner before leaving, regretting that he was not there to share it, to help her out with the menu and assist her in entertaining the guests. Her letter was brilliant and brimming with cheerfulness.

XXVII

"What is the matter with you?" asked Arobin that evening. "I never found you in such a happy mood." Edna was tired by that time, and was reclining on the lounge before the fire.

"Don't you know the weather prophet has told us we shall see the sun pretty soon?"

"Well, that ought to be reason enough," he acquiesced. "You wouldn't give me another if I sat here all night imploring you." He sat close to her on a low tabouret, and as he spoke his fingers lightly touched the hair that fell a little over her forehead. She liked the touch of his fingers through her hair, and closed her eyes sensitively.

"One of these days," she said, "I'm going to pull myself together for a while and think—try to determine what character of a woman I am; for, candidly, I don't know. By all the codes which I am acquainted with, I am a devilishly wicked specimen of the sex. But some way I can't convince myself that I am. I must think about it."

"Don't. What's the use? Why should you bother thinking about it when I can tell you what manner of woman you are." His fingers strayed occasionally down to her warm, smooth cheeks and firm chin, which was growing a little full and double.

"Oh, yes! You will tell me that I am adorable; everything that is captivating. Spare yourself the effort."

"No; I shan't tell you anything of the sort, though I shouldn't be lying if I did."

"Do you know Mademoiselle Reisz?" she asked irrelevantly.

"The pianist? I know her by sight. I've heard her play."

"She says queer things sometimes in a bantering way that you don't notice at the time and you find yourself thinking about afterward."

"For instance?"

"Well, for instance, when I left her to-day, she put her arms around me and felt my shoulder blades, to see if my wings were strong, she said. 'The bird that would soar above the level plain of tradition and prejudice must have strong wings. It is a sad spectacle to see the weaklings bruised, exhausted, fluttering back to earth.'"

"Whither would you soar?"

"I'm not thinking of any extraordinary flights. I only half comprehend her."

"I've heard she's partially demented," said Arobin.

"She seems to me wonderfully sane," Edna replied.

"I'm told she's extremely disagreeable and unpleasant. Why have you introduced her at a moment when I desired to talk of you?"

"Oh! talk of me if you like," cried Edna, clasping her hands beneath her head; "but let me think of something else while you do."

"I'm jealous of your thoughts to-night. They're making you a little kinder than usual; but some way I feel as if they were wandering, as if they were not here with me." She only looked at him and smiled. His eyes were very near. He leaned upon the lounge with an arm extended across her, while the other hand still rested upon her hair. They continued silently to look into each other's eyes. When he leaned forward and kissed her, she clasped his head, holding his lips to hers.

It was the first kiss of her life to which her nature had really responded. It was a flaming torch that kindled desire.

XXVIII

Edna cried a little that night after Arobin left her. It was only one phase of the multitudinous emotions which had assailed her. There was with her an overwhelming feeling of irresponsibility. There was the shock of the unexpected and the unaccustomed. There was her husband's reproach looking at her from the external things around her which he had provided for her external existence. There was Robert's reproach making itself felt by a quicker, fiercer, more overpowering love, which had awakened within her toward him. Above all, there was understanding. She felt as if a mist had been lifted from her eyes, enabling her to look upon and comprehend the significance of life, that monster made up of beauty and brutality. But among the conflicting sensations which assailed her, there was neither shame nor remorse. There was a dull pang of regret because it was not the kiss of love which had inflamed her, because it was not love which had held this cup of life to her lips.

XXIX

Without even waiting for an answer from her husband regarding his opinion or wishes in the matter, Edna hastened her preparations for quitting her home on Esplanade Street and moving into the little house around the block. A feverish anxiety attended her every action in that direction. There was no moment of deliberation, no interval of repose between the thought and its fulfillment. Early upon the morning following those hours passed in Arobin's society, Edna set about securing her new abode and hurrying her arrangements for occupying it. Within the precincts of her home she felt like one who has entered and lingered within the portals of some forbidden temple in which a thousand muffled voices bade her begone.

Whatever was her own in the house, everything she had acquired aside from her husband's bounty, she caused to be transported to the other house, supplying simple and meager deficiencies from her own resources.

Arobin found her with rolled sleeves, working in company with the housemaid when he looked in during the afternoon. She was splendid and robust, and had never appeared handsomer than in the old blue gown, with a red silk handkerchief knotted at random around her head to protect her hair from the dust. She was mounted upon a high step-ladder, unhooking a picture from the wall when he entered. He had found the front door open, and had followed his ring by walking in unceremoniously.

"Come down!" he said. "Do you want to kill yourself?" She greeted him with affected carelessness, and appeared absorbed in her occupation.

If he had expected to find her languishing, reproachful, or indulging in sentimental tears, he must have been greatly surprised.

He was no doubt prepared for any emergency, ready for any one of the foregoing attitudes, just as he bent himself easily and naturally to the situation which confronted him.

"Please come down," he insisted, holding the ladder and looking up at her.

"No," she answered; "Ellen is afraid to mount the ladder. Joe is working over at the 'pigeon house'—that's the name Ellen gives it, because it's so small and looks like a pigeon house—and some one has to do this."

Arobin pulled off his coat, and expressed himself ready and willing to tempt fate in her place. Ellen brought him one of her dust-caps, and went into contortions of mirth, which she found it impossible to control, when she saw him put it on before the mirror as grotesquely as he could. Edna herself could not refrain from smiling when she fastened it at his request. So it was he who in turn mounted the ladder, unhooking pictures and curtains, and dislodging ornaments as Edna directed. When he had finished he took off his dust-cap and went out to wash his hands.

Edna was sitting on the tabouret, idly brushing the tips of a feather duster along the carpet when he came in again.

"Is there anything more you will let me do?" he asked.

"That is all," she answered. "Ellen can manage the rest." She kept the young woman occupied in the drawing-room, unwilling to be left alone with Arobin.

"What about the dinner?" he asked; "the grand event, the *coup d'état?*"

"It will be day after to-morrow. Why do you call it the *coup d'état?* Oh! it will be very fine; all my best of everything—crystal, silver and gold, Sèvres, flowers, music, and champagne to swim in. I'll let Léonce pay the bills. I wonder what he'll say when he sees the bills."

"And you ask me why I call it a *coup d' état?*" Arobin put on his coat, and he stood before her and asked if his cravat was plumb. She told him it was, looking no higher than the tip of his collar.

"When do you go to the 'pigeon house?'—with all due acknowledgement to Ellen."

"Day after to-morrow, after the dinner. I shall sleep there."

"Ellen, will you very kindly get me a glass of water?" asked Arobin. "The dust in the curtains, if you will pardon me for hinting such a thing, has parched my throat to a crisp."

"While Ellen gets the water," said Edna, rising, "I will say good-by and let you go. I must get rid of this grime, and I have a million things to do and think of."

"When shall I see you?" asked Arobin, seeking to detain her, the maid having left the room.

"At the dinner, of course. You are invited."

"Not before?—not to-night or to-morrow morning or to-morrow noon or night? or the day after morning or noon? Can't you see yourself, without my telling you, what an eternity it is?"

He had followed her into the hall and to the foot of the stairway, looking up at her as she mounted with her face half turned to him.

"Not an instant sooner," she said. But she laughed and looked at him with eyes that at once gave him courage to wait and made it torture to wait.

XXX

Though Edna had spoken of the dinner as a grand affair, it was in truth a very small affair and very select, in so much as the guests invited were few and were selected with discrimination. She had counted upon an even dozen seating themselves at her round mahogany board, forgetting for the moment that Madame Ratignolle was to the last degree *souffrante*[67] and unpresentable, and not foreseeing that Madame Lebrun would send a thousand regrets at the last moment. So there were only ten, after all, which made a cozy, comfortable number.

There were Mr. and Mrs. Merriman, a pretty, vivacious little woman in the thirties; her husband, a jovial fellow, something of a shallow-pate, who laughed a good deal at other people's witticisms, and had thereby made himself extremely popular. Mrs. Highcamp had accompanied them. Of course, there was Alcée Arobin; and Mademoiselle Reisz had consented to come. Edna had sent her a fresh bunch of violets with black lace trimmings for her hair. Monsieur Ratignolle brought

[67] *souffrante:* ill

himself and his wife's excuses. Victor Lebrun, who happened to be in the city, bent upon relaxation, had accepted with alacrity. There was a Miss Mayblunt, no longer in her teens, who looked at the world through lorgnettes and with the keenest interest. It was thought and said that she was intellectual; it was suspected of her that she wrote under a *nom de guerre*.[68] She had come with a gentleman by the name of Gouvernail, connected with one of the daily papers, of whom nothing special could be said, except that he was observant and seemed quiet and inoffensive. Edna herself made the tenth, and at half-past eight they seated themselves at table, Arobin and Monsieur Ratignolle on either side of their hostess.

Mrs. Highcamp sat between Arobin and Victor Lebrun. Then came Mrs. Merriman, Mr. Gouvernail, Miss Mayblunt, Mr. Merriman, and Mademoiselle Reisz next to Monsieur Ratignolle.

There was something extremely gorgeous about the appearance of the table, an effect of splendor conveyed by a cover of pale yellow satin under strips of lace-work. There were wax candles in massive brass candelabra, burning softly under yellow silk shades; full, fragrant roses, yellow and red, abounded. There were silver and gold, as she had said there would be, and crystal which glittered like the gems which the women wore.

The ordinary stiff dining chairs had been discarded for the occasion and replaced by the most commodious and luxurious which could be collected throughout the house. Mademoiselle Reisz, being exceedingly diminutive, was elevated upon cushions, as small children are sometimes hoisted at table upon bulky volumes.

"Something new, Edna?" exclaimed Miss Mayblunt, with lorgnette directed toward a magnificent cluster of diamonds that sparkled, that almost sputtered, in Edna's hair, just over the center of her forehead.

"Quite new; 'brand' new, in fact; a present from my husband. It arrived this morning from New York. I may as well admit that this is my birthday, and that I am twenty-nine. In good time I expect you to drink my health. Meanwhile, I shall ask you to begin with this cocktail, composed—would you say 'composed?'" with an appeal to Miss Mayblunt—"composed by my father in honor of Sister Janet's wedding."

Before each guest stood a tiny glass that looked and sparkled like a garnet gem.

"Then, all things considered," spoke Arobin, "it might not be amiss to start out by drinking the Colonel's health in the cocktail which he composed, on the birthday of the most charming of women—the daughter whom he invented."

Mr. Merriman's laugh at this sally was such a genuine outburst and so contagious that it started the dinner with an agreeable swing that never slackened.

Miss Mayblunt begged to be allowed to keep her cocktail untouched before her, just to look at. The color was marvelous! She could compare it to nothing she had ever seen, and the garnet lights which it emitted were unspeakably rare. She pronounced the Colonel an artist, and stuck to it.

---

[68] *nom de guerre*: pseudonym (literally, "war name").

Monsieur Ratignolle was prepared to take things seriously: the *mets*, the *entre-mets*,[69] the service, the decorations, even the people. He looked up from his pompano[70] and inquired of Arobin if he were related to the gentleman of that name who formed one of the firm of Laitner and Arobin, lawyers. The young man admitted that Laitner was a warm personal friend, who permitted Arobin's name to decorate the firm's letterheads and to appear upon a shingle that graced Perdido Street.

"There are so many inquisitive people and institutions abounding," said Arobin, that one is really forced as a matter of convenience these days to assume the virtue of an occupation if he has it not."

Monsieur Ratignolle stared a little, and turned to ask Mademoiselle Reisz if she considered the symphony concerts up to the standard which had been set the previous winter. Mademoiselle Reisz answered Monsieur Ratignolle in French, which Edna thought a little rude, under the circumstances, but characteristic. Mademoiselle had only disagreeable things to say of the symphony concerts, and insulting remarks to make of all the musicians of New Orleans, singly and collectively. All her interest seemed to be centered upon the delicacies placed before her.

Mr. Merriman said that Mr. Arobin's remark about inquisitive people reminded him of a man from Waco the other day at the St. Charles Hotel—but as Mr. Merriman's stories were always lame and lacking point, his wife seldom permitted him to complete them. She interrupted him to ask if he remembered the name of the author whose book she had bought the week before to send to a friend in Geneva. She was talking "books" with Mr. Gouvernail and trying to draw from him his opinion upon current literary topics. Her husband told the story of the Waco man privately to Miss Mayblunt, who pretended to be greatly amused and to think it extremely clever.

Mrs. Highcamp hung with languid but unaffected interest upon the warm and impetuous volubility of her left-hand neighbor, Victor Lebrun. Her attention was never for a moment withdrawn from him after seating herself at table; and when he turned to Mrs. Merriman, who was prettier and more vivacious than Mrs. Highcamp, she waited with easy indifference for an opportunity to reclaim his attention. There was the occasional sound of music, of mandolins, sufficiently removed to be an agreeable accompaniment rather than an interruption to the conversation. Outside the soft, monotonous splash of a fountain could be heard; the sound penetrated into the room with the heavy odor of jessamine that came through the open windows.

The golden shimmer of Edna's satin gown spread in rich folds on either side of her. There was a soft fall of lace encircling her shoulders. It was the color of her skin, without the glow, the myriad living tints that one may sometimes discover in vibrant flesh. There was something in her attitude, in her whole appearance when she leaned her head against the high-backed chair and spread her arms, which suggested the regal woman, the one who rules, who looks on, who stands alone.

[69] *mets . . . entre-mets:* main courses . . . side dishes [70] *pompano:* kind of fish.

But as she sat there amid her guests, she felt the old ennui overtaking her; the hopelessness which so often assailed her, which came upon her like an obsession, like something extraneous, independent of volition. It was something which announced itself; a chill breath that seemed to issue from some vast cavern wherein discords wailed. There came over her the acute longing which always summoned into her spiritual vision the presence of the beloved one, overpowering her at once with a sense of the unattainable.

The moments glided on, while a feeling of good fellowship passed around the circle like a mystic cord, holding and binding these people together with jest and laughter. Monsieur Ratignolle was the first to break the pleasant charm. At ten o'clock he excused himself. Madame Ratignolle was waiting for him at home. She was *bien souffrante,*[71] and she was filled with vague dread, which only her husband's presence could allay.

Mademoiselle Reisz arose with Monsieur Ratignolle, who offered to escort her to the car. She had eaten well; she had tasted the good, rich wines, and they must have turned her head, for she bowed pleasantly to all as she withdrew from table. She kissed Edna upon the shoulder, and whispered: "*Bonne nuit, ma reine; soyez sage.*"[72] She had been a little bewildered upon rising, or rather, descending from her cushions, and Monsieur Ratignolle gallantly took her arm and led her away.

Mrs. Highcamp was weaving a garland of roses, yellow and red. When she had finished the garland, she laid it tightly upon Victor's black curls. He was reclining far back in the luxurious chair, holding a glass of champagne to the light.

As if a magician's wand had touched him, the garland of roses transformed him into a vision of Oriental beauty. His cheeks were the color of crushed grapes, and his dusky eyes glowed with a languishing fire.

"*Sapristi!*" exclaimed Arobin.

But Mrs. Highcamp had one more touch to add to the picture. She took from the back of her chair a white silken scarf, with which she had covered her shoulders in the early part of the evening. She draped it across the boy in graceful folds, and in a way to conceal his black, conventional evening dress. He did not seem to mind what she did to him, only smiled showing a faint gleam of white teeth, while he continued to gaze with narrowing eyes at the light through his glass of champagne.

"Oh! to be able to paint in color rather than in words!" exclaimed Miss Mayblunt, losing herself in a rhapsodic dream as she looked at him.

"'There was a graven image of Desire
Painted with red blood on a ground of gold.'"[73]

murmured Gouvernail, under his breath.

---

[71] *bien souffrante:* very ill. [72] *Bonne . . . sage.:* Good night, my love; be good. [73] *"There was . . . gold.":* first two lines of a sonnet entitled "A Cameo," by the English poet Algernon Charles Swinburne (1837–1909).

The effect of the wine upon Victor was to change his accustomed volubility into silence. He seemed to have abandoned himself to a reverie, and to be seeing pleasing visions in the amber bead.

"Sing," entreated Mrs. Highcamp. "Won't you sing to us?"

"Let him alone," said Arobin.

"He's posing," offered Mr. Merriman; "let him have it out."

"I believe he's paralyzed," laughed Mrs. Merriman. And leaning over the youth's chair, she took the glass from his hand and held it to his lips. He sipped the wine slowly, and when he had drained the glass she laid it upon the table and wiped his lips with her little filmy handkerchief.

"Yes, I'll sing for you," he said, turning in his chair toward Mrs. Highcamp. He clasped his hands behind his head, and looking up at the ceiling began to hum a little, trying his voice like a musician tuning an instrument. Then, looking at Edna, he began to sing:

"Ah! si tu savais!"

"Stop!" she cried, "don't sing that. I don't want you to sing it," and she laid her glass so impetuously and blindly upon the table as to shatter it against a carafe. The wine spilled over Arobin's legs and some of it trickled down upon Mrs. Highcamp's black gauze gown. Victor had lost all idea of courtesy, or else he thought his hostess was not in earnest, for he laughed and went on:

"Ah! si tu savais
Ce que tes yeux me disent"—[74]

"Oh! you mustn't! you mustn't," exclaimed Edna, and pushing back her chair she got up, and going behind him placed her hand over his mouth. He kissed the soft palm that pressed upon his lips.

"No, no, I won't, Mrs. Pontellier. I didn't know you meant it," looking up at her with caressing eyes. The touch of his lips was like a pleasing sting to her hand. She lifted the garland of roses from his head and flung it across the room.

"Come, Victor; you've posed long enough. Give Mrs. Highcamp her scarf."

Mrs. Highcamp undraped her scarf from about him with her own hands. Miss Mayblunt and Mr. Gouvernail suddenly conceived the notion that it was time to say good night. And Mr. and Mrs. Merriman wondered how it could be so late.

Before parting from Victor, Mrs. Highcamp invited him to call upon her daughter, who she knew would be charmed to meet him and talk French and sing French songs with him. Victor expressed his desire and intention to call upon Miss Highcamp at the first opportunity which presented itself. He asked if Arobin were going his way. Arobin was not.

The mandolin players had long since stolen away. A profound stillness had fallen upon the broad, beautiful street. The voices of Edna's disbanding guests jarred like a discordant note upon the quiet harmony of the night.

[74] *Ah! . . . disent:* "Oh, if you only knew what your eyes tell me."

XXXI

"Well?" questioned Arobin, who had remained with Edna after the others had departed.

"Well," she reiterated, and stood up, stretching her arms, and feeling the need to relax her muscles after having been so long seated.

"What next?" he asked.

"The servants are all gone. They left when the musicians did. I have dismissed them. The house has to be closed and locked, and I shall trot around to the pigeon house, and shall send Celestine over in the morning to straighten things up."

He looked around, and began to turn out some of the lights.

"What about upstairs?" he inquired.

"I think it is all right; but there may be a window or two unlatched. We had better look; you might take a candle and see. And bring me my wrap and hat on the foot of the bed in the middle room."

He went up with the light, and Edna began closing doors and windows. She hated to shut in the smoke and the fumes of the wine. Arobin found her cape and hat, which he brought down and helped her to put on.

When everything was secured and the lights put out, they left through the front door, Arobin locking it and taking the key, which he carried for Edna. He helped her down the steps.

"Will you have a spray of jessamine?" he asked, breaking off a few blossoms as he passed.

"No; I don't want anything."

She seemed disheartened, and had nothing to say. She took his arm, which he offered her, holding up the weight of her satin gown with the other hand. She looked down, noticing the black line of his leg moving in and out so close to her against the yellow shimmer of her gown. There was the whistle of a railway train somewhere in the distance, and the midnight bells were ringing. They met no one in their short walk.

The "pigeon-house" stood behind a locked gate, and a shallow *parterre*[75] that had been somewhat neglected. There was a small front porch, upon which a long window and the front door opened. The door opened directly into the parlor; there was no side entry. Back in the yard was a room for servants, in which old Celestine had been ensconced.

Edna had left a lamp burning low upon the table. She had succeeded in making the room look habitable and homelike. There were some books on the table and a lounge near at hand. On the floor was a fresh matting, covered with a rug or two; and on the walls hung a few tasteful pictures. But the room was filled with flowers. These were a surprise to her. Arobin had sent them, and had had Celestine distribute them during Edna's absence. Her bedroom was adjoining, and across a small passage were the dining-room and kitchen.

Edna seated herself with every appearance of discomfort.

---

[75] *parterre:* garden with geometric flower-beds and paths.

"Are you tired?" he asked.

"Yes, and chilled, and miserable. I feel as if I had been wound up to a certain pitch—too tight—and something inside of me had snapped."

She had rested her head against the table upon her bare arm.

"You want to rest," he said, "and to be quiet. I'll go; I'll leave you and let you rest."

"Yes," she replied.

He stood up beside her and smoothed her hair with his soft, magnetic hand. His touch conveyed to her a certain physical comfort. She could have fallen quietly asleep there if he had continued to pass his hand over her hair. He brushed the hair upward from the nape of her neck.

"I hope you will feel better and happier in the morning," he said. "You have tried to do too much in the past few days. The dinner was the last straw; you might have dispensed with it."

"Yes," she admitted; "it was stupid."

"No, it was delightful; but it has worn you out." His hand strayed to her beautiful shoulders, and he could feel the response of her flesh to his touch. He seated himself beside her and kissed her lightly on the shoulder.

"I thought you were going away," she said, in an uneven voice.

"I am, after I have said good night."

"Good night," she murmured.

He did not answer, except to continue to caress her. He did not say good night until she had become supple to his gentle, seductive entreaties.

XXXII

When Mr. Pontellier learned of his wife's intention to abandon her home and take up her residence elsewhere he immediately wrote her a letter of unqualified disapproval and remonstrance. She had given reasons which he was unwilling to acknowledge as adequate. He hoped she had not acted upon her rash impulse; and he begged her to consider first, foremost, and above all else, what people would say. He was not dreaming of scandal when he uttered this warning; that was a thing which would never have entered into his mind to consider in connection with his wife's name or his own. He was simply thinking of his financial integrity. It might get noised about that the Pontelliers had met with reverses, and were forced to conduct their *ménage*[76] on a humbler scale than heretofore. It might do incalculable mischief to his business prospects.

But remembering Edna's whimsical turn of mind of late, and foreseeing that she had immediately acted upon her impetuous determination, he grasped the situation with his usual promptness and handled it with his well-known business tact and cleverness.

The same mail which brought to Edna his letter of disapproval carried instructions—the most minute instructions—to a well known architect concerning the

[76] *ménage:* household.

remodeling of his home, changes which he had long contemplated, and which he desired carried forward during his temporary absence.

Expert and reliable packers and movers were engaged to convey the furniture, carpets, pictures—everything movable, in short—to places of security. And in an incredibly short time the Pontellier house was turned over to the artisans. There was to be an addition—a small snuggery; there was to be frescoing, and hardwood flooring was to be put into such rooms as had not yet been subjected to this improvement.

Furthermore, in one of the daily papers appeared a brief notice to the effect that Mr. and Mrs. Pontellier were contemplating a summer sojourn abroad, and that their handsome residence on Esplanade Street was undergoing sumptuous alterations, and would not be ready for occupancy until their return. Mr. Pontellier had saved appearances!

Edna admired the skill of his maneuver, and avoided any occasion to balk his intentions. When the situation as set forth by Mr. Pontellier was accepted and taken for granted, she was apparently satisfied that it should be so.

The pigeon-house pleased her. It at once assumed the intimate character of a home, while she herself invested it with a charm which it reflected like a warm glow. There was with her a feeling of having descended in the social scale, with a corresponding sense of having risen in the spiritual. Every step which she took toward relieving herself from obligations added to her strength and expansion as an individual. She began to look with her own eyes; to see and to apprehend the deeper undercurrents of life. No longer was she content to "feed upon opinion" when her own soul had invited her.

After a little while, a few days, in fact, Edna went up and spent a week with her children in Iberville. They were delicious February days, with all the summer's promise hovering in the air.

How glad she was to see the children! She wept for very pleasure when she felt their little arms clasping her; their hard, ruddy cheeks pressed against her own glowing cheeks. She looked into their faces with hungry eyes that could not be satisfied with looking. And what stories they had to tell their mother! About the pigs, the cows, the mules! About riding to the mill behind Gluglu; fishing back in the lake with their Uncle Jasper; picking pecans with Lidie's little black brood, and hauling chips in their little express wagon. It was a thousand times more fun to haul real chips for old lame Susie's real fire than to drag painted blocks along the banquette on Esplanade Street!

She went with them herself to see the pigs and the cows, to look at the darkies laying the cane, to thrash the pecan trees, and catch fish in the back lake. She lived with them a whole week long, giving them all of herself, and gathering and filling herself with their young existence. They listened, breathless, when she told them the house in Esplanade Street was crowded with workmen, hammering, nailing, sawing, and filling the place with clatter. They wanted to know where their bed was; what had been done with their rocking-horse; and where did Joe sleep, and where had Ellen gone, and the cook? But, above all, they were fired with a desire to see the little house around the block. Was there any place to play? Were there any boys next door? Raoul, with pessimistic foreboding, was convinced that there were only girls next door. Where would they sleep, and where would papa sleep? She told them the fairies would fix it all right.

The old Madame was charmed with Edna's visit, and showered all manner of delicate attentions upon her. She was delighted to know that the Esplanade Street house was in a dismantled condition. It gave her the promise and pretext to keep the children indefinitely.

It was with a wrench and a pang that Edna left her children. She carried away with her the sound of their voices and the touch of their cheeks. All along the journey homeward their presence lingered with her like the memory of a delicious song. But by the time she had regained the city the song no longer echoed in her soul. She was again alone.

XXXIII

It happened sometimes when Edna went to see Mademoiselle Reisz that the little musician was absent, giving a lesson or making some small necessary household purchase. The key was always left in a secret hiding-place in the entry, which Edna knew. If Mademoiselle happened to be away, Edna would usually enter and wait for her return.

When she knocked at Mademoiselle Reisz's door one afternoon there was no response; so unlocking the door, as usual, she entered and found the apartment deserted, as she had expected. Her day had been quite filled up, and it was for a rest, for a refuge, and to talk about Robert, that she sought out her friend.

She had worked at her canvas   a young Italian character study—all the morning, completing the work without the model; but there had been many interruptions, some incident to her modest housekeeping, and others of a social nature.

Madame Ratignolle had dragged herself over, avoiding the too public thoroughfares, she said. She complained that Edna had neglected her much of late. Besides, she was consumed with curiosity to see the little house and the manner in which it was conducted. She wanted to hear all about the dinner party; Monsieur Ratignolle had left *so* early. What had happened after he left? The champagne and grapes which Edna sent over were *too* delicious. She had so little appetite; they had refreshed and toned her stomach. Where on earth was she going to put Mr. Pontellier in that little house, and the boys? And then she made Edna promise to go to her when her hour of trial overtook her.

"At any time—any time of the day or night, dear," Edna assured her.

Before leaving Madame Ratignolle said:

"In some way you seem to me like a child, Edna. You seem to act without a certain amount of reflection which is necessary in this life. That is the reason I want to say you mustn't mind if I advise you to be a little careful while you are living here alone. Why don't you have some one come and stay with you? Wouldn't Mademoiselle Reisz come?"

"No; she wouldn't wish to come, and I shouldn't want her always with me."

"Well, the reason—you know how evil-minded the world is—some one was talking of Alcée Arobin visiting you. Of course, it wouldn't matter if Mr. Arobin had not such a dreadful reputation. Monsieur Ratignolle was telling me that his attentions alone are considered enough to ruin a woman's name."

"Does he boast of his successes?" asked Edna, indifferently, squinting at her picture.

"No, I think not. I believe he is a decent fellow as far as that goes. But his character is so well known among the men. I shan't be able to come back and see you; it was very, very imprudent to-day."

"Mind the step!" cried Edna.

"Don't neglect me," entreated Madame Ratignolle; "and don't mind what I said about Arobin, or having some one to stay with you."

"Of course not," Edna laughed. "You may say anything you like to me." They kissed each other good-by. Madame Ratignolle had not far to go, and Edna stood on the porch a while watching her walk down the street.

Then in the afternoon Mrs. Merriman and Mrs. Highcamp had made their "party call." Edna felt that they might have dispensed with the formality. They had also come to invite her to play *vingt-et-un*[77] one evening at Mrs. Merriman's. She was asked to go early, to dinner, and Mr. Merriman or Mr. Arobin would take her home. Edna accepted in a half-hearted way. She sometimes felt very tired of Mrs. Highcamp and Mrs. Merriman.

Late in the afternoon she sought refuge with Mademoiselle Reisz, and stayed there alone, waiting for her, feeling a kind of repose invade her with the very atmosphere of the shabby, unpretentious little room.

Edna sat at the window, which looked out over the house-tops and across the river. The window frame was filled with pots of flowers, and she sat and picked the dry leaves from a rose geranium. The day was warm, and the breeze which blew from the river was very pleasant. She removed her hat and laid it on the piano. She went on picking the leaves and digging around the plants with her hat pin. Once she thought she heard Mademoiselle Reisz approaching. But it was a young black girl, who came in, bringing a small bundle of laundry, which she deposited in the adjoining room, and went away.

Edna seated herself at the piano, and softly picked out with one hand the bars of a piece of music which lay open before her. A half-hour went by. There was the occasional sound of people going and coming in the lower hall. She was growing interested in her occupation of picking out the aria, when there was a second rap at the door. She vaguely wondered what these people did when they found Mademoiselle's door locked.

"Come in," she called, turning her face toward the door. And this time it was Robert Lebrun who presented himself. She attempted to rise; she could not have

---

[77] *vingt-et-un:* twenty-one (card game).

done so without betraying the agitation which mastered her at sight of him, so she fell back upon the stool, only exclaiming, "Why, Robert!"

He came and clasped her hand, seemingly without knowing what he was saying or doing.

"Mrs. Pontellier! How do you happen—oh! how well you look! Is Mademoiselle Reisz not here? I never expected to see you."

"When did you come back?" asked Edna in an unsteady voice, wiping her face with her handkerchief. She seemed ill at ease on the piano stool, and he begged her to take the chair by the window. She did so, mechanically, while he seated himself on the stool.

"I returned day before yesterday," he answered, while he leaned his arm on the keys, bringing forth a crash of discordant sound.

"Day before yesterday!" she repeated, aloud; and went on thinking to herself, "day before yesterday," in a sort of an uncomprehending way. She had pictured him seeking her at the very first hour, and he had lived under the same sky since day before yesterday; while only by accident had he stumbled upon her. Mademoiselle must have lied when she said, "Poor fool, he loves you."

"Day before yesterday," she repeated, breaking off a spray of Mademoiselle's geranium; "then if you had not met me here to-day you wouldn't—when—that is, didn't you mean to come and see me?"

"Of course, I should have gone to see you. There have been so many things—" he turned the leaves of Mademoiselle's music nervously. "I started in at once yesterday with the old firm. After all there is as much chance for me here as there was there—that is, I might find it profitable some day. The Mexicans were not very congenial."

So he had come back because the Mexicans were not congenial; because business was as profitable here as there; because of reason, and not because he cared to be near her. She remembered the day she sat on the floor, turning the pages of his letter, seeking the reason which was left untold.

She had not noticed how he looked—only feeling his presence; but she turned deliberately and observed him. After all, he had been absent but a few months, and was not changed. His hair—the color of hers—waved back from his temples in the same way as before. His skin was not more burned than it had been at Grand Isle. She found in his eyes, when he looked at her for one silent moment, the same tender caress, with an added warmth and entreaty which had not been there before—the same glance which had penetrated to the sleeping places of her soul and awakened them.

A hundred times Edna had pictured Robert's return, and imagined their first meeting. It was usually at her home, whither he had sought her out at once. She always fancied him expressing or betraying in some way his love for her. And here, the reality was that they sat ten feet apart, she at the window, crushing geranium leaves in her hand and smelling them, he twirling around on the piano stool, saying:

"I was very much surprised to hear of Mr. Pontellier's absence; it's a wonder Mademoiselle Reisz did not tell me; and your moving—mother told me yesterday.

I should think you would have gone to New York with him, or to Iberville with the children, rather than be bothered here with housekeeping. And you are going abroad, too, I hear. We shan't have you at Grand Isle next summer; it won't seem—do you see much of Mademoiselle Reisz? She often spoke of you in the few letters she wrote."

"Do you remember that you promised to write to me when you went away?" A flush overspread his whole face.

"I couldn't believe that my letters would be of any interest to you."

"That is an excuse; it isn't the truth." Edna reached for her hat on the piano. She adjusted it, sticking the hat pin through the heavy coil of hair with some deliberation.

"Are you not going to wait for Mademoiselle Reisz?" asked Robert.

"No; I have found when she is absent this long, she is liable not to come back till late." She drew on her gloves, and Robert picked up his hat.

"Won't you wait for her?" asked Edna.

"Not if you think she will not be back till late," adding, as if suddenly aware of some discourtesy in his speech, "and I should miss the pleasure of walking home with you." Edna locked the door and put the key back in its hiding-place.

They went together, picking their way across muddy streets and side-walks encumbered with the cheap display of small tradesmen. Part of the distance they rode in the car, and after disembarking, passed the Pontellier mansion, which looked broken and half torn asunder. Robert had never known the house, and looked at it with interest.

"I never knew you in your home," he remarked.

"I am glad you did not."

"Why?" She did not answer. They went on around the corner, and it seemed as if her dreams were coming true after all, when he followed her into the little house.

"You must stay and dine with me, Robert. You see I am all alone, and it is so long since I have seen you. There is so much I want to ask you."

She took off her hat and gloves. He stood irresolute, making some excuse about his mother who expected him; he even muttered something about an engagement. She struck a match and lit the lamp in the table; it was growing dusk. When he saw her face in the lamp-light, looking pained, with all the soft lines gone out of it, he threw his hat aside and seated himself.

"Oh! you know I want to stay if you will let me!" he exclaimed. All the softness came back. She laughed, and went and put her hand on his shoulder.

"This is the first moment you have seemed like the old Robert. I'll go tell Celestine." She hurried away to tell Celestine to set an extra place. She even sent her off in search of some added delicacy which she had not thought of for herself. And she recommended great care in dripping the coffee and having the omelet done to a proper turn.

When she reentered, Robert was turning over magazines, sketches and things that lay upon the table in great disorder. He picked up a photograph, and exclaimed:

"Alcée Arobin! What on earth is his picture doing here?"

"I tried to make a sketch of his head one day," answered Edna, "and he thought the photograph might help me. It was at the other house. I thought it had been left there. I must have picked it up with my drawing materials."

"I should think you would give it back to him if you have finished with it."

"Oh! I have a great many such photographs. I never think of returning them. They don't amount to anything." Robert kept on looking at the picture.

"It seems to me—do you think his head worth drawing? Is he a friend of Mr. Pontellier's? You never said you knew him."

"He isn't a friend of Mr. Pontellier's; he's a friend of mine. I always knew him—that is, it is only of late that I know him pretty well. But I'd rather talk about you, and know what you have been seeing and doing and feeling out there in Mexico." Robert threw aside the picture.

"I've been seeing the waves and the white beach of Grand Isle; the quiet, grassy street of the *Chênière Caminada;* the old fort at Grande Terre. I've been working like a machine, and feeling like a lost soul. There was nothing interesting."

She leaned her head upon her hand to shade her eyes from the light.

"And what have you been seeing and doing and feeling all these days?" he asked.

"I've been seeing the waves and the white beach of Grand Isle; the quiet, grassy street of the *Chênière;* the old sunny fort at Grande Terre. I've been working with a little more comprehension than a machine, and still feeling like a lost soul. There was nothing interesting."

"Mrs. Pontellier, you are cruel," he said, with feeling, closing his eyes and resting his head back in his chair. They remained in silence till old Celestine announced dinner.

XXXIV

The dining-room was very small. Edna's round mahogany would have almost filled it. As it was there was but a step or two from the little table to the kitchen, to the mantel, the small buffet, and the side door that opened out on the narrow brick-paved yard.

A certain degree of ceremony settled upon them with the announcement of dinner. There was no return to personalities. Robert related incidents of his sojourn in Mexico, and Edna talked of events likely to interest him, which had occurred during his absence. The dinner was of ordinary quality, except for the few delicacies which she had sent out to purchase. Old Celestine, with a bandana *tignon*[78] twisted about her head, hobbled in and out, taking a personal interest in everything; and she lingered occasionally to talk patois[79] with Robert, whom she had known as a boy.

He went out to a neighboring cigar stand to purchase cigarette papers, and when he came back he found that Celestine had served the black coffee in the parlor.

"Perhaps I shouldn't have come back," he said. "When you are tired of me, tell me to go."

---

[78] *bandana tignon:* hair tied in a scarf [79] *patois:* regional dialect of French, English, Spanish, and American Indian.

"You never tire me. You must have forgotten the hours and hours at Grand Isle in which we grew accustomed to each other and used to being together."

"I have forgotten nothing at Grand Isle," he said, not looking at her, but rolling a cigarette. His tobacco pouch, which he laid upon the table, was a fantastic embroidered silk affair, evidently the handiwork of a woman.

"You used to carry your tobacco in a rubber pouch, said Edna, picking up the pouch and examining the needle work.

"Yes; it was lost."

"Where did you buy this one? In Mexico?"

"It was given to me by a Vera Cruz girl; they are very generous," he replied, striking a match and lighting his cigarette.

"They are very handsome, I suppose, those Mexican women; very picturesque, with their black eyes and their lace scarfs."

"Some are; others are hideous. Just as you find women everywhere."

"What was she like—the one who gave you the pouch? You must have known her very well."

"She was very ordinary. She wasn't of the slightest importance. I knew her well enough."

"Did you visit at her house? Was it interesting? I should like to know and hear about the people you met, and the impressions they made on you."

"There are some people who leave impressions not so lasting as the imprint of an oar upon the water."

"Was she such a one?"

"It would be ungenerous for me to admit that she was of that order and kind." He thrust the pouch back in his pocket, as if to put away the subject with the trifle which had brought it up.

Arobin dropped in with a message from Mrs. Merriman, to say that the card party was postponed on account of the illness of one of her children.

"How do you do, Arobin?" said Robert, rising from the obscurity.

"Oh! Lebrun. To be sure! I heard yesterday you were back. How did they treat you down in Mexique?"

"Fairly well."

"But not well enough to keep you there. Stunning girls, though, in Mexico. I thought I should never get away from Vera Cruz when I was down there a couple of years ago."

"Did they embroider slippers and tobacco pouches and hat-bands and things for you?" asked Edna.

"Oh! my! no! I didn't get so deep in their regard. I fear they made more impression on me than I made on them."

"You were less fortunate than Robert, then."

"I am always less fortunate than Robert. Has he been imparting tender confidences?"

"I've been imposing myself long enough," said Robert, rising, and shaking hands with Edna. "Please convey my regards to Mr. Pontellier when you write."

He shook hands with Arobin and went away.

"Fine fellow, that Lebrun," said Arobin when Robert had gone. "I never heard you speak of him."

"I knew him last summer at Grand Isle," she replied. "Here is that photograph of yours. Don't you want it?"

"What do I want with it? Throw it away." She threw it back on the table.

"I'm not going to Mrs. Merriman's," she said. "If you see her, tell her so. But perhaps I had better write. I think I shall write now, and say that I am sorry her child is sick, and tell her not to count on me."

"It would be a good scheme," acquiesced Arobin. "I don't blame you; stupid lot!"

Edna opened the blotter, and having procured paper and pen, began to write the note. Arobin lit a cigar and read the evening paper, which he had in his pocket.

"What is the date?" she asked. He told her.

"Will you mail this for me when you go out?"

"Certainly." He read to her little bits out of the newspaper, while she straightened things on the table.

"What do you want to do?" he asked, throwing aside the paper. "Do you want to go out for a walk or a drive or anything? It would be a fine night to drive."

"No; I don't want to do anything but just be quiet. You go away and amuse yourself. Don't stay."

"I'll go away if I must; but I shan't amuse myself. You know that I only live when I am near you."

He stood up to bid her good night.

"Is that one of the things you always say to women?"

"I have said it before, but I don't think I ever came so near meaning it," he answered with a smile. There were no warm lights in her eyes; only a dreamy, absent look.

"Good night. I adore you. Sleep well," he said, and he kissed her hand and went away.

She stayed alone in a kind of reverie—a sort of stupor. Step by step she lived over every instant of the time she had been with Robert after he had entered Mademoiselle Reisz's door. She recalled his words, his looks. How few and meager they had been for her hungry heart! A vision—a transcendently seductive vision of a Mexican girl arose before her. She writhed with a jealous pang. She wondered when he would come back. He had not said he would come back. She had been with him, had heard his voice and touched his hand. But some way he had seemed nearer to her off there in Mexico.

XXXV

The morning was full of sunlight and hope. Edna could see before her no denial—only the promise of excessive joy. She lay in bed awake, with bright eyes full of speculation. "He loves you, poor fool." If she could but get that conviction firmly fixed in her mind, what mattered about the rest? She felt she had been childish and unwise the night before in giving herself over to despondency. She recapitulated the motives which no doubt explained Robert's reserve. They were not insurmountable; they would not hold if he really loved her; they could not hold against her own passion, which he must come to realize in time. She pictured him going to his business that morning. She even saw how he was dressed; how he walked down one street, and turned the corner of another; saw him bending over his desk, talking to people who entered the office, going to his lunch, and perhaps watching for her on the street. He would come to her in the afternoon or evening, sit and roll his cigarette, talk a little, and go away as he had done the night before. But how delicious it would be to have him there with her! She would have no regrets, nor seek to penetrate his reserve if he still chose to wear it.

Edna ate her breakfast only half dressed. The maid brought her a delicious printed scrawl from Raoul, expressing his love, asking her to send him some bonbons, and telling her they had found that morning ten tiny white pigs all lying in a row beside Lidie's big white pig.

A letter also came from her husband, saying he hoped to be back early in March, and then they would get ready for that journey abroad which he had promised her so long, which he felt now fully able to afford; he felt able to travel as people should, without any thought of small economies—thanks to his recent speculations in Wall Street.

Much to her surprise she received a note from Arobin, written at midnight from the club. It was to say good morning to her, to hope she had slept well, to assure her of his devotion, which he trusted she in some faintest manner returned.

All these letters were pleasing to her. She answered the children in a cheerful frame of mind, promising them bonbons, and congratulating them upon their happy find of the little pigs.

She answered her husband with friendly evasiveness,—not with any fixed design to mislead him, only because all sense of reality had gone out of her life; she had abandoned herself to Fate, and awaited the consequences with indifference.

To Arobin's note she made no reply. She put it under Celestine's stove-lid.

Edna worked several hours with much spirit. She saw no one but a picture dealer, who asked her if it were true that she was going abroad to study in Paris.

She said possibly she might, and he negotiated with her for some Parisian studies to reach him in time for the holiday trade in December.

Robert did not come that day. She was keenly disappointed. He did not come the following day, nor the next. Each morning she awoke with hope, and each night she was a prey to despondency. She was tempted to seek him out. But far from yielding to the impulse, she avoided any occasion which might throw her in his way. She did not go to Mademoiselle Reisz's nor pass by Madame Lebrun's, as she might have done if he had still been in Mexico.

When Arobin, one night, urged her to drive with him, she went—out to the lake, on the Shell Road. His horses were full of mettle, and even a little unmanageable. She liked the rapid gait at which they spun along, and the quick, sharp sound of the horses' hoofs on the hard road. They did not stop anywhere to eat or to drink. Arobin was not needlessly imprudent. But they ate and they drank when they regained Edna's little dining-room—which was comparatively early in the evening.

It was late when he left her. It was getting to be more than a passing whim with Arobin to see her and be with her. He had detected the latent sensuality, which unfolded under his delicate sense of her nature's requirements like a torpid, torrid, sensitive blossom.

There was no despondency when she fell asleep that night; nor was there hope when she awoke in the morning.

XXXVI

There was a garden out in the suburbs; a small, leafy corner, with a few green tables under the orange trees. An old cat slept all day on the stone step in the sun, and an old *mulatresse*[80] slept her idle hours away in her chair at the open window, till some one happened to knock on one of the green tables. She had milk and cream cheese to sell, and bread and butter. There was no one who could make such excellent coffee or fry a chicken so golden brown as she.

The place was too modest to attract the attention of people of fashion, and so quiet as to have escaped the notice of those in search of pleasure and dissipation. Edna had discovered it accidentally one day when the high-board gate stood ajar. She caught sight of a little green table, blotched with the checkered sunlight that filtered through the quivering leaves overhead. Within she had found the slumbering *mulatresse*, the drowsy cat, and a glass of milk which reminded her of the milk she had tasted in Iberville.

She often stopped there during her perambulations; sometimes taking a book with her, and sitting an hour or two under the trees when she found the place deserted. Once or twice she took a quiet dinner there alone, having instructed Celestine beforehand to prepare no dinner at home. It was the last place in the city where she would have expected to meet any one she knew.

Still she was not astonished when, as she was partaking of a modest dinner late in the afternoon, looking into an open book, stroking the cat, which had made friends with her—she was not greatly astonished to see Robert come in at the tall garden gate.

"I am destined to see you only by accident," she said, shoving the cat off the chair beside her. He was surprised, ill at ease, almost embarrassed at meeting her thus so unexpectedly.

"Do you come here often?" he asked.

"I almost live here," she said.

"I used to drop in very often for a cup of Catiche's good coffee. This is the first time since I came back."

"She'll bring you a plate, and you will share my dinner. There's always enough for two—even three." Edna had intended to be indifferent and as reserved as he when she met him; she had reached the determination by a laborious train of reasoning, incident to one of her despondent moods. But her resolve melted when

---

[80] *mulatresse:* woman of black and white ancestry.

she saw him before her, seated there beside her in the little garden, as if a designing Providence had led him into her path.

"Why have you kept away from me, Robert?" she asked, closing the book that lay open upon the table.

"Why are you so personal, Mrs. Pontellier? Why do you force me to idiotic subterfuges?" he exclaimed with sudden warmth. "I suppose there's no use telling you I've been very busy, or that I've been sick, or that I've been to see you and not found you at home. Please let me off with any of these excuses."

"You are the embodiment of selfishness," she said. "You save yourself something—I don't know what—but there is some selfish motive, and in sparing yourself you never consider for a moment what I think, or how I feel your neglect and indifference. I suppose this is what you would call unwomanly; but I have got into a habit of expressing myself. It doesn't matter to me, and you may think me unwomanly if you like."

"No; I only think you cruel, as I said the other day. Maybe not intentionally cruel; but you seem to be forcing me into disclosures which can result in nothing; as if you would have me bare a wound for the pleasure of looking at it, without the intention or power of healing it."

"I'm spoiling your dinner, Robert; never mind what I say. You haven't eaten a morsel."

"I only came in for a cup of coffee." His sensitive face was all disfigured with excitement.

"Isn't this a delightful place?" she remarked. "I am so glad it has never actually been discovered. It is so quiet, so sweet, here. Do you notice there is scarcely a sound to be heard? It's so out of the way; and a good walk from the car. However, I don't mind walking. I always feel so sorry for women who don't like to walk; they miss so much—so many rare little glimpses of life; and we women learn so little of life on the whole.

"Catiche's coffee is always hot. I don't know how she manages it, here in open air. Celestine's coffee gets cold bringing it from the kitchen to the dining-room. Three lumps! How can you drink it so sweet? Take some of the cress with your chop; it's so biting and crisp. Then there's the advantage of being able to smoke with your coffee out here. Now, in the city—aren't you going to smoke?"

"After a while," he said, laying a cigar on the table.

"Who gave it to you?" she laughed.

"I bought it. I suppose I'm getting reckless; I bought a whole box." She was determined not to be personal again and make him uncomfortable.

The cat made friends with him, and climbed into his lap when he smoked his cigar. He stroked her silky fur, and talked a little about her. He looked at Edna's book, which he had read; and he told her the end, to save her the trouble of wading through it, he said.

Again he accompanied her back to her home; and it was after dusk when they reached the little "pigeon-house." She did not ask him to remain, which he was grateful for, as it permitted him to stay without the discomfort of blundering through an excuse which he had no intention of considering. He helped her to light the lamp; then she went into her room to take off her hat and to bathe her face and hands.

When she came back Robert was not examining the pictures and magazines as before; he sat off in the shadow, leaning his head back on the chair as if in a reverie. Edna lingered a moment beside the table, arranging the books there. Then she went across the room to where he sat. She bent over the arm of his chair and called his name.

"Robert," she said, "are you asleep?"

"No," he answered, looking up at her.

She leaned over and kissed him—a soft, cool, delicate kiss, whose voluptuous sting penetrated his whole being—then she moved away from him. He followed, and took her in his arms, just holding her close to him. She put her hand up to his face and pressed his cheek against her own. The action was full of love and tenderness. He sought her lips again. Then he drew her down upon the sofa beside him and held her hand in both of his.

"Now you know," he said, "now you know what I have been fighting against since last summer at Grand Isle; what drove me away and drove me back again."

"Why have you been fighting against it?" she asked. Her face glowed with soft lights.

"Why? Because you were not free; you were Léonce Pontellier's wife. I couldn't help loving you if you were ten times his wife; but so long as I went away from you and kept away I could help telling you so." She put her free hand up to his shoulder, and then against his cheek, rubbing it softly. He kissed her again. His face was warm and flushed.

"There in Mexico I was thinking of you all the time, and longing for you."

"But not writing to me," she interrupted.

"Something put into my head that you cared for me; and I lost my senses. I forgot everything but a wild dream of your some way becoming my wife."

"Your wife!"

"Religion, loyalty, everything would give way if only you cared."

"Then you must have forgotten that I was Léonce Pontellier's wife."

"Oh! I was demented, dreaming of wild, impossible things, recalling men who had set their wives free, we have heard of such things."

"Yes, we have heard of such things."

"I came back full of vague, mad intentions. And when I got here—"

"When you got here you never came near me!" She was still caressing his cheek.

"I realized what a cur I was to dream of such a thing, even if you had been willing."

She took his face between her hands and looked into it as if she would never withdraw her eyes more. She kissed him on the forehead, the eyes, the cheeks, and the lips.

"You have been a very, very foolish boy, wasting your time dreaming of impossible things when you speak of Mr. Pontellier setting me free! I am no longer one of Mr. Pontellier's possessions to dispose of or not. I give myself where I choose. If he were to say, 'Here, Robert, take her and be happy; she is yours,' I should laugh at you both."

His face grew a little white. "What do you mean?" he asked.

There was a knock at the door. Old Celestine came in to say that Madame Ratignolle's servant had come around the back way with a message that Madame had been taken sick and begged Mrs. Pontellier to go to her immediately.

"Yes, yes," said Edna, rising; "I promised. Tell her yes—to wait for me. I'll go back with her."

"Let me walk over with you," offered Robert.

"No," she said; "I will go with the servant." She went into her room to put on her hat, and when she came in again she sat once more upon the sofa beside him. He had not stirred. She put her arms about his neck.

"Good-by, my sweet Robert. Tell me good-by." He kissed her with a degree of passion which had not before entered into his caress, and strained her to him.

"I love you," she whispered, "only you; no one but you. It was you who woke me last summer out of a life-long, stupid dream. Oh! you have made me so unhappy with your indifference. Oh! I have suffered, suffered! Now you are here we shall love each other, my Robert. We shall be everything to each other. Nothing else in the world is of any consequence. I must go to my friend; but you will wait for me? No matter how late; you will wait for me, Robert?"

"Don't go; don't go! Oh! Edna, stay with me," he pleaded. "Why should you go? Stay with me, stay with me."

"I shall come back as soon as I can; I shall find you here." She buried her face in his neck, and said good-by again. Her seductive voice, together with his great love for her, had enthralled his senses, had deprived him of every impulse but the longing to hold her and keep her.

XXXVII

Edna looked in at the drug store. Monsieur Ratignolle was putting up a mixture himself, very carefully, dropping a red liquid into a tiny glass. He was grateful to Edna for having come; her presence would be a comfort to his wife. Madame Ratignolle's sister, who had always been with her at such trying times, had not been able to come up from the plantation, and Adèle had been inconsolable until Mrs. Pontellier so kindly promised to come to her. The nurse had been with them at night for the past week, as she lived a great distance away. And Dr. Mandelet had been coming and going all the afternoon. They were then looking for him any moment.

Edna hastened upstairs by a private stairway that led from the rear of the store to the apartment above. The children were all sleeping in a back room. Madame Ratignolle was in the salon, whither she had strayed in her suffering impatience. She sat on the sofa, clad in an ample white *peignoir*, holding a handkerchief tight in her hand with a nervous clutch. Her face was drawn and pinched, her sweet blue eyes haggard and unnatural. All her beautiful hair had been drawn back and plaited. It lay in a long braid on the sofa pillow, coiled like a golden serpent. The nurse, a comfortable looking *Griffe*[81] woman in white apron and cap, was urging her to return to her bedroom.

"There is no use, there is no use," she said at once to Edna. "We must get rid of Mandelet; he is getting too old and careless. He said he would be here at half-past seven; now it must be eight. See what time it is, Joséphine."

The woman was possessed of a cheerful nature, and refused to take any situation too seriously, especially a situation with which she was so familiar. She urged Madame to have courage and patience. But Madame only set her teeth hard into her under lip, and Edna saw the sweat gather in beads on her white forehead. After a moment or two she uttered a profound sigh and wiped her face with the handkerchief rolled in a ball. She appeared exhausted. The nurse gave her a fresh handkerchief, sprinkled with cologne water.

"This is too much!" she cried. "Mandelet ought to be killed! Where is Alphonse? Is it possible I am to be abandoned like this—neglected by every one?"

"Neglected, indeed!" exclaimed the nurse. Wasn't she there? And here was Mrs. Pontellier leaving, no doubt, a pleasant evening at home to devote to her? And wasn't Monsieur Ratignolle coming that very instant through the hall? And Joséphine was quite sure she had heard Doctor Mandelet's coupé.[82] Yes, there it was, down at the door.

Adèle consented to go back to her room. She sat on the edge of a little low couch next to her bed.

Doctor Mandelet paid no attention to Madame Ratignolle's upbraidings. He was accustomed to them at such times, and was too well convinced of her loyalty to doubt it.

He was glad to see Edna, and wanted her to go with him into the salon and entertain him. But Madame Ratignolle would not consent that Edna should leave her for an instant. Between agonizing moments, she chatted a little, and said it took her mind off her sufferings.

Edna began to feel uneasy. She was seized with a vague dread. Her own like experiences seemed far away, unreal, and only half remembered. She recalled faintly an ecstasy of pain, the heavy odor of chloroform, a stupor which had deadened sensation, and an awakening to find a little new life to which she had given being, added to the great unnumbered multitude of souls that come and go.

She began to wish she had not come; her presence was not necessary. She might have invented a pretext for staying away; she might even invent a pretext now for going. But Edna did not go. With an inward agony, with a flaming, outspoken revolt against the ways of Nature, she witnessed the scene of torture.

She was still stunned and speechless with emotion when later she leaned over her friend to kiss her and softly say good-by. Adèle, pressing her cheek, whispered in an exhausted voice: "Think of the children, Edna. Oh, think of the children! Remember them!"

---

[81] *Griffe*: mixed-race   [82] *coupé*: closed four-wheel carriage.

XXXVIII

Edna still felt dazed when she got outside in the open air. The Doctor's coupé had returned for him and stood before the *porte cochère*. She did not wish to enter the coupé, and told Doctor Mandelet she would walk; she was not afraid, and would go alone. He directed his carriage to meet him at Mrs. Pontellier's, and he started to walk home with her.

Up—away up, over the narrow street between the tall houses, the stars were blazing. The air was mild and caressing, but cool with the breath of spring and the night. They walked slowly, the Doctor with a heavy, measured tread and his hands behind him; Edna, in an absent-minded way, as she had walked one night at Grand Isle, as if her thoughts had gone ahead of her and she was striving to overtake them.

"You shouldn't have been there, Mrs. Pontellier," he said. "That was no place for you. Adèle is full of whims at such times. There were a dozen women she might have had with her, unimpressionable women. I felt that it was cruel, cruel. You shouldn't have gone."

"Oh, well!" she answered, indifferently. "I don't know that it matters after all. One has to think of the children some time or other; the sooner the better."

"When is Léonce coming back?"

"Quite soon. Some time in March."

"And you are going abroad?"

"Perhaps—no, I am not going. I'm not going to be forced into doing things. I don't want to go abroad. I want to be let alone. Nobody has any right—except children, perhaps—and even then, it seems to me—or it did seem—" She felt that her speech was voicing the incoherency of her thoughts, and stopped abruptly.

"The trouble is," sighed the Doctor, grasping her meaning intuitively, "that youth is given up to illusions. It seems to be a provision of Nature; a decoy to secure mothers for the race. And Nature takes no account of moral consequences, or arbitrary conditions which we create, and which we feel obliged to maintain at any cost."

"Yes," she said. "The years that are gone seem like dreams—if one might go on sleeping and dreaming—but to wake up and find—oh! well! perhaps it is better to wake up after all, even to suffer, rather than to remain a dupe to illusions all one's life."

"It seems to me, my dear child," said the Doctor at parting, holding her hand, "you seem to me to be in trouble. I am not going to ask for your confidence. I will only say that if ever you feel moved to give it to me, perhaps I might help you. I know I would understand, and I tell you there are not many who would—not many, my dear."

"Some way I don't feel moved to speak of things that trouble me. Don't think I am ungrateful or that I don't appreciate your sympathy. There are periods of despondency and suffering which take possession of me. But I don't want anything but my own way. That is wanting a good deal, of course, when you have to trample upon the lives, the hearts, the prejudices of others—but no matter—still, I shouldn't want to trample upon the little lives. Oh! I don't know what I'm saying, Doctor. Good night. Don't blame me for anything."

"Yes, I will blame you if you don't come and see me soon. We will talk of things you never have dreamt of talking about before. It will do us both good. I don't want you to blame yourself, whatever comes. Good night, my child."

She let herself in at the gate, but instead of entering she sat upon the step of the porch. The night was quiet and soothing. All the tearing emotion of the last few hours seemed to fall away from her like a somber, uncomfortable garment, which she had but to loosen to be rid of. She went back to that hour before Adèle had sent for her; and her senses kindled afresh in thinking of Robert's words, the pressure of his arms, and the feeling of his lips upon her own. She could picture at the moment no greater bliss on earth than possession of the beloved one. His expression of love had already given him to her in part. When she thought that he was there at hand, waiting for her, she grew numb with the intoxication of expectancy. It was so late; he would be asleep perhaps. She would awaken him with a kiss. She hoped he would be asleep that she might arouse him with her caresses.

Still, she remembered Adèle's voice whispering, "Think of the children; think of them." She meant to think of them; that determination had driven into her soul like a death wound—but not to-night. To-morrow would be time to think of everything.

Robert was not waiting for her in the little parlor. He was nowhere at hand. The house was empty. But he had scrawled on a piece of paper that lay in the lamplight:

"I love you. Good-by—because I love you."

Edna grew faint when she read the words. She went and sat on the sofa. Then she stretched herself out there, never uttering a sound. She did not sleep. She did not go to bed. The lamp sputtered and went out. She was still awake in the morning, when Celestine unlocked the kitchen door and came in to light the fire.

XXXIX

Victor, with hammer and nails and scraps of scantling, was patching a corner of one of the galleries. Mariequita sat near by, dangling her legs, watching him work, and handing him nails from the tool-box. The sun was beating down upon them. The girl covered her head with her apron folded into a square pad. They had been talking for an hour or more. She was never tired of hearing Victor describe the dinner at Mrs. Pontellier's. He exaggerated every detail, making it appear a veritable Lucullean feast.[83] The flowers were in tubs, he said. The champagne was quaffed from huge golden goblets. Venus rising from the foam[84] could have presented no more entrancing a spectacle than Mrs. Pontellier, blazing with beauty and diamonds at the head of the board, while the other women were all of them youthful houris[85] possessed of incomparable charms.

---

[83] *Lucullean:* i.e., splendid, in the manner of the feasts given by the Roman general Lucius Licinius Lucullus. [84] *Venus rising from the foam:* goddess of love, said to have sprung from the foam of the sea. [85] *houris:* beautiful virgins of the Koranic paradise.

She got it into her head that Victor was in love with Mrs. Pontellier, and he gave her evasive answers, framed so as to confirm her belief. She grew sullen and cried a little, threatening to go off and leave him to his fine ladies. There were a dozen men crazy about her at the *Chénière;* and since it was the fashion to be in love with married people, why, she could run away any time she liked to New Orleans with Célina's husband.

Célina's husband was a fool, a coward, and a pig, and to prove it to her, Victor intended to hammer his head into a jelly the next time he encountered him. This assurance was very consoling to Mariequita. She dried her eyes, and grew cheerful at the prospect.

They were still talking of the dinner and the allurements of city life when Mrs. Pontellier herself slipped around the corner of the house. The two youngsters stayed dumb with amazement before what they considered to be an apparition. But it was really she in flesh and blood, looking tired and a little travel-strained.

"I walked up from the wharf," she said, "and heard the hammering. I supposed it was you mending the porch. It's a good thing. I was always tripping over those loose planks last summer. How dreary and deserted everything looks!"

It took Victor some time to comprehend that she had come in Beaudelet's lugger, that she had come alone, and for no purpose but to rest.

"There's nothing fixed up yet, you see. I'll give you my room; it's the only place."

"Any corner will do," she assured him.

"And if you can stand Philomel's cooking," he went on, "though I might try to get her mother while you are here. Do you think she would come?" turning to Mariequita.

Mariequita thought that perhaps Philomel's mother might come for a few days, and money enough.

Beholding Mrs. Pontellier make her appearance, the girl had at once suspected a lovers' rendezvous. But Victor's astonishment was so genuine, and Mrs. Pontellier's indifference so apparent, that the disturbing notion did not lodge long in her brain. She contemplated with the greatest interest this woman who gave the most sumptuous dinners in America, and who had all the men in New Orleans at her feet.

"What time will you have dinner?" asked Edna. "I'm very hungry; but don't get anything extra."

"I'll have it ready in little or no time," he said, bustling and packing away his tools. "You may go to my room to brush up and rest yourself. Mariequita will show you."

"Thank you," said Edna. "But, do you know, I have a notion to go down to the beach and take a good wash and even a little swim, before dinner?"

"The water is too cold!" they both exclaimed. "Don't think of it."

"Well, I might go down and try—dip my toes in. Why, it seems to me the sun is hot enough to have warmed the very depths of the ocean. Could you get me a couple of towels? I'd better go right away, so as to be back in time. It would be a little too chilly if I waited till this afternoon."

Mariequita ran over to Victor's room, and returned with some towels, which she gave to Edna.

"I hope you have fish for dinner," said Edna, as she started to walk away; "but don't do anything extra if you haven't."

"Run and find Philomel's mother," Victor instructed the girl. "I'll go to the kitchen and see what I can do. By Gimminy! Women have no consideration! She might have sent me word."

Edna walked on down to the beach rather mechanically, not noticing anything special except that the sun was hot. She was not dwelling upon any particular train of thought. She had done all the thinking which was necessary after Robert went away, when she lay awake upon the sofa till morning.

She had said over and over to herself: "To-day it is Arobin; to-morrow it will be some one else. It makes no difference to me, it doesn't matter about Léonce Pontellier—but Raoul and Etienne!" She understood now clearly what she had meant long ago when she said to Adèle Ratignolle that she would give up the unessential, but she would never sacrifice herself for her children.

Despondency had come upon her there in the wakeful night, and had never lifted. There was no one thing in the world that she desired. There was no human being whom she wanted near her except Robert; and she even realized that the day would come when he, too, and the thought of him would melt out of her existence, leaving her alone. The children appeared before her like antagonists who had overcome her; who had overpowered and sought to drag her into the soul's slavery for the rest of her days. But she knew a way to elude them. She was not thinking of these things when she walked down to the beach.

The water of the Gulf stretched out before her, gleaming with the million tights of the sun. The voice of the sea is seductive, never ceasing, whispering, clamoring, murmuring, inviting the soul to wander in abysses of solitude. All along the white beach, up and down, there was no living thing in sight. A bird with a broken wing was beating the air above, reeling, fluttering, circling disabled down, down to the water.

Edna had found her old bathing suit still hanging, faded, upon its accustomed peg.

She put it on, leaving her clothing in the bath-house. But when she was there beside the sea, absolutely alone, she cast the unpleasant, pricking garments from her, and for the first time in her life she stood naked in the open air, at the mercy of the sun, the breeze that beat upon her, and the waves that invited her.

How strange and awful it seemed to stand naked under the sky! how delicious! She felt like some new-born creature, opening its eyes in a familiar world that it had never known.

The foamy wavelets curled up to her white feet, and coiled like serpents above her ankles. She walked out. The water was chill, but she walked on. The water was deep, but she lifted her white body and reached out for a long, sweeping stroke. The touch of the sea is sensuous, enfolding the body in its soft, close embrace.

She went on and on. She remembered the night she swam far out, and recalled the terror that seized her at the fear of being unable to regain the shore. She did not look back now, but went on and on, thinking of the blue-grass meadow that she had traversed when a little child, believing that it had no beginning and no end.

Her arms and legs were growing tired.

She thought of Léonce and the children. They were a part of her life. But they need not have thought that they could possess her, body and soul. How Mademoiselle Reisz would have laughed, perhaps sneered, if she knew! "And you call yourself an artist! What pretensions, Madame! The artist must possess the courageous soul that dares and defies."

Exhaustion was pressing upon and overpowering her.

"Good-by—because I love you." He did not know; he did not understand. He would never understand. Perhaps Doctor Mandelet would have understood if she had seen him—but it was too late; the shore was far behind her, and her strength was gone.

She looked into the distance, and the old terror flamed up for an instant, then sank again. Edna heard her father's voice and her sister Margaret's. She heard the barking of an old dog that was chained to the sycamore tree. The spurs of the cavalry officer clanged as he walked across the porch. There was the hum of bees, and the musky odor of pinks filled the air.

Journal Entry

Record your responses to the conclusion of *The Awakening*. To what extent does it conform to or conflict with your assessment of Edna?

Textual Considerations

1. Characterize Adèle Ratignolle. Consider, for example, her attitudes toward her husband and children as well as toward Edna and Robert. To what extent is she a foil to Edna?
2. Analyze Edna's relationship with Mademoiselle Reisz. Consider, for example, what Edna admired about her. What kind of role does Mademoiselle Reisz play in Edna's relationship with Robert? Is she also a foil to Edna? Explain.
3. Analyze Edna's role as wife and mother. Do her husband and children contribute to her sense of identity?
4. Characterize Edna's relationship with Arobin. To which of Edna's awakenings does he contribute?
5. The sea is a dominant symbol in the novel. Analyze the role of the sea in Edna's awakening. Consider also Chopin's use of color and bird imagery to enhance theme and characterization.

6. Characterize Edna's father. How has he contributed to her sense of herself? Explain the significance of his reappearance in the novel's conclusion.
7. Chopin's original title for her novel was *A Solitary Soul*. How is Edna portrayed as an outsider in the story? Consider also the many scenes in which she appears alone. Was Chopin's original title more appropriate? Explain.

Cultural Contexts

1. To what extent are Edna and Léonce victims of social conditioning? Does society still expect men and women to accept prescribed gender roles? How do these roles contribute to or detract from personal identity? Do women today have more options than were available to Edna?
2. Debate with your group the thesis that Edna was unable to find personal freedom because she was unwilling to make personal commitments. Consider, for example, her comment to Doctor Mandelet in chapter XXXVIII, "I don't want anything but my own way." Is freedom possible without responsibility? What does Edna's comment reveal about her?

Charlotte Perkins Gilman

The Yellow Wallpaper

It is very seldom that mere ordinary people like John and myself secure ancestral halls for the summer.

A colonial mansion, a hereditary estate, I would say a haunted house, and reach the height of romantic felicity—but that would be asking too much of fate!

Still I will proudly declare that there is something queer about it.

Else, why should it be let so cheaply? And why have stood so long untenanted?

John laughs at me, of course, but one expects that in marriage.

John is practical in the extreme. He has not patience with faith, an intense horror of superstition, and he scoffs openly at any talk of things not to be felt and seen and put down in figures.

John is a physician, and *perhaps*—(I would not say it to a living soul, of course, but this is dead paper and a great relief to my mind)—*perhaps* that is one reason I do not get well faster.

You see he does not believe I am sick!

And what can one do?

If a physician of high standing, and one's own husband, assures friends and relatives that there is really nothing the matter with one but temporary nervous depression—a slight hysterical tendency—what is one to do?

My brother is also a physician, and also of high standing, and he says the same thing.

So I take phosphates or phosphites—whichever it is, and tonics, and journeys, and air, and exercise, and am absolutely forbidden to "work" until I am well again.

Personally, I disagree with their ideas.

Personally, I believe that congenial work, with excitement and change, would do me good.

But what is one to do?

I did write for a while in spite of them, but it *does* exhaust me a good deal—having to be so sly about it, or else meet with heavy opposition.

I sometimes fancy that in my condition if I had less opposition and more society and stimulus—but John says the very worst thing I can do is to think about my condition, and I confess it always makes me feel bad.

So I will let it alone and talk about the house.

The most beautiful place! It is quite alone, standing well back from the road, quite three miles from the village. It makes me think of English places that you read about, for there are hedges and walls and gates that lock, and lots of separate little houses for the gardeners and people.

There is a *delicious* garden! I never saw such a garden—large and shady, full of box-bordered paths, and lined with long grape-covered arbors with seats under them.

There were greenhouses, too, but they are all broken now.

There was some legal trouble, I believe, something about the heirs and coheirs; anyhow, the place has been empty for years.

That spoils my ghostliness, I am afraid, but I don't care—there is something strange about the house—I can feel it.

I even said so to John one moonlight evening, but he said what I felt was a *draught,* and shut the window.

I get unreasonably angry with John sometimes. I'm sure I never used to be so sensitive. I think it is due to this nervous condition.

But John says if I feel so, I shall neglect proper self-control; so I take pains to control myself—before him, at least, and that makes me very tired.

I don't like our room a bit. I wanted one downstairs that opened on the piazza and had roses all over the window, and such pretty old-fashioned chintz hangings! but John would not hear of it.

He said there was only one window and not room for two beds, and no near room for him if he took another.

He is very careful and loving, and hardly lets me stir without special direction.

I have a schedule prescription for each hour in the day; he takes all care from me, and so I feel basely ungrateful not to value it more.

He said we came here solely on my account, that I was to have perfect rest and all the air I could get. "Your exercise depends on your strength, my dear," said he, "and your food somewhat on your appetite, but air you can absorb all the time." So we took the nursery at the top of the house.

It is a big, airy room, the whole floor nearly, with windows that look all ways, and air and sunshine galore. It was nursery first and then playroom and gymnasium, I should judge; for the windows are barred for little children, and there are rings and things in the walls.

The paint and paper look as if a boys' school had used it. It is stripped off—the paper—in great patches all around the head of my bed, about as far as I can reach, and in a great place on the other side of the room low down. I never saw a worse paper in my life.

One of those sprawling flamboyant patterns committing every artistic sin.

It is dull enough to confuse the eye in following, pronounced enough to constantly irritate and provoke study, and when you follow the lame uncertain curves for a little distance they suddenly commit suicide—plunge off at outrageous angles, destroy themselves in unheard of contradictions.

The color is repellent, almost revolting; a smoldering unclean yellow, strangely faded by the slow-turning sunlight.

It is a dull yet lurid orange in some places, a sickly sulphur tint in others.

No wonder the children hated it! I should hate it myself if I had to live in this room long.

There comes John, and I must put this away,—he hates to have me write a word.

We have been here two weeks, and I haven't felt like writing before, since that first day.

I am sitting by the window now, up in this atrocioius nursery, and there is nothing to hinder my writing as much as I please, save lack of strength.

John is away all day, and even some nights when his cases are serious.

I am glad my case is not serious!

But these nervous troubles are dreadfully depressing.

John does not know how much I really suffer. He knows there is no *reason* to suffer, and that satisfies him.

Of course it is only nervousness. It does weigh on me so not to do my duty in any way!

I meant to be such a help to John, such a real rest and comfort, and here I am a comparative burden already!

Nobody would believe what an effort it is to do what little I am able,—to dress and entertain, and order things.

It is fortunate Mary is so good with the baby. Such a dear baby!

And yet I *cannot* be with him, it makes me so nervous.

I suppose John never was nervous in his life. He laughs at me so about this wall-paper!

At first he meant to repaper the room, but afterwards he said that I was letting it get the better of me, and that nothing was worse for a nervous patient than to give way to such fancies.

He said that after the wall-paper was changed it would be the heavy bedstead, and then the barred windows, and then that gate at the head of the stairs, and so on.

"You know the place is doing you good," he said, "and really, dear, I don't care to renovate the house just for a three months' rental."

"Then do let us go downstairs," I said, "there are such pretty rooms there."

Then he took me in his arms and called me a blessed little goose, and said he would go down to the cellar, if I wished, and have it whitewashed into the bargain.

But he is right enough about the beds and windows and things.

It is an airy and comfortable room as any one need wish, and, of course, I would not be so silly as to make him uncomfortable just for a whim.

I'm really getting quite fond of the big room, all but that horrid paper.

Out of one window I can see the garden, those mysterious deepshaded arbors, the riotous old-fashioned flowers, and bushes and gnarly trees.

Out of another I get a lovely view of the bay and a little private wharf belonging to the estate. There is a beautiful shaded lane that runs down there from the house. I always fancy I see people walking in these numerous paths and arbors, but John has cautioned me not to give way to fancy in the least. He says that with my imaginative power and habit of story-making, a nervous weakness like mine is sure to lead to all manner of excited fancies, and that I ought to use my will and good sense to check the tendency. So I try.

I think sometimes that if I were only well enough to write a little it would relieve the press of ideas and rest me.

But I find I get pretty tired when I try.

It is so discouraging not to have any advice and companionship about my work. When I get really well, John says we will ask Cousin Henry and Julia down for a long visit; but he says he would as soon put fireworks in my pillow-case as to let me have those stimulating people about now.

I wish I could get well faster.

But I must not think about that. This paper looks to me as if it *knew* what a vicious influence it had!

There is a recurrent spot where the pattern lolls like a broken neck and two bulbous eyes stare at you upside down.

I get positively angry with the impertinence of it and the everlastingness. Up and down and sideways they crawl, and those absurd, unblinking eyes are everywhere. There is one place where two breadths didn't match, and the eyes go all up and down the line, one a little higher than the other.

I never saw so much expression in an inanimate thing before, and we all know how much expression they have! I used to lie awake as a child and get more entertainment and terror out of blank walls and plain furniture than most children could find in a toy-store.

I remember what a kindly wink the knobs of our big, old bureau used to have, and there was one chair that always seemed like a strong friend.

I used to feel that if any of the other things looked too fierce I could always hop into that chair and be safe.

The furniture in this room is no worse than inharmonious, however, for we had to bring it all from downstairs. I suppose when this was used as a playroom they had to take the nursery things out, and no wonder! I never saw such ravages as the children have made here.

The wall-paper, as I said before, is torn off in spots, and it sticketh closer than a brother—they must have had perseverance as well as hatred.

Then the floor is scratched and gouged and splintered, the plaster itself is dug out here and there, and this great heavy bed which is all we found in the room, looks as if it had been through the wars.

But I don't mind it a bit—only the paper.

There comes John's sister. Such a dear girl as she is, and so careful of me! I must not let her find me writing.

She is a perfect and enthusiastic housekeeper, and hopes for no better profession. I verily believe she thinks it is the writing which made me sick!

But I can write when she is out, and see her a long way off from these windows.

There is one that commands the road, a lovely shaded winding road, and one that just looks off over the country. A lovely country, too, full of great elms and velvet meadows.

This wall-paper has a kind of sub-pattern in a different shade, a particularly irritating one, for you can only see it in certain lights, and not clearly then.

But in the places where it isn't faded and where the sun is just so—I can see a strange, provoking, formless sort of figure, that seems to skulk about behind that silly and conspicuous front design.

There's sister on the stairs!

Well, the Fourth of July is over! The people are all gone and I am tired out. John thought it might do me good to see a little company, so we just had mother and Nellie and the children down for a week.

Of course I didn't do a thing. Jennie sees to everything now.

But it tired me all the same.

John says if I don't pick up faster he shall send me to Weir Mitchell in the fall.

But I don't want to go there at all. I had a friend who was in his hands once, and she says he is just like John and my brother, only more so!

Besides, it is such an undertaking to go so far.

I don't feel as if it was worth while to turn my hand over for anything, and I'm getting dreadfully fretful and querulous.

I cry at nothing, and cry most of the time.

Of course I don't when John is here, or anybody else, but when I am alone.

And I am alone a good deal just now. John is kept in town very often by serious cases, and Jennie is good and lets me alone when I want her to.

So I walk a little in the garden or down that lovely lane, sit on the porch under the roses, and lie down up here a good deal.

I'm getting really fond of the room in spite of the wall-paper. Perhaps *because* of the wall-paper.

It dwells in my mind so!

I lie here on this great immovable bed—it is nailed down, I believe—and follow that pattern about by the hour. It is as good as gymnastics, I assure you. I start, we'll say, at the bottom, down in the corner over there where it has not been touched, and I determine for the thousandth time that I *will* follow that pointless pattern to some sort of a conclusion.

I know a little of the principle of design, and I know this thing was not arranged on any laws of radiation, or alternation, or repetition, or symmetry, or anything else that I ever heard of.

It is repeated, of course, by the breadths, but not otherwise.

Looked at in one way each breadth stands alone, the bloated curves and flourishes—a kind of "debased Romanesque" with *delirium tremens*—go waddling up and down in isolated columns of fatuity.

But, on the other hand, they connect diagonally, and the sprawling outlines run off in great slanting waves of optic horror, like a lot of wallowing seaweeds in full chase.

The whole thing goes horizontally, too, at least it seems so, and I exhaust myself in trying to distinguish the order of its going in that direction.

They have used a horizontal breadth for a frieze, and that adds wonderfully to the confusion.

There is one end of the room where it is almost intact, and there, when the crosslights fade and the low sun shines directly upon it, I can almost fancy radiation after all,—the interminable grotesques seem to form around a common centre and rush off in headlong plunges of equal distraction.

It makes me tired to follow it. I will take a nap I guess.

I don't know why I should write this.

I don't want to.

I don't feel able.

And I know John would think it absurd. But I *must* say what I feel and think in some way—it is such a relief!

But the effort is getting to be greater than the relief.

Half the time now I am awfully lazy, and lie down ever so much.

John says I mustn't lose my strength, and has me take cod liver oil and lots of tonics and things, to say nothing of ale and wine and rare meat.

Dear John! He loves me very dearly, and hates to have me sick. I tried to have a real earnest reasonable talk with him the other day, and tell him how I wish he would let me go and make a visit to Cousin Henry and Julia.

But he said I wasn't able to go, nor able to stand it after I got there; and I did not make out a very good case for myself, for I was crying before I had finished.

It is getting to be a great effort for me to think straight. Just this nervous weakness I suppose.

And dear John gathered me up in his arms, and just carried me upstairs and laid me on the bed, and sat by me and read to me till it tired my head.

He said I was his darling and his comfort and all he had, and that I must take care of myself for his sake, and keep well.

He says no one but myself can help me out of it, that I must use my will and self-control and not let any silly fancies run away with me.

There's one comfort, the baby is well and happy, and does not have to occupy this nursery with the horrid wall-paper.

If we had not used it, that blessed child would have! What a fortunate escape! Why, I wouldn't have a child of mine, an impressionable little thing, live in such a room for worlds.

I never thought of it before, but it is lucky that John kept me here after all, I can, stand it so much easier than a baby, you see.

Of course I never mention it to them any more—I am too wise,—but I keep watch of it all the same.

There are things in that paper that nobody knows but me, or ever will.

Behind that outside pattern the dim shapes get clearer every day.

It is always the same shape, only very numerous.

And it is like a woman stooping down and creeping about behind that pattern. I don't like it a bit. I wonder—I begin to think—I wish John would take me away from here!

It is so hard to talk with John about my case, because he is so wise, and because he loves me so.

But I tried it last night.

It was moonlight. The moon shines in all around just as the sun does.

I hate to see it sometimes, it creeps so slowly, and always comes in by one window or another.

John was asleep and I hated to waken him, so I kept still and watched the moonlight on that undulating wall-paper till I felt creepy.

The faint figure behind seemed to shake the pattern, just as if she wanted to get out.

I got up softly and went to feel and see if the paper *did* move, and when I came back John was awake.

"What is it, little girl?" he said. "Don't go walking about like that—you'll get cold."

I thought it was a good time to talk, so I told him that I really was not gaining here, and that I wished he would take me away.

"Why darling!" said he, "our lease will be up in three weeks, and I can't see how to leave before.

"The repairs are not done at home, and I cannot possibly leave town just now. Of course if you were in any danger, I could and would, but you really are better, dear, whether you can see it or not. I am a doctor, dear, and I know. You are gaining flesh and color, your appetite is better, I feel really much easier about you."

"I don't weigh a bit more," said I, "nor as much; and my appetite may be better in the evening when you are here, but it is worse in the morning when you are away!"

"Bless her little heart!" said he with a big hug, "she shall be as sick as she pleases! But now let's improve the shining hours by going to sleep, and talk about it in the morning!"

"And you won't go away?" I asked gloomily.

"Why, how can I, dear? It is only three weeks more and then we will take a nice little trip of a few days while Jennie is getting the house ready. Really dear you are better!"

"Better in body perhaps—" I began, and stopped short, for he sat up straight and looked at me with such a stern, reproachful look that I could not say another word.

"My darling," said he, "I beg of you, for my sake and for our child's sake, as well as for your own, that you will never for one instant let that idea enter your mind! There is nothing so dangerous, so fascinating, to a temperament like yours. It is a false and foolish fancy. Can you not trust me as a physician when I tell you so?"

So of course I said no more on that score, and we went to sleep before long. He thought I was asleep first, but I wasn't, and lay there for hours trying to decide whether that front pattern and the back pattern really did move together or separately.

On a pattern like this, by daylight, there is a lack of sequence, a defiance of law, that is a constant irritant to a normal mind.

The color is hideous enough, and unreliable enough, and infuriating enough, but the pattern is torturing.

You think you have mastered it, but just as you get well underway in following, it turns a back-somersault and there you are. It slaps you in the face, knocks you down, and tramples upon you. It is like a bad dream.

The outside pattern is a florid arabesque, reminding one of a fungus. If you can imagine a toadstool in joints, an interminable string of toadstools, budding and sprouting in endless convolutions—why, that is something like it.

That is, sometimes!

There is one marked peculiarity about this paper, a thing nobody seems to notice but myself, and that is that it changes as the light changes.

When the sun shoots in through the east window—I always watch for that first long, straight ray—it changes so quickly that I never can quite believe it.

That is why I watch it always.

By moonlight—the moon shines in all night when there is a moon—I wouldn't know it was the same paper.

At night in any kind of light, in twilight, candle light, lamplight, and worst of all by moonlight, it becomes bars! The outside pattern I mean, and the woman behind it is as plain as can be.

I didn't realize for a long time what the thing was that showed behind, that dim sub-pattern, but now I am quite sure it is a woman.

By daylight she is subdued, quiet. I fancy, it is the pattern that keeps her so still. It is so puzzling. It keeps me quiet by the hour.

I lie down ever so much now. John says it is good for me, and to sleep all I can.

Indeed he started the habit by making me lie down for an hour after each meal.

It is a very bad habit I am convinced, for you see I don't sleep.

And that cultivates deceit, for I don't tell them I'm awake—O no!

The fact is I am getting a little afraid of John.

He seems very queer sometimes, and even Jennie has an inexplicable look.

It strikes me occasionally, just as a scientific hypothesis,—that perhaps it is the paper!

I have watched John when he did not know I was looking, and come into the room suddenly on the most innocent excuses, and I've caught him several times *looking at the paper!* And Jennie too. I caught Jennie with her hand on it once.

She didn't know I was in the room, and when I asked her in a quiet, a very quiet voice, with the most restrained manner possible, what she was doing with the paper—she turned around as if she had been caught stealing, and looked quite angry—asked me why I should frighten her so!

Then she said that the paper stained everything it touched, that she had found yellow smooches on all my clothes and John's, and she wished we would be more careful!

Did not that sound innocent? But I know she was studying that pattern, and I am determined that nobody shall find it out but myself!

Life is very much more exciting now than it used to be. You see I have something more to expect, to look forward to, to watch. I really do eat better, and am more quiet than I was.

John is so pleased to see me improve! He laughed a little the other day, and said I seemed to be flourishing in spite of my wall-paper.

I turned it off with a laugh. I had no intention of telling him it was *because* of the wall-paper—he would make fun of me. He might even want to take me away.

I don't want to leave now until I have found it out. There is a week more, and I think that will be enough.

I'm feeling ever so much better! I don't sleep much at night, for it is so interesting to watch developments; but I sleep a good deal in the daytime.

In the daytime it is tiresome and perplexing.

There are always new shoots on the fungus, and new shades of yellow all over it. I cannot keep count of them, though I have tried conscientiously.

It is the strangest yellow, that wall-paper! It makes me think of all the yellow things I ever saw—not beautiful ones like buttercups, but old foul, bad yellow things.

But there is something else about that paper—the smell! I noticed it the moment we came into the room, but with so much air and sun it was not bad. Now we have had a week of fog and rain, and whether the windows are open or not, the smell is here.

It creeps all over the house.

I find it hovering in the dining-room, skulking in the parlor, hiding in the hall, lying in wait for me on the stairs.

It gets into my hair.

Even when I go to ride, if I turn my head suddenly and surprise it—there is that smell!

Such a peculiar odor, too! I have spent hours in trying to analyze it, to find what it smelled like.

It is not bad—at first, and very gentle, but quite the subtlest, most enduring odor I ever met.

In this damp weather it is awful, I wake up in the night and find it hanging over me.

It used to disturb me at first. I thought seriously of burning the house—to reach the smell.

But now I am used to it. The only thing I can think of that it is like is the *color* of the paper! A yellow smell.

There is a very funny mark on this wall, low down, near the mopboard. A streak that runs round the room. It goes behind every piece of furniture, except the bed, a long, straight, even *smooch,* as if it had been rubbed over and over.

I wonder how it was done and who did it, and what they did it for. Round and round and round—round and round and round—it makes me dizzy!

I really have discovered something at last.

Through watching so much at night, when it changes so, I have finally found out.

The front pattern *does* move—and no wonder! The woman behind shakes it!

Sometimes I think there are a great many women behind, and sometimes only one, and she crawls around fast, and her crawling shakes it all over.

Then in the very bright spots she keeps still, and in the very shady spots she just takes hold of the bars and shakes them hard.

And she is all the time trying to climb through. But nobody could climb through that pattern—it strangles so; I think that is why it has so many heads.

They get through, and then the pattern strangles them off and turns them upside down, and makes their eyes white!

If those heads were covered or taken off it would not be half so bad.

I think that woman gets out in the daytime!

And I'll tell you why—privately—I've seen her!

I can see her out of every one of my windows!

It is the same woman, I know, for she is always creeping, and most women do not creep by daylight.

I see her on that long road under the trees, creeping along, and when a carriage comes she hides under the blackberry vines.

I don't blame her a bit. It must be very humiliating to be caught creeping by daylight!

I always lock the door when I creep by daylight. I can't do it at night, for I know John would suspect something at once.

And John is so queer now, that I don't want to irritate him. I wish he would take another room! Besides, I don't want anybody to get that woman out at night but myself.

I often wonder if I could see her out of all the windows at once.

But, turn as fast as I can, I can only see out of one at one time.

And though I always see her, she *may* be able to creep faster than I can turn!

I have watched her sometimes away off in the open country, creeping as fast as a cloud shadow in a high wind.

If only that top pattern could be gotten off from the under one! I mean to try it, little by little.

I have found out another funny thing, but I shan't tell it this time! It does not do to trust people too much.

There are only two more days to get this paper off, and I believe John is beginning to notice. I don't like the look in his eyes.

And I heard him ask Jennie a lot of professional questions about me. She had a very good report to give.

She said I slept a good deal in the daytime.

John knows I don't sleep very well at night, for all I'm so quiet!

He asked me all sorts of questions, too, and pretended to be very loving and kind.

As if I couldn't see through him!

Still, I don't wonder he acts so, sleeping under this paper for three months.

It only interests me, but I feel sure John and Jennie are secretly affected by it.

Hurrah! This is the last day, but it is enough. John to stay in town over night, and won't be out until this evening.

Jennie wanted to sleep with me—the sly thing! but I told her I should undoubtedly rest better for a night all alone.

That was clever, for really I wasn't alone a bit! As soon as it was moonlight and that poor thing began to crawl and shake the pattern, I got up and ran to help her.

I pulled and she shook, I shook and she pulled, and before morning we had peeled off yards of that paper.

A strip about as high as my head and half around the room.

And then when the sun came and that awful pattern began to laugh at me, I declared I would finish it to-day!

We go away to-morrow, and they are moving all my furniture down again to leave things as they were before.

Jennie looked at the wall in amazement, but I told her merrily that I did it out of pure spite at the vicious thing.

She laughed and said she wouldn't mind doing it herself, but I must not get tired.

How she betrayed herself that time!

But I am here, and no person touches this paper but me,—not *alive!*

She tried to get me out of the room—it was too patent! But I said it was so quiet and empty and clean now that I believed I would lie down again and sleep all I could; and not to wake me even for dinner—I would call when I woke.

So now she is gone, and the servants are gone, and the things are gone, and there is nothing left but that great bedstead nailed down, with the canvas mattress we found on it.

We shall sleep downstairs to-night, and take the boat home to-morrow.

I quite enjoy the room, now it is bare again.

How those children did tear about here!

This bedstead is fairly gnawed!

But I must get to work.

I have locked the door and thrown the key down into the front path.

I don't want to go out, and I don't want to have anybody come in, till John comes.

I want to astonish him.

I've got a rope up here that even Jennie did not find. If that woman does get out, and tries to get away, I can tie her!

But I forgot I could not reach far without anything to stand on!

This bed will *not* move!

I tried to lift and push it until I was lame, and then I got so angry I bit off a little piece at one corner—but it hurt my teeth.

Then I peeled off all the paper I could reach standing on the floor. It sticks horribly and the pattern just enjoys it! All those strangled heads and bulbous eyes and waddling fungus growths just shriek with derision!

I am getting angry enough to do something desperate. To jump out of the window would be admirable exercise, but the bars are too strong even to try.

Besides I wouldn't do it. Of course not. I know well enough that a step like that is improper and might be misconstrued.

I don't like to *look* out of the windows even—there are so many of those creeping women, and they creep so fast.

I wonder if they all come out of that wall-paper as I did?

But I am securely fastened now by my well-hidden rope—you don't get *me* out in the road there!

I suppose I shall have to get back behind the pattern when it comes night, and that is hard!

It is so pleasant to be out in this great room and creep around as I please!

I don't want to go outside. I won't, even if Jennie asks me to.

For outside you have to creep on the ground, and everything is green instead of yellow.

But here I can creep smoothly on the floor, and my shoulder just fits in that long smooch around the wall, so I cannot lose my way.

Why there's John at the door!

It is no use, young man, you can't open it!

How he does call and pound!

Now he's crying for an axe.

It would be a shame to break down that beautiful door!

"John dear!" said I in the gentlest voice, "the key is down by the front steps, under a plantain leaf!"

That silenced him for a few moments.

Then he said—very quietly indeed, "Open the door, my darling!"

"I can't," said I. "The key is down by the front door under a plantain leaf!"

And then I said it again, several times, very gently and slowly, and said it so often that he had to go and see, and he got it of course, and came in. He stopped short by the door.

"What is the matter?" he cried. "For God's sake, what are you doing?"

I kept on creeping just the same, but I looked at him over my shoulder.

"I've got out at last," said I, "in spite of you and Jane. And I've pulled off most of the paper, so you can't put me back!"

Now why should that man have fainted? But he did, and right across my path by the wall, so that I had to creep over him every time!

Journal Entry

Analyze the role of the speaker's journal in "The Yellow Wallpaper."

Textual Considerations

1. Characterize the narrator's husband. To what extent is he responsible for his wife's emotional state?
2. Analyze the effectiveness of Gilman's use of symbolism in the story. Consider, for example, the physical description of the narrator's bedroom as well as the role of the wallpaper as the dominant symbol of the text.
3. Explain the narrator's statement "I've got out at last" in the next-to-last paragraph. To what extent is this true? Is there any sense in which madness can be liberating? Explain.

Cultural Contexts

1. Discuss with your group the reasons for the current popularity of "The Yellow Wallpaper."
2. The rest cure prescribed by the narrator's doctor and physician-husband was standard in Victorian medical theory for what is now known as postpartum depression. Discuss with your group how this "cure" might affect emotional depression and sense of identity.

Jean Toomer

Karintha

Her skin is like dusk on the eastern horizon,
O cant you see it, O cant you see it,
Her skin is like dusk on the eastern horizon
. . . When the sun goes down.

Men had always wanted her, this Karintha, even as a child, Karintha carrying beauty, perfect as dusk when the sun goes down. Old men rode her hobby-horse upon their knees. Young men danced with her at frolics when they should have been dancing with their grown-up girls. God grant us youth, secretly prayed the old men. The young fellows counted the time to pass before she would be old enough to mate with them. This interest of the male, who wishes to ripen a growing thing too soon, could mean no good to her.

Karintha, at twelve, was a wild flash that told the other folks just what it was to live. At sunset, when there was no wind, and the pinesmoke from over by the sawmill hugged the earth, and you couldnt see more than a few feet in front, her sudden darting past you was a bit of vivid color, like a black bird that flashes in light. With the other children one could hear, some distance off, their feet flopping in the two-inch dust. Karintha's running was a whir. It had the sound of the red dust that sometimes makes a spiral in the road. At dusk, during the hush just after the sawmill had closed down, and before any of the women had started their supper-getting-ready songs, her voice, high-pitched, shrill, would put one's ears to itching. But no one ever thought to make her stop because of it. She stoned the cows, and beat her dog, and fought the other children . . . Even the preacher, who caught her at mischief, told himself that she was as innocently lovely as a November cotton flower. Already, rumors were out about her. Homes in Georgia are most often built on the two-room plan. In one, you cook and eat, in the other you sleep, and there love goes on. Karintha had seen or heard, perhaps she had felt her parents loving. One could but imitate one's parents, for to follow them was the way of God. She played "home" with a small boy who was not afraid to do her bidding. That started the whole thing. Old men could no longer ride her hobby-horse upon their knees. But young men counted faster.

Her skin is like dusk,
O cant you see it,
Her skin is like dusk,
When the sun goes down.

Karintha is a woman. She who carries beauty, perfect as dusk when the sun goes down. She has been married many times. Old men remind her that a few years back they rode her hobby-horse upon their knees. Karintha smiles, and indulges them when she is in the mood for it. She has contempt for them. Karintha is a woman. Young men run stills to make her money. Young men go to the big cities and run on the road. Young men go away to college. They all want to bring her money. These are the young men who thought that all they had to do was to count time. But Karintha is a woman, and she has had a child. A child fell out of her womb onto a bed of pine-needles in the forest. Pine-needles are smooth and sweet. They are elastic to the feet of rabbits . . . A sawmill was nearby. Its pyramidal sawdust pile smouldered. It is a year before one completely burns. Meanwhile, the smoke curls up and hangs in odd wraiths about the trees, curls up, and spreads itself out over the valley . . . Weeks after Karintha returned home the smoke was so heavy you tasted it in water. Some one made a song:

> Smoke is on the hills. Rise up.
> Smoke is on the hills, O rise
> And take my soul to Jesus.

Karintha is a woman. Men do not know that the soul of her was a growing thing ripened too soon. They will bring their money; they will die not having found it out . . . Karintha at twenty, carrying beauty, perfect as dusk when the sun goes down. Karintha . . .

> Her skin is like dusk on the eastern horizon,
> O cant you see it, O cant you see it,
> Her skin is like dusk on the eastern horizon
> . . . When the sun goes down.

Goes down . . .

Journal Entry

Speculate on the reasons for Karintha's sense of solitude.

Textual Considerations

1. Toomer's poetic prose is rich in stylistic devices. Analyze the effects of his use of repetition, visual imagery, and parallel structure to portray Karintha's character and sense of identity.
2. Another stylistic feature of "Karintha" is Toomer's technique of alternating poetry with prose. Consider what the poetic passages reveal about Karintha. What do they otherwise contribute to the story?
3. How different would the story be in another setting? What aspects evoke a distinctly southern ambience?

Cultural Contexts

1. Analyze with your group the causes and effects of Karintha's sexual and personal alienation. Consider, for example, the fate of her child.

2. Working with your group, try to reach a consensus about the kinds of threats that menace Karintha. Do not overlook Toomer's uses of nature imagery in phrases such as "lovely as a November cotton flower" and "perfect as dusk when the sun goes down." Compare and contrast your group's responses to Karintha. To what extent do you each blame her or empathize with her?

Alifa Rifaat

Another Evening at the Club

In a state of tension, she awaited the return of her husband. At a loss to predict what would happen between them, she moved herself back and forth in the rocking chair on the wide wooden veranda that ran along the bank and occupied part of the river itself, its supports being fixed in the river bed, while around it grew grasses and reeds. As though to banish her apprehension, she passed her fingers across her hair. The specters of the eucalyptus trees ranged along the garden fence rocked before her gaze, with white egrets slumbering on their high branches like huge white flowers among the thin leaves.

The crescent moon rose from behind the eastern mountains and the peaks of the gently stirring waves glistened in its feeble rays, intermingled with threads of light leaking from the houses of Manfalout scattered along the opposite bank. The colored bulbs fixed to the trees in the garden of the club at the far end of the town stood out against the surrounding darkness. Somewhere over there her husband now sat, most likely engrossed in a game of chess.

It was only a few years ago that she had first laid eyes on him at her father's house, meeting his gaze that weighed up her beauty and priced it before offering the dowry. She had noted his eyes ranging over her as she presented him with the coffee in the Japanese cups that were kept safely locked away in the cupboard for important guests. Her mother had herself laid them out on the silver-plated tray with its elaborately embroidered spread. When the two men had taken their coffee, her father had looked up at her with a smile and had told her to sit down, and she had seated herself on the sofa facing them, drawing the end of her dress over her knees and looking through lowered lids at the man who might choose her as his wife. She had been glad to see that he was tall, well-built and clean-shaven except for a thin greying moustache. In particular she noticed the well-cut coat of English tweed and the silk shirt with gold links. She had felt herself blushing as she saw him returning her gaze. Then the man turned to her father and took out a gold case and offered him a cigarette.

"You really shouldn't, my dear sir," said her father, patting his chest with his left hand and extracting a cigarette with trembling fingers. Before he could bring out his box of matches Abboud Bey had produced his lighter.

"No, after you, my dear sir," said her father in embarrassment. Mingled with her sense of excitement at this man who gave out such an air of worldly self-confidence was a guilty shame at her father's inadequacy.

After lighting her father's cigarette Abboud Bey sat back, crossing his legs, and took out a cigarette for himself. He tapped it against the case before putting it in the corner of his mouth and lighting it, then blew out circles of smoke that followed each other across the room.

"It's a great honor for us, my son," said her father, smiling first at Abboud Bey, then at his daughter, at which Abboud Bey looked across at her and asked:

"And the beautiful little girl's still at secondary school?"

She lowered her head modestly and her father had answered:

"As from today she'll be staying at home in readiness for your happy life together. Allah permitting," and at a glance from her father she had hurried off to join her mother in the kitchen.

"You're a lucky girl," her mother had told her. "He's a real find. Any girl would be happy to have him. He's an Inspector of Irrigation though he's not yet forty. He earns a big salary and gets a fully furnished government house wherever he's posted, which will save us the expense of setting up a house—and I don't have to tell you what our situation is—and that's beside the house he owns in Alexandria where you'll be spending your holidays."

Samia had wondered to herself how such a splendid suitor had found his way to her door. Who had told him that Mr. Mahmoud Barakat, a mere clerk at the Court of Appeal, had a beautiful daughter of good reputation?

The days were then taken up with going the rounds of Cairo's shops and choosing clothes for the new grand life she would be living. This was made possible by her father borrowing on the security of his government pension. Abboud Bey, on his part, never visited her without bringing a present. For her birthday, just before they were married, he bought her an emerald ring that came in a plush box bearing the name of a well-known jeweler in Kasr el-Nil Street. On her wedding night, as he put a diamond bracelet round her wrist, he had reminded her that she was marrying someone with a brilliant career in front of him and that one of the most important things in life was the opinion of others, particularly one's equals and seniors. Though she was still only a young girl she must try to act with suitable dignity.

"Tell people you're from the well-known Barakat family and that your father was a judge," and he went up to her and gently patted her cheeks in a fatherly, reassuring gesture that he was often to repeat during their times together.

Then, yesterday evening, she had returned from the club somewhat light-headed from the bottle of beer she had been required to drink on the occasion of someone's birthday. Her husband, noting the state she was in, hurriedly took her back home. She had undressed and put on her nightgown, leaving her jewelry on the dressing table, and was fast asleep seconds after getting into bed. The following morning, fully recovered, she slept late, then rang the bell as usual and had breakfast brought to her. It was only as she was putting her jewelry away in the wooden and mother-of-pearl box that she realized that her emerald ring was missing.

Could it have dropped from her finger at the club? In the car on the way back? No, she distinctly remembered it last thing at night, remembered the usual difficulty she had in getting it off her finger. She stripped the bed of its sheets, turned over the mattress, looked inside the pillow cases, crawled on hands and knees under the bed. The tray of breakfast lying on the small bedside table caught her eye and she remembered the young servant coming in that morning with it, remembered the noise of the tray being put down, the curtain being drawn, the tray then being lifted up again and placed on the bedside table. No one but the servant had entered the room. Should she call her and question her?

Eventually, having taken two aspirins, she decided to do nothing and await the return of her husband from work.

Directly he arrived she told him what had happened and he took her by the arm and seated her down beside him:

"Let's calm down and go over what happened."

She repeated, this time with further details, the whole story.

"And you've looked for it?"

"Everywhere. Every possible and impossible place in the bedroom and the bathroom. You see, I remember distinctly taking it off last night."

He grimaced at the thought of last night, then said:

"Anybody been in the room since Gazia when she brought in the breakfast?"

"Not a soul. I've even told Gazia not to do the room today."

"And you've not mentioned anything to her?"

"I thought I'd better leave it to you."

"Fine, go and tell her I want to speak to her. There's no point in your saying anything but I think it would be as well if you were present when I talk to her."

Five minutes later Gazia, the young servant girl they had recently employed, entered behind her mistress. Samia took herself to a far corner of the room while Gazia stood in front of Abboud Bey, her hands folded across her chest, her eyes lowered.

"Yes, sir?"

"Where's the ring?"

"What ring are you talking about, sir?"

"Now don't make out you don't know. The one with the green stone. It would be better for you if you hand it over and then nothing more need be said."

"May Allah blind me if I've set eyes on it."

He stood up and gave her a sudden slap on the face. The girl reeled back, put one hand to her cheek, then lowered it again to her chest and made no answer to any of Abboud's questions. Finally he said to her:

"You've got just fifteen seconds to say where you've hidden the ring or else, I swear to you, you're not going to have a good time of it."

As he lifted up his arm to look at his watch the girl flinched slightly but continued in her silence. When he went to the telephone Samia raised her head and saw that the girl's cheeks were wet with tears. Abboud Bey got through to the Superintendent of Police and told him briefly what had occurred.

"Of course I haven't got any actual proof but seeing that no one else entered the room, it's obvious she's pinched it. Anyway I'll leave the matter in your capable hands—I know your people have their ways and means."

He gave a short laugh, then listened for a while and said: "I'm really most grateful to you."

He put down the receiver and turned to Samia:

"That's it, my dear. There's nothing more to worry about. The Superintendent has promised me we'll get it back. The patrol car's on the way."

The following day, in the late afternoon, she'd been sitting in front of her dressing-table rearranging her jewelry in its box when an earring slipped from her grasp and fell to the floor. As she bent to pick it up she saw the emerald ring stuck between the leg of the table and the wall. Since that moment she had sat in a state of panic awaiting her husband's return from the club. She even felt tempted to walk down to the water's edge and throw it into the river so as to be rid of the unpleasantness that lay ahead.

At the sound of the screech of tires rounding the house to the garage, she slipped the ring onto her finger. As he entered she stood up and raised her hand to show him the ring. Quickly, trying to choose her words but knowing that she was expressing herself clumsily, she explained what an extraordinary thing it was that it should have lodged itself between the dressing-table and the wall, what an extraordinary coincidence she should have dropped the earring and so seen it, how she'd thought of ringing him at the club to tell him the good news but . . .

She stopped in mid-sentence when she saw his frown and added weakly: "I'm sorry. I can't think how it could have happened. What do we do now?"

He shrugged his shoulders as though in surprise.

"Are you asking me, my dear lady? Nothing of course."

"But they've been beating up the girl—you yourself said they'd not let her be till she confessed."

Unhurriedly, he sat himself down as though to consider this new aspect of the matter. Taking out his case, he tapped a cigarette against it in his accustomed manner, then moistened his lips, put the cigarette in place and lit it. The smoke rings hovered in the still air as he looked at his watch and said:

"In any case she's not got all that long before they let her go. They can't keep her for more than forty-eight hours without getting any evidence or a confession. It won't kill her to put up with things for a while longer. By now the whole town knows the servant stole the ring—or would you like me to tell everyone: 'Look, folks, the fact is that the wife got a bit tiddly on a couple sips of beer and the ring took off on its own and hid itself behind the dressing-table'? What do you think?"

"I know the situation's a bit awkward . . ."

"Awkward? It's downright ludicrous. Listen, there's nothing to be done but to give it to me and the next time I go down to Cairo I'll sell it and get something else in its place. We'd be the laughing-stock of the town."

He stretched out his hand and she found herself taking off the ring and placing it in the outstretched palm. She was careful that their eyes should not meet. For a moment she was on the point of protesting and in fact uttered a few words:

"I'd just like to say we could . . ."

Putting the ring away in his pocket, he bent over her and with both hands gently patted her on the cheeks. It was gesture she had long become used to, a gesture that promised her that this man who was her husband and the father of her child had also taken the place of her father who, as though assured that he had found her a suitable substitute, had followed up her marriage with his own funeral. The gesture told her more eloquently than any words that he was the man, she the woman, he the one who carried the responsibilities, made the decisions, she the one whose role it was to be beautiful, happy, carefree. Now, though, for the first time in their life together the gesture came like a slap in the face.

Directly he removed his hands her whole body was seized with an uncontrollable trembling. Frightened he would notice, she rose to her feet and walked with deliberate steps towards the large window. She leaned her forehead against the comforting cold surface and closed her eyes tightly for several seconds. When she opened them she noticed that the café lights strung between the trees on the opposite shore had been turned on and that there were men seated under them and a waiter moving among the tables. The dark shape of a boat momentarily blocked out the café scene; in the light from the hurricane lamp hanging from its bow she saw it cutting through several of those floating islands of Nile waterlillies that, rootless, are swept along with the current.

Suddenly she became aware of his presence alongside her.

"Why don't you go and change quickly while I take the car out? It's hot and it would be nice to have supper at the club."

"As you like. Why not?"

By the time she had turned round from the window she was smiling.

Journal Entry

Imagine yourself as the wife of the Inspector of Irrigation. How would your responses to your husband be similar to or different from Samia's?

Textual Considerations

1. Analyze how Rifaat uses the language of gazes, glances, slaps, and gestures to reinforce the story's theme. What evidence can you find of the influence of other cultures on the characters' beliefs and behavior?

2. Analyze the story in terms of its narrative structure, considering Rifaat's use of flashbacks to create climax and conflict. Speculate also on the implications of the title and of the conclusion.

3. Examine the bonds that tie the young wife to her husband. To what extent has marriage enhanced her sense of identity and autonomy?

Cultural Contexts

1. Feminists, including the French writer Simone de Beauvoir, have suggested that while men have occupied the position of subject, or actor, women have occupied the position of marginalized object, or one acted upon. Identify and discuss with your group the cultural and economic forces that have contributed to a similar model of gender relations in Rifaat's text. Consider, too, how the wife's presence as object affects her husband's masculine identity.
2. Share with your classmates what you know about marriage traditions in different cultures. Then debate the merits of marriage customs centered on the "dowry" or the "sponsalia." Consider what the dowry tradition reveals about the structures of patriarchy. Consider, too, the extent to which traditions like these have affected Samia's and other women's views of themselves.

Barbara L. Greenberg

The Faithful Wife

But if I *were* to have a lover, it would be someone
who could take nothing from you. I would, in conscience,
not dishonor you. He and I would eat at Howard Johnson's

which you and I do not enjoy. With him I would go
fishing because it is not your sport. He would wear blue   5
which is your worst color; he would have none of your virtues.

Not strong, not proud, not just, not provident, my lover
would blame me for his heart's distress, which you would never
think to do. He and I would drink too much and weep together

and I would bruise his face as I would not bruise your face   10
even in my dreams. Yes I would dance with him, but to a music
you and I would never choose to hear, and in a place

where you and I would never wish to be. He and I would speak
Spanish, which is not your tongue, and we would take
long walks in fields of burdock, to which you are allergic.   15

We would make l

Adrienne Rich

Aunt Jennifer's Tigers

Aunt Jennifer's tigers prance across a screen,
Bright topaz denizens of a world of green.
They do not fear the men beneath the tree;
They pace in sleek chivalric certainty.

Aunt Jennifer's fingers fluttering through her wool   5
Find even the ivory needle hard to pull.
The massive weight of Uncle's wedding band
Sits heavily upon Aunt Jennifer's hand.

When Aunt is dead, her terrified hands will lie
Still ringed with ordeals she was mastered by.   10
The tigers in the panel that she made
Will go on prancing, proud and unafraid.

◆

Journal Entry

Argue for or against the thesis that the women in "The Faithful Wife" and "Aunt Jennifer's Tigers" are satisfied with their role as wife.

Textual Considerations

1. Investigate the meanings that the word *tigers* evokes in Aunt Jennifer's representation of herself. What other images of Aunt Jennifer does the poem contain? How does Aunt Jennifer differ from her tigers?
2. Speculate on the extent to which the speaker in "The Faithful Wife" is recording a fantasy. What does the poem imply about her sexual relationship with her husband? What does it imply about her sense of identity?
3. Discuss the degree to which the women in both poems are presented as subordinate to men.

Cultural Contexts

1. Imagine that you must defend the speaker's husband in "The Faithful Wife." Write a letter to the wife in response to her criticism of her husband.
2. Debate with your group the position that romantic love occupies in the lives of these female speakers. Would you refute or support the argument that these women replaced romantic love with a strong sense of self? Explain.

Maryfrances Wagner

Ragazza

A good Italian woman
will cover her dust-free house
with crocheted doilies,
bear dark-eyed sons,
know what to do   5
with artichokes and chick peas.
Her floors will shine.
She will serve tender brucaluni
in her perfect sauce,
make her own cannoli shells,   10
bake biscottas for every wedding.
Supper will be hot at six o'clock.
She will always wear dresses.
She will not balance the checkbook.
He can doze behind the paper   15
when she washes dishes.
Because she will never leave him,
he will forgive her bulging thighs.
Because he will never leave her,
she won't notice unfamiliar stains.   20

Italian men always know *ragazze*
who work the fields in Bivona.
For airfare one will come.
In time she will learn English.
In time they may learn to love.   25

Maria Mazziotti Gillan

Petals of Silence

The softness which comes to me at dawn
has petals made of silence
Upstairs, my husband, my children sleep,
dreaming their own shadows.

In these moments, stolen from the night, 5
no one needs me. I have my own quiet joys.
My notebook page is clean and white,
My pen moves across it almost by itself.
Even the cat sleeps content in the corner.

I collect the edges of myself around me, 10
curl in the flowers of my stillness
where I find the strength to emerge
into the world of this house,
your bubbling lives.

It is not that I love you less 15
or would wish you gone;
it is only this need
to gather my forces,
to drink from my own fountain
that causes these retreats from you, my loves. 20

Someday, perhaps my daughter will read this poem,
see her reflection in its glass,
as she sits alone, in the clarity of each morning,
with the sound of the crickets and her ghosts
and the place inside herself 25
that nothing, nothing can shatter.

◆

Journal Entry

Contrast the images of marriage in "Ragazza" and "Petals of Silence," both by Italian-American poets.

Textual Considerations

1. Identify images that express the speaker's concepts of personal identity in "Petals of Silence."
2. State the accomplishments of the "good Italian woman" in "Ragazza," and contrast them with what she will not do (ll. 14, 17, and 20).
3. Consider the implications of the titles of both poems. How do they contribute to the meaning of the texts?

Cultural Contexts

1. Discuss with your group the cultural and gender implications of the conclusion of both poems.

Pat Mora

Borders

My research suggests that men and women may
speak different languages that they
assume are the same. —Carol Gilligan

If we're so bright,
why didn't we notice?

I
The side-by-side translations
were the easy ones.
Our tongues tasted *luna*   5
chanting, chanting to the words
it touched; our lips circled
moon sighing its longing.
We knew: similar but different.

II
And we knew of grown-up talk,   10
how even in our own home
like became unlike,
how the child's singsong
                                        I want, I want
burned our mouth   15
when we whispered in the dark.

III
But us? You and I
who've talked for years
tossing words back and forth
                                        success, happiness   20
back and forth
over coffee, over wine
at parties, in bed
and I was sure you heard,
        understood,   25
though now I think of it
I can remember screaming
to be sure.

So who can hear
the words we speak   30
you and I, like but unlike,
and translate us to us
side by side?

Pat Mora

Elena

My Spanish isn't enough.
I remember how I'd smile
listening to my little ones,
understanding every word they'd say,
their jokes, their songs, their plots.   5
    Vamos a pedirle dulces a mamá. Vamos.
But that was in Mexico.
Now my children go to American high schools.
They speak English. At night they sit around
the kitchen table, laugh with one another.   10
I stand by the stove and feel dumb, alone.
I bought a book to learn English.
My husband frowned, drank more beer.
My oldest said, *"Mamá,* he doesn't want you
to be smarter than he is." I'm forty,   15
embarrassed at mispronouncing words,
embarrassed at the laughter of my children,
the grocer, the mailman. Sometimes I take
my English book and lock myself in the bathroom,
say the thick words softly,   20
for if I stop trying, I will be deaf
when my children need my help.

Robert Frost

Home Burial

He saw her from the bottom of the stairs
Before she saw him. She was starting down,
Looking back over her shoulder at some fear.
She took a doubtful step and then undid it
To raise herself and look again. He spoke   5
Advancing toward her: "What is it you see
From up there always?—for I want to know."
She turned and sank upon her skirts at that,
And her face changed from terrified to dull.
He said to gain time: "What is it you see?"   10
Mounting until she cowered under him.
"I will find out now—you must tell me, dear."
She, in her place, refused him any help,
With the least stiffening of her neck and silence.
She let him look, sure that he wouldn't see,   15
Blind creature; and awhile he didn't see.
But at last he murmured, "Oh," and again, "Oh."

"What is it—what?" she said.

                              "Just that I see."

"You don't," she challenged. "Tell me what it is."

"The wonder is I didn't see at once.   20
I never noticed it from here before.
I must be wonted to it—that's the reason.
The little graveyard where my people are!
So small the window frames the whole of it.
Not so much larger than a bedroom, is it?   25
There are three stones of slate and one of marble,
Broad-shouldered little slabs there in the sunlight
On the sidehill. We haven't to mind *those*.
But I understand: it is not the stones,
But the child's mound ——"

                    "Don't, don't, don't, don't," she cried.   30

She withdrew, shrinking from beneath his arm
That rested on the banister, and slid downstairs;
And turned on him with such a daunting look,
He said twice over before he knew himself:
"Can't a man speak of his own child he's lost?"   35

"Not you!—Oh, where's my hat? Oh, I don't need it!
I must get out of here. I must get air.—
I don't know rightly whether any man can."

"Amy! Don't go to someone else this time.
Listen to me. I won't come down the stairs."   40
He sat and fixed his chin between his fists.
"There's something I should like to ask you, dear."

"You don't know how to ask it."

                              "Help me, then."

Her fingers moved the latch for all reply.

"My words are nearly always an offense.   45
I don't know how to speak of anything
So as to please you. But I might be taught,
I should suppose. I can't say I see how.
A man must partly give up being a man
With womenfolk. We could have some arrangement   50
By which I'd bind myself to keep hands off
Anything special you're a-mind to name.
Though I don't like such things 'twixt those that love.
Two that don't love can't live together without them.
But two that do can't live together with them."   55
Don't carry it to someone else this time.
Tell me about it if it's something human.
Let me into your grief. I'm not so much
Unlike other folks as your standing there   60
Apart would make me out. Give me my chance.
I do think, though, you overdo it a little.
What was it brought you up to think it the thing
To take your mother-loss of a first child
So inconsolably—in the face of love.   65
You'd think his memory might be satisfied—"

"There you go sneering now!"

"I'm not, I'm not!
You make me angry. I'll come down to you.
God, what a woman! And it's come to this,
A man can't speak of his own child that's dead."   70

"You can't because you don't know how to speak.
If you had any feelings, you that dug
With your own hand—how could you?—his little grave;
I saw you from that very window there,
Making the gravel leap and leap in air,   75
Leap up, like that, like that, and land so lightly
And roll back down the mound beside the hole.
I thought, Who is that man? I didn't know you.
And I crept down the stairs and up the stairs
To look again, and still your spade kept lifting.   80
Then you came in. I heard your rumbling voice
Out in the kitchen, and I don't know why,
But I went near to see with my own eyes.
You could sit there with the stains on your shoes
Of the fresh earth from your own baby's grave   85
And talk about your everyday concerns.
You had stood the spade up against the wall
Outside there in the entry, for I saw it."

"I shall laugh the worst laugh I ever laughed.
I'm cursed. God, if I don't believe I'm cursed."   90

"I can repeat the very words you were saying:
'Three foggy mornings and one rainy day
Will rot the best birch fence a man can build.'
Think of it, talk like that at such a time!
What had how long it takes a birch to rot   95
To do with what was in the darkened parlor?
You *couldn't* care! The nearest friends can go
With anyone to death, comes so far short
They might as well not try to go at all.
No, from the time when one is sick to death,   100
One is alone, and he dies more alone.
Friends make pretense of following to the grave,
But before one is in it, their minds are turned
And making the best of their way back to life
And living people, and things they understand.   105
But the world's evil. I won't have grief so
If I can change it. Oh, I won't, I won't!"

"There, you have said it all and you feel better.
You won't go now. You're crying. Close the door.
The heart's gone out of it: why keep it up? 110
Amy! There's someone coming down the road!"

"*You*—oh, you think the talk is all. I must go—
Somewhere out of this house. How can I make you—"

"If—you—do!" She was opening the door wider.
"Where do you mean to go? First tell me that. 115
I'll follow and bring you back by force. I *will!*—"

Journal Entry

Analyze the causes of the lack of communication between the men and women in "Borders," "Elena," and "Home Burial."

Textual Considerations

1. Explain the dramatic situation of "Home Burial," citing in detail the events that lead to the confrontation on the stairs.
2. To what extent do you agree or disagree that the father in "Home Burial" feels the loss of the child less than does the mother? Explain.
3. Point out how the female speakers in "Borders" and "Elena" use direct speech and dialogue in an attempt to be understood. To what extent do they succeed in being "heard"?

Cultural Contexts

1. Reread lines 50–55 of "Home Burial." What do they suggest about the husband's attitude toward his wife, toward communication within their relationship, and toward love? Characterize your response to the husband.
2. Apply Carol Gilligan's thesis (see p. 525) to "Borders," and then discuss with your group its relevance to "Home Burial" and "Elena."

Claude McKay

The Harlem Dancer

Applauding youths laughed with young prostitutes
And watched her perfect, half-clothed body sway;
Her voice was like the sound of blended flutes
Blown by black players upon a picnic day.
She sang and danced on gracefully and calm,   5
The light gauze hanging loose about her form;
To me she seemed a proudly-swaying palm
Grown lovelier for passing through a storm.
Upon her swarthy neck black shiny curls
Luxuriant fell; and tossing coins in praise,   10
The wine-flushed, bold-eyed boys, and even the girls,
Devoured her shape with eager, passionate gaze;
But looking at her falsely-smiling face,
I knew her self was not in that strange place.

Edna St. Vincent Millay

What Lips My Lips Have Kissed

What lips my lips have kissed, and where, and why,
I have forgotten, and what arms have lain
Under my head till morning; but the rain
Is full of ghosts tonight, that tap and sigh
Upon the glass and listen for reply,   5
And in my heart there stirs a quiet pain
For unremembered lads that not again
Will turn to me at midnight with a cry.
Thus in the winter stands the lonely tree,
Nor knows what birds have vanished one by one,   10
Yet knows it boughs more silent than before:
I cannot say what loves have come and gone,
I only know that summer sang in me
A little while, that in me sings no more.

Journal Entry

Characterize the moods evoked by the speakers in "The Harlem Dancer" and "What Lips My Lips Have Kissed."

Textual Considerations

1. Contrast the speaker's perceptions of the dancer with those of her audience in McKay's poem.
2. Speculate on why "her self was not in that strange place."
3. State the theme of the first eight lines of Millay's poem, and speculate on audience response, given the speaker's gender.
4. Comment on the effectiveness of Millay's use of nature imagery to communicate meaning in the sonnet's sextet.

Cultural Contexts

1. Discuss with your group what both poems suggest about the relation between sexuality and identity, and between sexuality and youth.

Eliot and Browning

T. S. Eliot

The Love Song of J. Alfred Prufrock

S'io credesse che mia risposta fosse
A persona che mai tornasse al mondo,
Questa fiamma staria senza piu scosse.
Ma perciocche giammai di questo fondo
Non torno vivo alcun, s' i' odo il vero,
Senza tema d'infamia ti rispondo.*

Let us go then, you and I,
When the evening is spread out against the sky
Like a patient etherised upon a table;
Let us go, through certain half-deserted streets,
The muttering retreats   5
Of restless nights in one-night cheap hotels
And sawdust restaurants with oyster-shells:
Streets that follow like a tedious argument
Of insidious intent
To lead you to an overwhelming question . . .   10
Oh, do not ask, "What is it?"
Let us go and make our visit.

In the room the women come and go
Talking of Michelangelo.

The yellow fog that rubs its back upon the window-panes,   15
The yellow smoke that rubs its muzzle on the window-panes
Licked its tongue into the corners of the evening,
Lingered upon the pools that stand in drains,
Let fall upon its back the soot that falls from chimneys,
Slipped by the terrace, made a sudden leap,   20
And seeing that it was a soft October night,
Curled once about the house, and fell asleep.

And indeed there will be time
For the yellow smoke that slides along the street,
Rubbing its back upon the window-panes;   25
There will be time, there will be time
To prepare a face to meet the faces that you meet;
There will be time to murder and create,
And time for all the works and days of hands
That lift and drop a question on your plate;   30
Time for you and time for me,
And time yet for a hundred indecisions,
And for a hundred visions and revisions,
Before the taking of a toast and tea.

In the room the women come and go   35
Talking of Michelangelo

And indeed there will be time
To wonder, "Do I dare?" and, "Do I dare?"
Time to turn back and descend the stair,
With a bald spot in the middle of my hair—   40
[They will say: "How his hair is growing thin!"]
My morning coat, my collar mounting firmly to the chin,
My necktie rich and modest, but asserted by a simple pin—
[They will say: "But how his arms and legs are thin!"]
Do I dare   45
Disturb the universe?
In a minute there is time
For decisions and revisions which a minute will reverse.

For I have known them all already, known them all:—
Have known the evenings, mornings, afternoons,   50
I have measured out my life with coffee spoons;
I know the voices dying with a dying fall
Beneath the music from a farther room.
    So how should I presume?

And I have known the eyes already, known them all—   55
The eyes that fix you in a formulated phrase,
And when I am formulated, sprawling on a pin,
When I am pinned and wriggling on the wall,
Then how should I begin
To spit out all the butt-ends of my days and ways?   60
    And how should I presume?

And I have known the arms already, known them all
Arms that are braceleted and white and bare
[But in the lamplight, downed with light brown hair!]
Is it perfume from a dress   65
That makes me so digress?
Arms that lie along a table, or wrap about a shawl.
    And should I then presume?
    And how should I begin?

       . . . . .

Shall I say, I have gone at dusk through narrow streets   70
And watched the smoke that rises from the pipes
Of lonely men in shirt-sleeves, leaning out of windows? . . .

I should have been a pair of ragged claws
Scuttling across the floors of silent seas.

       . . . . .

And the afternoon, the evening, sleeps so peacefully!   75
Smoothed by long fingers,
Asleep . . . tired . . . or it malingers,
Stretched on the floor, here beside you and me.
Should I, after tea and cakes and ices,
Have the strength to force the moment to its crisis?   80
But though I have wept and fasted, wept and prayed,
Though I have seen my head [grown slightly bald] brought in upon a platter,
I am no prophet—and here's no great matter;
I have seen the moment of my greatness flicker,
And I have seen the eternal Footman hold my coat, and snicker,   85
And in short, I was afraid.

And would it have been worth it, after all,
After the cups, the marmalade, the tea,
Among the porcelain, among some talk of you and me,
Would it have been worth while,   90
To have bitten off the matter with a smile,
To have squeezed the universe into a ball
To roll it toward some overwhelming question,
To say: "I am Lazarus, come from the dead,
Come back to tell you all, I shall tell you all"—   95
If one, settling a pillow by her head,
    Should say: "That is not what I meant at all.
    That is not it, at all."

And would it have been worth it, after all,
Would it have been worth while,   100
After the sunsets and the dooryards and the sprinkled streets,
After the novels, after the teacups, after the skirts
    that trail along the floor—
And this, and so much more?—
It is impossible to say just what I mean!
But as if a magic lantern threw the nerves in patterns on a screen: 105
Would it have been worth while
If one, settling a pillow or throwing off a shawl,
And turning toward the window, should say:
    "That is not it at all,
    That is not what I meant, at all."   110

         . . . . .

No! I am not Prince Hamlet, nor was meant to be;
Am an attendant lord, one that will do
To swell a progress, start a scene or two,
Advise the prince; no doubt, an easy tool,
Deferential, glad to be of use,   115
Politic, cautious, and meticulous;
Full of high sentence, but a bit obtuse;
At times, indeed, almost ridiculous—
Almost, at times, the Fool.

I grow old . . . I grow old . . .   120
I shall wear the bottoms of my trousers rolled.

Shall I part my hair behind? Do I dare to eat a peach?
I shall wear white flannel trousers, and walk upon the beach.
I have heard the mermaids singing, each to each.

I do not think that they will sing to me.   125

I have seen them riding seaward on the waves
Combing the white hair of the waves blown back
When the wind blows the water white and black.

We have lingered in the chambers of the sea
By sea-girls wreathed with seaweed red and brown   130
Till human voices wake us, and we drown.

---

*In Dante's *Inferno* XXVII:61–66, a damned soul who had sought absolution before committing a crime addresses Dante, thinking that his words will never reach the earth: "If I believed that my answer were to a person who could ever return to the world, this flame would no longer quiver. But because no one ever returned from this depth, if what I hear is true, without fear of infamy, I answer you."

   Explanations of allusions in the poem may be helpful. "Works and days" (line 29) is the title of a poem on farm life by Hesiod (eighth century B.C.); "dying fall" (line 52) echoes Shakespeare's *Twelfth Night* I.i.4; lines 81–83 allude to John the Baptist (see Matthew 14:1–11); line 92 echoes lines 41–42 of Marvell's "To His Coy Mistress" . . . ; for "Lazarus" (line 94) see Luke 16 and John 11; lines 112–117 allude to Polonius and perhaps to other figures in *Hamlet;* "full of high sentence" (line 117) comes from Chaucer's description of the Clerk of Oxford in the *Canterbury Tales.*

Robert Browning

My Last Duchess

Ferrara
That's my last Duchess painted on the wall,
Looking as if she were alive; I call
That piece a wonder, now: Frà Pandolf's[1] hands
Worked busily a day, and there she stands.
Will't please you sit and look at her? I said   5
"Frà Pandolf" by design, for never read
Strangers like you that pictured countenance,
The depth and passion of its earnest glance,
But to myself they turned (since none puts by
The curtain I have drawn for you, but I)   10
And seemed as they would ask me, if they durst,
How such a glance came there; so, not the first
Are you to turn and ask thus. Sir, 'twas not
Her husband's presence only, called that spot
Of joy into the Duchess' cheek: perhaps   15
Frà Pandolf chanced to say "Her mantle laps

Over my Lady's wrist too much," or "Paint
Must never hope to reproduce the faint
Half-flush that dies along her throat": such stuff
Was courtesy, she thought, and cause enough   20
For calling up that spot of joy. She had
A heart—how shall I say?—too soon made glad,
Too easily impressed; she liked whate'er
She looked on, and her looks went everywhere.
Sir, 'twas all one! My favor at her breast,   25
The dropping of the daylight in the West,
The bough of cherries some officious fool
Broke in the orchard for her, the white mule
She rode with round the terrace—all and each
Would draw from her alike the approving speech,   30
Or blush, at least. She thanked men,—good; but thanked
Somehow—I know not how—as if she ranked
My gift of a nine-hundred-years-old name
With anybody's gift. Who'd stoop to blame
This sort of trifling? Even had you skill   35
In speech—(which I have not)—to make your will
Quite clear to such an one, and say, "Just this
Or that in you disgusts me; here you miss,
Or there exceed the mark"—and if she let
Herself be lessoned so, nor plainly set   40
Her wits to yours, forsooth, and made excuse,
—E'en then would be some stooping, and I choose
Never to stoop. Oh, Sir, she smiled, no doubt,
Whene'er I passed her; but who passed without
Much the same smile? This grew; I gave commands;   45
Then all smiles stopped together. There she stands
As if alive. Will't please you rise? We'll meet
The company below, then. I repeat,
The Count your Master's known munificence
Is ample warrant that no just pretence   50
Of mine for dowry will be disallowed;
Though his fair daughter's self, as I avowed
At starting, is my object. Nay, we'll go
Together down, Sir! Notice Neptune, though,
Taming a sea-horse, thought a rarity,   55
Which Claus of Innsbruck[2] cast in bronze for me.

[1] *Frà Pandolf's:* A fictitious artist.

[2] *Claus of Innsbruck:* Also a fictitious artist.

◆

Journal Entry

Compare and contrast the concepts of masculinity in "The Love Song of J. Alfred Prufrock" and "My Last Duchess."

Textual Considerations

1. Investigate how Eliot and Browning use internal monologue and dramatic monologue to portray the mental state of the speaker in each poem.
2. Speculate on the identity of the "you" in Eliot's poem—is Prufrock addressing his lover or his reader, or is he perhaps engaging in a dialogue with himself? Cite evidence to support your point of view.
3. Prufrock compares himself to various creatures or historical characters. Review lines 73–74, 82–83, 94, 111–112, and 119, and explain why these comparisons are appropriate and what they tell us about Prufrock's personality and attitude toward himself.
4. Characterize the dramatic situation in "My Last Duchess." Consider the setting and the purpose of the visit (ll. 47–53), and speculate on why Browning concludes the poem with the statue of Neptune taming a sea-horse.

Cultural Contexts

1. Discuss with your group the role that social class plays in each poem. Consider, for example, the extent to which the Duchess was aware of class distinctions and how her attitude toward people from lower classes affected the Duke. For "Prufrock," focus on the role of setting, the party he attends, the social class of the guests, their topics of conversation, and their attitudes toward Prufrock.
2. Debate with your group whether men are more trapped by gender stereotypes than are women. What does Eliot's poem, published in 1914, reveal about the male identity in that period? How closely does Prufrock reflect the conventional male model of men as physically strong, sexually active, competitive, and aggressive? How have such masculine stereotypes and taboos affected men in general? To what extent have concepts of masculinity changed since the poem was written?
3. Discuss with your group the extent to which Browning's use of dramatic irony results in our learning more about the Duke than he understands about himself. Consider, for example, his motivation for ordering his wife's death. Find evidence to show how the Duchess becomes a projection of her husband's fears and insecurities.

Gayle Two Eagles

The Young Warrior

The young warrior,
Seeing the world through brand-new eyes,
Brought up thinking she was special and good.

Lakota people can be proud again.

When an injustice is done to one of "the people,"   5
The warriors gather.

The woman warrior is among them,
Proud and strong,
Because she is a fighter.

The words flow off the tongues of the new orators,   10
Telling of the old ways,
And why being Indian is worth fighting for,
Mesmerized by the sense of strength and duty,
To become a warrior and keep the Lakota ways alive.

Tradition as told by men,   15
Written in history books by white men,
Religion didn't escape their influence.

Despite being told the women's squad is assigned the kitchen,
She guards the rooms and buildings from passing racists.

While the Lakota people make their stand,   20
Quiet defiance to the men who say, "respect your brother's vision,"
She mutters, "respect your sister's vision too."

She supported you in Wounded Knee,
She was with you at Sioux Falls,
Custer,   25
And Sturgis,
And has always remembered you,
Her Indian people,
In her prayers.

She has listened to women who were beaten by the men they love,   30
Or their husbands,
And gave strength to women who were raped,
As has the Sacred Mother Earth.

At some point asking where Tradition for women was being decided.

As a Traditional Lakota woman you are asked to approach a relative   35
or your spouse to speak your thoughts and feelings at a public meeting,
Not to touch a feather, or not to handle food at what the white culture
once referred to as the "sick time."

Woman warrior once told to break the stereotype of the white people,
She is also told to walk ten steps behind a man.   40

The new eyes that once were in awe at what the world had to offer,
Looks down at this new girl child,
The Lakota woman warrior knows her daughter also has a vision.

Anne Sexton

For My Lover,
Returning to His Wife

She is all there.
She was melted carefully down for you
and cast up from your childhood,
cast up from your one hundred favorite aggies.

She has always been there, my darling.   5
She is, in fact, exquisite.
Fireworks in the dull middle of February
and as real as a cast-iron pot.

Let's face it, I have been momentary.
A luxury. A bright red sloop in the harbor.   10
My hair rising like smoke from the car window.
Littleneck clams out of season.

She is more than that. She is your have to have,
has grown you your practical your tropical growth.
This is not an experiment. She is all harmony.   15
She sees to oars and oarlocks for the dinghy,

has placed wild flowers at the window at breakfast,
sat by the potter's wheel at midday,
set forth three children under the moon,
three cherubs drawn by Michelangelo,   20

done this with her legs spread out
in the terrible months in the chapel.
If you glance up, the children are there
like delicate balloons resting on the ceiling.

She has also carried each one down the hall   25
after supper, their heads privately bent,
two legs protesting, person to person,
her face flushed with a song and their little sleep.

I give you back your heart.
I give you permission—   30

for the fuse inside her, throbbing
angrily in the dirt, for the bitch in her
and the burying of her wound—
for the burying of her small red wound alive—

for the pale flickering flare under her ribs,   35
for the drunken sailor who waits in her left pulse,
for the mother's knee, for the stockings,
for the garter belt, for the call—

the curious call
when you will burrow in arms and breasts   40
and tug at the orange ribbon in her hair
and answer the call, the curious call.

She is so naked and singular.
She is the sum of yourself and your dream.
Climb her like a monument, step after step.   45
She is solid.

As for me, I am a watercolor.
I wash off.

◆

Journal Entry

To what extent do the speakers in "The Young Warrior" and "For My Lover, Returning to His Wife" challenge the patriarchal tradition in gender relationships?

Textual Considerations

1. Identify the various stages at which the narrative voice in Gayle Two Eagles's poem paints the portrait of the young Lakota warrior. How do tone and rhythm contribute to the dramatic effects of the poem?

2. Characterize the tone of Sexton's poem. Is the speaker sarcastic, angry, bitter, or resigned? Give reasons for your answer.
3. Discuss how Sexton's use of contrasting images of the wife and mistress contributes to your sense of the transience of the love affair described in the poem. With whom do you empathize—the mistress or the wife? Explain.

Cultural Contexts

1. Gloria Steinem, a contemporary feminist, defines "sisterhood" as a situation in which women who differ in age, race, and economic status share their experience as women. Apply the concept of sisterhood to "The Young Warrior" and "For My Lover, Returning to His Wife."
2. Discuss with your group what Sexton's poem reveals about the husband. What advantages and disadvantages does he enjoy as husband and lover? To what extent has the patriarchal tradition shaped his sexual identity? Characterize your attitude toward him.

Keats, Shakespeare, and de la Cruz ◆

John Keats

Bright Star

Bright star, would I were steadfast as thou art—
   Not in lone splendor hung aloft the night
And watching, with eternal lids apart,
   Like nature's patient, sleepless Eremite,[1]
The moving waters at their priestlike task   5
   Of pure ablution round earth's human shores,
Or gazing on the new soft fallen mask
   Of snow upon the mountains and the moors—
No—yet still steadfast, still unchangeable,
   Pillowed upon my fair love's ripening breast,   10
To feel forever its soft fall and swell,
   Awake forever in a sweet unrest,
Still, still to hear her tender-taken breath,
And so live ever—or else swoon to death.

[1] *Eremite:* hermit, devotee

William Shakespeare

My Mistress' Eyes Are Nothing like the Sun

My mistress' eyes are nothing like the sun;
Coral is far more red than her lips' red;
If snow be white, why then her breasts are dun;
If hairs be wires, black wires grow on her head.
I have seen roses damasked,[1] red and white,   5
But no such roses see I in her cheeks;
And in some perfumes is there more delight
Than in the breath that from my mistress reeks.
I love to hear her speak, yet well I know
That music hath a far more pleasing sound;   10
I grant I never saw a goddess go;[2]
My mistress, when she walks, treads on the ground.
And yet, by heaven, I think my love as rare
As any she belied with false compare.

[1] *damasked:* variegated

[2] *a goddess go:* walk

Sor Juana Inés de la Cruz

She Proves the Inconsistency of the Desires and Criticism of Men Who Accuse Women of What They Themselves Cause

Foolish men who accuse
women unreasonably,
you blame yet never see
you cause what you abuse.

You crawl before her, sad,   5
begging for a quick cure;
why ask her to be pure
when you have made her bad?

You combat her resistance
and then with gravity,   10
you call frivolity
the fruit of your intents.

In one heroic breath
your reason fails, like a wild
bogeyman made up by a child   15
who then is scared to death.

With idiotic pride
you hope to find your prize:
a regal whore like Thaïs
and Lucretia for a bride.   20

Has anyone ever seen
a stranger moral fervor:
you who dirty the mirror
regret it is not clean?

You treat favor and disdain   25
with the same shallow mock-
ing voice: love you and you squawk,
demur and you complain.

No answer at her door
will be a proper part: 30
say no—she has no heart,
say yes—and she's a whore.

Two levels to your game
in which *you* are the fool:
one you blame as cruel,   35
one who yields, you shame.

How can one not be bad
the way your love pretends
to be? Say no and she offends.
Consent and you are mad.   40

With all the fury and pain
your whims cause her, it's good
for her who has withstood
you. Now go and complain!

You let her grief take flight   45
and free her with new wings.
Then after sordid things
you say she's not upright.

Who is at fault in all
this errant passion? She   50
who falls for his pleas, or he
who pleads for her to fall?

Whose guilt is greater in
this raw erotic play?
The girl who sins for pay   55
or man who pays for sin?

So why be shocked or taunt
her for the steps you take?
Care for her as you make
her, or shape her as you want,   60

but do not come with pleas
and later throw them in
her face, screaming of sin
when you were at her knees.

You fight us from birth   65
with weapons of arrogance.
Between promise and pleading stance,
you are devil, flesh, and earth.

◆

Journal Entry

Consider how the romantic concept of the female as goddess or idealized being might affect a male's sense of identity.

Textual Considerations

1. Select three or four examples of similes and metaphors in the poems by Keats and Shakespeare, and discuss their appeal to the senses, the meanings they suggest, and the emotions they arouse in the reader. Comment also on the poets' use of comparison and contrast in relation to theme.

2. Summarize the key points of de la Cruz's arguments. To what extent do you agree or disagree with her logic and point of view?
3. Characterize the tone of each poem and discuss its appropriateness in relation to the poem's theme.

Cultural Contexts

1. Discuss the extent to which the views of the women in all three poems are relevant to women's position in society today.
2. Consider the effect of stereotypes such as "goddess," "madonna," or "whore" on women's identity. How might these stereotypes also affect gender relationships?

Euripides

Medea

CHARACTERS

NURSE
CREON, *King of Corinth*
CHILDREN OF MEDEA
MEDEA
TUTOR
JASON
CHORUS, *Corinthian Women*
AEGEUS, *King of Athens*
MESSENGER

The scene represents the home of Medea at Corinth.

Medea was acted 431 B.C.

(*Enter* NURSE.)

NURSE. How I wish that the ship Argo had never winged its way through the gray Clashing Rocks to the land of the Colchians! How I wish the pines had never been hewn down in the glens of Pelion, to put oars into the hands of the Heroes who went to fetch for Pelias the Golden Fleece! Then Medea my mistress would not have sailed to the towers of Iolcus, her heart pierced through and through with love for Jason, would not have prevailed on the daughters of Pelias to murder their father, would not now be dwelling here in Corinth with her husband and children. When she fled here she found favor with the citizens to whose land she had come and was herself a perfect partner in all things for Jason. (And therein lies a woman's best security, to avoid conflict with her husband.) But now there is nothing but enmity, a blight has come over their great love.

Jason has betrayed his own children and my mistress to sleep beside a royal bride, the daughter of Creon who rules this land, while Medea, luckless Medea, in her desolation invokes the promises he made, appeals to the pledges in which she put her deepest trust, and calls Heaven to witness the sorry recompense she has from Jason. Ever since she realized her husband's perfidy, she has been lying there prostrated, eating no food, her whole frame subdued to sorrow, wasting away with incessant weeping. She has not lifted an eye nor ever turned her face from the floor. The admonitions of her friends she receives with unhearing ears, like a rock or a wave of the sea. Only now and then she turns her white neck and talks to herself, in sorrow, of her dear father and her country and the home which she betrayed to come here with a husband who now holds her in contempt. Now she knows, from bitter experience, how sad a thing it is to lose one's fatherland. She hates her own children and has no pleasure at the sight of them. I fear she may form some new and horrible resolve. For hers is a dangerous mind, and she will not lie down to injury. I know her and she frightens me [lest she make her way stealthily into the palace where his couch is spread and drive a sharp sword into his vitals or even kill both the King and the bridegroom and then incur some greater misfortune.] She is cunning. Whoever crosses swords with her will not find victory easy, I tell you.

But here come the children, their playtime over. Little thought have they of their mother's troubles. Children do not like sad thoughts.

(*Enter* TUTOR, *with boys.*)

TUTOR. Ancient household chattel of my mistress, why are you standing here all alone at the gates, muttering darkly to yourself? What makes Medea want you to leave her alone?

NURSE. Aged escort of Jason's children, when their master's affairs go ill, good slaves find not only their misfortune but also their heart's grief. My sorrow has now become so great that a longing came over me to come out here and tell to earth and sky the story of my mistress's woes.

TUTOR. What? Is the poor lady not yet through with weeping?

NURSE. I wish I had your optimism. Why, her sorrow is only beginning, it's not yet at the turning point.

TUTOR. Poor foolish woman!—if one may speak thus of one's masters. Little she knows of the latest ills!

NURSE. What's that, old man? Don't grudge me your news.

TUTOR. It's nothing at all. I'm sorry I even said what I said.

NURSE. Please, I beg of you, don't keep it from a fellow slave. I'll keep it dark, if need be.

TUTOR. I had drawn near the checkerboards where the old men sit, beside the sacred water of Pirene, and there, when nobody thought I was listening, I heard somebody say that Creon the ruler of this land was planning to expel these children *and* their mother from Corinth. Whether the tale is true or not I do not know. I would wish it were not so.

NURSE. But will Jason ever allow his children to be so treated, even if he *is* at variance with their mother?

TUTOR. Old loves are weaker than new loves, and that man is no friend to this household.

NURSE. That's the end of us then, if we are to ship a second wave of trouble before we are rid of the first.

TUTOR. Meanwhile you keep quiet and don't say a word. This is no time for the mistress to be told.

NURSE. O children, do you hear what love your father bears you? Since he is my master, I do not wish him dead, but he is certainly proving enemy of those he should love.

TUTOR. Like the rest of the world. Are you only now learning that every man loves himself more than his neighbor? [Some justly, others for profit, as] now for a new bride their father hates these children.

NURSE. Inside, children, inside. It will be all right. (*To the* TUTOR.) And you keep them alone as much as you can, and don't let them near their mother when she's melancholy. I have already noticed her casting a baleful eye at them as if she would gladly do them mischief. She'll not recover from her rage, I know well, till the lightning of her fury has struck somebody to the ground. May it be enemies, not loved ones, that suffer!

MEDEA. (*within*) *Oh! my grief! the misery of it all! Why can I not die?*

NURSE. *What did I tell you, dear children? Your mother's heart is troubled, her anger is roused. Hurry indoors, quick. Keep out of her sight, don't go near her. Beware of her fierce manner, her implacable temper. Hers is a selfwilled nature. Go now, get you inside, be quick. Soon, it is clear, her sorrow like a gathering cloud will burst in a tempest of fury. What deed will she do then, that impetuous, indomitable heart, poisoned by injustice?*

(*Exeunt children with* TUTOR.)

MEDEA. (*within*) *O misery! the things I have suffered, cause enough for deep lamentations! O you cursed sons of a hateful mother, a plague on you! And on your father! Ruin seize the whole household!*

NURSE. *Ah me, unhappy me! Why will you have your sons partake of their father's guilt? Why hate them? Ah children, your danger overwhelms me with anxiety. The souls of royalty are vindictive; they do not easily forget their resentment, possibly because being used to command they are seldom checked. It is better to be used to living among equals. For myself, at any rate, I ask not greatness but a safe old age. Moderation! Firstly, the very name of it is excellent; to practise it is easily the best thing for mortals. Excess avails to no good purpose for men, and if the gods are provoked, brings greater ruin on a house.*

(*Enter* CHORUS.)

CHORUS. *I heard a voice, I heard a cry. It was the unhappy Colchian woman's. She is not yet calm. Pray tell us, old woman. From the court outside I heard her cries within. I do not rejoice, woman, in the griefs of this house. Dear, dear it is to me.*

NURSE. *It is a home no more; the life has gone out of it. Its master a princess' bed enthralls, while the mistress in her chamber is pining to death, and her friends have no words to comfort her heart.*

MEDEA. (*within*) *Oh! Would that a flaming bolt from Heaven might pierce my brain! What is the good of living any longer? O Misery! Let me give up this life I find so hateful. Let me seek lodging in the house of death.*

CHORUS. *O Zeus, O Earth, O Light, hear what a sad lament the hapless wife intones. What is this yearning, rash woman, after that fearful bed? Will you hasten to the end that is Death? Pray not for that. If your husband worships a new bride, it is a common event; be not exasperated. Zeus will support your cause. Do not let grief for a lost husband waste away your life.*

MEDEA. *(within) Great Zeus and Lady Themis, see you how I am treated, for all the strong oaths with which I bound my cursed husband? May I live to see him and his bride, palace and all, in one common destruction, for the wrongs that they inflict, unprovoked, on me! O father, O country, that I forsook so shamefully, killing my brother, my own!*

NURSE. *Hear what she says, how she cries out to Themis of Prayers and to Zeus whom mortals regard as the steward of oaths. With no small revenge will my mistress bate her rage.*

CHORUS. *I wish she would come into our presence and hear the sound of the words we would speak. Then she might forget the resentment in her heart and change her purpose. May my zeal be ever at the service of my friends. But bring her here, make her come forth from the palace. Tell her that here too are friends. Make haste before she does any harm to those within. Furious is the surge of such a sorrow.*

NURSE. *I shall do so, though I am not hopeful of persuading the mistress. But I freely present you with the gift of my labor. Yet she throws a hateful glare, like a lioness with cubs, at any servant who approaches her as if to speak. Blunderers and fools! that is the only proper name for the men of old who invented songs to bring the joy of life to feasts and banquets and festive boards, but never discovered a music of song or sounding lyre to dispel the weary sorrows of humanity, that bring death and fell havoc and destruction of homes. Yet what a boon to man, could these ills be cured by some! At sumptuous banquets why raise a useless strain? The food that is served and the satisfaction that comes to full men, that in itself is pleasure enough.*

(Exit NURSE.)

CHORUS. *I hear a cry of grief and deep sorrow. In piercing accents of misery she proclaims her woes, her ill-starred marriage and her love betrayed. The victim of grievous wrongs, she calls on the daughter of Zeus, even Themis, Lady of Vows, who led her through the night by difficult straits across the briny sea to Hellas.*

(Enter MEDEA.)

MEDEA. Women of Corinth, do not criticize me, I come forth from the palace. Well I know that snobbery is a common charge, that may be levelled against recluse and busy man alike. And the former, by their choice of a quiet life, acquire an extra stigma: they are deficient in energy and spirit. There is no justice in the eyes of men; a man who has never harmed them they may hate at sight, without ever knowing anything about his essential nature. An alien, to be sure, should adapt himself to the citizens with whom he lives. Even the citizen is to be condemned if he is too selfwilled or too uncouth to avoid offending his fellows. So I . . . but this unexpected blow which has befallen me has broken my heart.

It's all over, my friends; I would gladly die. Life has lost its savor. The man who was everything to me, well he knows it, has turned out to be the basest of men. Of all creatures that feel and think, we women are the unhappiest species. In the first place, we must pay a great dowry to a husband who will be the tyrant of our bodies (that's a further aggravation of the evil); and there is another fearful hazard: whether we shall get a good man or a bad. For separations bring disgrace on the woman and it is not possible to renounce one's husband. Then, landed among strange habits and regulations unheard of in her own home, a woman needs second sight to know how best to handle her bedmate. And if we manage this well and have a husband who does not find the yoke of intercourse too galling, ours is a life to be envied. Otherwise, one is better dead. When the man wearies of the company of his wife, he goes outdoors and relieves the disgust of his heart [having recourse to some friend or the companions of his own age], but we women have only one person to turn to.

They say that we have a safe life at home, whereas men must go to war. Nonsense! I had rather fight three battles than bear one child. But be that as it may, you and I are not in the same case. You have your city here, your paternal homes; you know the delights of life and association with you loved ones. But I, homeless and forsaken, carried off from a foreign land, am being wronged by a husband, with neither mother nor brother nor kinsman with whom I might find refuge from the storms of misfortune. One little boon I crave of you, if I discover any ways and means of punishing my husband for these wrongs: your silence. Woman in most respects is a timid creature, with no heart for strife and aghast at the sight of steel; but wronged in love, there is no heart more murderous than hers.

LEADER. Do as you say, Medea, for just will be your vengeance. I do not wonder that you bemoan your fate. But I see Creon coming, the ruler of this land, bringing tidings of new plans.

(*Enter* CREON.)

CREON. You there, Medea, looking black with rage against your husband; I have proclaimed that you are to be driven forth in exile from this land, you and your two sons. Immediately. I am the absolute judge of the case, and I shall not go back to my palace till I have cast you over the frontier of the land.

MEDEA. Ah! Destruction, double destruction is my unhappy lot. My enemies are letting out every sail and there is no harbor into which I may flee from the menace of their attack. But ill-treated and all, Creon, still I shall put the question to you: Why are you sending me out of the country?

CREON. I am afraid of you—there's no need to hide behind a cloak of words— afraid you will do my child some irreparable injury. There's plenty logic in that fear. You are a wizard possessed of evil knowledge. You are stung by the loss of your husbands's love. And I have heard of your threats—they told me of them—to injure bridegroom and bride and father of the bride. Therefore before anything happens to me, I shall take precautions. Better for me now to be hateful in your eyes than to relent and rue it greatly later.

MEDEA. Alas! Alas! Often ere now—this is not the first time—my reputation has hurt me and done me grievous wrong. If a man's really shrewd, he ought never to have his children taught too much. For over and above a name for uselessness that it will earn them, they incur the hostility and envy of their fellow men. Offer clever reforms to dullards, and you will be thought a useless fool yourself. And the reputed wiseacres, feeling your superiority, will dislike you intensely. I myself have met this fate. Because I have skill, some are jealous of me, others think me unsociable. But my wisdom does not go very far. However, you are afraid you may suffer something unpleasant at my hands, aren't you? Fear not, Creon; it is not my way to commit my crimes against kings. What wrong have you done me? You have only bestowed your daughter on the suitor of your choice. No, it is my husband I hate. You, I dare say, knew what you were doing in the matter. And now I don't grudge success to your scheme. Make your match, and good luck to you. But allow me to stay in this country. Though foully used, I shall keep my peace, submitting to my masters.

CREON. Your words are comforting to hear, but inside my heart there is a horrible fear that you are plotting some mischief, which makes me trust you even less than before. The hot-tempered woman, like the hot-tempered man, is easier to guard against than the cunning and silent. But off with you at once, make no speeches. My resolve is fixed; for all your skill you will not stay amongst us to hate me.

MEDEA. Please no, I beseech you, by your knees, by the young bride . . .

CREON. You are wasting your words; you will never convince me.

MEDEA. Will you drive me out and have no respect for my prayers?

CREON. Yes, for I love you less than I love my own family.

MEDEA. O fatherland, how strongly do I now remember you!

CREON. Yes, apart from my children, that is *my* dearest love.

MEDEA. Alas! the loves of men are a mighty evil.

CREON. In my opinion, that depends on the circumstances.

MEDEA. O Zeus, do not forget the author of this wickedness.

CREON. On your way, vain woman, and end my troubles.

MEDEA. The troubles are mine, I have no lack of troubles.

CREON. In a moment you will be thrust out by the hands of servants.

MEDEA. No, no, not that. But Creon I entreat you . . .

CREON. You seem to be bent on causing trouble, woman.

MEDEA. I shall go into exile. It is not *that* I beg you to grant me.

CREON. Why then are you clinging so violently to my hand?

MEDEA. Allow me to stay for this one day to complete my plans for departure and get together provision for my children, since their father prefers not to bother about his own sons. Have pity on them. You too are the father of children. It is natural that you should feel kindly. Stay or go, I care nothing for myself. It's them I weep for in their misfortune.

CREON. My mind is not tyrannical enough; mercy has often been my undoing. So now, though I know that it is a mistake, woman, you will have your request. But I give you warning: if tomorrow's divine sun sees you and your children inside the borders of this country, you die. True is the word I have spoken. [Stay, if you must, this one day. You'll not have time to do what I dread.]

(*Exit* CREON.)

CHORUS. *Hapless woman! overwhelmed by sorrow! Where will you turn? What stranger will afford you hospitality? God has steered you, Medea, into an unmanageable surge of troubles.*

MEDEA. Ill fortune's everywhere, who can gainsay it? But it is not yet as bad as that, never think so. There is still heavy weather ahead for the new bride and groom, and no little trouble for the maker of the match. Do you think I would ever have wheedled the king just now except to further my own plans? I would not even have spoken to him, nor touched him either. But he is such a fool that though he might have thwarted my plans by expelling me from the country he has allowed me to stay over for this one day, in which I shall make corpses of three of my enemies, father and daughter and my own husband.

My friends, I know several ways of causing their death, and I cannot decide which I should turn my hand to first. Shall I set fire to the bridal chamber or make my way in stealthily to where their bed is laid and drive a sword through their vitals? But there is one little difficulty. If I am caught entering the palace or devising my bonfire I shall be slain and my enemies shall laugh. Better take the direct way and the one for which I have the natural gift. Poison. Destroy them with poison. So be it.

But suppose them slain. What city will receive me? Whose hospitality will rescue me and afford me a land where I shall be safe from punishment, a home where I can live in security? It cannot be. I shall wait, therefore, a little longer and if any tower of safety shows up I shall carry out the murders in stealth and secrecy. However, if circumstances drive me to my wits' end, I shall take a sword in my own hands and face certain death to slay them. I shall not shirk the difficult adventure. No! by Queen Hecate who has her abode in the recesses of my hearth—her I revere above all gods and have chosen to assist me—never shall any one of them torture my heart with impunity. I shall make their marriage a torment and grief to them. Bitterly shall they rue the match they have made and the exile they inflict on me.

But enough! Medea, use all your wiles; plot and devise. Onward to the dreadful moment. Now is the test of courage. Do you see how you are being treated? It is not right that the seed of Sisyphus and Aeson should gloat over you, the daughter of a noble sire and descendant of the Sun. But you realize that. Moreover by our mere nature we women are helpless for good, but adept at contriving all manner of wickedness.

CHORUS. *Back to their sources flow the sacred rivers. The world and morality are turned upside-down. The hearts of* men *are treacherous; the sanctions of Heaven are undermined. The voice of time will change, and our glory will ring down the ages. Womankind will be honored. No longer will ill-sounding report attach to our sex.*

The strains of ancient minstrelsy will cease, that hymned our faithlessness. Would that Phoebus, Lord of Song, had put into woman's heart the inspired song of the lyre. Then I would have sung a song in answer to the tribe of males. History has much to tell of the relations of men with women.

You, Medea, in the mad passion of your heart sailed away from your father's home, threading your way through the twin rocks of the Euxine, to settle in a foreign land. Now, your bed empty, your lover lost, unhappy woman, you are being driven forth in dishonor into exile.

Gone is respect for oaths. Nowhere in all the breadth of Hellas is honor any more to be found; it has vanished into the clouds. Hapless one, you have no father's house to which you might fly for shelter from the gales of misfortune; and another woman, a princess, has charmed your husband away and stepped into your place.

(*Enter* JASON.)

JASON. Often and often ere now I have observed that an intractable nature is a curse almost impossible to deal with. So with you. When you might have stayed on in this land and in this house by submitting quietly to the wishes of your superiors, your forward tongue has got you expelled from the country. Not that your abuse troubles *me* at all. Keep on saying that Jason is a villain of the deepest dye. But for your insolence to royalty consider yourself more than fortunate that you are only being punished by exile. I was constantly mollifying the angry monarch and expressing the wish that you be allowed to stay. But in unabated folly you keep on reviling the king. That is why you are to be expelled.

But still, despite everything, I come here now with unwearied goodwill, to contrive on your behalf, Madam, that you and the children will not leave this country lacking money or anything else. Exile brings many hardships in its wake. And even if you do hate me, I could never think cruelly of you.

MEDEA. Rotten, heart-rotten, that is the word for you. Words, words, magnificent words. In reality a craven. You come to me, you come, my worst enemy! This isn't bravery, you know, this isn't valor, to come and face your victims. No! it's the ugliest sore on the face of humanity, Shamelessness. But I thank you for coming. It will lighten the weight on my heart to tell your wickedness, and it will hurt you to hear it. I shall begin my tale at the very beginning.

I saved your life, as all know who embarked with you on the Argo, when you were sent to master with the yoke the fire-breathing bulls and to sow with dragon's teeth that acre of death. The dragon, too, with wreathed coils, that kept safe watch over the Golden Fleece and never slept—I slew it and raised for you the light of life again. Then, forsaking my father and my own dear ones, I came to Iolcus where Pelias reigned, came with you, more than fond and less than wise. On Pelias too I brought death, the most painful death there is, at the hands of his own children. Thus I have removed every danger from your path.

And after all those benefits at my hands, you basest of men, you have betrayed me and made a new marriage, though I have borne you children. If you were still childless, I could have understood this love of yours for a new wife. Gone now is all reliance on pledges. You puzzle me. Do you believe that the gods of the old days are no longer in office? Do you think that men are now living under a new dispensation? For surely you know that you have broken all your oaths to me. Ah my hand, which you so often grasped, and oh my knees, how all for nothing have we been defiled by this false man, who has disappointed all our hopes.

But come, I shall confide in you as though you were my friend, not that I expect to receive any benefit from you. But let that go. My questions will serve to underline your infamy. As things are now, where am I to turn? Home to my father? But when I came here with you, I betrayed my home and my country. To the wretched daughters of Pelias? They would surely give me a royal welcome to their home; I only murdered their father. For it is how it is. My loved ones at home have learned to hate me; the others, whom I need not have harmed, I have made enemies to oblige you. And so in return for these services you have made me envied among the women of Hellas! A wonderful, faithful husband I have in you, if I must be expelled from the country into exile, deserted by my friends, alone with my friendless children! A fine story to tell of the new bridegroom, that his children and the woman who saved his life are wandering about in aimless beggary! O Zeus, why O why have you given to mortals sure means of knowing gold from tinsel, yet men's exteriors show no mark by which to descry the rotten heart?

LEADER. Horrible and hard to heal is the anger of friend at strife with friend.

JASON. It looks as if I need no small skill in speech if, like a skilful steersman riding the storm with close-reefed sheets, I am to escape the howling gale of your verbosity, woman. Well, since you are making a mountain out of the favors you have done me, I'll tell *you* what *I* think. It was the goddess of Love and none other, mortal or immortal, who delivered me from the dangers of my quest. You have indeed much subtlety of wit, but it would be an invidious story to go into, how the inescapable shafts of Love compelled you to save my life. Still, I shall not put too fine a point on it. If you helped me in some way or other, good and well. But as I shall demonstrate, in the matter of my rescue you got more than you gave.

In the first place, you have your home in Greece, instead of in a barbarian land. You have learned the blessings of Law and Justice, instead of the Caprice of the Strong. And all the Greeks have realized your wisdom, and you have won great fame. If you had been living on the edges of the earth, nobody would ever have heard of you. May I have neither gold in my house nor skill to sing a sweeter song than Orpheus if my fortune is to be hid from the eyes of men. That, then, is my position in the matter of the fetching of the Fleece. (It was you who proposed the debate.)

There remains my wedding with the Princess, which you have cast in my teeth. In this connection I shall demonstrate, one, my wisdom; two, my rightness; three, my great service of love to you and my children. (Be quiet please.) When I emigrated here from the land of Iolcus, dragging behind me an unmanageable chain of troubles, what greater windfall could I have hit upon, I an exile, than a marriage with the king's daughter? Not that I was weary of your charms (that's the thought that galls you) or that I was smitten with longing for a fresh bride; still less that I wanted to outdo my neighbors in begetting numerous children. Those I have are enough, there I have no criticism to make. No! what I wanted, first and foremost, was a good home where we would lack for nothing (well I knew that the poor man is shunned and avoided by all his friends); and secondly, I wanted to bring up the children in a style worthy of my house, and, begetting other children to be brothers to the children born of you, to bring them all together and unite the families. Then my happiness would be complete. What do *you* want with more children? As for me, it will pay me to advance the children I have by means of those I intend to beget. Surely that is no bad plan? You yourself would admit it, if jealousy were not pricking you.

You women have actually come to believe that, lucky in love, you are lucky in all things, but let some mischance befall that love, and you will think the best of all possible worlds a most loathsome place. There ought to have been some other way for men to beget their children, dispensing with the assistance of women. Then there would be no trouble in the world.

LEADER. Jason, you arrange your arguments very skillfully. And yet in my opinion, like it or not, you have acted unjustly in betraying your wife.

MEDEA. Yes! I do hold many opinions that are not shared by the majority of people. In my opinion, for example, the plausible scoundrel is the worst type of scoundrel. Confident in his ability to trick out his wickedness with fair phrases he shrinks from no depth of villainy. But there is a limit to his cleverness. As there is also to yours. You may well drop that fine front with me, and all that rhetoric. One word will floor you. If you had been an honorable man, you would have sought my consent to the new match and not kept your plans secret from your own family.

JASON. And if I had announced to you my intention to marry, I am sure I would have found you a most enthusiastic accomplice. Why! even now you cannot bring yourself to master your heart's deep resentment.

MEDEA. That's not what griped you. No! your foreign wife was passing into an old age that did you little credit.

JASON. Accept my assurance, it was not for the sake of a woman that I made the match I have made. As I told you once already, I wanted to save you and to beget princes to be brothers to my own sons, thereby establishing our family.

MEDEA.   May it never be mine . . . a happiness that hurts, a blessedness that frets my soul.

JASON.   Do you know how to change your prayer to show better sense? "May I regard nothing useful as grievous, no good fortune as ill."

MEDEA.   Insult me. *You* have a refuge, but I am helpless, faced with exile.

JASON.   It was your own choice. Don't blame anyone else.

MEDEA.   What did I do? Did I betray you and marry somebody else?

JASON.   You heaped foul curses on the king.

MEDEA.   And to your house also I shall prove a curse.

JASON.   Look here, I do not intend to continue this discussion any further. If you want anything of mine to assist you or the children in your exile, just tell me. I am ready to give it with an ungrudging hand and to send letters of introduction to my foreign friends who will treat you well. If you reject this offer, woman, you will be a great fool. Forget your anger, and you will find it greatly to your advantage.

MEDEA.   I would not use your friends on any terms or accept anything of yours. Do not offer it. The gifts of the wicked bring no profit.

JASON.   At any rate, heaven be my witness that I am willing to render every assistance to you and the children. But you do not like what is good for you. Your obstinacy repulses your friends; it will only aggravate your suffering.

MEDEA.   Be off with you. As you loiter outside here, you are burning with longing for the girl who has just been made your wife. Make the most of the union. Perhaps, god willing, you are making the kind of marriage you will some day wish unmade.

(*Exit* JASON.)

CHORUS.   *Love may go too far and involve men in dishonor and disgrace. But if the goddess comes in just measure, there is none so rich in blessing. May you never launch at me, O Lady of Cyprus, your golden bow's passion-poisoned arrows, which no man can avoid.*

May Moderation content me, the fairest gift of Heaven. Never may the Cyprian pierce my heart with longing for another's love and bring on me angry quarrelings and never-ending recriminations. May she have respect for harmonious unions and with discernment assort the matings of women.

O Home and Fatherland, never, never, I pray, may I be cityless. It is an intolerable existence, hopeless, piteous, grievous. Let me die first, die and bring this life to a close. There is no sorrow that surpasses the loss of country.

My eyes have seen it; not from hearsay do I speak. You have neither city nor friend to pity you in your most terrible trials. Perish, abhorred, the man who never brings himself to unbolt his heart in frankness to some honored friends! Never shall such a man be a friend of mine.

(*Enter* AEGEUS, *in traveler's dress.*)

AEGEUS. Medea, good health to you. A better prelude than that in addressing one's
　friends, no man knows.
MEDEA. Good health be yours also, wise Pandion's son, Aegeus. Where do you
　come from to visit this land?
AEGEUS. I have just left the ancient oracle of Phoebus.
MEDEA. What sent you to the earth's oracular hub?
AEGEUS. I was enquiring how I might get children.
MEDEA. In the name of Heaven, have you come thus far in life still childless?
AEGEUS. By some supernatural influence I am still without children.
MEDEA. Have you a wife or are you still unmarried?
AEGEUS. I have a wedded wife to share my bed.
MEDEA. Tell me, what did Phoebus tell you about offspring?
AEGEUS. His words were too cunning for a mere man to interpret.
MEDEA. Is it lawful to tell me the answer of the god?
AEGEUS. Surely. For, believe me, it requires a cunning mind to understand.
MEDEA. What then was the oracle? Tell me, if I may hear it.
AEGEUS. I am not to open the cock that projects from the skin . . .
MEDEA. Till you do what? Till you reach what land?
AEGEUS. Till I return to my ancestral hearth.
MEDEA. Then what errand brings your ship to this land?
AEGEUS. There is one Pittheus, king of Troezen . . .
MEDEA. The child of Pelops, as they say, and a most pious man.
AEGEUS. To him I will communicate the oracle of the god.
MEDEA. Yes, he is a cunning man and well-versed in such matters.
AEGEUS. Yes, and of all my comrades in arms the one I love most.
MEDEA. Well, good luck to you, and may you win your heart's desire.
AEGEUS. Why, what's the reason for those sad eyes, that wasted complexion?
MEDEA. Aegeus, I've got the basest husband in all the world.
AEGEUS. What do you mean? Tell me the reason of your despondency, tell me
　plainly.
MEDEA. Jason is wronging me; I never did him wrong.
AEGEUS. What has he done? Speak more bluntly.
MEDEA. He has another wife, to lord it over me in our home.
AEGEUS. You don't mean that he has done so callous, so shameful a deed!
MEDEA. Indeed he did. Me that used to be his darling he now despises.
AEGEUS. Has he fallen in love? Does he hate your embraces?
MEDEA. Yes, it's a grand passion! He was born to betray his loved ones.
AEGEUS. Let him go, then, since he is so base, as you say.
MEDEA. He became enamored of getting a king for a father-in-law.
AEGEUS. Who gave him the bride? Please finish your story.
MEDEA. Creon, the ruler of this Corinth.
AEGEUS. In that case, Madam, I can sympathize with your resentment.
MEDEA. My life is ruined. What is more, I am being expelled from the land.
AEGEUS. By whom? This new trouble is hard.

MEDEA. Creon is driving me out of Corinth into exile.

AEGEUS. And does Jason allow this? I don't like that either.

MEDEA. He says he does not, but he'll stand it. Oh! I beseech you by this beard, by these knees, a suppliant I entreat you, show pity, show pity for my misery. Do not stand by and see me driven forth to a lonely exile. Receive me into your land, into your home and the shelter of your hearth. So may the gods grant you the children you desire, to throw joy round your deathbed. You do not know what a lucky path you have taken to me. I shall put an end to your childlessness. I shall make you beget heirs of your blood. I know the magic potions that will do it.

AEGEUS. Many things make me eager to do this favor for you, Madam. Firstly, the gods, and secondly, the children that you promise will be born to me. In that matter I am quite at my wits' end. But here is how I stand. If you yourself come to Athens, I shall try to be your champion, as in duty bound. This warning, however, I must give you! I shall not consent to take you with me out of Corinth. If you yourself come to my palace, you will find a home and a sanctuary. Never will I surrender you to anybody. But your own efforts must get you away from this place. I wish to be free from blame in the eyes of my hosts also.

MEDEA. And so you shall. But just let me have a pledge for these services, and I shall have all I could desire of you.

AEGEUS. Do you not trust me? What is your difficulty?

MEDEA. I do trust you. But both the house of Pelias and Creon are my enemies. Bound by oaths, you would never hand me over to them if they tried to extradite me. But with an agreement of mere words, unfettered by any sacred pledge, you might be won over by their diplomatic advances to become *their* friend. For I have no influence or power, whereas they have the wealth of a royal palace.

AEGEUS. You take great precautions, Madam. Still, if you wish, I will not refuse to do your bidding. For me too it will be safer that way, if I have some excuse to offer to your enemies, and *you* will have more security. Dictate the oath.

MEDEA. Swear by the Floor of Earth, by the Sun my father's father, by the whole family of the gods, one and all——

AEGEUS. To do or not do what? Say on.

MEDEA. Never yourself to cast me out of your country and never, willingly, during your lifetime, to surrender me to any of my foes that desire to seize me.

AEGEUS. I swear by the Earth, by the holy majesty of the Sun, and by all the gods, to abide by the terms you propose.

MEDEA. Enough! And if you abide not by your oath, what punishment do you pray to receive?

AEGEUS. The doom of sacrilegious mortals.

MEDEA. Go and fare well. All is well. I shall arrive at your city as soon as possible, when I have done what I intend to do, and obtained my desire.

LEADER. (*as* AEGEUS *departs*) May Maia's son, the Lord of Journeys, bring you safe to Athens, and may you achieve the desire that hurries you homeward; for you are a generous man in my esteem.

MEDEA. O Zeus and his Justice, O Light of the Sun! The time has come, my friends, when I shall sing songs of triumph over my enemies. I am on my way. Now I can hope that my foes will pay the penalty. Just as my plans were most storm-tossed at sea, this man has appeared, a veritable harbor, where I shall fix my moorings, when I get to the town and citadel of Pallas.

Now I shall tell you all my plans; what you hear will not be said in fun. I shall send one of my servants to ask Jason to come and see me. When he comes, I shall make my language submissive, tell him I approve of everything else and am quite contented [with his royal marriage and his betrayal of me, that I agree it is all for the best]; I shall only ask him to allow my children to remain. Not that I wish to leave them in a hostile land [for my enemies to insult]. No! I have a cunning plan to kill the princess. I shall send them with gifts to offer to the bride, to allow them to stay in the land—a dainty robe and a headdress of beaten gold. If she takes the finery and puts it on her, she will die in agony. She and anyone who touches her. So deadly are the poisons in which I shall steep my gifts.

But now I change my tone. It grieves me sorely, the horrible deed I must do next. I shall murder my children, these children of mine. No man shall take them away from me. Then when I have accomplished the utter overthrow of the house of Jason, I shall flee from the land, to escape the consequences of my own dear children's murder and my other accursed crimes. My friends, I cannot bear being laughed at by my enemies.

So be it. Tell me, what has life to offer them. They have no father, no home, no refuge from danger.

My mistake was in leaving my father's house, won over by the words of a Greek. But, as god is my ally, he shall pay for his crime. Never, if I can help it, shall he behold his sons again in this life. Never shall he beget children by his new bride. She must die by my poisons, die the death she deserves. Nobody shall despise *me* or think me weak or passive. Quite the contrary. I am a good friend, but a dangerous enemy. For that is the type the world delights to honor.

LEADER. You have confided your plan in me, and I should like to help you, but since I also would support the laws of mankind, I entreat you not to do this deed.

MEDEA. It is the only way. But I can sympathize with your sentiments. You have not been wronged like me.

LEADER. Surely you will not have the heart to destroy your own flesh and blood?

MEDEA. I shall. It will hurt my husband most that way.

LEADER. But it will make you the unhappiest woman in the world.

MEDEA. Let it. From now on all words are superfluous. (*To the* NURSE.) Go now, please, and fetch Jason. Whenever loyalty is wanted, I turn to you. Tell him nothing of my intentions, as you are a woman and a loyal servant of your mistress.

(*Exit* NURSE.)

CHORUS. *The people of Erechtheus have been favored of Heaven from the beginning. Children of the blessed gods are they, sprung from a hallowed land that no foeman's foot has trodden. Their food is glorious Wisdom. There the skies are always clear, and lightly do they walk in that land where once on a time blonde Harmony bore nine chaste daughters, the Muses of Pieria.*

Such is the tale, which tells also how Aphrodite sprinkled the land with water from the fair steams of Cephissus and breathed over it breezes soft and fragrant. Ever on her hair she wears a garland of sweet-smelling roses, and ever she sends the Loves to assist in the court of Wisdom. No good thing is wrought without their help.

How then shall that land of sacred rivers, that hospitable land receive you the slayer of your children? It would be sacrilege for you to live with them. Think. You are stabbing your children. Think. You are earning the name of murderess. By your knees we entreat you, by all the world holds sacred, do not murder your children.

Whence got you the hardihood to conceive such a plan? And in the horrible act, as you bring death on your own children, how will you steel your heart and hand? When you cast your eyes on them, your own children, will you not weep that you should be their murderess? When your own children fall at your feet and beg for mercy, you will never be able to dye your hands with their blood. Your heart will not stand it.

(*Enter* JASON, *followed by the* NURSE.)

JASON. I come at your bidding. Though you hate me, I shall not refuse you an audience. What new favor have you to ask of me, woman?

MEDEA. Jason, please forgive me for all I said. After all the services of love you have rendered me before, I can count on you to put up with my fits of temper. I have been arguing the matter out with myself. Wretched woman (thus I scolded myself), why am I so mad as to hate those that mean me well, to treat as enemies the rulers of this land and my husband who, in marrying a princess and getting brothers for my children, is only doing what is best for us all? What is the matter with me? Why am I still furious, when the gods are showering their blessings on me? Have I not children of my own? Am I forgetting that I am an exile from my native land, in sore need of friends? These reflections let me see how very foolish I have been and how groundless is my resentment. Now, I want to thank you. I think you are only doing the right thing in making this new match. I have been the fool. I ought to have entered into your designs, helped you to accomplish them, even stood by your nuptial couch and been glad to be of service to the new bride. But I am what I am . . . to say no worse, a woman. You ought not therefore to imitate me in my error or to compete with me in childishness. I beg your pardon, and confess that I was wrong then. But now I have taken better counsel, as you see.

Children, children, come here, leave the house, come out and greet your father as I do. Speak to him. Join your mother in making friends with him, forgetting our former hate. It's a truce; the quarrel is over. Take his right hand. Alas! my imagination sickens strangely. My children, will you stretch out loving arms like that in the long hereafter? My grief! How quick my tears are! My fears brim over. It is that long quarrel with your father, now done with, that fills my tender eyes with tears.

LEADER. From my eyes, too, the burning tears gush forth. May Sorrow's advance proceed no further.

JASON. That is the talk I like to hear, woman. The past I can forgive. It is only natural for your sex to show resentment when their husbands contract another marriage. But your heart has now changed for the better. It took time, to be sure, but you have now seen the light of reason. That's the action of a wise woman. As for you, my children, your father has not forgotten you. God willing, he has secured your perfect safety. I feel sure that you will yet occupy the first place here in Corinth, with your brothers. Merely grow up. Your father, and any friends he has in heaven, will see to the rest. May I see you, sturdy and strong, in the flower of your youth, triumphant over my enemies.

You there, why wet your eyes with hot tears, and avert your pale cheek? Why are you not happy to hear me speak thus?

MEDEA. It's nothing. Just a thought about the children here.

JASON. Why all this weeping over the children? It's too much.

MEDEA. I am their mother. Just now when you were wishing them long life, a pang of sorrow came over me, in case things would not work out that way.

JASON. Cheer up, then. I shall see that they are all right.

MEDEA. Very well, I shall not doubt your word. Women are frail things and naturally apt to cry. But to return to the object of this conference, something has been said, something remains to be mentioned. Since it is their royal pleasure to expel me from the country—oh yes! it's the best thing for me too, I know well, not to stay on here in the way of you and the king; I am supposed to be their bitter enemy—*I* then shall go off into exile. But see that the children are reared by your own hand, ask Creon to let *them* stay.

JASON. I don't know if he will listen to me, but I shall try, as I ought.

MEDEA. At least you can get your wife to intercede with her father on their behalf.

JASON. Certainly, and I imagine I shall persuade her.

MEDEA. If she is a woman like the rest of us. In this task, I too shall play my part. I shall send the children with gifts for her, gifts far surpassing the things men make to-day [a fine robe, and a head-dress of beaten gold]. Be quick there. Let one of my maids bring the finery here. What joy will be hers, joys rather, joys innumerable, getting not only a hero like you for a husband, but also raiment which the Sun, my father's father, gave to his children. (MEDEA *takes the casket from a maid who has brought it, and hands it to the children.*) Here, my children, take these wedding gifts in your hands. Carry them to the princess, the happy bride, and give them to her. They are not the kind of gifts she will despise.

JASON.   Impetuous woman! Why leave yourself thus empty-handed? Do you think a royal palace lacks for raiment and gold? Keep these things for yourself, don't give them away. If my wife has any regard for me at all, she will prefer me to wealth, I'm sure.

MEDEA.   Please let me. They say that gifts persuade even the gods, and gold is stronger than ten thousand words. Hers is the fortune of the hour; her now is god exalting. She has youth, and a king for a father. And to save my children from exile, I would give my very life, let alone gold.

Away, my children, enter the rich palace and entreat your father's young wife, my mistress, to let you stay in Corinth. Give her the finery. That is most important. She must take these gifts in her hands. Go as fast as you can. Success attend your mission, and may you bring back to your mother the tidings she longs to hear.

(*Exeunt Children with* TUTOR *and* JASON.)

CHORUS.   *Now are my hopes dead. The children are doomed. Already they are on the road to death. She will take it, the bride will take the golden diadem, and with it will take her ruin, luckless girl. With her own hands she will put the precious circlet of death on her blonde hair.*

The beauty of it, the heavenly sheen, will persuade her to put on the robe and the golden crown. It is in the halls of death that she will put on her bridal dress forthwith. Into that fearful trap she will fall. Death will be her portion, hapless girl. She cannot overleap her doom.

And you, poor man. Little luck your royal father-in-law is bringing you. Unwittingly, you are bringing death on your children, and on your wife an awful end. Ill-starred man, what a way you are from happiness.

And now I weep for your sorrow, hapless mother of these children. You will slaughter them to avenge the dishonor of your bed betrayed, criminally betrayed by your husband who now sleeps beside another bride.

(*Enter Children with their* TUTOR.)

TUTOR.   Mistress, here are your children, reprieved from exile. Your gifts the royal bride took gladly in her hands. The children have made their peace with *her*. What's the matter? Why stand in such confusion, when fortune is smiling? [Why do you turn away your cheek? Why are you not glad to hear my message?]

MEDEA.   Misery!

TUTOR.   That note does not harmonize with the news I have brought.

MEDEA.   Misery, and again Misery!

TUTOR.   Have I unwittingly brought you bad news? I thought it was good. Was I mistaken?

MEDEA.   Your message was . . . your message. It is not you I blame.

TUTOR.   Why then are your eyes downcast and your tears flowing?

MEDEA.   Of necessity, old man, of strong necessity. This is the gods' doing, and mine, in my folly.

TUTOR.   Have courage. Some day your children will bring you too back home.

MEDEA.   Ah me! Before that day I shall bring others to another home.

TUTOR.   You are not the first woman to be separated from her children. We are mortals and must endure calamity with patience.

MEDEA.   That I shall do. Now go inside and prepare their usual food for the children.

(*Exit* TUTOR.)

O my children, my children. For you indeed a city is assured, and a home in which, leaving me to my misery, you will dwell for ever, motherless. But I must go forth to exile in a strange land, before I have ever tasted the joy of seeing *your* happiness, before I have got you brides and bedecked your marriage beds and held aloft the bridal torches. Alas! my own self-will has brought me to misery. Was it all for nothing, my children, the rearing of you, and all the agonizing labor, all the fierce pangs I endured at your birth? Ah me, there was a time when I had strong hopes, fool as I was, that you would tend my old age and with your own hands dress my body for the grave, a fate that the world might envy. Now the sweet dream is gone. Deprived of you, I shall live a life of pain and sorrow. And you, in another world altogether will never again see your mother with your dear, dear eyes.

O the pain of it! Why do your eyes look at me, my children? Why smile at me that last smile? Ah! What can I do? My heart is water, women, at the sight of my children's bright faces. I could never do it. Goodbye to my former plans. I shall take my children away with me. Why should I hurt their father by *their* misfortunes, only to reap a double harvest of sorrow myself? No! I cannot do it. Goodbye to my plans.

And yet . . . what is the matter with me? Do I want to make myself a laughing-stock by letting my enemies off scot-free? I must go through with it. What a coward heart is mine, to admit those soft pleas. Come, my children, into the palace. Those that may not attend my sacrifices can see to it that they are absent. I shall not let my hand be unnerved.

Ah! Ah! Stop, my heart. Do not you commit this crime. Leave them alone, unhappy one, spare the children. Even if they live far from us, they will bring you joy. No! by the unforgetting dead in hell, it cannot be! I shall not leave my children for my enemies to insult. [In any case they must die. And if die they must, *I* shall slay them, who gave them birth.] My schemes are crowned with success. She shall not escape. Already the diadem is on her head; wrapped in the robe the royal bride is dying, I know it well. And now I am setting out on a most sorrowful road [and shall send these on one still more sorrowful]. I wish to speak to my children. Give your mother your hands, my children, give her your hands to kiss.

O dear, dear hand. O dear, dear mouth, dear shapes, dear noble faces, happiness be yours, but not here. Your father has stolen this world from you. How sweet to touch! The softness of their skin, the sweetness of their breath, my babies! Away, away, I cannot bear to see you any longer. *(Children retire within.)* My misery overwhelms me. O I *do* realize how terrible is the crime I am about, but passion overrules my resolutions, passion that causes most of the misery in the world.

CHORUS. *Often ere now I have grappled with subtle subjects and sounded depths of argument deeper than woman may plumb. But, you see, we also have a Muse who teaches us philosophy. It is a small class—perhaps you might find one in a thousand—the women that love the Muse.*

And I declare that in this world those who have had no experience of paternity are happier than the fathers of children. Without children a man does not know whether they are a blessing or a curse, and so he does not miss a joy he has never had and he escapes a multitude of sorrows. But them that have in their home young, growing children that they love, I see them consumed with anxiety, day in day out, how they are to rear them properly, how they are to get a livelihood to leave to them. And, after all that, whether the children for whom they toil are worth it or not, who can tell?

And now I shall tell you the last and crowning sorrow for all mortals. Suppose they have found livelihood enough, their children have grown up, and turned out honest. Then, if it is fated that way, death carries their bodies away beneath the earth. What then is the use, when the love of children brings from the gods this crowning sorrow to top the rest?

MEDEA. My friends, all this time I have been waiting for something to happen, watching to see what they will do in the royal palace. Now I see one of Jason's attendants coming this way. His excited breathing shows that he has a tale of strange evils to tell.

(Enter MESSENGER.*)*

MESSENGER. What a horrible deed of crime you have done, Medea. Flee, flee. Take anything you can find, sea vessel or land carriage.

MEDEA. Tell me, what has happened that I should flee.

MESSENGER. The princess has just died. Her father Creon, too, killed by your poisons.

MEDEA. Best of news! From this moment and for ever you are one of my friends and benefactors.

MESSENGER. What's that? Are you sane and of sound mind, woman? You have inflicted a foul outrage on a king's home, yet you rejoice at the word of it and are not afraid.

MEDEA. I too have a reply that I might make to you. But take your time, my friend. Speak on. How did they die? You would double my delight, if they died in agony.

MESSENGER. When your children, both your offspring, arrived with their father and entered the bride's house, we rejoiced, we servants who had been grieved by your troubles. Immediately a whisper ran from ear to ear that you and your husband had patched up your earlier quarrel. And one kisses your children's hands, another their yellow hair. I myself, in my delight, accompanied the children to the women's rooms. The mistress, whom we now respect in your place, did not see the two boys at first, but cast a longing look at Jason. Then, however, resenting the entrance of the children, she covered her eyes with a veil and averted her white cheek.

Your husband tried to allay the maiden's angry resentment, saying, "You must not hate your friends. Won't you calm your temper, and turn your head this way? You must consider your husband's friends your own. Won't you accept the gifts and ask your father to recall their sentence of exile, for my sake?" Well, when she saw the finery, she could not refrain, but promised her husband everything, and before Jason and your children were far away from the house she took the elaborate robes and put them on her. She placed the golden diadem on her clustering locks and began to arrange her coiffure before a shining mirror, smiling at her body's lifeless reflection. Then she arose from her seat and walked through the rooms, stepping delicately with her fair white feet, overjoyed with the gifts. Time and time again, standing erect, she gazes with all her eyes at her ankles.

But then ensued a fearful sight to see. Her color changed, she staggered, and ran back, her limbs all atremble, and only escaped falling by sinking upon her chair. An old attendant, thinking, I suppose, it was a panic fit, or something else of divine sending, raised a cry of prayer, until she sees a white froth drooling from her mouth, sees her rolling up the pupils of her eyes, and all the blood leaving her skin. Then, instead of a cry of prayer, she let out a scream of lamentation. Immediately one maid rushed to Creon's palace, another to the new bridegroom, to tell of the bride's misfortune. From end to end, the house echoed to hurrying steps. A quick walker, stepping out well, would have reached the end of the two hundred yard track, when the poor girl, lying there quiet, with closed eyes, gave a fearful groan and began to come to. A double plague assailed her. The golden diadem on her head emitted a strange flow of devouring fire, while the fine robes, the gifts of your children, were eating up the poor girl's white flesh. All aflame, she jumps from her seat and flees, shaking her head and hair this way and that, trying to throw off the crown. But the golden band held firmly, and after she had shaken her hair more violently, the fire began to blaze twice as fiercely. Overcome by the agony she falls on the ground, and none but her father could have recognized her. The position of her eyes could not be distinguished, nor the beauty of her face. The blood, clotted with fire, dripped from the crown of her head, and the flesh melted from her bones, like resin from a pinetree, as the poisons ate their unseen way. It was a fearful sight. All were afraid to touch the corpse, taught by what had happened to her.

But her father, unlucky man, rushed suddenly into the room, not knowing what had happened, and threw himself on the body. At once he groaned, and embracing his daughter's form he kissed it and cried, "My poor, poor child, what god has destroyed you so shamefully? Who is it deprives this aged tomb of his only child? Ah! let me join you in death, my child." Then, when he ceased his weeping and lamentation and sought to lift his aged frame upright, he stuck to the fine robes, like ivy to a laurel bush. His struggles were horrible. He would try to free a leg, but the girl's body stuck to his. And if he pulled violently, he tore his shrunken flesh off his bones. At last his life went out; doomed, he gave up the ghost. Side by side lie the two bodies, daughter and old father. Who would not weep at such a calamity?

It seems to me . . . I need not speak of what's in store for you; you yourself will see how well the punishment fits the crime . . . it's not the first time the thought has come, that the life of a man is a shadow. [I might assert with confidence that the mortals who pass for philosophers and subtle reasoners are most to be condemned.] No mortal man has lasting happiness. When the tide of fortune flows his way, one man may have more prosperity than another, but happiness never.

(*Exit* MESSENGER.)

LEADER. It seems that this day Fate is visiting his sins on Jason. Unfortunate daughter of Creon, we pity your calamity. The love of Jason has carried you through the gates of death.

MEDEA. My friends, I am resolved to act, and act quickly [to slay the children and depart from the land]. I can delay no longer, or my children will fall into the murderous hands of those that love them less than I do. In any case they must die. And if they must, I shall slay them, who gave them birth. Now, my heart, steel yourself. Why do we still hold back? The deed is terrible, but necessary. Come, my unhappy hand, seize the sword, seize it. Before you is a course of misery, life-long misery; on now to the starting post. No flinching now, no thinking of the children, the darling children, that call you mother. This day, this one short day, forget your children. You have all the future to mourn for them. Aye, to mourn. Though you mean to kill them, at least you loved them. Oh! I am a most unhappy woman.

(*Exit* MEDEA.)

CHORUS. *O Earth, O glorious radiance of the Sun, look and behold the accursed woman. Stop her before she lays her bloody, murderous hands on her children. Sprung are they from your golden race, O Sun, and it is a fearful thing that the blood of a god should be spilt by mortals. Nay, stop her, skyborn light, prevent her. Deliver the house from the misery of slaughter, and the curse of the unforgetting dead.*

Gone, gone for nothing, are your maternal pangs. For nothing did you bear these lovely boys, O woman, who made the inhospitable passage through the gray Clashing Rocks! Why let your spleen poison your heart? Why this murderlust, where love was? On the man that spills the blood of kinsmen the curse of heaven descends. Go where he may, it rings ever in his ears, bringing sorrows and tribulations on his house.

(*The Children are heard within.*)

    Listen, listen. It is the cry of the children. O cruel, ill-starred woman.

ONE OF THE CHILDREN. (*within*) Ah me! What am I to do? Where can I escape my mothers murderous hands?

THE OTHER. (*within*) I know not, my dear, dear brother. She is killing us.

CHORUS. *Should we break in? Yes! I will save them from death.*

ONE OF THE CHILDREN. (*within*) Do, for god's sake. Save us. We need your help.

THE OTHER. (*within*) Yes, we are already in the toils of the sword.

CHORUS. *Heartless woman! Are you made of stone or steel? Will you slaughter the children, your own seed, slaughter them with your own hands?*

    Only one woman, only one in the history of the world, laid murderous hands on her children, Ino whom the gods made mad, driven from home to a life of wandering by the wife of Zeus. Hapless girl, bent on that foul slaughter, she stepped over a precipice by the shore and fell headlong into the sea, killing herself and her two children together. What crime, more horrible still, may yet come to pass? O the loves of women, fraught with sorrow, how many ills ere now have you brought on mortals!

(*Enter* JASON, *attended.*)

JASON. You women there, standing in front of this house, is Medea still within, who wrought these dreadful deeds? Or has she made her escape? I tell you, she had better hide under the earth or take herself off on wings to the recesses of the sky, unless she wishes to give satisfaction to the family of the king. Does she think she can slay the rulers of the land and get safely away from this house? But I am not so anxious about her as I am about the children. The victims of her crimes will attend to her. It's my own children I am here to save, in case the relatives of the king do them some injury, in revenge for the foul murders their mother has committed.

LEADER. Jason, poor Jason, you do not know the sum of your sorrows, or you would not have said these words.

JASON. What is it? She does not want to kill me too, does she?

LEADER. Your children are dead, slain by their mother's hand.

JASON. For pity's sake, what do you mean? You have slain me, woman.

LEADER. Your children are dead, make no mistake.

JASON. Why, where did she slay them? Indoors or out here?

LEADER. Open the doors and you will see their bodies.

JASON. Quick, servants, loosen the bolts, undo the fastenings. Let me see the double horror, the dead bodies of my children, and the woman who . . . oh! let me punish her.

MEDEA *appears aloft in a chariot drawn by winged dragons. She has the bodies of the children.*

MEDEA. What's all this talk of battering and unbarring? Are you searching for the bodies and me who did the deed? Spare yourself the trouble. If you have anything to ask of me, speak if you will, but never shall you lay a hand on me. I have a magic chariot, given me by the Sun, my father's father, to protect me against my enemies.

JASON. You abominable thing! You most loathsomest woman, to the gods and me and all mankind. You had the heart to take the sword to your children, you their mother, leaving me childless. And you still behold the earth and the sun, you who have done this deed, you who have perpetrated this abominable outrage. My curses on you! At last I have come to my senses, the senses I lost when I brought you from your barbarian home and country to a home in Greece, an evil plague, treacherous alike to your father and the land that reared you. There is a fiend in you, whom the gods have launched against me. In your own home you had already slain your brother when you came aboard the Argo, that lovely ship. Such was your beginning. Then you married me and bore me children, whom you have now destroyed because I left your bed. No Greek woman would ever have done such a deed. Yet I saw fit to marry you, rather than any woman of Greece, a wife to hate me and destroy me, not a woman at all, but a tigress, with a disposition more savage than Tuscan Scylla. But why all this? Ten thousand reproaches could not sting you; your impudence is too engrained. The devil take you, shameless, abominable murderess of your children. I must bemoan my fate; no joy shall I have of my new marriage, and I shall never see alive the children I begot and reared and lost.

MEDEA. I might have made an elaborate rebuttal of the speech you have made, but Zeus the Father knows what you received at my hands and what you have done. You could not hope, nor your princess either, to scorn my love, make a fool of me, and live happily ever after. Nor was Creon, the matchmaker, to drive me out of the country with impunity. Go ahead, then. Call me tigress if you like, or Scylla that haunts the Tuscan coast. I don't mind, now I have got properly under your skin.

JASON. You too are suffering. You have your share of the sorrow.

MEDEA. True, but it's worth the grief, since you cannot scoff.

JASON. O children, what a wicked mother you got!

MEDEA. O children, your father's sins have caused your death.

JASON. Yet it was not *my* hand that slew them.

MEDEA. No, it was your lust, and your new marriage.

JASON. Because your love was scorned you actually thought it right to murder.

MEDEA. Do you think a woman considers that a small injury?

JASON. Good women do. But you are wholly vicious.

MEDEA. The children here are dead. That will sting you.

JASON. No! they live to bring fierce curses on your head.

MEDEA. The gods know who began it all.

JASON. They know, indeed, they know the abominable wickedness of your heart.

MEDEA. Hate me then. I despise your bitter words.

JASON. And I yours. But it is easy for us to be quit of each other.

MEDEA. How, pray? Certainly I am willing.

JASON. Allow me to bury these bodies and lament them.

MEDEA. Certainly not. I shall bury them with my own hands, taking them to the sanctuary of Hera of the Cape, where no enemy may violate their tombs and do them insult. Here in the land of Sisyphus we shall establish a solemn festival, and appoint rites for the future to expiate their impious murder. I myself shall go to the land of Erechtheus, to live with Aegeus, the son of Pandion. You, as is proper, will die the death you deserve, [struck on the head by a fragment of the Argo,] now you have seen the bitter fruits of your new marriage.

JASON. May you be slain by the Curse of your children, and Justice that avenges murder!

MEDEA. What god or power above will listen to you, the breaker of oaths, the treacherous guest?

JASON. Oh! abominable slayer of children.

MEDEA. Get along to the palace and bury your wife.

JASON. I go, bereft of my two sons.

MEDEA. You have nothing yet to bemoan. Wait till you are old.

JASON. My dear, dear children!

MEDEA. Yes, dear to their mother, not to you.

JASON. And yet you slew them.

MEDEA. I did, to hurt you.

JASON. Alas! my grief! I long to kiss their dear mouths.

MEDEA. Now you speak to them, now you greet them, but in the past you spurned them.

JASON. For god's sake, let me touch my children's soft skin.

MEDEA. No! You have gambled and lost.

JASON. O Zeus, do you hear how I am repelled, how I am wronged by this foul tigress, that slew her own children? But such lament as I may and can make, I hereby make. I call upon the gods. I invoke the powers above to bear me witness that you slew my children and now prevent me from embracing their bodies and giving them burial. Would that I had never begotten them, to live to see them slain at your hands.

CHORUS. *Zeus on Olympus hath a wide stewardship. Many things beyond expectation do the gods fulfil. That which was expected has not been accomplished; for that which was unexpected has god found the way. Such was the end of this story.*

(*Exeunt.*)

Journal Entry

Cite evidence, if you can, to explain or justify Medea's actions.

Textual Considerations

1. Identify images in Medea's memorable language that are especially effective in communicating her love, hate, and violence. Analyze what such a language reveals about Medea's magical powers and her sense of self as lover, wife, and mother.
2. Study the **denouement** (see the glossary) of *Medea,* and analyze the kind of moral justice that Euripides explores at the end of his play. As a reader, do you feel satisfied or dissatisfied with the resolution of the drama?
3. Characterize Jason. To what extent do you consider his decision to abandon Medea justifiable? Are his arguments convincing? Why or why not?

Cultural Contexts

1. Make a list of movies, books, and fairy tales that present negative myths of woman as witch, stepmother, or femme fatale. Would you include Medea in this list of outcast women? Evaluate whether these women succeed or fail in creating a viable way of life for themselves through the use of their sexual and political powers.
2. Consider the psychological depth of *Medea* by applying to Medea's tragedy the definition of love as an irresistible passion that overpowers reason and eventually destroys itself.
3. According to Medea, women resort to evil when they are deprived of great deeds by men who reserve such deeds for themselves. Debate with your group the degree to which the identities of the women in *Medea* were derived solely from their roles as daughters, wives, and mothers. Consider also the extent to which they viewed themselves as powerless in the objective world. How might empowerment affect identity? Cite examples.

Henrik Ibsen

A Doll's House

TORVALD HELMER, *a lawyer*
NORA, *his wife*
DR. RANK
MRS. KRISTINE LINDE
NILS KROGSTAD
ANNE MARIE, *the nursemaid*
HELENE, *the maid*
The Helmers' three children
A porter

The action takes place in the Helmers' flat.

ACT ONE

A pleasant room, tastefully but not expensively furnished. On the back wall, one door on the right leads to the entrance hall, a second door on the left leads to HELMER'S *study. Between these two doors, a piano. In the middle of the left wall, a door; and downstage from it, a window. Near the window a round table with armchairs and a small sofa. In the right wall, upstage, a door; and on the same wall downstage, a porcelain stove with a couple of armchairs and a rocking-chair. Between the stove and the door a small table. Etchings on the walls. A whatnot with china and other small objets d'art; a small bookcase with books in handsome bindings. Carpet on the floor; a fire burns in the stove. A winter's day.*

The front door-bell rings in the hall; a moment later, there is the sound of the front door being opened. NORA *comes into the room, happily humming to herself. She is dressed in her outdoor things, and is carrying lots of parcels which she then puts down on the table, right. She leaves the door into the hall standing open; a* PORTER *can be seen outside holding a Christmas tree and a basket; he hands them to the* MAID *who has opened the door for them.*

NORA. Hide the Christmas tree away carefully, Helene. The children mustn't see it till this evening when it's decorated. [*To the* PORTER, *taking out her purse.*] How much?

PORTER. Fifty öre.

NORA. There's a crown. Keep the change.

[*The* PORTER *thanks her and goes.* NORA *shuts the door. She continues to laugh quietly and happily to herself as she takes off her things. She takes a bag of macaroons out of her pocket and eats one or two; then she walks stealthily across and listens at her husband's door.*]

NORA. Yes, he's in.

[*She begins humming again as she walks over to the table, right.*]

HELMER [*in his study*]. Is that my little sky-lark chirruping out there?

NORA [*busy opening some of the parcels*]. Yes, it is.

HELMER. Is that my little squirrel frisking about?

NORA. Yes!

HELMER. When did my little squirrel get home?

NORA. Just this minute. [*She stuffs the bag of macaroons in her pocket and wipes her mouth.*] Come on out, Torvald, and see what I've bought.

HELMER. I don't want to be disturbed! [*A moment later, he opens the door and looks out, his pen in his hand.*] 'Bought', did you say? All that? Has my little spendthrift been out squandering money again?

NORA. But, Torvald, surely this year we can spread ourselves just a little. This is the first Christmas we haven't had to go carefully.

HELMER. Ah, but that doesn't mean we can afford to be extravagant, you know.

NORA. Oh yes, Torvald, surely we can afford to be just a little bit extravagant now, can't we? Just a teeny-weeny bit. You are getting quite a good salary now, and you are going to earn lots and lots of money.

HELMER. Yes, after the New Year. But it's going to be three whole months before the first pay cheque comes in.

NORA. Pooh! We can always borrow in the meantime.

HELMER. Nora! [*Crosses to her and takes her playfully by the ear.*] Here we go again, you and your frivolous ideas! Suppose I went and borrowed a thousand crowns today, and you went and spent it all over Christmas, then on New Year's Eve a slate fell and hit me on the head and there I was. . . .

NORA [*putting her hand over his mouth*]. Sh! Don't say such horrid things.

HELMER. Yes, but supposing something like that did happen . . . what then?

NORA. If anything as awful as that did happen, I wouldn't care if I owed anybody anything or not.

HELMER. Yes, but what about the people I'd borrowed from?

NORA. Them? Who cares about them! They are only strangers!

HELMER. Nora, Nora! Just like a woman! Seriously though, Nora, you know what I think about these things. No debts! Never borrow! There's always something inhibited, something unpleasant, about a home built on credit and borrowed money. We two have managed to stick it out so far, and that's the way we'll go on for the little time that remains.

NORA [*walks over to the stove*]. Very well, just as you say, Torvald.

HELMER [*following her*]. There, there! My little singing bird mustn't go drooping her wings, eh? Has it got the sulks, that little squirrel of mine? [*Takes out his wallet.*] Nora, what do you think I've got here?

NORA [*quickly turning round*]. Money!

HELMER. There! [*He hands her some notes.*] Good heavens, I know only too well how Christmas runs away with the housekeeping.

NORA [*counts*]. Ten, twenty, thirty, forty. Oh, thank you, thank you, Torvald! This will see me quite a long way.

HELMER. Yes, it'll have to.

NORA. Yes, yes, I'll see that it does. But come over here, I want to show you all the things I've bought. And so cheap! Look, some new clothes for Ivar . . . and a little sword. There's a horse and a trumpet for Bob. And a doll and a doll's cot for Emmy. They are not very grand but she'll have them all broken before long anyway. And I've got some dress material and some handkerchiefs for the maids. Though, really, dear old Anne Marie should have had something better.

HELMER. And what's in this parcel here?

NORA [*shrieking*]. No, Torvald! You mustn't see that till tonight!

HELMER. All right. But tell me now, what did my little spendthrift fancy for herself?

NORA. For me? Puh, I don't really want anything.

HELMER. Of course you do. Anything reasonable that you think you might like, just
tell me.

NORA. Well, I don't really know. As a matter of fact, though, Torvald . . .

HELMER. Well?

NORA [*toying with his coat buttons, and without looking at him*]. If you did want to
give me something, you could . . . you could always . . .

HELMER. Well, well, out with it!

NORA [*quickly*]. You could always give me money, Torvald. Only what you think
you could spare. And then I could buy myself something with it later on.

HELMER. But Nora. . . .

NORA. Oh, please, Torvald dear! Please! I beg you. Then I'd wrap the money up in
some pretty gilt paper and hang it on the Christmas tree. Wouldn't that be fun?

HELMER. What do we call my pretty little pet when it runs away with all the money?

NORA. I know, I know, we call it a spendthrift. But please let's do what I said,
Torvald. Then I'll have a bit of time to think about what I need most. Isn't that
awfully sensible, now, eh?

HELMER [*smiling*]. Yes, it is indeed—that is, if only you really could hold on to the
money I gave you, and really did buy something for yourself with it. But it just
gets mixed up with the housekeeping and frittered away on all sorts of useless
things, and then I have to dig into my pocket all over again.

NORA. Oh but, Torvald. . . .

HELMER. You can't deny it, Nora dear. [*Puts his arm round her waist.*] My pretty
little pet is very sweet, but it runs away with an awful lot of money. It's
incredible how expensive it is for a man to keep such a pet.

NORA. For shame! How can you say such a thing? As a matter of fact I save
everything I can.

HELMER [*laughs*]. Yes, you are right there. Everything you *can*. But you simply
can't.

NORA [*hums and smiles quietly and happily*]. Ah, if you only knew how many
expenses the likes of us sky-larks and squirrels have, Torvald!

HELMER. What a funny little one you are! Just like your father. Always on the
look-out for money, wherever you can lay your hands on it; but as soon on as
you've got it, it just seems to slip through your fingers. You never seem to know
what you've done with it. Well, one must accept you as you are. It's in the
blood. Oh yes, it is, Nora. That sort of thing is hereditary.

NORA. Oh, I only wish I'd inherited a few more of Daddy's qualities.

HELMER. And I wouldn't want my pretty little song-bird to be the least bit different
from what she is now. But come to think of it, you look rather . . . rather . . .
how shall I put it? . . . rather guilty today. . . .

NORA. Do I?

HELMER. Yes, you do indeed. Look me straight in the eye.

NORA [*looks at him*]. Well?

HELMER [*wagging his finger at her*]. My little sweet-tooth surely didn't forget
herself in town today?

NORA. No, whatever makes you think that?

HELMER. She didn't just pop into the confectioner's for a moment?

NORA. No, I assure you, Torvald . . . !

HELMER. Didn't try sampling the preserves?

NORA. No, really I didn't.

HELMER. Didn't go nibbling a macaroon or two?

NORA. No, Torvald, honestly, you must believe me . . . !

HELMER. All right then! It's really just my little joke. . . .

NORA [*crosses to the table*]. I would never dream of doing anything you didn't want me to.

HELMER. Of course not, I know that. And then you've given me your word. . . . [*Crosses to her.*] Well then, Nora dearest, you shall keep your little Christmas secrets. They'll all come out tonight, I dare say, when we light the tree.

NORA. Did you remember to invite Dr. Rank?

HELMER. No. But there's really no need. Of course he'll come and have dinner with us. Anyway, I can ask him when he looks in this morning. I've ordered some good wine. Nora, you can't imagine how I am looking forward to this evening.

NORA. So am I. And won't the children enjoy it, Torvald!

HELMER. Oh, what a glorious feeling it is, knowing you've got a nice, safe job, and a good fat income. Don't you agree? Isn't it wonderful, just thinking about it?

NORA. Oh, it's marvellous!

HELMER. Do you remember last Christmas? Three whole weeks beforehand you shut yourself up every evening till after midnight making flowers for the Christmas tree and all the other splendid things you wanted to surprise us with. Ugh, I never felt so bored in all my life.

NORA. I wasn't the least bit bored.

HELMER [*smiling*]. But it turned out a bit of an anticlimax, Nora.

NORA. Oh, you are not going to tease me about that again! How was I to know the cat would get in and pull everything to bits?

HELMER. No, of course you weren't. Poor little Nora! All you wanted was for us to have a nice time—and it's the thought behind it that counts, after all. All the same, it's a good thing we've seen the back of those lean times.

NORA. Yes, really it's marvellous.

HELMER. Now there's no need for me to sit here all on my own, bored to tears. And you don't have to strain your dear little eyes, and work those dainty little fingers to the bone. . . .

NORA [*clapping her hands*]. No, Torvald, I don't, do I? Not any more. Oh, how marvellous it is to hear that! [*Takes his arm.*] Now I want to tell you how I've been thinking we might arrange things, Torvald. As soon as Christmas is over. . . . [*The door-bell rings in the hall.*] Oh, there's the bell. [*Tidies one or two things in the room.*] It's probably a visitor. What a nuisance!

HELMER. Remember I'm not at home to callers.

MAID [*in the doorway*]. There's a lady to see you, ma'am.

NORA. Show her in, please.

MAID [*to* HELMER]. And the doctor's just arrived, too, sir.

HELMER. Did he go straight into my room?

MAID. Yes, he did, sir.

> [HELMER *goes into his study. The* MAID *shows in* MRS. LINDE, *who is in travelling clothes, and closes the door after her.*]

MRS. LINDE [*subdued and rather hesitantly*]. How do you do, Nora?

NORA [*uncertainly*]. How do you do?

MRS. LINDE. I'm afraid you don't recognize me.

NORA. No, I don't think I . . . And yet I seem to. . . . [*Bursts out suddenly.*] Why! Kristine! Is it really you?

MRS. LINDE. Yes, it's me.

NORA. Kristine! Fancy not recognizing you again! But how was I to, when . . . [*Gently.*] How you've changed, Kristine!

MRS. LINDE. I dare say I have. In nine . . . ten years. . . .

NORA. Is it so long since we last saw each other? Yes, it must be. Oh, believe me these last eight years have been such a happy time. And now you've come up to town, too? All that long journey in wintertime. That took courage.

MRS. LINDE. I just arrived this morning on the steamer.

NORA. To enjoy yourself over Christmas, of course. How lovely! Oh, we'll have such fun, you'll see. Do take off your things. You are not cold, are you? [*Helps her.*] There now! Now let's sit down here in comfort beside the stove. No, here, you take the armchair, I'll sit here on the rocking-chair. [*Takes her hands.*] Ah, now you look a bit more like your old self again. It was just that when I first saw you. . . . But you are a little paler, Kristine . . . and perhaps even a bit thinner!

MRS. LINDE. And much, much older, Nora.

NORA. Yes, perhaps a little older . . . very, very little, not really very much. [*Stops suddenly and looks serious.*] Oh, what a thoughtless creature I am, sitting here chattering on like this! Dear, sweet Kristine, can you forgive me?

MRS. LINDE. What do you mean, Nora?

NORA [*gently*]. Poor Kristine, of course you're a widow now.

MRS. LINDE. Yes, my husband died three years ago.

NORA. Oh, I remember now. I read about it in the papers. Oh, Kristine, believe me I often thought at the time of writing to you. But I kept putting it off, something always seemed to crop up.

MRS. LINDE. My dear Nora, I understand so well.

NORA. No, it wasn't very nice of me, Kristine. Oh, you poor thing, what you must have gone through. And didn't he leave you anything?

MRS. LINDE. No.

NORA. And no children?

MRS. LINDE. No.

NORA. Absolutely nothing?

MRS. LINDE. Nothing at all . . . not even a broken heart to grieve over.

NORA [*looks at her incredulously*]. But, Kristine, is that possible?

MRS. LINDE [*smiles sadly and strokes* NORA'S *hair*]. Oh, it sometimes happens, Nora.

NORA. So utterly alone. How terribly sad that must be for you. I have three lovely children. You can't see them for the moment, because they're out with their nanny. But now you must tell me all about yourself. . . .

MRS. LINDE. No, no, I want to hear about you.

NORA. No, you start. I won't be selfish today. I must think only about your affairs today. But there's just one thing I really must tell you. Have you heard about the great stroke of luck we've had in the last few days?

MRS. LINDE. No. What is it?

NORA. What do you think? My husband has just been made Bank Manager!

MRS. LINDE. Your husband? How splendid!

NORA. Isn't it tremendous! It's not a very steady way of making a living, you know, being a lawyer, especially if he refuses to take on anything that's the least bit shady—which of course is what Torvald does, and I think he's quite right. You can imagine how pleased we are! He starts at the Bank straight after New Year, and he's getting a big salary and lots of commission. From now on we'll be able to live quite differently . . . we'll do just what we want. Oh, Kristine, I'm so happy and relieved. I must say it's lovely to have plenty of money and not have to worry. Isn't it?

MRS. LINDE. Yes. It must be nice to have enough, at any rate.

NORA. No, not just enough, but pots and pots of money.

MRS. LINDE [*smiles*]. Nora, Nora, haven't you learned any sense yet? At school you used to be an awful spendthrift.

NORA. Yes, Torvald still says I am. [*Wags her finger.*] But little Nora isn't as stupid as everybody thinks. Oh, we haven't really been in a position where I could afford to spend a lot of money. We've both had to work.

MRS. LINDE. You too?

NORA. Yes, odd jobs—sewing, crochet-work, embroidery and things like that. [*Casually.*] And one or two other things, besides. I suppose you know that Torvald left the Ministry when we got married. There weren't any prospects of promotion in his department, and of course he needed to earn more money than he had before. But the first year he wore himself out completely. He had to take on all kinds of extra jobs, you know, and he found himself working all hours of the day and night. But he couldn't go on like that; and he became seriously ill. The doctors said it was essential for him to go South.

MRS. LINDE. Yes, I believe you spent a whole year in Italy, didn't you?

NORA. That's right. It wasn't easy to get away, I can tell you. It was just after I'd had Ivar. But of course we had to go. Oh, it was an absolutely marvellous trip. And it saved Torvald's life. But it cost an awful lot of money, Kristine.

MRS. LINDE. That I can well imagine.

NORA. Twelve hundred dollars. Four thousand eight hundred crowns. That's a lot of money, Kristine.

MRS. LINDE. Yes, but in such circumstances, one is very lucky if one has it.

NORA. Well, we got it from Daddy, you see.

MRS. LINDE. Ah, that was it. It was just about then your father died, I believe, wasn't it?

NORA. Yes, Kristine, just about then. And do you know, I couldn't even go and look after him. Here was I expecting Ivar any day. And I also had poor Torvald, gravely ill, on my hands. Dear, kind Daddy! I never saw him again, Kristine. Oh, that's the saddest thing that has happened to me in all my married life.

MRS. LINDE. I know you were very fond of him. But after that you left for Italy?

NORA. Yes, we had the money then, and the doctors said it was urgent. We left a month later.

MRS. LINDE. And your husband came back completely cured?

NORA. Fit as a fiddle!

MRS. LINDE. But . . . what about the doctor?

NORA. How do you mean?

MRS. LINDE. I thought the maid said something about the gentleman who came at the same time as me being a doctor.

NORA. Yes, that was Dr. Rank. But this isn't a professional visit. He's our best friend and he always looks in at least once a day. No, Torvald has never had a day's illness since. And the children are fit and healthy, and so am I. [*Jumps up and claps her hands.*] Oh God, oh God, isn't it marvellous to be alive, and to be happy, Kristine! . . . Oh, but I ought to be ashamed of myself . . . Here I go on talking about nothing but myself. [*She sits on a low stool near* MRS. LINDE *and lays her arms on her lap.*] Oh, please, you musn't be angry with me! Tell me, is it really true that you didn't love your husband? What made you marry him, then?

MRS. LINDE. My mother was still alive; she was bedridden and helpless. And then I had my two young brothers to look after as well. I didn't think I would be justified in refusing him.

NORA. No, I dare say you are right. I suppose he was fairly wealthy then?

MRS. LINDE. He was quite well off, I believe. But the business was shaky. When he died, it went all to pieces, and there just wasn't anything left.

NORA. What then?

MRS. LINDE. Well, I had to fend for myself, opening a little shop, running a little school, anything I could turn my hand to. These last three years have been one long relentless drudge. But now it's finished, Nora. My poor dear mother doesn't need me any more, she's passed away. Nor the boys either; they're at work now, they can look after themselves.

NORA. What a relief you must find it. . . .

MRS. LINDE. No, Nora! Just unutterably empty. Nobody to live for any more. [*Stands up restlessly.*] That's why I couldn't stand it any longer being cut off up there. Surely it must be a bit easier here to find something to occupy your mind. If only I could manage to find a steady job of some kind, in an office perhaps. . . .

NORA. But, Kristine, that's terribly exhausting; and you look so worn out even before you start. The best thing for you would be a little holiday at some quiet little resort.

MRS. LINDE. [*crosses to the window*]. I haven't any father I can fall back on for the money, Nora.

NORA [*rises*]. Oh, please, you mustn't be angry with me!

MRS. LINDE [*goes to her*]. My dear Nora, you mustn't be angry with me either. That's the worst thing about people in my position, they become so bitter. One has nobody to work for, yet one has to be on the look-out all the time. Life has to go on, and one starts thinking only of oneself. Believe it or not, when you told me the good news about your step up, I was pleased not so much for your sake as for mine.

NORA. How do you mean? Ah, I see. You think Torvald might be able to do something for you.

MRS. LINDE. Yes, that's exactly what I thought.

NORA. And so he shall, Kristine. Just leave things to me. I'll bring it up so cleverly . . . I'll think up something to put him in a good mood. Oh, I do so much want to help you.

MRS. LINDE. It is awfully kind of you, Nora, offering to do all this for me, particularly in your case, where you haven't known much trouble or hardship in your own life.

NORA. When I . . . ? I haven't known much . . . ?

MRS. LINDE [*smiling*]. Well, good heavens, a little bit of sewing to do and a few things like that. What a child you are, Nora!

NORA [*tosses her head and walks across the room*]. I wouldn't be too sure of that, if I were you.

MRS. LINDE. Oh?

NORA. You're just like the rest of them. You all think I'm useless when it comes to anything really serious. . . .

MRS. LINDE. Come, come. . . .

NORA. You think I've never had anything much to contend with in this hard world.

MRS. LINDE. Nora dear, you've only just been telling me all the things you've had to put up with.

NORA. Pooh! They were just trivialities! [*Softly.*] I haven't told you about the really big thing.

MRS. LINDE. What big thing? What do you mean?

NORA. I know you rather tend to look down on me, Kristine. But you shouldn't, you know. You are proud of having worked so hard and so long for your mother.

MRS. LINDE. I'm sure I don't look down on anybody. But it's true what you say: I am both proud and happy when I think of how I was able to make Mother's life a little easier towards the end.

NORA. And you are proud when you think of what you have done for your brothers, too.

MRS. LINDE. I think I have every right to be.

NORA. I think so too. But now I'm going to tell you something, Kristine. I too have something to be proud and happy about.

MRS. LINDE. I don't doubt that. But what is it you mean?

NORA. Not so loud. Imagine if Torvald were to hear! He must never on any account . . . nobody must know about it, Kristine, nobody but you.

MRS. LINDE. But what is it?

NORA. Come over here. [*She pulls her down on the sofa beside her.*] Yes, Kristine, I too have something to be proud and happy about. I was the one who saved Torvald's life.

MRS. LINDE. Saved . . . ? How . . . ?

NORA. I told you about our trip to Italy. Torvald would never have recovered but for that. . . .

MRS. LINDE. Well? Your father gave you what money was necessary. . . .

NORA [*Smiles*]. That's what Torvald thinks, and everybody else. But . . .

MRS. LINDE. But . . . ?

NORA. Daddy never gave us a penny. I was the one who raised the money.

MRS. LINDE. You? All that money?

NORA. Twelve hundred dollars. Four thousand eight hundred crowns. What do you say to that!

MRS. LINDE. But, Nora, how was it possible? Had you won a sweepstake or something?

NORA. [*contemptuously*]. A sweepstake? Pooh! There would have been nothing to it then.

MRS. LINDE. Where did you get it from, then?

NORA [*hums and smiles secretively*]. H'm, tra-la-la!

MRS. LINDE. Because what you couldn't do was borrow it.

NORA. Oh? Why not?

MRS. LINDE. Well, a wife can't borrow without her husband's consent.

NORA [*tossing her head*]. Ah, but when it happens to be a wife with a bit of a sense for business . . . a wife who knows her way about things, then. . . .

MRS. LINDE. But, Nora, I just don't understand. . . .

NORA. You don't have to. I haven't said I did borrow the money. I might have got it some other way. [*Throws herself back on the sofa.*] I might even have got it from some admirer. Anyone as reasonably attractive as I am. . . .

MRS. LINDE. Don't be so silly!

NORA. Now you must be dying of curiosity, Kristine.

MRS. LINDE. Listen to me now, Nora dear—you haven't done anything rash, have you?

NORA [*sitting up again*]. Is it rash to save your husband's life?

MRS. LINDE. I think it was rash to do anything without telling him. . . .

NORA. But the whole point was that he mustn't know anything. Good heavens, can't you see! He wasn't even supposed to know how desperately ill he was. It was me the doctors came and told his life was in danger, that the only way to save him was to go South for a while. Do you think I didn't try talking him into it first? I began dropping hints about how nice it would be if I could be taken on a little trip abroad, like other young wives. I wept, I pleaded. I told him he ought to show some consideration for my condition, and let me have a bit of my own way. And then I suggested he might take out a loan. But at that he nearly lost his temper, Kristine. He said I was being frivolous, that it was his duty as a husband not to give in to all these whims and fancies of mine—as I do believe he called them. All right, I thought, somehow you've got to be saved. And it was then I found a way. . . .

MRS. LINDE. Did your husband never find out from your father that the money hadn't come from him?

NORA. No, never. It was just about the time Daddy died. I'd intended letting him into the secret and asking him not to give me away. But when he was so ill . . . I'm sorry to say it never became necessary.

MRS. LINDE. And you never confided in your husband?

NORA. Good heavens, how could you ever imagine such a thing! When he's so strict about such matters! Besides, Torvald is a man with a good deal of pride—it would be terribly embarrassing and humiliating for him if he owed anything to me. It would spoil everything between us; this happy home of ours would never be the same again.

MRS. LINDE. Are you never going to tell him?

NORA [*reflectively, half-smiling*]. Oh yes, some day perhaps . . . in many years time, when I'm no longer as pretty as I am now. You mustn't laugh! What I mean of course is when Torvald isn't quite so much in love with me as he is now, when he's lost interest in watching me dance, or get dressed up, or recite. Then it might be a good thing to have something in reserve. . . . [*Breaks off.*] What nonsense! That day will never come. Well, what have you got to say to my big secret, Kristine? Still think I'm not much good for anything? One thing, though, it's meant a lot of worry for me, I can tell you. It hasn't always been easy to meet my obligations when the time came. You know in business there is something called quarterly interest, and other things called instalments, and these are always terribly difficult things to cope with. So what I've had to do is save a little here and there, you see, wherever I could. I couldn't really save anything out of the housekeeping, because Torvald has to live in decent style. I couldn't let the children go about badly dressed either—I felt any money I got for them had to go on them alone. Such sweet little things!

MRS. LINDE. Poor Nora! So it had to come out of your own allowance?

NORA. Of course. After all, I was the one it concerned most. Whenever Torvald gave me money for new clothes and such-like, I never spent more than half. And always I bought the simplest and cheapest things. It's a blessing most things look well on me, so Torvald never noticed anything. But sometimes I did feel it was a bit hard, Kristine, because it is nice to be well dressed, isn't it?

MRS. LINDE. Yes, I suppose it is.

NORA. I have had some other sources of income, of course. Last winter I was lucky enough to get quite a bit of copying to do. So I shut myself up every night and sat and wrote through to the small hours of the morning. Oh, sometimes I was so tired, so tired. But it was tremendous fun all the same, sitting there working and earning money like that. It was almost like being a man.

MRS. LINDE. And how much have you been able to pay off like this?

NORA. Well, I can't tell exactly. It's not easy to know where you are with transactions of this kind, you understand. All I know is I've paid off just as much as I could scrape together. Many's the time I was at my wit's end. [*Smiles.*] Then I used to sit here and pretend that some rich old gentleman had fallen in love with me. . . .

MRS. LINDE. What! What gentleman?

NORA. Oh, rubbish! . . . and that now he had died, and when they opened his will, there in big letters were the words: 'My entire fortune is to be paid over, immediately and in cash, to charming Mrs. Nora Helmer.'

MRS. LINDE. But my dear Nora—who *is* this man?

NORA. Good heavens, don't you understand? There never was any old gentleman; it was just something I used to sit here pretending, time and time again, when I didn't know where to turn next for money. But it doesn't make very much difference; as far as I'm concerned, the old boy can do what he likes, I'm tired of him; I can't be bothered any more with him or his will. Because now all my worries are over. [*Jumping up.*] Oh God, what a glorious thought, Kristine! No more worries! Just think of being without a care in the world . . . being able to romp with the children, and making the house nice and attractive, and having things just as Torvald likes to have them! And then spring will soon be here, and blue skies. And maybe we can go away somewhere. I might even see something of the sea again. Oh yes! When you're happy, life is a wonderful thing!

[*The door-bell is heard in the hall.*]

MRS. LINDE [*gets up*]. There's the bell. Perhaps I'd better go.

NORA. No, do stay, please. I don't suppose it's for me; it's probably somebody for Torvald. . . .

MAID [*in the doorway*]. Excuse me, ma'am, but there's a gentleman here wants to see Mr. Helmer and I didn't quite know . . . because the Doctor is in there. . . .

NORA. Who is the gentleman?

KROGSTAD [*in the doorway*]. It's me, Mrs. Helmer.

[MRS. LINDE *starts, then turns away to the window.*]

NORA [*tense, takes a step towards him and speaks in a low voice*]. You? What is it? What do you want to talk to my husband about?

KROGSTAD. Bank matters . . . in a manner of speaking. I work at the bank, and I hear your husband is to be the new manager. . . .

NORA. So it's . . .

KROGSTAD. Just routine business matters, Mrs. Helmer. Absolutely nothing else.

NORA. Well then, please go into his study.

[*She nods impassively and shuts the hall door behind him; then she walks across and sees to the stove.*]

MRS. LINDE. Nora . . . who was that man?

NORA. His name is Krogstad.

MRS. LINDE. So it really was him.

NORA. Do you know the man?

MRS. LINDE. I used to know him . . . a good many years ago. He was a solicitor's clerk in our district for a while.

NORA. Yes, so he was.

MRS. LINDE. How he's changed!

NORA. His marriage wasn't a very happy one, I believe.

MRS. LINDE. He's a widower now, isn't he?

NORA. With a lot of children. There, it'll burn better now.

[*She closes the stove door and moves the rocking-chair a little to one side.*]

MRS. LINDE. He does a certain amount of business on the side, they say?

NORA. Oh? Yes, it's always possible. I just don't know. . . . But let's not think about business . . . it's all so dull.

[*DR. RANK comes in from HELMER's study.*]

DR. RANK [*still in the doorway*]. No, no, Torvald, I won't intrude. I'll just look in on your wife for a moment. [*Shuts the door and notices Mrs. Linde.*] Oh, I beg your pardon. I'm afraid I'm intruding here as well.

NORA. No, not at all! [*Introduces them.*] Dr. Rank . . . Mrs. Linde.

RANK. Ah! A name I've often heard mentioned in this house. I believe I came past you on the stairs as I came in.

MRS. LINDE. I have to take things slowly going upstairs. I find it rather a trial.

RANK. Ah, some little disability somewhere, eh?

MRS. LINDE. Just a bit run down, I think, actually.

RANK. Is that all? Then I suppose you've come to town for a good rest—doing the rounds of the parties?

MRS. LINDE. I have come to look for work.

RANK. Is that supposed to be some kind of sovereign remedy for being run down?

MRS. LINDE. One must live, Doctor.

RANK. Yes, it's generally thought to be necessary.

NORA. Come, come, Dr. Rank. You are quite as keen to live as anybody.

RANK. Quite keen, yes. Miserable as I am, I'm quite ready to let things drag on as long as possible. All my patients are the same. Even those with a moral affliction are no different. As a matter of fact, there's a bad case of that kind in talking with Helmer at this very moment. . . .

MRS. LINDE [*Softly*]. Ah!

NORA. Whom do you mean?

RANK. A person called Krogstad—nobody you would know. He's rotten to the core. But even he began talking about having to *live*, as though it were something terribly important.

NORA. Oh? And what did he want to talk to Torvald about?

RANK. I honestly don't know. All I heard was something about the Bank.

NORA. I didn't know that Krog . . . that this Mr. Krogstad had anything to do with the Bank.

RANK. Oh yes, he's got some kind of job down there. [*To* MRS. LINDE.] I wonder if you've got people in your part of the country too who go rushing round sniffing out cases of moral corruption, and then installing the individuals concerned in nice, well-paid jobs where they can keep them under observation. Sound, decent people have to be content to stay out in the cold.

MRS. LINDE. Yet surely it's the sick who most need to be brought in.

RANK [*shrugs his shoulders*]. Well, there we have it. It's that attitude that's turning society into a clinic.

> [NORA, *lost in her own thoughts, breaks into smothered laughter and claps her hands.*]

RANK. Why are you laughing at that? Do you know in fact what society is?

NORA. What do I care about your silly old society? I was laughing about something quite different . . . something frightfully funny. Tell me, Dr. Rank, are all the people who work at the Bank dependent on Torvald now?

RANK. Is *that* what you find so frightfully funny?

NORA [*smiles and hums*]. Never you mind! Never you mind! [*Walks about the room.*] Yes, it really is terribly amusing to think that we . . . that Torvald now has power over so many people. [*She takes the bag out of her pocket.*] Dr. Rank, what about a little macaroon?

RANK. Look at this, eh? Macaroons. I thought they were forbidden here.

NORA. Yes, but these are some Kristine gave me.

MRS. LINDE. What? I . . . ?

NORA. Now, now, you needn't be alarmed. You weren't to know that Torvald had forbidden them. He's worried in case they ruin my teeth, you know. Still . . . what's it matter once in a while! Don't you think so, Dr. Rank? Here! [*She pops a macaroon into his mouth.*] And you too, Kristine. And I shall have one as well; just a little one . . . or two at the most. [*She walks about the room again.*] Really I am so happy. There's just one little thing I'd love to do now.

RANK. What's that?

NORA. Something I'd love to say in front of Torvald.

RANK. Then why can't you?

NORA. No, I daren't. It's not very nice.

MRS. LINDE. Not very nice?

RANK. Well, in that case it might not be wise. But to us I don't see why. . . . What is this you would love to say in front of Helmer?

NORA. I would simply love to say: 'Damn'.

RANK. Are you mad!

MRS. LINDE. Good gracious, Nora.

RANK. Say it! Here he is!

NORA [*hiding the bag of macaroons*]. Sh! Sh!

> [HELMER *comes out of his room, his overcoat over his arm and his hat in his hand.*]

NORA [*going over to him*]. Well, Torvald dear, did you get rid of him?

HELMER. Yes, he's just gone.

NORA. Let me introduce you. This is Kristine, who has just arrived in town. . . .

HELMER. Kristine . . . ? You must forgive me, but I don't think I know . . .

NORA. Mrs. Linde, Torvald dear. Kristine Linde.

HELMER. Ah, indeed. A school-friend of my wife's, presumably.

MRS. LINDE. Yes, we were girls together.

NORA. Fancy, Torvald, she's come all this long way just to have a word with you.

HELMER. How is that?

MRS. LINDE. Well, it wasn't really. . . .

NORA. The thing is, Kristine is terribly clever at office work, and she's frightfully keen on finding a job with some efficient man, so that she can learn even more . . . .

HELMER. Very sensible, Mrs. Linde.

NORA. And then when she heard you'd been made Bank Manager— there was a bit in the paper about it—she set off at once. Torvald please! You will try and do something for Kristine, won't you? For my sake?

HELMER. Well, that's not altogether impossible. You are a widow, I presume?

MRS. LINDE. Yes.

HELMER. And you've had some experience in business?

MRS. LINDE. A fair amount.

HELMER. Well, it's quite probable I can find you a job, I think. . . .

NORA [*clapping her hands*]. There, you see!

HELMER. You have come at a fortunate moment, Mrs. Linde. . . .

MRS. LINDE. Oh, how can I ever thank you . . . ?

HELMER. Not a bit. [*He puts on his overcoat.*] But for the present I must ask you to excuse me. . . .

RANK. Wait. I'm coming with you.

> [*He fetches his fur coat from the hall and warms it at the stove.*]

NORA. Don't be long, Torvald dear.

HELMER. Not more than an hour, that's all.

NORA. Are you leaving too, Kristine?

MRS. LINDE [*putting on her things*]. Yes, I must go and see if I can't find myself a room.

HELMER. Perhaps we can all walk down the road together.

NORA [*helping her*]. What a nuisance we are so limited for space here. I'm afraid it just isn't possible. . . .

MRS. LINDE. Oh, you mustn't dream of it! Goodbye, Nora dear, and thanks for everything.

NORA. Goodbye for the present. But . . . you'll be coming back this evening, of course. And you too, Dr. Rank? What's that? If you are up to it? Of course you'll be up to it. Just wrap yourself up well.

> [*They go out, talking, into the hall; children's voices can be heard on the stairs.*]

NORA. Here they are! Here they are! [*She runs to the front door and opens it.* ANNE MARIE, *the nursemaid, enters with the children.*] Come in! Come in! [*She bends down and kisses them.*] Ah! my sweet little darlings. . . . You see them, Kristine? Aren't they lovely!

RANK. Don't stand here chattering in this draught!

HELMER. Come along, Mrs. Linde. The place now becomes unbearable for anybody except mothers.

> [DR. RANK, HELMER, *and* MRS. LINDE *go down the stairs: the* NURSEMAID *comes into the room with the children, then* NORA, *shutting the door behind her.*]

NORA. How fresh and bright you look! My, what red cheeks you've got! Like apples and roses. [*During the following, the children keep chattering away to her.*] Have you had a nice time? That's splendid. And you gave Emmy and Bob a ride on your sledge? Did you now! Both together! Fancy that! There's a clever boy, Ivar. Oh, let me take her a little while, Anne Marie. There's my sweet little baby-doll! [*She takes the youngest of the children from the nursemaid and dances with her.*] All right, Mummy will dance with Bobby too. What? You've been throwing snowballs? Oh, I wish I'd been there. No, don't bother, Anne Marie, I'll help them off with their things. No, please, let me—I like doing it. You go on in, you look frozen. You'll find some hot coffee on the stove. [*The nursemaid goes into the room, left.* NORA *takes off the children's coats and hats and throws them down anywhere, while the children all talk at once.*] Really! A great big dog came running after you? But he didn't bite. No, the doggies wouldn't bite my pretty little dollies. You mustn't touch the parcels, Ivar! What are they? Wouldn't you like to know! No, no, that's nasty. Now? Shall we play something? What shall we play? Hide and seek? Yes, let's play hide and seek. Bob can hide first. Me first? All right, let me hide first.

> [*She and the children play, laughing and shrieking, in this room and in the adjacent room on the right. Finally* NORA *hides under the table; the children come rushing in to look for her but cannot find her; they hear*

her stifled laughter, rush to the table, lift up the tablecloth and find her. Tremendous shouts of delight. She creeps out and pretends to frighten them. More shouts. Meanwhile there has been a knock at the front door, which nobody has heard. The door half opens, and KROGSTAD *can be seen. He waits a little; the game continues.*]

KROGSTAD. I beg your pardon, Mrs. Helmer. . . .

NORA [*turns with a stifled cry and half jumps up*]. Ah! What do you want?

KROGSTAD. Excuse me. The front door was standing open. Somebody must have forgotten to shut it. . . .

NORA [*standing up*]. My husband isn't at home, Mr. Krogstad.

KROGSTAD. I know.

NORA. Well . . . what are you doing here?

KROGSTAD. I want a word with you.

NORA. With . . . ? [*Quietly, to the children.*] Go to Anne Marie. What? No, the strange man won't do anything to Mummy. When he's gone we'll have another game. [*She leads the children into the room, left, and shuts the door after them; tense and uneasy.*] You want to speak to me?

KROGSTAD. Yes, I do.

NORA. Today? But it isn't the first of the month yet. . . .

KROGSTAD. No, it's Christmas Eve. It depends entirely on you what sort of Christmas you have.

NORA. What do you want? Today I can't possibly . . .

KROGSTAD. Let's not talk about that for the moment. It's something else. You've got a moment to spare?

NORA. Yes, I suppose so, though . . .

KROGSTAD. Good. I was sitting in Olsen's cafe, and I saw your husband go down the road . . .

NORA. Did you?

KROGSTAD. . . . with a lady.

NORA. Well?

KROGSTAD. May I be so bold as to ask whether that lady was a Mrs. Linde?

NORA. Yes.

KROGSTAD. Just arrived in town?

NORA. Yes, today.

KROGSTAD. And she's a good friend of yours?

NORA. Yes, she is. But I can't see . . .

KROGSTAD. I also knew her once.

NORA. I know.

KROGSTAD. Oh? So you know all about it. I thought as much. Well, I want to ask you straight: is Mrs. Linde getting a job in the Bank?

NORA. How dare you cross-examine me like this, Mr. Krogstad? You, one of my husband's subordinates? But since you've asked me, I'll tell you. Yes, Mrs.

Linde *has* got a job. And I'm the one who got it for her, Mr. Krogstad. Now you know.

KROGSTAD. So my guess was right.

NORA [*walking up and down*]. Oh, I think I can say that some of us have a little influence now and again. Just because one happens to be a woman, that doesn't mean. . . . People in subordinate positions, ought to take care they don't offend anybody . . . who . . . hm . . .

KROGSTAD. . . . has influence?

NORA. Exactly.

KROGSTAD [*changing his tone*]. Mrs. Helmer, will you have the goodness to use your influence on my behalf?

NORA. What? What do you mean?

KROGSTAD. Will you be so good as to see that I keep my modest little job at the Bank?

NORA. What do you mean? Who wants to take it away from you?

KROGSTAD. Oh, you needn't try and pretend to me you don't know. I can quite see that this friend of yours isn't particularly anxious to bump up against me. And I can also see now whom I can thank for being given the sack.

NORA. But I assure you. . . .

KROGSTAD. All right, all right. But to come to the point: there's still time. And I advise you to use your influence to stop it.

NORA. But, Mr. Krogstad, I *have* no influence.

KROGSTAD. Haven't you? I thought just now you said yourself . . .

NORA. I didn't mean it that way, of course. Me? What makes you think I've got any influence of that kind over my husband?

KROGSTAD. I know your husband from our student days. I don't suppose he is any more steadfast than other married men.

NORA. You speak disrespectfully of my husband like that and I'll show you the door.

KROGSTAD. So the lady's got courage.

NORA. I'm not frightened of you any more. After New Year I'll soon be finished with the whole business.

KROGSTAD [*controlling himself*]. Listen to me, Mrs. Helmer. If necessary I shall fight for my little job in the Bank as if I were fighting for my life.

NORA. So it seems.

KROGSTAD. It's not just for the money, that's the last thing I care about. There's something else . . . well, I might as well out with it. You see it's like this. You know as well as anybody that some years ago I got myself mixed up in a bit of trouble.

NORA. I believe I've heard something of the sort.

KROGSTAD. It never got as far as the courts; but immediately it was as if all paths were barred to me. So I started going in for the sort of business you know about. I had to do something, and I think I can say I haven't been one of the worst. But now I have to get out of it. My sons are growing up; for their sake

I must try and win back what respectability I can. That job in the Bank was like the first step on the ladder for me. And now your husband wants to kick me off the ladder again, back into the mud.

NORA. But in God's name, Mr. Krogstad, it's quite beyond my power to help you.

KROGSTAD. That's because you haven't the will to help me. But I have ways of making you.

NORA. You wouldn't go and tell my husband I owe you money?

KROGSTAD. Suppose I did tell him?

NORA. It would be a rotten shame. [*Half choking with tears.*] That secret is all my pride and joy—why should he have to hear about it in this nasty, horrid way . . . hear about it from *you*. You would make things horribly unpleasant for me. . . .

KROGSTAD. Merely unpleasant?

NORA [*vehemently*]. Go on, do it then! It'll be all the worse for you. Because then my husband will see for himself what a bad man you are, and then you certainly won't be able to keep your job.

KROGSTAD. I asked whether it was only a bit of domestic unpleasantness you were afraid of?

NORA. If my husband gets to know about it, he'll pay off what's owing at once. And then we'd have nothing more to do with you.

KROGSTAD [*taking a pace towards her*]. Listen, Mrs. Helmer, either you haven't a very good memory, or else you don't understand much about business. I'd better make the position a little bit clearer for you.

NORA. How do you mean?

KROGSTAD. When your husband was ill, you came to me for the loan of twelve hundred dollars.

NORA. I didn't know of anybody else.

KROGSTAD. I promised to find you the money. . . .

NORA. And you did find it.

KROGSTAD. I promised to find you the money on certain conditions. At the time you were so concerned about your husband's illness, and so anxious to get the money for going away with, that I don't think you paid very much attention to all the incidentals. So there is perhaps some point in reminding you of them. Well, I promised to find you the money against an IOU which I drew up for you.

NORA. Yes, and which I signed.

KROGSTAD. Very good, But below that I added a few lines, by which your father was to stand security. This your father was to sign.

NORA. Was to . . . ? He did sign it.

KROGSTAD. I had left the date blank. The idea was that your father was to add the date himself when he signed it. Remember?

NORA. Yes, I think. . . .

KROGSTAD. I then gave you the IOU to post to your father. Wasn't that so?

NORA. Yes.

KROGSTAD. Which of course you did at once. Because only about five or six days later you brought it back to me with your father's signature. I then paid out the money.

NORA. Well? Haven't I paid the instalments regularly?

KROGSTAD. Yes, fairly. But . . . coming back to what we were talking about . . . that was a pretty bad period you were going through then, Mrs. Helmer.

NORA. Yes, it was.

KROGSTAD. Your father was seriously ill, I believe.

NORA. He was very near the end.

KROGSTAD. And died shortly afterwards?

NORA. Yes.

KROGSTAD. Tell me, Mrs. Helmer, do you happen to remember which day your father died? The exact date, I mean.

NORA. Daddy died on 29 September.

KROGSTAD. Quite correct. I made some inquiries. Which brings up a rather curious point [*takes out a paper*] which I simply cannot explain.

NORA. Curious . . . ? I don't know . . .

KROGSTAD. The curious thing is, Mrs. Helmer, that your father signed this document three days after his death.

NORA. What? I don't understand. . . .

KROGSTAD. Your father died on 29 September. But look here. Your father has dated his signature 2 October. Isn't that rather curious, Mrs. Helmer? [NORA *remains silent.*] It's also remarkable that the words '2 October' and the year are not in your father's handwriting, but in a handwriting I rather think I recognize. Well, perhaps that could be explained. Your father might have forgotten to date his signature, and then somebody else might have made a guess at the date later, before the fact of your father's death was known. There is nothing wrong in that. What really matters is the signature. And *that* is of course genuine, Mrs. Helmer? It really was your father who wrote his name here?

NORA [*after a moment's silence, throws her head back and looks at him defiantly*]. No, it wasn't. It was me who signed father's name.

KROGSTAD. Listen to me. I suppose you realize that that is a very dangerous confession?

NORA. Why? You'll soon have all your money back.

KROGSTAD. Let me ask you a question: why didn't you send that document to your father?

NORA. It was impossible. Daddy was ill. If I'd asked him for his signature, I'd have had to tell him what the money was for. Don't you see, when he was as ill as that I couldn't go and tell him that my husband's life was in danger. It was simply impossible.

KROGSTAD. It would have been better for you if you had abandoned the whole trip.

NORA. No, that was impossible. This was the thing that was to save my husband's life. I couldn't give it up.

KROGSTAD. But did it never strike you that this was fraudulent . . . ?

NORA. That wouldn't have meant anything to me. Why should I worry about you? I couldn't stand you, not when you insisted on going through with all those cold-blooded formalities, knowing all the time what a critical state my husband was in.

KROGSTAD. Mrs. Helmer, it's quite clear you still haven't the faintest idea what it is you've committed. But let me tell you, my own offence was no more and no worse than that, and it ruined my entire reputation.

NORA. You? Are you trying to tell me that you once risked everything to save your wife's life?

KROGSTAD. The law takes no account of motives.

NORA. Then they must be very bad laws.

KROGSTAD. Bad or not, if I produce this document in court, you'll be condemned according to them.

NORA. I don't believe it. Isn't a daughter entitled to try and save her father from worry and anxiety on his deathbed? Isn't a wife entitled to save her husband's life? I might not know very much about the law, but I feel sure of one thing: it must say somewhere that things like this are allowed. You mean to say you don't know that—you, when it's your job? You must be a rotten lawyer, Mr. Krogstad.

KROGSTAD. That may be. But when it comes to business transactions— like the sort between us two—perhaps you'll admit I know something about *them?* Good. Now you must please yourself. But I tell you this: if I'm pitched out a second time, you are going to keep me company.

[*He bows and goes out through the hall.*]

NORA [*stands thoughtfully for a moment, then tosses her head*]. Rubbish! He's just trying to scare me. I'm not such a fool as all that. [*Begins gathering up the children's clothes; after a moment she stops.*] Yet . . . ? No, it's impossible! I did it for love, didn't I?

THE CHILDREN [*in the doorway, left*]. Mummy, the gentleman's just gone out of the gate.

NORA. Yes, I know. But you mustn't say anything to anybody about that gentleman. You hear? Not even to Daddy!

THE CHILDREN. All right, Mummy. Are you going to play again?

NORA. No, not just now.

THE CHILDREN. But Mummy, you promised!

NORA. Yes, but I can't just now. Off you go now, I have a lot to do. Off you go, my darlings. [*She herds them carefully into the other room and shuts the door behind them. She sits down on the sofa, picks up her embroidery and works a few stitches, but soon stops.*] No! [*She flings her work down, stands up, goes to the hall door and calls out.*] Helene! Fetch the tree in for me, please. [*She walks across to the table, left, and opens the drawer; again pauses.*] No, really, it's quite impossible!

MAID [*with the Christmas tree*]. Where shall I put it, Ma'am?

NORA. On the floor there, in the middle.

MAID. Anything else you want me to bring?

NORA. No, thank you. I've got what I want.

[*The* MAID *has put the tree down and goes out.*]

NORA [*busy decorating the tree*]. Candles here . . . and flowers here.—Revolting man! It's all nonsense! There's nothing to worry about. We'll have a lovely Christmas tree. And I'll do anything you want me to, Torvald; I'll sing for you, dance for you. . . .

[HELMER, *with a bundle of documents under his arm, comes in by the hall door.*]

NORA. Ah, back again already?

HELMER. Yes. Anybody been?

NORA. Here? No.

HELMER. That's funny. I just saw Krogstad leave the house.

NORA. Oh? O yes, that's right. Krogstad was here a minute.

HELMER. Nora, I can tell by your face he's been asking you to put a good word in for him.

NORA. Yes.

HELMER. And you were to pretend it was your own idea? You were to keep quiet about his having been here. He asked you to do that as well, didn't he?

NORA. Yes, Torvald. But . . .

HELMER. Nora, Nora, what possessed you to do a thing like that? Talking to a person like him, making him promises? And then on top of everything, to tell me a lie!

NORA. A lie . . . ?

HELMER. Didn't you say that nobody had been here? [*Wagging his finger at her.*] Never again must my little song-bird do a thing like that! Little song-birds must keep their pretty little beaks out of mischief; no chirruping out of tune! [*Puts his arm round her waist.*] Isn't that the way we want things to be? Yes, of course it is. [*Lets her go.*] So let's say no more about it. [*Sits down by the stove.*] Ah, nice and cosy here!

[*He glances through his papers.*]

NORA [*busy with the Christmas tree, after a short pause*]. Torvald!

HELMER. Yes.

NORA. I'm so looking forward to the fancy dress ball at the Stenborgs on Boxing Day.

HELMER. And I'm terribly curious to see what sort of surprise you've got for me.

NORA. Oh, it's too silly.

HELMER. Oh?

NORA. I just can't think of anything suitable. Everything seems so absurd, so pointless.

HELMER. Has my little Nora come to *that* conclusion?

NORA [*behind his chair, her arms on the chairback*]. Are you very busy, Torvald?
HELMER. Oh. . . .
NORA. What are all those papers?
HELMER. Bank matters.
NORA. Already?
HELMER. I have persuaded the retiring manager to give me authority to make any changes in organization or personnel I think necessary. I have to work on it over the Christmas week. I want everything straight by the New Year.
NORA. So that was why that poor Krogstad. . . .
HELMER. Hm!
NORA [*still leaning against the back of the chair, running her fingers through his hair*]. If you hadn't been so busy, Torvald, I'd have asked you to do me an awfully big favour.
HELMER. Let me hear it. What's it to be?
NORA. Nobody's got such good taste as you. And the thing is I do so want to look my best at the fancy dress ball. Torvald, couldn't you give me some advice and tell me what you think I ought to go as, and how I should arrange my costume?
HELMER. Aha! So my impulsive little woman is asking for somebody to come to her rescue, eh?
NORA. Please, Torvald, I never get anywhere without your help.
HELMER. Very well, I'll think about it. We'll find something.
NORA. That's sweet of you. [*She goes across to the tree again; pause.*] How pretty these red flowers look. Tell me, was it really something terribly wrong this man Krogstad did?
HELMER. Forgery. Have you any idea what that means?
NORA. Perhaps circumstances left him no choice?
HELMER. Maybe. Or perhaps, like so many others, he just didn't think. I am not so heartless that I would necessarily want to condemn a man for a single mistake like that.
NORA. Oh no, Torvald, of course not!
HELMER. Many a man might be able to redeem himself, if he honestly confessed his guilt and took his punishment.
NORA. Punishment?
HELMER. But that wasn't the way Krogstad chose. He dodged what was due to him by a cunning trick. And that's what has been the cause of his corruption.
NORA. Do you think it would . . . ?
HELMER. Just think how a man with a thing like that on his conscience will always be having to lie and cheat and dissemble; he can never drop the mask, not even with his own wife and children. And the children—*that's* the most terrible part of it, Nora.
NORA. Why?
HELMER. A fog of lies like that on a household, and it spreads disease and infection to every part of it. Every breath the children take in that kind of house is reeking with evil germs.

NORA [*closer behind him*]. Are you sure of that?

HELMER. My dear Nora, as a lawyer I know what I'm talking about. Practically all juvenile delinquents come from homes where the mother is dishonest.

NORA. Why mothers particularly?

HELMER. It's generally traceable to the mothers, but of course fathers can have the same influence. Every lawyer knows that only too well. And yet there's Krogstad been poisoning his own children for years with lies and deceit. That's the reason I call him morally depraved. [*Holds out his hands to her.*] That's why my sweet little Nora must promise me not to try putting in any more good words for him. Shake hands on it. Well? What's this? Give me your hand. There now! That's settled. I assure you I would have found it impossible to work with him. I quite literally feel physically sick in the presence of such people.

NORA [*draws her hand away and walks over to the other side of the Christmas tree*]. How hot it is in here! And I still have such a lot to do.

HELMER. [*stands up and collects his papers together*]. Yes, I'd better think of getting some of this read before dinner. I must also think about your costume. And I might even be able to lay my hands on something to wrap in gold paper and hang on the Christmas tree. [*He lays his hand on her head.*] My precious little singing bird.

[*He goes into his study and shuts the door behind him.*]

NORA [*quietly, after a pause*]. Nonsense! It can't be. It's impossible. It *must* be impossible.

MAID [*in the doorway, left*]. The children keep asking so nicely if they can come in and see Mummy.

NORA. No, no, don't let them in! You stay with them, Anne Marie.

MAID. Very well, ma'am.

[*She shuts the door.*]

NORA [*pale with terror*]. Corrupt my children. . . ! Poison my home? [*Short pause; she throws back her head.*] It's not true! It could never, never be true!

ACT TWO

The same room. In the corner beside the piano stands the Christmas tree, stripped, bedraggled and with its candles burnt out. NORA's outdoor things lie on the sofa. NORA, alone there, walks about restlessly; at last she stops by the sofa and picks up her coat.

NORA [*putting her coat down again*]. Somebody's coming! [*Crosses to the door, listens.*] No, it's nobody. Nobody will come today, of course, Christmas Day— nor tomorrow, either. But perhaps. . . . [*She opens the door and looks out.*] No, nothing in the letter box; quite empty. [*Comes forward.*] Oh, nonsense! He didn't mean it seriously. Things like that *can't* happen. It's impossible. Why, I have three small children.

[THE NURSEMAID *comes from the room, left, carrying a big cardboard box.*]

NURSEMAID. I finally found it, the box with the fancy dress costumes.

NORA. Thank you. Put it on the table, please.

NURSEMAID [*does this*]. But I'm afraid they are in an awful mess.

NORA. Oh, if only I could rip them up into a thousand pieces!

NURSEMAID. Good heavens, they can be mended all right, with a bit of patience.

NORA. Yes, I'll go over and get Mrs. Linde to help me.

NURSEMAID. Out again? In this terrible weather? You'll catch your death of cold, Ma'am.

NORA. Oh, worse things might happen.—How are the children?

NURSEMAID. Playing with their Christmas presents, poor little things, but . . .

NORA. Do they keep asking for me?

NURSEMAID. They are so used to being with their Mummy.

NORA. Yes, Anne Marie, from now on I can't be with them as often as I was before.

NURSEMAID. Ah well, children get used to anything in time.

NORA. Do you think so? Do you think they would forget their Mummy if she went away for good?

NURSEMAID. Good gracious—for good?

NORA. Tell me, Anne Marie—I've often wondered—how on earth could you bear to hand your child over to strangers?

NURSEMAID. Well, there was nothing else for it when I had to come and nurse my little Nora.

NORA. Yes but . . . how could you *bring* yourself to do it?

NURSEMAID. When I had the chance of such a good place? When a poor girl's been in trouble she must make the best of things. Because *he* didn't help, the rotter.

NORA. But your daughter will have forgotten you.

NURSEMAID. Oh no, she hasn't. She wrote to me when she got confirmed, and again when she got married.

NORA [*putting her arms round her neck*]. Dear old Anne Marie, you were a good mother to me when I was little.

NURSEMAID. My poor little Nora never had any other mother but me.

NORA. And if my little ones only had you, I know you would. . . . Oh, what am I talking about! [*She opens the box.*] Go in to them. I must . . . Tomorrow I'll let you see how pretty I am going to look.

NURSEMAID. Ah, there'll be nobody at the ball as pretty as my Nora.

[*She goes into the room, left.*]

NORA [*begins unpacking the box, but soon throws it down*]. Oh, if only I dare go out. If only I could be sure nobody would come. And that nothing would happen in the meantime here at home. Rubbish—nobody's going to come. I mustn't think about it. Brush this muff. Pretty gloves, pretty gloves! I'll put it right out of my mind. One, two, three, four, five, six. . . . [*Screams.*] Ah, they are coming. . . . [*She starts towards the door, but stops irresolute.* MRS. LINDE *comes from the hall, where she has taken off her things.*] Oh, it's you, Kristine. There's nobody else out there, is there? I'm so glad you've come.

MRS. LINDE. I heard you'd been over looking for me.

NORA. Yes, I was just passing. There's something you must help me with. Come and sit beside me on the sofa here. You see, the Stenborgs are having a fancy dress party upstairs tomorrow evening, and now Torvald wants me to go as a Neapolitan fisher lass and dance the tarantella. I learned it in Capri, you know.

MRS. LINDE. Well, well! So you are going to do a party piece?

NORA. Torvald says I should. Look, here's the costume, Torvald had it made for me down there. But it's got all torn and I simply don't know. . . .

MRS. LINDE. We'll soon have that put right. It's only the trimming come away here and there. Got a needle and thread? Ah, here's what we are after.

NORA. It's awfully kind of you.

MRS. LINDE. So you are going to be all dressed up tomorrow, Nora? Tell you what—I'll pop over for a minute to see you in all your finery. But I'm quite forgetting to thank you for the pleasant time we had last night.

NORA [*gets up and walks across the room*]. Somehow I didn't think yesterday was as nice as things generally are.—You should have come to town a little earlier, Kristine.—Yes, Torvald certainly knows how to make things pleasant about the place.

MRS. LINDE. You too, I should say. You are not your father's daughter for nothing. But tell me, is Dr. Rank always as depressed as he was last night?

NORA. No, last night it was rather obvious. He's got something seriously wrong with him, you know. Tuberculosis of the spine, poor fellow. His father was a horrible man, who used to have mistresses and things like that. That's why the son was always ailing, right from being a child.

MRS. LINDE [*lowering her sewing*]. But my dear Nora, how do you come to know about things like that?

NORA [*walking about the room*]. Huh! When you've got three children, you get these visits from . . . women who have had a certain amount of medical training. And you hear all sorts of things from them.

MRS. LINDE [*begins sewing again; short silence*]. Does Dr. Rank call in every day?

NORA. Every single day. He was Torvald's best friend as a boy, and he's a good friend of *mine,* too. Dr. Rank is almost like one of the family.

MRS. LINDE. But tell me—is he really genuine? What I mean is: doesn't he sometimes rather turn on the charm?

NORA. No, on the contrary. What makes you think that?

MRS. LINDE. When you introduced me yesterday, he claimed he'd often heard my name in this house. But afterwards I noticed your husband hadn't the faintest idea who I was. Then how is it that Dr. Rank should. . . .

NORA. Oh yes, it was quite right what he said, Kristine. You see Torvald is so terribly in love with me that he says he wants me all to himself. When we were first married, it even used to make him sort of jealous if I only as much as mentioned any of my old friends from back home. So of course I stopped doing it. But I often talk to Dr. Rank about such things. He likes hearing about them.

MRS. LINDE. Listen, Nora! In lots of ways you are still a child. Now, I'm a good deal older than you, and a bit more experienced. I'll tell you something: I think you ought to give up all this business with Dr. Rank.

NORA. Give up what business?

MRS. LINDE. The whole thing, I should say. Weren't you saying yesterday something about a rich admirer who was to provide you with money. . . .

NORA. One who's never existed, I regret to say. But what of it?

MRS. LINDE. Has Dr. Rank money?

NORA. Yes, he has.

MRS. LINDE. And no dependents?

NORA. No, nobody. But . . . ?

MRS. LINDE. And he comes to the house every day?

NORA. Yes, I told you.

MRS. LINDE. But how can a man of his position want to pester you like this?

NORA. I simply don't understand.

MRS. LINDE. Don't pretend, Nora. Do you think I don't see now who you borrowed the twelve hundred from?

NORA. Are you out of your mind? Do you really think that? A friend of ours who comes here every day? The whole situation would have been absolutely intolerable.

MRS. LINDE. It *really* isn't him?

NORA. No, I give you my word. It would never have occurred to me for one moment. . . . Anyway, he didn't have the money to lend then. He didn't inherit it till later.

MRS. LINDE. Just as well for you, I'd say, my dear Nora.

NORA. No, it would never have occurred to me to ask Dr. Rank. . . . All the same I'm pretty certain if I were to ask him. . . .

MRS. LINDE. But of course you won't.

NORA. No, of course not. I can't ever imagine it being necessary. But I'm quite certain if ever I were to mention it to Dr. Rank. . . .

MRS. LINDE. Behind your husband's back?

NORA. I have to get myself out of that other business. That's also behind his back. I must get myself out of that.

MRS. LINDE. Yes, that's what I said yesterday. But . . .

NORA [*walking up and down*]. A man's better at coping with these things than a woman. . . .

MRS. LINDE. Your own husband, yes.

NORA. Nonsense! [*Stops.*] When you've paid everything you owe, you do get your IOU back again, don't you?

MRS. LINDE. Of course.

NORA. And you can tear it up into a thousand pieces and burn it—the nasty, filthy thing!

MRS. LINDE [*looking fixedly at her, puts down her sewing and slowly rises*]. Nora, you are hiding something from me.

NORA. Is it so obvious?

MRS. LINDE. Something has happened to you since yesterday morning. Nora, what is it?

NORA [*going towards her*]. Kristine! [*Listens.*] Hush! There's Torvald back. Look, you go and sit in there beside the children for the time being. Torvald can't stand the sight of mending lying about. Get Anne Marie to help you.

MRS. LINDE [*gathering a lot of the things together*]. All right, but I'm not leaving until we have thrashed this thing out.

[*She goes into the room, left; at the same time* HELMER *comes in from the hall.*]

NORA [*goes to meet him*]. I've been longing for you to be back, Torvald, dear.

HELMER. Was that the dressmaker . . . ?

NORA. No, it was Kristine; she's helping me with my costume. I think it's going to look very nice. . . .

HELMER. Wasn't that a good idea of mine, now?

NORA. Wonderful! But wasn't it also nice of me to let you have your way?

HELMER [*taking her under the chin*]. Nice of you because you let your husband have his way? All right, you little rogue, I know you didn't mean it that way. But I don't want to disturb you. You'll be wanting to try the costume on, I suppose.

NORA. And I dare say you've got work to do?

HELMER. Yes. [*Shows her a bundle of papers.*] Look at this. I've been down at the Bank. . . .

[*He turns to go into his study.*]

NORA. Torvald!

HELMER. [*stopping*]. Yes.

NORA. If a little squirrel were to ask ever so nicely . . . ?

HELMER. Well?

NORA. Would you do something for it?

HELMER. Naturally I would first have to know what it is.

NORA. Please, if only you would let it have its way, and do what it wants, it'd scamper about and do all sorts of marvellous tricks.

HELMER. What is it?

NORA. And the pretty little sky-lark would sing all day long. . . .

HELMER. Huh! It does that anyway.

NORA. I'd pretend I was an elfin child and dance a moonlight dance for you, Torvald.

HELMER. Nora—I hope it's not that business you started on this morning?

NORA [*coming closer*]. Yes, it is, Torvald. I implore you!

HELMER. You have the nerve to bring that up again?

NORA. Yes, yes, you *must* listen to me. You must let Krogstad keep his job at the Bank.

HELMER. My dear Nora, I'm giving his job to Mrs. Linde.

NORA. Yes, it's awfully sweet of you. But couldn't you get rid of somebody else in the office instead of Krogstad?

HELMER. This really is the most incredible obstinacy! Just because you go and make some thoughtless promise to put in a good word for him, you expect me . . .

NORA. It's not that, Torvald. It's for your own sake. That man writes in all the nastiest papers, you told me that yourself. He can do you no end of harm. He terrifies me to death. . . .

HELMER. Aha, now I see. It's your memories of what happened before that are frightening you.

NORA. What do you mean?

HELMER. It's your father you are thinking of.

NORA. Yes . . . yes, that's right. You remember all the nasty insinuations those wicked people put in the papers about Daddy? I honestly think they would have had him dismissed if the Ministry hadn't sent you down to investigate, and you hadn't been so kind and helpful.

HELMER. My dear little Nora, there is a considerable difference between your father and me. Your father's professional conduct was not entirely above suspicion. Mine is. And I hope it's going to stay that way as long as I hold this position.

NORA. But nobody knows what some of these evil people are capable of. Things could be so nice and pleasant for us here, in the peace and quiet of our home—you and me and the children, Torvald! That's why I implore you. . . .

HELMER. The more you plead for him, the more impossible you make it for me to keep him on. It's already down at the Bank that I am going to give Krogstad his notice. If it ever got around that the new manager had been talked over by his wife. . . .

NORA. What of it?

HELMER. Oh, nothing! As long as the little woman gets her own stubborn way. . . ! Do you want me to make myself a laughing stock in the office? . . . Give people the idea that I am susceptible to any kind of outside pressure? You can imagine how soon I'd feel the consequences of that! Anyway, there's one other consideration that makes it impossible to have Krogstad in the Bank as long as I am manager.

NORA. What's that?

HELMER. At a pinch I might have overlooked his past lapses. . . .

NORA. Of course you could, Torvald!

HELMER. And I'm told he's not bad at his job, either. But we knew each other rather well when we were younger. It was one of those rather rash friendships that prove embarrassing in later life. There's no reason why you shouldn't know we were once on terms of some familiarity. And he, in his tactless way, makes no attempt to hide the fact, particularly when other people are present. On the contrary, he thinks he has every right to treat me as an equal, with his 'Torvald this' and 'Torvald that' every time he opens his mouth. I find it extremely irritating, I can tell you. He would make my position at the Bank absolutely intolerable.

NORA. Torvald, surely you aren't serious?

HELMER. Oh? Why not?

NORA. Well, it's all so petty.

HELMER. What's that you say? Petty? Do you think I'm petty?

NORA. No, not at all, Torvald dear! And that's why . . .

HELMER. Doesn't make any difference! . . . You call my motives petty; so I must be petty too. Petty! Indeed! Well, we'll put a stop to that, once and for all. [*He opens the hall door and calls.*] Helene!

NORA. What are you going to do?

HELMER. [*searching among his papers*]. Settle things. [*The* MAID *comes in.*] See this letter? I want you to take it down at once. Get hold of a messenger and get him to deliver it. Quickly. The address is on the outside. There's the money.

MAID. Very good, sir.

[*She goes with the letter.*]

HELMER. [*putting his papers together*]. There now, my stubborn little miss.

NORA [*breathless*]. Torvald . . . what was that letter?

HELMER. Krogstad's notice.

NORA. Get it back, Torvald! There's still time! Oh, Torvald, get it back! Please for my sake, for your sake, for the sake of the children! Listen, Torvald, please! You don't realize what it can do to us.

HELMER. Too late.

NORA. Yes, too late.

HELMER. My dear Nora, I forgive you this anxiety of yours, although it is actually a bit of an insult. Oh, but it is, I tell you! It's hardly flattering to suppose that anything this miserable pen-pusher wrote could frighten *me!* But I forgive you all the same, because it is rather a sweet way of showing how much you love me. [*He takes her in his arms.*] This is how things must be, my own darling Nora. When it comes to the point, I've enough strength and enough courage, believe me, for whatever happens. You'll find I'm man enough to take everything on myself.

NORA [*terrified*]. What do you mean?

HELMER. Everything, I said. . . .

NORA [*in command of herself*]. That is something you shall never, never do.

HELMER. All right, then we'll share it, Nora—as man and wife. That's what we'll do. [*Caressing her.*] Does that make you happy now? There, there, don't look at me with those eyes, like a little frightened dove. The whole thing is sheer imagination.—Why don't you run through the tarantella and try out the tambourine? I'll go into my study and shut both the doors, then I won't hear anything. You can make all the noise you want. [*Turns in the doorway.*] And when Rank comes, tell him where he can find me.

[*He nods to her, goes with his papers into his room, and shuts the door behind him.*]

NORA [*wild-eyed with terror, stands as though transfixed*]. He's quite capable of doing it! He would do it! No matter what, he'd do it.—No, never in this world! Anything but that! Help? Some way out . . . ? [*The door-bell rings in the hall.*] Dr. Rank . . . ! Anything but that, *anything!* [*She brushes her hands over her face, pulls herself together and opens the door into the hall.* DR. RANK *is standing outside hanging up his fur coat. During what follows it begins to grow dark.*] Hello, Dr. Rank. I recognized your ring. Do you mind not going in to Torvald just yet, I think he's busy.

RANK. And you?

[DR. RANK *comes into the room and she closes the door behind him.*]

NORA. Oh, you know very well I've always got time for you.

RANK. Thank you. A privilege I shall take advantage of as long as I am able.

NORA. What do you mean—as long as you are able?

RANK. Does that frighten you?

NORA. Well, it's just that it sounds so strange. Is anything likely to happen?

RANK. Only what I have long expected. But I didn't think it would come quite so soon.

NORA [*catching at his arm*]. What have you found out? Dr. Rank, you must tell me!

RANK. I'm slowly sinking. There's nothing to be done about it.

NORA [*with a sigh of relief*]. Oh, it's *you* you're . . . ?

RANK. Who else? No point in deceiving oneself. I am the most wretched of all my patients, Mrs. Helmer. These last few days I've made a careful analysis of my internal economy. Bankrupt! Within a month I shall probably be lying rotting up there in the churchyard.

NORA. Come now, what a ghastly thing to say!

RANK. The whole damned thing is ghastly. But the worst thing is all the ghastliness that has to be gone through first. I only have one more test to make; and when that's done I'll know pretty well when the final disintegration will start. There's something I want to ask you. Helmer is a sensitive soul; he loathes anything that's ugly. I don't want him visiting me. . . .

NORA. But Dr. Rank. . . .

RANK. On no account must he. I won't have it. I'll lock the door on him.—As soon as I'm absolutely certain of the worst, I'll send you my visiting card with a black cross on it. You'll know then the final horrible disintegration has begun.

NORA. Really, you are being quite absurd today. And here was I hoping you would be in a thoroughly good mood.

RANK. With death staring me in the face? Why should I suffer for another man's sins? What justice is there in that? Somewhere, somehow, every single family must be suffering some such cruel retribution. . . .

NORA [*stopping up her ears*]. Rubbish! Do cheer up!

RANK. Yes, really the whole thing's nothing but a huge joke. My poor innocent spine must do penance for my father's gay subaltern life.

NORA [*by the table, left*]. Wasn't he rather partial to asparagus and *pâté de foie gras*?

RANK. Yes, he was. And truffles.

NORA. Truffles, yes. And oysters, too, I believe?

RANK. Yes, oysters, oysters, of course.

NORA. And all the port and champagne that goes with them. It does seem a pity all these delicious things should attack the spine.

RANK. Especially when they attack a poor spine that never had any fun out of them.

NORA. Yes, that is an awful pity.

RANK [*looks at her sharply*]. Hm. . . .

NORA [*after a pause*]. Why did you smile?

RANK. No, it was you who laughed.

NORA. No, it was you who smiled, Dr. Rank!

RANK [*getting up*]. You are a bigger rascal than I thought you were.

NORA. I feel full of mischief today.

RANK. So it seems.

NORA [*putting her hands on his shoulders*]. Dear, dear Dr. Rank, you mustn't go and die on Torvald and me.

RANK. You wouldn't miss me for long. When you are gone, you are soon forgotten.

NORA [*looking at him anxiously*]. Do you think so?

RANK. People make new contacts, then . . .

NORA. Who make new contacts?

RANK. Both you and Helmer will, when I'm gone. You yourself are already well on the way, it seems to me. What was this Mrs. Linde doing here last night?

NORA. Surely you aren't jealous of poor Kristine?

RANK. Yes, I am. She'll be my successor in this house. When I'm done for, I can see this woman. . . .

NORA. Hush! Don't talk so loud, she's in there.

RANK. Today as well? There you are, you see!

NORA. Just to do some sewing on my dress. Good Lord, how absurd you are! [*She sits down on the sofa.*] Now Dr. Rank, cheer up. You'll see tomorrow how nicely I can dance. And you can pretend I'm doing it just for you—and for Torvald as well, of course. [*She takes various things out of the box.*] Come here, Dr. Rank. I want to show you something.

RANK [*sits*]. What is it?

NORA. Look!

RANK. Silk stockings.

NORA. Flesh-coloured! Aren't they lovely! Of course, it's dark here now, but tomorrow. . . . No, no, no, you can only look at the feet. Oh well, you might as well see a bit higher up, too.

RANK. Hm . . . .

NORA. Why are you looking so critical? Don't you think they'll fit?

RANK. I couldn't possibly offer any informed opinion about that.

NORA [*looks at him for a moment*]. Shame on you. [*Hits him lightly across the ear with the stockings.*] Take that! [*Folds them up again.*]

RANK. And what other delights am I to be allowed to see?

NORA. Not another thing. You are too naughty. [*She hums a little and searches among her things.*]

RANK [*after a short pause.*] Sitting here so intimately like this with you, I can't imagine . . . I simply cannot conceive what would have become of me if I had never come to this house.

NORA [*smiles*]. Yes, I rather think you do enjoy coming here.

RANK [*in a low voice, looking fixedly ahead*]. And the thought of having to leave it all . . .

NORA. Nonsense. You aren't leaving.

RANK [*in the same tone*]. . . . without being able to leave behind even the slightest token of gratitude, hardly a fleeting regret even . . . nothing but an empty place to be filled by the first person that comes along.

NORA. Supposing I were to ask you to . . . ? No . . .

RANK. What?

NORA. . . . to show me the extent of your friendship . . .

RANK. Yes?

NORA. I mean . . . to do me a tremendous favour. . . .

RANK. Would you really, for once, give me that pleasure?

NORA. You have no idea what it is.

RANK. All right, tell me.

NORA. No, really I can't, Dr. Rank. It's altogether too much to ask . . . because I need your advice and help as well. . . .

RANK. The more the better. I cannot imagine what you have in mind. But tell me anyway. You do trust me, don't you?

NORA. Yes, I trust you more than anybody I know. You are my best and my most faithful friend. I know that. So I will tell you. Well then, Dr. Rank, there is something you must help me to prevent. You know how deeply, how passionately Torvald is in love with me. He would never hesitate for a moment to sacrifice his life for my sake.

RANK [*bending towards her*]. Nora . . . do you think he's the only one who . . . ?

NORA [*stiffening slightly*]. Who . . . ?

RANK. Who wouldn't gladly give his life for your sake.

NORA [*sadly*]. Oh!

RANK. I swore to myself you would know before I went. I'll never have a better opportunity. Well, Nora! Now you know. And now you know too that you can confide in me as in nobody else.

NORA [*rises and speaks evenly and calmly*]. Let me past.

RANK [*makes way for her, but remains seated*]. Nora. . . .

NORA [*in the hall doorway*]. Helene, bring the lamp in, please. [*Walks over to the stove.*] Oh, my dear Dr. Rank, that really was rather horrid of you.

RANK [*getting up*]. That I have loved you every bit as much as anybody? Is *that* horrid?

NORA. No, but that you had to go and tell me. When it was all so unnecessary. . . .

RANK. What do you mean? Did you know . . . ?

[THE MAID *comes in with the lamp, puts it on the table, and goes out again.*]

RANK. Nora . . . Mrs. Helmer . . . I'm asking you if you knew?

NORA. How can I tell whether I did or didn't. I simply can't tell you. . . . Oh, how could you be so clumsy, Dr. Rank! When everything was so nice.

RANK. Anyway, you know now that I'm at your service, body and soul. So you can speak out.

NORA [*looking at him*]. After this?

RANK. I beg you to tell me what it is.

NORA. I can tell you nothing now.

RANK. You must. You can't torment me like this. Give me a chance—I'll do anything that's humanly possible.

NORA. You can do nothing for me now. Actually, I don't really need any help. It's all just my imagination, really it is. Of course! [*She sits down in the rocking chair, looks at him and smiles.*] I must say, you are a nice one, Dr. Rank! Don't you feel ashamed of yourself, now the lamp's been brought in?

RANK. No, not exactly. But perhaps I ought to go—for good?

NORA. No, you mustn't do that. You must keep coming just as you've always done. You know very well Torvald would miss you terribly.

RANK. And *you*?

NORA. I always think it's tremendous fun having you.

RANK. That's exactly what gave me wrong ideas. I just can't puzzle you out. I often used to feel you'd just as soon be with me as with Helmer.

NORA. Well, you see, there are those people you love and those people you'd almost rather *be* with.

RANK. Yes, there's something in that.

NORA. When I was a girl at home, I loved Daddy best, of course. But I also thought it great fun if I could slip into the maids' room. For one thing they never preached at me. And they always talked about such exciting things.

RANK. Aha! So it's their role I've taken over!

NORA [*jumps up and crosses to him*]. Oh, my dear, kind Dr. Rank, I didn't mean that at all. But you can see how it's a bit with Torvald as it was with Daddy. . . .

[THE MAID *comes in from the hall.*]

MAID. Please, ma'am . . . !

[*She whispers and hands her a card.*]

NORA [*glances at the card*]. Ah!

[*She puts it in her pocket.*]

RANK. Anything wrong?

NORA. No, no, not at all. It's just . . . it's my new costume. . . .

RANK. How is that? There's your costume in there.

NORA. That one, yes. But this is another one. I've ordered it. Torvald mustn't hear about it. . . .

RANK. Ah, so that's the big secret, is it!

NORA. Yes, that's right. Just go in and see him, will you? He's in the study. Keep him occupied for the time being. . . .

RANK. Don't worry. He shan't escape me.

[*He goes into* HELMER'S *study.*]

NORA [*to the maid*]. Is he waiting in the kitchen?

MAID. Yes, he came up the back stairs. . . .

NORA. But didn't you tell him somebody was here?

MAID. Yes, but it was no good.

NORA. Won't he go?

MAID. No, he won't till he's seen you.

NORA. Let him in, then. But quietly. Helene, you mustn't tell anybody about this. It's a surprise for my husband.

MAID. I understand, ma'am. . . .

[*She goes out.*]

NORA. Here it comes! What I've been dreading! No, no, it can't happen, it *can't* happen.

[*She walks over and bolts* HELMER'S *door. The maid opens the hall door for* KROGSTAD *and shuts it again behind him. He is wearing a fur coat, over-shoes, and a fur cap.*]

NORA [*goes towards him*]. Keep your voice down, my husband is at home.

KROGSTAD. What if he is?

NORA. What do you want with me?

KROGSTAD. To find out something.

NORA. Hurry, then. What is it?

KROGSTAD. You know I've been given notice.

NORA. I couldn't prevent it, Mr. Krogstad, I did my utmost for you, but it was no use.

KROGSTAD. Has your husband so little affection for you? He knows what I can do to you, yet he dares. . . .

NORA. You don't imagine he knows about it!

KROGSTAD. No, I didn't imagine he did. It didn't seem a bit like my good friend Torvald Helmer to show that much courage. . . .

NORA. Mr. Krogstad, I must ask you to show some respect for my husband.

KROGSTAD. Oh, sure! All due respect! But since you are so anxious to keep this business quiet, Mrs. Helmer, I take it you now have a rather clearer idea of just what it is you've done, than you had yesterday.

NORA. Clearer than *you* could ever have given me.

KROGSTAD. Yes, being as I am such a rotten lawyer. . . .

NORA. What do you want with me?

KROGSTAD. I just wanted to see how things stood, Mrs. Helmer. I've been thinking about you all day. Even a mere money-lender, a hack journalist, a—well, even somebody like me has a bit of what you might call feeling.

NORA. Show it then. Think of my little children.

KROGSTAD. Did you or your husband think of mine? But what does it matter now? There was just one thing I wanted to say: you needn't take this business too seriously. I shan't start any proceedings, for the present.

NORA. Ah, I knew you wouldn't.

KROGSTAD. The whole thing can be arranged quite amicably. Nobody need know. Just the three of us.

NORA. My husband must never know.

KROGSTAD. How can you prevent it? Can you pay off the balance?

NORA. No, not immediately.

KROGSTAD. Perhaps you've some way of getting hold of the money in the next few days.

NORA. None I want to make use of.

KROGSTAD. Well, it wouldn't have been very much help to you if you had. Even if you stood there with the cash in your hand and to spare, you still wouldn't get your IOU back from me now.

NORA. What are you going to do with it?

KROGSTAD. Just keep it—have it in my possession. Nobody who isn't implicated need know about it. So if you are thinking of trying any desperate remedies . . .

NORA. Which I am. . . .

KROGSTAD. . . . if you happen to be thinking of running away . . .

NORA. Which I am!

KROGSTAD. . . . or anything worse . . .

NORA. How did you know?

KROGSTAD. . . . forget it!

NORA. How did you know I was thinking of *that?*

KROGSTAD. Most of us think of *that,* to begin with. I did, too; but I didn't have the courage. . . .

NORA [*tonelessly*]. I haven't either.

KROGSTAD [*relieved*]. So you haven't the courage either, eh?

NORA. No, I haven't! I haven't!

KROGSTAD. It would also be very stupid. There'd only be the first domestic storm to get over. . . . I've got a letter to your husband in my pocket here. . . .

NORA. And it's all in there?

KROGSTAD. In as tactful a way as possible.

NORA [*quickly*]. He must never read that letter. Tear it up. I'll find the money somehow.

KROGSTAD. Excuse me, Mrs. Helmer, but I've just told you. . . .

NORA. I'm not talking about the money I owe you. I want to know how much you are demanding from my husband, and I'll get the money.

KROGSTAD. I want no money from your husband.

NORA. What do you want?

KROGSTAD. I'll tell you. I want to get on my feet again, Mrs. Helmer; I want to get to the top. And your husband is going to help me. For the last eighteen months I've gone straight; all that time it's been hard going; I was content to work my way up, step by step. Now I'm being kicked out, and I won't stand for being taken back again as an act of charity. I'm going to get to the top, I tell you. I'm going back into that Bank—with a better job. Your husband is to create a new vacancy, just for me. . . .

NORA. He'll never do that!

KROGSTAD. He will do it. I know him. He'll do it without so much as a whimper. And once I'm in there with him, you'll see what's what. In less than a year I'll be his right-hand man. It'll be Nils Krogstad, not Torvald Helmer, who'll be running that Bank.

NORA. You'll never live to see that day!

KROGSTAD. You mean you . . . ?

NORA. Now I have the courage.

KROGSTAD. You can't frighten me! A precious pampered little thing like you. . . .

NORA. I'll show you! I'll show you!

KROGSTAD. Under the ice, maybe? Down in the cold, black water? Then being washed up in the spring, bloated, hairless, unrecognizable. . . .

NORA. You can't frighten me.

KROGSTAD. You can't frighten me, either. People don't do that sort of thing, Mrs. Helmer. There wouldn't be any point to it, anyway, I'd still have him right in my pocket.

NORA. Afterwards? When I'm no longer . . .

KROGSTAD. Aren't you forgetting that your reputation would then be entirely in my hands? [NORA *stands looking at him, speechless.*] Well, I've warned you. Don't do anything silly. When Helmer gets my letter, I expect to hear from him. And don't forget: it's him who is forcing me off the straight and narrow again, your own husband! That's something I'll never forgive him for. Goodbye, Mrs. Helmer.

[*He goes out through the hall.* NORA *crosses to the door, opens it slightly, and listens.*]

NORA. He's going. He hasn't left the letter. No, no, that would be impossible! [*Opens the door further and further.*] What's he doing? He's stopped outside. He's not going down the stairs. Has he changed his mind? Is he . . . ? [*A letter falls into the letter-box. Then* KROGSTAD'S *footsteps are heard receding as he walks downstairs.* NORA *gives a stifled cry, runs across the room to the sofa table; pause.*] In the letter-box! [*She creeps stealthily across to the hall door.*] There it is! Torvald, Torvald! It's hopeless now!

MRS. LINDE [*comes into the room, left, carrying the costume*]. There, I think that's everything. Shall we try it on?

NORA [*in a low, hoarse voice*]. Kristine, come here.

MRS. LINDE [*throws the dress down on the sofa*]. What's wrong with you? You look upset.

NORA. Come here. Do you see that letter? *There,* look! Through the glass in the letter-box.

MRS. LINDE. Yes, yes, I can see it.

NORA. It's a letter from Krogstad.

MRS. LINDE. Nora! It was Krogstad who lent you the money!

NORA. Yes. And now Torvald will get to know everything.

MRS. LINDE. Believe me, Nora, it's best for you both.

NORA. But there's more to it than that. I forged a signature. . . .

MRS. LINDE. Heavens above!

NORA. Listen, I want to tell you something, Kristine, so you can be my witness.

MRS. LINDE. What do you mean 'witness'? What do you want me to . . . ?

NORA. If I should go mad . . . which might easily happen . . .

MRS. LINDE. Nora!

NORA. Or if anything happened to me . . . which meant I couldn't be here. . . .

MRS. LINDE. Nora, Nora! Are you out of your mind?

NORA. And if somebody else wanted to take it all upon himself, the whole blame, you understand. . . .

MRS. LINDE. Yes, yes. But what makes you think . . . ?

NORA. Then you must testify that it isn't true, Kristine. I'm not out of my mind; I'm quite sane now. And I tell you this: nobody else knew anything, I alone was responsible for the whole thing. Remember that!

MRS. LINDE. I will. But I don't understand a word of it.

NORA. Why should you? You see something miraculous is going to happen.

MRS. LINDE. Something miraculous?

NORA. Yes, a miracle. But something so terrible as well, Kristine—oh, it must *never* happen, not for anything.

MRS. LINDE. I'm going straight over to talk to Krogstad.

NORA. Don't go. He'll only do you harm.

MRS. LINDE. There was a time when he would have done anything for me.

NORA. Him!

MRS. LINDE. Where does he live?

NORA. How do I know . . . ? Wait a minute. [*She feels in her pocket.*] Here's his card. But the letter, the letter . . . !

HELMER. [*from his study, knocking on the door*]. Nora!

NORA [*cries out in terror*]. What's that? What do you want?

HELMER. Don't be frightened. We're not coming in. You've locked the door. Are you trying on?

NORA. Yes, yes, I'm trying on. It looks so nice on me, Torvald.

MRS. LINDE [*who has read the card*]. He lives just round the corner.

NORA. It's no use. It's hopeless. The letter is there in the box.

MRS. LINDE. Your husband keeps the key?

NORA. Always.

MRS. LINDE. Krogstad must ask for his letter back unread, he must find some sort of excuse. . . .

NORA. But this is just the time that Torvald generally . . .

MRS. LINDE. Put him off! Go in and keep him busy. I'll be back as soon as I can.

[*She goes out hastily by the hall door.* NORA *walks over to* HELMER'S *door, opens it and peeps in.*]

NORA. Torvald!

HELMER. [*in the study*]. Well, can a man get into his own living-room again now? Come along, Rank, now we'll see . . . [*In the doorway.*] But what's this?

NORA. What, Torvald dear?

HELMER. Rank led me to expect some kind of marvellous transformation.

RANK [*in the doorway*]. That's what I thought too, but I must have been mistaken.

NORA. I'm not showing myself off to anybody before tomorrow.

HELMER. Nora dear, you look tired. You haven't been practising too hard?

NORA. No, I haven't practised at all yet.

HELMER. You'll have to, though.

NORA. Yes, I certainly must, Torvald. But I just can't get anywhere without your help: I've completely forgotten it.

HELMER. We'll soon polish it up.

NORA. Yes, do help me, Torvald. Promise? I'm so nervous. All those people. . . . You must devote yourself exclusively to me this evening. Pens away! Forget all about the office! Promise me, Torvald dear!

HELMER. I promise. This evening I am wholly and entirely at your service . . . helpless little thing that you are. Oh, but while I remember, I'll just look first . . .

[*He goes towards the hall door.*]

NORA. What do you want out there?

HELMER. Just want to see if there are any letters.

NORA. No, don't, Torvald!

HELMER. Why not?

NORA. Torvald, *please!* There aren't any.

HELMER. Just let me see.

[*He starts to go.* NORA, *at the piano, plays the opening bars of the tarantella.*]

HELMER. [*at the door, stops*]. Aha!

NORA. I shan't be able to dance tomorrow if I don't rehearse it with you.

HELMER. [*walks to her*]. Are you really so nervous, Nora dear?

NORA. Terribly nervous. Let me run through it now. There's still time before supper. Come and sit here and play for me, Torvald dear. Tell me what to do, keep me right—as you always do.

HELMER. Certainly, with pleasure, if that's what you want.

[*He sits at the piano.* NORA *snatches the tambourine out of the box, and also a long gaily-coloured shawl which she drapes round herself, then with a bound she leaps forward.*]

NORA [*shouts*]. Now play for me! Now I'll dance!

[HELMER *plays and* NORA *dances;* DR. RANK *stands at the piano behind* HELMER *and looks on.*]

HELMER. [*playing*]. Not so fast! Not so fast!

NORA. I can't help it.

HELMER. Not so wild, Nora!

NORA. This is how it has to be.

HELMER. [*stops*]. No, no, that won't do at all.

NORA [*laughs and swings the tambourine*]. Didn't I tell you?

RANK. Let me play for her.

HELMER. [*gets up*]. Yes, do. Then I'll be better able to tell her what to do.

[RANK *sits down at the piano and plays.* NORA *dances more and more wildly.* HELMER *stands by the stove giving her repeated directions as she dances; she does not seem to hear them. Her hair comes undone and falls about her shoulders; she pays no attention and goes on dancing.* MRS. LINDE *enters.*]

MRS. LINDE [*standing as though spellbound in the doorway*]. Ah . . . !

NORA [*dancing*]. See what fun we are having, Kristine.

HELMER. But my dear darling Nora, you are dancing as though your life depended on it.

NORA. It does.

HELMER. Stop, Rank! This is sheer madness. Stop, I say.

[RANK *stops playing and* NORA *comes to a sudden halt.*]

HELMER. [*crosses to her*]. I would never have believed it. You have forgotten everything I ever taught you.

NORA [*throwing away the tambourine*]. There you are, you see.

HELMER. Well, some more instruction is certainly needed there.

NORA. Yes, you see how necessary it is. You must go on coaching me right up to the last minute. Promise me, Torvald?

HELMER. You can rely on me.

NORA. You mustn't think about anything else but me until after tomorrow . . . mustn't open any letters . . . mustn't touch the letter-box.

HELMER. Ah, you are still frightened of what that man might . . .

NORA. Yes, yes, I am.

HELMER. I can see from your face there's already a letter there from him.

NORA. I don't know. I think so. But you musn't read anything like that now. We don't want anything horrid coming between us until all this is over.

RANK [*softly to* HELMER]. I shouldn't cross her.

HELMER. [*puts his arm round her*]. The child must have her way. But tomorrow night, when your dance is done. . . .

NORA. Then you are free.

MAID [*in the doorway, right*]. Dinner is served, madam.

NORA. We'll have champagne, Helene.

MAID. Very good, madam.

> [*She goes.*]

HELMER. Aha! It's to be quite a banquet, eh?

NORA. With champagne flowing until dawn. [*Shouts.*] And some macaroons, Helene . . . lots of them, for once in a while.

HELMER. [*seizing her hands*]. Now, now, not so wild and excitable! Let me see you being my own little singing bird again.

NORA. Oh yes, I will. And if you'll just go in . . . you, too, Dr. Rank. Kristine, you must help me to do my hair.

RANK [*softly, as they leave*]. There isn't anything . . . anything as it were, impending, is there?

HELMER. No, not at all, my dear fellow. It's nothing but these childish fears I was telling you about.

> [*They go out to the right.*]

NORA. Well?

MRS. LINDE. He's left town.

NORA. I saw it in your face.

MRS. LINDE. He's coming back tomorrow evening. I left a note for him.

NORA. You shouldn't have done that. You must let things take their course. Because really it's a case for rejoicing, waiting like this for the miracle.

MRS. LINDE. What is it you are waiting for?

NORA. Oh, you wouldn't understand. Go and join the other two. I'll be there in a minute.

> [MRS. LINDE *goes into the dining-room.* NORA *stands for a moment as though to collect herself, then looks at her watch.*]

NORA. Five. Seven hours to midnight. Then twenty-four hours till the next midnight. Then the tarantella will be over. Twenty-four and seven? Thirty-one hours to live.

HELMER. [*in the doorway, right*] What's happened to our little sky-lark?

NORA [*running towards him with open arms*]. Here she is!

ACT THREE

The same room. The round table has been moved to the centre of the room, and the chairs placed round it. A lamp is burning on the table. The door to the hall stands open. Dance music can be heard coming from the floor above. MRS. LINDE *is sitting by the table, idly turning over the pages of a book; she tries to read, but does not seem able to concentrate. Once or twice she listens, tensely, for a sound at the front door.*

MRS. LINDE. [*looking at her watch*]. Still not here. There isn't much time left. I only hope he hasn't . . . [*She listens again.*] Ah, there he is. [*She goes out into the hall, and cautiously opens the front door. Soft footsteps can be heard on the stairs. She whispers.*] Come in. There's nobody here.

KROGSTAD. [*in the doorway*]. I found a note from you at home. What does it all mean?

MRS. LINDE. I *had* to talk to you.

KROGSTAD. Oh? And did it have to be here, in this house?

MRS. LINDE. It wasn't possible over at my place, it hasn't a separate entrance. Come in. We are quite alone. The maid's asleep and the Helmers are at a party upstairs.

KROGSTAD [*comes into the room*]. Well, well! So the Helmers are out dancing tonight! Really?

MRS. LINDE. Yes, why not?

KROGSTAD. Why not indeed!

MRS. LINDE. Well then, Nils. Let's talk.

KROGSTAD. Have we two anything more to talk about?

MRS. LINDE. We have a great deal to talk about.

KROGSTAD. I shouldn't have thought so.

MRS. LINDE. That's because you never really understood me.

KROGSTAD. What else was there to understand, apart from the old, old story? A heartless woman throws a man over the moment something more profitable offers itself.

MRS. LINDE. Do you really think I'm so heartless? Do you think I found it easy to break it off.

KROGSTAD. Didn't you?

MRS. LINDE. You didn't really believe that?

KROGSTAD. If that wasn't the case, why did you write to me as you did?

MRS. LINDE. There was nothing else I could do. If I had to make the break, I felt in duty bound to destroy any feeling that you had for me.

KROGSTAD. [*clenching his hands*]. So that's how it was. And all that . . . was for money!

MRS. LINDE. You mustn't forget I had a helpless mother and two young brothers. We couldn't wait for you, Nils. At that time you hadn't much immediate prospect of anything.

KROGSTAD. That may be. But you had no right to throw me over for somebody else.

MRS. LINDE. Well, I don't know. Many's the time I've asked myself whether I was justified.

KROGSTAD [*more quietly*]. When I lost you, it was just as if the ground had slipped away from under my feet. Look at me now a broken man clinging to the wreck of his life.

MRS. LINDE. Help might be near.

KROGSTAD. It was near. Then you came along and got in the way.

MRS. LINDE. Quite without knowing, Nils. I only heard today it's you I'm supposed to be replacing at the Bank.

KROGSTAD. If you say so, I believe you. But now you do know, aren't you going to withdraw?

MRS. LINDE. No, that wouldn't benefit you in the slightest.

KROGSTAD. Benefit, benefit . . . ! I would do it just the same.

MRS. LINDE. I have learned to go carefully. Life and hard, bitter necessity have taught me that.

KROGSTAD. And life has taught me not to believe in pretty speeches.

MRS. LINDE. Then life has taught you a very sensible thing. But deeds are something you surely must believe in?

KROGSTAD. How do you mean?

MRS. LINDE. You said you were like a broken man clinging to the wreck of his life.

KROGSTAD. And I said it with good reason.

MRS. LINDE. And I am like a broken woman clinging to the wreck of her life. Nobody to care about, and nobody to care for.

KROGSTAD. It was your own choice.

MRS. LINDE. At the time there was no other choice.

KROGSTAD. Well, what of it?

MRS. LINDE. Nils, what about us two castaways joining forces.

KROGSTAD. What's that you say?

MRS. LINDE. Two of us on *one* wreck surely stand a better chance than each on his own.

KROGSTAD. Kristine!

MRS. LINDE. Why do you suppose I came to town?

KROGSTAD. You mean, you thought of me?

MRS. LINDE. Without work I couldn't live. All my life I have worked, for as long as I can remember; that has always been my one great joy. But now I'm completely alone in the world, and feeling horribly empty and forlorn. There's no pleasure in working only for yourself. Nils, give me somebody and something to work for.

KROGSTAD. I don't believe all this. It's only a woman's hysteria, wanting to be all magnanimous and self-sacrificing.

MRS. LINDE. Have you ever known me hysterical before?

KROGSTAD. Would you really do this? Tell me—do you know all about my past?

MRS. LINDE. Yes.

KROGSTAD. And you know what people think about me?

MRS. LINDE. Just now you hinted you thought you might have been a different person with me.

KROGSTAD. I'm convinced I would.

MRS. LINDE. Couldn't it still happen?

KROGSTAD. Kristine! You know what you are saying, don't you? Yes, you do. I can see you do. Have you really the courage . . . ?

MRS. LINDE. I need someone to mother, and your children need a mother. We two need each other. Nils, I have faith in what, deep down, you are. With you I can face anything.

KROGSTAD [*seizing her hands*]. Thank you, thank you, Kristine. And I'll soon have everybody looking up to me, or I'll know the reason why. Ah, but I was forgetting. . . .

MRS. LINDE. Hush! The tarantella! You must go!

KROGSTAD. Why? What is it?

MRS. LINDE. You hear that dance upstairs? When it's finished they'll be coming.

KROGSTAD. Yes, I'll go. It's too late to do anything. Of course, you know nothing about what steps I've taken against the Helmers.

MRS. LINDE. Yes, Nils, I do know.

KROGSTAD. Yet you still want to go on. . . .

MRS. LINDE. I know how far a man like you can be driven by despair.

KROGSTAD. Oh, if only I could undo what I've done!

MRS. LINDE. You still can. Your letter is still there in the box.

KROGSTAD. Are you sure?

MRS. LINDE. Quite sure. But . . .

KROGSTAD. [*regards her searchingly*]. Is that how things are? You want to save your friend at any price? Tell me straight. Is that it?

MRS. LINDE. When you've sold yourself *once* for other people's sake, you don't do it again.

KROGSTAD. I shall demand my letter back.

MRS. LINDE. No, no.

KROGSTAD. Of course I will, I'll wait here till Helmer comes. I'll tell him he has to give me my letter back . . . that it's only about my notice . . . that he mustn't read it. . . .

MRS. LINDE. No, Nils, don't ask for it back.

KROGSTAD. But wasn't that the very reason you got me here?

MRS. LINDE. Yes, that was my first terrified reaction. But that was yesterday, and it's quite incredible the things I've witnessed in this house in the last twenty-four hours. Helmer must know everything. This unhappy secret must come out. Those two must have the whole thing out between them. All this secrecy and deception, it just can't go on.

KROGSTAD. Well, if you want to risk it. . . . But one thing I can do, and I'll do it at once. . . .

MRS. LINDE [*listening*]. Hurry! Go, go! The dance has stopped. We aren't safe a moment longer.

KROGSTAD. I'll wait for you downstairs.

MRS. LINDE. Yes, do. You must see me home.

KROGSTAD. I've never been so incredibly happy before.

> [*He goes out by the front door. The door out into the hall remains standing open.*]

MRS. LINDE [*tidies the room a little and gets her hat and coat ready*]. How things change! How things change! Somebody to work for . . . to live for. A home to bring happiness into. Just let me get down to it. . . . I wish they'd come. . . . [*Listens.*] Ah, there they are. . . . Get my things.

> [*She takes her coat and hat. The voices of* HELMER *and* NORA *are heard outside. A key is turned and* HELMER *pushes* NORA *almost forcibly into the hall. She is dressed in the Italian costume, with a big black shawl over it. He is in evening dress, and over it a black cloak, open.*]

NORA [*Still in the doorway, reluctantly*]. No, no, not in here! I want to go back up again. I don't want to leave so early.

HELMER. But my dearest Nora. . . .

NORA. Oh, please, Torvald, I beg you. . . . *Please,* just for another hour.

HELMER. Not another minute, Nora my sweet. You remember what we agreed. There now, come along in. You'll catch cold standing there.

> [*He leads her, in spite of her resistance, gently but firmly into the room.*]

MRS. LINDE. Good evening.

NORA. Kristine!

HELMER. Why, Mrs. Linde. You here so late?

MRS. LINDE. Yes. You must forgive me but I did so want to see Nora all dressed up.

NORA. Have you been sitting here waiting for me?

MRS. LINDE. Yes, I'm afraid I wasn't in time to catch you before you went upstairs. And I felt I couldn't leave again without seeing you.

HELMER [*removing* NORA'S *shawl*]. Well take a good look at her. I think I can say she's worth looking at. Isn't she lovely, Mrs. Linde?

MRS. LINDE. Yes, I must say. . . .

HELMER. Isn't she quite extraordinarily lovely? That's what everybody at the party thought, too. But she's dreadfully stubborn . . . the sweet little thing! And what shall we do about that? Would you believe it, I nearly had to use force to get her away.

NORA. Oh Torvald, you'll be sorry you didn't let me stay, even for half an hour.

HELMER. You hear that, Mrs. Linde? She dances her tarantella, there's wild applause—which was well deserved, although the performance was perhaps rather realistic . . . I mean, rather more so than was strictly necessary from the artistic point of view. But anyway! The main thing is she was a success, a tremendous success. Was I supposed to let her stay after that? Spoil the effect? No thank you! I took my lovely little Capri girl—my capricious little Capri girl,

I might say—by the arm, whisked her once round the room, a curtsey all round, and then—as they say in novels—the beautiful vision vanished. An exit should always be effective, Mrs. Linde. But I just can't get Nora to see that. Phew! It's warm in here. [*He throws his cloak over a chair and opens the door to his study.*] What? It's dark. Oh yes, of course. Excuse me. . . .

[*He goes in and lights a few candles.*]

NORA [*quickly, in a breathless whisper*]. Well?

MRS. LINDE [*softly*]. I've spoken to him.

NORA. And . . . ?

MRS. LINDE. Nora . . . you must tell your husband everything.

NORA [*tonelessly*]. I knew it.

MRS. LINDE. You've got nothing to fear from Krogstad. But you must speak.

NORA. I won't.

MRS. LINDE. Then the letter will.

NORA. Thank you, Kristine. Now I know what's to be done. Hush . . . !

HELMER [*comes in again*]. Well, Mrs. Linde, have you finished admiring her?

MRS. LINDE. Yes. And now I must say good night.

HELMER. Oh, already? Is this yours, this knitting?

MRS. LINDE [*takes it*]. Yes, thank you. I nearly forgot it.

HELMER. So you knit, eh?

MRS. LINDE. Yes.

HELMER. You should embroider instead, you know.

MRS. LINDE. Oh? Why?

HELMER. So much prettier. Watch! You hold the embroidery like this in the left hand, and then you take the needle in the right hand, like this, and you describe a long, graceful curve. Isn't that right?

MRS. LINDE. Yes, I suppose so. . . .

HELMER. Whereas knitting on the other hand just can't help being ugly. Look! Arms pressed into the sides, the knitting needles going up and down—there's something Chinese about it. . . . Ah, that was marvellous champagne they served tonight.

MRS. LINDE. Well, good night, Nora! And stop being so stubborn.

HELMER. Well said, Mrs. Linde!

MRS. LINDE. Good night, Mr. Helmer.

HELMER [*accompanying her to the door*]. Good night, good night! You'll get home all right, I hope? I'd be only too pleased to . . . But you haven't far to walk. Good night, good night! [*She goes; he shuts the door behind her and comes in again.*] There we are, got rid of her at last. She's a frightful bore, that woman.

NORA. Aren't you very tired, Torvald?

HELMER. Not in the least.

NORA. Not sleepy?

HELMER. Not at all. On the contrary, I feel extremely lively. What about you? Yes, you look quite tired and sleepy.

NORA. Yes, I'm very tired. I just want to fall straight off to sleep.

HELMER. There you are, you see! Wasn't I right in thinking we shouldn't stay any longer.

NORA. Oh, everything you do is right.

HELMER [*kissing her forehead*]. There's my little sky-lark talking common sense. Did you notice how gay Rank was this evening?

NORA. Oh, was he? I didn't get a chance to talk to him.

HELMER. I hardly did either. But it's a long time since I saw him in such a good mood. [*Looks at* NORA *for a moment or two, then comes nearer her.*] Ah, it's wonderful to be back in our own home again, and quite alone with you. How irresistibly lovely you are, Nora!

NORA. Don't look at me like that, Torvald!

HELMER. Can't I look at my most treasured possession? At all this loveliness that's mine and mine alone, completely and utterly mine.

NORA [*walks round to the other side of the table*]. You mustn't talk to me like that tonight.

HELMER [*following her*]. You still have the tarantella in your blood, I see. And that makes you even more desirable. Listen! The guests are beginning to leave now. [*Softly.*] Nora . . . soon the whole house will be silent.

NORA. I should hope so.

HELMER. Of course you do, don't you, Nora my darling? You know, whenever I'm out at a party with you . . . do you know why I never talk to you very much, why I always stand away from you and only steal a quick glance at you now and then . . . do you know why I do that? It's because I'm pretending we are secretly in love, secretly engaged and nobody suspects there is anything between us.

NORA. Yes, yes. I know your thoughts are always with me, of course.

HELMER. And when it's time to go, and I lay your shawl round those shapely, young shoulders, round the exquisite curve of your neck . . . I pretend that you are my young bride, that we are just leaving our wedding, that I am taking you to our new home for the first time . . . to be alone with you for the first time . . . quite alone with your young and trembling loveliness! All evening I've been longing for you, and nothing else. And as I watched you darting and swaying in the tarantella, my blood was on fire . . . I couldn't bear it any longer . . . and that's why I brought you down here with me so early. . . .

NORA. Go away, Torvald! Please leave me alone. I won't have it.

HELMER. What's this? It's just your little game isn't it, my little Nora. Won't! Won't! Am I not your husband . . . ?

[*There is a knock on the front door.*]

NORA [*startled*]. Listen . . . !

HELMER [*going towards the hall*]. Who's there?

RANK [*outside*]. It's me. Can I come in for a minute?

HELMER [*in a low voice, annoyed*]. Oh, what does he want now? [*Aloud.*] Wait a moment. [*He walks across and opens the door.*] How nice of you to look in on your way out.

RANK. I fancied I heard your voice and I thought I would just look in. [*He takes a quick glance round.*] Ah yes, this dear, familiar old place! How cosy and comfortable you've got things here, you two.

HELMER. You seemed to be having a pretty good time upstairs yourself.

RANK. Capital! Why shouldn't I? Why not make the most of things in this world? At least as much as one can, and for as long as one can. The wine was excellent. . . .

HELMER. Especially the champagne.

RANK. You noticed that too, did you? It's incredible the amount I was able to put away.

NORA. Torvald also drank a lot of champagne this evening.

RANK. Oh?

NORA. Yes, and that always makes him quite merry.

RANK. Well, why shouldn't a man allow himself a jolly evening after a day well spent?

HELMER. Well spent? I'm afraid I can't exactly claim that.

RANK [*clapping him on the shoulder*]. But I can, you see!

NORA. Dr. Rank, am I right in thinking you carried out a certain laboratory test today?

RANK. Exactly.

HELMER. Look at our little Nora talking about laboratory tests!

NORA. And may I congratulate you on the result?

RANK. You may indeed.

NORA. So it was good?

RANK. The best possible, for both doctor and patient—certainty!

NORA [*quickly and searchingly*]. Certainty?

RANK. Absolute certainty. So why shouldn't I allow myself a jolly evening after that?

NORA. Quite right, Dr. Rank.

HELMER. I quite agree. As long as you don't suffer for it in the morning.

RANK. Well, you never get anything for nothing in this life.

NORA. Dr. Rank . . . you are very fond of masquerades, aren't you?

RANK. Yes, when there are plenty of amusing disguises. . . .

NORA. Tell me, what shall we two go as next time?

HELMER. There's frivolity for you . . . thinking about the next time already!

RANK. We two? I'll tell you. You must go as Lady Luck. . . .

HELMER. Yes, but how do you find a costume to suggest *that*?

RANK. Your wife could simply go in her everyday clothes. . . .

HELMER. That was nicely said. But don't you know what you would be?

RANK. Yes, my dear friend, I know exactly what I shall be.

HELMER. Well?

RANK. At the next masquerade, I shall be invisible.

HELMER. That's a funny idea!

RANK. There's a big black cloak . . . haven't you heard of the cloak of invisibility? That comes right down over you, and then nobody can see you.

HELMER [*suppressing a smile*]. Of course, that's right.

RANK. But I'm clean forgetting what I came for. Helmer, give me a cigar, one of the dark Havanas.

HELMER. With the greatest of pleasure.

[*He offers his case.*]

RANK [*takes one and cuts the end off*]. Thanks.

NORA [*strikes a match*]. Let me give you a light.

RANK. Thank you. [*She holds out the match and he lights his cigar.*] And now, goodbye!

HELMER. Goodbye, goodbye, my dear fellow!

NORA. Sleep well, Dr. Rank.

RANK. Thank you for that wish.

NORA. Wish me the same.

RANK. You? All right, if you want me to. . . . Sleep well. And thanks for the light.

[*He nods to them both, and goes.*]

HELMER [*subdued*]. He's had a lot to drink.

NORA [*absently*]. Very likely.

[HELMER *takes a bunch of keys out of his pocket and goes out into the hall.*]

NORA. Torvald . . . what do you want there?

HELMER. I must empty the letter-box, it's quite full. There'll be no room for the papers in the morning. . . .

NORA. Are you going to work tonight?

HELMER. You know very well I'm not. Hello, what's this? Somebody's been at the lock.

NORA. At the lock?

HELMER. Yes, I'm sure of it. Why should that be? I'd hardly have thought the maids . . . ? Here's a broken hair-pin. Nora, it's one of yours. . . .

NORA [*quickly*]. It must have been the children. . . .

HELMER. Then you'd better tell them not to. Ah . . . there . . . I've managed to get it open. [*He takes the things out and shouts into the kitchen.*] Helene! . . . Helene, put the light out in the hall. [*He comes into the room again with the letters in his hand and shuts the hall door.*] Look how it all mounts up. [*Runs through them.*] What's this?

NORA. The letter! Oh no, Torvald, no!

HELMER. Two visiting cards . . . from Dr. Rank.

NORA. From Dr. Rank?

HELMER [*looking at them*]. Dr. Rank, Medical Practitioner. They were on top. He must have put them in as he left.

NORA. Is there anything on them?

HELMER. There's a black cross above his name. Look. What an uncanny idea. It's just as if he were announcing his own death.

NORA. He is.

HELMER. What? What do you know about it? Has he said anything to you?

NORA. Yes. He said when these cards came, he would have taken his last leave of us. He was going to shut himself up and die.

HELMER. Poor fellow! Of course I knew we couldn't keep him with us very long. But so soon. . . . And hiding himself away like a wounded animal.

NORA. When it has to happen, it's best that it should happen without words. Don't you think so, Torvald?

HELMER [*walking up and down*]. He had grown so close to us. I don't think I can imagine him gone. His suffering and his loneliness seemed almost to provide a background of dark cloud to the sunshine of our lives. Well, perhaps it's all for the best. For him at any rate. [*Pauses.*] And maybe for us as well, Nora. Now there's just the two of us. [*Puts his arms round her.*] Oh, my darling wife, I can't hold you close enough. You know, Nora . . . many's the time I wish you were threatened by some terrible danger so I could risk everything, body and soul, for your sake.

NORA [*tears herself free and says firmly and decisively*]. Now you must read your letters, Torvald.

HELMER. No, no, not tonight. I want to be with you, my darling wife.

NORA. Knowing all the time your friend is dying . . . ?

HELMER. You are right. It's been a shock to both of us. This ugly thing has come between us . . . thoughts of death and decay. We must try to free ourselves from it. Until then . . . we shall go our separate ways.

NORA [*her arms round his neck*]. Torvald . . . good night! Good night!

HELMER [*kisses her forehead*]. Goodnight, my little singing bird. Sleep well, Nora, I'll just read through my letters.

[*He takes the letters into his room and shuts the door behind him.*]

NORA [*gropes around her, wild-eyed, seizes* HELMER'S *cloak, wraps it round herself, and whispers quickly, hoarsely, spasmodically*]. Never see him again. Never, never, never. [*Throws her shawl over her head.*] And never see the children again either. Never, never. Oh, that black icy water. Oh, that bottomless . . . ! If only it were all over! He's got it now. Now he's reading it. Oh no, no! Not yet! Torvald, goodbye . . . and my children. . . .

[*She rushes out in the direction of the hall; at the same moment* HELMER *flings open his door and stands there with an open letter in his hand.*]

HELMER. Nora!

NORA [*shrieks*]. Ah!

HELMER. What is this? Do you know what is in this letter?

NORA. Yes, I know. Let me go! Let me out!

HELMER [*holds her back*]. Where are you going?

NORA [*trying to tear herself free*]. You mustn't try to save me, Torvald!

HELMER [*reels back*]. True! Is it true what he writes? How dreadful! No, no, it can't possibly be true.

NORA. It *is* true. I loved you more than anything else in the world.

HELMER. Don't come to me with a lot of paltry excuses!

NORA [*taking a step towards him*]. Torvald . . . !

HELMER. Miserable woman . . . what is this you have done?

NORA. Let me go. I won't have you taking the blame for me. You mustn't take it on yourself.

HELMER. Stop play-acting! [*Locks the front door.*] You are staying here to give an account of yourself. Do you understand what you have done? Answer me! Do you understand?

NORA [*looking fixedly at him, her face hardening*]. Yes, now I'm really beginning to understand.

HELMER [*walking up and down*]. Oh, what a terrible awakening this is. All these eight years . . . this woman who was my pride and joy . . . a hypocrite, a liar, worse than that, a criminal! Oh, how utterly squalid it all is! Ugh! Ugh! [NORA *remains silent and looks fixedly at him.*] I should have realized something like this would happen. I should have seen it coming. All your father's irresponsible ways. . . . Quiet! All your father's irresponsible ways are coming out in you. No religion, no morals, no sense of duty. . . . Oh, this is my punishment for turning a blind eye to him. It was for your sake I did it, and this is what I get for it.

NORA. Yes, this.

HELMER. Now you have ruined my entire happiness, jeopardized my whole future. It's terrible to think of. Here I am, at the mercy of a thoroughly unscrupulous person; he can do whatever he likes with me, demand anything he wants, order me about just as he chooses . . . and I daren't even whimper. I'm done for, a miserable failure, and it's all the fault of a feather-brained woman!

NORA. When I've left this world behind, you will be free.

HELMER. Oh, stop pretending! Your father was just the same, always ready with fine phrases. What good would it do me if you left this world behind, as you put it? Not the slightest bit of good. He can still let it all come out, if he likes; and if he does, people might even suspect me of being an accomplice in these criminal acts of yours. They might even think I was the one behind it all, that it was I who pushed you into it! And it's you I have to thank for this . . . and when I've taken such good care of you, all our married life. Now do you understand what you have done to me?

NORA [*coldly and calmly*]. Yes.

HELMER. I just can't understand it, it's so incredible. But we must see about putting things right. Take that shawl off. Take it off, I tell you! I must see if I can't find some way or other of appeasing him. The thing must be hushed up at all costs. And as far as you and I are concerned, things must appear to go on exactly as before. But only in the eyes of the world, of course. In other words you'll go on living here; that's understood. But you will not be allowed to bring up the children, I can't trust you with them. . . . Oh, that I should have to say this to the woman I loved so dearly, the woman I still. . . . Well, that must be all over and done with. From now on, there can be no question of happiness. All we can do is save the bits and pieces from the wreck, preserve appearances. . . . [*The front door-bell rings.* HELMER *gives a start.*] What's that? So late? How terrible, supposing. . . . If he should . . . ? Hide, Nora! Say you are not well.

[NORA *stands motionless.* HELMER *walks across and opens the door into the hall.*]

MAID [*half dressed, in the hall*]. It's a note for Mrs. Helmer.

HELMER. Give it to me. [*He snatches the note and shuts the door.*] Yes, it's from him. You can't have it. I want to read it myself.

NORA. You read it then.

HELMER [*by the lamp*]. I hardly dare. Perhaps this is the end, for both of us. Well, I *must* know. [*He opens the note hurriedly, reads a few lines, looks at another enclosed sheet, and gives a cry of joy.*] Nora! [NORA *looks at him inquiringly.*] Nora! I must read it again. Yes, yes, it's true! I am saved! Nora, I am saved!

NORA. And me?

HELMER. You too, of course, we are both saved, you as well as me. Look, he's sent your IOU back. He sends his regrets and apologies for what he has done. . . . His luck has changed. . . . Oh, what does it matter what he says. We are saved, Nora! Nobody can do anything to you now. Oh, Nora, Nora . . . but let's get rid of this disgusting thing first. Let me see. . . . [*He glances at the IOU.*] No, I don't want to see it. I don't want it to be anything but a dream. [*He tears up the IOU and both letters, throws all the pieces into the stove and watches them burn.*] Well, that's the end of that. He said in his note you'd known since Christmas Eve. . . . You must have had three terrible days of it, Nora.

NORA. These three days haven't been easy.

HELMER. The agonies you must have gone through! When the only way out seemed to be. . . . No, let's forget the whole ghastly thing. We can rejoice and say: It's all over! It's all over! Listen to me, Nora! You don't seem to understand: it's all over! Why this grim look on your face? Oh, poor little Nora, of course I understand. You can't bring yourself to believe I've forgiven you. But I have, Nora, I swear it. I forgive you everything. I know you did what you did because you loved me.

NORA. That's true.

HELMER. You loved me as a wife should love her husband. It was simply that you didn't have the experience to judge what was the best way of going about things. But do you think I love you any the less for that; just because you don't know how to act on your own responsibility? No, no, you just lean on me, I shall give you all the advice and guidance you need. I wouldn't be a proper man if I didn't find a woman doubly attractive for being so obviously helpless. You mustn't dwell on the harsh things I said in that first moment of horror, when

I thought everything was going to come crashing down about my ears. I have forgiven you, Nora, I swear it! I have forgiven you!

NORA. Thank you for your forgiveness.

[*She goes out through the door, right.*]

HELMER. No, don't go! [*He looks through the doorway.*] What are you doing in the spare room?

NORA. Taking off this fancy dress.

HELMER [*standing at the open door*]. Yes, do. You try and get some rest, and set your mind at peace again, my frightened little song-bird. Have a good long sleep; you know you are safe and sound under my wing. [*Walks up and down near the door.*] What a nice, cosy little home we have here, Nora! Here you can find refuge. Here I shall hold you like a hunted dove I have rescued unscathed from the cruel talons of the hawk, and calm your poor beating heart. And that will come, gradually, Nora, believe me. Tomorrow you'll see everything quite differently. Soon everything will be just as it was before. You won't need me to keep on telling you I've forgiven you; you'll feel convinced of it in your own heart. You don't really imagine me ever thinking of turning you out, or even of reproaching you? Oh, a real man isn't made that way, you know, Nora. For a man, there's something indescribably moving, and very satisfying in knowing that he has forgiven his wife—forgiven her, completely and genuinely, from the depths of his heart. It's as though it made her his property in a double sense: he has, as it were, given her a new life, and she becomes in a way both his wife and at the same time his child. That is how you will seem to me after today, helpless, perplexed little thing that you are. Don't you worry your pretty little head about anything, Nora. Just you be frank with me, and I'll take all the decisions for you. . . . What's this? Not in bed? You've changed your things?

NORA [*in her everyday dress*]. Yes, Torvald, I've changed.

HELMER. What for? It's late.

NORA. I shan't sleep tonight.

HELMER. But my dear Nora. . . .

NORA [*looks at her watch*]. It's not so terribly late. Sit down, Torvald. We two have a lot to talk about.

[*She sits down at one side of the table.*]

HELMER. Nora, what is all this? Why so grim?

NORA. Sit down. It'll take some time. I have a lot to say to you.

HELMER [*sits down at the table opposite her*]. You frighten me, Nora. I don't understand you.

NORA. Exactly. You don't understand me. And I have never understood you, either—until tonight. No, don't interrupt. I just want you to listen to what I have to say. We are going to have things out, Torvald.

HELMER. What do you mean?

NORA. Isn't there anything that strikes you about the way we two are sitting here?

HELMER. What's that?

NORA. We have now been married eight years. Hasn't it struck you this is the first time you and I, man and wife, have had a serious talk together?

HELMER. Depends what you mean by 'serious'.

NORA. Eight whole years—no, more, ever since we first knew each other—and never have we exchanged one serious word about serious things.

HELMER. What did you want me to do? Get you involved in worries that you couldn't possibly help me to bear?

NORA. I'm not talking about worries. I say we've never once sat down together and seriously tried to get to the bottom of anything.

HELMER. But, my dear Nora, would that have been a thing for you?

NORA. That's just it. You have never understood me . . . I've been greatly wronged, Torvald. First by my father, and then by you.

HELMER. What! Us two! The two people who loved you more than anybody?

NORA [*shakes her head*]. You two never loved me. You only thought how nice it was to be in love with me.

HELMER. But, Nora, what's this you are saying?

NORA. It's right, you know, Torvald. At home, Daddy used to tell me what he thought, then I thought the same. And if I thought differently, I kept quiet about it, because he wouldn't have liked it. He used to call me his baby doll, and he played with me as I used to play with my dolls. Then I came to live in your house. . . .

HELMER. What way is that to talk about our marriage?

NORA [*imperturbably*]. What I mean is: I passed out of Daddy's hands into yours. You arranged everything to your tastes, and I acquired the same tastes. Or I pretended to . . . I don't really know . . . I think it was a bit of both, sometimes one thing and sometimes the other. When I look back, it seems to me I have been living here like a beggar, from hand to mouth. I lived by doing tricks for you, Torvald. But that's the way you wanted it. You and Daddy did me a great wrong. It's your fault that I've never made anything of my life.

HELMER. Nora, how unreasonable . . . how ungrateful you are! Haven't you been happy here?

NORA. No, never. I thought I was, but I wasn't really.

HELMER. Not . . . not happy!

NORA. No, just gay. And you've always been so kind to me. But our house has never been anything but a play-room. I have been your doll wife, just as at home I was Daddy's doll child. And the children in turn have been my dolls. I thought it was fun when you came and played with me, just as they thought it was fun when I went and played with them. That's been our marriage, Torvald.

HELMER. There is some truth in what you say, exaggerated and hysterical though it is. But from now on it will be different. Play-time is over; now comes the time for lessons.

NORA. Whose lessons? Mine or the children's?

HELMER. Both yours and the children's, my dear Nora.

NORA. Ah, Torvald, you are not the man to teach me to be a good wife for you.

HELMER. How can you say that?

NORA. And what sort of qualifications have I to teach the children?

HELMER. Nora!

NORA. Didn't you say yourself, a minute or two ago, that you couldn't trust me with that job.

HELMER. In the heat of the moment! You shouldn't pay any attention to that.

NORA. On the contrary, you were quite right. I'm not up to it. There's another problem needs solving first. I must take steps to educate myself. You are not the man to help me there. That's something I must do on my own. That's why I'm leaving you.

HELMER [*jumps up*]. What did you say?

NORA. If I'm ever to reach any understanding of myself and the things around me, I must learn to stand alone. That's why I can't stay here with you any longer.

HELMER. Nora! Nora!

NORA. I'm leaving here at once. I dare say Kristine will put me up for tonight. . . .

HELMER. You are out of your mind! I won't let you! I forbid you!

NORA. It's no use forbidding me anything now. I'm taking with me my own personal belongings. I don't want anything of yours, either now or later.

HELMER. This is madness!

NORA. Tomorrow I'm going home—to what used to be my home, I mean. It will be easier for me to find something to do there.

HELMER. Oh, you blind, inexperienced . . .

NORA. I must set about *getting* experience, Torvald.

HELMER. And leave your home, your husband and your children? Don't you care what people will say?

NORA. That's no concern of mine. All I know is that this is necessary for *me*.

HELMER. This is outrageous! You are betraying your most sacred duty.

NORA. And what do you consider to be my most sacred duty?

HELMER. Does it take me to tell you that? Isn't it your duty to your husband and your children?

NORA. I have another duty equally sacred.

HELMER. You have not. What duty might *that* be?

NORA. My duty to myself.

HELMER. First and foremost, you are a wife and mother.

NORA. That I don't believe any more. I believe that first and foremost I am an individual, just as much as you are—or at least I'm going to try to be. I know most people agree with you, Torvald, and that's also what it says in books. But I'm not content any more with what most people say, or with what it says in books. I have to think things out for myself, and get things clear.

HELMER. Surely you are clear about your position in your own home? Haven't you an infallible guide in questions like these? Haven't you your religion?

NORA. Oh, Torvald, I don't really know what religion is.

HELMER. What do you say!

NORA. All I know is what Pastor Hansen said when I was confirmed. He said religion was this, that and the other. When I'm away from all this and on my own, I'll go into that, too. I want to find out whether what Pastor Hansen told me was right—or at least whether it's right for *me*.

HELMER. This is incredible talk from a young woman! But if religion cannot keep you on the right path, let me at least stir your conscience. I suppose you do have some moral sense? Or tell me—perhaps you don't?

NORA. Well, Torvald, that's not easy to say. I simply don't know. I'm really very confused about such things. All I know is my ideas about such things are very different from yours. I've also learnt that the law is different from what I thought; but I simply can't get it into my head that that particular law is right. Apparently a woman has no right to spare her old father on his death-bed, or to save her husband's life, even. I just don't believe it.

HELMER. You are talking like a child. You understand nothing about the society you live in.

NORA. No, I don't. But I shall go into that too. I must try to discover who is right, society or me.

HELMER. You are ill, Nora. You are delirious. I'm half inclined to think you are out of your mind.

NORA. Never have I felt so calm and collected as I do tonight.

HELMER. Calm and collected enough to leave your husband and children?

NORA. Yes.

HELMER. Then only one explanation is possible.

NORA. And that is?

HELMER. You don't love me any more.

NORA. Exactly.

HELMER. Nora! Can you say that!

NORA. I'm desperately sorry, Torvald. Because you have always been so kind to me. But I can't help it. I don't love you any more.

HELMER [*struggling to keep his composure*]. Is that also a 'calm and collected' decision you've made?

NORA. Yes, absolutely calm and collected. That's why I don't want to stay here.

HELMER. And can you also account for how I forfeited your love?

NORA. Yes, very easily. It was tonight, when the miracle didn't happen. It was then I realized you weren't the man I thought you were.

HELMER. Explain yourself more clearly. I don't understand.

NORA. For eight years I have been patiently waiting. Because, heavens, I knew miracles didn't happen every day. Then this devastating business started, and I became absolutely convinced the miracle *would* happen. All the time Krogstad's letter lay there, it never so much as crossed my mind that you would ever submit to that man's conditions. I was absolutely convinced you would say to him: Tell the whole wide world if you like. And when that was done . . .

HELMER. Yes, then what? After I had exposed my own wife to dishonour and shame . . . !

NORA. When that was done, I was absolutely convinced you would come forward and take everything on yourself, and say: I am the guilty one.

HELMER. Nora!

NORA. You mean I'd never let you make such a sacrifice for my sake? Of course not. But what would my story have counted for against yours?—That was the miracle I went in hope and dread of. It was to prevent it that I was ready to end my life.

HELMER. I would gladly toil day and night for you, Nora, enduring all manner of sorrow and distress. But nobody sacrifices his *honour* for the one he loves.

NORA. Hundreds and thousands of women have!

HELMER. Oh, you think and talk like a stupid child.

NORA. All right. But you neither think nor talk like the man I would want to share my life with. When you had got over your fright—and you weren't concerned about me but only about what might happen to you—and when all danger was past, you acted as though nothing had happened. I was your little sky-lark again, your little doll, exactly as before; except you would have to protect it twice as carefully as before, now that it had shown itself to be so weak and fragile. [*Rises.*] Torvald, that was the moment I realised that for eight years I'd been living with a stranger, and had borne him three children. . . . Oh, I can't bear to think about it! I could tear myself to shreds.

HELMER [*sadly*]. I see. I see. There is a tremendous gulf dividing us. But, Nora, is there no way we might bridge it?

NORA. As I am now, I am no wife for you.

HELMER. I still have it in me to change.

NORA. Perhaps . . . if you have your doll taken away.

HELMER. And be separated from you! No, no, Nora, the very thought of it is inconceivable.

NORA [*goes into the room, right*]. All the more reason why it must be done.

> [*She comes back with her outdoor things and a small travelling bag which she puts on the chair beside the table.*]

HELMER. Nora, Nora, not now! Wait till the morning.

NORA [*putting on her coat*]. I can't spend the night in a strange man's room.

HELMER. Couldn't we go on living here like brother and sister . . . ?

NORA [*tying on her hat*]. You know very well that wouldn't last. [*She draws the shawl round her.*] Goodbye, Torvald. I don't want to see the children. I know they are in better hands than mine. As I am now, I can never be anything to them.

HELMER. But some day, Nora, some day . . . ?

NORA. How should I know? I've no idea what I might turn out to be.

HELMER. But you are my wife, whatever you are.

NORA. Listen, Torvald, from what I've heard, when a wife leaves her husband's house as I am doing now, he is absolved by law of all responsibility for her. I can at any rate free you from all responsibility. You must not feel in any way bound, any more than I shall. There must be full freedom on both sides. Look, here's your ring back. Give me mine.

HELMER. That too?

NORA. That too.

HELMER. There it is.

NORA. Well, that's the end of that. I'll put the keys down here. The maids know where everything is in the house—better than I do, in fact. Kristine will come in the morning after I've left to pack up the few things I brought with me from home. I want them sent on.

HELMER. The end! Nora, will you never think of me?

NORA. I dare say I'll often think about you and the children and this house.

HELMER. May I write to you, Nora?

NORA. No, never. I won't let you.

HELMER. But surely I can send you . . .

NORA. Nothing, nothing.

HELMER. Can't I help you if ever you need it?

NORA. I said 'no'. I don't accept things from strangers.

HELMER. Nora, can I never be anything more to you than a stranger?

NORA [*takes her bag*]. Ah, Torvald, only by a miracle of miracles. . . .

HELMER. Name it, this miracle of miracles!

NORA. Both you and I would have to change to the point where . . . Oh, Torvald, I don't believe in miracles any more.

HELMER. But I *will* believe. Name it! Change to the point where . . . ?

NORA. Where we could make a real marriage of our lives together. Goodbye!

[*She goes out through the hall door.*]

HELMER [*sinks down on a chair near the door, and covers his face with his hands*]. Nora! Nora! [*He rises and looks round.*] Empty! She's gone! [*With sudden hope.*] The miracle of miracles . . . ?

[*The heavy sound of a door being slammed is heard from below.*]

Translated and edited by J. W. McFarlane

Journal Entry

Attack or defend Nora's decision to abandon her marriage and her children.

Textual Considerations

1. Characterize Torvald. To what extent does he fulfill his societal role?
2. Identify and discuss how Nora uses language to manipulate and validate her father's, Torvald's, and Dr. Rank's notions of authority and masculinity.
3. Analyze the implications of the play's title.

4. To what extent are Mrs. Linde and Nora foils for each other? What do her encounters with Krogstad reveal about Nora's character?

Cultural Contexts

1. Respond to the critical assessment that the play is not so much about the rights of women as about "the need of every individual to find out the kind of person he or she really is, and to strive to become that person."
2. To better understand the interplay of gender and power in *A Doll's House*, speculate with your group about who really holds the power in the Helmers' household. Is it Nora, who manipulates the patriarchal system but preserves its facade of stability, or Torvald, who claims to hold the real power?

PART ASSIGNMENTS

WRITING TOPICS

1. According to the French feminist Simone de Beauvoir, "The word *love* has by no means the same sense for both sexes, and this is one of the most serious misunderstandings that divide them." Apply this thesis to any three texts in Part Two.

2. Several texts in this part portray a male vision of gender relationships as fragmented and commercialized. Apply this concept to the text by Chekhov, Rifaat, Euripides, or Ibsen.

3. Assume the role of therapist, and write an essay on your first session with Prufrock. Use examples from his stream-of-consciousness monologue as the basis for your evaluation.

4. American linguist Deborah Tannen has observed that even though women usually start the conversation, it is men who control it. To what extent do you consider these linguistic differences a major factor in conversations between men and women? Select any three texts to support or refute Tannen's point of view.

5. Consider the functions that the myth of the perfect housewife or the cult of domesticity serves in society. In your discussion, consider the premise that such a myth, at its best, may fulfill women's highest aspirations and, at its worst, may contribute to women's low self-esteem. Use three texts from this part to support your arguments.

6. Analyze the sources of the wife's anger in "Home Burial," and write about the causes of her inability to accept that her husband also mourns their child's death. Review lines 92–93 and lines 100–105 before formulating your response.

7. Several authors representing diverse cultures focus on economics and gender. Compare and contrast the degree to which economics shapes gender relationships in any three of the following: "At Sea: A Sailor's Story," "Another Evening at the Club," "My Last Duchess," *Medea,* and *A Doll's House.*

8. Apply to any three texts in this part the concept that women's worst enemy is the enemy inside themselves or their inability to change their own ingrained psychological structures.

9. Several texts explore the issue of women's sexuality from different vantage points. Compare and contrast the attitudes toward this issue in the poems by Greenberg, Rich, Sexton, and de la Cruz.

10. To focus on changing aspects of masculinity, compare and contrast the condition of male power in the texts by Browning and Chekhov with indications of male powerlessness in the selection by Eliot. Analyze the sociohistorical forces that shape male identity in each text.

11. The tradition of the *mal mariee* (bad marriage) is an important theme in several culturally diverse texts in this part. To investigate the claim that marriage bestows upon women a sense of fixed identity, analyze three

texts that explore a married woman's sense of personal and societal alienation.

12. Compare and contrast the portrayals of husbands in the texts by Freeman, Chekhov, Chopin, and Rifaat. To what extent does each find fulfillment in his role? Cite evidence from the texts to support your point of view.

13. Woman as rebel is the focal point in the selections by Freeman, Toomer, Two Eagles, Sexton, and Ibsen. Analyze the causes and effects of the woman's rebellion on the gender relations in each text.

14. According to the French writer Charles Fourier, whenever men disgrace women, they end up degrading themselves. Choose two short stories from this unit to illustrate your agreement or disagreement with Fourier's idea.

15. Attack or defend the thesis that in *The Awakening* Chopin not only raises the right of a woman to become an individual and to abandon the roles of wife and mother, she also poses the problem of how a woman, once liberated, should use her freedom. To what extent is Edna prepared or unprepared to deal with her freedom and independence?

16. To what extent does Chopin, the author, approve or disapprove of Edna, her hero. Consider the author's editorializing in chapters VI and VII in formulating your response.

RESEARCH TOPICS

1. Several works in Part Two examine the history of women from different sociohistorical points of view. To understand what these texts portray in light of the women's liberation movement, investigate the history of one of the following: Mary Wollstonecraft's *A Vindication of the Rights of Women* (1790), Olympe de Gorges's *Declaration of the Rights of Women and Female Citizens* (1791), the suffragette movement in nineteenth-century England, the movement of the American feminists in the 1970s, or the black women's movement in America in the three last decades. Sources: Search under Women-History, Women-France, Feminism, Gender, American Women and Politics, African-American Women-History.

   You may also check:

   Krichmar, Albert. *The Women's Movement in the Seventies: An International English-Language Bibliography.*

   Sims, Janet. *The Progress of Afro-American Women: A Selected Bibliography and Resource Guide.*

   Williams, Ora. *American Black Women in the Arts and Social Sciences: A Bibliographic Survey,* revised and expanded edition.

2. To associate visual and verbal arts, look at how some world-famous paintings such as Adolf Rifino's *The Married Couple,* Mary Cassatt's paintings on maternity, and Picasso's *Portrait of Gertrude Stein* evoke specific images of women as wives, mothers, and intellectuals. Then investigate how women are represented in some of the literary portraits in this part. Consider also how these visual and literary texts reflect cultural revisions of women's images.

3. The passion of jealousy has been widely explored in literature. From Euripides' *Medea* to Shakespeare's *Othello,* from Molière's *L'Ecole des Femmes* to Robbe-Grillet's *Jealousie,* writers have analyzed different kinds of jealousy. With the help of a questionnaire you will distribute to your classmates, investigate first the sources of jealousy. Where are they centered? In the game of power that lovers play with each other? In lovers' narcissistic need for control and possession of the beloved and/or in their feelings of low self-esteem and insecurity? Then use the data provided by the survey to investigate the theme of jealousy in *Medea.*

4. The myth of the "warrior woman"—from the legend of the Amazons to Joan of Arc, and from the writings of Cervantes, Spenser, and Gayle Two Eagles to the actions of modern guerrillas—explores the images of women who have appropriated the great deeds traditionally attributed to the world of men. Examine three works in this part that incorporate, in one way or another, the image of the rebellious warrior woman.

5. To examine why different societies have developed rigid codes of masculinity, write a documented paper on three literary texts of your choice that portray stereotypical images of men as tough, powerful, stoic, successful, and sexually aggressive. Consider also their effects on personal identity. You may also use primary texts such as "Another Evening at the Club," "Ragazza," "Home Burial," and "She Proves the Inconsistency. . . ."

6. Use any three texts and your own experience to support or reject Carol Gilligan's statement that "relationships, and particularly issues of dependency, are experienced differently by women and by men. Since masculinity is defined through separation while femininity is defined through attachment, male gender identity is threatened by intimacy while female gender identity is threatened by separation."

PART THREE

War and Violence

Fiction

A Mystery of Heroism, Stephen Crane ◆ *The Sniper*, Liam O'Flaherty ◆ *Silence*, Tadeusz Borowski ◆ *The Hour of Truth*, Isabel Allende ◆ *Spoils of War*, Janice Mirikitani ◆ *The Curse*, Andre Dubus

Poetry

The Man He Killed, Thomas Hardy ◆ *What Were They Like?* Denise Levertov ◆ *Babiy Yar*, Yevgeny Yevtushenko ◆ *Prisons of Silence*, Janice Mirikitani ◆ *Disabled*, Wilfred Owen ◆ *The Dying Veteran*, Walt Whitman ◆ *First Practice*, Gary Gildner ◆ *Concord Hymn*, Ralph Waldo Emerson ◆ *The Charge of the Light Brigade*, Alfred, Lord Tennyson ◆ *Hope*, Ariel Dorfman ◆ *The Visitor*, Carolyn Forché ◆ *Cross Plains, Wisconsin*, Martín Espada ◆ *Quote from the Bureau of Information, from the* Argus, *August 27, 1986: "The Situation in Soweto Is Not Abnormal,"* Mavis Smallberg ◆ *Waking This Morning*, Muriel Rukeyser ◆ *The Artilleryman's Vision*, Walt Whitman

Drama

Lysistrata, Aristophanes ◆ *Picnic on the Battlefield*, Fernando Arrabal ◆ *Dutchman*, Amiri Baraka (LeRoi Jones)

Why do nations go to war? What causes individuals to engage in violence? What is the relation between power and violence? Why do poets, artists, musicians, and filmmakers create images celebrating the glories of war? What causes so many people to prefer conflict and tension to stability and calm? According to German-American social philosopher Hannah Arendt (1906–1975), a major cause of war throughout human history is the conflict between freedom and tyranny. Ironically, even in the name of freedom, innocent people are tortured, strangled, exiled, and murdered.

In fact, ordinary people often bear a greater share of the human costs of war than do their leaders who initiate the conflicts. The writers of many texts in Part Three try to make sense of a world where violence is perpetrated not only by the horrors of war but also by the racial and ethnic conflicts erupting almost daily in cities throughout the United States and other countries of the world.

Why has the human imagination always been captivated by heroism and the horrors of war? And why do so few literary works celebrate the virtues and possibilities of peace? The texts in this part pose many questions about the nature and consequences of war and violence. Some, such as Walt Whitman's "The Dying Veteran," celebrate the glory and victory of war, whereas others, such as Wilfred Owen's "Disabled," portray the alienation and rejection experienced by returning veterans wounded physically and psychologically in the trench warfare of World War I.

Another series of texts here explores the arbitrariness of war by attacking the tradition of "the blind hatred of the enemy." Although Thomas Hardy and Denise Levertov belong to different historical moments, each poet, in "The Man He Killed" and "What Were They Like?" evokes war's irrationality by attempting to portray the enemy as a human being with a personal and cultural identity. "The Sniper," a story that dramatizes the suspense of an urban guerrilla episode during civil war in Ireland, brings the concern of the "myth of the enemy" even closer to home.

One of the most devastating aspects of World War II was Hitler's attempt to exterminate the Jewish people in the death camps of the Third Reich. In "Silence," by Tadeusz Borowski, you will enter the bizarre world of the concentration camp, a terrifying reminder of human depravity, and in Yevtushenko's "Babiy Yar," you will share the courageous attempts of the poet to identify with the "enemy"—the Jewish victims of Stalin's massacre.

Other contemporary selections in Part Three focus on Latin America, re-creating conditions analogous to those of war: violence, torture, and dictatorship. In "Hope," for example, the Chilean poet Ariel Dorfman meditates on the "times," the "world," and the "land" that brutalized human beings through the use of torture. Isabel Allende's "The Hour of Truth" reminds us that the human spirit can sometimes transcend the tortured body.

To what extent can the violence of war abroad also become the catalyst for racial and sexual violence at home? Janice Mirikitani's "Spoils of War" portrays the effects of post-traumatic stress disorder on a Vietnam veteran and his civilian victim. Stanley Kubrick's film *Full Metal Jacket* explores the ramifications of a platoon's training slogan "Born to Kill."

It is generally acknowledged that alienation and apathy often lead to violence, and we read daily about gratuitous acts of violence, the subject of Andre Dubus's "The Curse." Another disturbing aspect of contemporary violence is that resulting from police brutality, whether in a small town in "Cross Plains, Wisconsin" or in Soweto, a black township in South Africa.

As you explore the complexities of war and violence in these and other texts, you may find yourself reexamining your presuppositions about both and considering alternative solutions to conflict. As Arendt again reminds us, "The end of war . . . is peace or victory; but to the question *and what is the end of peace?* there is no answer. Peace is an absolute, even though in recorded history persons of warfare have nearly always outlasted persons of peace." Perhaps it is time, in John Lennon's words, to "give peace a chance."

Stephen Crane

A Mystery of Heroism

The dark uniforms of the men were so coated with dust from the incessant wrestling of the two armies that the regiment almost seemed a part of the clay bank which shielded them from the shells. On the top of the hill a battery was arguing in tremendous roars with some other guns, and to the eye of the infantry, the artillerymen, the guns, the caissons, the horses, were distinctly outlined upon the blue sky. When a piece was fired, a red streak as round as a log flashed low in the heavens, like a monstrous bolt of lightning. The men of the battery wore white duck trousers, which somehow emphasized their legs; and when they ran and crowded in little groups at the bidding of the shouting officers, it was more impressive than usual to the infantry.

Fred Collins, of A Company, was saying: "Thunder! I wisht I had a drink. Ain't there any water round here?" Then somebody yelled, "There goes th' bugler!"

As the eyes of half the regiment swept in one machinelike movement there was an instant's picture of a horse in a great convulsive leap of a death wound and a rider leaning back with a crooked arm and spread fingers before his face. On the ground was the crimson terror of an exploding shell, with fibres of flame that seemed like lances. A glittering bugle swung clear of the rider's back as fell headlong the horse and the man. In the air was an odour as from a conflagration.

Sometimes they of the infantry looked down at a fair little meadow which spread at their feet. Its long, green grass was rippling gently in a breeze. Beyond it was the gray form of a house half torn to pieces by shells and by the busy axes of soldiers who had pursued firewood. The line of an old fence was now dimly marked by long weeds and by an occasional post. A shell had blown the well-house to fragments. Little lines of gray smoke ribboning upward from some embers indicated the place where had stood the barn.

From beyond a curtain of green woods there came the sound of some stupendous scuffle, as if two animals of the size of islands were fighting. At a distance there were occasional appearances of swift-moving men, horses, batteries, flags, and with the crashing of infantry volleys were heard, often, wild and frenzied cheers. In the midst of it all Smith and Ferguson, two privates of A Company, were engaged in a heated discussion, which involved the greatest questions of the national existence.

The battery on the hill presently engaged in a frightful duel. The white legs of the gunners scampered this way and that way, and the officers redoubled their shouts. The guns, with their demeanours of stolidity and courage, were typical of something infinitely self-possessed in this clamour of death that swirled around the hill.

One of a "swing" team was suddenly smitten quivering to the ground, and his maddened brethren dragged his torn body in their struggle to escape from this turmoil and danger. A young soldier astride one of the leaders swore and fumed in his saddle, and furiously jerked at the bridle. An officer screamed out an order so violently that his voice broke and ended the sentence in a falsetto shriek.

The leading company of the infantry regiment was somewhat exposed, and the colonel ordered it moved more fully under the shelter of the hill. There was the clank of steel against steel.

A lieutenant of the battery rode down and passed them, holding his right arm carefully in his left hand. And it was as if this arm was not at all a part of him, but belonged to another man. His sober and reflective charger went slowly. The officer's face was grimy and perspiring, and his uniform was tousled as if he had been in direct grapple with an enemy. He smiled grimly when the men stared at him. He turned his horse toward the meadow.

Collins, of A Company, said: "I wisht I had a drink. I bet there's water in that there ol' well yonder!"

"Yes; but how you goin' to git it?"

For the little meadow which intervened was now suffering a terrible onslaught of shells. Its green and beautiful calm had vanished utterly. Brown earth was being flung in monstrous handfuls. And there was a massacre of the young blades of grass. They were being torn, burned, obliterated. Some curious fortune of the battle had made this gentle little meadow the object of the red hate of the shells, and each one as it exploded seemed like an imprecation in the face of a maiden.

The wounded officer who was riding across this expanse said to himself, "Why, they couldn't shoot any harder if the whole army was massed here!"

A shell struck the gray ruins of the house, and as, after the roar, the shattered wall fell in fragments, there was a noise which resembled the flapping of shutters during a wild gale of winter. Indeed, the infantry paused in the shelter of the bank appeared as men standing upon a shore contemplating a madness of the sea. The angel of calamity had under its glance the battery upon the hill. Fewer white-legged men laboured about the guns. A shell had smitten one of the pieces, and after the flare, the smoke, the dust, the wrath of this blow were gone, it was possible to see white legs stretched horizontally on the ground. And at that interval to the rear, where it is the business of battery horses to stand with their noses to the fight awaiting the command to drag their guns out of the destruction or into it or wheresoever these incomprehensible humans demanded with whip and spur—in this line of passive and dumb spectators, whose fluttering hearts yet would not let them forget the iron laws of man's control of them—in this rank of brute-soldiers there had been relentless and hideous carnage. From the ruck of bleeding and prostrate horses, the men of the infantry could see one animal raising its stricken body with its fore legs, and turning its nose with mystic and profound eloquence toward the sky.

Some comrades joked Collins about his thirst. "Well, if yeh want a drink so bad, why don't yeh go git it!"

"Well, I will in a minnet, if yeh don't shut up!"

A lieutenant of artillery floundered his horse straight down the hill with as great concern as it were level ground. As he galloped past the colonel of the infantry, he threw up his hand in swift salute. "We've got to get out of that," he roared angrily. He was a black-bearded officer, and his eyes, which resembled beads, sparkled like those of an insane man. His jumping horse sped along the column of infantry.

The fat major, standing carelessly with his sword held horizontally behind him and with his legs far apart, looked after the receding horseman and laughed. "He wants to get back with orders pretty quick, or there'll be no batt'ry left," he observed.

The wise young captain of the second company hazarded to the lieutenant colonel that the enemy's infantry would probably soon attack the hill, and the lieutenant colonel snubbed him.

A private in one of the rear companies looked out over the meadow, and then turned to a companion and said, "Look there, Jim!" It was the wounded officer from the battery, who some time before had started to ride across the meadow, supporting his right arm carefully with his left hand. This man had encountered a shell apparently at a time when no one perceived him, and he could now be seen lying face downward with a stirruped foot stretched across the body of his dead horse. A leg of the charger extended slantingly upward precisely as stiff as a stake. Around this motionless pair the shells still howled.

There was a quarrel in A Company. Collins was shaking his fist in the faces of some laughing comrades. "Dern yeh! I ain't afraid t' go. If yeh say much, I will go!"

"Oh course, yeh will! You'll run through that there medder, won't yeh?"

Collins said, in a terrible voice, "You see now!" At this ominous threat his comrades broke into renewed jeers.

Collins gave them a dark scowl and went to find his captain. The latter was conversing with the colonel of the regiment.

"Captain," said Collins, saluting and standing at attention—in those days all trousers bagged at the knees—"captain, I want t' get permission to go git some water from that there well over yonder!"

The colonel and the captain swung about simultaneously and stared across the meadow. The captain laughed. "You must be pretty thirsty, Collins?"

"Yes sir, I am."

"Well—ah," said the captain. After a moment he asked, "Can't you wait?"

"No, sir."

The colonel was watching Collin's face. "Look here, my lad," he said, in a pious sort of voice—"look here, my lad"—Collins was not a lad—"don't you think that's taking pretty big risks for a little drink of water?"

"I dunno," said Collins uncomfortably. Some of the resentment toward his companions, which perhaps had forced him into this affair, was beginning to fade. "I dunno whether 'tis."

The colonel and the captain contemplated him for a time.

"Well," said the captain finally.

"Well," said the colonel, "if you want to go, why, go."

Collins saluted. "Much obliged t' yeh."

As he moved away the colonel called after him. "Take some of the other boys' canteens with you an' hurry back now."

"Yes, sir, I will."

The colonel and the captain looked at each other then, for it had suddenly occurred that they could not for the life of them tell whether Collins wanted to go or whether he did not.

They turned to regard Collins, and as they perceived him surrounded by gesticulating comrades, the colonel said: "Well, by thunder! I guess he's going."

Collins appeared as a man dreaming. In the midst of the questions, the advice, the warnings, all the excited talk of his company mates, he maintained a curious silence.

They were very busy in preparing him for his ordeal. When they inspected him carefully it was somewhat like the examination that grooms give a horse before a race; and they were amazed, staggered by the whole affair. Their astonishment found vent in strange repetitions.

"Are yeh sure a-goin'?" they demanded again and again.

"Certainly I am," cried Collins, at last furiously.

He strode sullenly away from them. He was swinging five or six canteens by their cords. It seemed that his cap would not remain firmly on his head, and often he reached up and pulled it down over his brow.

There was a general movement in the compact column. The long animal-like thing moved slightly. Its four hundred eyes were turned upon the figure of Collins.

"Well, sir, if that ain't th' dernest thing! I never thought Fred Collins had the blood in him for that kind of business."

"What's he goin' to do, anyhow?"

"He's goin' to that well there after water."

"We ain't dyin' of thirst, are we? That's foolishness."

"Well, somebody put him up to it, an' he's doin' it."

"Say, he must be a desperate cuss."

When Collins faced the meadow and walked away from the regiment, he was vaguely conscious that a chasm, the deep valley of all prides, was suddenly between him and his comrades. It was provisional, but the provision was that he return as a victor. He had blindly been led by quaint emotions, and laid himself under an obligation to walk squarely up to the face of death.

But he was not sure that he wished to make a retraction, even if he could do so without shame. As a matter of truth, he was sure of very little. He was mainly surprised.

It seemed to him supernaturally strange that he had allowed his mind to manoeuver his body into such a situation. He understood that it might be called dramatically great.

However, he had no full appreciation of anything, excepting that he was actually conscious of being dazed. He could feel his dulled mind grouping after the form and colour of this incident. He wondered why he did not feel some keen agony of fear cutting his sense like a knife. He wondered at this, because human expression had said loudly for centuries that men should feel afraid of certain things, and that all men who did not feel this fear were phenomena—heroes.

He was, then, a hero. He suffered that disappointment which we would all have if we discovered that we were ourselves capable of those deeds which we most admire in history and legend. This, then, was a hero. After all, heroes were not much.

No, it could not be true. He was not a hero. Heroes had no shames in their lives, and, as for him, he remembered borrowing fifteen dollars from a friend and promising to pay it back the next day, and then avoiding that friend for ten months. When at home his mother had aroused him for the early labour of his life on the farm, it had often been his fashion to be irritable, childish, diabolical; and his mother had died since he had come to the war.

He saw that, in this matter of the well, the canteens, the shells, he was an intruder in the land of fine deeds.

He was now about thirty paces from his comrades. The regiment had just turned its many faces toward him.

From the forest of terrific noises there suddenly emerged a little uneven line of men. They fired fiercely and rapidly at distant foliage on which appeared little puffs of white smoke. The spatter of skirmish firing was added to the thunder of the guns on the hill. The little line of men ran forward. A colour sergeant fell flat with his flag as if he had slipped on ice. There was a hoarse cheering from this distant field.

Collins suddenly felt that two demon fingers were pressed into his ears. He could see nothing but flying arrows, flaming red. He lurched from the shock of this explosion, but he made a mad rush for the house, which he viewed as a man submerged to the neck in a boiling surf might view the shore. In the air, little pieces of shell howled and the earthquake explosions drove him insane with the menace of their roar. As he ran the canteens knocked together with a rhythmical tinkling.

As he neared the house, each detail of the scene became vivid to him. He was aware of some bricks of the vanished chimney lying on the sod. There was a door which hung by one hinge.

Rifle bullets called forth by the insistent skirmishers came from the far-off bank of foliage. They mingled with the shells and the pieces of shells until the air was torn in all directions by hootings, yells, howls. The sky was full of fiends who directed all their wild rage at his head.

When he came to the well, he flung himself face downward and peered into its darkness. There were furtive silver glintings some feet from the surface. He grabbed one of the canteens and, unfastening its cap, swung it down by the cord. The water flowed slowly in with an indolent gurgle.

And now as he lay with his face turned away he was suddenly smitten with the terror. It came upon his heart like the grasp of claws. All the power faded from his muscles. For an instant he was no more than a dead man.

The canteen filled with maddening slowness, in the manner of all bottles. Presently he recovered his strength and addressed a screaming oath to it. He leaned over until it seemed as if he intended to try to push water into it with his hands. His eyes as he gazed down into the well shone like two pieces of metal and in their expression was a great appeal and a great curse. The stupid water derided him.

There was the blaring thunder of a shell. Crimson light shone through the swift-boiling smoke and made a pink reflection on part of the wall of the well. Collins jerked out his arm and canteen with the same motion that a man would use in withdrawing his head from a furnace.

He scrambled erect and glared and hesitated. On the ground near him lay the old well bucket, with a length of rusty chain. He lowered it swiftly into the well. The bucket struck the water and then, turning lazily over, sank. When, with hand reaching tremblingly over hand, he hauled it out, it knocked often against the walls of the well and spilled some of its contents.

In running with a filled bucket, a man can adopt but one kind of gait. So through this terrible field over which screamed practical angels of death Collins ran in the manner of a farmer chased out of a dairy by a bull.

His face went staring white with anticipation—anticipation of a blow that would whirl him around and down. He would fall as he had seen other men fall, the life knocked out of them so suddenly that their knees were no more quick to touch the ground than their heads. He saw the long blue line of the regiment, but his comrades were standing looking at him from the edge of an impossible star. He was aware of some deep wheel ruts and hoofprints in the sod beneath his feet.

The artillery officer who had fallen in this meadow had been making groans in the teeth of the tempest of sound. These futile cries, wrenched from him by his agony, were heard only by shells, bullets. When wild-eyed Collins came running, this officer raised himself. His face contorted and blanched from pain, he was about to utter some great beseeching cry. But suddenly his face straightened and he called: "Say, young man, give me a drink of water, will you?"

Collins had no room amid his emotions for surprise. He was mad from the threats of destruction.

"I can't," he screamed, and in his reply was a full description of his quaking apprehension. His cap was gone and his hair was riotous. His clothes made it appear that he had been dragged over the ground by the heels. He ran on.

The officer's head sank down and one elbow crooked. His foot in its brass bound stirrup still stretched over the body of his horse and the other leg was under the steed.

But Collins turned. He came dashing back. His face had now turned gray and in his eyes was all terror. "Here it is! here it is!"

The officer was as a man gone in drink. His arm bent like a twig. His head drooped as if his neck were of willow. He was sinking to the ground, to lie face downward.

Collins grabbed him by the shoulder. "Here it is. Here's your drink. Turn over. Turn over, man, for God's sake!"

With Collins hauling at his shoulder, the officer twisted his body and fell with his face turned toward that region where lived the unspeakable noises of the swirling missiles. There was the faintest shadow of a smile on his lips as he looked at Collins. He gave a sigh, a little primitive breath like that from a child.

Collins tried to hold the bucket steady, but his shaking hands caused the water to splash all over the face of the dying man. Then he jerked it away and ran on.

The regiment gave him a welcoming roar. The grimed faces were wrinkled in laughter.

His captain waved the bucket away. "Give it to the men!"

The two genial, skylarking young lieutenants were the first to gain possession of it. They played over it in their fashion.

When one tried to drink the other teasingly knocked his elbow. "Don't, Billie! You'll make me spill it," said the one. The other laughed.

Suddenly there was an oath, the thud of wood on the ground, and a swift murmur of astonishment among the ranks. The two lieutenants glared at each other. The bucket lay on the ground empty.

Journal Entry

Speculate on the motives that trigger Collins's act of heroism.

Textual Considerations

1. The opening paragraph contrasts the dark silhouettes on the hill of the artillerymen, the guns, the caissons, and the horses with the blue sky and the red streak when ammunition is fired with the white duck trousers of the battery men. At what other point in the story does Crane use color contrast to represent battle scenes? To what effect?
2. Irony is a key element in this text. Cite some particularly ironic actions in the narrative, and discuss their significance in relation to your understanding of the text's meaning and tone.
3. Reflect on the significance of the text's title. How does Crane define heroism—as an individual value or a social action dictated by circumstances? To what extent does Crane explain the "mystery"?

Cultural Contexts

1. Speculate on the political significance attached to individual heroism and the war hero. Imagine how you might respond to the hardships of war, given a background that places moral and political emphasis on the war hero.
2. Working with your group, construct a profile of Crane's protagonist. Chart the stages in his feelings about his fellow soldiers as well as his thoughts about heroism. To what extent does he consider himself heroic? Speculate on why he stops to give water to the dying lieutenant. Is this a heroic act? Explain.

Liam O'Flaherty

The Sniper

The long June twilight faded into night. Dublin lay enveloped in darkness but for the dim light of the moon that shone through fleecy clouds, casting a pale light as of approaching dawn over the streets and the dark waters of the Liffey. Around the beleaguered Four Courts the heavy guns roared. Here and there through the city, machine-guns and rifles broke the silence of the night, spasmodically, like dogs barking on lone farms. Republicans and Free Staters were waging civil war.

On a roof-top near O'Connell Bridge, a Republican sniper lay watching. Beside him lay his rifle and over his shoulders were slung a pair of field glasses. His face was the face of a student, thin and ascetic, but his eyes had the cold gleam of the fanatic. They were deep and thoughtful, the eyes of a man who is used to look at death.

He was eating a sandwich hungrily. He had eaten nothing since morning. He had been too excited to eat. He finished the sandwich, and, taking a flask of whiskey from his pocket, he took a short draught. Then he returned the flask to his pocket. He paused for a moment, considering whether he should risk a smoke. It was dangerous. The flash might be seen in the darkness and there were enemies watching. He decided to take the risk.

Placing a cigarette between his lips, he struck a match. There was a flash and a bullet whizzed over his head. He dropped immediately. He had seen the flash. It came from the opposite side of the street.

He rolled over the roof to a chimney stack in the rear, and slowly drew himself up behind it, until his eyes were level with the top of the parapet. There was nothing to be seen—just the dim outline of the opposite housetop against the blue sky. His enemy was under cover.

Just then an armored car came across the bridge and advanced slowly up the street. It stopped on the opposite of the street, fifty yards ahead. The sniper could hear the dull panting of the motor. His heart beat faster. It was an enemy car. He wanted to fire, but he knew it was useless. His bullets would never pierce the steel that covered the gray monster.

Then round the corner of a side street came an old woman, her head covered by a tattered shawl. She began to talk to the man in the turret of the car. She was pointing to the roof where the sniper lay. An informer.

The turret opened. A man's head and shoulders appeared, looking toward the sniper. The sniper raised his rifle and fired. The head fell heavily on the turret wall. The woman darted toward the side street. The sniper fired again. The woman whirled round and fell with a shriek into the gutter.

Suddenly from the opposite roof a shot rang out and the sniper dropped his rifle with a curse. The rifle clattered to the roof. The sniper thought the noise would wake the dead. He stopped to pick the rifle up. He couldn't lift it. His forearm was dead.

"Christ," he muttered, "I'm hit."

Dropping flat onto the roof, he crawled back to the parapet. With his left hand he felt the injured right forearm. There was no pain—just a deadened sensation, as if the arm had been cut off.

Quickly he drew his knife from his pocket, opened it on the breast-work of the parapet, and ripped open the sleeve. There was a small hole where the bullet had entered. On the other side there was no hole. The bullet had lodged in the bone. It must have fractured it. He bent the arm below the wound. The arm bent back easily. He ground his teeth to overcome the pain.

Then taking out the field dressing, he ripped open the packet with his knife. He broke the neck of the iodine bottle and let the bitter fluid drip into the wound. A paroxysm of pain swept through him. He placed the cotton wadding over the wound and wrapped the dressing over it. He tied the ends with his teeth.

Then he lay against the parapet, and, closing his eyes, he made an effort of will to overcome the pain.

In the street beneath all was still. The armored car had retired speedily over the bridge, with the machine-gunner's head hanging lifelessly over the turret. The woman's corpse lay still in the gutter.

The sniper lay still for a long time nursing his wounded arm and planning escape. Morning must not find him wounded on the roof. The enemy on the opposite roof covered his escape. He must kill that enemy and he could not use his rifle. He had only a revolver to do it. Then he thought of a plan.

Taking off his cap, he placed it over the muzzle of his rifle. Then he pushed the rifle slowly over the parapet, until the cap was visible from the opposite side of the street. Almost immediately there was a report, and a bullet pierced the center of the cap. The sniper slanted the rifle forward. The cap slipped down into the street. Then catching the rifle in the middle, the sniper dropped his left hand over the roof and let it hang, lifelessly. After a few moments he let the rifle drop to the street. Then he sank to the roof, dragging his hand with him.

Crawling quickly to the left, he peered up at the corner of the roof. His ruse had succeeded. The other sniper, seeing the cap and rifle fall, thought he had killed his man. He was now standing before a row of chimney pots, looking across, with his head clearly silhouetted against the western sky.

The Republican sniper smiled and lifted his revolver above the edge of the parapet. The distance was about fifty yards—a hard shot in the dim light, and his right arm was paining him like a thousand devils. He took a steady aim. His hand trembled with eagerness. Pressing his lips together, he took a deep breath through his nostrils and fired. He was almost deafened with the report and his arm shook with the recoil.

Then when the smoke cleared he peered across and uttered a cry of joy. His enemy had been hit. He was reeling over the parapet in his death agony. He struggled to keep his feet, but he was slowly falling forward, as if in a dream. The rifle fell from his grasp, hit the parapet, fell over, bounded off the pole of a barber's shop beneath and then clattered on the pavement.

Then the dying man on the roof crumpled up and fell forward. The body turned over and over in space and hit the ground with a dull thud. Then it lay still.

The sniper looked at his enemy falling and he shuddered. The lust of battle died in him. He became bitten by remorse. The sweat stood out in beads on his forehead. Weakened by his wound and the long summer day of fasting and watching on the roof, he revolted from the sight of the shattered mass of his dead enemy. His teeth chattered, he began to gibber to himself, cursing the war, cursing himself, cursing everybody.

He looked at the smoking revolver in his hand, and with an oath he hurled it to the roof at his feet. The revolver went off with the concussion and the bullet whizzed past the sniper's head. He was frightened back to his senses by the shock. His nerves steadied. The cloud of fear scattered from his mind and he laughed.

Taking the whiskey flask from his pocket, he emptied it at a draught. He felt reckless under the influence of the spirit. He decided to leave the roof now and look for his company commander, to report. Everywhere around was quiet. There was not much danger in going through the streets. He picked up his revolver and put it in his pocket. Then he crawled down through the sky-light to the house underneath.

When the sniper reached the laneway on the street level, he felt a sudden curiosity as to the identity of the enemy sniper whom he had killed. He decided that he was a good shot, whoever he was. He wondered did he know him. Perhaps he had been in his own company before the split in the army. He decided to risk going over to have a look at him. He peered round the corner into O'Connell Street. In the upper part of the street there was heavy firing, but around here all was quiet.

The sniper darted across the street. A machine-gun tore up the ground around him with a hail of bullets, but he escaped. He threw himself face downward beside the corpse. The machine-gun stopped.

Then the sniper turned over the dead body and looked into his brother's face.

Journal Entry

To what extent does "The Sniper" present both brothers as victims of the "myth of the enemy"?

Textual Considerations

1. Observe O'Flaherty's frequent use of irony in "The Sniper," and analyze its effects on the poem's meaning, style, and tone.
2. Investigate also the effects of the narrative point of view on the development of the story. To what extent does the narrator's stance affect your evaluation of the sniper?
3. Chart the stages in the sniper's responses to his situation, and evaluate their plausibility.

Cultural Contexts

1. To what extent do you share the sniper's commitment to a political cause? Engage in a dialogue with him about his commitment.
2. How does the violence of civil wars, like that in the war between the Republicans and the Free Staters in Ireland, compare to the violence that results from war among nations? Consider the extent to which family and religious ties continue to prevail in the midst of civil wars.

Tadeusz Borowski

Silence

At last they seized him inside the German barracks, just as he was about to climb over the window ledge. In absolute silence they pulled him down to the floor and panting with hate dragged him into a dark alley. Here, closely surrounded by a silent mob, they began tearing at him with greedy hands.

Suddenly from the camp gate a whispered warning was passed from one mouth to another. A company of soldiers, their bodies leaning forward, their rifles on the ready, came running down the camp's main road, weaving between the clusters of men in stripes standing in the way. The crowd scattered and vanished inside the blocks. In the packed, noisy barracks the prisoners were cooking food pilfered during the night from neighbouring farmers. In the bunks and in the passageways between them, they were grinding grain in small flour-mills, slicing meat on heavy slabs of wood, peeling potatoes and throwing the peels on to the floor. They were playing cards for stolen cigars, stirring batter for pancakes, gulping down hot soup, and lazily killing fleas. A stifling odour of sweat hung in the air, mingled with the smell of food, with smoke and with steam that liquefied along the ceiling beams and fell on the men, the bunks and the food in large, heavy drops, like autumn rain.

There was a stir at the door. A young American officer with a tin helmet on his head entered the block and looked with curiosity at the bunks and the tables. He wore a freshly pressed uniform; his revolver was hanging down, strapped in an open holster that dangled against his thigh. He was assisted by the translator who wore a yellow band reading "interpreter" on the sleeve of his civilian coat, and by the chairman of the Prisoners' Committee, dressed in a white summer coat, a pair of tuxedo trousers and tennis shoes. The men in the barracks fell silent. Leaning out of their bunks and lifting their eyes from the kettles, bowls and cups, they gazed attentively into the officer's face.

"Gentlemen," said the officer with a friendly smile, taking off his helmet—and the interpreter proceeded at once to translate sentence after sentence—"I know, of course, that after what you have gone through and after what you have seen, you must feel a deep hate for your tormentors. But we, the soldiers of America, and you, the people of Europe, have fought so that law should prevail over lawlessness. We must show our respect for the law. I assure you that the guilty will be punished, in this camp as well as in all the others. You have already seen, for example, that the S.S. men were made to bury the dead."

". . . right, we could use the lot at the back of the hospital. A few of them are still around," whispered one of the men in a bottom bunk.

". . . or one of the pits," whispered another. He sat straddling the bunk, his fingers firmly clutching the blanket.

"Shut up! Can't you wait a little longer? Now listen to what the American has to say," a third man, stretched across the foot of the same bunk, spoke in an angry whisper. The American officer was now hidden from their view behind the thick crowd gathered at the other end of the block.

"Comrades, our new Kommandant gives you his word of honour that all the criminals of the S.S. as well as among the prisoners will be punished," said the translator. The men in the bunks broke into applause and shouts. In smiles and gestures they tried to convey their friendly approval of the young man from across the ocean.

"And so the Kommandant requests," went on the translator, his voice turning somewhat hoarse, "that you try to be patient and do not commit lawless deeds, which may only lead to trouble, and please pass the sons of bitches over to the camp guards. How about it, men?"

The block answered with a prolonged shout. The American thanked the translator and wished the prisoners a good rest and an early reunion with their dear ones. Accompanied by a friendly hum of voices, he left the block and proceeded to the next.

Not until after he had visited all the blocks and returned with the soldiers to his headquarters did we pull our man off the bunk—where covered with blankets and half-smothered with the weight of our bodies he lay gagged, his face buried in the straw mattress—and dragged him on to the cement floor under the stove, where the entire block, grunting and growling with hatred, trampled him to death.

Journal Entry

Respond to the setting of the concentration camp in "Silence." Imagine yourself in the place of the survivors.

Textual Considerations

1. Explore the thematic nuances of the story's title. Consider, for example, the effects of juxtaposing the silence of the concentration camp survivors with the speech of the young American officer through his interpreter.

2. Review the story carefully, and discuss how Borowski uses the physical appearance and language of the survivors to reinforce their psychic distance from the outside world.
3. How successful is "Silence" in portraying not only the narrator's realistic re-creation of a concentration camp but also his own disillusionment and horror of war?

Cultural Contexts

1. Working with your group, support or challenge the thesis that in killing one of their former oppressors, the inmates in "Silence" perpetuate the violence that victimized them.
2. Analyze what "Silence" conveys about the survivors' need for revenge. Consider, too, what the text implies about the ability of the young American officer and other non-inmates to judge the actions of the inmates.

Isabel Allende

The Hour of Truth

Alba was curled up in the darkness. They had ripped the tape from her eyes and replaced it with a tight bandage. She was afraid. As she recalled her Uncle Nicolás's training, and his warning about the danger of being afraid of fear, she concentrated on trying to control the shaking of her body and shutting her ears to the terrifying sounds that reached her side. She tried to visualize her happiest moments with Miguel, groping for a means to outwit time and find the strength for what she knew lay ahead. She told herself that she had to endure a few hours without her nerves betraying her, until her grandfather was able to set in motion the heavy machinery of his power and influence to get her out of there. She searched her memory for a trip to the coast with Miguel, in autumn, long before the hurricane of events had turned the world upside down, when things were still called by familiar names and words had a single meaning; when people, freedom, and *compañero* were just that—people, freedom, and *compañero*—and had not yet become passwords. She tried to relive that moment—the damp red earth and the intense scent of the pine and eucalyptus forests in which a carpet of dry leaves lay steeping after the long hot summer and where the coppery sunlight filtered down through the treetops. She tried to recall the cold, the silence, and that precious feeling of owning the world, of being twenty years old and having her whole life ahead of her, of making love slowly and calmly, drunk with the scent of the forest and their love, without a past, without suspecting the future, with just the incredible richness of that present moment in which they stared at each other, smelled each other, kissed each other, and explored each other's bodies, wrapped in the whisper of the wind among the trees and the sound of the nearby waves breaking against the rocks at the foot of the cliff, exploding in a crash of pungent surf, and the two of them embracing underneath a single poncho like Siamese twins, laughing and swearing that this would last forever, that they were the only ones in the whole world who had discovered love.

Alba heard the screams, the long moans, and the radio playing full blast. The woods, Miguel, and love were lost in the deep well of her terror and she resigned herself to facing her fate without subterfuge.

She calculated that a whole night and the better part of the following day had passed when the door was finally opened and two men took her from her cell. With insults and threats they led her in to Colonel García, whom she could recognize blindfolded by his habitual cruelty, even before he opened his mouth. She felt his hands take her face, his thick fingers touch her ears and neck.

"Now you're going to tell me where your lover is," he told her. "That will save us both a lot of unpleasantness."

Alba breathed a sigh of relief. That meant they had not arrested Miguel!

"I want to go to the bathroom," Alba said in the strongest voice she could summon up.

"I see you're not planning to cooperate, Alba. That's too bad." García sighed. "The boys will have to do their job. I can't stand in their way."

There was a brief silence and she made a superhuman effort to remember the pine forest and Miguel's love, but her ideas got tangled up and she no longer knew if she was dreaming or where this stench of sweat, excrement, blood, and urine was coming from, or the radio announcer describing some Finnish goals that had nothing to do with her in the middle of other, nearer, more clearly audible shouts. A brutal slap knocked her to the floor. Violent hands lifted her to her feet. Ferocious fingers fastened themselves to her breasts, crushing her nipples. She was completely overcome by fear. Strange voices pressed in on her. She heard Miguel's name but did not know what they were asking her, and kept repeating a monumental *no* while they beat her, manhandled her, pulled off her blouse, and she could no longer think, could only say *no, no,* and *no* and calculate how much longer she could resist before her strength gave out, not knowing this was only the beginning, until she felt herself begin to faint and the men left her alone, lying on the floor, for what seemed to her a very short time.

She soon heard García's voice again and guessed it was his hands that were helping her to her feet, leading her toward a chair, straightening her clothes, and buttoning her blouse.

"My God!" he said. "Look what they've done to you! I warned you, Alba. Try to relax now, I'm going to give you a cup of coffee."

Alba began to cry. The warm liquid brought her back to life, but she could not taste it because when she swallowed it was mixed with blood. García held the cup, guiding it carefully toward her lips like a nurse.

"Do you want a cigarette?"

"I want to go to the bathroom," she said, pronouncing each syllable with difficulty with her swollen lips.

"Of course, Alba. They'll take you to the bathroom and then you can get some rest. I'm your friend. I understand your situation perfectly. You're in love, and that's why you want to protect him. I know you don't have anything to do with the guerrillas. But the boys don't believe me when I tell them. They won't be satisfied until you tell them where Miguel is. Actually they've already got him surrounded. They know exactly where he is. They'll catch him, but they want to be sure that you have nothing to do with the guerrillas. You understand? If you protect him and refuse to talk, they'll continue to suspect you. Tell them what they want to know and then I'll personally escort you home. You'll tell them, right?"

"I want to go to the bathroom," Alba repeated.

"I see you're just as stubborn as your grandfather. All right. You can go to the bathroom. I'm going to give you a chance to think things over," García said.

They took her to a toilet and she was forced to ignore the man who stood beside her, holding on to her arm. After that they returned her to her cell. In the tiny, solitary cube where she was being held, she tried to clarify her thoughts, but she was tortured by the pain of her beating, her thirst, the bandage pressing on her temples, the drone of the radio, the terror of approaching footsteps and her relief when they moved away, the shouts and the orders. She curled up like a fetus on the floor and surrendered to her pain. She remained in that position for hours, perhaps days. A man came twice to take her to the bathroom. He led her to a fetid lavatory where she was unable to wash because there was no water. He allowed her a minute, placing her on the toilet seat next to another person as silent and sluggish as herself. She could not tell if it was a woman or a man. At first she wept, wishing her Uncle Nicolás had given her a special course in how to withstand humiliation, which she found worse than pain, but she finally resigned herself to her own filth and stopped thinking about her unbearable need to wash. They gave her boiled corn, a small piece of chicken, and a bit of ice cream, which she identified by their taste, smell, and temperature, and which she wolfed down with her hands, astonished to be given such luxurious food, unexpected in a place like that. . . .

The third time they took her in to Esteban García, Alba was more prepared, because through the walls of her cell she could hear what was going on in the next room, where they were interrogating other prisoners, and she had no illusions. She did not even try to evoke the woods where she had shared the joy of love.

"Well, Alba, I've given you time to think things over. Now the two of us are going to talk and you're going to tell me where Miguel is and we're going to get this over with quickly," García said.

"I want to go to the bathroom," Alba answered.

"I see you're making fun of me, Alba," he said. "I'm sorry, but we don't have any time to waste."

Alba made no response.

"Take off your clothes!" García ordered in another voice.

She did not obey. They stripped her violently, pulling off her slacks despite her kicking. The memory of her adolescence and Miguel's kiss in the garden gave her the strength of hatred. She struggled against him, until they got tired of beating her and gave her a short break, which she used to invoke the understanding spirits of her grandmother, so that they would help her die. But no one answered her call for help. Two hands lifted her up, and four laid her on a cold, hard metal cot with springs that hurt her back, and bound her wrists and ankles with leather thongs.

"For the last time, Alba. Where is Miguel?" García asked.

She shook her head in silence. They had tied her head down with another thong.

"When you're ready to talk, raise a finger," he said.

Alba heard another voice.

"I'll work the machine," it said.

Then she felt the atrocious pain that coursed through her body, filling it completely, and that she would never forget as long as she lived. She sank into darkness.

"Bastards! I told you to be careful with her!" she heard Esteban García say from far away. She felt them opening her eyelids, but all she saw was a misty brightness. Then she felt a prick in her arm and sank back into unconsciousness.

A century later Alba awoke wet and naked. She did not know if she was bathed with sweat, or water, or urine. She could not move, recalled nothing, and had no idea where she was or what had caused the intense pain that had reduced her to a heap of raw meat. She felt the thirst of the Sahara and called out for water.

"Wait, *compañera*," someone said beside her. "Wait until morning. If you drink water, you'll get convulsions, and you could die."

She opened her eyes. They were no longer bandaged. A vaguely familiar face was leaning over her, and hands were wrapping her in a blanket.

"Do you remember me? I'm Ana Díaz. We went to the university together. Don't you recognize me?"

Alba shook her head, closed her eyes, and surrendered to the sweet illusion of death. But she awakened a few hours later, and when she moved she realized that she ached to the last fiber of her body.

"You'll feel better soon," said a woman who was stroking her face and pushing away the locks of damp hair that hid her eyes. "Don't move, and try to relax. I'll be here next to you. You need to rest."

"What happened?" Alba whispered.

"They really roughed you up, *compañera*," the other woman said sadly.

"Who are you?" Alba asked.

"Ana Díaz. I've been here for a week. They also got my *compañero*, Andrés, but he's still alive. I see him once a day, when they take them to the bathroom."

"Ana Díaz?" Alba murmured.

"That's right. We weren't so close back then, but it's never too late to start. The truth is, you're the last person I expected to meet here, Countess," the woman said gently. "Don't talk now. Try to sleep. That way the time will go faster for you. Your memory will gradually come back. Don't worry. It's because of the electricity."

But Alba was unable to sleep, for the door of her cell opened and a man walked in.

"Put the bandage back on her!" he ordered Ana Díaz.

"Please . . . can't you see how weak she is? Let her rest a little while. . . ."

"Do as I say!"

Ana bent over the cot and put the bandage over her eyes. Then she removed the blanket and tried to dress her, but the guard pulled her away, lifted the prisoner by her arms, and sat her up. Another man came in to help him, and between them they carried her out because she could not walk. Alba was sure that she was dying, if she was not already dead. She could tell they were walking down a hallway in which the sound of their footsteps echoed. She felt a hand on her face, lifting her head.

"You can give her water. Wash her and give her another shot. See if she can swallow some coffee and bring her back to me," García said.

"Do you want us to dress her?"

"No."

Alba was in García's hands a long time. After a few days, he realized she had recognized him, but he did not abandon his precaution of keeping her blindfolded, even when they were alone. Every day new prisoners arrived and others were led away. Alba heard the vehicles, the shouts, and the gate being closed. She tried to keep track of the number of prisoners, but it was almost impossible. Ana Díaz thought there were close to two hundred. García was very busy, but he never let a day go by without seeing Alba, alternating unbridled violence with the pretense that he was her good friend. At times he appeared to be genuinely moved, personally spooning soup into her mouth, but the day he plunged her head into a bucket full of excrement until she fainted from disgust, Alba understood that he was not trying to learn Miguel's true whereabouts but to avenge himself for injuries that had been inflicted on him from birth, and that nothing she could confess would have any effect on her fate as the private prisoner of Colonel García. This allowed her to venture slowly out of the private circle of her terror. Her fear began to ebb and she was able to feel compassion for the others, for those they hung by their arms, for the newcomers, for the man whose shackled legs were run over by a truck. They brought all the prisoners into the courtyard at dawn and forced them to watch, because this was also a personal matter between the colonel and his prisoner. It was the first time Alba had opened her eyes outside the darkness of her cell, and the gentle splendor of the morning and the frost shining on the stones, where puddles of rain had collected overnight, seemed unbearably radiant to her. They dragged the man, who offered no resistance, out into the courtyard. He could not stand, and they left him lying on the ground. The guards had covered their faces with handkerchiefs so no one would ever be able to identify them in the improbable event that circumstances changed. Alba closed her eyes when she heard the truck's engine, but she could not close her ears to the sound of his howl, which stayed in her memory forever. . . .

One day Colonel García was surprised to find himself caressing Alba like a lover and talking to her of his childhood in the country, when he would see her walking hand in hand with her grandfather, dressed in her starched pinafores and with the green halo of her hair, while he, barefoot in the mud, swore that one day he would make her pay for her arrogance and avenge himself for his cursed bastard fate. Rigid and absent, naked and trembling with disgust and cold, Alba neither heard nor felt him, but that crack in his eagerness to torture her sounded an alarm in the colonel's mind. He ordered Alba to be thrown in the doghouse, and furiously prepared to forget that she existed.

The doghouse was a small, sealed cell like a dark, frozen, airless tomb. There were six of them altogether, constructed in an empty water tank especially for punishment. They were used for relatively short stretches of time, because no one could withstand them very long, at most a few days, before beginning to ramble—to lose the sense of things, the meaning of words, and the anxiety of passing time—or simply, beginning to die. At first, huddled in her sepulcher, unable either to stand up or sit down despite her small size, Alba managed to stave off madness. Now that she was alone, she realized how much she needed Ana Díaz. She thought she heard an imperceptible tapping in the distance, as if someone were sending her coded messages from another cell, but she soon stopped paying attention to it because she realized that all attempts at communication were completely hopeless. She gave up, deciding to end this torture once and for all. She stopped eating, and only when her feebleness became too much for her did she take a sip of water. She tried not to breathe or move, and began eagerly to await her death. She stayed like this for a long time. . . . Word went out that she was dying. The guards opened the hatch of the doghouse and lifted her effortlessly, because she was very light. They took her back to Colonel García, whose hatred had returned during these days, but she did not recognize him. She was beyond his power.

Translated by Magda Bogin

Journal Entry

Explain how the forces that Colonel García unleashes to subdue Alba paradoxically set her free.

Textual Considerations

1. Analyze the dynamics of the narrative in "The Hour of Truth." Focus on how the author organizes time, space, narrative gaps, narrative closure, dialogues, and sequential order. How do these techniques affect meaning?
2. Allende juxtaposes fantasy and reality in the story. How does that technique affect the portrayal of Alba's character and her ability to endure torture?
3. Evaluate the role of social class in the political conflicts of the story. Cite evidence from the text to support your point of view.
4. Dictatorships like the one Allende describes in "The Hour of Truth" did not rule out the use of torture to combat the alleged communist threat in Latin America. Quote from the text to show the kind of threat that a young woman like Alba might pose to such a political system.

Cultural Contexts

1. Debate with your group what circumstances might justify the use of institutionalized violence. Consider some concrete episodes involving police brutality (such as the beating of Rodney King in Los Angeles in 1991), as well as the defense of violence invoked by various military dictatorships.

Janice Mirikitani

Spoils of War

Violet ran up the familiar path of Telman Park determined today to make five miles. She knew the exact spot of her destination, through the eucalyptus, past the emergency telephone box, up to the twin boulders where she would sit triumphantly and rest in the warm sun.

He watched her from his green volkswagen van. Her black hair bouncing at her shoulder blades, her sturdy thighs and sleek runner's calves. Her small breasts jousled with each step under the sweatshirt that read, "Lotus Blossom Doesn't Live Here."

Spirit of the bayonet.
red/march
white/hup
blue/eyes front
square your piece
left/right
kill 'em
thrust/jab
jab
jab/kill 'em,
"hey mamasan,
joto mate ichiban"
poontang one/two
poontang three/four
when we're done
we'll kill some more.

Of all the joggers he saw, this was the one he wanted. He would park and watch the several who, at the same time each day, would run the path up into the wooded hills of the park.

Violet started running after she had met Josh. In fact, she started doing a lot of things. All her life she had been introverted, studious, conscientious, shy. During her last graduate year, life revolted around her. There were so many demonstrations on campus against the Vietnam war, she didn't pay attention to the noises—the speeches, doomsday messages from wild-eyed street preachers and twitching pan-handlers. So when the police stormed the gathered protestors, Violet did not move out of the way in time as the sweep of billyclubs and helmets picked her up like a wave. Violet hit the cement with her elbow, and curled up reflexively to protect her head from the stampede of legs and feet. Josh had stumbled over her and scrambling up, lifted her with him.

In the months of their new friendship, the world she had pulled around herself like a narrow corridor began to swell and pulse as they talked of civil rights, the war, military tycoonism, racism that had many faces. They saw and touched their com-mon wounds.

Josh talked about his war. He who escaped the draft, his mother's endless work to help him through college, his father whose heart was crushed by the humiliation of worklessness. His father's death gave him life, the circumstance for exemption from the military, and the freedom to revolt, protest.

Violet talked about her war. The sheets of silence that covered history from the moment the gates slammed her parents into concentration camps in Arkansas. Her mother distant and forgetful. Her father demanding, critical. It didn't seem to matter what Violet achieved. They kept their silence like blades beneath their tongues.

Violet passed the old eucalyptus, branching high, its constant falling leaves and shedding bark making the air smell pungent. She noticed the green van, dismissed it in the glaring light of afternoon.

He crouched lower behind the wheel as she passed, seeing her closer, the dark sloping eyes, her olive skin browned by the sun, her delicate mouth and bones above her cheek. The beads of sweat popping around her brow.

They all had Vietnamese women.
None like mine.
She was bamboo thin,
her fingers clutching
the hem of her sleeve
like a child.
I felt red flame
licking the nape of my neck burning
deeper than napalm.
She was quiet,

her eyes, darker than night
helped me forget my My Lais.
Her beautiful body
curling around me,
flesh cocooned me against the
jungle where eyes were like rain,
Her arms like ivory bracelets
encircling my pain.
Flesh whole, sensual, shining
amidst the stench of rotting wounds
that fed the fat flies.
The insatiable flies of Vietnam.

Violet felt her anger draining with each step. The pounds shed, the tightening of her thighs, the new curves at her hips, and the thoughts of leaving home soon. Free as the wind in her face. Free from the jagged silences of her mother, the brooding disapproval of her father. Violet had informed them that she would be moving in with Josh. Perhaps they would live in Oregon where he was interviewing for a job at the University. She smiled, thinking of Josh's return, his sardonic grin when she told him of her parent's reaction. Josh who encouraged her to run, to strengthen herself, to speak her mind, to open her body, so long wrapped in years of suffocation. Her body that she had felt pitifully shapeless, small, powerless, burdened with blame and fault. If only he had not died. He was not due for another month. Her mother's face, pinched in pain as water and blood ran from her, rushed to the hospital. Her mother's body, wracked, gray, heaving and bellowing. The child tearing to exit too soon. She could still hear the screams from her mother's bones. The son, born dead. She remembered feeling alone. The weight of their grief, the sense of regret that she remained alive, on her small shoulders. All these years, the weight like boulders, the weight now shedding with each step.

The sun was a hot hand on her back as Violet ran through the threaded leaves, cracking beneath her steady feet.

He could feel the drugs wearing off. His skin twitching. He imagined the sores popping anew, the smell from jungle rot seeping from his pale flesh, tinted blue. He knew he would vomit.

She never withheld her warm thighs,
even when gorged with woman blood,
hot blood
sucking me deeper into her.
All the blood that would fill
a river.
Those jungles, villages like
a body split, slit, gouged.
Blood on me.

Swelling within her,
my blade, gleaming in the moonlight
exits flesh, flashes in her eyes.
She licks the blood from the shaft.
Deep, I thrust it past her teeth.
She took it all
her throat tightening on it
blood bubbling from the edges
of her lips.
Her arms circling my hips,
her hands moving in my groin
with grenade.
My blade cuts the arm away,
splits her womb
that spumes hot blood.

Violet noticed the day emptier, the sun hotter. No wind. She would reach her boulders today. Her mouth opened slightly as she pushed her breath. The path became clearer, the trees very still. Like entering a strange new place. She remembered her corridor where she withdrew, compressed by whispers of guilt, mother's unhappiness, father's loneliness. Her narrow corridor, airless. Dark. Her flesh lined the walls. Josh's hands touching, warming her surfaces, expanding. His long runner's body entering her corners. Breathing. She discovers sensation. Muscles moving, sinews of desire. Nerve endings alive.

Violet stood before her parents and shouted. Her mother threatened to kill herself. Her father informed her she could never bring Josh into his house. It was bad enough to marry outside her race, but to live in sin with someone especially *that* color is endless disgrace. Violet's fury unleashed like exploding walls. She would leave this week. Run free of them. Lift it all from her like the wind picking up leaves and spinning them to the sky.

The son, blue and breathless, wrinkled like a raisin. Mother gave up back then, switched off her eyes. Her dull face all these years never saw her daughter's pain. Well, Violet didn't want to take it on anymore. Can't bring him back to life. Can't trade places, can't be what they want, no matter what she did. Had he lived, he'd be in college or a soldier drafted, maybe dead anyway in Southeast Asia.

Violet running faster. She'd live her own life. She could see the boulders now.

He, crouching behind the trees, watched her lengthening shadow climbing the boulder where she lay down, stretched her bare arms and legs glistening with sweat. Her body lifted by her panting breath.

He pulls her by both legs onto the ground. She is surprised, not knowing how she fell. He pulls her to him, hand over her mouth and drags her into the trees. Her legs are strong, digging into the soft earth, resisting, thrashing. He reveals the long knife unsheathed, whispers that he will cut her throat if she screams. Violet retreats into her corridor, breathing quietly through her nose. He leads her far from the path, under brush and thicket of trees. He commands her to kneel in the leaves. Violet, terror exploding, screams, her fists beating against his pressing body, suffocating, scarred, distorted flesh. He falls upon her like a rock. His fists beat her again, brutally again, until she is unconscious. He pulls her shorts off, and gently. Gently. Caressing, kisses her slightly open mouth, her neck, her still arms. Inserts his blade in her womb and makes her bleed.

After, he carefully dresses himself. With a wide arched swing of his sharp knife, he severs her arm above the elbow.

Wiping the blood from his blade, gently he wraps the arm in his flak jacket. Carries it like a child to his van and leaves.

The wind is still, the sun falling, casting long shadows from the boulders, the trees. In the thicket, the faint hum of flies gathering.

> Spirit of the bayonet.
> red/march
> white/hup
> blue/eyes front
> Square your piece
> left/right
> kill 'em
> thrust/jab
> jab
> jab/kill 'em
> "hey mamasan
> joto mate ichiban"
> poontang one/two
> poontang three/four
> when we're done
> we'll kill some more.

Journal Entry

Freewrite about your responses to the rape in "Spoils of War."

Textual Considerations

1. The narrative structure of "Spoils of War" evokes a rich intersection of voices—from Violet and the Vietnam veteran to Josh and Violet's mother—carefully orchestrated to contrast and highlight one another. Explore the meaning of the interconnections among these voices. To what extent does each come to terms with his or her individual experience?

2. Mirikitani uses irony throughout the story to reinforce theme. Contrast, for example, the discrepancies between Violet's expectations for her jog through the park, expressed in the first paragraph, with the climactic events of the story's conclusion. Cite other examples of irony, and show how they contribute to the relation between war and sexual violence implicit in the story.

3. Speculate on the levels of meaning in the story's title. To what extent do you consider both Violet and the veteran victims of war? Characterize your attitude toward the veteran.

Cultural Contexts

1. Review the story carefully, looking for examples that support or challenge the image of the Vietnam veteran as antihero.
2. Can you reach a consensus about the image of America that emerges from the intersection of the postwar world of the Vietnam veteran and the world of peace that Violet and Josh are trying to build for themselves? To what extent does Mirikitani's story point to the political impact of the Vietnam War on the home front?

Andre Dubus

The Curse

Mitchell Hayes was forty-nine years old, but when the cops left him in the bar with Bob, the manager, he felt much older. He did not know what it was like to be very old, a shrunken and wrinkled man, but he assumed it was like this: fatigue beyond relieving by rest, by sleep. He also was not a small man. His weight moved up and down in the 170s, and he was five feet, ten inches tall. But now his body seemed short and thin. Bob stood at one end of the bar; he was a large, black-haired man, and there was nothing in front of him but an ashtray he was using. He looked at Mitchell at the cash register and said, "Forget it. You heard what Smitty said."

Mitchell looked away, at the front door. He had put the chairs upside down on the tables. He looked from the door past Bob to the empty space of floor at the rear; sometimes people danced there, to the jukebox. Opposite Bob, on the wall behind the bar, was a telephone; Mitchell looked at it. He had told Smitty there were five guys, and when he moved to the phone, one of them stepped around the corner of the bar and shoved him, one hand against Mitchell's chest, and it pushed him backward; he nearly fell. That was when they were getting rough with her at the bar. When they took her to the floor, Mitchell looked once toward her sounds, then looked down at the duckboard he stood on, or at the belly or chest of a young man in front of him.

He knew they were not drunk. They had been drinking before they came to his place, a loud popping of motorcycles outside, then walking into the empty bar, young and sunburned and carrying helmets and wearing thick leather jackets in August. They stood in front of Mitchell and drank drafts. When he took their first order, he thought they were on drugs, and later, watching them, he was certain.

They were not relaxed in the way of most drinkers near closing time. Their eyes were quick, alert as wary animals, and they spoke loudly, with passion, but their passion was strange and disturbing, because they were only chatting, bantering. Mitchell knew nothing of the effects of drugs, so could not guess what was in their blood. He feared and hated drugs because of his work and because he was the stepfather of teenagers: a boy and a girl. He gave last call and served them and leaned against the counter behind him.

Then the door opened and the girl walked in from the night, a girl he had never seen, and she crossed the floor toward Mitchell. He stepped forward to tell her she had missed last call; but before he spoke, she asked for change for the cigarette machine. She was young—he guessed nineteen to twenty-one—and deeply tanned and had dark hair. She was sober and wore jeans and a dark-blue T-shirt. He gave her the quarters, but she was standing between two of the men and she did not get to the machine.

When it was over and she lay crying on the cleared circle of floor, he left the bar and picked up the jeans and T-shirt beside her and crouched and handed them to her. She did not look at him. She laid the clothes across her breasts and what Mitchell thought of now as her wound. He left her and dialed 911, then Bob's number. He woke up Bob. Then he picked up her sneakers from the floor and placed them beside her and squatted near her face, her crying. He wanted to speak to her and touch her, hold a hand or press her brow, but he could not.

The cruiser was there quickly, the siren coming east from town, then slowing and deepening as the car stopped outside. He was glad Smitty was one of them; he had gone to high school with Smitty. The other was Dave, and Mitchell knew him because it was a small town. When they saw the girl, Dave went out to the cruiser to call for an ambulance; and when he came back, he said two other cruisers had those scumbags and were taking them in. The girl was still crying and could not talk to Smitty and Dave. She was crying when a man and a woman lifted her onto a stretcher and rolled her out the door and she vanished forever in a siren.

Bob came in while Smitty and Dave were sitting at the bar drinking coffee and Smitty was writing his report; Mitchell stood behind the bar. Bob sat next to Dave as Mitchell said, "I could have stopped them, Smitty."

"That's our job," Smitty said. "You want to be in the hospital now?"

Mitchell did not answer. When Smitty and Dave left, he got a glass of Coke from the cobra and had a cigarette with Bob. They did not talk. Then Mitchell washed his glass and Bob's cup and they left, turning off the lights. Outside, Mitchell locked the front door, feeling the sudden night air after almost ten hours of air conditioning. When he had come to work, the day had been very hot, and now he thought it would not have happened in winter. They had stopped for a beer on their way somewhere from the beach; he had heard them say that. But the beach was not the reason. He did not know the reason, but he knew it would not have happened in winter. The night was cool, and now he could smell trees. He turned and looked at the road in front of the bar. Bob stood beside him on the small porch.

"If the regulars had been here . . ." Bob said.

He turned and with his hand resting on the wooden rail, he walked down the ramp to the ground. At his car, he stopped and looked over its roof at Mitchell.

"You take it easy," he said.

Mitchell nodded. When Bob got into his car and left, he went down the ramp and drove home to his house on a street that he thought was neither good nor bad. The houses were small, and there were old large houses used now as apartments for families. Most of the people had work, most of the mothers cared for their children and most of the children were clean and looked like they lived in homes, not caves like some he saw in town. He worried about the older kids, one group of them, anyway. They were idle. When he was a boy in a town farther up the Merrimack River, he and his friends committed every mischievous act he could recall on afternoons and nights when they were idle. His stepchildren were not part of that group. They had friends from the high school. The front-porch light was on for him and one in the kitchen at the rear of the house. He went in the front door and switched off the porch light and walked through the living and dining rooms to the kitchen. He got a can of beer from the refrigerator, turned out the light, and sat at the table. When he could see, he took a cigarette from Susan's pack in front of him.

Down the hall, he heard Susan move on the bed, then get up, and he hoped it wasn't for the bathroom but for him. He had met her eight years ago, when he had given up on ever marrying and having kids; then, one night, she came into the bar with two of her girlfriends from work. She made six dollars an hour going to homes of invalids, mostly what she called her little old ladies, and bathing them. She got the house from her marriage, and child support the guy paid for a few months till he left town and went south. She came barefoot down the hall and stood in the kitchen doorway and said, "Are you all right?"

"No."

She sat across from him, and he told her. Very soon, she held his hand. She was good. He knew if he had fought all five of them and was lying in pieces in the hospital bed, she would tell him he had done the right thing, as she was telling him now. He liked her strong hand on his. It was a professional hand, and he wanted from her something he had never wanted before: to lie in bed while she bathed him. When they went to bed, he did not think he would be able to sleep, but she knelt beside him and massaged his shoulders and rubbed his temples and pressed her hands on his forehead. He woke to the voices of Marty and Joyce in the kitchen. They had summer jobs, and always when they woke him, he went back to sleep till noon, but now he got up and dressed and went to the kitchen door. Susan was at the stove, her back to him, and Marty and Joyce were talking and smoking. He said, "Good morning," and stepped into the room.

"What are you doing up?" Joyce said.

She was a pretty girl with her mother's wide cheekbones, and Marty was a tall, good-looking boy, and Mitchell felt as old as he had before he slept. Susan was watching him. Then she poured him a cup of coffee and put it at his place and he sat. Marty said, "You getting up for the day?"

"Something happened last night. At the bar." They tried to conceal their excitement, but he saw it in their eyes. "I should have stopped it. I think I *could* have stopped it. That's the point. There were these five guys. They were on motorcycles, but they weren't bikers. Just punks. They came in late, when everybody else had gone home. It was a slow night, anyway. Everybody was at the beach."

"They rob you?" Marty asked.

"No. A girl came in. Young. Nice-looking. You know: just a girl, minding her business."

They nodded, and their eyes were apprehensive.

"She wanted cigarette change; that's all. Those guys were on dope. Coke or something. You know: They were flying in place."

"Did they rape her?" Joyce said.

"Yes, honey."

"The *fuck*ers."

Susan opened her mouth, then closed it, and Joyce reached quickly for Susan's pack of cigarettes. Mitchell held his lighter for her and said, "When they started getting rough with her at the bar, I went for the phone. One of them stopped me. He shoved me; that's all. I should have hit him with a bottle."

Marty reached over the table with his big hand and held Mitchell's shoulder.

"No, Mitch. Five guys that mean. And coked up or whatever. No way. You wouldn't be here this morning."

"I don't know. There was always a guy with me. But just one guy, taking turns."

"Great," Joyce said. Marty's hand was on Mitchell's left shoulder; she put hers on his right hand.

"They took her to the hospital," he said. "The guys are in jail."

"They are?" Joyce said.

"I called the cops. When they left."

"You'll be a good witness," Joyce said.

He looked at her proud face.

"At the trial," she said.

The day was hot, but that night, most of the regulars came to the bar. Some of the younger ones came on motorcycles. They were a good crowd: They all worked, except the retired ones, and no one ever bothered the women, not even the young ones with their summer tans. Everyone talked about it: Some had read the newspaper story, some had heard the story in town, and they wanted to hear it from Mitchell. He told it as often as they asked, but he did not finish it, because he was working hard and could not stay with any group of customers long enough.

He watched their faces. Not one of them, even the women, looked at him as if he had not cared enough for the girl or was a coward. Many of them even appeared sympathetic, making him feel for moments that he was a survivor of something horrible; and when that feeling left him, he was ashamed. He felt tired and old, making drinks and change, talking and moving up and down the bar. At the stool at the far end, Bob drank coffee; and whenever Mitchell looked at him, he smiled or nodded and once raised his right fist, with the thumb up.

Reggie was drinking too much. He did that two or three times a month, and Mitchell had to shut him off, and Reggie always took it humbly. He was a big, gentle man with a long brown beard. But tonight, shutting off Reggie demanded from Mitchell an act of will, and when the eleven-o'clock news came on the television and Reggie ordered another shot and a draft, Mitchell pretended not to hear him. He served the customers at the other end of the bar, where Bob was. He could hear Reggie calling, "Hey, Mitch; shot and a draft, Mitch."

Mitchell was close to Bob now. Bob said softly, "He's had enough."

Mitchell nodded and went to Reggie, leaned closer to him, so he could speak quietly, and said, "Sorry, Reggie. Time for coffee. I don't want you dead out there."

Reggie blinked at him.

"OK, Mitch." He pulled some bills from his pocket and put them on the bar. Mitchell glanced at them and saw at least a ten-dollar tip. When he ran up Reggie's tab, the change was $16.50, and he dropped the coins and shoved the bills into the beer mug beside the cash register. The mug was full of bills, as it was on most nights, and he kept his hand in there, pressing Reggie's into the others, and saw the sun-burned young men holding her down on the floor and one kneeling between her legs, spread and held, and he heard their cheering voices and her screaming and groaning and finally weeping and weeping and weeping, until she was the siren crying, then fading into the night. From the floor behind him, far across the room, he felt her pain and terror and grief, then her curse upon him. The curse moved into his back and spread down and up his spine, into his stomach and legs and arms and shoulders until he quivered with it. He wished he were alone so he could kneel to receive it.

Journal Entry

To what extent are the woman and Mitchell both victims of the rapists in "The Curse"?

Textual Considerations

1. Analyze the character of Mitchell. Do you agree with his family and friends that his intervention would have accomplished nothing? Why, or why not?
2. Discuss how the author's use of a third-person narration affects the meaning and tone of the story.
3. Review the last paragraph. What does it reveal about Mitchell's psychological state? How does it add to the implications of the story's title?

Cultural Contexts

1. Discuss with your group the effects of being a witness to violence. To what extent should people get involved? Is action or inaction most likely to result in the psychological suffering of the witness? How might you have responded in Mitchell's situation?

Thomas Hardy

The Man He Killed

"Had he and I but met
  By some old ancient inn,
We should have sat us down to wet
  Right many a nipperkin!

"But ranged as infantry,   5
  And staring face to face,
I shot at him as he at me,
  And killed him in his place.

"I shot him dead because—
  Because he was my foe,   10
Just so: my foe of course he was;
  That's clear enough; although

"He thought he'd 'list, perhaps,
  Off-hand like—just as I—
Was out of work—had sold his traps—   15
  No other reason why.

"Yes; quaint and curious war is!
  You shoot a fellow down
You'd treat if met where any bar is,
  Or help to half-a-crown."   20

Denise Levertov

What Were They Like?

1) Did the people of Viet Nam
   use lanterns of stone?
2) Did they hold ceremonies
   to reverence the opening of buds?
3) Were they inclined to quiet laughter?   5
4) Did they use bone and ivory,
   jade and silver, for ornament?
5) Had they an epic poem?
6) Did they distinguish between speech and singing?

1) Sir, their light hearts turned to stone.   10
   It is not remembered whether in gardens
   stone lanterns illumined pleasant ways.
2) Perhaps they gathered once to delight in blossom,
   but after the children were killed
   there were no more buds.   15
3) Sir, laughter is bitter to the burned mouth.
4) A dream ago, perhaps. Ornament is for joy.
   All the bones were charred.
5) It is not remembered. Remember,
   most were peasants; their life   20
   was in rice and bamboo.
   When peaceful clouds were reflected in the paddies
   and the water buffalo stepped surely along terraces,
   maybe fathers told their sons old tales.
   When bombs smashed those mirrors   25
   there was time only to scream.
6) There is no echo yet
   of their speech which was like a song.
   It was reported their singing resembled
   the flight of moths in moonlight.   30
   Who can say? It is silent now.

Yevgeny Yevtushenko

Babiy Yar

Over Babiy Yar
there are no memorials.
The steep hillside like a rough inscription.
I am frightened.
Today I am as old as the Jewish race. 5
I seem to myself a Jew at this moment.
I, wandering in Egypt.
I, crucified. I perishing.
Even today the mark of the nails.
I think also of Dreyfus. I am he. 10
The Philistine my judge and my accuser.
Cut off by bars and cornered,
ringed round, spat at, lied about;
the screaming ladies with the Brussels lace
poke me in the face with parasols. 15
I am also a boy in Belostok,
the dropping blood spreads across the floor,
the public-bar heroes are rioting
in an equal stench of garlic and of drink.
I have no strength, go spinning from a boot, 20
shriek useless prayers that they don't listen to;
with a cackle of "Thrash the kikes and save Russia!"
the corn-chandler is beating up my mother.
I seem to myself like Anna Frank
to be transparent as an April twig 25
and am in love, I have no need for words,
I need for us to look at one another.
How little we have to see or to smell
separated from foliage and the sky,
how much, how much in the dark room 30
gently embracing each other.
They're coming. Don't be afraid.
The booming and banging of the spring.
It's coming this way. Come to me.
Quickly, give me your lips. 35
They're battering in the door. Roar of the ice.

Over Babiy Yar
rustle of the wild grass.
The trees look threatening, look like judges.
And everything is one silent cry.   40
Taking my hat off
I feel myself slowly going grey.
And I am one silent cry
over the many thousands of the buried;
am every old man killed here,   45
every child killed here.
O my Russian people, I know you.
Your nature is international.
Foul hands rattle your clean name.
I know the goodness of my country.   50
How horrible it is that pompous title
the anti-semites calmly call themselves,
Society of the Russian People.
No part of me can ever forget it.
When the last anti-semite on the earth   55
is buried for ever
let the International ring out.
No Jewish blood runs among my blood,
But I am as bitterly and hardly hated
by every anti-semite   60
as if I were a Jew. By this
I am a Russian.

Journal Entry

Explore the significance of the settings in "The Man He Killed," "What Were They Like?" and "Babiy Yar."

Textual Considerations

1. Investigate how Yevtushenko uses literary conventions such as flashbacks and a first-person narrator to reinforce the meanings of "Babiy Yar."
2. The poem is divided into two relatively long stanzas. What aspects of its thematic organization justify this division?
3. In the latter part of "Babiy Yar," Yevtushenko addresses the Russian people. Characterize his attitude toward them. Does it surprise you that Yevtushenko's poem was originally banned in Russia because he was regarded as a traitor? Explain.
4. Consider how the sentence structure of "The Man He Killed" conveys the attitude of the speaker toward his so-called foe. What indications are there that the speaker is

trying to clarify for himself his reasons for killing? Characterize your response to his situation.

5. What is the effect of Levertov's raising a series of questions followed by a series of answers? Who might the questioner be? Is his occupation important?
6. Who is answering? Does his nationality matter? Characterize the attitude of the person answering the questions, the questions themselves, the people of Vietnam, and the war.

Cultural Contexts

1. In "Babiy Yar," Yevtushenko refers to historical places and people. Review the poem and research the significance of his allusions to Dreyfus, Brussels, Belostok, and so on. Discuss with your group what these references have in common.
2. What kinds of responses do poems like "The Man He Killed," "What Were They Like?" and "Babiy Yar" elicit? To what extent, for example, do you agree with Hardy's speaker that war "is quaint and curious"? Explain.

Mirikitani and Owen

Janice Mirikitani

Prisons of Silence

1.
The strongest prisons are built
with walls of silence.

2.
Morning light falls between us
like a wall.
We have laid beside each other   5
as we have for years.
Before the war, when life
would clamor through our windows,
we woke joyfully to the work.

I keep those moments   10
like a living silent seed.

After day's work, I would
smell the damp soil in his hands,
his hands that felt the outlines
of my body in the velvet   15
night of summers.

I hold his warm hands to this
cold wall of flesh
as I have for years.

3.
Jap!   20
Filthy Jap!

Who lives within me?

Abandoned homes, confiscated land,
loyalty oaths, barbed wire prisons
in a strange wasteland.   25

Go home, Jap!
Where is home?

A country of betrayal.
No one speaks to us.

We would not speak to each other.   30

We were accused.

Hands in our hair,
hands that spread our legs
and searched our thighs for secret weapons,
hands that knit barbed wire   35
to cripple our flight.

Giant hot hands flung me,
fluttering, speechless into
barbed wire, thorns in a broken wing.

The strongest prisons are built   40
with walls of silence.

4.

I watched him depart that day
from the tedious wall of wire,
the humps of barracks,
handsome in his uniform.   45

I would look each day for letters
from a wall of time,
waiting for approach of my deliverance
from a wall of dust.

I do not remember   50
reading about his death
only the wall of wind
that encased me, as I turned my head.

5.

U.S. Japs hailed as heroes!

I do not know the face of this country   55
it is inhabited by strangers
who call me obscene names.

Jap. Go home.
Where is home?

I am alone wandering   60
in this desert.

Where is home?
Who lives within me?

A stranger with a knife in her tongue
and broken wing,   65
mad from separations and losses cruel
as hunger.

Walls suffocate her as a tomb,
encasing history.

6.

I have kept myself contained   70
within these walls shaped to my body
and buried my rage.
I rebuilt my life
like a wall, unquestioning.
Obeyed their laws . . . their laws.   75

7.
All persons of Japanese ancestry
    filthy jap.
Both alien and non-alien
    japs are enemy aliens.
To be incarcerated   80
    for their own good
A military necessity
    The army to handle only the japs
Where is home?
A country of betrayal.   85

8.
This wall of silence crumbles
from the bigness of their crimes.
This silent wall
crushed by living memory.

He awakens from the tomb   90
I have made for myself
and unearths my rage.

I must speak.

9.
He faces me in this small
room of myself.   95
I find the windows
where light escapes.

From this cell of history
this mute grave,
we birth our rage.   100

We heal our tongues.

We listen to ourselves

    Korematsu, Hirabayashi, Yasui.

We ignite the syllables of our names.

We give testimony.   105

We hear the bigness of our sounds freed
like many clapping hands,
thundering for reparations.

We give testimony.

Our noise is dangerous.   110

10.
We beat our hands
like wings healed.

We soar
from these walls of silence.

Wilfred Owen

Disabled

He sat in a wheeled chair, waiting for dark,
And shivered in his ghastly suit of grey,
Legless, sewn short at elbow. Through the park
Voices of boys rang saddening like a hymn,
Voices of play and pleasure after day,   5
Till gathering sleep had mothered them from him.

    . . .

About this time Town used to swing so gay
When glow-lamps budded in the light blue trees,
And girls glanced lovelier as the air grew dim,—
In the old times, before he threw away his knees.   10
Now he will never feel again how slim
Girls' waists are, or how warm their subtle hands.
All of them touch him like some queer disease.

    . . .

There was an artist silly for his face,
For it was younger than his youth, last year.   15
Now, he is old; his back will never brace;
He's lost his colour very far from here,
Poured it down shell-holes till the veins ran dry,
And half his lifetime lapsed in the hot race
And leap of purple spurted from his thigh.   20

    . . .

One time he liked a blood-smear down his leg,
After the matches, carried shoulder-high.
It was after football, when he'd drunk a peg,
He thought he'd better join.—He wonders why.
Someone had said he'd look a god in kilts,   25
That's why; and maybe, too, to please his Meg,
Aye, that was it, to please the giddy jilts
He asked to join. He didn't have to beg;
Smiling they wrote his lie: aged nineteen years.
Germans he scarcely though of; all their guilt,   30
And Austria's, did not move him. And no fears
Of Fear came yet. He thought of jewelled hilts
For daggers in plaid socks; of smart salutes;
And care of arms; and leave; and pay arrears;
Esprit de corps; and hints for young recruits.   35
And soon, he was drafted out with drums and cheers.

                    . . .

Some cheered him home, but not as crowds cheer Goal.
Only a solemn man who brought him fruits
Thanked him; and then enquired about his soul.

                    . . .

Now, he will spend a few sick years in institutes,   40
And do what things the rules consider wise,
And take whatever pity they may dole.
Tonight he noticed how the women's eyes
Passed from him to the strong men that were whole.
How cold and late it is! Why don't they come   45
And put him into bed? Why don't they come?

Journal Entry

Speculate on the physical and psychological effects of being wounded in war.

Textual Considerations

1. Review sections 3, 8, and 9 of "Prisons of Silence" and find examples from the poem to answer the following questions: What enables the victims to break through their silence? To what extent does their testimony make possible their transformation from victims to victors?
2. The narrator of "Prisons of Silence" frequently juxtaposes the discourses of silence and speech. Investigate the various relationships between silence and powerlessness and between speech and power in the poem.

3. Analyze the effects of Owen's juxtaposing images from the soldier's past and present life.
4. Characterize the tone of "Disabled." Is the speaker angry, bitter, resigned? How does tone reinforce theme?
5. How does society's attitude toward the soldier change after his injury? On what aspects of war and people's attitude toward war does the speaker comment?

Cultural Contexts

1. "Prisons of Silence" dramatizes the decision of the United States to relegate Americans of Japanese ancestry to prison camps after the Japanese attack on Pearl Harbor during World War II. Identify the images that most effectively chart the progression of their physical displacement and psychological alienation.
2. Examine the relationship between war and sex by analyzing the gender-related issues explored in lines 9–13, 25–28, and 43–44 of "Disabled." To what extent is the military uniform still considered a magnet of sexual attraction?

Whitman and Gildner

◆

Walt Whitman

The Dying Veteran

(A Long Island incident—early part of the nineteenth century)

Amid these days of order, ease, prosperity,
Amid the current songs of beauty, peace, decorum,
I cast a reminiscence—(likely 'twill offend you,
I heard it in my boyhood;)—More than a generation since,
A queer old savage man, a fighter under Washington himself,   5
(Large, brave, cleanly, hot-blooded, no talker, rather spiritualistic,
Had fought in the ranks—fought well—had been all through the
     Revolutionary war,)
Lay dying—sons, daughters, church-deacons, lovingly tending him,
Sharping their sense, their ears, towards his murmuring, half-caught words:
"Let me return again to my war-days,   10
To the sights and scenes—to forming the line of battle,
To the scouts ahead reconnoitering,
To the cannons, the grim artillery,
To the galloping aids, carrying orders,
To the wounded, the fallen, the heat, the suspense,   15
The perfume strong, the smoke, the deafening noise;
Away with your life of peace!—your joys of peace!
Give me my old wild battle-life again!"

Gary Gildner

First Practice

After the doctor checked to see
we weren't ruptured,
the man with the short cigar took us
under the grade school,
where we went in case of attack   5
or storm, and said
he was Clifford Hill, he was
a man who believed dogs
ate dogs, he had once killed
for his country, and if   10
there were any girls present
for them to leave now.
                  No one
left. OK, he said, he said I take
that to mean you are hungry   15
men who hate to lose as much
as I do. OK. Then
he made two lines of us
facing each other,
and across the way, he said,   20
is the man you hate most
in the world,
and if we are to win
that title I want to see how.
But I don't want to see   25
any marks when you're dressed,
he said. He said, *Now.*

Journal Entry

What significance do you see in the speakers in "The Dying Veteran" and "First Practice" being war veterans?

Textual Considerations

1. Discuss the comparisons that Whitman's speaker makes between war and peace. To what extent do you agree with his perspective on peace?

2. "First Practice" does not express directly the effects of the forces put in motion by "the man with the short cigar." These effects, however, are the real subject of the poem. What are they?
3. Gildner's poem bristles with tense drama. Characterize some of the dramatic effects, and analyze how the poet achieves them. Consider, for example, the meaning of the command "But I don't want to see / any marks when you're dressed."

Cultural Contexts

1. Discuss with your group the concept of masculinity expressed in each poem. What does each poem suggest about the relation between war and violence?
2. Characterize Gildner's attitude toward the incident in "First Practice" and speculate on what the poem implies about sports and violence.

Emerson and Tennyson

Ralph Waldo Emerson

Concord Hymn

Sung At the Completion of the Battle
Monument, July 4, 1837

By the rude bridge that arched the flood,
    Their flag to April's breeze unfurled,
Here once the embattled farmers stood
    And fired the shot heard round the world.

The foe long since in silence slept;   5
    Alike the conqueror silent sleeps;
And Time the ruined bridge has swept
    Down the dark stream which seaward creeps.

On this green bank, by this soft stream,
    We set to-day a votive stone;   10
That memory may their deed redeem,
    When, like our sires, our sons are gone.

Spirit, that made those heroes dare
    To die, and leave their children free,
Bid Time and Nature gently spare   15
    The shaft we raise to them and thee.

Alfred, Lord Tennyson

The Charge of the Light Brigade

I

Half a league, half a league,
Half a league onward,
All in the valley of Death
 Rode the six hundred.
"Forward, the Light Brigade!   5
Charge for the guns!" he said.
Into the valley of Death
 Rode the six hundred.

II

"Forward, the Light Brigade!"
Was there a man dismay'd?   10
Not tho' the soldier knew
 Some one had blunder'd.
Theirs not to make reply,
Theirs not to reason why,
Theirs but to do and die.   15
Into the valley of Death
 Rode the six hundred.

III

Cannon to right of them,
Cannon to left of them,
Cannon in front of them   20
 Volley'd and thunder'd;
Storm'd at with shot and shell,
Boldly they rode and well,
Into the jaws of Death,
Into the mouth of hell   25
 Rode the six hundred.

IV

Flash'd all their sabres bare,
Flash'd as they turn'd in air
Sabring the gunners there,
Charging an army, while   30
   All the world wonder'd.
Plunged in the battery-smoke
Right thro' the line they broke;
Cossack and Russian
Reel'd from the sabre-stroke   35
   Shatter'd and sunder'd.
Then they rode back, but not,
   Not the six hundred.

V

Cannon to right of them,
Cannon to left of them,   40
Cannon behind them
   Volley'd and thunder'd;
Storm'd at with shot and shell,
While horse and hero fell,
They that had fought so well   45
Came thro' the jaws of Death,
Back from the mouth of hell,
All that was left of them,
   Left of six hundred.

VI

When can their glory fade?   50
O the wild charge they made!
   All the world wonder'd.
Honour the charge they made!
Honour the Light Brigade,
   Noble six hundred!   55

◆

Journal Entry

Compare and contrast your view of patriotism with the views of Emerson and Tennyson.

Textual Considerations

1. How does Emerson's use of alliteration contribute to the unity of the poem? Characterize the poem's tone.

2. What is the poem's theme? What is the effect of waiting until the last stanza to introduce it?
3. Consider how Tennyson explores the effects of sound and rhythm to convey the emotional intensity of the charge of the light brigade. Focus specifically on the patterns of rhythm and the phonic symbolism of the galloping of the horses in stanzas 1 and 3.
4. Discuss with your group whether "The Charge of the Light Brigade" may be considered an expression of chivalric patriotism or a piece of social criticism meant to encourage the British to adopt a more critical attitude toward the Crimean War (1854–1856).

Cultural Contexts

1. In "Concord Hymn," Emerson suggests that war memorials can serve as reminders to future generations of the heroic deeds of the past. Can your group reach a consensus about the need to build memorials?

Dorfman and Forché ◆

Ariel Dorfman

Hope

My son has been
missing
since May 8
of last year.

They took him   5
just for a few hours
they said
just for some routine
questioning.

After the car left,   10
the car with no license plate,
we couldn't

find out

anything else
about him.   15

But now things have changed.
We heard from a compañero
who just got out
that five months later
they were torturing him   20
in Villa Grimaldi,
at the end of September
they were questioning him
in the red house
that belonged to the Grimaldis.   25

    They say they recognized
    his voice his screams
    they say.

Somebody tell me frankly
what times are these   30
what kind of world
what country?
What I'm asking is
how can it be
that a father's   35
joy
a mother's
joy
is knowing
that they   40
that they are still
torturing
their son?
Which means
that he was alive   45
five months later
and our greatest
hope
will be to find out
next year   50
that they're still torturing him
eight months later

and he may   might   could
still be alive.

Carolyn Forché

The Visitor

In Spanish he whispers there is no time left.
It is the sound of scythes arcing in wheat,
the ache of some field song in Salvador.
The wind along the prison, cautious
as Francisco's hands on the inside, touching   5
the walls as he walks, it is his wife's breath
slipping into his cell each night while he
imagines his hand to be hers. It is a small country.

There is nothing one man will not do to another.

Journal Entry

Discuss "Hope" and "The Visitor" as voices of dissent. To what extent are they also calls for action? Explain.

Textual Considerations

1. In "The Visitor," Forché juxtaposes images of peace and human intimacy with an image of impending violence in the last line of the poem. Comment on the poetic and thematic effects of this technique.
2. Explore the implications of the speakers' voices in "Hope" and "The Visitor," and discuss the effects of their engaging in internal dialogue. Point out examples to illustrate how they narrate, question, or address an audience in order to reach their own inner consciousness.
3. Speculate on the several levels of meaning in Dorfman's title.

Cultural Contexts

1. Share with your group your ideas about violence and suffering. Begin with your response to the speaker's statement in "The Visitor" that "there is nothing one man will not do to another." Make a list of the strategies you would develop to cope with political and urban violence.

2. With the help of your group, generate ideas about the different ways we can read "Hope" and "The Visitor." Consider what these poems articulate about the relationship between parents and children, the conflict between authorities and individuals, the suspension of civil rights, and humankind's capacity to inflict cruelty.

Espada and Smallberg

Martín Espada

Cross Plains, Wisconsin

Blue bandanna
across the forehead,
beard bristling
like a straw broom,
sleeveless T-shirt   5
of the Puerto Rican flag
with Puerto Rico stamped
across the chest,
a foreign name on the license,
evidence enough   10
for the cop to announce
that the choice is cash or jail,
that today
the fine for speeding
is exactly   15
sixty-seven dollars,
and his car
will follow my car
out of town

Mavis Smallberg

Quote from the Bureau of Information, from the Argus, August 27, 1986: "The Situation in Soweto Is Not Abnormal"

Everything's normal in Soweto today.
We reasonably killed eleven.
They were making a fuss in the street
You know us,
We don't stand any fuss   5
Not us
So we typically killed eleven
And wounded an average sixty-two
And you?

Went on a regular patrol to a school.   10
Some children were breaking a rule.
They burned their identity cards.
White kids don't carry 'em
Don't need to, you know
Black kids don't carry 'em   15
Don't want to, you know
The whole thing was just about to erupt,
When we routinely went to beat them up.
Cornered a few of 'em and rained down the blows
Split one's head. She's dead,   20
But nobody knows.
Naturally the children ran all around
So we just shot down those that we found.
Bullets, birdshot, buckshot,
What the hell? It's all run-of-the-mill!   25
Saw this "comrade" walking alone,
Shot him down before he got home.
Ja, he died.
You should've seen the ones that we fried.

What a fire! What a blaze!   30
Children crying, people dying.
One woman got shot in the hip
That really shut up her lip!
Now she can't walk. Mmm, there was some talk.
Ja, the situation in Soweto is not   35
Abnormal today.

What's abnormal, anyway?
What's monstrous, deviant, abhorrent,
weird about gassing a baby
Shooting a child, raping a mother   40
or crippling a father?
What's odd about killing the people we fear?
No, the situation in Soweto
is quite normal today.

Journal Entry

Evaluate the role of the authorities in each poem. To what extent does authority usually assume these roles?

Textual Considerations

1. Analyze the effects of Espada's withholding the use of the personal pronoun until the end of his poem. What factors contributed to the fine imposed by the policeman?
2. Comment on the tone of Smallberg's poem, and discuss the effects of having the authorities state directly their accounts of the day's activities.
3. Review the last segment of Smallberg's poem, and discuss how change in point of view affects meaning and tone.

Cultural Contexts

1. Discuss with your group the extent to which racism is a major cause of violence not only in each poem but in contemporary society as well. What other causes of violence can you cite?
2. Police brutality is often cited as a cause of urban alienation and violence. What ideas does your group have for promoting better understanding between the police and young people in your community? How could Espada's poem be used in this context?

Rukeyser and Whitman

Muriel Rukeyser

Waking This Morning

Waking this morning,
a violent woman in the violent day
Laughing.

           Past the line of memory
along the long body of your life   5
in which move childhood, youth, your lifetime of touch,
eyes, lips, chest, belly, sex, legs, to the waves of the sheet.
I look past the little plant
on the city windowsill
to the tall towers bookshaped, crushed together in greed,   10
the river flashing flowing corroded,
the intricate harbor and the sea, the wars, the moon, the planets, all who
          people space
in the sun visible invisible.
African violets in the light
breathing, in a breathing universe.   I want strong peace, and delight,   15
the wild good.
I want to make my touch poems:
to find my morning, to find you entire
alive moving among the anti-touch people.

           I say across the waves of the air to you: 20
today once more
I will try to be non-violent
one more day
this morning, waking the world away
in the violent day.   25

Walt Whitman

The Artilleryman's Vision *

While my wife at my side lies slumbering, and the wars are over long,
And my head on the pillow rests at home, and the vacant midnight passes,
And through the stillness, through the dark, I hear, just hear, the breath of my
    infant,
There in the room as I wake from sleep this vision presses upon me;
The engagement opens there and then in fantasy unreal,   5
The skirmishers begin, they crawl cautiously ahead, I hear the irregular snap!
    snap!
I hear the sounds of the different missiles, the short *t-h-t! t-h-t!* of the rifle-balls,
I see the shells exploding leaving small white clouds, I hear the great shells
    shrieking as they pass,
The grape like the hum and whirr of wind through the trees, (tumultuous now
    the contest rages,)
All the scenes at the batteries rise in detail before me again,   10
The crashing and smoking, the pride of the men in their pieces,
The chief-gunner ranges and sights his piece and selects a fuse of the right time,
After firing I see him lean aside and look eagerly off to note the effect;
Elsewhere I hear the cry of a regiment charging, (the young colonel leads
    himself this time with brandish'd sword,)
I see the gaps cut by the enemy's volleys, (quickly fill'd up, no delay,)   15
I breathe the suffocating smoke, then the flat clouds hover low concealing all;
Now a strange lull for a few seconds, not a shot fired on either side,
Then resumed the chaos louder than ever, with eager calls and orders of officers,
While from some distant part of the field the wind wafts to my ears a shout of
    applause, (some special success,)
And ever the sound of the cannon far or near, (rousing even in dreams a
    devilish exultation and all the old mad joy in the depths of my soul,)   20
And ever the hastening of infantry shifting positions, batteries, cavalry, moving
    hither and thither,
(The falling, dying, I heed not, the wounded dripping and red I heed not,
    some to the rear are hobbling,)
(Grime, heat, rush, aide-de-camps galloping by or on a full run,
With the patter of small arms, the warning *s-s-t* of the rifles, (these in my vision
    I hear or see,)
And bombs bursting in air, and at night the vari-color'd rockets.   25

---

*First published as "The Veteran's Vision" in the 1865 edition of *Leaves of Grass* and with this title
in the 1871 edition.

Journal Entry

To what extent are "Waking This Morning" and "The Artilleryman's Vision" critical of war?

Textual Considerations

1. Discuss the effects on meaning of the speaker's juxtaposing images of past and present, violence and antiviolence, touch and antitouch in "Waking This Morning."
2. Evaluate Whitman's use of visual imagery. To what other senses does the poem appeal?
3. Explain the effects of the contrasting images of war and peace in Whitman's poem.

Cultural Contexts

1. Discuss with your group your responses to the veteran's "vision." To what extent has he "survived" the war?

Aristophanes

Lysistrata

CHARACTERS

LYSISTRATA
KALONIKE
MYRRHINE
LAMPITO
Chorus
Magistrate
KINESIAS
Spartan Herald
Spartan Ambassador
A Sentry
Athenian Drunkard

SCENE: *Athens. First, a public square; later, beneath the walls of the Akropolis; later, a courtyard within the Akropolis. Time: early in*
411 B.C.

Until the éxodos, *the* CHORUS *is divided into two hemichori: the first, of Old Men; the second, of Old Women. Each of these has its* CHORAGOS. *In the* éxodos, *the hemichori return as Athenians and Spartans.*

The supernumeraries include the BABY SON *of* KINESIAS; STRATYLLIS, *a member of the hemichorus of Old Women; various individual speakers, both Spartan and Athenian.*

PROLOGUE

Athens; a public square; early morning; LYSISTRATA *sola*

LYSISTRATA. If someone had invited them to a festival—
   Bacchos's, say, or Pan's, or Aphroditê's, or
   that Genetyllis business—, you couldn't get through the streets,
   what with the drums and the dancing. But now,
   not a woman in sight!
                    Except—oh, yes!

Enter KALONIKE

Here's one, at last. Good
morning, Kalonikê.

KALONIKE.   Good morning, Lysistrata.

             Darling,
don't frown so! You'll ruin your face!

LYSISTRATA.   Never mind my face.
Kalonikê,
the way we women behave! Really, I don't blame the men
for what they say about us.

KALONIKE.   No; I imagine they're right.

LYSISTRATA. For example: I call a meeting
to think out a most important matter—and what happens?
The women all stay in bed!

KALONIKE.   Oh, they'll be along.
It's hard to get away, you know: a husband, a cook,
a child . . . Home life can be *so* demanding!

LYSISTRATA. What I have in mind is even more demanding.

KALONIKE. Tell me: what is it?

LYSISTRATA.   Something big.

KALONIKE.   Goodness! *How* big?

LYSISTRATA. Big enough for all of us.

KALONIKE.   But we're not all here!

LYSISTRATA. We would be, if *that's* what was up!

           No Kalonikê,
this is something I've been turning over for nights;
and, I may say, sleepless nights.

KALONIKE.   Can't be so hard, then,
if you've spent so much time on it.

LYSISTRATA.   Hard or not,
it comes to this: Only we women can save Greece!

KALONIKE. Only we women? Poor Greece!

LYSISTRATA.   Just the same,
it's up to us. First, we must liquidate
the Peloponnesians—

KALONIKE.   Fun, fun!

LYSISTRATA.   —and then the Boiotians.

KALONIKE. Oh! But not those heavenly eels!

LYSISTRATA.   You needn't worry.
Athens shall have her sea food. —But here's the point:
If we can get the women from those places
to join us women here, why, we can save
all Greece!

KALONIKE. But dearest Lysistrata!
    How can women do a thing so austere, so
    political? We belong at home. Our only armor's
    our transparent saffron dresses and
    our pretty little shoes!
LYSISTRATA.   That's it exactly.
    Those transparent saffron dresses, those little shoes—
    well, there we are!
KALONIKE.   Oh?
LYSISTRATA.   Not a single man would lift
    his spear—
KALONIKE. I'll get my dress from the dyer's tomorrow!
LYSISTRATA. —or need a shield—
KALONIKE.   The sweetest little negligée—
LYSISTRATA. —or bring out his sword.
KALONIKE.   I know where I can buy
    the dreamiest sandals!
LYSISTRATA. Well, so you see. Now, shouldn't
    the women have come?
KALONIKE.   Come? They should have *flown!*
LYSISTRATA. Athenians are always late.
                            But imagine!
    There's no one here from the South Shore.
KALONIKE.   They go to work early,
    I can swear to that.
LYSISTRATA.   And nobody from Acharnai.
    They should have been here hours ago!
KALONIKE.   Well, you'll get
    that awful Theagenês woman: she's been having
    her fortune told at Hekatês shrine.
                        But look!
    Someone at last! Can you see who they are?

Enter MYRRHINE *and other women*

LYSISTRATA. People from the suburbs.
KALONIKE.   Yes! The entire
    membership of the Suburban League!
MYRRHINE. Sorry to be late, Lysistrata.
                        Oh come,
    don't scowl so! Say something!
LYSISTRATA. My dear Myrrhinê,
    what is there to say? After all,
    you've been pretty casual about the whole thing.

MYRRHINE. Couldn't find
my girdle in the dark, that's all.
But what *is*
'the whole thing'?
LYSISTRATA. Wait for the rest of them.
KALONIKE. I suppose so. But, look!
Here's Lampitô!

Enter LAMPITO *with other women
from Sparta*

LYSISTRATA. Darling Lampitô
how pretty you are today! What a nice color!
Goodness, you look as though you could strangle a bull!
LAMPITO. Ah think Ah could! It's the work-out
in the gym every day; and, of co'se that dance of ahs
where y' kick yo' own tail.
LYSISTRATA. What lovely breasts!
LAMPITO. Lawdy, when y'touch me lahk that,
Ah feel lahk a heifer at the altar!
LYSISTRATA. And this young lady?
Where is she from?
LAMPITO. Boiotia. Social-Register type.
LYSISTRATA. Good morning, Boiotian. You're as pretty as green grass.
KALONIKE. And if you look,
you'll find that the lawn has just been cut.
LYSISTRATA. And this lady?
LAMPITO. From Korinth. But a good woman.
LYSISTRATA. Well, in Korinth
anything's possible.
LAMPITO. But let's get to work. Which one of you
called this meeting, and why?
LYSISTRATA. *I* did.
LAMPITO. Well, then:
what's up?
MYRRHINE. Yes, what *is* 'the whole thing,' after all?
LYSISTRATA. I'll tell you. —But first, one question.
MYRRHINE. Ask away!
LYSISTRATA. It's your husbands. Fathers of your children. Doesn't it bother you
that they're always off with the Army? I'll stake my life,
not one of you has a man in the house this minute!
KALONIKE. Mine's been in Thrace the last five months, keeping an eye on that
General.
MYRRHINE. Mine's been in Pylos for seven.

LAMPITO.   And mahn,
   whenever he gets a *dis*charge, he goes raht back
   with that li'l ole speah of his, and enlists again!
LYSISTRATA. And not the ghost of a lover to be found!
   From the very day the war began—
                      those Milesians!
   I could skin them alive!
               —I've not seen so much, even,
   as one of those devices they call Widow's Delight.
   But there! What's important is: If I've found a way
   to end the war, are you with me?
MYRRHINE.   I should *say* so!
   Even if I have to pawn my best dress and
   drink up the proceeds.
KALONIKE.   Me, too! Even if they split me
   right up the middle, like a flounder.
LAMPITO.   Ah'm shorely with you.
   Ah'd crawl up Taygetos on mah knees
   if that'd bring peace.
LYSISTRATA. Then here it is.
   Women! Sisters!
   If we really want our men to make an armistice,
   we must be ready to give up—
MYRRHINE.   Give up what?
   Quick, tell us!
LYSISTRATA.   But *will* you?
MYRRHINE.   We will, even if it kills us.
LYSISTRATA. Then we must give up sleeping with our men. (*Long silence*)
   Oh? So now you're sorry? Won't look at me?
   Doubtful? Pale? All teary-eyed?
               But come: be frank with me,
   as I've certainly been with you. Will you do it?
MYRRHINE.   I couldn't. No.
   Let the war go on.
KALONIKE.   Nor I. Let the war go on.
LYSISTRATA. You, you little flounder,
   ready to be split up the middle?
KALONIKE.   Lysistrata, no!
   I'd walk through fire for you—you *know* I would!—but don't
   ask us to give up *that!* Why, there's nothing like it!
LYSISTRATA. And you?
BOIOTIAN.   No. I must say *I'd* rather walk through fire.
LYSISTRATA. You little salamanders!

No wonder poets write tragedies about women.
All we want's a quick tumble!
                             But you from Sparta:
if you stand by me, we may win yet! Will you?
It means to much!
LAMPITO.   Ah sweah, it means *too* much!
By the Two Goddesses, it does! Asking a girl
to sleep—Heaven knows how long!—in a great big bed
with nobody there but herself! But Ah'll stay with you!
Peace comes first!
LYSISTRATA.   Spoken like a true Spartan!
KALONIKE. But if—
                oh dear!
                      —if we give up what you tell us to,
will there *be* any peace?
LYSISTRATA.   Why, mercy, of course there will!
We'll just sit snug in our very thinnest gowns,
perfumed and powdered from top to bottom, and those men
simply won't stand still! And when we say No,
they'll go out of their minds! And there's your peace.
You can take my word for it.
LAMPITO.   Ah seem to remember
that Colonel Menelaos threw his sword away
when he saw Helen's breast all bare.
KALONIKE.   But, goodness me!
What if they just get up and leave us?
LYSISTRATA.   Well,
we'd have to fall back on ourselves, of course.
But they won't.
KALONIKE. What if they drag us into the bedroom?
LYSISTRATA.   Hang on to the door.
KALONIKE. What if they slap us?
LYSISTRATA.   If they do, you'd better give in.
But be sulky about it. Do I have to teach you how?
You know there's no fun for men when they have to force you.
There are millions of ways of getting them to see reason.
Don't you worry: a man
doesn't like it unless the girl cooperates.
KALONIKE. I suppose so. Oh, all right! We'll go along!
LAMPITO. Ah imagine us Spahtans can arrange a peace. But you
Athenians! Why, you're just war-mongerers!
LYSISTRATA.   Leave that to me.
I know how to make them listen.

LAMPITO.   Ah don't see how.
   After all, they've got their boats; and there's lots of money
   piled up in the Akropolis.
LYSISTRATA.   The Akropolis? Darling,
   we're taking over the Akropolis today!
   That's the older women's job. All the rest of us
   are going to the Citadel to sacrifice—you understand me?
   And once there, we're in for good!
LAMPITO.   Whee! Up the rebels!
   Ah can see you're a good strat*ee*gist.
LYSISTRATA.   Well, then, Lampitô,
   let's take the oath.
LAMPITO.   Say it. We'll sweah.
LYSISTRATA.   This is it.
   —But Lord! Where's our Inner Guard? Never mind. —You see this
   shield? Put it down there. Now bring me the victim's entrails.
KALONIKE. But the oath?
LYSISTRATA.   You remember how in Aischylos' *Seven*
   they killed a sheep and swore on a shield? Well, then?
KALONIKE. But I don't see how you can swear for peace on a shield.
LYSISTRATA. What else do you suggest?
KALONIKE.   Why not a white horse?
   We could swear by that.
LYSISTRATA. And where will you get a white horse?
KALONIKE. I never thought of that. *What* can we do?
MYRRHINE.   I have it!
   Let's set this big black wine-bowl on the ground
   and pour in a gallon or so of Thasian, and swear
   not to add one drop of water.
LAMPITO.   Ah lahk *that* oath!
LYSISTRATA. Bring the bowl and the wine-jug.
KALONIKE.   Oh, what a simply *huge* one!
LYSISTRATA. Set it down; and, women, place your hands on the gift-offering.
   O Goddess of Persuasion! And thou, O Loving-cup!
   Look upon this our sacrifice, and
   be gracious!
KALONIKE. It spills out like blood. How red and pretty it is!
LAMPITO. And Ah must say it smells good.
MYRRHINE.   Let me swear first.
KALONIKE. No, by Aphroditê, let's toss for it!
LYSISTRATA. Lampitô: all of you women: come, touch the bowl,
   and repeat after me:
   I WILL HAVE NOTHING TO DO WITH MY HUSBAND OR MY
      LOVER

KALONIKE. *I will have nothing to do with my husband or my lover*
LYSISTRATA. THOUGH HE COME TO ME IN PITIABLE CONDITION
KALONIKE. *Though he come to me in pitiable condition*
(Oh Lysistrata! This is killing me!)
LYSISTRATA. I WILL STAY IN MY HOUSE UNTOUCHABLE
KALONIKE. *I will stay in my house untouchable*
LYSISTRATA. IN MY THINNEST SAFFRON SILK
KALONIKE. *In my thinnest saffron silk*
LYSISTRATA. AND MAKE HIM LONG FOR ME.
KALONIKE. *And make him long for me.*
LYSISTRATA. I WILL NOT GIVE MYSELF
KALONIKE. *I will not give myself*
LYSISTRATA. AND IF HE CONSTRAINS ME
KALONIKE. *And if he constrains me*
LYSISTRATA. I WILL BE AS COLD AS ICE AND NEVER MOVE
KALONIKE. *I will be as cold as ice and never move*
LYSISTRATA. I WILL NOT LIFT MY SLIPPERS TOWARD THE CEILING
KALONIKE. *I will not lift my slippers toward the ceiling*
LYSISTRATA. OR CROUCH ON ALL FOURS LIKE THE LIONESS IN THE
CARVING
KALONIKE. *Or crouch on all fours like the lioness in the carving*
LYSISTRATA. AND IF I KEEP THIS OATH LET ME DRINK FROM THIS
BOWL
KALONIKE. *And if I keep this oath let me drink from this bowl*
LYSISTRATA. IF NOT, LET MY OWN BOWL BE FILLED WITH WATER.
KALONIKE. *If not, let my own bowl be filled with water.*
LYSISTRATA. You have all sworn?
MYRRHINE. We have.
LYSISTRATA. Then thus
I sacrifice the victim. (*Drinks largely*)
KALONIKE. Save some for us!
Here's to you, darling, and to you, and to you! It's all
for us women. (*Loud cries off-stage*)
LAMPITO. What's all *that* whoozy-goozy?
LYSISTRATA. Just what I told you.
The older women have taken the Akropolis. Now you, Lampitô,
rush back to Sparta. We'll take care of things here. And
be sure you get organized!
The rest of you girls,
up to the Citadel: and mind you push in the bolts.
KALONIKE. But the men? Won't they be after us?
LYSISTRATA. Just you leave
the men to me. There's not fire enough in the world
to make me open *my* door.

KALONIKE.   I hope so, by Aphroditê!
  At any rate,
  let's remember the League's reputation for hanging on! (*Exeunt*)

PÁRADOS: CHORAL EPISODE

The hillside just under the Akropolis. Enter CHORUS OF OLD MEN *with burning
torches and braziers; much puffing and coughing*

CHORAGOS^m. Easy, Drakês, old friend! Don't skin your shoulders
  with those damnable big olive-branches. What a job!
CHORUS^m. Forward, forward, comrades! Whew!   [STROPHE 1
  The things that old age does to you!
  Neighbor Strymodoros, would you have thought it?
  We've caught it—
             And from women, too!
  Women that used to board with us, bed with us—
  Now, by the gods, they've got ahead of us,
  Taken the Akropolis (Heaven knows why!),
  Profanèd the sacred statuar-y,
         And barred the doors,
         The aggravating whores!
CHORAGOS^m. Come, Philourgos, quick, pile your brushwood
  next to the wall there.
            These traitors to Athens and to us,
  we'll fry each last one of them! And the very first
  will be old Lykôn's wife.
CHORUS^m. By Deméter I swear it—(ouch!),   [ANTISTROPHE 1
  I'll not perform the Kleomenês-crouch!
  How he looked—and a good soldier, too—
  When out he flew,
         that filthy pouch
  Of a body of his all stinking and shaggy,
  Bare as an eel, except for the bag he
  Covered his rear with. Lord, what a mess!
  Never a bath in six years, I'd guess!
         Unhappy Sparta,
         With such a martyr!
CHORAGOS^m. What a siege, friends! Seventeen ranks strong
  we stood at the Gate, and never a chance for a nap.
  And all because of women, whom the gods hate
  (and so does Euripidês).
         It's enough to make a veteran
  turn in his medals from Marathon!

CHORUS^m.   Forward, men! Just up the hillside,   [STROPHE 2
  And we're there!
  Keep to the path! A yoke of oxen
  Wouldn't care
   To haul this lumber. Mind the fire,
   Or it'll die before we're higher!
    Puff! Puff!
   This smoke will strangle me; sure enough!

  Holy Heraklés, I'm blinded,   [ANTISTROPHE 2
  Sure as fate!
  It's Lemnos-fire we've been toting;
   And isn't it great
   To be singed by this infernal flame?
   (Lachês, remember the Goddess: for shame!)
    Woof! Woof!
   A few steps more, and we're under the roof!

CHORAGOS^m.   It catches! It's blazing!
Down with your loads!
We'll sizzle 'em now,
By all the gods!
Vine-branches here, quick!
Light 'em up,
And in through the gate with 'em!
If that doesn't stop
Their nonsense—well,
We'll smoke 'em to Hell.
Ker*shoo!*
(What we really need
Is a grad-u-ate,
Top of his class,
From Samos Military State.
A*choo!*)
Come, do
Your duty, you!
Pour out your braziers,
Embers ablaze!
But first, Gentlemen, allow me to raise
The paian:
   Lady
Victory, now
Assist thine adherents
Here below!
Down with women!

Up with men!
Iô triumphe!
CHORUS^m. Amen!

Enter CHORUS OF OLD WOMEN *on the walls of the Akropolis, carrying jars of water to*
extinguish the fire set by the CHORUS OF OLD MEN

CHORAGOS^W. Fire, fire!
  Quickly, quickly, women, if we're to save ourselves!
CHORUS^W. Nikodikê, run!   [STROPHE
      Or Kalykês done
      To a turn, and poor Kratylla's
      Smoked like a ham.
                    Damn
  These man and their wars,
  Their hateful ways!
  I nearly died before I got to the place
  Where we fill our jars:
      Slaves pushing and jostling—
      Such a hustling
  I never saw in all my days!

  But here's water as last.   [ANTISTROPHE
  Sisters, make haste
  And slosh it down on them,
  The silly old wrecks!
                  Sex
  Almighty! What they want's
  A hot bath? Send it down!
  And thou, Athenê of Athens town,
  Assist us in drowning their wheezy taunts!
      O Trito-born! Helmet of Gold!
      Help us to cripple their backs, the old
  Foods with their semi-incendiary brawn!

          The OLD MEN *capture a woman,* STRATYLLIS

STRATYLLIS. Let me go! Let me go!
CHORAGOS^W.   You walking corpses,
  have you no shame?
CHORAGOS^m.   I wouldn't have believed it!
  An army of women in the Akropolis!
CHORAGOS^W. So we scare you, do we? Grandpa, you've seen
  only our pickets yet!

CHORAGOS^m.   Hey Phaidrias!
  Help me with the necks of these jabbering hens!

CHORAGOS^w. Down with your pots, girls! We'll need both hands
  if those antiques attack us.

CHORAGOS^m.   Want your face kicked in?

CHORAGOS^w. Want to try my teeth?

CHORAGOS^m.   Look out! I've got a stick!

CHORAGOS^w. You lay a half-inch of your stick on Strayllis,
  and you'll never stick again!

CHORAGOS^m. Fall apart!

CHORAGOS^w. I'll chew your guts!

CHORAGOS^m.   Euripedês! Master!
  How well you knew women!

CHORAGOS^w.   Listen to him! Rhodippê.
  up with the pots!

CHORAGOS^m. Demolition of God,
  what good are your pots?

CHORAGOS^w.   You refugee from the tomb,
  what good is your fire?

CHORAGOS^m.   Good enough to make a pyre
  to barbecue you!

CHORAGOS^w.   We'll squizzle your kindling!

CHORAGOS^m. You think so?

CHORAGOS^w.   Yah! Just hang around a while!

CHORAGOS^m. Want a touch of my torch?

CHORAGOS^w.   Your torch needs a bath.

CHORAGOS^m. How about you?

CHORAGOS^w.   Soap for a senile bridegroom!

CHORAGOS^m. Senile? Hold your trap!

CHORAGOS^w.   Just *you* try to hold it!

CHORAGOS^m. The yammer of women!

CHORAGOS^w.   The yatter of men!
  But you'll never sit in the jury-box again.

CHORAGOS^m. Gentlemen, I beg you, burn off that woman's hair!

CHORAGOS^w. Let it come down! (*They empty their pots on the men*)

CHORAGOS^m. What a way to drown!

CHORAGOS^w. Hot, hey?

CHORAGOS^m.   Say,
  enough!

CHORAGOS^w. Dandruff
  needs watering. I'll make you
  nice and fresh.

CHORAGOS^m.   For God's sake, you
  sluts, hold off!

SCENE 1.

Enter a MAGISTRATE *accompanied by four constables*

MAGISTRATE. These degenerate women! What a racket of little drums,
   what a yapping for Adonis on every house-top!
   It's like the time in the Assembly when I was listening
   to a speech—out of order, as usual—by that fool
   Demostratos, all about troops for Sicily,
   that kind of nonsense—
                              and there was his wife
   trotting around in circles howling
   Alas for Adonis!—
                         and Demostratos insisting
   we must draft every last Zakynthian that can walk—
   and his wife up there on the roof,
   drunk as an owl, yowling
   Oh weep for Adonis!—
                            and that damned ox Demostratos
   mooing away through the rumpus. That's what we get
   for putting up with this wretched woman-business!
CHORAGOS^m. Sir, you haven't heard the half of it. They laughed at us!
   Insulted us! They took pitchers of water
   and nearly drowned us! We're still wringing out our clothes,
   for all the world like unhousebroken brats.
MAGISTRATE. And a good thing, by Poseidon!
   Whose fault is it if these women-folk of ours
   get out of hand? We coddle them,
   we teach them to be wasteful and loose. You'll see a husband
   go into a jeweler's. 'Look,' he'll say,
   'jeweler,' he'll say, 'you remember that gold choker
   'you made for my wife? Well, she went to a dance last night
   'and broke the clasp. Now, I've got to go to Salamis,
   'and can't be bothered. Run over to my house tonight,
   'will you, and see if you can put it together for her.'
   Or another one
   goes to a cobbler—a good strong workman, too,
   with an awl that was never meant for child's play. 'Here,'
   he'll tell him, 'one of my wife's shoes is pinching
   'her little toe. Could you come up about noon
   'and stretch it out for her?'
                                  Well, what do you expect?
   Look at me, for example. I'm a Public Officer,
   and it's one of my duties to pay off the sailors.
   And where's the money? Up there in the Akropolis!

And those blasted women slam the door in my face!
But what are we waiting for?
                                        —Look here, constable,
stop sniffing around for a tavern, and get us
some crowbars. We'll force their gates! As a matter of fact,
I'll do a little forcing myself.

> *Enter* LYSISTRATA, *above, with* MYRRHINE, KALONIKE, *and
> the* BOIOTIAN

LYSISTRATA.   No need of forcing.
   Here I am, of my own accord. And all this talk
   about locked doors—! We don't need locked doors,
   but just the least bit of common sense.
MAGISTRATE. Is that so, ma'am!
                                 —Where's my constable?
                                                —Constable,
   arrest that woman, and tie her hands behind her.
LYSISTRATA. If he touches me, I swear by Artemis
   there'll be one scamp dropped from the public pay-roll tomorrow!
MAGISTRATE. Well, constable? You're not afraid, I suppose? Grab her,
   two of you, around the middle!
KALONIKE.   No, by Pándrosos!
   Lay a hand on her, and I'll jump on you so hard
   your guts will come out the back door!
MAGISTRATE.   That's what *you* think!
   Where's the sergeant?—Here, you: tie up that trollop first,
   the one with the pretty talk!
MYRRHINE.   By the Moon-Goddess!
   Just you try it, and you'd better call a surgeon!
MAGISTRATE. Another one!
                  Officer, seize that woman!
                                              I swear
   I'll put an end to this riot!
BOIOTIAN.   By the Taurian,
   one inch closer and you won't have a hair on your head!
MAGISTRATE. Lord, what a mess! And my constables seem to have left me.
   But—women get the best of us? By God, no!
                                        —Skythians!
   Close ranks and forward march!
LYSISTRATA.   'Forward,' indeed!
   By the Two Goddesses, what's the sense in *that*?
   They're up against four companies of women
   armed from top to bottom.
MAGISTRATE.   Forward, my Skythians!

LYSISTRATA. Forward, yourselves, dear comrades!
  You grainlettucebeanseedmarket girls!
  You garlicandonionbreadbakery girls!
  Give it to 'em! Knock 'em down! Scratch 'em!
  Tell 'em what you think of 'em! (*General mêlée; the Skythians yield*)
                    —Ah, that's enough!
  Sound a retreat: good soldiers don't rob the dead!
MAGISTRATE. A nice day *this* has been for the police!
LYSISTRATA. Well, there you are.—Did you really think we women
  would be driven like slaves? Maybe now you'll admit
  that a women knows something about glory.
MAGISTRATE.   Glory enough,
  especially glory in bottles! Dear Lord Apollo!
CHORAGOS^m. Your Honor, there's no use talking to them. Words
  mean nothing whatever to wild animals like these.
  Think of the sousing they gave us! and the water
  was not, I believe, of the purest.
CHORAGOS^w. You shouldn't have come after us. And if you try it again,
  you'll be one eye short!—Although, as a matter of fact,
  what I like best is just to stay at home and read,
  like a sweet little bride: never hurting a soul, no,
  never going out. But if you *must* shake hornets' nests,
  look out for the hornets!
CHORUS^m. Good God, what can we do?   [STROPHE
          What are we coming to?
  These women! Who could bear it? But, for that matter, who
          Will find
          What they had in mind,
          When they seized Kranaos' city
          And held it (more's the pity!)
  Against us men of Athens, and our police force, too?
CHORAGOS^m. We might question them, I suppose. But I warn you, sir,
  don't believe anything you hear! It would be un-Athenian
  not to get to the bottom of this plot.
MAGISTRATE.   Very well.
  My first question is this: Why, so help you God,
  did you bar the gates of the Akropolis?
LYSISTRATA.   Why?
  To keep the money, of course. No money, no war.
MAGISTRATE. You think that money's the cause of war?
LYSISTRATA.   I do.
  Money brought about that Peisandros business
  and all the other attacks on the State. Well and good!
  They'll not get another cent here!

MAGISTRATE. And what will you do?

LYSISTRATA. What a question! From now on, we intend
to control the Treasury.

MAGISTRATE. Control the Treasury!

LYSISTRATA. Why not? Does that seem strange? After all,
we control our household budgets.

MAGISTRATE. But that's different!

LYSISTRATA. 'Different'? What do you mean?

MAGISTRATE. I mean simply this:
it's the Treasury that pays for National Defense.

LYSISTRATA. Unnecessary. We propose to abolish war!

MAGISTRATE. Good God.—And National Security?

LYSISTRATA. Leave that to us.

MAGISTRATE. You?

LYSISTRATA. Us.

MAGISTRATE. We're done for, then!

LYSISTRATA. Never mind.
We women will save you in spite of yourselves.

MAGISTRATE. What nonsense!

LYSISTRATA. If you like. But you must accept it, like it or not.

MAGISTRATE. Why, this is downright subversion!

LYSISTRATA. Maybe it is.
But we're going to save you, Judge.

MAGISTRATE. I don't *want* to be saved!

LYSISTRATA. Tut. The death-wish. All the more reason.

MAGISTRATE. But the idea
of women bothering themselves about peace and war!

LYSISTRATA. Will you listen to me?

MAGISTRATE. Yes. But be brief, or I'll—

LYSISTRATA. This is no time for stupid threats.

MAGISTRATE. By the gods,
I'm losing my mind!

AN OLD WOMAN. That's nice. If you do, remember
you've less to lose than *we* have.

MAGISTRATE. Quiet, you old buzzard!
Now, Lysistrata: tell me what you're thinking.

LYSISTRATA. Glad to.
Ever since this war began
we women have been watching you men, agreeing with you,
keeping our thoughts to ourselves. That doesn't mean
we were happy: we weren't, for we saw how things were going;
but we'd listen to you at dinner
arguing this way and that.
—Oh you, and your big

Top Secrets!—
                    And then we'd grin like little patriots
(though goodness knows we didn't feel like grinning) and ask you:
'Dear, did the Armistice come up in Assembly today?'
And you'd say, 'None of your business! Pipe down!', you'd say.
And so we would.
AN OLD WOMAN.   *I* wouldn't have, by God!
MAGISTRATE.   You'd have taken a beating, then!
                                        —Please go on.
LYSISTRATA.   Well, we'd be quiet. But then, you know, all at once
you men would think up something worse than ever.
Even *I* could see it was fatal. And, 'Darling,' I'd say,
'have you gone completely mad?' And my husband would look at me
and say, 'Wife, you've got your weaving to attend to.
'Mind your tongue, if you don't want a slap. "War's
'"a man's affair!"'

MAGISTRATE.   Good words, and well pronounced!
LYSISTRATA.   You're a fool if you think so.
                                   It was hard enough
to put up with all this banquet-hall strategy.
But then we'd hear you out in the public square:
'Nobody left for the draft-quota here in Athens?'
you'd say; and, 'No,' someone else would say, 'not a man!'
And so we women decided to rescue Greece.
You might as well listen to us now: you'll have to, later.
MAGISTRATE.   *You* rescue Greece? Absurd!
LYSISTRATA.   You're the absurd one!
MAGISTRATE.   You expect me to take orders from a woman?
LYSISTRATA.   Heavens, if that's what's bothering you, take my veil,
here, and my girdle, and my market-basket. Go home
to your weaving and your cooking! I tell you, 'War's
a woman's affair!'
CHORAGOS^W.   Down with your pitchers, comrades,
but keep them close at hand. It's time for a rally!
CHORUS^W.   Dance, girls, dance for peace!   [ANTISTROPHE
                 Who cares if our knees
Wobble and creak? Shall we not dance for such allies as these?
                      Their wit! Their grace! Their beauty!
                      It's a municipal duty
To dance them luck and happiness who risk their all for Greece!
CHORAGOS^W.   Women, remember your grandmothers! Remember, you were born
among brambles and nettles! Dance for victory!
LYSISTRATA.   O Erôs, god of delight! O Aphroditê! Kyprian!
Drench us now with the savor of love!

Let these men, getting wind of us, dream such joy
that they'll tail us through all the provinces of Hellas!

MAGISTRATE.   And if we do?

LYSISTRATA.   Well, for one thing, we shan't have to watch you
going to market, a spear in one hand, and heaven knows
what in the other.

CHORAGOS^w.   Nicely said, by Aphroditê!

LYSISTRATA.   As things stand now, you're neither men nor women.
Armor clanking with kitchen pans and pots—
you sound like a pack of Korybantês!

MAGISTRATE.   A man must do what a man must do.

LYSISTRATA.   So I'm told.
But to see a General, complete with Gorgon-shield,
jingling along the dock to buy a couple of herrings!

CHORAGOS^w.   *I* saw a Captain the other day—lovely fellow he was,
nice curly hair—sitting on his horse; and—can you believe it?—
he'd just bought some soup, and was pouring it into his helmet!
And there was a soldier from Thrace
swishing his lance like something out of Euripidês
and the poor fruit-store woman got so scared
that she ran away and let him have his figs free!

MAGISTRATE.   All this is beside the point.
                              Will you be so kind
as to tell me how you mean to save Greece?

LYSISTRATA.   Of course!
Nothing could be simpler.

MAGISTRATE.   I assure you, I'm all ears.

LYSISTRATA.   Do you know anything about weaving?
Say the yarn gets tangled: we thread it
this way and that through the skein, up and down,
until it's free. And it's like that with war.
We'll send our envoys
up and down, this way and that, all over Greece,
until it's finished.

MAGISTRATE.   Yarn? Thread? Skein?
Are you out of your mind? I tell you,
war is a serious business.

LYSISTRATA.   So serious
That I'd like to go on talking about weaving.

MAGISTRATE.   All right. Go ahead.

LYSISTRATA.   The first thing we have to do
is to wash our yarn, get the dirt out of it.
You see? Isn't there too much dirt here in Athens?
You must wash those men away.

Then our spoiled wool—
that's like your job-hunters, out for a life
of no work and big pay. Back to the basket,
citizens or not, allies or not,
or friendly immigrants!

And your colonies?
Hanks of wool lost in various places. Pull them
together, weave them into one great whole,
and our voters are clothed for ever.

MAGISTRATE. It would take a women
to reduce state questions to a matter of carding and weaving!

LYSISTRATA. You fool! Who were the mothers whose sons sailed off
to fight for Athens in Sicily?

MAGISTRATE. Enough!
I beg you, do not call back those memories.

LYSISTRATA. And then,
instead of the love that every woman needs,
we have only our single beds, where we can dream
of our husbands off with the Army.

Bad enough for wives!
But what about our girls, getting older every day,
and older, and no kisses?

MAGISTRATE. Men get older, too.

LYSISTRATA. Not in the same sense.
A soldier's discharged,
and he may be bald and toothless, yet he'll find
a pretty young thing to go to bed with.

But a woman!
Her beauty is gone with the first grey hair.
She can spend her time
consulting the oracles and the fortune-tellers,
but they'll never send her a husband.

MAGISTRATE. Still, if a man can rise to the occasion—

LYSISTRATA. Rise? Rise, yourself! (*Furiously*)
Go invest in a coffin!
You've money enough.
I'll bake you
a cake for the Underworld.
And here's your funeral
wreath! (*She pours water upon him*)

MYRRHINE. And here's another! (*More water*)

KALONIKE. And here's
my contribution! (*More water*)

LYSISTRATA.   What are you waiting for?
All aboard the Styx Ferry!
                   Charôn's calling for you!
It's sailing-time: don't disrupt the schedule!
MAGISTRATE. The insolence of women! And to me!
No, by God, I'll go back to court and show
the rest of the Bench the things that might happen to them! *Exit* MAGISTRATE
LYSISTRATA. Really, I suppose we should have laid out his corpse
on the doorstep, in the usual way.
                      But never mind!
We'll give him the rites of the dead tomorrow morning! *Exit* LYSISTRATA *with*
    MYRRHINE *and* KALONIKE

CHORAL EPISODE

CHORUS^m. Sons of Liberty, strip off your clothes for action!   [STROPHE 1
    Men, arise!
Shall we stand here limp and useless while old Kleisthenês' allies
Prod a herd of furious grandmas to attempt to bring to pass
A female restoration of the Reign of Hippias?
            Forbid it, gods misogynist!
            Return our Treasury, at least!
We must clothe ourselves and feed ourselves to face these civic rages,
And who can do a single thing if they cut off our wages?
CHORAGOS^m. Gentlemen, we are disgraced forever it we allow
these madwomen to jabber about spears and shields
and make friends with the Spartans. What's a Spartan? a wild
wolf's a safer companion any day! No; their plan's
to bring back Dictatorship; and we won't stand for that!
From now on, let's go armed, each one of us
a new Aristogeiton!
              And to begin with,
I propose to poke a number of teeth
down the gullet of that harridan over there.
CHORUS^w. Hold your tongues, you senile bravoes, or I   [ANTISTROPHE 1
    swear, when you get home
Your own mothers wouldn't know you! Strip for action, ladies, come!
I bore the holy vessels in my eighth year, and at ten
I was pounding out the barley for Athenê Goddess; then
            They elected me Little Bear
            For Artemis at Brauron Fair;
I'd been made a Basket-Carrier by the time I came of age:
So trust me to advise you in this feminist rampage!

CHORAGOS[W]. As a woman, I pay my taxes to the State,
though I pay them in baby boys. What do you contribute,
you impotent horrors? Nothing but waste:
our treasury, the so-called Glory of the Persian Wars,
gone! rifled! parceled out for privilege! And you
have the insolence to control public policy,
leading us all to disaster!
                              No, don't answer back
unless you want the heel of my slipper
slap against that ugly jaw of yours!

CHORUS[m].   What impuence!   [STROPHE 2
                             What malevolence!
                             Comrades, make haste,
All those of you who still are sensitive below the waist!
                             Off with your clothes, men!
                             Nobody knows when
                               We'll put them back on.
                               Remember Leipsydrion!
                             We may be old,
                             But let's be bold!

CHORAGOS[m]. Give them an inch, and we're done for! We'll have them
launching boats next and planning naval strategy.
Or perhaps they fancy themselves as cavalry!
That's fair enough: women know how to ride,
they're good in the saddle. Just think of Mikôn's paintings,
all those Amazons wrestling with men! No, it's time
to bridle these wild mares!

CHORUS[W]. Hold on, or   [ANTISTROPHE 2
        You *are* done for,
        By the Two Goddesses above!
Strip, strip, my women: we've got the veterans on the move!
        Tangle with me, Gramps,
        And you'll have cramps
          For the rest of your days!
          No more beans! No more cheese!
        My two legs
        Will scramble your eggs!

CHORAGOS[W]. If Lampitô stands by me, and that elegant
Theban girl, Ismenia—what good are *you*?
                                        Pass your laws!
Laws upon laws, you decrepit legislators!
At the worst you're just a nuisance, rationing Boiotian eels
on the Feast of Hekatê, making our girls go without!

That was statesmanship! And we'll have to put up with it
until some patriot slits your silly old gizzards! (*Exeunt omnes*)

SCENE 2

The scene shifts to a court within the Akropolis. Re-enter LYSISTRATA

CHORAGOS^W. But Lysistrata! Leader! Why such a grim face?
LYSISTRATA. Oh the behavior of these idiotic women!
 There's something about the female temperament
 that I can't bear!
CHORAGOS^W.   What in the world do you mean?
LYSISTRATA. Exactly what I say.
CHORAGOS^W.   What dreadful thing has happened?
 Come, tell us, we're all your friends.
LYSISTRATA.   It isn't easy
 to say it; yet, God knows, we can't hush it up.
CHORAGOS^W. Well, then? Out with it!
LYSISTRATA.   To put it bluntly,
 we're desperate for men.
CHORAGOS^W.   Almighty God!
LYSISTRATA. Why bring God into it? No, it's just as I say.
 I can't manage them any longer: they've gone man-crazy,
 they're all trying to get out.
                Why, look:
 one of them was sneaking out the back door
 over there by Pan's cave; another
 was sliding down the walls with rope and tackle;
 another was climbing aboard a sparrow, ready to take off
 for the nearest brothel—I dragged *her* back by the hair!
 They're all finding some reason to leave.
                        Look there!
 There goes another one.
                —Just a minute, you!
 Where are you off to so fast?
FIRST WOMAN.   I've got to get home!
 I've a lot of Milesian wool, and the worms are spoiling it.
LYSISTRATA. Oh bother you and your worms! Get back inside!
FIRST WOMAN. I'll be back right away, I swear I will!
 I just want to get it stretched out on my bed.
LYSISTRATA. You'll do no such thing. You'll stay right here.
FIRST WOMAN.   And my wool?
 You want it ruined?
LYSISTRATA.   Yes, for all I care.

SECOND WOMAN. Oh dear! My lovely new flax from Amorgos—
  I left it at home, all uncarded!
LYSISTRATA.   Another one!
  And all she wants is someone to card her flax.
  Get back in there!
SECOND WOMAN.   But I swear by the Moon-Goddess,
  the minute I get it done, I'll be back!
LYSISTRATA.   I say No!
  If you, why not all the other women as well?
THIRD WOMAN. O Lady Eileithyia! Radiant goddess! Thou
  intercessor for women in childbirth! Stay, I pray thee,
  oh stay this parturition! Shall I pollute
  a sacred spot?
LYSISTRATA.   And what's the matter with *you*?
THIRD WOMAN. I'm having a baby—any minute now!
LYSISTRATA. But you weren't pregnant yesterday.
THIRD WOMAN.   Well, I am today!
  Let me go home for a midwife, Lysistrata:
  there's not much time.
LYSISTRATA.   I never heard such nonsense.
  What's that bulging under your cloak?
THIRD WOMAN.   A little baby boy.
LYSISTRATA. It certainly isn't. But it's something hollow,
  like a basin or—Why, it's the helmet of Athenê!
  And you said you were having a baby!
THIRD WOMAN.   Well, I am! So there!
LYSISTRATA. Then why the helmet?
THIRD WOMAN.   I was afraid that my pains
  might begin here in the Akropolis; and I wanted
  to drop my chick into it, just as the dear doves do.
LYSISTRATA. Lies! Evasions!—But at least one thing's clear:
  you can't leave the place before your purification.
THIRD WOMAN. But I can't stay here in the Akropolis! Last night I dreamed
  of a snake.
FIRST WOMAN. And those horrible owls, the noise they make!
  I can't get a bit of sleep; I'm just about dead.
LYSISTRATA. You useless girls, that's enough: Let's have no more lying.
  Of course you want your men. But don't you imagine
  that they want you just as much? I'll give you my word,
  their nights must be pretty hard.
                              Just stick it out!
  A little patience, that's all, and our battle's won.
  I have heard an Oracle. Should you like to hear it?
FIRST WOMAN. An Oracle? Yes, tell us!

LYSISTRATA.   Quiet, then.—Here
  is what it said:
IF EVER THE SWALLOWS, ESCHEWING HOOPOE-BIRDS,
SHALL CONSPIRE TOGETHER TO DENY THEM ALL ACCESS
THEIR GRIEF IS FOREVER OVER.
                                                    These are the words
from the Shrine itself.
                              AYE, AND ZEUS WILL REDRESS
    THEIR WRONGS, AND SET THE LOWER ABOVE THE HIGHER.
FIRST WOMAN.   Does that mean we'll be on top?
LYSISTRATA.   BUT IF THEY RETIRE
EACH SWALLOW HER OWN WAY, FROM THIS HOLY PLACE
LET THE WORLD PROCLAIM NO BIRD OF SORRIER GRACE
THAN THE SWALLOW.
FIRST WOMAN.   I swear, *that* Oracle makes sense!
LYSISTRATA.   Now, then, by all the gods,
  let's show that we're bigger than these annoyances.
  Back to your places! Let's not disgrace the Oracle.   *Exeunt* LYSISTRATA *and the*
    dissident women; the CHORUSES *renew their conflict.*

CHORAL EPISODE

CHORUS^m.   I know a little story that I learned way back in school   [STROPHE 1
  Goes like this:
  Once upon a time there was a young man—and no fool—
  Named Melanion; and his
  One aversi-on was marriage. He loathed the very thought!
  So he ran off to the hills, and in a special grot
  Raised a dog, and spent his days
  Hunting rabbits. And it says
  That he never never never did come home.
  It might be called a refuge *from* the womb.
  All right,
            all right,
                  all right!
  We're as pure as young Melanion, and we hate the very sight
  Of you sluts!
A MAN.   How about a kiss, old woman?
A WOMAN.   Here's an onion in your eye!
A MAN.   A kick in the guts, then?
A WOMAN.   Try, old bristle-tail, just try!
A MAN.   Yet they say Myronidês
  On hands and knees
  Looked just as shaggy fore and aft as I!

CHORUS^W. Well, *I* know a little story, and it's just as good as yours.   [ANTISTROPHE
  Goes like this:
  Once there was a man named Timon—a rough diamond, of course,
  And that whiskery face of his
  Looked like murder in the shrubbery. By God, he was a son
  Of the Furies, let me tell you! And what did he do but run
  From the world and all its ways,
  Cursing mankind! And it says
  That his choicest execrations as of then
  Were leveled almost wholly at *old* men.
  All right,
         all right,
               all right!
  But there's one thing about Timon: he could always stand the sight
  Of us 'sluts'!
A WOMAN. How about a crack in the jaw, Pop?
A MAN. I can take it, Ma—no fear!
A WOMAN. How about a kick in the face?
A MAN. You'd show your venerable rear.
A WOMAN. I may be old;
  But I've been told
  That I've nothing to worry about down there!

SCENE 3

Re-enter LYSISTRATA

LYSISTRATA. Oh, quick, girls, quick! Come here!
CHORAGOS^W.   What is it?
LYSISTRATA.   A man!
  A man simply bulging with love!
                          O Kyprian Queen,
  O Paphian, O Kythereian! Hear us and aid us!
CHORAGOS^W. Where is this enemy?
LYSISTRATA.   Over there, by Deméter's shrine.
CHORAGOS^W. Damned if he isn't. But who *is* he?
MYRRHINE.   My husband.
  Kinesias.
LYSISTRATA. Oh then, get busy! Tease him! Undermine him!
  Wreck him! Give him everything—kissing, tickling, nudging,
  whatever you generally torture him with—: give him everything
  except what we swore on the wine we would not give.
MYRRHINE. Trust me!
LYSISTRATA. I do. But I'll help you get him started.
  The rest of you women, stay back.

Enter KINESIAS

KINESIAS.   Oh God! Oh my God!
  I'm stiff for lack of exercise. All I can do to stand up!
LYSISTRATA.   Halt! Who are you, approaching our lines?
KINESIAS.   Me? I.
LYSISTRATA.   A man?
KINESIAS.   You have eyes, haven't you?
LYSISTRATA.   Go away.
KINESIAS.   Who says so?
LYSISTRATA.   Officer of the Day.
KINESIAS.   Officer, I beg you,
  by all the gods at once, bring Myrrhinê out!
LYSISTRATA.   Myrrhinê? And who, my good sir, are you?
KINESIAS.   Kinesias. Last name's Pennison. Her husband.
LYSISTRATA.   Oh, of course. I beg your pardon. We're glad to see you.
  We've heard so much about you. Dearest Myrrhinê
  is always talking about 'Kinesias'— never nibbles an egg
  or an apple without saying
  'Here's to Kinesias!'
KINESIAS.   Do you really mean it?
LYSISTRATA.   I do.
  When we're discussing men, she always says,
  'Well, after all, there's nobody like Kinesias!'
KINESIAS.   Good God.—Well, then, please send her down here.
LYSISTRATA.   And what do *I* get out of it?
KINESIAS.   A standing promise.
LYSISTRATA.   I'll take it up with her. (*Exit* LYSISTRATA)
KINESIAS.   But be quick about it!
  Lord, what's life without a wife? Can't eat. Can't sleep.
  Every time I go home, the place is so empty, so
  insufferably sad! Love's killing me! Oh,
  hurry!

Enter MANES, *a slave, with* KINESIAS' *baby; the voice of* MYRRHINE
is heard off-stage

MYRRHINE.   But of course I love him! Adore him!—But no,
  he hates love. No. I won't go down.

Enter MYRRHINE, *above*

KINESIAS.   Myrrhinê!
  Darlingest little Myrrhinê! Come down quick!
MYRRHINE.   Certainly not.
KINESIAS.   Not? But why, Myrrhinê?
MYRRHINE.   Why? You don't need me.

KINESIAS.   Need you? My God, *look* at me!
MYRRHINE.   So long!   (*Turns to go*)
KINESIAS.   Myrrhinê, Myrrhinê, Myrrhinê!
If not for my sake, for our child!   (*Pinches baby*)
                              —All right, you: pipe up!
BABY.   Mummie! Mummie! Mummie!
KINESIAS.   You hear that?
Pitiful, I call it. Six days now
with never a bath; no food, enough to break your heart!
MYRRHINE.   My darlingest child! What a father *you* acquired!
KINESIAS.   At least come down for his sake!
MYRRHINE.   I suppose I must.
Oh, this mother business!   (*Exit*)
KINESIAS.   How pretty she is! And younger!
She's so much nicer when she's bothered!

MYRRHINE *enters, below*

MYRRHINE.   Dearest child,
you're as sweet as your father's horrid. Give me a kiss.
KINESIAS.   Now you see how wrong it was to get involved
in this scheming League of women. All this agony
for nothing!
MYRRHINE.   Keep your hands to yourself!
KINESIAS.   But our house
going to rack and ruin?
MYRRHINE.   *I* don't care.
KINESIAS.   And your knitting
all torn to pieces by the chickens? Don't you care?
MYRRHINE.   Not at all.
KINESIAS.   And our vows to Aphroditê?
Oh, *won't* you come back?
MYRRHINE.   No.—At least, not until you men
make a treaty to end the war.
KINESIAS.   Why, if that's all you want,
by God, we'll make your treaty!
MYRRHINE.   Oh? Very well.
When you've done that, I'll come home. But meanwhile,
I've sworn an oath.
KINESIAS.   Don't worry.—Now, let's have fun.
MYRRHINE.   No! Stop it! I said no!
                              —Although, of course,
I *do* love you.
KINESIAS.   I know you do. Darling Myrrhinê:
come, shall we?
MYRRHINE.   Are your out of your mind? In front of the child?

KINESIAS. Take him home, Manês. (*Exit* MANES *with baby*)
                                    There. He's gone.
                                                      Come on!
There's nothing to stop us now.
MYRRHINE.   You devil! But where?
KINESIAS. In Pan's cave. What could be snugger than that?
MYRRHINE. But my purification before I go back to the Citadel?
KINESIAS. There's always the Klepsydra.
MYRRHINE.   And my oath?
KINESIAS.   Leave the oath to me.
  After all, I'm the man.
MYRRHINE.   Well . . . if you say so! I'll go find a bed.
KINESIAS. Oh, bother a bed! The ground's good enough for me!
MYRRHINE. No. You're a bad man, but you deserve something better than
    dirt. (*Exit* MYRRHINE)
KINESIAS. What a love she is! And how thoughtful!

Re-enter MYRRHINE

MYRRHINE.   Here's your bed.
  Now let me get my clothes off.
                         But, good horrors!
  We haven't a mattress!
KINESIAS.   Oh, forget the mattress!
MYRRHINE.   No.
  Just lying on blankets? Too sordid!
KINESIAS.   Give me a kiss.
MYRRHINE. Just a second. (*Exit* MYRRHINE)
KINESIAS.   I swear, I'll explode!

Re-enter MYRRHINE

MYRRHINE.   Here's your mattress.
  Go to bed now. I'll just take my dress off.
                           But look—
  where's our pillow?
KINESIAS.   I don't need a pillow!
MYRRHINE.   Well, *I* do. (*Exit* MYRRHINE)
KINESIAS. I don't suppose even Hereklês
  would stand for this!

Re-enter MYRRHINE

MYRRHINE.   There we are. Ups-a-daisy!
KINESIAS. So we are. Well, come to bed.
MYRRHINE.   But I wonder:
  is everything ready now?

KINESIAS.   I can swear to that. Come, darling!
MYRRHINE. Just getting out of my girdle.

                                     But remember, now,
what you promised about the treaty!
KINESIAS.   I'll remember.
MYRRHINE. But no coverlet!
KINESIAS.   Damn it, I'll be
your coverlet!
MYRRHINE.   Be right back. (*Exit* MYRRHINE)
KINESIAS.   This girl and her coverlets
will be the death of me.

               Re-enter MYRRHINE

MYRRHINE.   Here we are. Up you go!
KINESIAS. Up? I've been up for ages!
MYRRHINE.   Some perfume?
KINESIAS. No, by Apollo!
MYRRHINE.   Yes, by Aphroditê!
  I don't care whether you want it or not. (*Exit* MYRRHINE)
KINESIAS. For love's sake, hurry!

               Re-enter MYRRHINE

MYRRHINE. Here, in your hand. Rub it right in.
KINESIAS.   Never cared for perfume.
  And this is particularly strong. Still, here goes!
MYRRHINE. What a nitwit I am! I brought you the Rhodian bottle!
KINESIAS. Forget it.
MYRRHINE. No trouble at all. You just wait here. (*Exit* MYRRHINE)
KINESIAS. God damn the man who invented perfume!

               Re-enter MYRRHINE

MYRRHINE. At last! The right bottle!
KINESIAS.   I've got the rightest
bottle of all, and it's right here waiting for you.
  Darling, forget everything else. Do come to bed!
MYRRHINE. Just let me get my shoes off.

                      —And, by the way,
you'll vote for the treaty?
KINESIAS.   I'll think about it.

            MYRRHINE *runs away*

There! That's done it! Off she runs,
with never a thought for the way I'm feeling. I must
have *someone,* or I'll go mad! Myrrhinê

has just about ruined me.
                           And you, strutting little soldier:
what about you? There's nothing for it, I guess,
but an expedition to old Dog-fox's bordello.

CHORUS^m.   She's left you in a sorry state:
               You have my sympathy.
        What upright citizen could bear
           Your pain? I swear, not I!
Just the look of you, with never a woman
To come to your aid! It isn't human!

KINESIAS. The agony!

CHORAGOS^m.   Well, why not?
          She has you on the spot!

CHORAGOS^w. A lovelier girl never breathed, you old sot!

KINESIAS. A lovelier girl? Zeus! Zeus!
          Produce a hurricane
       To hoist these lovely girls aloft
          And drop them down again
Bump on our lances! Then they'd know
What they do that makes men suffer so. (*Exit* KINESIAS)

SCENE 4

Enter a SPARTAN HERALD

HERALD. Gentlemen, Ah beg you will be so kind
  as to direct me to the Central Committee
  Ah have a communication.

Re-enter MAGISTRATE

MAGISTRATE.   Are you a man,
  or a fertility symbol?

HERALD.   Ah refuse to answer that question!
  Ah'm a certified herald from Spahta, and Ah've come
  to talk about an ahmistice.

MAGISTRATE.   Then why
  that spear under your cloak?

HERALD.   Ah have no speah!

MAGISTRATE. You don't walk naturally, with your tunic
  poked out so. You have a tumor, maybe,
  or a hernia?

HERALD.   No, by Kastor!

MAGISTRATE.   Well,
  something's wrong, I can see that. And I don't like it.

HERALD. Colonel, Ah resent this.

MAGISTRATE.   So I see. But what *is* it?
HERALD.   A scroll
   with a message from Spahta.
MAGISTRATE.   Oh. I've heard about these scrolls.
   Well, then, man, speak out: How are things in Sparta?
HERALD. Hard, Colonel, hard! We're at a standstill.
   Can't seem to think of anything but women.
MAGISTRATE. How curious! Tell me, do you Spartans think
   that maybe Pan's to blame?
HERALD. Pan? No. Lampitô and her little naked friends.
   They won't let a man come near them.
MAGISTRATE. How are you handling it?
HERALD.   Losing our minds,
   if you want to know, and walking around hunched over
   like men carrying candles in a gale.
   The women have sworn they'll have nothing to do with us
   until we get a treaty.
MAGISTRATE.   Yes. I know.
   It's a general uprising, sir, in all parts of Greece.
   But as for the answer—
                Sir: go back to Sparta
   and have them send us your Armistice Commission.
   I'll arrange things in Athens.
                And I may say
   that my standing is good enough to make them listen.
HERALD. A man after mah own heart! Sir, Ah thank you! (*Exit* HERALD)

CHORAL EPISODE

CHORUS^m. Oh these women! Where will you find   [STROPHE
         A slavering beast that's more unkind?
           Where a hotter fire?
         Give me a panther, any day!
         He's not so merciless as they,
           And panthers don't conspire!
CHORUS^w. We may be hard, you silly old ass,   [ANTISTROPHE
         But who brought you to this stupid pass?
           You're the ones to blame.
         Fighting with us, your oldest friends,
         Simply to serve your selfish ends—
           Really, you have no shame!
CHORAGOS^m. No, I'm through with women for ever!
CHORAGOS^w.   If you say so.
   Still, you might put some clothes on. You look too absurd
   standing around naked. Come, get into this cloak.

CHORAGOS[m]. Thank you; you're right. I merely took it off
because I was in such a temper.
CHORAGOS[w].   That's much better
Now you resemble a man again.

                                                  Why have you been so horrid?
And look: there's some sort of insect in your eye!
Shall I take it out?
CHORAGOS[m].   An insect, is it? So that's
what's been bothering me. Lord, yes: take it out!
CHORAGOS[w]. You might be more polite.

                                                  —But, heavens!
What an enormous gnat!
CHORAGOS[m].   You've saved my life.
That gnat was drilling an artesian well
in my left eye.
CHORAGOS[w].   Let me wipe
those tears away!—And now: one little kiss?
CHORAGOS[m]. Over my dead body!
CHORAGOS[w].   You're so difficult!
CHORAGOS[m]. These impossible women! How they do get around us!
The poet was right: Can't live with them, or without them!
But let's be friends.
And to celebrate, you might lead off with an Ode.
CHORUS[w]. Let it never be said   [STROPHE
            That my tongue is malicious:
            Both by word and by deed
I would set an example that's noble and gracious.
            We've had sorrow and care
            Till we're sick of the tune.
            Is there anyone here
            Who would like a small loan?
              My purse is crammed,
              As you'll soon find;
As you needn't pay me back if the Peace gets signed!
            I've invited to lunch
            Some Karystian rips—
            An esurient bunch,
But I've ordered a menu to water their lips!
            I can still make soup
            And slaughter a pig.
            You're all coming, I hope?
            But a bath first, I beg!
              Walk right up
              As though you owned the place,
And you'll get the front door slammed to in your face!

SCENE 5

Enter SPARTAN AMBASSADOR, *with entourage*

CHORAGOS^m. The Commission has arrived from Sparta.

                                           How oddly

  they're walking!

                    Gentlemen, welcome to Athens!

  How is life in Lakonia?

AMBASSADOR.   Need we discuss that?

  Simply use your eyes.

CHORUS^m.   The poor man's right:

                  What a sight!

AMBASSADOR.   Words fail me.

  But come, gentlemen, call in your Commissioners,

  and let's get down to a Peace.

CHORAGOS^m.   The state we're in! Can't bear

  a stitch below the waist. It's a kind of pelvic

  paralysis.

AN ATHENIAN. Won't somebody call Lysistrata?

  She has the answer.

A SPARTAN.   Yes, there, look at him.

  Same thing.

          Seh, do y'all feel a certain strain

  early in the morning?

ATHENIAN.   I do, sir. It's worse than a strain.

  A few more days, and there's nothing for us but Kleisthenês,

  that broken blossom!

CHORAGOS^m.   But you'd better get dressed again.

  You know these prudes who go around Athens with chisels,

  looking for prominent statues.

ATHENIAN.   Sir, you are right.

SPARTAN. He certainly is! Ah'll put mah own clothes back on.

Enter ATHENIAN COMMISIONERS

AN ATHENIAN. They're no better off than we are!

                    —Greetings, Lakonians!

SPARTAN. (*To one of his own group:*) Colonel, we got dressed just in time.

  Ah sweah,

  if they'd seen us the way we were, there'd have been a new war

  between the states.

ATHENIAN. Call the meeting to order.

               Now, Lakonians,

  what's your proposal?

AMBASSADOR. We'd lahk to consider peace.
ATHENIAN. Good. That's on our minds, too.
—Summon Lysistrata.
We'll never get anywhere without her.
AMBASSADOR. Lysistrata?
Summon Lysis-*any*body! Only, summon!
CHORAGOS[m]. No need to summon:
here she is, herself.

Enter LYSISTRATA

Lysistrata! Lion of women!
This is your hour to be
hard and yielding, outspoken and sly, austere and
gentle. You see here
the best brains of Hellas (confused, I admit,
by your devious charming) met as one man
to turn the future over to you.
LYSISTRATA. That's fair enough,
unless you men take it into your heads
to turn to each other instead of to me. But I'd know
soon enough if you did!
—Where is that goddess of Peace?
Go, some of you: bring her here. (*Exeunt two* SERVANTS)
And now,
summon the Spartan Commission. Treat them courteously:
our husbands have been lax in that respect.
Take them by the hand, women,
or by anything else, if they seem unwilling.
—Spartans:
you stand here. Athenians: on this side. Now listen to me.

Re-enter SERVANTS, *staggering under the weight of a more than life-size statue of a
naked woman: this is* PEACE.

I'm only a woman, I know, but I've a mind,
and I can distinguish between sense and foolishness.
I owe the first to my father; the rest
to the local politicians. So much for that.
Now, then.
What I have to say concerns both sides in this war.
We are all Greeks.
Must I remind you of Thermopylai? of Olympia?
of Delphoi? names deep in all our hearts?

And yet you men go raiding through the country,
Greek killing Greek, storming down Greek cities—
and all the time the Barbarian across the sea
is waiting for his chance.—That's my first point.

AN ATHENIAN. Lord! I can hardly contain myself!

LYSISTRATA.   And you Spartans:
Was it so long ago that Perikleidês
came here to beg our help? I can see him still,
his white face, his sombre gown. And what did he want?
An army from Athens! Messenia
was at your heels, and the sea-god splitting your shores.
Well, Kimòn and his men,
four thousand infantry, marched out of here to save you.
What thanks do we get? You come back to murder us.

ATHENIAN. Can't trust a Spartan, Lysistrata!

A SPARTAN.   Ah admit it.
When Ah look at those legs, Ah sweah Ah can't trust mahself!

LYSISTRATA. And you, men of Athens:
you might remember that bad time when we were down,
and an army came from Sparta
and sent Hippias and the Thessalians
whimpering back to the hills. That was Sparta,
and only Sparta; without Sparta, we'd now be
cringing helots, not walking about like free men!

> *From this point, the male responses are less to* LYSISTRATA *than to the
> statue of* PEACE.

A SPARTAN. An eloquent speech!

AN ATHENIAN.   An elegant construction!

LYSISTRATA. Why are we fighting each other? Why not make peace?

AMBASSADOR. Spahta is ready, ma'am,
so long as we get that place back.

LYSISTRATA.   Place? What place?

AMBASSADOR. Ah refer to Pylos.

MAGISTRATE.   Not while I'm alive, by God!

LYSISTRATA. You'd better give in.

MAGISTRATE.   But—what were we fighting about?

LYSISTRATA. Lots of places left.

MAGISTRATE.   All right. Well, then:
Hog Island first, and that gulf behind there, and the land between
the Legs of Megara.

AMBASSADOR.   Mah government objects.

LYSISTRATA. Over-ruled. Why fuss about a pair of legs?

General assent; the statue of PEACE *is removed*

AN ATHENIAN. Let's take off our clothes and plow our fields.

A SPARTAN. Ah'll fertilize mahn first, by the Heavenly Twins!

LYSISTRATA. And so you shall,
  once we have peace. If you are serious,
  go, both of you, and talk with your allies.

ATHENIAN. Too much talk already. We'll stand together!
  We've only one end in view. All that we want
  is our women: and I speak for our allies.

AMBASSADOR. Mah government concurs.

ATHENIAN.   So does Karystos.

LYSISTRATA. Good.—But before you come inside
  to join your wives at supper, you must perform
  the usual lustration. Then we'll open
  our baskets for you, and all that we have is yours.
  But you must promise upright good behavior
  from this day on. Then each man home with his woman!

ATHENIAN. Let's get it over with!

SPARTAN.   Lead on: Ah follow!

ATHENIAN. Quick as a cat can wink! (*Exeunt all but the* CHORUSES)

CHORUS^W. Embroideries ánd   [ANTISTROPHE
           Twinkling ornaments ánd
           Pretty dresses—I hand
Them all over to you, and with never a qualm.
           They'll be nice for your daughters
           On festival days
           When the girls bring the Goddess
           The ritual prize.
             Come in, one and all:
             Take what you will.
I've nothing here so tightly corked that you can't make it spill!
           You may search my house,
           But you'll not find
           The least thing of use,
Unless your two eyes are keener than mine.
           Your numberless brats
           Are half starved? and your slaves?
           Courage, grandpa! I've lots
           Of grain left, and big loaves.
             I'll fill your guts,
             I'll go the whole hog;
           But if you come too close to me, remember: 'ware the dog! *Exeunt*
CHORUSES

EXODOS

An ATHENIAN DRUNKARD *approaches the gate and is halted by a* SENTRY

DRUNKARD. Open. The. Door.

SENTRY. Now, friend, just shove along!
So you want to sit down! If it weren't such an old joke,
I'd tickle your tail with this torch. Just the sort of thing
that this kind of audience appreciates.

DRUNKARD. I. Stay. Right. Here.

SENTRY. Oh, all right. But you'll see some funny sights!

DRUNKARD. Bring. Them. On.

SENTRY. No, what am I thinking of?
The gentlemen from Sparta are just coming back from supper.
Get out of here, or I'll scalp you! *Exit* DRUNKARD; *the general company*
re-enters; the two CHORUSES *now represent* SPARTANS *and* ATHENIANS

MAGISTRATE. I must say,
I've never tasted a better meal. And those Lakonians!
They're gentlemen, by the Lord! Just goes to show:
a drink to the wise is sufficient. And why not?
A sober man's an ass.
Men of Athens, mark my words: the only efficient
Ambassador's a drunk Ambassador. Is that clear?
Look: we go to Sparta,
and when we get there we're dead sober. The result?
Everyone cackling at everyone else. They make speeches;
and even if we understand, we get it all wrong
when we file our reports in Athens. But today—!
Everybody's happy. Couldn't tell the difference
between *Drink to Me Only* and
the *Star Spangled Athens.*
What's a few lies,
washed down in good strong drink?

Re-enter DRUNKARD

SENTRY. God almighty,
he's back again!

DRUNKARD. I. Resume. My. Place.

A SPARTAN (*To an* ATHENIAN): I beg you, seh,
take your instrument in your hand and play for us.
Ah'm told
you understand the in*tri*cacies of the floot?
Ah'd lahk to execute a song and dance
in honor of Athens,
and of course, of Spahta.

The following song is a solo—an aria—accompanied by flute. The Chorus of Spartans *begins a slow dance.*

Drunkard. Toot. On. Your. Flute.
Choragos⁵. Mnemosynê,
  Inspire once more the Grecian Muse
  To sing of glory glory glory without end.
  Sing Artemesion's shore,
  Where Athens fluttered the Persian fleet—
  Alalaí, that great
  Victory! Sing Leonidas and his men,
  Those wild boars, sweat and blood
  Down in a red drench. Then, then
  The barbarians broke, though they had stood
  A myriad strong before!
                    O Artemis,
  Virgin Goddess, whose darts
  Flash in our forests: approve
  This pact of peace, and join our hearts,
  From this day on, in love.
  Huntress, descend!
Lysistrata. All that will come in time.
                    But now, Lakonians,
  take home your wives. Athenians, take yours.
  Each man be kind to his woman; and you, women,
  be equally kind. Never again, pray God,
  shall we lose our way in such madness.
                    —And now
  let's dance our joy! (*From this point the dance becomes general*)
Chorus of Athenians. Dance!
                    Dance!
                    Dance, you Graces!
  Artemis, dance!
                    Dance, Phoibos, Lord of dancing!
  Dance, Dionysos, in a scurry of Maenads!
                    Dance, Zeus Thunderer!
                    Dance! Lady Herê,
  Queen of the Sky!
                    Dance, dance, all you gods!
  Dance for the dearest, the bringer of peace,
  Deathless Aphroditê!
Lysistrata. Now let us have another song from Sparta.
Chorus of Spartans. From Taÿgetos' skyey summit,
    Lakonian Muse, come down!

Sing the glories of Apollo,
　　Regent of Amyklai Town.
Sing of Leda's Twins,
Those gallant songs,
On the banks of Eurotas—
　　Alalaí Evohé!
Here's to our girls
　　With their tangling curls,
　　　Legs a-wriggle,
　　　Bellies a-jiggle.
　　　　　A riot of hair,
　　A fury of feet,
Evohé! Evohaí! Evohé!
　　　　　　　　as they pass
　　Dancing,
　　　　　dancing,
　　　　　　　dancing,
　　　　　　　　　to greet
Athenê of the House of Brass!

　　　　　　　　　　　Translated by Dudley Fitts

Journal Entry

React to the statement that Lysistrata opposes war because "war's a man's affair" that brings with it the glorification of male competitiveness.

Textual Considerations

1. Analyze the function of the choruses in Aristophanes' play. To what extent do the male and female choruses in *Lysistrata* stimulate the comic action of the play? How do they reinforce the relationship between sex and war? In what manner do they provoke a confrontation between male and female values?
2. Examine characterization by analyzing the role that Lysistrata plays in Aristophanes' comedy. Don't overlook the fact that Lysistrata's name means "Dismisser of Armies." Consider how she reacts to the women who attempt to desert.
3. Investigate the issue of power relations in *Lysistrata*. Quote from the text to defend your position on who wins and who holds the real power in Lysistrata's society.

Cultural Contexts

1. Quote from the text to initiate a discussion on the way the women in *Lysistrata* use their bodies and their sexuality to undermine the traditional notions of masculinity.
2. To generate a debate about the battle of the sexes in *Lysistrata*, write some arguments in defense of both: Lysistrata's position as women's leader and a guardian of Athens' values, versus men's feelings about being deprived of sex and leadership. Which position do you support?
3. In Greek plays such as *Lysistrata*, as well as in Shakespeare's plays, female roles were played by males. What kinds of responses might the theatrical convention of an all-male cast evoke from a modern audience?

Fernando Arrabal

Picnic on the Battlefield

CHARACTERS

ZAPO, *a soldier*
MONSIEUR TÉPAN, *the soldier's father*
MADAME TÉPAN, *the soldier's mother*
ZÉPO, *an enemy soldier*
First Stretcher Bearer
Second Stretcher Bearer

A battlefield. The stage is covered with barbed wire and sandbags. The battle is at its height. Rifle shots, exploding bombs and machine guns can be heard.

ZAPO is alone on the stage; flat on his stomach, hidden among the sandbags. He is very frightened. The sound of the fighting stops. Silence.

ZAPO takes a ball of wool and some needles out of a canvas workbag and starts knitting a pullover, which is already quite far advanced. The field telephone, which is by his side, suddenly starts ringing.

ZAPO. Hallo, hallo . . . yes, Captain . . . yes, I'm the sentry of sector 47 . . . Nothing new, Captain . . . Excuse me, Captain, but when's the fighting going to start again? And what am I supposed to do with the hand-grenades? Do I chuck them in front of me or behind me? . . . Don't get me wrong. I didn't mean to annoy you . . . Captain, I really feel terribly lonely, couldn't you send me someone to keep me company? . . . even if it's only a nanny-goat? [*The* CAPTAIN *is obviously severely reprimanding him.*] Whatever you say, Captain, whatever you say. [ZAPO *hangs up. He mutters to himself. Silence. Enter* MONSIEUR *and* MADAME TÉPAN *carrying baskets as if they were going on a picnic. They address their son, who has his back turned and doesn't see them come in.*]

MONS. T. [*ceremoniously.*] Stand up, my son, and kiss your mother on the brow. [ZAPO, *surprised, gets up and kisses his mother very respectfully on the forehead. He is about to speak, but his father doesn't give him a chance.*] And now, kiss *me.*

ZAPO. But, dear Father and dear Mother, how did you dare to come all this way, to such a dangerous place? You must leave at once.

MONS. T. So you think you've got something to teach your father about war and danger, do you? All this is just a game to me. How many times—to take the first example that comes to mind—have I got off an underground train while it was still moving.

MME. T. We thought you must be bored, so we came to pay you a little visit. This war must be a bit tedious, after all.

ZAPO. It all depends.

MONS. T. I know exactly what happens. To start with you're attracted by the novelty of it all. It's fun to kill people, and throw hand-grenades about, and wear uniforms—you feel smart, but in the end you get bored stiff. You'd have found it much more interesting in my day. Wars were much more lively, much more highly colored. And then, the best thing was that there were horses, plenty of horses. It was a real pleasure; if the Captain ordered us to attack, there we all were immediately, on horseback, in our red uniforms. It was a sight to be seen. And then there were the charges at the gallop, sword in hand, and suddenly you found yourself face to face with the enemy, and he was equal to the occasion too—with his horses—there were always horses, lots of horses, with their well-rounded rumps—in his highly-polished boots, and his green uniform.

MME. T. No, no, the enemy uniform wasn't green. It was blue. I remember distinctly that it was blue.

MONS. T. I tell you it was green.

MME. T. When I was little, how many times did I go out to the balcony to watch the battle and say to the neighbour's little boy: 'I bet you a gum-drop the blues win.' And the blues were our enemies.

MONS. T. Oh, well, you must be right, then.

MME. T. I've always liked battles. As a child I always said that when I grew up I wanted to be a Colonel of dragoons. But my mother wouldn't hear of it, you know how she will stick to her principles at all costs.

MONS. T. Your mother's just a half-wit.

ZAPO. I'm sorry, but you really must go. You can't come into a war unless you're a soldier.

MONS. T. I don't give a damn, we came here to have a picnic with you in the country and to enjoy our Sunday.

MME. T. And I've prepared an excellent meal, too. Sausage, hard-boiled eggs—you know how you like them!—ham sandwiches, red wine, salad, and cakes.

ZAPO. All right, let's have it your way. But if the Captain comes he'll be absolutely furious. Because he isn't at all keen on us having visits when we're at the front. He never stops telling us: 'Discipline and hand-grenades are what's wanted in war, not visits.'

MONS. T. Don't worry, I'll have a few words to say to your Captain.

ZAPO. And what if we have to start fighting again?

MONS. T. You needn't think that'll frighten me, it won't be the first fighting I've seen. Now if only it was battles on horseback! Times have changed, you can't understand. [*Pause.*] We came by motor bike. No one said a word to us.

ZAPO. They must have thought you were the referees.

MONS. T. We had enough trouble getting through, though. What with all the tanks and jeeps.

MME. T. And do you remember the bottle-neck that cannon caused, just when we got here?

MONS. T. You mustn't be surprised at anything in wartime, everyone knows that.

MME. T. Good, let's start our meal.

MONS. T. You're quite right, I feel as hungry as a hunter. It's the smell of gunpowder.

MME. T. We'll sit on the rug while we're eating.

ZAPO. Can I bring my rifle with me?

MME. T. You leave your rifle alone. It's not good manners to bring your rifle to table with you. [*Pause.*] But you're absolutely filthy, my boy. How on earth did you get into such a state? Let's have a look at your hands.

ZAPO [*ashamed, holding out his hands*]. I had to crawl about on the ground during the manoeuvres.

MME. T. And what about your ears?

ZAPO. I washed them this morning.

MME. T. Well that's all right, then. And your teeth? [*He shows them.*] Very good. Who's going to give her little boy a great big kiss for cleaning his teeth so nicely? [*To her husband.*] Well, go on, kiss your son for cleaning his teeth so nicely. [*M. Tépan kisses his son.*] Because, you know, there's one thing I *will* not have, and that's making fighting a war an excuse for not washing.

ZAPO. Yes, mother. [*They eat.*]

MONS. T. Well, my boy, did you make a good score?

ZAPO. When?

MONS. T. In the last few days, of course.

ZAPO. Where?

MONS. T. At the moment, since you're fighting a war.

ZAPO. No, nothing much. I didn't make a good score. Hardly ever scored a bull.

MONS. T. Which are you best at shooting, enemy horses or soldiers?

ZAPO. No, not horses, there aren't any horses any more.

MONS. T. Well, soldiers then?

ZAPO. Could be.

MONS. T. Could be? Aren't you sure?

ZAPO. Well you see . . . I shoot without taking aim, [*pause*] and at the same time I say a Pater Noster for the chap I've shot.

MONS. T. You must be braver than that. Like your father.

MME. T. I'm going to put a record on. [*She puts a record on the gramophone—a pasodoble. All three are sitting on the ground, listening.*]

MONS. T. That really *is* music. Yes indeed, ole! [*The music continues. Enter an enemy soldier: ZÉPO. He is dressed like ZAPO. The only difference is the colour of their uniforms. ZÉPO is in green and ZAPO is in grey. ZÉPO listens to the music openmouthed. He is behind the family so they can't see him. The record ends. As he gets up ZAPO discovers ZÉPO. Both put their hands up. M. and MME. TÉPAN look at them in surprise.*] What's going on? [*ZAPO reacts—he hesitates. Finally, looking as if he's made up his mind, he points his rifle at ZÉPO.*]

ZAPO. Hands up! [*ZÉPO puts his hands up even higher, looking even more terrified. ZAPO doesn't know what to do. Suddenly he goes over quickly to ZÉPO and touches him gently on the shoulder, like a child playing a game of 'tag'.*] Got you! [*To his father, very pleased.*] There we are! A prisoner!

MONS. T.   Fine. And now what're you going to do with him?

ZAPO.   I don't know, but, well, could be—they might make me a corporal.

MONS. T.   In the meantime, you'd better tie him up.

ZAPO.   Tie him up? Why?

MONS. T.   Prisoners always get tied up!

ZAPO.   How?

MONS. T.   Tie up his hands.

MME. T.   Yes, there's no doubt about it, you must tie up his hands, I've always seen them do that.

ZAPO.   Right. [*To his prisoner.*] Put your hands together, if you please.

ZÉPO.   Don't hurt me too much.

ZAPO.   I won't.

ZÉPO.   Ow! You're hurting me.

MONS. T.   Now, now, don't maltreat your prisoner.

MME. T.   Is that the way I brought you up? How many times have I told you that we must be considerate of our fellow-men?

ZAPO.   I didn't do it on purpose. [*To* ZÉPO.] And like that, does it hurt?

ZÉPO.   No, it's all right like that.

MONS. T.   Tell him straight out, say what you mean, don't mind us.

ZÉPO.   It's all right like that.

MONS. T.   Now his feet.

ZAPO.   His feet as well, whatever next?

MONS. T.   Didn't they teach you the rules?

ZAPO.   Yes.

MONS. T.   Well then!

ZAPO [*very politely, to* ZÉPO].   Would you be good enough to sit on the ground, please?

ZÉPO.   Yes, but don't hurt me.

MME. T.   You'll see, he'll take a dislike to you.

ZAPO.   No he won't, no he won't. I'm not hurting you, am I?

ZÉPO.   No, that's perfect.

ZAPO.   Papa, why don't you take a photo of the prisoner on the ground and me with my foot on his stomach?

MONS. T.   Oh, yes that'd look good.

ZÉPO.   Oh no, not that!

MME. T.   Say yes, don't be obstinate.

ZÉPO.   No, I said no, and no it is.

MME. T.   But just a little teeny weeny photo, what harm could that do you? And we could put it in the dining room, next to the life-saving certificate my husband won thirteen years ago.

ZÉPO.   No—you won't shift me.

ZAPO.   But why won't you let us?

ZÉPO.   I'm engaged. And if she sees the photo one day, she'll say I don't know how to fight a war properly.

ZAPO. No she won't, all you'll need to say is that it isn't you, it's a panther.

MME. T. Come on, do say yes.

ZÉPO. All right then. But only to please you.

ZAPO. Lie down flat. [ZÉPO *lies down.* ZAPO *puts a foot on his stomach and grabs his rifle with a martial air.*]

MME. T. Stick your chest out a bit further.

ZAPO. Like this?

MME. T. Yes like that, and don't breathe.

MONS. T. Try to look like a hero.

ZAPO. What d'you mean, like a hero?

MONS. T. It's quite simple; try and look like the butcher does when he's boasting about his successes with the girls.

ZAPO. Like this?

MONS. T. Yes, like that.

MME. T. The most important thing is to puff your chest out and not breathe.

ZÉPO. Have you nearly finished?

MONS. T. Just be patient a moment. One . . . two . . . three.

ZAPO. I hope I'll come out well.

MME. T. Yes, you looked very martial.

MONS. T. You were fine.

MME. T. It makes me want to have my photo taken with you.

MONS. T. Now there's a good idea.

ZAPO. Right. I'll take it if you like.

MME. T. Give me your helmet to make me look like a soldier.

ZÉPO. I don't want any more photos. Even one's far too many.

ZAPO. Don't take it like that. After all, what harm can it do you?

ZÉPO. It's my last word.

MONS. T. [*to his wife*]. Don't press the point, prisoners are always very sensitive. If we go on he'll get cross and spoil our fun.

ZAPO. Right, what're we going to do with him, then?

MME. T. We could invite him to lunch. What do you say?

MONS. T. I don't see why not.

ZAPO [*to* ZÉPO]. Well, will you have lunch with us, then?

ZÉPO. Er . . .

MONS. T. We brought a good bottle with us.

ZÉPO. Oh well, all right then.

MME. T. Make yourself at home, don't be afraid to ask for anything you want.

ZÉPO. All right.

MONS. T. And what about you, did you make a good score?

ZÉPO. When?

MONS. T. In the last few days, of course.

ZÉPO. Where?

MONS. T. At the moment, since you're fighting a war.

ZÉPO. No, nothing much. I didn't make a good score, hardly ever scored a bull.

MONS. T. Which are you best at shooting? Enemy horses or soldiers?

ZÉPO. No, not horses, they aren't any horses any more.

MONS. T. Well, soldiers, then?

ZÉPO. Could be.

MONS. T. Could be? Aren't you sure?

ZÉPO. Well you see . . . I shoot without taking aim, [*pause*] and at the same time I say an Ave Maria for the chap I've shot.

ZAPO. An Ave Maria? I'd have thought you'd have said a Pater Noster.

ZÉPO. No, always an Ave Maria. [*Pause*] It's shorter.

MONS. T. Come come, my dear fellow, you must be brave.

MME. T. [*to* ZÉPO]. We can untie you if you like.

ZÉPO. No, don't bother, it doesn't matter.

MONS. T. Don't start getting stand-offish with us now. If you'd like us to untie you, say so.

MME. T. Make yourself comfortable.

ZÉPO. Well, if that's how you feel, you can untie my feet, but it's only to please you.

MONS. T. Zapo, untie him. [ZAPO *unties him.*]

MME. T. Well, do you feel better?

ZÉPO. Yes, of course. I really am putting you to a lot of inconvenience.

MONS. T. Not at all, just make yourself at home. And if you'd like us to untie your hands you only have to say so.

ZÉPO. No, not my hands, I don't want to impose upon you.

MONS. T. No no, my dear chap, no no. I tell you, it's no trouble at all.

ZÉPO. Right . . . Well then, untie my hands too. But only for lunch, eh? I don't want you think that you give me an inch and I take an ell.[1]

MONS. T. Untie his hands, son.

MME. T. Well, since our distinguished prisoner is so charming, we're going to have a marvelous day in the country.

ZÉPO. Don't call me your distinguished prisoner; just call me your prisoner.

MME. T. Won't that embarrass you?

ZÉPO. No, no, not at all.

MONS. T. Well, I must say you're modest. [*Noise of aeroplanes.*]

ZAPO. Aeroplanes. They're sure to be coming to bomb us. [ZAPO *and* ZÉPO *throw themselves on the sandbags and hide.*] [*To his parents.*] Take cover. The bombs will fall on you. [*The noise of the aeroplanes overpowers all the other noises. Bombs immediately start to fall. Shells explode very near the stage but not on it. A deafening noise.* ZAPO *and* ZÉPO *are cowering down between the sandbags.* M. TÉPAN *goes on talking calmly to his wife, and she answers in the same unruffled way. We can't hear what they are saying because of the bombing.* MME. TÉPAN *goes over to one of the baskets and takes an umbrella out of it. She opens it.* M. *and* MME. TÉPAN *shelter under it as if it were raining. They are standing up. They shift rhythmically from one foot to the other and talk about their personal affairs. The*

---

[1] *ell:* A unit of measure equal to 45 inches.

bombing continues. Finally the aeroplanes go away. Silence. M. Tépan *stretches an arm outside the umbrella to make sure that nothing more is falling from the heavens.*]

Mons. T. [*to his wife*]. You can shut your umbrella. [Mme. Tépan *does so. They both go over to their son and tap him lightly on the behind with the umbrella.*] Come on, out you come. The bombing's over. [Zapo *and* Zépo *come out of their hiding place.*]

Zapo. Didn't you get hit?

Mons. T. What d'you think could happen to your father? [*Proudly.*] Little bombs like that! Don't make me laugh! [*Enter, left, two Red Cross Soldiers. They are carrying a stretcher.*]

1st Stretcher Bearer. Any dead here?

Zapo. No, no one around these parts.

1st Stretcher Bearer. Are you sure you've looked properly?

Zapo. Sure.

1st Stretcher Bearer. And there isn't a single person dead?

Zapo. I've already told you there isn't.

1st Stretcher Bearer. No one wounded, even?

Zapo. Not even that.

2nd Stretcher Bearer [*to the* 1st S. B.]. Well, now we're in a mess! [*To* Zapo *persuasively.*] Just look again, search everywhere, and see if you can't find us a stiff.

1st Stretcher Bearer. Don't keep on about it, they've told you quite clearly there aren't any.

2nd Stretcher Bearer. What a lousy trick!

Zapo. I'm terribly sorry. I promise you I didn't do it on purpose.

2nd Stretcher Bearer. That's what they all say. That no one's dead and that they didn't do it on purpose.

1st Stretcher Bearer. Oh, let the chap alone!

Mons. T. [*obligingly*]. We should be only too pleased to help you. At your service.

2nd Stretcher Bearer. Well, really, if things go on like this I don't know what the Captain will say to us.

Mons. T. But what's it all about?

2nd Stretcher Bearer. Quite simply that the others' wrists are aching with carting so many corpses and wounded men about, and that we haven't found any yet. And it's not because we haven't looked!

Mons. T. Well, yes, that really is annoying. [*To* Zapo.] Are you quite sure no one's dead?

Zapo. Obviously, Papa.

Mons. T. Have you looked under all the sandbags?

Zapo. Yes, Papa.

Mons. T. [*angrily*]. Well then, you might as well say straight out that you don't want to lift a finger to help these gentlemen, when they're so nice, too!

1st Stretcher Bearer. Don't be angry with him. Let him be. We must just hope we'll have more luck in another trench and that all the lot'll be dead.

MONS. T.   I should be delighted.

MME. T.   Me too. There's nothing I like more than people who put their hearts into their work.

MONS. T.   [*indignantly, addressing his remarks to the wings*].   Then is no one going to do anything for these gentlemen?

ZAPO.   If it only rested with me, it'd already be done.

ZÉPO.   I can say the same.

MONS. T.   But look here, is neither of you even wounded?

ZAPO [*ashamed*].   No, not me.

MONS. T.   [*to* ZÉPO].   What about you?

ZÉPO [*ashamed*].   Me neither. I never have any luck.

MME. T.   [*pleased*].   Now I remember! This morning, when I was peeling the onions, I cut my finger. Will that do you?

MONS. T.   Of course it will!   [*Enthusiastically.*]   They'll take you off at once!

1ST STRETCHER BEARER.   No, that won't work. With ladies it doesn't work.

MONS. T.   We're no further advanced, then.

1ST STRETCHER BEARER.   Never mind.

2ND STRETCHER BEARER.   We may be able to make up for it in the other trenches.   [*They start to go off.*]

MONS. T.   Don't worry! If we find a dead man we'll keep him for you! No fear of us giving him to anyone else!

2ND STRETCHER BEARER.   Thank you very much, sir.

MONS. T.   Quite all right, old chap, think nothing of it.   [*The two stretcher bearers say goodbye. All four answer them. The stretcher bearers go out.*]

MME. T.   That's what's so pleasant about spending a Sunday in the country. You always meet such nice people.

MONS. T.   [*pause*].   But why are you enemies?

MME. T.   Your father is the only one who's capable of thinking such ideas; don't forget he's a former student of the Ecole Normale, *and* a philatelist.[2]

ZÉPO.   I don't know, I'm not very well educated.

MME. T.   Was it by birth, or did you become enemies afterwards?

ZÉPO.   I don't know, I don't know anything about it.

MONS. T.   Well then, how did you come to be in the war?

ZÉPO.   One day, at home, I was just mending my mother's iron, a man came and asked me: 'Are you Zépo?' 'Yes.' 'Right, you must come to the war.' And so I asked him: 'But what war?' and he said: 'Don't you read the papers then? You're just a peasant!' I told him I did read the papers but not the war bits. . . .

ZAPO.   Just how it was with me—exactly how it was with me.

MONS. T.   Yes, they came to fetch you too.

MME. T.   No, it wasn't quite the same; that day you weren't mending an iron, you were mending the car.

MONS. T.   I was talking about the rest of it.   [*To* ZÉPO.]   Go on, what happened then?

---

[2] *Ecole Normale . . . philatelist:* Student of the Teacher's College and a stamp collector.

ZÉPO. Then I told him I had a fiancée and that if I didn't take her to the pictures on Sundays she wouldn't like it. He said that wasn't the least bit important.

ZAPO. Just how it was with me—exactly how it was with me.

ZÉPO. And then my father came down, and he said I couldn't go to the war because I didn't have a horse.

ZAPO. Just what my father said.

ZÉPO. The man said you didn't need a horse any more, and I asked him if I could take my fiancée with me. He said no. Then I asked whether I could take my aunt with me so that she could make me one of her custards on Thursdays; I'm very fond of them.

MME. T. [*realizing that she'd forgotten it*]. Oh! The custard!

ZÉPO. He said no again.

ZAPO. Same as with me.

ZÉPO. And ever since then I've been alone in the trench nearly all the time.

MME. T. I think you and your distinguished prisoner might play together this afternoon, as you're as close to each other and so bored.

ZAPO. Oh no, Mother, I'm too afraid, he's an enemy.

MONS. T. Now now, you mustn't be afraid.

ZAPO. If you only knew what the General was saying about the enemy!

MME. T. What did he say?

ZAPO. He said the enemy are very nasty people. When they take prisoners they put little stones in their shoes so that it hurts them to walk.

MME. T. How awful! What barbarians!

MONS. T. [*indignantly, to* ZÉPO]. And aren't you ashamed to belong to an army of criminals?

ZÉPO. I haven't done anything. I don't do anybody any harm.

MME. T. He was trying to take us in, pretending to be such a little saint!

MONS. T. We oughtn't to have untied him. You never know, we only need to turn our backs and he'll be putting a stone in our shoes.

ZÉPO. Don't be so nasty to me.

MONS. T. What'd you think we *should* be, then? I'm indignant. I know what I'll do. I'll go and find the Captain and ask him to let me fight in the war.

ZAPO. He won't let you, you're too old.

MONS. T. Then I'll buy myself a horse and a sword and come and fight on my own account.

MME. T. Bravo! If I were a man I'd do the same.

ZÉPO. Don't be like that with me, Madame. Anyway I'll tell you something—our General told us the same thing about you.

MME. T. How could he dare tell such a lie!

ZAPO. No—but the same thing really?

ZÉPO. Yes, the same thing.

MONS. T. Perhaps it was the same man who talked to you both?

MME. T. Well if it was the same man he might at least have said something different. That's a fine thing—saying the same thing to everyone!

MONS. T. [*to* ZÉPO *in a different tone of voice*]. Another little drink?

MME. T. I hope you liked our lunch?

MONS. T. In any case, it was better than last Sunday.

ZÉPO. What happened?

MONS. T. Well, we went to the country and we put the food on the rug. While we'd got our backs turned a cow ate up all our lunch, and the napkins as well.

ZÉPO. What a greedy cow!

MONS. T. Yes, but afterwards, to get our own back, we ate the cow. [*They laugh.*]

ZAPO [*to* ZÉPO]. They couldn't have been very hungry after that!

MONS. T. Cheers! [*They all drink.*]

MME. T. [*to* ZÉPO]. And what do you do to amuse yourself in the trench?

ZÉPO. I spend my time making flowers out of rags, to amuse myself. I get terribly bored.

MME. T. And what do you do with the flowers?

ZÉPO. At the beginning I used to send them to my fiancée, but one day she told me that the greenhouse and the cellar were already full of them and that she didn't know what to do with them any more, and she asked me, if I didn't mind, to send her something else.

MME. T. And what did you do?

ZÉPO. I go on making rag flowers to pass the time.

MME. T. Do you throw them away afterwards, then?

ZÉPO. No, I've found a way to use them now. I give one flower for each pal who dies. That way I know that even if I make an awful lot there'll never be enough.

MONS. T. That's a good solution you've hit on.

ZÉPO [*shyly*]. Yes.

ZAPO. Well, what I do is knit, so as not to get bored.

MME. T. But tell me, are all the soldiers as bored as you?

ZÉPO. It all depends on what they do to amuse themselves.

ZAPO. It's the same on our side.

MONS. T. Then let's stop the war.

ZÉPO. How?

MONS. T. It's very simple. [*To* ZAPO.] You just tell your pals that the enemy soldiers don't want to fight a war, and you [*to* ZÉPO] say the same to your comrades. And then everyone goes home.

ZAPO. Marvellous!

MME. T. And then you'll be able to finish mending the iron.

ZAPO. How is it that no one thought of such a good idea before?

MME. T. Your father is the only one who's capable of thinking such ideas; don't forget he's a former student of the Ecole Normale, *and* a philatelist.

ZÉPO. But what will the sergeant-majors and corporals do?

MONS. T. We'll give them some guitars and castanets to keep them quiet!

ZÉPO. Very good idea.

MONS. T. You see how easy it is. Everything's fixed.

ZÉPO. We shall have a tremendous success.

ZAPO. My pals will be terribly pleased.

MME. T. What d'you say to putting on the pasodoble we were playing just now, to celebrate?

ZÉPO. Perfect.

ZAPO. Yes, put the record on, Mother. [MME. TÉPAN *puts a record on. She turns the handle. She waits. Nothing can be heard.*]

MONS. T. I can't hear a thing.

MME. T. Oh, how silly of me! Instead of putting a record on I put on a beret. [*She puts the record on. A gay pasodoble is heard.* ZAPO *dances with* ZÉPO *and* MME. TÉPAN *with her husband. They are all very gay. The field telephone rings. None of the four hears it. They go on dancing busily. The telephone rings again. The dance continues.*

The battle starts up again with a terrific din of bombs, shots and bursts of machine-gun fire. None of the four has seen anything and they go on dancing merrily. A burst of machine-gun fire mows them all down. They fall to the ground, stone dead. A shot must have grazed the gramophone; the record keeps repeating the same thing, like a scratched record. The music of the scratched record can be heard till the end of the play. The two STRETCHER BEARERS *enter left. They are carrying the empty stretcher.*]

SUDDEN CURTAIN

Journal Entry

React to the idea that war may be seen as a private game dramatizing individual conflicts and a public game involving warfare among nations.

Textual Considerations

1. The sense of the absurdity of life in *Picnic on the Battlefield* is usually ascribed to the characters' inability to control their own lives. To examine how Arrabal communicates his view of the absurd to the audience, make a list of the contradictions, paradoxes, and other devices that dominate his characters' use of language.

2. What role does Zépo play in the dramatic development of *Picnic on the Battlefield*? Analyze the degree to which his presence advances or increases the dramatic action. Then consider Zépo's relationship to Zapo, and explain how these characters double and mirror each other.

3. To what extent do you agree with the statement that *Picnic on the Battlefield* portrays war as a private, social, and political game devoid of any moral purpose? Quote from the text to support your point of view.

Cultural Contexts

1. Madame Tépan's defense of polite social manners at the battlefield illustrates one way in which Arrabal juxtaposes the activities that belong to the world of peace with those of the battlefield. Make a list of other events that also indicate Arrabal's point of view on war.

2. Consider your attitude toward war. Cite some examples of prowar or antiwar ideology depicted in *Picnic on the Battlefield*. Don't overlook the cultural conventions (the virtues of heroism, patriotism, and the war myths) and the different sensibilities that characters like Monsieur and Madame Tépan, Zapo, Zépo, and government officials exhibit regarding war.

Amiri Baraka (LeRoi Jones)

Dutchman

CHARACTERS

CLAY, *twenty-year-old Negro*
LULA, *thirty-year-old white woman*
Riders of Coach, *white and black*
Young Negro
Conductor

In the flying underbelly of the city. Steaming hot, and summer on top, outside. Underground. The subway heaped in modern myth.

Opening scene is a man sitting in a subway seat, holding a magazine but looking vacantly just above its wilting pages. Occasionally he looks blankly toward the window on his right. Dim lights and darkness whistling by against the glass. (Or paste the lights, as admitted props, right on the subway windows. Have them move, even dim and flicker. But give the sense of speed. Also stations, whether the train is stopped or the glitter and activity of these stations merely flash by the windows.)

The man is sitting alone. That is, only his seat is visible, though the rest of the car is outfitted as a complete subway car. But only his seat is shown. There might be, for a time, as the play begins, a loud scream of the actual train. And it can recur throughout the play, or continue on a lower key once the dialogue starts.

The train slows after a time, pulling to a brief stop at one of the stations. The man looks idly up, until he sees a woman's face staring at him through the windows; when it realizes that the man has noticed the face, it begins very premeditatedly to smile. The man smiles too, for a moment, without a trace of self-consciousness. Almost an instinctive though undesirable response. Then a kind of awkwardness or embarrassment sets in, and the man makes to look away, is further embarrassed, so he brings back his eyes to where the face was, but by now the train is moving again, and the face would seem to be left behind by the way the man turns his head to look back through the other windows at the slowly fading platform. He smiles then; more comfortably confident, hoping perhaps that his memory of this brief encounter will be pleasant. And then he is idle again.

SCENE I

Train roars. Lights flash outside the windows.

   LULA *enters from the rear of the car in bright, skimpy summer clothes and sandals. She carries a net bag full of paper books, fruit, and other anonymous articles. She is wearing sunglasses, which she pushes up on her forehead from time to time.* LULA *is a tall, slender, beautiful woman with long red hair hanging straight down her back, wearing only loud lipstick in somebody's good taste. She is eating an apple, very daintily. Coming down the car toward* CLAY.

   She stops beside CLAY'S *seat and hangs languidly from the strap, still managing to eat the apple. It is apparent that she is going to sit in the seat next to* CLAY *and that she is only waiting for him to notice her before she sits.*

   CLAY *sits as before, looking just beyond his magazine, now and again pulling the magazine slowly back and forth in front of his face in a hopeless effort to fan himself. Then he sees the woman hanging there beside him and he looks up into her face, smiling quizzically.*

LULA. Hello.
CLAY. Uh, hi're you?
LULA. I'm going to sit down. . . . O.K.?
CLAY. Sure.
LULA.

   [*Swings down onto the seat, pushing her legs straight out as if she is very weary*]

   Oooof! Too much weight.
CLAY. Ha, doesn't look like much to me.

   [*Leaning back against the window, a little surprised and maybe stiff*]

LULA. It's so anyway.

   [*And she moves her toes in the sandals, then pulls her right leg up on the left knee, better to inspect the bottoms of the sandals and the back of her heel. She appears for a second not to notice that* CLAY *is sitting next to her or that she has spoken to him just a second before.* CLAY *looks at the magazine, then out the black window. As he does this, she turns very quickly toward him*]

Weren't you staring at me through the window?

CLAY.

[*Wheeling around and very much stiffened*]

What?

LULA. Weren't you staring at me through the window? At the last stop?

CLAY. Staring at you? What do you mean?

LULA. Don't you know what staring means?

CLAY. I saw you through the window . . . if that's what it means. I don't know if I was staring. Seems to me you were staring through the window at me.

LULA. I was. But only after I'd turned around and saw you staring through that window down in the vicinity of my ass and legs.

CLAY. Really?

LULA. Really. I guess you were just taking those idle pot-shots. Nothing else to do. Run your mind over people's flesh.

CLAY. Oh boy. Wow, now I admit I was looking in your direction. But the rest of that weight is yours.

LULA. I suppose.

CLAY. Staring through train windows is weird business. Much weirder than staring very sedately at abstract asses.

LULA. That's why I came looking through the window . . . so you'd have more than that to go on. I even smiled at you.

CLAY. That's right.

LULA. I even got into this train, going some other way than mine. Walked down the aisle . . . searching you out.

CLAY. Really? That's pretty funny.

LULA. That's pretty funny. . . . God, you're dull.

CLAY. Well, I'm sorry, lady, but I really wasn't prepared for party talk.

LULA. No, you're not. What are you prepared for?

[*Wrapping the apple core in a Kleenex and dropping it on the floor*]

CLAY.

[*Takes her conversation as pure sex talk. He turns to confront her squarely with this idea*]

I'm prepared for anything. How about you?

LULA.

[*Laughing loudly and cutting it off abruptly*]

What do you think you're doing?

CLAY. What?

LULA. You think I want to pick you up, get you to take me somewhere and screw me, huh?

CLAY. Is that the way I look?

LULA. You look like you been trying to grow a beard. That's exactly what you look like. You look like you live in New Jersey with your parents and are trying to grow a beard. That's what. You look like you've been reading Chinese poetry and drinking lukewarm sugarless tea.

> [*Laughs, uncrossing and recrossing her legs*]

You look like death eating a soda cracker.

CLAY.

> [*Cocking his head from one side to the other, embarrassed and trying to make some comeback, but also intrigued by what the woman is saying . . . even the sharp city coarseness of her voice, which is still a kind of gentle sidewalk throb*]

Really? I look like all that?

LULA. Not all of it.

> [*She feints a seriousness to cover an actual somber tone*]

I lie a lot.

> [*Smiling*]

It helps me control the world.

CLAY.

> [*Relieved and laughing louder than the humor*]

Yeah, I bet.

LULA. But it's true, most of it, right? Jersey? Your bumpy neck?

CLAY. How'd you know all that? Huh? Really, I mean about Jersey . . . and even the beard. I met you before? You know Warren Enright?

LULA. You tried to make it with your sister when you were ten.

> [CLAY *leans back hard against the back of the seat, his eyes opening now, still trying to look amused*]

But I succeeded a few weeks ago.

> [*She starts to laugh again*]

CLAY. What're you talking about? Warren tell you that? You're a friend of Georgia's?

LULA. I told you I lie. I don't know your sister. I don't know Warren Enright.

CLAY. You mean you're just picking these things out of the air?

LULA. Is Warren Enright a tall skinny black black boy with a phony English accent?

CLAY. I figured you knew him.

LULA. But I don't. I just figured you would know somebody like that.

> [*Laughs*]

CLAY. Yeah, yeah.

LULA. You're probably on your way to his house now.
CLAY. That's right.
LULA.

> [*Putting her hand on* CLAY'S *closest knee, drawing it from the knee up to the thigh's hinge, then removing it, watching his face very closely, and continuing to laugh, perhaps more gently than before*]

Dull, dull, dull. I bet you think I'm exciting.
CLAY. You're O.K.
LULA. Am I exciting you now?
CLAY. Right. That's not what's supposed to happen?
LULA. How do I know?

> [*She returns her hand, without moving it, then takes it away and plunges it in her bag to draw out an apple*]

You want this?
CLAY. Sure.
LULA.

> [*She gets one out of the bag for herself*]

Eating apples together is always the first step. Or walking up uninhabited Seventh Avenue in the twenties on weekends.

> [*Bites and giggles, glancing at* CLAY *and speaking in loose sing-song*]

Can get you involved . . . boy! Get us involved. Um-huh.

> [*Mock seriousness*]

Would you like to get involved with me, Mister Man?
CLAY.

> [*Trying to be as flippant as* LULA, *whacking happily at the apple*]

Sure. Why not? A beautiful woman like you. Huh, I'd be a fool not to.
LULA. And I bet you're sure you know what you're talking about.

> [*Taking him a little roughly by the wrist, so he cannot eat the apple, then shaking the wrist*]

I bet you're sure of almost everything anybody ever asked you about . . . right?

> [*Shakes his wrist harder*]

Right?
CLAY. Yeah, right . . . Wow, you're pretty strong, you know? Whatta you, a lady wrestler or something?
LULA. What's wrong with lady wrestlers? And don't answer because you never knew any. Huh.

[*Cynically*]

That's for sure. They don't have any lady wrestlers in that part of Jersey. That's for sure.

CLAY. Hey, you still haven't told me how you know so much about me.

LULA. I told you I didn't know anything about *you* . . . you're a well-known type.

CLAY. Really?

LULA. Or at least I know the type very well. And your skinny English friend too.

CLAY. Anonymously?

LULA.

[*Settles back in seat, single-mindedly finishing her apple and humming snatches of rhythm and blues song*]

What?

CLAY. Without knowing us specifically?

LULA. Oh boy.

[*Looking quickly at* CLAY]

What a face. You know, you could be a handsome man.

CLAY. I can't argue with you.

LULA.

[*Vague, off-center response*]

What?

CLAY.

[*Raising his voice, thinking the train noise has drowned part of his sentence*]

I can't argue with you.

LULA. My hair is turning gray. A gray hair for each year and type I've come through.

CLAY. Why do you want to sound so old?

LULA. But it's always gentle when it starts.

[*Attention drifting*]

Hugged against tenements, day or night.

CLAY. What?

LULA.

[*Refocusing*]

Hey, why don't you take me to that party you're going to?

CLAY. You must be a friend of Warren's to know about the party.

LULA. Wouldn't you like to take me to the party?

[*Imitates clinging vine*]

Oh, come on, ask me to your party.

CLAY. Of course I'll ask you to come with me to the party. And I'll bet you're a friend of Warren's.

LULA. Why not be a friend of Warren's? Why not?

[*Taking his arm*]

Have you asked me yet?

CLAY. How can I ask you when I don't know your name?

LULA. Are you talking to my name?

CLAY. What is it, a secret?

LULA. I'm Lena the Hyena.

CLAY. The famous woman poet?

LULA. Poetess! The same!

CLAY. Well, you know so much about me . . . what's my name?

LULA. Morris the Hyena.

CLAY. The famous woman poet?

LULA. The same.

[*Laughing and going into her bag*]

You want another apple?

CLAY. Can't take it, lady. I only have to keep one doctor away a day.

LULA. I bet your name is . . . something like . . . uh, Gerald or Walter. Huh?

CLAY. God, no.

LULA. Lloyd, Norman? One of those hopeless colored names creeping out of New Jersey. Leonard? Gag. . . .

CLAY. Like Warren?

LULA. Definitely. Just exactly like Warren. Or Everett.

CLAY. Gag. . . .

LULA. Well, for sure, it's not Willie.

CLAY. It's Clay.

LULA. Clay? Really? Clay what?

CLAY. Take your pick. Jackson, Johnson, or Williams.

LULA. Oh, really? Good for you. But it's got to be Williams. You're too pretentious to be a Jackson or Johnson.

CLAY. Thass right.

LULA. But Clay's O.K.

CLAY. So's Lena.

LULA. It's Lula.

CLAY. Oh?

LULA. Lula the Hyena.

CLAY. Very good.

LULA.

[*Starts laughing again*]

Now you say to me, "Lula, Lula, why don't you go to this party with me tonight?" It's your turn, and let those be your lines.

CLAY. Lula, why don't you go to this party with me tonight, Huh?

LULA. Say my name twice before you ask, and no huh's.

CLAY. Lula, Lula, why don't you go to this party with me tonight?

LULA. I'd like to go, Clay, but how can you ask me to go when you barely know me?

CLAY. That is strange, isn't it?

LULA. What kind of reaction is that? You're supposed to say, "Aw, come on, we'll get to know each other better at the party."

CLAY. That's pretty corny.

LULA. What are you into anyway?

> [*Looking at him half sullenly but still amused*]

What thing are you playing at, Mister? Mister Clay Williams?

> [*Grabs his thigh, up near the crotch*]

What are *you* thinking about?

CLAY. Watch it now, you're gonna excite me for real.

LULA.

> [*Taking her hand away and throwing her apple core through the window*]

I bet.

> [*She slumps in the seat and is heavily silent*]

CLAY. I thought you knew everything about me? What happened?

> [LULA *looks at him, then looks slowly away, then over where the other aisle would be. Noise of the train. She reaches in her bag and pulls out one of the paper books. She puts it on her leg and thumbs the pages listlessly.* CLAY *cocks his head to see the title of the book. Noise of the train.* LULA *flips pages and her eyes drift. Both remain silent*]

Are you going to the party with me, Lula?

LULA.

> [*Bored and not even looking*]

I don't even know you.

CLAY. You said you know my type.

LULA.

> [*Strangely irritated*]

Don't get smart with me, Buster. I know you like the palm of my hand.

CLAY. The one you eat the apples with?

LULA. Yeh. And the one I open doors late Saturday evening with. That's my door. Up at the top of the stairs. Five flights. Above a lot of Italians and lying Americans. And scrape carrots with. Also . . .

[*Looks at him*]

the same hand I unbutton my dress with, or let my skirt fall down. Same hand. Lover.

CLAY. Are you angry about anything? Did I say something wrong?

LULA. Everything you say is wrong.

[*Mock smile*]

That's what makes you so attractive. Ha. In that funnybook jacket with all the buttons.

[*More animate, taking hold of his jacket*]

What've you got that jacket and tie on in all this heat for? Any why're you wearing a jacket and tie like that? Did your people ever burn witches or start revolutions over the price of tea? Boy, those narrow-shoulder clothes come from a tradition you ought to feel oppressed by. A three-button suit. What right do you have to be wearing a three-button suit and striped tie? Your grandfather was a slave, he didn't go to Harvard.

CLAY. My grandfather was a night watchman.

LULA. And you went to a colored college where everybody thought they were Averell Harriman.

CLAY. All except me.

LULA. And who did you think you were? Who do you think you are now?

CLAY.

[*Laughs as if to make light of the whole trend of the conversation*]

Well, in college I thought I was Baudelaire. But I've slowed down since.

LULA. I bet you never once thought you were a black nigger.

[*Mock serious, then she howls with laughter. CLAY is stunned but after initial reaction, he quickly tries to appreciate the humor. LULA almost shrieks*]

A black Baudelaire.

CLAY. That's right.

LULA. Boy, are you corny. I take back what I said before. Everything you say is not wrong. It's perfect. You should be on television.

CLAY. You act like you're on television already.

LULA. That's because I'm an actress.

CLAY. I thought so.

LULA. Well, you're wrong. I'm no actress. I told you I always lie. I'm nothing, honey, and don't you ever forget it.

[*Lighter*]

Although my mother was a Communist. The only person in my family ever to amount to anything.

CLAY. My mother was a Republican.

LULA. And your father voted for the man rather than the party.

CLAY. Right!

LULA. Yea for him. Yea, yea for him.

CLAY. Yea!

LULA. And yea for America where he is free to vote for the mediocrity of his choice! Yea!

CLAY. Yea!

LULA. And yea for both your parents who even though they differ about so crucial a matter as the body politic still forged a union of love and sacrifice that was destined to flower at the birth of the noble Clay . . . what's your middle name?

CLAY. Clay.

LULA. A union of love and sacrifice that was destined to flower at the birth of the noble Clay Clay Williams. Yea! And most of all yea yea for you, Clay Clay. The Black Baudelaire! Yes!

[*And with knifelike cynicism*]

My Christ. My Christ.

CLAY. Thank you, ma'am.

LULA. May the people accept you as a ghost of the future. And love you, that you might not kill them when you can.

CLAY. What?

LULA. You're a murderer, Clay, and you know it.

[*Her voice darkening with significance*]

You know goddamn well what I mean.

CLAY. I do?

LULA. So we'll pretend the air is light and full of perfume.

CLAY.

[*Sniffing at her blouse*]

It is.

LULA. And we'll pretend the people cannot see you. That is, the citizens. And that you are free of your own history. And I am free of my history. We'll pretend that we are both anonymous beauties smashing along through the city's entrails.

[*She yells as loud as she can*]

GROOVE!

Black

SCENE II

Scene is the same as before, though now there are other seats visible in the car. And throughout the scene other people get on the subway. There are maybe one or two seated in the car as the scene opens, though neither CLAY *nor* LULA *notices them.* CLAY'*s tie is open.* LULA *is hugging his arm.*

CLAY. The party!

LULA. I know it'll be something good. You can come in with me, looking causal and significant. I'll be strange, haughty, and silent, and walk with long slow strides.

CLAY. Right.

LULA. When you get drunk, pat me once, very lovingly on the flanks, and I'll look at you cryptically, licking my lips.

CLAY. It sounds like something we can do.

LULA. You'll go around talking to young men about your mind, and to old men about your plans. If you meet a very close friend who is also with someone like me, we can stand together, sipping our drinks and exchanging codes of lust. The atmosphere will be slithering in love and half-love and very open moral decision.

CLAY. Great. Great.

LULA. And everyone will pretend they don't know your name, and then . . .

[*She pauses heavily*]

later, when they have to, they'll claim a friendship that denies your sterling character.

CLAY.

[*Kissing her neck and fingers*]

And then what?

LULA. Then? Well, then we'll go down the street, late night, eating apples and winding very deliberately toward my house.

CLAY. Deliberately?

LULA. I mean, we'll look in all the shopwindows, and make fun of the queers. Maybe we'll meet a Jewish Buddhist and flatten his conceits over some very pretentious coffee.

CLAY. In honor of whose God?

LULA. Mine.

CLAY. Who is . . . ?

LULA. Me . . . and you?

CLAY. A corporate Godhead.

LULA. Exactly. Exactly.

[*Notices one of the other people entering*]

CLAY. Go on with the chronicle. Then what happens to us?

LULA.

[*A mild depression, but she still makes her description triumphant and increasingly direct*]

To my house, of course.

CLAY. Of course.

LULA. And up the narrow steps of the tenement.

CLAY. You live in a tenement?

LULA. Wouldn't live anywhere else. Reminds me specifically of my novel form of insanity.

CLAY. Up the tenement stairs.

LULA. And with my apple-eating hand I push open the door and lead you, my tender big-eyed prey, into my . . . God, what can I call it . . . into my hovel.

CLAY. Then what happens?

LULA. After the dancing and games, after the long drinks and long walks, the real fun begins.

CLAY. Ah, the real fun.

[*Embarrassed, in spite of himself*]

Which is . . . ?

LULA.

[*Laughs at him*]

Real fun in the dark house. Hah! Real fun in the dark house, high up above the street and the ignorant cowboys. I lead you in, holding your wet hand gently in my hand . . .

CLAY. Which is not wet?

LULA. Which is dry as ashes.

CLAY. And cold?

LULA. Don't think you'll get out of your responsibility that way. It's not cold at all. You Fascist! Into my dark living room. Where we'll sit and talk endlessly, endlessly.

CLAY. About what?

LULA. About what? About your manhood, what do you think? What do you think we've been talking about all this time?

CLAY. Well, I didn't know it was that. That's for sure. Every other thing in the world but that.

[*Notices another person entering, looks quickly, almost involuntarily up and down the car, seeing the other people in the car*]

Hey, I didn't even notice when those people got on.

LULA. Yeah, I know.

CLAY. Man, this subway is slow.

LULA. Yeah, I know.

CLAY. Well, go on. We were talking about my manhood.

LULA. We still are. All the time.

CLAY. We were in your living room.

LULA. My dark living room. Talking endlessly.

CLAY. About my manhood.

LULA. I'll make you a map of it. Just as soon as we get to my house.

CLAY. Well, that's great.

LULA. One of the things we do while we talk. And screw.

CLAY.

[*Trying to make his smile broader and less shaky*]

We finally got there.

LULA. And you'll call my rooms black as a grave. You'll say, "This place is like Juliet's tomb."

CLAY.

[*Laughs*]

I might.

LULA. I know. You've probably said it before.

CLAY. And is that all? The whole grand tour?

LULA. Not all. You'll say to me very close to my face, many, many times, you'll say, even whisper, that you love me.

CLAY. Maybe I will.

LULA. And you'll be lying.

CLAY. I wouldn't lie about something like that.

LULA. Hah. It's the only kind of thing you will lie about. Especially if you think it'll keep me alive.

CLAY. Keep you alive? I don't understand.

LULA.

[*Bursting out laughing, but too shrilly*]

Don't understand? Well, don't look at me. It's the path I take, that's all. Where both feet take me when I set them down. One in front of the other.

CLAY. Morbid. Morbid. You sure you're not an actress? All that self-aggrandizement.

LULA. Well, I told you I wasn't an actress . . . but I also told you I lie all the time. Draw your own conclusions.

CLAY. Morbid. Morbid. You sure you're not an actress? All scribed? There's no more?

LULA. I've told you all I know. Or almost all.

CLAY. There's no funny parts?

LULA. I thought it was all funny.

CLAY. But you mean peculiar, not ha-ha.

LULA. You don't know what I mean.

CLAY. Well, tell me the almost part then. You said almost all. What else? I want the whole story.

LULA.

> [*Searching aimlessly through her bag. She begins to talk breathlessly, with a light and silly tone*]

All stories are whole stories. All of 'em. Our whole story . . . nothing but change. How could things go on like that forever? Huh?

> [*Slaps him on the shoulder, begins finding things in her bag, taking them out and throwing them over her shoulder into the aisle*]

Except I do go on as I do. Apples and long walks with deathless intelligent lovers. But you mix it up. Look out the window, all the time. Turning pages. Change change change. Till, shit, I don't know you. Wouldn't, for that matter. You're too serious. I bet you're even too serious to be psychoanalyzed. Like all those Jewish poets from Yonkers, who leave their mothers looking for other mothers, or others' mothers, on whose baggy tits they lay their fumbling heads. Their poems are always funny, and all about sex.

CLAY. They sound great. Like movies.

LULA. But you change.

> [*Blankly*]

And things work on you till you hate them.

> [*More people come into the train. They come closer to the couple, some of them not sitting, but swinging drearily on the straps, staring at the two with uncertain interest*]

CLAY. Wow. All these people, so suddenly. They must all come from the same place.

LULA. Right. That they do.

CLAY. Oh? You know about them too?

LULA. Oh yeah. About them more than I know about you. Do they frighten you?

CLAY. Frighten me? Why should they frighten me?

LULA. 'Cause you're an escaped nigger.

CLAY. Yeah?

LULA. 'Cause you crawled through the wire and made tracks to my side.

CLAY. Wire?

LULA. Don't they have wire around plantations?

CLAY. You must be Jewish. All you can think about is wire. Plantations didn't have any wire. Plantations were big open whitewashed places like heaven, and everybody on 'em was grooved to be there. Just strummin' and hummin' all day.

LULA. Yes, yes.

CLAY. And that's how the blues was born.

LULA. Yes, yes. And that's how the blues was born.

[*Begins to make up a song that becomes quickly hysterical. As she sings she rises from her seat, still throwing things out of her bag into the aisle, beginning a rhythmical shudder and twistlike wiggle, which she continues up and down the aisle, bumping into many of the standing people and tripping over the feet of those sitting. Each time she runs into a person she lets out a very vicious piece of profanity, wiggling and stepping all the time*]

And that's how the blues was born. Yes. Yes. Son of a bitch, get out of the way. Yes. Quack. Yes. Yes. And that's how the blues was born. Ten little niggers sitting on a limb, but none of them ever looked like him.

[*Points to* CLAY, *returns toward the seat, with her hands extended for him to rise and dance with her*]

And that's how blues was born. Yes. Come on, Clay. Let's do the nasty. Rub bellies. Rub bellies.

CLAY.

[*Waves his hands to refuse. He is embarrassed, but determined to get a kick out of the proceedings*]

Hey, what was in those apples? Mirror, mirror on the wall, who's the fairest one of all? Snow White, baby, and don't you forget it.

LULA.

[*Grabbing for his hands, which he draws away*]

Come on, Clay. Let's rub bellies on the train. The nasty. The nasty. Do the gritty grind, like your ol' rag-head mammy. Grind till you lose your mind. Shake it, shake it, shake it, shake it! OOOOweeee! Come on, Clay. Let's do the choo-choo train shuffle, the navel scratcher.

CLAY. Hey, you coming on like the lady who smoked up her grass skirt.

LULA.

[*Becoming annoyed that he will not dance, and becoming more animated as if to embarrass him still further*]

Come on, Clay . . . let's do the thing. Uhh! Uhh! Clay! Clay! You middle-class black bastard. Forget your social-working mother for a few seconds and let's knock stomachs. Clay, you liver-lipped white man. You would-be Christian. You ain't no nigger, you're just a dirty white man. Get up, Clay. Dance with me, Clay.

CLAY. Lula! Sit down, now. Be cool.

LULA.

[*Mocking him, in wild dance*]

Be cool. Be cool. That's all you know . . . shaking that wildroot cream-oil on your knotty head, jackets buttoning up to your chin, so full of white man's words. Christ. God. Get up and scream at these people. Like scream meaning-less shit in these hopeless faces.

> [*She screams at people in train, still dancing*]

Red trains cough Jewish underwear for keeps! Expanding smells of silence. Gravy snot whistling like sea birds. Clay. Clay, you got to break out. Don't sit there dying the way they want you to die. Get up.

CLAY. Oh, sit the fuck down.

> [*He moves to restrain her*]

Sit down, goddamn it.

LULA.

> [*Twisting out of his reach*]

Screw yourself, Uncle Tom. Thomas Woolly-head.

> [*Begins to dance a kind of jig, mocking* CLAY *with loud forced humor*]

There is Uncle Tom . . . I mean, Uncle Thomas Woolly-Head. With old white matted mane. He hobbles on his wooden cane. Old Tom. Old Tom. Let the white man hump his ol' mama, and he jes' shuffle off in the woods and hide his gentle gray head. Ol' Thomas Woolly-Head.

> [*Some of the other riders are laughing now. A drunk gets up and joins* LULA *in her dance, singing, as best he can, her "song."* CLAY *gets up out of his seat and visibly scans the faces of the other riders*]

CLAY. Lula! Lula!

> [*She is dancing and turning, still shouting as loud as she can. The drunk too is shouting, and waving his hands wildly*]

Lula . . . you dumb bitch. Why don't you stop it?

> [*He rushes half stumbling from his seat, and grabs one of her flailing arms*]

LULA. Let me go! You black son of a bitch.

> [*She struggles against him*]

Let me go! Help!

> [CLAY *is dragging her towards her seat, and the drunk seeks to interfere. He grabs* CLAY *around the shoulders and begins wrestling with him.* CLAY *clubs the drunk to the floor without releasing* LULA, *who is still screaming.* CLAY *finally gets her to the seat and throws her into it*]

CLAY. Now you shut the hell up.

[*Grabbing her shoulders*]

Just shut up. You don't know what you're talking about. You don't know anything. So just keep your stupid mouth closed.

LULA. You're afraid of white people. And your father was. Uncle Tom Big Lip!

CLAY.

[*Slaps her as hard as he can, across the mouth.* LULA's *head bangs against the back of the seat. When she raises it again,* CLAY *slaps her again*]

Now shut up and let me talk.

[*He turns toward the other riders, some of whom are sitting on the edge of their seats. The drunk is on one knee, rubbing his head, and singing softly the same song. He shuts up too when he sees* CLAY *watching him. The others go back to newspapers or stare out the windows*]

Shit, you don't have any sense, Lula, nor feelings either. I could murder you now. Such a tiny ugly throat. I could squeeze it flat, and watch you turn blue, on a humble. For dull kicks. And all these weak-faced ofays squatting around here, staring over their papers at me. Murder them too. Even if they expected it. That man there . . .

[*Points to well-dressed man*]

I could rip that *Times* right out of his hand, as skinny and middle-classed as I am, I could rip that paper out of his hand and just as easily rip out his throat. It takes no great effort. For what? To kill you soft idiots? You don't understand anything but luxury.

LULA. You fool!

CLAY.

[*Pushing her against the seat*]

I'm not telling you again, Tallulah Bankhead! Luxury. In your face and your fingers. You telling me what I ought to do.

[*Sudden scream frightening the whole coach*]

Well, don't! Don't you tell me anything! If I'm a middle-class fake white man . . . let me be. And let me be in the way I want.

[*Through his teeth*]

I'll rip your lousy breasts off! Let me be who I feel like being. Uncle Tom. Thomas. Whoever. It's none of your business. You don't know anything except what's there for you to see. An act. Lies. Device. Not the pure heart, the pumping black heart. You don't ever know that. And I sit here, in this buttoned-up suit, to keep myself from cutting all your throats. I mean wantonly. You great liberated whore! You fuck some black man, and right away you're an expert on black people. What a lotta shit that is. The only thing you know is that you come if he bangs you hard enough. And that's all. The belly rub? You wanted to do the belly rub? Shit, you don't even know how. You don't know how. That ol' dipty-dip shit you do, rolling your ass like an elephant. That's not my kind of belly rub. Belly rub is not Queens. Belly rub is dark places, with big hats and overcoats held up with one arm. Belly rub hates you. Old bald-headed four-eyed ofays popping their fingers . . . and don't know yet what they're doing. They say, "I love Bessie Smith." And don't even understand that Bessie Smith is saying, "Kiss my ass, kiss my black unruly ass." Before love, suffering, desire, anything you can explain, she's saying, and very plainly, "Kiss my black ass." And if you don't know that, it's you that's doing the kissing.

Charlie Parker? Charlie Parker. All the hip white boys scream for Bird. And Bird saying, "Up your ass, feeble-minded ofay! Up your ass." And they sit there talking about the tortured genius of Charlie Parker. Bird would've played not a note of music if he just walked up to East Sixty-seventh Street and killed the first ten white people he saw. Not a note! And I'm the great would-be poet. Yes. That's right! Poet. Some kind of bastard literature . . . all it needs is a simple knife thrust. Just let me bleed you, you loud whore, and one poem vanished. A whole people of neurotics, struggling to keep from being sane. And the only thing that would cure the neurosis would be your murder. Simple as that. I mean if I murdered you, then other white people would begin to understand me. You understand? No. I guess not. If Bessie Smith had killed some white people she wouldn't have needed that music. She could have talked very straight and plain about the world. No metaphors. No grunts. No wiggles in the dark of her soul. Just straight two and two are four. Money. Power. Luxury. Like that. All of them. Crazy niggers turning their backs on sanity. When all it needs is that simple act. Murder. Just murder! Would make us all sane.

[*Suddenly weary*]

Ahhh. Shit. But who needs it? I'd rather be a fool. Insane. Safe with my words, and no deaths, and clean, hard thoughts, urging me to new conquests. My people's madness. Hah! That's a laugh. My people. They don't need me to claim them. They got legs and arms of their own. Personal insanities. Mirrors. They don't need all those words. They don't need any defense. But listen, though, one more thing. And you tell this to your father, who's probably the kind of man who needs to know at once. So he can plan ahead. Tell him not to preach so much rationalism and cold logic to these niggers. Let them alone. Let them sing curses at you in code and see your filth as simple lack of style. Don't make the mistake, through some irresponsible surge of Christian charity, of talking too much about the advantages of Western rationalism, or the great intellectual legacy of the white man, or maybe they'll begin to listen. And then, maybe one day, you'll find they actually do understand exactly what you are talking about, all these fantasy people. All these blues people. And on that day, as sure as shit, when you really believe you can "accept" them into your fold, as half-white trusties late of the subject peoples. With no more blues, except the very old ones, and not a watermelon in sight, the great missionary heart will have triumphed, and all of those ex-coons will be stand-up Western men, with eyes for clean hard useful lives, sober, pious and sane, and they'll murder you. They'll murder you, and have very rational explanations. Very much like your own. They'll cut your throats, and drag you out to the edge of your cities so the flesh can fall away from your bones, in sanitary isolation.

LULA.

> [*Her voice takes on a different, more businesslike quality*]

I've heard enough.

CLAY.

> [*Reaching for his books*]

I bet you have. I guess I better collect my stuff and get off this train. Looks like we won't be acting out that little pageant you outlined before.

LULA.   No. We won't. You're right about that, at least.

> [*She turns to look quickly around the rest of the car*]

All right!

> [*The others respond*]

CLAY.

> [*Bending across the girl to retrieve his belongings*]

Sorry, baby, I don't think we could make it.

> [*As he is bending over her, the girl brings up a small knife and plunges it into* CLAY'S *chest. Twice. He slumps across her knees, his mouth working stupidly*]

LULA.   Sorry is right.

> [*Turning to the others in the car who have already gotten up from their seats*]

Sorry is the rightest thing you've said. Get this man off me! Hurry, now!

> [*The others come and drag* CLAY'S *body down the aisle*]

Open the door and throw his body out.

> [*They throw him off*]

And all of you get off at the next stop.

[LULA *busies herself straightening her things. Getting everything in order. She takes out a notebook and makes a quick scribbling note. Drops it in her bag. The train apparently stops and all the others get off, leaving her alone in the coach.*

Very soon a young Negro of about twenty comes into the coach, with a couple of books under his arms. He sits a few seats in back of LULA. *When he is seated she turns and gives him a long slow look. He looks up from his book and drops the book on his lap. Then an old Negro conductor comes into the car, doing a sort of restrained soft shoe, and half mumbling the words of some song. He looks at the young man, briefly, with a quick greeting*]

CONDUCTOR. Hey, brother!
YOUNG MAN. Hey.

[*The conductor continues down the aisle with his little dance and the mumbled song.* LULA *turns to stare at him and follows his movements down the aisle. The conductor tips his hat when he reaches her seat, and continues out the car*]

Curtain

Journal Entry

Speculate on your responses had you been a passenger in the subway at the time of the stabbing.

Textual Considerations

1. Consult a dictionary for various definitions of "Dutchman" and comment on its significance as the play's title.
2. The playwright describes the setting as the "flying underbelly of the city . . . the subway heaped in modern myth." Analyze the functions of setting, and comment on the appropriateness of the playwright's metaphor.
3. To what extent are Clay and Lula representative of their races? Does the playwright present both as victims of a racist society? Explain?

Cultural Contexts

1. Discuss with your group the thematic implications of the play. Consider what the drama suggests about the relation between race and sexuality and between sexuality and violence.

PART ASSIGNMENTS

WRITING TOPICS

1. According to the Russian-American pacifist Emma Goldman, "Organized violence at the top . . . creates individual violence at the bottom." Test the validity of her hypothesis by applying it to any three texts in Part Three.

2. All of the short stories in this part make use of the literary convention of the surprise ending. Review the last paragraph of each story, and write an analysis of the new meanings they introduce or the ironies they reinforce.

3. Analyze the roles and portrayals of gender in three texts of your choice. To what extent do these texts also explore the connection between gender and war?

4. The conflict of Alba and García in "The Hour of Truth" focuses on the debate between the torturer and his prisoner. Examine the terms of this debate by analyzing Alba's act of defiance ("I want to go to the bathroom") in light of García's need to subjugate her through torture. To what extent does Alba's conduct support the claim that human beings are free even when they are born in chains?

5. How is the theme of the mutilated body that is presented in "Disabled" relevant to the experiences of the Vietnam War veterans in the film *Coming Home* or *Born on the Fourth of July*? What gender-related issues are implicit in the film as well as in the text?

6. Apply the notion of the "myth of the enemy" to "The Sniper," "The Man He Killed," and/or *Picnic on the Battlefield*. To what extent does each text reinforce the arbitrary nature of war? How does war also alter the normal order of things?

7. Investigate the dialectic of fantasy and reality in "The Hour of Truth" and/or "Spoils of War." To what extent do the stories succeed in making the protagonists' individual experiences of torture part of the collective consciousness of readers?

8. Several texts explore the relationship between the discourses of speech and silence. To what extent do Yevtushenko and Allende make it possible for you to listen to the "voice of silence"? Write a postscript expressing what you "heard."

9. The Roman poet Lucan stated that the true soldier should be ready not only to die for his country but also to "entomb [his] sword within [his] brother's bowels." Apply his admonition to two texts in Part Three. What does each text suggest about the relation between patriotism and heroism?

10. Apply the following defense of human rights by the Roman Catholic church to the circumstances surrounding Alba's imprisonment: "Whatever violates the integrity of the human person—such as mutilations,

physical or moral tortures and attempts at psychological domination is effectively worthy of censure, for it greatly contradicts the honor of the Creator" (*Gaudium et Spes*, 1965). Then watch the film *Romero*, the account of a Salvadoran archbishop's personal struggles to reconcile the stance of the church with the torture and death of his parishioners. What new meanings can you now apply to the church's defense of human rights?

11. Consider the relationship of gender and violence in "The Hour of Truth," "Spoils of War," and/or "The Curse" or *Dutchman*. What does each story imply about the relationship between sexuality and violence?

12. Traditionally, antiwar dramas portray images of suffering and death caused by war. Debate the degree to which *Lysistrata* may be considered an antiwar drama.

13. Write an essay on the relationship between gender and war in *Lysistrata*. Examine whether male-female relations determine the creation of a prowar and an antiwar sensibility. Consider Lysistrata's position, as well as the point of view of the old men.

RESEARCH TOPICS

1. War songs such as "Lili Marlene," "For Johnny," "When This Bleeding War Is Over," and "Hymn of Hate"—and many others that emphasize either the patriotic view of war or various forms of war protest—became an important part of the tradition of World Wars I and II. Research some lyrics from World Wars I and II, the Vietnam War, and the Persian Gulf War, and write a documented paper analyzing their function as war poetry. Speculate on other functions they may have served.

2. Write a documented paper summarizing the history of women in World Wars I and II, the Vietnam War, and/or the Persian Gulf War. Starting with the domestic view of women as lovers, mothers, and peacemakers, and the image of women as the "stepdaughters" of war—nurses, doctors, ambulance drivers—move to the modern view of women as actively engaged in war.

3. To investigate the relationship between race and war, write a documented paper on the history of African-American soldiers. Examine the contributions they made to American history from the time of the Civil War to the time of the Vietnam War. You may need to rely on testimonials of slaves, abolitionists, and veterans from the two world wars and the Vietnam War. Among other sources, you might check:

McPherson, James M. *The Negro's Civil War: How American Blacks Felt and Acted During the War for the Union.*

Wallace, Terry. *Bloods: An Oral History of the Vietnam War by Black Veterans.*

4. Scholar Arthur A. Cohen comments that

> the stripping of language of its subtlety and moral intention is a procedure which begins in the West long before Hitler and continues after he is gone. It will help us explain a kind of cauterization of conscience by the use of metaphor and euphemism to understand that in official Nazi language the extermination of Jews was precisely that—the disinfectant of lice, the burning of garbage, the incineration of trash, and hence language never had to say exactly what its words commanded: kill, burn, murder that old Jew, that middle-aged Jew, that child Jew.

Test the validity of Cohen's hypothesis by investigating the significance of the following words and phrases used during Hitler's regime: "the Jewish question," "yellow badge," "ghetto," "crematoria," "work camps," and "final solution." Then make a list of recent war terms, such as "friendly fire" and "collateral damage," and discuss their effects on our emotional and moral responses to genocide and war enemies. To what extent does the language of the Persian Gulf War support or contradict Cohen's hypothesis?

PART FOUR

Race and Difference

Fiction

The Test, Angelica Gibbs ◆ *The Loudest Voice*, Grace Paley ◆
I Stand Here Ironing, Tillie Olsen ◆ *The Stolen Party*, Liliana
Heker ◆ *Puertoricanness*, Aurora Levins Morales ◆ *Jasmine*,
Bharati Mukherjee

Poetry

I Hear America Singing, Walt Whitman ◆ *Poet Power*, Denise
Levertov ◆ *The Melting Pot*, Dudley Randall ◆ *Federico's Ghost*,
Martín Espada ◆ *First Day of Work*, Luis Rodriguez ◆ *Poem by a
Yellow Woman*, Sook Lyol Ryu ◆ *Public School No. 18: Paterson,
New Jersey*, Maria Mazziotti Gillan ◆ *Telephone Conversation*,
Wole Soyinka ◆ *On the Subway*, Sharon Olds ◆ *Poem for the
Young White Man Who Asked Me How I, an Intelligent, Well-
Read Person Could Believe in the War Between Races*, Lorna Dee
Cervantes ◆ *My Blackness Is the Beauty of This Land*, Lance Jeffers
◆ *Richard Cory*, Edwin Arlington Robinson ◆ *Latero Story*, Tato
Laviera ◆ *AIDS*, May Sarton ◆ *How to Watch Your Brother Die*,
Michael Lassell

Drama

Othello, The Moor of Venice, William Shakespeare ◆ *Florence*, Alice
Childress ◆ *Los Vendidos*, Luis Valdez ◆ *On Tidy Endings*, Harvey
Fierstein

"**O**urs is the only nation to have a dream and give its name to one—the American Dream," wrote the literary critic Lionel Trilling almost fifty years ago. Although the United States continues to be a nation of immigrants in search of that dream, many groups have felt excluded from the right to equality promised in the Declaration of Independence of 1776. These groups are challenging the ideal of the "melting pot," which was first expressed in Hector St. Jean de Crevecoeur's 1781 statement that "individuals of all nations are melted down in a new race of men" and which has shaped the collective consciousness of North Americans for almost two centuries.

In fact, in a 1991 interview, the Asian-American writer Bharati Mukherjee proposed that the metaphor of a "fusion chamber," in which elements interact but do not melt, has perhaps become a more appropriate metaphor to describe the new, multiracial democracy of the present time and that of the approaching twenty-first century. The African-American novelist Toni Morrison concurs: "We have to acknowledge that the thing we call 'literature' is pluralistic now, just as society ought to be. The melting pot never worked."

Much of the literature in Part Four portrays the irrationality of racism and the politics of exclusion and examines their effects on the marginalized groups that continue to challenge myths of assimilation and justice for all. Walt Whitman's poem "I Hear America Singing" (1867), for instance, celebrates the delight of diversity in what Whitman envisions as a truly democratic America. In a strong epic voice, Whitman communicates to all Americans, regardless of class and race, the idealized vision of democracy engraved in the Declaration of Independence (1776) and the Gettysburg Address (1863). However, in Lance Jeffers's poem "My Blackness Is the Beauty of This Land," written almost 150 years after Whitman's poem, we can see the failure of Whitman's idealistic dream in the images of blackness and whiteness that constitute the racial consciousness of the United States. And Dudley Randall's vivid image of the melting pot as one in which "*Johann* and *Jan* and *Jean* and *Juan,* / *Giovanni* and *Ivan* / step in and then step out again / all freshly christened *John,*" while Sam is repeatedly thrown out because of his "black stain," reinforces two of the myth's most fundamental failures: its inability to accommodate ethnic diversity and difference, and its historical exclusion of African Americans.

To what extent can we say that perceptions of race, ethnicity, and class have also shaped the identities of Chicanos, Asian Americans, Italian Americans, Native Americans, and Latinos, who live on the fringes of both worlds? Does ethnic identity preclude cultural assimilation in the United States? Several texts, including "Latero Story" and "Puertoricanness," record how bilingual and bicultural differences have determined their speakers' identities and contributed to a double consciousness with which they confront their feelings of linguistic, geographical, and emotional displacement. In "Public School No. 18: Paterson, New Jersey," the Italian-American speaker finally learns as an adult to find her own voice and an identity strong enough to confront and challenge the myth of Anglo-Saxon superiority reinforced by the educational institutions she attended.

That personal and social inequities resulting in emotional exclusion and entrapment are not confined to the United States is apparent in the South-African poet Wole Soyinka's "Telephone Conversation," set in London, and in the Argentinian writer Liliana Heker's "The Stolen Party," set in Argentina.

Cultural attitudes toward homosexuals and lesbians have also resulted in social and political exclusion. Some texts included here address the issue of AIDS and attempt to explore new definitions of and meanings for the concept of love. Two poems, "AIDS" and "How to Watch Your Brother Die," focus on the issue of sexual preference and the gay community's capacity for grief, rage, and desire for connection.

As you read these and other texts in this part, consider how factors such as ethnicity, gender, and class have contributed to or detracted from your own position of privilege in U.S. society. As you read Walt Whitman's poem, you might consider formulating a new definition of the American Dream appropriate to the more diverse and complex society of the approaching twenty-first century.

Angelica Gibbs

The Test

On the afternoon Marian took her second driver's test, Mrs. Ericson went with her. "It's probably better to have someone a little older with you," Mrs. Ericson said as Marian slipped into the driver's seat beside her. "Perhaps the last time your Cousin Bill made you nervous, talking too much on the way."

"Yes, Ma'am," Marian said in her soft unaccented voice. "They probably do like it better if a white person shows up with you."

"Oh, I don't think it's *that*," Mrs. Ericson began, and subsided after a glance at the girl's set profile. Marian drove the car slowly through the shady suburban streets. It was one of the first hot days in June, and when they reached the boulevard they found it crowded with cars headed for the beaches.

"Do you want me to drive?" Mrs. Ericson asked. "I'll be glad to if you're feeling jumpy." Marian shook her head. Mrs. Ericson watched her dark, competent hands and wondered for the thousandth time how the house had ever managed to get along without her, or how she had lived through those earlier years when her household had been presided over by a series of slatternly white girls who had considered housework demeaning and the care of children an added insult. "You drive beautifully, Marian," she said. "Now, don't think of the last time. Anybody would slide on a steep hill on a wet day like that."

"It takes four mistakes to flunk you," Marian said. "I don't remember doing all the things the inspector marked down on my blank."

"People say that they only want you to slip them a little something," Mrs. Ericson said doubtfully.

"*No,*" Marian said. "That would only make it worse, Mrs. Ericson, I know."

The car turned right, at a traffic signal, into a side road and slid up to the curl at the rear of a short line of parked cars. The inspectors had not arrived yet.

"You have the papers," Mrs. Ericson asked. Marian took them out of her bag, her learner's permit, the car registration, and her birth certificate. They settled down to the dreary business of waiting.

"It will be marvelous to have someone dependable to drive the children to school every day," Mrs. Ericson said.

Marian looked up from the list of driving requirements she had been studying. "It'll make things simpler at the house, won't it?" she said.

"Oh, Marian," Mrs. Ericson exclaimed, "if I could only pay you half of what you're worth!"

"Now, Mrs. Ericson," Marian said firmly. They looked at each other and smiled with affection.

Two cars with official insignia on their doors stopped across the street. The inspectors leaped out, very brisk and military in their neat uniforms. Marian's hand tightened on the wheel. "There's the one who flunked me last time," she whispered, pointing to a stocky, self-important man who had begun to shout directions at the driver at the head of the line. "Oh, Mrs. Ericson."

"Now, Marian," Mrs. Ericson said. They smiled at each other again, rather weakly.

The inspector who finally reached their car was not the stocky one but a genial middle-aged man who grinned broadly as he thumbed over their papers. Mrs. Ericson started to get out of the car. "Don't you want to come along?" the inspector asked. "Mandy and I don't mind company."

Mrs. Ericson was bewildered for a moment. "No," she said, and stepped to the curb. "I might make Marian self-conscious. She's a fine driver, Inspector."

"Sure thing," the inspector said, winking at Mrs. Ericson. He slid into the seat beside Marian. "Turn right at the corner, Mandy-Lou."

From the curb, Mrs. Ericson watched the car move smoothly up the street.

The inspector made notations in a small black book. "Age?" he inquired presently, as they drove along.

"Twenty-seven."

He looked at Marian out of the corner of his eye. "Old enough to have quite a flock of pickaninnies, eh?"

Marian did not answer.

"Left at this corner," the inspector said, "and park between that truck and the green Buick."

The two cars were very close together, but Marian squeezed in between them without too much maneuvering. "Driven before, Mandy-Lou?" the inspector asked.

"Yes, sir. I had a license for three years in Pennsylvania."

"Why do you want to drive a car?"

"My employer needs me to take her children to and from school."

"Sure you don't really want to sneak out nights to meet some young blood?" the inspector asked. He laughed as Marian shook her head.

"Let's see you take a left at the corner and then turn around in the middle of the next block," the inspector said. He began to whistle "Swanee River." "Make you homesick?" he asked.

Marian put out her hand, swung around neatly in the street, and headed back in the direction from which they had come. "No," she said. "I was born in Scranton, Pennsylvania."

The inspector feigned astonishment. "You-all ain't Southern?" he said. "Well, dog my cats if I didn't think you-all came from down yondah."

"No, sir," Marian said.

"Turn onto Main Street and let's see how you-all does in heavier traffic."

They followed a line of cars along Main Street for several blocks until they came in sight of a concrete bridge which arched high over the railroad tracks.

"Read that sign at the end of the bridge," the inspector said.

"'Proceed with caution. Dangerous in slippery weather,'" Marian said.

"You-all sho can read fine," the inspector exclaimed. "Where d'you learn to do that, Mandy?"

"I got my college degree last year," Marian said. Her voice was not quite steady.

As the car crept up the slope of the bridge the inspector burst out laughing. He laughed so hard he could scarcely give his next direction. "Stop here," he said, wiping his eyes, "then start'er up again. Mandy got her degree, did she? Dog my cats!"

Marian pulled up beside the curb. She put the car in neutral, pulled on the emergency, waited a moment, and then put the car into gear again. Her face was set. As she released the brake her foot slipped off the clutch pedal and the engine stalled.

"Now, Mistress Mandy," the inspector said, "remember your degree."

"*Damn* you!" Marian cried. She started the car with a jerk.

The inspector lost his joviality in an instant. "Return to the starting place, please," he said, and made four very black crosses at random in the squares on Marian's application blank.

Mrs. Ericson was waiting at the curb where they had left her. As Marian stopped the car, the inspector jumped out and brushed past her, his face purple, "What happened?" Mrs. Ericson asked, looking after him with alarm.

Marian stared down at the wheel and her lip trembled.

"Oh, Marian, *again?*" Mrs. Ericson said.

Marian nodded. "In a sort of different way," she said, and slid over to the right hand side of the car.

Journal Entry

Respond to the ramifications of the story's title, "The Test." Consider, for example, the implications of using "The" instead of "A."

Textual Considerations

1. Characterize Marian. What facets of her personality might have appealed to Mrs. Ericson? What portrait of Mrs. Ericson emerges through the language she uses to address Marian?
2. Analyze the forces at play in the examiner's language by listing examples of the comments and questions he addresses to Marian.
3. Characterize the mood of the story. How does it contribute to meaning and purpose?

Cultural Contexts

1. Gibbs's story takes place in the 1940s. To what extent are women like Marian who hold a college degree still disempowered in the 1990s? To what extent do the ethnic stereotypes expressed by the driving inspector still hold today?

2. Examine with your group the degree to which racial inequality is affected by competition. What happens, for example, when different ethnic groups compete for key resources, such as jobs and housing?

Grace Paley

The Loudest Voice

There is a certain place where dumb-waiters[1] boom, doors slam, dishes crash; every window is a mother's mouth bidding the street shut up, go skate somewhere else, come home. My voice is the loudest.

There, my own mother is still as full of breathing as me and the grocer stands up to speak to her. "Mrs. Abramowitz," he says, "people should not be afraid of their children."

"Ah, Mr. Bialik," my mother replies, "if you say to her or her father 'Ssh,' they say, 'In the grave it will be quiet.' "

"From Concy Island to the cemetery," says my papa. "It's the same subway; it's the same fare."

I am right next to the pickle barrel. My pinky is making tiny whirlpools in the brine. I stop a moment to announce: "Campbell's Tomato Soup. Campbell's Vegetable Beef Soup. Campbell's S-c-otch Broth . . . "

"Be quiet," the grocer says, "the labels are coming off."

"Please, Shirley, be a little quiet," my mother begs me.

In that place the whole street groans: Be quiet! Be quiet! but steals from the happy chorus of my inside self not a tittle or a jot.

There, too, but just around the corner, is a red brick building that has been old for many years. Every morning the children stand before it in double lines which must be straight. They are not insulted. They are waiting anyway.

I am usually among them. I am, in fact, the first, since I begin with "A."

One cold morning the monitor tapped me on the shoulder. "Go to Room 409, Shirley Abramowitz," he said. I did as I was told. I went in a hurry up a down staircase to Room 409, which contained sixth-graders. I had to wait at the desk without wiggling until Mr. Hilton, their teacher, had time to speak.

After five minutes he said, "Shirley?"

"What?" I whispered.

He said, "My! My! Shirley Abramowitz! They told me you had a particularly loud, clear voice and read with lots of expression. Could that be true?"

---

[1] A small elevator for moving food, garbage, etc. between floors.

"Oh yes," I whispered.

"In that case, don't be silly; I might very well be your teacher someday. Speak up, speak up."

"Yes," I shouted.

"More like it," he said. "Now, Shirley, can you put a ribbon in your hair or a bobby pin? It's too messy."

"Yes!" I bawled.

"Now, now, calm down." He turned to the class. "Children, not a sound. Open at page 39. Read till 52. When you finish, start again." He looked me over once more. "Now, Shirley, you know, I suppose, that Christmas is coming. We are preparing a beautiful play. Most of the parts have been given out. But I still need a child with a strong voice, lots of stamina. Do you know what stamina is? You do? Smart kid. You know, I heard you read 'The Lord is my shepherd'[2] in Assembly yesterday. I was very impressed. Wonderful delivery. Mrs. Jordan, your teacher, speaks highly of you. Now listen to me, Shirley Abramowitz, if you want to take the part and be in the play, repeat after me, 'I swear to work harder than I ever did before.' "

I looked to heaven and said at once, "Oh, I swear." I kissed my pinky and looked at God.

"That is an actor's life, my dear," he explained: "Like a soldier's, never tardy or disobedient to his general, the director. Everything," he said, "absolutely everything will depend on you."

That afternoon, all over the building, children scraped and scrubbed the turkeys and the sheaves of corn off the schoolroom windows. Goodbye Thanksgiving. The next morning a monitor brought red paper and green paper from the office. We made new shapes and hung them on the walls and glued them to the doors.

The teachers became happier and happier. Their heads were ringing like the bells of childhood. My best friend Evie was prone to evil, but she did not get a single demerit for whispering. We learned "Holy Night" without an error. "How wonderful!" said Miss Glacé, the student teacher. "To think that some of you don't even speak the language!" We learned "Deck the Halls" and "Hark! The Herald Angels." . . . They weren't ashamed and we weren't embarrassed.

Oh, but when my mother heard about it all, she said to my father: "Misha, you don't know what's going on there. Cramer is the head of the Tickets Committee."

"Who?" asked my father. "Cramer? Oh yes, an active woman."

"Active? Active has to have a reason. Listen," she said sadly, "I'm surprised to see my neighbors making tra-la-la for Christmas."

My father couldn't think of what to say to that. Then he decided: "You're in America! Clara, you wanted to come here. In Palestine the Arabs would be eating you alive. Europe you had pogroms.[3] Argentina is full of Indians. Here you got Christmas. . . . Some joke, ha?"

---

[2] Psalm 23: A Psalm of David.   [3] An organized and often officially encouraged massacre or persecution of a minority group, especially one conducted against the Jews.

"Very funny, Misha. What is becoming of you? If we came to a new country a long time ago to run away from tyrants, and instead we fall into a creeping pogrom, that our children learn a lot of lies, so what's the joke? Ach, Misha, your idealism is going away."

"So is your sense of humor."

"That I never had, but idealism you had a lot of."

"I'm the same Misha Abramovitch, I didn't change an iota. Ask anyone."

"Only ask me," says my mama, may she rest in peace. "I got the answer."

Meanwhile the neighbors had to think of what to say too.

Marty's father said: "You know, he has a very important part, my boy."

"Mine also," said Mr. Sauerfeld.

"Not my boy!" said Mrs. Klicg. "I said to him no. The answer is no. When I say no! I mean no!"

The rabbi's wife said, "It's disgusting!" But no one listened to her. Under the narrow sky of God's great wisdom she wore a strawberry-blond wig.[4]

Everyday was noisy and full of experience. I was Right-hand Man. Mr. Hilton said: "How could I get along without you, Shirley?"

He said: "Your mother and father ought to get down on their knees every night and thank God for giving them a child like you."

He also said: "You're absolutely a pleasure to work with, my dear, dear child."

Sometimes he said: "For God's sakes, what did I do with the script? Shirley! Shirley! Find it."

Then I answered quietly: "Here it is, Mr. Hilton."

Once in a while, when he was very tired, he would cry out: "Shirley, I'm just tired of screaming at those kids. Will you tell Ira Pushkov not to come in till Lester points to that star the second time?"

Then I roared: "Ira Pushkov, what's the matter with you? Dope! Mr. Hilton told you five times already, don't come in till Lester points to that star the second time."

"Ach, Clara," my father asked, "what does she do there till six o'clock she can't even put the plates on the table?"

"Christmas," said my mother coldly.

"Ho! Ho!" my father said. "Christmas. What's the harm? After all, history teaches everyone. We learn from reading this is a holiday from pagan times also, candles, lights, even Chanukah.[5] So we learn it's not altogether Christian. So if they think it's a private holiday, they're only ignorant, not patriotic. What belongs to history, belongs to all men. You want to go back to the Middle Ages? Is it better to shave your head with a secondhand razor? Does it hurt Shirley to learn to speak up? It does not. So maybe someday she won't live between the kitchen and the shop.[6] She's not a fool."

---

[4] Wigs are worn by orthodox Jewish women after they marry. [5] An eight-day Jewish festival celebrated in December or late November, commemorating the Maccabees' victory over the Syrians in 165 B.C. and the rededication of the Temple at Jerusalem. [6] Jewish immigrant women who worked in sweatshops.

I thank you, Papa, for your kindness. It is true about me to this day. I am foolish but I am not a fool.

That night my father kissed me and said with great interest in my career, "Shirley, tomorrow's your big day. Congrats."

"Save it," my mother said. Then she shut all the windows in order to prevent tonsillitis.

In the morning it snowed. On the street corner a tree had been decorated for us by a kind city administration. In order to miss its chilly shadow our neighbors walked three blocks east to buy a loaf of bread. The butcher pulled down black window shades to keep the colored lights from shining on his chickens. Oh, not me. On the way to school, with both my hands I tossed it a kiss of tolerance. Poor thing, it was a stranger in Egypt.[7]

I walked straight into the auditorium past the staring children. "Go ahead. Shirley!" said the monitors. Four boys, big for their age, had already started work as propmen and stagehands.

Mr. Hilton was very nervous. He was not even happy. Whatever he started to say ended in a sideward look of sadness. He sat slumped in the middle of the first row and asked me to help Miss Glacé. I did this, although she thought my voice too resonant and said, "Show-off!"

Parents began to arrive long before we were ready. They wanted to make a good impression. From among the yards of drapes I peeked out at the audience. I saw my embarrassed mother.

Ira, Lester, and Meyer were pasted to their beards by Miss Glacé. She almost forgot to thread the star on its wire, but I reminded her. I coughed a few times to clear my throat. Miss Glacé looked around and saw that everyone was in costume and on line waiting to play his part. She whispered, "All right. . . . " Then:

Jackie Sauerfeld, the prettiest boy in first grade, parted the curtains with his skinny elbow and in a high voice sang out:

"Parents dear
We are here
To make a Christmas play in time.
It we give
In narrative
And illustrate with pantomime."

He disappeared.

My voice burst immediately from the wings to the great shock of Ira, Lester, and Meyer, who were waiting for it but were surprised all the same.

"I remember, I remember, the house where I was born . . . "[8]

Miss Glacé yanked the curtain open and there it was, the house—an old hayloft, where Celia Kornbluh lay in the straw with Cindy Lou, her favorite doll. Ira, Lester,

---

[7] An allusion to Moses' sojourn in Egypt. See Exodus 2:2. As the persecuted Israelites were out of place in Egypt, so was the Christmas tree in an all-Jewish neighborhood. [8] A sentimental poem by Thomas Hood (1798–1845).

and Meyer moved slowly from the wings toward her, sometimes pointing to a moving star and sometimes ahead to Cindy Lou.

It was a long story and it was a sad story. I carefully pronounced all the words about my lonesome childhood, while little Eddie Braunstein wandered upstage and down with his shepherd's stick, looking for sheep. I brought up lonesomeness again, and not being understood at all except by some women everybody hated. Eddie was too small for that and Marty Graff took his place, wearing his father's prayer shawl. I announced twelve friends, and half the boys in the fourth grade gathered round Marty, who stood on an orange crate while my voice harangued. Sorrowful and loud, I declaimed about love and God and Man, but because of the terrible deceit of Abie Stock we came suddenly to a famous moment. Marty, whose remembering tongue I was, waited at the foot of the cross. He stared desperately at the audience. I groaned, "My God, my God, why hast thou forsaken me?"[9] The soldiers who were sheiks grabbed poor Marty to pin him up to die, but he wrenched free, turned again to the audience, and spread his arms aloft to show despair and the end. I murmured at the top of my voice, "The rest is silence,[10] but as everyone in this room, in this city—in this world—now knows, I shall have life eternal."

That night Mrs. Kornbluh visited our kitchen for a glass of tea.

"How's the virgin?"[11] asked my father with a look of concern.

"For a man with a daughter, you got a fresh mouth, Abramovitch."

"Here," said my father kindly, "have some lemon, it'll sweeten your disposition."

They debated a little in Yiddish, then fell in a puddle of Russian and Polish. What I understood next was my father, who said, "Still and all, it was certainly a beautiful affair, you have to admit, introducing us to the beliefs of a different culture."

"Well, yes," said Mrs. Kornbluh. "The only thing . . . you know Charlie Turner—that cute boy in Celia's class—a couple others? They got very small parts or no part at all. In very bad taste, it seemed to me. After all, it's their religion."

"Ach," explained my mother, "what could Mr. Hilton do? They got very small voices: after all, why should they holler? The English language they know from the beginning by heart. They're blond like angels. You think it's so important they should get in the play? Christmas . . . the whole piece of goods . . . they own it."

I listened and listened until I couldn't listen any more. Too sleepy, I climbed out of bed and kneeled. I made a little church of my hands and said, "Hear, O Israel[12] . . . " Then I called out in Yiddish, "Please, good night, good night. Ssh." My father said, "Ssh yourself," and slammed the kitchen door.

I was happy. I fell asleep at once. I had prayed for everybody: my talking family, cousins far away, passersby, and all the lonesome Christians. I expected to be heard. My voice was certainly the loudest.

---

[9] Psalm 22, A Psalm of David. Also the fourth of the seven last words of Christ on the cross.
[10] *Hamlet*, V, ii. [11] The virgin Mary portrayed by Mrs. Kornbluh's daughter in the school play.
[12] "Hear, O Israel, the Lord Our God, the Lord is One." The most often recited Jewish prayer.

Journal Entry

Speculate on the significance of the story's title, "The Loudest Voice."

Textual Considerations

1. Characterize Shirley's father. To what extent do you agree with him that "history teaches everyone" and that "what belongs to history, belongs to all"?
2. How does Shirley's mother view the relation between immigrants and the dominant culture? To what extent do you agree with her assessment?
3. How does Paley's use of fragments, ellipses, and humor contribute to the story's meaning and characterizations?

Cultural Contexts

1. Discuss with your group the dilemmas that immigrant parents confront in trying to preserve their ethnic heritage for their children while wishing them to assimilate and succeed in their new land. Consider also the role of language in this situation.

Tillie Olsen

I Stand Here Ironing

I stand here ironing, and what you asked me moves tormented back and forth with the iron.

"I wish you would manage the time to come in and talk with me about your daughter. I'm sure you can help me understand her. She's a youngster who needs help and whom I'm deeply interested in helping."

"Who needs help." Even if I came, what good would it do? You think because I am her mother I have a key, or that in some way you could use me as a key? She has lived for nineteen years. There is all that life that has happened outside of me, beyond me.

And when is there time to remember, to sift, to weigh, to estimate, to total? I will start and there will be an interruption and I will have to gather it all together again. Or I will become engulfed with all I did or did not do, with what should have been and what cannot be helped.

She was a beautiful baby. The first and only one of our five that was beautiful at birth. You do not guess how new and uneasy her tenancy in her now-loveliness. You did not know her all those years she was thought homely, or see her poring over her baby pictures, making me tell her over and over how beautiful she had been— and would be, I would tell her—and was now, to the seeing eye. But the seeing eyes were few or non-existent. Including mine.

I nursed her. They feel that's important nowadays. I nursed all the children, but with her, with all the fierce rigidity of first motherhood, I did like the books then said. Though her cries battered me to trembling and my breasts ached with swollenness, I waited till the clock decreed.

Why do I put that first? I do not even know if it matters, or if it explains anything.

She was a beautiful baby. She blew shining bubbles of sound. She loved motion, loved light, loved colour and music and textures. She would lie on the floor in her blue overalls patting the surface so hard in ecstasy her hands and feet would blur. She was a miracle to me, but when she was eight months old I had to leave her daytimes with the woman downstairs to whom she was no miracle at all, for I worked or looked for work and for Emily's father, who "could no longer endure" (he wrote in his good-bye note) "sharing want with us."

I was nineteen. It was the pre-relief, pre-WPA world of the depression. I would start running as soon as I got off the street-car, running up the stairs, the place smelling sour, and awake or asleep to startle awake, when she saw me she would break into a clogged weeping that could not be comforted, a weeping I can yet hear.

After a while I found a job hashing at night so I could be with her days, and it was better. But it came to where I had to bring her to his family and leave her.

It took a long time to raise the money for her fare back. Then she got chicken pox and I had to wait longer. When she finally came, I hardly knew her, walking quick and nervous like her father, looking like her father, thin, and dressed in a shoddy red that yellowed her skin and glared at the pock marks. All the baby loveliness gone.

She was two. Old enough for nursery school they said, and I did not know then what I know now—the fatigue of the long day, and the lacerations of group life in nurseries that are only parking places for children.

Except that it would have made no difference if I had known. It was the only place there was. It was the only way we could be together, the only way I could hold a job.

And even without knowing, I knew. I knew the teacher that was evil because all these years it has curdled into my memory, the little boy hunched in the corner, her rasp, "why aren't you outside, because Alvin hits you? that's no reason, go out, scaredy." I knew Emily hated it even if she did not clutch and implore "don't go Mommy" like the other children, mornings.

She always had a reason why we should stay home. Momma, you look sick, Momma. I feel sick. Momma, the teachers aren't there today, they're sick. Momma, we can't go, there was a fire there last night. Momma, it's a holiday today, no school, they told me.

But never a direct protest, never rebellion. I think of our others in their three-, four-year-oldness—the explosions, the tempers, the denunciations, the demands— and I feel suddenly ill. I put the iron down. What in me demanded that goodness in her? And what was the cost, the cost to her of such goodness?

The old man living in the back once said in his gentle way: "You should smile at Emily more when you look at her." What *was* in my face when I looked at her? I loved her. There were all the acts of love.

It was only with the others I remembered what he said, and it was the face of joy, and not of care or tightness or worry I turned to them—too late for Emily. She does not smile easily, let alone almost always as her brothers and sisters do. Her face is closed and sombre, but when she wants, how fluid. You must have seen it in her pantomimes, you spoke of her rare gift for comedy on the stage that rouses a laughter out of the audience so dear they applaud and applaud and do not want to let her go.

Where does it come from, that comedy? There was none of it in her when she came back to me that second time, after I had had to send her away again. She had a new daddy now to learn to love, and I think perhaps it was a better time. Except when we left her alone nights, telling ourselves she was old enough.

"Can't you go some other time, Mommy, like tomorrow?" she would ask. "Will it be just a little while you'll be gone? Do you promise?"

The time we came back, the front door open, the clock on the floor in the hall. She rigid awake. "It wasn't just a little while. I didn't cry. Three times I called you, just three times, and then I ran downstairs to open the door so you could come faster. The clock talked loud. I threw it away, it scared me what it talked."

She said the clock talked loud again that night I went to the hospital to have Susan. She was delirious with the fever that comes before red measles, but she was fully conscious all the week I was gone and the week after we were home when she could not come near the new baby or me.

She did not get well. She stayed skeleton thin, not wanting to eat, and night after night she had nightmares. She would call for me, and I would rouse from exhaustion to sleepily call back: "You're all right, darling, go to sleep, it's just a dream," and if she still called, in a sterner voice, "now go to sleep, Emily, there's nothing to hurt you." Twice, only twice, when I had to get up for Susan anyhow, I went in to sit with her.

Now when it is too late (as if she would let me hold and comfort her like I do the others) I get up and go to her at once at her moan or restless stirring. "Are you awake, Emily? Can I get you something, dear?" And the answer is always the same: "No, I'm all right, go back to sleep, Mother."

They persuaded me at the clinic to send her away to a convalescent home in the country where "she can have the kind of food and care you can't manage for her, and you'll be free to concentrate on the new baby." They still send children to that place. I see pictures on the society page of sleek young women planning affairs to raise money for it, or dancing at the affairs, or decorating Easter eggs or filling Christmas stockings for the children.

They never have a picture of the children so I do not know if the girls still wear those gigantic red bows and the ravaged looks on the every other Sunday when parents can come to visit "unless otherwise notified"—as we were notified the first six weeks.

Oh it is a handsome place, green lawns and tall trees and fluted flower beds. High up on the balconies of each cottage the children stand, the girls in their red bows and white dresses, the boys in white suits and giant red ties. The parents stand below shrieking up to be heard and the children shriek down to be heard, and between them the invisible wall "Not To Be Contaminated by Parental Germs or Physical Affection."

There was a tiny girl who always stood hand in hand with Emily. Her parents never came. One visit she was gone. "They moved her to Rose Cottage," Emily shouted in explanation. "They don't like you to love anybody here."

She wrote once a week, the laboured writing of a seven-year-old. "I am fine. How is the baby. If I write my leter nicely I will have a star. Love." There never was a star. We wrote every other day, letters she could never hold or keep but only hear read—once. "We simply do not have room for children to keep any personal possessions," they patiently explained when we pieced one Sunday's shrieking together to plead how much it would mean to Emily, who loved so to keep things, to be allowed to keep her letters and cards.

Each visit she looked frailer. "She isn't eating," they told us.

(They had runny eggs for breakfast or mush with lumps, Emily said later, I'd hold it in my mouth and not swallow. Nothing ever tasted good, just when they had chicken.)

It took us eight months to get her released home, and only the fact that she gained back so little of her seven lost pounds convinced the social worker.

I used to try to hold and love her after she came back, but her body would stay stiff, and after a while she'd push away. She ate little. Food sickened her, and I think much of life too. Oh she had physical lightness and brightness, twinkling by on skates, bouncing like a ball up and down up and down over the jump rope, skimming over the hill; but these were momentary.

She fretted about her appearance, thin and dark and foreign-looking at a time when every little girl was supposed to look or thought she should look a chubby blonde replica of Shirley Temple. The door-bell sometimes rang for her, but no one seemed to come and play in the house or be a best friend. Maybe because we moved so much.

There was a boy she loved painfully through two school semesters. Months later she told me how she had taken pennies from my purse to buy him candy. "Liquorice was his favourite and I brought him some every day, but he still liked Jennifer better'n me. Why, Mommy?" The kind of question for which there is no answer.

School was a worry to her. She was not glib or quick in a world where glibness and quickness were easily confused with ability to learn. To her overworked and exasperated teachers she was an overconscientious "slow learner" who kept trying to catch up and was absent entirely too often.

I let her be absent, though sometimes the illness was imaginary. How different from my now-strictness about attendance with the others. I wasn't working. We had a new baby, I was home anyhow. Sometimes, after Susan grew old enough, I would keep her home from school, too, to have them all together.

Mostly Emily had asthma, and her breathing, harsh and laboured, would fill the house with a curiously tranquil sound. I would bring the two old dresser mirrors and her boxes of collections to her bed. She would select beads and single ear-rings, bottle tops and shells, dried flowers and pebbles, old postcards and scraps, all sorts of oddments; then she and Susan would play Kingdom, setting up landscapes and furniture, peopling them with action.

Those were the only times of peaceful companionship between her and Susan. I have edged away from it, that poisonous feeling between them, that terrible balancing of hurts and needs I had to do between the two, and did so badly, those earlier years.

Oh there are conflicts between the others too, each one human, needing, demanding, hurting, taking—but only between Emily and Susan, no Emily toward Susan that corroding resentment. It seems so obvious on the surface, yet it is not obvious. Susan, the second child, Susan, golden- and curly-haired and chubby, quick and articulate and assured, everything in appearance and manner Emily was not; Susan, not able to resist Emily's precious things, losing or sometimes clumsily breaking them; Susan telling jokes and riddles to company for applause while Emily sat silent (to say to me later: that was *my* riddle, Mother, I told it to Susan); Susan, who for all the five years' difference in age was just a year behind Emily in developing physically.

I am glad for that slow physical development that widened the difference between her and her contemporaries, though she suffered over it. She was too vulnerable for that terrible world of youthful competition, of preening and parading, of constant measuring of yourself against every other, of envy, "If I had that copper hair," or "If I had that skin. . . . " She tormented herself enough about not looking like the others, there was enough of the unsureness, the having to be conscious of words before you speak, the constant caring—what are they thinking of me? What kind of an impression am I making?—there was enough without having it all magnified by the merciless physical drives.

Ronnie is calling. He is wet and I change him. It is rare there is such a cry now. That time of motherhood is almost behind me when the ear is not one's own but must always be racked and listening for the child cry, the child call. We sit for a while and I hold him, looking out over the city spread in charcoal with its soft aisles of light. "*Shoogily*," he breathes and curls closer. I carry him back to bed, asleep. *Shoogily*. A funny word, a family word, inherited from Emily, invented by her to say: *comfort.*

In this and other ways she leaves her seal, I say aloud. And startle at my saying it. What do I mean? What did I start to gather together, to try and make coherent? I was at the terrible, growing years. War years. I do not remember them well. I was working, there were four smaller ones now, there was not time for her. She had to help be a mother, and housekeeper, and shopper. She had to set her seal. Mornings of crisis and near hysteria trying to get lunches packed, hair combed, coats and shoes found, everyone to school or Child Care on time, the baby ready for transportation.

And always the paper scribbled on by a smaller one, the book looked at by Susan then mislaid, the homework not done. Running out to that huge school where she was one, she was lost, she was a drop; suffering over the unpreparedness, stammering and unsure in her classes.

There was so little time left at night after the kids were bedded down. She would struggle over books, always eating (it was in those years she developed her enormous appetite that is legendary in our family) and I would be ironing, or preparing food for the next day, or writing V-mail to Bill, or tending the baby. Sometimes, to make me laugh, or out of her despair, she would imitate happenings or types at school.

I think I said once: "Why don't you do something like this in the school amateur show?" One morning she phoned me at work, hardly understandable through the weeping: "Mother, I did it. I won, I won; they gave me first prize; they clapped and clapped and wouldn't let me go."

Now suddenly she was Somebody, and as imprisoned in her difference as she had been in anonymity.

She began to be asked to perform at other high schools, even in colleges, then at city and state-wide affairs. The first one we went to, I only recognized her that first moment when thin, shy, she almost drowned herself into the curtains. Then: Was this Emily? The control, the command, the convulsing and deadly clowning, the spell, then the roaring, stamping audience, unwilling to let this rare and precious laughter out of their lives.

Afterwards: You ought to do something about her with a gift like that—but without money or knowing how, what does one do? We have left it all to her, and the gift has as often eddied inside, clogged and clotted, as been used and growing.

She is coming. She runs up the stairs two at a time with her light graceful step, and I know she is happy tonight. Whatever it was that occasioned your call did not happen today.

"Aren't you ever going to finish the ironing, Mother? Whistler painted his mother in a rocker. I'd have to paint mine standing over an ironing-board." This is one of her communicative nights and she tells me everything and nothing as she fixes herself a plate of food out of the icebox.

She is so lovely. Why did you want me to come in at all? Why were you concerned? She will find her way.

She starts up the stairs to bed. "Don't get me up with the rest in the morning." "But I thought you were having midterms." "Oh, those," she comes back in, kisses me, and says quite lightly, "in a couple of years when we'll all be atom-dead they won't matter a bit."

She has said it before. She *believes* it. But because I have been dredging the past, and all that compounds a human being is so heavy and meaningful in me, I cannot endure it tonight.

I will never total it all. I will never come in to say: She was a child seldom smiled at. Her father left me before she was a year old. I had to work her first six years when there was work, or I sent her home and to his relatives. There were years she had care she hated. She was dark and thin and foreign-looking in a world where the prestige went to blondness and curly hair and dimples, she was slow where glibness was prized. She was a child of anxious, not proud, love. We were poor and could not afford for her the soil of easy growth. I was a young mother, I was a distracted mother. There were the other children pushing up, demanding. Her younger sister seemed all that she was not. There were years she did not want me to touch her. She kept too much in herself, her life was such she had to keep too much in herself. My wisdom came too late. She has much to her and probably nothing will come of it. She is a child of her age, of depression, of war, of fear.

Let her be. So all that is in her will not bloom—but in how many does it? There is still enough left to live by. Only help her to know—help make it so there is cause for her to know that she is more than this dress on the ironing-board, helpless before the iron.

Journal Entry

React to the narrator's idea that the poor can't afford "the soil of easy growth" for their children.

Textual Considerations

1. Relate the title of the story to the events that occur. To what extent is the iron the dominant symbol of the story? What does it symbolize? What other symbols can you identify?
2. Examine the bonds that tie mother and daughter in Olsen's text. How well does the mother succeed in building a good relationship with her daughter? What kind of resentment might Emily feel toward her mother?
3. How does point of view function in the story? To what extent might the narrative be considered an interior monologue? What does the narrator reveal about herself? About her understanding of Emily?

Cultural Contexts

1. Olsen's story is set partly during the depression, when the child star Shirley Temple dominated American movies. Share with your group what you feel about the narrator's criticism of that time in expressions such as "She was dark and thin and foreign-looking in a world where the prestige went to blondness and curly hair and dimples" and "She is a child of her age, of depression, of war, of fear." To what extent do you consider Emily a victim of socioeconomic circumstances?
2. Emily's mother represents the plight of single parents in the 1930s. Debate with your group what can be done to help the young, distracted mothers of the 1990s who are trying to raise children by themselves. Consider also what these mothers might do to help themselves.

Liliana Heker

The Stolen Party

As soon as she arrived she went straight to the kitchen to see if the monkey was there. It was: what a relief! She wouldn't have liked to admit that her mother had been right. *Monkeys at a birthday?* her mother had sneered. *Get away with you, believing any nonsense you're told!* She was cross, but not because of the monkey, the girl thought; it's just because of the party.

"I don't like you going," she told her. "It's a rich people's party."

"Rich people go to Heaven too," said the girl, who studied religion at school.

"Get away with Heaven," said the mother. "The problem with you, young lady, is that you like to fart higher than your ass."

The girl didn't approve of the way her mother spoke. She was barely nine, and one of the best in her class.

"I'm going because I've been invited," she said. "And I've been invited because Luciana is my friend. So there."

"Ah yes, your friend," her mother grumbled. She paused. "Listen, Rosaura," she said at last. "That one's not your friend. You know what you are to them? The maid's daughter, that's what."

Rosaura blinked hard: she wasn't going to cry. Then she yelled: "Shut up! You know nothing about being friends!"

Every afternoon she used to go to Luciana's house and they would both finish their homework while Rosaura's mother did the cleaning. They had their tea in the kitchen and they told each other secrets. Rosaura loved everything in the big house, and she also loved the people who lived there.

"I'm going because it will be the most lovely party in the whole world, Luciana told me it would. There will be a magician, and he will bring a monkey and everything."

The mother swung around to take a good look at her child, and pompously put her hands on her hips.

"Monkeys at a birthday?" she said. "Get away with you, believing any nonsense you're told!"

Rosaura was deeply offended. She thought it unfair of her mother to accuse other people of being liars simply because they were rich. Rosaura too wanted to be rich, of course. If one day she managed to live in a beautiful palace, would her mother stop loving her? She felt very sad. She wanted to go to that party more than anything else in the world.

"I'll die if I don't go," she whispered almost without moving her lips.

And she wasn't sure whether she had been heard, but on the morning of the party, she discovered that her mother had starched her Christmas dress. And in the afternoon, after washing her hair, her mother rinsed it in apple vinegar so that it would be all nice and shiny. Before going out, Rosaura admired herself in the mirror, with her white dress and glossy hair, and thought she looked terribly pretty.

Señora Ines also seemed to notice. As soon as she saw her, she said:

"How lovely you look today, Rosaura."

Rosaura gave her starched skirt a slight toss with her hands and walked into the party with a firm step. She said hello to Luciana and asked about the monkey. Luciana put on a secretive look and whispered into Rosaura's ear: "He's in the kitchen. But don't tell anyone, because it's a surprise."

Rosaura wanted to make sure. Carefully she entered the kitchen and there she saw it: deep in thought, inside its cage. It looked so funny that the girl stood there for a while, watching it, and later, every so often, she would slip out of the party unseen and go and admire it. Rosaura was the only one allowed into the kitchen. Señora Ines had said: "You yes, but not the others, they're much too boisterous, they might break something." Rosaura had never broken anything. She even managed the jug of orange juice, carrying it from the kitchen into the dining room. She held it carefully and didn't spill a single drop. And Señora Ines had said: "Are you sure you can manage a jug as big as that?" Of course she could manage. She wasn't a butterfingers, like the others. Like that blonde girl with the bow in her hair. As soon as she saw Rosaura, the girl with the bow had said:

"And you? Who are you?"

"I'm a friend of Luciana," said Rosaura.

"No," said the girl with the bow, "you are not a friend of Luciana because I'm her cousin and I know all her friends. And I don't know you."

"So what," said Rosaura. "I come here every afternoon with my mother and we do our homework together."

"You and your mother do your homework together?" asked the girl, laughing.

"I and Luciana do our homework together," said Rosaura, very seriously.

The girl with the bow shrugged her shoulders.

"That's not being friends," she said. "Do you go to school together?"

"No."

"So where do you know her from?" said the girl, getting impatient.

Rosaura remembered her mother's words perfectly. She took a deep breath.

"I'm the daughter of the employee," she said.

Her mother had said very clearly: "If someone asks, you say you're the daughter of the employee; that's all." She also told her to add: "And proud of it." But Rosaura thought that never in her life would she dare say something of the sort.

"What employee?" said the girl with the bow. "Employee in a shop?"

"No," said Rosaura angrily. "My mother doesn't sell anything in any shop, so there."

"So how come she's an employee?" said the girl with the bow.

Just then Señora Ines arrived saying *shh shh,* and asked Rosaura if she wouldn't mind helping serve out the hotdogs, as she knew the house so much better than the others.

"See?" said Rosaura to the girl with the bow, and when no one was looking she kicked her in the shin.

Apart from the girl with the bow, all the others were delightful. The one she liked best was Luciana, with her golden birthday crown; and then the boys. Rosaura won the sack race, and nobody managed to catch her when they played tag. When they split into two teams to play charades, all the boys wanted her for their side. Rosaura felt she had never been so happy in all her life.

But the best was still to come. The best came after Luciana blew out the candles. First the cake. Señora Ines had asked her to help pass the cake around, and Rosaura had enjoyed the task immensely, because everyone called out to her, shouting "Me, me!" Rosaura remembered a story in which there was a queen who had the power of life or death over her subjects. She had always loved that, having the power of life or death. To Luciana and the boys she gave the largest pieces, and to the girl with the bow she gave a slice so thin one could see through it.

After the cake came the magician, tall and bony, with a fine red cape. A true magician: he could untie handkerchiefs by blowing on them and make a chain with links that had no openings. He could guess what cards were pulled out from a pack, and the monkey was his assistant. He called the monkey "partner." "Let's see here, partner," he would say, "turn over a card." And, "Don't run away, partner: time to work now."

The final trick was wonderful. One of the children had to hold the monkey in his arms and the magician said he would make him disappear.

"What, the boy?" they all shouted.

"No, the monkey!" shouted back the magician.

Rosaura thought that this was truly the most amusing party in the whole world.

The magician asked a small fat boy to come and help, but the small fat boy got frightened almost at once and dropped the monkey on the floor. The magician picked him up carefully, whispered something in his ear, and the monkey nodded almost as if he understood.

"You mustn't be so unmanly, my friend," the magician said to the fat boy.

"What's unmanly?" said the fat boy.

The magician turned around as if to look for spies.

"A sissy," said the magician. "Go sit down."

Then he stared at all the faces, one by one. Rosaura felt her heart tremble.

"You, with the Spanish eyes," said the magician. And everyone saw that he was pointing at her.

She wasn't afraid. Neither holding the monkey, nor when the magician made him vanish; not even when, at the end, the magician flung his red cape over Rosaura's head and uttered a few magic words . . . and the monkey reappeared, chattering happily, in her arms. The children clapped furiously. And before Rosaura returned to her seat, the magician said:

"Thank you very much, my little countess."

She was so pleased with the compliment that a while later, when her mother came to fetch her, that was the first thing she told her.

"I helped the magician and he said to me, 'Thank you very much, my little countess.' "

It was strange because up to then Rosaura had thought that she was angry with her mother. All along Rosaura had imagined that she would say to her: "See that the monkey wasn't a lie?" But instead she was so thrilled that she told her mother all about the wonderful magician.

Her mother tapped her on the head and said: "So now we're a countess!"

But one could see that she was beaming.

And now they both stood in the entrance, because a moment ago Señora Ines, smiling, had said: "Please wait here a second."

Her mother suddenly seemed worried.

"What is it?" she asked Rosaura.

"What is what?" said Rosaura. "It's nothing; she just wants to get the presents for those who are leaving, see?"

She pointed at the fat boy and at a girl with pigtails who were also waiting there, next to their mothers. And she explained about the presents. She knew, because she had been watching those who left before her. When one of the girls was about to leave, Señora Ines would give her a bracelet. When a boy left, Señora Ines gave him a yo-yo. Rosaura preferred the yo-yo because it sparkled, but she didn't mention that to her mother. Her mother might have said: "So why don't you ask for one, you blockhead?" That's what her mother was like. Rosaura didn't feel like explaining that she'd be horribly ashamed to be the odd one out. Instead she said:

"I was the best-behaved at the party."

And she said no more because Señora Ines came out into the hall with two bags, one pink and one blue.

First she went up to the fat boy, gave him a yo-yo out of the blue bag, and the fat boy left with mother. Then she went up to the girl and gave her a bracelet out of the pink bag, and the girl with the pigtails left as well.

Finally she came up to Rosaura and her mother. She had a big smile on her face and Rosaura liked that. Señora Ines looked down at her, then looked up at her mother, and then said something that made Rosaura proud:

"What a marvelous daughter you have, Herminia."

For an instant, Rosaura thought that she'd give her two presents: the bracelet and the yo-yo. Señora Ines bent down as if about to look for something. Rosaura also leaned forward, stretching out her arm. But she never completed the movement.

Señora Ines didn't look in the pink bag. Nor did she look in the blue bag. Instead she rummaged in her purse. In her hand appeared two bills.

"You really and truly earned this," she said handing them over. "Thank you for all your help, my pet."

Rosaura felt her arms stiffen, stick close to her body, and then she noticed her mother's hand on her shoulder. Instinctively she pressed herself against her mother's body. That was all. Except her eyes. Rosaura's eyes had a cold, clear look that fixed itself on Señora Ines's face.

Señora Ines, motionless, stood there with her hand outstretched. As if she didn't dare draw it back. As if the slightest change might shatter an infinitely delicate balance.

Journal Entry

Analyze the significance of the story's title, "The Stolen Party."

Textual Considerations

1. Explore the mother-daughter relationship. How does it change during the course of the story? What lesson does each learn?
2. Examine the narrative structure of the story. Consider, for example, the author's use of flashback as well as her plot construction of rising action, climax, and dénouement.
3. Explain the significance of the last paragraph. If the story were told from the point of view of Señora Ines, would we see that the problem was also hers and not only Rosaura's? Explain.

Cultural Contexts

1. React to the idea that people like Rosaura are judged not by their character but by their position in society. Debate whether this mode of differentiation by class is as unfair as differentiation by skin color.
2. Heker's story is set in Latin America. Could it have taken place in the United States instead? Why or why not?

Aurora Levins Morales

Puertoricanness

It was Puerto Rico waking up inside her. Puerto Rico waking her up at 6:00 a.m., remembering the rooster that used to crow over on 59th Street and the neighbors all cursed "that damn rooster," but she loved him, waited to hear his harsh voice carving up the Oakland sky and eating it like chopped corn, so obliviously sure of himself, crowing all alone with miles of houses around him. She was like that rooster.

Often she could hear them in her dreams. Not the lone rooster of 59th Street (or some street nearby . . . she had never found the exact yard though she had tried), but the wild careening hysterical roosters of 3:00 a.m. in Bartolo, screaming at the night and screaming again at the day.

It was Puerto Rico waking up inside her, uncurling and showing open the door she had kept neatly shut for years and years. Maybe since the first time she was an immigrant, when she refused to speak Spanish in nursery school. Certainly since the last time, when at thirteen she found herself between languages, between countries, with no land feeling at all solid under her feet. The mulberry trees of Chicago, that first summer, had looked so utterly pitiful beside her memory of flamboyan and banana and. . . . No, not even the individual trees and bushes but the mass of them, the overwhelming profusion of green life that was the home of her comfort and nest of her dreams.

The door was opening. She could no longer keep her accent under lock and key. It seeped out, masquerading as dyslexia, stuttering, halting, unable to speak the word which will surely come out in the wrong language, wearing the wrong clothes. Doesn't that girl know how to dress? Doesn't she know how to date, what to say to a professor, how to behave at a dinner table laid with silver and crystal and too many forks?

Yesterday she answered her husband's request that she listen to the whole of his thoughts before commenting by screaming. "This is how we talk. I will not wait sedately for you to finish. Interrupt me back!" She drank pineapple juice three or four times a day. Not Lotus, just Co-op brand, but it was *piña*,[1] and it was sweet and yellow. And she was letting the clock slip away from her into a world of morning and afternoon and night, instead of "five-forty-one-and-twenty seconds—beep."

There were things she noticed about herself, the Puertoricanness of which she had kept hidden all these years, but which had persisted as habits, as idiosyncrasies of her nature. The way she left a pot of food on the stove all day, eating out of it whenever hunger struck her, liking to have something ready. The way she had lacked food to offer Elena in the old days and had stamped on the desire to do so because it *was* Puerto Rican: Come, mija . . . ¿quieres café?[2] The way she was embarrassed and irritated by Ana's unannounced visits, just dropping by, keeping the country habits after a generation of city life. So unlike the cluttered datebooks of all her friends, making appointments to speak to each other on the phone days in advance. Now she yearned for that clocklessness, for the perpetual food pots of her childhood. Even in the poorest houses a plate of white rice and brown beans with calabaza[3] or green bananas and oil.

---

[1] Pineapple.   [2] "Eat, darling, you want some coffee?"   [3] Pumpkin.

She had told Sally that Puerto Ricans lived as if they were all in a small town still, a small town of six million spread out over tens of thousands of square miles, and that the small town that was her country needed to include Manila Avenue in Oakland now, because she was moving back into it. She would not fight the waking early anymore, or the eating all day, or the desire to let time slip between her fingers and allow her work to shape it. Work, eating, sleep, lovemaking, play—to let them shape the day instead of letting the day shape them. Since she could not right now, in the endless bartering of a woman with two countries, bring herself to trade in one-half of her heart for the other, exchange this loneliness for another perhaps harsher one, she would live as a Puerto Rican lives en la isla,[4] right here in north Oakland, plant the bananales[5] and cafetales[6] of her heart around her bedroom door, sleep under the shadow of their bloom and the carving hoarseness of the roosters, wake to blue-rimmed white enamel cups of jugo de piña[7] and plates of guineo verde,[8] and heat pots of rice with bits of meat in them on the stove all day.

There was a woman in her who had never had the chance to move through this house the way she wanted to, a woman raised to be like those women of her childhood, hardworking and humorous and clear. That woman was yawning up out of sleep and into this cluttered daily routine of a Northern California writer living at the edges of Berkeley. She was taking over, putting doilies on the word processor, not bothering to make appointments, talking to the neighbors, riding miles on the bus to buy bacalao,[9] making her presence felt . . . and she was all Puerto Rican, every bit of her.

Journal Entry

Respond to the protagonist's desire to live again in a "clockless" world.

Textual Considerations

1. Discuss Morales's use of repetition to reinforce the story's theme. Cite examples of repetition that you found particularly effective.
2. Make a list of the protagonist's associations with Puertoricanness. Why had she felt compelled to hide her ethnicity?
3. Review the last paragraph of the story. What does it suggest about the cost of cultural displacement?

Cultural Contexts

1. Discuss with your group the speaker's point of view on whether ethnic identity and cultural assimilation are mutually exclusive. To what extent do you agree with her? Explain.

---

[4] On the island. [5] Banana plants. [6] Coffee trees. [7] Pineapple juice. [8] Green bananas, or Plantains.
[9] Codfish.

Bharati Mukherjee

Jasmine

Jasmine came to Detroit from Port-of-Spain, Trinidad, by way of Canada. She crossed the border at Windsor in the back of a gray van loaded with mattresses and box springs. The plan was for her to hide in an empty mattress box if she heard the driver say, "All bad weather seems to come down from Canada, doesn't it?" to the customs man. But she didn't have to crawl into a box and hold her breath. The customs man didn't ask to look in.

The driver let her off at a scary intersection on Woodward Avenue and gave her instructions on how to get to the Plantations Motel in Southfield. The trick was to keep changing vehicles, he said. That threw off the immigration guys real quick.

Jasmine took money for cab fare out of the pocket of the great big raincoat that the van driver had given her. The raincoat looked like something that nuns in Port-of-Spain sold in church bazaars. Jasmine was glad to have a coat with wool lining, though; and anyway, who would know in Detroit that she was Dr. Vassanji's daughter?

All the bills in her hand looked the same. She would have to be careful when she paid the cabdriver. Money in Detroit wasn't pretty the way it was back home, or even in Canada, but she liked this money better. Why should money be pretty, like a picture? Pretty money is only good for putting on your walls maybe. The dollar bills felt businesslike, serious. Back home at work, she used to count out thousands of Trinidad dollars every day and not even think of them as real. Real money was worn and green, American dollars. Holding the bills in her fist on a street corner meant she had made it in okay. She'd outsmarted the guys at the border. Now it was up to her to use her wits to do something with her life. As her Daddy kept saying, "Girl, is opportunity come only once." The girls she'd worked with at the bank in Port-of-Spain had gone green as bananas when she'd walked in with her ticket on Air Canada. Trinidad was too tiny. That was the trouble. Trinidad was an island stuck in the middle of nowhere. What kind of place was that for a girl with ambition?

The Plantations Motel was run by a family of Trinidad Indians who had come from the tuppenny-ha'penny country town, Chaguanas. The Daboos were nobodies back home. They were lucky, that's all. They'd gotten here before the rush and bought up a motel and an ice cream parlor. Jasmine felt very superior when she saw Mr. Daboo in the motel's reception area. He was a pumpkin-shaped man with very black skin and Elvis Presley sideburns turning white. They looked like earmuffs. Mrs. Daboo was a bumpkin, too; short, fat, flapping around in house slippers. The Daboo daughters seemed very American, though. They didn't seem to know that they were nobodies, and kept looking at her and giggling.

She knew she would be short of cash for a great long while. Besides, she wasn't sure she wanted to wear bright leather boots and leotards like Viola and Loretta. The smartest move she could make would be to put a down payment on a husband.

Her Daddy had told her to talk to the Daboos first chance. The Daboos ran a service fixing up illegals with islanders who had made it in legally. Daddy had paid three thousand back in Trinidad, with the Daboos and the mattress man getting part of it. They should throw in a good-earning husband for that kind of money.

The Daboos asked her to keep books for them and to clean the rooms in the new wing, and she could stay in 16B as long as she liked. They showed her 16B. They said she could cook her own roti; Mr. Daboo would bring in a stove, two gas rings that you could fold up in a metal box. The room was quite grand, Jasmine thought. It had a double bed, a TV, a pink sink and matching bathtub. Mrs. Daboo said Jasmine wasn't the big-city Port-of-Spain type she'd expected. Mr. Daboo said that he wanted her to stay because it was nice to have a neat, cheerful person around. It wasn't a bad deal, better than stories she'd heard about Trinidad girls in the States.

All day every day except Sundays Jasmine worked. There wasn't just the book-keeping and the cleaning up. Mr. Daboo had her working on the match-up marriage service. Jasmine's job was to check up on social security cards, call clients' bosses for references, and make sure credit information wasn't false. Dermatologists and engineers living in Bloomfield Hills, store owners on Canfield and Woodward: she treated them all as potential liars. One of the first things she learned was that Ann Arbor was a magic word. A boy goes to Ann Arbor and gets an education, and all the barriers come crashing down. So Ann Arbor was the place to be.

She didn't mind the work. She was learning about Detroit, every side of it. Sunday mornings she helped unload packing crates of Caribbean spices in a shop on the next block. For the first time in her life, she was working for a black man, an African. So what if the boss was black? This was a new life, and she wanted to learn everything. Her Sunday boss, Mr. Anthony, was a courtly, Christian, church-going man, and paid her the only wages she had in her pocket. Viola and Loretta, for all their fancy American ways, wouldn't go out with blacks.

One Friday afternoon she was writing up the credit info on a Guyanese Muslim who worked in an assembly plant when Loretta said that enough was enough and there was no need for Jasmine to be her father's drudge.

"Is time to have fun," Viola said, "We're going to Ann Arbor."

Jasmine filed the sheet on the Guyanese man who probably now would never get a wife and got her raincoat. Loretta's boyfriend had a Cadillac parked out front. It was the longest car Jasmine had ever been in and louder than a country bus. Viola's boyfriend got out of the front seat. "Oh, oh, sweet things," he said to Jasmine. "Get in front." He was a talker. She'd learned that much from working on the matrimonial match-ups. She didn't believe him for a second when he said that there were dudes out there dying to ask her out.

Loretta's boyfriend said, "You have eyes I could leap into, girl."

Jasmine knew he was just talking. They sounded like Port-of-Spain boys of three years ago. It didn't surprise her that these Trinidad country boys in Detroit were still behind the times, even of Port-of-Spain. She sat very stiff between the two men, hands on her purse. The Daboo girls laughed in the back seat.

On the highway the girls told her about the reggae night in Ann Arbor. Kevin and the Krazee Islanders. Malcolm's Lovers. All the big reggae groups in the Midwest were converging for the West Indian Students Association fall bash. The ticket didn't come cheap but Jasmine wouldn't let the fellows pay. She wasn't that kind of girl.

The reggae and steel drums brought out the old Jasmine. The rum punch, the dancing, the dreadlocks, the whole combination. She hadn't heard real music since she got to Detroit, where music was supposed to be so famous. The Daboo girls kept turning on rock stuff in the motel lobby whenever their father left the area. She hadn't danced, really *danced,* since she'd left home. It felt so good to dance. She felt hot and sweaty and sexy. The boys at the dance were more than sweet talkers; they moved with assurance and spoke of their futures in America. The bartender gave her two free drinks and said, "Is ready when you are, girl." She ignored him but she felt all hot and good deep inside. She knew Ann Arbor was a special place.

When it was time to pile back into Loretta's boyfriend's Cadillac, she just couldn't face going back to the Plantations Motel and to the Daboos with their accounting books and messy files.

"I don't know what happen, girl," she said to Loretta. "I feel all crazy inside. Maybe is time for me to pursue higher studies in this town."

"This Ann Arbor, girl, they don't just take you off the street. It *cost* like hell."

She spent the night on a bashed-up sofa in the Student Union. She was a well-dressed, respectable girl, and she didn't expect anyone to question her right to sleep on the furniture. Many others were doing the same thing. In the morning, a boy in an army parka showed her the way to the Placement Office. He was a big, blond, clumsy boy, not bad-looking except for the blond eyelashes. He didn't scare her, as did most Americans. She let him buy her a Coke and a hotdog. That evening she had a job with the Moffitts.

Bill Moffitt taught molecular biology and Lara Hatch-Moffitt, his wife, was a performance artist. A performance artist, said Lara, was very different from being an actress, though Jasmine still didn't understand what the difference might be. The Moffitts had a little girl, Muffin, whom Jasmine was to look after, though for the first few months she might have to help out with the housework and the cooking because Lara said she was deep into performance rehearsals. That was all right with her, Jasmine said, maybe a little too quickly. She explained she came from a big family and was used to heavy-duty cooking and cleaning. This wasn't the time to say anything about Ram, the family servant. Americans like the Moffitts wouldn't understand about keeping servants. Ram and she weren't in similar situations. Here mother's helpers, which is what Lara had called her— Americans were good with words to cover their shame—seemed to be as good as anyone.

Ann Arbor was a huge small town. She couldn't imagine any kind of school the size of the University of Michigan. She meant to sign up for courses in the spring. Bill brought home a catalogue bigger than the phonebook for all of Trinidad. The university had courses in everything. It would be hard to choose; she'd have to get help from Bill. He wasn't like a professor, not the ones back home where even high school teachers called themselves professors and acted like little potentates. He wore blue jeans and thick sweaters with holes in the elbows and used phrases like "in vitro" as he watched her curry up fish. Dr. Parveen back home—he called himself "doctor" when everybody knew he didn't have even a Master's degree—was never seen without his cotton jacket which had gotten really ratty at the cuffs and lapel edges. She hadn't learned anything in the two years she'd put into college. She'd learned more from working in the bank for two months than she had at college. It was the assistant manager, Personal Loans Department, Mr. Singh, who had turned her on to the Daboos and to smooth, bargain-priced emigration.

Jasmine liked Lara. Lara was easygoing. She didn't spend the time she had between rehearsals telling Jasmine how to cook and clean American-style. Mrs. Daboo did that in 16B. Mrs. Daboo would barge in with a plate of stale samosas and snoop around giving free advice on how mainstream Americans did things. As if she were dumb or something! As if she couldn't keep her own eyes open and make her mind up for herself. Sunday mornings she had to share the butcher-block workspace in the kitchen with Bill. He made the Sunday brunch from new recipes in *Gourmet* and *Cuisine*. Jasmine hadn't seen a man cook who didn't have to or wasn't getting paid to do it. Things were topsy-turvy in the Moffitt house. Lara went on two- and three-day road trips and Bill stayed home. But even her Daddy, who'd never poured himself a cup of tea, wouldn't put Bill down as a woman. The mornings Bill tried out something complicated, a Cajun shrimp, sausage, and beans dish, for instance, Jasmine skipped church services. The Moffitts didn't go to church, though they seemed to be good Christians. They just didn't talk church talk, which suited her fine.

Lara showed her the room she would have all to herself in the finished basement. There was a big, old TV, not in color like the motel's and a portable typewriter on a desk which Lara said she would find handy when it came time to turn in her term papers. Jasmine didn't say anything about not being a student. She was a student of life, wasn't she? There was a scary moment after they'd discussed what she could expect as salary, which was three times more than anything Mr. Daboo was supposed to pay her but hadn't. She thought Bill Moffitt was going to ask her about her visa or her green card[1] number and social security. But all Bill did was smile and smile at her—he had a wide, pink, baby face—and play with a button on his corduroy jacket. The button would need sewing back on, firmly.

Lara said, "I think I'm going to like you, Jasmine. You have a something about you. A something real special. I'll just bet you've acted, haven't you?" The idea amused her, but she merely smiled and accepted Lara's hug. The interview was over.

Then Bill opened a bottle of Soave and told stories about camping in northern Michigan. He'd been raised there. Jasmine didn't see the point in sleeping in tents; the woods sounded cold and wild and creepy. But she said, "Is exactly what I want to try out come summer, man. Campin and huntin."

---

[1] Work permit issued only to immigrants who have permanent resident status in the U.S.

Lara asked about Port-of-Spain. There was nothing to tell about her hometown that wouldn't shame her in front of nice white American folk like the Moffitts. The place was shabby, the people were grasping and cheating and lying and life was full of despair and drink and wanting. But by the time she finished, the island sounded romantic. Lara said, "It wouldn't surprise me one bit if you were a writer, Jasmine."

Two months passed. Jasmine knew she was lucky to have found a small, clean, friendly family like the Moffitts to build her new life around. "Man!" she'd exclaim as she vacuumed the wide-plank wood floors or ironed (Lara wore pure silk or pure cotton). "In this country Jesus givin out good luck only!" By this time they knew she wasn't a student, but they didn't care and said they wouldn't report her. They never asked if she was illegal on top of it.

To savor her new sense of being a happy, lucky person, she would put herself through a series of "what ifs": what if Mr. Singh in Port-of-Spain hadn't turned her on to the Daboos and loaned her two thousand! What if she'd been ugly like the Mintoo girl and the manager hadn't even offered! What if the customs man had unlocked the door of the van! Her Daddy liked to say, "You is a helluva girl, Jasmine."

"Thank you, Jesus," Jasmine said, as she carried on.

Christmas Day the Moffitts treated her just like family. They gave her a red cashmere sweater with a V neck so deep it made her blush. If Lara had worn it, her bosom wouldn't hang out like melons. For the holiday weekend Bill drove her to the Daboos in Detroit. "You work too hard," Bill said to her. "Learn to be more selfish. Come on, throw your weight around." She'd rather not have spent time with the Daboos, but that first afternoon of the interview she'd told Bill and Lara that Mr. Daboo was her mother's first cousin. She had thought it shameful in those days to have no papers, no family, no roots. Now Loretta and Viola in tight, bright pants seemed trashy like girls at Two-Johnny Bissoondath's Bar back home. She was stuck with the story of the Daboos being family. Village bumpkins, ha! She would break out. Soon.

Jasmine had Bill drop her off at the RenCen. The Plantations Motel, in fact, the whole Riverfront area, was too seamy. She'd managed to cut herself off mentally from anything too islandy. She loved her Daddy and Mummy, but she didn't think of them that often anymore. Mummy had expected her to be homesick and come flying right back home. "Is blowin sweat-of-brow money is what you doin, Pa," Mummy had scolded. She loved them, but she'd become her own person. That was something that Lara said: "I am my own person."

The Daboos acted thrilled to see her back. "What you drinkin, Jasmine girl?" Mr. Daboo kept asking. "You drinkin sherry or what?" Pouring her little glasses of sherry instead of rum was a sure sign he thought she had become whitefolk-fancy. The Daboo sisters were very friendly, but Jasmine considered them too wild. Both Loretta and Viola had changed boyfriends. Both were seeing black men they'd danced with in Ann Arbor. Each night at bedtime, Mr. Daboo cried. "In Trinidad we stayin we side, they stayin they side. Here, everything mixed up. Is helluva confusion, no?"

On New Year's Eve the Daboo girls and their black friends went to a dance. Mr. and Mrs. Daboo and Jasmine watched TV for a while. Then Mr. Daboo got out a brooch from his pocket and pinned it on Jasmine's red sweater. It was a Christmasy brooch, a miniature sleigh loaded down with snowed-on mistletoe. Before she could pull away, he kissed her on the lips. "Good luck for the New Year!" he said. She lifted her head and saw tears. "Is year for dreams comin true."

Jasmine started to cry, too. There was nothing wrong, but Mr. Daboo, Mrs. Daboo, she, everybody was crying.

What for? This is where she wanted to be. She'd spent some damned uncomfortable times with the assistant manager to get approval for her loan. She thought of Daddy. He would be playing poker and fanning himself with a magazine. Her married sisters would be rolling out the dough for stacks and stacks of roti, and Mummy would be steamed purple from stirring the big pot of goat curry on the stove. She missed them. But. It felt strange to think of anyone celebrating New Year's Eve in summery clothes.

In March Lara and her performing group went on the road. Jasmine knew that the group didn't work from scripts. The group didn't use a stage, either; instead, it took over supermarkets, senior citizens' centers, and school halls, without notice. Jasmine didn't understand the performance world. But she was glad that Lara said, "I'm not going to lay a guilt trip on myself. Muffie's in super hands," before she left.

Muffie didn't need much looking after. She played Trivial Pursuit all day, usually pretending to be two persons, sometimes Jasmine, whose accent she could imitate. Since Jasmine didn't know any of the answers, she couldn't help. Muffie was a quiet, precocious child with see-through blue eyes like her dad's, and red braids. In the early evenings Jasmine cooked supper, something special she hadn't forgotten from her island days. After supper she and Muffie watched some TV, and Bill read. When Muffie went to bed, Bill and she sat together for a bit with their glasses of Soave. Bill, Muffie, and she were a family, almost.

Down in her basement room that late, dark winter, she had trouble sleeping. She wanted to stay awake and think of Bill. Even when she fell asleep it didn't feel like sleep because Bill came barging into her dreams in his funny, loose-jointed, clumsy way. It was mad to think of him all the time, and stupid and sinful; but she couldn't help it. Whenever she put back a book he'd taken off the shelf to read or whenever she put his clothes through the washer and dryer, she felt sick in a giddy, wonderful way. When Lara came back things would get back to normal. Meantime she wanted the performance group miles away.

Lara called in at least twice a week. She said things like, "We've finally obliterated the margin between realspace and performancespace." Jasmine filled her in on Muffie's doings and the mail. Bill always closed with, "I love you. We miss you, hon."

One night after Lara had called—she was in Lincoln, Nebraska—Bill said to Jasmine, "Let's dance."

She hadn't danced since the reggae night she'd had too many rum punches. Her toes began to throb and clench. She untied her apron and the fraying, knotted-up laces of her running shoes.

Bill went around the downstairs rooms turning down lights. "We need atmosphere," he said. He got a small, tidy fire going in the living room grate and pulled the Turkish scatter rug closer to it. Lara didn't like anybody walking on the Turkish rug, but Bill meant to have his way. The hissing logs, the plants in the dimmed light, the thick patterned rug: everything was changed. This wasn't the room she cleaned every day.

He stood close to her. She smoothed her skirt down with both hands.

"I want you to choose the record," he said.

"I don't know your music."

She brought her hand high to his face. His skin was baby smooth.

"I want *you* to pick," he said. "You are your own person now."

"You got island music?"

He laughed, "What do you think?" The stereo was in a cabinet with albums packed tight alphabetically into the bottom three shelves. "Calypso has not been a force in my life."

She couldn't help laughing. "Calypso? Oh, man." She pulled dust jackets out at random. Lara's records. The Flying Lizards. The Violent Femmes. There was so much still to pick up on!

"This one," she said, finally.

He took the record out of her hand. "God!" he laughed. "Lara must have found this in a garage sale!" He laid the old record on the turntable. It was "Music for Lovers," something the nuns had taught her to foxtrot to way back in Port-of-Spain.

They danced so close that she could feel his heart heaving and crashing against her head. She liked it, she liked it very much. She didn't care what happened.

"Come on," Bill whispered. "If it feels right, do it." He began to take her clothes off.

"Don't Bill," she pleaded.

"Come on, baby," he whispered again. "You're a blossom, a flower."

He took off his fisherman's knit pullover, the corduroy pants, the blue shorts. She kept pace. She'd never had such an effect on a man: He nearly flung his socks and Adidas into the fire. "You feel so good," he said. "You smell so good. You're really something, flower of Trinidad."

"Flower of Ann Arbor," she said, "not Trinidad."

She felt so good she was dizzy. She'd never felt this good on the island where men did this all the time, and girls went along with it always for favors. You couldn't feel really good in a nothing place. She was thinking this as they made love on the Turkish carpet in front of the fire: she was a bright, pretty girl with no visa, no papers, and no birth certificate. No nothing other than what she wanted to invent and tell. She was a girl rushing wildly into the future.

His hand moved up her throat and forced her lips apart and it felt so good, so right, that she forgot all the dreariness of her new life and gave herself up to it.

Journal Entry

What does the future hold for Jasmine? What do you imagine she would be doing in five years?

Textual Considerations

1. Jasmine is described as "a girl with ambition." What is she ambitious for? Does she accomplish her ambition? How? What are her other outstanding characteristics? Compare her experiences in Michigan with those in Trinidad.
2. Jasmine thinks what she learned about "bargain-priced emigration" from the assistant bank manager in Trinidad more important than anything she learned in two years of college. What does this tell us about Jasmine? What is the tone of the phrase "bargain-priced emigration"? How do you interpret the sentence "She'd spent some damned uncomfortable times with the assistant manager to get approval for her loan"?
3. Stories develop mainly from conflict: between two or more characters, within a character as the result of some psychological force (guilt, jealousy), or between a character and some impersonal force such as poverty or disease. What is the main conflict in this story? Between what or whom? Is the struggle resolved?

Cultural Contexts

1. "In this country Jesus givin out good luck only!" Why did Jasmine think Ann Arbor was "the place to be"? To what extent was she captured by the promise of the American Dream? Was she lucky to work for the Moffitts? Why or why not?
2. Examine with your group the portrait of the American family as exemplified by the Moffitts. Consider their attitudes toward marriage, child raising, and careers. To what extent does your group share their values?

Whitman, Levertov, and Randall

Walt Whitman

I Hear America Singing

I hear America singing, the varied carols I hear,
Those of mechanics, each one singing his as it should be blithe and strong,
The carpenter singing his as he measures his plank or beam,
The mason singing his as he makes ready for work, or leaves off work,
The boatman singing what belongs to him on his boat, the deck-hand singing
    on the steamboat deck,   5
The shoemaker singing as he sits on his bench, the hatter singing as he stands,
The wood-cutter's song, the ploughboy's on his way in the morning, or at
    noon intermission or at sundown,
The delicious singing of the mother, or of the young wife at work, or of the
    girl sewing or washing,
Each singing what belongs to him or her and to none else,
The day what belongs to the day—at night the party of young fellows,
    robust, friendly,   10
Singing with open mouths their strong melodious songs.

Denise Levertov

Poet Power

Riding by taxi, Brooklyn to Queens,
a grey spring day. The Hispanic driver,
when I ask, 'Es usted Mexicano?' tells me
No, he's an exile for Uruguay. And I say,
'The only other Uraguayan I've met   5
was a writer—maybe
you know his name?—
           Mario Benedetti?
And he takes both hands

off the wheel and swings round,   10
glittering with joy: *'Benedetti!*
Mario Benedetti!!'*
                    There are
hallelujahs in his voice—
we execute a perfect   15
figure 8 on the shining highway,
and rise aloft, high above traffic, flying
all the rest of the way in the blue sky, azul, azul!

Dudley Randall

The Melting Pot

There is a magic melting pot
where any girl or man
can step in Czech or Greek or Scot,
step out American.

Johann and *Jan* and *Jean* and *Juan,*   5
Giovanni and *Ivan*
step in and then step out again
all freshly christened *John.*

Sam, watching, said, "Why, I was here
even before they came,"   10
and stepped in too, but was tossed out
before he passed the brim.

And every time Sam tried that pot
they threw him out again.

"Keep out. This is our private pot   15
We don't want your black stain."

At last, thrown out a thousand times,
Sam said, "I don't give a damn.
Shove your old pot. You can like it or not,
but I'll be just what I am."   20

Journal Entry

Contrast the speakers' views on cultural diversity and equality in the three poems.

Textual Considerations

1. Analyze the effectiveness of the metaphor of song to reinforce meaning in Whitman's poem.
2. Examine the structural pattern of "The Melting Pot" from the point of view of poetic form, imagery, and narrative voice.
3. Evaluate the effectiveness of the melting pot as the dominant symbol in Randall's poem.

Cultural Contexts

1. Discuss with your group Sam's rejection of the concept of the melting pot in Randall's poem. What forces make it possible for him to reinforce his personal and ethnic identity despite the hostility and rejection he encounters? Try to reach a consensus about the ability (or inability) of people to respect cultural and ethnic diversity and gender difference.

Espada and Rodriguez

Martín Espada

Federico's Ghost

The story is
that whole families of fruitpickers
still crept between the furrows
of the field at dusk,
when for reasons of whiskey or whatever   5
the cropduster plane sprayed anyway,
floating a pesticide drizzle
over the pickers
who thrashed like dark birds
in a glistening white net,   10
except for Federico,
a skinny boy who stood apart
in his own green row,
and, knowing the pilot
would not understand in Spanish   15
that he was the son of a whore,
instead jerked his arm
and thrust an obscene finger.

The pilot understood.
He circled the plane and sprayed again,   20
watching a fine gauze of poison
drift over the brown bodies
that cowered and scurried on the ground,
and aiming for Federico,
leaving the skin beneath his shirt   25
wet and blistered,
but still pumping his finger at the sky.

After Federico died,
rumors at the labor camp
told of tomatoes picked and smashed at night,   30
growers muttering of vandal children
or communists in camp,
first threatening to call Immigration,
then promising every Sunday off
if only the smashing of tomatoes would stop.   35

Still tomatoes were picked and squashed
in the dark,
and the old women in camp
said it was Federico,
laboring after sundown   40
to cool the burns on his arms,
flinging tomatoes
at the cropduster
that hummed like a mosquito
lost in his ear,   45
and kept his soul awake.

Luis Rodriguez

First Day of Work

My dark-eyed wife
saw me off in the new
green work clothes.
Me—proud in shiny hard hat
and steel-tipped shoes.   5

First day of work.
What a day! What a dream.
Our *barrio Florencia* flat
never ached so good.

Days before this place stunk   10
of newlywed poor.
I couldn't find work.
Oh, I had tried:
Trouncing the rows
of factories,   15
warehouses,
and construction sites.

Come back next month,
        they'd say.
You ain't got experience,   20
        they'd say.
How the hell was I
supposed to get some,
        I'd say.

She was tired. I was tired.   25
We were tired of each other.
Then a friend of a friend,
who I met standing in line
for an application one morning,
told me to check out   30
the construction site
on Alameda Street near Wilmington.

I went. I was tired.

Then they called back. Great day!
They needed helpers. They needed   35
young backs like mine
to haul and pull and drag.
I'm your man. For sure!

I got the shoes: the Sears workingman's special.
I borrowed the money . . . but hey   40
I was working again.

So off I went. Kinda nervous.
My wife almost looked happy.

I worked with a journeyman
millwright; putting together   45
a conveyor system—a whirl
of gears, electric motors,
rubber belts, and hoses
full of oil.

At one point he had to arc-weld   50
two pieces of metal.
Hold this for me while I weld,
        he said.

Okay. Anything. I can do it.
It was great, watching that   55
little sun glow on the steel,
fusing it with another rod
held in an electric claw.
It looked sharp, bright
—powerful.   60

Lunch came. Jokes about new dudes,
Mexicans, blacks—
I didn't know what to say, but hey,
it was work.

Most of the day went fine.   65
But then came a burning in my eyes.
I tried to ignore it.
But something tore at them
from the inside.

I didn't know what to do.   70
I told the journeyman, finally,
when I couldn't see
the end of the crescent wrench
I was pulling on.

Did you look at the spark   75
when I was welding?
        he asked.
Well, yeah . . .

Damn it, man!
        he shouted.   80
Don't you know not to look
at an arc-weld!

Great. My first day at work
and I could go blind.

The pain became unbearable.   85
Every time I exposed the eyes,
the sting, like fire,
cut through them.
That afternoon
my dark-eyed wife   90
came for me.

At the industrial clinic,
I got the official word:
I had seared the lubrication
off the eyes—   95
that precious oil that protected
the sensitive cornea and iris
from dirt and debris.

Without this, I felt
every hint of dust, lint, smog   100
slicing into me.

First day of work!

That evening, I lay cradled
in my wife's arms;
my eyes in bandages.   105

Journal Entry

Respond to the images of entrapment in both poems.

Textual Considerations

1. Follow the development of the speaker's voice in "First Day of Work" as it moves from joy, hope, and expectation to despair. How does the poet's use of devices such as repetition, dashes, and ellipses contribute to the poem's meaning?
2. What portrait of the speaker's wife emerges in "First Day of Work"? What does the poem suggest about the effects of economics on gender relationships?
3. Characterize Federico. What images best portray him? What is the speaker's attitude toward him? How does it compare to yours?

Cultural Contexts

1. Debate with your group the issues of unemployment and the situation of migrant workers presented in both poems. What ramifications besides economic deprivation are implicit in their situations? Consider, for example, images of violence in the poems.

Sook Lyol Ryu

Poem by a Yellow Woman

When I first saw America,
it was like a huge giant,
and I was like a pygmy woman.
I made a desperate struggle with this giant
not to fall. He whistled merrily, waving his hands.   5
He was a huge man, but a man like a snake.

Now, here I am in America, where
people drink Coca-Cola, where
people are crazy about Spielberg's silly films, where
people chase endless desires, where   10
people choose an old anachronistic
movie star as their president, where
people enjoy powerful wealth,
but keep homeless people in the street, where
people shout, "ladies first,"   15
and don't allow a woman to be president.
Now here I am from the country, where
the people are burning American flags,
singing, "Yankee, go home!"
Now here I am in America, where   20
most of my yellow people are hungry
for McDonald's and greedy for "Made in U.S.A."
My brother, who has a master's degree in English literature
thinks about Norman Mailer's American Dream
while selling fishes and vegetables   25
to his white neighbors 24 hours a day.
My sister, who liked paintings of
Picasso's Blue Period
is working on a sewing machine, with dyed blond hair.

When colored friends are making a rainbow coalition,   30
my yellow people wonder whether yellow is on the rainbow.
They think the lighter the skin, the closer to heaven,
the darker the skin, the closer to hell.
They decide yellow is in between.
So they smile at white and frown at black.   35
They make money in the hope of becoming a majority
and forget about the minority.

Maria Mazziotti Gillan

Public School No. 18: Paterson, New Jersey

Miss Wilson's eyes, opaque
as blue glass, fix on me:
"We must speak English.
We're in America now."
I want to say, "I am American,"   5
but the evidence is stacked against me.

My mother scrubs my scalp raw, wraps
my shining hair in white rags
to make it curl; Miss Wilson
drags me to the window, checks my hair   10
for lice. My face wants to hide.

At home, my words smooth in my mouth,
I chatter and am proud. In school,
I am silent; I grope for the right English
words, fear the Italian word will sprout   15
from my mouth like a rose.

I fear the progression of teachers
in their sprigged dresses,
their Anglo-Saxon faces.

Without words, they tell me   20
to be ashamed.
I am.
I deny that booted country
even from myself,
want to be still   25
and untouchable
as these women
who teach me to hate myself.

Years later, in a white
Kansas City house,   30
the psychology professor tells me
I remind him of the Mafia leader
on the cover of *Time* magazine.

My anger spits
venomous from my mouth: 35

I am proud of my mother,
dressed all in black,
proud of my father
with his broken tongue,
proud of the laughter   40
and noise of our house.

Remember me, ladies,
the silent one?
I have found my voice
and my rage will blow   45
your house down.

Journal Entry

Respond to the critique of American values in both poems.

Textual Considerations

1. Identify images of power and powerlessness in each poem, and analyze their causes and effects.
2. Analyze the functions of skin color in both poems, and assess the extent to which awareness of color affects the speakers' sense of exclusion. What other factors contribute to their alienation?
3. Identify effective examples of figurative language in both poems, and discuss their contribution to theme.

Cultural Contexts

1. Discuss what "Poem by a Yellow Woman" reveals about the socioeconomic and educational status of many Asian-American immigrants in the United States.
2. Discuss the link between perception of race and presentation of the self in both poems. To what extent do the speakers' perceptions of their ethnic roots determine the way they view themselves?

Wole Soyinka

Telephone Conversation

The price seemed reasonable, location
Indifferent. The landlady swore she lived
Off premises. Nothing remained
But self-confession. "Madam," I warned,
"I hate a wasted journey—I am African."   5
Silence. Silenced transmission of
Pressurized good-breeding. Voice, when it came,
Lipstick coated, long gold-rolled
Cigarette-holder pipped. Caught I was, foully.
"HOW DARK?" . . . I had not misheard . . . "ARE YOU LIGHT   10
OR VERY DARK?" Button B. Button A. Stench
Of rancid breath of public hide-and-speak.
Red booth. Red pillar-box. Red double-tiered
Omnibus squelching tar. It *was* real! Shamed
By ill-mannered silence, surrender   15
Pushed dumbfoundment to beg simplification.
Considerate she was, varying the emphasis—
"ARE YOU DARK? OR VERY LIGHT?" Revelation came.
"You mean—like plain or milk chocolate?"
Her assent was clinical, crushing in its light   20
Impersonality. Rapidly, wave-length adjusted,
I chose. "West African sepia"—and as afterthought,
"Down in my passport." Silence for spectroscopic
Flight of fancy, till truthfulness clanged her accent
Hard on the mouthpiece. "WHAT'S THAT?" conceding   25
"DON'T KNOW WHAT THAT IS." "Like brunette."
"THAT'S DARK, ISN'T IT?" "Not altogether.
Facially, I am brunette, but madam, you should see
The rest of me. Palm of my hand, soles of my feet
Are a peroxide blonde. Friction, caused—   30
Foolishly madam—by sitting down, has turned
My bottom raven black—One moment madam!"—sensing
Her receiver rearing on the thunderclap
About my ears—"Madam," I pleaded, "wouldn't you rather
See for yourself?"   35

Sharon Olds

On the Subway

The boy and I face each other.
His feet are huge, in black sneakers
laced with white in a complex pattern like a
set of intentional scars. We are stuck on
opposite sides of the car, a couple of   5
molecules stuck in a rod of light
rapidly moving through darkness. He has the
casual cold look of a mugger,
alert under hooded lids. He is wearing
red, like the inside of the body   10
exposed. I am wearing dark fur, the
whole skin of an animal taken and
used. I look at his raw face,
he looks at my fur coat, and I don't
know if I am in his power—   15
he could take my coat so easily, my
briefcase, my life—
or if he is in my power, the way I am
living off his life, eating the steak
he does not eat, as if I am taking   20
the food from his mouth. And he is black
and I am white, and without meaning or
trying to I must profit from his darkness,
the way he absorbs the murderous beams of the
nation's heart, as black cotton   25
absorbs the heat of the sun and holds it. There is
no way to know how easy this
white skin makes my life, this
life he could take so easily and
break across his knee like a stick the way his   30
own back is being broken, the
rod of his soul that at birth was dark and
fluid and rich as the heart of a seedling
ready to thrust up into any available light.

Journal Entry

Analyze the functions of setting in both poems.

Textual Considerations

1. Explore the concepts of power and powerlessness as expressed in "On the Subway" (ll. 15–18).
2. Analyze the references to skin color in "On the Subway." Explain the meaning of lines 20–23.
3. Consider the landlady's perception of race in "Telephone Conversation," starting with her degree of tolerance toward skin pigmentation. What images does she envision to define blackness? Identify the specific statements or questions that escalate the racial tension of the conversation.
4. Examine the structural pattern of "Telephone Conversation" from the point of view of poetic form, imagery, and narrative voice.

Cultural Contexts

1. How does your group view the statement by Martin Luther King, Jr., that "white America must assume the guilt for the Black man's inferior status"? Is this a fair or unfair attempt to force a feeling of guilt on the consciousness of white America?
2. Review the last four lines of "Telephone Conversation," and discuss their implications for the speaker's identity.

Cervantes and Jeffers

Lorna Dee Cervantes

Poem for the Young White Man Who Asked Me How I, an Intelligent, Well-Read Person Could Believe in the War Between Races

In my land there are no distinctions.
The barbed wire politics of oppression
have been torn down long ago. The only reminder
of past battles, lost or won, is a slight
rutting in the fertile fields.   5

In my land
people write poems about love,
full of nothing but contented childlike syllables.
Everyone reads Russian short stories and weeps.
There are no boundaries.   10
There is no hunger, no
complicated famine or greed.

I am not revolutionary.
I don't even like political poems.
Do you think I can believe in a war between races?   15
I can deny it. I can forget about it
when I'm safe,
living on my own continent of harmony
and home, but I am not
there.   20

I believe in revolution
because everywhere the crosses are burning,
sharp-shooting goose-steppers round every corner,
there are snipers in schools . . .
(I know you don't believe this.   25
You think this is nothing
but faddish exaggeration. But they
are not shooting at you.)

I'm marked by the color of my skin.
The bullets are discrete and designed to kill slowly.   30
They are aiming at my children.
These are facts.
Let me show you my wounds: my stumbling mind, my
"excuse me" tongue, and this
nagging preoccupation   35
with the feeling of not being good enough.

These bullets bury deeper than logic.
Racism is not intellectual.
I can not reason these scars away.

Outside my door   40
there is a real enemy
who hates me.

I am a poet
who yearns to dance on rooftops,
to whisper delicate lines about joy   45
and the blessings of human understanding.
I try. I go to my land, my tower of words and
bolt the door, but the typewriter doesn't fade out
the sounds of blasting and muffled outrage.
My own days bring me slaps on the face.   50
Every day I am deluged with reminders
that this is not
my land
and this is my land.

I do not believe in the war between races.   55

but in this country
there is war.

Lance Jeffers

My Blackness Is the Beauty of This Land

My blackness is the beauty of this land,
my blackness,
tender and strong, wounded and wise,
my blackness:
I, drawing black grandmother, smile muscular and sweet,   5
unstraightened white hair soon to grow in earth,
work thickened hand thoughtful and gentle on grandson's
        head,
my heart is bloody-razored by a million memories' thrall:

    remembering the crook-necked cracker who spat   10
        on my naked body,
    remembering the splintering of my son's spirit
        because he remembered to be proud
    remembering the tragic eyes in my daughter's
        dark face when she learned her color's   15
        meaning,

and my own dark rage a rusty knife with teeth to gnaw
    my bowels,
my agony ripped loose by anguished shouts in Sunday's
    humble church,   20
my agony rainbowed to ecstasy when my feet oversoared
    Montgomery's slime,
ah, this hurt, this hate, this ecstasy before I die,
and all my love a strong cathedral!
My blackness is the beauty of this land!   25

Lay this against my whiteness, this land!
Lay me, young Brutus stamping hard on the cat's tail,
gutting the Indian, gouging the nigger,
booting Little Rock's Minniejean Brown in the buttocks and
    boast,   30
    my sharp white teeth derision-bared as I the
        conqueror crush!
Skyscraper-I, white hands burying God's human clouds
    beneath
            the dust!   35
Skyscraper-I, slim blond young Empire
        thrusting up my loveless bayonet to rape the
            sky,
then shrink all my long body with filth and in the gutter lie
as lie I will to perfume this armpit garbage,   40

While I here standing black beside
wrench tears from which the lies would suck the salt
to make me more American than America . . .
But yet my love and yet my hate shall civilize this land,
this land's salvation.   45

Journal Entry

Characterize and respond to the tone of both poems.

Textual Considerations

1. Compare and contrast both poets' concepts of their "land." Explain the paradoxes in the last stanza of Jeffers's poem and in the last seven lines of Cervantes's poem.
2. Comment on Jeffers's imagery of the cathedral and the skyscraper. Why are these images appropriate for his meaning?

3. Comment on Jeffers's line arrangement. How does it contribute to the poem's meaning? Point out examples of repetition and discuss their effectiveness.
4. Characterize Cervantes's style. To what extent is it appropriate for her audience? Who is her primary audience?

Cultural Contexts

1. To develop your critical awareness about the stereotypes associated with skin color in the United States, discuss with your group the degree to which our assumptions about people are based on skin color. What consensus did you reach?

Robinson and Laviera ◆

Edwin Arlington Robinson

Richard Cory

Whenever Richard Cory went down town,
We people on the pavement looked at him:
He was a gentleman from sole to crown,
Clean favored, and imperially slim.

And he was always quietly arrayed,   5
And he was always human when he talked;
But still he fluttered pulses when he said,
"Good-morning," and he glittered when he walked.

And he was rich—yes, richer than a king—
And admirably schooled in every grace: 10
In fine, we thought that he was everything
To make us wish that we were in his place.

So on we worked, and waited for the light,
And went without the meat, and cursed the bread;
And Richard Cory, one calm summer night,   15
Went home and put a bullet through his head.

Tato Laviera

Latero[1] Story

i am a twentieth-century welfare recipient
moonlighting in the sun as a latero
a job invented by national state laws
designed to re-cycle aluminum cans
returned to consumer's acid laden   5
gastric inflammation pituitary glands
coca diet rites low cal godsons
of artificially flavored malignant
indigestions somewhere down the line
of a cancerous cell   10

i collect garbage cans in outdoor facilities
congested with putrid residues
my hands shelving themselves
opening plastic bags never knowing
what they'll encounter   15

several times a day i touch evil rituals
cut throats of chickens
tongues of poisoned rats
salivating my index finger
smells of month old rotten foods   20
next to pamper's diarrhea
    dry blood infectious diseases
hypodermic needles tissued with
heroin water drops pilfered in
slimy greases hazardous waste materials   25
but i cannot use rubber gloves
they undermine my daily profits

i am twentieth-century welfare recipient
moonlighting in the day as a latero
that is the only opportunity i have   30
to make it big in america
some day i might become experienced enough
to offer technical assistance
to other lateros
i am thinking of publishing   35
my own guide to latero's collection
and a latero's union offering
medical dental benefits

i am a twentieth-century welfare recipient
moonlighting in the night as a latero   40
i am considered some kind of expert
at collecting cans during fifth avenue parades
i can now hire workers at twenty
five cents an hour guaranteed salary
and fifty per cent two and one half cents   45
profit on each can collected

i am a twentieth-century welfare recipient
moonlighting in midnight as a latero
i am becoming an entrepreneur
an american success story   50
i have hired bag ladies to keep peddlers
from my territories
i have read in some guide to success
that in order to get rich
to make it big   55
i have to sacrifice myself
moonlighting until dawn by digging
deeper into the extra can
margin of profit
i am on my way up the opportunistic   60
ladder of success
in ten years i will quit welfare
to become a legitimate businessman
i'll soon become a latero executive
with corporate conglomerate intents   65
god bless america

¹ From Spanish *lata:* can. A man who picks up cans from garbage containers and the streets.

Journal Entry

React to the issue of social class as both poems convey it.

Textual Considerations

1. Cite words or phrases associating Richard Cory with wealth or royalty, and discuss how these affect your response to him.
2. Comment on Robinson's use of irony.
3. Characterize the tone of Laviera's poem, and comment on its appropriateness to his theme.
4. Much of Laviera's poetry belongs to the oral tradition. What does that suggest about his purpose and audience? How do you respond to his style?

Cultural Contexts

1. Discuss with your group the treatment of success in both poems. Why did Richard Cory commit suicide, despite his wealth and social status? What kind of success does the Latero envisage for himself? To what extent does your concept of success resemble his?

Sarton and Lassell ◆

May Sarton

AIDS

We are stretched to meet a new dimension
Of love, a more demanding range
Where despair and hope must intertwine.
How grow to meet it? Intention
Here can neither move nor change   5
The raw truth. Death is on the line.
It comes to separate and estrange
Lover from lover in some reckless design.
Where do we go from here?

Fear. Fear. Fear. Fear.   10

Our world has never been more stark
Or more in peril.
It is very lonely now in the dark.
Lonely and sterile.

And yet in the simple turn of a head   15
Mercy lives. I heard it when someone said
"I must go now to a dying friend.
Every night at nine I tuck him into bed,
And give him a shot of morphine,"
And added, "I go where I have never been."   20
I saw he meant into a new discipline
He had not imagined before, and a new grace.

Every day now we meet face to face.
Every day now devotion is the test.
Through the long hours, the hard, caring nights   25
We are forging a new union. We are blest.

As closed hands open to each other
Closed lives open to strange tenderness.
We are learning the hard way how to mother.
Who says it is easy? But we have the power.   30
I watch the faces deepen all around me.
It is the time of change, the saving hour.
The word is not fear, the word we live,
But an old word suddenly made new,
As we learn it again, as we bring it alive: 35

Love. Love. Love. Love.

Michael Lassell

How to Watch Your Brother Die

When the call comes, be calm
Say to your wife, "My brother is dying. I have
to fly to California."
Try not to be shocked that he already looks like a cadaver.
Say to the young man sitting by your brother's side,   5
"I'm his brother."
Try not to be shocked when the young man says,
"I'm his lover. Thanks for coming."

Listen to the doctor with a steel face on.
Sign the necessary forms.   10
Tell the doctor you will take care of everything.
Wonder why doctors are so remote.

Watch the lover's eyes as they stare into
your brother's eyes as they stare into
space.   15
Wonder what they see there.
Remember the time he was jealous and
opened your eyebrows with a sharp stick.
Forgive him out loud
even if he can't understand you.   20
Realize the scar will be
all that's left of him.

Over coffee in the hospital cafeteria
say to the lover, "You're an extremely good-looking
young man."   25
Hear him say,
"I never I thought I was good enough looking to
deserve your brother."
Watch the tears well up in his eyes. Say,
"I'm sorry. I don't know what it means to be   30
the lover of another man."
Hear him say,
"It's just like a wife, only the commitment is
deeper because the odds against you are so much
greater."   35
Say nothing, but
take his hand like a brother's.

Drive to Mexico for unproven drugs that might
help him live longer.
Explain what they are to the border guard.   40
Fill with rage when he informs you,
"You can't bring those across."
Begin to grow loud.
Feel the lover's hand on your arm,
restraining you. See in the guard's eye   45
how much a man can hate another man.
Say to the lover, "How can you stand it?"
Hear him say, "You get used to it."
Think of one of your children getting used to
another man's hatred.   50

Call your wife on the telephone. Tell her
"He hasn't much time.
I'll be home soon." Before you hang up, say,
"How could anyone's commitment be deeper than
a husband and wife?" Hear her say,   55
"Please, I don't want to know all the details."

When he slips into an irrevocable coma
hold his lover in your arms while he sobs,
no longer strong. Wonder how much longer
you will be able to be strong.   60
Feel how it feels to hold a man in your arms
whose arms are used to holding men.
Offer God anything to bring your brother back.
Know you have nothing God could possibly want.
Curse God, but do not   65
abandon Him.

Stare at the face of the funeral director
when he tells you he will not
embalm the body for fear of
contamination. Let him see in your eyes   70
how much a man can hate a man.

Stand beside a casket covered in flowers,
white flowers. Say,
"Thank you for coming" to each of several hundred men
who file past in tears, some of them   75
holding hands. Know that your brother's life
was not what you imagined. Overhear two mourners say,
"I wonder who'll be next."

Arrange to take an early flight home.
His lover will drive you to the airport.   80
When your flight is announced say,
awkwardly, "If I can do anything, please
let me know." Do not flinch when he says,
"Forgive yourself for not wanting to know him
after he told you. He did."   85
Stop and let it soak in. Say,
"He forgave me, or he knew himself?"
"Both," the lover will say, not knowing what else
to do. Hold him like a brother while he
kisses you on the cheek. Think that   90
you haven't been kissed by a man since
your father died. Think,
"This is no moment not to be strong." Fly
first class and drink scotch. Stroke
your split eyebrow with a finger   95
and think of your brother alive. Smile
at the memory and think
how your children will feel in your arms,
warm and friendly and without challenge.

Journal Entry

Respond to the contrasting images of love and hate in Lassell's poem.

Textual Considerations

1. To what extent do you agree with the speaker in Sarton's poem that words like *fear,*
   mercy, and *love* evoke new meanings in the context of AIDS?

2. Evaluate which of the speakers' voices in the two poems is more effective in communicating the sense of fear and insecurity connected with the AIDS epidemic. Which is more successful in presenting a message of hope and solidarity to the audience? What factors might account for differences in the speakers' points of view?
3. Analyze the functions of dialogue in Lassell's poem. Consider, for example, what the speaker's dialogues reveal about himself, his wife, his relationship to his brother, and his relationship to his brother's lover. What do the various conversations suggest about the relationship of the gay community to the larger society?

Cultural Contexts

1. Working with your group, make a list of the images that you associate with AIDS. To what extent has this issue affected your lives?
2. Can your group find any justification for the marginalized position that gays and lesbians occupy in U.S. society? Where do you stand on the issue of whether people should be free to express their sexual preferences? Debate with your group whether the freedom to express sexual preference may be viewed as the embodiment of the democratic spirit and whether true equality can exist without this freedom.

William Shakespeare

Othello, the Moor of Venice

THE NAMES OF THE ACTORS

OTHELLO, *the Moor*
BRABANTIO, *a senator, father to* DESDEMONA
CASSIO, *an honourable lieutenant to* OTHELLO
IAGO, OTHELLO's *ancient, a villain*
RODERIGO, *a gulled gentleman*
DUKE OF VENICE
SENATORS *of Venice*
MONTANTO, *governor of Cyprus*
LODOVICO *and* GRATIANO, *kinsmen to* BRABANTIO, *two noble Venetians*
Sailors
Clown
DESDEMONA, *daughter to* BRABANTIO *and wife to* OTHELLO
EMILIA, *wife to* IAGO
BIANCA, *a courtezan and mistress to* CASSIO
Messenger, Herald, Officers, Gentlemen, Musicians, *and* Attendants

[SCENE: *Venice: a sea-port in Cyprus*]

ACT I

SCENE I. *Venice. A street.*

[*Enter* RODERIGO *and* IAGO.]

ROD. Tush! never tell me; I take it much unkindly
  That thou, Iago, who hast had my purse
  As if the strings were thine, shouldst know of this.
IAGO. 'Sblood,[1] but you'll not hear me:
  If ever I did dream of such a matter,
  Abhor me.
ROD. Thou told'st me thou didst hold him in thy hate.
IAGO. Despise me, if I do not. Three great ones of the city,[2]
  In personal suit to make me his lieutenant,

---

[1] *'Sblood* an oath, "by God's blood" [2] *great ones of the city* Iago means to indicate his importance in the community; this is suggested also by his use of the word *worth* in line 11

Off-capp'd to him:[3] and, by the faith of man,   10
I know my price, I am worth no worse a place:
But he, as loving his own pride and purposes,
Evades them, with a bombast circumstance
Horribly stuff'd with epithets of war;
And, in conclusion,
Nonsuits[4] my mediators; for, "Certes," says he,
"I have already chose my officer."
And what was he?
Forsooth, a great arithmetician,[5]
One Michael Cassio, a Florentine,   20
A fellow almost damn'd in a fair wife;[6]
That never set a squadron in the field,
Nor the division[7] of a battle knows
More than a spinster; unless the bookish theoric,[8]
Wherein the toged[9] consuls can propose[10]
As masterly as he: mere prattle, without practice,
Is all his soldiership. But he, sir, had th' election:
And I, of whom his eyes had seen the proof
At Rhodes, at Cyprus[11] and on other grounds
Christian and heathen, must be be-lee'd and calm'd   30
By debitor and creditor: this counter-caster,[12]
He, in good time,[13] must his lieutenant be,
And I—God bless the mark![14]—his Moorship's ancient.[15]
Rod.   By heaven, I rather would have been his hangman.
Iago.   Why, there's no remedy; 'tis the curse of service,
Preferment goes by letter and affection,
And not by old gradation,[16] where each second
Stood heir to th' first. Now, sir, be judge yourself,
Whether I in any just term am affin'd[17]
To love the Moor.
Rod.   I would not follow then.   40
Iago.   O, sir, content you;
I follow him to serve my turn upon him:
We cannot all be masters, nor all masters

---

[3] *him* Othello   [4] *Nonsuits* rejects   [5] *arithmetician* a man whose military knowledge was merely theoretical, based on books of tactics   [6] *A . . . wife* Cassio does not seem to be married, but his counterpart in Shakespear's source did have a wife   [7] *division* disposition of a battle line   [8] *theoric* theory   [9] *toged* wearing the toga   [10] *propose* discuss   [11] *Rhodes, Cyprus* islands in the Mediterranean south of Asia Minor, long subject to contention between the Venetians and the Turks
[12] *counter-caster* a sort of bookkeeper; contemptuous term   [13] *in good time* forsooth   [14] *God bless the mark* anciently, a pious interjection to avert evil omens   [15] *ancient* standardbearer, ensign
[16] *old gradation* seniority; Iago here expresses a characteristic prejudice of professional soldiers
[17] *affin'd* bound

Cannot be truly follow'd. You shall mark
Many a duteous and knee-crooking knave,
That, doting on his own obsequious bondage,
Wears out his time, much like his master's ass,
For nought but provender, and when he's old, cashier'd:
Whip me such honest knaves. Others there are
Who, trimm'd in forms and visages of duty,   50
Keep yet their hearts attending on themselves,
And, throwing but shows of service on their lords,
Do well thrive by them and when they have lin'd their coats
Do themselves homage: these fellow have some soul;
And such a one do I profess myself. For, sir,
It is as sure as you are Roderigo,
Were I the Moor, I would not be Iago:[18]
In following him, I follow but myself;
Heaven is my judge, nor I for love and duty,
But seeming so, for my peculiar end: 60
For when my outward action doth demonstrate
The native act and figure of my heart
In compliment extern,[19] 'tis not long after
But I will wear my heart upon my sleeve
For daws to peck at: I am not what I am.
ROD. What a full fortune does the thick-lips[20] owe,
  If he can carry 't thus!
IAGO.   Call up her father,
  Rouse him: make after him, poison his delight,
  Proclaim him in the streets; incense her kinsmen,
  And, though he in a fertile climate dwell,   70
  Plague him with flies: though that his joy be joy,
  Yet throw such changes of vexation on 't,
  As it may lose some colour.
ROD. Here is her father's house; I'll call aloud.
IAGO. Do, with like timorous[21] accent and dire yell
  As when, by night and negligence, the fire
  Is spied in populous cities.
ROD. What, ho, Brabantio! Signior Brabantio, ho!
IAGO. Awake! what, ho, Brabantio! thieves! thieves! thieves!
  Look to your house, your daughter and your bags!   80
  Thieves! thieves!

[BRABANTIO *appears above at a window.*]

---

[18] *Were . . . Iago* Were I in the position of the Moor, I should not feel as Iago feels   [19] *compliment extern* outward civility   [20] *thick-lips* Elizabethans often applied the term *Moor* to Negroes
[21] *timorous* frightening

BRA. What is the reason of this terrible summons?
  What is the matter there?
ROD. Signior, is all your family within?
IAGO. Are your doors lock'd?
BRA.   Why, wherefore ask you this?
IAGO. 'Zounds, sir, y' are robb'd; for shame, put on your gown;
  Your heart is burst, you have lost half your soul;
  Even now, now, very now, an old black ram
  Is tupping your white ewe. Arise, arise:
  Awake the snorting[22] citizens with the bell,   90
  Or else the devil will make a grandsire of you:
  Arise, I say.
BRA.   What, have you lost your wits?
ROD. Most reverend signior, do you know my voice?
BRA. Not I: what are you?
ROD. My name is Roderigo.
BRA.   The worser welcome:
  I have charg'd thee not to haunt about my doors:
  In honest plainness thou has heard me say
  My daughter is not for thee; and now, in madness,
  Being full of supper and distemp'ring draughts,
  Upon malicious bravery,[23] doest thou come   100
  To start[24] my quiet.
ROD. Sir, sir, sir,—
BRA.   But thou must needs be sure
  My spirit and my place have in them power
  To make this bitter to thee.
ROD.   Patience, good sir.
BRA. What tell'st thou me of robbing? this is Venice;
  My house is not a grange.[25]
ROD.   Most grave Brabantio,
  In simple and pure soul I come to you.
IAGO. 'Zounds, sir, you are one of those that will not serve God, if the devil bid
  you. Because we come to do you service and you think we are ruffians, you'll
  have your daughter covered with a Barbary horse, you'll have your nephews[26]   110
  neigh to you; you'll have coursers for cousins and gennets[27] for germans.[28]
BRA. What profane wretch art thou?
IAGO. I am one, sir, that comes to tell you your daughter and the Moor are now
  making the beast with two backs.
BRA. Thou art a villain.
IAGO.   You are—a senator.
BRA. This thou shalt answer; I know thee, Roderigo.

---

[22] *snorting* snoring   [23] *bravery* defiance, bravado   [24] *start* disrupt   [25] *grange* isolated farmhouse
[26] *nephews* grandsons   [27] *gennets* small Spanish horses   [28] *germans* near relatives

Rod.   Sir, I will answer any thing. But, I beseech you,
  If 't be your pleasure and most wise consent,
  As partly I find it is, that your fair daughter,
At this odd-even[29] and dull watch o' th' night,   120
  Transported, with no worse nor better guard
  But with a knave of common hire, a gondolier,
  To the gross clasps of a lascivious Moor,—
  If this be known to you and your allowance,[30]
  We then have done you bold and saucy wrongs;
  But if you know not this, my manners tell me
  We have your wrong rebuke. Do not believe
  That, from[31] the sense of all civility,
  I thus would play and trifle with your reverence:
  Your daughter, if you have not given her leave,   130
  I say again, hath made a gross revolt;
  Tying her duty, beauty, wit and fortunes
  In an extravagant[32] and wheeling[33] stranger
  Of here and every where. Straight satisfy yourself:
  If she be in her chamber or your house,
  Let loose on me the justice of the state
  For thus deluding you.
Bra.   Strike on the tinder,[34] ho!
  Give me a taper! call up my people!
  This accident[35] is not unlike my dream:
  Belief of it oppresses me already.   140
  Light, I say! light? [*Exit above.*]
Iago.   Farewell; for I must leave you:
  If seems not meet, nor wholesome to my place,
  To be produc'd—as, if I stay, I shall—
  Against the Moor: for, I do know, the state,
  However this may gall him with some check,[36]
  Cannot with safety cast[37] him, for he's embark'd
  With such loud reason to the Cyprus wars,
  Which even now stand in act,[38] that, for their souls,
  Another of his fathom[39] they have none,
  To lead their business: in which regard,   150
  Though I do hate him as I do hell-pains,
  Yet, for necessity of present life,
  I must show out a flag and sign of love,

---

[29] *odd-even* between night and morning   [30] *allowance* permission   [31] *from* contrary to
[32] *extravagant* wandering   [33] *wheeling* vagabond   [34] *tinder* charred linen kept in a metal box, and
ignited by a spark from flint and steel   [35] *accident* occurrence, event   [36] *check* rebuke
[37] *cast* dismiss   [38] *stand in act* are going on   [39] *fathom* ability

Which is indeed but sign. That you shall surely find him,
Lead to the Sagittary[40] the raised search:
And there will I be with him. So, farewell. [*Exit.*]

[*Enter below* BRABANTIO *with* SERVANTS *and torches.*]

BRA. It is too true an evil; gone she is;
   And what's to come of my despised time
   Is nought but bitterness. Now, Roderigo,
   Where didst thou see her? O unhappy girl!   160
   With the Moor, say'st thou? Who would be a father!
   How didst thou know 'twas she? O, she deceives me
   Past thought! What said she to you? Get moe[41] tapers:
   Raise all my kindred. Are they married, think you?
ROD. Truly, I think they are.
BRA. O heaven! How got she out? O treason of the blood!
   Fathers, from hence trust not your daughters' minds
   By what you see them act. Is[42] there not charms
   By which the property[43] of youth and maidhood
   May be abus'd? Have you not read, Roderigo,   170
   Of some such thing?
ROD.   Yes, sir, I have indeed.
BRA. Call up my brother. O, would you[44] had had her!
   Some one way, some another. Do you know
   Where we may apprehend her and the Moor?
ROD. I think I can discover him, if you please
   To get good guard and go along with me.
BRA. Pray you, lead on. At every house I'll call;
   I may command at most. Get weapons, ho!
   And raise some special officers of night.[45]
   On, good Roderigo: I will deserve your pains. [*Exeunt.*]   180

SCENE II. *Another street.*

[*Enter* OTHELLO, IAGO, ATTENDANTS *with torches.*]

IAGO. Though in the trade of war I have slain men,
   Yet do I hold it very stuff o' th' conscience
   To do no contriv'd murder: I lack iniquity
   Sometime to do me service: nine or ten times
   I had thought t' have yerk'd[46] him here under the ribs.
OTH. 'Tis better as it is.
IAGO.   Nay, but he prated,
   And spoke such scurvy and provoking terms

---

[40] *Sagittary* probably an inn [41] *moe* more [42] *Is* are [43] *property* special quality [44] *you* Roderigo
[45] *officers of night* police [46] *yerk'd* stabbed

Against your honour
That, with the little godliness I have,
I did full hard forbear him. But, I pray you, sir,   10
Are you fast married? Be assur'd of this,
That the magnifico[47] is much belov'd,
And hath in his effect[48] a voice potential[49]
As double[50] as the duke's: he will divorce you;
Or put upon you what restraint and grievance
The law, with all his might to enforce it on,
Will give him cable.

OTH.   Let him do his spite;
My services, which I have done the signiory[51]
Shall out-tongue his complaints. 'Tis yet to know—
Which, when I know that boasting is an honour,   20
I shall promulgate—I fetch my life and being
From men of royal siege,[52] and my demerits[53]
May speak unbonneted[54] as to proud a fortune
As this that I have reach'd: for know, Iago,
But that I love the gentle Desdemona,
I would not my unhoused free condition
Put into circumscription and confine
For the sea's worth. But, look! what lights come yond?

IAGO. Those are the raised father and his friends:
You were best go in.

OTH.   Not I; I must be found: 30
My parts, my title and my perfect soul[55]
Shall manifest my rightly. Is it they?

IAGO. By Janus, I think no.

[*Enter* CASSIO *and certain* OFFICERS *with torches.*]

OTH. The servants of the duke, and my lieutenant.
The goodness of the night upon you, friends!
What is the news?

CAS.   The duke does greet you, general,
And he requires your haste-post-haste appearance,
Even on the instant.

OTH.   What is the matter, think you?

CAS. Something from Cyprus, as I may divine:

---

[47] *magnifico* Venetian grandee (i.e., Brabantio)   [48] *effect* influence   [49] *potential* powerful
[50] *double* twice as influential as most men's   [51] *signiory* Venetian government   [52] *siege* rank
[53] *demerits* deserts   [54] *unbonneted* on equal terms   [55] *perfect soul* unflawed conscience

It is a business of some heat: the galleys   40
Have sent a dozen sequent[56] messengers
This very night at one another's heels,
And many of the consuls,[57] rais'd and met,
Are at the duke's already: you have been hotly call'd for;
When, being not at your lodging to be found,
The senate hath sent about three several[58] quests
To search you out.
OTH.   'Tis well I am found by you.
I will but spend a word here in the house.
And go with you. [*Exit.*]
CAS.   Ancient, what makes he here?
IAGO. 'Faith, he to-night hath boarded a land carack:[59]   50
If it prove lawful prize, he's made for ever.
CAS. I do not understand.
IAGO.   He's married.
CAS.   To who?

[*Enter* OTHELLO.]

IAGO. Marry, to—Come, captain, will you?
OTH.   Have with you.
CAS. Here comes another troop to seek for you.

[*Enter* BRABANTIO, RODERIGO, *with* OFFICERS *and torches.*]

IAGO. It is Brabantio. General, be advis'd;
   He comes to bad intent.
OTH.   Holla! stand there!
ROD. Signior, it is the Moor.
BRA.   Down with him, thief! [*They draw on both sides.*]
IAGO. You, Roderigo! come, sir, I am for you.
OTH. Keep up your bright swords, for the dew will rust them.
   Good Signior, you shall more command with years   60
   Than with your weapons.
BRA. O thou foul thief, where hast thou stow'd my daughter?
   Damn'd as thou art, thou has enchanted her;
   For I'll refer me to all things of sense,[60]
   If she in chains of magic were not bound,
   Whether a maid so tender, fair and happy,

---

[56] *sequent* successive [57] *consuls* senators [58] *several* separate [59] *carack* large merchant ship
[60] *things of sense* commonsense understandings of the natural order

So opposite to marriage that she shunn'd
The wealthy curled darlings of our nation,
Would ever have, t' incur a general mock
Run from her guardage⁶¹ to the sooty bosom   70
Of such a thing as thou, to fear, not to delight
Judge me the world, if 'tis not gross in sense⁶²
That thou has practis'd on her with foul charms,
Abus'd her delicate youth with drugs or minerals⁶³
That weaken motion:⁶⁴ I'll have't disputed on;⁶⁵
'Tis probable and palpable to thinking.
I therefore apprehend and do attach thee
For an abuser of the world,⁶⁶ a practiser
Of arts inhibited⁶⁷ and out of warrant.
Lay hold upon him: if he do resist,   80
Subdue him at his peril.
OTH.   Hold your hands,
Both you of my inclining,⁶⁸ and the rest:
Were it my cue to fight, I should have known it
Without a prompter. Wither will you that I go
To answer this charge?
BRA.   To prison, till fit time
Of law and course of direct session⁶⁹
Call thee to answer.
OTH.   What if I do obey?
How may the duke be therewith satisfied,
Whose messengers are here about my side,
Upon some present business of the state   90
To bring me to him?
FIRST OFF.   'Tis true, most worthy signior;
The duke's in council, and your noble self,
I am sure, is sent for.
BRA.   How! the duke in council!
In this time of night! Bring him away:
Mine's not an idle cause: the duke himself,
Or any of my brothers of the state
Cannot but feel this wrong as 'twere their own;
For if such actions may have passage free,
Bond-slaves and pagans⁷⁰ shall our statesmen be. [*Exeunt.*]

---

⁶¹ *guardage* guardianship   ⁶² *gross in sense* easily discernible in apprehension or perception
⁶³ *minerals* medicine, poison   ⁶⁴ *motion* thought, reason   ⁶⁵ *disputed on* argued in court by
professional counsel   ⁶⁶ *abuser of the world* corrupter of society   ⁶⁷ *inhibited* prohibited
⁶⁸ *inclining* following, party   ⁶⁹ *course of direct session* regular legal proceedings
⁷⁰ *Bond-slaves and pagans* contemptuous reference to Othello's past history

SCENE III. *A council-chamber.*

[*Enter* DUKE, SENATORS *and* OFFICERS *set at a table, with lights and* ATTENDANTS.]

DUKE. There is no composition in these news
    That gives them credit.
FIRST SEN.   Indeed, they are disproportion'd;[71]
    My letters say a hundred and seven galleys.
DUKE. And mine, a hundred forty.
SEC. SEN.   And mine, two hundred:
    But though they jump[72] not on a just account,—
    As in these cases, where the aim[73] reports,
    'Tis oft with difference—yet do they all confirm
    A Turkish fleet, and bearing up to Cyprus.
DUKE. Nay, it is possible enough to judgment:
    I do not so secure me[74] in the error,   10
    But the main article[75] I do approve
    In fearful sense.
SAILOR [*Within*]. What, ho! what, ho! what, ho!
FIRST OFF. A messenger from the galleys.

[*Enter* SAILOR.]

DUKE.   Now, what's the business?
SAIL. The Turkish preparation makes for Rhodes;
    So was I bid report here to the state
    By Signior Angelo.
DUKE. How say you by this change?
FIRST SEN.   This cannot be,
    By no assay[76] of reason: 'tis a pageant,
    To keep us in false gaze. When we consider
    Th' importancy of Cyprus to the Turk,   20
    And let ourselves again but understand,
    That as it more concerns the Turk than Rhodes,
    So may he with more facile question[77] bear it,
    For that it stands not in such warlike brace,[78]
    But altogether lacks th' abilities
    That Rhodes is dress'd in: if we make thought of this,
    We must not think the Turk is so unskilful
    To leave that latest which concerns him first,
    Neglecting an attempt of ease and gain,
    To wake and wage a danger profitless.   30

---

[71] *disproportion'd* inconsistent [72] *jump* agree [73] *aim* conjecture [74] *secure me* feel myself secure
[75] *main article* i.e., that the Turkish fleet is threatening [76] *assay* test [77] *more facile question* greater
facility of effort [78] *brace* state of defense

DUKE.   Nay, in all confidence, he's not for Rhodes.
FIRST OFF.   Here is more news.

[Enter a MESSENGER.]

MESS.   The Ottomites, reverend and gracious,
 Steering with due course toward the isle of Rhodes,
 Have there injointed them with an after fleet.
FIRST SEN.   Ay, so I thought. How many, as you guess?
MESS.   Of thirty sail: and now they do re-stem[79]
 Their backward course, bearing with frank appearance
 Their purposes toward Cyprus. Signior Montano,
 Your trusty and most valiant servitor,   40
 With his free duty recommends you thus,
 And prays you to believe him.
DUKE.   'Tis certain, then, for Cyprus.
 Marcus Luccicos, is not he in town?
FIRST SEN.   He's now in Florence.
DUKE.   Write from us to him; post-post-haste dispatch.
FIRST SEN.   Here comes Brabantio and the valiant Moor.

[Enter BRABANTIO, OTHELLO, CASSIO, IAGO, RODERIGO, *and* OFFICERS.]

DUKE.   Valiant, Othello, we must straight employ you
 Against the general enemy Ottoman.
 [To BRABANTIO] I did not see you; welcome, gentle signior; 50
 We lack'd your counsel and your help to-night.
BRA.   So did I yours. Good your grace, pardon me;
 Neither my place nor aught I heard of business
 Hath rais'd me from my bed, nor does the general care
 Take hold on me, for my particular grief
 Is of so flood-gate and o'erbearing nature
 That it engluts[80] and swallows other sorrows
 And it is still itself.
DUKE.   Why, what's the matter?
BRA.   My daughter! O, my daughter!
DUKE *and* SEN.   Dead?
BRA.   Ay, to me;
 She is abus'd, stol'n from me, and corrupted   60
 By spells and medicines bought of mountebanks;
 For nature so preposterously to err,
 Being not deficient, blind, or lame of sense,
 Sans witchcraft could not.

[79] *re-stem* steer again [80] *engluts* engulfs

DUKE. Whoe'er he be that in this foul proceeding
  Hath thus beguil'd your daughter of herself
  And you of her, the bloody book of law
  You shall yourself read in the bitter letter
  After your own sense, yea, though our proper son
  Stood in your action.[81]

BRA.   Humbly I thank your grace.   70
  Here is the man, this Moor, whom now, it seems,
  Your special mandate for the state-affairs
  Hath hither brought.

DUKE *and* SEN.   We are very sorry for 't.

DUKE [*To* OTHELLO]. What, in your own part, can you say to this?

BRA. Nothing, but this is so.

OTH. Most potent, grave, and reverend signiors,
  My very noble and approv'd good masters,
  That I have ta'en away this old man's daughter,
  It is most true; true, I have married her:
  The very head and front of my offending   80
  Hath this extent, no more. Rude am I in my speech,
  And little bless'd with the soft phrase of peace;
  For since these arms of mine had seven years' pith,[82]
  Till now some nine moons wasted, they have us'd
  Their dearest action in the tented field,
  And little of this great world can I speak,
  More than pertains to feats of broil and battle,
  And therefore little shall I grace my cause
  In speaking for myself. Yet, by your gracious patience,[83]
  I will a round unvarnish'd tale deliver   90
  Of my whole course of love; what drugs, what charms,
  What conjuration and what mighty magic,
  For such proceeding I am charg'd withal,
  I won his daughter.

BRA.   A maiden never bold;
  Of spirit so still and quiet, that her motion
  Blush'd at herself;[84] and she, in spite of nature,
  Of years, of country, credit, every thing,
  To fall in love with what she fear'd to look on!
  It is a judgement maim'd and most imperfect
  That will confess perfection so could err   100
  Against all rules of nature, and must be driven
  To find our practices of cunning hell,

---

[81] *Stood . . . action* was under your accusation   [82] *pith* strength, vigor   [83] *patience* suffering, permission   [84] *motion . . . herself* inward impulses blushed at themselves

Why this should be. I therefore vouch[85] again
That with some mixtures pow'rful o'er the blood,
Or with some dram conjur'd to this effect,
He wrought upon her.
DUKE.   To vouch this, is no proof,
Without more wider and more overt test
Than these thin habits and poor likelihoods
Of modern seeming do prefer against him.
FIRST SEN.   But, Othello, speak: 110
Did you by indirect and forced courses
Subdue and poison this young maid's affections?
Or came it by request and such fair question
As soul to soul affordeth?
OTH.   I do beseech you,
Send for the lady to the Sagittary,
And let her speak of me before her father:
If you do find me foul in her report,
The trust, the office I do hold of you,
Not only take away, but let your sentence
Even fall upon my life.
DUKE.   Fetch Desdemona hither.   120
OTH.   Ancient, conduct them; you best know the place. [*Exeunt* IAGO *and*
    ATTENDANTS.]
And, till she come, as truly as to heaven
I do confess the vices of my blood,
So justly to your grave ear I'll present
How I did thrive in this fair lady's love,
And she in mine.
DUKE.   Say it, Othello.
OTH.   Her father lov'd me; oft invited me;
Still question'd me the story of my life,
From year to year, the battles, sieges, fortunes,   130
That I have pass'd.
I ran it through, even from my boyish days,
To th' very moment that he bade me tell it;
Wherein I spake of most disastrous chances,
Of moving accidents by flood and field,
Of hair-breadth scapes i' th' imminent[86] deadly breach,
Of being taken by the insolent foe
And sold to slavery, of my redemption thence
And portance[87] in my travels' history:

---

[85] *vouch* assert   [86] *imminent* i.e., impending parts when a gap has been made in a fortification
[87] *portance* conduct

Wherein of antres[88] vast and deserts idle,[89]   140
Rough quarries, rocks and hills whose heads touch heaven,
It was my hint[90] to speak,—such was the process;
And of the Cannibals that each other eat,[91]
The Anthropophagi[92] and men whose heads
Do grow beneath their shoulders. This to hear
Would Desdemona seriously incline:
But still the house-affairs would draw her thence:
Which ever as she could with haste dispatch,
She 'ld come again, and with a greedy ear
Devour up my discourse: which I observing,   150
Took once a pliant hour, and found good means
To draw from her a prayer of earnest heart
That I would all my pilgrimage dilate,[93]
Whereof by parcels she had something heard,
But not intentively;[94] I did consent,
And often did beguile her of her tears,
When I did speak some distressful stroke
That my youth suffer'd. My story being done,
She gave me for my pains a world of sighs:
She swore, in faith, 'twas strange, 'twas passing strange,   160
'Twas pitiful, 'twas wondrous pitiful:
She wish'd she had not heard it, yet she wish'd
That heaven had made her such a man: she thank'd me,
And bade me, if I had a friend that lov'd her,
I should but teach him how to tell my story,
And that would woo her. Upon this hint I spake:
She lov'd me for the dangers I had pass'd,
And I lov'd her that she did pity them.
This only is the witchcraft I have us'd:
Here comes the lady; let her witness it.   170

    [*Enter* DESDEMONA, IAGO *and* ATTENDANTS.]

DUKE. I think this tale would win my daughter too.
 Good Brabantio,
 Take up this mangled matter at the best:
 Men do their broken weapons rather use
 Than their bare hands.
BRA.   I pray you, hear her speak:
 If she confess that she was half the wooer,
 Destruction on my head, if my bad blame

---

[88] *antres* caverns [89] *idle* barren, unprofitable [90] *hint* occasion
[91] *eat* ate [92] *Anthropophagi* man-eaters [93] *dilate* relate in detail [94] *intentively* with full attention

Light on the man! Come hither, gentle mistress:
Do you perceive in all this noble company
Where most you owe obedience?

DES.   My noble father,   180
  I do perceive here a divided duty:[95]
To you I am bound for life and education;
My life and education both do learn me
How to respect you; you are the lord of duty;
I am hitherto your daughter: but here's my husband,
And so much duty as my mother show'd
To you, preferring you before her father,
So much I challenge that I may profess
Due to the Moor my lord.

BRA.   God be with you! I have done.
  Please it your grace, on to[96] the state-affairs: 190
I had rather to adopt a child than get[97] it.
Come hither, Moor:
I here do give thee that with all my heart
Which, but thou hast already, with all my heart
I would keep from thee. For your sake,[98] jewel,
I am glad at soul I have no other child;
For thy escape would teach me tyranny,
To hang clogs on them. I have done, my lord.

DUKE. Let me speak like yourself,[99] and lay a sentence,[100]
  Which, as a grise[101] or step, may help these lovers   200
Into your favour.
When remedies are past, the griefs are ended
By seeing the worst, which late on hopes depended.
To mourn a mischief that is past and gone
Is the next[102] way to draw new mischief on.
Which cannot be preserv'd when fortune takes,
Patience her injury a mock'ry makes.
The robb'd that smiles steals something from the thief;
He robs himself that spends a bootless grief.

BRA. So let the Turk of Cyprus us beguile;   210
  We lost it now, so long as we can smile.
He bears the sentence well that nothing bears
But the free comfort[103] which from thence he hears,
But he bears both the sentence and the sorrow

---

[95] *divided duty* Desdemona recognizes that she still owes a duty to her father even after marriage
[96] *on to* i.e., proceed with [97] *get* beget [98] *For your sake* on your account [99] *like yourself* i.e., as you
would, in your proper temper [100] *sentence* maxim [101] *grise* step [102] *next* nearest [103] *comfort* i.e.,
the consolation that it may be borne with patience

That, to pay grief, must of poor patience borrow.
These sentences, to sugar, or to gall,
Being strong on both sides, are equivocal:
But words are words; I never yet did hear
That the bruis'd heart was pierced through the ear.
I humbly beseech you, proceed to th' affairs of state.   220

DUKE. The Turk with a most mighty preparation makes for Cyprus. Othello, the
    fortitude[104] of the place is best known to you; and though we have there a
    substitute of most allowed[105] sufficiency, yet opinion, a sovereign mistress of
    effects, throws a more safer voice on you:[106] you must therefore be content to
    slubber[107] the gloss of your new fortunes with this more stubborn and bois-
    trous expedition.

OTH. The tyrant custom, most grave senators,
    Hath made the flinty and steel couch of war
    My thrice-driven[108] bed of down: I do agnize[109]
    A natural and prompt alacrity   230
    I find in hardness[110] and do undertake
    These present wars against the Ottomites.
    Most humbly therefore bending to your state,
    I crave fit disposition for my wife,
    Due reference of place and exhibition,[111]
    With such accommodation and besort[112]
    As levels with her breeding.

DUKE.   If you please,
    Be 't at her father's.

BRA.   I'll not have it so.

OTH. Nor I.

DES.   Nor I; I would not there reside,
    To put my father in impatient thoughts   240
    By being in his eye. Most gracious duke,
    To my unfolding lend your prosperous[113] ear
    And let me find a charter[114] in your voice,
    T' assist my simpleness.[115]

DUKE. What would you, Desdemona?

DES. That I did love the Moor to live with him,
    My downright violence and storm of fortunes
    May trumpet to the world: my heart's subdu'd
    Even to the very quality of my lord:
    I saw Othello's visage in his mind,   250

---

[104] *fortitude* strength [105] *allowed* acknowledged [106] *opinion . . . on you* public opinion, an important
determiner of affairs, chooses you as the best man [107] *slubber* soil, sully [108] *thrive-driven* thrice
sifted [109] *agnize* know in myself [110] *hardness* hardship [111] *exhibition* allowance [112] *besort* suitable
company [113] *prosperous* propitious [114] *charter* privilege [115] *simpleness* simplicity

And to his honours and his valiant parts
Did I my soul and fortunes consecrate.
So that, dear lords, if I be left behind,
A moth of peace, and he go to the war,
The rites for why I love him are bereft me,
And I a heavy interim shall support
By his dear absence. Let me go with him.
OTH. Let her have your voices.
Vouch with me, heaven, I therefore beg it not,
To please the palate of my appetite,   260
Nor to comply with heat—the young affects[116]
In me defunct—and proper satisfaction,
But to be free and bounteous to her mind:
And heaven defend your good souls, that you think
I will your serious and great business scant
When she is with me: no, when light-wing'd toys
Of feather'd Cupid seel[117] with wanton dullness
My speculative and offic'd instruments,[118]
That[119] my disports[120] corrupt and taint[121] my business,
Let housewives make a skillet of my helm,   270
And all indign[122] and base adversities
Make head against my estimation![123]
DUKE. Be it as you shall privately determine,
Either for her stay or going: th' affair cries haste,
And speed must answer for it.
FIRST SEN. You must away to-night.
OTH.   With all my heart.
DUKE. At nine i' th' morning here we'll meet again.
Othello, leave some officer behind,
And he shall our commission bring to you;
With such things else of quality and respect   280
As doth import[124] you.
OTH.   So please your grace, my ancient;
A man he is of honesty and trust:
To his conveyance I assign my wife,
With what else needful your good grace shall think
To be sent after me.
DUKE.   Let it be so.
Good night to every one. [*To* BRA.] And, noble signior,

---

[116] *affects* inclinations, desires   [117] *seel* in falconry, to make blind by sewing up the eyes of the hawk
in training   [118] *speculative . . . instruments* ability to see and reason clearly   [119] *That* so that
[120] *disports* pastimes   [121] *taint* impair   [122] *indign* unworthy, shameful   [123] *estimation* reputation
[124] *import* concern

If virtue no delighted[125] beauty lack,
Your son-in-law is far more fair than black.
FIRST SEN. Adieu, brave Moor; use Desdemona well.
BRA. Look to her, Moor, if thou hast eyes to see;   290
  She has deceiv'd her father, and may thee. [*Exeunt* DUKE, SENATORS,
    OFFICERS, &c.]
OTH. My life upon her faith! Honest Iago,[126]
  My Desdemona must I leave to thee:
  I prithee, let thy wife attend on her;
  And bring them after in the best advantage.
  Come, Desdemona; I have but an hour
  Of love, of worldly matters and direction,
  To spend with thee: we must obey the time. [*Exit with* DESDEMONA.]
ROD. Iago—
IAGO. What say'st thou, noble heart?   300
ROD. What will I do, thinkest thou?
IAGO. Why, go to bed, and sleep.
ROD. I will incontinently[127] drown myself.
IAGO. If thou dost, I shall never love thee after. Why, thou silly gentleman!
ROD. It is silliness to live when to live is torment; and then have we a prescription
  to die when death is our physician.
IAGO. O villanous! I have looked upon the world for four times seven years; and
  since I could distinguish betwixt a benefit and an injury, I never found man that
  knew how to love himself. Ere I would say, I would drown myself for the love
  of a guinea-hen, I would change my humanity with a baboon.   310
ROD. What should I do? I confess it is my shame to be so fond; but it is not in my
  virtue[128] to amend it.
IAGO. Virtue! a fig! 'tis in ourselves that we are thus or thus. Our bodies are our
  gardens, to the which our wills are gardeners; so that if we will plant nettles, or
  sow lettuce, let hyssop[129] and weed up thyme, supply it with one gender[130] of
  herbs, or distract it with many, either to have it sterile with idleness,[131] or
  manured with industry, why, the power and corrigible authority[132] of this lies
  in our wills. If the balance of our lives had not one scale of reason to poise
  another of sensuality, the blood and baseness of our natures would conduct us
  to most preposterous conclusions:[133] but we have reason to cool our raging   320
  motions,[134] our carnal stings, our unbitted[135] lusts, whereof I take this that you
  call love to be a sect[136] or scion.

---

[125] *delighted* delightful   [126] *Honest Iago* an evidence of Iago's carefully built reputation
[127] *incontinently* immediately   [128] *virtue* strength   [129] *hyssop* an herb of the mint family
[130] *gender* kind   [131] *idleness* want of cultivation   [132] *corrigible authority* the power to correct
[133] *reason . . . motions* Iago understands the warfare between reason and sensuality, but his
ethics are totally inverted; reason works in him not good, as it should according to natural law,
but evil, which he has chosen for his good   [134] *motions* appetites   [135] *unbitted* uncontrolled
[136] *sect* cutting

ROD. It cannot be.

IAGO. It is merely a lust of the blood and a permission of the will. Come, be a man. Drown thyself! drown cats and blind puppies. I have professed me thy friend and I confess me knit to thy deserving with cables of perdurable[137] toughness; I could never better stead thee than now. Put money in thy purse; follow thou the wars; defeat the favour[138] with an usurped beard; I say, put money in thy purse. It cannot be that Desdemona should long continue her love to the Moor,—put money in thy purse,—nor he his to her: it was a violence com- 330
mencement in her, and thou shalt see an answerable sequestration:[139]—put but money in thy purse. These Moors are changeable in their wills:—fill thy purse with money:—the food that to him now is as luscious as locusts,[140] shall be to him shortly as bitter as colquintida.[141] She must change for youth: when she is sated with his body, she will find the error of her choice: she must have change, she must: therefore put money in thy purse. If thou wilt needs damn thyself, do it a more delicate way than drowning. Make all the money thou canst: if sanctimony and a frail vow betwixt an erring[142] barbarian and a super-subtle Venetian be too hard for my wits and all the tribe of hell, thou shalt enjoy her; therefore make money. A pox of drowning thyself! it is clean out of the way: 340
seek thou rather to be hanged in compassing thy joy than to be drowned and go without her.

ROD. Wilt thou be fast to my hopes, if I depend on the issue?

IAGO. Thou art sure of me:—go, make money:—I have told thee often, and I re-tell thee again and again, I hate the Moor: my cause is hearted;[143] thine hath no less reason. Let us be conjunctive[144] in our revenge against him; if thou canst cuckold him, thou dost thyself a pleasure, me a sport. There are many events in the womb of time which will be delivered. Traverse![145] go, provide thy money. We shall have more of this to-morrow. Adieu.

ROD. Where shall we meet i' the morning? 350

IAGO. At my lodging.

ROD. I'll be with thee betimes.

IAGO. Go to; farewell. Do you hear, Roderigo?

ROD. What say you?

IAGO. No more of drowning, do you hear?

ROD. I am changed: I'll go sell all my land. [*Exit*]

IAGO. Thus do I ever make my fool my purse;
   For I mine own gain'd knowledge should profane,
   If I would time expend with such a snipe,[146]
   But for my sport and profit. I hate the Moor; 360

---

[137] *perdurable* very durable [138] *defeat thy favour* disguise and disfigure thy face [139] *answerable sequestration* a separation corresponding [140] *locusts* of doubtful meaning; defined as fruit of the carob tree, as honeysuckle, and as lollipops or sugar sticks [141] *coloquintida* colocynth, or bitter apple, a purgative [142] *erring* wandering [143] *hearted* fixed in the heart [144] *conjunctive* united [145] *Traverse* go (military term) [146] *snipe* gull, fool

And it is thought abroad, that 'twixt my sheets
H' as done my office: I know not if 't be true;
But I, for mere suspicion in that kind,
Will do as if for surety. He holds me well;
The better shall my purpose work on him.
Cassio's a proper man: let me see now:
To get his place and to plume up[147] my will
In double knavery—How, how?—Let's see:—
After some time, to abuse Othello's ears
That he[148] is too familiar with his wife. 370
He hath a person and a smooth dispose[149]
To be suspected, fram'd to make women false.
The Moor is of a free[150] and open nature,
That thinks men honest that but seem to be so,
And will as tenderly be led by th' nose
As asses are.
I have 't. It is engend'red. Hell and night
Must bring this monstrous birth to the world's light. [*Exit.*]

ACT II

SCENE I. *A Sea-port in Cyprus. An open place near the quay.*

[*Enter* MONTANO *and two* GENTLEMEN.]

MON. What from the cape can you discern at sea?
FIRST GENT. Nothing at all: it is a high-wrought flood;
  I cannot, 'twixt the heaven and the main,
  Descry a sail.
MON. Methinks the wind hath spoke aloud at land;
  A fuller blast ne'er shook our battlements:
  If it hath ruffian'd[1] so upon the sea,
  What ribs of oak, what mountains melt on them,
  Can hold the mortise?[2] What shall we hear of this?
SEC. GENT. A segregation[3] of the Turkish fleet: 10
  For do but stand upon the foaming shore,
  The chidden billow seems to pelt the clouds:
  The wind-shak'd surge, with high and monstrous mane,
  Seems to cast water on the burning bear,[4]
  And quench the guards[5] of th' ever-fixed pole:

---

[147] *plume up* glorify, gratify [148] *he* i.e., Cassio [149] *dispose* external manner [150] *free* frank
ACT II [1] *ruffian'd* raged [2] *mortise* the socket hollowed out in fitting timbers [3] *segregation* dispersion [4] *bear* a constellation [5] *quench the guards* overwhelm the stars near the polestar

I never did like molestation view
On the enchafed[6] flood.

MON.   If that the Turkish fleet
Be not enshelter'd and embay'd, they are drown'd;
It is impossible they bear it out.

[*Enter a third* GENTLEMAN.]

THIRD GENT. News, lads! our wars are done   20
The desperate tempest hath so bang'd the Turks,
That their designment[7] halts: a noble ship of Venice
Hath seen a grievous wrack and sufferance[8]
On most part of their fleet.

MON. How! is this true?

THIRD GENT.   The ship is here put in,
A Veronesa; Michael Cassio,
Lieutenant to the warlike Moor Othello,
Is come on shore: the Moor himself at sea,
And is in full commission here for Cyprus.

MON. I am glad on 't; 'tis a worthy governor.   30

THIRD GENT. But this same Cassio, though he speak of comfort
Touching the Turkish loss, yet he looks sadly,
And prays the Moor be safe; for they were parted
With foul and violent tempest.

MON.   Pray heavens he be;
For I have serv'd him, and the man commands
Like a full[9] soldier. Let's to the seaside, ho!
As well to see the vessel that's come in
As to throw out our eyes for brave Othello,
Even till we make the main and th' aerial blue
And indistinct regard.[10]

THIRD GENT.   Come, let's do so;   40
For every minute is expectancy
Of more arrivance.[11]

[*Enter* CASSIO.]

CAS. Thanks, you the valiant of this warlike isle,
That so approve the Moor! O, let the heavens
Give him defence against the elements,
For I have lost him on a dangerous sea.

MON. Is he well shipp'd?

---

[6] *enchafed* angry [7] *designment* enterprise [8] *sufferance* disaster [9] *full* perfect [10] *make . . . regard*
cause the blue of the sea and the air to grow indistinguishable in our view [11] *arrivance* arrival

CAS. His bark is stoutly timber'd, and his pilot
Of very expert and approv'd allowance;[12]
Therefore my hopes, not surfeited to death, 50
Stand in bold cure. [*A cry within.*] "A sail, a sail, a sail!"

[*Enter a fourth* GENTLEMAN.]

CAS. What noise?
FOURTH GENT. The town is empty; on the brow o' th' sea
Stand ranks of people, and they cry "A sail!"
CAS. My hopes do shape him for the governor. [*Guns heard.*]
SEC. GENT. They do discharge their shot of courtesy:
Our friends at least.
CAS.   I pray you, sir, go forth,
And give us truth who 'tis that is arriv'd.
SEC. GENT. I shall. [*Exit.*]
MON. But, good lieutenant, is your general wiv'd? 60
CAS. Most fortunately: he hath achiev'd a maid
That paragons[13] description and wild fame;
One that excels the quirks[14] of blazoning[15] pens,
And in th' essential vesture of creation[16]
Does tire the ingener.[17]

[*Enter second* GENTLEMAN.]

                         How now! who has put in?
SEC. GENT. 'Tis one Iago, ancient to the general.
CAS. Has had most favourable and happy speed:
Tempests themselves, high seas and howling winds,
The gutter'd[18] rocks and congregated sands,—
Traitors ensteep'd[19] to clog the guiltless keel,— 70
As having sense of beauty, do omit
Their mortal[20] natures, letting go safely by
The divine Desdemona.
MON.   What is she?
CAS. She that I spake of, our great captain's captain,
Left in the conduct of the bold Iago,
Whose footing here anticipates our thoughts
A se'nnight's[21] speed. Great Jove, Othello guard,
And swell his sail with thine own powr'ful breath,

---

[12] *allowance* reputation   [13] *paragons* surpasses   [14] *quirks* witty conceits   [15] *blazoning* setting forth
honorably in words   [16] *vesture of creation* the real qualities with which creation has invested her
[17] *ingener* inventor, praiser   [18] *gutter'd* jagged, trenched   [19] *ensteep'd* lying under water
[20] *mortal* deadly   [21] *se'nnight's* week's

That he may bless this bay with his tall ship,
Make love's quick pants in Desdemona's arms,   80
Give renew'd fire to our extincted spirits,
And bring all Cyprus comfort!

[*Enter* DESDEMONA, IAGO, RODERIGO, *and* EMILIA *with* ATTENDANTS.]

                    O, behold!
The riches of the ship is come on shore!
You men of Cyprus, let her have your knees.
Hail to thee, lady! and the grace of heaven,
Before, behind thee and on every hand,
Enwheel thou round!
DES.   I thank you, valiant Cassio.
What tidings can you tell me of my lord?
CAS. He is not yet arriv'd: nor know I aught
But that he's well and will be shortly here.   90
DES. O, but I fear—How lost you company?
CAS. The great contention of the sea and skies
Parted our fellowship—But, hark! a sail.
[*Within*] "A sail, a sail!" [*Guns heard.*]
SEC. GENT. They give their greeting to the citadel:
This likewise is a friend.
CAS.   See for the news. [*Exit* GENTLEMAN.]
Good ancient, you are welcome. [*To* EMILIA] Welcome, mistress:
Let is not gall your patience, good Iago,
That I extend my manners; 'tis my breeding
That gives me this bold show of courtesy. [*Kissing her.*]   100
IAGO. Sir, would she give you so much of her lips
As of her tongue she oft bestows on me,
You would have enough.
DES.   Alas, she has no speech.
IAGO. In faith, too much;
I find it still, when I have list to sleep:
Marry, before your ladyship, I grant,
She puts her tongue a little in her heart,
And chides with thinking.
EMIL. You have little cause to say so.
IAGO. Come on, come on; you are pictures out of doors,   110
Bells in your parlours, wild-cats in your kitchens,
Saints in your injuries, devils being offended,
Players in your housewifery, and housewives[22] in your beds.
DES. O, fie upon thee, slanderer!

---

[22] *housewives* hussies

IAGO. Nay, it is true, or else I am a Turk:
  You rise to play and go to bed to work.
EMIL. You shall not write my praise.
IAGO.   No, let me not.
DES. What wouldst thou write of me, if thou shouldst praise me?
IAGO. O gentle lady, do not put me to 't;
  For I am nothing, if not critical.[23]   120
DES. Come on, assay. There's one gone to the harbour?
IAGO. Ay, madam.
DES. I am not merry; but I do beguile
  The thing I am, by seeming otherwise.
  Come, how wouldst thou praise me?
IAGO. I am about it; but indeed my invention
  Comes from my pate as birdlime[24] does from frieze;[25]
  It plucks out brains and all: but my Muse labours,
  And thus she is deliver'd.
  If she be fair and wise, fairness and wit,   130
  The one's for use, the other useth it.
DES. Well praised! How if she be black and witty?
IAGO. If she be black, and thereto have a wit,
  She'll find a white[26] that shall her blackness fit.
DES. Worse and worse.
EMIL. How if fair and foolish?
IAGO. She never yet was foolish that was fair;
  For even her folly help'd her to an heir.
DES. These are old fond[27] paradoxes to make fools laugh i' the alehouse.
  What miserable praise hast thou for her that's foul and foolish?   140
IAGO. There's none so foul and foolish thereunto,
  But does foul pranks which fair and wise ones do.
DES. O heavy ignorance! thou praisest the worst best. But what praise couldst thou
    bestow on a deserving woman indeed, one that, in the authority of her merit,
    did justly put on the vouch[28] of her malice itself?
IAGO. She that was ever fair and never proud,
  Had tongue at will and yet was never loud,
  Never lack'd gold and yet went never gay,
  Fled from her wish and yet said "Now I may,"
  She that being ang'rd, her revenge being nigh,   150
  Bade her wrong stay and her displeasure fly,
  She that in wisdom never was so frail
  To change the cod's head for the salmon's tail,[29]

---

[23] *critical* censorious   [24] *birdlime* sticky substance smeared on twigs to catch small birds
[25] *frieze* coarse woolen cloth   [26] *white* a fair person, with a wordplay on *wight*   [27] *fond* foolish   [28] *put on the vouch* compel the approval   [29] *To change . . . tail* to exchange a delicacy for mere refuse

She that could think and ne'er disclose her mind,
See suitors following and not look behind,
She was a wight, if ever such wight were,—
DES. To do what?
IAGO. To suckle fools and chronicle small beer.[30]
DES. O most lame and impotent conclusion! Do not learn of him, Emilia,
though he be thy husband. How say you, Cassio? is he not a most profane and   160
liberal[31] counsellor?
CAS. He speaks home,[32] madam: you may relish him more in the soldier than in
the scholar.
IAGO. [*Aside*]. He takes her by the palm: ay, well said, whisper: with as little a web
as this will I ensnare as great a fly as Cassio. Ay, smile upon her, do; I will gyve[33]
thee in thine own courtship.[34] You say true; 'tis so, indeed: if such tricks as these
strip you out of your lieutenantry, it had been better you had not kissed your
three fingers[35] so oft, which now again you are most apt to play the sir[36] in.
Very good; well kissed! an excellent courtesy! 'tis so, indeed. Yet again your
fingers to your lips? would they were clyster-pipes[37] for your sake. [*Trumpet*   170
within.] The Moor! I know his trumpet.
CAS. 'Tis truly so.
DES. Let's meet him and receive him.
CAS. Lo, where he comes!

[*Enter* OTHELLO *and* ATTENDANTS.]

OTH. O my fair warrior!
DES.   My dear Othello!
OTH. It gives me wonder great as my content
To see you here before me. O my soul's joy!
If after every tempest come such calms,
May the winds blow till they have waken'd death!
And let the labouring bark climb hills of seas   180
Olympus-high and duck again as low
As hell 's from heaven! If it were now to die,
'Twere now to be most happy; for, I fear,
My soul hath her content so absolute
That not another comfort like to this
Succeeds in unknown fate.
DES.   The heavens forbid
But that our loves and comforts should increase,
Even as our days grow!

---

[30] *chronicle small beer* keep petty household accounts   [31] *liberal* licentious   [32] *speaks home* i.e.,
without reserve   [33] *gyve* fetter, shackle   [34] *courship* courtesy   [35] *kissed your three fingers* he kisses his
own hand as a token of reverence   [36] *the sir* i.e., the fine gentleman   [37] *clyster-pipes* tubes used for
enemas

OTH.   Amen to that, sweet powers!
  I cannot speak enough of this content;
  It stops me here; it is too much of joy;   190
  And this, and this, the greatest discords be [*Kissing her*]
  That e'er our hearts shall make!
IAGO   [*Aside*]. O, you are well run'd now!
  But I'll set down the pegs[38] that make this music,
  As honest as I am.
OTH.   Come, let us to the castle.
  News, friends, our wars are done, the Turks are drowned.
  How does my old acquaintance of this isle?
  Honey, you shall be well desir'd in Cyprus;
  I have found greatest love amongst them. O my sweet,
  I prattle out of fashion, and I dote
  In mine own comforts. I prithee, good Iago,   200
  Go to the bay and disembark my coffers:
  Bring thou the master to the citadel;
  He is a good one, and his worthiness
  Does challenge much respect. Come, Desdemona,
  Once more, well met at Cyprus. [*Exeunt* OTHELLO *and* DESDEMONA *and all
  but* IAGO *and* RODERIGO.]
IAGO [*to an* ATTENDANT]. Do thou meet me presently at the harbour. [*To* ROD.]
  Come hither. If thou be'st valiant,—as, they say, base men being in love have
  then a nobility in their natures more than is native to them,—list me. The
  lieutenant tonight watches on the court of guard.[39]—First, I must tell thee
  this—Desdemona is directly in love with him.   210
ROD. With him! why 'tis not possible.
IAGO. Lay thy finger thus, and let thy soul be instructed. Mark me with what
  violence she first loved the Moor, but for bragging and telling her fantastical
  lies: and will she love him still for prating? let not thy discreet heart think it.
  Her eye must be fed; and what delight shall she have to look on the devil? When
  the blood is made dull with the act of sport, there should be, again to inflame
  it and to give satiety a fresh appetite, loveliness in favour, sympathy in years,
  manners and beauties; all which the Moor is defective in: now, for want of these
  required conveniences, her delicate tenderness will find itself abused, begin to
  heave the gorge, disrelish and abhor the Moor; very nature will instruct her in 220
  it and compel her to some second choice. Now, sir, this granted,—as it is a most
  pregnant and unforced position—who stands so eminent in the degree of this
  fortune as Cassio does? a knave very voluble; no further conscionable[40] than in
  putting on the mere form of a civil and humane seeming, for the better
  compassing of his salt[41] and most hidden loose affection? why, none; why, none:

---

[38] *set down the pegs* lower the pitch of the strings, i.e., disturb the harmony [39] *court of guard*
guardhouse [40] *conscionable* conscientious [41] *salt* licentious

a slipper[42] and subtle knave, a finder of occasions, that has an eye can stamp and counterfeit advantages, though true advantage never present itself; a devilish knave. Besides, the knave is handsome, young, and hath all those requisites in him that folly and green minds look after: a pestilent complete knave; and the woman hath found him already.   230

ROD.   I cannot believe that in her; she's full of most blessed condition.

IAGO.   Blessed fig's-end! the wine she drinks is made of grapes: if she had been blessed, she would never have loved the Moor. Blessed pudding! Didst thou not see her paddle with the palm of his hand? didst not mark that?

ROD.   Yes, that I did; but that was but courtesy.

IAGO.   Lechery, by this hand; an index and obscure prologue to the history of lust and foul thoughts. They met so near with their lips that their breaths embraced together. Villainous thoughts, Roderigo! when these mutualities so marshall the way, hard at hand comes the master and main exercise, the incorporate conclusion. Pish! But, sir, be you ruled by me: I have brought you from Venice.   240 Watch you to-night; for the command, I'll lay't upon you. Cassio knows you not. I'll not be far from you: do you find some occasion to anger Cassio, either by speaking too loud, or tainting[43] his discipline; or from what other course you please, which the time shall more favourably minister.

ROD.   Well.

IAGO.   Sir, he is rash and very sudden in choler, and haply may strike at you: provoke him, that he may; for even out of that will I cause these of Cyprus to mutiny; whose qualification[44] shall come into no true taste again but by the displanting of Cassio. So shall you have a shorter journey to your desires by the means I shall then have to prefer them; and the impediment most profitably removed,   250 without the which there were no expectation of our prosperity.

ROD.   I will do this if I can bring it to any opportunity.

IAGO.   I warrant thee. Meet me by and by[45] at the citadel: I must fetch his necessaries ashore. Farewell.

ROD.   Adieu. [*Exit*]

IAGO.   That Cassio loves her, I do well believe 't;
That she loves him, 'tis apt[46] and of great credit:[47]
The Moor, howbeit that I endure him not,
Is of a constant, loving, noble nature,
And I dare think he'll prove to Desdemona   260
A most dear husband. Now I do love her too;
Not out of absolute lust, through peradventure
I stand accountant for as great a sin,
But partly led to diet my revenge,
For that I do suspect the lusty Moor
Hath leap'd into my seat; the thought whereof

---

[42] *slipper* slippery   [43] *tainting* disparaging   [44] *qualification* appeasement   [45] *by and by* immediately
[46] *apt* probable   [47] *credit* credibility

Doth, like a poisonous mineral, gnaw my inwards;
And nothing can or shall content my soul
Till I am even'd with him, wife for wife,
Or failing so, yet that I put the Moor   270
At least into a jealousy so strong
That judgement cannot cure. Which thing to do,
If this poor trash[48] of Venice, whom I trash[49]
For his quick hunting, stand the putting on,[50]
I'll have Michael Cassio on the hip,[51]
Abuse him to the Moor in the rank garb—
For I fear Cassio with my night-cap too—
Make the Moor thank me, love me and reward me,
For making him egregiously an ass
And practicing upon his peace and quiet   280
Even to madness. 'Tis here, but yet confus'd:
Knavery's plain face is never seen till us'd. [*Exit.*]

SCENE II. A street.

[Enter Othello's HERALD with a proclamation.]

HER. It is Othello's pleasure, our noble and valiant general, that, upon certain
tidings now arrived, importing the mere perdition[52] of the Turkish fleet, every
man put himself into triumph; some to dance, some to make bonfires, each man
to what sport and revels his addiction leads him: for, besides these beneficial
news, it is the celebration of his nuptial. So much was his pleasure should be
proclaimed. All offices[53] are open, and there is full liberty of feasting from this
present hour of five till the bell have told eleven. Heaven bless the isle of Cyprus
and our general Othello! [*Exit.*]

SCENE III. A hall in the castle.

[Enter OTHELLO, DESDEMONA, CASSIO, and ATTENDANTS.]

OTH. Good Michael, look you to the guard to-night:
Let's teach ourselves that honourable stop,[54]
Not to outsport discretion.
CAS. Iago hath direction what to do;
But, notwithstanding, with my personal eye
Will I look to 't.
OTH.   Iago is most honest.
Michael, goodnight: to-morrow with your earliest
Let me have speech with you. [*To* DESDEMONA] Come, my dear love,

---

[48] *trash* worthless thing (Roderigo)   [49] *trash* hold in check   [50] *putting on* incitement to quarrel
[51] *on the hip* at my mercy (wrestling term)   [52] *mere perdition* complete destruction   [53] *offices* rooms
where food and drink were kept   [54] *stop* restraint

The purchase made, the fruits to ensue;
That profit's yet to come 'tween me and you.   10
Good night. [*Exit* OTHELLO, *with* DESDEMONA *and* ATTENDANTS.]

[*Enter* IAGO.]

CAS. Welcome, Iago; we must to the watch.
IAGO. Not this hour, lieutenant; 'tis not yet ten o' the clock. Our general cast[55] us
thus early for the love of his Desdemona; who let us not therefore blame: he
hath not yet made wanton the night with her; and she is sport for Jove.
CAS. She's a most exquisite lady.
IAGO. And, I'll warrant her, full of game.
CAS. Indeed, she's a most fresh and delicate creature.
IAGO. What an eye she has! methinks it sounds a parley of provocation.
CAS. An inviting eye; and yet methinks right modest.   20
IAGO. And when she speaks, is it not an alarum to love?
CAS. She is indeed perfection.
IAGO. Well, happiness to their sheets! Come, lieutenant, I have a stoup[56] of wine;
and here without are a brace of Cyprus gallants that would fain have a measure
to the health of black Othello.
CAS. Not to-night, good Iago: I have very poor and unhappy brains for drinking: I
could well wish courtesy would invent some other custom of entertainment.
IAGO. O, they are our friends; but one cup: I'll drink for you.
CAS. I have drunk but one cup to-night, and that was craftily qualified[57] too, and,
behold, what innovation[58] it makes here:[59] I am unfortunate in the infirmity, 30
and dare not task my weakness with any more.
IAGO. What, man! 'tis a night of revels: the gallants desire it.
CAS. Where are they?
IAGO. Here at the door; I pray you, call them in.
CAS. I'll do 't; but it dislikes me. [*Exit.*]
IAGO. If I can fasten but one cup upon him,
    With that which he hath drunk to-night already,
    He'll be as full of quarrel and offence
    As my young mistress' dog. Now, my sick fool Roderigo,
    Whom love hath turn'd almost the wrong side out,   40
    To Desdemona hath to-night carous'd
    Potations pottle-deep;[60] and he's to watch:
    Three lads of Cyprus, noble swelling spirits,
    That hold their honours in a wary distance,[61]
    The very elements[62] of this warlike isle,

---

[55] *cast* dismissed [56] *stoup* measure of liquor, two quarts [57] *qualified* diluted [58] *innovation*
disturbance [59] *here* i.e., in Cassio's head [60] *pottle-deep* to the bottom of the tankard [61] *bold . . .
distance* i.e., are extremely sensitive of their honor [62] *very elements* true representatives

Have I to-night fluster'd with flowing cups,
And they watch[63] too. Now, 'mongst this flock of drunkards,
Am I to put our Cassio in some action
That may offend the isle.—But here they come:

[*Enter* CASSIO, MONTANO, *and* GENTLEMEN; SERVANTS *following with wine.*]

If consequence do but approve[64] my dream,   50
My boat sails freely, both with wind and stream.
CAS. 'Fore God, they have given me a rouse[65] already.
MON. Good faith, a little one; not past a pint, as I am a soldier.
IAGO. Some wine, ho!
[*Sings*] And let me the canakin[66] clink, clink;
And let me the canakin clink:
A soldier's a man;
A life's but a span;
Why, then, let a soldier drink.
Some wine, boys!   60
CAS. 'Fore God, an excellent song.
IAGO. I learned it in England, where, indeed, they are most potent in potting: your
Dane, your German, and your swag-bellied Hollander—Drink, ho!—are noth-
ing to your English.
CAS. Is your Englishman so expert in his drinking?
IAGO. Why, he drinks you, with facility, your Dane dead drunk; he sweats not to
overthrow your Almain;[67] he gives your Hollander a vomit, ere the next pottle
can be filled.
CAS. To the health of our general!
MON. I am for it, lieutenant; and I'll do you justice.[68]   70
IAGO. O sweet England! [*Sings.*]
King Stephen was a worthy peer,
His breeches cost him but a crown;
He held them sixpence all too dear,
With that he call'd the tailor lown.[69]

He was a wight of high renown,
And thou art but of low degree:
'Tis pride that pulls the country down;
Then take thine auld cloak about thee.
Some wine, ho!   80
CAS. Why, this is a more exquisite song than the other.

---

[63] *watch* are members of the guard [64] *approve* confirm [65] *rouse* full draft of liquor
[66] *canakin* small drinking vessel [67] *Almain* German [68] *I'll . . . justice* i.e., drink as much as you
[69] *lown* lout, loon

IAGO. Will you hear't again?

CAS. No; for I hold him to be unworthy of his place that does those things. Well, God's above all; and there be souls must be saved, and there be souls must not be saved.

IAGO. It's true, good lieutenant.

CAS. For mine own part,—no offence to the general, nor any man of quality,—I hope to be saved.

IAGO. And so do I too, lieutenant.

CAS. Ay, but, by your leave, not before me; the lieutenant is to be saved before the 90
ancient. Let's have no more of this; let 's to our affairs.—God forgive us our sins!—Gentlemen, let's look to our business. Do not think, gentlemen, I am drunk: this is my ancient; this is my right hand, and this is my left: I am not drunk now; I can stand well enough, and speak well enough.

ALL. Excellent well.

CAS. Why, very well then; you must not think then that I am drunk. [*Exit*]

MON. To th' platform, masters; come, let's set the watch.

IAGO. You see this fellow that is gone before;
  He's soldier fit to stand by Caesar
  And give direction: and do but see his vice; 100
  'Tis to his virtue a just equinox,[70]
  The one as long as th' other: 'tis pity of him.
  I fear the trust Othello puts him in,
  On some odd time of his infirmity,
  Will shake this island.

MON.   But is he often thus?

IAGO. 'Tis evermore the prologue to his sleep:
  He'll watch the horologe[71] a double set,[72]
  If drink rock not his cradle.

MON.   It were well
  The general were put in mind of it.
  Perhaps he sees it not; or his good nature 110
  Prizes the virtue that appears in Cassio,
  And looks not on his evils: is not this true?

[*Enter* RODERIGO.]

IAGO. [*Aside to him*]. How now, Roderigo!
  I pray you, after the lieutenant; go. [*Exit* RODERIGO.]

MON. And 'tis great pity that the noble Moor
  Should hazard such a place as his own second
  With one of an ingraft[73] infirmity:

---

[70] *equinox* equal length of days and nights; used figuratively to mean "counterpart"   [71] *horologe* clock   [72] *double set* twice around   [73] *ingraft* ingrafted, inveterate

It were an honest action to say
So to the Moor.
IAGO.   Not I, for this fair island:
I do love Cassio well; and would do much   120
To cure him of this evil—But, hark! what noise? [*Cry within:* "Help! help!"]

[*Enter* CASSIO, *pursuing* RODERIGO.]

CAS. 'Zounds, you rogue! you rascal!
MON.   What's the matter, lieutenant?
CAS. A knave teach me my duty!
I'll beat the knave into a twiggen[74] bottle.
ROD. Beat me!
CAS.   Dost thou prate, rogue? [*Striking* RODERIGO.]
MON.   Nay, good lieutenant; [*Staying him.*]
I pray you, sir, hold your hand.
CAS.   Let me go, sir,
Or I'll knock you o'er the mazzard.[75]
MON.   Come, come, you're drunk.
CAS. Drunk! [*They fight.*]
IAGO. [*aside to* RODERIGO]. Away, I say; go out, and cry a mutiny. [*Exit*
    RODERIGO.]
Nay, good lieutenant,—God's will, gentlemen;—   130
Help, ho!—Lieutenant,—sir,—Montano,—sir,—
Help, masters!—Here's a goodly watch indeed! [*Bell rings.*]
Who's that which rings the bell?—Diablo,[76] ho!
The town will rise:[77] God's will, lieutenant, hold!
You'll be asham'd for ever.

[*Enter* OTHELLO *and* ATTENDANTS.]

OTH.   What is the matter here?
MON. 'Zounds, I bleed still; I am hurt to th' death
He dies! [*Thrusts at* CASSIO.]
OTH. Hold, for your lives!
IAGO. Hold, ho! Lieutenant,—sir,—Montano,—gentlemen,—
Have your forgot all sense of place and duty?   140
Hold! the general speaks to you; hold, for shame!
OTH. Why, how now, ho! from whence ariseth this?
Are we turn'd Turks[78] and to ourselves do that
Which heaven hath forbid the Ottomites?

---

[74] *twiggen* covered with woven twigs [75] *mazzard* head [76] *Diablo* the devil [77] *rise* grow riotous
[78] *turn'd Turks* changed completely for the worse; proverbial

For Christian shame, put by this barbarous brawl:
He that stirs next to carve for[79] his own rage
Holds his soul light; he dies upon his motion.
Silence that dreadful bell: it frights the isle
From her propriety.[80] What is the matter, masters?
Honest Iago, that looks dead with grieving,   150
Speak, who began this? on thy love, I charge thee.
IAGO. I do not know: friends all but now, even now,
In quarter,[81] and in terms like bride and groom
Devesting them for bed; and then, but now—
As if some planet had unwitted men—
Swords out, and tilting one at other's breast,
In opposition bloody. I cannot speak
Any beginning to this peevish odds;[82]
And would in action glorious I had lost
Those legs that brought me to a part of it!   160
OTH. How comes it, Michael, you are thus forgot?
CAS. I pray you, pardon me; I cannot speak.
OTH. Worthy Montano, you were wont be civil;
The gravity and stillness of your youth
The world hath noted, and your name is great
In mouths of wisest censure:[83] what's the matter,
That you unlace[84] your reputation thus
And spend your rich opinion for the name
Of a night-brawler? give me answer to it.
MON. Worthy Othello, I am hurt to danger: 170
Your officer, Iago, can inform you,—
While I spare speech, which something now offends me,—
Of all that I do know: nor know I aught
By me that's said or done amiss this night;
Unless self-charity be sometimes a vice,
And to defend ourselves it be a sin
When violence assails us.
OTH.   Now, by heaven,
My blood begins my safer guides to rule;
And passion, having my best judgement collied,[85]
Assays to lead the way: if I once stir,   180
Or do but lift this arm, the best of you
Shall sink in my rebuke. Give me to know
How this foul rout began, who set it on;
And he that is approv'd in[86] this offence,

---

[79] *carve for* indulge   [80] *propriety* proper state or condition   [81] *In quarter* on terms   [82] *peevish odds* childish quarrel   [83] *censure* judgment   [84] *unlace* degrade   [85] *collied* darkened   [86] *approv'd in* found guilty of

Though he had twinn'd with me, both at birth,
Shall lose me. What! in a town of war,
Yet wild, the people's hearts brimful of fear,
To manage private and domestic quarrel,
In night, and on the court and guard[87] of safety!
'Tis monstrous. Iago, who began 't? 190
MON. If partially affin'd,[88] or leagu'd in office,
Thou dost deliver more or less than truth,
Thou art no soldier.
IAGO. Touch me not so near:
I had rather have this tongue cut from my mouth
Than it should do offence to Michael Cassio;
Yet, I persuade myself, to speak the truth,
Shall nothing wrong him. Thus it is, general.
Montano and myself being in speech,
There comes a fellow crying out for help;
And Cassio following him with determin'd sword, 200
To execute[89] upon him. Sir, this gentleman
Steps in to Cassio, and entreats his pause:
Myself the crying fellow did pursue,
Lest by his clamour—as it so fell out—
The town might fall in fright: he, swift of foot,
Outran my purpose; and I return'd the rather
For that I heard the clink and fall of swords,
And Cassio high in oath; which till to-night
I ne'er might say before. When I came back—
For this was brief—I found them close together, 210
At blow and thrust; even as again they were
When you yourself did part them.
More of this matter cannot I report:
But men are men; the best sometimes forget:
Though Cassio did some little wrong to him,
As men in rage strike those that wish them best,
Yet surely, Cassio, I believe, receive'd
From him that fled some strange indignity,
Which patience could not pass.
OTH. I know, Iago,
Thy honesty and love doth mince this matter, 220
Making it light to Cassio. Cassio, I love thee;
But never more be officer of mine.

[*Enter* DESDEMONA, *attended.*]

---

[87] *court and guard* spot and guarding place, i.e., the main guardhouse [88] *affin'd* bound by a tie
[89] *execute* give effect to (his anger)

Look, if my gentle love be not rais'd up!
I'll make thee an example.
DES.   What's the matter?
OTH. All's well now, sweeting; come away to bed.
Sir, for your hurts, myself will be your surgeon:
Lead him off. [To MONTANO, *who is led off.*]
Iago, look with care about the town,
And silence those whom this vile brawl distracted.
Come, Desdemona: 'tis the soldier's life   230
To have their balmy slumbers wak'd with strife. [*Exit with all but* IAGO *and*
    CASSIO.]
IAGO. What, are you hurt, lieutenant?
CAS. Ay, past all surgery.
IAGO. Marry, God forbid!
CAS. Reputation, reputation, reputation! O, I have lost my reputation! I have lost
    the immortal part of myself, and what remains is bestial. My reputation, Iago,
    my reputation!
IAGO. As I am an honest man, I thought you had received some bodily wound;
    there is more sense in that than in reputation. Reputation is an idle and most
    false imposition; oft got without merit, and lost without deserving: you have 240
    lost no reputation at all, unless you repute yourself such a loser. What, man!
    there are ways to recover the general again: you are but now cast in his mood,
    a punishment more in policy than in malice; even so as one would beat his
    offenceless dog to affright an imperious lion: sue to him again, and he 's yours.
CAS. I will rather sue to be despised than to deceive so good a commander with so
    slight, so drunken, and so indiscreet an officer. Drunk? and speak parrot?[90] and
    squabble? swagger? swear? and discourse fustian[91] with one's own shadow? O
    thou invisible spirit of wine, if thou has no name to be known by, let us call
    thee devil!
IAGO. What was he that you followed with your sword? What had he done to you? 250
CAS. I know not.
IAGO. Is't possible?
CAS. I remember a mass of things, but nothing distinctly; a quarrel, but nothing
    wherefore. O God, that men should put an enemy in their mouths to steal away
    their brains! that we should, with joy, pleasance, revel and applause, transform
    ourselves into beasts!
IAGO. Why, but you are now well enough: how came you thus recovered?
CAS. It hath pleased the devil drunkenness to give place to the devil wrath: one
    unperfectness[92] shows me another, to make me frankly despise myself.
IAGO. Come, you are too severe a moraler: as the time, the place, and the condition 260
    of this country stands, I could heartily wish this had not befallen; but, since it
    is as it is, mend it for your own good.

---

[90] *speak parrot* talk nonsense   [91] *discourse fustian* talked nonsense   [92] *unperfectness* imperfection

CAS. I will ask him for my place again; he shall tell me I am a drunkard! Had I as
many mouths as Hydra,[93] such an answer would stop them all. To be now a
sensible man, by and by a fool, and presently a beast! O strange! Every
inordinate cup is unblessed and the ingredient is a devil.

IAGO. Come, come, good wine is a good familiar creature, if it be well used: exclaim
no more against it. And, good lieutenant, I think you think I love you.

CAS. I have well approved[94] it, sir. I drunk!

IAGO. You or any man living may be a drunk at a time, man. I'll tell you what you 270
shall do. Our general's wife is now the general: I may say so in this respect, for
that he hath devoted and given up himself to the contemplation, mark, and
denotement[95] of her parts and graces: confess yourself freely to her; importune
her help to put you in your place again: she is of so free, so kind, so apt, so
blessed a dispositon, she holds it a vice in her goodness not to do more than
she is requested: this broken joint between you and her husband entreat her to
splinter;[96] and, my fortunes against any lay[97] worth naming, this crack of your
love shall grow stronger than it was before.

CAS. You advise me well.

IAGO. I protest, in the sincerity of love and honest kindness. 280

CAS. I think it freely; and betimes in the morning I will beseech the virtuous
Desdemona to undertake for me: I am desperate of my fortunes if they check[98]
me here.

IAGO. You are in the right. Good night, lieutenant; I must to the watch.

CAS. Good night, honest Iago. [*Exit* CASSIO.]

IAGO. And what 's he then that says I play the villain?
When this advice is free I give the honest,
Probal[99] to thinking and indeed the course
To win the Moor again? For 'tis most easy
Th' inclining[100] Desdemona to subdue[101] 290
In any honest suit: she 's fram'd as fruitful
As the free elements. And then for her
To win the Moor—were 't to renounce his baptism,
All seals and symbols of redeemed sin,
His soul is so enfetter'd to her love,
That she may make, unmake, do what she list,
Even as her appetite shall play the god
With his weak function. How am I then a villain
To counsel Cassio to this parallel[102] course,
Directly to his good? Divinity of hell! 300
When devils will the blackest sins put on,[103]

---

[93] *Hydra* a monster with many heads, slain by Hercules as the second of his twelve labors
[94] *approved* proved [95] *denotement* observation [96] *splinter* bind with splints [97] *lay* stake, wager
[98] *check* repulse [99] *Probal* probable [100] *inclining* favorably disposed [101] *subdue* persuade
[102] *parallel* probably, corresponding to his best interest [103] *put on* further

They do suggest[104] at first with heavenly shows,
As I do now; for whiles this honest fool
Plies Desdemona to repair his fortunes
And she for him pleads strongly to the Moor,
I'll pour this pestilence into his ear,
That she repeals him[105] for her body's lust;
And by how much she strives to do him good,
She shall under her credit with the Moor,
So will I turn her virtue into pitch,   310
And out of her own goodness make the net
That shall enmesh them all.

[*Enter* RODERIGO.]

How now, Roderigo!

ROD. I do not follow here in the chase, not like a hound that hunts, but one that
fills up the cry.[106] My money is almost spent; I have been tonight exceedingly
well cudgellèd; and I think the issue will be, I shall have so much experience for
my pains, and so, with no money at all and a little more wit, return again to
Venice.

IAGO. How poor are they that have not patience!
What wound did ever heal but by degrees?
Thou know'st we work by wit, and not by witchcraft;   320
And wit depends on dilatory time.
Does 't not go well? Cassio hath beaten thee,
And thou, by that small hurt, hast cashier'd[107] Cassio:
Though other things grow fair against the sun,
Yet fruits that blossom first will first be ripe:
Content thyself awhile. By th' mass, 'tis morning;
Pleasure and action make the hours seem short.
Retire thee; go where thou art billeted:
Away, I say; thou shalt know more hereafter:
Nay, get thee gone. [*Exit* RODERIGO.]
                        Two things are to be done: 330
My wife must move for Cassio to her mistress;
I'll set her on;
Myself the while to draw the Moor apart,
And bring him jump[108] when he may Cassio find
Soliciting his wife: ay, that's the way:
Dull not device by coldness and delay. [*Exit.*]

---

[104] *suggest* tempt [105] *repeals him* i.e., attempts to get him restored [106] *cry* pack [107] *cashier'd*
dismissed from service [108] *jump* precisely

ACT III

SCENE I. *Before the castle.*

[*Enter* CASSIO *and* MUSICIANS.]

CAS. Masters, play here; I will content[1] your pains;
  Something that's brief; and bid "Good morrow, general." [*They play.*]

[*Enter* CLOWN.]

CLO. Why, masters, have your instruments been in Naples, that they speak i' the
  nose[2] thus?
FIRST MUS. How, sir, how!
CLO. Are these, I pray you, wind-instruments?
FIRST MUS. Ay, marry, are they, sir.
CLO. O, thereby hangs a tail.
FIRST MUS. Whereby hangs a tale,[3] sir?
CLO. Marry, sir, by many a wind-instrument that I know. But, masters, here 's   10
  money for you: and the general so likes your music, that he desires you, for
  love's sake, to make no more noise with it.
FIRST MUS. Well, sir, we will not.
CLO. If you have any music that may not be heard, to 't again: but, as they say, to
  hear music the general does not greatly care.
FIRST MUS. We have none such, sir.
CLO. Then put up your pipes in your bag, for I'll away: go; vanish into air;
  away! [*Exeunt* MUSICIANS.]
CAS. Dost thou hear, my honest friend?
CLO. No, I hear not your honest friend; I hear you.   20
CAS. Prithee, keep up thy quillets. There's a poor piece of gold for thee: if the
  gentlewoman that attends the general's wife be stirring, tell her there 's one
  Cassio entreats her a little favour of speech: wilt thou do this?
CLO. She is stirring, sir: if she will stir hither, I shall seem to notify unto her.
CAS. Do, good my friend. [*Exit* CLOWN.]

[*Enter* IAGO.]

          In happy time, Iago.
IAGO. You have not been a-bed, then?
CAS. Why, no; the day had broke
  Before we parted. I have made bold, Iago,
  To send in to your wife: my suit to her

ACT III [1] *content* reward [2] *speak i' the nose* i.e., like Neapolitans, who spoke a nasal dialect (with a
joke on syphillis, which attacks the nose) [3] *tale* pun on *tail,* a wind instrument of sorts

Is, that she will to virtuous Desdemona   30
 Procure me some access.
IAGO.   I'll send her to you presently;
 And I'll devise a means to draw the Moor
 Out of the way, that your converse and business
 May be more free.
CAS. I humbly thank you for 't. [*Exit* IAGO.]
         I never knew
 A Florentine more kind and honest.

      [*Enter* EMILIA.]

EMIL. Good morrow, good lieutenant: I am sorry
 For your displeasure; but all will sure be well.
 The general and his wife are talking of it;
 And she speaks for you stoutly: the Moor replies,   40
 That he you hurt is of great fame in Cyprus
 And great affinity[4] and that in wholesome wisdom
 He might not but refuse you, but he protests he loves you
 And needs no other suitor but his likings
 To take the safest occasion by the front[5]
 To bring you in again.
CAS.   Yet, I beseech you,
 If you think fit, or that it may be done,
 Give me advantage of some brief discourse
 With Desdemona alone.
EMIL.   Pray you, come in:
 I will bestow you where you shall have time   50
 To speak your bosom freely.
CAS. I am much bound to you. [*Exeunt.*]

    SCENE II. *A room in the castle.*

   [*Enter* OTHELLO, IAGO, *and* GENTLEMEN.]

OTH. These letters give, Iago, to the pilot;
 And by him do my duties to the senate:
 That done, I will be walking on the works:[6]
 Repair there to me.
IAGO.   Well, my good lord, I'll do 't.
OTH. This fortification, gentlemen, shall we see 't?
GENT. We'll wait upon your lordship. [*Exeunt.*]

---

[4] *affinity* kindred, family connection [5] *by the front* i.e., by the forelock [6] *works* earthworks, fortifications

SCENE III. *The garden of the castle.*

[*Enter* DESDEMONA, CASSIO, *and* EMILIA.]

DES. Be thou assur'd, good Cassio, I will do
  All my abilities in thy behalf.
EMIL. Good madam, do: I warrant it grieves my husband,
  As if the case were his.
DES. O, that 's an honest fellow. Do not doubt, Cassio,
  But I will have my lord and you again
  As friendly as you were.
CAS.   Bounteous madam,
  Whatever shall become of Michael Cassio,
  He's never any thing but your true servant.
DES. I know 't; I thank you. You do love my lord: 10
  You have known him long; and be you well assur'd
  He shall in strangeness[7] stand no farther off
  Than in a politic distance.
CAS.   Ay, but lady,
  That policy may either last so long
  Or feed upon such nice and waterish diet,
  Or breed itself so out of circumstance,[8]
  That, I being absent and my place supplied,
  My general will forget my love and service.
DES. Do not doubt[9] that; before Emilia here
  I give thee warrant of thy place: assure thee,   20
  If I do vow a friendship, I'll perform it
  To the last article: my lord shall never rest;
  I'll watch him tame[10] and talk him out of patience;
  His bed shall seem a school, his board a shrift;[11]
  I'll intermingle every thing he does
  With Cassio's suit: therefore be merry, Cassio;
  For thy solicitor shall rather die
  Than give thy cause away.[12]

[*Enter* OTHELLO *and* IAGO *at a distance.*]

EMIL. Madam, here comes my lord.
CAS. Madam, I'll take my leave.   30
DES. Why, stay, and hear me speak.
CAS. Madam, not now: I am very ill at ease,
  Unfit for mine own purposes.

---

[7] *strangeness* distant behavior   [8] *breed . . . circumstance* increase itself so on account of accidents
[9] *doubt* fear   [10] *watch him tame* tame him by keeping him from sleeping (a term from falconry)
[11] *shrift* confessional   [12] *away* up

DES. Well, do your discretion. [*Exit* CASSIO.]
IAGO. Ha! I like not that.
OTH.   What dost thou say?
IAGO. Nothing, my lord: or if—I know not what.
OTH. Was not that Cassio parted from my wife?
IAGO. Cassio, my lord! No, sure, I cannot think it,
  That he would steal away so guilty-like,
  Seeing you coming.
OTH.   I do believe 'twas he.   40
DES. How now, my lord!
  I have been talking with a suitor here,
  A man that languishes in your displeasure.
OTH. Who is 't you mean?
DES. Why, your lieutenant, Cassio. Good my lord,
  If I have any grace or power to move you,
  His present reconciliation take;
  For if he be not one that truly loves you,
  That errs in ignorance and not in cunning,
  I have no judgement in an honest face: 50
  I prithee, call him back.
OTH.   Went he hence now?
DES. Ay, sooth; so humbled
  That he hath left part of his grief with me,
  To suffer with him. Good love, call him back.
OTH. Not now, sweet Desdemon; some other time.
DES. But shall 't be shortly?
OTH.   The sooner, sweet, for you.
DES. Shall 't be to-night at supper?
OTH.   No, not to-night.
DES. To-morrow dinner, then?
OTH.   I shall not dine at home;
  I meet the captains at the citadel.
DES. Why, then, to-morrow night; or Tuesday morn;   60
  On Tuesday noon, or night; on Wednesday morn:
  I prithee, name the time, but let it not
  Exceed three days: in faith, he's penitent;
  And yet his trespass, in our common reason[13]—
  Save that, they say, the wars must make examples
  Out of their best—is not almost a fault
  T' incur a private check. When shall he come?
  Tell me, Othello: I wonder in my soul,
  What you would ask me, that I should deny,

[13] *common reason* everyday judgments

Or stand so mamm'ring on.[14] What! Michael Cassio,   70
  That came a-wooing with you, and so many a time,
  When I have spoke of you dispraisingly,
  Hath ta'en your part; to have so much to do
  To bring him in! Trust me, I could do much,—
OTH.   Prithee, no more: let him come when he will;
  I will deny thee nothing.
DES.   Why, this is not a boon;
  'Tis as I should entreat you wear your gloves,
  Or feed on nourishing dishes, or keep you warm,
  Or sue to you to do a peculiar profit
  To your own person: nay, when I have a suit   80
  Wherein I mean to touch your love indeed,
  It shall be full of poise[15] and difficult weight
  And fearful to be granted.
OTH.   I will deny thee nothing:
  Whereon, I do beseech thee, grant me this,
  To leave me but a little to myself.
DES.   Shall I deny you? no: farewell, my lord.
OTH.   Farewell, my Desdemona. I'll come to thee straight.
DES.   Emilia, come. Be as your fancies teach you;
  Whate'er you be, I am obedient. [*Exit with* EMILIA.]
OTH.   Excellent wretch![16] Perdition catch my soul,   90
  But I do love thee! and when I love thee not,
  Chaos is come again.
IAGO.   My noble lord,—
OTH.   What dost thou say, Iago?
IAGO.   Did Michael Cassio, when you woo'd my lady,
  Know of your love?
OTH.   He did, from first to last: why dost thou ask?
IAGO.   But for a satisfaction of my thought;
  No further harm.
OTH.   Why of thy thought, Iago?
IAGO.   I did not think he had been acquainted with her.
OTH.   O, yes; and went between us very oft.   100
IAGO.   Indeed!
OTH.   Indeed! ay, indeed: discern'st thou aught in that?
  Is he not honest?
IAGO.   Honest, my lord!
OTH.   Honest! ay, honest.
IAGO.   My lord, for aught I know.

---

[14] *mamm'ring on* wavering   [15] *poise* weight, heaviness   [16] *wretch* term of affectionate endearment
with a connotation of pity

OTH. What dost thou think?
IAGO.   Think, my lord!
OTH.   Think, my lord!
   By heaven, he echoes me,
   As if there were some monster in his thought
   Too hideous to be shown. Thou dost mean something:
   I heard thee say even now, thou lik'st not that,
   When Cassio left my wife: what didst not like?   110
   And when I told thee he was of my counsel
   In my whole course of wooing, thou criedst "Indeed!"
   And didst contract and purse thy brow together,
   As if thou then hadst shut up in thy brain
   Some horrible conceit: if thou dost love me,
   Show me thy thought.
IAGO. My lord, you know I love you.
OTH.   I think thou dost;
   And, for I know thou 'rt full of love and honesty,
   And weigh'st thy words before thou giv'st them breath,
   Therefore these stops of thine fright me more: 120
   For such things in a false disloyal knave
   Are tricks of custom, but in a man that's just
   They 're close delations,[17] working from the heart
   That passion cannot rule.
IAGO.   For Michael Cassio,
   I dare be sworn I think that he is honest.
OTH. I think so too.
IAGO.   Men should be what they seem;
   Or those that be not, would they might seem none!
OTH. Certain, men should be what they seem.
IAGO. Why, then, I think Cassio 's an honest man.
OTH. Nay, yet there 's more in this: 130
   I prithee, speak to me as to thy thinkings,
   As thou dost ruminate, and give thy worst of thoughts
   The worst of words.
IAGO.   Good my lord, pardon me:
   Though I am bound to every act of duty,
   I am not bound to that all slaves are free to.
   Utter my thoughts? Why, say they are vile and false:
   As where 's that palace whereinto foul things
   Sometimes intrude not? who has a breast so pure,
   But some uncleanly apprehensions

---

[17] *close delations* secret or involuntary accusations

Keep leets[18] and law-days[19] and in sessions sit   140
   With meditations lawful?
OTH. Thou dost conspire against thy friend, Iago,
   If thou but think'st him wrong'd and mak'st his ear
   A stranger to thy thoughts.
IAGO.   I do beseech you—
   Though I perchance am vicious[20] in my guess,
   As, I confess, it is my nature's plague
   To spy into abuses, and oft my jealousy[21]
   Shapes faults that are not—that your wisdom yet,
   From one that so imperfectly conceits,[22]
   Would take no notice, nor build yourself a trouble   150
   Out of his scattering and unsure observance.
   It were not for your quiet nor your good,
   Nor for my manhood, honesty, or wisdom,
   To let you know my thoughts.
OTH.   What dost thou mean?
IAGO. Good name in man and woman, dear my lord,
   Is the immediate jewel of their souls:
   Who steals my purse steals trash: 'tis something, nothing;
   'Twas mine, 'tis his, and has been slave to thousands;
   But he that filches from me my good name
   Robs me of that which not enriches him   160
   And makes me poor indeed.
OTH. By heaven, I'll know thy thoughts.
IAGO. You cannot, if my heart were in your hand;
   Nor shall not, whilst 'tis in my custody.
OTH. Ha!
IAGO.   Oh, beware, my lord, of jealousy;
   It is the green-ey'd monster which doth mock
   The meat it feeds on: that cuckhold lives in bliss
   Who certain of his fate, loves not his wronger;
   But, O, what damned minutes tells her o'er
   Who dotes, yet doubts, suspects, yet strongly loves!   170
OTH. O misery!
IAGO. Poor and content is rich and rich enough,
   But riches fineless[23] is as poor as winter
   To him that ever fears he shall be poor.
   Good God, the souls of all my tribe defend
   From jealousy!

---

[18] *Keep leets* hold courts [19] *law-days* court days [20] *vicious* wrong [21] *jealousy* suspicion of evil
[22] *conceits* judges [23] *fineless* boundless

OTH.   Why, why is this?
 Think'st thou I'd make a life of jealousy,
 To follow still the changes of the moon
 With fresh suspicions? No; to be once in doubt
 Is once to be resolv'd: exchange me for a goat,   180
 When I shall turn the business of my soul
 To such exsufflicate and blown[24] surmises,
 Matching thy inference. 'Tis not to make me jealous
 To say my wife is fair, feeds well, loves company,
 Is free of speech, sings, plays and dances well;
 Where virtue is, these are more virtuous;
 Nor from mine own weak merits will I draw
 The smallest fear or doubt of her revolt:
 For she had eyes, and chose me. No, Iago;
 I'll see before I doubt; when I doubt, prove;   190
 And on the proof, there is no more but this,—
 Away at once with love or jealousy!
IAGO. I am glad of this; for now I shall have reason
 To show the love and duty that I bear you
 With franker spirit: therefore, as I am bound,
 Receive it from me. I speak not yet of proof.
 Look to your wife; observe her well with Cassio;
 Wear your eye thus, not jealous nor secure.[25]
 I would not have your free and noble nature,
 Out of self-bounty,[26] be abus'd; look to 't: 200
 I know our country disposition well;
 In Venice they do let heaven see the pranks
 They dare not show their husbands; their best conscience
 Is not to leave 't undone, but keep 't unknown.
OTH. Dost thou say so?
IAGO. She did deceive her father, marrying you;
 And when she seem'd to shake and fear your looks,
 She lov'd them most.
OTH.   And so she did.
IAGO.   Why, go to then;
 She that, so young, could give out such a seeming,[27]
 To seel[28] her father's eyes up close as oak—   210
 He thought 'twas witchcraft—but I am much to blame;
 I humbly do beseech you of your pardon
 For too much loving you.

---

[24] *exsufflicate and blown* unsubstantial and inflated, flyblown [25] *secure* free from uneasiness
[26] *self-bounty* inherent or natural goodness [27] *seeming* false appearance [28] *seel* blind (a term from falconry)

OTH.   I am bound to thee for ever.

IAGO. I see this hath a little dash'd your spirits.

OTH. Not a jot, not a jot.

IAGO.   I' faith, I fear it has.
  I hope you will consider what is spoke
  Comes from my love. But I do see y' are mov'd:
  I am to pray you not to strain my speech
  To grosser issues nor to larger reach[29]
  Than to suspicion.   220

OTH. I will not.

IAGO.   Should you do so, my lord,
  My speech would fall into such vile success
  As my thoughts aim not at. Cassio 's my worthy friend—
  My lord, I see y' are mov'd.

OTH.   No, not much mov'd:
  I do not think but Desdemona's honest.

IAGO. Long live she so! and long live you to think so!

OTH. And yet, how nature erring from itself,—

IAGO. Ay, there's the point: as—to be bold with you—
  Not to affect many proposed matches
  Of her own clime, complexion, and degree,   230
  Whereto we see in all things nature tends—
  Foh! one may smell in such a will[30] most rank,
  Foul disproportion,[31] thoughts unnatural.
  But pardon me; I do not in position[32]
  Distinctly speak of her; though I may fear
  Her will, recoiling to[33] her better judgment,
  May fall to match you with her country forms[34]
  And happily repent.[35]

OTH.   Farewell, farewell:
  If more thou dost perceive, let me know more;
  Set on they wife to observe: leave me, Iago.   240

IAGO [*going*]. My lord take my leave.

OTH. Why did I marry? This honest creature doubtless
  Sees and knows more, much more, than he unfolds.

IAGO [*returning*]. My Lord, I would I might entreat your honour
  To scan this thing no farther; leave it to time:
  Although 'tis fit that Cassio have his place,
  For, sure, he fills it up with great ability,
  Yet, if you please to hold him off awhile,

---

[29] *reach* meaning [39] *will* sensuality [31] *disproportion* abnormality [32] *position* general argument
[33] *recoiling to* falling back upon, or recoiling against [34] *fall . . . forms* happen to compare you with
Venetian norms of handsomeness [35] *repent* i.e., of her marriage

You shall by that perceive him and his means:
Note, if your lady strain his entertainment[36]   250
With any strong or vehement importunity;
Much will be seen in that. In the mean time,
Let me be thought too busy in my fears—
As worthy cause I have to fear I am—
And hold her free,[37] I do beseech your honour.
OTH. Fear not my government.[38]
IAGO. I once more take my leave. [*Exit.*]
OTH. This fellow 's of exceeding honesty,
And knows all qualities, with a learned spirit,
Of human dealings. If I do prove her haggard,[39]   260
Though that her jesses[40] were my dear heartstrings,
I 'ld whistle her off and let her down the wind,
To prey at fortune.[41] Haply, for I am black
And have not those soft parts of conversation
That chamberers[42] have, or for I am declin'd
Into the vale of years,—yet that 's not much—
She 's gone. I am abus'd: and my relief
Must be to loathe her. O curse of marriage,
That we can call these delicate creatures ours,
And not their appetites! I had rather be a toad,   270
And live upon the vapour of a dungeon,
Than keep a corner in the thing I love
For others' uses. Yet, 'tis the plague of great ones;
Prerogativ'd[43] are they less than the base;
'Tis destiny unshunnable, like death:
Even then this forked[44] plague is fated to us
When we do quicken.[45] Look where she comes:

[*Enter* DESDEMONA *and* EMILIA.]

If she be false, O, then heaven mocks itself!
I'll not believe 't.
DES.   How now, my dear Othello!
You dinner, and the generous[46] islanders   280
By you invited, do attend your presence.
OTH. I am to blame.

---

[36] *strain his entertainment* urge his reinstatement   [37] *hold her free* regard her as innocent
[38] *government* self-control   [39] *haggard* a wild female duck   [40] *jesses* straps fastened around
the legs of a trained hawk   [41] *at fortune* at random   [42] *chamberers* gallants   [43] *Prerogativ'd*
privileged   [44] *forked* an allusion to the horns of the cuckold   [45] *quicken* receive life
[46] *generous* noble

DES.   Why do you speak so faintly?
  Are you not well?

OTH. I have a pain upon my forehead here.

DES. 'Faith, that 's with watching;[47] 'twill away again:
  Let me but bind it hard, within this hour
  It will be well.

OTH.   Your napkin is too little: [*He puts the handkerchief from him;
  and it drops.*]
  Let it alone. Come, I'll go in with you.

DES. I am very sorry that you are not well. [*Exit with* OTHELLO.]

EMIL. I am glad I have found this napkin: 290
  This was her first remembrance from the Moor:
  My wayward husband hath a hundred times
  Woo'd me to steal it; but she so loves the token,
  For he conjur'd her she should ever keep it,
  That she reserves it evermore about her
  To kiss and talk to. I'll have the work ta'en out,[48]
  And give 't Iago: what he will do with it
  Heaven knows, not I;
  I nothing but to please his fantasy.

      [*Enter* IAGO.]

IAGO. How now! what do you here alone?   300

EMIL. Do not you chide; I have a thing for you.

IAGO. A thing for me? it is a common thing[49]—

EMIL. Ha!

IAGO. To have a foolish wife.

EMIL. O, is that all? What will you give me now
  For that same handkerchief?

IAGO.   What handkerchief?

EMIL. What handkerchief!
  Why, that the Moor first gave Desdemona;
  That which so often you did bid me steal.

IAGO. Hast stol'n it from her?   310

EMIL. No, 'faith; she let it drop by negligence,
  And, to th' advantage, I, being here, took 't up.
  Look, here it is.

IAGO.   A good wench; give it to me.

EMIL. What will you do with 't, that you have been so earnest
  To have me filch it?

---

[47] *watching* working late [48] *work ta'en out* design copied [49] *common thing common* suggests
coarseness and availability to all, and *thing* is slang for female sexual organs

IAGO.   [*Snatching it*] Why, what is that to you?
EMIL. If it be not for some purpose of import,
   Give 't me again: poor lady, she'll run mad
   When she shall lack it.
IAGO. Be not acknown on 't;[50] I have use for it.
   Go, leave me. [*Exit* EMILIA.]   320
   I will in Cassio's lodging lose this napkin,
   And let him find it. Trifles light as air
   Are to the jealous confirmations strong
   As proofs of holy writ: this may do something.
   The Moor already changes with my poison:
   Dangerous conceits are, in their natures, poisons,
   Which at the first are scarce found to distaste,
   But with a little act[51] upon the blood,
   Burn like the mines of sulphur. I did say so:

                [*Enter* OTHELLO.]

   Look, where he comes! Not poppy, nor mandragora,   330
   Nor all the drowsy syrups of the world,
   Shall ever medicine thee to that sweet sleep
   Which thou owedst yesterday.
OTH.   Ha! ha! false to me?
IAGO. Why, how now, general! no more of that.
OTH. Avaunt! be gone! thou has set me on the rack;
   I swear 'tis better to be much abus'd
   Than but to know 't a little.
IAGO.   How now, my lord!
OTH. What sense had I of her stol'n hours of lust?
   I saw 't not, thought it not, it harm'd not me:
   I slept the next night well, fed well, was free and merry;   340
   I found not Cassio's kisses on her lips:
   He that is robb'd, not wanting what is stol'n,
   Let him not know 't, and he 's not robb'd at all.
IAGO. I am sorry to hear this.
OTH. I had been happy, if the general camp,
   Pioners[52] and all, had tasted her sweet body,
   So I had nothing known. O, now, for ever
   Farewell the tranquil mind! farewell content!
   Farewell the plumed troop, and the big wars,
   That make ambition virtue! O, farewell!   350
   Farewell the neighing steed, and the shrill trump,

---

[50] *Be . . . on 't* do not confess knowledge of it   [51] *act* action, working   [52] *Pioners* sappers, a low grade
of soldiers

The spirit-stirring drum, th' ear-piercing fife,
The royal banner, and all quality,
Pride, pomp and circumstance[53] of glorious war!
And, O you mortal engines,[54] whose rude throats
Th' immortal Jove's dread clamours counterfeit,
Farewell! Othello's occupation 's gone!

IAGO. Is 't possible, my lord?

OTH. Villain, be sure thou prove my love a whore,
Be sure of it; give me the ocular proof;   360
Or, by the worth of mine eternal soul,
Thou hadst been better have been born a dog
Than answer my wak'd wrath!

IAGO.   Is 't come to this?

OTH. Make me to see 't; or, at the least, so prove it,
That the probation bear no hinge nor loop
To hang a doubt on; or woe upon thy life!

IAGO. My noble lord,—

OTH. If thou dost slander her and torture me,
Never pray more; abandon all remorse;
On horror's head horrors[55] accumulate;   370
Do deeds to make heaven weep, all earth amaz'd;
For nothing canst thou to damnation add
Greater than that.

IAGO.   O grace! O heaven forgive me!
Are you a man? have you a soul or sense?
God be wi' you; take mine office. O wretched fool,
That liv'st to make thine honesty a vice!
O monstrous world! Take note, take note, O world,
To be direct and honest is not safe.
I thank you for this profit; and from hence
I'll love no friend, sith love breeds such offence.   380

OTH. Nay, stay: thou shouldst be honest.

IAGO. I should be wise, for honesty 's a fool
and loses that it works for.

OTH.   By the world,
I think my wife be honest and think she is not;
I think thou are just and think thou are not.
I'll have some proof. Her name, that was as fresh
As Dian's visage, is now begrim'd and black
As mine own face. If there be cords, or knives,
Poison, or fire, or suffocating streams,

---

[53] *circumstance* attendant fact; here, formal display [54] *mortal engines* i.e., cannon [55] *horrors* object of *accumulate*

I'll not endure it. Would I were satisfied! 390
IAGO. I see, sir, you are eaten up with passion:
  I do repent me that I put it to you.
  You would be satisfied!
OTH.   Would! nay, I will.
IAGO. And may: but, how? how satisfied, my lord?
  Would you, the supervisor, grossly gape on—
  Behold her topp'd?
OTH.   Death and damnation! O!
IAGO. It were a tedious difficulty, I think,
  To bring them to that prospect: damn them then,
  If ever mortal eyes do see them bolster[56]
  More than their own! What then? how then? 400
  What shall I say? Where 's satisfaction?
  It is impossible you should see this,
  Were they as prime as goats, as hot as monkeys,
  As salt[57] as wolves in pride, and fools as gross
  As ignorance made drunk. But yet, I say,
  If imputation[58] and strong circumstances,
  Which lead directly to the door of truth,
  Will give you satisfaction, you may have 't.
OTH. Give me a living reason she 's disloyal.
IAGO. I do not like the office: 410
  But, sith I am ent'red in this cause so far,
  Prick'd to 't by foolish honesty and love,
  I will go on. I lay with Cassio lately;
  And, being troubled with a raging tooth,
  I could not sleep.
  There are a kind of men so loose of soul,
  That in their sleeps will mutter their affairs:
  One of this kind is Cassio:
  In sleep I heard him say "Sweet Desdemona,
  Let us be wary, let us hide our loves"; 420
  And then, sir, would he grip and wring my hand,
  Cry, "O sweet creature!" and then kiss me hard,
  As if he pluck'd up kisses by the roots
  That grew upon my lips: then laid his leg
  Over my thigh, and sigh'd, and kiss'd; and then
  Cried "Cursed fate that gave thee to the Moor!"
OTH. O monstrous! monstrous!
IAGO.   Nay, this was but his dream.

---

[56] *bolster* lie together   [57] *salt* wanton, sexual   [58] *imputation* i.e., opinion founded on strong circumstantial evidence

OTH. But this denoted a foregone conclusion:[59]
  'Tis a shrewd doubt, though it be but a dream.
IAGO. And this may help to thicken other proofs   430
  That do demonstrate thinly.
OTH.   I'll tear her all to pieces.
IAGO. Nay, but be wise; yet we see nothing done;
  She may be honest yet. Tell me but this,
  Have you not sometimes seen a handkerchief
  Spotted with strawberries in your wife's hand?
OTH. I gave her such a one; 'twas my first gift.
IAGO. I know not that: but such a handkerchief—
  I am sure it was your wife's—did I to-day
  See Cassio wipe his beard with.
OTH.   If it be that,—
IAGO. If it be that, or any that was hers,   440
  It speaks against her with the other proofs.
OTH. O, that the slave had forty thousand lives!
  One is too poor, too weak for my revenge.
  Now do I see 'tis true. Look here, Iago;
  All my fond love thus do I blow to heaven.
  'Tis gone.
  Arise, black vengeance, from the hollow hell!
  Yield up, O love, thy crown and hearted[60] throne
  To tyrannous hate! Swell, bosom, with thy fraught,[61]
  For 'tis of apsics'[62] tongues!
IAGO.   Yet be content   450
OTH. O, blood, blood, blood!
IAGO. Patience, I say; your mind perhaps may change.
OTH. Never, Iago. Like to the Pontic sea,
  Whose icy current and compulsive course
  Ne'er feels retiring ebb, but keeps due on
  To the Propontic and the Hellespont,
  Even so my bloody thoughts, with violent pace,
  Shall ne'er look back, ne'er ebb to humble love,
  Till that a capable and wide revenge
  Swallow them up. Now, by yond marble[63] heaven,   460
  [*Kneels*] In the due reverence of a sacred vow
  I here engage my words.
IAGO.   Do not rise yet.
  [*Kneels*] Witness, you ever-burning lights above,
  You elements that clip us round about,

---

[59] *foregone conclusion* previous trial or experience (not used in our sense)   [60] *hearted* fixed in the heart   [61] *fraught* freight, burden   [62] *aspics'* venemous serpents'   [63] *marble* i.e., gleaming like marble

Witness that here Iago doth give up
The execution[64] of his wit, hands, heart,
To wrong'd Othello's service! Let him command,
And to obey shall be in me remorse,[65]
What bloody business ever. [*They rise.*]

OTH.   I greet thy love,
Not with vain thanks, but with acceptance bounteous,   470
And will upon the instant put thee to 't:
Within these three days let me hear thee say
That Cassio 's not alive.

IAGO. My friend is dead; 'tis done at your request:
But let her live.

OTH. Damn her, lewd minx! O, damn her! damn her!
Come, go with me apart; I will withdraw,
To furnish me with some swift means of death
For the fair devil. Now art thou my lieutenant.

IAGO. I am your own for ever. [*Exeunt.*]   480

SCENE IV. *Before the castle.*

[*Enter* DESDEMONA, EMILIA, *and* CLOWN.]

DES. Do you know, sirrah, where Lieutenant Cassio lies?

CLO. I dare not say he lies any where.

DES. Why, man?

CLO. He's a soldier, and for one to say a soldier lies, is stabbing.

DES. Go to; where lodges he?

CLO. To tell you where he lodges, is to tell you where I lie.

DES. Can any thing be made of this?

CLO. I know not where he lodges, and for me to devise a lodging and say he lies
   here or he lies there, were to lie in mine own throat.

DES. Can you inquire him out, and be edified by report?   10

CLO. I will catechize the world for him, that is, make questions, and by them
   answer.

DES. Seek him, bid him come hither: tell him I have moved my lord on his behalf,
   and hope all will be well.

CLO. To do this is within the compass of man's wit; and therefore I will attempt the
   doing it. [*Exit* Clown.]

DES. Where should I lose that handkerchief, Emilia?

EMIL. I know not, madam.

DES. Believe me, I had rather lost my purse
Full of crusadoes:[66] and, but my noble Moor   20
Is true of mind and made of no such baseness

---

[64] *execution* exercise [65] *remorse* pity for Othello's wrongs [66] *crusadoes* Portugese gold coins

As jealous creatures are, it were enough
To put him to ill thinking.
EMIL.   Is he not jealous?
DES. Who, he? I think the sun where he was born
Drew all such humours from him.
EMIL.   Look, where he comes.

[*Enter* OTHELLO.]

DES. I will not leave him now till Cassio
Be call'd to him.—How is 't with you, my lord?
OTH. Well, my good lady. [*Aside*] O, hardness, to dissemble!—
How do you do, Desdemona?
DES.   Well, my good lord.
OTH. Give me your hand: this hand is moist, my lady.   30
DES. It yet hath felt no age nor known no sorrow.
OTH. This argues fruitfulness and liberal heart:
Hot, hot, and moist: this hand of yours requires
A sequester[67] from liberty, fasting and prayer,
Much castigation, exercise devout;
For here 's a young and sweating devil here,
That commonly rebels. 'Tis a good hand,
A frank one.
DES.   You may, indeed, say so:
For 'twas that hand that gave away my heart.
OTH. A liberal hand: the hearts of old gave hands;   40
But our new heraldry is hands, not hearts.[68]
DES. I cannot speak of this. Come now, your promise.
OTH. What promise, chuck?
DES. I have sent to bid Cassio come speak with you.
OTH. I have a salt and sorry rheum[69] offends me;
Lend my thy handkerchief.
DES.   Here, my lord.
OTH. That which I gave you.
DES.   I have it not about me.
OTH. Not?
DES.   No, indeed, my lord.
OTH.   That 's a fault.
That handkerchief
Did an Egyptian[70] to my mother give;   50

---

[67] *sequester* separation, sequestration [68] *new . . . hearts* a current expression referring to marriages in which there is a joining of hands without the giving of hearts [69] *sorry rheum* distressful head cold
[70] *Egyptian* gypsy

She was a charmer, and could almost read
The thoughts of people: she told her, while she kept it,
'Twould make her amiable and subdue my father
Entirely to her love, but if she lost it
Or made a gift of it, my father's eye
Should hold her loathed and his spirits should hunt
After new fancies: she, dying, gave it me;
And bid me, when my fate would have me wive,
To give it her. I did so: and take heed on 't;
Make it a darling like your precious eye;   60
To lose 't or give 't away were such perdition
As nothing else could match.
DES.   Is 't possible?
OTH. 'Tis true: there 's magic in the web of it:
   A sibyl, that had numb'red in the world
   The sun to course two hundred compasses,
   In her prophetic fury sew'd the work;
   The worms were hallow'd that did breed the silk;
   And it was dy'd in mummy[71] which the skilful
   Conserv'd of[72] maidens' hearts.
DES.   Indeed! is 't true?
OTH. Most veritable; therefore look 't well.   70
DES. Then would to God that I had never seen 't!
OTH. Ha! wherefore?
DES. Why do you speak so startingly and rash?
OTH. Is 't lost? is 't gone? speak, is it out o' the' way?
DES. Heaven bless us!
OTH. Say you?
DES. It is not lost; but what if it were?
OTH. How!
DES. I say, it is not lost.
OTH.   Fetch 't, let me see 't.
DES. Why, so I can sir, but I will not now.   80
   This is a trick to put me from my suit:
   Pray you, let Cassio be receiv'd again.
OTH. Fetch me the handkerchief: my mind misgives.
DES. Come, come:
   You'll never meet a more sufficient man.
OTH. The handkerchief!
DES.   I pray, talk me of Cassio.
OTH. The handkerchief!

---

[71] *mummy* medicinal or magical preparation drained from the flesh of mummified bodies
[72] *Conserv'd of* preserved out of

DES.   A man that all his time
  Hath founded his good fortunes on your love,
  Shar'd dangers with you,—
OTH. The handkerchief!   90
DES. In sooth, you are to blame.
OTH. Away! [*Exit* OTHELLO.]
EMIL. Is not this man jealous?
DES. I ne'er saw this before.
  Sure, there 's some wonder in this handkerchief:
  I am most unhappy in the loss of it.
EMIL. 'Tis not a year or two shows us a man:
  They are all but stomachs, and we all but food;
  They eat us hungerly, and when they are full,
  They belch us.

[*Enter* IAGO *and* CASSIO.]

        Look you, Cassio and my husband!   100
IAGO. There is not other way; 'tis she must do 't:
  And, lo, the happiness! go, and importune her.
DES. How now, good Cassio! what 's the news with you?
CAS. Madam, my former suit: I do beseech you
  That by your virtuous means I may again
  Exist, and be a member of his love
  Whom I with all the office of my heart
  Entirely honour: I would not be delay'd.
  If my offence be of such mortal kind
  That nor my service past, nor present sorrows,   110
  Nor purpos'd merit in futurity,
  Can ransom me into his love again,
  But to know so much be my benefit;[73]
  So shall I clothe me in a forc'd content,
  And shut myself up in some other course,
  To fortune's alms.
DES.   Alas, thrice-gentle Cassio!
  My advocation[74] is not now in tune;
  My lord is not my lord; nor should I know him,
  Were he in favour as in humour alter'd.
  So help me every spirit sanctified   120
  As I have spoken for you all my best
  And stood within the blank[75] of his displeasure

---

[73] *to know . . . benefit* to know that my case is hopeless will end my vain endeavor [74] *advocation* advocacy [75] *blank* white spot in the center of a target; here, range

For my free speech! You must awhile be patient:
What I can do I will; and more I will
Than for myself I dare: let that suffice you.
IAGO. Is my lord angry?
EMIL.   He went hence but now,
  And certainly in strange unquietness.
IAGO. Can he be angry? I have seen the cannon,
  When it hath blown his ranks into the air,
  And, like the devil, from his very arm   130
  Puff'd his own brother:—and can he be angry?
  Something of moment then: I will go meet him:
  There 's matter in 't indeed, if he be angry.
DES. I prithee, do so. [*Exit* IAGO.]
                               Something, sure, of state,
  Either from Venice, or some unhatch'd practice
  Made demonstrable here in Cyprus to him,
  Hath puddled[76] his clear spirit; and in such cases
  Men's natures wrangle with inferior things,
  Though great ones are their object. 'Tis even so;
  For let our finger ache, and it indues[77]   140
  Our other healthful members even to a sense
  Of pain: nay, we must think men are not gods,
  Nor of them look for such observancy
  As fits the bridal. Beshrew me much, Emilia,
  I was, unhandsome[78] warrior as I am,
  Arraigning his unkindness with my soul;
  But now I find I had suborn'd the witness,
  And he 's indicted falsely.
EMIL. Pray heaven it be state-matters, as you think,
  And no conception[79] nor no jealous toy   150
  Concerning you.
DES. Alas the day! I never gave him cause.
EMIL. But jealous souls will not be answer'd so;
  They are not ever jealous for the cause,
  But jealous for they are jealous: 'tis a monster
  Begot upon itself, born on itself.
DES. Heaven keep that monster from Othello's mind!
EMIL. Lady, amen.
DES. I will go seek him. Cassio, walk here about:
  If I do find him fit, I'll move your suit   160
  And seek to effect it to my uttermost.
CAS. I humbly thank your ladyship. [*Exit* DESDEMONA *with* EMILIA.]

---

[76] *puddled* sullied the purity of [77] *indues* brings to the same condition [78] *unhandsome* unfair
[79] *conception* mere fancy

[*Enter* BIANCA.]

BIAN. Save you, friend Cassio!

CAS.   What make you from home?

  How is 't with you, my most fair Bianca?

  I' faith, sweet love, I was coming to your house.

BIAN. And I was going to your lodging, Cassio.

  What, keep a week away? seven days and nights?

  Eight score eight hours? and lovers' absent hours,

  More tedious than the dial eight score times?

  O weary reck'ning!

CAS.   Pardon me, Bianca.   170

  I have this while with leaden thoughts been press'd;

  But I shall, in a more continuate[80] time,

  Strike off this score of absence. Sweet Bianca,   [*Giving her* DESDEMONA'S

    handkerchief.]

  Take me this work out.[81]

BIAN.   O Cassio, whence came this?

  This is some token from a newer friend:

  To the felt absence now I feel a cause:

  Is 't come to this? Well, well.

CAS.   Go to, woman!

  Throw your vile guesses in the devil's teeth,

  From whence you have them. You are jealous now

  That this is from some mistress, some remembrance: 180

  No, in good troth, Bianca.

BIAN.   Why, whose is it?

CAS. I know not, sweet: I found it in my chamber.

  I like the work well: ere it be demanded—

  As like enough it will—I would have it copied:

  Take it, and do 't; and leave me for this time.

BIAN. Leave you! wherefore?

CAS. I do attend here on the general;

  And think it no addition, nor my wish,

  To have him see me woman'd.

BIAN.   Why, I pray you?

CAS. Not that I love you not.

BIAN.   But that you do not love me.   190

  I pray you, bring me on the way a little,

  And say if I shall see you soon at night.

CAS. 'Tis but a little way that I can bring you;

  For I attend here: but I'll see you soon.

BIAN. 'Tis very good; I must be circumstance'd.[82]   [*Exeunt omnes.*]

---

[80] *continuate* uninterrupted   [81] *Take . . . out* i.e., copy this embroidery for me   [82] *circumstance'd*
governed by circumstances

ACT IV

SCENE I. *Cyprus. Before the castle.*

[*Enter* OTHELLO *and* IAGO.]

IAGO. Will you think so?

OTH.   Think so, Iago!

IAGO.   What,
   To kiss in private?

OTH.   An unauthoriz'd kiss.

IAGO. Or to be naked with her friend in bed
   An hour or more, not meaning any harm?

OTH. Naked in bed, Iago, and not mean harm!
   It is hypocrisy against the devil:
   They that mean virtuously, and yet do so,
   The devil their virtue tempts, and they tempt heaven.

IAGO. So[1] they do nothing, 'tis a venial slip:
   But if I give my wife a handkerchief,—   10

OTH. What then?

IAGO. Why, then, 'tis hers, my lord: and, being hers,
   She may, I think, bestow 't on any man.

OTH. She is protectress of her honour too:
   May she give that?

IAGO. Her honour is an essence that 's not seen;
   They have it very oft that have it not:
   But, for the handkerchief,—

OTH. By heaven, I would most gladly have forgot it.
   Thou said'st—O, it comes o'er my memory,   20
   As doth the raven o'er the infected house,[2]
   Boding to all—he had my handkerchief.

IAGO. Ay, what of that?

OTH.   That's not so good now.

IAGO.   What,
   If I had said I had seen him do you wrong?
   Or hear him say,—as knaves be such abroad,
   Who having, by their own importunate suit,
   Or voluntary dotage of some mistress,
   Convinced or supplied[3] them, cannot choose
   But they must blab—

OTH.   Hath he said any thing?

ACT IV [1] *So* as long as [2] *raven . . . house* allusion to the belief that the raven hovered over a house of sickness or infection [3] *Convinced or supplied* i.e., mistresses gained by importunity and those who doted voluntarily

IAGO. He hath, my lord; but be you well assur'd,   30
No more than he'll unswear.

OTH.   What hath he said?

IAGO. 'Faith, that he did—I know not what he did.

OTH. What? What?

IAGO. Lie—

OTH.   With her?

IAGO.   With her, on her; what you will.

OTH. Lie with her! lie on her! We say lie on her, when they belie her. Lie with her!
that's   fulsome.—Handkerchief—confessions—handkerchief!—To   confess,
and be hanged for his labour;—first, to be hanged, and then to confess.—I
tremble at it. Nature would not invest herself in such shadowing passion
without some instruction.[4] It is not words that shakes me thus. Pish! Noses,
ears, and lips.—Is 't possible?—Confess—handkerchief—O devil! [*Falls in a* 40
trance.]

IAGO. Work on,
My medicine, work! Thus credulous fools are caught;
And many worthy and chaste dames even thus,
All guiltless, meet reproach. What, ho! my lord!
My lord, I say! Othello!

[*Enter* CASSIO.]

How now, Cassio!

CAS. What 's the matter?

IAGO. My lord is fall'n into an epilepsy:
This is his second fit; he had one yesterday.

CAS. Rub him about the temples.

IAGO.   No, forbear;
The lethargy[5] must have his quiet course: 50
If not, he foams at mouth and by and by
breaks out to savage madness. Look, he stirs:
Do you withdraw yourself a little while,
He will recover straight: when he is gone,
I would on great occasion speak with you. [*Exit* CASSIO.]
How is it, general? have you not hurt your head?

OTH. Dost thou mock me?

IAGO.   I mock you! no, by heaven.
Would you would bear your fortune like a man!

OTH. A horned man 's a monster and a beast.

IAGO. There 's many a beast then in a populous city,   60
And many a civil[6] monster.

---

[4] *Nature . . . instruction* i.e., my jealousy cannot be merely the result of natural imagination, but
must have some foundation in fact [5] *lethargy* unconscious condition [6] *civil* i.e., in civilized society

OTH. Did he confess it?

IAGO.   Good sir, be a man;
  Think every bearded fellow that 's but yok'd
  May draw with you:[7] there 's millions now alive
  That nightly lie in those unproper[8] beds
  Which they dare swear peculiar:[9] your case is better.
  O, 'tis the spite of hell, the fiend's arch-mock,
  To lip a wanton in a secure couch,
  And to suppose her chaste! No, let me know;
  And knowing what I am, I know what she shall be.   70

OTH. O, thou are wise; 'tis certain.

IAGO.   Stand you awhile apart;
  Confine yourself but in a patient list.[10]
  Whilst you were here o'erwhelmed with your grief—
  A passion most unsuiting such a man—
  Cassio came hither: I shifted him away,
  And laid good 'scuse upon your ecstasy,
  Bade him anon return and here speak with me;
  The which he promis'd. Do but encave[11] yourself,
  And mark the fleers,[12] the gibes, and notable scorns,
  That dwell in every region of his face;   80
  For I will make him tell the tale anew,
  Where, how, how oft, how long ago, and when
  He hath, and is again to cope your wife:
  I say, but mark his gesture. Marry, patience;
  Or I shall say y' are all in all in spleen,
  And nothing of a man.

OTH.   Dost thou hear, Iago?
  I will be found most cunning in my patience;
  But—dost thou hear?—most bloody.

IAGO.   That 's not amiss;
  But yet keep time[13] in all. Will you withdraw? [OTHELLO *retires.*]
  Now will I question Cassio of Bianca,   90
  A housewife that by selling her desires
  Buys herself bread and clothes: it is a creature
  That dotes on Cassio; as 'tis the strumpet's plague
  To beguile many and be beguil'd by one:
  He, when he hears of her, cannot refrain
  From the excess of laughter. Here he comes:

---

[7] *draw with you* i.e., share your fate as cuckold [8] *unproper* not belonging exclusively to an individual
[9] *peculiar* private, one's own [10] *patient list* within the bounds of patience [11] *encave* conceal
[12] *fleers* sneers [13] *keep time* use judgment and order

[*Enter* CASSIO.]

As he shall smile, Othello shall go mad;
And his unbookish[14] jealousy must conster[15]
Poor Cassio's smiles, gestures and light behaviour,
Quite in the wrong. How do you know, lieutenant?   100
CAS. The worser that you give me the addition[16]
Whose want even kills me.
IAGO. Ply Desdemona well, and you are sure on 't
[*Speaking lower*] Now, if this suit lay in Bianca's power,
How quickly should you speed!
CAS.   Alas, poor caitiff!
OTH. Look, how he laughs already!
IAGO. I never knew woman love man so.
CAS. Alas, poor rogue! I think, i' faith, she loves me.
OTH. Now he denies it faintly, and laughs it out.
IAGO. Do you hear, Cassio?
OTH.   Now he importunes him   110
To tell o'er: go to; well said, well said.
IAGO. She gives it out that you shall marry her:
Do you intend it?
CAS. Ha, ha, ha!
OTH. Do you triumph, Roman?[17] do you triumph?
CAS. I marry her! what? a customer![18] Prithee, bear some charity to my wit; do not
think it so unwholesome. Ha, ha, ha!
OTH. So, so, so, so: they laugh that win.
IAGO. 'Faith, the cry goes that you shall marry her.
CAS. Prithee, say true.   120
IAGO. I am a very villain else.
OTH. Have you scored me?[19] Well.
CAS. This is the monkey's own giving out: she is persuaded I will marry her, out of
her own love and flattery, not out of my promise.
OTH. Iago beckons me; now he begins the story.
CAS. She was here even now; she haunts me in every place. I was the other day
talking on the seabank with certain Venetians; and thither comes the bauble,[20]
and, by this hand, she falls me thus about my neck—
OTH. Crying, 'O dear Cassio!' as it were: his gesture imports it.
CAS. So hangs, and lolls, and weeps upon me; so shakes, and pulls me: ha, ha, ha!   130
OTH. Now he tells how she plucked him to my chamber. O, I see that nose of yours,
but not that dog I shall throw it to.

---

[14] *unbookish* uninstructed [15] *conster* construe [16] *addition* title [17] *Roman* epithet arising from the
association of the Romans with the idea of triumph [18] *customer* prostitute [19] *scored me* made up my
reckoning, or branded me [20] *bauble* plaything

CAS. Well, I must leave her company.
IAGO. Before me![21] look, where she comes.

[*Enter* BIANCA.]

CAS. 'Tis such another fitchew![22] marry, a perfumed one.—What do you mean by this haunting of me?
BIAN. Let the devil and his dam haunt you! What did you mean by that same handkerchief you gave me even now? I was a fine fool to take it. I must take out the work?—A likely piece of work, that you should find it in your chamber, and not know who left it there! This is some minx's token, and I must take out 140 the work? There; give it your hobby-horse:[23] wheresoever you had it, I'll take out no work on 't.
CAS. How now, my sweet Bianca! how now! how now!
OTH. By heaven, that should be my handkerchief!
BIAN. An you'll come to supper to-night, you may; an you will not, come when you are next prepared for. [*Exit.*]
IAGO. After her, after her.
CAS. 'Faith, I must; she'll rail in the street else.
IAGO. Will you sup there?
CAS. Yes, I intend so. 150
IAGO. Well, I may chance to see you; for I would very fain speak with you.
CAS. Prithee, come; will you?
IAGO. Go to; say no more. [*Exit* CASSIO.]
OTH [*advancing*]. How shall I murder him, Iago?
IAGO. Did you perceive how he laughed at his vice?
OTH. O Iago!
IAGO. And did you see the handkerchief?
OTH. Was that mine?
IAGO. Yours, by this hand: and to see how he prizes the foolish woman your wife! She gave it him, and he hath given it his whore. 160
OTH. I would have him nine years a-killing. A fine woman! a fair woman! a sweet woman!
IAGO. Nay, you must forget that.
OTH. Ay, let her rot, and perish, and be damned to-night; for she shall not live: no, my heart is turned to stone; I strike it, and it hurts my hand. O, the world hath not a sweeter creature: she might lie by an emperor's side and command him tasks.
IAGO. Nay, that 's not your way.[24]
OTH. Hang her! I do but say what she is: so delicate with her needle: an admirable musician: O! she will sing the savageness out of a bear: of so high and plenteous 170 wit and invention:—

---

[21] *Before me!* On my soul! [22] *fitchew* polecat (because of her strong perfume; also, slang word for a prostitute) [23] *hobby-horse* harlot [24] *your way* i.e., the way you should think of her

IAGO. She 's the worse for all this.

OTH. O, a thousand thousand times: and then, of so gentle a condition!

IAGO. Ay, too gentle.

OTH. Nay, that 's certain: but yet the pity of it, Iago! O Iago, the pity of it, Iago!

IAGO. If you are so fond over her iniquity, give her patent[25] to offend; for, if it touch not you, it comes near nobody.

OTH. I will chop her into messes;[26] cuckold me!

IAGO. O, 'tis foul in her

OTH. With mine officer!   180

IAGO. That 's fouler.

OTH. Get me some poison, Iago; this night: I'll not expostulate with her, lest her body and beauty unprovide[27] my mind again: this night, Iago.

IAGO. Do it not with poison, strangle her in her bed, even the bed she hath contaminated.

OTH. Good, good: the justice of it pleases: very good.

IAGO. And for Cassio, let me be his undertaker:[28] you shall hear more by midnight.

OTH. Excellent good. [*A trumpet within.*] What trumpet is that same?

IAGO. I warrant something from Venice.

[*Enter* LODOVICO, DESDEMONA, *and* ATTENDANTS.]

                   'Tis Lodovico.

This comes from the duke: and, see, your wife's with him.   190

LOD. God save you, worthy general!

OTH.   With all my heart, sir.

LOD. The duke and the senators of Venice greet you. [*Gives him a letter.*]

OTH. I kiss the instrument of their pleasures. [*Opens the letter, and reads.*]

DES. And what 's the news, good cousin Lodovico?

IAGO. I am very glad to see you, signior;
Welcome to Cyprus.

LOD. I thank you. How does Lieutenant Cassio?

IAGO. Lives, sir.

DES. Cousin, there 's fall'n between him and my lord
An unkind breach: but you shall make all well.   200

OTH. Are you sure of that?

DES. My lord?

OTH [*reads*]. "This fail you not to do, as you will—"

LOD. He did not call; he 's busy in the paper.
Is there division 'twixt my lord and Cassio?

DES. A most unhappy one: I would do much
T' atone them, for the love I bear to Cassio.

OTH. Fire and brimstone!

---

[25] *patent* license   [26] *messes* dishes of food   [27] *unprovide* weaken, unfit   [28] *let . . . undertaker* i.e., let me settle with him

DES.   My lord?
OTH.   Are you wise?
DES. What, is he angry?
LOD.   May be the letter mov'd him:
  For, as I think, they do command him home,
  Deputing Cassio in his government.²⁹   210
DES. Trust me, I am glad on 't.
OTH.   Indeed!
DES.   My lord?
OTH. I am glad to see you mad.
DES.   Why, sweet Othello,—
OTH [*striking her*]. Devil!
DES. I have not deserv'd this.
LOD. My lord, this would not be believ'd in Venice,
  Though I should swear I saw 't; 'tis very much:
  Make her amends; she weeps.
OTH.   O devil, devil!
  If that the earth could teem with woman's tears,
  Each drop she falls would prove a crocodile.³⁰
  Out of my sight!
DES.   I will not stay to offend you. [*Going.*]   220
LOD. Truly, an obedient lady:
  I do beseech your lordship, call her back.
OTH. Mistress!
DES.   My lord?
OTH.   What would you with her, sir?
LOD. Who, I, my lord?
OTH. Ay; you did wish that I would make her turn:
  Sir, she can turn, and turn, and yet go on,
  And turn again; and she can weep, sir, weep;
  And she 's obedient, as you say, obedient,
  Very obedient. Proceed you in your tears.
  Concerning this, sir,—O well-painted passion,³¹!—   230
  I am commanded home. Get you away;
  I'll send for you anon. Sir, I obey the mandate,
  And will return to Venice. Hence, avaunt! [*Exit* DESDEMONA.]
  Cassio shall have my place. And, sir, to-night,
  I do entreat that we may sup together:
  You are welcome, sir, to Cyprus.—Goats and monkeys! [*Exit.*]

---

²⁹ *government* office   ³⁰ *prove a crocodile* i.e., by weeping crocodile tears; it was believed the crocodile shed tears over the body of the person it was eating   ³¹ *well-painted passion* well-simulated emotion

LOD. Is this the noble Moor whom our full senate
   Call all in all sufficient? Is this the nature
   Whom passion could not shake? whose solid virtue
   The shot of accident, nor dart of chance,   240
   Could neither graze nor pierce?
IAGO.   He is much chang'd.
LOD. Are his wits safe? is he not light of brain?
IAGO. He 's that he is: I may not breathe my censure
   What he might be: if what he might he is not,
   I would to heaven he were!
LOD.   What, strike his wife!
IAGO. 'Faith, that was not so well; yet would I knew
   That stroke would prove the worst!
LOD.   Is it his use?
   Or did the letters work upon his blood,
   And new-create this fault?
IAGO.   Alas, alas!
   It is not honesty in me to speak   250
   What I have seen and known. You shall observe him,
   And his own courses will denote him so
   That I may save my speech: do but go after,
   And mark how he continues.
LOD. I am sorry that I am deceiv'd in him. [*Exeunt.*]

SCENE II. *A room in the castle.*

[*Enter* OTHELLO *and* EMILIA.]

OTH. You have seen nothing then?
EMIL. Nor ever heard, nor ever did suspect.
OTH. Yes, you have seen Cassio and she together.
EMIL. But then I saw no harm, and then I heard
   Each syllable that breath made up between them.
OTH. What, did they never whisper?
EMIL.   Never, my lord.
OTH. Nor send you out 'o th' way?
EMIL. Never.
OTH. To fetch her fan, her gloves, her mask, nor nothing?
EMIL. Never, my lord.   10
OTH. That 's strange.
EMIL. I durst, my lord, to wager she is honest,
   Lay down my soul at stake: if you think other,
   Remove your thought: it doth abuse your bosom.
   If any wretch have put this in your head,

Let heaven requite it with the serpent's curse!
For, if she be not honest, chaste, and true,
There's no man happy; the purest of their wives
Is foul as slander.
OTH.   Bid her come hither: go. [*Exit* EMILIA.]   20
She says enough; yet she's a simple bawd
That cannot say as much. This is a subtle whore,
A closet lock and key[32] of villanous secrets:
And yet she'll kneel and pray; I have seen her do 't.

[*Enter* DESDEMONA *and* EMILIA.]

DES. My lord, what is your will?
OTH.   Pray, chuck, come hither.
DES. What is your pleasure?
OTH.   Let me see your eyes;
   Look in my face.
DES.   What horrible fancy 's this?
OTH [*to* EMILIA]. Some of your function,[33] mistress;
   Leave procreants[34] alone and shut the door;
   Cough, or cry "hem," if any body come:
   Your mystery, your mystery:[35] nay, dispatch. [*Exit* EMILIA.]   30
DES. Upon my knees, what doth your speech import?
   I understand a fury in your words,
   But not the words.
OTH. Why, what art thou?
DES.   Your wife, my lord; your true
   And loyal wife.
OTH.   Come, swear it, damn thyself;
   Lest, being like one of heaven, the devils themselves
   Should fear to seize thee: therefore be double damn'd:
   Swear thou are honest.
DES.   Heaven doth truly know it.
OTH. Heaven truly knows that thou are false as hell.
DES. To whom, my lord? with whom? how am I false?   40
OTH. O Desdemon! away! away! away!
DES. Alas the heavy day! Why do you weep?
   Am I the motive of these tears, my lord?
   If haply you my father do suspect
   An instrument of this your calling back,
   Lay not your blame on me: if you have lost him,
   Why, I have lost him too.

---

[32] *closet lock and key* complete storeroom   [33] *Some . . . function* i.e., set to work in your chosen
profession, that of bawd   [34] *procreants* mating couples   [35] *mystery* trade, occupation

OTH.   Had it pleas'd heaven
    To try me with affliction; had they[36] rain'd
    All kinds of sores and shames on my bare head,
    Steep'd me in poverty to the very lips,   50
    Given to captivity me and my utmost hopes,
    I should have found in some place of my soul
    A drop of patience: but, alas, to make me
    A fixed figure for the time of scorn
    To point his slow unmoving finger at![37]
    Yet could I bear that too; well, very well:
    But there, where I have garner'd up my heart,
    Where either I must live, or bear no life;
    The fountain from the which my current runs,
    Or else dries up; to be discarded thence!   60
    Or keep it as a cistern for foul toads
    To knot and gender[38] in! Turn thy complexion[39] there,
    Patience, thou young and rose-lipp'd cherubin,—
    Ay, there, look grim as hell!
DES. I hope my noble lord esteems me honest.
OTH. O, ay; as summer flies are in the shambles,[40]
    That quicken[41] even with blowing. O thou weed,
    Who are so lovely fair and smell'st so sweet
    That the sense aches at thee, would thou hads't ne'er been born!
DES. Alas, what ignorant sin have I committed?   70
OTH. Was this fair paper, this most goodly book,
    Made to write "whore" upon? What committed!
    Committed! O thou public commoner![42]
    I should make very forges of my cheeks,
    That would to cinders burn up modesty,
    Did I but speak they deeds. What committed!
    Heaven stops the nose at it and the moon winks,
    The bawdy wind that kisses all it meets
    Is hush'd within the hollow mine of earth,
    And will not hear it. What committed!   80
    Impudent strumpet!
DES.   By heaven, you do me wrong.
OTH. Are not you a strumpet?
DES.   No, as I am a Christian:
    If to preserve this vessel[43] for my lord

---

[36] *they* heavenly powers [37] *A . . . at* Othello possibly thinks of himself as a man set in a pillory at whom the scornful world points in mockery. There seems to be a comparison with the sundial, whose gnomon, or indicator, becomes the finger of scornful time [38] *gender* engender [39] *Turn thy complexion* grow pale [40] *shambles* slaughterhouse [41] *quicken* come to life [42] *commoner* prostitute [43] *vessel* body

From any other foul unlawful touch
Be not to be a strumpet, I am none.
OTH. What, not a whore?
DES.   No, as I shall be sav'd.
OTH. Is 't possible?
DES. O, heaven forgive us!
OTH.   I cry you mercy, then:
     I took you for the cunning whore of Venice
     That married with Othello. [*Raising his voice.*] You, mistress,   90
     That have the office opposite to Saint Peter,
     And keep the gate of hell!

[*Enter* EMILIA.]

                You, you, ay, you!
     We have done our course; there 's money for your pains:
     I pray you, turn the key and keep our counsel. [*Exit.*]
EMIL. Alas, what does this gentleman conceive?
     How do you, madam? how do you, my good lady?
DES. 'Faith, half asleep.
EMIL. Good madam, what 's the matter with my lord?
DES. With who?
EMIL. Why, with my lord, madam.   100
DES. Who is thy lord?
EMIL.   He that is yours, sweet lady.
DES. I have none: do not talk to me, Emilia;
     I cannot weep; nor answers have I none,
     But what should go by water.[44] Prithee, tonight
     Lay on my bed my wedding sheets: remember;
     And call thy husband hither.
EMIL.   Here 's a change indeed! [*Exit.*]
DES. 'Tis meet I should be us'd so, very meet.
     How have I been behav'd, that he might stick
     The small'st opinion on my least misuse?[45]

[*Enter* IAGO *and* EMILIA.]

IAGO. What is your pleasure, madam? How is 't with you?   110
DES. I cannot tell. Those that do teach young babes
     Do it with gentle means and easy tasks:
     He might have chid me so; for, in good faith,
     I am a child to chiding.

---

[44] *go by water* be expressed by tears   [45] *misuse* evil conduct

IAGO.   What is the matter, lady?

EMIL. Alas, Iago, my lord hath so bewhor'd her,
   Thrown such despite[46] and heavy terms upon her,
   As true hearts cannot bear.

DES. Am I that name, Iago?

IAGO.   What name, fair lady?

DES. Such as she said my lord did say I was.

EMIL. He call'd her whore: a beggar in his drink   120
   Could not have laid such terms upon his callet.[47]

IAGO. Why did he so?

DES. I do not know; I am sure I am none such.

IAGO. Do not weep, do not weep. Alas the day!

EMIL. Hath she forsook so many noble matches,
   Her father and her country and her friends,
   To be call'd whore? would it not make one weep?

DES. It is my wretched fortune.

IAGO.   Beshrew him for 't!
   How comes this trick upon him?

DES.   Nay, heaven doth know.

EMIL. I will be hang'd, if some eternal villain,   130
   Some busy and insinuating rogue,
   Some cogging,[48] cozening slave, to get some office,
   Have not devis'd this slander; I will be hang'd else.

IAGO. Fie, there is no such man; it is impossible.

DES. If any such there be, heaven pardon him!

EMIL. A halter pardon him! and hell gnaw his bones!
   Why should he call her whore? who keeps her company?
   What place? what time? what form? what likelihood?
   The Moor's abus'd by some most villainous knave,
   Some base notorious knave, some scurvy fellow.   140
   O heaven, that such companions thou 'ldst unfold,
   And put in every honest hand a whip
   To lash the rascals naked through the world
   Even from the east to th' west!

IAGO.   Speak within door.[49]

EMIL. O, fie upon them! Some such squire he was
   That turn'd your wit the seamy side without,
   And made you to suspect me with the Moor.

IAGO. You are a fool; go to.

DES.   Alas, Iago.
   What shall I do to win my lord again?

---

[46] *despite* contempt, scorn [47] *callet* lewd woman [48] *coggin* cheating [49] *Speak . . . door* i.e., not so loud

Good friend, go to him; for, by this light of heaven,   150
I know not how I lost him. Here I kneel:
If e'er by will did trespass 'gainst his love,
Either in discourse of thought or actual deed,
Or that mine eyes, mine ears, or any sense,
Delighted them in any other form;
Or that I do not yet, and ever did,
And ever will—though he do shake me off
To beggarly divorcement—love him dearly,
Comfort forswear me! Unkindness may do much;
And his unkindness may defeat my life,   160
But never taint my lord. I cannot say "whore":
It doth abhor me now I speak the word;
To do the act that might the addition[50] earn
Not the world's mass of vanity could make me.
IAGO. I pray you, be content; 'tis but his humour:
The business of the state does him offence,
And he does chide with you.
DES. If 'twere no other,—
IAGO.   'Tis but so, I warrant. [*Trumpets within.*]
Hark, how these instruments summon to supper!
The messengers of Venice stay the meat;[51]   170
Go in, and weep not; all things shall be well. [*Exeunt* DESDEMONA *and* EMILIA.]

[*Enter* RODERIGO.]

How now, Roderigo!
ROD. I do not find that thou dealest justly with me.
IAGO. What in the contrary?
ROD. Everyday thou daffest me[52] with some device, Iago; and rather, as it seems to
    me now, keepest from me all conveniency[53] than suppliest me with the least
    advantage of hope. I will indeed no longer endure it, nor am I yet persuaded
    to put up[54] in peace what already I have foolishly suffered.
IAGO. Will you hear me, Roderigo?
ROD. 'Faith, I have heard too much, for your words and performances are no kin 180
    together.
IAGO. You charge me most unjustly.
ROD. With nought but truth. I have wasted myself out of my means. The jewels
    you have had from me to deliver to Desdemona would half have corrupted a
    votarist:[55] you have told me she hath received them and returned me expecta-
    tions and comforts of sudden respect and acquaintance, but I find none.

---

[50] *addition* title [51] *stay the meat* are waiting for supper [52] *daffest me* puts me off with an excuse
[53] *conveniency* advantage, opportunity [54] *put up* submit to [55] *votarist* nun

IAGO. Well; go to; very well.

ROD. Very well! go to! I cannot go to, man; nor 'tis not very well: nay, I think it is scurvy, and begin to find myself fopped[56] in it.

IAGO. Very well.   190

ROD. I tell you 'tis not very well. I will make myself known to Desdemona: if she will return me my jewels, I will give over my suit and repent my unlawful solicitation; if not, assure yourself I will seek satisfaction of you.

IAGO. You have said now.[57]

ROD. Ay, and said nothing but what I protest intendment[58] of doing.

IAGO. Why, now I see there 's mettle in thee, and even from this instant do build on thee a better opinion than ever before. Give my thy hand, Roderigo: thou hast taken against me a most just exception; but yet, I protest, I have dealt most directly in thy affair.

ROD. It hath not appeared.   200

IAGO. I grant indeed it had not appeared, and your suspicion is not without wit and judgement. But, Roderigo, if thou hast that in thee indeed, which I have greater reason to believe now than ever, I mean purpose, courage and valour, this night show it: if thou the next night following enjoy not Desdemona, take me from this world with treachery and devise engines for[59] my life.

ROD. Well, what is it? is it within reason and compass?

IAGO. Sir, there is especial commission come from Venice to depute Cassio in Othello's place.

ROD. Is that true? why, then Othello and Desdemona return again to Venice.

IAGO. O, no; he goes into Mauritania[60] and takes away with him the fair Desde-   210
mona, unless his abode be lingered here by some accident: wherein none can be so determinate[62] as the removing of Cassio.

ROD. How do you mean, removing of him?

IAGO. Why, by making him uncapable of Othello's place; knocking out his brains.

ROD. And that you would have me to do?

IAGO. Ay, if you dare do yourself a profit and a right. He sups to-night with a harlotry,[63] and thither will I go to him: he knows not yet of his honourable fortune. If you will watch his going thence, which I will fashion to fall out between twelve and one, you may take him at your pleasure: I will be near to second your attempt, and he shall fall between us. Come, stand not amazed at   220
it, but go along with me; I will show you such a necessity in his death that you shall think yourself bound to put it to him. It is now high[63] supper-time, and the night grows to waste: about it.

ROD. I will hear further reason for this.

IAGO. And you shall be satisfied. [*Exeunt.*]

---

[56] *fopped* fooled [57] *You . . . now* well said, quite right [58] *intendment* purpose, intention [59] *engines for* plots against [60] *Mauritania* Roman name of northwest Africa, supposed land of the Moors
[61] *determinate* decisive [62] *harlotry* courtesan [63] *high* quite

SCENE III. *Another room in the castle.*

[*Enter* OTHELLO, LODOVICO, DESDEMONA, EMILIA, *and* ATTENDANTS.]

LOD. I do beseech you, sir, trouble yourself no further.
OTH. O, pardon me; 'twill do me good to walk.
LOD. Madam, good night; I humbly thank your ladyship.
DES. Your honour is most welcome.
OTH.   Will you walk, sir?
   O,—Desdemona,—
DES. My lord?
OTH. Get you to bed on th' instant; I will be returned forthwith: dismiss your
   attendant there: look 't be done.
DES. I will, my lord. [*Exit* OTHELLO, *with* LODOVICO *and* ATTENDANTS.]
EMIL. How goes it now? he looks gentler than he did.   10
DES. He says he will return incontinent:[64]
   He hath commanded me to go to bed,
   And bade me to dismiss you.
EMIL.   Dismiss me!
DES. It was his bidding; therefore, good Emilia,
   Give me my nightly wearing, and adieu:
   We must not now displease him.
EMIL. I would you had never seen him!
DES. So would not I: my love doth so approve him,
   That even his stubbornness,[65] his checks,[66] his frowns,—
   Prithee, unpin me,—have grace and favour in them.   20
EMIL. I have laid those sheets you bade me on the bed.
DES. All 's one. Good faith, how foolish are our minds!
   If I do die before thee, prithee, shroud me
   In one of those same sheets.
EMIL.   Come, come, you talk.
DES. My mother had a maid call'd Barbary:
   She was in love, and he she lov'd prov'd mad
   And did forsake her: she had a song of 'willow';
   An old thing 'twas, but it express'd her fortune,
   And she died singing it: that song to-night
   Will not go from my mind; I have much to do,   30
   But to[67] go hang my head all at one side,
   And sing it like poor Barbary. Prithee, dispatch.
EMIL. Shall I go fetch your night-gown?[68]
DES.   No, unpin me here.
   This Lodovico is a proper man.

---

[64] *incontinent* immediately [65] *stubbornness* harshness [66] *checks* rebukes [67] *But to* not to
[68] *night-gown* dressing gown

EMIL. A very handsome man.

DES. He speaks well.

EMIL. I know a lady in Venice would have walked barefoot to Palestine for a touch
of his nether lip.

DES [*Singing*]. The poor soul sat sighing by a sycamore tree,
  Sing all a green willow;   40
 Her hand on her bosom, her head on her knee,
  Sing willow, willow, willow:
 The fresh streams ran by her, and murmur'd her moans;
  Sing willow, willow, willow;
 Her salt tears fell from her, and soft'ned the stones;—

Lay by these:—

[*Singing*] Sing willow, willow, willow;

Prithee, hie thee; he'll come anon:—

[*Singing*] Sing all a green willow must be my garland.
 Let nobody blame him; his scorn I approve,—   50

Nay, that 's not next.—Hark! who is 't that knocks?

EMIL. It 's the wind.

DES [*Singing*]. I call'd my love false love; but what said he then?
  Sing willow, willow, willow:
 If I court moe women, you'll couch with moe men.—

So, get thee gone; good night. Mine eyes do itch;

Doth that bode weeping?

EMIL.   'Tis neither here nor there.

DES. I have heard it said so. O, these men, these men!

Dost thou in conscience think,—tell me, Emilia,—

That there be women do abuse their husbands   60

In such gross kind?

EMIL.   There be some such, no question.

DES. Wouldst thou do such a deed for all the world?

EMIL. Why, would not you?

DES.   No, by this heavenly light!

EMIL. Nor I neither by this heavenly light; I might do't as well i' the dark.

DES. Wouldst thou do such a deed for all the world?

EMIL. The world 's a huge thing: it is a great price

For a small vice.

DES. In troth, I think thou wouldst not.

EMIL. In troth, I think I should; and undo 't when I had done. Marry, I would not
do such a thing for a joint-ring,[69] nor for measures of lawn, nor for gowns, 70
petticoats, nor caps, nor any petty exhibition;[70] but, for all the whole world,—
why, who would not make her husband a cuckold to make him a monarch? I
should venture purgatory for 't.

---

[69] *joint-ring* a ring made in separable halves as a lover's token   [70] *exhibition* gift, present

DES. Beshrew me, if I would do such a wrong
   For the whole world.
EMIL. Why, the wrong is but a wrong i' the world; and having the world for your
   labour, 'tis a wrong in your own world, and you might quickly make it right.
DES. I do not think there is any such woman.
EMIL. Yes, a dozen; and as many to the vantage[71] as would store the world they
   played for.   80
   But I do think it is their husband's faults
   If wives do fall: say that they slack their duties,
   And pour our treasures into foreign laps,[72]
   Or else break out in peevish jealousies,
   Throwing restraint upon us; or say they strike us,
   Or scant our former having in despite;[73]
   Why, we have galls,[74] and though we have some grace,
   Yet have we some revenge. Let husbands know
   Their wives have sense like them: they see and smell
   And have their palates both for sweet and sour,   90
   As husbands have. What is it that they do
   When they change us for others? Is it sport?
   I think it is: and doth affection breed it?
   I think it doth: is 't frailty that thus errs?
   It is so too: and have not we affections,
   Desires for sport, and frailty, as men have?
   Then let them use us well: else let them know,
   The ills we do, their ills instruct us so.
DES. Good night, good night: heaven me such uses send,
   Not to pick bad from bad, but by bad mend! [*Exeunt.*]   100

ACT V

SCENE I. *Cyprus. A street.*

[*Enter* IAGO *and* RODERIGO.]

IAGO. Here stand behind this bulk;[1] straight will he come:
   Wear thy good rapier bare, and put it home:
   Quick, quick; fear nothing; I'll be at they elbow:
   It makes us, or it mars us; think on that,
   And fix most firm thy resolution.
ROD. Be near at hand; I may miscarry in 't.
IAGO. Here, at thy hand: be bold, and take thy stand. [*Retires.*]

[71] *to the vantage* in addition   [72] *pour . . . laps* i.e., are unfaithful   [73] *scant . . . despite* reduce our allowance to spite us   [74] *have galls* are capable of resenting injury and insult   ACT V [1] *bulk* framework projecting from the front of a shop

ROD. I have no great devotion to the deed;
  And yet he hath given me satisfying reasons:
  'Tis but a man gone. Forth, my sword: he dies.   10
IAGO. I have rubb'd this young quat[2] almost to the sense,[3]
  And he grows angry. Now, whether he kill Cassio,
  Or Cassio him, or each do kill the other,
  Every way makes my gain: live Roderigo,
  He calls me to a restitution large
  Of gold and jewels that I bobb'd[4] from him,
  As gifts to Desdemona;
  It must not be: if Cassio do remain,
  He hath a daily beauty in his life
  That makes me ugly; and, besides, the Moor   20
  May unfold me to him; there stand I in much peril:
  No, he must die. But so: I hear him coming.

               [*Enter* CASSIO.]

ROD. I know his gait, 'tis he.—Villain, thou diest! [*Makes a pass at* CASSIO.]
CAS. That thrust had been mine enemy indeed,
  But that my coat[5] is better than thou know'st:
  I will make proof of thine. [*Draws, and wounds* RODERIGO.]
ROD.   O, I am slain!

    [IAGO *from behind wounds* CASSIO *in the leg, and exits.*]

CAS. I am maim'd for ever. Help, ho! murder! murder! [*Falls.*]

             [*Enter* OTHELLO.]

OTH. The voice of Cassio: Iago keeps his word.
ROD. O, villain that I am!
OTH.   It is even so.
CAS. O, help, ho! light! a surgeon!   30
OTH. 'Tis he:—O brave Iago, honest and just,
  That hast such noble sense of they friends's wrong!
  Thou teachest me. Minion, your dear lies dead,
  And your unblest fate hies: strumpet, I come.
  Forth of my heart those charms, thine eyes, are blotted;
  Thy bed, lust-stain'd, shall with lust's blood be spotted. [*Exit* OTHELLO.]

        [*Enter* LODOVICO *and* GRATIANO.]

CAS. What, ho! no watch? no passage?[6] murder! murder!
GRA. 'Tis some mischance; the cry is very direful.

---

[2] *quat* pimple, pustule; used contemptuously [3] *to the sense* to the quick [4] *bobb'd* filched cunningly
[5] *coat* coat of mail [6] *passage* people passing

CAS. O, help!
LOD. Hark!   40
ROD. O wretched villain!
LOD. Two or three groan: it is a heavy[7] night;
   These may be counterfeits: let 's think 't unsafe
   To come in to the cry without more help.
ROD. Nobody come? then shall I bleed to death.
LOD. Hark!

[Enter IAGO *with a light.]*

GRA. Here 's one comes in his shirt, with light and weapons.
IAGO. Who 's there? whose noise is this that cries on[8] murder?
LOD. We do not know.
IAGO.   Did not you hear a cry?
CAS. Here, here! for heaven's sake, help me!
IAGO.   What's the matter?   50
GRA. This is Othello's ancient, as I take it.
LOD. The same indeed; a very valiant fellow.
IAGO. What are you here that cry so grievously?
CAS. Iago? O, I am spoil'd, undone by villains!
   Give me some help.
IAGO. O me, lieutenant! what villains have done this?
CAS. I think that one of them is hereabout,
   And cannot make away.
IAGO.   O treacherous villains!
   What are you there? come in, and give some help. *[To* LODOVICO *and*
     GRATIANO.]
ROD. O, help me here!   60
CAS. That 's one of them.
IAGO.   O murd'rous slave! O villain! *[Stabs* RODERIGO.]
ROD. O damn'd Iago! O inhuman dog!
IAGO. Kill men i' th' dark!—Where be these bloody thieves?—
   How silent in this town!—Ho! murder! murder!—
   What[9] may you be? are you of good or evil?
LOD. As you shall prove us, praise us.
IAGO. Signior Lodovico?
LOD. He, sir.
IAGO. I cry you mercy. Here 's Cassio hurt by villains.
GRA. Cassio!   70
IAGO. How is 't, brother!
CAS. My leg is cut in two.

---

[7] *heavy* thick, cloudy   [8] *cries on* cries out   [9] *What* who

IAGO.   Marry, heaven forbid!
  Light, gentlemen: I'll bind it with my shirt.

[*Enter* BIANCA.]

BIAN. What is the matter, ho? who is 't that cried?
IAGO. Who is 't that cried?
BIAN. O my dear Cassio! my sweet Cassio!
  O Cassio, Cassio, Cassio!
IAGO. O notable strumpet! Cassio, may you suspect
  Who they should be that have thus mangled you?
CAS. No.   80
GRA. I am sorry to find you thus: I have been to seek you.
IAGO. Lend me a garter. So. O, for a chair,[10]
  To bear him easily hence!
BIAN. Alas, he faints! O Cassio, Cassio, Cassio!
IAGO. Gentlemen all, I do suspect this trash[11]
  To be a party in this injury.
  Patience awhile, good Cassio. Come, come;
  Lend me a light. Know we this face or no?
  Alas, my friend and my dear countryman
  Roderigo! no:—yes, sure:—O heaven! Roderigo.   90
GRA. What, of Venice?
IAGO. Even he, sir: did you know him?
GRA.   Know him! ay.
IAGO. Signior Gratiano? I cry your gentle pardon;
  These bloody accidents must excuse my manners,
  That so neglected you.
GRA.   I am so glad to see you.
IAGO. How do you, Cassio? O, a chair, a chair!
GRA. Roderigo!
IAGO. He, he, 'tis he. [*A chair brought in.*] O, that's well said; the chair.
  Some good man bear him carefully from hence;
  I'll fetch the general's surgeon. [*To* BIANCA] For you, mistress,   100
  Save you your labour. He that lies slain here, Cassio,
  Was my dear friend: what malice was between you?
CAS. None in the world; nor do I know the man.
IAGO [*To* BIAN.]. What, look you pale? O, bear him out o' th' air.

[CASSIO *and* RODERIGO *are borne off.*]

  Stay you, good gentlemen. Look you pale, mistress?
  Do you perceive the gastness[12] of her eye?

---

[10] *chair* sedan chair [11] *trash* worthless thing, i.e., Bianca [12] *gastness* terror, ghastliness

Nay, if you stare, we shall hear more anon.
Behold her well; I pray you, look upon her:
Do you see, gentlemen? nay, guiltiness will speak,
Though tongues were out of use.   110

[Enter EMILIA.]

EMIL. 'Las, what 's the matter? what 's the matter, husband?
IAGO. Cassio hath here been set on in the dark
  By Roderigo and fellows that are scap'd:
  He 's almost slain, and Roderigo dead.
EMIL. Alas, good gentlemen! alas, good Cassio!
IAGO. This is the fruit of whoring. Prithee, Emilia.
  Go know of Cassio where he supp'd to-night.
  [*To* BIANCA] What, do you shake at that?
BIAN. He supp'd at my house; but I therefore shake not.
IAGO. O, did he so? I charge you, go with me.   120
EMIL. Fie, fie upon thee, strumpet!
BIAN. I am no strumpet; but of life as honest
  As you that thus abuse me.
EMIL.   As I! foh! fie upon thee!
IAGO. Kind gentlemen, let 's go see poor Cassio dress'd.
  Come, mistress, you must tell 's another tale.
  Emilia, run you to the citadel,
  And tell my lord and lady what hath happ'd.
  Will you go on afore? [*Aside*] This is the night
  That either mades me or fordoes[13] me quite. [*Exeunt.*]

SCENE II. A bedchamber in the castle.

[Enter OTHELLO with a light; DESDEMONA in her bed.]

OTH. It is the cause, it is the cause,[14] my soul,—
  Let me not name it to you, you chaste stars!—
  It is the cause. Yet I'll not shed her blood;
  Nor scar that whiter skin of hers than snow,
  And smooth as monumental alabaster.
  Yet she must die, else she'll betray more men.
  Put out the light, and then put out the light:
  If I quench thee, thou flaming minister,
  I can again thy former light restore,
  Should I repent me: but once put out thy light,   10
  Thou cunning'st pattern of excelling nature,

---

[13] *fordoes* undoes, ruins [14] *It is the cause* i.e., the cause of justice on which Othello must act,
Desdemona's deed, which is too unmentionable to be named to the chaste stars

I know not where is that Promethean heat[15]
That can thy light relume.[16] When I have pluck'd the rose,
I cannot give it vital growth again,
It needs must wither: I'll smell thee on the tree. [*Kissing her.*]
O balmy breath, that dost almost persuade
Justice to break her sword! One more, one more.
Be thus when thou art dead, and I will kill thee,
And love thee after. One more, and that 's the last:
So sweet was ne'er so fatal. I must weep,   20
But they are cruel tears: this sorrow 's heavenly;[17]
It strikes where it doth love. She wakes.

DES. Who 's there? Othello?

OTH.   Ay, Desdemona.

DES. Will you come to bed, my lord?

OTH. Have you pray'd to-night, Desdemon?

DES.   Ay, my lord.

OTH. If you bethink yourself of any crime
Unreconcil'd as yet to heaven and grace,
Solicit for it straight.

DES. Alack, my lord, what may you mean by that?

OTH. Well, do it, and be brief; I will walk by: 30
I would not kill thy unprepared spirit;
No; heaven forfend! I would not kill thy soul.

DES. Talk you of killing?

OTH.   Ay, I do.

DES.   Then heaven
Have mercy on me!

OTH.   Amen, with all my heart!

DES. If you say so, I hope you will not kill me.

OTH. Hum!

DES. And yet I fear you; for you 're fatal then
When your eyes roll so: why I should fear I know not,
Since guiltiness I know not; but yet I feel I fear.

OTH. Think on thy sins.

DES.   They are loves I bear to you.   40

OTH. Ay, and for that thou diest.

DES. That death 's unnatural that kills for loving.
Alas, why gnaw you so your nether lip?
Some bloody passion shakes your very frame:
These are portents; but yet I hope, I hope,
They do not point on me.

---

[15] *Promethean heat* divine fire; allusion to the theft of fire from heaven by Prometheus
[16] *relume* rekindle   [17] *this . . . heavenly* this tenderness, with which I lament the punishment which justice compels me to inflict, is a holy passion

OTH.   Peace, and be still!
DES. I will so. What 's the matter?
OTH. That handkerchief which I so lov'd and gave thee
    Thou gav'st to Cassio.
DES.   No, by my life and soul!
    Send for the man, and ask him.
OTH.   Sweet soul, take heed,   50
    Take heed of perjury; thou are on thy deathbed.
DES. Ay, but not yet to die.
OTH.   Yes, presently:
    Therefore confess thee freely of thy sin;
    For to deny each article with oath
    Cannot remove nor choke the strong conception[18]
    That I do groan withal. Thou art to die.
DES. Then Lord have mercy on me!
OTH.   I say, amen.
DES. And have you mercy too! I never did
    Offend you in my life; never lov'd Cassio
    But with such general warranty of heaven   60
    As I might love; I never gave him token.
OTH. By heaven, I saw my handkerchief in 's hand.
    O perjur'd woman! thou dost stone[19] my heart,
    And makest me call what I intend to do
    A murder, which I thought a sacrifice:
    I saw the handkerchief.
DES.   He found it then;
    I never gave it him: send for him hither;
    Let him confess a truth.
OTH.   He hath confess'd.
DES. What, my Lord?
OTH. That he hath us'd thee.
DES.   How? unlawfully?
OTH.   Ay.   70
DES. He will not say so.
OTH.   No, his mouth is stopp'd;
    Honest Iago hath ta'en order[20] for 't.
DES. O! my fear interprets: what, is he dead?
OTH. Had all his hairs been lives, my great revenge
    Had stomach for them all.
DES. Alas! he is betray'd and I undone.
OTH. Out, strumpet! weep'st thou for him to my face?

---

[18] *conception* plan, intention   [19] *stone* turn to stone, harden; Othello means that he will be tempted to kill her in sheer anger because of her perjury   [20] *ta'en order* taken measures

DES. O, banish me, my lord, but kill me not!

OTH. Down, strumpet!

DES. Kill me to-morrow: let me live to-night! 80

OTH. Nay, if you strive,—

DES. But half an hour!

OTH.   Being done, there is no pause.[21]

DES. But while I say one prayer!

OTH.   It is too late. [*Smothers her.*]

EMIL [*at the door*]. My lord, my lord! what, ho! my lord, my lord!

OTH. What noise is this? Not dead? not yet quite dead?
  I that am cruel am yet merciful;
  I would not have thee linger in thy pain:
  So, so.

EMIL [*within*]. What, ho! my lord, my lord!

OTH.   Who's there?

EMIL [*within*]. O, good my lord, I would speak a word with you! 90

OTH. Yes: 'tis Emilia. By and by. She 's dead.
  'Tis like she comes to speak of Cassio's death.—
  The noise was here. Ha! no more moving?
  Still as the grave. Shall she come in? were 't good?—
  I think she stirs again:—no. What 's best to do?
  If she come in, she'll sure speak to my wife:
  My wife! my wife! what wife? I have no wife.
  O, insupportable! O heavy hour!
  Methinks it should be now a huge eclipse
  Of sun and moon, and that th' affrighted globe 100
  Should yawn[22] at alteration.[23]

EMIL.   [*Within*] I do beseech you
  That I may speak with you, O, good my lord!

OTH. I had forgot thee: O, come in, Emilia:
  Soft; by and by. Let me the curtains draw.
  Where art thou? [*Closes bed-curtains and opens door.*]

[*Enter* EMILIA.]

                    What 's the matter with thee now?

EMIL. O, my good lord, yonder's foul murders done!

OTH. What, now?

EMIL. But now, my lord.

OTH. It is the very error[24] of the moon;
  She comes more nearer earth than she was wont, 110
  And makes men mad.

---

[21] *Being . . . pause* i.e., when the execution of the deed has once begun, there is no stopping
[22] *yawn* gape in amazement [23] *at alteration* at the change [24] *error* irregularity

EMIL. Cassio, my lord, hath kill'd a young Venetian
   Call'd Roderigo.
OTH.   Roderigo kill'd!
   And Cassio kill'd!
EMIL.   No, Cassio is not kill'd.
OTH. Not Cassio kill'd! then murder 's out of tune,
   And sweet revenge grows harsh.
DES. O, falsely, falsely murder'd!
EMIL.   Alas, what cry is that?
OTH. That! what!
EMIL. Out, and alas! that was my lady's voice.
   Help, help, ho! help. O lady, speak again!   120
   Sweet Desdemona! O sweet mistress, speak!
DES. A guiltless death I die.
EMIL. O, who hath done this deed?
DES. Nobody; I myself. Farewell:
   Commend me to my kind lord: O, farewell! [*Dies*]
OTH. Why, how should she be murd'red?
EMIL.   Alas, who knows?
OTH. You heard her say herself, it was not I.
EMIL. She said so: I must needs report the truth.
OTH. She's, like a liar, gone to burning hell:
   'Twas I that kill'd her.
EMIL.   O, the more angel she,   130
   And you the blacker devil!
OTH. She turn'd to folly,[25] and she was a whore.
EMIL. Thou dost belie her, and thou art a devil.
OTH. She was false as water.
EMIL.   Thou art rash as fire, to say
   That she was false: O, she was heavenly true!
OTH. Cassio did top her; ask thy husband else.
   O, I were damned beneath all depth in hell,
   But that I did proceed upon just grounds
   To this extremity. Thy husband knew it all.
EMIL. My husband!   140
OTH. Thy husband.
EMIL. That she was false to wedlock?
OTH. Ay, with Cassio. Nay, had she been true,
   If heaven would make me such another world
   Of one entire and perfect chrysolite,[26]
   I'ld not have sold her for it.

---

[25] *folly* unchastity [26] *chrysolite* the golden stone; a name given to various precious stones of green
color

EMIL. My husband!

OTH.   Ay, 'twas he that told me first:
  An honest man he is, and hates the slime
  That sticks on filthy deeds.

OTH.   My husband!

OTH. What needs this iterance,[27] woman? I say thy husband.   150

EMIL. O mistress, villainy hath made mocks with[28] love!
  My husband say that she was false!

OTH.   He, woman;
  I say thy husband: dost understand the word?
  My friend, thy husband, honest, honest Iago.

EMIL. If he say so, may his pernicious soul
  Rot half a grain a day! he lies to th' heart:
  She was too fond of her most filthy bargain.

OTH. Ha!

EMIL. Do thy worst:
  This deed of thine is no more worthy heaven   160
  Than thou wast worthy her.

OTH.   Peace, you were best.

EMIL. Thou hast not half that power to do me harm
  As I have to be hurt.[29] O gull! O dolt!
  As ignorant as dirt! thou hast done a deed—
  I care not for thy sword; I'll make thee known,
  Though I lost twenty lives.—Help! help, ho! help!
  The Moor hath kill'd my mistress! Murder! murder!

[*Enter* MONTANO, GRATIANO, *and* IAGO *with others.*]

MON. What is the matter! How now, general!

EMIL. O, are you come, Iago? you have done well,
  That men must lay their murders on your neck.   170

GRA. What is the matter?

EMIL. Disprove this villain, if thou be'st a man:
  He says thou told'st him that his wife was false:
  I know thou didst not, thou 'rt not such a villain:
  Speak, for my heart is full.

IAGO. I told him what I thought, and told no more
  Than what he found himself was apt[30] and true.

EMIL. But did you ever tell him she was false?

IAGO. I did.

---

[27] *iterance* iteration, repetition   [28] *made mocks with* derided, made sport of   [29] *to be hurt* i.e., to endure hurting   [30] *apt* natural, likely

EMIL. You told a lie; an odious, damned lie;   180
  Upon my soul, a lie, a wicked lie.
  She false with Cassio!—did you say with Cassio?
IAGO. With Cassio, mistress. Go to, charm[31] your tongue.
EMIL. I will not charm my tongue; I am bound to speak:
  My mistress here lies murdered in her bed,—
ALL. O heavens forfend!
EMIL. And your reports have set the murder on.
OTH. Nay, stare not, masters: it is true, indeed.
GRA. 'Tis a strange truth.
MON. O monstrous act!
EMIL.   Villainy, villainy, villainy!   190
  I think upon 't, I think: I smell 't: O villainy—
  I thought so then:[32] I'll kill myself for grief:—
  O villainy, villainy!
IAGO. What, are you mad? I charge you, get you home.
EMIL. Good gentlemen, let me have leave to speak:
  'Tis proper I obey him, but not now.
  Perchance, Iago, I will ne'er go home.
OTH. O! O! O! [*He falls on the bed.*]
EMIL.   Nay, lay thee down and roar;
  For thou hast kill'd the sweetest innocent
  That e'er did lift up eye.
OTH.   [*Rising*] O, she was foul!   200
  I scarce did know you, uncle: there lies your niece,
  Whose breath, indeed, these hands have newly stopp'd:
  I know this act shows horrible and grim.
GRA. Poor Desdemon! I am glad thy father 's dead:
  Thy match was mortal to him, and pure grief
  Shore[33] his old thread in twain: did he live now,
  This sight would make him do a desperate turn,
  Yea, curse his better angel from his side,
  And fall to reprobation.[34]
OTH. 'Tis pitiful; but yet Iago knows   210
  That she with Cassio hath the act of shame
  A thousand times committed; Cassio confess'd it:
  And she did gratify his amorous works
  With that recognizance[35] and pledge of love
  Which I first gave her; I saw it in his hand:

---

[31] *charm* keep silent [32] *then* i.e., at some earlier time, probably IV, ii, when she suspected the machinations of *some eternal villain;* she did not, however, know that villain to be Iago until this moment [33] *Shore* cut [34] *reprobation* damnation, rejection by God [35] *recognizance* token

It was a handkerchief, an antique token
My father gave my mother.

EMIL. O heaven! O heavenly pow'rs!

IAGO. Come, hold your peace.

EMIL.   'Twill out, 'twill out:I peace!
No, I will speak as liberal as the north:[36]   220
Let heaven and men and devils, let them all,
All, all, cry shame against me, yet I'll speak.

IAGO. Be wise, and get you home.

EMIL.   I will not! [IAGO *offers to stab* EMILIA.]

GRA.   Fie!
Your sword upon a woman?

EMIL. O thou dull Moor! that handkerchief thou speak'st of
I found by fortune[37] and did give my husband;
For often, with solemn earnestness,
More than indeed belong'd to such a trifle,
He begg'd me to steal it.

IAGO.   Villainous whore!

EMIL. She give it Cassio! no, alas! I found it,   230
And I did give 't my husband.

IAGO.   Filth, thou liest!

EMIL. By heaven, I do not, I do not, gentlemen.
O murd'rous coxcomb![38] what should such a fool
Do with so a good a wife!

OTH.   Are there no stones in heaven[39]
But what serves for the thunder?—Precious villain! [*He runs at* IAGO: IAGO,
    from behind, stabs EMILIA, *and exits.*]

GRA. The woman falls; sure, he hath kill'd his wife.

EMIL. Ay, ay: O, lay me by my mistress' side.

GRA. He 's gone, but his wife 's kill'd.

MON. 'Tis a notorious villain. Take you this weapon,
Which I have here recover'd from the Moor: 240
Come, guard the door without; let him not pass,
But kill him rather. I'll after that same villain,
For 'tis a damned slave. [*Exit with all but* OTHELLO *and* EMILIA.]

OTH.   I am not valiant neither,
But every puny whipster[40] gets my sword:
But why should honour outlive honesty?[41]
Let it go all.

---

[36] *liberal as the north* freely as the north wind   [37] *fortune* chance   [38] *coxcomb* fool; addressed to
Othello   [39] *stones in heaven* thunderbolts. It was supposed that real stones fell with the thunder and
caused the damage   [40] *whipster* contemptible fellow   [41] *honour outlive honesty* Othello realizes that he
has done a shameful deed; he asks why his reputation for valor should endure

EMIL.   What did thy song bode, lady?
  Hark, canst thou hear me? I will play the swan,
  And die in music. [*Singing*] Willow, willow, willow.—
  Moor, she was chaste; she lov'd thee, cruel Moor;
  So come my soul to bliss, as I speak true;   250
  So speaking as I think, I die, I die. [*Dies.*]
OTH. I have another weapon in this chamber;
  It is a sword of Spain, the ice-brook's temper[42]:—
  O, here it is. Uncle, I must come forth.
GRA [*within*]. If thou attempt it, it will cost thee dear:
  Thou hast no weapon, and perforce must suffer.
OTH. Look in upon me then and speak with me,
  Or, naked[43] as I am, I will assault thee.

                            [*Enter* GRATIANO.]

GRA. What is the matter?
OTH.   Behold, I have a weapon;
  A better never did itself sustain   260
  Upon a soldier's thigh: I have seen the day,
  That, with this little arm and this good sword,
  I have made my way through more impediments
  Than twenty times your stop:[44] but, O vain boast!
  Who can control his fate? 'tis not so now.
  Be not afraid, though you do see me weapon'd;
  Here is my journey's end, here is my butt,[45]
  And very sea-mark[46] of my utmost sail.
  Do you go back dismay'd? 'tis a lost fear;
  Man[47] but a rush[48] against Othello's breast,   270
  And he retires. Where should Othello go?
  Now, how dost thou look now? O ill-starr'd wench!
  Pale as thy smock! when we shall meet at compt,[49]
  This look of thine will hurl my soul from heaven,
  And fiends will snatch at it. Cold, cold, my girl!
  Even like thy chastity. O cursed, cursed slave!
  Whip me, ye devils,
  From the possession of this heavenly sight!
  Blow me about in winds! roast me in sulphur!
  Wash me in steep-down gulfs of liquid fire!   280
  O Desdemon! Dead Desdemon! dead!
  Oh! Oh!

---

[42] *ice-brook's temper* usually defined as "tempered in ice-cold water" [43] *naked* unarmed [44] *stop*
power [45] *butt* mark for archery, goal, limit [46] *sea-mark* beacon (marking his destination or limit)
[47] *Man* provide, as in manning a gun [48] *rush* reed [49] *compt* account, judgment day

[*Enter* LODOVICO, CASSIO, *carried in a chair*, MONTANO, *and* IAGO, *prisoner*,
With OFFICERS.]

LOD. Where is this rash and most unfortunate man?

OTH. That 's he that was Othello: here I am.

LOD. Where is that viper? bring the villian forth.

OTH. I look down towards his feet;[50] but that 's a fable.
If that thou be'st a devil, I cannot kill thee. [*Wounds* IAGO.]

LOD. Wrench his sword from him.

IAGO.   I bleed sir; but not kill'd.

OTH. I am not sorry neither: I 'ld have thee live;
For, in my sense, 'tis happiness to die.   290

LOD. O thou Othello, that wert once so good,
Fall'n in the practice of a damned slave,
What shall be said to thee?

OTH.   Why, any thing:
An honourable murder, if you will;
For nought I did in hate, but all in honour.

LOD. This wretch hath part confess'd his villainy:
Did you and he consent in Cassio's death?

OTH. Ay.

CAS. Dear general, I never gave you cause.

OTH. I do believe it, and I ask your pardon.   300
Will you, I pray, demand that demi-devil
Why he hath thus ensnar'd my soul and body?

IAGO. Demand me nothing: what you know, you know:
From this time forth I never will speak word.

LOD. What, not to pray?

GRA.   Torments will ope your lips.

OTH. Well, thou dost best.

LOD. Sir, you shall understand what hath befall'n,
Which, as I think, you know not. Here is a letter
Found in the pocket of the slain Roderigo;
And here another: the one of them imports   310
The death of Cassio to be undertook
By Roderigo

OTH. O villain!

CAS.   Most heathenish and most gross!

LOD. Now here 's another discontented[51] paper,
Found in his pocket too; and this, it seems,
Roderigo meant t' have sent this damned villain;

---

[50] *towards his feet* i.e., to see if they were cloven like a devil's [51] *discontented* expressing
dissatisfaction

But that belike Iago in the interim
Came in and satisfied him.

OTH.   O thou pernicious caitiff[52]!—
How came you, Cassio, by that handkerchief
That was my wife's?

CAS.   I found it in my chamber: 320
And he himself confess'd but even now
That there he dropp'd it for a special purpose
Which wrought to his desire.

OTH.   O fool! O fool! fool!

CAS. There is besides in Roderigo's letter,
How he upbraids Iago, that he made him
Brave[53] me upon the watch; whereon it came
That I was cast:[54] and even but now he spake,
After long seeming dead, Iago hurt him,
Iago set him on.

LOD. You must forsake this room, and go with us: 330
Your power and your command is taken off,[55]
And Cassio rules in Cyprus. For this slave,
If there be any cunning cruelty
That can torment him much and hold him long,
It shall be his. You shall close prisoner rest,
Till that the nature of your fault be known
To the Venetian state. Come, bring him away.

OTH. Soft you; a word or two before you go.
I have done the state some service, and they know 't.
No more of that. I pray you, in your letters,   340
When you shall these unlucky deeds relate,
Speak of me as I am; nothing extenuate,[56]
Nor set down aught in malice: then must you speak
Of one that lov'd not wisely but too well;
Of one not easily jealous, but being wrought,
Perplex'd[57] in the extreme; of one whose hand,
Like the base Judean,[58] threw a pearl away
Richer than all his tribe; of one whose subdu'd eyes,
Albeit unused to the melting mood,
Drop tears as fast as the Arabian trees   350
Their medicinable gum. Set you down this;

---

[52] *caitiff* wretch [53] *Brave* defy [54] *cast* dismissed [55] *taken off* taken away [56] *extenuate* diminish, depreciate; the idea is contrasted with the thought of *malice* in the following line [57] *Perplex'd* confounded, distracted [58] *Judean* infidel or disbeliever

And say besides, that in Aleppo[59] once,
Where a malignant and a turban'd Turk
Beat a Venetian and traduc'd the state,
I took by th' throat the circumcised dog,
And smote him, thus. [*Stabs himself.*]
LOD. O bloody period![60]
GRA.   All that is spoke is marr'd.
OTH. I kiss'd thee ere I kill'd thee: no way but this;
Killing myself, to die upon a kiss.

[*Falls on the bed, and dies.*]

CAS. This did I fear, but thought he had no weapon;   360
For he was great of heart.
LOD.   [*To* IAGO] O Spartan dog,[61]
More fell than anguish, hunger, or the sea!
Look on the tragic loading of this bed;
This is thy work: the object poisons sight;
Let it be hid, Gratiano, keep the house,
And seize upon the fortunes of the Moor,
For they succeed on you. To you, lord governor,
Remains the censure of this hellish villain;
The time, the place, the torture: O, enforce it!
Myself will straight abroad; and to the state   370
This heavy act with heavy heart relate. [*Exeunt.*]

Journal Entry

How effective is Shakespeare's play in portraying the presence of a black moor in a white society? Consider Brabantio's, the Duke's, Iago's, and Othello's various attitudes toward the issue of race relations.

Textual Considerations

1. To analyze the structural development of *Othello*, consider Othello's autobiographical speeches in act 1, scene 3. Explain how Othello's portrait of himself and his cultural background might have contributed to his manipulation by Iago.
2. Analyze the images of women in *Othello* from the viewpoint of social class and the position women occupied in Venetian society. Don't overlook Cassio's treatment of Desdemona and Bianca, as well as the various images of women with which Iago entertains his audience in act 2, scene 1.

---

[59] *Aleppo* a Turkish city where the Venetians had special trading privileges. It is stated that it was immediate death for a Christian to strike a Turk in Aleppo; Othello risked his life for the honor of Venice   [60] *period* termination, conclusion   [61] *Spartan dog* Spartan dogs were noted for their savagery

3. Consider the extent to which the settings of the play suggest a symbolic contrast between the social and political order of Venice and Cyprus. To what extent do these symbolic settings reflect psychological changes in Othello?
4. What kinds of responses do Iago's soliloquies and asides evoke from the audience? Consider the audience's feelings of comfort, discomfort, fear, sympathy, repulsion, expectation, and suspense.
5. Analyze the images of women that Desdemona uses in act 1, scene 3, lines 185–88, and in act 4, scene 3, lines 25–32. To what extent do these images help Desdemona justify her actions and communicate her feelings and emotions? How effective is Desdemona's use of language in both passages?

Cultural Contexts

1. The explanations behind Iago's motives for destroying Othello have ranged from Iago's dissatisfaction with Othello's poor distribution of power within the ranks of his army, to Iago's pleasure and excitement in manipulating people, to Iago's "motiveless malignity." What other motives can you and your classmates attribute to Iago? How effective are these motives in view of the closure Iago imposes on this issue at the end of the play: "what you know, you know. / From this time forth I will never speak a word" (act 5, scene 2, ll. 304–305)?
2. Some of the lines in *Othello,* such as "Were I the moor, I would not be Iago" (act 1, scene 1, l. 57), suggest Iago's dissatisfaction with his sense of self. Identify other lines and speeches that support the viewpoint that Iago needs to fashion a new identity for himself.

Alice Childress

Florence

PLACE: *A very small town in the South.*
TIME: *The present.*

SCENE: *A railway station waiting room. The room is divided in two sections by a low railing. Upstage center is a double door which serves as an entrance to both sides of the room. Over the doorway stage right is a sign "Colored," over the doorway stage left is another sign "White." Stage right are two doors . . . one marked "Colored men" . . . the other "Colored women." Stage left two other doorways are "White ladies" and "White gentlemen." There are two benches . . . one on each side. The room is drab and empty looking. Through the double doors upstage center can be seen a gray lighting which gives the effect of early evening and open platform.*

*At rise of curtain the stage remains empty for about twenty seconds. . . .
A middle aged Negro woman enters, looks offstage . . . then crosses to the
"Colored" side and sits on the bench. A moment later she is followed by a
young Negro woman about twenty-one years old. She is carrying a large
new cardboard suitcase and a wrapped shoebox. She is wearing a shoulder
strap bag and a newspaper protrudes from the flap. She crosses to the Colored side and rests the suitcase at her feet as she looks at her mother with
mild annoyance.*

MARGE. You didn't have to get here so early mama. Now you got to wait!

MAMA. If I'm going someplace . . . I like to get there in plenty time. You don't have
to stay.

MARGE. You shouldn't wait 'round here alone.

MAMA. I ain't scared. Ain't a soul going to bother me.

MARGE. I got to get back to Ted. He don't like to be in the house by himself. (*She
picks up the bag and places it on the bench by* MAMA.)

MAMA. You'd best go back. (*Smiles*) You know I think he misses Florence.

MARGE. He's just a little fellow. He needs his mother. You make her come home!
She shouldn't be way up there in Harlem. She ain't got nobody there.

MAMA. You know Florence don't like the South.

MARGE. It ain't what we like in this world! You tell her that.

MAMA. If Mr. Jack ask about the rent. You tell him we gonna be a little late on
account of the trip.

MARGE. I'll talk with him. Don't worry so about everything. (*Places suitcase on
floor.*) What you carryin', mama . . . bricks?

MAMA. If Mr. Jack won't wait . . . write to Rudley. He oughta send a little somethin'.

MARGE. Mama . . . Rudley ain't got nothin' fo himself. I hate to ask him to give us.

MAMA. That's your brother! If push comes to shove, we got to ask.

MARGE (*Places box on bench*). Don't forget to eat your lunch . . . and try to get a
seat near the window so you can lean on your elbow and get a little rest.

MAMA. Hmmmm . . . mmmph. Yes.

MARGE. Buy yourself some coffee when the man comes through. You'll need
something hot and you can't go to the diner.

MAMA. I know that. You talk like I'm a northern greenhorn.

MARGE. You got handkerchiefs?

MAMA. I got everything, Marge.

MARGE (*Wanders upstage to the railing division line*). I know Florence is real bad
off or she wouldn't call on us for money. Make her come home. She ain't gonna
get rich up there and we can't afford to do for her.

MAMA. We talked all of that before.

MARGE (*Touches rail*). Well, you got to be strict on her. She got notions a Negro
woman don't need.

MAMA. But she was in a real play. Didn't she send us twenty-five dollars a week?

MARGE. For two weeks.

MAMA. Well the play was over.

MARGE (*Crosses to* MAMA *and sits beside her*). It's not money, Mama. Sarah wrote us about it. You know what she said Florence was doin'! Sweepin' the stage!

MAMA. She was *in* the play!

MARGE. Sure she was in it! Sweepin'! Them folks ain't gonna let her be no actress. You tell her to wake up.

MAMA. I . . . I . . . think.

MARGE. Listen Ma. . . . She won't wanna come. We know that . . . but she gotta!

MAMA. Maybe we shoulda told her to expect me. It's kind of mean to just walk in like this.

MARGE. I bet she's livin' terrible. What's the matter with her? Don't she know we're keepin' her son?

MAMA. Florence don't feel right 'bout down here since Jim got killed.

MARGE. Who does? I should be the one goin' to get her. You tell her she ain't gonna feel right no place. Mama, honestly! She must think she's white!

MAMA. Florence is brownskin.

MARGE. I don't mean that. I'm talkin' about her attitude. Didn't she go into Strumley's down here and ask to be a sales girl? (*Rises*) Now ain't that somethin'? They don't hire no Colored folks.

MAMA. Others besides Florence been talkin' about their rights.

MARGE. I know it . . . but there's things we can't do cause they ain't gonna let us. (*She wanders over to the "White" side of the stage*) Don't feel a damn bit different over here than it does on our side.

(*Silence*)

MAMA. Maybe we shoulda just sent her the money this time. This one time.

MARGE (*Coming back to "Colored" side*). Mama! Don't you let her cash that check for nothin' but to bring her back home.

MAMA. I know.

MARGE (*Restless . . . fidgets with her hair . . . patting it in place*). I oughta go now.

MAMA. You best get back to Ted. He might play with the lamp.

MARGE. He better not let me catch him! If you got to go to the ladies' room take your grip.

MAMA. I'll be alright. Make Ted get up on time for school.

MARGE (*Kisses her quickly and gives her the newspaper*). Here's something to read. So long Mama.

MAMA. G'bye, Margie baby.

MARGE (*Goes to door . . . stops and turns to her mother*). You got your smelling salts?

MAMA. In my pocketbook.

MARGE (*Wistfully*). Tell Florence I love her and I miss her too.

PORTER (*Can be heard singing in the distance.*)

MAMA. Sure.

MARGE (*Reluctant to leave*). Pin that check in your bosom, Mama. You might fall asleep and somebody'll rob you.

MAMA. I got it pinned to me. (*Feels for the check which is in her blouse*)

MARGE (*Almost pathetic*). Bye, Ma.

MAMA (*Sits for a moment looking at her surroundings. She opens the paper and begins to read.*)

PORTER (*Offstage*). Hello, Marge. What you doin' down here?

MARGE. I came to see Mama off.

PORTER. Where's she going?

MARGE. She's in there; she'll tell you. I got to get back to Ted.

PORTER. Bye now . . . Say, wait a minute, Marge.

MARGE. Yes?

PORTER. I told Ted he could have some of my peaches and he brought all them Brandford boys over and they picked 'em all. I wouldn't lay a hand on him but I told him I was gonna tell you.

MARGE. I'm gonna give it to him!

PORTER (*Enters and crosses to white side of waiting room. He carries a pail of water and a mop. He is about fifty years old. He is obviously tired but not lazy*). Every peach off my tree!

MAMA. There wasn't but six peaches on that tree.

PORTER (*Smiles . . . glances at* MAMA *as he crosses to white side and begins to mop*). How d'ye do, Mrs. Whitney . . . you going on a trip?

MAMA. Fine, I thank you. I'm going to New York.

PORTER. Wish it was me. You gonna stay?

MAMA. No, Mr. Brown. I'm bringing Florence . . . I'm visiting Florence.

PORTER. Tell her I said hello. She's a fine girl.

MAMA. Thank you.

PORTER. My brother Bynum's in Georgia now.

MAMA. Well now, that's nice.

PORTER. Atlanta.

MAMA. He goin' to school?

PORTER. Yes'm. He saw Florence in a Colored picture. A moving picture.

MAMA. Do tell! She didn't say a word about it.

PORTER. They got Colored moving picture theatres in Atlanta.

MAMA. Yes. Your brother going to be a doctor?

PORTER (*With pride*). No. He writes things.

MAMA. Oh.

PORTER. My son is goin' back to Howard next year.

MAMA. Takes an awful lot of goin' to school to be anything. Lot of money leastways.

PORTER (*Thoughtfully*). Yes'm, it sure do.

MAMA. That sure was a nice church sociable the other night.

PORTER. Yes'm. We raised 87 dollars.

MAMA. That's real nice.

PORTER. I won your cake at the bazaar.

MAMA. The chocolate one?

PORTER (*As he wrings mop*). Yes'm . . . was light as a feather. That old train is gonna be late this evenin'. It's number 42.

MAMA. I don't mind waitin'.

PORTER (*Lifts pail, tucks mop handle under his arm. Looks about in order to make certain no one is around. Leans over and addresses* MAMA *in a confidential tone*). Did you buy your ticket from that Mr. Daly?

MAMA (*In a low tone*). No. Marge bought it yesterday.

PORTER (*Leaning against railing*). That's good. That man is mean. Especially if he thinks you're goin' north. (*He starts to leave . . . then turns back to* MAMA): If you go to the rest room use the Colored men's . . . the other one is out of order.

MAMA. Thank you, sir.

MRS. CARTER (*A white woman . . . well dressed, wearing furs and carrying a small, expensive overnight bag. She breezes in . . . breathless . . . flustered and smiling. She addresses the porter as she almost collides with him*). Boy! My bags are out there. The taxi driver just dropped them. Will they be safe?

PORTER. Yes, mam. I'll see after them.

MRS. CARTER. I thought I'd missed the train.

PORTER. It's late, mam.

MRS. CARTER (*Crosses to bench on the White side and rests her bag*). Fine! You come back here and get me when it comes. There'll be a tip in it for you.

PORTER. Thank you, mam. I'll be here. (*As he leaves*) Miss Whitney, I'll take care of your bag too.

MAMA. Thank you, sir.

MRS. CARTER (*Wheels around . . . notices* MAMA). Oh. . . . Hello there. . . .

MAMA. Howdy, mam. (*She opens her newspaper and begins to read.*)

MRS. CARTER (*Paces up and down rather nervously. She takes a cigarette from her purse, lights it. Takes a deep draw. She looks at her watch. Speaks to* MAMA *across the railing*). Have you any idea how late the train will be?

MAMA. No mam. (*Starts to read again.*)

MRS. CARTER. I can't leave this place fast enough. Two days of it and I'm bored to tears. Do you live here?

MAMA (*Rests paper on her lap*). Yes, mam.

MRS. CARTER. Where are you going?

MAMA. New York City, mam.

MRS. CARTER. Good for you! You can stop "maming" me. My name is Mrs. Carter. I'm not a southerner really.

MAMA. Yes'm . . . Mrs. Carter.

MRS. CARTER (*Takes handkerchief from her purse and covers her nose for a moment*). My God! Disinfectant! This is a frightful place. My brother's here writing a book. Wants atmosphere. Well he's got it. I'll never come back here ever.

MAMA. That's too bad, mam . . . Mrs. Carter.

MRS. CARTER. That's good. I'd die in this place. Really die. Jeff . . . Mr. Wiley . . . my brother. . . . He's tied in knots, a bundle of problems . . . positively knots.

MAMA (*Amazed*). That so, mam?

MRS. CARTER. You don't have to call me mam. It's so southern. Mrs. Carter! These people are still fighting the Civil War. I'm really a New Yorker now. Of course I was born here . . . in the South I mean. Memphis. Listen . . . am I annoying you? I've simply got to talk to someone.

MAMA (*Places newspaper on bench*). No, Mrs. Carter. It's perfectly alright.

MRS. CARTER. Fine! You see Jeff has ceased writing. Stopped! Just like that! (*Snaps fingers.*)

MAMA (*Turns to her*). That so?

MRS. CARTER. Yes. The reviews came out on his last book. Poor fellow.

MAMA. I'm sorry, mam . . . Mrs. Carter. They didn't like his book?

MRS. CARTER. Well enough . . . but Jeff's . . . well Mr. Wiley is a genius. He says they missed the point! Lost the whole message! Did you read . . . do you . . . have you heard of *Lost My Lonely Way*?

MAMA. No, mam. I can't say I have.

MRS. CARTER. Well it doesn't matter. It's profound. Real . . . you know. (*Stands at railing upstage.*) It's about your people.

MAMA. That's nice.

MRS. CARTER. Jeff poured his complete self into it. Really delved into the heart of the problem, pulled no punches! He hardly stopped for his meals. . . . And of course I wasn't here to see that he didn't overdo. He suffers so with his characters.

MAMA. I guess he wants to do his best.

MRS. CARTER. Zelma! . . . That's his heroine. . . . Zelma! A perfect character.

MAMA (*Interested . . . coming out of her shell eagerly*). She was colored, mam?

MRS. CARTER. Oh yes! . . . But of course you don't know what it's about do you?

MAMA. No, miss . . . Would you tell me?

MRS. CARTER (*Leaning on railing*). Well . . . she's almost white, see? Really you can't tell except in small ways. She wants to be a lawyer . . . and . . . well, there she is full of complexes and this deep shame you know.

MAMA (*Excitedly but with curiosity*). Do tell! What shame has she got?

MRS. CARTER (*Takes off her fur neckpiece and places it on bench with overnight bag*). It's obvious! This lovely creature . . . intelligent, ambitious, and well . . . she's a Negro!

MAMA (*Waiting eagerly*). Yes'm. you said that. . . .

MRS. CARTER. Surely you understand? She's constantly hating herself. Just before she dies she says it! . . . Right on the bridge. . . .

MAMA (*Genuinely moved*). How sad. Ain't it a shame she had to die?

MRS. CARTER. It was inevitable . . . couldn't be any other way!

MAMA. What did she say on the bridge?

MRS. CARTER. Well . . . just before she jumped. . . .

MAMA (*Slowly straightening*). You mean she killed *herself*?

MRS. CARTER. Of course. Close your eyes and picture it!

MAMA (*Turns front and closes her eyes tightly with enthusiasm*). Yes'm.

MRS. CARTER (*Center stage of white side*). Now . . .! She's standing on the bridge in the moonlight. . . . Out of her shabby purse she takes a mirror . . . and by the light of the moon she looks at her reflection in the glass.

MAMA (*Clasps her hands together gently*). I can see her just as plain.

MRS. CARTER (*Sincerely*). Tears roll down her cheeks as she says . . . almost! almost white . . . but I'm black! I'm a Negro! and then . . . (*Turns to Mama*) she jumps and drowns herself!

MAMA (*Opens her eyes. Speaks quietly*). Why?

MRS. CARTER. She can't face it! Living in a world where she almost belongs but not quite. (*Drifts upstage*) Oh it's so . . . so . . . tragic.

MAMA (*Carried away by her convictions . . . not anger . . . she feels challenged. She rises*). That ain't so. Not one bit it ain't!

MRS. CARTER (*Surprised*). But it is!

MAMA (*During the following she works her way around the railing until she crosses about one foot over to the white side and is face to face with MRS. CARTER*). I know it ain't! Don't my friend Essie Kitredge daughter look just like a German or somethin'? She didn't kill herself! She's teachin' the third grade in the colored school right here. Even the bus drivers ask her to sit in the front seats cause they think she's white! . . . an . . . an . . . she just says clear as you please . . . "I'm sittin' where my people got to sit by law. I'm a Negro woman!"

MRS. CARTER (*Uncomfortable but not knowing why*). . . . But there you have it. The exception makes the rule. That's proof!

MAMA. No such a thing! My cousin Hemsly's as white as you! . . . an' . . . an' he never. . . .

MRS. CARTER (*Flushed with anger . . . yet lost . . . because she doesn't know why*). Are you losing your temper? (*Weakly*) Are you angry with me?

MAMA (*Stands silently trembling as she looks down and notices she is on the wrong side of the railing. She looks up at the "White Ladies Room" sign and slowly works her way back to the "Colored" side. She feels completely lost*). No, mam. Excuse me please. (*With bitterness*) I just meant Hemsly works in the colored section of the shoe store. . . . He never once wanted to kill his self! (*She sits down on the bench and fumbles for her newspaper.*)

(*Silence*)

MRS. CARTER (*Caught between anger and reason . . . she laughs nervously*). Well! Let's not be upset by this. It's entirely my fault you know. This whole thing is a completely controversial subject. (*Silence*) If it's too much for Jeff . . . well naturally I shouldn't discuss it with you. (*Approaching railing*) I'm sorry. Let *me* apologize.

MAMA (*Keeps her eyes on the paper*). No need for that, mam. (*Silence*)

MRS. CARTER (*Painfully uncomfortable*). I've drifted away from . . . What started all of this?

MAMA (*No comedy intended or allowed on this line*). Your brother, mam.

MRS. CARTER (*Trying valiantly to brush away the tension*). Yes. . . . Well I had to come down and sort of hold his hand over the reviews. He just thinks too much . . . and studies. He knows the Negro so well that sometimes our friends tease him and say he almost seems like . . . well you know. . . .

MAMA (*Tightly*). Yes'm.

MRS. CARTER (*Slowly walks over to the colored side near the top of the rail*). You know I try but it's really difficult to understand you people. However . . . I keep trying.

MAMA (*Still tight*). Thank you, mam.

MRS. CARTER (*Retreats back to white side and begins to prove herself*). Last week . . . Why do you know what I did? I sent a thousand dollars to a Negro college for scholarships.

MAMA. That was right kind of you.

MRS. CARTER (*Almost pleading*). I know what's going on in your mind . . . and what you're thinking is wrong. I've . . . I've . . . eaten with Negroes.

MAMA. Yes, mam.

MRS. CARTER (*Trying to find a straw*). . . . And there's Malcom! If it weren't for the guidance of Jeff he'd never written his poems. Malcom is a Negro.

MAMA (*Freezing*). Yes, mam.

MRS. CARTER (*Gives up, crosses to her bench, opens her overnight bag and takes out a book and begins to read. She glances at* MAMA *from time to time.* MAMA *is deeply absorbed in her newspaper.* MRS. CARTER *closes her book with a bang . . . determined to penetrate the wall that* MAMA *has built around her*). Why are you going to New York?

MAMA (*Almost accusingly*). I got a daughter there.

MRS. CARTER. I lost my son in the war. (*Silence . . .* MAMA *is ill at ease*). Your daughter . . . what is she doing . . . studying?

MAMA. No'm. She's trying to get on the stage.

MRS. CARTER (*Pleasantly*). Oh . . . a singer?

MAMA. No, mam. She's . . .

MRS. CARTER (*Warmly*). Your people have such a gift. I love spirituals . . . "Steal Away," "Swing Low, Sweet Chariot."

MAMA. They are right nice. But Florence wants to act. Just say things in plays.

MRS. CARTER. A dramatic actress?

MAMA. Yes, that's what it is. She been in a Colored moving picture, and a big show for two weeks on Broadway.

MRS. CARTER. The dear, precious child! . . . But this is funny . . . no! it's pathetic. She must be bitter . . . *really* bitter. Do you know what I do?

MAMA. I can't rightly say.

MRS. CARTER. I'm an actress! A dramatic actress. . . . And I haven't really worked in six months. . . . And I'm pretty well known. . . . And everyone knows Jeff. I'd like to work. Of course, there are my committees, but you see, they don't need me. Not really . . . not even Jeff.

MAMA. Now that's a shame.

MRS. CARTER. Your daughter . . . you must make her stop before she's completely unhappy. Make her stop!

MAMA. Yes'm . . . why?

MRS. CARTER. I have the best contacts and *I've* only done a few *broadcasts* lately. Of course, I'm not counting the things I just wouldn't do. Your daughter . . . make her stop.

MAMA. A drama teacher told her she has real talent.

MRS. CARTER. A drama teacher! My dear woman, there are loads of unscrupulous whites up there that just hand out opinions for. . . .

MAMA. This was a colored gentleman down here.

MRS. CARTER. Oh well! . . . And she went up there on the strength of that? This makes me very unhappy. (*Puts book away in case, and snaps lock.*)

(*Silence*)

MAMA (*Getting an idea*). Do you really, truly feel that way, mam?

MRS. CARTER. I do. Please . . . I want you to believe me.

MAMA. Could I ask you something?

MRS. CARTER. Anything.

MAMA. You won't be angry mam?

MRS. CARTER (*Remembering*). I won't. I promise you.

MAMA (*Gathering courage*). Florence is proud . . . but she's having it hard.

MRS. CARTER. I'm sure she is.

MAMA. Could you help her out some, mam? Knowing all the folks you do . . . maybe. . . .

MRS. CARTER (*Rubs the outside of the case*). Well . . . it isn't that simple . . . but . . . you're very sweet. If I only could. . . .

MAMA. Anything you did, I feel grateful. I don't like to tell it, but she can't even pay her rent and things. And she's used to my cooking for her. . . . I believe my girl goes hungry sometime up there . . . and yet she'd like to stay so bad.

MRS. CARTER (*Looks up, resting case on her knees*). How can I refuse? You seem like a good woman.

MAMA. Always lived as best I knew how and raised my children up right. We got a fine family, mam.

MRS. CARTER. And I've no family at all. I've got to! It's clearly my duty. Jeff's books . . . guiding Malcom's poetry. . . . It isn't enough . . . oh I know it isn't! Have you ever heard of Melba Rugby?

MAMA. No, mam. I don't know anybody much . . . except right here.

MRS. CARTER (*Brightening*). She's in California, but she's moving East again . . . hates California.

MAMA. Yes'm.

MRS. CARTER. A most versatile woman. Writes, directs, acts . . . everything!

MAMA. That's nice, mam.

MRS. CARTER. Well, she's uprooting herself and coming back to her first home . . . New York . . . to direct "Love Flowers" . . . it's a musical.

MAMA. Yes'm.

MRS. CARTER. She's grand . . . helped so many people . . . and I'm sure she'll help your . . . what's her name.

MAMA. Florence.

MRS. CARTER (*Turns back to bench, opens her bag, takes out pencil and address book*). Yes, Florence. She'll have to *make* a place for her.

MAMA. Bless you, mam.

MRS. CARTER (*Holds handbag steady on rail as she uses it to write on*). Now let's see . . . the best thing to do would be to give you the telephone number . . . since you're going there.

MAMA. Yes'm.

MRS. CARTER (*Writing address on paper*). Your daughter will love her . . . and if she's a deserving girl. . . .

MAMA (*Looking down as* MRS. CARTER *writes*). She's a good child. Never a bit of trouble. Except about her husband, and neither one of them could help that.

MRS. CARTER (*Stops writing, raises her head questioning*). Oh?

MAMA. He got killed at voting time. He was a good man.

MRS. CARTER (*Embarrassed*). I guess that's worse than losing him in the war.

MAMA. We all got our troubles passing through here.

MRS. CARTER (*Gives her the address*). Tell your dear girl to call this number about a week from now.

MAMA. Yes, mam.

MRS. CARTER. Her experience won't matter with Melba. I know she'll understand. I'll call her too.

MAMA. Thank you, mam.

MRS. CARTER. I'll just tell her . . . no heavy washing or ironing . . . just light cleaning and a little cooking . . . does she cook?

MAMA. Mam? (*Slowly backs away from* MRS. C. *and sits down on bench.*)

MRS. CARTER. Don't worry. That won't matter with Melba. (*Silence. Moves around rail to "Colored" side, leans over* MAMA.) I'd take your daughter myself, but I've got Binnie. She's been with me for years, and I can't just let her go . . . can I?

MAMA (*Looks at* MRS. C. *closely*). No, mam.

MRS. CARTER. Of course she must be steady. I couldn't ask Melba to take a fly-by-night. (*Touches* MAMA's *arm*). But she'll have her own room and bath, and above all . . . security.

MAMA (*Reaches out, clutches* MRS. C.'s *wrist almost pulling her off balance*). Child!

MRS. CARTER (*Frightened*). You're hurting my wrist.

MAMA (*Looks down, realizes how tight she's clutching her, and releases her wrist*). I mustn't hurt you, must I.

MRS. CARTER (*Backs away rubbing her wrist*). It's all right.

MAMA (*Rises*). You better get over on the other side of that rail. It's against the law for you to be here with me.

MRS. CARTER (*Frightened and uncomfortable*). If you think so.

MAMA. I don't want to break the law.

MRS. CARTER (*Keeps her eye on* MAMA *as she drifts around railing to bench on her side. Gathers overnight bag*). I know I must look a fright. The train should be along soon. When it comes, I won't see you until New York. These silly laws. (*Silence*) I'm going to powder my nose. (*Exits into "White Ladies" room.*)

PORTER (*Singing offstage*).

MAMA (*Sits quietly, staring in front of her . . . then looks at the address for a moment . . . tears the paper into little bits and lets them flutter to the floor. She opens the suitcase, takes out notebook, an envelope and a pencil. She writes a few words on the paper.*)

PORTER (*Enters with broom and dust pan*). Number 42 will be coming along in nine minutes. (*When* MAMA *doesn't answer him, he looks up and watches her. She reaches in her bosom, unpins the check, smooths it out, places it in the envelope with her letter. She closes the suitcase*). I said the train's coming. Where's the lady?

MAMA. She's in the *ladies'* room. You got a stamp?

PORTER. No. But I can get one out the machine. Three for a dime.

MAMA (*Hands him the letter*). Put one on here and mail it for me.

PORTER (*Looks at it*). Gee . . . you writing to Florence when you're going to see her?

MAMA (*Picks up the shoe box and puts it back on the bench*). You want a good lunch? It's chicken and fruit.

PORTER. Sure . . . thank you . . . but won't you . . .

MAMA (*Rises, paces up and down*). I ain't gonna see Florence for a long time. Might be never.

PORTER. How's that, Mrs. Whitney?

MAMA. She can be anything in the world she wants to be! That's her right. Marge can't make her turn back, Mrs. Carter can't make her turn 'cause they look white but be black. They just don't know do they, Mr. Brown?

PORTER. Whatever happened don't you fret none. Life is too short.

MAMA. Oh, I'm gonna fret plenty! You know what I wrote Florence?

PORTER. No, mam. But you don't have to tell me.

MAMA. I said "Keep trying." . . . Oh, I'm going home.

PORTER. I'll take your bag. (*Picks up bag and starts out.*) Come on, Mrs. Whitney. (PORTER *exits.*)

MAMA (*moves around to "White" side, stares at signs over door. Starts to knock on "White Ladies" door, changes her mind. As she turns to leave, her eye catches the railing; she approaches it gently, touches it, turns, exits.*) (*Stage is empty for about six or seven seconds. Sound of train whistle in distance. Slow curtain.*)

Journal Entry

React to the thematic implications for *Florence* of Jeff Wiley's novel *Lost My Lonely Way* (p. 807).

Textual Considerations

1. Consider the functions of chronology and setting in the play.
2. Characterize the porter, and comment on his role in the play.

3. To what extent is Mrs. Carter's offer to find Florence a job as a domestic a deliberate misunderstanding of Mama's request of her to help Florence?
4. Comment on the appropriateness of the play's title.

Cultural Contexts

1. *Florence* takes place in the South in the 1950s. Discuss with your group the extent to which the racial stereotypes evidenced in the play are still relevant in the 1990s. Explain.

Luis Valdez

*LOS VENDIDOS**

LIST OF CHARACTERS

HONEST SANCHO
SECRETARY
FARM WORKER
JOHNNY
REVOLUCIONARIO
MEXICAN-AMERICAN

> SCENE: *Honest Sancho's Used Mexican Lot and Mexican Curio Shop. Three models are on display in* HONEST SANCHO'S *shop: to the right, there is a Revolucionario, complete with sombrero, carrilleras[1] and carabina 30–30. At center, on the floor, there is the Farm Worker, under a broad straw sombrero. At stage left is the Pachuco,[2] filero[3] in hand.*
>
> (HONEST SANCHO *is moving among his models, dusting them off and preparing for another day of business.*)

SANCHO.   Bueno, bueno, mis monos, vamos a ver a quien vendemos ahora. ¿no?[4] (*To audience.*) ¡Quihubo! I'm Honest Sancho and this is my shop. Antes fui contratista pero ahora logré tener mi negocito[5] All I need now is a customer. (*A bell rings offstage.*) Ay, a customer!
SECRETARY (*Entering*).   Good morning, I'm Miss Jiménez from—
SANCHO.   ¡Ah, una chicana! Welcome, welcome Señorita Jiménez.

---

* *Los Vendidos* the sellouts   [1] *carrilleras* cartridge belts   [2] *Pachuco* an urban tough guy   [3] *filero* blade   [4] *Bueno . . . ¿no?* Well, well, darlings, let's see who we can sell now, O.K.?   [5] *Antes . . . negocito* I used to be a contractor, but now I've succeeded in having my little business.

SECRETARY (*Anglo prounciation*). JIM-enez.

SANCHO. ¿Qué?

SECRETARY. My name is Miss JIM-enez. Don't you speak English? What's wrong with you?

SANCHO. Oh, nothing. Señorita JIM-enez. I'm here to help you.

SECRETARY. That's better. As I was starting to say, I'm a secretary from Governor Reagan's office, and we're looking for a Mexican type for the administration.

SANCHO. Well, you come to the right place, lady. This is Honest Sancho's Used Mexican lot, and we got all types here. Any particular type you want?

SECRETARY. Yes, we were looking for somebody suave—

SANCHO. Suave.

SECRETARY. Debonair.

SANCHO. De buen aire.

SECRETARY. Dark.

SANCHO. Prieto.

SECRETARY. But of course not too dark.

SANCHO. No muy prieto.

SECRETARY. Perhaps, beige.

SANCHO. Beige, just the tone. Así como cafecito con leche,[6] ¿no?

SECRETARY. One more thing. He must be hard-working.

SANCHO. That could only be one model. Step right over here to the center of the shop, lady. (*They cross to the* FARM WORKER.) This is our standard farm worker model. As you can see, in the words of our beloved Senator George Murphy, he is "built close to the ground." Also take special notice of his four-ply Goodyear huaraches, made from the rain tire. This wide-brimmed sombrero is an extra added feature—keeps off the sun, rain, and dust.

SECRETARY. Yes, it does look durable.

SANCHO. And our farmworker model is friendly. Muy amable.[7] Watch. (*Snaps his fingers.*)

FARM WORKER (*Lifts up head*). Buenos días, señorita. (*His head drops.*)

SECRETARY. My, he's friendly.

SANCHO. Didn't I tell you? Loves his patrones! But his most attractive feature is that he's hard-working. Let me show you. (*Snaps fingers.* FARM WORKER *Stands.*)

FARM WORKER. ¡El jale![8] (*He begins to work.*)

SANCHO. As you can see, he is cutting grapes.

SECRETARY. Oh, I wouldn't know.

SANCHO. He also picks cotton. (*Snap.* FARM WORKER *begins to pick cotton.*)

SECRETARY. Versatile isn't he?

SANCHO. He also picks melons. (*Snap.* FARM WORKER *picks melons.*) That's his slow speed for late in the season. Here's his fast speed. (*Snap.* FARM WORKER *picks faster.*)

SECRETARY. ¡Chihuahua! . . . I mean, goodness, he sure is a hard worker.

---

[6] *Así . . . leche* like coffee with milk [7] *Muy amable* very friendly [8] *El jale* The job

SANCHO (*Pulls the* FARM WORKER *to his feet*). And that isn't the half of it. Do you see these little holes on his arms that appear to be pores? During those hot sluggish days in the field, when the vines or the branches get so entangled, it's almost impossible to move; these holes emit a certain grease that allow our model to slip and slide right through the crop with no trouble at all.

SECRETARY. Wonderful. But is he economical?

SANCHO. Economical? Señorita, you are looking at the Volkswagen of Mexicans. Pennies a day is all it takes. One plate of beans and tortillas will keep him going all day. That, and chile. Plenty of chile. Chile jalapenos, chile verde, chile colorado. But, of course, if you do give him chile (*Snap.* FARM WORKER *turns left face. Snap.* FARM WORKER *bends over.*) then you have to change his oil filter once a week.

SECRETARY. What about storage?

SANCHO. No problem. You know these new farm labor camps our Honorable Governor Reagan has built out by Parlier or Raisin City? They were designed with our model in mind. Five, six, seven, even ten in one of those shacks will give you no trouble at all. You can also put him in old barns, old cars, river banks. You can even leave him out in the field overnight with no worry!

SECRETARY. Remarkable.

SANCHO. And here's an added feature: Every year at the end of the season, this model goes back to Mexico and doesn't return, automatically, until next Spring.

SECRETARY. How about that. But tell me: does he speak English?

SANCHO. Another outstanding feature is that last year this model was programmed to go out on STRIKE! (*Snap.*)

FARM WORKER. ¡HUELGA! ¡HUELGA! Hermanos, sálganse de esos files.[9] (*Snap. He stops.*)

SECRETARY. No! Oh no, we can't strike in the State Capitol.

SANCHO. Well, he also scabs. (*Snap.*)

FARM WORKER. Me vendo barato, ¿y qué?[10] (*Snap.*)

SECRETARY. That's much better, but you didn't answer my question. Does he speak English?

SANCHO. Bueno . . . no, pero[11] he has other—

SECRETARY. No.

SANCHO. Other features.

SECRETARY. NO! He just won't do!

SANCHO. Okay, okay pues. We have other models.

SECRETARY. I hope so. What we need is something a little more sophisticated.

SANCHO. Sophisti—¿qué?

SECRETARY. An urban model.

SANCHO. Ah, from the city! Step right back. Over here in this corner of the shop is exactly what you're looking for. Introducing our new 1969 JOHNNY

---

[9] *¡Huelga . . . files.* Strike! Strike! Brothers, leave those rows. [10] *Me . . . qué* I come cheap. So what?
[11] *Bueno . . . no, pero* Well, no, but

PACHUCO model! This is our fast-back model. Streamlined. Built for speed, low-riding, city life. Take a look at some of these features. Mag shoes, dual exhausts, green chartreuse paint-job, dark-tint windshield, a little poof on top. Let me just turn him on. (*Snap.* JOHNNY *walks to stage center with a pachuco bounce.*)

SECRETARY. What was that?

SANCHO. That, señorita, was the Chicano shuffle.

SECRETARY. Okay, what does he do?

SANCHO. Anything and everything necessary for city life. For instance survival: He knife fights. (*Snap.* JOHNNY *pulls out switch blade and swings at* SECRETARY.)

(SECRETARY *screams.*)

SANCHO. He dances. (*Snap.*)

JOHNNY. (*Singing*). "Angel Baby, my Angel Baby . . . " (*Snap.*)

SANCHO. And here's a feature no city model can be without. He gets arrested, but not without resisting, of course. (*Snap.*)

JOHNNY. ¡En la madre, la placa!¹² I didn't do it! I didn't do it! (JOHNNY *turns and stands up against an imaginary wall, legs spread out, arms behind his back.*)

SECRETARY. Oh no, we can't have arrests! We must maintain law and order.

SANCHO. But he's bilingual!

SECRETARY. Bilingual?

SANCHO. Simón que yes.¹³ He speaks English! Johnny, give us some English. (*Snap.*)

JOHNNY (*Comes downstage*). Fuck-you!

SECRETARY (*Gasps*). Oh! I've never been so insulted in my whole life!

SANCHO. Well, he learned it in your school.

SECRETARY. I don't care where he learned it.

SANCHO. But he's economical!

SECRETARY. Economical?

SANCHO. Nickels and dimes. You can keep Johnny running on hamburgers, Taco Bell tacos, Lucky Lager beer, Thunderbird wine, yesca—

SECRETARY. Yesca?

SANCHO. Mota.

SECRETARY. Mota?

SANCHO. Leños¹⁴ . . . Marijuana. (*Snap;* JOHNNY *inhales on an imaginary joint.*)

SECRETARY. That's against the law!

JOHNNY (*Big smile, holding his breath*). Yeah.

SANCHO. He also sniffs glue. (*Snap.* JOHNNY *inhales glue, big smile.*)

JOHNNY. Tha's too much man, ése.¹⁵

SECRETARY. No, Mr. Sancho, I don't think this—

---

¹² *¡En . . . la placa!* Wow, the cops! ¹³ *Simón que yes.* Yea, sure. ¹⁴ *Leños* joints (marijuana) ¹⁵ *ése* fellow

SANCHO. Wait a minute, he has other qualities I know you'll love. For example, an inferiority complex. (*Snap.*)

JOHNNY. (*To Sancho*). You think you're better than me, huh ése? (*Swings switch blade.*)

SANCHO. He can also be beaten and he bruises, cut him and he bleeds; kick him and he—(*He beats, bruises and kicks* PACHUCO.) would you like to try it?

SECRETARY. Oh, I couldn't

SANCHO. Be my guest. He's a great scapegoat.

SECRETARY. No, really.

SANCHO. Please.

SECRETARY. Well, all right. Just once. (*She kicks* PACHUCO.) Oh, he's so soft.

SANCHO. Wasn't that good? Try again.

SECRETARY (*Kicks* PACHUCO.) Oh, he's so wonderful! (*She kicks him again.*)

SANCHO. Okay, that's enough, lady. You ruin the merchandise. Yes, our Johnny Pachuco model can give you many hours of pleasure. Why, the L.A.P.D. just bought twenty of these to train their rookie cops on. And talk about maintenance. Señorita, you are looking at an entirely self-supporting machine. You're never going to find our Johnny Pachuco model on the relief rolls. No, sir, this model knows how to liberate.

SECRETARY. Liberate?

SANCHO. He steals. (*Snap.* JOHNNY *rushes the* SECRETARY *and steals her purse.*)

JOHNNY. ¡Dame esa bolsa, vieja!¹⁶ (*He grabs the purse and runs. Snap by* SANCHO. *He stops.*)

(SECRETARY *runs after* JOHNNY *and grabs purse away from him, kicking him as she goes.*)

SECRETARY. No, no, no! We can't have any *more* thieves in the State Administration. Put him back.

SANCHO. Okay, we still got other models. Come on, Johnny, we'll sell you to some old lady. (SANCHO *takes* JOHNNY *back to his place.*)

SECRETARY. Mr. Sancho, I don't think you quite understand what we need. What we need is something that will attract the women voters. Something more traditional, more romantic.

SANCHO. Ah, a lover. (*He smiles meaningfully.*) Step right over here, señorita. Introducing our standard Revolucionario and/or Early California Bandit type. As you can see he is well-built, sturdy, durable. This is the International Harvester of Mexicans.

SECRETARY. What does he do?

SANCHO. You name it, he does it. He rides horses, stays in the mountains, crosses deserts, plains, rivers, leads revolutions, follows revolutions, kills, can be killed, serves as a martyr, hero, movie star—did I say movie star? Did you ever see *Viva*

---

¹⁶ *Dame . . . vieja* Give me that bag, old lady!

*Zapata? Viva Villa? Villa Rides? Pancho Villa Returns? Pancho Villa Goes Back?
Pancho Villa Meets Abbott and Costello—*

SECRETARY. I've never seen any of those.

SANCHO. Well, he was in all of them. Listen to this. (*Snap.*)

REVOLUCIONARIO (*Scream*). ¡VIVA VILLAAAAA!

SECRETARY. That's awfully loud.

SANCHO. He has a volume control. (*He adjusts volume. Snap.*)

REVOLUCIONARIO (*Mousey voice*). ¡Viva Villa!

SECRETARY. That's better.

SANCHO. And even if you didn't see him in the movies, perhaps you saw him on TV. He makes commercials. (*Snap.*)

REVOLUCIONARIO. Is there a Frito Bandito in your house?

SECRETARY. Oh yes, I've seen that one!

SANCHO. Another feature about this one is that he is economical. He runs on raw horsemeat and tequila!

SECRETARY. Isn't that rather savage?

SANCHO. Al contrario,[17] it makes him a lover. (*Snap.*)

REVOLUCIONARIO (*To* SECRETARY). ¡Ay, mamasota, cochota, ven pa'ca![18] (*He grabs* SECRETARY *and folds her back—Latin-Lover style.*)

SANCHO (*Snap.* REVOLUCIONARIO *goes back upright*). Now wasn't that nice?

SECRETARY. Well, it was rather nice.

SANCHO. And finally, there is one outstanding feature about this model I KNOW the ladies are going to love: He's a GENUINE antique! He was made in Mexico in 1910!

SECRETARY. Made in Mexico?

SANCHO. That's right. Once in Tijuana, twice in Guadalajara, three times in Cuernavaca.

SECRETARY. Mr. Sancho, I thought he was an American product.

SANCHO. No, but—

SECRETARY. No, I'm sorry. We can't buy anything but American-made products. He just won't do.

SANCHO. But he's an antique!

SECRETARY. I don't care. You still don't understand what we need. It's true we need Mexican models such as these, but it's more important that he be *American*.

SANCHO. American?

SECRETARY. That's right, and judging from what you've shown me, I don't think you have what we want. Well, my lunch hour's almost over; I better—

SANCHO. Wait a minute! Mexican but American?

SECRETARY. That's correct.

SANCHO. Mexican but . . . (*A sudden flash.*) AMERICAN! Yeah, I think we've got exactly what you want. He just came in today! Give me a minute. (*He exits.*

---

[17] *Al contrario* On the contrary [18] *¡Ay . . . pa'ca!* —, get over here!

Talks from backstage.) Here he is in the shop. Let me just get some papers off. There. Introducing our new 1970 Mexican-American! Ta-ra-ra-ra-ra-ra-RA-RAAA!

(SANCHO *brings out the Mexican-American model, a clean-shaven mid-dle-class type in a business suit, with glasses.*)

SECRETARY. (*Impressed*). Where have you been hiding this one?

SANCHO. He just came in this morning. Ain't he a beauty? Feast your eyes on him! Sturdy US STEEL frame, streamlined, modern. As a matter of fact, he is built exactly like our Anglo models except that he comes in a variety of darker shades: naugahyde, leather, or leatherette.

SECRETARY. Naugahyde.

SANCHO. Well, we'll just write that down. Yes, señorita, this model represents the apex of American engineering! He is bilingual, college educated, ambitious! Say the word "acculturate" and he accelerates. He is intelligent, well-mannered, clean—did I say clean? (*Snap*. MEXICAN-AMERICAN *raises his arm.*) Smell.

SECRETARY (*Smells.*) Old Sobaco, my favorite.

SANCHO. (*Snap*. MEXICAN-AMERICAN *turns toward Sancho*). Eric! (*To Secretary.*) We call him Eric García. (*To* ERIC.) I want you to meet Miss JIM-enez, Eric.

MEXICAN-AMERICAN. Miss JIM-enez, I am delighted to make your acquaintance. (*He kisses her hand.*)

SECRETARY. Oh, my, how charming!

SANCHO. Did you feel the suction? He has seven especially engineered suction cups right behind his lips. He's a charmer all right!

SECRETARY. How about boards? Does he function on boards?

SANCHO. You name them, he is on them. Parole boards, draft boards, school boards, taco quality control boards, surf boards, two-by-fours.

SECRETARY. Does he function in politics?

SANCHO. Senorita, you are looking at a political MACHINE. Have you ever heard of the OEO, EOC, COD, WAR ON POVERTY? That's our model! Not only that, he makes political speeches.

SECRETARY. May I hear one?

SANCHO. With pleasure. (*Snap*.) Eric, give us a speech.

MEXICAN-AMERICAN. Mr. Congressman, Mr. Chairman, members of the board, honored guests, ladies and gentlemen. (SANCHO *and* SECRETARY *applaud.*) Please, please. I come before you as a Mexican-American to tell you about the problems of the Mexican. The problems of the Mexican stem from one thing and one thing alone: He's stupid. He's uneducated. He needs to stay in school. He needs to be ambitious, forward-looking, harder-working. He needs to think American, American, American, AMERICAN, AMERICAN AMERICAN. GOD BLESS AMERICA! GOD BLESS AMERICA! GOD BLESS AMER-ICA!! (*He goes out of control.*)

(SANCHO *snaps frantically and the* MEXICAN-AMERICAN *finally slumps forward, bending at the waist.*)

SECRETARY. Oh my, he's patriotic too!

SANCHO. Sí, Señorita, he loves his country. Let me just make a little adjustment here. (*Stands* MEXICAN-AMERICAN *up.*)

SECRETARY. What about upkeep? Is he economical?

SANCHO. Well, no, I won't lie to you. The Mexican-American costs a little bit more, but you get what you pay for. He's worth every extra cent. You can keep him running on dry Martinis, Langendorf bread.

SECRETARY. Apple pie?

SANCHO. Only Mom's. Of course, he's also programmed to eat Mexican food on ceremonial functions, but I must warn you: an overdose of beans will plug up his exhaust.

SECRETARY. Fine! There's just one more question: HOW MUCH DO YOU WANT FOR HIM?

SANCHO. Well, I tell you what I'm gonna do. Today and today only, because you've been so sweet, I'm gonna let you steal this model from me! I'm gonna let you drive him off the lot for the simple price of—let's see taxes and licence included—$15,000.

SECRETARY. Fifteen thousand DOLLARS? For a MEXICAN!

SANCHO. Mexican? What are you talking, lady? This is a Mexican-AMERICAN! We had to melt down two pachucos, a farm worker and three gabachos[19] to make this model! You want quality, but you gotta pay for it! This is no cheap run-about. He's got class!

SECRETARY. Okay, I'll take him.

SANCHO. You will?

SECRETARY. Here's your money.

SANCHO. You mind if I count it?

SECRETARY. Go right ahead.

SANCHO. Well, you'll get your pink slip in the mail. Oh, do you want me to wrap him up for you? We have a box in the back.

SECRETARY. No, thank you. The Governor is having a luncheon this afternoon, and we need a brown face in the crowd. How do I drive him?

SANCHO. Just snap your fingers. He'll do anything you want.

(SECRETARY *snaps.* MEXICAN-AMERICAN *steps forward.*)

MEXICAN-AMERICAN. RAZA QUERIDA, ¡VAMOS LEVANTANDO ARMAS PARA LIBERARNOS DE ESTOS DESGRACIADOS GABACHOS QUE NOS EXPLOTAN! VAMOS.[20]

---

[19] *gabachos* whites [20] *Raza . . . Vamos.* Beloved Raza [persons of Mexican descent], let's take up arms to liberate ourselves from those damned whites who exploit us. Let's get going.

SECRETARY. What did he say?

SANCHO. Something about lifting arms, killing white people, etc.

SECRETARY. But he's not supposed to say that!

SANCHO. Look, lady, don't blame me for bugs from the factory. He's your Mexican-American; you bought him, now drive him off the lot!

SECRETARY. But he's broken!

SANCHO. Try snapping another finger.

(SECRETARY *snaps.* MEXICAN-AMERICAN *comes to life again.*)

MEXICAN-AMERICAN. ¡ESTA GRAN HUMANIDAD HA DICHO BASTA! Y SE HA PUESTO EN MARCHA! ¡BASTA! ¡BASTA! ¡VIVA LA RAZA! ¡VIVA LA CAUSA! ¡VIVA LA HUELGA! ¡VIVAN LOS BROWN BERETS! ¡VIVAN LOS ESTUDIANTES!²¹ ¡CHICANO POWER!

(*The* MEXICAN-AMERICAN *turns toward the* SECRETARY, *who gasps and backs up. He keeps turning toward the* PACHUCO, FARM WORKER, *and* REVOLUCIONARIO, *snapping his fingers and turning each of them on, one by one.*)

PACHUCO (*Snap. To* SECRETARY). I'm going to get you, baby! ¡Viva La Raza!

FARM WORKER (*Snap. To* SECRETARY). ¡Viva la huelga! ¡Viva la Huelga! ¡VIVA LA HUELGA!

REVOLUCIONARIO (*Snap. To* SECRETARY). ¡Viva la revolución! ¡VIVA LA REVOLUCIÓN!

(*The three models join together and advance toward the* SECRETARY *who backs up and runs out of the shop screaming.* SANCHO *is at the other end of the shop holding his money in his hand. All freeze. After a few seconds of silence, the* PACHUCO *moves and stretches, shaking his arms and loosening up. The* FARM WORKER *and* REVOLUCIANARIO *do the same.* SANCHO *stays where he is, frozen to the spot.*)

JOHNNY. Man, that was a long one, ése.²² (*Others agree with him.*)

FARM WORKER. How did we do?

JOHNNY. Perty good, look at all that lana,²³ man! (*He goes over to* SANCHO *and removes the money from his hand.* SANCHO *stays where he is.*)

REVOLUCIONARIO. En la madre, look at all the money.

JOHNNY. We keep this up, we're going to be rich.

---

²¹ *¡Esta . . . Estudiantes!* This great mass of humanity has said enough! And it has begun to march. Enough! Enough! Long live La Raza! Long live the Cause! Long live the strike! Long live the Brown Berets! Long live the students! ²² Man ²³ Money

FARM WORKER. They think we're machines.

REVOLUCIONARIO. Burros.

JOHNNY. Puppets.

MEXICAN-AMERICAN. The only thing I don't like is—how come I always got to play the godamn Mexican-American?

JOHNNY. That's what you get for finishing high school.

FARM WORKER. How about our wages, ése?

JOHNNY. Here it comes right now. $3,000 for you, $3,000 for you, $3,000 for you, and $3,000 for me. The rest we put back into the business.

MEXICAN-AMERICAN. Too much, man. Heh, where you vatos[24] going tonight?

FARM WORKER. I'm going over to Concha's. There's a party.

JOHNNY. Wait a minute, vatos. What about our salesman? I think he needs an oil job.

REVOLUCIONARIO. Leave him to me.

> (*The* PACHUCO, FARM-WORKER *and* MEXICAN-AMERICAN *exit, talking loudly about their plans for the night. The* REVOLUCIONARIO *goes over to* SANCHO, *removes his derby hat and cigar, lifts him up and throws him over his shoulder.* SANCHO *hangs loose, lifeless.*)

REVOLUCIONARIO. (*To audience*). He's the best model we got! ¡Ajua![25] (*Exit.*)

> (*End.*)

Journal Entry

Respond to the implications of the play's title, *"Los Vendidos."*

Textual Considerations

1. What stereotypes of Mexican Americans does the play present?
2. Contrast the image of Mexican Americans at the end of the play with the stereotypes presented earlier.
3. How does Valdez use irony and humor to reinforce theme? Cite examples.
4. Comment on the play's effectiveness as a drama of social protest.

Cultural Contexts

1. Compare your group's responses to the play. To what extent did they find it entertaining? offensive? dated?

---

[24] Guys [25] Wow!

Harvey Fierstein

On Tidy Endings

The curtain rises on a deserted, modern Upper West Side apartment. In the bright daylight that pours in through the windows we can see the living room of the apartment. Far Stage Right is the galley kitchen, next to it the multilocked front door with intercom. Stage Left reveals a hallway that leads to the two bedrooms and baths.

Though the room is still fully furnished (couch, coffee table, etc.), there are boxes stacked against the wall and several photographs and paintings are on the floor leaving shadows on the wall where they once hung. Obviously someone is moving out. From the way the boxes are neatly labeled and stacked, we know that this is an organized person.

From the hallway just outside the door we hear the rattling of keys and two arguing voices:

JIM (*Offstage*). I've got to be home by four. I've got practice.

MARION (*Offstage*). I'll get you to practice, don't worry.

JIM. (*Offstage*). I don't want to go in there.

MARION. (*Offstage*). Jimmy, don't make Mommy crazy, alright? We'll go inside, I'll call Aunt Helen and see if you can go down and play with Robbie.

(*The door opens.* MARION *is a handsome woman of forty. Dressed in a business suit, her hair conservatively combed,* SHE *appears to be going to a business meeting. Jim is a boy of eleven. His playclothes are typical, but someone has obviously just combed his hair.* MARION *recovers the key from the lock.*)

JIM. Why can't I just go down and ring the bell?

MARION. Because I said so.

(*As* MARION *steps into the room she is struck by some unexpected emotion. She freezes in her path and stares at the empty apartment.* JIM *lingers by the door.*)

JIM. I'm going downstairs.

MARION. Jimmy, please.

JIM. This place gives me the creeps.

MARION. This was your father's apartment. There's nothing creepy about it.

JIM. Says you.

MARION. You want to close the door, please?

(JIM *reluctantly obeys.*)

MARION. Now, why don't you go check your room and make sure you didn't leave anything.

JIM. It's empty.

MARION. Go look.

JIM. I looked last time.

MARION. (*Trying to be patient*). Honey, we sold the apartment. You're never going to be here again. Go make sure you have everything you want.

JIM. But Uncle Arthur packed everything.

MARION. (*Less patiently*). Go make sure.

JIM. There's nothing in there.

MARION. (*Exploding*). I said make sure!

(JIM *jumps, then realizing that she's not kidding, obeys.*)

MARION. Everything's an argument with that one. (*She looks around the room and breathes deeply. There is sadness here. Under her breath:*) I can still smell you. (*Suddenly not wanting to be alone*) Jimmy? Are you okay?

JIM (*Returning*). Nothing. Told you so.

MARION. Uncle Arthur must have worked very hard. Make sure you thank him.

JIM. What for? Robbie says, (*Fey mannerisms*) "They love to clean up things!"

MARION. Sometimes you can be a real joy.

JIM. Did you call Aunt Helen?

MARION. Do I get a break here? (*Approaching the boy understandingly*) Wouldn't you like to say good-bye?

JIM. To who?

MARION. To the apartment. You and your daddy spent a lot of time here together. Don't you want to take one last look around?

JIM. Ma, get a real life.

MARION. "Get a real life." (*Going for the phone*) Nice. Very nice.

JIM. Could you call already?

MARION. (*Dialing*). Jimmy, what does this look like I'm doing?

(JIM *kicks at the floor impatiently. Someone answers the phone at the other end.*)

MARION. (*Into the phone*). Helen? Hi, we're upstairs. . . . No, we just walked in the door. Jimmy wants to know if he can come down. . . . Oh, thanks.

(*Hearing that,* JIM *breaks for the door.*)

MARION. (*Yelling after him*). Don't run in the halls! And don't play with the elevator buttons!

(*The door slams shut behind him.*)

MARION. (*Back to the phone*). Hi. . . . No, I'm okay. It's a little weird being here. . . . No. Not since the funeral, and then there were so many people. Jimmy told me to get "a real life." I don't think I could handle anything realer. . . . No, please.

Stay where you are. I'm fine. The doorman said Arthur would be right back and my lawyer should have been here already. . . . Well, we've got the papers to sign and a few other odds and ends to clean up. Shouldn't take long.

(*The intercom buzzer rings.*)

MARION. Hang on, that must be her. (MARION *goes to the intercom and speaks*) Yes? . . . Thank you. (*Back to the phone*) Helen? Yeah, it's the lawyer. I'd better go. . . . Well, I could use a stiff drink, but I drove down. Listen, I'll stop by on my way out. Okay? Okay. 'Bye.

(SHE *hangs up the phone, looks around the room. That uncomfortable feeling returns to her quickly.* SHE *gets up and goes to the front door, opens it and looks out. No one there yet.* SHE *closes the door, shakes her head knowing that she's being silly and starts back into the room.* SHE *looks around, can't make it and retreats to the door.* SHE *opens it, looks out, closes it, but stays right there, her hand on the doorknob.*
The bell rings. SHE *throws open the door.*)

MARION. That was quick.

(JUNE LOWELL *still has her finger on the bell. Her arms are loaded with contracts.* MARION's *contemporary,* JUNE *is less formal in appearance and more hyper in her manner.*)

JUNE. *That* was quicker. What, were you waiting by the door?
MARION. (*Embarrassed*). No. I was just passing it. Come on in.
JUNE. Have you got your notary seal?
MARION. I think so.
JUNE. Great. Then you can witness. I left mine at the office and thanks to gentrification I'm double-parked downstairs. (*Looking for a place to dump her load*) Where?
MARION. (*Definitely pointing to the coffee table*). Anywhere. You mean you're not staying?
JUNE. If you really think you need me I can go down and find a parking lot. I think there's one over on Columbus. So, I can go down, park the car in the lot and take a cab back if you really think you need me.
MARION. Well . . . ?
JUNE. But you shouldn't have any problems. The papers are about as straightforward as papers get. Arthur is giving you power of attorney to sell the apartment and you're giving him a check for half the purchase price. Everything else is just signing papers that state that you know that you signed the other papers. Anyway, he knows the deal, his lawyers have been over it all with him, it's just a matter of signatures.
MARION. (*Not fine*). Oh, fine.
JUNE. Unless you just don't want to be alone with him . . . ?
MARION. With Arthur? Don't be silly.

JUNE. (*Laying out the papers*). Then you'll handle it solo? Great. My car thanks you, the parking lot thanks you, and the cab driver that wouldn't have gotten a tip thanks you. Come have a quick look-see.

MARION. (*Joining her on the couch*). There are a lot of papers here.

JUNE. Copies. Not to worry. Start here.

(MARION *starts to read.*)

JUNE. I ran into Jimmy playing Elevator Operator.

(MARION *jumps.*)

JUNE. I got him off at the sixth floor. Read on.

MARION. This is definitely not my day for dealing with him.

(JUNE *gets up and has a look around.*)

JUNE. I don't believe what's happening to this neighborhood. You made quite an investment when you bought this place.

MARION. Collin was always very good at figuring out those things.

JUNE. Well, he sure figured this place right. What, have you tripled your money in ten years?

MARION. More.

JUNE. It's a shame to let it go.

MARION. We're not ready to be a two-dwelling family.

JUNE. So, sublet it again.

MARION. Arthur needs the money from the sale.

JUNE. Arthur got plenty already. I'm not crying for Arthur.

MARION. I don't hear you starting in again, do I?

JUNE. Your interests and your wishes are my only concern.

MARION. Fine.

JUNE. I still say we should contest Collin's will.

MARION. June! . . .

JUNE. You've got a child to support.

MARION. And a great job, and a husband with a great job. Tell me what Arthur's got.

JUNE. To my thinking, half of everything that should have gone to you. And more. All of Collin's personal effects, his record collection . . .

MARION. And I suppose their three years together meant nothing.

JUNE. When you compare them to your sixteen-year marriage? Not nothing, but not half of everything.

MARION. (*Trying to change the subject*). June, who gets which copies?

JUNE. Two of each to Arthur. One you keep. The originals and anything else come back to me. (*Looking around*) I still say you should've sublet the apartment for a year and then sold it. You would've gotten an even better price. Who wants to buy an apartment when they know someone died in it. No one. And certainly no one wants to buy an apartment when they know the person died of AIDS.

MARION. (*Snapping*). June. Enough!

JUNE. (*Catching herself*). Sorry. That was out of line. Sometimes my mouth does that to me. Hey, that's why I'm a lawyer. If my brain worked as fast as my mouth I would have gotten a real job.

MARION. (*Holding out a stray paper*). What's this?

JUNE. I forgot. Arthur's lawyer sent that over yesterday. He found it in Collin's safety-deposit box. It's an insurance policy that came along with some consulting job he did in Japan. He either forgot about it when he made out his will or else he wanted you to get the full payment. Either way, it's yours.

MARION. Are you sure we don't split this?

JUNE. Positive.

MARION. But everything else . . . ?

JUNE. Hey, Arthur found it, his lawyer sent it to me. Relax, it's all yours. Minus my commission, of course. Go out and buy yourself something. Anything else before I have to use my cut to pay the towing bill?

MARION. I guess not.

JUNE (*Starting to leave*). Great. Call me when you get home. (*Stopping at the door and looking back*) Look, I know that I'm attacking this a little coldly. I am aware that someone you loved has just died. But there's a time and place for everything. This is about tidying up loose ends, not holding hands. I hope you'll remember that when Arthur gets here. Call me.

> (*And she's gone.*)
> (MARION *looks ill at ease to be alone again. She nervously straightens the papers into neat little piles, looks at them and then remembers:*)

MARION. Pens. We're going to need pens.

> (*At last a chore to be done.* SHE *looks in her purse and finds only one.* SHE *goes to the kitchen and opens a drawer where she finds two more.* SHE *starts back to the table with them but suddenly remembers something else.* SHE *returns to the kitchen and begins going through the cabinets until* SHE *finds what* SHE'S *looking for: a blue Art Deco teapot. Excited to find it,* SHE *takes it back to the couch.*
> *Guilt strikes.* SHE *stops, considers putting it back, wavers, then:*)

MARION. (*To herself*). Oh, he won't care. One less thing to pack.

> (SHE *takes the teapot and places it on the couch next to her purse.* SHE *is happier. Now* SHE *searches the room with her eyes for any other treasures* SHE *may have overlooked. Nothing here.* SHE *wanders off into the bedroom.*
> *We hear keys outside the front door.* ARTHUR *lets himself into the apartment carrying a load of empty cartons and a large shopping bag.*)

ARTHUR *is in his mid-thirties, pleasant looking though sloppily dressed in work clothes and slightly overweight.*

ARTHUR *enters the apartment just as* MARION *comes out of the bedroom carrying a framed watercolor painting. They jump at the sight of each other.*)

MARION. Oh, hi, Arthur. I didn't hear the door.

ARTHUR. (*Staring at the painting*). Well hello, Marion.

MARION. (*Guiltily*). I was going to ask you if you were thinking of taking this painting because if you're not going to then I'll take it. Unless, of course, you want it.

ARTHUR. No. You can have it.

MARION. I never really liked it, actually. I hate cats. I didn't even like the show. I needed something for my college dorm room. I was never the rock star poster type. I kept it in the back of a closet for years until Collin moved in here and took it. He said he liked it.

ARTHUR. I do too.

MARION. Well, then you keep it.

ARTHUR. No. Take it.

MARION. We've really got no room for it. You keep it.

ARTHUR. I don't want it.

MARION. Well, if you're sure.

ARTHUR. (*Seeing the teapot*). You want the teapot?

MARION. If you don't mind.

ARTHUR. One less thing to pack.

MARION. Funny, but that's exactly what I thought. One less thing to pack. You know, my mother gave it to Collin and me when we moved in to our first apartment. Silly sentimental piece of junk, but you know.

ARTHUR. That's not the one.

MARION. Sure it is. Hall used to make them for Westinghouse back in the thirties. I see them all the time at antiques shows and I always wanted to buy another, but they ask such a fortune for them.

ARTHUR. We broke the one your mother gave you a couple of years ago. That's a reproduction. You can get them almost anywhere in the Village for eighteen bucks.

MARION. Really? I'll have to pick one up.

ARTHUR. Take this one. I'll get another.

MARION. No, it's yours. You bought it.

ARTHUR. One less thing to pack.

MARION. Don't be silly. I didn't come here to raid the place.

ARTHUR. Well, was there anything else of Collin's that you thought you might like to have?

MARION. Now I feel so stupid, but actually I made a list. Not for me. But I started thinking about different people; friends, relatives, you know, that might want to have something of Collin's to remember him by. I wasn't sure just what you were taking and what you were throwing out. Anyway, I brought the list. (*Gets it from her purse*) Of course these are only suggestions. You probably thought of a few of these people yourself. But I figured it couldn't hurt to write it all down. Like I said, I don't know what you are planning on keeping.

ARTHUR. (*Taking the list*). I was planning on keeping it all.

MARION. Oh, I know. But most of these things are silly. Like his high school yearbooks. What would you want with them?

ARTHUR. Sure. I'm only interested in his Gay period.

MARION. I didn't mean it that way. Anyway, you look it over. They're only suggestions. Whatever you decide to do is fine with me.

ARTHUR. (*Folding the list*). It would have to be, wouldn't it. I mean, it's all mine now. He did leave this all to me.

> (MARION *is becoming increasingly nervous, but tries to keep a light approach as* SHE *takes a small bundle of papers from her bag.*)

MARION. While we're on the subject of what's yours. I brought a batch of condolence cards that were sent to you care of me. Relatives mostly.

ARTHUR (*Taking them*). More cards? I'm going to have to have another printing of thank-you notes done.

MARION. I answered these last week, so you don't have to bother. Unless you want to.

ARTHUR. Forge my signature?

MARION. Of course not. They were addressed to both of us and they're mostly distant relatives or friends we haven't seen in years. No one important.

ARTHUR. If they've got my name on them, then I'll answer them myself.

MARION. I wasn't telling you not to, I was only saying that you don't have to.

ARTHUR. I understand.

> (MARION *picks up the teapot and brings it to the kitchen.*)

MARION. Let me put this back.

ARTHUR. I ran into Jimmy in the lobby.

MARION. Tell me you're joking.

ARTHUR. I got him to Helen's.

MARION. He's really racking up the points today.

ARTHUR. You know, he still can't look me in the face.

MARION. He's reacting to all of this in strange ways. Give him time. He'll come around. He's really very fond of you.

ARTHUR. I know. But he's at that awkward age: under thirty. I'm sure in twenty years we'll be the best of friends.

MARION. It's not what you think.

ARTHUR. What do you mean?

MARION. Well, you know.

ARTHUR. No I don't know. Tell me.

MARION. I thought that you were intimating something about his blaming you for Collin's illness and I was just letting you know that it's not true. (*Foot in mouth, she braves on*) We discussed it a lot and . . . uh . . . he understands that his father was sick before you two ever met.

ARTHUR. I don't believe this.

MARION. I'm just trying to say that he doesn't blame you.

ARTHUR. First of all, who asked you? Second of all, that's between him and me. And third and most importantly, of course he blames me. Marion, he's eleven years old. You can discuss all you want, but the fact is that his father died of a "fag" disease and I'm the only fag around to finger.

MARION. My son doesn't use that kind of language.

ARTHUR. Forget the language. I'm talking about what he's been through. Can you imagine the kind of crap he's taken from his friends? That poor kid's been chased and chastised from one end of town to the other. He's got to have someone to blame just to survive. He can't blame you, you're all he's got. He can't blame his father; he's dead. So, Uncle Arthur gets the shaft. Fine, I can handle it.

MARION. You are so wrong, Arthur. I know my son and that is not the way his mind works.

ARTHUR. I don't know what you know. I only know what I know. And all I know is what I hear and see. The snide remarks, the little smirks . . . And it's not just the illness. He's been looking for a scapegoat since the day you and Collin first split up. Finally he has one.

MARION. (*Getting very angry now*). Wait. Are you saying that if he's going to blame someone it should be me?

ARTHUR. I think you should try to see things from his point of view.

MARION. Where do you get off thinking you're privy to my son's point of view?

ARTHUR. It's not that hard to imagine. Life's rolling right along, he's having a happy little childhood, when suddenly one day his father's moving out. No explanations, no reasons, none of the fights that usually accompany such things. Divorce is hard enough for a kid to understand when he's listened to years of battles, but yours?

MARION. So what should we have done? Faked a few months' worth of fights before Collin moved out?

ARTHUR. You could have told him the truth, plain and simple.

MARION. He was seven years old at the time. How the hell do you tell a seven-year-old that his father is leaving his mother to go sleep with other men?

ARTHUR. Well, not like that.

MARION. You know, Arthur, I'm going to say this as nicely as I can: Butt out. You're not his mother and you're not his father.

ARTHUR. Thank you. I wasn't acutely aware of that fact. I will certainly keep that in mind from now on.

MARION. There's only so much information a child that age can handle.

ARTHUR. So it's best that he reach his capacity on the street.

MARION. He knew about the two of you. We talked about it.

ARTHUR. Believe me, he knew before you talked about it. He's young, not stupid.

MARION. It's very easy for you to stand here and criticize, but there are aspects that you will just never be able to understand. You weren't there. You have no idea what it was like for me. You're talking to someone who thought that a girl went to college to meet a husband. I went to protest rallies because I liked the music. I bought a guitar because I thought it looked good on the bed! This lifestyle, this knowledge that you take for granted, was all a little out of left field for me.

ARTHUR. I can imagine.

MARION. No. I don't think you can. I met Collin in college, married him right after graduation and settled down for a nice quiet life of Kids and Careers. You think I had any idea about this? Talk about life's little surprises. You live with someone for sixteen years, you share your life, your bed, you have a child together, and then you wake up one day and he tells you that to him it's all been a lie. A lie. Try that on for size. Here you are the happiest couple you know, fulfilling your every life fantasy and he tells you he's living a lie.

ARTHUR. I'm sure he never said that.

MARION. Don't be so sure. There was a lot of new ground being broken back then and plenty of it was muddy.

ARTHUR. You know that he loved you.

MARION. What's that supposed to do, make things easier? It doesn't. I was brought up to believe, among other things, that if you had love that was enough. So what if I wasn't everything he wanted. Maybe he wasn't exactly everything I wanted either. So, you know what? You count your blessings and you settle.

ARTHUR. No one has to settle. Not him. Not you.

MARION. Of course not. You can say, "Up yours!" to everything and everyone who depends and needs you, and go off to make yourself happy.

ARTHUR. It's not that simple.

MARION. No. This is simpler. Death is simpler. (*Yelling out*) Happy now?

(*They stare at each other.* MARION *calms the rage and catches her breath.* ARTHUR *holds his emotions in check.*)

ARTHUR. How about a nice hot cup of coffee? Tea with lemon? Hot cocoa with a marshmallow floating in it?

MARION. (*Laughs*). I was wrong. You *are* a mother.

(ARTHUR *goes into the kitchen and starts preparing things.* MARION *loafs by the doorway.*)

MARION. I lied before. He *was* everything I ever wanted.

(ARTHUR *stops, looks at her, and then changes the subject as he goes on with his work.*)

ARTHUR. When I came into the building and saw Jimmy in the lobby I absolutely freaked for a second. It's amazing how much they look alike. It was like seeing a little miniature Collin standing there.

MARION. I know. He's like Collin's clone. There's nothing of me in him.

ARTHUR. I always kinda hoped that when he grew up he'd take after me. Not much chance, I guess.

MARION. Don't do anything fancy in there.

ARTHUR. Please. Anything we can consume is one less thing to pack.

MARION. So you've said.

ARTHUR. So *we've* said.

MARION. I want to keep seeing you and I want you to see Jim. You're still part of this family. No one's looking to cut you out.

ARTHUR. Ah, who'd want a kid to grow up looking like me anyway. I had enough trouble looking like this. Why pass on the misery?

MARION. You're adorable.

ARTHUR. Is that like saying I have a good personality?

MARION. I think you are one of the most naturally handsome men I know.

ARTHUR. Natural is right, and the bloom is fading.

MARION. All you need is a few good nights' sleep to kill those rings under your eyes.

ARTHUR. Forget the rings under my eyes, (*Grabbing his middle*) . . . how about the rings around my moon?

MARION. I like you like this.

ARTHUR. From the time that Collin started using the wheelchair until he died, about six months, I lost twenty-three pounds. No gym, no diet. In the last seven weeks I've gained close to fifty.

MARION. You're exaggerating.

ARTHUR. I'd prove it on the bathroom scale, but I sold it in working order.

MARION. You'd never know.

ARTHUR. Marion, *you'd* never know, but ask my belt. Ask my pants. Ask my underwear. Even my stretch socks have stretch marks. I called the ambulance at five A.M., he was gone at nine and by nine-thirty, I was on a first-name basis with Sara Lee. I can quote the business hours of every ice-cream parlor, pizzeria and bakery on the island of Manhattan. I know the location of every twenty-four-hour grocery in the greater New York area, and I have memorized the phone numbers of every Mandarin, Szechuan and Hunan restaurant with free delivery.

MARION. At least you haven't wasted your time on useless hobbies.

ARTHUR. Are you kidding? I'm opening my own Overeater's Hotline. We'll have to start small, but expansion is guaranteed.

MARION. You're the best, you know that? If I couldn't be everything that Collin wanted then I'm grateful that he found someone like you.

ARTHUR. (*Turning on her without missing a beat*). Keep your goddamned gratitude to yourself. I didn't go through any of this for you. So your thanks are out of line. And he didn't find "someone like" me. It was me.

MARION. (*Frightened*). I didn't mean . . .

ARTHUR. And I wish you'd remember one thing more: He died in my arms, not yours.

> (MARION *is totally caught off guard. She stares disbelieving, open-mouthed.* ARTHUR *walks past her as he leaves the kitchen with place mats. He puts them on the coffee table. As he arranges the papers and place mats he speaks, never looking at her.*)

ARTHUR. Look, I know you were trying to say something supportive. Don't waste your breath. There's nothing you can say that will make any of this easier for me. There's no way for you to help me get through this. And that's your fault. After three years you still have no idea or understanding of who I am. Or maybe you do know but refuse to accept it. I don't know and I don't care. But at least understand, from my point of view, who you are: You are my husband's *ex*-wife. If you like, the mother of *my* stepson. Don't flatter yourself into thinking you're any more than that. And whatever you are, you're certainly not my friend.

> (*He stops, looks up at her, then passes her again as he goes back to the kitchen.*
> MARION *is shaken, working hard to control herself.* SHE *moves toward the couch.*)

MARION. Why don't we just sign these papers and I'll be out of your way.

ARTHUR. Shouldn't you say *I'll* be out of *your* way? After all, I'm not just signing papers, I'm signing away my home.

MARION. (*Resolved not to fight, she gets her purse*). I'll leave the papers here. Please have them notarized and returned to my lawyer.

ARTHUR. Don't forget my painting.

MARION. (*Exploding*). What do you want from me, Arthur?

ARTHUR. (*Yelling back*). I want you the hell out of my apartment! I want you out of my life! And I want you to leave Collin alone!

MARION. The man's dead. I don't know how much more alone I can leave him.

> (ARTHUR *laughs at the irony, but behind the laughter is something much more desperate.*)

ARTHUR. Lots more, Marion. You've got to let him go.

MARION. For the life of me, I don't know what I did, or what you think I did, for you to treat me like this. But you're not going to get away with it. You will not take your anger out on me. I will not stand here and be badgered and insulted by you. I know you've been hurt and I know you're hurting but you're not the only one who lost someone here.

ARTHUR. (*Topping her*). Yes I am! You didn't just lose him. I did! You lost him five years ago when he divorced you. This is not your moment of grief and loss, it's mine! (*Picking up the bundle of cards and throwing it toward her*) These condolences do not belong to you, they're mine. (*Tossing her list back to her*)

His things are not yours to give away, they're mine! This death does not belong to you, it's mine! Bought and paid for outright. I suffered for it, I bled for it. I was the one who cooked his meals. I was the one who spoon-fed them. I pushed his wheelchair. I carried and bathed him. I wiped his backside and changed his diapers. I breathed life into and wrestled fear out of his heart. I kept him alive for two years longer than any doctor thought possible and when it was time I was the one who prepared him for death.

I paid in full for my place in his life and I will *not* share it with you. We are not the two widows of Collin Redding. Your life was not here. Your husband didn't just die. You've got a son and a life somewhere else. Your husband's sitting, waiting for you at home, wondering, as I am, what the hell you're doing here and why you can't let go.

> (MARION *leans back against the couch.* SHE'S *blown away.* ARTHUR *stands staring at her.*)

ARTHUR. (*Quietly*). Let him go, Marion. He's mine. Dead or alive; mine.

> (*The teakettle whistles.* ARTHUR *leaves the room, goes to the kitchen and pours the water as* MARION *pulls herself together.*
> ARTHUR *carries the loaded tray back into the living room and sets it down on the coffee table. He sits and pours a cup.*)

ARTHUR. One marshmallow or two?

> (MARION *stares, unsure as to whether the attack is really over or not.*)

ARTHUR. (*Placing them in her cup*). Take three, they're small.

> (MARION *smiles and takes the offered cup.*)

ARTHUR. (*Campily*). Now let me tell you how I *really* feel.

> (MARION *jumps slightly, then they share a small laugh. Silence as they each gather themselves and sip their refreshments.*)

MARION. (*Calmly*). Do you think that I sold the apartment just to throw you out?
ARTHUR. I don't care about the apartment . . .
MARION. . . . Because I really didn't. Believe me.
ARTHUR. I know.
MARION. I knew the expenses here were too much for you, and I knew you couldn't afford to buy out my half . . . I figured if we sold it, that you'd at least have a nice chunk of money to start over with.
ARTHUR. You could've given me a little more time.
MARION. Maybe. But I thought the sooner you were out of here, the sooner you could go on with your life.
ARTHUR. Or the sooner you could go on with yours.
MARION. Maybe. (*Pause to gather her thoughts*) Anyway, I'm not going to tell you that I have no idea what you're talking about. I'd have to be worse than deaf

and blind not to have seen the way you've been treated. Or mistreated. When I read Collin's obituary in the newspaper and saw my name and Jimmy's name and no mention of you . . . (*Shakes her head, not knowing what to say*) You know that his secretary was the one who wrote that up and sent it in. Not me. But I should have done something about it and I didn't. I know.

ARTHUR. Wouldn't have made a difference. I wrote my own obituary for him and sent it to the smaller papers. They edited me out.

MARION. I'm sorry. I remember, at the funeral, I was surrounded by all of Collin's family and business associates while you were left with your friends. I knew it was wrong. I knew I should have said something but it felt good to have them around me and you looked like you were holding up . . . Wrong. But saying that it's all my fault for not letting go? . . . There were other people involved.

ARTHUR. Who took their cue from you.

MARION. Arthur, you don't understand. Most people that we knew as a couple had no idea that Collin was Gay right up to his death. And even those that did know only found out when he got sick and the word leaked out that it was AIDS. I don't think I have to tell you how stupid and ill-informed most people are about homosexuality. And AIDS . . . ? The kinds of insane behavior that word inspires? . . .

Those people at the funeral, how many times did they call to see how he was doing over these years? How many of them ever went to see him in the hospital? Did any of them even come here? So, why would you expect them to act any differently after his death?

So, maybe that helps to explain their behavior, but what about mine, right? Well, maybe there is no explanation. Only excuses. And excuse number one is that you're right, I have never really let go of him. And I am jealous of you. Hell, I was jealous of anyone that Collin ever talked to, let alone slept with . . . let alone loved.

The first year, after he moved out, we talked all the time about the different men he was seeing. And I always listened and advised. It was kind of fun. It kept us close. It kept me a part of his intimate life. And the bottom line was always that he wasn't happy with the men he was meeting. So, I was always allowed to hang on to the hope that one day he'd give it all up and come home. Then he got sick.

He called me, told me he was in the hospital and asked if I'd come see him. I ran. When I got to his door there was a sign, INSTRUCTIONS FOR VISITORS OF AN AIDS PATIENT. I nearly died.

ARTHUR. He hadn't told you?

MARION. No. And believe me a sign is not the way to find these things out. I was so angry . . . And he was so sick . . . I was sure that he'd die right then. If not from the illness then from the hospital staff's neglect. No one wanted to go near him and I didn't bother fighting with them because I understood that they were scared. I was scared. That whole month in the hospital I didn't let Jimmy visit him once.

You learn.

Well, as you know, he didn't die. And he asked if he could come stay with me until he was well. And I said yes. Of course, yes. Now, here's something I never thought I'd ever admit to anyone: had he asked to stay with me for a few weeks I would have said no. But he asked to stay with me until he was well and knowing there was no cure I said yes. In my craziness I said yes because to me that meant forever. That he was coming back to me forever. Not that I wanted him to die, but I assumed from everything I'd read . . . And we'd be back together for whatever time he had left. Can you understand that?

> (ARTHUR *nods.*)

MARION. (*Gathers her thoughts again*). Two weeks later he left. He moved in here. Into this apartment that we had bought as an investment. Never to live in. Certainly never to live apart in. Next thing I knew, the name Arthur starts appearing in every phone call, every dinner conversation.

"Did you see the doctor?"

"Yes. Arthur made sure I kept the appointment."

"Are you going to your folks for Thanksgiving?"

"No. Arthur and I are having some friends over."

I don't know which one of us was more of a coward, he for not telling or me for not asking about you. But eventually you became a given. Then, of course, we met and became what I had always thought of as friends.

> (ARTHUR *winces in guilt.*)

MARION. I don't care what you say, how could we not be friends with something so great in common: love for one of the most special human beings there ever was. And don't try and tell me there weren't times when you enjoyed my being around as an ally. I can think of a dozen occasions when we ganged up on him, teasing him with our intimate knowledge of his personal habits.

> (ARTHUR *has to laugh.*)

MARION. Blanket stealing? Snoring? Excess gas, no less? (*Takes a moment to enjoy this truce*) I don't think that my loving him threatened your relationship. Maybe I'm not being truthful with myself. But I don't. I never tried to step between you. Not that I ever had the opportunity. Talk about being joined at the hip! And that's not to say I wasn't jealous. I was. Terribly. Hatefully. But always lovingly. I was happy for Collin because there was no way to deny that he was happy. With everything he was facing, he was happy. Love did that. You did that.

> He lit up with you. He came to life. I envied that and all the time you spent together, but more, I watched you care for him (sometimes *overcare* for him), and I was in awe. I could never have done what you did. I never would have survived. I really don't know how you did.

ARTHUR. Who said I survived?

MARION. Don't tease. You did an absolutely incredible thing. It's not as if you met him before he got sick. You entered a relationship that you knew in all probability would end this way and you never wavered.

ARTHUR. Of course I did. Don't have me sainted, Marion. But sometimes you have no choice. Believe me, if I could've gotten away from him I would've. But I was a prisoner of love.

(*He makes a campy gesture and pose.*)

MARION. Stop.

ARTHUR. And there were lots of pluses. I got to quit a job I hated, stay home all day and watch game shows. I met a lot of doctors and learned a lot of big words. (ARTHUR *jumps up and goes to the pile of boxes where he extracts one and brings it back to the couch*) And then there was all the exciting traveling I got to do. This box has a souvenir from each one of our trips. Wanna see?

(MARION *nods. He opens the box and pulls things out one by one.*)

ARTHUR. (*Continued*) (*Holding up an old bottle*). This is from the house we rented in Reno when we went to clear out his lungs. (*Holding handmade potholders*) This is from the hospital in Reno. Collin made them. They had a great arts and crafts program (*Copper bracelets*) These are from a faith healer in Philly. They don't do much for a fever, but they look great with a green sweater. (*Glass ashtrays*) These are from our first visit to the clinic in France. Such lovely people. (*A Bible*) This is from our second visit to the clinic in France. (*A bead necklace*) A Voodoo doctor in New Orleans. Next time we'll have to get there earlier in the year. I think he sold all the pretty ones at Mardi Gras. (*A tiny piñata*) Then there was Mexico. Black market drugs and empty wallets. (*Now pulling things out at random*) L.A., San Francisco, Houston, Boston . . . We traveled everywhere they offered hope for sale and came home with souvenirs. (ARTHUR *quietly pulls a few more things out and then begins to put them all back into the box slowly. Softly as he works:*)

Marion, I would have done anything, traveled anywhere to avoid . . . or delay . . . Not just because I loved him so desperately, but when you've lived the way we did for three years . . . the battle becomes your life. (*He looks at her and then away*)

His last few hours were beyond any scenario I had imagined. He hadn't walked in nearly six months. He was totally incontinent. If he spoke two words in a week I was thankful. Days went by without his eyes ever focusing on me. He just stared out at I don't know what. Not the meals as I fed him. Not the TV I played constantly for company. Just out. Or maybe in.

It was the middle of the night when I heard his breathing become labored. His lungs were filling with fluid again. I knew the sound. I'd heard it a hundred times before. So, I called the ambulance and got him to the hospital. They hooked him up to the machines, the oxygen, shot him with morphine and told me that they would do what they could to keep him alive.

But, Marion, it wasn't the machines that kept him breathing. He did it himself. It was that incredible will and strength inside him. Whether it came from his love of life or fear of death, who knows. But he'd been counted out a hundred times and a hundred times he fought his way back.

I got a magazine to read him, pulled a chair up to the side of his bed and holding his hand, I wondered whether I should call Helen to let the cleaning lady in or if he'd fall asleep and I could sneak home for an hour. I looked up from the page and he was looking at me. Really looking right into my eyes. I patted his cheek and said, "Don't worry, honey, you're going to be fine."

But there was something else in his eyes. He wasn't satisfied with that. And I don't know why, I have no idea where it came from, I just heard the words coming out of my mouth, "Collin, do you want to die?" His eyes filled and closed, he nodded his head.

I can't tell you what I was thinking, I'm not sure I was. I slipped off my shoes, lifted his blanket and climbed into bed next to him. I helped him to put his arms around me, and mine around him, and whispered as gently as I could into his ear, "It's alright to let go now. It's time to go on." And he did.

Marion, you've got your life and his son. All I have is an intangible place in a man's history. Leave me that. Respect that.

MARION. I understand.

> (ARTHUR *suddenly comes to life, running to get the shopping bag that he'd left at the front door.*)

ARTHUR. Jeez! With all the screamin' and sad storytelling I forget something. (*He extracts a bouquet of flowers from the bag*) I brung you flowers and everything.

MARION. You brought *me* flowers?

ARTHUR. Well, I knew you'd never think to bring me flowers and I felt that on an occasion such as this somebody oughta get flowers from somebody.

MARION. You know, Arthur, you're really making me feel like a worthless piece of garbage.

ARTHUR. So what else is new? (*He presents the flowers*) Just promise me one thing: Don't press one in a book. Just stick them in a vase and when they fade just toss them out. No more memorabilia.

MARION. Arthur, I want to do something for you and I don't know what. Tell me what you want.

ARTHUR. I want little things. Not much. I want to be remembered. If you get a Christmas card from Collin's mother, make sure she sent me one too. If his friends call to see how you are, ask if they've called me. Have me to dinner so I can see Jimmy. Let me take him out now and then. Invite me to his wedding.

> (*They both laugh.*)

MARION. You've got it.

ARTHUR. (*Clearing the table*). Let me get all this cold cocoa out of the way. We still have the deed to do.

MARION. (*Checking her watch*). And I've got to get Jimmy home in time for practice.

ARTHUR. Band practice?

MARION. Baseball. (*Picking her list off the floor*) About this list, you do what you want.

ARTHUR. Believe me, I will. But I promise to consider your suggestions. Just don't rush me. I'm not ready to give it all away. (ARTHUR *is off to the kitchen with his tray and the phone rings. He answers it in the kitchen*) Hello? . . . just a minute. (*Calling out*) It's your eager Little Leaguer.

(MARION *picks up the living room extension and* ARTHUR *hangs his up.*)

MARION. (*Into phone*). Hello, honey . . . I'll be down in five minutes. No. You know what? You come up here and get me. . . . No, I said you should come up here. . . . I said I want you to come up here. . . . Because I said so. . . . Thank you.

(SHE *hangs the receiver.*)

ARTHUR. (*Rushing to the papers*). Alright, where do we start on these?

MARION. (*Getting out her seal*). I guess you should just start signing everything and I'll stamp along with you. Keep one of everything on the side for yourself.

ARTHUR. Now I feel so rushed. What am I signing?

MARION. You want to do this another time?

ARTHUR. No. Let's get it over with. I wouldn't survive another session like this.

(HE *starts to sign and she starts her job.*)

MARION. I keep meaning to ask you; how are you?

ARTHUR. (*At first puzzled and then*). Oh, you mean my health? Fine. No, I'm fine. I've been tested, and nothing. We were very careful. We took many precautions. Collin used to make jokes about how we should invest in rubber futures.

MARION. I'll bet.

ARTHUR. (*Stops what he's doing*). It never occurred to me until now. How about you?

MARION. (*Not stopping*). Well, we never had sex after he got sick.

ARTHUR. But before?

MARION. (*Stopping but not looking up*). I have the antibodies in my blood. No signs that it will ever develop into anything else. And it's been five years so my chances are pretty good that I'm just a carrier.

ARTHUR. I'm so sorry. Collin never told me.

MARION. He didn't know. In fact, other than my husband and the doctors, you're the only one I've told.

ARTHUR. You and your husband . . . ?

MARION. Have invested in rubber futures. There'd only be a problem if we wanted to have a child. Which we do. But we'll wait. Miracles happen every day.

ARTHUR. I don't know what to say.

MARION. Tell me you'll be there if I ever need you.

(ARTHUR *gets up, goes to her and puts his arms around her. They hold each other. He gently pushes her away to make a joke.*)

ARTHUR. Sure! Take something else that should have been mine.
MARION. Don't even joke about things like that.

(*The doorbell rings. They pull themselves together.*)

ARTHUR. You know we'll never get these done today.
MARION. So, tomorrow.

(ARTHUR *goes to open the door as* MARION *gathers her things. He opens the door and Jimmy is standing in the hall.*)

JIM. C'mon, Ma. I'm gonna be late.
ARTHUR. Would you like to come inside?
JIM. We've gotta go.
MARION. Jimmy, come on.
JIM. Ma!

(*She glares. He comes in.* ARTHUR *closes the door.*)

MARION. (*Holding out the flowers*). Take these for Mommy.
JIM. (*Taking them*). Can we go?
MARION. (*Picking up the painting*). Say good-bye to your Uncle Arthur.
JIM. 'Bye, Arthur. Come on.
MARION. Give him a kiss.
ARTHUR. Marion, don't.
MARION. Give your uncle a kiss good-bye.
JIM. He's not my uncle.
MARION. No. He's a hell of a lot more than your uncle.
ARTHUR. (*Offering his hand*). A handshake will do.
MARION. Tell Uncle Arthur what your daddy told you.
JIM. About what?
MARION. Stop playing dumb. You know.
ARTHUR. Don't embarrass him.
MARION. Jimmy, please.
JIM. (*He regards his mother's softer tone and then speaks*). He said that after me and Mommy he loved you the most.
MARION. (*Standing behind him*). Go on.
JIM. And that I should love you too. And make sure that you're not lonely or very sad.
ARTHUR. Thank you.

(ARTHUR *reaches down to the boy and they hug.* JIM *gives him a little peck on the cheek and then breaks away.*)

MARION. (*Going to open the door*). Alright, kid, you done good. Now let's blow this joint before you muck it up.

(JIM *rushes out the door.* MARION *turns to* ARTHUR .)

MARION. A child's kiss is magic. Why else would they be so stingy with them. I'll call you.

(ARTHUR *nods understanding.* MARION *pulls the door closed behind her.* ARTHUR *stands quietly as the lights fade to black.*)

THE END

NOTE: *If being performed on film, the final image should be of* ARTHUR *leaning his back against the closed door on the inside of the apartment and* MARION *leaning on the outside of the door. A moment of thought and then they both move on.*

Journal Entry

Comment on the significance of the lawyer's role in *On Tidy Endings.*

Textual Considerations

1. Characterize Marion. To what extent do you find her concern for Arthur believable?
2. Arthur says that Marion should have told Jimmy the real reason his father decided to leave. Do you agree? Why or why not?
3. Characterize Arthur. What do we learn about his relationship with Collin through his conversation with Marion? How would you describe his attitude toward Marion?
4. What does the title of the play contribute to your understanding of the play's meaning?

Cultural Contexts

1. Discuss with your group what you learned about AIDS and its effects on individual and family lives. With which character did your group members empathize most, and why?
2. Speculate on Fierstein's purpose in writing *On Tidy Endings.* Is he interested in informing or persuading his audience? Is *On Tidy Endings* a protest drama? Why or why not?

PART ASSIGNMENTS

WRITING TOPICS

1. "To be an American means something more than to belong to a specific group of Americans. To be an American is to acknowledge a collective identity that simultaneously transcends and encompasses our disparate identities and communities" (Elizabeth Fox-Genovese). Examine any two texts from Part Four that contradict or affirm this point of view.

2. Using at least two texts, explain how gender, ethnicity, and class have shaped the identities of Puerto Ricans in the United States.

3. Identify and analyze the sources of racial hostility in "The Melting Pot," "Telephone Conversation," and "Poem by a Yellow Woman." Consider too whether these texts reinforce or negate the idea that people can modify ingrained assumptions about race.

4. Several selections use stereotypes to show how one racial group envisions the other. Write an essay in which you test these stereotypes against reality by comparing them to facts or to your own observations about racial groups.

5. Choose two or three texts that support or refute the African-American critic Shelby Steele's thesis that "black anger always in a way flatters white power."

6. Several selections, including "Poem by a Yellow Woman," "Jasmine," and "First Day of Work," address the issue of immigration in the United States. To what extent do they suggest that immigrants can expect inclusion in the larger community? What other aspects of immigrant life do they address?

7. Explore the causes and effects of cultural displacement in any three texts.

8. Make a list of the common cultural and ethnic stereotypes that you encountered in any three texts, and discuss the causes and effects of the prejudices they embody.

9. Lack of awareness of cultural differences or the assumption by one cultural group that another is inferior often results in painful personal and social encounters. Apply this thesis to any three texts.

10. Personal and cultural alienation is a recurring motif in several selections. Analyze the causes and effects of the protagonists' sense of exclusion.

11. Several texts focus on the relation between exclusion and social class. Discuss their portrayal in "The Stolen Party," "I Stand Here Ironing," "Latero Story," and/or "On the Subway."

12. Using the selection by Mukherjee, Espada, or Ryu, write an analysis of the emotional cost of being an immigrant, migrant worker, or illegal alien in the United States.

13. Write an essay on the issue of race in *Othello*. To what extent are Othello's actions attributable to his being black in a predominantly white Venetian society?

14. Discuss the issue of gender relations in *Othello*. Consider, for example, how social class and the patriarchal tradition have shaped the personal identities of Iago, Emilia, and Desdemona.
15. Discuss Venetian attitudes toward duplicity and deception. Consider how Othello, Iago, Brabantio, Desdemona, and Emilia react to the idea that the outward apperance one gives to the world bears no relation to the reality inside oneself.

RESEARCH TOPICS

1. In a documented paper, analyze Walt Whitman's concept of the expansive self and his democratic vision of humanity in his poem *Song of Myself*. To what extent is Whitman considered naive in believing that American ideals of freedom and brotherhood are possible?
2. To understand better the cultural background for the chronology and setting of Grace Paley's "The Loudest Voice," view the film *Ellis Island* or *Hester Street* and/or read *A Bintel Brief: A Bundle of Letters to the Jewish Daily Forward* (New York: Ballantine, 1971). Write an essay on what you learned about the Jewish immigrant experience, including the conflict between first- and second-generation immigrants.
3. To explore further themes of African-American drama performed in the 1950s, read either William Branch's *Medal for Willie* (1951) or *In Splendid Error* (1955), Alice Childress's *Trouble in Mind* (1955), or Lorraine Hansberry's *A Raisin in the Sun* (1959). Write a paper on what you learned about the effects of racism on the dreams of many African Americans, about marginalization as a result of segregation, and about the role of the civil rights movement of the 1950s, including the Montgomery bus boycott and the civil disobedience of Rosa Parks (1955).
4. The literature of AIDS has flourished in the last decade, providing readers with new voices and perspectives with which to view the epidemic and its inherent sense of loss. Examine at least three works—poems, short stories, or plays—that explore the AIDS issue. Investigate the premises these texts advance in relation to the epidemic, the discourse of AIDS, and the emotional outlets that help people deal with the presence and absence of AIDS victims.

PART FIVE

Individualism and Community

Fiction

Poetry

Drama

"Postmodern life will place a premium on relationships, not individualism," predicts a contemporary psychologist as he looks ahead
to the next century. Cross-cultural studies show marked variations in social
relationships, but one theme remains constant: we are social beings. Not
many of us could or would want to live a life of isolation. Many questions
haunt us, however, about the relation between our private and communal
selves. How can we reconcile our individual quests for identity with the
sometimes conflicting demands of social responsibility? To what extent
should we rebel against social conformity? What kind of threats, if any, do
individuals pose to the community? Are individual rights and social responsibility irreconcilable? What are the necessary preconditions for individual
participation in any society?

Culture, according to anthropologist Bronislaw Malinowski, is the "artificial, secondary environment" that human beings superimpose on nature.
We human beings, then, are in both nature and culture, and both influence
our choices. A diversity of cultures, which the following selections illustrate,
creates many opportunities for choices and sometimes leads to great difficulty in actually choosing. While nature is passively selecting the fittest or-
ganisms for survival, we humans are actively, sometimes painfully, making
a variety of choices—personal, ethical, political, economic—for a number
of reasons both rational and emotional. Many of these choices concern
other people and our relations with them; others involve coming to terms
with our cultural or institutional pasts. Are cultural and historical factors limitations on freedom of choice, or do they allow more opportunity for individual action and imagination? Do we increase our individual choices to the
degree that we free ourselves from history and culture?

Several texts in Part Five will engage you also in the various debates
raised by the voices of individuals and of the community in different historical and cross-cultural contexts. These voices speak out personally and po-
litically through the conversations they re-create among racially and
socially diverse groups. The stories "Eveline" and "A Red Sweater," for example, explore the degree to which the individual identities of the Irish and
Chinese-American female protagonists have been shaped by their social
and cultural environments. The way in which communities deal with threats
against their autonomy is the subject of "Call Me Not a Man," "Hands," and
"Dead Men's Path." These stories also evaluate various forces that lead the
different cross-cultural communities of the American Midwest and Africa to
defend themselves against the external threats imposed on them by nature, political authority, and their own fellow beings.

Poems such as "People," "Street Kid," and "Black Jackets" extend the
discussion of individualism and community through the claim they place

on the uniqueness of human beings, despite their obscure or alienated condition. Others, such as "History," "To My Father," and "Those Winter Sundays," explore the complex role of the family as a mediating element between individuals and their collective worlds. And "Mending Wall" and "Summer Solstice" focus on the concept of boundaries in relationships, addressing our desires for both solitude and solidarity, personal space and social interaction.

The dramas in Part Five are concerned with civil disobedience, a subject debated by artists and philosophers throughout human history. Although Sophocles, in his Greek tragedy *Antigone,* presents conflicts such as between male and female, youth and age, and religious and secular beliefs, his main concern is the decision of Antigone, who insists on obeying her conscience even if it means violating the laws of the state. Susan Glaspell's play *Trifles,* set on an isolated midwestern farm in the late nineteenth century, also addresses conflicts between men and women, but her primary focus is on the two female protagonists' decision to choose in favor of their own concept of justice, even if that choice involves disobeying the law.

As you read these and other texts in this part, you too will be asked to make judgments about issues such as personal freedom and social responsibility, rebellion and conformity, the right of an individual to participate in acts of civil disobedience, the conflicting demands of individual preference and familial obligation, and the extent to which personal identity is shaped by external social forces.

Franz Kafka

The Metamorphosis

I

As Gregor Samsa awoke one morning from uneasy dreams he found himself transformed in his bed into a gigantic insect. He was lying on his hard, as it were armor-plated, back and when he lifted his head a little he could see his dome-like brown belly divided into stiff arched segments on top of which the bed quilt could hardly keep in position and was about to slide off completely. His numerous legs, which were pitifully thin compared to the rest of his bulk, waved helplessly before his eyes.

What has happened to me? he thought. It was no dream. His room, a regular human bedroom, only rather too small, lay quiet between the four familiar walls. Above the table on which a collection of cloth samples was unpacked and spread out—Samsa was a commercial traveler—hung the picture which he had recently cut out of an illustrated magazine and put into a pretty gilt frame. It showed a lady, with a fur cap on and a fur stole, sitting upright and holding out to the spectator a huge fur muff into which the whole of her forearm had vanished!

Gregor's eyes turned next to the window, and the overcast sky—one could hear rain drops beating on the window gutter—made him quite melancholy. What about sleeping a little longer and forgetting all this nonsense, he thought, but it could not be done, for he was accustomed to sleep on his right side and in his present condition he could not turn himself over. However violently he forced himself towards his right side he always rolled on to his back again. He tried it at least a hundred times, shutting his eyes to keep from seeing his struggling legs, and only desisted when he began to feel in his side a faint dull ache he had never experienced before.

Oh God, he thought, what an exhausting job I've picked on! Traveling about day in, day out. It's much more irritating work than doing the actual business in the office, and on top of that there's the trouble of constant traveling, of worrying about train connections, the bed and irregular meals, casual acquaintances that are always new and never become intimate friends. The devil take it all! He felt a slight itching up on his belly; slowly pushed himself on his back nearer to the top of the bed so that he could lift his head more easily; identified the itching place which was surrounded by many small white spots the nature of which he could not understand and made to touch it with a leg, but drew the leg back immediately, for the contact made a cold shiver run through him.

He slid down again into his former position. This getting up early, he thought, makes one quite stupid. A man needs his sleep. Other commercials live like harem women. For instance, when I come back to the hotel of a morning to write up the orders I've got, these others are only sitting down to breakfast. Let me just try that with my chief; I'd be sacked on the spot. Anyhow, that might be quite a good thing for me, who can tell? If I didn't have to hold my hand because of my parents I'd have given notice long ago. I'd have gone to the chief and told him exactly what I think of him. That would knock him endways from his desk! It's a queer way of doing, too, this sitting on high at a desk and talking down to employees, especially when they have to come quite near because the chief is hard of hearing. Well, there's still hope; once I've saved enough money to pay back my parents' debts to him— that should take another five or six years—I'll do it without fail. I'll cut myself completely loose then. For the moment, though, I'd better get up, since my train goes at five.

He looked at the alarm clock ticking on the chest. Heavenly Father! he thought. It was half-past six o'clock and the hands were quietly moving on, it was even past the half-hour, it was getting on toward a quarter to seven. Had the alarm clock not gone off? From the bed one could see that it had been properly set for four o'clock; of course it must have gone off. Yes, but was it possible to sleep quietly through that ear-splitting noise? Well, he had not slept quietly, yet apparently all the more soundly for that. But what was he to do now? The next train went at seven o'clock; to catch that he would need to hurry like mad and his samples weren't even packed up, and he himself wasn't feeling particularly fresh and active. And even if he did catch the train he wouldn't avoid a row with the chief, since the firm's porter would have been waiting for the five o'clock train and would long since have reported his failure to turn up. The porter was a creature of the chief's, spineless and stupid. Well, supposing he were to say he was sick? But that would be most unpleasant and would look suspicious, since during his five years' employment he had not been ill once. The chief himself would be sure to come with the sick-insurance doctor, would reproach his parents with their son's laziness and would cut all excuses short by referring to the insurance doctor, who of course regarded all mankind as perfectly healthy malingerers. And would he be so far wrong on this occasion? Gregor really felt quite well, apart from a drowsiness that was utterly superfluous after such a long sleep, and he was even unusually hungry.

As all this was running through his mind at top speed without his being able to decide to leave his bed—the alarm clock had just struck a quarter to seven—there came a cautious tap at the door behind the head of his bed. "Gregor," said a voice—it was his mother's—"it's a quarter to seven. Hadn't you a train to catch?" That gentle voice! Gregor had a shock as he heard his own voice answering hers, unmistakably his own voice, it was true, but with a persistent horrible twittering squeak behind it like an undertone, that left the words in their clear shape only for the first moment and then rose up reverberating round them to destroy their sense, so that one could not be sure one had heard them rightly. Gregor wanted to answer at length and explain everything, but in the circumstances he confined himself to saying: "Yes, yes, thank you, Mother, I'm getting up now." The wooden door between them must have kept the change in his voice from being noticeable outside, for his mother contented herself with this statement and shuffled away. Yet this brief exchange of words had made the other members of the family aware that Gregor was still in the house, as they had not expected, and at one of the side doors his father was already knocking, gently, yet with his fist. "Gregor, Gregor," he called, "what's the matter with you?" And after a little while he called again in a deeper voice: "Gregor! Gregor!" At the other side door his sister was saying in a low, plaintive tone: "Gregor? Aren't you well? Are you needing anything?" He answered them both at once: "I'm just ready," and did his best to make his voice sound as normal as possible by enunciating the words very clearly and leaving long pauses between them. So his father went back to his breakfast, but his sister whispered: "Gregor, open the door, do." However, he was not thinking of opening the door, and felt thankful for the prudent habit he had acquired in traveling of locking all doors during the night, even at home.

His immediate attention was to get up quietly without being disturbed, to put on his clothes and above all eat his breakfast, and only then to consider what else was to be done, since in bed, he was well aware, his meditations would come to no sensible conclusion. He remembered that often enough in bed he had felt small aches and pains, probably caused by awkward postures, which had proved purely imaginary once he got up, and he looked forward eagerly to seeing this morning's delusions gradually fall away. That the change in his voice was nothing but the precursor of a severe chill, a standing ailment of commercial travelers, he had not the least possible doubt.

To get rid of the quilt was quite easy; he had only to inflate himself a little and it fell off by itself. But the next move was difficult, especially because he was so uncommonly broad. He would have needed arms and hands to hoist himself up; instead he had only the numerous little legs which never stopped waving in all directions and which he could not control in the least. When he tried to bend one of them it was the first to stretch itself straight; and did he succeed at last in making it do what he wanted, all the other legs meanwhile waved the more wildly in a high degree of unpleasant agitation. "But what's the use of lying idle in bed," said Gregor to himself.

He thought that he might get out of bed with the lower part of his body first, but this lower part, which he had not yet seen and of which he could form no clear conception, proved too difficult to move; it shifted so slowly, and when finally, almost wild with annoyance, he gathered his forces together and thrust out recklessly, he had miscalculated the direction and bumped heavily against the lower end of the bed, and the stinging pain he felt informed him that precisely this lower part of his body was at the moment probably the most sensitive.

So he tried to get the top part of himself out first, and cautiously moved his head towards the edge of the bed. That proved easy enough, and despite its breadth and mass the bulk of his body at last slowly followed the movement of his head. Still, when he finally got his head free over the edge of the bed he felt too scared to go on advancing, for after all if he let himself fall in this way it would take a miracle to keep his head from being injured. And at all costs he must not lose consciousness now, precisely now; he would rather stay in bed.

But when after a repetition of the same efforts he lay in his former position again, sighing, and watched his little legs struggling against each other more wildly than ever, if that were possible, and saw no way of bringing any order into this arbitrary confusion, he told himself again that it was impossible to stay in bed and that the most sensible course was to risk everything for the smallest hope of getting away from it. At the same time he did not forget meanwhile to remind himself that cool reflection, the coolest possible, was much better than desperate resolves. In such moments he focused his eyes as sharply as possible on the window, but, unfortunately, the prospect of the morning fog, which muffled even the other side of the narrow street, brought him little encouragement and comfort. "Seven o'clock already," he said to himself when the alarm clock chimed again, "seven o'clock already and still such a thick fog." And for a little while he lay quiet, breathing lightly, as if perhaps expecting such complete repose to restore all things to their real and normal condition.

But then he said to himself: "Before it strikes a quarter past seven I must be quite out of this bed, without fail. Anyhow, by that time someone will have come from the office to ask for me, since it opens before seven." And he set himself to rocking his whole body at once in a regular rhythm, with the idea of swinging it out of the bed. If he tipped himself out in that way he could keep his head from injury by lifting it at an acute angle when he fell. His back seemed to be hard and was not likely to suffer from a fall on the carpet. His biggest worry was the loud crash he would not be able to help making, which would probably cause anxiety, if not terror, behind all the doors. Still, he must take the risk.

When he was already half out of the bed—the new method was more a game than an effort, for he needed only to hitch himself across by rocking to and fro—it struck him how simple it would be if he could get help. Two strong people—he thought of his father and the servant girl—would be amply sufficient; they would only have to thrust their arms under his convex back, lever him out of the bed, bend down with their burden and then be patient enough to let him turn himself right over on to the floor, where it was to be hoped his legs would then find their proper function. Well, ignoring the fact that the doors were all locked, ought he really to call for help? In spite of his misery he could not suppress a smile at the very idea of it.

He had got so far that he could barely keep his equilibrium when he rocked himself strongly, and he would have to nerve himself very soon for the final decision since in five minutes' time it would be a quarter past seven—when the front door bell rang. "That's someone from the office," he said to himself, and grew almost rigid, while his little legs jigged about all the faster. For a moment everything stayed quiet. "They're not going to open the door," said Gregor to himself, catching at some kind of irrational hope. But then of course the servant girl went as usual to the door with her heavy tread and opened it. Gregor needed only to hear the first good morning of the visitor to know immediately who it was—the chief clerk himself. What a fate, to be condemned to work for a firm where the smallest omission at once gave rise to the gravest suspicion! Were all employees in a body nothing but scoundrels, was there not among them one single loyal devoted man who, had he wasted only an hour or so of the firm's time in a morning, was so tormented by conscience as to be driven out of his mind and actually incapable of leaving his bed? Wouldn't it really have been sufficient to send an apprentice to inquire—if any inquiry were necessary at all—did the chief clerk himself have to come and thus indicate to the entire family, an innocent family, that this suspicious circumstance could be investigated by no one less versed in affairs than himself? And more through the agitation caused by these reflections than through any act of will Gregor swung himself out of bed with all his strength. There was a loud thump, but it was not really a crash. His fall was broken to some extent by the carpet, his back, too, was less stiff than he thought, and so there was merely a dull thud, not so very startling. Only he had not lifted his head carefully enough and had hit it; he turned it and rubbed it on the carpet in pain and irritation.

"That was something falling down in there," said the chief clerk in the next room to the left. Gregor tried to suppose to himself that something like what had happened to him today might some day happen to the chief clerk; one really could not deny that it was possible. But as if in brusque reply to this supposition the chief clerk took a couple of firm steps in the next-door room and his patent leather boots creaked. From the right-hand room his sister was whispering to inform him of the situation: "Gregor, the chief clerk's here." "I know," muttered Gregor to himself; but he didn't dare to make his voice loud enough for his sister to hear it.

"Gregor," said his father now from the left-hand room, "the chief clerk has come and wants to know why you didn't catch the early train. We don't know what to say to him. Besides, he wants to talk to you in person. So open the door, please. He will be good enough to excuse the untidiness of your room." "Good morning, Mr. Samsa," the chief clerk was calling amiably meanwhile. "He's not well," said his mother to the visitor, while his father was still speaking through the door, "he's not well, sir, believe me. What else would make him miss a train! The boy thinks about nothing but his work. It makes me almost cross the way he never goes out in the evenings; he's been here the last eight days and has stayed at home every single evening. He just sits there quietly at the table reading a newspaper or looking through railway timetables. The only amusement he gets is doing fretwork. For instance, he spent two or three evenings cutting out a little picture frame; you would be surprised to see how pretty it is; it's hanging in his room; you'll see it in a minute when Gregor opens the door. I must say I'm glad you've come, sir; we should never have got him to unlock the door by ourselves; he's so obstinate; and I'm sure he's unwell, though he wouldn't have it to be so this morning." "I'm just coming," said Gregor slowly and carefully, not moving an inch for fear of losing one word of the conversation. "I can't think of any other explanation, madam," said the chief clerk, "I hope it's nothing serious. Although on the other hand I must say that we men of business—fortunately or unfortunately—very often simply have to ignore any slight indisposition, since business must be attended to." "Well, can the chief clerk come in now?" asked Gregor's father impatiently, again knocking on the door. "No," said Gregor. In the left-hand room a painful silence followed this refusal, in the right-hand room his sister began to sob.

Why didn't his sister join the others? She was probably newly out of bed and hadn't even begun to put on her clothes yet. Well, why was she crying? Because he wouldn't get up and let the chief clerk come in, because he was in danger of losing his job, and because the chief would begin dunning his parents again for the old debts? Surely these were things one didn't need to worry about for the present. Gregor was still at home and not in the least thinking of deserting the family. At the moment, true, he was lying on the carpet and no one who knew the condition he was in could seriously expect him to admit the chief clerk. But for such a small discourtesy, which could plausibly be explained away somehow later on, Gregor could hardly be dismissed on the spot. And it seemed to Gregor that it would be much more sensible to leave him in peace for the present than to trouble him with tears and entreaties. Still, of course, their uncertainty bewildered them all and excused their behavior.

"Mr. Samsa," the chief clerk called now in a louder voice, "what's the matter with you? Here you are, barricading yourself in your room, giving only 'yes' and 'no' for answers, causing your parents a lot of unnecessary trouble and neglecting—I mention this only in passing—neglecting your business duties in an incredible fashion. I am speaking here in the name of your parents and of your chief, and I beg you quite seriously to give me an immediate and precise explanation. You amaze me, you amaze me. I thought you were a quiet, dependable person, and now all at once you seem bent on making a disgraceful exhibition of yourself. The chief did hint to me early this morning a possible explanation for your disappearance—with reference to the cash payments that were entrusted to you recently—but I almost pledged my solemn word of honor that this could not be so. But now that I see how incredibly obstinate you are, I no longer have the slightest desire to take your part at all. And your position in the firm is not so unassailable. I came with the intention of telling you all this in private, but since you are wasting my time so needlessly I don't see why your parents shouldn't hear it too. For some time past your work has been most unsatisfactory; this is not the season of the year for a business boom, of course, we admit that, but a season of the year for doing no business at all, that does not exist, Mr. Samsa, must not exist."

"But sir," cried Gregor, beside himself and in his agitation forgetting everything else, "I'm just going to open the door this very minute. A slight illness, an attack of giddiness, has kept me from getting up. I'm still lying in bed. But I feel all right again. I'm getting out of bed now. Just give me a moment or two longer! I'm not quite so well as I thought. But I'm all right, really. How a thing like that can suddenly strike one down! Only last night I was quite well, my parents can tell you, or rather I did have a slight presentiment. I must have showed some sign of it. Why didn't I report it at the office! But one always thinks that an indisposition can be got over without staying in the house. Oh sir, do spare my parents! All that you're reproaching me with now has no foundation; no one has ever said a word to me about it. Perhaps you haven't looked at the last orders I sent in. Anyhow, I can still catch the eight o'clock train, I'm much the better for my few hours' rest. Don't let me detain you here, sir; I'll be attending to business very soon, and do be good enough to tell the chief so and to make my excuses to him!"

And while all this was tumbling out pell-mell and Gregor hardly knew what he was saying, he had reached the chest quite easily, perhaps because of the practice he had had in bed, and was now trying to lever himself upright by means of it. He meant actually to open the door, actually to show himself and speak to the chief clerk; he was eager to find out what the others, after all their insistence, would say at the sight of him. If they were horrified then the responsibility was no longer his and he could stay quiet. But if they took it calmly, then he had no reason either to be upset, and could really get to the station for the eight o'clock train if he hurried. At first he slipped down a few times from the polished surface of the chest, but at length with a last heave he stood upright; he paid no more attention to the pains in the lower part of his body, however they smarted. Then he let himself fall against the back of a near-by chair, and clung with his little legs to the edges of it. That brought him into control of himself again and he stopped speaking, for now he could listen to what the chief clerk was saying.

"Did you understand a word of it?" the chief clerk was asking; "surely he can't be trying to make fools of us?" "Oh dear," cried his mother, in tears, "perhaps he's terribly ill and we're tormenting him. Grete! Grete!" she called out then. "Yes Mother?" called his sister from the other side. They were calling to each other across Gregor's room. "You must go this minute for the doctor. Gregor is ill. Go for the doctor, quick. Did you hear how he was speaking?" "That was no human voice," said the chief clerk in a voice noticeably low beside the shrillness of the mother's. "Anna! Anna!" his father was calling through the hall to the kitchen, clapping his hands, "get a locksmith at once!" And the two girls were already running through the hall with a swish of skirts—how could his sister have got dressed so quickly?— and were tearing the front door open. There was no sound of its closing again; they had evidently left it open, as one does in houses where some great misfortune has happened.

But Gregor was now much calmer. The words he uttered were no longer understandable, apparently, although they seemed clear enough to him, even clearer than before, perhaps because his ear had grown accustomed to the sound of them. Yet at any rate people now believed that something was wrong with him, and were ready to help him. The positive certainty with which these first measures had been taken comforted him. He felt himself drawn once more into the human circle and hoped for great and remarkable results from both the doctor and the locksmith, without really distinguishing precisely between them. To make his voice as clear as possible for the decisive conversation that was now imminent he coughed a little, as quietly as he could, of course, since this noise too might not sound like a human cough for all he was able to judge. In the next room meanwhile there was complete silence. Perhaps his parents were sitting at the table with the chief clerk, whispering, perhaps they were all leaning against the door and listening.

Slowly Gregor pushed the chair towards the door, then let go of it, caught hold of the door for support—the soles at the end of his little legs were somewhat sticky—and rested against it for a moment after his efforts. Then he set himself to turning the key in the lock with his mouth. It seemed, unhappily, that he hadn't really any teeth—what could he grip the key with?—but on the other hand his jaws were certainly very strong; with their help he did manage to set the key in motion, heedless of the fact that he was undoubtedly damaging them somewhere, since a brown fluid issued from his mouth, flowed over the key and dripped on the floor. "Just listen to that," said the chief clerk next door; "he's turning the key." That was a great encouragement to Gregor; but they should all have shouted encouragement to him, his father and mother too: "Go on, Gregor," they should have called out, "keep going, hold on to that key!" And in the belief that they were all following his efforts intensely, he clenched his jaws recklessly on the key with all the force at his command. As the turning of the key progressed he circled round the lock, holding on now only with his mouth, pushing on the key, as required, or pulling it down again with all the weight of his body. The louder click of the finally yielding lock literally quickened Gregor. With a deep breath of relief he said to himself: "So I didn't need the locksmith," and laid his head on the handle to open the door wide.

Since he had to pull the door towards him, he was still invisible when it was really wide open. He had to edge himself slowly round the near half of the double door, and to do it very carefully if he was not to fall plump upon his back just on the threshold. He was still carrying out this difficult manoeuvre, with no time to observe anything else, when he heard the chief clerk utter a loud "Oh!"—it sounded like a gust of wind—and now he could see the man, standing as he was nearest to the door, clapping one hand before his open mouth and slowly backing away as if driven by some invisible steady pressure. His mother—in spite of the chief clerk's being there her hair was still undone and sticking up in all directions—first clasped her hands and looked at his father, then took two steps towards Gregor and fell on the floor among her outspread skirts, her face quite hidden on her breast. His father knotted his fist with a fierce expression on his face as if he meant to knock Gregor back into his room, then looked uncertainly round the living room, covered his eyes with his hands and wept till his great chest heaved.

Gregor did not go now into the living room, but leaned against the inside of the firmly shut wing of the door, so that only half his body was visible and his head above it bending sideways to look at the others. The light had meanwhile strengthened; on the other side of the street one could see clearly a section of the endlessly long, dark gray building opposite—it was a hospital—abruptly punctuated by its row of regular windows; the rain was still falling, but only in large singly discernible and literally singly splashing drops. The breakfast dishes were set out on the table lavishly, for breakfast was the most important meal of the day to Gregor's father, who lingered it out for hours over various newspapers. Right opposite Gregor on the wall hung a photograph of himself on military service, as a lieutenant, hand on sword, a carefree smile on his face, inviting one to respect his uniform and military bearing. The door leading to the hall was open, and one could see that the front door stood open too, showing the landing beyond and the beginning of the stairs going down.

"Well," said Gregor, knowing perfectly that he was the only one who had retained any composure, "I'll put my clothes on at once, pack up my samples and start off. Will you only let me go? You see, sir, I'm not obstinate, and I'm willing to work; traveling is a hard life, but I couldn't live without it. Where are you going, sir? To the office? Yes? Will you give a true account of all this? One can be temporarily incapacitated, but that's just the moment for remembering former services and bearing in mind that later on, when the incapacity has been got over, one will certainly work with all the more industry and concentration. I'm loyally bound to serve the chief, you know that very well. Besides, I have to provide for my parents and my sister. I'm in great difficulties, but I'll get out of them again. Don't make things any worse for me than they are. Stand up for me in the firm. Travelers are not popular there, I know. People think they earn sacks of money and just have a good time. A prejudice there's no particular reason for revising. But you, sir, have a more comprehensive view of affairs than the rest of the staff, yes, let me tell you in confidence, a more comprehensive view than the chief himself, who, being the owner, lets his judgment easily be swayed against one of his employees. And you know very well that the traveler, who is never seen in the office almost the whole year round, can so easily fall a victim to gossip and ill luck and unfounded complaints, which he mostly knows nothing about, except when he comes back exhausted from his rounds, and only then suffers in person from their evil consequences, which he can no longer trace back to the original causes. Sir, sir, don't go away without a word to me to show that you think me in the right at least to some extent!"

But at Gregor's very first words the chief clerk had already backed away and only stared at him with parted lips over one twitching shoulder. And while Gregor was speaking he did not stand still one moment but stole away towards the door, without taking his eyes off Gregor, yet only an inch at a time, as if obeying some secret injunction to leave the room. He was already at the hall, and the suddenness with which he took his last step out of the living room would have made one believe he had burned the sole of his foot. Once in the hall he stretched his right arm before him towards the staircase, as if some supernatural power were waiting there to deliver him.

Gregor perceived that the chief clerk must on no account be allowed to go away in this frame of mind if his position in the firm were not to be endangered to the utmost. His parents did not understand this so well; they had convinced themselves in the course of years that Gregor was settled for life in this firm, and besides they were so occupied with their immediate troubles that all foresight had forsaken them. Yet Gregor had this foresight. The chief clerk must be detained, soothed, persuaded and finally won over; the whole future of Gregor and his family depended on it! If only his sister had been there! She was intelligent; she had begun to cry while Gregor was still lying on his back. And no doubt the chief clerk, so partial to ladies, would have been guided by her; she would have shut the door of the flat and in the hall talked him out of his horror. But she was not there, and Gregor would have to handle the situation himself. And without remembering that he was still unaware what powers of movement he possessed, without even remembering that his words in all possibility, indeed in all likelihood, would again be unintelligible, he let go of the wing of the door, pushed himself through the opening, started to walk towards the chief clerk, who was already ridiculously clinging with both hands to the railing on the landing; but immediately, as he was feeling for a support, he fell down with a little cry upon all his numerous legs. Hardly was he down when he experienced for the first time a sense of physical comfort; his legs had firm ground under them; they were completely obedient, as he noted with joy; they even strove to carry him forward in whatever direction he chose; and he was inclined to believe that a final relief from all his sufferings was at hand. But in the same moment as he found himself on the floor, rocking with suppressed eagerness to move, not far from his mother, indeed just in front of her, she, who had seemed so completely crushed, sprang all at once to her feet, her arms and fingers outspread, cried: "Help, for God's sake, help!" bent her head down as if to see Gregor better, yet on the contrary kept backing senselessly away; had quite forgotten that the laden table stood behind her; sat upon it hastily, as if in absence of mind, when she bumped into it; and seemed altogether unaware that the big coffee pot beside her was upset and pouring coffee in a flood over the carpet.

"Mother, Mother," said Gregor in a low voice, and looked up at her. The chief clerk, for the moment, had quite slipped from his mind; instead, he could not resist snapping his jaws together at the sight of the streaming coffee. That made his mother scream again, she fled from the table and fell into the arms of his father, who hastened to catch her. But Gregor had now no time to spare for his parents; the chief clerk was already on the stairs; with his chin on the banisters he was taking one last backward look. Gregor made a spring, to be as sure as possible of overtaking him; the chief clerk must have divined his intention, for he leaped down several steps and vanished; he was still yelling "Ugh!" and it echoed through the whole staircase.

Unfortunately, the flight of the chief clerk seemed completely to upset Gregor's father, who had remained relatively calm until now, for instead of running after the man himself, or at least not hindering Gregor in his pursuit, he seized in his right hand the walking stick which the chief clerk had left behind on a chair, together with a hat and greatcoat, snatched in his left hand a large newspaper from the table and began stamping his feet and flourishing the stick and the newspaper to drive Gregor back into his room. No entreaty of Gregor's availed, indeed no entreaty was even understood, however humbly he bent his head his father only stamped on the floor the more loudly. Behind his father his mother had torn open a window, despite the cold weather, and was leaning far out of it with her face in her hands. A strong draught set in from the street to the staircase, the window curtains blew in, the newspapers on the table fluttered, stray pages whisked over the floor. Pitilessly Gregor's father drove him back, hissing and crying "Shoo!" like a savage. But Gregor was quite unpracticed in walking backwards, it really was a slow business. If he only had a chance to turn round he could get back to his room at once, but he was afraid of exasperating his father by the slowness of such a rotation and at any moment the stick in his father's hand might hit him a fatal blow on the back or on the head. In the end, however, nothing else was left for him to do since to his horror he observed that in moving backwards he could not even control the direction he took; and so, keeping an anxious eye on his father all the time over his shoulder, he began to turn round as quickly as he could, which was in reality very slowly. Perhaps his father noted his good intentions, for he did not interfere except every now and then to help him in the manouevre from a distance with the point of the stick. If only he would have stopped making that unbearable hissing noise! It made Gregor quite lose his head. He had turned almost completely round when the hissing noise so distracted him that he even turned a little the wrong way again. But when at last his head was fortunately right in front of the doorway, it appeared that his body was too broad simply to get through the opening. His father, of course, in his present mood was far from thinking of such a thing as opening the other half of the door, to let Gregor have enough space. He had merely the fixed idea of driving Gregor back into his room as quickly as possible. He would never have suffered Gregor to make the circumstantial preparations for standing up on end and perhaps slipping his way through the door. Maybe he was now making more noise than ever to urge Gregor forward, as if no obstacle impeded him; to Gregor, anyhow, the noise in his rear sounded no longer like the voice of one single father; this was really no joke, and Gregor thrust himself—come what might—into the doorway. One side of his body rose up, he was tilted at an angle in the doorway, his flank was quite bruised, horrid blotches stained the white door, soon he was stuck fast and, left to himself, could not have moved at all, his legs on one side fluttered trembling in the air, those on the other were crushed painfully to the floor—when from behind his father gave him a strong push which was literally a deliverance and he flew far into the room, bleeding freely. The door was slammed behind him with the stick, and then at last there was silence.

II

Not until it was twilight did Gregor awake out of a deep sleep, more like a swoon than a sleep. He would certainly have waked up of his own accord not much later, for he felt himself sufficiently rested and well-slept, but it seemed to him as if a fleeting step and a cautious shutting of the door leading into the hall had aroused him. The electric lights in the street cast a pale sheen here and there on the ceiling and the upper surfaces of the furniture, but down below, where he lay, it was dark. Slowly, awkwardly trying out his feelers, which he now first learned to appreciate, he pushed his way to the door to see what had been happening there. His left side felt like one single long, unpleasantly tense scar, and he had actually to limp on his two rows of legs. One little leg, moreover, had been severely damaged in the course of that morning's events—it was almost a miracle that only one had been damaged—and trailed uselessly behind him.

He had reached the door before he discovered what had really drawn him to it: the smell of food. For there stood a basin filled with fresh milk in which floated little sops of white bread. He could almost have laughed with joy, since he was now still hungrier than in the morning, and he dipped his head almost over the eyes straight into the milk. But soon in disappointment he withdrew it again; not only did he find it difficult to feed because of his tender left side—and he could only feed with the palpitating collaboration of his whole body—he did not like the milk either, although milk had been his favorite drink and that was certainly why his sister had set it there for him, indeed it was almost with repulsion that he turned away from the basin and crawled back to the middle of the room.

He could see through the crack of the door that the gas was turned on in the living room, but while usually at this time his father made a habit of reading the afternoon newspaper in a loud voice to his mother and occasionally to his sister as well, not a sound was now to be heard. Well, perhaps his father had recently given up this habit of reading aloud, which his sister had mentioned so often in conversation and in her letters. But there was the same silence all around, although the flat was certainly not empty of occupants. "What a quiet life our family has been leading," said Gregor to himself, and as he sat there motionless staring into the darkness he felt great pride in the fact that he had been able to provide such a life for his parents and sister in such a fine flat. But what if all the quiet, the comfort, the contentment were now to end in horror? To keep himself from being lost in such thoughts Gregor took refuge in movement and crawled up and down the room.

Once during the long evening one of the side doors was opened a little and quickly shut again, later the other side door too; someone had apparently wanted to come in and then thought better of it. Gregor now stationed himself immediately before the living room door, determined to persuade any hesitating visitor to come in or at least to discover who it might be; but the door was not opened again and he waited in vain. In the early morning, when the doors were locked, they had all wanted to come in, now that he had opened one door and the other had apparently been opened during the day, no one came in and even the keys were on the other side of the doors.

It was late at night before the gas went out in the living room, and Gregor could easily tell that his parents and his sister had all stayed awake until then, for he could clearly hear the three of them stealing away on tiptoe. No one was likely to visit him, not until the morning, that was certain; so he had plenty of time to meditate at his leisure on how he was to arrange his life afresh. But the lofty, empty room in which he had to lie flat on the floor filled him with an apprehension he could not account for, since it had been his very own room for the past five years—and with a half-unconscious action, not without a slight feeling of shame, he scuttled under the sofa, where he felt comfortable at once, although his back was a little cramped and he could not lift his head up, and his only regret was that his body was too broad to get the whole of it under the sofa.

He stayed there all night, spending his time partly in a light slumber, from which his hunger kept waking him up with a start, and partly in worrying and sketching vague hopes, which all led to the same conclusion, that he must lie low for the present and, by exercising patience and the utmost consideration, help the family to bear the inconvenience he was bound to cause them in his present condition.

Very early in the morning, it was still almost night, Gregor had the chance to test the strength of his new resolutions, for his sister, nearly fully dressed, opened the door from the hall and peered in. She did not see him at once, yet when she caught sight of him under the sofa—well, he had to be somewhere, he couldn't have flown away, could he?—she was so startled that without being able to help it she slammed the door shut again. But as if regretting her behavior she opened the door again immediately and came in on tiptoe, as if she were visiting an invalid or even a stranger. Gregor had pushed his head forward to the very edge of the sofa and watched her. Would she notice that he had left the milk standing, and not for lack of hunger, and would she bring in some other kind of food more to his taste? If she did not do it of her own accord, he would rather starve than draw her attention to the fact, although he felt a wild impulse to dart out from under the sofa, throw himself at her feet and beg her for something to eat. But his sister at once noticed, with surprise, that the basin was still full, except for a little milk that had been spilt all around it, she lifted it immediately, not with her bare hands, true, but with a cloth and carried it away. Gregor was wildly curious to know what she would bring instead, and made various speculations about it. Yet what she actually did next, in the goodness of her heart, he could never have guessed at. To find out what he liked she brought him a whole selection of food, all set out on an old newspaper. There were old, half-decayed vegetables, bones from last night's supper covered with a white sauce that had thickened; some raisins and almonds; a piece of cheese that Gregor would have called uneatable two days ago; a dry roll of bread, a buttered roll, and a roll both buttered and salted. Besides all that, she set down again the same basin, into which she had poured some water, and which was apparently to be reserved for his exclusive use. And with fine tact, knowing that Gregor would not eat in her presence, she withdrew quickly and even turned the key, to let him understand that he could take his ease as much as he liked. Gregor's legs all whizzed towards the food. His wounds must have healed completely, moreover, for he felt no disability, which amazed him and made him reflect how more than a month ago he had cut one finger a little with a knife and had still suffered pain from the wound only the day before yesterday. Am I less sensitive now? he thought, and sucked greedily at the cheese, which above all the other edibles attracted him at once and strongly. One after another and with tears of satisfaction in his eyes he quickly devoured the cheese, the vegetables and the sauce; the fresh food, on the other hand, had no charms for him, he could not even stand the smell of it and actually dragged away to some little distance the things he could eat. He had long finished his meal and was only lying lazily on the same spot when his sister turned the key slowly as a sign for him to retreat. That roused him at once, although he was nearly asleep, and he hurried under the sofa again. But it took considerable self-control for him to stay under the sofa, even for the short time his sister was in the room, since the large meal had swollen his body somewhat and he was so cramped he could hardly breathe. Slight attacks of breathlessness afflicted him and his eyes were starting a little out of his head as he watched his unsuspecting sister sweeping together with a broom not only the remains of what he had eaten but even the things he had not touched, as if these were now of no use to anyone, and hastily shoveling it all into a bucket, which she covered with a wooden lid and carried away. Hardly had she turned her back when Gregor came from under the sofa and stretched and puffed himself out.

In this manner Gregor was fed, once in the early morning while his parents and the servant girl were still asleep, and a second time after they had all had their midday dinner, for then his parents took a short nap and the servant girl could be sent out on some errand or other by his sister. Not that they would have wanted him to starve, of course, but perhaps they could not have borne to know more about his feeding than from hearsay, perhaps too his sister wanted to spare them such little anxieties wherever possible, since they had quite enough to bear as it was.

Under what pretext the doctor and the locksmith had been got rid of on that first morning Gregor could not discover, for since what he said was not understood by the others it never struck any of them, not even his sister, that he could understand what they said, and so whenever his sister came into his room he had to content himself with hearing her utter only a sigh now and then and an occasional appeal to the saints. Later on, when she had got a little used to the situation—of course she could never get completely used to it—she sometimes threw out a remark which was kindly meant or could be so interpreted. "Well, he liked his dinner today," she would say when Gregor had made a good clearance of his food; and when he had not eaten, which gradually happened more and more often, she would say almost sadly: "Everything's been left standing again."

But although Gregor could get no news directly, he overheard a lot from the neighboring rooms, and as soon as voices were audible, he would run to the door of the room concerned and press his whole body against it. In the first few days especially there was no conversation that did not refer to him somehow, even if only indirectly. For two whole days there were family consultations at every mealtime about what should be done; but also between meals the same subject was discussed, for there were always at least two members of the family at home, since no one wanted to be alone in the flat and to leave it quite empty was unthinkable. And on the very first of these days the household cook—it was not quite clear what and how much she knew of the situation—went down on her knees to his mother and begged leave to go, and when she departed, a quarter of an hour later, gave thanks for her dismissal with tears in her eyes as if for the greatest benefit that could have been conferred on her, and without any prompting swore a solemn oath that she would never say a single word to anyone about what had happened.

Now Gregor's sister had to cook too, helping her mother; true, the cooking did not amount to much, for they ate scarcely anything. Gregor was always hearing one of the family vainly urging another to eat and getting no answer but: "Thanks, I've had all I want," or something similar. Perhaps they drank nothing either. Time and again his sister kept asking his father if he wouldn't like some beer and offered kindly to go and fetch it herself, and when he made no answer suggested that she could ask the concierge to fetch it, so that he need feel no sense of obligation, but then a round "No" came from his father and no more was said about it.

In the course of that very first day Gregor's father explained the family's financial position and prospects to both his mother and his sister. Now and then he rose from the table to get some voucher or memorandum out of the small safe he had rescued from the collapse of his business five years earlier. One could hear him opening the complicated lock and rustling papers out and shutting it again. This statement made by his father was the first cheerful information Gregor had heard since his imprisonment. He had been of the opinion that nothing at all was left over from his father's business, at least his father had never said anything to the contrary, and of course he had not asked him directly. At that time Gregor's sole desire was to do his utmost to help the family to forget as soon as possible the catastrophe which had overwhelmed the business and thrown them all into a state of complete despair. And so he had set to work with unusual ardor and almost overnight had become a commercial traveler instead of a little clerk, with of course much greater chances of earning money, and his success was immediately translated into good round coin which he could lay on the table for his amazed and happy family. These had been fine times, and they had never recurred, at least not with the same sense of glory, although later on Gregor had earned so much money that he was able to meet the expenses of the whole household and did so. They had simply got used to it, both the family and Gregor; the money was gratefully accepted and gladly given, but there was no special uprush of warm feeling. With his sister alone had he remained intimate, and it was a secret plan of his that she, who loved music, unlike himself, and could play movingly on the violin, should be sent next year to study at the Conservatorium, despite the great expense that would entail, which must be made up in some other way. During his brief visits home the Conservatorium was often mentioned in the talks he had with his sister, but always merely as a beautiful dream which could never come true, and his parents discouraged even those innocent references to it; yet Gregor had made up his mind firmly about it and meant to announce the fact with due solemnity on Christmas Day.

Such were the thoughts, completely futile in his present condition, that went through his head as he stood clinging upright to the door and listening. Sometimes out of sheer weariness he had to give up listening and let his head fall negligently against the door, but he always had to pull himself together again at once, for even the slight sound his head made was audible next door and brought all conversation to a stop. "What can he be doing now?" his father would say after a while, obviously turning towards the door, and only then would the interrupted conversation gradually be set going again.

Gregor was now informed as amply as he could wish—for his father tended to repeat himself in his explanations, partly because it was a long time since he had handled such matters and partly because his mother could not always grasp things at once—that a certain amount of investments, a very small amount it was true, had survived the wreck of their fortunes and had even increased a little because the dividends had not been touched meanwhile. And besides that, the money Gregor brought home every month—he had kept only a few dollars for himself—had never been quite used up and now amounted to a small capital sum. Behind the door Gregor nodded his head eagerly, rejoiced at this evidence of unexpected thrift and foresight. True, he could really have paid off some more of his father's debts to the chief with his extra money, and so brought much nearer the day on which he could quit his job, but doubtless it was better the way his father had arranged it.

Yet this capital was by no means sufficient to let the family live on the interest of it; for one year, perhaps, or at the most two, they could live on the principal, that was all. It was simply a sum that ought not to be touched and should be kept for a rainy day; money for living expenses would have to be earned. Now his father was still hale enough but an old man, and he had done no work for the past five years and could not be expected to do much; during these five years, the first years of leisure in his laborious though unsuccessful life, he had grown rather fat and become sluggish. And Gregor's old mother, how was she to earn a living with her asthma, which troubled her even when she walked through the flat and kept her lying on a sofa every other day panting for breath beside an open window? And was his sister to earn her bread, she who was still a child of seventeen and whose life hitherto had been so pleasant, consisting as it did in dressing herself nicely, sleeping long, helping in the housekeeping, going out to a few modest entertainments and above all playing the violin? At first whenever the need for earning money was mentioned Gregor let go his hold on the door and threw himself down on the cool leather sofa beside it, he felt so hot with shame and grief.

Often he just lay there the long nights through without sleeping at all, scrabbling for long hours on the leather. Or he nerved himself to the great effort of pushing an armchair to the window, then crawled up over the window sill and, braced against the chair, leaned against the window panes, obviously in some recollection of the sense of freedom that looking out of a window always used to give him. For in reality day by day things that were even a little way off were growing dimmer to his sight; the hospital across the street, which he used to execrate for being all too often before his eyes, was now quite beyond his range of vision, and if he had not known that he lived in Charlotte Street, a quiet street but still a city street, he might have believed that his window gave on a desert waste where gray sky and gray land blended indistinguishably into each other. His quick-witted sister only needed to observe twice that the armchair stood by the window; after that whenever she had tidied the room she always pushed the chair back to the same place at the window and even left the inner casements open.

If he could have spoken to her and thanked her for all she had to do for him, he could have borne her ministrations better; as it was, they oppressed him. She certainly tried to make as light as possible of whatever was disagreeable in her task, and as time went on she succeeded, of course, more and more, but time brought more enlightenment to Gregor too. The very way she came in distressed him. Hardly was she in the room when she rushed to the window, without even taking time to shut the door, careful as she was usually to shield the sight of Gregor's room from the others, and as if she were almost suffocating tore the casements open with hasty fingers, standing then in the open draught for a while even in the bitterest cold and drawing deep breaths. This noisy scurry of hers upset Gregor twice a day; he would crouch trembling under the sofa all the time, knowing quite well that she would certainly have spared him such a disturbance had she found it at all possible to stay in his presence without opening the window.

On one occasion, about a month after Gregor's metamorphosis, when there was surely no reason for her to be still startled at his appearance, she came a little earlier than usual and found him gazing out the window, quite motionless, and thus well placed to look like a bogey. Gregor would not have been surprised had she not come in at all, for she could not immediately open the window while he was there, but not only did she retreat, she jumped back as if in alarm and banged the door shut; a stranger might well have thought that he had been lying in wait for her there meaning to bite her. Of course he hid himself under the sofa at once, but he had to wait until midday before she came again, and seemed more ill at ease than usual. This made him realize how repulsive the sight of him still was to her, and that it was bound to go on being repulsive, and what an effort it must cost her not to run away even from the sight of the small portion of his body that stuck out from under the sofa. In order to spare her that, therefore, one day he carried a sheet on his back to the sofa—it cost him four hours' labor—and arranged it there in such a way as to hide him completely, so that even if she were to bend down she could not see him. Had she considered the sheet unnecessary, she would certainly have stripped it off the sofa again, for it was clear enough that this curtaining and confining of himself was not likely to conduce Gregor's comfort, but she left it where it was, and Gregor even fancied that he caught a thankful glance from her eye when he lifted the sheet carefully a very little with his head to see how she was taking the new arrangement.

For the first fortnight his parents could not bring themselves to the point of entering his room, and he often heard them expressing their appreciation of his sister's activities, whereas formerly they had frequently scolded her for being as they thought a somewhat useless daughter. But now, both of them often waited outside the door, his father and his mother, while his sister tidied his room, and as soon as she came out she had to tell them exactly how things were in the room, what Gregor had eaten, how he had conducted himself this time and whether there was not perhaps some slight improvement in his condition. His mother, moreover, began relatively soon to want to visit him, but his father and sister dissuaded her at first with arguments which Gregor listened to very attentively and altogether approved. Later, however, she had to be held back by main force, and when she cried out: "Do let me in to Gregor, he is my unfortunate son! Can't you understand that I must go in to him?" Gregor thought that it might be well to have her come in, not every day, of course, but perhaps once a week; she understood things, after all, much better than his sister, who was only a child despite the efforts she was making and had perhaps taken on so difficult a task merely out of childish thoughtlessness.

Gregor's desire to see his mother was soon fulfilled. During the daytime he did not want to show himself at the window, out of consideration for his parents, but he could not crawl very far around the few square yards of floor space he had, nor could he bear lying quietly at rest all during the night, while he was fast losing any interest he had ever taken in food, so that for mere recreation he had formed the habit of crawling crisscross over the walls and ceiling. He especially enjoyed hanging suspended from the ceiling; it was much better than lying on the floor; one could breathe more freely; one's body swung and rocked lightly; and in the almost blissful absorption induced by this suspension it could happen to his own surprise that he let go and fell plump on the floor. Yet he now had his body much better under control than formerly, and even such a big fall did him no harm. His sister at once remarked the new distraction Gregor had found for himself—he left traces behind him of the sticky stuff on his soles wherever he crawled—and she got the idea in her head of giving him as wide a field as possible to crawl in and of removing the pieces of furniture that hindered him, above all the chest of drawers and the writing desk. But that was more than she could manage all by herself; she did not dare ask her father to help her; and as for the servant girl, a young creature of sixteen who had had the courage to stay on after the cook's departure, she could not be asked to help, for she had begged as an especial favor that she might keep the kitchen door locked and open it only on a definite summons; so there was nothing left but to apply to her mother at an hour when her father was out. And the old lady did come, with exclamations of joyful eagerness, which, however, died away at the door of Gregor's room. Gregor's sister, of course, went in first, to see that everything was in order before letting his mother enter. In great haste Gregor pulled the sheet lower and rucked it more in folds so that it really looked as if it had been thrown accidentally over the sofa. And this time he did not peer out from under it; he renounced the pleasure of seeing his mother on this occasion and was only glad that she had come at all. "Come in, he's out of sight," said his sister, obviously leading her mother in by the hand. Gregor could now hear the two women struggling to shift the heavy old chest from its place, and his sister claiming the greater part of the labor for herself, without listening to the admonitions of her mother who feared she might overstrain herself. It took a long time. After at least a quarter of an hour's tugging his mother objected that the chest had better be left where it was, for in the first place it was too heavy and could never be got out before his father came home, and standing in the middle of the room like that it would only hamper Gregor's movements, while in the second place it was not at all certain that removing the furniture would be doing a service to Gregor. She was inclined to think to the contrary; the sight of the naked walls made her own heart heavy, and why shouldn't Gregor have the same feeling, considering that he had been used to his furniture for so long and might feel forlorn without it. "And doesn't it look," she concluded in a low voice—in fact she had been almost whispering all the time as if to avoid letting

Gregor, whose exact whereabouts she did not know, hear even the tones of her voice, for she was convinced that he could not understand her words—"doesn't it look as if we were showing him, by taking away his furniture, that we have given up hope of his ever getting better and are just leaving him coldly to himself? I think it would be best to keep his room exactly as it has always been, so that when he comes back to us he will find everything unchanged and be able all the more easily to forget what has happened in between."

On hearing these words from his mother Gregor realized that the lack of all direct human speech for the past two months together with the monotony of family life must have confused his mind, otherwise he could not account for the fact that he had quite earnestly looked forward to having his room emptied of furnishing. Did he really want his warm room, so comfortably fitted with old family furniture, to be turned into a naked den in which he would certainly be able to crawl unhampered in all directions but at the price of shedding simultaneously all recollection of his human background? He had indeed been so near the brink of forgetfulness that only the voice of his mother, which he had not heard for so long, had drawn him back from it. Nothing should be taken out of his room; everything must stay as it was; he could not dispense with the good influence of the furniture on his state of mind; and even if the furniture did hamper him in his senseless crawling round and round, that was no drawback but a great advantage.

Unfortunately his sister was of the contrary opinion; she had grown accustomed, and not without reason, to consider herself an expert in Gregor's affairs as against her parents, and so her mother's advice was now enough to make her determined on the removal not only of the chest and the writing desk, which had been her first intention, but of all the furniture except the indispensable sofa. This determination was not, of course, merely the outcome of childish recalcitrance and of the self-confidence she had recently developed so unexpectedly and at such cost; she had in fact perceived that Gregor needed a lot of space to crawl about in, while on the other hand he never used the furniture at all, so far as could be seen. Another factor might have been also the enthusiastic temperament of an adolescent girl, which seeks to indulge itself on every opportunity and which now tempted Grete to exaggerate the horror of her brother's circumstances in order that she might do all the more for him. In a room where Gregor lorded it all alone over empty walls no one save herself was likely ever to set foot.

And so she was not to be moved from her resolve by her mother who seemed moreover to be ill at ease in Gregor's room and therefore unsure of herself, was soon reduced to silence and helped her daughter as best she could to push the chest outside. Now, Gregor could do without the chest, if need be, but the writing desk he must retain. As soon as the two women had got the chest out of his room, groaning as they pushed it, Gregor stuck his head out from under the sofa to see how he might intervene as kindly and cautiously as possible. But as bad luck would have it, his mother was the first to return, leaving Grete clasping the chest in the room next door where she was trying to shift it all by herself, without of course moving it from the spot. His mother however was not accustomed to the sight of him, it might sicken her and so in alarm Gregor backed quickly to the other end of the sofa, yet could not prevent the sheet from swaying a little in front. That was enough to put her on the alert. She paused, stood still for a moment and then went back to Grete.

Although Gregor kept reassuring himself that nothing out of the way was happening, but only a few bits of furniture were being changed around, he soon had to admit that all this trotting to and fro of the two women, their little ejaculations and the scraping of furniture along the floor affected him like a vast disturbance coming from all sides at once, and however much he tucked in his head and legs and cowered to the very floor he was bound to confess that he would not be able to stand it for long. They were clearing his room out; taking away everything he loved; the chest in which he kept his fret saw and other tools was already dragged off; they were now loosening the writing desk which had almost sunk into the floor, the desk at which he had done all his homework when he was at the commercial academy, at the grammar school before that, and, yes, even at the primary school—he had no more time to waste in weighing the good intentions of the two women, whose existence he had by now forgotten, for they were so exhausted that they were laboring in silence and nothing could be heard but the heavy scuffling of their feet.

And so he rushed out—the women were just leaning against the writing desk in the next room to give themselves a breather—and four times changed his direction, since he really did not know what to rescue first, then on the wall opposite, which was already otherwise cleared, he was struck by the picture of the lady muffled in so much fur and quickly crawled up to it and pressed himself to the glass, which was a good surface to hold on to and comforted his hot belly. This picture at least, which was entirely hidden beneath him, was going to be removed by nobody. He turned his head towards the door of the living room so as to observe the women when they came back.

They had not allowed themselves much of a rest and were already coming; Grete had twined her arm round her mother and was almost supporting her. "Well, what shall we take now?" said Grete, looking round. Her eyes met Gregor's from the wall. She kept her composure, presumably because of her mother, bent her head down to her mother, to keep her from looking up, and said, although in a fluttering, unpremeditated voice: "Come, hadn't we better go back to the living room for a moment?" Her intentions were clear enough to Gregor, she wanted to bestow her mother in safety and then chase him down from the wall. Well, just let her try it! He clung to his picture and would not give it up. He would rather fly in Grete's face.

But Grete's words had succeeded in disquieting her mother, who took a step to one side, caught sight of the huge brown mass on the flowered wallpaper, and before she was really conscious that what she saw was Gregor screamed in a loud, hoarse voice: "Oh God, oh God!" fell with outspread arms over the sofa as if giving up and did not move. "Gregor!" cried his sister, shaking her fist and glaring at him. This was the first time she had directly addressed him since his metamorphosis. She ran into the next room for some aromatic essence with which to rouse her mother from her fainting fit. Gregor wanted to help too—there was still time to rescue the picture—but he was stuck fast to the glass and had to tear himself loose; he then ran after his sister into the next room as if he could advise her, as he used to do; but then had to stand helplessly behind her; she meanwhile searched among various small bottles and when she turned round started in alarm at the sight of him; one bottle fell on the floor and broke; a splinter of glass cut Gregor's face and some kind of corrosive medicine splashed him; without pausing a moment longer Grete gathered up all the bottles she could carry and ran to her mother with them; she banged the door shut with her foot. Gregor was now cut off from his mother, who was perhaps nearly dying because of him; he dared not open the door for fear of frightening away his sister, who had to stay with her mother; there was nothing he could do but wait; and harassed by self-reproach and worry he began now to crawl to and fro, over everything, walls, furniture, and ceiling, and finally in his despair, when the noble room seemed to be reeling round him, fell down on to the middle of the big table.

A little while lapsed. Gregor was still lying there feebly and all around was quiet, perhaps that was a good omen. Then the doorbell rang. The servant girl was of course locked in her kitchen, and Grete would have to open the door. It was his father. "What's been happening?" were his first words; Grete's face must have told him everything. Grete answered in a muffled voice, apparently hiding her head on his breast: "Mother has been fainting, but she's better now. Gregor's broken loose." "Just what I expected," said his father, "just what I've been telling you, but you women would never listen." It was clear to Gregor that his father had taken the worst interpretation of Grete's all too brief statement and was assuming that Gregor had been guilty of some violent act. Therefore Gregor must now try to propitiate his father, since he had neither time nor means for an explanation. And so he fled to the door of his own room and crouched against it, to let his father see as soon as he came in from the hall that his son had the good intention of getting back into his room immediately and that it was not necessary to drive him there, but that if only the door were opened he would disappear at once.

Yet his father was not in the mood to perceive such fine distinctions. "Ah!" he cried as soon as he appeared, in a tone which sounded at once angry and exultant. Gregor drew his head back from the door and lifted it to look at his father. Truly, this was not the father he had imagined to himself; admittedly he had been too absorbed of late in his new recreation of crawling over the ceiling to take the same interest as before in what was happening elsewhere in the flat, and he ought really to be prepared for some changes. And yet, and yet, could that be his father? The man who used to lie wearily sunk in bed whenever Gregor set out on a business journey; who welcomed him back of an evening lying in a long chair in a dressing gown; who could not really rise to his feet but only lifted his arms in greeting, and on the rare occasions when he did go out with his family, on one or two Sundays a year and on high holidays, walked between Gregor and his mother, who were slow walkers anyhow, even more slowly than they did, muffled in his old greatcoat, shuffling laboriously forward with the help of his crook-handled stick which he set down most cautiously at every step and, whenever he wanted to say anything, nearly always came to a full stop and gathered his escort around him? Now he was standing there in fine shape; dressed in a smart blue uniform with gold buttons, such as bank messengers wear; his strong double chin bulged over the stiff high collar of his jacket; from under his bushy eyebrows his black eyes darted fresh and penetrating glances; his onetime tangled white hair had been combed flat on either side of a shining and carefully exact parting. He pitched his cap, which bore a gold monogram, probably the badge of some bank, in a wide sweep across the whole room on to a sofa and with the tail-ends of his jacket thrown back, his hands in his trouser pockets, advanced with a grim visage towards Gregor. Likely enough he did not himself know what he meant to do; at any rate he lifted his feet uncommonly high, and Gregor was dumbfounded at the enormous size of his shoe soles. But Gregor could not risk standing up to him, aware as he had been from the very first day of his new life that his father believed only the severest measures suitable for dealing with him. And so he ran before his father, stopping when he stopped and scuttling forward again when his father made any kind of move. In this way they circled the room several times without anything decisive happening; indeed the whole operation did not even look like a pursuit because it was carried out so slowly. And so Gregor did not leave the floor, for he feared that his father might take as a piece of peculiar wickedness any excursion of his over the walls or the ceiling. All the same, he could not stay this course much longer, for while his father took one step he had to carry out a whole series of movements. He was already beginning to feel breathless, just as in his former life his lungs had not been very dependable. As he was staggering along, trying to concentrate his energy on running, hardly keeping his eyes open; in his dazed state never even thinking of any other escape than simply going forward; and having almost forgotten that the walls were free to him, which in this room were well provided with finely carved pieces of furniture full of knobs and crevices—suddenly something lightly flung landed close behind him and rolled before him. It was an apple; a second apple followed immediately; Gregor came to a stop in alarm; there was no point in running on, for his father was determined to bombard him. He had filled his pockets with fruit from the dish on the sideboard and was now shying apple after apple, without taking particularly good aim for the moment. The small red apples rolled about the floor as if magnetized and cannoned into each other. An apple thrown without much force grazed Gregor's back and glanced off harmlessly. But another following immediately landed right on his back and sank in; Gregor wanted to drag himself forward, as if this startling, incredible pain could be left behind him; but he felt as if nailed to the spot and flattened himself out in a complete derangement of all his senses. With his last conscious look he saw the door of his room being torn open and his mother rushing out ahead of his screaming sister, in her underbodice, for her daughter had loosened her clothing to let her breathe more freely and recover from her swoon, he saw his mother rushing towards his father, leaving one after another behind behind her on the floor her loosened petticoats, stumbling over her petticoats straight to his father and embracing him, in complete union with him—but here Gregor's sight began to fail—with her hands clasped round his father's neck as she begged for her son's life.

III

The serious injury done to Gregor, which disabled him for more than a month—the apple went on sticking in his body as a visible reminder, since no one bothered to remove it—seemed to have made even his father recollect that Gregor was a member of the family, despite his present unfortunate and repulsive shape, and ought not to be treated as an enemy, that, on the contrary, family duty required the suppression of disgust and the exercise of patience, nothing but patience.

And although his injury had impaired, probably for ever, his power of movement, and for the time being it took him long, long minutes to creep across his room like an old invalid—there was no question now of crawling up the wall—yet in his own opinion he was sufficiently compensated for this worsening of his condition by the fact that towards evening the living-room door, which he used to watch intently for an hour or two beforehand, was always thrown open, so that lying in the darkness of his room, invisible to the family, he could see them all at the lamp-lit table and listen to their talk, by general consent as it were, very different from his earlier eavesdropping.

True, their intercourse lacked the lively character of former times, which he had always called to mind with a certain wistfulness in the small hotel bedrooms where he had been wont to throw himself down, tired out, on damp bedding. They were now mostly very silent. Soon after supper his father would fall asleep in his armchair; his mother and sister would admonish each other to be silent; his mother, bending low over the lamp, stitched at fine sewing for an underwear firm; his sister, who had taken a job as a salesgirl, was learning shorthand and French in the evenings on the chance of bettering herself. Sometimes his father woke up, and as if quite unaware that he had been sleeping said to his mother: "What a lot of sewing you're doing today!" and at once fell asleep again, while the two women exchanged a tired smile.

With a kind of mulishness his father persisted in keeping his uniform on even in the house; his dressing gown hung uselessly on its peg and he slept fully dressed where he sat, as if he were ready for service at any moment and even here only at the beck and call of his superior. As a result, his uniform, which was not brand-new to start with, began to look dirty, despite all the loving care of the mother and sister to keep it clean, and Gregor often spent whole evenings gazing at the many greasy spots on the garment, gleaming with gold buttons always in a high state of polish, in which the old man sat sleeping in extreme discomfort and yet quite peacefully.

As soon as the clock struck ten his mother tried to rouse his father with gentle words and to persuade him after that to get into bed, for sitting there he could not have a proper sleep and that was what he needed most, since he had to go to duty at six. But with the mulishness that had obsessed him since he became a bank messenger he always insisted on staying longer at the table, although he regularly fell asleep again and in the end only with the greatest trouble could be got out of his armchair and into his bed. However insistently Gregor's mother and sister kept urging him with gentle reminders, he would go on slowly shaking his head for a quarter of an hour, keeping his eyes shut, and refuse to get to his feet. The mother plucked at his sleeve, whispering endearments in his ear, the sister left her lessons to come to her mother's help, but Gregor's father was not to be caught. He would only sink down deeper in his chair. Not until the two women hoisted him up by the armpits did he open his eyes and look at them both, one after the other, usually with the remark: "This is a life. This is the peace and quiet of my old age." And leaning on the two of them he would heave himself up, with difficulty, as if he were a great burden to himself, suffer them to lead him as far as the door and then wave them off and go on alone, while the mother abandoned her needlework and the sister her pen in order to run after him and help him farther.

Who could find time, in this overworked and tired-out family, to bother about Gregor more than was absolutely needful? The household was reduced more and more; the servant girl was turned off; a gigantic bony charwoman with white hair flying round her head came in morning and evening to do the rough work; everything else was done by Gregor's mother, as well as great piles of sewing. Even various family ornaments, which his mother and sister used to wear with pride at parties and celebrations, had to be sold, as Gregor discovered of an evening from hearing them all discuss the prices obtained. But what they lamented most was the fact that they could not leave the flat which was much too big for their present circumstances, because they could not think of any way to shift Gregor. Yet Gregor saw well enough that consideration for him was not the main difficulty preventing the removal, for they could have easily shifted him in some suitable box with a few air holes in it; what really kept them from moving into another flat was rather their own complete hopelessness and the belief that they had been singled out for a misfortune such as had never happened to any of their relations or acquaintances. They fulfilled to the uttermost all that the world demands of poor people, the father fetched breakfast for the small clerks in the bank, the mother devoted her energy to making underwear for strangers, the sister trotted to and fro behind the counter at the behest of customers, but more than this they had not the strength to do. And the wound in Gregor's back began to nag at him afresh when his mother and sister, after getting his father into bed, came back again, left their work lying, drew close to each other and sat cheek by cheek; when his mother, pointing towards his room, said: "Shut that door now, Grete," and he was left again in darkness, while next door the women mingled their tears or perhaps sat dry-eyed staring at the table.

Gregor hardly slept at all by night or by day. He was often haunted by the idea that next time the door opened he would take the family's affairs in hand again just as he used to do; once more, after this long interval, there appeared in his thoughts the figures of the chief and the chief clerk, the commercial travelers and the apprentices, the porter who was so dull-witted, two or three friends in other firms, a chambermaid in one of the rural hotels, a sweet and fleeting memory, a cashier in a milliner's shop, whom he had wooed earnestly but too slowly—they all appeared, together with strangers or people he had quite forgotten, but instead of helping him and his family they were one and all unapproachable and he was glad when they vanished. At other times he would not be in the mood to bother about his family, he was only filled with rage at the way they were neglecting him, and although he had no clear idea of what he might care to eat he would make plans for getting into the larder to take the food that was after all his due, even if he were not hungry. His sister no longer took thought to bring him what might especially please him, but in the morning and at noon before she went to business hurriedly pushed into his room with her foot any food that was available, and in the evening cleared it out again with one sweep of the broom, heedless of whether it had been merely tasted, or—as most frequently happened—left untouched. The cleaning of his room, which she now always did in the evenings, could not have been more hastily done. Streaks of dirt stretched along the walls, here and there lay balls of dust and filth. At first Gregor used to station himself in some particularly filthy corner when his sister arrived, in order to reproach her with it, so to speak. But he could have sat there for weeks without getting her to make any improvements; she could see the dirt as well as he did, but she had simply made up her mind to leave it alone. And yet, with a touchiness that was new to her, which seemed anyhow to have infected the whole family, she jealously guarded her claim to be the sole caretaker of Gregor's room. His mother once subjected his room to a thorough cleaning, which was achieved only by means of several buckets of water—all this dampness of course upset Gregor too and he lay widespread, sulky and motionless on the sofa—but she was well punished for it. Hardly had his sister noticed the changed aspect of his room that evening than she rushed in high dudgeon into the living room and, despite the imploringly raised hands of her mother, burst into a storm of weeping, while her parents—her father had of course been startled out of his chair—looked on at first in helpless amazement; then they too began to go into action; the father reproached the mother on his right for not having left the cleaning of Gregor's room to his sister; shrieked at the sister on his left that never again was she allowed to clean Gregor's room; while the mother tried to pull the father into his bedroom, since he was beyond himself with agitation; the sister, shaken with sobs, then beat upon the table with her small fists; and Gregor hissed loudly with rage because not one of them thought of shutting the door to spare him such a spectacle and so much noise.

Still, even if the sister, exhausted by her daily work, had grown tired of looking after Gregor as she did formerly, there was no need for his mother's intervention or for Gregor's being neglected at all. The charwoman was there. This old widow, whose strong bony frame had enabled her to survive the worst a long life could offer, by no means recoiled from Gregor. Without being in the least curious she had once by chance opened the door of his room and at the sight of Gregor, who, taken by surprise, began to rush to and fro although no one was chasing him, merely stood there with her arms folded. From that time she never failed to open his door a little for a moment, morning and evening, to have a look at him. At first she even used to call him to her, with words which apparently she took to be friendly, such as: "Come along, then, you old dung beetle!" or "Look at the old dung beetle, then!" To such allocutions Gregor made no answer, but stayed motionless where he was, as if the door had never been opened. Instead of being allowed to disturb him so senselessly whenever the whim took her, she should rather have been ordered to clean out his room daily, that charwoman! Once, early in the morning—heavy rain was lashing on the windowpanes, perhaps a sign that spring was on the way—

Gregor was so exasperated when she began addressing him again that he ran at her, as if to attack her, although slowly and feebly enough. But the charwoman instead of showing fright merely lifted high a chair that happened to be beside the door, and as she stood there with her mouth wide open it was clear that she meant to shut it only when she brought the chair down on Gregor's back. "So you're not coming any nearer?" she asked, as Gregor turned away again, and quietly put the chair back into the corner.

Gregor was now eating hardly anything. Only when he happened to pass the food laid out for him did he take a bit of something in his mouth as a pastime, kept it there for an hour at a time and usually spat it out again. At first he thought it was chagrin over the state of his room that prevented him from eating, yet he soon got used to the various changes in his room. It had become a habit in the family to push into his room things there was no room for elsewhere, and there were plenty of these now, since one of the rooms had been let to three lodgers. Three serious gentlemen—all three of them with full beards, as Gregor once observed through a crack in the door—had a passion for order, not only in their own room but, since they were now members of the household, in all its arrangements, especially in the kitchen. Superfluous, not to say dirty, objects they could not bear. Besides, they had brought with them most of the furnishings they needed. For this reason many things could be dispensed with that it was no use trying to sell but that should not be thrown away either. All of them found their way into Gregor's room. The ash can likewise and the kitchen garbage can. Anything that was not needed for the moment was simply flung into Gregor's room by the charwoman, who did everything in a hurry; fortunately Gregor usually saw only the object, whatever it was, and the hand that held it. Perhaps she intended to take the things away again as time and opportunity offered, or to collect them until she could throw them all out in a heap, but in fact they just lay wherever she happened to throw them, except when Gregor pushed his way through the junk heap and shifted it somewhat, at first out of necessity, because he had not room enough to crawl, but later with increasing enjoyment, although after such excursions, being sad and weary to death, he would lie motionless for hours. And since the lodgers often ate their supper at home in the common living room, the living-room door stayed shut many an evening, yet Gregor reconciled himself quite easily to the shutting of the door, for often enough on evenings when it was opened he had disregarded it entirely and lain in the darkest corner of his room, quite unnoticed by the family. But on one occasion the charwoman left the door open a little and it stayed ajar even when the lodgers came in for supper and the lamp was lit. They set themselves at the top end of the table where formerly Gregor and his father and mother had eaten their meals, unfolded their napkins and took knife and fork in hand. At once his mother appeared in the other doorway with a dish of meat and close behind her his sister with a dish of potatoes piled high. The food steamed with a thick vapor. The lodgers bent over the food set before them as if to scrutinize it before eating, in fact the man in the middle, who seemed to pass for an authority with the other two, cut a piece of meat as it lay on the dish, obviously to discover if it were tender or should be sent back to the kitchen. He showed satisfaction, and Gregor's mother and sister, who had been watching anxiously, breathed freely and began to smile.

The family itself took its meals in the kitchen. None the less, Gregor's father came into the living room before going into the kitchen and with one prolonged bow, cap in hand, made a round of the table. The lodgers all stood up and murmured something in their beards. When they were alone again they ate their food in almost complete silence. It seemed remarkable to Gregor that among the various noises coming from the table he could always distinguish the sound of their masticating teeth, as if this were a sign to Gregor that one needed teeth in order to eat, and that with toothless jaws even of the finest make one could do nothing. "I'm hungry enough," said Gregor sadly to himself, "but not for that kind of food. How these lodgers are stuffing themselves, and here am I dying of starvation!"

On that very evening—during the whole of his time there Gregor could not remember ever having heard the violin—the sound of violin-playing came from the kitchen. The lodgers had already finished their supper, the one in the middle had brought out a newspaper and given the other two a page apiece, and now they were leaning back at ease reading and smoking. When the violin began to play they pricked up their ears, got to their feet, and went on tiptoe to the hall door where they stood huddled together. Their movements must have been heard in the kitchen, for Gregor's father called out: "Is the violin-playing disturbing you, gentlemen? It can be stopped at once." "On the contrary," said the middle lodger, "could not Fräulein Samsa come and play in this room, beside us, where it is much more convenient and comfortable?" "Oh certainly," cried Gregor's father, as if he were the violin-player. The lodgers came back into the living room and waited. Presently Gregor's father arrived with the music stand, his mother carrying the music and his sister with the violin. His sister quietly made everything ready to start playing; his parents, who had never let rooms before and so had an exaggerated idea of the courtesy due to lodgers, did not venture to sit down on their own chairs; his father leaned against the door, the right hand thrust between two buttons of his livery coat, which was formally buttoned up; but his mother was offered a chair by one of the lodgers and, since she left the chair just where he had happened to put it, sat down in a corner to one side.

Gregor's sister began to play; the father and mother, from either side, intently watched the movements of her hands. Gregor, attracted by the playing, ventured to move forward a little until his head was actually inside the living room. He felt hardly any surprise at his growing lack of consideration for the others; there had been a time when he prided himself on being considerate. And yet just on this occasion he had more reason than ever to hide himself, since owing to the amount of dust which lay thick in his room and rose into the air at the slightest movement, he too was covered with dust; fluff and hair and remnants of food trailed with him, caught on his back and along his sides; his indifference to everything was much too great for him to turn on his back and scrape himself clean on the carpet, as once he had several times a day. And in spite of his condition, no shame deterred him from advancing a little over the spotless floor of the living room.

To be sure, no one was aware of him. The family was entirely absorbed in the violin-playing; the lodgers, however, who first of all had stationed themselves, hands in pockets, much too close behind the music stand so that they could all have read the music, which must have bothered his sister, had soon retreated to the window, half-whispering with downbent heads, and stayed there while his father turned an anxious eye on them. Indeed, they were making it more than obvious that they had been disappointed in their expectation of hearing good or enjoyable violin-playing, that they had had more than enough of the performance and only out of courtesy suffered a continued disturbance of their peace. From the way they all kept blowing the smoke of their cigars high in the air through nose and mouth one could divine their irritation. And yet Gregor's sister was playing so beautifully. Her face leaned sideways, intently and sadly her eyes followed the notes of music. Gregor crawled a little farther forward and lowered his head to the ground so that it might be possible for his eyes to meet hers. Was he an animal, that music had such an effect upon him? He felt as if the way were opening before him to the unknown nourishment he craved. He was determined to push forward till he reached his sister, to pull at her skirt and so let her know that she was to come into his room with her violin, for no one here appreciated her playing as he would appreciate it. He would never let her out of his room, at least, not so long as he lived; his frightful appearance would become, for the first time, useful to him; he would watch all the doors of his room at night and spit at intruders; but his sister should need no constraint, she should stay with him of her own free will; she should sit beside him on the sofa, bend down her ear to him and hear him confide that he had had the firm intention of sending her to the Conservatorium, and that, but for his mishap, last Christmas—surely Christmas was long past?—he would have announced it to everybody without allowing a single objection. After this confession his sister would be so touched that she would burst into tears, and Gregor would then raise himself to her shoulder and kiss her on the neck, which, now that she went to business, she kept free of any ribbon or collar.

"Mr. Samsa!" cried the middle lodger, to Gregor's father, and pointed, without wasting any more words, at Gregor, now working himself slowly forwards. The violin fell silent, the middle lodger first smiled to his friends with a shake of the head and then looked at Gregor again. Instead of driving Gregor out, his father seemed to think it more needful to begin by soothing the lodgers, although they were not at all agitated and apparently found Gregor more entertaining than the violin-play-ing. He hurried towards them and, spreading out his arms, tried to urge them back into their own room and at the same time to block their view of Gregor. They now began to be really a little angry, one could not tell whether because of the old man's behavior or because it had just dawned on them that all unwittingly they had such a neighbor as Gregor next door. They demanded explanations of his father, they waved their arms like him, tugged uneasily at their beards, and only with reluctance backed towards their room. Meanwhile Gregor's sister, who stood there as if lost when her playing was so abruptly broken off, came to life again, pulled herself together all at once after standing for a while holding violin and bow in nervelessly hanging hands and staring at her music, pushed her violin into the lap of her mother, who was still sitting in her chair fighting asthmatically for breath, and ran into the lodgers' room to which they were now being shepherded by her father more quickly than before. One could see the pillows and blankets on the beds flying under her accustomed fingers and being laid in order. Before the lodgers had actually reached their room she had finished making the beds and slipped out.

The old man seemed once more to be so possessed by his mulish self-assertive-ness that he was forgetting all the respect he should show to his lodgers. He kept driving them on and driving them on until in the very door of the bedroom the middle lodger stamped his foot loudly on the floor and so brought him to a halt. "I beg to announce," said the lodger, lifting one hand and looking also at Gregor's mother and sister, "that because of the disgusting conditions prevailing in this household and family"—here he spat on the floor with emphatic brevity—"I give you notice on the spot. Naturally I won't pay you a penny for the days I have lived here, on the contrary I shall consider bringing an action for damages against you, based on claims—believe me—that will be easily susceptible of proof." He ceased and stared straight in front of him, as if he expected something. In fact his two friends at once rushed into the breach with these words: "And we too give notice on the spot." On that he seized the door-handle and shut the door with a slam.

Gregor's father, groping with his hands, staggered forward and fell from his chair; it looked as if he were stretching himself there for his ordinary evening nap, but the marked jerkings of his head, which was as if uncontrollable, showed that he was far from asleep. Gregor had simply stayed quietly all the time on the spot where the lodgers had espied him. Disappointment at the failure of his plan, perhaps also the weakness arising from extreme hunger, made it impossible for him to move. He feared, with a fair degree of certainty, that at any moment the general tension would discharge itself in a combined attack upon him, and he lay waiting. He did not react even to the noise made by the violin as it fell off his mother's lap from under her trembling fingers and gave out a resonant note.

"My dear parents," said his sister, slapping her hand on the table by way of introduction, "things can't go on like this. Perhaps you don't realize that, but I do. I won't utter my brother's name in the presence of this creature, and so all I say is: we must try to get rid of it. We've tried to look after it and to put up with it as far as is humanly possible, and I don't think anyone could reproach us in the slightest."

"She is more than right," said Gregor's father to himself. His mother, who was still choking for lack of breath, began to cough hollowly into her hand with a wild look in her eyes.

His sister rushed over to her and held her forehead. His father's thoughts seemed to have lost their vagueness at Grete's words, he sat more upright, fingering his service cap that lay among the plates still lying on the table from the lodgers' supper, and from time to time looked at the still form of Gregor.

"We must try to get rid of it," his sister now said explicitly to her father, since her mother was coughing too much to hear a word, "it will be the death of both of you, I can see that coming. When one has to work as hard as we do, all of us, one can't stand this continual torment at home on top of it. At least I can't stand it any longer." And she burst into such a passion of sobbing that her tears dropped on her mother's face, where she wiped them off mechanically.

"My dear," said the old man sympathetically, and with evident understanding, "but what can we do?"

Gregor's sister merely shrugged her shoulders to indicate the feeling of helplessness that had now overmastered her during her weeping fit, in contrast to her former confidence.

"If he could understand us," said her father, half questioningly; Grete, still sobbing, vehemently waved a hand to show how unthinkable that was.

"If he could understand us," repeated the old man, shutting his eyes to consider his daughter's conviction that understanding was impossible, "then perhaps we might come to some agreement with him. But as it is—"

"He must go," cried Gregor's sister, "that's the only solution, Father. You must just try to get rid of the idea that this is Gregor. The fact that we've believed it for so long is the root of all our trouble. But how can it be Gregor? If this were Gregor, he would have realized long ago that human beings can't live with such a creature, and he'd have gone away on his own accord. Then we wouldn't have any brother, but we'd be able to go on living and keep his memory in honor. As it is, this creature persecutes us, drives away our lodgers, obviously wants the whole apartment to himself and would have us all sleep in the gutter. Just look, Father," she shrieked all at once, "he's at it again!" And in an access of panic that was quite incomprehensible to Gregor she even quitted her mother, literally thrusting the chair from her as if she would rather sacrifice her mother than stay so near to Gregor, and rushed behind her father, who also rose up, being simply upset by her agitation, and half-spread his arms out as if to protect her.

Yet Gregor had not the slightest intention of frightening anyone, far less his sister. He had only begun to turn round in order to crawl back to his room, but it was certainly a startling operation to watch, since because of his disabled condition he could not execute the difficult turning movements except by lifting his head and then bracing it against the floor over and over again. He paused and looked round. His good intentions seemed to have been recognized; the alarm had been only momentary. Now they were all watching him in melancholy silence. His mother lay in her chair, her legs stiffly outstretched and pressed together, her eyes almost closing for sheer weariness; his father and his sister were sitting beside each other, his sister's arm around the old man's neck.

Perhaps I can go on turning round now, thought Gregor, and began his labors again. He could not stop himself from panting with the effort, and had to pause now and then to take breath. Nor did anyone harass him, he was left entirely to himself. When he had completed the turn-round he began at once to crawl straight back. He was amazed at the distance separating him from his room and could not understand how in his weak state he had managed to accomplish the same journey so recently, almost without remarking it. Intent on crawling as fast as possible, he barely noticed that not a single word, not an ejaculation from his family, interfered with his progress. Only when he was already in the doorway did he turn his head round, not completely, for his neck muscles were getting stiff, but enough to see that nothing had changed behind him except that his sister had risen to her feet. His last glance fell on his mother, who was not quite overcome by sleep.

Hardly was he well inside his room when the door was hastily pushed shut, bolted and locked. The sudden noise in his rear startled him so much that his little legs gave beneath him. It was his sister who had shown such haste. She had been standing ready waiting and had made a light spring forward, Gregor had not even heard her coming, and she cried "At last!" to her parents as she turned the key in the lock.

"And what now?" said Gregor to himself, looking round in the darkness. Soon he made the discovery that he was unable to stir a limb. This did not surprise him, rather it seemed unnatural that he should ever actually have been able to move on these feeble little legs. Otherwise he felt relatively comfortable. True, his whole body was aching, but it seemed that the pain was gradually growing less and would finally pass away. The rotting apple in his back and the inflamed area around it, all covered with soft dust, already hardly troubled him. He thought of his family with tenderness and love. The decision that he must disappear was one that he held to even more strongly than his sister, if that were possible. In this state of vacant and peaceful meditation he remained until the tower clock struck three in the morning. The first broadening of light in the world outside the window entered his consciousness once more. Then his head sank to the floor of its own accord and from his nostrils came the last faint flicker of his breath.

When the charwoman arrived early in the morning—what between her strength and her impatience she slammed all the doors so loudly, never mind how often she had been begged not to do so, that no one in the whole apartment could enjoy any quiet sleep after her arrival—she noticed nothing unusual as she took her customary peep into Gregor's room. She thought he was lying motionless on purpose, pretending to be in the sulks; she credited him with every kind of intelligence. Since she happened to have the long-handled broom in her hand she tried to tickle him up with it from the doorway. When that too produced no reaction she felt provoked and poked at him a little harder, and only when she had pushed him along the floor without meeting any resistance was her attention aroused. It did not take her long to establish the truth of the matter, and her eyes widened, she let out a whistle, yet did not waste much time over it but tore open the door of the Samsas' bedroom and yelled into the darkness at the top of her voice: "Just look at this, it's dead; it's lying here dead and done for!"

Mr. and Mrs. Samsa started up in their double bed and before they realized the nature of the charwoman's announcement had some difficulty in overcoming the shock of it. But then they got out of bed quickly, one on either side, Mr. Samsa throwing a blanket over his shoulders, Mrs. Samsa in nothing but her nightgown; in this array they entered Gregor's room. Meanwhile the door of the living room

s slowly but
turn of the
o; the more
and when a
udly with a
and as if a

ey had not
so they sat
s board of
firm. While
w, since her
up, but as
amsa. The
apart to the
nall ostrich
r since she
asked Mrs.
"Oh," said
"just this,
been seen
eoccupied;
in detail,
story, she
ed: "Bye,
slamming

is wife nor
shattered
ndow and
ok at them
now, do.
The two
shed their

they had
own. The
sunshine.
he future,
jobs they
all three
mmediate
another

leeping since the advent of the lodgers; she was
been to bed, which seemed to be confirmed
ad?" said Mrs. Samsa, looking questioningly at
have investigated for herself, and the fact was
ion. "I should say so," said the charwoman,
gor's corpse a long way to one side with her
vement as if to stop her, but checked it. "Well,"
God." He crossed himself, and the three women
eyes never left the corpse, said: "Just see how
ce he's eaten anything. The food came out again
body was completely flat and dry, as could only
r supported by the legs and nothing prevented

a little while," said Mrs. Samsa with a tremulous
ing back at the corpse, followed her parents into
shut the door and opened the window wide.
ning a certain softness was perceptible in the fresh
of March.
from their room and were surprised to see no
. "Where's our breakfast?" said the middle lodger
she put her finger to her lips and hastily, without
they should go into Gregor's room. They did so
ockets of their somewhat shabby coats, around
re it was now fully light.
sas' bedroom opened and Mr. Samsa appeared in
, his daughter on the other. They all looked a little
ime to time Grete hid her face on her father's arm.
said Mr. Samsa, and pointed to the door without
men. "What do you mean by that?" said the middle
with a feeble smile. The two others put their hands
them together, as if in gleeful expectation of a fine
l to come off the winners. "I mean just what I say,"
nced in a straight line with his two companions
s ground at first quietly, looking at the floor as if his
tern in his head. "Then let us go, by all means," he
msa as if in a sudden access of humility he were
on for this decision. Mr. Samsa merely nodded briefly
yes. Upon that the lodger really did go with long
friends had been listening and had quite stopped
noments and now went scuttling after him as if afraid
the hall before them and cut them off from their
e took their hats from the rack, their sticks from the
ce and quitted the apartment. With a suspiciousness
d Mr. Samsa and the two women followed them out

to the landing; leaning over the banister they watched the three figur
surely going down the long stairs, vanishing from sight at a certair
staircase on every floor and coming into view again after a moment or
they dwindled, the more the Samsa family's interest in them dwindled
butcher's boy met them and passed them on the stairs coming up pr
tray on his head, Mr. Samsa and the two women soon left the landin
burden had been lifted from them went back into their apartment.

They decided to spend this day in resting and going for a stroll;
only deserved such a respite from work, but absolutely needed it. An
down at the table and wrote three notes of excuse, Mr. Samsa to
management, Mrs. Samsa to her employer and Grete to the head of he
they were writing, the charwoman came in to say that she was going n
morning's work was finished. At first they only nodded without lookin
she kept hovering there they eyed her irritably. "Well?" said Mr.
charwoman stood grinning in the doorway as if she had good news to i
family but meant not to say a word unless properly questioned. The s
feather standing upright on her hat, which had annoyed Mr. Samsa ev
was engaged, was waving gaily in all directions. "Well, what is it, then?"
Samsa, who obtained more respect from the charwoman than the others
the charwoman, giggling so amiably that she could not at once continu
you don't need to bother about how to get rid of the thing next door. It
to already." Mrs. Samsa and Grete bent over their letters again, as if p
Mr. Samsa, who perceived that she was eager to begin describing it a
stopped her with a decisive hand. But since she was not allowed to tell h
remembered the great hurry she was in, being obviously deeply hu
everybody," she said, whirling off violently, and departed with a frightfu
of doors.

"She'll be given notice tonight," said Mr. Samsa, but neither from
his daughter did he get any answer, for the charwoman seemed to hav
again the composure they had barely achieved. They rose, went to the w
stayed there, clasping each other tight. Mr. Samsa turned in his chair to lo
and quietly observed them for a little. Then he called out: "Come along
Let bygones be bygones. And you might have some consideration for me
of them complied at once, hastened to him, caressed him and quickly fin
letters.

Then they all three left the apartment together, which was more tha
done for months, and went by tram into the open country outside the
tram, in which they were the only passengers, was filled with warm
Leaning comfortably back in their seats they canvassed their prospects for
and it appeared on closer inspection that these were not at all bad, for the
had got, which so far they had never really discussed with each other, wer
admirable and likely to lead to better things later on. The greatest i
improvement in their condition would of course arise from moving t

house; they wanted to take a smaller and cheaper but also better situated and more easily run apartment than the one they had, which Gregor had selected. While they were thus conversing, it struck both Mr. and Mrs. Samsa, almost at the same moment, as they became aware of their daughter's increasing vivacity, that in spite of all the sorrow of recent times, which had made her cheeks pale, she had bloomed into a pretty girl with a good figure. They grew quieter and half unconsciously exchanged glances of complete agreement, having come to the conclusion that it would soon be time to find a good husband for her. And it was like a confirmation of their new dreams and excellent intentions that at the end of their journey their daughter sprang to her feet first and stretched her young body.

Journal Entry

Record your responses to the first sentence of "The Metamorphosis." Characterize the narrator's tone.

Textual Considerations

1. Characterize the narrator's attitude toward Gregor. What does he reveal about Gregor's job and relationship with his boss?
2. Analyze Gregor's relationship with his sister. How does her treatment of him change as the story continues? To what extent is her final betrayal inevitable?
3. Food plays an important role in the story. Analyze its effects on theme.
4. Characterize Gregor's father. To what extent has he exploited Gregor? Why is it ironic that as Gregor's situation deteriorates that of his family improves?
5. Consider the roles of the three lodgers and the charwoman. How are their attitudes toward Gregor similar to or different from those of his family?
6. Compare and contrast Kafka's treatment of time in parts one and two. How is it reflective of Gregor's psychological state?
7. How many "metamorphoses" occur in the story? Consider, for example, the final scene. How does it differ stylistically from the rest of the story?

Cultural Contexts

1. Discuss with your group the extent to which Gregor is responsible for his sense of alienation. Does he deserve his fate? Of what is he guilty? Is he a victim of the selfishness or manipulation of others? What might Kafka be implying about one's relationship to oneself versus responsiblity to family and community?
2. Many critics attribute Kafka's thematic preoccupation with exile and alienation to his biographical circumstances. Kafka was a Jew raised in a Gentile world, he suffered from tuberculosis, was terrified of his domineering and judgmental father, and was a sensitive artist in a typical middle-class society. Debate with your group the degree to which Gregor's sense of isolation may be explained solely by these circumstances.

Sherwood Anderson

Hands

Upon the half decayed veranda of a small frame house that stood near the edge of a ravine near the town of Winesburg, Ohio, a fat little old man walked nervously up and down. Across a long field that had been seeded for clover but that had produced only a dense crop of yellow mustard weeds, he could see the public highway along which went a wagon filled with berry pickers returning from the fields. The berry pickers, youths and maidens, laughed and shouted boisterously. A boy clad in a blue shirt leaped from the wagon and attempted to drag after him one of the maidens, who screamed and protested shrilly. The feet of the boy in the road kicked up a cloud of dust that floated across the face of the departing sun. Over the long field came a thin girlish voice. "Oh, you Wing Biddlebaum, comb your hair, it's falling into your eyes," commanded the voice to the man, who was bald and whose nervous little hands fiddled about the bare white forehead as though arranging a mass of tangled locks.

Wing Biddlebaum, forever frightened and beset by a ghostly band of doubts, did not think of himself as in any way a part of the life of the town where he had lived for twenty years. Among all the people of Winesburg but one had come close to him. With George Willard, son of Tom Willard, the proprietor of the New Willard House, he had formed something like a friendship. George Willard was the reporter on the *Winesburg Eagle* and sometimes in the evenings he walked out along the highway to Wing Biddlebaum's house. Now as the old man walked up and down on the veranda, his hands moving nervously about, he was hoping that George Willard would come and spend the evening with him. After the wagon containing the berry pickers had passed, he went across the field through the tall mustard weeds and climbing a rail fence peered anxiously along the road to the town. For a moment he stood thus, rubbing his hands together and looking up and down the road, and then, fear overcoming him, ran back to walk again upon the porch on his own house.

In the presence of George Willard, Wing Biddlebaum, who for twenty years had been the town mystery, lost something of his timidity, and his shadowy personality, submerged in a sea of doubts, came forth to look at the world. With the young reporter at his side, he ventured in the light of day into Main Street or strode up and down on the rickety front porch of his own house, talking excitedly. The voice that had been low and trembling became shrill and loud. The bent figure straightened. With a kind of wriggle, like a fish returned to the brook by the fisherman, Biddlebaum the silent began to talk, striving to put into words the ideas that had been accumulated by his mind during long years of silence.

Wing Biddlebaum talked much with his hands. The slender expressive fingers, forever active, forever striving to conceal themselves in his pockets or behind his back, came forth and became the piston rods of his machinery of expression.

The story of Wing Biddlebaum is a story of hands. Their restless activity, like unto the beating of the wings of an imprisoned bird, had given him his name. Some obscure poet of the town had thought of it. The hands alarmed their owner. He wanted to keep them hidden away and looked with amazement at the quiet inexpressive hands of other men who worked beside him in the fields, or passed, driving sleepy teams on country roads.

When he talked to George Willard, Wing Biddlebaum closed his fists and beat with them upon a table or on the walls of his house. The action made him more comfortable. If the desire to talk came to him when the two were walking in the fields, he sought out a stump or the top board of a fence and with his hands pounding busily talked with renewed ease.

The story of Wing Biddlebaum's hands is worth a book in itself. Sympathetically set forth it would tap many strange, beautiful qualities in obscure men. It is a job for a poet. In Winesburg the hands had attracted attention merely because of their activity. With them Wing Biddlebaum had picked as high as a hundred and forty quarts of strawberries in a day. They became his distinguishing feature, the source of his fame. Also they made more grotesque an already grotesque and elusive individuality. Winesburg was proud of the hands of Wing Biddlebaum in the same spirit in which it was proud of Banker White's new stone house and Wesley Moyer's bay stallion, Tony Tip, that had won the two-fifteen trot at the fall races in Cleveland.

As for George Willard, he had many times wanted to ask about the hands. At times an almost overwhelming curiosity had taken hold of him. He felt that there must be a reason for their strange activity and their inclination to keep hidden away and only a growing respect for Wing Biddlebaum kept him from blurting out the questions that were often in his mind.

Once he had been on the point of asking. The two were walking in the fields on a summer afternoon and had stopped to sit upon a grassy bank. All afternoon Wing Biddlebaum had talked as one inspired. By a fence he had stopped and beating like a giant woodpecker upon the top board had shouted at George Willard, condemning his tendency to be too much influenced by the people about him. "You are destroying yourself," he cried. "You have the inclination to be alone and to dream and you are afraid of dreams. You want to be like others in town here. You hear them talk and you try to imitate them."

On the grassy bank Wing Biddlebaum had tried again to drive his point home. His voice became soft and reminiscent, and with a sigh of contentment he launched into a long rambling talk, speaking as one lost in a dream.

Out of the dream Wing Biddlebaum made a picture for George Willard. In the picture men lived again in a kind of pastoral golden age. Across a green open country came clean-limbed young men, some afoot, some mounted upon horses. In crowds the young men came to gather about the feet of an old man who sat beneath a tree in a tiny garden and who talked to them.

Wing Biddlebaum became wholly inspired. For once he forgot the hands. Slowly they stole forth and lay upon George Willard's shoulders. Something new and bold came into the voice that talked. "You must try to forget all you have learned," said the old man. "You must begin to dream. From this time on you must shut your ears to the roaring of the voices."

Pausing in his speech, Wing Biddlebaum looked long and earnestly at George Willard. His eyes glowed. Again he raised the hands to caress the boy and then a look of horror swept over his face.

With a convulsive movement of his body, Wing Biddlebaum sprang to his feet and thrust his hands deep into his trousers pockets. Tears came to his eyes. "I must be getting along home. I can talk no more with you," he said nervously.

Without looking back, the old man had hurried down the hillside and across a meadow, leaving George Willard perplexed and frightened upon the grassy slope. With a shiver of dread the boy arose and went along the road toward town. "I'll not ask him about his hands," he thought, touched by the memory of the terror he had seen in the man's eyes. "There's something wrong, but I don't want to know what it is. His hands have something to do with his fear of me and of everyone."

And George Willard was right. Let us look briefly into the story of the hands. Perhaps our talking of them will arouse the poet who will tell the hidden wonder story of the influence for which the hands were but fluttering pennants of promise.

In his youth Wing Biddlebaum had been a school teacher in a town in Pennsylvania. He was not then known as Wing Biddlebaum, but went by the less euphonic name of Adolph Myers. As Adolph Myers he was much loved by the boys of his school.

Adolph Myers was meant by nature to be a teacher of youth. He was one of those rare, little-understood men who rule by a power so gentle that it passes as a lovable weakness. In their feeling for the boys under their charge such men are not unlike the finer sort of women in their love of men.

And yet that is but crudely stated. It needs the poet there. With the boys of his school, Adolph Myers had walked in the evening or had sat talking until dusk upon the schoolhouse steps lost in a kind of dream. Here and there went his hands, caressing the shoulders of the boys, playing about the tousled heads. As he talked his voice became soft and musical. There was a caress in that also. In a way the voice and the hands, the stroking of the shoulders and the touching of the hair were a part of the schoolmaster's effort to carry a dream into the young minds. By the caress that was in his fingers he expressed himself. He was one of those men in whom the force that creates life is diffused, not centralized. Under the caress of his hands doubt and disbelief went out of the minds of the boys and they began also to dream.

And then the tragedy. A half-witted boy of the school became enamored of the young master. In his bed at night he imagined unspeakable things and in the morning went forth to tell his dreams as facts. Strange, hideous accusations fell from his loose-hung lips. Through the Pennsylvania town went a shiver. Hidden, shadowy doubts that had been in men's minds concerning Adolph Myers were galvanized into beliefs.

The tragedy did not linger. Trembling lads were jerked out of bed and questioned. "He put his arms about me," said one. "His fingers were always playing in my hair," said another.

One afternoon a man of the town, Henry Bradford, who kept a saloon, came to the schoolhouse door. Calling Adolph Myers into the school yard he began to beat him with his fists. As his hard knuckles beat down into the frightened face of the schoolmaster, his wrath, became more and more terrible. Screaming with dismay, the children ran here and there like disturbed insects. "I'll teach you to put your hands on my boy, you beast," roared the saloon keeper, who tired of beating the master, had begun to kick him about the yard.

Adolph Myers was driven from the Pennsylvania town in the night. With lanterns in their hands a dozen men came to the door of the house where he lived alone and commanded that he dress and come forth. It was raining and one of the men had a rope in his hands. They had intended to hang the schoolmaster, but something in his figure, so small, white, and pitiful, touched their hearts and they let him escape. As he ran away into the darkness they repented of their weakness and ran after him, swearing and throwing sticks and great balls of soft mud at the figure that screamed and ran faster and faster into the darkness.

For twenty years Adolph Myers had lived alone in Winesburg. He was but forty but looked sixty-five. The name of Biddlebaum he got from a box of goods seen at a freight station as he hurried through an eastern Ohio town. He had in aunt in Winesburg, a black-toothed old woman who raised chickens, and with her he lived until she died. He had been ill for a year after the experience in Pennsylvania, and after his recovery worked as a day laborer in the fields, going timidly about and striving to conceal his hands. Although he did not understand what had happened he felt that the hands must be to blame. Again and again the fathers of the boys talked of the hands. "Keep your hands to yourself," the saloon keeper had roared, dancing with fury in the schoolhouse yard.

Upon the veranda of his house by the ravine, Wing Biddlebaum continued to walk up and down until the sun had disappeared and the road beyond the field was lost in the grey shadows. Going into his house he cut slices of bread and spread honey upon them. When the rumble of the evening train that took away the express cars loaded with the day's harvest of berries had passed and restored the silence of the summer night, he went again to walk upon the veranda. In the darkness he could not see the hands and they became quiet. Although he still hungered for the presence of the boy, who was the medium through which he expressed his love of man, the hunger became again a part of his loneliness and his waiting. Lighting a lamp, Wing Biddlebaum washed the few dishes soiled by his simple meal and, setting up a folding cot by the screen door that led to the porch, prepared to undress for the night. A few stray white bread crumbs lay on the cleanly washed floor by the table; putting the lamp upon a low stool he began to pick up the crumbs, carrying them to his mouth one by one with unbelievable rapidity. In the dense blotch of light beneath the table, the kneeling figure looked like a priest engaged in some service of his church. The nervous expressive fingers, flashing in and out of the light, might well have been mistaken for the fingers of the devotee going swiftly through decade after decade of his rosary.

Journal Entry

Respond to the Pennsylvania community's treatment of Wing Biddlebaum.

Textual Considerations

1. How does "Hands" allow readers to see the reality of Biddlebaum's identity for themselves, whereas Biddlebaum himself "did not understand what had happened [and] he felt that the hands must be to blame"? Focus on the role that the narrator plays in Anderson's story.
2. Anderson juxtaposes Biddlebaum, a fat little old man, with the community of "youths and maidens, [who] laughed and shouted boisterously." Analyze the encounter of these opposing characters in terms of the relationship between the individual and the community.
3. Consider whether the issue of power fits into the overall development of the plot in "Hands." Investigate this issue in relation to the two communities in "Hands," as well as to Biddlebaum himself, whom the narrator describes as "one of those rare, little-understood men who rule by a power so gentle that it passes as a lovable weakness."
4. Respond to the religious imagery at the end of the story by analyzing what it suggests in terms of Biddlebaum's value as an individual.

Cultural Contexts

1. Some psychologists now see humankind as fundamentally divided beings who are split biologically, sexually, linguistically, and socially. Discuss with your group whether one can apply the concept of the split individual to Wing Biddlebaum in "Hands."
2. "Hands" offers a dynamic investigation into the way a community reacts to an individual's potential threat. Can your group reach a consensus on whether there is any foundation for this threat? How would you characterize it?

James Joyce

Eveline

She sat at the window watching the evening invade the avenue. Her head was leaned against the window curtains and in her nostrils was the odor of dusty cretonne. She was tired.

Few people passed. The man out of the last house passed on his way home; she heard his footsteps clicking along the concrete pavement and afterwards crunching on the cinder path before the new red houses. One time there used to be a field there in which they used to play every evening with other people's children. Then a man from Belfast bought the field and built houses in it—not like their little brown houses but bright brick houses with shining roofs. The children of the avenue used to play together in that field—the Devines, the Waters, the Dunns, little Keogh the cripple, she and her brothers and sisters. Ernest, however, never played: he was too grown up. Her father used often to hunt them in out of the field with his blackthorn stick; but usually little Keogh used to keep *nix* and call out when he saw her father coming. Still they seemed to have been rather happy then. Her father was not so bad then; and besides, her mother was alive. That was a long time ago; she and her brothers and sisters were all grown up; her mother was dead. Tizzie Dunn was dead, too, and the Waters had gone back to England. Everything changes. Now she was going to go away like the others, to leave her home.

Home! She looked round the room, reviewing all its familiar objects which she had dusted once a week for so many years, wondering where on earth all the dust came from. Perhaps she would never see again those familiar objects from which she had never dreamed of being divided. And yet during all those years she had never found out the name of the priest whose yellowing photograph hung on the wall above the broken harmonium beside the colored print of the promises made to Blessed Margaret Mary Alacoque. He had been a school friend of her father. Whenever he showed the photograph to a visitor her father used to pass it with a casual word:

—He is in Melbourne now.

She had consented to go away, to leave her home. Was that wise? She tried to weigh each side of the question. In her home anyway she had shelter and food; she had those whom she had known all her life about her. Of course she had to work hard both in the house and at business. What would they say of her in the Stores when they found out that she had run away with a fellow? Say she was a fool, perhaps; and her place would be filled up by advertisement. Miss Gavan would be glad. She had always had an edge on her, especially whenever there were people listening.

—Miss Hill, don't you see these ladies are waiting?

—Look lively, Miss Hill, please.

She would not cry many tears at leaving the Stores.

But in her new home, in a distant unknown country, it would not be like that. Then she would be married—she, Eveline. People would treat her with respect then. She would not be treated as her mother had been. Even now, though she was over nineteen, she sometimes felt herself in danger of her father's violence. She knew it was that that had given her the palpitations. When they were growing up he had never gone for her, like he used to go for Harry and Ernest, because she was a girl; but latterly he had begun to threaten her and say what he would do to her only for her dead mother's sake. And now she had nobody to protect her. Ernest was dead and Harry, who was in the church decorating business, was nearly always down somewhere in the country. Besides, the invariable squabble for money on Saturday nights had begun to weary her unspeakably. She always gave her entire wages—seven shillings—and Harry always sent up what he could but the trouble was to get any money from her father. He said she used to squander the money, that she had no head, that he wasn't going to give her his hard-earned money to throw about the streets, and much more, for he was usually fairly bad of a Saturday night. In the end he would give her the money and ask her had she any intention of buying Sunday's dinner. Then she had to rush out as quickly as she could and do her marketing, holding her black leather purse tightly in her hand as she elbowed her way through the crowds and returning home late under her load of provisions. She had hard work to keep the house together and to see that the two young children who had been left to her charge went to school regularly and got their meals regularly. It was hard work—a hard life—but now that she was about to leave it she did not find it a wholly undesirable life.

She was about to explore another life with Frank. Frank was very kind, manly, open-hearted. She was to go away with him by the night-boat to be his wife and to live with him in Buenos Ayres where he had a home waiting for her. How well she remembered the first time she had seen him; he was lodging in a house on the main road where she used to visit. It seemed a few weeks ago. He was standing at the gate, his peaked cap pushed back on his head and his hair tumbled forward over a face of bronze. Then they had come to know each other. He used to meet her outside the Stores every evening and see her home. He took her to see *The Bohemian Girl* and she felt elated as she sat in an unaccustomed part of the theatre with him. He was awfully fond of music and sang a little. People knew that they were courting and, when he sang about the lass that loves a sailor, she always felt pleasantly confused. He used to call her Poppens out of fun. First of all it had been an excitement for her to have a fellow and then she had begun to like him. He had tales of distant countries. He had started as a deck boy at a pound a month on a ship of the Allan Line going out to Canada. He told her the names of the ships he had been on and the names of the different services. He had sailed through the Straits of Magellan and he told her stories of the terrible Patagonians. He had fallen on his feet in Buenos Ayres, he said, and had come over to the old country just for a holiday. Of course, her father had found out the affair and had forbidden her to have anything to say to him.

—I know these sailor chaps, he said.

One day he had quarrelled with Frank and after that she had to meet her lover secretly.

The evening deepened in the avenue. The white of two letters in her lap grew indistinct. One was to Harry; the other was to her father. Ernest had been her favorite but she liked Harry too. Her father was becoming old lately, she noticed; he would miss her. Sometimes he could be very nice. Not long before, when she had been laid up for a day, he had read her out a ghost story and made toast for her at the fire. Another day, when their mother was alive, they had all gone for a picnic to the Hill of Howth. She remembered her father putting on her mother's bonnet to make the children laugh.

Her time was running out but she continued to sit by the window, leaning her head against the window curtain, inhaling the odor of dusty cretonne. Down far in the avenue she could hear a street organ playing. She knew the air. Strange that it should come that very night to remind her of the promise to her mother, her promise to keep the home together as long as she could. She remembered the last night of her mother's illness; she was again in the close dark room at the other side of the hall and outside she heard a melancholy air of Italy. The organ-player had been ordered to go away and given sixpence. She remembered her father strutting back into the sickroom saying:

—Damned Italians! coming over here!

As she mused, the pitiful vision of her mother's life laid its spell on the very quick of her being—that life of commonplace sacrifices closing in final craziness. She trembled as she heard again her mother's voice saying constantly with foolish insistence:

—Derevaun Seraun! Derevaun Seraun!

She stood up in a sudden impulse of terror. Escape! She must escape! Frank would save her. He would give her life, perhaps love, too. But she wanted to live. Why should she be unhappy? She had a right to happiness. Frank would take her in his arms, fold her in his arms. He would save her.

She stood among the swaying crowd in the station at the North Wall. He held her hand and she knew that he was speaking to her, saying something about the passage over and over again. The station was full of soldiers with brown baggages. Through the wide doors of the sheds she caught a glimpse of the black mass of the boat, lying in beside the quay wall, with illumined portholes. She answered nothing. She felt her cheek pale and cold and, out of a maze of distress, she prayed to God to direct her, to show her what was her duty. The boat blew a long mournful whistle into the mist. If she went, tomorrow she would be on the sea with Frank, steaming towards Buenos Ayres. Their passage had been booked. Could she still draw back after all he had done for her? Her distress awoke a nausea in her body and she kept moving her lips in silent fervent prayer.

A bell clanged upon her heart. She felt him seize her hand:

—Come!

All the seas of the world tumbled about her heart. He was drawing her into them: he would drown her. She gripped with both hands at the iron railing.

—Come!

No! No! No! It was impossible. Her hands clutched the iron in frenzy. Amid the seas she sent a cry of anguish!

—Eveline! Evvy!

He rushed beyond the barrier and called to her to follow. He was shouted at to go on but he still called to her. She set her white face to him, passive, like a helpless animal. Her eyes gave him no sign of love or farewell or recognition.

Journal Entry

Write a journal entry about the interplay of power and gender in "Eveline."

Textual Considerations

1. Analyze Eveline's definition of the word *home* in paragraphs 3–5 of Joyce's story. To what extent does her definition of *home* differ or contrast with her definition of *new home*?
2. Reflect on the roles of religion and romance in "Eveline." List the words and phrases that relate to these issues, and then analyze the extent to which both issues represent different ways of responding to the patriarchal structure of families like Eveline's.
3. To what extent is Eveline's inability to choose her own happiness attributable to her role as daughter and as a single woman in an Irish Catholic environment at the turn of the century? What other factors might have contributed to her sense of paralysis?
4. Discuss the appropriateness of dust as the dominant symbol in the story. Can you find other symbols in the text?

Cultural Contexts

1. Initiate a group discussion on "Eveline" by locating the forces of tradition and change that shape Joyce's story.
2. Discuss Joyce's story as a social document that reflects or criticizes the values of the Irish community.

Fae Myenne Ng

A Red Sweater

I chose red for my sister. Fierce, dark red. Made in Hong Kong. Hand Wash Only because it's got that skin of fuzz. She'll look happy. That's good. Everything's perfect, for a minute. That seems enough.

Red. For Good Luck. Of course. This fire-red sweater is swollen with good cheer. Wear it, I will tell her. You'll look lucky.

We're a family of three girls. By Chinese standards, that's not lucky. "Too bad," outsiders whisper, " . . . nothing but daughters. A failed family."

First, Middle, and End girl. Our order of birth marked us. That came to tell more than our given names.

My eldest sister, Lisa, lives at home. She quit San Francisco State, one semester short of a psychology degree. One day she said, "Forget about it, I'm tired." She's working full time at Pacific Bell now. Nine hundred a month with benefits. Mah and Deh think it's a great deal. They tell everybody, "Yes, our Number One makes good pay, but that's not even counting the discount. If we call Hong Kong, China even, there's forty percent off!" As if anyone in their part of China had a telephone.

Number Two, the in-between, jumped off the "M" floor three years ago. Not true! What happened? Why? Too sad! All we say about that is, "It was her choice."

We sent Mah to Hong Kong. When she left Hong Kong thirty years ago, she was the envy of all: "Lucky girl! You'll never have to work." To marry a sojourner was to have a future. Thirty years in the land of gold and good fortune, and then she returned to tell the story: three daughters, one dead, one unmarried, another who-cares-where, the thirty years in sweatshops, and the prince of the Golden Mountain turned into a toad. I'm glad I didn't have to go with her. I felt her shame and regret. To return, seeking solace and comfort, instead of offering banquets and stories of the good life.

I'm the youngest. I started flying with American the year Mah returned to Hong Kong, so I got her a good discount. She thought I was good for something then. But when she returned, I was pregnant.

"Get an abortion," she said. "Drop the baby," she screamed.

"No."

"Then get married."

"No. I don't want to."

I was going to get an abortion all along. I just didn't like the way they talked about the whole thing. They made me feel like dirt, that I was a disgrace. Now I can see how I used it as an opportunity. Sometimes I wonder if there wasn't another way. Everything about those years was so steamy and angry. There didn't seem to be any answers.

"I have no eyes for you," Mah said.

"Don't call us," Deh said.

They wouldn't talk to me. They ranted idioms to each other for days. The apartment was filled with images and curses I couldn't perceive. I got the general idea: I was a rotten, no-good, dead thing. I would die in a gutter without rice in my belly. My spirit—if I had one—wouldn't be fed. I wouldn't see good days in this life or the next.

My parents always had a special way of saying things.

Now I'm based in Honolulu. When our middle sister jumped, she kind of closed the world. The family just sort of fell apart. I left. Now, I try to make up for it; the folks still won't see me, but I try to keep in touch with them through Lisa. Flying cuts up your life, hits hardest during the holidays. I'm always sensitive then. I feel like I'm missing something, that people are doing something really important while I'm up in the sky, flying through time zones.

So I like to see Lisa around the beginning of the year. January, New Year's, and February, New Year's again, double luckiness with our birthdays in between. With so much going on, there's always something to talk about.

"You pick the place this year," I tell her.

"Around here?"

"No," I say. "Around here" means the food is good and the living hard. You eat a steaming rice plate, and then you feel like rushing home to sew garments or assemble radio parts or something. We eat together only once a year, so I feel we should splurge. Besides, at the Chinatown places, you have nothing to talk about except the bare issues. In American restaurants, the atmosphere helps you along. I want nice light and a view and handsome waiters.

"Let's go somewhere with a view," I say.

We decide to go to Following Sea, a new place on the Pier 39 track. We're early, the restaurant isn't crowded. It's been clear all day, so I think the sunset will be nice. I ask for a window table. I turn to talk to my sister, but she's already talking to a waiter. He's got that dark island tone that she likes. He's looking her up and down. My sister does not blink at it. She holds his look and orders two Johnny Walkers. I pick up a fork, turn it around in my hand. I seldom use chopsticks now. At home, I eat my rice in a plate, with a fork. The only chopsticks I own, I wear in my hair. For a moment, I feel strange sitting here at this unfamiliar table. I don't know this tablecloth, this linen, these candles. Everything seems foreign. It feels like we should be different people. But each time I look up, she's the same. I know this person. She's my sister. We sat together with chopsticks, mismatched bowls, braids, and braces, across the formica tabletop.

"I like three-pronged forks," I say, pressing my thumb against the sharp points.

My sister rolls her eyes. She lights a cigarette.

I ask for one.

I finally say, "So, what's new?"

"Not much." Her voice is sullen. She doesn't look at me. Once a year, I come in, asking questions. She's got the answers, but she hates them. For me, I think she's got the peace of heart, knowing that she's done her share for Mah and Deh. She thinks I have the peace, not caring. Her life is full of questions, too, but I have no answers.

I look around the restaurant. The sunset is not spectacular, and we don't comment on it. The waiters are lighting candles. Ours is bringing the drinks. He stops very close to my sister, seems to breathe her in. She raises her face toward him. "Ready?" he asks. My sister orders for us. The waiter struts off.

"Tight ass," I say.

"The best," she says.

My scotch tastes good. It reminds me of Deh. Johnny Walker or Seagrams 7, that's what they served at Chinese banquets. Nine courses and a bottle. No ice. We learned to drink it Chinese style, in teacups. Deh drank from his rice bowl, sipping it like hot soup. By the end of the meal, he took it like cool tea, in bold mouthfuls. We sat watching, our teacups in our laps, his three giggly girls.

Relaxed, I'm thinking there's a connection. Johnny Walker then and Johnny Walker now. I ask for another cigarette and this one I enjoy. Now my Johnny Walker pops with ice. I twirl the glass to make the ice tinkle.

We clink glasses. Three times for good luck. She giggles. I feel better.

"Nice sweater," I say.

"Michael Owyang," she says. She laughs. The light from the candle makes her eyes shimmer. She's got Mah's eyes. Eyes that make you want to talk. Lisa is reed-thin and tall. She's got a body that clothes look good on. My sister slips something on, and it wraps her like skin. Fabric has pulse on her.

"Happy birthday, soon," I say.

"Thanks, and to yours too, just as soon."

"Here's to Johnny Walker in shark's fin soup," I say.

"And squab dinners."

" 'I Love Lucy,' " I say.

We laugh. It makes us feel like children again. We remember how to be sisters. I raise my glass, "To 'I Love Lucy,' squab dinners, and brown bags."

"To bones," she says.

"Bones," I repeat. This is a funny story that gets sad, and knowing it, I keep laughing. I am surprised how much memory there is in one word. Pigeons. Only recently did I learn they're called squab. Our word for them was pigeon—on a plate or flying over Portsmouth Square. A good meal at forty cents a bird. In line by dawn, we waited at the butcher's listening for the slow churning motor of the trucks. We watched the live fish flushing out of the tanks into the garbage pails. We smelled the honey-crushed cha sui bows baking. When the white laundry truck turned into Wentworth, there was a puffing trail of feathers following it. A stench filled the alley. The crowd squeezed in around the truck. Old ladies reached into the crates, squeezing and tugging for the plumpest pigeons.

My sister and I picked the white ones, those with the most expressive eyes. Dove birds, we called them. We fed them leftover rice in water, and as long as they stayed plump, they were our pets, our baby dove birds. And then one day we'd come home from school and find them cooked. They were a special, nutritious treat. Mah let us fill our bowls high with little pigeon parts: legs, breasts, and wings, and take them out to the front room to watch "I Love Lucy." We took brown bags for the bones. We balanced our bowls on our laps and laughed at Lucy. We leaned forward, our chopsticks crossed in mid-air, and called out, "Mah! Mah! Come watch! Watch Lucy cry!"

But she always sat alone in the kitchen sucking out the sweetness of the lesser parts: necks, backs, and the head. "Bones are sweeter than you know," she always said. She came out to check the bags. "Clean bones," she said, shaking the bags. "No waste," she said.

Our dinners come with a warning. "Plate's hot. Don't touch." My sister orders a carafe of house white. "Enjoy," he says, smiling at my sister. She doesn't look up.

I can't remember how to say scallops in Chinese. I ask my sister, she doesn't know either. The food isn't great. Or maybe we just don't have the taste buds in us to go crazy over it. Sometimes I get very hungry for Chinese flavors: black beans, garlic and ginger, shrimp paste and sesame oil. These are tastes we grew up with, still dream about. Crave. Run around town after. Duck liver sausage, bean curd, jook, salted fish, and fried dace with black beans. Western flavors don't stand out, the surroundings do. Three pronged forks. Pink tablecloths. Fresh flowers. Cute waiters. An odd difference.

"Maybe we should have gone to Sun Hung Heung. At least the vegetables are real," I say.

"Hung toh-yee-foo-won-tun!" she says.

"Yeah, yum!" I say.

I remember Deh teaching us how to pick bok choy, his favorite vegetable. "Stick your fingernail into the stem. Juicy and firm, good. Limp and tough, no good." The three of us followed Deh, punching our thumbnails into every stem of bok choy we saw.

"Deh still eating bok choy?"

"Breakfast, lunch and dinner." My sister throws her head back, and laughs. It is Deh's motion. She recites in a mimic tone. "Your Deh, all he needs is a good hot bowl of rice and a plate full of greens. A good monk."

There was always bok choy. Even though it was nonstop for Mah—rushing to the sweatshop in the morning, out to shop on break, and then home to cook by evening—she did this for him. A plate of bok choy, steaming with the taste of ginger and garlic. He said she made good rice. Timed full-fire until the first boil, medium until the grains formed a crust along the sides of the pot, and then low-flamed to let the rice steam. Firm, that's how Deh liked his rice.

The waiter brings the wine, asks if everything is all right.

"Everything," my sister says.

There's something else about this meeting. I can hear it in the edge of her voice. She doesn't say anything and I don't ask. Her lips make a contorting line; her face looks sour. She lets out a breath. It sounds like she's been holding it in too long.

"Another fight. The bank line," she says. "He waited four times in the bank line. Mah ran around outside shopping. He was doing her a favor. She was doing him a favor. Mah wouldn't stop yelling. 'Get out and go die! Useless Thing! Stinking Corpse!' "

I know he answered. His voice must have had that fortune teller's tone to it. You listened because you knew it was a warning.

He always threatened to disappear, jump off the Golden Gate. His thousand-year-old threat. I've heard it all before. "I will go. Even when dead, I won't be far enough away. Curse the good will that blinded me into taking you as wife!"

I give Lisa some of my scallops. "Eat," I tell her.

She keeps talking. "Of course, you know how Mah thinks, that nobody should complain because she's been the one working all these years."

I nod. I start eating, hoping she'll follow.

One bite and she's talking again. "You know what shopping with Mah is like, either you stand outside with the bags like a servant, or inside like a marker, holding a place in line. You know how she gets into being frugal—saving time because it's the one free thing in her life. Well, they're at the bank and she had him hold her place in line while she runs up and down Stockton doing her quick shopping maneuvers. So he's in line, and it's his turn, but she's not back. So he has to start all over at the back again. Then it's his turn but she's still not back. When she finally comes in, she's got bags in both hands, and he's going through the line for the fourth time. Of course she doesn't say sorry or anything."

I interrupt. "How do you know all this?" I tell myself not to come back next year. I tell myself to apply for another transfer, to the East Coast.

"She told me. Word for word." Lisa spears a scallop, puts it in her mouth. I know it's cold by now. "Word for word," she repeats. She cuts a piece of chicken. "Try," she says.

I think about how we're sisters. We eat slowly, chewing carefully like old people. A way to make things last, to fool the stomach.

Mah and Deh both worked too hard; it's as if their marriage was a marriage of toil—of toiling together. The idea is that the next generation can marry for love.

In the old country, matches were made, strangers were wedded, and that was fate. Those days, sojourners like Deh were considered princes. To become the wife to such a man was to be saved from the war-torn villages.

Saved to work. After dinner, with the rice still in between her teeth, Mah sat down at her Singer. When we pulled out the wall-bed, she was still there, sewing. The street noises stopped long before she did. The hot lamp made all the stitches blur together. And in the mornings, long before any of us awoke, she was already there, sewing again.

His work was hard, too. He ran a laundry on Polk Street. He sailed with the American President Lines. Things started to look up when he owned the take-out place in Vallejo, and then his partner ran off. So he went to Alaska and worked the canneries.

She was good to him, too. We remember. How else would we have known him all those years he worked in Guam, in the Fiji Islands, in Alaska? Mah always gave him majestic welcomes home. It was her excitement that made us remember him.

I look around. The restaurant is full. The waiters move quickly.

I know Deh. His words are ugly. I've heard him. I've listened. And I've always wished for the street noises, as if in the traffic of sound, I believe I can escape. I know the hard color of his eyes and the tightness of his jaw. I can almost hear his teeth grind. I know this. Years of it.

Their lives weren't easy. So is their discontent without reason?

What about the first one? You didn't even think to come to the hospital. The first one, I say! Son or daughter, dead or alive, you didn't even come!

What about living or dying? Which did you want for me that time you pushed me back to work before my back brace was off?

Money! Money! Money to eat with, to buy clothes with, to pass this life with!

Don't start that again! Everything I make at that dead place I hand . . .

How come . . .
What about . . .
So . . .

It was obvious. The stories themselves mean little. It was how hot and furious they could become.

Is there no end to it? What makes their ugliness so alive, so thick and impossible to let go of?

"I don't want to think about it anymore." The way she says it surprises me. This time I listen. I imagine what it would be like to take her place. It will be my turn one day.

"Ron," she says, wiggling her fingers above the candle. "A fun thing."

The opal flickers above the flame. I tell her that I want to get her something special for her birthday, " . . . next trip I get abroad." She looks up at me, smiles.

For a minute, my sister seems happy. But she won't be able to hold onto it. She grabs at things out of despair, out of fear. Gifts grow old for her. Emotions never ripen, they sour. Everything slips away from her. Nothing sustains her. Her beauty has made her fragile.

We should have eaten in Chinatown. We could have gone for coffee in North Beach, then for jook at Sam Wo's.

"No work, it's been like that for months, just odd jobs," she says.

I'm thinking, it's not like I haven't done my share. I was a kid once, I did things because I felt I should. I helped fill out forms at the Chinatown employment agencies. I went with him to the Seaman's Union. I waited too, listening and hoping for those calls: "Busboy! Presser! Prep Man!" His bags were packed, he was always ready to go. "On standby," he said.

Every week. All the same. Quitting and looking to start all over again. In the end, it was like never having gone anywhere. It was like the bank line, waiting for nothing.

How many times did my sister and I have to hold them apart? The flat *ting!* sound as the blade slapped onto the linoleum floor, the wooden handle of the knife slamming into the corner. Was it she or I who screamed, repeating all of their ugliest words? Who shook them? Who made them stop?

The waiter comes to take the plates. He stands by my sister for a moment. I raise my glass to the waiter.

"You two Chinese?" he asks.

"No," I say, finishing off my wine. I roll my eyes. I wish I had another Johnny Walker. Suddenly I don't care.

"We're two sisters," I say. I laugh. I ask for the check, leave a good tip. I see him slip my sister a box of matches.

Outside, the air is cool and brisk. My sister links her arm into mine. We walk up Bay onto Chestnut. We pass Galileo High School and then turn down Van Ness to head toward the pier. The bay is black. The foghorns sound far away. We walk the whole length of the pier without talking.

The water is white where it slaps against the wooden stakes.

For a long time Lisa's wanted out. She can stay at that point of endurance forever. Desire that becomes old feels too good, it's seductive. I know how hard it is to go.

The heart never travels. You have to be heartless. My sister holds that heart, too close and for too long. This is her weakness, and I like to think, used to be mine. Lisa endures too much.

We're lucky, not like the bondmaids growing up in service, or the newborn daughters whose mouths were stuffed with ashes. Courtesans with the three-inch feet, beardless, soft-shouldered eunuchs, and the frightened child-brides, they're all stories to us. We're the lucky generation. Our parents forced themselves to live through the humiliation in this country so that we could have it better. We know so little of the old country. We repeat names of Grandfathers and Uncles, but they will always be strangers to us. Family exists only because somebody has a story, and knowing the story connects us to a history. To us, the deformed man is oddly compelling, the forgotten man is a good story. A beautiful woman suffers.

I want her beauty to buy her out.

The sweater cost two weeks pay. Like the forty cent birds that are now a delicacy, this is a special treat. The money doesn't mean anything. It is, if anything, time. Time is what I would like to give her.

A red sweater. One hundred percent angora. The skin of fuzz will be a fierce rouge on her naked breasts.

Red. Lucky. Wear it. Find that man. The new one. Wrap yourself around him. Feel the pulsing between you. Fuck him and think about it. One hundred percent. Hand Wash Only. Worn Once.

Journal Entry

Explore the concepts of family presented in "A Red Sweater."

Textual Considerations

1. Locate the climax of the story, and analyze it in terms of the conflict that erupts externally on the level of events and internally within the protagonist's mind.
2. Speculate on the different meanings, both conscious and unconscious, that the red sweater acquires throughout the story. Remember that what the text implies may be as important as what it states directly.
3. Analyze the conversations in which the female character engages over the course of the story. To what extent do these conversations reflect the story of her personal life, and to what extent do they connect to the historical story of her family and ethnic group?

Cultural Contexts

1. React to the protagonist's statement that "I am surprised how much memory there is in one word." How does memory contribute to her sense of self? Investigate also whether she is able to reconcile her memories with the advice she gives to her sister at the end of the story.
2. To appreciate better the sense of cultural displacement experienced by some Asian immigrants in America, investigate the social conditions behind the narrator's assessment that "we're the lucky generation. Our parents forced themselves to live through the humiliation in this country so that we could have it better." Are they, in fact, the "lucky ones"? Explain. Consider, for example, the extent to which the narrator and her sister have achieved a sense of community in the United States.

Ruth Prawer Jhabvala

The Englishwoman

The Englishwoman—her name is Sadie—was fifty-two years old when she decided to leave India. She could hardly believe it. She felt young and free. At fifty-two! Her bag is packed and she is running away. She is eloping, leaving everything behind her—husband, children, grandchildren, thirty years of married life. Her heart is light and so is her luggage. It is surprising how few things she has to take with her. Most of her clothes are not worth taking. These last years she has been mostly wearing dowdy cotton frocks sewn by a little turbaned tailor. She still has a few saris but she is not taking them with her. She doesn't ever intend to wear those again.

The person who is crying the most at her impending departure is Annapurna, her husband's mistress. Annapurna has a very emotional nature. She looks into the packed bag; like Sadie, she is surprised by its meager contents. "Is that all you are taking with you?" she asks. Sadie answers, "It's all I've got." Annapurna breaks into a new storm of tears.

"But that's good," Sadie urges. "Not to accumulate things, to travel light—what could be better?"

"Oh, you're so spiritual," Annapurna tells her, wiping her eyes on the other's sleeve. "Really you are far more Indian than I am."

"Nonsense," Sadie says, and she means it. What nonsense.

But it is true that if Indian means "spiritual"—as so many people like to believe—then Annapurna is an exception. She is a very, very physical sort of person. She is stout, with a tight glowing skin, and shining eyes and teeth, and hair glossy with black dye. She loves clothes and jewelry and rich food. Although she is about the same age as the Englishwoman, she is far more vigorous, and when she moves, her sari rustles and her bracelets jingle.

"But are you really going?"

Annapurna keeps asking this question. And Sadie keeps asking it of herself too. But they ask it in two very different ways. Annapurna is shocked and grieved (yes, grieved—she loves the Englishwoman). But Sadie is incredulous with happiness. Can it really be true? she keeps asking herself. I'm going? I'm leaving India? Her heart skips with joy and she has difficulty in repressing her smiles. She doesn't want anyone to suspect her feelings. She is ashamed of her own callousness—and yet she goes on smiling, more and more, and happiness wells up in her like a spring.

Last week she went to say goodbye to the children. They are both settled in Bombay now with their families. Dev, her son, has been married for two years and has a baby girl; Monica, the daughter, has three boys. Dev has a fine job with an advertising company; and Monica is working too, for she has too much to drive to be content with just staying at home. She calls herself a go-go girl and that is what she is, charging around town interviewing people for the articles she writes for a women's magazine, talking in the latest slang current in Bombay, throwing parties of which she herself is the life and soul. Monica looks quite Indian—her eyes are black, her skin glows; she is really more like Annapurna than like the Englishwoman, who is gaunt and pale.

Although so gay, Monica also likes to have serious discussions. She attempted to have such a discussion with her mother. She said, "But, Mummy, *why* are you going?" and she looked at her with the special serious face she has for serious moments.

Sadie didn't know what to answer. What could she say? But she had to say something, or Monica would be hurt. So she too became solemn, and she explained to her daughter that when people get older they begin to get very homesick for the place in which they were born and grew up and that this homesickness becomes worse and worse till in the end life becomes almost unbearable. Monica understood what she said and sympathised with it. She made plans how they would all come and visit her in England. She promised that when the boys became bigger, she would send them to her for long holidays. She was now in full agreement with her mother's departure, so Sadie was glad she told her what she did. She was prepared to tell Dev the same thing if he asked her, but he didn't ask. He and his wife were rather worried in those days because there was an outbreak of chicken pox in their apartment building and they were afraid Baby might catch it. But they too promised frequent visits to her in England.

Only Annapurna is still crying. She looks at Sadie's little suitcase and cries, and then she looks at Sadie and cries. She keeps asking, "But why, *why?*" Sadie tries to tell her what she told Monica, but Annapurna waves her aside; for her it is not a good enough reason and she is right, Sadie herself knows it isn't. She asks wouldn't Sadie miss all of them and their love for her, and wouldn't she miss the life she has lived and the place in which she has lived it, her whole past, everything she has been and done for thirty years? Thirty years! she cries, again and again, appalled—and

Sadie too is appalled, it is such a long time. Annapurna says that an Indian wife also yearns for her father's house, and at the beginning of her marriage she is always waiting to go off there to visit; but as the years progress and she becomes deeper and deeper embedded in her husband's home, these early memories fade till they are nothing more than a sweet sensation enshrined in the heart. Sadie knows that what Annapurna is saying is true, but also that it does not in the least apply in her own case because her feelings are not ones of gentle nostalgia.

The Englishwoman doesn't like to remember the early years when she first came to live here. It is as if she wished to disown her happiness then. How she loved everything! She never gave a backward glance to home or England. Her husband's family enjoyed and abetted her attempts to become Indian. A whole lot of them—mother-in-law, sister-in-law, aunts, cousins and friends—would cram into the family car (with blue silk curtains discreetly drawn to shield them from view) and drive to the bazaar to buy saris for Sadie. She was never much consulted about their choice, and when they got home, she was tugged this way and that while they argued with each other about the best way to drape it round her. When they had finished, they stood back to admire, only instead of admiring they often could not help sailing at her appearance. She didn't care. Yes, she knew she was too tall for the sari, and too thin, and too English, but she loved wearing it and to feel herself Indian. She also made attempts to learn Hindi, and this too amused everyone and they never tired of making her repeat certain words, going into peals of laughter at her pronunciation. Everyone, all the ladies of the household, had a lot of fun. They were healthy, rich and gay. They were by no means a tradition-bound family, and although their life in the house did have something of the enclosed, languorous quality of purdah living, the minds flowering within it were full of energy and curiosity. The mother-in-law herself, at that time well over sixty, spent a lot of her time reading vernacular novels, and she also attempted to write some biographical sketches of her own, describing life in a high-caste household in the 1880s. She took to smoking cigarettes quite late in life and liked them so much that she ended up as a chain-smoker. When Sadie thinks of her, she sees her reclining on an embroidered mat spread on the floor, one elbow supported on a bolster, some cushions at her back, reading a brown tattered little volume through her glasses and enveloping herself in clouds of scented cigarette smoke.

Annapurna often speaks about those days. Annapurna was a relative, some sort of cousin. She had run away from her husband (who drank and, it was whispered, went in for unnatural practices) and had come to live with them in the house. When Annapurna speaks about those distant times, she does so as if everyone were still alive and all of them as young and gay as they were then. Often she says, "If only Srilata [or Radhika—or Raksha—or Chandralekha] were here now, how she would laugh!" But Srilata died of typhoid twenty years ago; Raksha married a Nepalese general and has gone to live in Kathmandu; Chandralekha poisoned herself over an unhappy love affair. To Annapurna, however, it is as if everyone is still there and she recalls and brings to life every detail of a distant event so that to Sadie too it begins to appear that she can hear the voices of those days. Till Annapurna returns to the present and with an outstretched hand, her plump palm turned up to heaven, she acknowledges that they are all gone and many of them are dead; and she turns and looks at the Englishwoman and says, "And now you are going too," and her eyes are full of reproach.

It may seem strange that the mistress should reproach the wife, but Annapurna is within her rights to do so. For so many years now it is she who has taken over from the Englishwoman all the duties of a wife. There has never been any bitterness or jealousy between them. On the contrary, Sadie has always been grateful to her. She knows that before her husband became intimate with Annapurna, he used to go to other women. He *had* to go; he was such a healthy man and needed women as strong and healthy as he was. These were often young prostitutes. But for a long time now he has been content with Annapurna. He has put on an enormous amount of weight in these last years. It is Annapurna's fault; she feeds him too well and panders to his passion for good food. His meals are frequent and so heavy that in between them, he is not capable of moving. He lies on a couch arranged for him on a verandah and breathes heavily. Sometimes he puffs at a hookah which stands within easy reach. He lies there for hours while Annapurna sits on the other end of the couch and entertains him with lively gossip. He enjoys that, but doesn't mind at all if she has no time for him. When he feels like talking, he summons one of the servants to come and squat on the carpet near his couch.

When Sadie first knew him, as a student at Oxford, he was a slim boy with burning eyes and a lock of hair on his forehead. He was always smiling and always on the go. He loved being a student, and though he never managed to graduate, got a lot out of it. He gave breakfast parties and had his own wine merchant and a red car in which he drove up to London several times a week; he was always discovering new pleasures, like hampers from Fortnum and Mason's and champagne parties on the river. Sadie had grown up in rather an austere atmosphere. Her family were comfortably off but had high principles of self-restraint and preferred lofty thought to lavish living. Sadie herself—a serious girl, a spare, stringent, high-bred English beauty—thought she had the same principles, but the young Indian made her see another side to her nature. When he went back to India, it was impossible to stay behind. She followed him, married him, and loved him even more than she had in England. He belonged here so completely. Sometimes Sadie didn't see him for days on end—when he went on shooting parties and other expeditions with his friends—but she didn't mind. She stayed at home with the other women and enjoyed life as much as he did. There were summer nights when they all sat out in the garden by the fountain, and Chandralekha, who had a very sweet voice, sang sad songs from the hills while Radhika accompanied her on a lutelike instrument; and the moon shone, and Annapurna cut up mangoes for all of them, and the smell of these mangoes mingled with that exuding from the flowering bushes in a mixture so pungent, so heady, that when the Englishwoman recalls those nights now, it is always by their scent that they become physical and present to her.

Annapurna and Sadie's husband play cards every evening. They play for money and Annapurna usually loses and then she gets cross; she always refuses to pay up, and the next evening they conveniently forget her debt and start again from scratch. But if he loses, then she insists on immediate payment: she laughs in triumph, and holding out her hand, opens and shuts it greedily and shouts, "Come on, pay up!" She also calls to Sadie and the servants to witness his discomfiture; those evenings are always merry. But sooner or later, and often in the middle of a game, she falls asleep. Once Annapurna is asleep, everything is very quiet. The servants turn off the lights and go to their quarters; the husband sits on his couch and looks out into the garden and takes a few puffs at his hookah; Sadie is upstairs in her bedroom. Nothing stirs, there isn't a sound, until the husband gives a loud sigh as he heaves himself up. He wakes Annapurna and they support each other up the stairs to their bedroom, where they sink onto their large, soft bed and are asleep immediately and totally until it is morning. It is a long time before Sadie can get to sleep. She walks up and down the room. She argues with herself to and fro, and her mind heaves in turmoil like a sea in storm. The fact that everything else is calm and sleeping exacerbates her restlessness. She longs for some response, for something or someone other than herself to be affected by what is going on within her. But there is only silence and sleep. She steps out of her room and onto the verandah. The garden is in imperfect darkness, dimly and fitfully lit by the moon. Occasionally—very, very occasionally—a bird wakes up and rustles in a tree.

It was during these hours of solitude that she came to her decision to leave. To others—and at the actual moment of making it, even to herself—it seemed like a sudden decision, but in fact, looking back, she realizes that she has been preparing for it for twenty years. She can even mark the exact day, twenty years ago, when first she knew that she did not want to go on living here. It was when her son was sick with one of those sudden mysterious illnesses that so often attack children in India. He lay burning in the middle of a great bed, with his eyes full of fever; he was very quiet except for an occasional groan. All the women in the house had gathered round his bedside and all were giving advice and different remedies. Some sat on chairs, some on the floor; the mother-in-law squatted crosslegged on the end of his bed; her spectacles on her nose, smoking cigarettes and turning the pages of a novel; from time to time she made soothing noises at Dev and squeezed his ankles. Annapurna sat by his side and rubbed ice on his head. Every time Dev groaned they all said, "Oh, poor Baba, poor Baba." The servants moved in and out; they too said, "Oh, poor Baba," and looked at him pityingly. The Englishwoman remembered the sickbeds of her own childhood, how she lay for hours comfortable and bored with nothing to do except watch the tree outside the window and the fat wet raindrops squashing against and sliding down the window-pane. The only person who ever came in was her mother, when it was time for her medicine. But Dev wouldn't have liked that. He wanted everyone with him, and if one of the aunts was out of the room for too long a time, he would ask for her in a weak voice and someone would have to go and fetch her.

Sadie went out onto the verandah. But it was no better there. The day was one of these murky yellow ones when the sun is stifled in vapours of dust. She felt full of fears, for Dev and for herself, as if they were both being sucked down by—what was it? the heat? the loving women inside? the air thick as a swamp in which fevers breed? She longed to be alone with her sick child in some cool place. But she knew this was not possible and that they belonged here in this house crammed full with relatives and choking under a yellow sky. She could never forget the despair of that moment, though in the succeeding years there were many like it. But that was the first.

As she stood there on the verandah, she saw her husband arrive home. He was a very bright spot in that murky day. He was dressed in a starched white kurta with little jewels for buttons, and his face was raised towards her as she stood up on the verandah, and he was smiling. He was no longer the slim boy she had first known but neither was he as fat as he is today: no, he was in the prime of life then, and what a prime! He came bounding up the outside staircase toward her and said, "How is he?"

"How can he be," she answered, "with all of them in there?"

Surprised at her tone, he stopped smiling and looked at her anxiously. Her anger mounted, and there were other things mixed in with it now: not only the heat and the overcrowded room but also that he was so sleek and smiling and young while she—oh, she felt worn out, wrung out, and knew she looked it. She thought of the prostitutes he went to. It seemed to her that she could see and smell their plump, brown, wriggling young bodies greasy with scented oil.

In a shaking voice she said, "They're stifling that poor boy—they won't let him breathe. No one seems to have the least idea of hygiene."

He knew it was more than she was saying and continued to look at her anxiously. "Are you ill?" he asked and put out his hand to feel her forehead. When she drew back, he asked, "What is it?" full of sympathy.

They had been speaking in low voices, but all the same from inside the crowded room Annapurna had sensed that something was wrong. She left the bedside and came out to join them. She looked enquiringly at Sadie's husband. They were not yet lovers at the time, but there was that instinctive understanding between them there was between all the members of that household.

"She is not well," he said.

"I *am* well! I'm perfectly well!" Sadie burst into tears. She had no control over this. Furiously she wiped the foolish tears from her cheeks.

Both of them melted with tenderness. Annapurna folded her in an embrace; the husband stroked her back. When she struggled to get free, they thought it was a new outbreak of anguish and redoubled their attentions. At last she cried, "It's so *hot!*" and indeed she could hardly breathe and perspiration ran down her in runnels from her being squashed against fat Annapurna. Then Annapurna let her go. They both stood and looked at her, full of anxiety for her; and these two round healthy shining faces looking at her with love, *pitying* her, were so unbearable to her that, to prevent herself from bursting into the tears that she despised but that they, she knew, not only awaited but even expected, she turned and, hurrying along the verandah that ran like a gallery all round the house, she hid herself in her bedroom and locked the door. They followed and knocked urgently and begged to be allowed to enter. She refused to open. She could hear them discussing her outside the door: they were full of understanding; they realized that people did get upset like this and that then it was the duty of others to soothe and help them.

She was always being soothed and helped. She is still being soothed and helped. Annapurna has taken everything out of her suitcase and is repacking it in what she considers is a better way. She has had special shoe bags sewn. As a matter of fact, she would like to have a completely new outfit of clothes made for her. She says how will it look if Sadie arrives with nothing better than those few shabby rags in that little suitcase? Sadie thinks silently to herself: Look to whom? She knows almost no one there. A few distant relatives, one old school friend; she hasn't been there for thirty years, she has no contacts, no correspondence—and yet she is going home! Home! And again happiness rushes over her in waves, and she takes a deep breath to be able to bear it.

"And not a single piece of jewelry," Annapurna grumbles.

Sadie laughs. She has given it all away long ago to Monica and to Dev's wife: and very glad she was to get rid of all those heavy costly gold ornaments. They were her share of the family jewels, but she never knew what to do with them. Certainly she couldn't wear them—she was always too thin and pale to be able to carry off those pieces fit for a barbarian queen; so she had left them lying around for years in a cupboard till Annapurna had taken them away from her to lock up in a safe.

"At least *one* piece you could have let me keep for you," Annapurna now says. "Then you would have had something to show them. What will they think of us?"

"What will *who* think?" Sadie asks, and the idea of the distant relatives and her poor school friend (Clare, still unmarried and still teaching) having any thoughts on the subject of what properties she has brought back with her from India makes her laugh again. And there is a lightheartedness in her laughter that hasn't been there for a long time, and Annapurna hears it and is hurt by it.

They are both hurt by her attitude. It has been years since Sadie saw her husband so upset; but then it has been years since anything really upset him. He has led a very calm life lately. Not that his life was not always calm and comfortable, but there were times in his younger days when he, like everyone else in the house, had his outbursts. She particularly remembers one he had with his sister Chandralekha. Actually, at that time, the whole house was in upheaval. Chandralekha had formed an unfortunate attachment to a man nobody approved of. They were not a rigid family that way—there had been several love matches—but it seemed Chandralekha's choice was entirely unsuitable. Sadie had met the man, who struck her as intelligent and of a strong character. In fact, she thought Chandralekha had shown excellent taste. But when she told her husband so, he waved her aside and said she didn't understand. And it was true, she didn't; everything that went on in the house during those days was a mystery to her. Oh, she understood vaguely what it was all about—the man was of *low birth,* and all his virtues of character and self-made position could not wipe that stain away—but the passions that were aroused, the issues that were thought to be at stake, were beyond her comprehension. Yet she could see that all of them were suffering deeply, and Chandralekha was in a torment of inner conflict (indeed, she later committed suicide).

One day Chandralekha came in carrying a dish of sweet rice which she had made herself. She said, "Just wait till you taste this," and she lovingly ladled a spoonful onto her brother's plate. He began to eat with relish, but quite suddenly he pushed the plate away and began to cry out loud. Everyone at once knew why, of course. The only person who was surprised was Sadie— both at the suddenness of the outburst and at the lengths to which he went. He banged his head against the wall, flung himself on the ground at Chandralekha's feet, and at one point he snatched up a knife and held it at his own throat and had to have it wrested away from him by all the women there surrounding him. "The children, the children!" he kept crying, and at first Sadie thought he meant their own children, Monica and Dev, and she couldn't understand what was threatening them; but everyone else knew he meant Chandralekha's children who were yet unborn but who would be born, and if she married this man, born with polluted blood. Sadie didn't know how that scene ended; she went away and locked herself up in her bedroom. She covered her ears with her hands to shut out the noise and cries that echoed through the house.

When he learned of her decision to leave, Sadie's husband begged and pleaded with her in the same way he had done with Chandralekha all those years ago. The Englishwoman felt embarrassed and ashamed for him. He looked so ridiculous, being so heavy and fat, with his great bulk heaving, and emitting cries like those of a hysterical woman. No one else found him ridiculous—on the contrary, the servants and Annapurna were deeply affected by his strong emotions and tried to comfort him. But he wouldn't be comforted till in the end his passion spent itself. Then he became resigned and even quite practical and sent for his lawyer to make a settlement. He was very generous toward his wife, and indeed keeps pressing her to accept more and is distressed because she doesn't need it. So now she feels ashamed not of him but of herself and her own lack of feeling.

It is her last night in India. As usual, her husband and Annapurna are playing cards together. When she joins them, they look at her affectionately and treat her like a guest. Annapurna offers tea, sherbet, lime water, and is distressed when she declines all these suggestions. She is always distressed by the fact that Sadie needs less food than she does. She says, "How can you live like that?" After a moment's thought, she adds, "How will you live *there?* Who will look after you and see that you don't starve yourself to death?" When Sadie looks at her it is as she feared: tears are again flowing down Annapurna's cheeks. A sob also breaks from out of her bosom. It is echoed by another sob: Sadie looks up and sees that tears are also trickling down her husband's face. Neither of them speaks, and in fact they go on playing cards. The Englishwoman lowers her eyes away from them; she sits there, silent, prim, showing no emotion. She hopes they think she *has* no emotion; she does her best to hide it—the happiness that will not be suppressed, even at the sight of their tears.

Annapurna has had enough of playing. She flings down the cards (she has been losing). She wipes her tears away with her forearm like a child, yawns, sighs, says, "Well, time to go to bed," in resignation. He says, "Yes, it's time," with the same sigh and the same resignation. They have accepted the Englishwoman's departure; it grieves them, but they submit to it, as human beings have to submit to everything, such as old age and disease and loss of every kind. They walk upstairs slowly, leaning on each other.

When Sadie goes up to her own room, she is almost running in her excitement. She looks in the mirror and is surprised at the drained face that looks back at her. She doesn't feel like that at all—no, she feels the way she used to do, so that now she expects her bright eyes back again and her pink cheeks. She turns away from the mirror, laughing at her own foolishness; and she can hear her own laughter and it is just the way it used to be. She knows she won't sleep tonight. She doesn't want to sleep. She loves this feeling of excitement and youth and to pace the room with her heart beating and wild thoughts storming in her head. The servants have turned out the lights downstairs and gone to bed. The lights are out in her husband and Annapurna's room too; they must be fast asleep, side by side on their bed.

The Englishwoman can't see the moon, but the garden is lit up by some sort of faint silver light. She can make out the fountain with the stone statue, and the lime trees, and the great flowering bush of Queen of the Night; there is the bench where they used to sit in the evenings when Chandralekha sang in her sweet voice. But as she goes on looking, the moonlit scene brightens until it is no longer that silver garden but English downs spreading as far as the eye can see, yellow on one side, green on another. The green side is being rained upon by mild soft rain coming down like a curtain, and the yellow side is being shone upon by a sun as mild and soft as that rain. On a raised knoll in the foreground there is an oak tree with leaves and acorns, and she is standing by this tree; and as she stands there, on that eminence overlooking the downs, strong winds blow right through her. They are as cold and fresh as the waters of a mountain torrent. They threaten to sweep her off her feet so that she has to plant herself down very firmly and put out her hand to support herself against the trunk of the tree (she can feel the rough texture of its bark). She raises her face, and her hair—not *her* hair but the shining hair of her youth—flies wild and free in that strong wind.

Journal Entry

Speculate on why Jhabvala uses the generic term "Englishwoman" as a title. Why doesn't she use "Sadie," the Englishwoman's name? What is the difference in implication?

Textual Considerations

1. The story's protagonist is ambivalent about India, her adopted country. How does her ambivalence affect her family, her own personality, and the choices that she makes? What aspects of Indian culture does she find most difficult to accept?

2. To what extent does her husband's relationship with Annapurna contribute to her decision? Why is the husband never given a name or allowed to speak, except in one scene?
3. According to the Englishwoman, she and Annapurna had never been jealous of each other. Do you find this plausible? To what extent does the account of their social interactions refute or support her assertion?

Cultural Contexts

1. Analyze with your group the causes and effects of the Englishwoman's alienation in India. To what extent do you empathize with her decision to return to England?
2. The caste system is an integral part of Indian society. Discuss its role in the social interactions in Jhabvala's story.

Mtutuzeli Matshoba

Call Me Not a Man

For neither am I a man in the eyes of the law,
Nor am I a man in the eyes of my fellow man.

By dodging, lying, resisting where it is possible, bolting when I'm already cornered, parting with invaluable money, sometimes calling my sisters into the game to get amorous with my captors, allowing myself to be slapped on the mouth in front of my womenfolk and getting sworn at with my mother's private parts, that component of me which is man has died countless times in one lifetime. Only a shell of me remains to tell you of the other man's plight, which is in fact my own. For what is suffered by another man in view of my eyes is suffered also by me. The grief he knows is a grief I know. Out of the same bitter cup do we drink. To the same chain-gang do we belong.

Friday has always been their chosen day to go plundering, although they come only occasionally, maybe once a month. Perhaps they have found better pastures elsewhere, where their prey is more predictable than at Mzimhlope, the place which has seen the tragic demise of three of their accomplices who had taken the game a bit too far by entering the hostel on the northern side of our location and fleecing the people right in the midst of their disgusting labour camps. Immediately after this there was a notable abatement in the frequency of their visits to both the location and the adjacent hostel. However the lull was short-lived, lasting only until the storm had died down, because the memory tarnishes quickly in the locations, especially the memory of death. We were beginning to emit sighs of relief and to mutter "good riddance" when they suddenly reappeared and made their presence in our lives felt once again. June 'seventy-six had put them out of the picture for the next year, during which they were scarcely seen. Like a recurring pestilence they refuse to vanish absolutely from the scene.

A person who has spent some time in Soweto will doubtless have guessed by now that the characters I am referring to are none other than some of the so-called police reservists who roam our dirty streets at weekends, robbing every timid, unsuspecting person, while masquerading as peace officers to maintain law and order in the community. There are no greater thieves than these men of the law, men of justice, peace officers and volunteer public protectors in the whole of the slum complex because, unlike others in the same trade of living off the sweat of their victims, they steal out in the open, in front of everybody's eyes. Of course nothing can be done about it because they go out on their pillaging exploits under the banners of the law, and to rise in protest against them is analogous to defiance of the powers that be.

So, on this Friday too we were standing on top of the station bridge at Mzimhlope. It was about five in the afternoon and the sun hung over the western horizon of spectacularly identical coalsmoke-puffing rooftops like a gigantic, glowing red ball which dyed the foamy clouds with the crimson sheen of its rays. The commuter trains in from the city paused below us every two or three minutes to regurgitate their infinite human cargo, the greater part of whom were hostel-dwellers who hurried up Mohale Street to cook their meagre suppers on primus stoves. The last train we had seen would now be leaving Phefeni, the third station from Mzimhlope. The next train had just emerged from the bridge this side of New Canada, junction to East and West Soweto. The last group of the hostel people from the train now leaving Phefeni had just turned the bend at Mohale Street where it intersects with Elliot. The two-hundred-metre stretch to Elliot was therefore relatively empty, and people coming towards the station could be clearly made out.

As the wheels of the train from New Canada squealed on the iron tracks and it came to a jerking stop, four men, two in overalls and the others in dustcoats, materialized around the Mohale Street bend. There was no doubt who they were, from the way they filled the whole width of the street and walked as if they owned everything and everybody in their sight. When they came to the grannies selling vegetables, fruit and fried mealies along the ragged, unpaved sides of the street, they grabbed what they fancied and munched gluttonously the rest of the way towards us. Again nothing could be done about it, because the poverty-stricken vendors were not licensed to scrape together some crumbs to ease the gnawing stomachs of their fatherless grandchildren at home, which left them wide open for plunder by the indifferent "reserves." "*Awu!* The Hellions," remarked Mandla next to me, "Let's get away from here, my friend."

He was right. They reminded one of the old western film; but I was not moving from where I was simply because the reservists were coming down the street like a bunch of villains. One other thing I knew was that the railway constable who was on guard duty that Friday at the station did not allow the persecution of the people on his premises. I wanted to have my laugh when they were chased off the station.

"Don't worry about them. Just wait and see how they're going to be chased away by this copper. He won't allow them on the station," I answered.

They split into twos when they arrived below us. Two of them, a tall chap with a face corroded by skin-lightening cream and wearing a yellow golf cap on his shaven head, and another stubby, shabbily dressed, middle-aged man with a bald frontal lobe and a drunk face, chewing at a cooked sheep's foot that he had taken from one of the grannies, climbed the stairs on our right-hand side. The younger man took the flight in fours. The other two chose to waylay their unsuspecting victims on the street corner at the base of the left-hand staircase. The first wave of the people who had alighted from the train was in the middle of the bridge when the second man reached the top of the stars.

Maybe they knew the two reservists by sight, maybe they just smelt cop in the smoggy air, or it being a Friday, they were alert for such possibilities. Three to four of the approaching human wall turned suddenly in their tracks and ran for their dear freedom into the mass behind them. The others were caught unawares by this unexpected movement and they staggered in all directions trying to regain balance. In a split second there was commotion on the station, as if a wild cat had found its way into a fowl-run. Two of those who had not been quick enough were grabbed by their sleeves, and their passes demanded. While they were producing their books the wolves went over their pockets, supposedly feeling for dangerous weapons, *dagga*[1] and other illegal possessions that might be concealed in the clothes, but really to ascertain whether they had caught the right people for their iniquitous purposes. They were paging through the booklets when the Railway policeman appeared.

"Wha . . . ? Don't you fools know that you're not supposed to do that shit here? Get off! Get off and do that away from Railway property. Fuck off!" He screamed at the two reservists so furiously that the veins threatened to burst in his neck.

"Arrest the dogs, *baba!* Give them a chance also to taste jail!" Mandla shouted.

"*Ja,*" I said to Mandla, "you bet, they've never been where they are so prepared to send others."

The other people joined in and we jeered the cowards off the station. They descended the stairs with their tails tucked between their legs and joined their companions below the station. Some of the commuters who had been alerted by the uproar returned to the platform to wait there until the reservists had gone before they would dare venture out of the station.

We remained where we had been and watched the persecution from above. I doubted if they even read the passes (if they could), or whether the victims knew if their books were right or out of order. Most likely the poor hunted men believed what they were told by the licensed thieves. The latter demanded the books, after first judging their prey to be weak propositions, flicked through the pages, put the passes into their own pockets, without which the owners could not continue on their way, and told the dumbfounded hostel men to stand aside while they accosted other

---

[1] *dagga* marijuana

victims. Within a very short while there was a group of confused men to one side of the street, screaming at their hostel mates to go to room so-and-so and tell so-and-so that they had been arrested at the station, and to bring money quickly to release them. Few of those who were being sent heard the messages since they were only too eager to leave the danger zone. Those who had money shook hands with their captors, received their books back and ran up Mohale Street. If they were unlucky they came upon another "roadblock" three hundred metres up the street where the process was repeated. Woe unto them who had paid their last money to the first extortionists, for this did not matter. The police station was their next stopover before the Bantu Commissioners, and thence their final destination, Modderbee Prison, where they provided the farmers with ready cheap labour until they had served their terms for breaking the law. The terms vary from a few days to two years for *loaferskap*,[2] which is in fact mere unemployment, for which the unfortunate men are not to blame. The whole arrangement stinks of forced labour.

The large *kwela-kwela*[3] swayed down Mohale Street at breakneck speed. The multitudes scattered out of its way and hung on to the sagging fences until it had passed. To be out of sight of the people on the station bridge, it skidded and swerved into the second side street from the station. More reservists poured out of it and went immediately to their dirty job with great zeal. The chain-gang which had been lined up along the fence of the house nearest the station was kicked and shoved to the *kwela-kwela* into which the victims were bundled under a rain of fists and boots, all of them scrambling to go in at the same time through the small door. The driver of the *kwela-kwela*, the only uniformed constable among the group, clanged the door shut and secured it with the locking lever. He went to stand authoritatively near one of the vendors, took a small avocado pear, peeled it and put it whole into a gargantuan mouth, spitting out the large stone later. He did not have to take the trouble of accosting anyone himself. His gangsters would all give him a lion's share of whatever they made, and moreover buy him some beers and brandy. He kept adjusting his polished belt over his potbelly as the .38 police special in its leather holster kept tugging it down. He probably preferred to wear his gun unconventionally, cowboy style.

A boy of about seventeen was caught with a knife in his pocket, a dangerous weapon. They slapped him a few times and let him stand handcuffed against the concrete wall of the station. Ten minutes later his well-rounded sister alighted from the train to find her younger brother among the prisoners. As she was inquiring from him why he had been arrested, and reprimanding him for carrying a knife, one of the younger reservists came to stand next to her and started pawing her. She let him carry on, and three minutes later her brother was free. The reservist was beaming all over his face, glad to have won himself a beautiful woman in the course of his duties and little knowing that he had been given the wrong address. Some of our

[2] *loaferskap* vagrancy [3] *kwela-kwela* police van

Black sisters are at times compelled to go all the way to save their menfolk, and, as always, nothing can be done about it.

There was a man coming down Mohale Street, conspicuous amidst the crowd because of the bag and baggage that was loaded on his overall-clad frame. On his right shoulder was a large suitcase with a grey blanket strapped to it with flaxen strings. From his left hand hung a bulging cardboard box, only a few inches from the ground, and tilting him to that side. He walked with the bounce of someone used to walking in gumboots or on uneven ground. There was the urgency of someone who had a long way to travel in his gait. It was doubtless a *goduka* on his way home to his family after many months of work in the city. It might even have been years since he had visited the countryside.

He did not see the hidden *kwela-kwela*, which might have forewarned him of the danger that was lurking at the station. Only when he had stumbled into two reservists, who stepped into his way and ordered him to put down his baggage, did he perhaps remember that it was Friday and raid-day. A baffled expression sprang into his face as he realized what he had walked into. He frantically went through the pockets of his overalls. The worried countenance deepened on his dark face. He tried again to make sure, but he did not find what he was looking for. The men who had stopped him pulled him to one side, each holding him tightly by the sleeve of his overall. He obeyed meekly like a tame animal. They let him lift his arms while they searched him all over the body. Finding nothing hidden on him, they demanded the inevitable book, although they had seen that he did not have it. He gesticulated with his hands as he explained what had caused him not to be carrying his pass with him. A few feet above them, I could hear what was said.

"Strue, *madoda*,"[4] he said imploringly, "I made a mistake. I luggaged the pass with my trunk. It was a jacket that I forgot to search before I packed it into the trunk."

"How do we know that you're not lying?" asked one of the reservists in a querulous voice.

"I'm not lying, *mfowethu*.[5] I swear by my mother, that's what happened," explained the frightened man.

The second reservist had a more evil and uncompromising attitude. "That was your own stupidity, mister. Because of it you're going to jail now; no more to your wife."

"Oh, my brother. Put yourself in my shoes. I've not been home to my people for two years now. It's the first chance I have to go and see my twin daughters who were born while I've been here. Feel for another poor Black man, please, my good brother. Forgive me only for this once."

"What? Forgive you? And don't give us that slush about your children. We've also got our own families, for whom we are at work right now, at this very moment," the obstinate one replied roughly.

---

[4] *madola* [5] *mfowethu* terms of respect

"But, *mfo*. Wouldn't you make a mistake too?"

That was a question the cornered man should not have asked. The reply this time was a resounding slap on the face. "You think I'm stupid like you, huh? Bind this man, Mazibuko, put the bloody irons on the dog."

"No, man. Let us talk to the poor bloke. Perhaps he can do something for us in exchange for the favour of letting him proceed on his way home," the less volatile man suggested, and pulled the hostel man away from the rest of the arrested people.

"*Ja*. Speak to him yourself, Mazibuko. I can't bear talking to rural fools like him. I'll kill him with my bare hands if he thinks that I've come to play here in Johannesburg!" The anger in the man's voice was faked, the fury of a coward trying to instill fear in a person who happened to be at his mercy. I doubted if he could face up to a mouse. He accosted two boys and ran his hands over their sides, but he did not ask for their passes.

"You see, my friend, you're really in trouble. I'm the only one who can help you. This man who arrested you is not in his best mood today. How much have you got on you? Maybe if you give something he'll let you go. You know what wonders money can do for you. I'll plead for you; but only if I show him something can he understand." The reservist explained the only way out of the predicament for the trapped man, in a smooth voice that sounded rotten through and through with corruption, the sole purpose for which he had joined the "force."

"I haven't got a cent in my pocket. I bought provisions, presents for the people at home and the ticket with all the money they gave me at work. Look, *nkosi*,[6] I have only the ticket and the papers with which I'm going to draw my money when I arrive at home." He took out his papers, pulled the overall off his shoulders and lowered it to his thighs so that the brown trousers he wore underneath were out in the open. He turned the dirty pockets inside out. "There's nothing else in my pockets except these, mister, honestly."

"Man!"

"Yessir?"

"You want to go home to your wife and children?"

"Yes, *please*, good man of my people. Give me a break."

"Then why do you show me these damn papers? They will feed your own children, but not mine. When you get to your home you're going to draw money and your kids will be scratching their tummies and dozing after a hectic meal, while I lose my job for letting you go and my own children join the dogs to scavenge the trashbins. You're mad, *mos.*" He turned to his mate. "Hey, Baloyi. Your man says he hasn't got anything, but he's going to his family which he hasn't seen for two years."

"I told you to put the irons on him. He's probably carrying a little fortune in his underpants. Maybe he's shy to take it out in front of the people. It'll come out at the police station, either at the charge office or in the cells when the small boys shake him down."

---

[6] *nkosi* term of respect

"Come on, you. Your hands, maan!"

The other man pulled his arms away from the manacles. His voice rose desperately, "*Awu* my people. You mean you're really arresting me? Forgive me! I pray do."

A struggle ensued between the two men.

"You're resisting arrest? You—" and a stream of foul vitriolic words concerning the anatomy of the hostel man's mother gushed out of the reservist's mouth.

"I'm not, I'm not! But please listen!" The hostel man heaved and broke loose from the reservist's grip. The latter was only a lump of fat with nothing underneath. He staggered three steps back and flopped on his rump. When he bounced back to his feet, unexpectedly fast for his bulk, his eyes were blazing murder. His companions came running from their own posts and swarmed upon the defenceless man like a pack of hyenas upon a carcass. The other people who had been marooned on the bridge saw a chance to go past while the wolves were still preoccupied. They ran down the stairs and up Mohale like racehorses. Two other young men who were handcuffed together took advantage of the diversion and bolted down the first street in tandem, taking their bracelets with them. They ran awkwardly with their arms bound together, but both were young and fit and they did their best in the circumstances.

We could not stand the sickening beating that the other man was receiving any more.

"Hey! Hey. *Sies,* maan. Stop beating the man like that. Arrest him if you want to arrest him. You're killing him, dogs!" we protested loudly from the station. An angry crowd was gathering.

"Stop it or we'll stop you from doing anything else forever!" someone shouted.

The psychopaths broke their rugger scrum and allowed us to see their gruesome handiwork. The man was groaning at the base of the fence, across the street where the dirt had gathered. He twisted painfully to a sitting position. His face was covered with dirt and blood from where the manacles that were slipped over the knuckles had found their marks, and his features were grotesquely distorted. In spite of that, the fat man was not satisfied. He bent and gathered the whimpering man's wrists with the intention of fastening them to the fence with the handcuffs.

"Hey, hey, hey, Satan! Let him go. Can't you see that you've hurt that man enough?"

The tension was building up to explosion point and the uniformed policeman sensed it.

"Let him go, boys. Forgive him. Let him go," he said, shooting nervous glances in all directions.

Then the beaten-up man did the most unexpected and heart-rending thing. He knelt before the one ordering his release and held his dust-covered hands with the palms together in the prayer position, and still kneeling he said, "Thank you very much, my lord. God bless you. Now I can go and see my twins and my people at home."

He would have done it. Only it never occurred in his mind at that moment of thanksgiving to kiss the red gleaming boots of the policeman.

The miserable man beat the dust off his clothes as best he could, gathered his two parcels and clambered up the stairs, trying to grin his thanks to the crowd that had raised its voice of protest on his behalf. The policeman decided to call it a day. The other unfortunates were shepherded to the waiting *kwela-kwela.*

I tried to imagine how the man would explain his lumps to his wife. In the eye of my mind I saw him throwing his twins into the air and gathering them again and again as he played with them.

"There's still a long way to cover, my friend," I heard Mandla saying into my ear.

"Before?" I asked.

"Before we reach hell. Ha, ha, ha! Maybe there we'll be men."

"Ha, we've long been there. We've long been in hell."

"Before we get out, then."

Journal Entry

React to the statement "For neither am I a man in the eyes of the law, / Nor am I a man in the eyes of my fellow man."

Textual Considerations

1. Choose examples from the story to investigate the functions of the unnamed narrator of "Call Me Not a Man." Consider, for example, his relation to the events he narrates.
2. To explore the meaning that the word *man* acquires in the story, analyze the title, the epigraph, and the first paragraph. What is implied by Matshoba's recurrent use of this word? Can you apply the values related to the concept of manhood to the Black sisters of Soweto? What does Matshoba's story say about women's oppression under apartheid political codes?
3. Characterize the tone of the story. Consider what is implied by the use of three different terms to suggest respect.

Cultural Contexts

1. Can you relate the dialogue between Mandla and the narrator at the end of Matshoba's story to the kind of political commitment that led to the official collapse of South African apartheid in 1992? Explain.
2. Discuss whether it is the oppressive political system in "Call Me Not a Man" that creates corrupted people like the reservists, or whether it is the reservists' arbitrary use of power that abuses and corrupts the system. Can your group reach a consensus about this issue?

Chinua Achebe

Dead Men's Path

Michael Obi's hopes were fulfilled much earlier than he had expected. He was appointed headmaster of Ndume Central School in January 1949. It had always been an unprogressive school, so the Mission authorities decided to send a young and energetic man to run it. Obi accepted this responsibility with enthusiasm. He had many wonderful ideas and this was an opportunity to put them into practice. He had had sound secondary school education which designated him a "pivotal teacher" in the official records and set him apart from the other headmasters in the mission field. He was outspoken in his condemnation of the narrow views of these older and often less-educated ones.

"We shall make a good job of it, shan't we?" he asked his young wife when they first heard the joyful news of his promotion.

"We shall do our best," she replied. "We shall have such beautiful gardens and everything will be just *modern* and delightful . . . " In their two years of married life she had become completely infected by his passion for "modern methods" and his denigration of "these old and superannuated people in the teaching field who would be better employed as traders in the Onitsha market." She began to see herself already as the admired wife of the young headmaster, the queen of the school.

The wives of the other teachers would envy her position. She would set the fashion in everything . . . Then, suddenly, it occurred to her that there might not be other wives. Wavering between hope and fear, she asked her husband, looking anxiously at him.

"All our colleagues are young and unmarried," he said with enthusiasm which for once she did not share. "Which is a good thing," he continued.

"Why?"

"Why? They will give all their time and energy to the school."

Nancy was downcast. For a few minutes she became sceptical about the new school; but it was only for a few minutes. Her little personal misfortune could not blind her to her husband's happy prospects. She looked at him as he sat folded up in a chair. He was stoop-shouldered and looked frail. But he sometimes surprised people with sudden bursts of physical energy. In his present posture, however, all his bodily strength seemed to have retired behind his deep-set eyes, giving them an extraordinary power of penetration. He was only twenty-six, but looked thirty or more. On the whole, he was not unhandsome.

"A penny for your thoughts, Mike," said Nancy after a while, imitating the woman's magazine she read.

"I was thinking what a grand opportunity we've got at last to show these people how a school should be run."

Ndume School was backward in every sense of the word. Mr. Obi put his whole life into the work, and his wife hers too. He had two aims. A high standard of teaching was insisted upon, and the school compound was to be turned into a place of beauty. Nancy's dream-gardens came to life with the coming of the rains, and blossomed. Beautiful hibiscus and allamanda hedges in brilliant red and yellow marked out the carefully tended school compound from the rank neighbourhood bushes.

One evening as Obi was admiring his work he was scandalized to see an old woman from the village hobble right across the compound, through a marigold flower-bed and the hedges. On going up there he found faint signs of an almost disused path from the village across the school compound to the bush on the other side.

"It amazes me," said Obi to one of his teachers who had been three years in the school, "that you people allowed the villagers to make use of this footpath. It is simply incredible." He shook his head.

"The path," said the teacher apologetically, "appears to be very important to them. Although it is hardly used, it connects the village shrine with their place of burial."

"And what has that got to do with the school?" asked the headmaster.

"Well, I don't know," replied the other with a shrug of the shoulders. "But I remember there was a big row some time ago when we attempted to close it."

"That was some time ago. But it will not be used now," said Obi as he walked away. "What will the Government Education Officer think of this when he comes to inspect the school next week? The villagers might, for all I know, decide to use the schoolroom for a pagan ritual during the inspection."

Heavy sticks were planted closely across the path at the two places where it entered and left the school premises. These were further strengthened with barbed wire.

Three days later the village priest of *Ani* called on the headmaster. He was an old man and walked with a slight stoop. He carried a stout walking-stick which he usually tapped on the floor, by way of emphasis, each time he made a new point in his argument.

"I have heard," he said after the usual exchange of cordialities, "that our ancestral footpath has recently been closed . . . "

"Yes," replied Mr. Obi. "We cannot allow people to make a highway of our school compound."

"Look here, my son," said the priest bringing down his walking-stick, "this path was here before you were born and before your father was born. The whole life of this village depends on it. Our dead relatives depart by it and our ancestors visit us by it. But most important, it is the path of children coming in to be born . . . "

Mr. Obi listened with a satisfied smile on his face.

"The whole purpose of our school," he said finally, "is to eradicate just such beliefs as that. Dead men do not require footpaths. The whole idea is just fantastic. Our duty is to teach your children to laugh at such ideas."

"What you say may be true," replied the priest, "but we follow the practices of our fathers. If you re-open the path we shall have nothing to quarrel about. What I always say is: let the hawk perch and let the eagle perch." He rose to go.

"I am sorry," said the young headmaster. "But the school compound cannot be a thoroughfare. It is against our regulations. I would suggest your constructing another path, skirting our premises. We can even get our boys to help in building it. I don't suppose the ancestors will find the little detour too burdensome."

"I have no more words to say," said the old priest, already outside.

Two days later a young woman in the village died in childbed. A diviner was immediately consulted and he prescribed heavy sacrifices to propitiate ancestors insulted by the fence.

Obi woke up next morning among the ruins of his work. The beautiful hedges were torn up not just near the path but right round the school, the flowers trampled to death and one of the school buildings pulled down . . . That day, the white Supervisor came to inspect the school and wrote a nasty report on the state of the premises but more seriously about the "tribal-war situation developing between the school and the village, arising in part from the misguided zeal of the new headmaster."

Journal Entry

React to Obi's reverence for modern things.

Textual Considerations

1. Characterize Obi's attitude toward the teachers and the people in the community.
2. Speculate on the implications of the story's title. To what extent do you agree with Obi's reasons for closing the path?
3. Explain what the supervisor means by "misguided zeal." Does Obi's race play a role in the supervisor's evaluation? Did Obi deserve his censure? Why or why not?

Cultural Considerations

1. Consider with your group why Obi and the village priest are unable to negotiate a compromise. Explain the implications of the priest's plea to "let the hawk perch and let the eagle perch."
2. The conflict between individual aspirations and communal rites is central to this story. With whom do you empathize—Obi, who insisted on "civilizing the pagans," or the villagers, who used the path that "connects the village shrine with their place of burial"?

Wallace Stevens

Disillusionment of Ten O'Clock

The houses are haunted
By white night-gowns.
None are green,
Or purple with green rings,
Or green with yellow rings,   5
Or yellow with blue rings.
None of them are strange,
With socks of lace
And beaded ceintures.
People are not going   10
To dream of baboons and periwinkles.
Only, here and there, an old sailor,
Drunk and asleep in his boots,
Catches tigers
In red weather.   15

Emily Dickinson

Much Madness Is Divinest Sense—

Much Madness is divinest Sense—
To a discerning Eye—
Much Sense—the starkest Madness—
'Tis the Majority
In this, as All, prevail—   5
Assent—and you are sane—
Demur—you're straightway dangerous—
And handled with a Chain—

Emily Dickinson

The Soul Selects Her Own Society—

The Soul selects her own Society—
Then—shuts the Door—
To her divine Majority—
Present no more—

Unmoved—she notes the Chariots—pausing—   5
At her low Gate—
Unmoved—an Emperor be kneeling
Upon her Mat—

I've known her—from an ample nation—
Choose One—   10
Then—close the Valves of her attention—
Like Stone—

Journal Entry

Respond to the portrayals of society in the three poems.

Textual Considerations

1. Explain how Dickinson's use of door imagery contributes to the unity and meaning of "The Soul Selects Her Own Society—."
2. How does Stevens use color to convey his concepts of individuality and conformity? What function does the old sailor have in the poem?
3. Analyze Dickinson's use of paradox in "Much Madness Is Divinest Sense—."
4. Analyze the argumentative development of "Disillusionment of Ten O'Clock" in relation to what the poem suggests about illusions and disillusionment. Don't overlook the importance of the negative images in lines 3–7.

Cultural Contexts

1. Discuss with your group what all three poems imply about the relationship between the individual and society. Identify the images that most effectively characterize this relationship.
2. Under what circumstances can you imagine choosing the common good as opposed to choosing individual rights? Use examples from your own experience or from current events to argue your point of view.

Yevtushenko, Niatum, and Gunn

Yevgeny Yevtushenko

People

No people are uninteresting.
Their fate is like the chronicle of planets.

Nothing in them is not particular,
and planet is dissimilar from planet.

And if a man lived in obscurity   5
making his friends in that obscurity
obscurity is not uninteresting.

To each his world is private,
and in that world one excellent minute.

And in that world one tragic minute.   10
These are private.

In any man who dies there dies with him
his first snow and kiss and fight.
It goes with him.

They are left books and bridges   15
and painted canvas and machinery.

Whose fate is to survive.
But what has gone is also not nothing:

by the rule of the game something has gone.
Not people die but worlds die in them.   20

Whom we knew as faulty, the earth's creatures.
Of whom, essentially, what did we know?

Brother of a brother? Friend of friends?
Lover of lover?

We who knew our fathers   25
in everything, in nothing.

They perish. They cannot be brought back.
The secret worlds are not regenerated.

And every time again and again
I make my lament against destruction.   30

Duane Niatum

Street Kid

I stand before the window that opens
to a field of sagebrush—
California country northeast of San Francisco.
Holding to the earth and its shield of silence,
The sun burns my thirteen years into the hill.   5
The white breath of twilight
Whirrs with insects crawling down the glass
Between the bars. But it is the meadowlark
Warbling at the end of the fence
That sets me apart from the rest of the boys,   10
The cool toughs playing ping pong
And cards before lock-up.
When this new home stops calling on memory,
As well as my nickname, Injun Joe,
Given to me by the brothers,   15
The Blacks, the Chicanos, the others growing
Lean as this solitude, I step
From the window into the darkness
Reach my soul building a nest against the wall.

Thom Gunn

Black Jackets

In the silence that prolongs the span
Rawly of music when the record ends,
   The red-haired boy who drove a van
In weekday overalls but, like his friends,

   Wore cycle boots and jacket here   5
To suit the Sunday hangout he was in,
   Heard, as he stretched back from his beer,
Leather creak softly round his neck and chin.

Before him, on a coal-black sleeve
Remote exertion had lined, scratched, and burned   10
   Insignia that could not revive
The heroic fall or climb where they were earned.

   On the other drinkers bent together,
Concocting selves for their impervious kit,
   He saw it as no more than leather   15
Which, taut across the shoulders grown to it,

   Sent through the dimness of a bar
As sudden and anonymous hints of light
   As those that shipping give, that are
Now flickers in the Bay, now lost in night.   20

   He stretched out like a cat, and rolled
The bitterish taste of beer upon his tongue,
   And listened to a joke being told:
The present was the things he stayed among.

   If it was only loss he wore,   25
He wore it to assert, with fierce devotion,
   Complicity and nothing more.
He recollected his initiation,

   And one especially of the rites:
For on his shoulders they had put tattoos: 30
   The group's name on the left, The Knights,
And on the right the slogan Born To Lose.

◆

Journal Entry

Reflect on Yevtushenko's idea that "obscurity is not uninteresting" as you examine the theme of private versus communal selves in the three poems.

Textual Considerations

1. Analyze Yevtushenko's use of symbolism in "People." To what events might the "excellent minute" and the "tragic minute" refer? What other examples reinforce the poem's meanings about individual uniqueness, mortality, and our ability to know another person?

2. Comment on the effectiveness of Niatum's use of nature imagery to suggest his protagonist's emotional state. How does his identification with the meadowlark, for example, help us to understand better his protagonist?
3. How does Gunn use setting to enhance meaning in "Black Jackets"? Discuss also the implications of the tattoos in the poem's last stanza.
4. Quote from each poem to support your opinion as to whether the poetic voices they raise verge entirely on disillusionment, loss, violence, and marginalized identities, or whether they also raise voices of protest and hope against despondency.

Cultural Contexts

1. The protagonists of "Black Jackets" and "Street Kid" are struggling to find their individual and collective identities in cultures from which they feel essentially alienated. To what extent do they succeed? Use quotes from the poems to support your position. With which protagonist do you most empathize? Why?
2. Use "Black Jackets" and "Street Kid" to debate the extent to which these poems challenge traditional concepts of success and individual fulfillment.

Frost, Olds, and Romero ◆

Robert Frost

Mending Wall

Something there is that doesn't love a wall,
That sends the frozen-ground-swell under it
And spills the upper boulders in the sun,
And makes gaps even two can pass abreast.
The work of hunters is another thing: 5
I have come after them and made repair
Where they have left not one stone on a stone,
But they would have the rabbit out of hiding,
To please the yelping dogs. The gaps I mean,
No one has seen them made or heard them made, 10
But at spring mending-time we find them there.
I let my neighbor know beyond the hill;
And on a day we meet to walk the line

And set the wall between us once again.
We keep the wall between us as we go.   15
To each the boulders that have fallen to each.
And some are loaves and some so nearly balls
We have to use a spell to make them balance:
'Stay where you are until our backs are turned!'
We wear our fingers rough with handling them.   20
Oh, just another kind of outdoor game,
One on a side. It comes to little more:
There where it is we do not need the wall:
He is all pine and I am apple orchard.
My apple trees will never get across   25
And eat the cones under his pines, I tell him.
He only says, 'Good fences make good neighbors.'
Spring is the mischief in me, and I wonder
If I could put a notion in his head:
'*Why* do they make good neighbors? Isn't it   30
Where there are cows? But here there are no cows.
Before I built a wall I'd ask to know
What I was walling in or walling out,
And to whom I was like to give offense.
Something there is that doesn't love a wall,   35
That wants it down.' I could say 'Elves' to him,
But it's not elves exactly, and I'd rather
He said it for himself. I see him there,
Bringing a stone grasped firmly by the top
In each hand, like an old-stone savage armed.   40
He moves in darkness as it seems to me,
Not of woods only and the shade of trees.
He will not go behind his father's saying,
And he likes having thought of it so well
He says again, 'Good fences make good neighbors.'   45

Sharon Olds

Summer Solstice, New York City

By the end of the longest day of the year he could not stand it,
he went up the iron stairs through the roof of the building
and over the soft, tarry surface
to the edge, put one leg over the complex green tin cornice
and said if they came a step closer that was it.   5
Then the huge machinery of the earth began to work for his life,
the cops came in their suits blue-gray as the sky on a cloudy evening,
and one put on a bulletproof vest, a
black shell around his own life,
life of his children's father, in case   10
the man was armed, and one, slung with a
rope like the sign of his bounden duty,
came up out of a hole in the top of the neighboring building,
like the gold hole they say is in the top of the head,
and began to lurk toward the man who wanted to die.   15
The tallest cop approached him directly,
softly, slowly, talking to him, talking, talking,
while the man's leg hung over the lip of the next world,
and the crowd gathered in the street, silent, and the
dark hairy net with its implacable grid was   20
unfolded near the curb and spread out and
stretched as the sheet is prepared to receive at a birth.
Then they all came a little closer
where he squatted next to his death, his shirt
glowing its milky glow like something   25
growing in a dish at night in the dark in a lab, and then
everything stopped
as his body jerked and he
stepped down from the parapet and went toward them
and they closed on him, I thought they were going to   30
beat him up, as a mother whose child has been
lost will scream at the child when it's found, they
took him by the arms and held him up and
leaned him against the wall of the chimney and the
tall cop lit a cigarette   35
in his own mouth, and gave it to him, and
then they all lit cigarettes, and the
red glowing ends burned like the
tiny campfires we lit at night
back at the beginning of the world.   40

Leo Romero

What the Gossips Saw

Everyone pitied Escolastica, her leg
had swollen like a watermelon in the summer
It had practically happened over night
She was seventeen, beautiful and soon
to be married to Guillermo who was working   5
in the mines at Terreros, eighty miles away
far up in the mountains, in the wilderness
Poor Escolastica, the old women would say
on seeing her hobble to the well with a bucket
carrying her leg as if it were the weight   10
of the devil, surely it was a curse from heaven
for some misdeed, the young women who were
jealous would murmur, yet they were grieved too
having heard that the doctor might cut
her leg, one of a pair of the most perfect legs   15
in the valley, and it was a topic of great
interest and conjecture among the villagers
whether Guillermo would still marry her
if she were crippled, a one-legged woman—
as if life weren't hard enough for a woman   20
with two legs—how could she manage

Guillermo returned and married Escolastica
even though she had but one leg, the sound
of her wooden leg pounding down the wooden aisle
stayed in everyone's memory for as long   25
as they lived, women cried at the sight
of her beauty, black hair so dark
that the night could get lost in it, a face
more alluring than a full moon

Escolastica went to the dances with her husband 30
and watched and laughed but never danced
though once she had been the best dancer
and could wear holes in a pair of shoes
in a matter of a night, and her waist had been
as light to the touch as a hummingbird's flight 35
And Escolastica bore five children, only half
what most women bore, yet they were healthy
In Escolastica's presence, no one would mention
the absence of her leg, though she walked heavily
And it was not long before the gossips 40
spread their poison, that she must be in cohorts
with the devil, had given him her leg
for the power to bewitch Guillermo's heart
and cloud his eyes so that he could not see
what was so clear to them all 45

Journal Entry

Compare and contrast the concepts of community in each poem.

Textual Considerations

1. Frost's, Olds's, and Romero's poetic styles are rich in simple, direct language. Choose examples of natural speech patterns from each poem and analyze the way in which these poets' conversational styles invite comparison with one another.
2. Analyze Frost's use of the word *fences,* Old's use of the phrase *machinery of the earth,* and Romero's use of the term *a one-legged woman*. Explain what each suggests about the relationship of the individual to society.
3. Consider the importance of the word *saw* in the title "What the Gossips Saw." What other allusions to sight can you find in Romero's poem? Analyze what this poem both articulates and implies about communal opinion.
4. Frost and Olds address the issues of boundaries or fences in relationships: our often conflicting needs for solitude and solidarity, identity and community, and personal space and relatedness. What new meanings about relationships can you draw from these poems?

Cultural Contexts

1. Take a position about the role the community plays in molding people's identity and destiny. What issues seem of greatest concern to the community in "What the Gossips Saw"? Chart the progress of the community's reaction to Escolastica and Guillermo.
2. Working with your group, reconstruct the circumstances under which each of you would risk your life to save another's. Can you imagine yourself in the place of the cops in Olds's poem? How does the poem address the conflict between individual rights and the claims of communal obligation? Were the cops only doing their jobs? Explain.

Soto, di Prima, and Hayden

Gary Soto

History

Grandma lit the stove.
Morning sunlight
Lengthened in spears
Across the linoleum floor.
Wrapped in a shawl,   5
Her eyes small
With sleep.
She sliced papas,[1]
Pounded chiles
With a stone   10
Brought from Guadalajara.[2]
                               After
Grandpa left for work,
She hosed down
The walk her sons paved   15
And in the shade
Of a chinaberry,
Unearthed her
Secret cigar box
Of bright coins   20
And bills, counted them
In English,
Then in Spanish,
And buried them elsewhere.
Later, back   25
From the market,
Where no one saw her,
She pulled out
Pepper and beet, spines
Of asparagus   30
From her blouse,
Tiny chocolates
From under a paisley bandana,
And smiled.

That was the '50s,   35
And Grandma in her '50s.
A face streaked
From cutting grapes
And boxing plums.
I remember her insides   40
Were washed of tapeworm.
Her arms swelled into knobs
Of small growths—
Her second son
Dropped from a ladder   45
And was dust.
And yet I do not know
The sorrows
That sent her praying
In the dark of a closet,   50
The tear that fell
At night
When she touched
Loose skin
Of belly and breasts.   55
I do not know why
Her face shines
Or what goes beyond this shine,
Only the stories
That pulled her   60
From Taxco[3] to San Joaquin,
Delano to Westside,[4]
The places
In which we all begin.

[1] Potatoes.

[2] A city in Mexico.

[3] A city in Mexico.

[4] Places in California.

Diane di Prima

To My Father

In my dreams you stand among roses.
You are still the fine gardener you were.
You worry about mother.
You are still the fierce wind, the intolerable force
that almost broke me.   5
Who forced my young body into awkward and proper clothes
Who spoke of his standing in the community.
And men's touch is still a little absurd to me
because you trembled when you touched me.
What external law were you expounding?   10
How can I take your name like prayer?
My youngest son has your eyes.
Why are you knocking at the doors of my brain?
You kept all their rules and more.
What were you promised that you cannot rest?   15
What fierce, angry honesty in the darkness?
What can you hope who had preferred my death
to the birth of my oldest daughter?
O fierce hummer of tunes
Forget, eat the black seedcake.   20
In my dreams you stand at the door of your house
and weep for your wife, my mother.

Robert Hayden

Those Winter Sundays

Sundays too my father got up early
and put his clothes on in the blueblack cold,
then with cracked hands that ached
from labor in the weekday weather made
banked fires blaze. No one ever thanked him.   5

I'd wake and hear the cold splintering, breaking.
When the rooms were warm, he'd call,
and slowly I would rise and dress,
fearing the chronic angers of that house,

Speaking indifferently to him,   10
who had driven out the cold
and polished my good shoes as well.

What did I know, what did I know
of love's austere and lonely offices?

◆

Journal Entry

Analyze the function of memory in the portrayals of family relationships in each poem.

Textual Considerations

1. To what extent are the speakers in these poems emotionally involved or detached? Examine their narrative strategies. To whom are the poems addressed, and do the speakers talk directly or indirectly about the intensity of their emotions? Discuss the significance of the differences in their methods of address.
2. Characterize the father in Hayden's poem. How does he attempt to subdue the "chronic angers" of the house? How does Hayden's use of repetition in line 13 reinforce his meaning?
3. Di Prima addresses a series of questions to her dead father. How do they contribute to your understanding of their relationship? To what extent does gender affect her memories of him?
4. Characterize Soto's grandmother, and explain how his relationship with her has affected his self-concept.

Cultural Contexts

1. Discuss how the family context of support, rejection, or solidarity affects the making of the individual self in "History," "To My Father," and "Those Winter Sundays." Expand your discussion by evaluating the role of the family as a mediating element between the individual and his or her collective world.
2. Working with your group, list the various images of family members in these poems. Then discuss the reasons for the paradoxical relationship between solitude and solidarity that pervades each poem.

Langston Hughes

Theme for English B

The instructor said,

> *Go home and write*
> *a page tonight.*
> *And let that page come out of you—*
> *Then, it will be true.* 5

I wonder if it's that simple?
I am twenty-two, colored, born in Winston-Salem.
I went to school there, then Durham, then here
to this college[1] on the hill above Harlem.
I am the only colored student in my class. 10
The steps from the hill lead down into Harlem,
through a park, then I cross St. Nicholas,[2]
Eighth Avenue, Seventh, and I come to the Y,
the Harlem Branch Y, where I take the elevator
up to my room, sit down, and write this page: 15

It's not easy to know what is true for you or me
at twenty-two, my age. But I guess I'm what
I feel and see and hear, Harlem, I hear you:
hear you, hear me—we two—you, me, talk on this page.
(I hear New York, too.) Me—who? 20

Well, I like to eat, sleep, drink, and be in love.
I like to work, read, learn, and understand life.
I like a pipe for a Christmas present,
or records—Bessie,[3] bop, or Bach.
I guess being colored doesn't make me *not* like 25
the same things other folks like who are other races.
So will my page be colored that I write?

Being me, it will not be white.
But it will be
a part of you, instructor. 30
You are white—
yet a part of me, as I am a part of you.
That's American.
Sometimes perhaps you don't want to be a part of me.
Nor do I often want to be a part of you. 35
But we are, that's true!
As I learn from you,
I guess you learn from me—
although you're older—and white—
and somewhat more free. 40

This is my page for English B.

[1] *this college* Columbia University
[2] *St. Nicholas* St. Nicholas Avenue, a street in Harlem
[3] *Bessie* Bessie Smith (1898–1937) African-American Blues singer

Cherríe Moraga

The Welder

I am a welder.
Not an alchemist.
I am interested in the blend
of common elements to make
a common thing. 5

No magic here.
Only the heat of my desire to fuse
what I already know
exists. Is possible.

We plead to each other, 10
we all come from the same rock
we all come from the same rock
ignoring the fact that we bend
at different temperatures
that each of us is malleable 15
up to a point.

Yes, fusion *is* possible
but only if things get hot enough—
all else is temporary adhesion,
patching up. 20

It is the intimacy of steel melting
into steel, the fire of our individual
passion to take hold of ourselves
that makes sculpture of our lives,
builds buildings.   25

And I am not talking about skyscrapers,
merely structures that can support us
without fear
of trembling.

For too long a time   30
the heat of my heavy hands,
has been smoldering
in the pockets of other
people's business—
they need oxygen to make fire.   35

I am now
coming up for air.
Yes, I *am*
picking up the torch.

I am the welder.   40
I understand the capacity of heat
to change the shape of things.
I am suited to work
within the realm of sparks
out of control.   45

I am the welder.
I am taking the power
into my own hands.

Journal Entry

Respond to the concept of individual identity in each poem.

Textual Considerations

1. Comment on the effectiveness of the welding metaphor in Moraga's poem. Cite other powerful images that reinforce the poem's theme.
2. Review stanza 7 of "The Welder," and explain the speaker's meaning.
3. Analyze the functions of color in relation to the speaker's identity in "Theme for English B."
4. Review lines 28–40 in Hughes's poem, and explain their relevance to the relationship between the speaker and the instructor, and, by implication, the larger community.

Cultural Contexts

1. Discuss what each poem implies about the ability of the individual to form his or her own identity. What does each suggest also about the concept of solidarity?
2. Discuss with your group the relation between learning and teaching expressed by both speakers. What power do learners hold? What is the relationship between power and education? How has learning contributed to both speakers' awareness of community?

Walsh and Ferlinghetti ◆

Chad Walsh

Port Authority Terminal: 9 A.M. Monday

From buses beached like an invasion fleet
They fill the waiting room with striding feet.

Their faces, white, and void of hate or pity,
Move on tall bodies toward the conquered city.

Among the lesser breeds of black and brown   5
They board their taxis with an absent frown,

Each to his concrete citadel,
To rule the city and to buy and sell.

At five o'clock they ride the buses back,
Leaving their Irish to guard the brown and black.   10

At six a drink, at seven dinner's served.
At ten or twelve, depressed, undressed, unnerved,

They mount their wives, dismount, they doze and dream
Apocalyptic Negroes in a stream

Of moving torches, marching from the slums,   15
Beating a band of garbage pails for drums,

Marching, with school-age children in their arms,
Advancing on the suburbs and the farms,

To integrate the schools and burn the houses . . .
The normal morning comes, the clock arouses   20

Junior and senior executive alike.
Back on the bus, and down the usual pike.

From buses beached like an invasion fleet
They fill the waiting room with striding feet.

Lawrence Ferlinghetti

Constantly Risking Absurdity

Constantly risking absurdity
                and death
      whenever he performs
               above the heads
                     of his audience   5
     the poet like an acrobat
               climbs on rime
                  to a high wire of his own making
    and balancing on eyebeams
              above a sea of faces   10
        paces his way
            to the other side of day
     performing entrechats
           and sleight-of-foot tricks
  and other high theatrics   15
          and all without mistaking
     any thing
         for what it may not be

   For he's the super realist
           who must perforce perceive   20
      taut truth
         before the taking of each stance or step
   in his supposed advance
        toward that still higher perch
 where Beauty stands and waits   25
        with gravity
           to start her death-defying leap
And he
    a little charleychaplin man
          who may or may not catch   30
     her fair eternal form
         spreadeagled in the empty air
     of existence

Journal Entry

Consider how the structure of each poem contributes to its meaning.

Textual Considerations

1. Comment on Walsh's image of commuters as soldiers and New York City as a battlefield.
2. What is implied in the speaker's description of the commuters' faces as "void of hate or pity" and as containing "an absent frown"?
3. Ferlinghetti's poem is based on the simile of the poet as acrobat. Why is it an appropriate comparison for the poem's subject?
4. Respond to the concept of the poet as a super-realist. Why does the poet sometimes miss beauty? Explain why beauty's leap is death-defying.

Cultural Considerations

1. Discuss with your group the relationships of the various ethnic groups described in Walsh's poem. To what extent is this poem, written in the late 1960s, still relevant? Do your group members have similar responses to the speaker's comments about the home lives of the commuters?
2. Characterize the poet's relationship to his audience in "Constantly Risking Absurdity." What attitude toward himself is the speaker expressing in calling himself "a little charleychaplin man"? Why is he "constantly risking absurdity"? Explain his concept of community.

Sophocles

Antigone

PERSONS REPRESENTED

ANTIGONE
ISMENE
EURYDICE
CREON
HAIMON
TEIRESIAS
A Sentry
A Messenger
Chorus

SCENE: *Before the palace of* CREON, *King of Thebes. A central double door, and two lateral doors. A platform extends the length of the façade, and from this platform three steps lead down into the "orchestra," or chorus-ground.* TIME: *dawn of the day after the repulse of the Argive army from the assault on Thebes.*

PROLOGUE

[ANTIGONE *and* ISMENE *enter from the central door of the Palace.*]

ANTIGONE. Ismenê, dear sister,
　You would think that we had already suffered enough
　For the curse on Oedipus:
　I cannot imagine any grief
　That you and I have not gone through. And now—
　Have they told you of the new decree of our King Creon?
ISMENE. I have heard nothing: I know
　That two sisters lost two brothers, a double death
　In a single hour; and I know that the Argive army
　Fled in the night; but beyond this, nothing.
ANTIGONE. I thought so. And that is why I wanted you
　To come out here with me. There is something we must do.
ISMENE. Why do you speak so strangely?
ANTIGONE. Listen, Ismenê:
　Creon buried our brother Eteoclês
　With military honors, gave him a soldier's funeral,

And it was right that he should; but Polyneicês,
Who fought as bravely and died as miserably,—
They say that Creon has sworn
No one shall bury him, no one mourn for him,
But his body must lie in the fields, a sweet treasure
For carrion birds to find as they search for food.
That is what they say, and our good Creon is coming here
To announce it publicly; and the penalty—
Stoning to death in the public square!
                         There it is,
And now you can prove what you are:
A true sister, or a traitor to your family.

ISMENE. Antigonê, you are mad! What could I possibly do?
ANTIGONE. You must decide whether you will help me or not.
ISMENE. I do not understand you. Help you in what?
ANTIGONE. Ismenê, I am going to bury him. Will you come?
ISMENE. Bury him! You have just said the new law forbids it.
ANTIGONE. He is my brother. And he is your brother, too.
ISMENE. But think of the danger! Think what Creon will do!
ANTIGONE. Creon is not strong enough to stand in my way.
ISMENE. Ah sister!
Oedipus died, everyone hating him
For what his own search brought to light, his eyes
Ripped out by his own hand; and Iocastê died,
His mother and wife at once: she twisted the cords
That strangled her life; and our two brothers died,
Each killed by the other's sword. And we are left:
But oh, Antigonê!
Think how much more terrible than these
Our own death would be if we should go against Creon
And do what he has forbidden! We are only women,
We cannot fight with men, Antigonê!
The law is strong, we must give in to the law
In this thing, and in worse. I beg the Dead
To forgive me, but I am helpless: I must yield
To those in authority. And I think it is dangerous business
To be always meddling.

ANTIGONE.   If that is what you think,
I should not want you, even if you asked to come.
You have made your choice, you can be what you want to be.
But I will bury him; and if I must die,
I say that this crime is holy: I shall lie down
With him in death, and I shall be as dear
To him as he to me.

It is the dead,

Not the living, who make the longest demands:
We die for ever . . .

You may do as you like,

Since apparently the laws of the gods mean nothing to you.
ISMENE. They mean a great deal to me; but I have no strength
To break laws that were made for the public good.
ANTIGONE. That must be your excuse, I suppose. But as for me,
I will bury the brother I love.
ISMENE. Antigonê,
I am so afraid for you!
ANTIGONE. You need not be:
You have yourself to consider, after all.
ISMENE. But no one must hear of this, you must tell no one!
I will keep it a secret, I promise!
ANTIGONE. Oh tell it! Tell everyone!
Think how they'll hate you when it all comes out
If they learn that you knew about it all the time!
ISMENE. So fiery! You should be cold with fear.
ANTIGONE. Perhaps. But I am only doing what I must.
ISMENE. But can you do it? I say that you cannot.
ANTIGONE. Very well: when my strength gives out, I shall do no more.
ISMENE. Impossible things should not be tried at all.
ANTIGONE. Go away, Ismenê:
I shall be hating you soon, and the dead will too,
For your words are hateful. Leave me my foolish plan:
I am not afraid of the danger; if it means death,
It will not be the worst of deaths—death without honor.
ISMENE. Go then, if you feel that you must.
You are unwise,
But a loyal friend indeed to those who love you. [*Exit into the Palace.*
ANTIGONE *goes off, L. Enter the* CHORUS.]

PÁRODOS

CHORUS. Now the long blade of the sun, lying   [STROPHE 1]
Level east to west, touches with glory
Thebes of the Seven Gates. Open, unlidded
Eye of golden day! O marching light
Across the eddy and rush of Dircê's stream,
Striking the white shields of the enemy
Thrown headlong backward from the blaze of morning!
CHORAGOS. Polyneicês their commander
Roused them with windy phrases,

He the wild eagle screaming
Insults above our land,
His wings their shields of snow,
His crest their marshalled helms.

CHORUS. Against our seven gates in a yawning ring   [ANTISTROPHE 1]
   The famished spears came onward in the night;
   But before his jaws were sated with our blood,
   Or pinefire took the garland of our towers,
   He was thrown back; and as he turned, great Thebes—
   No tender victim for his noisy power—
   Rose like a dragon behind him, shouting war.

CHORAGOS. For God hates utterly
   The bray of bragging tongues;
   And when he beheld their smiling,
   Their swagger of golden helms,
   The frown of his thunder blasted
   Their first man from our walls.

CHORUS. We heard his shout of triumph high in the air   [STROPHE 2]
   Turn to a scream; far out in a flaming arc
   He fell with his windy torch, and the earth struck him.
   And others storming in fury no less than his
   Found shock of death in the dusty joy of battle.

CHORAGOS. Seven captains at seven gates
   Yielded their clanging arms to the god
   That bends the battle-line and breaks it.
   These two only, brothers in blood,
   Face to face in matchless rage,
   Mirroring each the other's death,
   Clashed in long combat.

CHORUS. But now in the beautiful morning of victory   [ANTISTROPHE 2]
   Let Thebes of the many chariots sing for joy!
   With hearts for dancing we'll take leave of war:
   Our temples shall be sweet with hymns of praise,
   And the long night shall echo with our chorus.

SCENE I

CHORAGOS. But now at last our new King is coming:
   Creon of Thebes, Menoikeus' son.
   In this auspicious dawn of his reign
   What are the new complexities
   That shifting Fate has woven for him?
   What is his counsel? Why has he summoned
   The old men to hear him?

[*Enter* CREON *from the Palace, C. He addresses the* CHORUS *from the top step.*]

CREON. Gentlemen: I have the honor to inform you that our Ship of State, which recent storms have threatened to destroy, has come safely to harbor at last, guided by the merciful wisdom of Heaven. I have summoned you here this morning because I know that I can depend upon you: your devotion to King Laïos was absolute; you never hesitated in your duty to our late ruler Oedipus; and when Oedipus died, your loyalty was transferred to his children. Unfortunately, as you know, his two sons, the princes Eteoclês and Polyneicês, have killed each other in battle; and I, as the next in blood, have succeeded to the full power of the throne.

   I am aware, of course, that no Ruler can expect complete loyalty from his subjects until he has been tested in office. Nevertheless, I say to you at the very outset that I have nothing but contempt for the kind of Governor who is afraid, for whatever reason, to follow the course that he knows is best for the State; and as for the man who sets private friendship above the public welfare,—I have no use for him, either. I call God to witness that if I saw my country headed for ruin, I should not be afraid to speak out plainly; and I need hardly remind you that I would never have any dealings with an enemy of the people. No one values friendship more highly than I; but we must remember that friends made at the risk of wrecking our Ship are not real friends at all.

   These are my principles, at any rate, and that is why I have made the following decision concerning the sons of Oedipus: Eteoclês, who died as a man should die, fighting for his country, is to be buried with full military honors, with all the ceremony that is usual when the greatest heroes die; but his brother Polyneicês, who broke his exile to come back with fire and sword against his native city and the shrines of his fathers' gods, whose one idea was to spill the blood of his blood and sell his own people into slavery—Polyneicês, I say, is to have no burial: no man is to touch him or say the least prayer for him; he shall lie on the plain, unburied; and the birds and the scavenging dogs can do with him whatever they like.

   This is my command, and you can see the wisdom behind it. As long as I am King, no traitor is going to be honored with the loyal man. But whoever shows by word and deed that he is on the side of the State,—he shall have my respect while he is living, and my reverence when he is dead.

CHORAGOS. If that is your will, Creon son of Menoikeus,
   You have the right to enforce it: we are yours.

CREON. That is my will. Take care that you do your part.

CHORAGOS. We are old men: let the younger ones carry it out.

CREON. I do not mean that: the sentries have been appointed.

CHORAGOS. Then what is it that you would have us do?

CREON. You will give no support to whoever breaks this law.

CHORAGOS. Only a crazy man is in love with death!

CREON. And death it is; yet money talks, and the wisest
  Have sometimes been known to count a few coins too many. [*Enter* SENTRY
  from L.]
SENTRY. I'll not say that I'm out of breath from running, King, because every time
  I stopped to think about what I have to tell you, I felt like going back. And all
  the time a voice kept saying, "You fool, don't you know you're walking straight
  into trouble?"; and then another voice: "Yes, but if you let somebody else get
  the news to Creon first, it will be even worse than that for you!" But good sense
  won out, at least I hope it was good sense, and here I am with a story that makes
  no sense at all; but I'll tell it anyhow, because, as they say, what's going to
  happen's going to happen, and—
CREON. Come to the point. What have you to say?
SENTRY. I did not do it. I did not see who did it. You must not punish me for what
  someone else has done.
CREON. A comprehensive defense! More effective, perhaps,
  If I knew its purpose. Come: what is it?
SENTRY. A dreadful thing . . . I don't know how to put it—
CREON. Out with it!
SENTRY.   Well, then;
  The dead man—
              Polyneicês—

[*Pause. The* SENTRY *is overcome, fumbles for words.* CREON *waits impassively.*]

                    out there—
                            someone,—
New dust on the slimy flesh!

            [*Pause. No sign from* CREON]

Someone has given it burial that way, and
Gone . . .

          [*Long pause.* CREON *finally speaks with deadly control:*]

CREON. And the man who dared do this?
SENTRY.   I swear I
  Do not know! You must believe me!
                            Listen:
  The ground was dry, not a sign of digging, no,
  Not a wheeltrack in the dust, no trace of anyone.
  It was when they relieved us this morning: and one of them,
  The corporal, pointed to it.
                      There it was,
  The strangest—
            Look:

The body, just mounded over with light dust: you see?
Not buried really, but as if they'd covered it
Just enough for the ghost's peace. And no sign
Of dogs or any wild animal that had been there.

And then what a scene there was! Every man of us
Accusing the other: we all proved the other man did it,
We all had proof that we could not have done it.
We were ready to take hot iron in our hands,
Walk through fire, swear by all the gods,
It was not I!
I do not know who it was, but it was not I!

[CREON'S *rage has been mounting steadily, but the* SENTRY *is too intent upon
his story to notice it*]

And then, when this came to nothing, someone said
A thing that silenced us and made us stare
Down at the ground: you had to be told the news,
And one of us had to do it! We threw the dice,
And the bad luck fell to me. So here I am,
No happier to be here than you are to have me:
Nobody likes the man who brings bad news.
CHORAGOS. I have been wondering, King: can it be that the gods have done this?
CREON. [*Furiously*] Stop!
Must you doddering wrecks
Go out of your heads entirely? "The gods!"
Intolerable!
The gods favor this corpse? Why? How had he served them?
Tried to loot their temples, burn their images,
Yes, and the whole State, and its laws with it!
Is it your senile opinion that the gods love to honor bad men?
A pious thought!—
No, from the very beginning
There have been those who have whispered together,
Stiff-necked anarchists, putting their heads together,
Scheming against me in alleys. These are the men,
And they have bribed my own guard to do this thing.

Money! [*Sententiously*]
There's nothing in the world so demoralizing as money.
Down go your cities,
Homes gone, men gone, honest hearts corrupted,
Crookedness of all kinds, and all for money! [*To* SENTRY]

But you—!

I swear by God and by the throne of God,
The man who has done this thing shall pay for it!
Find that man, bring him here to me, or your death
Will be the least of your problems: I'll string you up
Alive, and there will be certain ways to make you
Discover your employer before you die;
And the process may teach you a lesson you seem to have missed:
The dearest profit is sometimes all too dear:
That depends on the source. Do you understand me?
A fortune won is often misfortune.

SENTRY. King, may I speak?

CREON.   Your very voice distresses me.

SENTRY. Are you sure that it is my voice, and not your conscience?

CREON. By God, he wants to analyze me now!

SENTRY. It is not what I say, but what has been done, that hurts you.

CREON. You talk too much.

SENTRY.   Maybe; but I've done nothing.

CREON. Sold your soul for some silver: that's all you've done.

SENTRY. How dreadful it is when the right judge judges wrong!

CREON. Your figures of speech
May entertain you now; but unless you bring me the man,
You will get little profit from them in the end. [*Exit* CREON *into the Palace.*]

SENTRY. "Bring me the man"—!
I'd like nothing better than bringing him the man!
But bring him or not, you have seen the last of me here.
At any rate, I am safe! [*Exit* SENTRY]

ODE I

CHORUS.   [STROPHE 1]

  Numberless are the world's wonders, but none
  More wonderful than man; the stormgray sea
  Yields to his prows, the huge crests bear him high;
  Earth, holy and inexhaustible, is graven
  With shining furrows where his plows have gone
  Year after year, the timeless labor of stallions.

  The lightboned birds and beasts that cling to cover,   [ANTISTROPHE 1]
  The lithe fish lighting their reaches of dim water,
  All are taken, tamed in the net of his mind;
  The lion on the hill, the wild horse windy-maned,
  Resign to him; and his blunt yoke has broken
  The sultry shoulders of the mountain bull.

Words also, and thought as rapid as air,   [STROPHE 2]
He fashions to his good use; statecraft is his,
And his the skill that deflects the arrows of snow,
The spears of winter rain: from every wind
He has made himself secure—from all but one:
In the late wind of death he cannot stand.

O clear intelligence, force beyond all measure!   [ANTISTROPHE 2]
O fate of man, working both good and evil!
When the laws are kept, how proudly his city stands!
When the laws are broken, what of his city then?
Never may the anárchic man find rest at my hearth,
Never be it said that my thoughts are his thoughts.

SCENE II

[Re-enter SENTRY *leading* ANTIGONE.*]*

CHORAGOS. What does this mean? Surely this captive woman
    Is the Princess, Antigonê. Why should she be taken?
SENTRY. Here is the one who did it! We caught her
    In the very act of burying him.—Where is Creon?
CHORAGOS. Just coming from the house.

[Enter CREON, *C.]*

CREON. What has happened?
    Why have you come back so soon?
SENTRY.   *[Expansively]* O King,
    A man should never be too sure of anything:
    I would have sworn
    That you'd not see me here again: your anger
    Frightened me so, and the things you threatened me with;
    But how could I tell then
    That I'd be able to solve the case so soon?

No dice-throwing this time: I was only too glad to come!

Here is this woman. She is the guilty one:
We found her trying to bury him.
Take her, then; question her; judge her as you will.
I am through with the whole thing now, and glád óf it.
CREON. But this is Antigonê! Why have you brought her here?
SENTRY. She was burying him, I tell you!
CREON.   *[Severely]* Is this the truth?

SENTRY. I saw her with my own eyes. Can I say more?
CREON. The details: come, tell me quickly!
SENTRY.   It was like this:
　After those terrible threats of yours, King,
　We went back and brushed the dust away from the body.
　The flesh was soft by now, and stinking,
　So we sat on a hill to windward and kept guard.
　No napping this time! We kept each other awake.
　But nothing happened until the white round sun
　Whirled in the center of the round sky over us:
　Then, suddenly,
　A storm of dust roared up from the earth, and the sky
　Went out, the plain vanished with all its trees
　In the stinging dark. We closed our eyes and endured it.
　The whirlwind lasted a long time, but it passed;
　And then we looked, and there was Antigonê!
　I have seen
　A mother bird come back to a stripped nest, heard
　Her crying bitterly a broken note or two
　For the young ones stolen. Just so, when this girl
　Found the bare corpse, and all her love's work wasted,
　She wept, and cried on heaven to damn the hands
　That had done this thing.
　　　　　　　　And then she brought more dust
　And sprinkled wine three times for her brother's ghost.

　We ran and took her at once. She was not afraid,
　Not even when we charged her with what she had done.
　She denied nothing.
　　　　　　　　And this was a comfort to me,
　And some uneasiness: for it is a good thing
　To escape from death, but it is no great pleasure
　To bring death to a friend.
　　　　　　　　Yet I always say
　There is nothing so comfortable as your own safe skin!
CREON. [*Slowly, dangerously*] And you, Antigonê,
　You with your head hanging,—do you confess this thing?
ANTIGONE. I do. I deny nothing.
CREON.   [*To* SENTRY:] You may go. [*Exit* SENTRY]

　　　　　　[*To* ANTIGONE:]

　Tell me, tell me briefly:
　Had you heard my proclamation touching this matter?
ANTIGONE. It was public. Could I help hearing it?

CREON. And yet you dared defy the law.
ANTIGONE.   I dared.
  It was not God's proclamation. That final Justice
  That rules the world below makes no such laws.

  Your edict, King, was strong,
  But all your strength is weakness itself against
  The immortal unrecorded laws of God.
  They are not merely now: they were, and shall be,
  Operative for ever, beyond man utterly.

  I knew I must die, even without your decree:
  I am only mortal. And if I must die
  Now, before it is my time to die,
  Surely this is no hardship: can anyone
  Living, as I live, with evil all about me,
  Think Death less than a friend? This death of mine
  Is of no importance; but if I had left my brother
  Lying in death unburied, I should have suffered.
  Now I do not.
                    You smile at me. Ah Creon,
  Think me a fool, if you like; but it may well be
  That a fool convicts me of folly.
CHORAGOS. Like father, like daughter: both headstrong, deaf to reason!
  She has never learned to yield.
CREON.   She has much to learn.
  The inflexible heart breaks first, the toughest iron
  Cracks first, and the wildest horses bend their necks
  At the pull of the smallest curb.
                              Pride? In a slave?
  This girl is guilty of double insolence,
  Breaking the given laws and boasting of it.
  Who is the man here,
  She or I, if this crime goes unpunished?
  Sister's child, or more than sister's child,
  Or closer yet in blood—she and her sister
  Win bitter death for this!

                  [*To servants:*]

                  Go, some of you,
  Arrest Ismenê. I accuse her equally.
  Bring her: you will find her sniffling in the house there.

  Her mind's a traitor: crimes kept in the dark
  Cry for light, and the guardian brain shudders;

But how much worse than this
Is brazen boasting of barefaced anarchy!
ANTIGONE.   Creon, what more do you want than my death?
CREON.   Nothing.
That gives me everything.
ANTIGONE.   Then I beg you: kill me.
This talking is a great weariness: your words
Are distasteful to me, and I am sure that mine
Seem so to you. And yet they should not seem so:
I should have praise and honor for what I have done.
All these men here would praise me
Were their lips not frozen shut with fear of you. [*Bitterly*]
Ah the good fortune of kings,
Licensed to say and do whatever they please!
CREON.   You are alone here in that opinion.
ANTIGONE.   No, they are with me. But they keep their tongues in leash.
CREON.   Maybe. But you are guilty, and they are not.
ANTIGONE.   There is no guilt in reverence for the dead.
CREON.   But Eteoclês—was he not your brother too?
ANTIGONE.   My brother too.
CREON.   And you insult his memory?
ANTIGONE.   [*Softly*]   The dead man would not say that I insult it.
CREON.   He would: for you honor a traitor as much as him.
ANTIGONE.   His own brother, traitor or not, and equal in blood.
CREON.   He made war on his country. Eteoclês defended it.
ANTIGONE.   Nevertheless, there are honors due all the dead.
CREON.   But not the same for the wicked as for the just.
ANTIGONE.   Ah Creon, Creon,
Which of us can say what the gods hold wicked?
CREON.   An enemy is an enemy, even dead.
ANTIGONE.   It is my nature to join in love, not hate.
CREON.   [*Finally losing patience*]   Go join him, then; if you must have your love,
Find it in hell!
CHORAGOS.   But see, Ismenê comes:

[*Enter* ISMENE, *guarded*]

Those tears are sisterly, the cloud
That shadows her eyes rains down gentle sorrow.
CREON.   You, too, Ismenê,
Snake in my ordered house, sucking my blood
Stealthily—and all the time I never knew
That these two sisters were aiming at my throne!

                                                      Ismenê,
Do you confess your share in this crime, or deny it?
Answer me.

ISMENE. Yes, if she will let me say so. I am guilty.

ANTIGONE. [*Coldly*] No, Ismenê. You have no right to say so.
  You would not help me, and I will not have you help me.

ISMENE. But now I know what you meant; and I am here
  To join you, to take my share of punishment.

ANTIGONE. The dead man and the gods who rule the dead
  Know whose act this was. Words are not friends.

ISMENE. Do you refuse me, Antigonê? I want to die with you:
  I too have a duty that I must discharge to the dead.

ANTIGONE. You shall not lessen my death by sharing it.

ISMENE. What do I care for life when you are dead?

ANTIGONE. Ask Creon. You're always hanging on his opinions.

ISMENE. You are laughing at me. Why, Antigonê?

ANTIGONE. It's a joyless laughter, Ismenê.

ISMENE.   But can I do nothing?

ANTIGONE. Yes. Save yourself. I shall not envy you.
  There are others who will praise you; I shall have honor, too.

ISMENE. But we are equally guilty!

ANTIGONE.   No more, Ismenê.
  You are alive, but I belong to Death.

CREON. [*To the* CHORUS:] Gentlemen, I beg you to observe these girls:
  One has just now lost her mind; the other,
  It seems, has never had a mind at all.

ISMENE. Grief teaches the steadiest minds to waver, King.

CREON. Yours certainly did, when you assumed guilt with the guilty!

ISMENE. But how could I go on living without her?

CREON.   You are.
  She is already dead.

ISMENE.   But your own son's bride!

CREON. There are places enough for him to push his plow.
  I want no wicked women for my sons!

ISMENE. O dearest Haimon, how your father wrongs you!

CREON. I've had enough of your childish talk of marriage!

CHORAGOS. Do you really intend to steal this girl from your son?

CREON. No; Death will do that for me.

CHORAGOS.   Then she must die?

CREON. [*Ironically*] You dazzle me.

                              —But enough of this talk!

[*To* GUARDS:]

You, there, take them away and guard them well:
For they are but women, and even brave men run
When they see Death coming. [*Exeunt* ISMENE, ANTIGONE, *and* GUARDS]

ODE II

CHORUS. Fortunate is the man who has never tasted God's vengeance! [STROPHE 1]
 Where once the anger of heaven has struck, that house is shaken
 For ever: damnation rises behind each child
 Like a wave cresting out of the black northeast,
 When the long darkness under sea roars up
 And bursts drumming death upon the whirlwhipped sand.

 I have seen this gathering sorrow from time long past [ANTISTROPHE 1]
 Loom upon Oedipus' children: generation from generation
 Takes the compulsive rage of the enemy god.
 So lately this last flower of Oedipus' line
 Drank the sunlight! but now a passionate word
 And a handful of dust have closed up all its beauty.

  What mortal arrogance [STROPHE 2]
  Transcends the wrath of Zeus?
 Sleep cannot lull him, nor the effortless long months
 Of the timeless gods: but he is young for ever,
 And his house is the shining day of high Olympos.
  All that is and shall be,
  And all the past, is his.
 No pride on earth is free of the curse of heaven.

  The straying dreams of men [ANTISTROPHE 2]
  May bring them ghosts of joy:
 But as they drowse, the waking embers burn them;
 Or they walk with fixed éyes, as blind men walk.
 But the ancient wisdom speaks for our own time:
  Fate works most for woe
  With Folly's fairest show.
 Man's little pleasure is the spring of sorrow.

SCENE III

CHORAGOS. But here is Haimon, King, the last of all your sons.
 Is it grief for Antigonê that brings him here,
 And bitterness at being robbed of his bride?

[*Enter* HAIMON]

CREON. We shall soon see, and no need of diviners.
       —Son,

You have heard my final judgment on that girl:
Have you come here hating me, or have you come
With deference and with love, whatever I do?
HAIMON. I am your son, father. You are my guide.
You make things clear for me, and I obey you.
No marriage means more to me than your continuing wisdom.
CREON. Good. That is the way to behave: subordinate
Everything else, my son, to your father's will.
This is what a man prays for, that he may get
Sons attentive and dutiful in his house,
Each hating his father's enemies,
Honoring his father's friends. But if his sons
Fail him, if they turn out unprofitably,
What has he fathered but trouble for himself
And amusement for the malicious?

                                        So you are right
Not to lose your head over this woman.
Your pleasure with her would soon grow cold, Haimon,
And then you'd have a hellcat in bed and elsewhere.
Let her find her husband in Hell!
Of all the people in this city, only she
Has had contempt for my law and broken it.

Do you want me to show myself weak before the people?
Or to break my sworn word? No, and I will not.
The woman dies.
I suppose she'll plead "family ties." Well, let her.
If I permit my own family to rebel,
How shall I earn the world's obedience?
Show me the man who keeps his house in hand,
He's fit for public authority.

                                  I'll have no dealings
With law-breakers, critics of the government:
Whoever is chosen to govern should be obeyed—
Must be obeyed, in all things, great and small,
Just and unjust! O Haimon,
The man who knows how to obey, and that man only,
Knows how to give commands when the time comes.
You can depend on him, no matter how fast
The spears come: he's a good soldier, he'll stick it out.

Anarchy, anarchy! Show me a greater evil!
This is why cities tumble and the great houses rain down,
This is what scatters armies!

No, no: good lives are made so by discipline.
We keep the laws then, and the lawmakers,
And no woman shall seduce us. If we must lose,
Let's lose to a man, at least! Is a woman stronger than we?
CHORAGOS. Unless time has rusted my wits,
  What you say, King, is said with point and dignity.
HAIMON. [*Boyishly earnest*] Father:
  Reason is God's crowning gift to man, and you are right
  To warn me against losing mine. I cannot say—
  I hope that I shall never want to say!—that you
  Have reasoned badly. Yet there are other men
  Who can reason too; and their opinions might be helpful.
  You are not in a position to know everything
  That people say or do, or what they feel:
  Your temper terrifies them—everyone
  Will tell you only what you like to hear.
  But I, at any rate, can listen; and I have heard them
  Muttering and whispering in the dark about this girl.
  They say no woman has ever, so unreasonably,
  Died so shameful a death for a generous act:
  "She covered her brother's body. Is this indecent?
  She kept him from dogs and vultures. Is this a crime?
  Death?—She should have all the honor that we can give her!"

This is the way they talk out there in the city.

You must believe me:
Nothing is closer to me than your happiness.
What could be closer? Must not any son
Value his father's fortune as his father does his?
I beg you, do not be unchangeable:
Do not believe that you alone can be right.
The man who thinks that,
The man who maintains that only he has the power
To reason correctly, the gift to speak, the soul—
A man like that, when you know him, turns out empty.

It is not reason never to yield to reason!

In flood time you can see how some trees bend,
And because they bend, even their twigs are safe,
While stubborn trees are torn up, roots and all.
And the same thing happens in sailing:

Make your sheet fast, never slacken,—and over you go,
Head over heels and under: and there's your voyage.

Forget you are angry! Let yourself be moved!
I know I am young; but please let me say this:
The ideal condition
Would be, I admit, that men should be right by instinct;
But since we are all too likely to go astray,
The reasonable thing is to learn from those who can teach.
CHORAGOS. You will do well to listen to him, King,
If what he says is sensible. And you, Haimon,
Must listen to your father.—Both speak well.
CREON. You consider it right for a man of my years and experience
To go to school to a boy?
HAIMON.   It is not right
If I am wrong. But if I am young, and right,
What does my age matter?
CREON. You think it right to stand up for an anarchist?
HAIMON. Not at all. I pay no respect to criminals.
CREON. Then she is not a criminal?
HAIMON. The City would deny it, to a man.
CREON. And the City proposes to teach me how to rule?
HAIMON. Ah. Who is it that's talking like a boy now?
CREON. My voice is the one voice giving orders in this City!
HAIMON. It is no City if it takes orders from one voice.
CREON. The State is the King!
HAIMON.   Yes, if the State is a desert. [*Pause*]
CREON. This boy, it seems, has sold out to a woman.
HAIMON. If you are a woman: my concern is only for you.
CREON. So? Your "concern"! In a public brawl with your father!
HAIMON. How about you, in a public brawl with justice?
CREON. With justice, when all that I do is within my rights?
HAIMON. You have no right to trample on God's right.
CREON. [*Completely out of control*] Fool, adolescent fool! Taken in by a woman!
HAIMON. You'll never see me taken in by anything vile.
CREON. Every word you say is for her!
HAIMON.   [*Quietly darkly*] And for you.
And for me. And for the gods under the earth.
CREON. You'll never marry her while she lives.
HAIMON. Then she must die.—But her death will cause another.
CREON. Another?
Have you lost your senses? Is this an open threat?
HAIMON. There is no threat in speaking to emptiness.

CREON. I swear you'll regret this superior tone of yours!
   You are the empty one!
HAIMON.   If you were not my father,
   I'd say you were perverse.
CREON. You girlstruck fool, don't play at words with me!
HAIMON. I am sorry. You prefer silence.
CREON.   Now, by God—!
   I swear, by all the gods in heaven above us,
   You'll watch it, I swear you shall!

[To the SERVANTS:]

                  Bring her out!
  Bring the woman out! Let her die before his eyes!
  Here, this instant, with her bridegroom beside her!
HAIMON. Not here, no; she will not die here, King.
   And you will never see my face again.
   Go on raving as long as you've a friend to endure you. [*Exit* HAIMON]
CHORAGOS. Gone, gone.
   Creon, a young man in a rage is dangerous!
CREON. Let him do, or dream to do, more than a man can.
   He shall not save these girls from death.
CHORAGOS.   These girls?
   You have sentenced them both?
CREON.   No, you are right.
   I will not kill the one whose hands are clean.
CHORAGOS. But Antigonê?
CREON.   [*Somberly*] I will carry her far away
   Out there in the wilderness, and lock her
   Living in a vault of stone. She shall have food,
   As the custom is, to absolve the State of her death.
   And there let her pray to the gods of hell:
   They are her only gods:
   Perhaps they will show her an escape from death
   Or she may learn,
              though late,
  That piety shown the dead is pity in vain. [*Exit* CREON]

ODE III

CHORUS. Love, unconquerable   [STROPHE]
   Waster of rich men, keeper
   Of warm lights and all-night vigil

In the soft face of a girl:
Sea-wanderer, forest-visitor!
Even the pure Immortals cannot escape you,
And mortal man, in his one day's dusk,
Trembles before your glory.

Surely you swerve upon ruin   [ANTISTROPHE]
The just man's consenting heart,
As here you have made bright anger
Strike between father and son—
And none has conquered but Love!
A girl's glánce wórking the will of heaven:
Pleasure to her alone who mocks us,
Merciless Aphroditê.

SCENE IV

CHORAGOS. [*As* ANTIGONE *enters guarded*] But I can no longer stand in awe of
    this,
    Nor, seeing what I see, keep back my tears.
    Here is Antigonê, passing to that chamber
    Where we all find sleep at last.
ANTIGONE. Look upon me, friends, and pity me   [STROPHE 1]
    Turning back at the night's edge to say
    Good-by to the sun that shines for me no longer;
    Now sleepy Death
    Summons me down to Acheron, that cold shore:
    There is no bridesong there, nor any music.
CHORUS. Yet not unpraised, not without a kind of honor,
    You walk at last into the underworld;
    Untouched by sickness, broken by no sword.
    What woman has ever found your way to death?
ANTIGONE. How often I have heard the story of Niobê,   [ANTISTROPHE 1]
    Tantalos' wretched daughter, how the stone
    Clung fast about her, ivy-close: and they say
    The rain falls endlessly
    And sifting soft snow; her tears are never done.
    I feel the loneliness of her death in mine.
CHORUS. But she was born of heaven, and you
    Are woman, woman-born. If her death is yours,
    A mortal woman's, is this not for you
    Glory in our world and in the world beyond?
ANTIGONE. You laugh at me. Ah, friends, friends,   [STROPHE 2]
    Can you not wait until I am dead? O Thebes,

O men many-charioted, in love with Fortune,
Dear springs of Dircê, sacred Theban grove,
Be witnesses for me, denied all pity,
Unjustly judged! and think a word of love
For her whose path turns
Under dark earth, where there are no more tears.
CHORUS. You have passed beyond human daring and come at last
  Into a place of stone where Justice sits.
  I cannot tell
  What shape of your father's guilt appears in this.
ANTIGONE. You have touched it at last: that bridal bed   [ANTISTROPHE 2]
  Unspeakable, horror of son and mother mingling:
  Their crime, infection of all our family!
  O Oedipus, father and brother!
  Your marriage strikes from the grave to murder mine.
  I have been a stranger here in my own land:
  All my life
  The blasphemy of my birth has followed me.
CHORUS. Reverence is a virtue, but strength
  Lives in established law: that must prevail.
  You have made your choice,
  Your death is the doing of your conscious hand.
ANTIGONE. Then let me go, since all your words are bitter,   [EPODE]
  And the very light of the sun is cold to me.
  Lead me to my vigil, where I must have
  Neither love nor lamentation; no song, but silence.

[CREON *interrupts impatiently*]

CREON. If dirges and planned lamentations could put off death,
  Men would be singing for ever.

[*To the* SERVANTS:]

        Take her, go!
You know your orders: take her to the vault
And leave her alone there. And if she lives or dies,
That's her affair, not ours: our hands are clean.
ANTIGONE. O tomb, vaulted bride-bed in eternal rock,
  Soon I shall be with my own again
  Where Persephonê welcomes the thin ghosts underground:
  And I shall see my father again, and you, mother,
  And dearest Polyneicês—
             dearest indeed

To me, since it was my hand
That washed him clean and poured the ritual wine:
And my reward is death before my time!

And yet, as men's hearts know, I have done no wrong,
I have not sinned before God. Or if I have,
I shall know the truth in death. But if the guilt
Lies upon Creon who judged me, then, I pray,
May his punishment equal my own.

CHORAGOS.   O passionate heart,
   Unyielding, tormented still by the same winds!
CREON.   Her guards shall have good cause to regret their delaying.
ANTIGONE.   Ah! That voice is like the voice of death!
CREON.   I can give you no reason to think you are mistaken.
ANTIGONE.   Thebes, and you my fathers' gods,
   And rulers of Thebes, you see me now, the last
   Unhappy daughter of a line of kings,
   Your kings, led away to death. You will remember
   What things I suffer, and at what men's hands,
   Because I would not transgress the laws of heaven.

[*To the* GUARDS, *simply:*]

Come: let us wait no longer. [*Exit* ANTIGONE, *L., guarded*]

ODE IV

CHORUS.   All Danaê's beauty was locked away   [STROPHE 1]
   In a brazen cell where the sunlight could not come:
   A small room, still as any grave, enclosed her.
   Yet she was a princess too,
   And Zeus in a rain of gold poured love upon her.
   O child, child,
   No power in wealth or war
   Or tough sea-blackened ships
   Can prevail against untiring Destiny!

And Dryas' son also, that furious king,   [ANTISTROPHE 1]
   Bore the god's prisoning anger for his pride:
   Sealed up by Dionysos in deaf stone,
   His madness died among echoes.
   So at the last he learned what dreadful power
   His tongue had mocked:
   For he had profaned the revels,

And fired the wrath of the nine
Implacable Sisters that love the sound of the flute.

And old men tell a half-remembered tale   [STROPHE 2]
Of horror done where a dark ledge splits the sea
And a double surf beats on the gráy shóres:
How a king's new woman, sick
With hatred for the queen he had imprisoned,
Ripped out his two sons' eyes with her bloody hands
While grinning Arês watched the shuttle plunge
Four times: four blind wounds crying for revenge,

Crying, tears and blood mingled.—Piteously born,   [ANTISTROPHE 2]
Those sons whose mother was of heavenly birth!
Her father was the god of the North Wind
And she was cradled by gales,
She raced with young colts on the glittering hills
And walked untrammeled in the open light:
But in her marriage deathless Fate found means
To build a tomb like yours for all her joy.

SCENE V

[*Enter blind* TEIRESIAS, *led by a boy. The opening speeches of* TEIRESIAS *should be in singsong contrast to the realistic lines of* CREON.]

TEIRESIAS. This is the way the blind man comes, Princes, Princes,
    Lock-step, two heads lit by the eyes of one.
CREON. What new thing have you to tell us, old Teiresias?
TEIRESIAS. I have much to tell you: listen to the prophet, Creon.
CREON. I am not aware that I have ever failed to listen.
TEIRESIAS. Then you have done wisely, King, and ruled well.
CREON. I admit my debt to you. But what have you to say?
TEIRESIAS. This, Creon: you stand once more on the edge of fate.
CREON. What do you mean? Your words are a kind of dread.
TEIRESIAS. Listen, Creon:
    I was sitting in my chair of augury, at the place
    Where the birds gather about me. They were all a-chatter,
    As is their habit, when suddenly I heard
    A strange note in their jangling, a scream, a
    Whirring fury; I knew that they were fighting,
    Tearing each other, dying
    In a whirlwind of wings clashing. And I was afraid.
    I began the rites of burnt-offering at the altar,

But Hephaistos failed me: instead of bright flame,
There was only the sputtering slime of the fat thigh-flesh
Melting: the entrails dissolved in gray smoke,
The bare bone burst from the welter. And no blaze!

This was a sign from heaven. My boy described it,
Seeing for me as I see for others.

I tell you, Creon, you yourself have brought
This new calamity upon us. Our hearths and altars
Are stained with the corruption of dogs and carrion birds
That glut themselves on the corpse of Oedipus' son.
The gods are deaf when we pray to them, their fire
Recoils from our offering, their birds of omen
Have no cry of comfort, for they are gorged
With the thick blood of the dead.
                                        O my son,
These are no trifles! Think: all men make mistakes,
But a good man yields when he knows his course is wrong,
And repairs the evil. The only crime is pride.

Give in to the dead man, then: do not fight with a corpse—
What glory is it to kill a man who is dead?
Think, I beg you:
It is for your own good that I speak as I do.
You should be able to yield for your own good.

CREON. It seems that prophets have made me their especial province.
All my life long
I have been a kind of butt for the dull arrows
Of doddering fortune-tellers!
                                        No, Teiresias:
If your birds—if the great eagles of God himself
Should carry him stinking bit by bit to heaven,
I would not yield. I am not afraid of pollution:
No man can defile the gods.
                                        Do what you will,
Go into business, make money, speculate
In India gold or that synthetic gold from Sardis,
Get rich otherwise than by my consent to bury him.
Teiresias, it is a sorry thing when a wise man
Sells his wisdom, lets out his words for hire!

TEIRESIAS. Ah Creon! Is there no man left in the world—

CREON. To do what?—Come, let's have the aphorism!

TEIRESIAS. No man who knows that wisdom outweighs any wealth?

CREON. As surely as bribes are baser than any baseness.

TEIRESIAS. You are sick, Creon! You are deathly sick!
CREON. As you say: it is not my place to challenge a prophet.
TEIRESIAS. Yet you have said my prophecy is for sale.
CREON. The generation of prophets has always loved gold.
TEIRESIAS. The generation of kings has always loved brass.
CREON. You forget yourself! You are speaking to your King.
TEIRESIAS. I know it. You are a king because of me.
CREON. You have a certain skill; but you have sold out.
TEIRESIAS. King, you will drive me to words that—
CREON.   Say them, say them!
   Only remember: I will not pay you for them.
TEIRESIAS. No, you will find them too costly.
CREON.   No doubt. Speak:
   Whatever you say, you will not change my will.
TEIRESIAS. Then take this, and take it to heart!
   The time is not far off when you shall pay back
   Corpse for corpse, flesh of your own flesh.
   You have thrust the child of this world into living night,
   You have kept from the gods below the child that is theirs:
   The one in a grave before her death, the other,
   Dead, denied the grave. This is your crime:
   And the Furies and the dark gods of Hell
   Are swift with terrible punishment for you.

   Do you want to buy me now, Creon?

                           Not many days,
   And your house will be full of men and women weeping,
   And curses will be hurled at you from far
   Cities grieving for sons unburied, left to rot
   Before the walls of Thebes.

   These are my arrows, Creon: they are all for you.

   But come, child: lead me home. [*To* BOY:]
   Let him waste his fine anger upon younger men.
   Maybe he will learn at last
   To control a wiser tongue in a better head. [*Exit* TEIRESIAS]
CHORAGOS. The old man has gone, King, but his words
   Remain to plague us. I am old, too,
   But I cannot remember that he was ever false.
CREON. That is true. . . . It troubles me.
   Oh it is hard to give in! but it is worse
   To risk everything for stubborn pride.
CHORAGOS. Creon: take my advice.

CREON.   What shall I do?
CHORAGOS.   Go quickly: free Antigonê from her vault
   And build a tomb for the body of Polyneicês.
CREON.   You would have me do this?
CHORAGOS.   Creon, yes!
   And it must be done at once: God moves
   Swiftly to cancel the folly of stubborn men.
CREON.   It is hard to deny the heart! But I
   Will do it: I will not fight with destiny.
CHORAGOS.   You must go yourself, you cannot leave it to others.
CREON.   I will go.
                     —Bring axes, servants:
   Come with me to the tomb. I buried her, I
   Will set her free.
                     Oh quickly!
   My mind misgives—
   The laws of the gods are mighty, and a man must serve them
   To the last day of his life! [*Exit* CREON]

PÆAN

CHORAGOS.   God of many names   [STROPHE 1]
CHORUS.   O Iacchos
                              son
   of Kadmeian Sémelê
                     O born of the Thunder!
   Guardian of the West
                     Regent
   of Eleusis' plain
                     O Prince of maenad Thebes
   and the Dragon Field by rippling Ismenos:
CHORAGOS.   God of many names   [ANTISTROPHE 1]
CHORUS.   the flame of torches
   flares on our hills
                     the nymphs of Iacchos
   dance at the spring of Castalia:

   from the vine-close mountain
                              come ah come in ivy:
   Evohé evohé! sings through the streets of Thebes
CHORAGOS.   God of many names   [STROPHE 2]
CHORUS.   Iacchos of Thebes
   heavenly Child

           of Sémelê bride of the Thunderer!
The shadow of plague is upon us:
                         come
with clement feet
                oh come from Parnasos
down the long slopes
                 across the lamenting water

CHORAGOS. Iô Fire! Chorister of the throbbing stars!   [ANTISTROPHE 2]
  O purest among the voices of the night!
  Thou son of God, blaze for us!
CHORUS. Come with choric rapture of circling Maenads
  Who cry *Iô Iacche!*
              God of many names!

ÉXODOS

[*Enter* MESSENGER, *L.*]

MESSENGER. Men of the line of Kadmos, you who live
  Near Amphion's citadel:
                  I cannot say
Of any condition of human life "This is fixed,
This is clearly good, or bad." Fate raises up,
And Fate casts down the happy and unhappy alike:
No man can foretell his Fate.
                    Take the case of Creon:
Creon was happy once, as I count happiness:
Victorious in battle, sole governor of the land,
Fortunate father of children nobly born.
And now it has all gone from him! Who can say
That a man is still alive when his life's joy fails?
He is a walking dead man. Grant him rich,
Let him live like a king in his great house:
If his pleasure is gone, I would not give
So much as the shadow of smoke for all he owns.
CHORAGOS. Your words hint at sorrow: what is your news for us?
MESSENGER. They are dead. The living are guilty of their death.
CHORAGOS. Who is guilty? Who is dead? Speak!
MESSENGER.   Haimon.
  Haimon is dead; and the hand that killed him
  Is his own hand.
CHORAGOS.   His father's? or his own?
MESSENGER. His own, driven mad by the murder his father had done.
CHORAGOS. Teiresias, Teiresias, how clearly you saw it all!
MESSENGER. This is my news: you must draw what conclusions you can from it.

CHORAGOS. But look: Eurydicê, our Queen:
Has she overheard us?

[*Enter* EURYDICE *from the Palace, C.*]

EURYDICE. I have heard something, friends:
As I was unlocking the gate of Pallas' shrine,
For I needed her help today, I heard a voice
Telling of some new sorrow. And I fainted
There at the temple with all my maidens about me.
But speak again: whatever it is, I can bear it:
Grief and I are no strangers.
MESSENGER.   Dearest Lady,
I will tell you plainly all that I have seen.
I shall not try to comfort you: what is the use,
Since comfort could lie only in what is not true?
The truth is always best.

                               I went with Creon
To the outer plain where Polyneicês was lying,
No friend to pity him, his body shredded by dogs.
We made our prayers in that place to Hecatê
And Pluto, that they would be merciful. And we bathed
The corpse with holy water, and we brought
Fresh-broken branches to burn what was left of it,
And upon the urn we heaped up a towering barrow
Of the earth of his own land.

                               When we were done, we ran
To the vault where Antigonê lay on her couch of stone.
One of the servants had gone ahead,
And while he was yet far off he heard a voice
Grieving within the chamber, and he came back
And told Creon. And as the King went closer,
The air was full of wailing, the words lost,
And he begged us to make all haste. "Am I a prophet?"
He said, weeping, "And must I walk this road,
The saddest of all that I have gone before?
My son's voice calls me on. Oh quickly, quickly!
Look through the crevice there, and tell me
If it is Haimon, or some deception of the gods!"

We obeyed; and in the cavern's farthest corner
We saw her lying:
She had made a noose of her fine linen veil
And hanged herself. Haimon lay beside her,
His arms about her waist, lamenting her,

His love lost under ground, crying out
That his father had stolen her away from him.

When Creon saw him the tears rushed to his eyes
And he called to him: "What have you done, child? Speak to me.
What are you thinking that makes your eyes so strange?
O my son, my son, I come to you on my knees!"
But Haimon spat in his face. He said not a word,
Staring—
        And suddenly drew his sword
And lunged. Creon shrank back, the blade missed; and the boy,
Desperate against himself, drove it half its length
Into his own side, and fell. And as he died
He gathered Antigonê close in his arms again,
Choking, his blood bright red on her white cheek.
And now he lies dead with the dead, and she is his
At last, his bride in the houses of the dead. [*Exit* EURYDICE *into the Palace*]
CHORAGOS. She has left us without a word. What can this mean?
MESSENGER. It troubles me, too; yet she knows what is best,
  Her grief is too great for public lamentation,
  And doubtless she has gone to her chamber to weep
  For her dead son, leading her maidens in his dirge.
CHORAGOS. It may be so: but I fear this deep silence. [*Pause*]
MESSENGER. I will see what she is doing. I will go in. [*Exit* MESSENGER *into the Palace*]

[*Enter* CREON *with attendants, bearing* HAIMON'S *body*]

CHORAGOS. But here is the King himself: oh look at him,
  Bearing his own damnation in his arms.
CREON. Nothing you say can touch me any more.
  My own blind heart has brought me
  From darkness to final darkness. Here you see
  The father murdering, the murdered son—
  And all my civic wisdom!

  Haimon my son, so young, so young to die,
  I was the fool, not you; and you died for me.
CHORAGOS. That is the truth; but you were late in learning it.
CREON. This truth is hard to bear. Surely a god
  Has crushed me beneath the hugest weight of heaven,
  And driven me headlong a barbaric way
  To trample out the thing I held most dear.

  The pains that men will take to come to pain!

[*Enter* MESSENGER *from the Palace*]

MESSENGER. The burden you carry in your hands is heavy,
But it is not all: you will find more in your house.
CREON. What burden worse than this shall I find there?
MESSENGER. The Queen is dead.
CREON. O port of death, deaf world,
Is there no pity for me? And you, Angel of evil,
I was dead, and your words are death again.
Is it true, boy? Can it be true?
Is my wife dead? Has death bred death?
MESSENGER. You can see for yourself.

[*The doors are opened, and the body of* EURYDICE *is disclosed within.*]

CREON. Oh pity!
All true, all true, and more than I can bear!
O my wife, my son!
MESSENGER. She stood before the altar, and her heart
Welcomed the knife her own hand guided,
And a great cry burst from her lips for Megareus dead,
And for Haimon dead, her sons; and her last breath
Was a curse for their father, the murderer of her sons.
And she fell, and the dark flowed in through her closing eyes.
CREON. O god, I am sick with fear.
Are there no swords here? Has no one a blow for me?
MESSENGER. Her curse is upon you for the deaths of both.
CREON. It is right that it should be. I alone am guilty.
I know it, and I say it. Lead me in,
Quickly, friends.
I have neither life nor substance. Lead me in.
CHORAGOS. You are right, if there can be right in so much wrong.
The briefest way is best in a world of sorrow.
CREON. Let it come,
Let death come quickly, and be kind to me.
I would not ever see the sun again.
CHORAGOS. All that will come when it will; but we, meanwhile,
Have much to do. Leave the future to itself.
CREON. All my heart was in that prayer!
CHORAGOS. Then do not pray any more: the sky is deaf.
CREON. Lead me away. I have been rash and foolish.
I have killed my son and my wife.
I look for comfort; my comfort lies here dead.
Whatever my hands have touched has come to nothing.
Fate has brought all my pride to a thought of dust.

[*As* CREON *is being led into the house, the* CHORAGOS *advances and speaks
directly to the audience*]

CHORAGOS.   There is no happiness where there is no wisdom;
   No wisdom but in submission to the gods.
   Big words are always punished,
   And proud men in old age learn to be wise.

English version by Dudley Fitts and Robert Fitzgerald

Journal Entry

Identify the concerns, themes, or problems of your generation that emerge in *Antigone*.
Quote from the play as you develop your entry.

Textual Considerations

1. To what extent is Ismene a foil for Antigone? What is your evaluation of Ismene's
   point of view that individuals must obey the law?
2. Analyze the function of Teiresias in the play, and define the nature of the conflict
   between him and Creon.
3. Investigate the interplay of gender and power in the play.
4. To what extent are Antigone and Creon responsible for their individual tragedies, and
   to what extent are they victims of fate?

Cultural Contexts

1. Discuss with your group the political implications of the debate between Creon and
   Haimon. Split your group into two, and debate the merits and fallacies of Haimon's
   and Creon's political points of view on the role of the people.
2. Debate also whether, according to Sophocles, Antigone and Creon might represent
   equal dangers to the state.

Susan Glaspell

Trifles

CHARACTERS

GEORGE HENDERSON, *County attorney*
HENRY PETERS, *Sheriff*
LEWIS HALE, *A neighboring farmer*
MRS. PETERS
MRS. HALE

> SCENE. *The kitchen in the now abandoned farmhouse of* JOHN WRIGHT, *a gloomy kitchen, and left without having been put in order—unwashed pans under the sink, a loaf of bread outside the breadbox, a dish towel on the table—other signs of incompleted work. At the rear the outer door opens and the* SHERIFF *comes in followed by the* COUNTY ATTORNEY *and* HALE. *The* SHERIFF *and* HALE *are men in middle life, the* COUNTY ATTORNEY *is a young man; all are much bundled up and go at once to the stove. They are followed by two women—the* SHERIFF's *wife first; she is a slight wiry woman, a thin nervous face.* MRS. HALE *is larger and would ordinarily be called more comfortable looking, but she is disturbed now and looks fearfully about as she enters. The women have come in slowly, and stand close together near the door.*

COUNTY ATTORNEY. [*Rubbing his hands.*] This feels good. Come up to the fire, ladies.

MRS. PETERS. [*After taking a step forward.*] I'm not—cold.

SHERIFF. [*Unbuttoning his overcoat and stepping away from the stove as if to mark the beginning of official business.*] Now, Mr. Hale, before you move things about, you explain to Mr. Henderson just what you saw when you came here yesterday morning.

COUNTY ATTORNEY. By the way, has anything been moved? Are things just as you left them yesterday?

SHERIFF. [*Looking about.*] It's just the same. When it dropped below zero last night I thought I'd better send Frank out this morning to make a fire for us—no use getting pneumonia with a big case on, but I told him not to touch anything except the stove—and you know Frank.

COUNTY ATTORNEY. Somebody should have been left here yesterday.

SHERIFF. Oh—yesterday. When I had to send Frank to Morris Center for that man who went crazy—I want you to know I had my hands full yesterday, I knew you could get back from Omaha by today and as long as I went over everything here myself—

COUNTY ATTORNEY. Well, Mr Hale, tell just what happened when you came here yesterday morning.

HALE. Harry and I had started to town with a load of potatoes. We came along the road from my place and as I got here I said, "I'm going to see if I can't get John Wright to go in with me on a party telephone." I spoke to Wright about it once before and he put me off, saying folks talked to much anyway, and all he asked was peace and quiet—I guess you know how much he talked himself; but I though maybe if I went to the house and talked about it before his wife, though I said to Harry I didn't know as what his wife wanted made much difference to John—

COUNTY ATTORNEY. Let's talk about that later, Mr. Hale. I do want to talk about that, but tell now just what happened when you got to the house.

HALE. I didn't hear or see anything; I knocked at the door, and still it was all quiet inside. I knew they must be up, it was past eight o'clock. So I knocked again, and I thought I heard somebody say, "Come in." I wasn't sure, I'm not sure yet, but I opened the door—this door [*Indicating the door by which the two women are still standing.*] and there in that rocker— [*Pointing to it.*] sat Mrs. Wright.

[*They all look at the rocker.*]

COUNTY ATTORNEY. What—was she doing?

HALE. She was rockin' back and forth. She had her apron in her hand and was kind of—pleating it.

COUNTY ATTORNEY. And how did she—look?

HALE. Well, she looked queer.

COUNTY ATTORNEY. How do you mean—queer?

HALE. Well, as if she didn't know what she was going to do next. And kind of done up.

COUNTY ATTORNEY. How did she seem to feel about your coming?

HALE. Why, I don't think she minded—one way or other. She didn't pay much attention. I said, "How do, Mrs. Wright, it's cold, ain't it?" And she said, "Is it?"—and went on kind of pleating at her apron. Well, I was surprised; she didn't ask me to come up to the stove, or to set down, but just sat there, not even looking at me, so I said, "I want to see John." And then she—laughed. I guess you would call it a laugh. I thought of Harry and the team outside, so I said a little sharply "Can't I see John?" "No," she says, kind o' dull like. "Ain't he home?" says I. "Yes," says she, "he's home." "Then why can't I see him?" I asked her, out of patience. "'Cause he's dead," says she. "*Dead?*" says I. She just nodded her head, not getting a bit excited, but rockin' back and forth. "Why—where is he?" says I, not knowing what to say. She just pointed upstairs—like that [*Himself pointing to the room above*]. I got up, with the idea of going up there. I walked from there to here—then I says, "Why, what did he die of?" "He died of a rope round his neck," says she, and just went on pleating at her apron. Well, I went out and called Harry. I thought I might—need help. We went upstairs and there he was lyin'—

COUNTY ATTORNEY. I think I'd rather have you go into that upstairs, where you can point it all out. Just go on now with the rest of the story.

HALE. Well, my first thought was to get that rope off. It looked . . . [*Stops, his face twitches.*] . . . but Harry, he went up to him, and he said, "No, he's dead all right, and we'd better not touch anything." So we went back down stairs. She was still sitting that same way. "Has anybody been notified?" I asked. "No," she says, unconcerned. "Who did this, Mrs. Wright?" said Harry. He said it businesslike—and she stopped pleatin' of her apron. "I don't know," she says. "You don't *know*?" says Harry. "No," says she. "Weren't you sleepin in the bed with him?" says Harry. "Yes," says she, "but I was on the inside." "Somebody slipped a rope around his neck and strangled him and you didn't wake up?" says Harry. "I didn't wake up," she said after him. We must 'a looked as if we didn't see how that could be, for after a minute she said, "I sleep sound." Harry was going to ask her more questions but I said maybe we ought to let her tell her story first to the coroner, or the sheriff, so Harry went fast as he could to Rivers' place, where there's a telephone.

COUNTY ATTORNEY. And what did Mrs. Wright do when she knew that you had gone for the coroner?

HALE. She moved from that chair to this one over here [*Pointing to small chair in the corner.*] and just sat there with her hands together and looking down. I got a feeling that I ought to make some conversation, so I said I had come in to see if John wanted to put in a telephone, and at that she started to laugh, and the she stopped and looked at me—scared. [*The* COUNTY ATTORNEY, *who has had his notebook out, makes a note.*] I dunno, maybe it wasn't scared. I wouldn't like to say it was. Soon Harry got back, and then Dr. Lloyd came, and you, Mr. Peters, and so I guess that's all I know that you don't.

COUNTY ATTORNEY. [*Looking around.*] I guess we'll go upstairs first—and then out to the barn and around there. [*To the* SHERIFF] You're convinced that there was nothing important here—nothing that would point to any motive.

SHERIFF. Nothing here but kitchen things.

[*The* COUNTY ATTORNEY, *after again looking around the kitchen, opens the door of a cupboard closet. He gets up on a chair and looks on a shelf. Pulls his hand away, sticky.*]

COUNTY ATTORNEY. Here's a nice mess.

[*The women draw nearer.*]

MRS. PETERS [*To the other woman.*]. Oh, her fruit, it did freeze. [*To the* COUNTY ATTORNEY] She worried about that when it turned so cold. She said the fire'd go out and her jars would break.

SHERIFF. Well, can you beat the women! Held for murder and worryin' about her preserves.

COUNTY ATTORNEY. I guess before we're through she may have something more serious than preserves to worry about.

HALE. Well, women are used to worrying over trifles.

[*The two women move a little closer together.*]

COUNTY ATTORNEY. [*With the gallantry of a young politician.*] And yet, for all their worries, what would we do without the ladies? [*The women do not unbend. He goes to the sink, takes a dipperful of water from the pail and pouring it into a basin, washes his hands. Starts to wipe them on the roller towel, turns it for a cleaner place.*] Dirty towels! [*Kicks his foot against the pans under the sink.*] Not much of a housekeeper, would you say, ladies?

MRS. HALE. [*Stiffly.*] There's a great deal of work to be done on a farm.

COUNTY ATTORNEY. To be sure. And yet [*With a little bow to her*] I know there are some Dickson county farmhouses which do not have such roller towels.

[*He gives it a pull to expose its full length again.*]

MRS. HALE. Those towels get dirty awful quick. Men's hands aren't always as clean as they might be.

COUNTY ATTORNEY. Ah, loyal to your sex, I see. But you and Mrs. Wright were neighbors. I suppose you were friends, too.

MRS. HALE. [*Shaking her head.*] I've not seen much of her of late years. I've not been in this house—it's more than a year.

COUNTY ATTORNEY. And why was that? You didn't like her?

MRS. HALE. I liked her all well enough. Farmers's wives have their hands full, Mr. Henderson. And then—

COUNTY ATTORNEY. Yes—?

MRS. HALE. [*Looking about.*] It never seemed a cheerful place.

COUNTY ATTORNEY. No—it's not cheerful. I shouldn't say she had the homemaking instinct.

MRS. HALE. Well, I don't know as Wright had, either.

COUNTY ATTORNEY. You mean that they didn't get on very well?

MRS. HALE. No, I don't mean anything. But I don't think a place'd be any cheerfuller for John Wright's being in it.

COUNTY ATTORNEY. I'd like to talk more of that a little later. I want to get the lay of things upstairs now.

[*He goes to the left, where three steps lead to a door.*]

SHERIFF. I suppose anything Mrs. Peter does'll be all right. She was to take in some clothes for her, you know, and a few little things. We left in such a hurry yesterday.

COUNTY ATTORNEY. Yes, but I would like to see what you take, Mrs. Peters, and keep an eye out for anything that might be of use to us.

MRS. PETERS. Yes, Mr. Henderson.

[*The women listen to the men's steps on the stairs, then look about the kitchen.*]

MRS. HALE. I'd hate to have men coming into my kitchen, snooping around and criticising.

[*She arranges the pans under the sink which the* COUNTY ATTORNEY *had shoved out of place.*]

MRS. PETERS. Of course it's no more than their duty.

MRS. HALE. Duty's all right, but I guess that deputy sheriff that came out to make the fire might have got a little of this on. [*Gives the roller towel a pull.*] Wish

I'd thought of that sooner. Seems mean to talk about her for not having things slicked up when she had to come away in such a hurry.

MRS. PETERS. [*Who has gone to a small table in the left rear corner of the room and lifted one end of a towel that covers a pan.*] She had bread set.

    [*Stands still.*]

MRS. HALE. [*Eyes fixed on a loaf of bread beside the breadbox, which is on a low shelf at the other side of the room. Moves slowly toward it.*] She was going to put this in there. [*Picks up loaf, then abruptly drops it. In a manner of returning to familiar things.*] It's a shame about her fruit. I wonder if it's all gone. [*Gets up on the chair and looks.*] I think there's some here that's all right, Mrs. Peters. Yes—here; [*Holding it toward the window.*] this is cherries, too. [*Looking again.*] I declare I believe that's the only one. [*Gets down, bottle in her hand. Goes to the sink and wipes it off on the outside.*] She'll feel awful after all her hard work in the hot weather. I remember the afternoon I put up my cherries last summer. [*She puts the bottle on the big kitchen table, center of the room. With a sigh, is about to sit down in the rocking-chair. Before she is seated realizes what chair it is; with a slow look at it, steps back. The chair which she has touched rocks back and forth.*]

MRS. PETERS. Well, I must get those things from the front room closet. [*She goes to the door at the right, but after looking into the other room, steps back.*] You coming with me, Mrs. Hale? You could help me carry them.

    [*They go in the other room; reappear,* MRS. PETERS *carrying a dress and skirt,* MRS. HALE *following with a pair of shoes.*]

MRS. PETERS. My, it's cold in there.

    [*She puts the clothes on the big table, and hurries to the stove.*]

MRS. HALE. [*Examining her skirt.*] Wright was close. I think maybe that's why she kept so much to herself. She didn't even belong to the Ladies Aid. I suppose she felt she couldn't do her part, and then you don't enjoy things when you feel shabby. She used to wear pretty clothes and be lively, when she was Minnie Foster, one of the town girls singing in the choir. But that—oh, that was thirty years ago. This all you was to take in?

MRS. PETERS. She said she wanted an apron. Funny thing to want, for there isn't much to get you dirty in jail, goodness knows. But I suppose just to make her feel more natural. She said they was in the top drawer in this cupboard. Yes, here. And then her little shawl that always hung behind the door. [*Opens stair door and looks.*] Yes, here it is.

    [*Quickly shuts door leading upstairs.*]

MRS. HALE. [*Abruptly moving toward her.*] Mrs. Peters?

MRS. PETERS. Yes, Mrs. Hale?

MRS. HALE. Do you think she did it?

MRS. PETERS. [*In a frightened voice.*] Oh, I don't know.

MRS. HALE. Well, I don't think she did. Asking for an apron and her little shawl. Worrying about her fruit.

MRS. PETERS. [*Starts to speak, glances up, where footsteps are heard in the room above. In a low voice*]. Mr. Peters says it looks bad for her. Mr. Henderson is awful sarcastic in a speech and he'll make fun of her sayin' she didn't wake up.

MRS. HALE. Well, I guess John Wright didn't wake when they was slipping that rope under his neck.

MRS. PETERS. No, it's strange. It must have been done awful crafty and still. They say it was such a—funny way to kill a man, rigging it all up like that.

MRS. HALE. That's just what Mr. Hale said. There was a gun in the house. He says that's what he can't understand.

MRS. PETERS. Mr. Henderson said coming out that what was needed for the case was a motive; something to show anger, or—sudden feeling.

MRS. HALE. [*Who is standing by the table.*] Well, I don't see any signs of anger around here. [*She puts her hand on the dish towel which lies on the table, stands looking down at table, one half of which is clean, the other half messy.*] It's wiped to here. [*Makes a move as if to finish work, then turns and looks at loaf of bread outside the breadbox. Drops towel. In that voice of coming back to familiar things.*] Wonder how they are finding things upstairs. I hope she had it a little more red-up up there. You know, it seems kind of *sneaking*. Locking her up in town and then coming out here and trying to get her own house to turn against her!

MRS. PETERS. But Mrs. Hale, the law is the law.

MRS. HALE. I s'pose 'tis. [*Unbuttoning her coat.*] Better loosen up your things, Mrs. Peters. You won't feel them when you go out.

> [MRS. PETERS *takes off her fur tippet, goes to hang it on hook at back of room, stands looking at the under part of the small corner table.*]

MRS. PETERS. She was piecing a quilt.

> [*She brings the large sewing basket and they look at the bright pieces.*]

MRS. HALE. It's log cabin pattern. Pretty, isn't it? I wonder if she was goin' to quilt it or just knot it?

> [*Footsteps have been heard coming down the stairs. The* SHERIFF *enters followed by* HALE *and the* COUNTY ATTORNEY.]

SHERIFF. They wonder if she was going to quilt it or just knot it!

> [*The men laugh; the women look abashed.*]

COUNTY ATTORNEY. [*Rubbing his hands over the stove.*] Frank's fire didn't do too much up there, did it? Well, let's go out to the barn and get that cleared up.

> [*The men go outside.*]

MRS. HALE. [*Resentfully.*] I don't know as there's anything so strange, our takin' up our time with little things while we're waiting for them to get the evidence. [*She sits down at the big table smoothing out a block with decision.*] I don't see as it's anything to laugh about.

MRS. PETERS. [*Apologetically.*] Of course they've got awful important things on their minds.

> [*Pulls up a chair and joins* MRS. HALE *at the table.*]

MRS. HALE. [*Examining another block.*] Mrs. Peters, look at this one. Here, this is the one she was working on, and look at the sewing. All the rest of it has been so nice and even. And look at this! It's all over the place. Why, it looks as if she didn't know what she was about!

> [*After she has said this they look at each other, then start to glance back at the door. After an instant* MRS. HALE *has pulled at a knot and ripped the sewing.*]

MRS. PETERS. Oh, what are you doing, Mrs. Hale?

MRS. HALE. [*Mildly.*] Just pulling out a stitch or two that's not sewed very good. [*Threading a needle.*] Bad sewing always makes me fidgety.

MRS. PETERS. [*Nervously.*] I don't think we ought to touch things.

MRS. HALE. I'll just finish up this end. [*Suddenly stopping and leaning forward.*] Mrs. Peters?

MRS. PETERS. Yes, Mrs. Hale?

MRS. HALE. What do you suppose she was so nervous about?

MRS. PETERS. Oh—I don't know. I don't know as she was nervous. I sometimes sew awful queer when I'm just tired. [MRS. HALE *starts to say something, looks at* MRS. PETERS, *then goes on sewing.*] Well, I must get these things wrapped up. They may be through sooner than we think. [*Putting apron and other things together.*] I wonder where I can find a piece of paper, and string.

MRS. HALE. In that cupboard, maybe.

MRS. PETERS. [*Looking in cupboard.*] Why, here's a birdcage. [*Holds it up.*] Did she have a bird, Mrs. Hale?

MRS. HALE. Why, I don't know whether she did or not—I've not been here for so long. There was a man around last year selling canaries cheap, but I don't know as she took one; maybe she did. She used to sing real pretty herself.

MRS. PETERS [*Glancing around.*]. Seems funny to think of a bird here. But she must have had one, or why would she have a cage? I wonder what happened to it.

MRS. HALE. I s'pose maybe the cat got it.

MRS. PETERS. No, she didn't have a cat. She's got that feeling some people have about cats—afraid of them. My cat got in her room and she was real upset and asked me to take it out.

MRS. HALE. My sister Bessie was like that. Queer, ain't it?

MRS. PETERS. [*Examining the cage.*] Why, look at this door. It's broke. One hinge is pulled apart.

MRS. HALE. [*Looking too.*] Looks as if someone must have been rough with it.

MRS. PETERS. Why, yes.

[*She brings the cage forward and puts it on the table.*]

MRS. HALE. I wish if they're going to find any evidence they'd be about it. I don't like this place.

MRS. PETERS. But I'm awful glad you came with me, Mrs. Hale. It would be lonesome for me sitting here alone.

MRS. HALE. It would, wouldn't it? [*Dropping her sewing.*] But I tell you what I do wish, Mrs. Peters. I wish I had come over sometimes when *she* was here. I— [*Looking around the room.*] —wish I had.

MRS. PETERS. But of course you were awfully busy, Mrs. Hale—your house and your children.

MRS. HALE. I could've come. I stayed away because it weren't cheerful—and that's why I ought to have come. I—I've never like this place. Maybe because it's down in a hollow and you don't see the road. I dunno what it is but it's a lonesome place and always was. I wish I had come over to see Minnie Foster sometimes. I can see now—

[*Shakes her head.*]

MRS. PETERS. Well, you musn't reproach yourself, Mrs. Hale. Somehow we just don't see how it is with other folks until—something comes up.

MRS. HALE. Not having children makes less work—but it makes a quiet house, and Wright out to work all day, and no company when he did come in. Did you know John Wright, Mrs. Peters?

MRS. PETERS. Not to know him; I've seen him in town. They say he was a good man.

MRS. HALE. Yes—good; he didn't drink, and kept his word as well as most, I guess, and paid his debts. But he was a hard man, Mrs. Peters. Just to pass the time of day with him— [*Shivers.*] Like a raw wind that gets to the bone. [*Pauses, her eye falling on the cage.*] I should think she would 'a wanted a bird. But what do you suppose went with it?

MRS. PETERS. I don't know, unless it got sick and died.

[*She reaches over and swings the broken door, swings it again. Both women watch it.*]

MRS. HALE. You weren't raised round here, were you? [MRS. PETERS *shakes her head.*] You didn't know—her?

MRS. PETERS. Not till they brought her yesterday.

MRS. HALE. She—come to think of it, she was kind of like a bird herself—real sweet and pretty, but kind of timid and—fluttery. How—she—did—change.

[*Silence; then as if struck by a happy thought and relieved to get back to every day things.*] Tell you what, Mrs. Peters, why don't you take the quilt in with you? It might take up her mind.

MRS. PETERS. Why, I think that's a real nice idea, Mrs. Hale. There couldn't possibly be any objection to it, could there? Now, just what would I take? I wonder if her patches are in here—and her things. [*They look in the sewing basket.*]

MRS. HALE. Here's some red. I expect this has got sewing things in it. [*Brings out a fancy box.*] What a pretty box. Looks like something somebody would give you. Maybe her scissors are in here. [*Opens box. Suddenly puts her hand to her nose.*] Why— [MRS. PETERS *bends nearer, then turns her face away.*] There's something wrapped up in this piece of silk.

MRS. PETERS. Why, this isn't her scissors.

MRS. HALE. [*Lifting the silk.*] Oh, Mrs. Peters—its—

[MRS. PETERS *bends closer.*]

MRS. PETERS. It's the bird.

MRS. HALE. [*Jumping up.*] But, Mrs. Peters—look at it! Its neck! Look at its neck. It's all—other side *to.*

MRS. PETERS. Somebody—wrung—its—neck.

[*Their eyes meet. A look of growing comprehension, of horror. Steps are heard outside.* MRS. HALE *slips box under quilt pieces, and sinks into her chair. Enter* SHERIFF *and* COUNTY ATTORNEY. MRS. PETERS *rises.*]

COUNTY ATTORNEY. [*As one turning from serious things to little pleasantries.*] Well, ladies, have you decided whether she was going to quilt it or knot it?

MRS. PETERS. We think she was going to—knot it.

COUNTY ATTORNEY. Well, that's interesting, I'm sure. [*Seeing the bird cage.*] Has the bird flown?

MRS. HALE. [*Putting more quilt pieces over the box.*] We think the—cat got it.

COUNTY ATTORNEY. [*Preoccupied.*] Is there a cat?

[MRS. HALE *glances in a quick covert way at* MRS. PETERS.]

MRS. PETERS. Well, not *now.* They're superstitious, you know. They leave.

COUNTY ATTORNEY. [*To* SHERIFF PETERS, *continuing an interrupted conversation.*] No sign at all of anyone having come from the outside. Their own rope. Now let's go up again and go over it piece by piece. [*They start upstairs.*] It would have to have been someone who knew just the—

[MRS. PETERS *sits down. The two women sit there not looking at one another, but as if peering into something and at the same time holding back. When they talk now it is in the manner of feeling their way over strange ground, as if afraid of what they are saying, but as if they can not help saying it.*]

MRS. HALE. She liked the bird. She was going to bury it in that pretty box.

MRS. PETERS. [*In a whisper.*] When I was a girl—my kitten—there was a boy took a hatchet, and before my eyes—and before I could get there— [*Covers her face an instant.*] If they hadn't held me back I would have— [*Catches herself, looks upstairs where steps are heard, falters weakly.*] —hurt him.

MRS. HALE. [*With a slow look around her.*] I wonder how it would seem never to have had any children around. [*Pause.*] No, Wright wouldn't like the bird—a thing that sang. She used to sing. He killed that, too.

MRS. PETERS. [*Moving uneasily.*] We don't know who killed the bird.

MRS. HALE. I knew John Wright.

MRS. PETERS. It was an awful thing was done in this house that night, Mrs. Hale. Killing a man while he slept, slipping a rope around his neck that choked the life out of him.

MRS. HALE. His neck. Choked the life out of him.

[*Her hand goes out and rests on the birdcage.*]

MRS. PETERS. [*With rising voice.*] We don't know who killed him. We don't *know.*

MRS. HALE. [*Her own feeling not interrupted.*] If there'd been years and years of nothing, then a bird to sing to you, it would be awful—still, after the bird was still.

MRS. PETERS. [*Something within her speaking.*] I know what stillness is. When we homesteaded in Dakota, and my first baby died—after he was two years old, and me with no other then—

MRS. HALE. [*Moving.*] How soon do you suppose they'll be through, looking for the evidence?

MRS. PETERS. I know what stillness is. [*Pulling herself back.*] The law has got to punish crime, Mrs. Hale.

MRS. HALE. [*Not as if answering that.*] I wish you'd seen Minnie Foster when she wore a white dress and blue ribbons and stood up there in the choir and sang. [*A look around the room.*] Oh, I *wish* I'd come over here once in awhile! That was a crime! That was a crime! Who's going to punish that?

MRS. PETERS. [*Looking upstairs.*] We mustn't—take on.

MRS. HALE. I might have known she needed help! I know how things can be—for women. I tell you, it's queer, Mrs. Peters. We live close together and we live far apart. We all go through the same things—it's all just a different kind of the same thing. [*Brushes her eyes; noticing the bottle of fruit, reaches out for it.*] If I was you I wouldn't tell her her fruit was gone. Tell her it *ain't.* Tell her it's all right. Take this in to prove it to her. She—she may never know whether it was broke or not.

MRS. PETERS. [*Takes the bottle, looks about for something to wrap it in; takes petticoat from the clothes brought from the other room, very nervously begins winding this around the bottle. In a false voice.*] My, it's a good thing the men couldn't hear us. Wouldn't they just laugh! Getting all stirred up over a little thing like a—dead canary. As if that could have anything to do with—with—wouldn't they *laugh!*

[*The men are heard coming down stairs.*]

MRS. HALE. [*Under her breath.*] Maybe they would—maybe they wouldn't.

COUNTY ATTORNEY. No, Peters, it's all perfectly clear except a reason for doing it. But you know juries when it comes to women. If there was some definite thing. Something to show—something to make a story about—a thing that would connect up with this strange way of doing it—

[*The women's eyes meet for an instant. Enter* HALE *from outer door.*]

HALE. Well, I've got the team around. Pretty cold out there.

COUNTY ATTORNEY. I'm going to stay here a while by myself. [*To the* SHERIFF] You can send Frank out for me, can't you? I want to go over everything. I'm not satisfied we can't do better.

SHERIFF. Do you want to see what Mrs. Peters is going to take in?

[*The* COUNTY ATTORNEY *goes to the table, picks up the apron, laughs.*]

COUNTY ATTORNEY. Oh, I guess they're not very dangerous things the ladies have picked out. [*Moves a few things about, disturbing the quilt pieces which cover the box. Steps back.*] No, Mrs. Peters doesn't need supervising. For that matter, a sheriff's wife is married to the law. Ever think of it that way, Mrs. Peters?

MRS. PETERS. Not—just that way.

SHERIFF. [*Chuckling.*] Married to the law. [*Moves toward the other room.*] I just want you to come here a minute, George. We ought to take a look at these windows.

COUNTY ATTORNEY. [*Scoffingly.*] Oh, windows!

SHERIFF. We'll be right out, Mr. Hale.

[HALE *goes outside. The* SHERIFF *follows the* COUNTY ATTORNEY *into the other room. Then* MRS. HALE *rises, hands tight together, looking intensely at* MRS. PETERS, *whose eyes make a slow turn, finally meeting* MRS. HALE'*s. A moment* MRS. HALE *holds her, then her own eyes point to where the box is concealed. Suddenly* MRS. PETERS *throws back quilt pieces and tries to put the box in the bag she is wearing. It is too big. She opens box, starts to take bird out, cannot touch it, goes to pieces, stands there help-less. Sound of a knob turning in the other room.* MRS. HALE *snatches the box and puts it in the pocket of her big coat. Enter* COUNTY ATTORNEY *and* SHERIFF.]

COUNTY ATTORNEY. [*Facetiously.*] Well, Henry, at least we found out that she was not going to quilt it. She was going to—what is it you call it, ladies?

MRS. HALE. [*Her hand against her pocket.*] We call it—knot it, Mr. Henderson.

CURTAIN

Journal Entry

Respond to the concept of female bonding in *Trifles*.

Textual Considerations

1. Discuss the significance of the bird cage and the quilt as the dominant symbols of the play, and explain their relationship to the theme.
2. What does *Trifles* reveal about traditional male and female roles in marriage? Analyze the kind of marriage the Wrights might have had.
3. Using evidence from the text, investigate the charge against Mrs. Hale's and Mrs. Peters's capacity to subvert the law through passive resistance and compromise.

Cultural Contexts

1. Consider with your group how fair or unfair Susan Glaspell is in her portrayal of the male characters in *Trifles*. List the traits Glaspell connects with the male characters, and discuss them in light of the feminist focus Glaspell adopts in *Trifles*.
2. Discuss with your group the moral and legal questions raised in the play. Consider, for example, how many crimes have been committed and what kind of punishment seems appropriate for Mrs. Wright's crime. Evaluate also Mrs. Hale's and Mrs. Peters's decision to withhold evidence.

WRITING TOPICS

1. Examine the images or metaphors of fences, boundaries, or walls in any three poems in Part Five. Consider, for example, walls within families as well as those between or within groups.

2. To what extent do you agree that "the personal is political" or that "there cannot be any individual freedom unrooted in community discipline"? How do these concepts apply to individual choices in *Antigone* and *Trifles,* or in other selections included here?

3. Would it be fair to describe the protagonists in any Part Five texts as rebels? Write an essay justifying your response and conveying your attitudes toward their rebellion.

4. Reflect on the representation of the forces of authority in the selections by Matshoba, Olds, and Glaspell. What positions do they take? How do they enhance or impede the dialogue between our private and communal selves? What did you learn about the law from these texts?

5. Investigate the extent to which physical boundaries limit the choices of the protagonists of *Trifles,* "The Englishwoman," or another text in this part. Analyze each woman's relationship to her environment, and speculate on how some change in her surroundings might increase her sense of personal autonomy.

6. Several texts, including "Hands" and "What the Gossips Saw," present the community as a hostile force with power to decrease or even to destroy individuals' rights and options. Analyze the causes and the effects of a community's behavior in these or other selections. How can such behavior limit individual participation in the social order? Under what circumstances, if any, should individual rights be considered more important than social consensus?

7. Several texts also address civil disobedience and the historical right of the individual to engage in social protest. Re-create a dialogue between the voice of the community and the voice of the individual in any two selections in this part. Given a choice between a society in which individual rights come first and one in which community needs have priority, which would you choose?

8. Apply the theory of "the melting pot" to "Street Kid" and another selection in this part. What do the texts imply about assimilation among ethnic groups? What might the protagonists of the texts have learned about one another had they engaged in dialogue?

9. Drawing on the stories you have read in Part Five, argue whether the conflict between individualism and community is irreconcilable.

10. A notation in Kafka's diary reads, "I have powerfully assumed the negativity of times." To what extent does this apply to "The Metamorphosis"? Consider, for example, the portrayal of the family and their interrelationships.

PART ASSIGNMENTS

RESEARCH TOPICS

1. To examine racism and the sociopolitical conditions produced by apartheid in South Africa, write a documented paper discussing how literary texts, such as Alan Paton's *Cry, the Beloved Country* and Donald Woods's *Biko*, assumed an active role in awakening South African consciousness. Consult bibliographic sources in your library and see this book's "Researching Literary Sources" appendix for the uses of secondary sources and the Modern Language Association (MLA) style of documentation.

2. In a documented paper, explore the relationship between the individual and the community in any three short stories from James Joyce's *Dubliners* or from Sherwood Anderson's *Winesburg, Ohio*.

3. Using two or three sources on ancient Greek culture, write a research paper on Greek religion, with particular references to burial customs and belief in the afterlife.

4. Write a documented paper on the relationship between the individual and society in any four poems by one of the following poets: Dickinson, Frost, Gunn, Romero, or Hughes.

An Introduction to the Elements of Fiction, Poetry, and Drama

FICTION

What do we mean by *fiction?* For the novelist Toni Morrison, "fiction, by definition, is distinct from fact. Presumably it's the product of imagination—invention—and it claims the freedom to dispense with 'what really happened' or where it really happened, or when it really happened, and nothing in it needs to be publicly verifiable, although much of it can be verified." Morrison goes on to say, however, that as a storyteller she is less interested in the distinction between fiction and fact than in that between fact and truth, "because facts can exist without human intelligence, but truth cannot." Fiction, then, is concerned with what the novelist William Faulkner calls "the verities and truths of the heart."

Tales, fables, parables, epic poems, and romances, and even the fairy tales you heard as a child, rank among the most ancient modes of fiction, kept alive by the power of the human voice to narrate and transmit the excitement and authenticity of imaginary actions and events. Short stories, however, belong to a more contemporary mode of narrative fiction and gained in recognition through the works of nineteenth-century American and European writers, including Edgar Allan Poe, Mary E. Wilkins Freeman, Anton Chekhov, and Guy de Maupassant.

This appendix introduces several technical terms, such as *character, plot, setting, theme, narrator,* and *style and tone,* that are used to describe the formal elements of a short story. Getting acquainted with these terms will help you to understand how short stories are put together and make it easier for you both to read them and to write about them.

Character

A *character* is a fictional person in a story, and readers' first reactions to him or her are usually based on their subjective capacity to empathize with the character's experiences. A character is often revealed through his or her actions, which provide readers with clues about the character's personality, motives, and expectations. Many stories present a conflict between the protagonist (the story's central character) and the antagonist (the opposing character or force); the conflict is revealed through the author's use of dialogue and narrative. In Alifa Rifaat's story "Another Evening at the Club" (p. 408) for instance, the main character or protagonist, Samia, is in conflict with her husband, the antagonist, because of her inability to liberate herself from his dominating behavior.

Fictional characters are sometimes referred to as *round* or *flat, static* or *dynamic*. A round character is usually more fully developed, challenging readers to analyze the character's motives and evaluate his or her actions. Round characters change, grow, and possess a credible personality, like the mother in Mary E. Wilkins Freeman's short story "The Revolt of 'Mother.'" Flat characters, in contrast, usually play a minor role in a story, act predictably, and are often presented as stereotypes. The minister in Freeman's story, for example, is presented as an unimaginative and inflexible individual. In fact, he is in many ways a foil to Mrs. Penn, because he has a totally opposite personality.

Plot

Plot is the arrangement of the events in a story according to a pattern devised by the writer and inferred by the reader. Often the plot develops when characters and situations oppose each other, creating conflicts that grow and eventually reach a climax, the point of highest intensity of the story. After this climatic turning point, the action of the story finally declines, moving toward a resolution of the conflict.

Although the time frame in a story may vary from recapturing an intense, momentary experience to narrating an event that covers a much longer period, the storyteller must focus on what Poe terms the "single effect" as the action of the story moves toward a resolution of the conflict.

"Another Evening at the Club" provides an example of a plot centered on a conflict between Samia and her husband. The action starts to rise in dramatic intensity (*the rising action*) when Samia's loss of her emerald ring destabilizes her relationship with her husband. After this initial exposition, or narrative introduction of characters and situation, the action reaches its crisis (the *climax* of the action) when Samia's husband refuses to exonerate the maid, even though he knows she is innocent. Notice that this external conflict also parallels the internal conflict of the protagonist when she recognizes the degree of the husband's control over her and her inability to oppose him. The action of the story moves toward the resolution of its conflict (*the falling action*) when Samia yields to her husband's authority.

While many writers continue to follow this traditional model of plot development, some contemporary authors deviate from it. Liam O'Flaherty, in "The Sniper" (p. 537), for example, and Stephen Crane, in "A Mystery of Heroism" (p. 530), prefer the surprise ending, while Rosemary Cho Leyson, in "The Visit Home" (p. 130), ends her story without a resolution of the protagonist's inner conflict.

Although the typical fictional plot has a beginning, a middle, and an end, authors may also vary their patterns of narration. In "The Sniper," the story's events unfold in the order in which they took place, following a *chronological* development. In "Another Evening at the Club," Rifaat uses *flashbacks*, selecting a few episodes to build a plot that moves backward and forward in time: the action begins in the present with Samia's anguish at her husband's decision to blame the maid for the theft of the ring; then, through the use of flashbacks, the author reports past events that illustrate the position that women like Samia occupy in a patriarchal culture. Rifaat also uses *suspense* or uncertainty, creating a sense of anticipation and curiosity about what the protagonist will do next. Will she defend the servant accused of stealing the ring? How will her husband react when he finds out that the ring was not stolen? Many stories also use *foreshadowing*, providing details and hints about what will happen next. In William Shakespeare's play (p. 170), the title "The Tragedy of Hamlet" functions as a foreshadowing, anticipating the outcome of the story.

Fictional devices such as flashback and foreshadowing do not operate in isolation but rather work together with characterization, setting, point of view, style, and tone to create a unified effect.

Setting

The time, place, and social context of a story constitute its *setting*. In Mtutuzeli Matshoba's "Call Me Not a Man" (p. 907), the theme emerges from the description of the station bridge at Mzimhlope on a Friday afternoon at five o'clock, when workers are commuting home with their weekly pay and the police are out to make some extra money. By situating the time, place, and social context of the action, Matshoba prepares the reader for the brutal conflict that erupts between the police reservists and the commuters at Mzimhlope station. Other stories reconstruct historical moments with great precision. The setting of "The Sky Is Gray" (p. 108) transports readers to the American South in the 1940s, and the mythical narrative of "A Power Struggle" (p. 100) describes primeval times. Still others tell of events that could have taken place anywhere and at any time.

As you read a short story, watch for details related to time, place, and social context that reveal the motivation of the protagonist and establish the story's credibility. Pay particular attention to the writer's use of visual imagery aimed at helping you to create mental pictures of the setting and assessing its effects on the characters' actions.

Theme

Theme may be defined as the central or dominant idea of the story reinforced by the interaction of fictional devices such as character, plot, setting, and point of view. The theme is the overall generalization we can make about the story's meaning and significance. Sometimes the theme can be stated in a short phrase. For instance, "the rights of the community versus those of an individual" is one theme that emerges in Achebe's short story "Dead Men's Path." The theme of "The Sky Is Gray" is complex, because the story is concerned not only with the relationship between the narrator and his mother but also with the complexity of race relationships in the American South in the 1940s.

To define the theme of a story, look for clues provided by the author, such as the title, imagery, symbolism, and dialogue between the characters. A story may evoke a range of meanings. And readers—because of their diverse interests, cultural backgrounds, and expectations—will react individually and produce varied meanings. Meanings should be supported by evidence from the story, however.

Narrator

The voice that narrates a story is not necessarily the writer's; while the author writes the story, the narrator tells it. The *narrator* is a technique that writers use to create a particular point of view from which they will tell the story, present the actions, and shape the readers' responses. Narrators can report external and internal events, but most important, they express the narrative angle that writers use to tell the story.

Narrators are *omniscient* when they know everything or almost everything that happens in the story, including what goes on inside the minds of the characters. They are presumed to be *reliable*. In "The Visit Home" (p. 130), the narrator penetrates two minds: Maree's, the daughter who left her home, and her father's, a minor character, briefly sketched, who is in inner turmoil over his daughter's decision. By exposing their interior thoughts, the omniscient narrator provides glimpses of a dramatic dialogue between two opposing points of view. Omniscient narrators tend to be objective, emotionally removed from the action, and to use the third-person *he, she, it,* and *they* to create a *third-person* point of view.

Narrators are *first person* when they report the events from the point of view of the *I*, or first person. A first-person narrator differs from an omniscient narrator because the *I* both participates in the action and communicates a single point of view. This type of narrator usually creates a greater degree of intimacy with the reader, as in "At Sea: A Sailor's Story" (p. 294) and "A Red Sweater" (p. 890). The writer's choice of a narrator is important because it determines the *point of view* (or the voice and angle from which the narrator tells the story) and thereby affects the story's tone and meaning.

Narrators are *unreliable* when they do not possess a full understanding of the events they narrate and when the reader can see more than they do. In "The Sky Is

Gray," the reader encounters implications of issues related to race and class that escape the young African-American narrator. The narrator's lack of awareness is evident in the dentist's office scene when a college student disagrees with an older preacher about the existence of God and racial injustices.

Style and Tone

Style refers to the way writers express themselves. Style depends on *diction* (the writer's choice of vocabulary), *syntax* (grammar and sentence structure), and well as *voice* and *rhythm*. Style reveals the writers' linguistic choices or preferences and therefore is as private and unique as their personalities and identities. Note the sharp contrast, for example, between Jean Toomer's poetic style, infused with similes and metaphors, in "Karintha" (p. 406) and Fae Myenne Ng's straight, concise style, created to evoke the rhythm of a colloquial conversation, in "A Red Sweater." To make their language unique and particular, writers also use devices such as the following:

Irony is the discrepancy between what is expected and what actually happens. The title of Franz Kafka's story "The Metamorphosis" (p. 848) is ironic because it reverses the reader's expectations of a positive change from an inferior to a superior transformation. Verbal irony is the descrepancy between what the words convey and what they actually mean, as in the title of Stephen Crane's "A Mystery of Heroism."

A *symbol* is something—a word or an object—that stands for an idea beyond a literal meaning. In "A Red Sweater," the red sweater may function as a symbol that evokes ideas about female identity and sexuality.

A *metaphor* is a figure of speech that compares two dissimilar elements without using *like* or *as:* "Karintha at twelve, was a wild flash" (p. 406). A *simile* is a comparison using *like* or *as:* "Her skin is like dusk on the eastern horizon" (p. 407).

Tone is the manner, mood, pervading attitude, or tone of voice that writers establish in relation to the characters, situations, and readers. You may think of tone as the various tones of voice that fiction writers establish through style. Authors use a variety of different tones, including intimate or distant, ironic or direct, hostile or sympathetic, formal or casual, humorous or serious, and emotional or objective.

In "First Confession" (p. 93), for example, Frank O'Connor uses humor to communicate his young protagonist's terror, reinforced by his sister's threats of punishment, as he faces his first religious confession. In "Jasmine" (p. 680), Bharati Mukherjee uses irony to portray her protagonist's experiences as an illegal alien in the United States.

That successful creators of short fiction must be involved with the intricacies of their craft is clear, but remember also that their primary purpose is to use language to communicate to you. As the novelist William Faulkner reminds us, in his 1950 Nobel prize acceptance speech, writers like to tell and retell stories about "love and honor and pity and pride and compassion and sacrifice"—in other words, stories about the lives and experiences of all human beings.

POETRY

What is poetry? The nineteenth-century poet William Wordsworth defines it as "an overflow of powerful feelings"; for the contemporary poet Adrienne Rich, "poems are like dreams; in them you put what you don't know you know." Many other contemporary poets extend the power of poetry to a cultural context. Javier Heraud, for example, speaks of "the songs of oppressed peoples, / the new songs of liberated peoples."

Poets, like other artists, regardless of their historical moment, write for a variety of different reasons, but they share an imaginative view of language and a belief in the power of words. Compare, for example, Emily Dickinson's thoughts on words expressed in her poem number 1212:

A word is dead
When it is said,
Some say.
I say it just
Begins to live
That day.

with those of Anne Sexton in her poem "Words," written a century later:

Words and eggs must be handled with care,
Once broken they are impossible
things to repair.

Both poets focus on the possibilities and power of words, emphasizing the ability of language to shape and express human experiences. Despite the contradictory claims and concerns with which different generations define poetry, there is some consensus that poetry combines emotional expression, meanings, and experiences through rhythm, images, structural form, and, above all, words.

Voice and Tone

The voice that communicates the feelings, emotions, and meanings of the poem is called the speaker. The speaker's voice is not the voice of the poet but a created voice, or *persona*. Shakespeare, in his love sonnets, often uses the persona of a lover to express his views on love. Robert Browning, in "My Last Duchess" (p. 429), assumes the persona of a Renaissance duke to communicate a portrait of his former wife. The speaker's voice, like that of a real person, may change and express different tones throughout the poem as his or her attitudes vary toward the subject, him- or herself, and the reader. In "Those Winter Sundays," by Robert Hayden (p. 930), the speaker's tone is at first meditative, but in the last lines ("What did I know / of love's austere and lonely offices?") his tone becomes more remorseful.

The Poetic Elements: Images, Simile, Metaphor, Symbol, Personification, Paradox

Notice that the language of poetry is especially rich in creating images that evoke the senses of sight, smell, taste, and touch. To achieve their purposes, writers use not only language that communicates images literally but also figurative language that compares objects, describes emotions, and appeals to the reader's imagination through figures of speech such as simile, metaphor, symbol, personification, and paradox. To become an effective reader of poetry, you should learn to recognize how these elements reinforce poetic meaning.

Images are words and phrases that communicate sensory experiences and convey moods and emotions. Notice how in "Fern Hill" (p. 159), for example, Dylan Thomas uses visual images such as "All the sun long," "All the moon long," and "the lamb white days" to capture a vision of childhood embedded in the idyllic bright, white colors of joy and innocence.

A *simile* is a direct comparison between two explicit terms, usually introduced by "like" or "as." In "For My Lover, Returning to His Wife" (p. 433), the ironic speaker of Anne Sexton's poem compares her lover's wife to a "cast-iron pot" and his children to "delicate balloons." Through these similes, the speaker comes to terms with the solid presence of the wife and the vulnerable existence of the children in her lover's life as opposed to the fragility of her own claim on him.

A *metaphor* is an implicit comparison that omits *like* or *as*. "For My Lover, Returning to His Wife" also ends with the metaphor "I am a watercolor. / I wash off." Much of the meaning of this poem depends on the contrast that the speaker, the lover of a married man, establishes between the wife's permanent position in her husband's life and her own transient presence.

A *symbol* is a sign that points to meanings beyond its literal significance. The cross, for instance, is an archetype universally accepted as a symbol of Christianity. In T. S. Eliot's "The Love Song of J. Alfred Prufrock" (p. 425), the "mermaids" (l. 124) point beyond the literal meaning the word suggests to function as a symbol of Prufrock's unfulfilled sexuality.

Personification is the attribution of human qualities to animals, ideas, or inanimate things. It is used in these lines from Henry Wadsworth Longfellow's "The Jewish Cemetery at Newport" (p. 157):

Pride and humiliation hand in hand
Walked with them through the world wherever they went.

A *paradox* is a statement that appears to be contradictory and absurd but displays an element of truth. In Yevgeny Yevtushenko's poem "People" (p. 920), the paradox "We who knew our fathers / in everything, in nothing" suggests our inability to know or understand fully another human being, even a parent.

Types of Poetry—Lyric, Dramatic, and Narrative

A *lyric poem* is usually a short composition depicting the speaker's deepest emotions and feelings. Lyric poems are especially effective in arousing personal participation of readers and in stirring their sensations, feelings, and emotions. Songs, elegies, odes, and sonnets fall into this category.

A *dramatic poem* uses dramatic monologue or dialogue and assumes the presence of another character besides the speaker of the poem. In Eliot's "The Love Song of J. Alfred Prufrock" and in Robert Browning's "My Last Duchess" (p. 429), for instance, the speakers seem to assume the presence of an audience.

A *narrative poem* usually emphasizes action or the plot. "The Young Warrior" (p. 432), by Gayle Two Eagles, may be considered a short narrative poem in which the speaker narrates through brief biographical data the elements that constitute her identity as a young Lakota warrior.

Many contemporary poets merge the lyric, dramatic, and narrative modes in the same poem, ignoring the traditional distinctions between them. See elements of all three in Eliot's "The Love Song of J. Alfred Prufrock."

The Forms of Poetry

Some poems in this anthology use structural forms long established by literary history and tradition. In fact, for many poets a vision of poetic completion revolves around an idea of poetic structure or the formal beauty of a poetic pattern. Thus, to read a poem effectively and establish a dialogue with its poetic voice, you should be able to recognize some of the elements related to poetic form.

Meter is the recurrent pattern of stressed and unstressed syllables in a poetic line. Together with elements such as rhyme and pause, meter determines the rhythm of the poem. One way to identify the metrical pattern of a poem is to mark the accented and unaccented syllables of the poetic line, as in the example below from a sonnet by Shakespeare:

My mistress' eyes are nothing like the sun

Next, divide the line into feet, the basic unit of measurement, according to patterns of accented and unaccented syllables. These are the five most common types of poetic feet:

iambic   (˘ ´)   forget
trochee   (´ ˘)   morning
anapest   (˘ ˘ ´)   at a house
dactyl   (´ ˘ ˘)   separate
spondee   (´ ´)   come, now

Shakespeare's line thus marked becomes five feet of iambs:

˘ ´ / ˘ ´ / ˘ ´ / ˘ ´ / ˘ ´ /
My mis/tress' eyes/are no/thing like/the sun/
  1   2   3   4   5

Notice that the length of the poetic lines depends on the number of poetic feet they possess, and they are defined by the following terms:

one foot = monometer
two feet = dimeter
three feet = trimeter
four feet = tetrameter
five feet = pentameter
six feet = hexameter

Shakespeare's line "My mistress' eyes are nothing like the sun," is a good example of iambic pentameter, one of the most common patterns in English poetry.

Two other terms you should recognize in relation to meter are *caesura*, a pause or pauses within the poetic line, and *enjambment*, a poetic line that carries its meaning and sound to the next line. The lines below, from the poem "The Faithful Wife," by Barbara L. Greenberg (p. 414), provide us with a good example of a caesura followed by an enjambment:

But if I *were* to have a lover, it would be someone
who could take nothing from you.

Notice that the caesura occurs after the first phrase "But if I *were* to have a lover," and the enjambment occurs when the following sentence spills over into the next line. If the poet had broken the first line after the comma, the second line as it now stands would have lost its emphasis.

A *stanza* is a group of two or more poetic lines forming the same metrical pattern or a closely similar pattern that is repeated throughout the poem. Most stanzas combine a fixed pattern of poetic lines with a fixed *rhyme scheme*. Thomas Hardy's poem "The Man He Killed" (p. 558) follows the traditional pattern of the **ballad stanza:** a quatrain (four-line stanza) with alternating tetrameter (four-feet line) and trimeter (three-feet line):

Had he and I but met
By some old ancient inn,
We should have sat us down to wet
Right many a nipperkin!

Notice, however, that Hardy varies the typical rhyme scheme of the ballad stanza, in which only the second and fourth lines rhyme (which is called an *abcb* scheme), by also rhyming his first and third lines, for an *abab* scheme.

Conventionally, the English *sonnet* is a poem of fourteen iambic pentameter lines. Immortalized by the fourteenth-century Italian poet Petrarch, the sonnet spread throughout Europe, becoming a major cultural form with which sonneteers represented and explored the terms of their inward self and public life. Shakespeare and many other English poets used the *abab cdcd efef gg* rhyme scheme, which marks the division of a sonnet into three quatrains (four lines) and a couplet (two rhyming lines). John Keats also uses this Shakespearean sonnet pattern in "Bright Star" (p. 435).

Blank verse is unrhymed iambic pentameter. Because it is very close to human speech, blank verse became an ideal dramatic medium and was used by Shakespeare in many of his plays.

Free verse is poetry that does not follow a fixed pattern of rhythm, rhyme, and stanzaic arrangements. Like Walt Whitman, many poets have abandoned any kind of poetic structure for free verse, relying instead on a pattern based largely on repetition and parallel grammatical structure. The primary focus of free verse is not the external poetic form but the presence of an internal voice of address. One example is Whitman's "Song of Myself":

> I celebrate myself, and sing myself,
> And what I assume you shall assume,
> For every atom belonging to me as good belongs to you.

Most contemporary poets either use free verse or combine traditional and new patterns.

Poetry as Performance: The Sounds of Poetry

Reading a poem aloud is more than encountering actions and situations that the poet's creative imagination reshaped as meanings, rhythms, and emotions; it is an act of oral delivery conveying to the poetic discourse a special kind of situation and point of view comparable to the performance of a play. In fact, in most ancient cultures, and in some contemporary ones, poetry had strong ties to the oral tradition, and it was often meant to be sung and accompanied by musical instruments like the lyre. Although the oral delivery of poetry has been widely replaced by silent reading, reading a poem aloud will allow you to recover the emotional and phonic potential through which poetry expresses its relation to music and to life's dramatic possibilities. You will encounter the poetic voice—the voice that speaks the poem—in the act of expressing the poem's full potentiality.

To form layers of poetic meaning, poets throughout the centuries have explored several phonic devices, such as alliteration, repetition, onomatopoeia, assonance, as well as effects of orchestration, the clash of consonants. Here are some of the most common poetic devices.

Alliteration is the repetition of the initial sounds of the words in a poetic line. In "Moving Away [1]," Gary Soto combines alliteration (repetition of the plosive sound {k}) and *assonance* (repetition of vowel sounds) along three poetic lines:

From a <u>c</u>oldness I
<u>C</u>ould not understand
And <u>c</u>upped the <u>c</u>rucifix beneath the <u>c</u>overs.

Repetition refers to the repetition of a single word or phrase; the repetition of a refrain or a specific line or lines in a poem; or the repetition of a slightly changed version of a poetic line.

Onomatopoeia is the use of words that evoke or imitate the sounds they describe, such as *slam, murmur,* and *splash.*

DRAMA

Unlike fiction and most poetry, plays are intended to be performed before an audience, making drama primarily a communal art form in which the playwright collaborates with actors, director, set, lighting, and costume designers to produce an aural, visual, and social experience. If you are unable to see a performance of the plays included in this book, try to view a video production of *Antigone, Medea, Hamlet,* or *A Doll's House.*

What is the function of drama? Although its purpose and functions have evolved from ancient Greece to the present, according to contemporary playwright Arthur Miller, "all plays we call great, let alone those we call serious, are ultimately involved with some aspects of a single problem. It is this. How may man make of the outside world a home?" Unlike Greek playwrights or Shakespeare, many modern dramatists, like Miller, are most concerned with presenting social issues onstage. In the last decade, for example, several dramas have focused on the suffering and death caused by two contemporary forms of plague, cancer and AIDS, demonstrating the playwright's commitment to exploring the relation between the individual and society and to urging the audience to consider its personal and social commitment.

The Basic Elements of Drama

Characterization. *Dramatis personae* are the characters in a play. Usually the names of the persons who appear in a play, the dramatic characters, are listed at the beginning, often with a brief description. Read this list carefully to understand who the characters are.

As you read the play, pay attention not only to the dialogue of the characters but also to what the *stage directions* say about their entrances and exits, clothing, tone of voice, facial expressions, gestures, and movements.

As in fiction, the *protagonist,* or main character, of a play opposes the *antagonist,* or the character or other elements that defy his or her stability. In some plays there is a fairly simple contrast, as between Medea and Jason and between Medea and

Athenian law, whereas in others, as in *Antigone,* there is a more complex or involved contrast—not just between Antigone and Creon but also between Antigone and Ismene and Creon and Haimon and between religious and civil law. Often, if you recognize different sides of the conflict between a protagonist and an antagonist, you will be able to identify the core of the dramatic action of the play.

It is also important to notice that characters and dramatic action are intrinsically connected with each other. In Susan Glaspell's *Trifles,* for instance, dramatic action emerges from the inner motivation and goals, which account for the inability of the characters—the female protagonists and male antagonists—to abide by the same set of gender-related assumptions.

Plot. *Plot* may be defined as the arrangement of the dramatic action of a play. A typical plot structure follows a pattern of rising and falling action along five major steps: the exposition (or presentation of the dramatic situation), the rising action, the climax, the falling action, and the conclusion. The arrangement of the dramatic action in *Hamlet* may be illustrated by the so-called pyramid pattern, which is not always as symmetrical as the diagram below suggests.

Exposition	Rising action	Climax	Falling action	Conclusion
Death of old Hamlet	Appearance of ghost	From the play within the play to the killing of Polonius	Ophelia's death	Hamlet's death
Accession of Claudius	Hamlet's promise of revenge		Hamlet's return	
Marriage of Claudius				

To understand how the plot develops, consider the dramatic crisis that follows the major conflict, as well as *subplots,* or secondary lines of action connected with the main plot. In *A Doll's House,* for instance, the crisis involving Christine Linde and Nils Krogstad reflects and comments on the major conflict centered on Nora and Torvald Helmer.

One can look at the plot arrangement of Greek plays such as *Antigone* and *Medea* from the point of view of the conventions of *time, place,* and *action.* According to these conventions, traditionally attributed to Aristotle and the later dramatic theorists of the Renaissance (although Shakespeare did not observe them), the action of a play should not exceed a period of twenty-four hours (unity of time). Its locale should always remain the same (unity of place), and its actions and incidents should all contribute to the resolution of the plot (unity of action). An analysis of *Antigone* and *Medea* from the viewpoint of these conventions will reveal the dramatic freedom taken in the film versions of these classical plays.

Theme. *Theme* is the central idea or ideas dramatized in a play. Although you can look for a play's theme in the title, conflict, characters, or scenery, the ideas and the meanings you identify will depend on your own set of beliefs, assumptions, and experiences. The play *On Tidy Endings,* for instance, explores what happens when a character's ex-wife and son as well as his male lover must cope with the tragedy of AIDS. However, if you are especially concerned with the question of the validity of homosexual love, you might react most strongly to that specific theme.

Types of Plays: Tragedy and Comedy

According to Aristotle, whose *Poetics* provides an analysis of the nature of classical drama, *tragedy* is the highest form of literary art. It deals with protagonists who are better than we are because of their engagement in honorable or dignified actions and their capacity to maintain their human dignity when withstanding adversity and suffering. Tragic protagonists are often also somehow connected with the religious and political destiny of their country. *Antigone,* for example, asks deeply religious questions about an individual's responsibility to the laws of God and the laws of the state. Greek and Shakespearean tragedies such as *Antigone, Medea,* and *Hamlet* are centered on the struggle that the protagonists, the *tragic heroes* and **heroines,** conduct against antagonistic forces.

The major event in a tragedy is the downfall that the protagonist suffers as a result of external causes (fate, coincidence), internal causes (ambition, excessive pride or hubris), or some error or frailty for which he or she is at least partially responsible. According to Aristotle, the spectators are purged of the emotions of "pity and fear" as they watch the hero or the heroine fall from greatness and as they witness the self-knowledge that the tragic protagonist gains in the process. The term *catharsis* refers to the emotional process that spectators undergo when they view a tragedy.

For modern playwrights, the protagonists of tragedies are no longer extraordinary beings but ordinary human beings caught in the struggle to shape their identities amid the crude realities of external and internal circumstances. In *Dutchman,* for instance, Amiri Baraka explores the causes and effects of racial and sexual violence on Lula and Clay. In the modern tragedy, the audience is urged to confront the corresponding social issues. Sometimes, in contemporary plays, the audience is also asked to participate in the actual performance of the play, or to construct meanings that determine the conclusion of the play.

In its ancient origins, *comedy* was a type of drama, designed to celebrate the renewal of life. Classical comedies usually dealt with the lives of ordinary people caught in personal and social conflicts, which they attempted to overcome through wit and humor. Unlike classical tragedies, which focus on heroes and heroines who are greater than ordinary human beings, classical comedies explore the lives of ordinary people facing the realities of love, sex, and class. Tragedies usually lead to a sense of wasted human potential in the death of the protagonist, whereas comedies tend to promote a happy ending through the reestablishment of social norms. Most contemporary plays, however, combine the hilarious ingredients of comedy with the dramatic overtones of tragedy, as seen in *Picnic on the Battlefield*, Fernando Arrabal's humorous portrayal of the irrationality of war.

Kinds of Theater

Greek theater developed in Athens in connection with religious celebrations in honor of Dionysus, the god of wine and revelry. Athenian drama festivals also gained social and political meaning, becoming an intrinsic part of Athenian cultural life.

Plays such as *Medea* and *Antigone* were performed in large, semicircular amphitheaters like the Theater of Dionysus at Athens, which could hold about seventeen thousand spectators. To cope with the physical conditions of such huge amphitheaters, actors had to look larger than life by wearing masks, padded costumes, elevated shoes, and mouthpieces that amplified their voices. Women's roles were performed by male actors because in Greek culture, as in many other early cultures, performances by women were taboo.

Greek plays such as *Antigone* usually alternate dramatic episodes with choral odes, following a five-part dramatic structure:

Prologue	Parados	Episodia/Stasimon	Exodus
Background information	Chorus, Evaluation of situation	Debates followed by choral odes	Last scene

The *chorus* consisted of a group of about twelve actors (often led by a leader, or *choragos*) who sang and danced in the *orchestra,* an area at the foot of the amphitheater. The chorus served several other functions as well: it represented the voice of the community, commented on the events of the play, provided background information about the story, and sometimes participated in the dramatic action. As part of its choreography, the chorus moved from right to left across the orchestra, the "dancing place" of the stage, as they sang the *strophe,* or the choral lyric, of the ode, and from left to right as they sang the *antistrophe.*

When reading a Greek play, keep in mind the following theatrical conventions:

Comic relief is provided by comic speeches or scenes that occur in a serious play. Consider, for example, the relief from dramatic action that the character of the sentry provides in *Antigone.*

Dramatic irony is a double meaning that occurs when the audience possesses foreknowledge of the situation and is therefore better informed than the characters. An effective example of dramatic irony occurs when Creon says after Haimon's death that nothing else could hurt him. However, he speaks this moments before he finds out about his wife's death, of which the audience is already aware.

Elizabethan theater, including Shakespearean theater, refers to plays written during the reign of Queen Elizabeth I of England, (1558–1603). Compared to the huge Greek amphitheaters, the Elizabethan playhouse was small, seating a maximum of three thousand spectators. Its stage, as the illustration on page 998 shows, protruded into the orchestra so that the audience and actors could enjoy a more intimate theatrical atmosphere. Since Elizabethan theater used little setting, it was the power of Shakespeare's poetic language that stimulated the spectators to exercise their imagination and visualize places like the platform of the watch at the royal castle at Elsinore in *Hamlet.*

Although the text of *Hamlet* shows a series of structural divisions into acts and scenes, in Shakespeare's day *Hamlet* and the other Shakespearean plays were performed without any intermission. In Elizabethan theater, as in Greek theater, female roles were performed by male actors. The first actresses appeared on the English stage only after the Restoration of Charles II in 1660.

Shakespearean plays employ the theatrical conventions of soliloquy and aside:

A *soliloquy* is a speech delivered by a character who is alone on the stage. Through these speeches, such as Hamlet's famous soliloquy "O, what a rogue and peasant slave am I!" (2.2.475), actors reveal their thoughts, feelings, inner struggles, and psychological complexity, securing their ties with the audience. The critic Ralph Berry believes that soliloquies permit the actors to establish a special kind of relationship with the audience. It is in his sequence of soliloquies, Berry argues, that Hamlet manages to seduce the audience.

An *aside* is a short speech that a character delivers in an undertone directly to the audience and that is not heard by the other actors onstage. For instance,

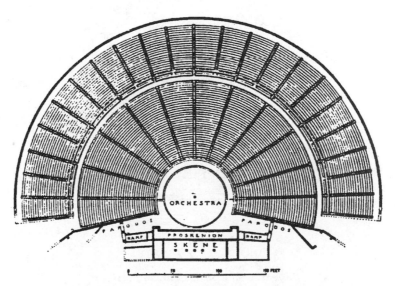

Illustration of a Greek Amphitheater at Epidaurus

Hamlet's aside "A little more than kin, and less than kind!" (1.2.65) invites the audience to share the state of mind he has adopted against Claudius.

Realistic Theater dates from nineteenth-century Europe. One of its purposes was to set the daily reality of middle-class life against antagonistic social conventions. The physical conditions of the picture-frame stage, with its proscenium arch, favored the exhibiting of realistic, lifelike pictures of everyday life. *A Doll's House,* by Henrik Ibsen, is a good example of a play that relies on the conditions of a specific realistic setting: the Helmers' drawing room conveys to the audience the degree to which Nora's life is influenced and dominated by her husband's presence.

Theater of the absurd, which has developed in the second half of the twentieth century, portrays human beings as antiheroes caught in a world that is basically irrational, unpredictable, and illogical. Playwright Eugene Ionesco (b. 1912) defined theater of the absurd as "that which has no purpose or goal or objective." Two major techniques of absurdist drama include the lack of logically connected events and the presence of characters whose fragmented language, personalities, and nihilistic attitudes undermine their ability to control their own destiny. *Picnic on the Battlefield,* Fernando Arrabal's absurdist play, provides a good example of a drama whose challenges to a rational view of life verge on the absurd. Instead of constructing a classical plot or creating characters with developed personalities, Arrabal presents one dramatic episode in which the characters Zapo and Zepo are so similar that they are practically interchangeable. Although absurdist theater can be per-

Illustration of a Shakespearean Playhouse

formed on any kind of stage, twentieth-century dramatists prefer a stage with only a few props that are suggestive of a realistic setting or symbolic of the play's meaning.

FICTION, POETRY, AND DRAMA AS CULTURAL PRODUCTIONS

As part of your reading experience, *Literature Across Cultures* asks you not only to analyze the formal aspects of literature but also to integrate your study of the literary genres with a cultural focus that attempts to discover connections among literature, film, culture, and society. Such interactions will enable you not only to consider the interpretation of the literary text but to understand also its historical and cultural significance.

In addition to the Cultural Contexts questions after each reading selection in this anthology, the following list of topics will help you to initiate a culturally oriented discussion of literature and film.

1. To examine the relation between the text and its social reality, consider the relation between writers and the cultural and historical issues of their times. Your focus here should be the literary text and its cultural (philosophical, religious, sociohistorical, and political) perspectives.

2. Focus on the physical and social aspects of the setting, attempting to define the tensions and relations between the setting and the speaker.

3. Notice how many plots, especially in fiction, tend to challenge or reinforce the conventional focus concerning the quest for individual identity and the sometimes competing values of the community.

4. When you study characterization, explore private and public attitudes toward race, class, gender, law, economics, and justice.

5. Think about the extent to which social and psychological forces such as heredity, environment, or fate control the action of individuals. Are individuals presented as victims of society? What kinds of responses do they develop to counteract the influence of society?

YOU MAY ALSO CONSIDER THE FOLLOWING TOPICS:

6. The interplay of gender and power.

7. Gender differences.

8. Male gender construction.

9. The male patriarchal psyche and its definition of masculinity.

10. Sex role stereotypes supporting traditional notions of masculine aggression and feminine passivity.

11. The conflict between the individual and the social self.

12. Individuality and community as the core of American character.

13. Individual aspirations and community responsibility.

14. The psychological drama of the individual self.

15. The presence of the self in social, sexual, and cultural contexts.

16. The relation between war and violence.

17. Issues of cultural identity, gender, politics, and class. Their effects on individual and social identity.

18. Individuality and identity as products of a fixed historical era.

19. The forces of tradition and change and their effects on individual and communal lives.

20. The politics of domestic life; the organization of the family; the separation of private and public responsibility.

21. Changing concepts of the role of the family.

22. The politics of domestic life as affected by gender and class.

23. The significance of single-parent households.

24. The nature of mother-daughter, father-daughter, father-son, mother-son relations.

25. The role of the family in validating or manipulating one's sense of self.

26. The ethnic structure of the family and its effects on gender identity and communal relationships.

27. The literary text as a protest against racism or sexism.

28. The relation between war and sexual violence.

29. Immigration and its influence on contemporary culture.

30. The dominant ideology of the text: who has power, who benefits from portrayal of power.

31. The dynamics of male-female relations both within and outside of conventional social roles.

32. Women as creators and shapers of culture and history.

33. Evolving images and representations of women and men.

34. The causes and effects of sexism and domestic violence.

35. The sexual division of labor and its effects on gender relations.

36. Class distinction and class mobility within society; the causes of exclusion from the mainstream.

37. The interplay of class, race, and economics.

38. The causes and effects of segregation and integration.

39. Racial stereotypes, racial differences, and racial dominance; their effects on individuals and group identity.

40. Causes and effects of racial, sexual, and economic oppression.

41. Stereotypes of sexuality and race; the function of color in literary and social contexts.

42. The relation among racism, sexism, and violence; attitudes toward sexual preferences and sexual differences.

43. Concepts of the melting pot versus ethnic identity.

44. The notion of tragedy, moving away from Aristotelian stress on character and tragic flaw toward a concern for the sociopolitical roles of men and women.

45. Causes and effects of sociopolitical order and disorder.

46. AIDS; the discrimination imposed on AIDS victims; the effects of AIDS on the family and on gender relationships.

47. The attempt to understand our individualism and participate in it.

48. How writers situate their work in relation to the collective past.

49. The role that movies have assumed as powerful cultural agents in rewriting the past.

50. Films as articulators of gender roles; films, in which male-female relationships are central to the story, as a reflection of traditional and/or social perspectives on gender roles.

51. Gender, race, sex, violence, and identity as prominent cultural issues in films.

52. How a film that you believe addresses an important issue in contemporary society either endorses the standard criteria of values or questions how standards of behavior are created and applied.

53. Portrayals of World War II and the Vietnam war in film.

54. Literature and film as articulators of male and female experiences of war.

55. Consider a popular film genre (e.g., western, melodrama, war, science fiction) as a reflection of certain accepted norms of behavior and traditional values of American society.

Researching Literary Sources

WHAT IS A RESEARCH PAPER?

A research paper is a writing assignment in which the writer poses a specific question or problem and then investigates, analyzes, and evaluates that issue, documenting the sources used.

If your instructor does not assign a specific topic for your literary research paper, browse through a few articles or books in which your author and his or her works are discussed.

SOME AREAS TO EXPLORE IN FICTION: characters, plot, setting, the role of the narrator, style, tone, and symbolism

SOME AREAS TO EXPLORE IN POETRY: voice, tone, sound, symbolism, poetic elements such as images, similes, metaphors, symbols, paradoxes, diction, and irony

SOME AREAS TO EXPLORE IN DRAMA: plot, structure, characterization, theme, theatrical conventions such as comic relief, dramatic irony, soliloquy, the dramatic genres (tragedy, comedy), and different kinds of theater staging

SOME CULTURAL AREAS TO EXPLORE: topics related to issues, such as race, class, gender, construction of the self, power relations, the politics of inclusion and exclusion, attitudes toward authority

Notice that comparison-and-contrast topics, involving characters in the same work or in different works, as well as topics related to plot, setting, dramatic structure, voice, tone, and cultural issues, are usually very effective. See pages 999–1001 for a list of cultural issues.

WHAT ARE PRIMARY AND SECONDARY SOURCES?

The poem, short story, or play you are discussing is considered a primary source; the books, articles, and any other material you consult at the library during the investigation of your thesis are known as secondary sources. If you are writing a research paper on *Hamlet,* the text of Shakespeare's play is considered your primary source; the current scholarship on *Hamlet* that you will consult at the library will be your secondary sources.

Secondary Sources: Using the Library

Your goal in using the library for literary research may be

1. simply to get a better idea of what a poem, short story, or play is about.

2. to research an author's life.

3. to write an in-depth paper on what you have read.

In any of these cases you can obtain help from books and articles in the library.

Where to Start. The library's card catalog, which lists all the books the library owns, is the place to begin. Many libraries now have their catalog in computer form rather than on cards. In either case, the library's catalog should be your first stop.

How to Locate a Book. Locate a book by looking under one of three categories in the catalog: subject, author, or title.

1. **Subject.** If you do not know the name of a specific book, look up a subject:

   American Literature, 20th Century
   Puerto Rican Authors
   Women in Literature

   Help with the exact wording of subject headings can be found in the *Library of Congress Subject Headings* list, a set of books usually kept near the catalog or the reference desk. The author may also be the subject of a book and can be found by consulting the subject file. Along with biographical information, there will be critical and analytical works concerning the author and his or her writings.

2. **Author.** Under the author's name you will find all the books he or she has written. Look up the author's last name first—for example, Hayden, Robert. If a last name begins with *Mc,* it is interfiled with authors whose names begin with *Mac.*

3. **Title.** If you know the title of a book, look for the first word of the title—for *Tell Me a Riddle,* look for *Tell.* Disregard initial articles such as *A, An,* or *The*—for *A Doll's House,* look for *Doll's.*

You will rarely find a poem or short story listed in the catalog under its name. Refer to the list of author's books and look for the individual poem or short story in the index or contents pages.

To find information on the author, consult general and specialized encyclopedias. An example of the latter is *Contemporary Authors,* a multivolume set that presents biographical information about thousands of twentieth-century writers representing a variety of nationalities. Each entry includes personal and career details about the author, a short critical comment, bibliographies of his or her works, and sources of additional information.

For authors prior to the twentieth century, consult works such as:

American Authors, 1600–1900
British Authors Before 1800
British Authors of the 19th Century
European Authors, 1000–1900
The Reader's Encyclopedia

Other specialized biographical information can be found in

Mexican-American Biographies: A Historical Dictionary, 1836–1987
Asian-American Literature: An Annotated Bibliography
Black American Writers Past and Present
American Women Writers: Bibliographical Essays

Five important sources of criticism of poems, short stories, and plays are the following multivolume sets:

Humanities Index
MLA International Bibliography of Books and Articles
Essay and General Literature Index
Contemporary Literary Criticism
Twentieth-Century Literary Criticism

Humanities Index is a cumulative index to articles in English language periodicals on literature as well as history, linguistics, language, and philology. Because of its wide range of subject matter, it is less comprehensive than others in this category. The entries are listed by author and subject and arranged in one alphabet.

MLA (Modern Language Association) *International Bibliography of Books and Articles* is the most comprehensive index (published since 1921) to scholarly discussions of literary works. Volumes are arranged by country and then by century and author. Genres, themes, and other topics are also included.

Essay and General Literature Index provides a means of finding essays in anthologies. Its coverage extends back to 1900 and continues to the present.

Contemporary Literary Criticism contains excerpts from criticism of works by living authors of poems, short stories, novels and plays. Critical evaluations are taken from scholarly journals, general magazines, book review periodicals and books spanning periods from a writer's first works to the present. Because an author may be represented in more than one volume, use the master index.

Twentieth-Century Literary Criticism presents significant passages from criticism of the works of poets, short-story writers, novelists, and playwrights who died between 1900 and 1960.

Two excellent sources of detailed descriptions of reference books that can aid in literary investigations are *A Reference Guide for English Studies* and *Literary Research Guide*.

HOW TO FIND YOUR SOURCES

A discussion of the poem "My Last Duchess," by Robert Browning, may be included in a collection of essays on poetry in general or in a book about all of Browning's works. How do you find it?

One way is to use *Essay and General Literature Index*, which is designed to help you find a specific subject in chapters or parts of books (see previous discussion). Under Browning, Robert, you will find studies of his works under the subdivision "About Individual Works."

Reference books that may help you find sources of poetry criticism are

> *Poetry Explication: A Checklist of Interpretations Since 1925 of British and American Poems Past and Present*
> *Crowell's Handbook of Contemporary American Poetry*
> *American and British Poetry: A Guide to the Criticism 1925–1978*
> *Explicator Cyclopedia*
> *Magill's Critical Survey of Poetry*

Sherwood Anderson's short story "Hands" can be looked up in *Essay and General Literature Index* in the same manner as Browning's poem. *Twentieth-Century Short Story Explication* is another source of criticism on short stories.

For further help, see also

> *American Short Fiction Criticism and Scholarship*
> *Explicator Cyclopedia, Prose*
> *Magill's Critical Survey of Short Fiction*

Sophocles' play *Antigone* can be researched in a manner similar to a poem or short story. Additional drama sources include

> *Drama Criticism Index*
> *Drama Criticism*
> *Modern Drama*
> *European Drama Criticism*
> *American Drama Criticism: Interpretations 1890–1977*
> *The Major Shakespearean Tragedies*

Keep in mind these general guidelines as you research literary sources:

1. Be aware of whether a reference book contains the critique itself or offers only a list of places to find criticism.

2. Don't judge a book by its title. Investigate what information can be found in the book by reading the preface or introduction. "Recent" or "Modern" in the title may be misleading.

3. Find out what time period, countries, and genres are included in each reference book.

4. Use more than one book as a source of information.

5. Copy complete information (title, author, publisher and year of publication) as you use the book.

Ask the librarian for help if you can't find information on your own!

HOW TO DOCUMENT A RESEARCH PAPER

Giving Credit to All Your Sources

Any information from books and articles used in your paper must be documented. Common knowledge, however, such as the fact that Shakespeare wrote comedies and tragedies, need not be credited. To document your sources efficiently, learn to take notes on all the information you may need later.

Taking Notes

To record information about your sources, use 4" × 6" note cards and write the following bibliographical details:

- ◆ name of author, editor, or translator (if any)
- ◆ title of the work and subtitle
- ◆ editions (if not the first)
- ◆ place of publication
- ◆ publishing company
- ◆ date

If working with periodicals, you must also write down volume and page numbers. You will need this information when you write the list of Works Cited, which will appear at the end of your paper.

Write each quotation that interests you on a separate card. Read it a few times, and then try to write it in your own words as if you were explaining it to someone.

If you do copy word for word from the source and use the passage in your paper, put quotation marks around it.

Quoting

Use an introductory phrase before citing sources in the body of your essay:

> As Sigmund Freud has noted, " . . . "
> In the words of Toni Morrison, " . . . "
> In the late 1940s, Simone de Beauvoir offered the argument that " . . . "
> " . . . , " suggests Stephen J. Greenblatt.

Verbs such as the following may help you to communicate a fact, advance an idea, refute an argument, make suggestions, and draw conclusions:

agree	confirm	insist	report
argue	deny	note	suggest
claim	emphasize	refute	think
communicate	endorse	reject	write

Short Quotations. Quotations from other sources need not always be complete sentences. You can integrate phrases or parts of a sentence into your own text:

```
Among many other things, Barbara Christian suggests the im-
portance of "practical slave culture without which black
people as an abused race would not have been able to sur-
vive" (72).
```

In the example above, (72) refers to the page number. A reader of your paper can refer to your list of Works Cited to find out that this quotation came from

```
Christian, Barbara.  Black Women Novelists: The Development
     of a Tradition, 1892-1976.  Westport, Conn.: Green-
     wood, 1980.
```

Use ellipsis marks (three spaced periods) to indicate that something has been omitted from the text:

```
Among many other things, Barbara Christian suggests the im-
portance of "practical slave culture without which black
people . . . would not have been able to survive" (72).
```

The format for parenthetical citation used above follows the guidelines that the Modern Language Association of America (MLA) established for research papers on literary subjects. See also the *MLA Handbook for Writers of Research Papers* (third edition) published by the Modern Language Association.

Long Quotations. A long quotation of more than three lines should be indented ten spaces. Since the indented format indicates that the words are taken from a secondary source, a long quotation does not need quotation marks.

Randall Jarrell demonstrates his enthusiasm for Robert Frost's poetry when he asserts in *Poetry and the Age*:

> Frost's virtues are extraordinary. No other living poet has written so well about the actions of ordinary men; his wonderful dramatic monologues or dramatic scenes come out of a knowledge of people that few poets have had, and they are written in a verse that uses, sometimes with absolute mastery, the rhythms of actual speech. (28)

In MLA style, used here, the parenthetical citation comes two spaces after the period that ends the long quotation.

Quoting from a Poem. When quoting from poetry, use slash marks to designate the end of a line, and duplicate the capitalization and punctuation of the poem:

Yevgeny Yevtushenko creates images that stimulate our imagination when he writes, "Here I plod through ancient Egypt / Here I perish crucified, on the cross."

If quoting more than a few lines of poetry, indent but do not use quotation marks.

In the example below, Martin Espada uses alliteration to paint a vivid picture of his protagonist:

> Blue bandanna
> across the forehead,
> beard bristling
> like a straw broom
> sleeveless T-shirt
> of the Puerto Rican flag

Quoting from a Play. When quoting from a play, always give act, scene, and lines in Arabic (not Roman) numerals:

Hamlet observes Claudius and says, "Now might I do it pat, now he is praying, / And now I'll do it" (3.3.73-74).

OR

Hamlet hesitates as he observes Claudius:

> Now might I do it pat, now he is praying,
> And now I'll do it. And so he goes to Heaven,
> And so I am revenged. That would be scanned:

```
A villain kill my father, and for that
I, his sole son, do this same villain send
To Heaven.  (3.3.73-78)
```

When quoting from plays that are not divided into acts, such as *Antigone,* give the scenes and line numbers:

```
You have heard my final judgment on that girl:
Have you come here hating me, or have you come
With deference and with love, whatever I do?
(3.5-8)
```

Also indicate the speakers if you are quoting dialogue or a passage in which more than two characters speak:

```
Hamlet. Ha, ha! Are you honest?
Ophelia. My lord?
Hamlet. Are you fair?
Ophelia. What means your lordship?
Hamlet. That if you be honest and fair, your honesty should
        admit not discourse to your beauty?  (3.1.103-107)
```

Paraphrasing

When you do not quote exactly from a source, you can paraphrase or report the information in your own words, using roughly the same number of words you found in the source.

The following quote by R. W. B. Lewis

```
A certain Melvillian grandeur went into the con-
figuration of her tragically conceived hero.
Despite her early disclaimers, the spirit of
Nathaniel Hawthorne pervades the New England land-
scape of the novella. . . . The role of the in-
quisitive city-born narrator is deployed with a
good deal of cunning and artistry of Henry
James.  (307)
```

could be paraphrased in your paper in the following form:

```
    R. W. B. Lewis notes the influence of Herman Melville,
Nathaniel Hawthorne, and Henry James on Edith Wharton's
novel Ethan Frome.  The nobility of the hero derives from
the epic characters of Melville's style with the added ur-
ban outlook of the Jamesian protagonist.  The atmosphere is
similar to that found in Hawthorne's depiction of New Eng-
land.  (309)
```

The source would be listed at the end of the paper as

> Lewis, R. W. B. <u>Edith Wharton: A Biography</u>. New York:
> Harper, 1975.

Works Cited

The list of Works Cited, containing the names of the authors and works you referred to or cited in your paper, should be arranged alphabetically and typed on a separate page at the end of your essay.

Sample Entries

BOOK BY ONE AUTHOR

> Meier, Matt S. <u>Mexican American Bibliography: A Historical
> Dictionary, 1836–1987</u>. Westport, Conn.: Greenwood,
> 1988.

BOOK BY TWO OR THREE AUTHORS

> Gilbert, Sandra M., and Susan Gubar. <u>The Madwoman in the
> Attic: The Woman Writer and the Nineteenth-Century Lit-
> erary Imagination</u>. New Haven: Yale UP, 1979.

BOOK BY FOUR OR MORE AUTHORS

> Gatto, Joseph, et al. <u>Exploring Visual Design</u>. 2nd ed.
> Worcester: Davis, 1987.

BOOK WITH AN EDITOR

> Stetson, Erlene, ed. <u>Black Sister: Poetry by Black Ameri-
> can Women, 1746–1980</u>. Bloomington: Indiana UP, 1981.

TWO OR MORE BOOKS BY THE SAME AUTHOR

> Frye, Northrup. <u>Anatomy of Criticism: Four Essays</u>. Prince-
> ton: Princeton UP, 1957.

> ---. <u>The Myth of Deliverance: Reflections on Shakespeare's
> Problem Comedies</u>. Toronto: U of Toronto P, 1983.

WORK IN AN ANTHOLOGY OR COLLECTION

> Berghahn, Marion. "Images of Africa in the Writings of
> James Baldwin." <u>James Baldwin</u>. Ed. Harold Bloom.
> New York: Chelsea, 1986.

MULTIVOLUME WORK

> Wimsatt, William K., and Cleanth Brooks. <u>Literary Criti-
> cism: A Short History</u>. 2 vols. Chicago: Chicago UP,
> 1979.

**ARTICLE IN A JOURNAL THAT PAGES
EACH ISSUE SEPARATELY**

> Giles, Ronald K. "Archetype and Irony in <u>The Natural</u>."
> <u>English Journal</u> 75.4 (1986): 49-54.

**ARTICLE IN A JOURNAL THAT USES CONTINUOUS
PAGE NUMBERS FROM JANUARY TO DECEMBER**

> Conboy, Sheila C. "Exhibition and Inhibition: The Body
> Scene in <u>Dubliners</u>." <u>Twentieth-Century Literature</u> 37
> (1991): 405-414.

ARTICLE IN A NEWSPAPER

> McDowell, Edwin. "Black Writers Gain Audiences and Visibil-
> ity in Publishing." <u>New York Times</u> 12 Feb. 1991: C11.

See the *MLA Handbook for Writers of Research Papers* for more information.

TWO SAMPLE RESEARCH PAPERS: MLA STYLE

DeAngeli 1

Patricia DeAngeli

Professor Shaw

English 102

April 8, 1994

Wall, Cracked or Broken: Female Roles
in "The Yellow Wallpaper"

A wall, however cracked or broken, can appear as smooth and flawless or as ripped and
torn as the paper upon it. Only by peeling
away the paper can we see what truly lurks beneath. In Charlotte Perkins Gilman's "The Yellow Wallpaper," the wallpaper covers the wall
beneath as the expectations of the protagonist's husband cover her true self. The very
pattern of the wallpaper is representative of
the contradictory and erratic restrictions society places upon the protagonist and women in
general: "when you follow the lame, uncertain
curves for a little distance they suddenly commit suicide--plunge off at outrageous angles,
destroy themselves in unheard of
contradictions" (395).

Society usually demands that women accept
their assigned roles and not deviate from them.
Yet to some, like the protagonist of "The Yellow Wallpaper," such roles are unfulfilling or
meaningless. Her husband in "The Yellow Wallpaper" has thrust on her the roles of wife,
mother, and housekeeper. However, those roles
are empty: the baby has a nanny, her sister-in-

Last name:
1/2 inch from
the top of
each page

Heading:
double-spaced
1 inch from
the top

Title:
centered
double-spaced

Short citation:
– quotation
 marks
– page
 numbers
– the period at
 the end

DeAngeli 2

law keeps the house, and her husband treats her
like a child, not a wife. The one role she
wants and needs--that of writer--is denied her.

    Besides the traditional roles assigned to
the protagonist, her husband, discounting her
fears about her health, acts as if she were an
invalid by giving her "a schedule prescription
for each hour in the day" (394). As the protagonist acknowledges, "he takes all care from
me" (394). The room he chooses for her, the
nursery, merely reinforces her dependent
status. He expects her to do as she is told
and, in effect, to behave as an invalid or a
child. When she tries to discuss her worries
about her illness with him, he lovingly patron-
izes her: "Bless her little heart, she shall be
as sick as she pleases!" (400).

    The protagonist struggles to break free of
the role into which society has cast her and
to express herself creatively. However, as she
is forbidden to write, to create stories, and
to occupy her mind in any meaningful way, she
starts to occupy herself with the wallpaper.
As Haney-Peritz suggests, "Ironically, it is
precisely because the narrator is patient
enough to follow some of the doctor's orders
[her husband's] that she finds it necessary to
deal with the yellow wallpaper" (115).

    The way that the protagonist sees the pa-
per, by sight and scent, may be taken as a re-

Short citation

Short citation

Short citation introduced by a phrase

Brackets indicate that words are not in the original text

DeAngeli 3

flection of the oppressive roles society imposed on women in Gilman's time. The patriar
chal structure in "The Yellow Wallpaper" shows
the limited use women were allowed to make of
themselves in a male-dominated society. Like
the smell the protagonist is obsessed with,
women's limitations were also encountered everywhere, permeating every aspect of a woman's life:

> . . . the smell is here. It creeps
> all over the house. I find it hover-
> ing in the dining-room, skulking in
> the parlor, hiding in the hall, lying
> in wait for me on the stairs. . . .
> It is not bad--at first, and very gen-
> tle, but quite the subtlest, most en-
> during odor I have ever met. (402)

At first the wallpaper pattern merely irri-
tates the protagonist, but, as she begins to
study it, she concludes that there is something
beneath the design: "I didn't realize for a
long time what the thing was that showed behind, that dim sub-pattern, but now I am quite
sure it is a woman" (401). She is now fascinated by the paper, and the woman behind it.
In Bader's words, "[T]he narrative pauses to
suggest that an external reality hitherto objec-
tively perceived and transparently visible can
blur and dissolve, that the firm, knowable texture of a familiar world can be shaken and
lost" (176).

Long citation:
– no quotation
  marks
– indented ten
  spaces
– followed by
  the period
  and page
  numbers in
  parentheses

DeAngeli 4

She starts to identify with the woman behind the paper because the wallpaper and its in-
habitant parallel her own situation. Both are
trapped by bars and must creep in order to do
what they desire. Both are also trying to free
themselves. The tragedy of one woman mirrors
and reflects the tragedy of the other: "And she
is all the time trying to climb through. But nobody could climb through that pattern--it strangles so" (402).

The protagonist can't reconcile her husband's kind and gentle treatment of her with
the jailer of her imagination. Once she has escaped from the paper, she seems proud that she
has finally escaped from her roles and outwit-
ted her husband. Yet she is mistrustful and
fearful of being returned to the prison of social expectations: "I've got out at last . . .
in spite of you and Jane. And I've pulled off
most of the paper, so you can't put me
back!" (405).

Short citation

Short citation

DeAngeli 5

Works Cited

Bader, J. "The Dissolving Vision: Realism in
　　Jewett, Freeman and Gilman." American Re-
　　alism: New Essays. Ed. Eric J. Sandquist.
　　Baltimore: Johns Hopkins UP, 1982.

Gilman, Charlotte Perkins. "The Yellow Wallpa-
　　per." Literature Across Cultures. Ed.
　　Sheena Gillespie, Terezinha Fonseca, and
　　Carol Sanger. Boston: Allyn, 1994: 393-
　　405.

Haney-Peritz, Janice. "Monumental Feminism and
　　Literature's Ancestral House: Another Look
　　at 'The Yellow Wallpaper.'" Women's Stud-
　　ies 12 (1986): 113-28.

List of Works
Cited:
– typed on a
　separate page
– double-
　spaced
– heading is
　centered and
　typed 1 inch
　from the top
　of the page
– in alpha-
　betical order
– after first line,
　all lines
　indented five
　spaces

Pipolo 1

Isabel Pipolo

Professor Robson

Introduction to Literature

January 17, 1995

Antigone: the Woman, the Heroine, the Role Model

The character of Antigone in Sophocles'
play has many different facets. She represents
something as a woman, as a heroine, and as a
role model. However, on closer examination,
can we say that all these facets come together
to form a unique character and personality? Or
can we say that if taken separately, any one
of these individual personal traits would be
enough to describe her?

As a Greek woman, Antigone is very different even within Sophocles' play. She especially contrasts with the law-abiding Ismene.
As Ismene is overwhelmed by Creon's power, she
expects Antigone to behave as a typical woman
and submit to men: "we must be sensible. Remember we are women, / we're not born to contend
with men. Then too, / we're underlings, ruled
by much stronger hands, / so we must submit in
this, and things still worse" (2.74-77). Antigone, however, is independent and believes
that she has a right to her own opinions.
Moreover, she is willing to defend them at all
costs even if it means forsaking the roles--tra-
ditionally assigned to women--of marriage and
children.

Pipolo 2

Thus, while Ismene views her womanhood in traditional ways, Antigone discovers strength in her female nature and uses it to her own advantage. Unlike Ismene, Antigone is not afraid to defy her king. As the passage below shows, she values marriage and children, but she is willing to give them up for the honor of burying her brother:

> And now he leads me off, a captive
> in his hands, with no part in the bri-
> dal-song, the bridal-bed, denied all
> joy of marriage, raising children--
> deserted so by loved ones, struck by
> fate, I descend alive to the caverns
> of the dead. (2.1008-12)

Unlike Creon's, Antigone's values seem to be deeply rooted in her duties to the dead members of her family. She values her emotional ties to brother Polyneices over her ties to country and king.

As a woman, too, Antigone resents the way Creon sexualizes the power hierarchy in Thebes. As Segal writes in his essay "Sophocles' Praise of Man and the Conflicts of the *Antigone*," "Antigone's struggle is the woman's emotional resistance to the ordered male reason of the state" (66). However, the conflict between Antigone and Creon can go beyond the debate between a woman and a man. It can be further defined, as Segal mentions, as Creon's inabil-

Pipolo 3

ity to grasp the reasons, the motives, and the nature of the "woman's resistance." In such a debate, Antigone comes out as more typically "female" or at least as representing the emotional side of human nature.

Antigone's display of her female nature in such a rash and unrelenting way can be better understood when we realize that Antigone is still a very young, impetuous woman. Bowra remarks in his book <u>Sophoclean Tragedy</u> that Antigone "is young, a girl on the verge of womanhood, not yet married, with a girl's directness and refusal to compromise" (90). Because of her age, Antigone expresses her love for her brother in a less "rational" way than we might expect.

Antigone can also be considered a heroine, not only in the context of the play but also in a more universal sense. Even though she is oppressed and stifled by Creon and his laws, which she considers unjust, she shows a heroic kind of resilience, courage, and determination to fight him to death to defend her own principles. If we see Creon representing the "state" in a more general sense, then Antigone symbolizes the heroic moral claims of individual conscience.

In the play, Creon is often portrayed as the blind, stubborn leader who is drunk on his own power: "The city is the king's--that's the

Pipolo 4

law!" (1.825). As Rebecca Bushnell writes in
her book <u>Prophesying Tragedy</u>, "Creon is tyrannical in his belief in the power of his own
voice and his separation of himself from the
claims of humanity" (54). He also raises the
power of the city and his rule above the religious traditions of the people. According to
the critic Gerald Else, this empowerment of the
state defied what the Greeks considered the
natural order: "Creon [exalts] the city above
the gods and their laws, thus subverting the hi-
erarchical order" (12).

 Antigone is also portrayed in the play as
an oppressed member of society who envisions
power and glory as the outcome of her heroic
struggle against impossible odds:

   Give me glory! What greater glory
   could I win then to give my own
   brother decent burial? These citizens here would all agree, they would
   praise me too if their lips weren't
   locked in fear. (2.562-65)

Antigone is a representative of the common people who are unable to voice their opinions because of the threat of political dictatorship.
As she rises as a heroic figure, she becomes
an ideal for those who are not strong enough
to stand up on their own and fight. Because
of her strength, obstinate personality, and
moral convictions, she also becomes a role

model for her sister Ismene and for those who
believe she is right.

Even though Antigone has some influence
over Ismene, this is not enough to convince her
sister to defy Creon, his patriarchal system,
and his public policy. By the end of the
play, however, after Ismene has been convinced
of the heroic purpose of Antigone's madness and
is willing to die with her, Antigone will not
let her. She feels that Ismene would be sharing the glory for a courageous act in which
she had no part: "Never share my dying, /
don't lay claim to what you never touched. /
My death will be enough" (2.615-17).

Antigone also becomes a role model for
Haimon, her cousin and husband-to-be. In spite
of his initial assurance of his loyalty to his
father, Haimon proves that he and the people of
Thebes support Antigone. He tries to lend his
support to her by discussing the situation with
his father, but he fails to convince Creon of
his error. As Ruth Scodel writes in her book
Sophocles, "Haemon can join [Antigone] only by
joining in her death" (50). Haimon's suicide,
in fact, may be seen as his final act in support of Antigone.

What is most remarkable about Antigone's
influence over Haimon is that her actions motivate him to challenge his father's private and
public authority. It is to Antigone that Hai-

Pipolo 6

mon owes his loyalty. Not only does Haimon betray his father to someone else, but he also
betrays him for a woman, which is exactly what
Creon seems to fear throughout. As Segal remarks in his essay,

> [Creon] sees in Antigone a challenge
> to his whole way of living and his ba-
> sic attitudes toward the world. And
> of course he is right, for Antigone's
> full acceptance of her womanly na-
> ture, her absolute valuation of the
> bonds of blood and affection, is a to-
> tal denial of Creon's obsessively mas-
> culine rationality. (70)

In betraying his father, therefore, and
siding with Antigone, Haimon not only breaks
his bonds of loyalty to father and family, but
breaks them in conjunction with his affirmation
of female power. His attitude especially an-
tagonizes his father. The fact that Haimon
takes such action against Creon's powerful
voice may be considered a sign that Antigone
functioned as a role model to him.

The individual traits that make up Antigone's character, portraying her as a woman,
a heroine, and a role model, are all important
factors in understanding her motivations and
what she symbolizes as a whole. None of them
on their own, however, is enough to completely
explain her, since she has so many different

Pipolo 7

sides. Bowra describes her character as a complex one that can be seen from different perspectives at different times:

> She is a human being, moved by
> deep affection and capable of true
> love. . . . She is no embodiment of
> abstract devotion to duty, no martyr
> for martyrdom's sake, but a girl of
> strong character and strong feelings.
> Her motives are fundamentally simple,
> but are displayed now in one light,
> now in another, as her circumstances
> or her needs vary. (90)

However, together with each one of her individual facets, Antigone also shows a dark and complex side to her personality. It is this darkness and complexity, in fact, that makes her so interesting. She is also guided by what we might consider some self-centered, negative drives.

She is inspired by her loyalty to her family and to the gods, but what really drives her and what enables her to stand resolute against Creon's decree is her tragic inability to negotiate, compromise, or see any kind of virtue in somebody else's argument. Such personality traits make Antigone inflexible and unable to relate well to others. Eventually they lead her to death. However, they also are what really makes Antigone different and notice-

Pipolo 8

able in this play. She is fighting for what
she believes in, and even though she is far
from perfect, she is carrying out her fight
her own way.

Therefore, as a whole, we could say that
what Antigone really represents is a complete
human being. She means well when she defends
her individual conscience against Creon's public policy. However, she is undone by her own
frailties and cannot overcome them. She becomes a heroine because she is able to fight
for what she believes in, and in this process,
she shows much strength as a woman. She also
becomes a role model for several of the characters in the play. However, as she cannot and
does not try to meet anyone's expectations of
her, eventually her inability to compromise
causes her undoing.

Pipolo 9

Works Cited

Bowra, C. M. Sophoclean Tragedy. Oxford:
    Oxford UP, 1944.

Bushnell, Rebecca W. Prophesying Tragedy.
    Ithaca: Cornell UP, 1988.

Else, Gerald. The Madness of Antigone. Heidel-
    berg: Carl Winter, 1976.

Scodel, Ruth. Sophocles. Boston: Twayne, 1984.

Segal, Charles Paul. "Sophocles' Praise of Man
    and the Conflicts of the Antigone." Sopho-
    cles. Ed. Thomas Woodard. Englewood
    Cliffs: Prentice, 1966.

Sophocles. Antigone. The Three Theban Plays.
    Trans. Robert Fagles. Middlesex, Eng.:
    Penguin, 1984.

Critical Approaches: A Case Study *of* Hamlet

You have probably noticed that at times your response to a literary text may differ greatly from that of your classmates. Sometimes as you listen to these various voices in your literature class, you may even wonder whether you have all read the same text. Diverse factors such as your personalities, lifestyles, social environments, and experiences may lead you to adopt various kinds of value judgments, and to react differently to the stories, poems, and plays that you read. Like you, literary critics also come up with different responses to and diverse interpretations of the same literary work. Often they also adopt reading strategies that reflect a personal affiliation to various critical theories, such as formalism, psychoanalytic criticism, reader-response criticism, feminist criticism, and the New Historicism.

The selections following highlight five different ways that literary critics have chosen to interpret Shakespeare's *Hamlet.* As you read them, you will discover how each can illuminate your reading of *Hamlet,* making you aware of new ways to reach its literary complexity. Sigmund Freud once said that the poets and artists of the past had anticipated most of his findings about the unconscious. Freud's thesis may also be applied to *Hamlet,* the literary complexity of which seems to have anticipated the possibilities of various critical interpretations.

Notice that while none of the interpretations in this appedix claims to express an ideal evaluation of *Hamlet,* each will help you to uncover the rich complexity, ambiguity, and suggestiveness of Shakespeare's play.

PSYCHOANALYTIC CRITICISM

What Is the Focus of Psychoanalytic Criticism?

Psychoanalytic criticism takes the methods used to analyze the behavior of people in real-life situations and applies them to the dramatized patterns of human behavior in literature. Overall, it explores some basic assumptions devised by the pioneer of psychoanalysis, Sigmund Freud (1856–1939). Most important among these are Freud's fundamental ideas about the structure of the human psyche, his theory of repression, and the Oedipus complex model that Freud applied to his reading of *Hamlet*.

Freud's Theory of Repression.   Freud viewed one part of the human psyche, the **id** or unconscious, as the site of our instincts, or the unconscious part of ourselves that is biologically rooted and is always pressing for some kind of satisfaction. For Freud, the id basically fulfilled the principle of life he called the "pleasure principle." The **ego** or the "I," on the other hand, forms the rational part of the psyche. The ego opposes the id, as well as the **superego** or conscience. In a simplified view, the superego is that part of ourselves that regulates our moral judgment, telling us what is right or wrong. Based on this structural model, Freud developed his theory of **repression.** In his theory, the id becomes the repository of repressed material, such as pain, sexual desires, wishes, and fears that the ego and superego tend to censor because of social mores, taboos, and other factors. As Freud viewed it, such repressed forces might eventually be reactivated to emerge either through our creative activities or through our fantasies, dreams, language, slips of the tongue, neuroses, repressed fears, and other sorts of mental conflicts.

The Oedipus Complex.   The name "Oedipus" takes us back to the Greek hero Oedipus who unwittingly kills his father and marries his mother. By **Oedipus complex** Freud meant to define one of the major repressed wishes of a boy's childhood: his desire to identify with the father and replace him in the affection of the mother. Psychoanalysts who came after Freud constructed a feminine version of the Oedipus complex, called the Electra complex. Named after a Greek legend in which the heroine Electra kills her mother to avenge the death of her father, the Electra complex describes a girl's unconscious wish to take the mother's place in the affection of the father.

A Psychoanalytic Reading of *Hamlet*

In his analysis of *Hamlet,* which was later amplified by his disciple and biographer Ernest Jones, Freud used his theory of repression and his overall assessment of the Oedipus complex to raise the issue of how Hamlet's strong repressed desire for his mother prevents him from fulfilling the task assigned to him by his father's ghost.

Sigmund Freud

"The Interpretation of Dreams"

Another of the great creations of tragic poetry, Shakespeare's *Hamlet,* has its roots in the same soil as *Oedipus Rex.* But the changed treatment of the same material reveals the whole difference in the mental life of these two widely separated epochs of civilization: the secular advance of repression in the emotional life of mankind. In the *Oedipus* the child's wishful phantasy that underlies it is brought into the open and realized as it would be in a dream. In *Hamlet* it remains repressed; and—just as in the case of a neurosis—we only learn of its existence from its inhibiting consequences. Strangely enough, the overwhelming effect produced by the more modern tragedy has turned out to be compatible with the fact that people have remained completely in the dark as to the hero's character. The play is built up on Hamlet's hesitations over fulfilling the task of revenge that is assigned to him; but its text offers no reasons or motives for these hesitations and an immense variety of attempts at interpreting them have failed to produce a result. According to the view which was originated by Goethe and is still the prevailing one to-day, Hamlet represents the type of man whose power of direct action is paralysed by an excessive development of his intellect. (He is "sicklied o'er with the pale cast of thought.") According to another view, the dramatist has tried to portray a pathologically irresolute character which might be classed as neurasthenic. The plot of the drama shows us, however, that Hamlet is far from being represented as a person incapable of taking any action. We see him doing so on two occasions: first in a sudden outburst of temper, when he runs his sword through the eavesdropper behind the arras, and secondly in a premeditated and even crafty fashion, when, with all the callousness of a Renaissance prince, he sends the two courtiers to the death that had been planned for himself. What is it, then, that inhibits him in fulfilling the task set him by his father's ghost? The answer, once again, is that it is the peculiar nature of the task. Hamlet is able to do anything—except take vengeance on the man who did away with his father and took that father's place with his mother, the man who shows him the repressed wishes of his own childhood realized. Thus the loathing which should drive him on to revenge is replaced in him by self-reproaches, by scruples of conscience, which remind him that he himself is literally no better than the sinner whom he is to punish.

Freud's psychoanalytic theories have been complemented, disputed, and revised by many of his followers. For instance, Carl Gustav Jung (1875–1961), Freud's student and later opponent, replaced Freud's main focus on "sex" with a theory of the **collective unconscious.** Unlike Freud, who highlights the individual history of repressed wishes, Jung emphasizes the importance of the collective unconscious, also known as racial memory, or the collective desires of the human race. The French psychoanalyst Jacques Lacan (1901–1981) shifted Freud's view from mental processes to argue that the unconscious is structured like a language.

A Psychosocial Reading of *Hamlet*

Recent psychoanalytic thought, as well as some post-Freudian development in psychoanalysis, has opened up the criticism of *Hamlet* to different approaches. One such approach is known as the psychosocial. Without ignoring the psycho-sexual implications of the play, a psychosocial approach to *Hamlet,* such as the one David Leverenz adopts in his article "The Women in *Hamlet:* An Interpersonal View," emphasizes the role that culture plays in shaping Hamlet's identity. On the basis of such a rationale, Leverenz argues that the real tragedy of *Hamlet* is that Hamlet finally does act. He assumes the aggressive masculine role that the patriarchal structure of power imposes on him, even though he views it as quite meaningless.

David Leverenz

"The Women in Hamlet: *An Interpersonal View"*

       Hamlet's tragedy is the forced triumph of filial duty over sensitivity to his own heart. To fulfil various fathers' commands, he has to deny his self-awareness, just as Gertrude and Ophelia have done. That denial is equivalent to suicide, as the language of the last act shows. His puritanical cries about whoredom in himself and others, his hysterical outbursts to Ophelia about nunneries and painted women, are the outer shell of a horror at what the nurtured, loving, and well-loved soul has been corrupted to. From a more modern perspective than the play allows, we can sense that the destruction of good mothering is the real issue, at least from Hamlet's point of view.

       Freudians, too many of whom have their own paternal answers to "Who's there," see Hamlet as an unconscious Claudius-Oedipus, or as a man baffled by pre-Oedipal ambivalences about his weak-willed, passionate, fickle mother. While acknowledging Hamlet's parricidal and matricidal impulses, we should see these inchoate feelings as responses, not innate drives. Interpersonal expectations, more than self-contained desires, are what divide Hamlet from himself and con-script him to false social purposes. In this perspective, taken from Harry Stack Sullivan, R. D. Laing, and D. W. Winnicott, Hamlet's supposed delay is a natural reaction to overwhelming interpersonal confusion. His self-preoccupation is para-doxically grounded not so much in himself as in the extraordinary and unremitting array of "mixed signals" that separate role from self, reason from feeling, duty from love.

Hamlet has no way of unambiguously understanding what anyone says to him. The girl who supposedly loves him inexplicably refuses his attentions. His grieving mother suddenly marries. His dead father, suddenly alive, twice tells him to deny his anger at his mother's shocking change of heart. Two of his best friends 'make love to this employment' of snooping against him (V.ii.57). Polonius, Claudius, and the Ghost all manifest themselves as loving fathers, yet expect the worst from their sons and spy on their children, either directly or through messengers. Who is this "uncle-father" and "aunt-mother" (II.ii.366), or this courtier-father, who preach the unity of being true to oneself and others yet are false to everyone, who can "smile, smile, and be a villain" (I.v.108)? Gertrude's inconstancy not only brings on disgust and incestuous feelings, it is also the sign of diseased doubleness in everyone who has accommodated to his or her social role. Usurping Claudius is the symbol of all those "pretenders," who are now trying to bring Hamlet into line. No wonder Hamlet weeps at the sight of a genuine actor—the irony reveals the problem—playing Hecuba's grief. The male expressing a woman's constancy once again mirrors Hamlet's need. And the role, though feigned, at least is openly played. The actor's tears are the play's one unambigious reflection of the grief Hamlet thought his mother shared with him before the onset of so many multitudinous double-dealings.

To kill or not to kill cannot be entertained when one is not even sure of existing with any integrity. Being, not desiring or revenging, is the question. Freudians assume that everyone has strong desires blocked by stronger repressions, but contemporary work with schizophrenics reveals the tragic variety of people whose voices are only amalgams of other people's voices, with caustic self-observation or a still more terrifying vacuum as their incessant inward reality. This is Hamlet to a degree, as it is Ophelia completely. As Laing says of her in *The Divided Self,* "in her madness, there is no one there. She is not a person. There is no integral selfhood expressed through her actions or utterances. Incomprehensible statements are said by nothing. She has already died. There is now only a vacuum where there was once a person." Laing misrepresents her state only because there are many voices in Ophelia's madness speaking through her, all making sense, and none of them her own. She becomes the mirror for a madness-inducing world. Hamlet resists these pressures at the cost of a terrifying isolation. Once he thinks his mother has abandoned him, there is nothing and no one to "mirror" his feelings, as Winnicott puts it. Hamlet is utterly alone, beyond the loving semi-understanding of reasonable Horatio or obedient Ophelia.

A world of fathers and sons, ambition and lust, considers grief "unmanly," as Claudius preaches (I.ii.94). Hamlet seems to agree, at least to himself, citing his "whorish" doubts as the cause of his inability to take manly filial action. This female imagery, which reflects the play's male-centered world view, represents a covert homosexual fantasy, according to Freudian interpretation. Certainly Hamlet's idealisations of his father and of Horatio's friendship show a hunger for male closeness. Poisoning in the ear may unconsciously evoke anal intercourse. And the climactic swordplay with Laertes does lead to a brotherly understanding. But these instances of covert homosexual desire are responses to a lack. Poisoning in the ear evokes conscious and unconscious perversity to intimate the perversion of communication, especially between men. The woman in Hamlet is the source of his most acute perceptions about the diseased, disordered patriarchal society that tries to "play upon this pipe" of Hamlet's soul (III.ii.336), even as a ghost returning from the dead.

Reading Contexts

FREUD'S TEXT

1. Why, according to Freud, have Shakespeare's readers and critics remained completely in the dark in their attempts to interpret Hamlet's character?
2. Freud mentions that the Hamlet theory developed by the German poet Goethe (1749–1832) still prevailed in his time. Describe Goethe's theory, and summarize the arguments that Freud developed to refute Goethe's romantic interpretation of Hamlet's character. How does Freud's psychoanalytic interpretation differ from Goethe's romantic one?

LEVERENZ'S TEXT

1. Explain the distinction between Freud's psychosexual interpretation and Leverenz's psychosocial interpretation of *Hamlet,* which highlights the idea that we are creatures of culture.
2. Leverenz argues that "interpersonal expectations, more than self-contained desires, are what divide Hamlet from himself and conscript him to false social purposes." In your opinion, is Leverenz's argument complex enough to explain the Hamlet problem?
3. One of the major arguments running through Leverenz's article supports the idea that Hamlet is manipulated and ultimately controlled by the male roles that patriarchal society imposes on him. Do you agree or disagree with Leverenz?

Psychoanalytic Criticism: Reading References. The reading references in this section include a series of works that, although not directly connected with *Hamlet,* highlight some of the critical ideas that inform the modern reading of *Hamlet.*

Erlich, Avi. *Hamlet's Absent Father.* Princeton: Princeton UP, 1977.

Freud, Sigmund. "The Interpretation of Dreams." *The Standard Edition of the Complete Psychological Works.* Ed. James Strachey. London: Hogarth, 1953–1974.

Kurtzweil, Edith, and William Philips, eds. *Literature and Psychoanalysis.* New York: Columbia UP, 1983.

Lacan, Jacques. "Desire and the Interpretation of Desire in *Hamlet." Literature and Psychoanalysis: The Question of Reading: Otherwise.* Ed. Shoshana Felman. Baltimore: Johns Hopkins UP, 1982.

Leverenz, David. "The Woman in *Hamlet:* An Interpersonal View." *Hamlet: Contemporary Critical Essays.* Ed. Martin Coyle. New York: St. Martin's, 1992.

Skura, Meredith. *The Literary Use of the Psychoanalytic Process.* New Haven: Yale UP, 1981.

Wright, Elizabeth. *Psychoanalytic Criticism.* London: Methuen, 1984.

FORMALISM/NEW CRITICISM

What Is the Major Focus of Formalism?

Formalism seeks to emphasize the importance of the formal elements of literature or the formal qualities related to the language, form, and content of a literary text. It directly opposes any extrinsic kind of criticism that views the literary text as a product of the author's intentions or as a reflection of ethical and sociocultural forces. In modern formalist criticism, especially in the works of formalist critics known as New Critics, literature is alienated and isolated from the actual world, seeking to fulfill the purposes of revealing deeper truths and embodying a unified vision of life in the shaped structure of a work of art.

Formalism flourished from the 1940s to the 1960s. To some extent, the close reading it advocates has remained a major goal not only for formalists but for all readers who rely on formal devices, such as imagery, irony, paradox, symbols, diction, plot, characterization, and narrative techniques, to understand the meanings of a literary text. A formalist reading of poetry can show, for instance, how a poem can integrate an ideal order of form and content by relating its phonic devices (aspects related to sounds, rhythm, and meter) to its images, symbols, and overall mode of poetic construction.

A New Critical Reading of *Hamlet*

Since a major focus of the New Critical method or formalism is the construction of literary craft, formalist critics have explored Shakespeare's use of character, language, and staging to validate the dramatic world of *Hamlet.* In "Hamlet and His Problems," T. S. Eliot applies formalist strategies to argue that feelings and emotions can be viewed as an objective mode of construction and be formally channeled in art. Shakespeare fails in *Hamlet,* Eliot argues, because he is unable to find "an objective correlative" or "a set of objects, a situation, a chain of events which shall be the formula of that *particular* emotion." Thus, as Eliot sees it, emotions and feelings in *Hamlet* exceed the literary form of Shakespeare's tragedy and cannot be expressed in art—they are "in excess of the facts." As to Gertrude, Eliot remarks that she "arouses in Hamlet the feeling which she is incapable of representing."

T. S. Eliot

"Hamlet and His Problems"

The only way of expressing emotion in the form of art is by finding an "objective correlative": in other words, a set of objects, a situation, a chain of events which shall be the formula of that *particular* emotion; such that when the external facts, which must terminate in sensory experience, are given, the emotion is immediately evoked. If you examine any of Shakespeare's more successful tragedies, you will find this exact equivalence; you will find that the state of mind of Lady Macbeth walking in her sleep has been communicated to you by a skilful accumulation of imagined sensory impressions; the words of Macbeth on hearing of his wife's death strike us as if, given the sequence of events, these words were automatically released by the last event in the series. The artistic "inevitability" lies in this complete adequacy of the external to the emotion; and this is precisely what is deficient in *Hamlet*. Hamlet (the man) is dominated by an emotion which is inexpressible, because it is in *excess* of the facts as they appear. And the supposed identity of Hamlet with his author is genuine to this point: that Hamlet's bafflement at the absence of objective equivalent to his feelings is a prolongation of the bafflement of his creator in the face of his artistic problem. Hamlet is up against the difficulty that his disgust is occasioned by his mother, but that his mother is not an adequate equivalent for it; his disgust envelops and exceeds her. It is thus a feeling which he cannot understand; he cannot objectify it, and it therefore remains to poison life and obstruct action. None of the possible actions can satisfy it; and nothing that Shakespeare can do with the plot can express Hamlet for him. And it must be noticed the the very nature of the *données* of the problem precludes objective equivalence. To have heightened the criminality of Gertrude would have been to provide the formula for a totally different emotion in Hamlet; it is just *because* her character is so negative and insignificant that she arouses in Hamlet the feeling which she is incapable of representing.

Reading Contexts

1. New Criticism or formalism attempts to present a unified vision of a work of art in which every element, such as a word, an image, or a situation, contributes to a formal view of unity. With this in mind, analyze the use that Eliot makes of words like *deficient, excess, not adequate,* and *negative* to support his reading of *Hamlet*.

2. According to Hazard Adams, what Eliot really meant by the "objective correlative" is not very clear. Examine Eliot's definition of this concept in the beginning of the first paragraph of Eliot's essay, and then decide whether you agree or disagree with Adams.

Formalism/New Criticism: Reading References

Brooks, Cleanth, and Robert Penn Warren. *Understanding Poetry.* New York: Henry Holt, 1938.

Crane, Ronald Salmon. *The Languages of Criticism and the Structure of Poetry.* Toronto: U of Toronto P, 1953.

Eliot, T. S. "Hamlet and His Problems." *Selected Essays.* New York: Harcourt, 1960.

Warren, Austin. *Rage for Order: Essays in Criticism.* Ann Arbor: U of Michigan P, 1948.

READER-RESPONSE CRITICISM

What Is the Focus of Reader-Response Criticism?

Reader-response criticism places much emphasis on the literary experience of individual readers not only as interpreters of texts but as producers of meanings. One of its basic assumptions is that each reading of a text by a single reader will be different because the dynamic and subjective scope of the reader's responses makes each reader react in different ways. Thus, the major focus of reader-response criticism is the diversity and plurality of the reader's interpretive experiences. As individual readers are apt to be influenced by social, communal, cultural, and political values, reader-response criticism also focuses on how women, individuals, and groups, in different social settings and in different time periods, read texts. Some studies show, for instance, how readers can interact with the texts' gaps, ambiguities, and pluralities or use the reading process itself to revise and build up their own expectations as readers.

A Reader-Response Analysis of *Hamlet*

Reader-response criticism can make us understand why we encounter such diverse interpretive responses to our study of *Hamlet.* The critic Norman N. Holland, for instance, explains how three different readers can respond to *Hamlet* and construct the meaning of this play according to their emotional and psychological reactions to the concept of authority. For Holland, as for most reader-response critics, whenever a text threatens the identity of its readers, the readers question, rewrite, and project their feelings on it.

In the following passage, another reader-response critic, Stephen Booth, analyzes *Hamlet* in terms of the audience's response to the play. For Booth, the audience not only is involved in constructing the meaning of *Hamlet* but is also affected when its character and experience are altered and revised by the reading process itself. Thus, at times *Hamlet*'s audience is invited to settle its mind, to get information, to develop double and contrary responses to Claudius, while at other times it gets frustrated, finding its focus shifted and its understanding threatened. At least once the audience is taken to the brink of intellectual terror. Most important, according to Booth, the audience never knows what it would have done in Hamlet's situation. Notice how Booth focuses on the position that the audience occupies in shaping the literary experience of act 2 of *Hamlet.*

Stephen Booth

"On the Value of Hamlet*"*

The audience sets out into Act II knowing what Hamlet knows, knowing Hamlet's plans, and secure in its superiority to the characters who do not. (Usually an audience is superior to the central characters: it knows that Desdemona is innocent, Othello does not; it knows what it would do when Lear foolishly divides his kingdom; it knows how Birnam Wood came to come to Dunsinane. In *Hamlet,* however, the audience never knows what it would have done in Hamlet's situation; in fact, since the King's successful plot in the duel with Laertes changes Hamlet's situation so that he becomes as much the avenger of his own death as of his father's, the audience never knows what Hamlet would have done. Except for brief periods near the end of the play, the audience never has insight or knowledge superior to Hamlet's or, indeed, different from Hamlet's. Instead of having superiority *to* Hamlet, the audience goes into the second act to share the superiority *of* Hamlet.) The audience knows that Hamlet will play mad, and its expectations are quickly confirmed. Just seventy-five lines into Act II, Ophelia comes in and describes a kind of behavior in Hamlet that sounds like the behavior of a young man of limited theatrical ability who is pretending to be mad (II.i.77–84). Our confidence that this behavior so puzzling to others is well within our grasp is strengthened by the reminder of the ghost, the immediate cause of the promised pretense, in Ophelia's comparison of Hamlet to a creature "loosed out of hell / To speak of horrors."

Before Ophelia's entrance, II.ii has presented an example of the baseness and foolishness of Polonius, the character upon whom both the audience and Hamlet exercise their superiority throughout Act II. Polonius seems base because he is arranging to spy on Laertes. He instructs his spy in ways to use the "bait of falsehood"—to find out directions by indirections (II.i.74). He is so sure that he knows everything, and so sure that his petty scheme is not only foolproof but brilliant, that he is as contemptible mentally as he is morally. The audience laughs at him because he loses his train of thought in pompous byways, so that, eventually, he forgets what he set out to say: "What was I about to say? . . . I was about to say something! Where did I leave?" (II.i.50–51). When Ophelia reports Hamlet's behavior, Polonius takes what is apparently Hamlet's bait: "Mad for thy love?" (II.i.85). He also thinks of (and then spends the rest of the act finding evidence for) a specific cause for Hamlet's madness: he is mad for love of Ophelia. The audience knows (1) Hamlet will pretend madness, (2) Polonius is a fool, and (3) what is actually bothering Hamlet. Through the rest of the act, the audience laughs at Polonius for being fooled by Hamlet. It continues to laugh at Polonius' inability to keep his mind on a track (II.ii.85–130); it also laughs at him for the opposite fault—he has a one-track mind and sees anything and everything as evidence that Hamlet is mad for love (II.ii.173–212; 394–402). Hamlet, whom the audience knows and understands, spends a good part of the rest of the scene making Polonius demonstrate his foolishness.

Reading Contexts

1. What kind of argument is Booth trying to make when he mentions that the audience in *Hamlet* "never knows what it would have done in Hamlet's situation"? Notice that while the formalist or New Critical approach to *Hamlet* privileges character analysis, Booth's overall assumptions privilege the position of the audience.
2. How would you characterize Booth's portrayal of the audience in *Hamlet*? To what extent does the audience in *Hamlet* function as a reflection and a mirror of Hamlet's own frustrations and contradictions? Where do you stand in relation to this reader-response reading of *Hamlet*?

Reader-Response Criticism: Reference Readings

Booth, Stephen. "On the Value of *Hamlet*." *Reinterpretations of Elizabethan Drama*. Ed. Norman Rabkin. New York: Columbia UP, 1969.

Eco, Umberto. *The Role of the Reader*. Bloomington: Indiana UP, 1979.

Iser, Wolfgang. *The Implied Reader: Patterns of Communication in Prose Fiction from Bunyan to Beckett*. Baltimore: Johns Hopkins UP, 1974.

Suleiman, Susan R., and Inge Crossman, eds. *The Reader in the Text: Essays on Audience and Interpretation*. Princeton: Princeton UP, 1980.

Tompkins, Jane P. "An Introduction to Reader-Response Criticism." *Reader-Response Criticism: From Formalism to Post-Structuralism*. Ed. Jane P. Tompkins. Baltimore: Johns Hopkins UP, 1980.

FEMINIST CRITICISM

What Is the Focus of Feminist Criticism?

Modern feminist criticism emerged in the late 1960s and early 1970s out of a socio-political movement aimed at the defense of women's rights. It addressed the need women felt to reinterpret literature, to rewrite history, and to change the power structure that has traditionally defined male and female relationships in patriarchal societies. Like Marxist, African-American, and the New Historical Criticism, the socially oriented perspective of feminist criticism has spread its voice in many directions. Among other things, it has promoted a reevaluation of the Freudian theory of sexual differences, a reassessment of female and male writing, a revision of the role of gender in literature, and a critique of the oppressive rationale of patriarchal ideology.

In her essay "This Sex Which Is Not One," the feminist critic Luce Irigaray has revised Freud's theory of sex difference, protesting against the view of woman as a biological version of the male model. In following the assumptions of Jacques Lacan, French feminists have also criticized, among other things, the logic of language that associates positive qualities such as those related to creativity, light, logic, and power with masculinity. Many feminists like Hélène Cixous, who tend to draw a relationship between women's writing and women's bodies, have also attempted to create a language or a specific kind of women's writing (*ecriture feminine*) that refuses participation in masculine discourse.

Other feminists have promoted a feminist critique of masculine ideology, protesting against the political marginalization women have suffered as blacks, chicanos, Asian Americans, and lesbians. For the feminist critic Catharine R. Stimpson, the defiance of sexual difference, the celebration of sexual difference, and the recognition of differences constitute the three major principles of feminist criticism.

Many of the critical efforts of feminists have also been aimed at the study of women's history and the role of women in literary tradition.

A Feminist Reading of *Hamlet*

One of the major contributions that feminist literary criticism has made to our reading of *Hamlet* has been its revisionist affirmation that female characters such as Gertrude and Ophelia possess a narrative of their own or a form of feminine discourse.

Notice in the following passage that Diane Elizabeth Dreher's feminist analysis of *Hamlet* opens new possibilities for an evaluation of Ophelia. By analyzing the forces that shaped Ophelia's identity as a "dominated daughter," Dreher liberates Ophelia from the rigid stereotypes that traditional criticism has ascribed to her. According to Dreher, because of the "fearful domination" that Polonius, Laertes, and Hamlet exercised on Ophelia, which cast her in the role of the "other," Ophelia is unable to grasp the full complexity of her self and resolve the crisis of her identity. As Dreher sees it, Ophelia is defined as a simpleminded creature only when evaluated from a male-oriented viewpoint.

Diane Elizabeth Dreher

"Dominated Daughters"

A feminist analysis of Ophelia's behavior demonstrates that she is not the simpleminded creature she seems. Traditional readings of her character have been as superficial as nineteenth-century productions, which portrayed her as a simple, pretty girl of flowers whose mad scenes were artfully sung and danced. As Helena

Faucit realized and dared to play her to a stunned audience in 1844–45, Ophelia actually does go mad. There is pain and struggle beneath that sweet surface. Her misfortune merits not only our pity but our censure of traditional mores that make women repress themselves and behave like automatons.

Contrary to prevailing opinion, Ophelia is more than a simple girl, living in "a world of dumb ideas and feelings." The pity of it is that Ophelia *does* think and feel. A careful examination of the text in I.iii reveals that she loves Hamlet and thinks for herself, but is forced to repress all this at her father's command, conforming to the stifling patriarchal concept of female behavior that subordinates women to their "honor," their procreative function in male society.

Torn between what she feels and what she is told to be, Ophelia is tormented by the crisis of identity. As one critic pointed out long ago, "she is not aware of the nature of her own feelings; they are prematurely developed in their full force before she has strength to bear them." Caught in adolescent uncertainty between child-hood and adulthood, she cannot enter the stage of intimacy and adult commitment because she does not yet know who she is. Carol Gilligan has pointed to the difficulties young women have in individuation. Raised with an emphasis on empathy rather than autonomy, girls tend to subordinate their own needs to those of others. Ophelia experiences severe role confusion in which her personal feelings are suppressed in favor of external expectations. . . .

Ophelia has been condemned for letting her father dominate her, for failing to "observe the fundamental responsibilities that hold together an existence." But let us consider the situation from her point of view. As a young woman, she is, first of all, more inclined to defer to the wishes of others than follow her own feelings. Ophelia errs in trusting her father, but she is not the only person in the play who has taken a parent at face value. Hamlet failed to recognize his mother's moral weakness until her marriage to Claudius. Furthermore, reverence for one's parents was expected of Renaissance youth. As Harley Granville-Barker emphasized, "we may call her docility a fault, when, as she is bid, she shuts herself away from Hamlet; but how not to trust to her brother's care for her and her father's wisdom?" Like Othello, Ophelia errs in trusting the wrong moral guide: in his case a friend who had shared dangers on the battlefield, in hers a father to whom convention bound her duty and obedience. Polonius' warning, seconded by her brother's, gains greater credibility. But most significant, her moral guides have not only told her how to behave; they have redefined her entire universe, inculcating in Ophelia a view of human sexuality as nasty and brutish as that which infects Othello. Ophelia sees herself in a world in which sexuality transforms human beings into beasts, with men the predators and women their prey.

Reading Contexts

1. Describe the traditional critical assumptions about Ophelia, and then contrast them with Dreher's. Explain how Dreher collapses the traditional view of Ophelia, offering insights into a new representation of this character.

2. To what extent does Dreher's argument about the rival claims of individuation and external expectations help to explain Ophelia's identity crisis? Where do you stand in relation to this argument?

Feminist Literary Criticism: Reading References

Abel, Elizabeth, ed. *Writing and Sexual Difference*. Chicago: U of Chicago P, 1982.

Carby, Hazel V. *Reconstructing Womanhood: The Emergence of the Afro-American Woman Novelist*. New York: Oxford UP, 1987.

de Beauvoir, Simone. *The Second Sex*. Trans. and ed. H. M. Parshley. New York: Knopf, 1953.

Dreher, Diane Elizabeth. *Dominance and Defiance: Fathers and Daughters in Shakespeare*. Kentucky: U of Kentucky P, 1986.

Showalter, Elaine. "Representing Ophelia: Women, Madness and the Responsibilities of Feminist Criticism." *Shakespeare and the Question of Theory* Ed. Patricia Parker and Geoffrey Hartman. London: Methuen, 1985.

THE NEW HISTORICISM

What Is the Focus of the New Historicism?

The New Historicism, or cultural poetics, may be defined as a form of political criticism closely related to Marxist criticism. One of its main goals is to focus on the critical study of power relations, politics, and ideology. For the New Historicist critics, such as Stephen Greenblatt, who coined the term "New Historical" in the early 1980s, this criticism displaces the traditional view of history as a discipline committed to an altruistic search for truth and to a faithful reconstruction of the dates and events of the past. Instead, the New Historicist perspective advocates a focus on a historical dynamic or a view of history in action. Its aim is to erase the boundaries among disciplines such as literature, history, and the social sciences. The ideas of the French philosopher and historian Michel Foucault (1926–1984) seem to inform much of the rationale that New Historicism established for the complex relation among language, power, and knowledge.

New Historical critics tend to view Shakespeare's plays as political acts reflecting and shaping the collective codes and beliefs of Shakespeare's times. New Historicists also affirm the reciprocity between the text and the world, which they attempt to rewrite by showing how sociopolitical practices and institutions such as the theater can shape and transform cultural meanings. When considering the relation between text and reader, the New Historicists advocate the reciprocity between these two elements, viewing them as dynamic forces interacting with and responding to each other.

A New Historical Reading of *Hamlet*

Leonard Tennenhouse's reading of *Hamlet* shows Shakespeare's play as a critique of power relations centered on a struggle for power between Hamlet and Claudius. According to Tennenhouse, the political struggle in *Hamlet* emerges from the clash between two different claims to the throne of Denmark: Hamlet's, which is based on blood and popular support, and Claudius's, which is based on his marriage to Gertrude and his use of force.

By approaching Shakespeare's tragedy through the critical lens traditionally applied in the criticism of history plays such as *Richard III, Richard II,* and *Henry IV,* Tennenhouse has erased the boundaries that traditional and formalist criticism insisted on establishing between Shakespeare's tragedies and his history plays. In his critique of the play-within-the-play in *Hamlet,* Tennenhouse also shifts the focus from Hamlet's goal of "catch[ing] the conscience of the King" to Hamlet's crime against the state. Tennenhouse also argues that in the play-within-the-play Hamlet fails because the political force he generates amounts to a mere symbolic gesture.

Leonard Tennenhouse

"Power in Hamlet*"*

Hamlet rehearses [the] dilemma of a state torn between two competitors, neither of whom can embody the mystical power of blood and land associated with the natural body. Hamlet's claim to power derives from his position as son in a patrilinear system as well as from "popular support." It is this support which Claudius consistently lacks and which, at the same time, prevents him from moving openly against Hamlet. Following the murder of Polonius, for example, Claudius says of Hamlet, "Yet must not we put the strong law on him. / He's lov'd of the distracted multitude . . . " (IV.iii.3–4). But this alone does not guarantee authority. Hamlet is not by nature capable of exercising force. To signal this lack, Shakespeare has given him the speech of Stoical writing, which shifts all action onto a mental plane where any show of force becomes self-inflicted aggression. We find this identification of force with self-assault made explicit in Hamlet's speeches on suicide as well as those in which he berates himself for his inability to act.

In contrast with Hamlet, Claudius's authority comes by way of his marriage to Gertrude. Where he would be second to Hamlet and Hamlet's line in a patrilineal system, the queen's husband and uncle of the king's son occupies the privileged male position in a matrilineal system. Like one of the successful figures from a history play, Claudius overthrew the reigning patriarch. Like one of the successful courtiers in a romantic comedy, he married into the aristocratic community. What is perhaps more important, he has taken the position through the effective use of force. Thus Shakespeare sets in opposition the two claims to authority—the exercise of force and the magic of blood—by means of these two members of the royal family. Because each has a claim, neither Hamlet nor Claudius achieves legitimate control over Denmark. Each one consequently assaults the aristocratic body in attempting to acquire the crown. It is to be expected that Claudius could not legally possess the crown, the matrilinear succession having the weaker claim on British political thinking. Thus the tragedy resides not in his failure but in the impossibility of Hamlet's rising according to Elizabethan strategies of state. This calls the relationship between the metaphysics of patriarchy and the force of law into question.

Reading Contexts

1. Find the sentences that best describe the two rival claims to power that Tennenhouse discusses in his text. Analyze the way these images of power reflect Tennenhouse's political views of *Hamlet*.
2. What conclusions can you draw from Tennenhouse's reading of this scene? Decide whether or not you agree or disagree with Tennenhouse's interpretation of *Hamlet*.

The New Historicism: Reading References

Greenblatt, Stephen J. *Renaissance Self-Fashioning: From More to Shakespeare.* Chicago: U of Chicago P, 1980.

———, ed. *Representing the English Renaissance.* Berkeley: U of California P, 1988.

Hunt, Lynn, ed. *The New Cultural History.* Berkeley: U of California P, 1989.

Lindenberger, Herbert. "Toward a New History in Literature Studies." *Profession: Selected Articles from the Bulletin of the Association of Departments of English and the Association of Departments of Foreign Languages.* New York: MLA, 1984.

Tennenhouse, Leonard. "Power in Hamlet." *Hamlet.* Ed. Martin Coyle. New York: St. Martin's, 1992.

Veeser, H. Aram, ed. *The New Historicism.* New York: Routledge, 1989.

FILM VERSIONS OF *HAMLET*

Some Celebrated Film Versions of *Hamlet*

Many versions of Shakespeare's *Hamlet* have been produced. In the early days of film history, it was fashionable to film famous stage actors in their famous roles so that movie audiences, primarily composed of working- and middle-class people who might never see a live performance, would be exposed to what was once thought an experience available only to the elite. Thus, producers filmed selective parts or abridged versions of Sarah Bernhardt's or John Barrymore's Hamlet. Of course, before sound this made the experience a bit pointless, since the essence of the play—Shakespeare's language—was not heard coming from the actors' mouths but was abbreviated and provided in the form of intertitles.

In the sound era, at least five film versions of the play have appeared, one of them a moody Russian film of 1964. The three best-known English language films are Laurence Olivier's 1948 version, which the actor also produced and directed and which won the Academy Award as best picture of that year; a British film of 1969 starring Nicol Williamson as Hamlet; and in 1990 the Franco Zeffirelli production with Mel Gibson. A teleplay of the Richard Burton version, directed by the great English actor John Gielgud in 1964, is also available.

There are as many variations in approach and interpretation among the films as there have been among the many stage productions.

The Olivier Version of *Hamlet*. Olivier's is undoubtedly the most respected version, but because it is so celebrated one tends to forget that it is still a specific reading of the play, and not necessarily the only legitimate one. His is very much a Freudian Hamlet: key scenes and speeches are composed and delivered in ways that make the Oedipal conflict central to the action and the primary cause of Hamlet's delay in avenging his father's murder. Olivier is also a more sensitive prince than either Williamson or Gibson. His affinity with the arts and culture and the best of human instincts is completely credible, making the vengeful task before him seem even more intolerable.

The Zeffirelli Version of *Hamlet*. The Zeffirelli film does not provide an interpretation that embraces the contradictions within the character. It evades the problem by deleting many of the richest and most complex lines in Hamlet's speeches, substituting whirling action scenes that attempt to depict a man of rugged determination. In the clinch, however, Zeffirelli still seems unable to escape the Oedipal implications, and in what is perhaps the boldest and most tasteless moment in the film, he has Hamlet kiss his mother passionately on the mouth in close-up at the very moment the father's ghost enters the bedchamber. We might wonder how this version accords with the character as perceived in Shakespeare's play.

A Note About Film

Throughout the history of film—which will reach its centennial in 1995—movies have served a number of purposes and assumed a number of roles in the development of twentieth-century culture. No history of this century, no serious consideration of the forces that have helped to shape it, could conceivably ignore the impact of movies.

From the birth of film, movies have documented events, personalities, and places, providing not only invaluable sources of information to scholars but a sense of how things looked and felt. The French brothers August and Louis Lumiere were among the very first in the late 1890s to film the world around them, and the often spectacular results of their efforts still exist for anyone to behold. We can walk into virtually any film museum in the world and see "living" testimony of what New York or Paris or San Francisco looked like at the time of our grandparents or great-grandparents; we can see how people dressed and in what vehicles they traveled. We can view actual footage of immigrants aboard ships taking them to United States at the turn of the century. If we are celebrity conscious, we can gaze at Czar Nicholas of Russia long before the Russian Revolution, or at writers Leo Tolstoy and George Bernard Shaw walking through their gardens.

Also from the first, movies have played tricks on our imaginations. In the films of George Melies, a contemporary of the Lumiere brothers, things disappear, illusory composites of people and objects are created before our eyes, feats that would be the envy of any stage magician are performed.

In a different application of imagination, photographers with an artistic inclination saw new possibilities to re-create the world, rather than merely record it, by finding abstract and lyrical designs in nature. In none of these examples did stories

1043

or narratives play major roles, although they often provided a minimal structure to anecdotal and incidental sketches.

The most popular line of development for movies, however, was certainly the one that made storytelling the primary goal. Narrative films emerged so quickly and became so commonplace that most people don't realize they were not the first kind of movies made and are not necessarily superior to the others.

FILM AND LITERATURE

Narrative films occupy an appropriate place in a literature anthology because they share with dramatic and prose literature many common features, such as theme, plot, characterization, the use of imagery, narrative point of view, and a number of rhetorical devices that have film and literary equivalents, such as metaphors and symbols.

Films have always looked to literature—to novels, plays, short stories, even poems—for sources and subject matter. Some filmmakers believed that the primary goal of movies was to introduce larger audiences to classic plays and performances they would otherwise never have a chance to see. While filmmakers continue to adapt works of literature to the screen (Stanley Kubrick's *Full Metal Jacket,* for example, is based on Gustav Hasford's novel of Vietnam, *The Short-timers*), many films do not rely on preexisting literary texts.

Films have been inspired by literature in ways other than that of direct adaptation. Many films, like works of literature, are rereadings or reimaginings of famous myths and tales. Steven Spielberg's *Hook,* for example, presumes the audience's familiarity with the Peter Pan story, but creates an entirely new contemporary allegory inspired by the original tale's themes of growing up and maturity.

Whatever their origins, however, most films must be tailored so as to be accessible to many people and to observe a relatively clear narrative structure. A film cannot be taken in at our leisure, or mulled over, or put aside as one might a novel. We are a captive audience when we watch a movie for the first time—at least if this occurs in a theater. We are bound to the pacing and flow of information, which have been preset by the filmmaker. If our attention lapses, or if we chat with the person next to us, we may—and invariably do—miss something crucial. Of course, in the age of the VCR we can view and review movies dozens of times to get to know them better, but this luxury was unavailable throughout most of film history.

Furthermore, ideas can be more fully explained in a novel or in a play, and characters often more fully developed. One has only to think of most film versions of Shakespeare's plays to realize this. This does not mean that narrative films are more shallow than literary works; it means that most great works of literature are great precisely because they can accomplish things that other art forms cannot. Hence, a great novel or play will rarely be made into a great film. But the obverse is also true. Great films could never be translated into literature since they have undoubtedly utilized the visual and audio powers of the film medium to achieve their impact. Alfred Hitchcock, one of film history's greatest directors, remarked that he never attempted to film a serious work of literature because to the degree that it was great literature it would be impossible to translate it into film terms. Instead, he took a French potboiler and a horror novel and made the classic films *Vertigo* and *Psycho,* respectively.

This leads us to a consideration of how best to approach a study of film. To ensure a clarity of structure for the viewer to find his or her way, Hollywood developed genres that have proved to be more durable and elastic than one might have thought.

GENRE

By definition, *genre* movies follow certain formulaic conventions, such as conforming to certain patterns of structuring stories and creating heroes, heroines, and villains. Horror films, westerns, musicals, science fiction, crime and detective stories, and melodramas are all examples of the most readily recognized movie genres. But the concept of genre is hardly limited to these more popular examples. American and European filmmakers have also been attracted to historical epics and biographical dramas for half a century. Much as the word *genre* may not instantly form on our lips when we think of films such as *Lawrence of Arabia, Gandhi, Hoffa,* or *Malcolm X,* all of these films are examples of the biographical drama, a genre that has as long a history as any other and as many conventions and formulas. One of its conventions is that we must see how the central figure was singled out and marked for greatness, even if we question the morality of that figure's actions. Specific thresholds and moments of crisis and transformation are normally a part of the life being chronicled because they help to crystallize the important stages of the character's evolution and therefore justify the narrative development toward the specific goal. The biographical genre "explains" a life by giving it a familiar shape, structure, and purpose.

The question of genre is both unavoidable and productive because it allows us to recognize ways in which a particular film resembles or differs from others. A consideration of a film's place within a genre tradition highlights the ways in which it conforms to familiar—and therefore safe—patterns, as well as the ways in which it may be unique. Genre study also reveals the expectations that audiences bring to the movies, as well as their capacity and willingness to accept revisions of cherished formulas. *Full Metal Jacket* and *Thelma and Louise* are two films that are unconventional in their relation to their generic bases, but their most striking and important features are best seen in the context of the conventions of their respective genres. In that way we can appreciate how these films point toward new and enlightened ways of perceiving characters, situations, and reality.

PSYCHOLOGY AND CHARACTER

In addition to relying on words and dialogue and other traditional literary methods of perceiving characterization, films can convey or reinforce certain behavioral traits through nonliterary means. One of these is the undeniable influence of actors and actresses. Audiences form relationships with film performers and expect certain traits of character regardless of the specific role a performer is playing. We have, presumably, moved away from such restrictions, but they have not entirely disappeared.

A good case in point is Clint Eastwood, who has been engaged in genre movies—particularly westerns and crime thrillers—for his entire career, and has a clearly established persona and mode of interaction with which his considerable international audience is familiar. While he was never a conventional hero of morally unimpeachable character, he has in recent years often broken entirely with the concept of the hero, challenging his audience's preconceived notions of those genres in which heroes play so crucial a part.

In *Unforgiven,* for example, Eastwood demythicizes the concept of the hero and, by disrupting the conventions of the western genre, creates a disturbing allegory of modern times. In this film the law is represented by a sadistic and self-righteous sheriff. When the Eastwood character with a shady past takes revenge on the sheriff for beating his friend to death, the audience may feel some satisfaction. But the avenger's angry and bloodthirsty behavior is hardly the stuff of heroism. We are left with an unpleasant taste in our mouths and the conviction that violence simply begets more violence, that justice has not really been accomplished.

Studying a film from the perspective of its relationship to genre conventions is revealing in terms of character psychology as well. A typical western or war film, for example, often relies on character *types* rather than fully rounded human beings. We can predict the behavior of a character *type,* but not always that of a more complex character. When a genre film shows us characters behaving in unfamiliar ways, it is revising a concept of genre and character.

POINT OF VIEW

In literature, *point of view* refers to the perspective through which an action, an event, or an entire story is seen and/or told. While it is often carelessly applied or overlooked in film analysis, point of view can be a key to understanding the entire structure and look of a film. Most films employ a combination of a kind of omniscient third person with intermittent moments or passages in which a particular character may govern the perspective on an action. This is because a first-person point of view is more difficult to sustain in a movie than in literature, where the dominating voice is constantly reinforced by the simple use of pronouns such as *I* or *we*. In films, however, unless a character is constantly narrating on the soundtrack, we tend to accept what we see as objective given reality, rather than as the exclusive or restrictive view of a particular character.

Nevertheless, there *are* cinematic ways of conveying and reinforcing a first-person narrative point of view in a film. For example, if we seem to be following and watching the actions and behavior of one character more than another, this *may* indicate that we are supposed to experience the film's events from this character's perspective. Generally, we need more evidence before we can say that this was the intention of the filmmaker.

Often camera angles, camera movements, and editing have a great deal to do with establishing a point of view and allowing the spectator to share the experience with a character, or in some cases, a group of characters. In the film *E.T.*, for example, there is a tendency to frame images at a camera angle consistent with the height of E.T. and the children who adopt the creature. Frontal shots of male adults are also consciously avoided in the film. Together, these techniques tend to privilege the child's perspective as the dominant fictional point of view in the film.

If we find that the way a character looks at other characters and things becomes the way *we* look at them, it is usually a sign that the character's point of view is being represented. If the camera often sides with a character instead of showing us things the character cannot witness, then we can assume that the camera's eye at such times is identified with the character's eyes and mind. If the character is excluded from a specific action and remains ignorant, the audience is also excluded and remains ignorant.

LANGUAGE

Language is naturally a significant part of a film's composition. As in literature, it reflects the cultural and social circumstances of characters as well as their abilities or limitations in dealing with the world. There was a time when most characters spoke a uniform literary English in American and British films, no matter what their backgrounds were. As films became more committed to reflecting social reality, this rule gave way to a more heterogeneous representation of linguistic differences.

Contemporary films are especially vital sources of the impact and variety of language experiences, since they cover such a range of worldly experience and give us views of cultures, subcultures, alien cultures, and foreign cultures that would normally be completely beyond the average filmgoer's life experience.

The way in which language affects or even constructs certain realities can also be especially dramatically and compellingly demonstrated in films. Language, for example, plays an important part in creating the claustrophobic militaristic atmosphere in *Full Metal Jacket*. During the basic training of the marines, the sergeant berates and humiliates them with a constant barrage of sexist and scatological imagery, reinforcing the artificial machismo and conformist thinking that is the focus of the film's bitter critique. The onslaught lets the viewer *feel* the relentless brainwashing at work.

The language in recent films by young African-American filmmakers about various African-American experiences—*Boyz 'n the Hood*, *New Jack City*, and *Juice*, to name a few—is a significant part of those experiences. Not only does it provide non-African-American viewers with a clear sense of black culture, but it allows African-American viewers to have a more authentic connection to the stories, characters, and experiences in films—something African-American audiences were sorely deprived of for the better part of film history.

GENDER

The issue of gender has become prominent in cultural studies in general, and has been an active part of literary and film scholarship for the past dozen years. As the issue enters more and more into the nonacademic, social sphere, it naturally affects the kinds of movies that are made. Some films raise the subject directly, placing in the foreground some aspect of the theme of the relations between the sexes. This might be the exposing of sexist behavior or attitudes in various contexts, such as the workplace (e.g., *Working Girl*), or it might be the reversing of assumptions of a genre by having women behave and play roles normally associated with men.

For example, *Thelma and Louise* is a road movie set in the majestic West, the genre and turf that traditionally belonged to the rugged western hero, yet its protagonists are female. *Alien* and *Aliens* upturned the conventions of science-fiction/horror films by killing off the male characters, leaving a bold, courageous woman the lone survivor who must fight the monster to the death.

Some films, however, go beyond a mere revising of genre expectations to probe the deeper psychological underpinnings of sexist behavior. Such a work is *Full Metal Jacket,* a staggering revision of the war film in that its climactic sequence depicts a company of hard-core marines being attacked by and then tracking down and killing an enemy sniper who turns out to be a young Vietnamese woman.

IMAGERY AND TECHNIQUE

Last but not least, any serious consideration of how narrative movies do their work must note the simple fact that they are primarily *visual* and *audio* experiences. Everything—settings, costumes, actors, camera angles, lighting, the use of color, and the way shots are framed, composed, and edited—has a powerful visual impact on the viewer. Dialogue, music, and sound effects have similarly powerful effects. In both cases, these important dimensions of the film experience are often unconsciously absorbed or entirely ignored by spectators. Too many media reviewers discuss or review films as if they were nothing but illustrations of preexisting literary texts with good or bad performances.

Most good movies and certainly all great ones are so not because they have great plots or themes and memorable lines. They leave their mark because they have effectively used the elements of the medium. Just as any great poem or play must convey its important ideas through great and imaginative language, the single most important element of literature, any great film must convey its ideas and its emotional and psychological force through the elements unique to film.

When Stanley Kubrick repeatedly frames the shots inside of the marine barracks in *Full Metal Jacket* with perfectly symmetrical compositions—the recruits lined up on either side of the screen as the bullying sergeant walks between them in screen center telling them what they must do to make the grade—we witness a visual metaphor that captures the idea and the feelings associated with rigid conformity.

When the protagonists of *Thelma and Louise* drive through Monument Valley, it is hardly a mere backdrop to the action, for the connotative dimensions of this setting are steeped in the conventions of what was once a privileged male genre. Thus, the atmosphere, the mood, and the meaning of the film are all affected by the way the setting and its reference to film history are used.

Francis Ford Coppola concludes *The Godfather* by juxtaposing the scene in church in which Michael Corleone witnesses the baptism of his sister's child with various scenes in different places in which men are being killed on his orders. We are forced to note that a parallel is being drawn, particularly when similar gestures are made by the priest and the killers and that the irony of such parallels exposes the hypocrisy of the character's life. This is almost entirely conveyed through the power of editing.

Biographical Endnotes

Achebe, Chinua (b. 1930)

Born in Nigeria, Achebe is considered one of Africa's most accomplished writers. He was educated at the University College of Ibadan and London University, and then took up a career in radio broadcasting. Dismayed with European writers' depiction of African life, he decided that Africans should tell their own stories and proceeded to write his first novel, *Things Fall Apart* (1958). This book has been translated into forty-five languages; has been adapted for stage, television, and radio; has won awards for its author; and is considered a classic in English. The novel's theme reflects Achebe's belief that outside influences eradicate traditional culture and values. When military forces took over Nigeria's government, Achebe left for the United States, taught at the University of Massachusetts, and lectured around the country. "Dead Men's Path" takes up his themes of loss of respect for tradition, and the past versus the present. His latest work includes *The Trouble with Nigeria* (1984), *Anthills of the Savannah* (1988), *Arrow of God* (1989), *A Man of the People* (1989), *Hopes and Impediments: Selected Essays* (1990), and *Girls at War: And Other Stories* (1991).

Allende, Isabel (b. 1942)

Born in Chile, Allende fled to Venezuela when her uncle, President Salvador Allende, was assassinated. She was detained and tortured by Augusto Pinochet's government. The chapter included in this anthology is from her first novel, *The House of Spirits* (1982). It recounts the lives of four generations of a Latin American family who are oppressed by rich landowners and a military dictatorship. Allende now lives in California. She has also authored *Of Love and Shadows* (1988) and *The Stories of Eva Luna* (1991).

Anderson, Sherwood (1876–1941)

Born in Camden, Ohio, Anderson was a self-educated man who, at the age of thirty-six, left his wife and business to resettle in Chicago and become a writer. His masterpiece, a collection of short stories titled *Winesburg, Ohio,* portrays life in a typical small midwestern town where many inhabitants are frustrated creatively and emotionally. "Hands" is the first story in that collection.

Aristophanes (445–380 B.C.)

Born in Greece, Aristophanes became a comic playwright at the age of eighteen. Of the more than forty plays he wrote, only eleven remain. The targets of his humor were people from all walks of life: philosophers, politicians, poets, warriors, the young and old, the rich and poor. *Lysistrata* was written during the twenty-seven-year war between Athens and Sparta.

Arrabal, Fernando (b. 1932)

Arrabal, born in Spanish Morocco, lived his early years in Madrid. At the age of twenty-three, finding life in Spain intolerable because of parental problems and the atmosphere of political oppression, he moved to Paris, where he still resides. Tuberculosis sapped his strength and his early works mirror the despair he experienced because of his illness. He regained his health after an operation in 1957, and his plays were soon produced in Paris theaters. He refers to his work as "panic theater" in the tradition of the theater of the absurd. *Picnic on the Battlefield* was written when he was fourteen and is the most frequently performed of his plays. Arrabal's concerns are the horrors of civil war, betrayal, torture, tyranny, and human helplessness in an alien universe.

Baraka, Amiri (b. 1934)

Born in Newark, New Jersey, as Everett LeRoi Jones, Baraka had a conventional middle-class upbringing and attended Howard University. There he became disillusioned with student conformity to white men's ideas. After three years in the air force, he settled on the Lower East Side of New York in the 1950s when the Beat movement in poetry was flourishing. Association with Allen Ginsberg, Jack Kerouac, and Gregory Corso introduced him to divergent forms of poetry. In 1968, he became a Muslim and changed his name to Imamu Amiri Baraka. (He later dropped the title Imamu, which means spiritual leader.) Slowly he drew away from the Beats and evolved his own theories concerning black nationalism. His first volume of poetry, *Preface to a Twenty Volume Suicide Note* (1961), was followed by other plays, poems, and essays delineating his belief in the need for blacks to find their true identities, which would bring about the separation of the races. Baraka received an

Obie Award for *Dutchman* as the best off-Broadway play in 1964. Some of his other works include *The Slave* (1964), *Black Magic* (1969), *Hard Facts* (1976), *Selected Plays and Prose* (1979), *Selected Poems* (1979), and *The Autobiography of LeRoi Jones/Amiri Baraka* (1984).

Borowski, Tadeusz (1922–1951)

Born of Polish parents in the Soviet Ukraine, Borowski lived a life of poverty and oppression. When he was four, his father was sent to an Arctic labor camp. Four years later, his mother was sent to Siberia. The family was reunited in Warsaw before World War II. Borowski wrote poetry and managed to take classes, despite the ban on education for Jews. He was eventually arrested by the Gestapo and sent to the concentration camp at Auschwitz. There he observed the horror and brutality perpetrated on the victims. He also witnessed prisoners betraying each other in order to survive. Borowski became a hospital orderly to escape extermination. The American forces freed him and his fellow prisoners in 1945. Borowski returned to Warsaw where he wrote short stories based on his experiences. His work has been criticized because he portrays some of the victims who resorted to betrayal and other criminal acts. Ironically, Borowski committed suicide using gas when he was twenty-nine.

Browning, Robert (1812–1889)

Born in England, Browning was a relatively unrecognized poet until his middle age. In fact, for a time he was better known for his dramatic rescue of Elizabeth Barrett from her tyrannical father. The couple had carried on a love affair through poetry and letters until they eloped and escaped to Italy, where they lived until her death in 1861. During his life in Italy, Browning developed his dramatic monologues, in which a person reveals his or her motives and thoughts through speech. Browning researched many subjects of the Italian Renaissance. His most famous work is *The Ring and the Book* (1868–1869), one of the longest poems in English literature.

Cervantes, Lorna Dee (b. 1954)

Cervantes, born in San Francisco, is a descendant of an old Californian Mexican family. With the breakup of her parents' marriage, she and her mother and brother moved to San Jose. Unhappy experiences in the public schools led her to seek an outlet in poetry when she was eight. In her teens she became active in the Chicano movement and the American Indian movement. In 1980, her poems were published under the title *Emplumada*. She continues to express the conflicts experienced by those of Chicano heritage who try to coexist with the white majority.

Chekhov, Anton (1860–1904)

Born in Russia, Chekhov was the third of six children. He supported himself and contributed to his family's welfare by writing short stories. Although he graduated from medical school, he chose the life of a writer. Before he was thirty, he had written six hundred short stories. He turned to playwriting in the latter part of his life, and revolutionized the theater with his realistic and sensitive depiction of life in plays such as *The Seagull, The Three Sisters,* and *The Cherry Orchard.* His work is peopled with characters who convey the sadness and hopelessness of life because of lack of communication. He died at forty-four of tuberculosis.

Childress, Alice (b. 1920)

Born in Charleston, South Carolina, Childress was raised in New York City. Her plays include *Florence* (1950), *Gold Through the Trees* (1952), and *Wine in the Wilderness* (1969). She has also written two books for adolescents, *A Hero Ain't Nothin' But a Sandwich* (1973) and *Rainbow Jordan* (1981). Although the struggle for racial equality is a recurring theme in her work, she develops it with humor and irony.

Chopin, Kate (1851–1904)

Chopin was born in St. Louis, and moved to New Orleans when she married a Louisiana Creole. Her short stories and novels usually take place in that locale. Her last novel, *The Awakening* (1899), found a new audience during the women's movement of the 1960s, not only because it examined a woman's search for personal identity but also for its interest in financial and sexual autonomy.

Crane, Stephen (1871–1900)

Born in Newark, New Jersey, Crane was a journalist, short-story writer, novelist, and poet. He is best known for *The Red Badge of Courage* (1895), a realistic study of the mind of a soldier in the Civil War. This classic is remarkable for its accuracy because Crane had not experienced war when he wrote it. Later, as a war correspondent, he covered the Spanish-American War and the Greco-Turkish War. He died of tuberculosis at twenty-eight in self-imposed exile. His war stories reflected his wish to shatter the beliefs of those who saw war as a romantic and idealized experience. Among the best known of his many short stories are "The Open Boat," "The Blue Hotel," and "The Bride Comes to Yellow Sky."

Cruz, Sor (Sister) Juana Inés de la (1651?–1695)

Born in Nepantla, Mexico, to a Spanish father and a Creole mother, Cruz was one of the earliest authors in the Americas. At the age of three, she followed her sister to school and learned to read and write. With the guidance of her learned grandfather, she became educated far beyond any of her contemporaries. Cruz attracted the attention of the royal court in Mexico City, where she became a lady-in-waiting to the viceroy's wife. During those two years, she started writing poetry. Abruptly, at nineteen, she entered a convent. She continued to study and write, but her superiors demanded that she devote herself to churchly duties. When she refused to comply, and argued that women should not have to submit to men's orders, she was accused of heresy. Sor Juana yielded and gave up her intellectual pursuits. While nursing her sister nuns during a plague in 1695, she contracted the disease and died.

Dickinson, Emily (1830–1886)

Born in Amherst, Massachusetts, Dickinson was educated at schools for females, and then retired to her home. She rarely left it, and saw only family and a few friends during her lifetime. Although she wrote almost two thousand poems, only two were published while she lived. Many of her poems reflect her interest in the dialectic of private and public selves.

di Prima, Diane (b. 1934)

Di Prima, born in Brooklyn, New York, now lives in San Francisco and is a member of the faculty at New College of California. She was educated at Swarthmore College but left before graduation to settle in Greenwich Village and take up a bohemian lifestyle. There she became part of the countercultural community that included poets of the Beat Generation such as Allen Ginsberg and Jack Kerouac. She and Amiri Baraka edited a monthly literary journal, the *Floating Bear,* in which avant-garde and nontraditional work found an audience. In subsequent years, her poetry reflected her interests in the Vietnam War protests, Buddhism, Hinduism, Zen, and the women's movement. She has also explored the influence of her Italian-American heritage on her personal experience as a woman and as an artist. Di Prima has written twenty-one books of prose and poetry, among them *Pieces of a Song: Selected Poems* (1989), *Memoirs of a Beatnik* (1989), and *ZipCode: Selected Plays* (1992).

Dorfman, Ariel (b. 1942)

Born in Argentina, Dorfman relocated to Chile, became a citizen, and worked as a teacher, journalist, and author. When Salvador Allende, the elected president of Chile, was assassinated in 1973, Augusto Pinochet became the military dictator. Because of Dorfman's repeated denunciations of the government and its methods of ruling, he was exiled. He eventually settled in the United States, and travels to Europe, where he lectures and writes. His play *Death and the Maiden* (1992) takes place in a South American dictatorship. He has also authored *Last Waltz in Santiago* (1988) and *My House Is on Fire: Short Stories* (1991).

Doro, Sue (b. 1937)

Born in Berlin, Wisconsin, Doro was writing by the age of twelve. She was a machinist for thirteen years and is the mother of five children. Her poems and prose have been published in the *Village Voice, Chicano Tribune,* and various women's and union magazines as well as working-class anthologies such as *Paper Work* (1992) and *If I Had a Hammer* (1992). She is also the author of three books of poetry and prose on the subject of her blue-collar work experience and its relationship to family and personal life: *Of Birds and Factories* (1982), *Heart, Home and Hard-Hats* (1986), and *Blue Collar Goodbyes* (1993).

Dubus, Andre (b. 1936)

Born in Lake Charles, Louisiana, and educated in his home state, Dubus became an officer in the United States Marine Corps at age twenty-two. After five years, he resigned, resumed his education, and became a teacher of fiction and creative writing at Bradford College in Massachusetts. In 1970, one of his stories was chosen for the annual volume of *Best American Short Stories*. Dubus has written seven short-story collections, including *The Times Are Never So Bad* (1983), *The Last Worthless Evening* (1986), and *Collected Stories* (1988). His novel *Voices from the Moon* was published in 1984. "The Curse" was written while he was convalescing from the loss of his leg in a highway accident. The themes of frailty and fallibility can be noted in Dubus's works.

Eliot, T(homas) S(tearns) (1888–1965)

Born in St. Louis and educated at Harvard, the Sorbonne, and Oxford, Eliot resettled in England in 1914 and eventually became a British citizen. He was a poet, critic, and dramatist. His revolutionary break in subject matter and technique with the poetic traditions of the Victorian and romantic eras influenced poetry of the twentieth century. The spiritual decay, boredom, and emotional stagnation of all of society dominated his work. Later, his conversion to Anglicanism led him to express the hope that Christian values and beliefs would regenerate the soul. He was awarded the Nobel Prize in Literature in 1948. *The Waste Land* (1922) and *Four Quartets* are among his most famous poems. His plays include *Murder in the Cathedral* (1935), *Family Reunion* (1939), and *The Cocktail Party* (1949).

Emanuel, James A. (b. 1921)

Born in Alliance, Nebraska, Emanuel was educated at Howard, Northwestern, and Columbia universities, and is professor emeritus at City College of the City University of New York. Poet, biographer, and critic, he has published several volumes of poetry, including *The Treehouse and Other Poems* (1961), *Panther Man* (1970), and *The Broken Bowl: New and Uncollected Poems* (1983). In the last decade, he has written most of his poetry and prose in Europe.

Emerson, Ralph Waldo (1803–1882)

Emerson was born in Boston and graduated from Harvard. He became a minister, but resigned because he could not accept certain doctrines of the church. After traveling in Europe, where he met English philosophers and poets, he formulated the theory of transcendentalism, which stressed the divinity of humankind and relied on intuition to reveal life's truths. Although his prose writings were revolutionary, his poetry followed traditional form and content.

Espada, Martín (b. 1957)

Born in Brooklyn, New York, Espada is considered one of the leading poets of Latino heritage. Educated at the University of Wisconsin and Northeastern University, his work experience encompasses a variety of jobs from bouncer to radio journalist in Nicaragua. At present he is a tenant lawyer in Boston. The themes of his poetry include immigrants, hard work, and poverty. His published works include *The Immigrant's Iceboy's Bolero* (1982), *Trumpets from the Islands of Their Eviction* (1987), and *Rebellion Is the Circle of a Lover's Hands* (1990).

Euripides (480–406 B.C.)

Born on the Greek island of Salamis, Euripides was a writer of tragedies. Today he is considered as great a dramatist as Sophocles and Aeschylus, although during his lifetime he was not popular. His themes reflected a pessimistic view of life, and his criticism of social matters was not viewed approvingly. He attacked the inequalities of women's status in *Medea,* the emphasis on the glories of war in *The Trojan Women,* and the unjust treatment of illegitimate children in *Hippolytus.* Only nineteen of his eighty or ninety plays exist today, among them *Alcestis, Electra,* and *Ion.*

Ferlinghetti, Lawrence (b. 1919)

Poet, playwright, and editor, Ferlinghetti is co-owner of City Lights Books in San Francisco and founder and editor of City Lights Publishing House. He was an important figure in the Beat movement of the 1950s, whose adherents were primarily concerned with rebelling against society and taking strong stands on political issues. Ferlinghetti writes in the language and speech rhythms of ordinary people rather than in formal poetic language and structures. In his poem "Constantly Risking Absurdity" (1958), he speculates on the poet's responsibility to society.

Fierstein, Harvey (b. 1954)

Born in Brooklyn, New York, of parents who had emigrated from Eastern Europe, Fierstein studied painting at New York's Pratt Institute. He acted in various Broadway plays before writing his own drama, *Torch Song Trilogy* (1982), which won the Theater World Award, the Tony Award for best play, and the Drama Desk Award; Fierstein also won the Tony for best actor in this play. In 1983, he won a third Tony Award for his musical version of *La Cage Aux Folles.*

Forché, Carolyn (b. 1950)

Born in Detroit, Michigan, and educated at Michigan State University, Forché is a poet, journalist, and educator. While a journalist in El Salvador from 1978 to 1980, she reported on human rights conditions for Amnesty International. This experience greatly affected her poetry, and she also lectured extensively on the subject when she returned to the United States. Two of her poetry collections are *Gathering the Tribes* (1976) and *The Country Between Us* (1981). She is the editor of *Against Forgetting: Twentieth Century Poetry of Witness* (1993).

Freeman, Mary E. Wilkins (1852–1930)

Freeman, born in Randolph, Maine, is one of the few women of her time who earned her living through writing. When she was fifty years old, she married Dr. Charles Freeman and moved with him to New Jersey, but their marriage failed because of his alcoholism. She specialized in stories of people in remote New England villages, and her characters were often determined individualists, particularly the women who endured despite lack of possibilities and economic security. Her work, which was popular during her lifetime, lost favor after her death but has been revived in the last twenty years. Her best known works are: *A Humble Romance and Other Stories* (1887) and *A New England Nun and Other Stories* (1891).

Frost, Robert (1874–1963)

Born in San Francisco, Frost moved east with his family when he was a child, and his poems reflect New England life and people. He attended Dartmouth and Harvard for short periods, held a variety of jobs, and tried farming in New Hampshire. During these years, he wrote poetry but was rejected by publishers. Finally, he went to England where his poems were published. On his return to the United States, he met with more success. During his long life, he received four Pulitzer prizes and many other awards. At President John F. Kennedy's inauguration in 1961, he read his poem "The Gift Outright." In many of his poems, Frost uses nature as the backdrop for his reflections on human behavior.

Gaines, Ernest J. (b. 1933)

Born in Louisiana, Gaines spent his childhood working in the fields. When he moved to California, he attended San Francisco College and Stanford University. His work recounts the everyday lives of poor people whose experiences reflect the violence and deprivation of slavery and segregation. "The Sky Is Gray" is from his short-story collection *Bloodline* (1968). His many novels include *A Gathering of Old Men* (1983) and *A Lesson before Dying* (1993). Gaines's novel, *The Autobiography of Miss Jane Pittman* (1971) was made into a movie.

Gildner, Gary (b. 1938)

A teacher of creative writing at the University of Iowa, Gildner has published a number of works, among them *First Practice* (1970) and *Digging for Indians* (1972). His latest novel, *The Warsaw Sparks* (1990), was written after teaching American literature in Poland on a Fulbright scholarship.

Gillan, Maria Mazziotti

Born in New Jersey, Gillan has taught at a number of colleges. She is presently director of the Poetry Center of Passaic County Community College and editor of *Footwork* magazine. Her poetry has been collected in *Flowers from the Tree of Night* (1981). Her work reflects her interest in exploring her Italian heritage.

Gilman, Charlotte Perkins (1860–1935)

Born in Hartford, Connecticut, and educated at the Rhode Island School of Design, Gilman was a social critic and feminist who wrote prolifically about the necessity of social and sexual equality, particularly about women's need for economic independence. Following a nervous breakdown after the birth of her daughter, Gilman divorced her husband and devoted her time to lecturing and writing about feminist issues. Her nonfiction includes *Women and Economics* (1898) and *The Man-Made World* (1911). Her novels include *Herland* (1915) and *With Her in Ourland* (1916). "The Yellow Wallpaper" (1899) is a fictionalized account of Gilman's own postpartum depression.

Gilyard, Keith (b. 1952)

Gilyard has been a lifelong resident of New York City. Poet, prose writer, and educator, he has read and taught before various audiences for over twenty years. Since 1981 he has served on the faculty of Medgar Evers College of the City University of New York, where he is an associate professor of English. Gilyard, who holds graduate degrees from Columbia University and New York University, is on the editorial board of the National Council of Teachers of English, and is serving a four-year term on the executive committee of the Conference on English Education.

His writings have appeared in *Before Columbus Review, Black American Literature Forum, College English, Community Review, Emerge, Essence, Johari II, Transition Press, The Treehouse: An Introduction to Literature,* and *White Paper, Black Poem.* He received a 1992 American Book Award for his educational memoir, *Voices of the Self: A Study of Language Competence.*

Giovanni, Nikki (b. 1943)

Giovanni was born in Knoxville, Tennessee, and raised in Cincinnati. She attended Fisk University and the University of Pennsylvania. During the 1960s, she wrote poetry and spoke out for revolutionary social change. Giovanni's poetry readings increased the popularity of her work. Today she teaches writing at universities, and her subjects continue to be pride in family, ethnic concerns, and relationships. Her books include *Black Feeling, Black Talk/Black Judgment* (1968), *My House* (1972), *The Women and the Men* (1979), *Those Who Ride the Night Winds* (1983), and *Sacred Cows and Other Edibles* (1988).

Glaspell, Susan (1882?–1948)

Born in Davenport, Iowa, Glaspell began her writing career as a reporter in Des Moines. Soon she was writing novels and plays. With her husband, George Cram Cook, she founded the Provincetown Players in 1915 as an alternative to the commercialism of Broadway. This group encouraged and produced drama by Eugene O'Neill and other American writers. In 1931, Glaspell was awarded the Pulitzer Prize in Drama for *Alison's House,* based on the life of the poet Emily Dickinson. Much of her art, like that of Sherwood Anderson, is concerned with the effect of confining environments on personal autonomy.

Greenberg, Barbara L. (b. 1932)

Greenberg was born in Boston and received a bachelor's degree from Wellesley College and a master's degree from Simmons College. Living in Massachusetts with her husband and two children, she finds the themes for her short stories, plays, and poems in women's experiences of everyday life. Her published books include *The Spoils of August* (1974), *Fire Drills: Stories* (1982), and *The Never-Not Sonnets* (1989).

Gunn, Thom (b. 1929)

Born in England, Gunn was schooled in many different locations because of his father's journalistic profession and the wartime bombings. He served two years in the army, went to Paris to write, and finally returned to England, where he entered Cambridge University. With the publication of his book *Fighting Terms,* in 1954, he was considered one of the most promising young English poets. In the same year he was awarded a fellowship at Stanford University and has resided in California since then. His many collections include *Jack Straw's Castle* (1976), *Selected Poems 1950–1975* (1979), *The Passages of Joy* (1982), and *The Man with Night Sweats: Poems* (1992). Many of his poems portray the often-thwarted attempts of marginalized adolescents to find personal identity.

Hardy, Thomas (1860–1928)

Born in Dorset, England, Hardy became an architect but started writing in 1867. The success of one of his novels, *Far from the Madding Crowd* (1874), enabled him to give up architecture for a literary career. After two more successful novels, *Tess of the D'Urbervilles* (1891) and *Jude the Obscure* (1896), he gave up fiction for poetry. A reliance on language close to that of speech, and the subjects of fate, character, and environment (which characterized his novels), continued to permeate his poetry.

Hayden, Robert (1913–1980)

Born and reared in a Detroit ghetto, Hayden not only suffered from the indignities of poverty but was ridiculed because of his poor eyesight. He immersed himself in books and attended Detroit City College and the University of Michigan, where he studied with the poet W. H. Auden. His poetry was not widely appreciated until the 1960s. He was the first African-American writer to serve as poetry consultant to the Library of Congress, and was a member of the American Academy and Institute of Arts and Letters. Among his important works are *Heart-Shape in the Dust* (1940), *Angle of Ascent* (1975), and *American Journal* (1979), in which he celebrates the triumphs of his people despite their years of slavery in the American South.

Head, Bessie (1937–1986)

Head, born in Natal, South Africa, to a white mother and a black father, was ostracized for her mixed parentage. Her mother was condemned to an insane asylum by her family and subsequently committed suicide. Head's childhood was unhappy in the care of foster parents and missionaries. She was educated and became a teacher, then a journalist. In the 1960s, when apartheid was the rule in South Africa, and violence and oppression reigned, Head attempted to obtain a passport to travel internationally. The permit was denied, and she accepted a teaching position in neighboring Botswana in 1964. Head and her son lived there but were refused citizenship until 1979. She wrote *When Rain Clouds Gather* (1968), *Maru* (1971), *A Question of Power* (1973), and many short stories. In her position as public historian, she grew increasingly interested in the traditions and background of her adopted country. It led her to interview the inhabitants of a village, about which she wrote *Serowe: Village of the Rain Wind* (1981). Her fervent belief was that every-one—white and black—must abandon power struggles. She died suddenly of hepatitis in 1986.

Heker, Liliana (b. 1943)

Born in Argentina, Heker has been a successful writer in her native country since she was a teenager. Although her country has been oppressed by military govern-ments that brought death and strife, she urged her colleagues not to flee for safety. She has stayed to edit the literary magazine *El Ornitorrinco (The Platypus)*. Her works include *Those Who Beheld the Burning Bush* and *Zona de Clivage* (1989). The latter novel won the Buenos Aires Municipal Prize.

Hogan, Linda (b. 1947)

Hogan was born in Denver of Chickasaw heritage, and earned a bachelor's degree from the University of Colorado. Her honors include the Five Civilized Tribes Playwriting Award in 1980 for *A Piece of Moon* and the 1986 Before Columbus Foundation's American Book Award for *Seeing Through the Sun*. Presently, Hogan is an associate professor of American Indian studies at the University of Minnesota. Her poems reflect her interest in preserving the Chickasaw culture. She works as a volunteer with environmental and wildlife groups. Her published works include *Mean Spirit* (1990), *Savings* (1988), and *Eclipse* (1983).

Hughes, Langston (1902–1967)

Born in Joplin, Missouri, and educated at Lincoln University in Pennsylvania, Hughes was variously employed as a seaman, waiter, gardener, and busboy. The joys and sorrows of black life dominate his writings. The rhythms of jazz and blues and black speech patterns characterize his style. Among his many books are *The Weary Blues* (1926), *Not Without Laughter* (1930), *The Dream Keeper* (1932), *The Big Sea* (1940), *Simple Speaks His Mind* (1950), and *Tambourines to Glory* (1958).

Ibsen, Henrik (1828–1906)

Born in Skien, Norway, Ibsen worked as an apothecary's apprentice, stage manager, and playwright. His plays did not find favor in Norway because of their nontraditional subject matter, so he left his native country and found acceptance in Italy and Germany. The social criticism he voiced in his work encompassed such modern themes as women's rights and society's hypocrisy. His subject matter and his realistic depiction of life have earned him the title "father of modern drama." His most famous plays are *A Doll's House* (1879), *Ghosts* (1881), *An Enemy of the People* (1882), *The Wild Duck* (1884), and *Hedda Gabler* (1890).

Jeffers, Lance (1919–1985)

Jeffers was born in Nebraska and received his bachelor's and master's degrees from Columbia University. He taught college English in many American universities and ultimately became chairman of the English Department at Bowie State College in Maryland. His poetry was published in numerous journals and anthologies. Among his collected works are *When I Knew the Power of My Black Hand* (1975), *O Africa, Where I Baked My Black Bread* (1977), and *Grandshire* (1979).

Jhabvala, Ruth Prawer (b. 1927)

Jhabvala was born in Cologne, Germany, emigrated to England in 1939, and became a British citizen in 1948. She married C. S. H. Jhabvala, an architect, in 1951, and currently lives in New York. They have three children. She has published many novels—among them *Amrita* (1956), *The Nature of Passion* (1956), *The Householder* (1960), and *Three Continents* (1988)—and many collections of stories. Her screenplays include *A Passage to India* and *Room with a View*, which won an Academy Award in 1987. In "The Englishwoman" she returns to a prevalent theme in her writings, that of being an outsider in an Indian family.

Joyce, James (1882–1941)

Born in Dublin, Ireland, the eldest in a family of ten children, Joyce knew a life of poverty and efforts to maintain respectability. He was educated in Jesuit schools, where he was trained in Catholicism and the classics. However, he rebelled against his religion, his country, and his family, and at twenty he left Dublin for a life in Europe as an exile. By teaching languages and doing clerical work, he eked out a living for his common-law wife and their two children. His novel *Ulysses,* written in an innovative style, took seven years to complete. *Finnegans Wake,* his most experimental work, is written in a language he created. He also wrote poems, short stories, and one play. Despite his years of exile, all of his fiction is set in his native Dublin and portrays his attempt to free himself of religious and geographic restrictions.

Kafka, Franz (1883–1924)

Born in Prague, Czechoslovakia, Kafka spent an unhappy life as a victim of anti-Semitism and in a job he detested in an insurance company. His stories, such as "The Metamorphosis," (1915), and his three novels, *The Trial* (1925), *The Castle* (1926), and *Amerika* (1927), reflect his feelings of alienation from the community. When he died of tuberculosis at forty-one, he left his unpublished manuscripts to a friend with instructions that they be destroyed. Instead, the friend edited and published them, thereby establishing the obscure clerk as a world-renowned author.

Keats, John (1795–1821)

Born in London, Keats studied to be a doctor but he never practiced medicine. His early interest in literature and his friendship with poets inspired him to write poetry. Along with Lord Byron and Percy Bysshe Shelley, he established romantic poetry, with its emphasis on emotion and the imagination over reason and intelligence. Idealized love was the subject of many of his poems. At twenty-six, he died of tuberculosis.

Kenny, Maurice (b. 1929)

Born near the St. Lawrence River, the ancestral home of the Mohawk Indians, Kenny lived in New Jersey and in Watertown, New York, as a child. After high school he worked at a variety of jobs and lived in Mexico, Puerto Rico, and Chicago. Finally, he settled in Brooklyn and continued writing poetry until he experienced a near-fatal heart attack in 1974. Thereafter, he focused on his Native American roots as subjects for his poetry, and is now considered one of the leading Native American poets. As editor of a magazine and a publishing company, Kenny encourages other Native American writers. In 1984, he received the Before Columbus Foundation's American Book Award for *The Mama Poems.* He has taught writing in Oklahoma and is now a professor at North Country Community College in Saranac Lake, New York. Some of his two dozen books include *Between Two Rivers: Selected Poems* (1987), *Greyhounding This America* (1987), and *Rain and Other Fictions* (1990).

Lassell, Michael (b. 1947)

Born in New York City, Lassell has earned degrees from Colgate University, California Institute of the Arts, and the Yale School of Drama. Now living in Los Angeles, he is managing editor of *LA Style* magazine and has worked as a critic, photographer, teacher, and writer. His book *Poems for Lost and Un-Lost Boys* won the Amelia Chapbook Award in 1986. *Decade Dance* (1990) is his latest published collection.

Laviera, Tato (b. 1951)

Laviera, born in Puerto Rico, has lived in New York City since 1960. He has taught creative writing at several northeastern universities, including Rutgers. His poetry and drama celebrate the ethnic diversity of New York City, and he often writes in English and Spanish as well as in "Spanglish," a mixture of the two languages used by several bilingual poets. He is deeply committed to preserving the oral traditions of Puerto Rico and the Caribbean, and, although his poetry is published in written form, it is meant to be sung and celebrated by the community.

Levertov, Denise (b. 1923)

Born in England of Welsh and Jewish parents, Levertov was a nurse in World War II. She married an American writer and moved to the United States in 1948. Her poetic style was influenced by her affiliation with the Black Mountain poets of North Carolina, who advocated verse form that duplicates everyday speech patterns. Some of her poems focus on human relationships; many others express her commitment to social and environmental issues.

Leyson, Rosemary Cho

Born in the Philippines, Leyson lived in Korea but now resides in San Francisco. In addition to her career as a short-story writer, she is an experienced carpenter. Leyson frequently explores conflicts among Asian Americans of different generations.

Longfellow, Henry Wadsworth (1807–1882)

Longfellow was born in Portland, Maine, graduated from Bowdoin College, and studied languages in Europe. On his return, he taught at Bowdoin and at Harvard University until he resigned to devote his life to writing poetry. He is best known for his narrative poems dramatizing American history and legend in a simple and sentimental style. Longfellow was responsible for making poetry popular in this country through poems such as "Evangeline" (1847), "Song of Hiawatha" (1885), "The Courtship of Miles Standish" (1858), and "Paul Revere's Ride" (1863).

Lorde, Audre (1934–1992)

Born in New York City, Lorde was educated at Hunter College of the City University of New York and at Columbia University. She taught at various branches of the City University. Her publications include nine volumes of poetry, among them *Between Ourselves* (1976), *Chosen Poems* (1982), and *Our Dead Behind Us* (1987). In her autobiography, *Zami: A New Spelling of My Name* (1982), Lorde compares her expectations as an African American with those of her African-Caribbean immigrant parents. In 1991, she was named the official state poet of New York.

Lum, Wing Tek (b. 1946)

Born in Honolulu, Hawaii, Lum attended Brown University and Union Theological Seminary. Although primarily a businessman, Lum continues to write poetry as an avocation, treating familial and domestic experiences as well as sociopolitical issues. He received the Poetry Center's Discovery Award in 1970, the Creative Literature Award from the Association for Asian American Studies in 1988, and the Before Columbus Foundation Book Award in 1989. In his most recent work, he has moved on to a more complex understanding of pluralism, evoking Chinese pride, American patriotism and Hawaiian sensibilities.

McElroy, Colleen J. (b. 1935)

McElroy, born in St. Louis, has engaged in two careers—speech clinician at Western Washington University and professor of creative writing at the University of Missouri in Kansas City. Her poems illuminate African culture and heritage. She was the recipient of the Best of the Small Presses Award for poetry in 1976 and the Before Columbus Foundation's 1984 American Book Award for *The Queen of the Ebony Isles*. McElroy has also written *The Mules Done Long Since Gone* (1973), *Music from Home: Selected Poems* (1976), *Winters without Snow* (1980), and *A Country Under Its Original Name* (1985).

McKay, Claude (1890–1948)

Born on the island of Jamaica to peasant farmers, McKay heard African folk tales when he was a child and came to appreciate his racial heritage. He was encouraged in his literary ambitions by an Englishman through whose efforts two of his poetry collections were published in England. In 1912, he came to the United States to study agriculture. After a few years of school, he left for New York City to become a writer. Although he had experienced discrimination in Jamaica, he was unprepared for the extreme racism he encountered in America. McKay channeled his anger into a collection of poetry, *Harlem Shadows* (1922), which heralded the Harlem Renaissance (a period of unprecedented creativity by black writers centered in Harlem). His poetry reflects his concern over the treatment of African Americans in American society. His other works include *Home to Harlem* (1928), *Banjo* (1929), *Songs of Jamaica* (1911), *Constab Ballads* (1912), and *Spring in New Hampshire and Other Poems* (1920).

Matshoba, Mtutuzeli (b. 1950)

Matshoba was born in South Africa and educated at the University of Fort Hare, an institution founded specifically for the education of blacks. He is the author of a novel, *Seeds of War,* and a collection of short stories, *Call Me Not a Man,* from which the selection in this anthology is taken. Most of his stories express his critical attitude toward apartheid.

Millay, Edna St. Vincent (1892–1950)

Born in Rockland, Maine, Millay began to write poetry at an early age. Her first poem, "Renascence," was published during her senior year in college. During the 1920s, she lived a bohemian life in Greenwich Village, where she acted in plays and continued to write poetry. Her love sonnets, which advocated sexual and emotional freedom for women, were particularly popular. In 1923, she won the Pulitzer Prize in Poetry for *The Harp-Weaver and Other Poems*. She wrote infrequently during the last years of her life, and she died in relative obscurity.

Mirikitani, Janice (b. 1942)

A third-generation Japanese American, Mirikitani is program director and president of the Corporation at Glide Church/Urban Center, a community organization in California. Her poetry illuminates contemporary urban life and also focuses on the injustices experienced by Japanese Americans who were interned in U.S. camps during World War II. Her published books include *Awake in the River* and *Shedding Silence: Poetry and Prose* (1987).

Mora, Pat (b. 1942)

Born in El Paso, Texas, Mora now lives in Cincinnati. She received a bachelor's degree from Texas Western College and a master's degree from the University of Texas at El Paso. Her poetry reflects her Hispanic perspective, and she writes frequently on gender and political issues. Her work has been collected in *Chants* (1984), *Borders* (1986), and *Communion* (1991).

Moraga, Cherríe (b. 1952)

Moraga, born in Los Angeles, is co-editor of *This Bridge Called My Back: Writings by Radical Women of Color* (1981) and *Cuentos: Stories by Latinas* (1983). She also has published two collections of her own writing, *Loving in the War Years: Lo que nunca paso por sus labios* (1983) and *Giving Up the Ghost* (1986). Recurrent themes in many of her poems include the connectedness between individual and community and the working woman's struggle to gain a sense of personal identity. She teaches Chicano studies at the University of California at Berkeley.

Morales, Aurora Levins (b. 1954)

Born in Indiera Baja, Puerto Rico, to a Jewish father and a Puerto Rican mother, Morales began writing poetry at seven. Her parents' love of literature and commitment to social justice have influenced her poetry, fiction, and nonfiction. Morales's work has been included in many anthologies, journals, and magazines. *Getting Home Alive* (1986) was written in collaboration with her mother, Rosario Morales. She now resides in California.

Mukherjee, Bharati (b. 1940)

Born in Calcutta, India, Mukherjee has lived in Canada but is now a permanent resident of the United States. She received her doctorate from the University of Iowa and has taught at several academic institutions, including Skidmore College and Columbia University. Her novels include *The Tiger's Daughter* (1972), *The Wire* (1975), *The Middleman and Other Stories* (1988), and *Jasmine* (1989), an expansion of the story appearing in this anthology. Her themes often deal with immigrants adjusting to life in a new society.

Ng, Fae Myenne (b. 1967)

Born in San Francisco, Ng as a child helped her mother in a sweatshop, noting that "one of my duties was to write the little code number of my mother's sewing machine onto the laundering tabs." She studied English at the University of California at Berkeley and received an M.F.A. from Columbia University; she now resides in Brooklyn. Her prose has been published in numerous anthologies and periodicals including *Harper's, The American Voice,* and *The City Lights Review.* Her novel *Bone* (1993) is an account of the attempts of an Asian-American family in San Francisco's Chinatown to cope with the suicide of the second of three daughters. Ng says of her novel "The whole ritual of sending the bones back to China was fascinating to me," a reference to the desire of many early Asian immigrants to be buried in their homeland. "Bone is what lasts, and I wanted to honor the quality of endurance in the human spirit."

Niatum, Duane (b. 1938)

Born in Seattle, this Native American poet was educated at the University of Washington and Johns Hopkins University. Niatum has worked as an editor, librarian, and teacher. The Pacific Northwest Writers Conference has awarded him first prize in poetry twice. His books include *Ascending Red Cedar Moon* (1969), *Songs for the Harvester of Dreams* (1982), and *Pieces* (1981). His poems express the disappointments and dreams of his people as they attempt to reconcile their private and communal selves.

O'Connor, Frank (1903–1966)

O'Connor was born in Cork, Ireland. His real name was Michael O'Donovan. During his imprisonment in Ireland's 1923 civil war, he educated himself by reading Irish literature. He became a director of the Abbey Theatre in Dublin during the Irish Renaissance, a period in the 1920s when the Irish people awakened to the realization of the richness and value of their own culture. Subsequently, he moved to the United States, but his themes remained the Irish-English troubles and a realistic picture of contemporary life in Ireland. Two of his short-story collections are *Guests of the Nation* (1931) and *Dutch Interior* (1940). His autobiographical works include *An Only Child* (1960) and *My Father's Son* (1968).

O'Flaherty, Liam (1896–1984)

Born in the Aran Islands off the west coast of Ireland, O'Flaherty was educated for the priesthood but abandoned it and joined the Irish Guard before World War I. He was wounded and discharged in 1918. After completing his education, he traveled for several years, returning to Ireland in 1921 to fight with the Republicans against the Free Staters in the Irish civil war. He was exiled soon after, and while living in England he published his first short story, "The Sniper." His best-known novel, *The Informer* (1925), became an Academy Award–winning film. However, *Famine* (1937), a novel based on the potato famine that claimed more than one million lives in Ireland during the 1840s, is considered his greatest work. Ireland's poor people were often the main characters in his stories.

Olds, Sharon (b. 1942)

Born in San Francisco, Olds, who now resides in New York City, graduated from Stanford University and received a doctorate from Columbia University. She has authored *Satan Says* (1980); *The Dead and the Living* (1984), for which she was awarded a National Book Critics Circle Award in poetry; and *The Gold Cell* (1987). Much of her work expresses her involvement with contemporary social issues and their effects on private and public selves.

Olsen, Tillie (b. 1913)

Olsen, born in Omaha, Nebraska, was determined to be a writer although she worked at many jobs and raised four children. She began working on her novel *Yonnondio* in the 1920s and finished it in the 1970s. The subjects of her short stories and novels are people who have been denied their chance at creativity because of their sex, race, or class. Olsen's work is often anthologized. *Tell Me a Riddle* (1961) and *Silences* (1978) are among her published works.

Owen, Wilfred (1893–1918)

Born in Shropshire, England, Owen is considered the most famous of the English poets of World War I. He expressed his hatred of war in descriptions of brutality and horror that he experienced on the battlefield. Owen died in action a week before the Armistice. "Above all this book is not concerned with Poetry, the subject of it is War, and the pity of War. The Poetry is in the pity. All a poet can do is warn," he said.

Paley, Grace (b. 1922)

Born in New York City, Paley attended Hunter College and New York University. As a child of Russian-Jewish immigrants, she grew up influenced by Russian literature and social activism. Her three short-story collections, *The Little Disturbances of Man* (1953), *Enormous Changes at the Last Minute* (1974), and *Later the Same Day* (1985), reflect her interest in the lives of working people in New York City. Critics have commented on her ability to record the cadences of New York speech as well as her humor and compassion for her characters. She remains actively involved in feminist and pacifist issues. Among the many honors she has received the latest is the 1993 Rea Award for the short story.

Randall, Dudley (b. 1914)

Randall, born in Washington, D.C., was encouraged by his parents to follow intellectual pursuits and earned degrees at Wayne State University and the University of Michigan. He became a librarian but maintained his lifelong interest in poetry. In the 1960s, Randall started the publishing company Broadside Press, which introduced hundreds of unknown black poets to the world. Gwendolyn Brooks, Margaret Walker, Amiri Baraka, Robert Hayden, Nikki Giovanni, Don Lee, and Audre Lorde are a few of the distinguished poets for whom Randall provided a forum. Many of these authors remained loyal to Broadside Press after their reputations were established, even though more lucrative contracts were offered by other publishing companies. *For Malcolm: Poems on the Life and Death of Malcolm X* remains one of Randall's most successful editorial accomplishments. His own poetry often points out the irony of the American Dream for black Americans and calls for survival through individuality.

Rich, Adrienne (b. 1929)

Rich was born in Baltimore. Her first book, *A Change of World*, was published during her senior year at Radcliffe College, and since then she has devoted her life to writing. She has been an author and a spokesperson for political and social causes, including the antiwar crusade of the 1960s and the women's movement. Among her much-praised books are *Necessities of Life: Poems 1962–65* (1966), *Diving into the Wreck: Poems 1971–72* (1973), *The Dream of a Common Language: Poems 1974–77* (1978), and a collection comprising her life's work, *The Fact of a Door-frame: Poems 1950–84* (1984).

Rifaat, Alifa (b. 1930)

Born in Cairo, Egypt, Rifaat still resides there. She wrote a short story when she was nine, but was punished for doing so. Although opposition to her writing continued in her Muslim family, her first short stories were published in 1955. Obstacles prevented her from writing for fifteen years during her marriage, but she resumed work in 1975 and has published hundreds of stories and a few novels. Themes related to the sexual and emotional problems encountered by married women in the Middle East dominate her fiction.

Robinson, Edwin Arlington (1869–1935)

Born in Gardiner, Maine, Robinson wrote poetry at an early age. He studied at Harvard University but had to drop out when his family's fortunes declined. Moving to New York City, he worked at a number of unrewarding jobs but continued to write. President Theodore Roosevelt praised one of his books and secured him a post at the New York custom house. Poems like "Richard Cory" were written during his early years of creativity, when his themes focused on the isolation and loneliness of characters in small towns.

Rodriguez, Luis (b. 1954)

Rodriguez, a Chicano poet, was born in El Paso, Texas. He spent his formative years in Watts and east Los Angeles. He held a number of jobs, from truck driver to steelworker. His poems derive from his experience, and often focus on the disappointments, discrimination, and frustrations of an immigrant's life. Rodriguez's books include *The Concrete River* (1991) and *Poems Across the Pavement* (1991).

Romero, Leo (b. 1950)

Born in New Mexico, Romero uses his home state as the setting for many of his poems. Educated at the University of New Mexico and New Mexico State University, he is a leading writer of Chicano poetry. His works include *During the Growing Season* (1978), *Celso* (1985), *Desert Nights* (1989), and *Going Home Away Indian* (1990).

Rukeyser, Muriel (1913–1980)

Born in New York City, Rukeyser was educated at Vassar College and Columbia University. A journalist as well as a poet, she reported from Spain on the Spanish civil war and was one of the journalists arrested at the Scottsboro Trial in 1931, an important moment in the history of civil rights in the United States. Her poems, published over a period of forty years, reflect her commitment to her Jewish heritage, civil rights, and the antiwar movement.

Ryu, Sook Lyol (b. 1954)

Ryu was born in South Korea. She became a journalist and was exiled when she and her colleagues tried to establish a free press movement in the 1980s. She is currently a journalist with the Korean press in New York.

Sarton, May (b. 1912)

Born in Belgium, Sarton was brought to the United States at the outbreak of World War I. Her early enthusiasms were poetry and acting. She joined Eva Le Gallienne's repertory theater in New York and later directed her own company. In the 1930s, she began to write poetry while supporting herself with teaching jobs, lecturing, and book reviewing. Sarton's main theme is the effect that love, in all its forms, has on personal relationships. Some of her works are *Encounter in April* (1937), *A Grain of Mustard Seed* (1971), *Journal of a Solitude* (1973), *Collected Poems 1930–1973* (1974), *Halfway to Silence* (1980), and *The Silence Now: New and Uncollected Earlier Poems* (1988).

Sexton, Anne (1928–1974)

Born in Newton, Massachusetts, Sexton was one of a group of successful modern "confessional" poets. After one of her nervous breakdowns, a psychiatrist suggested that she try writing as therapy. Her work is highly personal and reflects her preoccupation with suicide. She wrote several poems about her daughters, and explored gender relationships in many of her works. In 1966, she received the Pulitzer prize for *Live or Die*. *The Death Notebooks* (1974) was her last published volume before she took her life at age forty-five.

Shakespeare, William (1564–1616)

Born in Stratford-on-Avon, England, Shakespeare was a poet and dramatist of the Elizabethan Age. Relatively little is known about his personal life. He received a grammar school education and in 1594 was a member of the Lord Chamberlain's company of actors. By 1597, Shakespeare had written at least a dozen plays, including comedies, histories, and one tragedy. His greatest plays include the tragedies *Julius Caesar* (1600), *Hamlet* (1601), *Othello* (1604), *King Lear* (1605), and *Macbeth* (1606). He also composed a series of 154 sonnets between 1593 and 1601.

Smallberg, Mavis (b. 1945)

A poet and a teacher, Smallberg lives in South Africa. Her works, which have appeared in underground journals, were banned in her country.

Song, Cathy (b. 1955)

Song was born in Honolulu. She attended the University of Hawaii, received a bachelor's degree from Wellesley College, and earned a master's degree at Boston University. Her first book, *Picture Bride* (1983), won the Yale Series of Younger Poets Award and was nominated for a National Book Critics Circle Award. Her poems reflect a deep awareness of her Asian heritage and the struggles of her people to find their own voices in contemporary culture. Her latest book is *Frameless Windows, Squares of Light* (1988).

Sophocles (496–406 B.C.)

Born near Athens, Greece, Sophocles was the most popular playwright of his day. He also held posts in the military and political life of Athens. Of the more than one hundred plays that he wrote, only seven survive, among them three about Oedipus and his children, *Oedipus the King, Oedipus at Colonus,* and *Antigone.* Using mythology as the backdrop for his complex exploration of our private and public selves, Sophocles expressed the continuity of human experience.

Soto, Gary (b. 1952)

Soto was born in California's San Joaquin Valley to a family of migrant workers who toiled in the fruit and vegetable fields. Often the theme of his fiction, poetry, and nonfiction is the plight of the poor, especially Mexican Americans who have endured despite social inequities. He now teaches at the University of California. *Living Up the Street* received the 1985 Before Columbus Foundation's American Book Award. Among his other works are *The Elements of San Joaquin* (1977), *Father Is a Pillow Tied to a Broom* (1980), *Small Faces* (1986), *Who Will Know Us?* (1990), and *Home Course in Religion* (1991).

Soyinka, Wole (b. 1934)

Born in Nigeria, Soyinka, a poet, playwright, novelist, and essayist, was educated in his homeland and in England. Through his efforts, the theater in Nigeria has flourished. For his role in the political life of his country, he was imprisoned. Although denied the chance to write while in jail, he used scraps of cigarette and toilet papers to compose a collection of poems, which was smuggled out and published as *Poems from Prison* (1969). In 1986, he was awarded the Nobel Prize in Literature. His themes, social injustice and the preservation of individual freedom, are developed with humor and satire.

Stevens, Wallace (1879–1955)

Born in Pennsylvania and educated at Harvard, Stevens became a lawyer and for forty years worked for the Hartford (Connecticut) Accident and Indemnity Company. In his spare time he wrote poetry, but he was not recognized as a major poet until the latter part of his life. Many of his poems explore the issues of individuality and conformity. His *Collected Poems* (1954) won a Pulitzer prize. Among his poems are "The Emperor of Ice Cream," "Sunday Morning," and "Peter Quince at the Clavier."

Tapahonso, Luci (b. 1951)

Luci Tapahonso is a Navajo who lives in Albuquerque, New Mexico. A mother and a writer, she is currently working on a collection of poems.

Tennyson, Alfred (1st Baron Tennyson, commonly called Alfred, Lord Tennyson) (1809–1892)

Born in Somersby, Lincolnshire, England, Tennyson is considered representative of the Victorian era in his native country. His work encompasses the gamut of lyric, elegaic, dramatic, and epic poetry. His subject matter includes Arthurian legends, classical mythology, and the moral values of the upper classes. Among his best-known poems are "The Lady of Shalott," "In Memorium," and "Crossing the Bar."

Thomas, Dylan (1914–1953)

Thomas, born in Swansea, Wales, avoided formal education but began to write poems at an early age. By the age of twenty, he was a published poet. His voice impressed audiences who heard him read his works in lecture halls, on radio, and through recordings. His pastoral poems frequently reflect his joy in the frightening but beautiful processes of nature. "Do Not Go Gentle into That Good Night," "And death shall have no dominion," "A Refusal to Mourn Death, by Fire of a Child in London," and "Fern Hill" are among his best-known poems. *Portrait of the Artist As a Young Dog* (1940) recalls his childhood and youth in Wales. *Under Milk Wood* (1954) is an inventive radio play for voices.

Toomer, Jean (1894–1967)

Born in Washington, D.C., Toomer attended the University of Wisconsin and City College of New York. During the 1920s, he was a leading writer in the Harlem Renaissance, a time of creativity by black artists centered in Harlem. Toomer and others sought their identities through a celebration of their race and a recognition of their brothers' and sisters' tribulations and triumphs. "Karintha" is from *Cane,* Toomer's best-known work. *Cane* is a collection of short stories, poems, and sketches. Among his themes is the inequity of southern culture as personified by the exploitation of black women. After the publication of *Cane* in 1923, Toomer continued to write, but publishers rejected his work. He sought spiritual help from various philosophies and spent his last days as a recluse.

Two Eagles, Gayle

Two Eagles is a Lakota Indian living in South Dakota. She is the mother of two adopted children, is finishing her college degree, and writes of feminist concerns from a Native American perspective.

Valdez, Luis (b. 1950)

Valdez was born in Delano, California, and spent much of his early life working in the fields with his parents. Despite years of interrupted schooling as a child of migrant workers, he graduated from San Jose State University in 1964. A year later, he founded El Teatro Compesino (the Farm Workers' Theater) and put on plays in community centers and in the fields where he had worked. In 1987, Valdez wrote and directed the movie *La Bamba,* a biography of the Chicano rock singer Ritchie Valens. His PBS production of *Corridos: Tales of Passion and Revolution* won the Peabody Award.

Vigil, Evangelina (b. 1952)

Vigil, a Latina, produced a volume of poetry, *Thirty an' Seen a Lot* (1982), that reflects her explanations of the relation between past and present as it pertains to the preservation of family, myth, culture, and history. The role of the woman as lifegiver, literally as well as metaphorically, is central to her poetic vision. Her anthology, *Woman of Her Word: Hispanic Women Writers,* was published in 1983.

Wagner, Maryfrances Cusumano (b. 1947)

Born in Kansas City, Missouri, Wagner teaches high school English. Like many second-generation Italian-Americans, she learned the Italian language during her adult life. Her poetry reflects her interest in traditional and present-day attitudes toward her ethnic heritage. She has written *Bandaged Watermelon and Other Rusty Ducks* (1976) and *Tonight Cicadas Sing* (1981).

Walsh, Chad (b. 1914–1991)

Born in South Boston and educated at the University of Virginia and the University of Michigan, Walsh was an ordained Episcopal priest. He taught English for many years at Beloit College. He published several volumes of poetry, including *The Unknown Dance* (1964) and *Hand Me Up My Begging Bowl* (1981) and received many literary awards. In an interview, he stated that his purpose in writing was to speak to his readers: "I assume that they and I have our ordinary humanity in common, and that what interests me ought to interest them."

Wharton, Edith (1862–1937)

Wharton, born in New York City to wealthy and socially prominent parents, married a Boston banker in 1885. However, resenting the restrictions of a society matron, she pursued her own intellectual interests. She wrote novels such as *The House of Mirth* (1902) and *The Custom of the Country* (1913), which probed the emptiness of life in aristocratic New York society. A favorite theme was the rigid code of manners and conventions that denied personal happiness to both men and women. In 1907, she moved permanently to Europe but continued to write books with American settings and themes of the ironies and tragedies of life. *The Age of Innocence* (1920) won a Pulitzer prize. The Cross of the Legion of Honor was awarded to her for relief work in World War I.

Whitman, Walt (1819–1892)

Born near Huntington, Long Island, in New York, Whitman held a variety of jobs, including office boy, carpenter, printer, schoolteacher, journalist, and editor. In 1855, he published a volume of poems entitled *Leaves of Grass,* but it was unfavorably reviewed because of its radical form and content. During the next thirty-five years, he revised and added to it in nine editions. When his brother was wounded in the Civil War, Whitman went to Virginia to nurse him. He stayed on in Washington, D.C., as a nurse in army hospitals. After the war, he was a clerk in a government office but was fired because *Leaves of Grass* was considered an immoral book. His verse was appreciated in Europe, however, and eventually he received recognition in his own country. "When Lilacs Last in the Dooryard Bloom'd" and "O Captain! My Captain!" commemorated the death of Abraham Lincoln. His war impressions appear in *Drum Taps and Specimen Days.* Some of his war poems reflect a nostalgic or romantic vision of war.

Wiesel, Elie (b. 1928)

Born in Rumania, Wiesel is a survivor of the Nazi concentration camps at Auschwitz and Buchenwald, where his parents and sister were killed. François Mauriac, the French novelist and essayist, urged Wiesel to write of the horrors of the war, and Wiesel produced *Night* in 1956. This memoir-novel recounts his family's death-camp sufferings and his own guilt at surviving. Since then, he has completed twenty-five books on Holocaust themes. Man's inhumanity to man, survival, and injustice are his subjects. In 1986, he was awarded the Nobel Peace Prize.

Yevtushenko, Yevgeny (b. 1933)

Yevtushenko was born in Zima, Siberia, and had his first volume of poetry published when he was nineteen. He became prominent as the leader of the Soviet younger generation in its criticism of his country's policies. "Babiy Yar," his poem condemning the Nazi's murder of ninety-six thousand Jews in the Ukraine, caused consternation because it implied complicity on the part of the Soviet leadership. During the cold-war thaw in the late 1950s, he was allowed to travel to the United States to give poetry readings that attracted large audiences. In recent years, he again gained prominence for his support of Soviet president Mikhail Gorbachev's policy of *glasnost*. Some of his poems celebrate the everyday life of ordinary people. His works include *The Poetry of Yevgeny Yevtushenko* (1981), *Wild Berries* (1989), and *Fatal Half Measures: The Cultures of Democracy in the Soviet Union* (1991).

Glossary of Literary and Cultural Terms

Alienation Emotional or intellectual separation from peer groups and/or society.

Allegory A narrative that has a second meaning in addition to the obvious one. The meaning may be religious, moral, or political.

Allusion A reference to a familiar mythical, historical, or literary person, place, or thing.

Ambiguity Uncertainty or lack of clarity about meaning, where more than one meaning is possible, usually intended by the author.

Ambivalence The existence of mutually conflicting attitudes or feelings.

Anachronism Wrongful assignment of an event, person, or scene to a time when it did not exist.

Anecdote Brief, unadorned narrative of an event or happening. It differs from a short story in that it is shorter, is a single episode, and has a simple plot.

Antihero A protagonist who is deficient in attributes usually attributed to a hero.

Anti-semitism Hostility toward Jews as a religious or racial minority group, often accompanied by social, economic, and/or political discrimination.

Archetype A universal theme, image, or narrative that occurs often in literature.

Assonance In a line, sentence, or stanza, the repetition of similar vowel sounds although the consonants differ, for example, *penitent* and *reticence*.

Atmosphere The overall mood of a literary work, often created by the setting or landscape.

Ballad A narrative poem in which the second and fourth lines rhyme. It often contains a refrain that is the repetition of the last line of each stanza.

Burlesque A form of comedy characterized by ridiculous and exaggerated actions.

Canon A criterion or standard of measurement; the generally accepted list of great works of literature or accepted list of an author's work.

Canto A division or section of a long poem.

Catharsis The effect of tragedy in relieving or purging the emotions of an audience. Aristotle explains the theory in his *Poetics*.

Classical tragedy Refers to the tragedy of the ancient Greeks and Romans. The rules of tragic composition are derived from Aristotle and Horace.

Collective unconscious A Jungian term arguing that racially inherited images and ideas persist in individual consciousness, and unconscious motivations are therefore collectively shared as well as personal.

Comedy A play of a light and humorous nature with a happy ending.

Conceit A comparison between two very different objects.

Connotation The implication(s) and overtones, qualities, feelings, and ideas a word suggests. Connotation goes beyond literal meaning or dictionary definition.

Consensus General agreement and/or collective opinion of a group.

Convention Any device, style, or subject matter that has become, through its recurring use, an accepted element of technique.

Couplet Two successive lines of verse that rhyme.

Culture The total pattern of human (learned) behavior embodied in thought, speech, action, and artifacts. It is dependent on the human capacity for learning and transmitting knowledge to succeeding generations through the use of tools, language, and systems of abstract thought.

Denotation The literal meaning of a word as defined in a dictionary. It is the opposite of *connotation*.

Denouement The dramatic climax to the main conflict in a literary work.

Discourse Sets of statements that hold together around languages; any statements across culture that organize a mechanism, discipline, or sexuality; the social use of language.

Ego The rational and conscious part of the psyche that opposes the id as well as the superego.

Elegy A poem expressing sadness, often a lament for the dead.

Elizabethan Age The English literary period named after Queen Elizabeth, lasting from 1558 until 1642, the year of the closing of the theaters. Notable names of the period include Shakespeare, Sidney, Spenser, and Marlowe.

Epic A long narrative poem, dignified in theme and style with a hero who, through experiences of great adventure, accomplishes important deeds.

Epigram A witty or clever saying, concisely expressed.

Epigraph A quotation at the beginning of a work that is related to the theme.

Epilogue A concluding statement, sometimes in verse, summarizing the themes of the work.

Epiphany A moment of insight for a character, often resulting in a turning point.

Episode An incident in the course of a series of events.

Erotic Tending to excite sexual pleasure or desire.

Ethnicity Ethnic quality or affiliation; physical or cultural characteristics that identify an individual with a particular race or religion.

Ethnocentrism The tendency to judge other cultures by the standards of one's own.

Exclusion The act of deliberately not including someone or something, or preventing entry into a place or activity.

Existentialism A twentieth-century philosophy that denies the existence of a transcendent meaning to life and places the burden of justifying existence on individuals.

Exposition A mode or form of discourse that conveys information, gives directions, or explains an idea that is difficult to understand.

Fable A simple tale, either in prose or verse, told to illustrate a moral. The subject matter may be drawn from folklore.

Fantasy An imaginative or fanciful work concerning supernatural or unnatural events or characters.

Farce A dramatic piece intended to generate laughter through exaggerated or improbable situations.

Feminist criticism A mode of analysis, a method of approaching life and politics, rather than a set of political conclusions about the oppression of women; examines representations of the feminine in all literature and often focuses on works written by women.

Foil A term for any character who, through extreme contrast, intensifies the character of another.

Gender Characteristics and roles assigned to preferred patterns of behavior based on sex; sets of social attributions, characteristics, behavior, appearance, dress, expectations, roles, and so on made to individuals according to their gender assignment at birth.

Genre The division of literature into difference categories, each distinguishable from the other, such as play, short story, poem, novel.

Hero/Heroine (see TRAGIC HERO/HEROINE).

Heterocentrism The tendency to judge or treat as invisible any sexual/affectional relationship that does not conform to the dominant heterosexual/marriage standard.

Heterosexism The dominant ideology that maintains that heterosexuality is "natural" and superior to any other form of social/sexual relationship.

Hubris The excessive arrogance or pride that results in the downfall of the protagonist.

Hyperbole Obvious exaggeration, an extravagant statement, intentionally designed to give the reader a memorable image.

Id The driving force of the unconscious mind that is endowed with energy and is capable of motivating our actions.

Identity The set of behavioral or personal characteristics by which an individual is recognizable as a member of a group.

Ideology A system of beliefs used overtly or covertly to justify or legitimize preferred patterns of behavior.

Imagery The formation of pictures drawn with words, a reproduction of persons, objects, or sensations that are perceived through sight, sound, touch, taste, or smell.

Imperialism The imposition of the power of one state over the territories of another, normally by military means, in order to exploit subjugated populations to extract economic and political advantages.

Institution That which is established or constituted in society; an established way of behaving; an established procedure characteristic of group activity—schools, for example.

Internal rhyme Rhyming words that appear within a line of poetry.

Irony The undermining or contradicting of someone's expectations. Irony may be either verbal or dramatic. Verbal irony arises from a discrepancy, sometimes intentional and sometimes not, between what is said and what is meant, as when a dog jumps forward to bite you, and you say, "What a friendly dog!" Dramatic irony arises from a discrepancy between what someone expects to happen and what does happen, for example, if the dog that seemed so unfriendly to you saved your life.

Journal A daily written record of ideas, memories, experiences, or dreams. A journal can be used for prewriting and as a source for formal writing.

Literal The ordinary or primary meaning of a word or expression. Strict language without imagination or embellishment.

Marginalized Not fully explored or realized.

Melodrama A play written in a sensational manner pitting a stereotypical hero and villain against one another in violent, suspenseful, and emotional scenes.

Misogyny Women-hating; the belief that women are inferior to men mentally, emotionally, and physically.

Mixed metaphor An implied comparison between two things that are inconsistent and incongruous.

Modernism A movement of the early twentieth century against the conventions of romantic literary representation. The modernists rejected the flowery and artificial language of Victorian literature and began using techniques such as stream of consciousness in fiction and free verse in poetry.

Monoculturalism Pertaining to one culture to the exclusion of all other cultures.

Motif A recurring character, theme, or situation that appears in many types of literature.

Motive Whatever prompts a person to act in a particular way.

Multiculturalism Assimilation of several cultures while allowing each culture to retain its separate identity.

Myth A traditional or legendary story with roots in folk beliefs.

Naturalism A school of writing that tries to show that human fate is controlled by environment and heredity, both of which humans do not understand.

Neurosis Emotional disturbance due to unresolved unconscious conflicts and typically involving anxiety and depression.

New Criticism An approach to criticism of literature that concentrates on textual criticism without referring to biographical or historical study.

Ode A lyric poem that expresses exalted or enthusiastic emotion and often commemorates a person or event.

Oedipus complex Repressed wishes of childhood to identify with the parent of one's own sex and to take his place in the affections of the parent of the opposite sex.

Oppression The conditions and experience of subordination and injustice. Oppression is the condition of being overwhelmed by the exercise of wrongful authority or power in a burdensome, wrongful manner, for example, the unjust or cruel treatment of subjects or inferiors; the imposition of unreasonable or unjust burdens.

Oxymoron A figure of speech that produces an effect of seeming contradiction, for example, "Make haste slowly."

Parable A short allegorical story designed to convey a truth or a moral lesson.

Pastoral Any literary work that celebrates the simple rural life or those who live close to nature.

Pathos The power of literature to evoke feelings of pity or compassion from the reader.

Patriarchy A system in which men have all or most of the power and importance in a society or group. The patriarchal system is preserved through marriage and the family; it is rooted in biology rather than in economics or history.

Persona The mask or voice that the author creates to tell a story.

Poetic justice The ideal judgment that rewards virtue and punishes evil.

Postmodernism Literary and artistic philosophy that rejects all formal constraints. The postmodern artist tends to accept the world as fragmented and incoherent and to represent those characteristics in art, typically in a comic and self-reflexive style.

Projection The unconscious process of attributing one's own feelings and/or attitudes to others, especially as defense against guilt or feelings of inferiority.

Psyche The aggregate of the mental components of an individual, including both conscious and unconscious states and often regarded as an entity functioning apart from or independently of the body.

Realism A literary movement that lasted from approximately the mid-nineteenth century to the early twentieth century in America, England, and France. Realism is characterized by the attempt to truthfully depict the lives of ordinary people through the accurate description of details and psychologically realistic characters.

Refrain A phrase or verse consisting of one or more lines repeated at intervals in a poem, usually at the end of a stanza.

Repression The exclusion from consciousness of painful, unpleasant, or unacceptable memories, desires, and impulses.

Rhetorical question A question not requiring a response. The answer is obvious and is intended to produce an effect.

Romanticism An artistic revolt of the late-eighteenth and early-nineteenth centuries against the traditional, formal, and orderly neoclassicism. The writers of this time dropped conventional poetic diction and forms in favor of freer forms and bolder language, and explored the grotesque, nature, mysticism, and emotional psychology in their art.

Satire A literary work in poetry or prose in which a subject or person is held up to scorn, derision, or ridicule with the intent of bringing about an improvement in a situation.

Scene An episode that relates one part of a play's story. Acts are usually composed of more than one scene. It may also refer to the setting of a work.

Sex The anatomical and physiological characteristics that distinguish males from females.

Social class Those having similar shares of power or wealth can be grouped together in a class, thus forming a stratum in the hierarchy of possessions.

Social structure The organized patterns of human behavior in a society.

Stream of consciousness A technique of writing in which a character's thoughts are presented as they occur in random sequence.

Subjectivity The personal element in writing. The more subjective a piece of writing, the more likely it is to be focused on the writer's opinions and feelings.

Superego The part of the unconscious that regulates our moral judgment.

Suspense Uncertainty or excitement resulting from the reader's anxiety in awaiting a decision or outcome.

Textual criticism A form of scholarship that attempts to establish an authentic text in the exact form the author wrote it.

Theater of the absurd Drama that points to the absurdity of the human condition, frequently employing unrealistic, untraditional dramatic devices.

Theory A way of making sense of or explaining some social phenomenon.

Tragic hero/heroine In classical Greek drama, a noble character who possesses a tragic flaw that leads to his or her destruction.

Verisimilitude The appearance or semblance of truth.

Acknowledgments continued from p. iv.

Frank O'Connor. "First Confession" from *Collected Stories* by Frank O'Connor. Copyright © 1951 by Frank O'Connor. Reprinted by permission of Alfred A. Knopf, Inc.

Bessie Head. "A Power Struggle" from *Tales of Tenderness* by Bessie Head. Copyright © 1989 by the Estate of Bessie Head. Reprinted by permission of Jean Johnson (Authors' Agent) Ltd. on behalf of the author.

Elie Wiesel. "The Watch" from *One Generation After* by Elie Wiesel. Copyright © 1965 by Elie Wiesel. Reprinted by permission of Random House, Inc.

Ernest J. Gaines. "The Sky Is Gray" from *Bloodline* by Ernest J. Gaines. Copyright © 1963 by Ernest J. Gaines. Reprinted by permission of Doubleday, a division of Bantam Doubleday Dell Publishing Group, Inc.

Rosemary Cho Leyson. "The Visit Home" from *Making Face, Making Soul*, ed. by Gloria Anzaldúa. Copyright © 1990 by Gloria Anzaldúa. Reprinted by permission of Aunt Lute Books.

Luis Rodriguez. "Chained Time" from *The Concrete River* by Luis Rodriguez. Copyright © 1991 by Luis J. Rodriguez. Reprinted by permission of Curbstone Press.

Sue Doro. "The Father Poem Two" originally published in a slightly different version in *Women: A Journal of Liberation* 8, no. 3 (1983). Also printed by Midwest Village & Voices in *Heart, Home & Hard Hats* by Sue Doro. Copyright 1972, 1992. Reprinted by permission of the author.

Keith Gilyard. "The Hatmaker" from *American Forty* by Keith Gilyard. Copyright 1993 by Keith Gilyard. Reprinted by permission of the author.

Maurice Kenny. "Going Home" from *Between Two Rivers: Selected Poems* by Maurice Kenny. Copyright 1987 by White Pine Press. Reprinted by permission of White Pine Press.

Denise Levertov. "During a Son's Dangerous Illness" from *Breathing the Water* by Denise Levertov. Copyright © 1987 by Denise Levertov. Reprinted by permission of New Directions Publishing Corporation.

Cathy Song. "Lost Sister" from *Picture Bride* by Cathy Song. Copyright 1983 by Cathy Song. Reprinted by permission of Yale University Press.

Linda Hogan. "Song for My Name" from *Calling Myself Home* by Linda Hogan. First published by the Greenfield Review Press. Reprinted by permission of the author.

Gary Soto. "Moving Away" from *The Elements of San Joaquin* by Gary Soto. Copyright © 1977 by Gary Soto. Reprinted by permission of the University of Pittsburgh Press.

Robert Hayden. "Runagate Runagate" from *Collected Poems* by Robert Hayden, ed. by Frederick Glaysher. Copyright © 1985 by Erma Hayden. Reprinted by permission of Liveright Publishing Corporation.

Nikki Giovanni. " Nikki-Rosa" from *Black Feeling, Black Talk, Black Judgment* by Nikki Giovanni. Copyright © 1968, 1970 by Nikki Giovanni. Reprinted by permission of William Morrow & Company, Inc.

Dylan Thomas. "Fern Hill" from *Poems of Dylan Thomas*. Copyright 1945 by The Trustees for the Copyrights of Dylan Thomas. Reprinted by permission of New Directions Publishing Corporation.

Luci Tapahonso. "A Breeze Swept Through" from *A Gathering of Spirit*, ed. by Beth Brant. Copyright © 1984, 1988 by Firebrand Books. Reprinted by permission of Firebrand Books.

Colleen J. McElroy. "This Is the Poem I Never Meant to Write" from *Queen of the Ebony Isles* by Colleen J. McElroy. Copyright 1984 by Colleen J. McElroy. Reprinted by permission of the University Press of New England.

Wing Tek Lum. "It's Something Our Family Has Always Done" from *Expounding the Doubtful Points* by Wing Tek Lum. Copyright © 1987 by Wing Tek Lum. Reprinted by permission of the author.

Evangelina Vigil. "warm heart contains life" is reprinted with permission of the publisher from *Thirty an' Seen a Lot*. Copyright 1982 by Arte Publico Press–University of Houston. Reprinted by permission of Arte Publico Press–University of Houston.

James A. Emanuel. "Fishermen" from *Whole Grain: Collected Poems* by James A. Emanuel. Copyright 1991 by Lotus Press Inc. Reprinted by permission of the author.

Audre Lorde. "What My Child Learns of the Sea" is reprinted from *Undersong, Chosen Poems Old and New,* revised edition, by Audre Lorde, by permission of W. W. Norton & Company, Inc. Copyright © 1992, 1982, 1976, 1974, 1973, 1970, 1968 by Audre Lorde.

William Shakespeare. "The Tragedy of Hamlet, Prince of Denmark" by William Shakespeare, ed. by Edward Hubler. Copyright © 1963 by Edward Hubler. Copyright © 1963, 1986, 1987 by Sylvan Barnet. Reprinted by permission of New American Library, a division of Penguin Books USA Inc.

PART TWO

Anton Chekhov. "At Sea: A Soldier's Story" from *Selected Stories of Anton Chekhov,* trans. Ann Dunnigan. Translation copyright © 1960 by Ann Dunnigan. Reprinted by permission of New American Library, a division of Penguin Books USA Inc.

Jean Toomer. "Karintha" is reprinted from *Cane* by Jean Toomer, by permission of Liveright Publishing Corporation. Copyright 1923 by Boni & Liveright. Copyright renewed 1951 by Jean Toomer.

PART FOUR

Michael Lassell. "How to Watch Your Brother Die" from *Poems for Lost and Un-Lost Boys* Michael Lassell. Copyright 1985 by Michael Lassell. Reprinted by permission of the author.

William Shakespeare. "Othello, the Moor of Venice" from *The Complete Works of Shakespeare* by David Bevington. Copyright © 1980, 1973 by Scott, Foresman and Company. Reprinted by permission of HarperCollins Publishers.

Alice Childress. "Florence" copyright © 1950. Renewed 1978 by Alice Childress. Reprinted by permission of Flora Roberts, Inc.

Luis Valdez. "Los Vendidos" from *Luis Valdez—Early Works: Actos, Bernabe and Pensamiento Serpentino,* by Luis Valdez. Copyright © 1990 by Arte Publico Press–University of Houston. Reprinted by permission of Arte Publico Press–University of Houston.

Harvey Fierstein. "On Tidy Endings" is reprinted with the permission of Atheneum Publishers, an imprint of Macmillan Publishing Company from *Safe Sex* by Harvey Fierstein. Copyright © 1987 by Harvey Fierstein. This play may not be reproduced in whole or in part without permission of the publisher. No performance of any kind, including readings, may be given without permission in writing from the author's agents, William Morris Agency, 1350 Avenue of the Americas, New York, NY 10019.

PART FIVE

Franz Kafka. "The Metamorphosis" from *Franz Kafka: The Complete Stories by Franz Kafka,* ed. Nahum N. Glatzer. Copyright 1946, 1947, 1948, 1949, 1954 © 1958, 1971 by Schocken Books Inc. Reprinted by permission of Schocken Books, published by Pantheon Books, a division of Random House, Inc.

Sherwood Anderson. "Hands" from *Winesburg, Ohio* by Sherwood Anderson. Copyright 1919 by B. W Huebsch. Copyright 1947 by Eleanor Copenhaver Anderson. Reprinted by permission of Viking Penguin, a division of Penguin Books USA Inc.

James Joyce. "Eveline" from *Dubliners* by James Joyce. Copyright 1916 by B. W. Heubsch. Definitive text copyright © 1967 by the Estate of James Joyce. Reprinted by permission of Viking Penguin, a division of Penguin Books USA Inc.

Fae Myenne Ng. "A Red Sweater" from *The American Voice* by Fae Myenne Ng. Copyright © 1987 by Fae Myenne Ng. Reprinted by permission of Donadio & Ashworth, Inc.

Ruth Prawer Jhabvala. "The Englishwoman" first appeared in *Cosmopolitan* Magazine. Copyright © 1972 by Ruth Prawer Jhabvala. Reprinted by permission of Harriet Wasserman Literary Agent, as agents for the author.

Mtutuzeli Matshoba. "Call Me Not a Man" from *Call Me Not a Man* by Mtutuzeli Matshoba. Copyright 1981 by Mtutuzeli Matshoba. Reprinted by permission of Longman Group UK.

Chinua Achebe. "Dead Man's Path" from *Girls at War and Other Stories* by Chinua Achebe. Copyright © 1972, 1973 by Chinua Achebe. Reprinted by permission of Doubleday, a division of Bantam Doubleday Dell Publishing Group, Inc.

Wallace Stevens. "Disillusionment of Ten O'Clock" from *Collected Poems* by Wallace Stevens. Copyright © 1923 and renewed 1951 by Wallace Stevens. Reprinted by permission of Alfred A. Knopf, Inc.

Emily Dickinson. "Much Madness Is Divinest Sense—" from *The Poems of Emily Dickinson,* ed. Thomas H. Johnson, Cambridge, MA: The Belknap Press of Harvard University Press. Copyright © 1951, 1955, 1979, 1983 by the President and Fellows of Harvard College. Reprinted by permission of the publishers and the Trustees of Amherst College. "The Soul Selects Her Own Society—" from *The Poems of Emily Dickinson,* ed. Thomas H. Johnson, Cambridge, MA: The Belknap Press of Harvard University Press. Copyright © 1951, 1955, 1979, 1983 by the President and Fellows of Harvard College. Reprinted by permission of the publishers and the Trustees of Amherst College.

Yevgeny Yevtushenko. "People" from *Selected Poems* by Yevgeny Yevtushenko, trans. Robin Milner-Gulland and Peter Levi. Translation copyright © 1962 by Robin Milner-Gulland and Peter Levi. Reprinted by permission of Penguin Books Ltd, UK.

Duane Niatum. "Street Kid" from *Digging Out the Roots* by Duane Niatum. Copyright © 1978 by Duane Niatum. Reprinted by permission of HarperCollins Publishers.

Thom Gunn. "Black Jackets" from *Moly and My Sad Captains* by Thom Gunn. Copyright © 1973 by Thom Gunn. Reprinted by permission of Farrar, Straus and Giroux, Inc.

Robert Frost. "Mending Wall" published by Henry Holt and Company, Inc.

Sharon Olds. "Summer Solstice, New York City" from *The Gold Cell* by Sharon Olds. Copyright © 1987 by Sharon Olds. Reprinted by permission of Alfred A. Knopf, Inc.

Leo Romero. "What the Gossips Saw" from *Aqua Negra* by Leo Romero. Copyright © 1981 by Leo Romero. Reprinted by permission of Ahsahta Press at Boise State Univelisty.

Gary Soto. "History" from *The Elements of San Joaquin* by Gary Soto. Copyright © 1977 by Gary Soto. Reprinted by permission of the University of Pittsburgh Press.

APPENDIX

Index of Authors and Titles

Index of First Lines

Index of Terms